Melonee Paschal

JOURNEYS

Program Consultants

Shervaughnna Anderson · Marty Hougen
Carol Jago · Erik Palmer · Shane Templeton
Sheila Valencia · MaryEllen Vogt

Consulting Author · Irene Fountas

Cover illustration by Valeria Docampo.

Copyright © 2017 by Houghton Mifflin Harcourt Publishing Company

Printed in the U.S.A.

ISBN 978-0544-54335-5

9 10 0868 23 22 21 20 19 18 17
4500649861   B C D E F G

UNIT 1 Neighborhood Visit 9

UNIT 2 Nature Watch 185

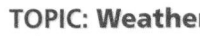

Poppleton in Winter
FANTASY

by Cynthia Rylant • illustrated by Mark Teague

5

Be a Reading Detective!

Welcome, Reader!

Your help is needed to find clues in texts. As a **Reading Detective,** you will need to **ask a lot of questions** to understand what you are reading. You also need to read carefully to find **evidence,** or **clues,** to figure things out.

myNotebook

As you read, mark up the text. Save your work to **myNotebook.**

- Highlight details.
- Add notes and questions.
- Add new words to **myWordList.**

- Ask questions that start with *who*, *what*, *where*, *why*, and *how*.

- Figure out the meanings of words you do not know.

- Look for clues in the author's words, the pictures, and the captions.

Let's do it!

UNIT 1
Neighborhood Visit

Stream to Start

66 Alone we can do so little; together we can do so much. 99

— Helen Keller

Performance Task Preview

At the end of this unit, you will think about two of the texts you have read. Then you will use information from the texts to write a story about a family who gets a dog!

hmhfyi.com

Channel One News®

HENRY AND MUDGE
The First Book

Story by Cynthia Rylant
Pictures by Suçie Stevenson

All in the Family

Q LANGUAGE DETECTIVE

Talk About Words
Work with a partner.
Take turns asking and
answering questions
about the photos. Use
the Vocabulary words
in your questions and
answers.

🗒 myNotebook

Add new words to
myWordList. Use them
in your speaking
and writing.

Vocabulary in Context

▶ **Read each Context Card.**

▶ **Use a Vocabulary word to tell about something you did.**

1 curly

A poodle is a dog that has very curly hair.

2 straight

Some kinds of dogs have long, straight hair.

3 floppy

Hound dogs have floppy ears. The ears hang down very low.

4 drooled

The Saint Bernard drooled all over the place!

5 weighed

A dog can be weighed on a scale. Then the vet knows how heavy the dog is.

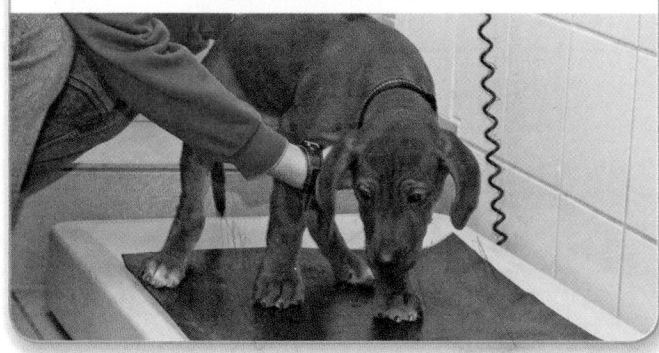

6 stood

The children measured the dog. He stood one foot tall.

7 collars

Collars come in different styles. A collar goes around a dog's neck.

8 row

The dog treats are lined up in a row on the shelf.

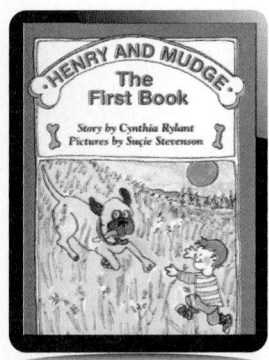

Read and Comprehend

Sequence of Events In *Henry and Mudge,* one event happens and then another and another. The order of events in a story is called the **sequence of events.** You can use a chart like this one to show the order of story events.

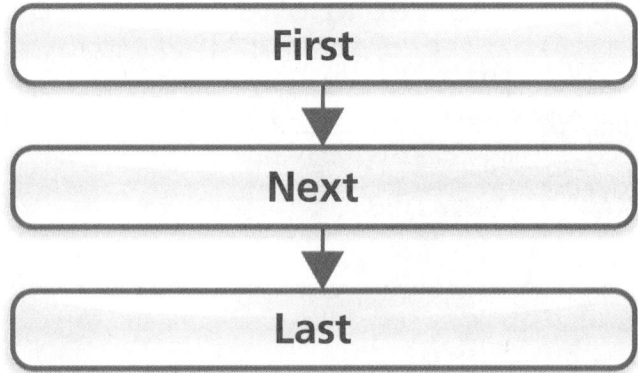

First

↓

Next

↓

Last

☑ **TARGET STRATEGY**

Infer/Predict Use clues, or text evidence, to figure out more about story parts.

ELA RL.2.2, RL.2.5, SL.2.1a, SL.2.1c, SL.2.3

Animal Traits

All dogs are alike in some ways. Dogs are also different in some ways. Some dogs are short. Some dogs are tall. Some have long, skinny tails. Some have short, fluffy tails. The different ways a dog can look are called traits. Each dog's traits make it special.

In *Henry and Mudge,* you will read about one dog who looks different from all the others.

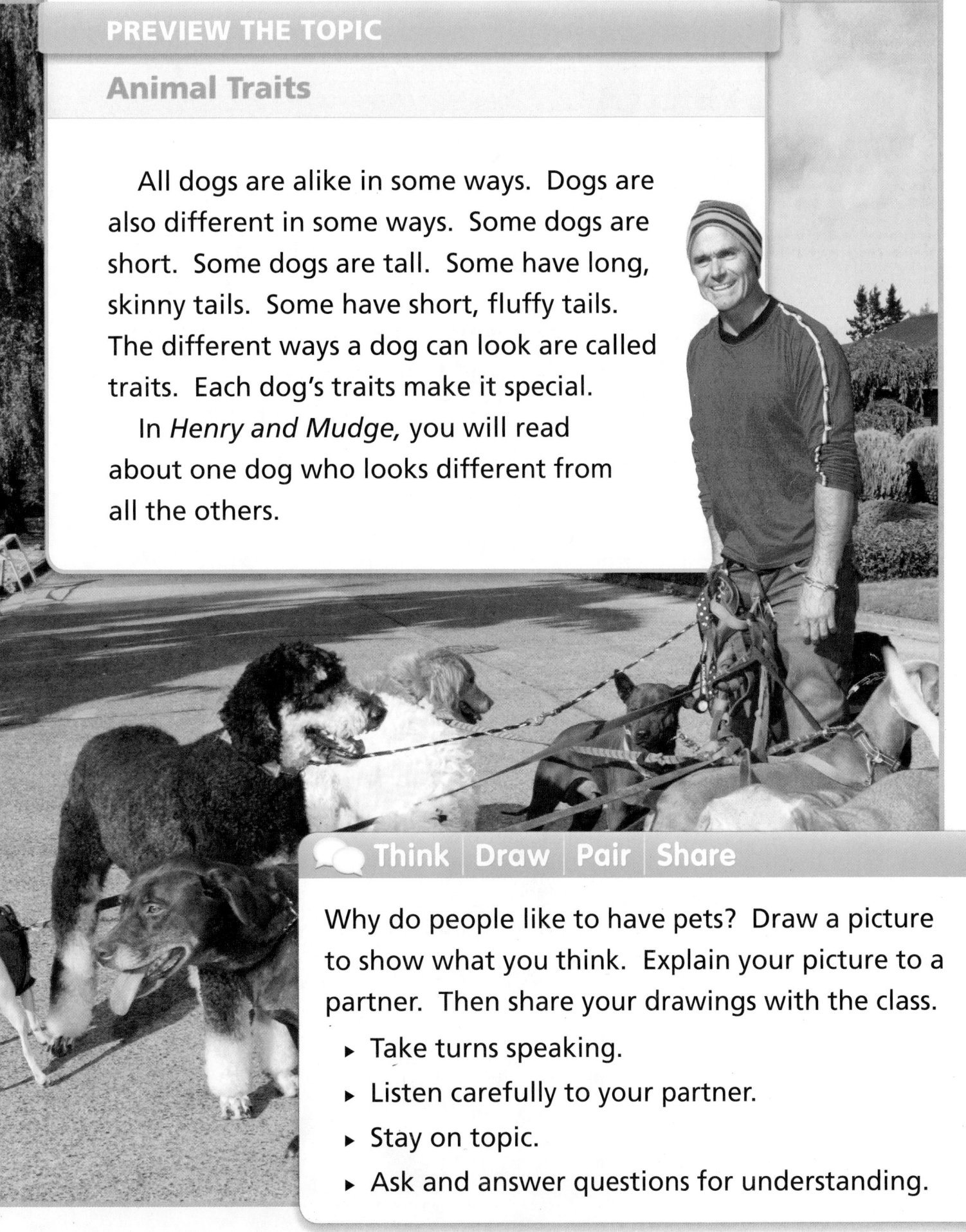

Think | Draw | Pair | Share

Why do people like to have pets? Draw a picture to show what you think. Explain your picture to a partner. Then share your drawings with the class.

- ▸ Take turns speaking.
- ▸ Listen carefully to your partner.
- ▸ Stay on topic.
- ▸ Ask and answer questions for understanding.

13

ANCHOR TEXT

✓ GENRE

Realistic fiction is a story that could happen in real life. As you read, look for:

▶ characters who act like real people

▶ story events that could happen to you or to someone you know

MEET THE AUTHOR

Cynthia Rylant

Henry and Mudge have starred in more than twenty-five books by Cynthia Rylant. A musical based on their adventures once toured the United States. The part of Mudge was played by a grown man in a dog costume!

MEET THE ILLUSTRATOR

Suçie Stevenson

Suçie Stevenson loves drawing the character of Mudge. In fact, she has two big dogs of her own. "They don't drool as much as Mudge," she says.

HENRY and MUDGE

by Cynthia Rylant

illustrated by Suçie Stevenson

ESSENTIAL QUESTION

What is a perfect
pet like?

Henry had no brothers and no sisters.
"I want a brother," he told his parents.
"Sorry," they said.
Henry had no friends on his street.

"I want to live on a different street,"
he told his parents.
"Sorry," they said.
Henry had no pets at home.
"I want to have a dog," he told his parents.
"Sorry," they *almost* said.

But first they looked at their house
with no brothers and sisters.
Then they looked at their street
with no children.
Then they looked at Henry's face.

Then they looked at each other.
"Okay," they said.
"I want to hug you!" Henry told
his parents.
And he did.

ANALYZE THE TEXT

Sequence of Events What
happens after Henry's parents
look at each other?

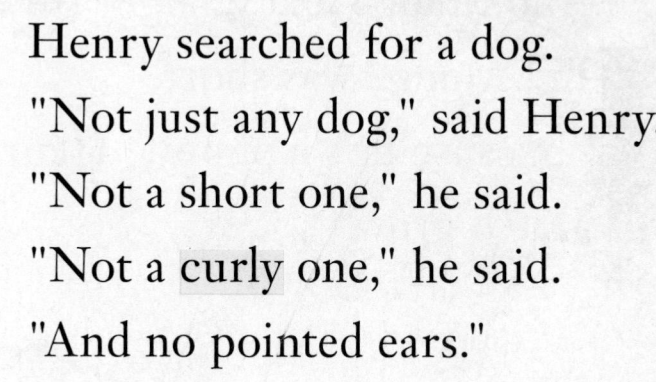

Henry searched for a dog.
"Not just any dog," said Henry.
"Not a short one," he said.
"Not a curly one," he said.
"And no pointed ears."

Then he found Mudge.

Mudge had floppy ears, not pointed.

And Mudge had straight fur, not curly.

But Mudge was short.

"Because he's a puppy," Henry said.

"He'll grow."

ANALYZE THE TEXT

Author's Word Choice What words does the author use to describe Mudge?

And did he ever!
He grew out of his puppy cage.
He grew out of his dog cage.

He grew out of seven collars in a row.
And when he finally stopped growing . . .

he weighed
one hundred eighty pounds,
he stood three feet tall,
and he drooled.
"I'm glad you're not short,"
Henry said.
And Mudge licked him,
then sat on him.

Dig Deeper

Use Clues to Analyze the Text

Use these pages to learn about Sequence of Events and Author's Word Choice. Then read *Henry and Mudge* again. Use what you learn to understand it better.

Sequence of Events

In *Henry and Mudge,* you read about how Henry's family gets Mudge. The author writes about what happens in a certain order. The order of what happens in a story is called the **sequence of events.**

Think about what happens first, next, and last in the story. You can show sequence of events in a chart like the one below.

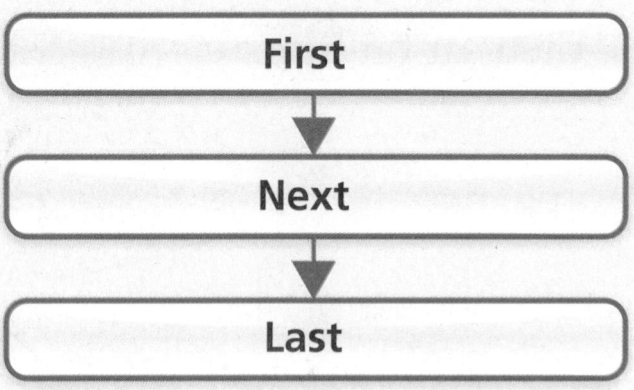

Author's Word Choice

Authors think about which words and phrases to use in a story. Choosing strong words makes the story interesting. Some strong words can help you picture what is happening and what things look like. As you reread the story, think about the words the author uses to tell about Mudge.

Your Turn

What is a perfect pet like? Talk about your ideas with a partner. Take turns talking. Use text evidence from *Henry and Mudge* to tell your ideas. Listen carefully to what your partner says, and ask questions if you don't understand something.

Classroom Conversation

Now talk about these questions with the class.

1 Why did Henry want a dog?

2 What happens as Mudge grows? Find text evidence to explain. Use the words and pictures to tell what happens in order.

3 Do you think Henry and his parents knew how big Mudge would get? Why or why not?

28   ELA RL.2.7, W.2.1, SL.2.1a

WRITE ABOUT READING ·········

Response Think about what Henry asks for at the beginning of the story. Do you think that Henry's parents are right to let him get a dog? Write a few sentences to explain your opinion. Use text evidence from the story to help tell your reasons.

Writing Tip

Use a capital letter at the beginning of each sentence. Use an end mark at the end of each sentence.

INFORMATIONAL TEXT

All in the Family

☑ **GENRE**

Informational text gives facts about a topic.

☑ **TEXT FOCUS**

Headings are titles for different parts of a selection.

All in the Family

by Katherine Mackin

At the San Antonio Zoo, you can see many amazing animals. Some of these animals may have a family member living in your neighborhood!

Different Kinds of **Dogs**

Bush dogs live in Central America and South America. They have straight, brown fur. In the wild, they eat large rodents.

Pet dogs come in all shapes and sizes. They may have floppy ears or curly hair. They eat food made for dogs. Pet dogs should wear collars.

Cats of All Sizes

Lions belong to the cat family. They can grow up to eight feet long. Some have stood four feet tall. Lions hunt big animals in the wild.

Most house cats do not weigh more than fifteen pounds. They mostly eat special food for cats. However, some cats like to hunt for mice or birds.

Large Lizards

Komodo dragons are the largest lizards. They can grow to ten feet long. Some have weighed five hundred pounds! The saliva of a Komodo dragon is dangerous. You would not want to be drooled on by a Komodo dragon!

Little Lizards

Geckos belong to the lizard family. They are about eight inches long. Adult geckos weigh about one to two ounces. Geckos eat insects. They can eat ten crickets in a row.

Compare Texts

TEXT TO TEXT

Compare and Contrast With a partner, pick one of the animals from *All in the Family*. Discuss how that animal is the same as and different from Mudge. Ask questions if you don't understand something your partner says.

TEXT TO SELF

Make a List Henry convinces his parents to get a dog. What reasons does he give? Imagine you want a new pet. List your reasons.

TEXT TO WORLD

Connect to Science Choose an animal from *All in the Family* to research. Make a list of questions and find the answers. Then share the answers with a partner.

ELA RI.2.9, W.2.8

Grammar

Subjects and Predicates The **subject** of a sentence is the naming part. It tells who or what did or does something.

Pam walks her dog.
The boy chooses a pet.

The **predicate** of a sentence is the action part. It tells what the subject did or does.

The dogs pull on a rope.
Ben plays with his dog.

 **Write each sentence. Then circle the subject.**

1 Mel grew tall.

2 My father hugs the dog.

Write each sentence. Draw a line under the predicate.

1 The boys play ball.

2 Susan fed her dog.

When two short sentences have the same predicate, you can put the sentences together. Join them to make one longer sentence. Write *and* between the two subjects. This will make your writing smoother.

Short Sentences

Jim liked the park.

Spot liked the park.

New Sentence with Joined Subjects

Jim and Spot liked the park.

Connect Grammar to Writing

When you revise your sentences, try joining sentences that have the same predicate.

Narrative Writing

☑ **Elaboration** Use details when you write a **true story** about something that happened. Details help your reader picture what you are telling about.

Megan drafted some sentences for a true story. See how she revised her writing to add details.

Writing Checklist

☑ **Organization**
Did I tell about events in an order that makes sense?

☑ **Development**
Does my writing sound like the way I would tell the story?

☑ **Elaboration**
Did I use details to tell the reader more?

☑ **Conventions**
Did I use complete sentences?

Revised Draft

My friend Lucy gave me a beautiful bracelet
with many colorful beads ∧
. She made it. She
∧
calls it a friendship bracelet.

When I wear it I think of my

best friend Lucy.
∧
I love my bracelet!

A Gift

by Megan Stiles

My friend Lucy gave me a beautiful bracelet. She made it with many colorful beads. She calls it a friendship bracelet. When I wear it I think of my best friend Lucy. I love my bracelet!

Reading as a Writer

How do the words that Megan added help you picture what she is telling about? Where can you add details to your true story?

I added details to my final paper to make it more interesting.

mi familia
my family

Family Poetry

Talk About Words
Work with a partner. Choose two Vocabulary words. Use them together in a sentence. Share your sentence with the class.

Vocabulary in Context

▶ Read each **Context Card**.

▶ Place the Vocabulary words in alphabetical order.

1 **remembered**

Mom remembered my birthday. She never forgets.

2 **porch**

They sat outside and talked on the front porch.

3 crown

This girl wears a crown on her head for her birthday.

4 spend

These girls spend time together. They play every day.

5 stuck

While on vacation, their car got stuck in the mud. It can't move.

6 visit

These grandparents like to visit. They see their grandchildren a lot.

7 cousin

My aunt and uncle have three children. Each child is my cousin.

8 piano

The father teaches his child to play the piano, a musical instrument.

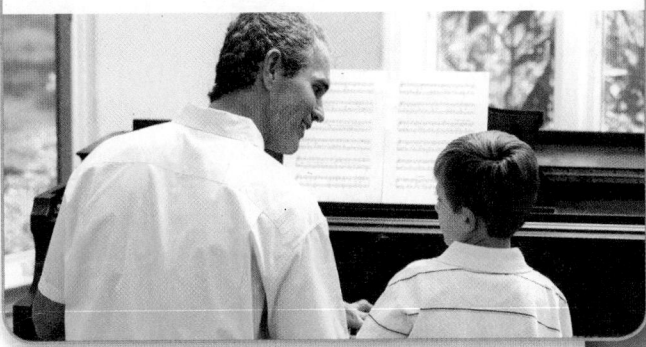

Read and Comprehend

TARGET SKILL

Compare and Contrast In *My Family*, you will find out how the people in a family are alike and different. When you think about how things are alike, you **compare** them. When you think about how things are different, you **contrast** them. You can use a diagram like this one to show how things are alike and different.

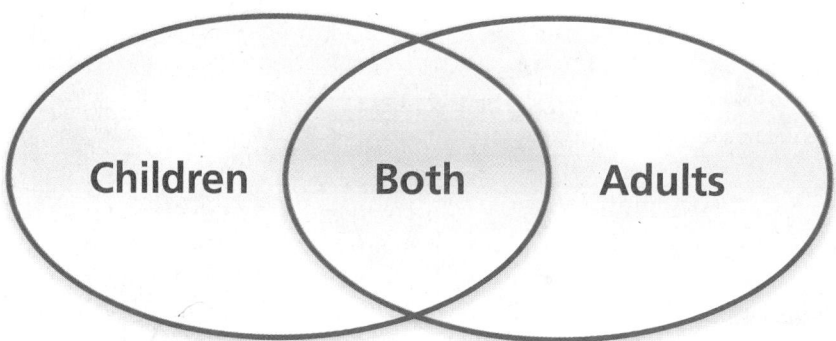

✓ **TARGET STRATEGY**

Question Ask questions about what you are reading.

ELA RI.2.1

Family Time

Families spend time together. They can do many different things. Some families play board games. Some families like to go to the zoo. Others enjoy playing outside. Sometimes families make and eat dinner together. What does your family like to do together?

My Family is about a girl named Camila. You will read about what she likes to do with her family.

Think | Pair | Share

Think about a fun day you spent with your family. Use the sentences below to tell a partner about your fun day. Then share them with the class.

▶ My family had fun when we _____.

▶ It was fun because _____.

▶ My favorite part was when we _____.

41

ANCHOR TEXT

Informational text gives facts about a topic. As you read, look for:

▸ photos
▸ information about real events and people

MEET THE AUTHOR AND PHOTOGRAPHER

George Ancona

George Ancona is often asked if he keeps in touch with the people he photographs. The answer is yes! Not long ago, he heard from the father of the young boy he had photographed for *Pablo Remembers*. Pablo, now grown, was getting married. Mr. Ancona went back to Mexico to go to Pablo's wedding!

My Family

by George Ancona

ESSENTIAL QUESTION

What are some things that families like to do together?

I am Camila. I live in Miami with my
mother, Damaris, my father, Roberto, and my
brother, René. My mother came from Cuba.
My father came from Puerto Rico.

My mother and I go to school together. That's because she teaches Spanish in my school. When we are at home, I like to help her cook dinner.

Sometimes when my Grandma Marta comes to visit, I dress up and put on a show for her. Today she is teaching me a song. It goes like this:

There once was a sailor at sea
who liked to play the guitar.
When he remembered his far away land
he picked his guitar, and started to sing:
On the high sea, on the high sea, on the
high sea. [repeat]

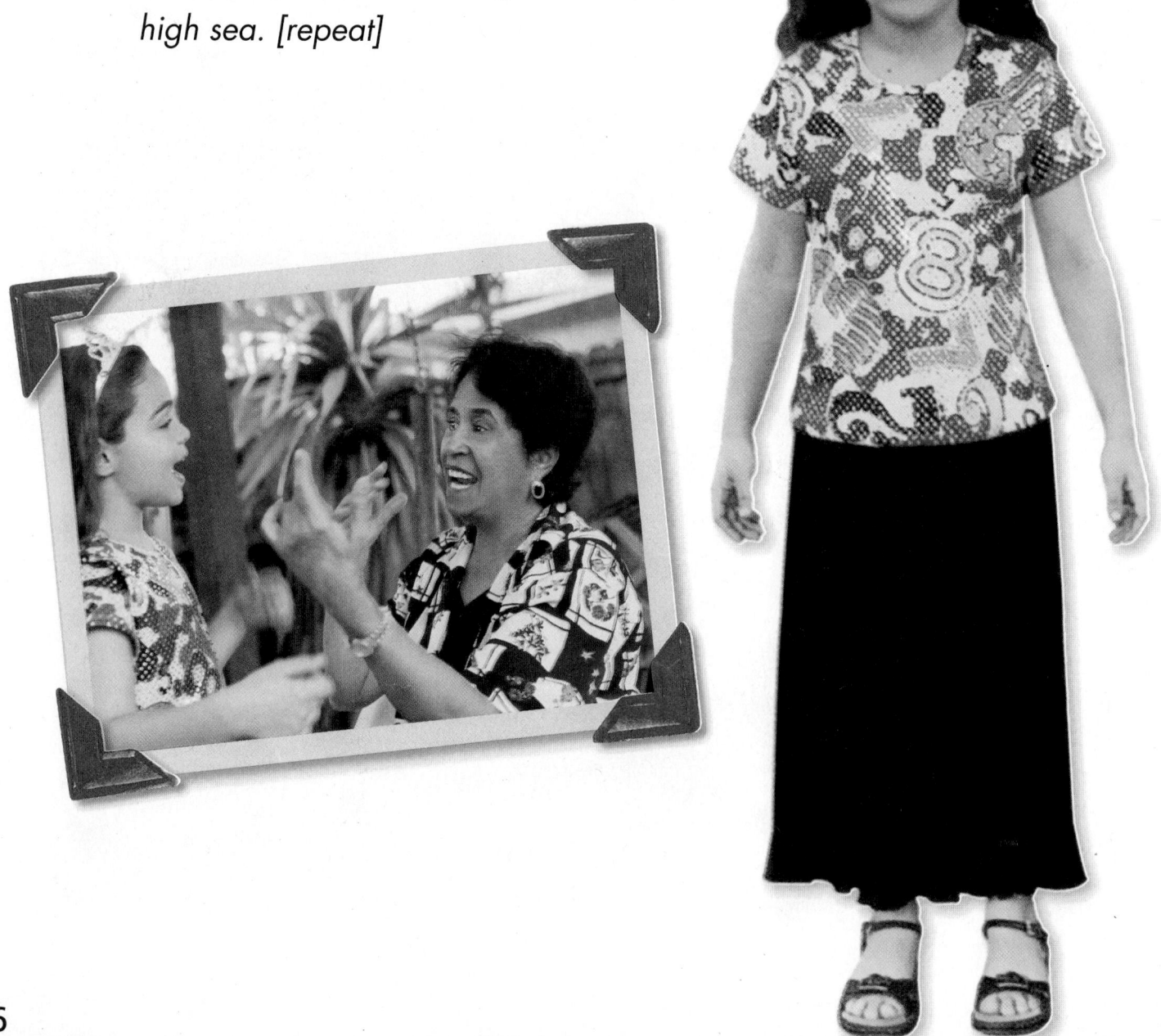

René is my little brother. Our friends and family come to the house for his birthday. We play games, eat, and sing "Happy Birthday" to him.

Here is my family: Grandmother Marta and Grandfather Rigoberto had four children. Almost all of them came to René's birthday party.

Marta & Rigoberto

Andrés & Darleen	María Irene & Victor	Martica & Miguel	Damaris & Roberto	◀ They married:
Victor Mar Isabel	Victoria Valeria Vanesa	Gabriela Leticia	René Camila	And they had these ◀ children:

49

Grandma came with Aunt María Irene and
Victoria. Uncle Andrés came with Victor and Mar
Isabel. Aunt Martica, Uncle Miguel, Gabriela, and
Leticia came too. Soon the house was full.

We played many games. Aunt María Irene showed us how to play hopscotch. Little Leticia put on a crown to dance. Grandpa Rigoberto danced with cousin Mar Isabel.

ANALYZE THE TEXT

Genre: Informational Text
What do you learn about Camila's family from the photos?

51

On Sundays we go to church with Grandma.
Then we all go to Aunt Martica and Uncle Miguel's
house. After lunch we play music and sing.

Uncle Miguel plays the double bass. Uncle Andrés plays the violin. Aunt Darleen plays the piano. Victor plays the clarinet and Mar Isabel plays the flute.

We spend the rest of the day in the backyard. The grown-ups play dominoes while Uncle Andrés tells funny stories. Gabriela and I sit on the porch and paint pictures.

ANALYZE THE TEXT

Compare and Contrast How are the activities of the adults the same as and different from the activities of the children on this page?

What I like best is when Papi takes us fishing. Most of the time my hook gets stuck on a rock. I can't wait to catch my first fish.

Dig Deeper

Use Clues to Analyze the Text

Use these pages to learn about Compare and Contrast and Informational Text. Then read *My Family* again. Use what you learn to understand it better.

Compare and Contrast

In *My Family*, you read about the people in Camila's family. You can **compare** the people in her family by thinking about how they are alike. You can **contrast** them by thinking about how they are different.

Comparing and contrasting can help you understand more about people or ideas. Use a diagram like this one to compare and contrast the children and adults in Camila's family.

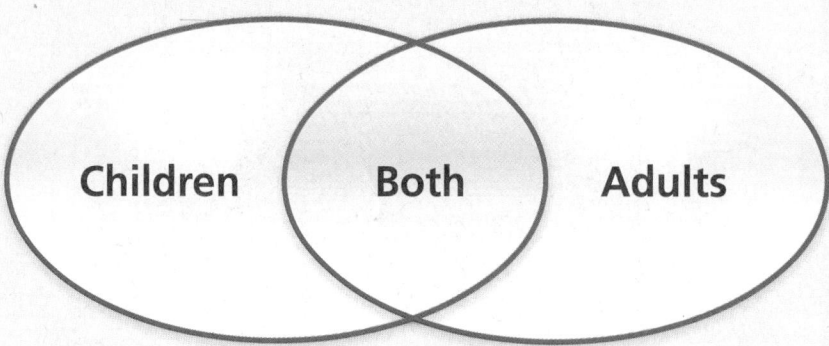

Children   Both   Adults

Genre: Informational Text

The author of an **informational text** tells real information about a topic. Informational text often has photos instead of illustrations. Authors choose photos that tell more about the topic. You can use photos to get more information than you find in the words. Look at page 46. The photos show that Camila is happy to sing the song that Grandma Marta teaches her.

Your Turn

 **What are some things that families like to do together?** Discuss your ideas with a partner. Use text evidence from *My Family* to explain. Take turns talking, and listen carefully when it is your partner's turn to speak.

 **Classroom Conversation**

Now talk about these questions with the class.

1. How are the mother and father in the family the same and different?

2. How does the family tree help you understand Camila's family?

3. What parts of the selection tell you that Camila has a large family?

WRITE ABOUT READING

Response Write about how you think Camila and her family feel about spending time together. Use the words and photos to give text evidence for your answer.

Writing Tip

Make sure that each sentence has a subject and a predicate.

POETRY

Family Poetry

Family Poetry

A family may have parents, brothers, sisters, grandparents, cousins, and more. People in a family visit one another and spend time together. Poets write about these remembered times. Listen to the rhythm of these family poems as you read them.

Everybody Says

Everybody says
I look just like my mother.
Everybody says
I'm the image of Aunt Bee.
Everybody says
My nose is like my father's.
But *I* want to look like *ME!*

by Dorothy Aldis

Abuelita's Lap

I know a place where I can sit
and tell about my day,
tell every color that I saw
from green to cactus gray.

I know a place where I can sit
and hear a favorite beat,
her heart and *cuentos* from the past,
the rhythms honey-sweet.

I know a place where I can sit
and listen to a star,
listen to its silent song
gliding from afar.

I know a place where I can sit
and hear the wind go by,
hearing it spinning round my house,
my whirling lullaby.

by Pat Mora

Grandpa's Stories

The pictures on the television
Do not make me dream as well
As the stories without pictures
Grandpa knows how to tell.

Even if he does not know
What makes a Spaceman go,
Grandpa says back in his time
Hamburgers only cost a dime,
Ice cream cones a nickel,
And a penny for a pickle.

by Langston Hughes

Write a Family Poem

What do you like to do with your family?
Do you tell stories on the porch?
Do you play the piano and sing?
Write a poem about your family.
Use words and phrases that give
your poem rhythm.

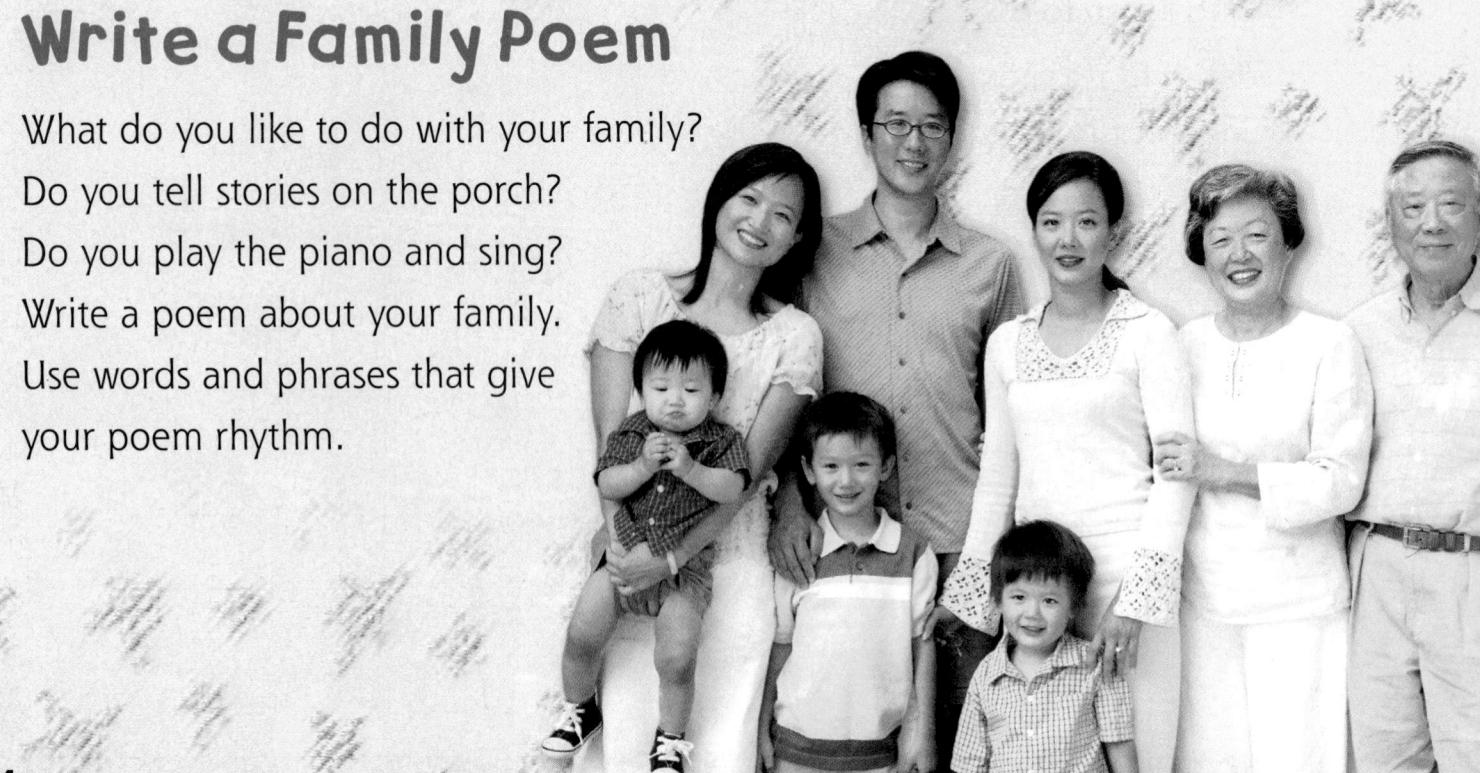

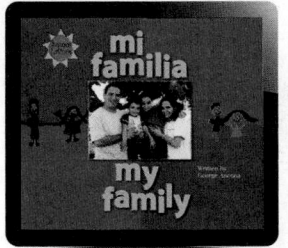

Compare Texts

TEXT TO TEXT

Select a Poem Which poem from *Family Poetry* do you think Camila would say best tells about her family? Share your ideas with a partner.

TEXT TO SELF

Select an Activity Think about what Camila and her family do in *My Family*. Which of these activities would you like to do with a family member? Tell why.

TEXT TO WORLD

Connect to Social Studies Camila's mother came from Cuba. Her father came from Puerto Rico. Now her family lives in Miami. With a partner, find these places on a map. Talk about where you could look to find out more about these places.

ELA RI.2.1

Grammar

Complete Simple Sentences A complete **simple sentence** has both a **subject** and a **predicate.** The subject tells who or what did or does something. The predicate tells what the subject did or does.

Subject	Predicate
Ana	sings.
My older brother	plays the drums.

Try This! **Work with a partner. Read each group of words aloud. Tell which groups of words are sentences.**

❶ Dad cooked.

❷ Harry's birthday.

❸ Ate three slices of cake!

❹ Jen and Bobbi danced.

When you write, use complete sentences. Be sure that simple sentences have a subject and a predicate.

Not Complete Simple Sentences

My family.

Was Auntie Lu's birthday.

Complete Simple Sentences

My family had a party. It was Auntie Lu's birthday.

Connect Grammar to Writing

When you revise your friendly letter, fix any sentences that are not complete. Add a subject or a predicate.

Narrative Writing

✓Development When you write a **friendly letter,** the voice of your letter shows what you are like.

Nestor drafted a letter to his uncle. Then he added words to make the letter sound more like the way he would talk to his uncle.

Writing Checklist

✓ Organization
Did I use the five parts of a friendly letter? Did I tell things in order?

✓ Development
Does the letter sound like me?

✓ Elaboration
Did I use words that tell how I fell?

✓ Conventions
Did I capitalize and punctuate the date, greeting, and closing correctly?

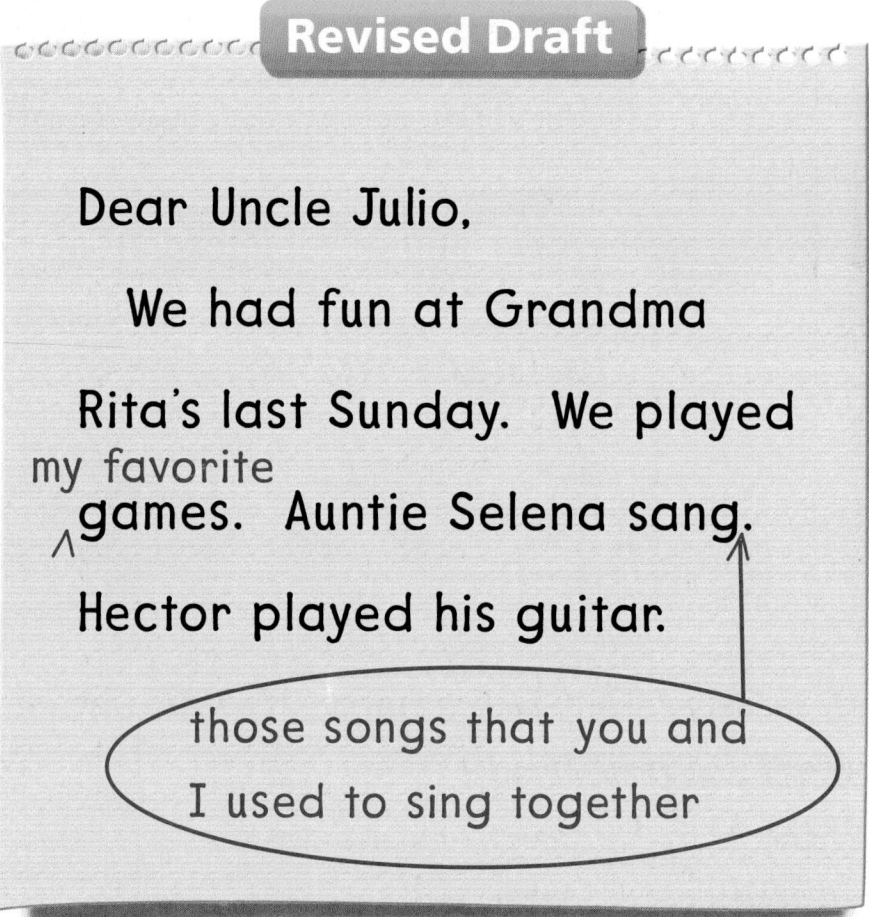

Revised Draft

Dear Uncle Julio,

We had fun at Grandma

Rita's last Sunday. We played
my favorite
∧ games. Auntie Selena sang.

Hector played his guitar.

those songs that you and
I used to sing together

68   ELA W.2.3, L.2.2b

September 24, 2015

Dear Uncle Julio,

We had fun at Grandma Rita's last Sunday. We played my favorite games. Auntie Selena sang those songs that you and I used to sing together. Hector played his guitar. I wish you had been there. Maybe you can come the next time we go to Grandma Rita's. I miss you!

Love,
Nestor

Reading as a Writer

What did Nestor add to let you know how he feels? What can you add to your letter to show your thoughts and feelings?

I added words so my letter sounds like me and shows how I feel.

🔍 **LANGUAGE DETECTIVE**

Talk About Words
Work with a partner. Take turns asking and answering questions about the photos. Share your questions and answers with the class.

Vocabulary in Context

▶ **Read each Context Card.**

▶ **Talk about a picture. Use a different Vocabulary word from the one on the card.**

1 hairy

This dog is very hairy. It has a lot of long fur.

2 mammals

Cats are mammals, but fish are not.

3 litter

These puppies are different colors, but they are from the same litter.

4 stayed

My dog stayed at my cousin's house while we were on vacation.

5 canned

This man chose canned dog food at the pet store.

6 chews

My older brother gets upset when our puppy chews on his shoes!

7 clipped

The lost dog had a name tag clipped to her collar. It helped us find her owner.

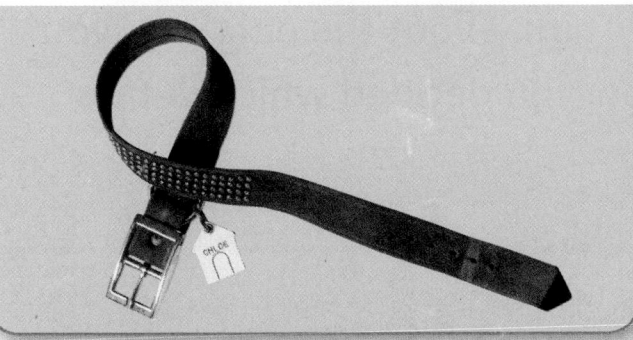

8 coat

This fox has a thick coat that helps it keep warm in the winter.

Read and Comprehend

Author's Purpose An author may write for different reasons. The reason an author writes a selection is called the **author's purpose**. An author's purpose may be to explain something. It could also be to tell a story or to make the reader laugh.

Use text evidence as clues to help you figure out why an author wrote something. You can use a chart like this one to help you.

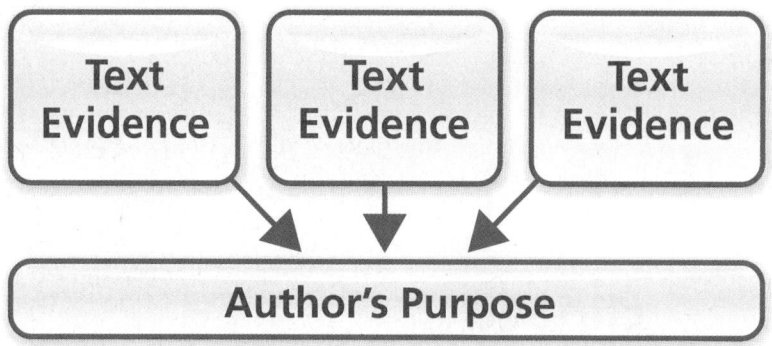

☑ **TARGET STRATEGY**

Analyze/Evaluate Think about the details as you read. Then tell how you decided which details are important.

Animal Traits

Different kinds of pets have different traits. A trait tells something about the way a pet looks or acts. Pets need different kinds of care depending on their traits. For example, a pet cat might have long fur. That cat's owner must brush the fur often. A pet fish lives in water. A fish owner must make sure the water is clean.

Dogs is about having a pet dog. You will read about how to take care of that kind of pet.

💬 Talk About It

Do you think dogs make good pets? Write your opinion. Then talk about your ideas in a group. Be sure to take turns and listen carefully to everyone's ideas.

ANCHOR TEXT

 GENRE

Informational text gives facts about a topic. As you read, look for:

▸ photos
▸ facts and details about a topic
▸ headings that begin a section

MEET THE AUTHOR

Jennifer Blizin Gillis

Jennifer Blizin Gillis wrote her first story in the third grade. It was a mystery story that was four pages long! She has now written lots of books. She has written about pets, people, and even ballroom dancing. Besides writing, she likes to read, work in her garden, and cook. She also takes care of some pets of her own. She has two dogs and a cat.

Dogs

by Jennifer Blizin Gillis

ESSENTIAL QUESTION

What do pets need to be healthy and happy?

75

What Kind of Pet Is This?

Pets are animals that live with us. Some pets are small and have feathers. My pet is big and hairy. Can you guess what kind of pet this is?

What Are Dogs?

Dogs are mammals. Mammals make milk for their babies. Dogs are cousins of wolves and coyotes. Most dogs live with people as pets.

Where Did My Dog Come From?

A mother dog had a litter of puppies. At first, the puppies could not see. The puppies stayed with their mother for eight weeks. Then I took a puppy home.

How Big Is My Dog?

At first, my dog was as small as a cat. It weighed as much as a big bag of sugar. Now my puppy is a dog. It weighs as much as a bicycle.

Where Does My Dog Live?

My dog lives in the house with us. It sleeps on a special dog bed. Sometimes my dog sleeps in my room. It may even sleep on my bed.

What Does My Dog Eat?

My dog eats canned dog food. Sometimes my dog eats dry dog food. My dog chews special bones, too. Chewing the bones helps keep its teeth strong and clean.

What Else Does My Dog Need?

My dog needs a collar and a nametag. These can help me find it if it gets lost. My dog needs a leash, too. The leash is clipped to the collar so my dog can go for a walk.

ANALYZE THE TEXT

Author's Purpose What question does the author want to answer on this page?

What Can I Do For My Dog?

I play with my dog every day. Playing is good exercise for dogs. I brush my dog with a special brush. This keeps its coat clean and smooth.

What Can My Dog Do?

My dog can play fetch. When I throw a ball, it brings it back. My dog can help at home. It can bring in the newspaper.

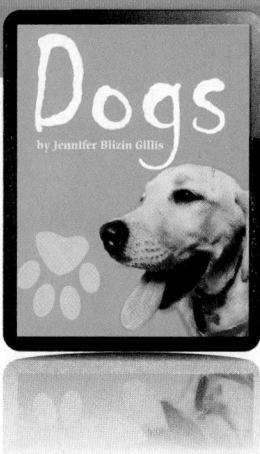

Dig Deeper

Use Clues to Analyze the Text

Use these pages to learn about Author's Purpose and Compare and Contrast. Then read *Dogs* again. Use what you learn to understand it better.

Author's Purpose

Dogs is about how to care for a pet dog. The author wrote this selection for a reason. The reason an author writes is the **author's purpose.** The author may write to help you learn about something or to make you smile.

As you read, think about why the author wrote *Dogs*. Use a chart like the one below to list text evidence. Use the evidence to help you figure out what the author wants you to know.

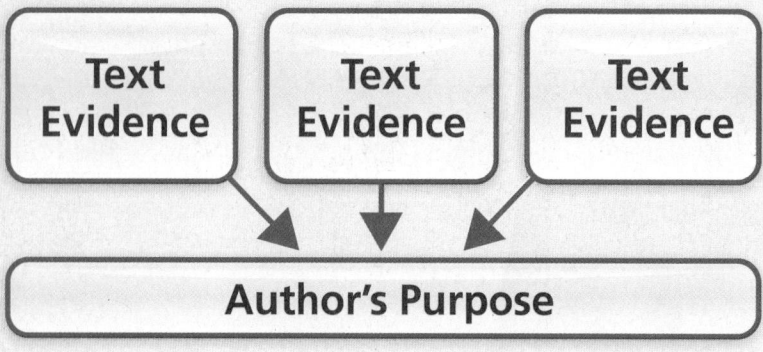

ELA RI.2.3, RI.2.6

Compare and Contrast

Sometimes an author tells how things are the same and different. For example, an author may tell how two animals are the same and different. Telling how things are the same is called **comparing**. Telling how things are different is called **contrasting**. As you read, compare and contrast to help you understand ideas from the text.

Your Turn

What do pets need to be healthy and happy?
Think about what you read in *Dogs*. Then talk with a partner about your ideas. Use text evidence to explain your thoughts. Ask questions if you do not understand what your partner says.

Classroom Conversation

Now talk about these questions with the class.

1 What does the author want you to learn about dogs? Give text evidence to explain.

2 How do people take care of their dogs?

3 Why do people have dogs as pets?

WRITE ABOUT READING

Response Would you like to care for a dog as a pet? Write a few sentences to tell your opinion. Use evidence from the text to help you explain.

Writing Tip

In the first sentence, tell if you would or would not like a dog. Tell your reasons in the other sentences.

Helping Paws

Helping Paws

Most people think of dogs as pets. For many people, dogs are family helpers! Some dogs help people who have disabilities. They give care to people who need it.

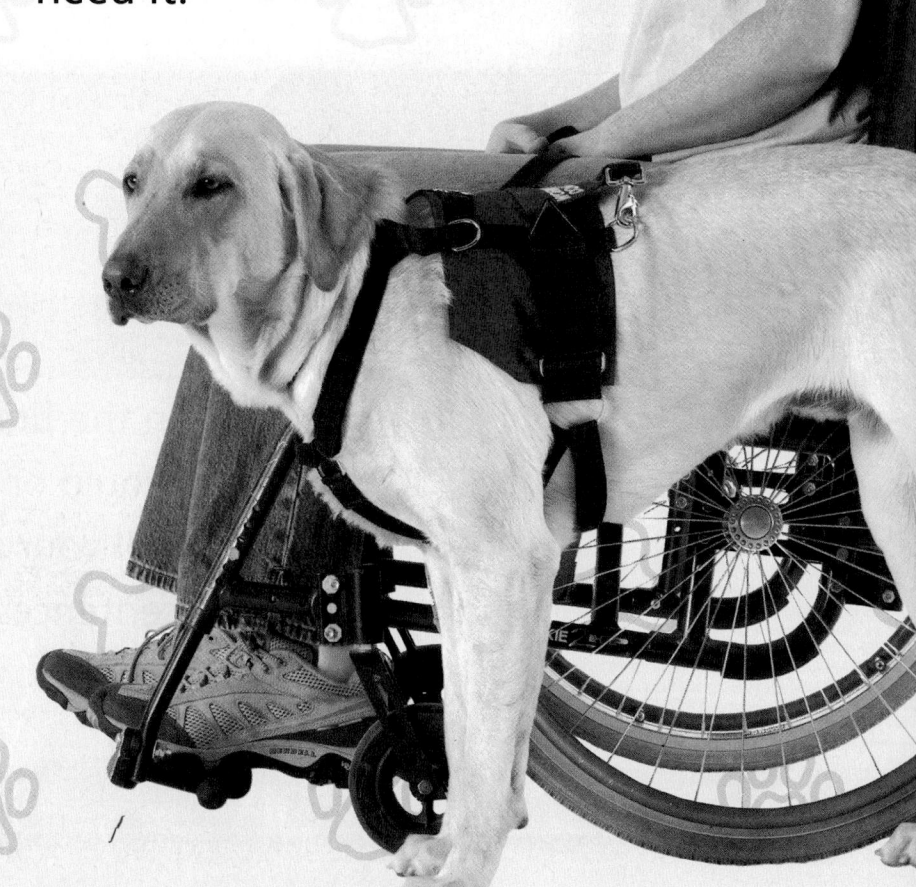

Hearing Ear Dogs

Hearing ear dogs help people who are deaf or who cannot hear well. These dogs listen for important sounds at home. An alarm clock and a doorbell are important sounds. When the dogs hear these sounds, they touch their owners with their noses. This gets their owners' attention. When hearing ear dogs are outside with their owners, they listen for sounds that could mean danger. They help keep their owners safe.

Hearing Ear Dogs Are Helpers

- They listen for important sounds inside and outside.

- They let their owners know if there is danger.

Hearing ear dogs listen for the ring of a telephone or the sound of a smoke detector.

Guide Dogs Are Helpers

- Guide dogs help their owners walk safely.
- They follow directions to help their owners.

Guide Dogs

Guide dogs help people who are blind or cannot see well. A guide dog learns sights, sounds, and smells of busy places. Guide dogs can go anywhere their owners need to go. They follow directions from their owners.

Make sure not to pet a guide dog when it is working.

Compare Texts

TEXT TO TEXT

Write a Paragraph How would page 81 of *Dogs* be written if the selection were about Mudge? With a partner, rewrite the paragraph to be about Mudge.

TEXT TO SELF

Share Experiences Think about the dogs in *Helping Paws*. How do the pets that live with you or near you help people? Share your ideas with a partner.

TEXT TO WORLD

Share Ideas What else can pets do to help their owners? Write a few sentences to tell your ideas.

ELA W.2.2, W.2.3, SL.2.4

Grammar

Digital Resources

▶ Multimedia Grammar Glossary

▶ GrammarSnap Videos

Kinds of Sentences A **statement** tells something. A **command** gives an order. They each end with a period. An **exclamation** shows strong feeling. It ends with an exclamation point. A **question** asks something. It ends with a question mark.

Statement	Some dogs can be trained to help people.
Question	Can a dog help a person who is deaf?
Command	Do not pet a working guide dog.
Exclamation	She is a great guide dog!

Try This! **Decide whether each sentence is a statement, a command, an exclamation, or a question. Write each sentence with the correct end mark.**

1 What did the dog hear

2 Be careful when you cross a street

3 Guide dogs help keep their owners safe

4 His guide dog is so helpful

Using different kinds of sentences makes your writing more interesting to read. You can change one kind of sentence to another by moving or adding words.

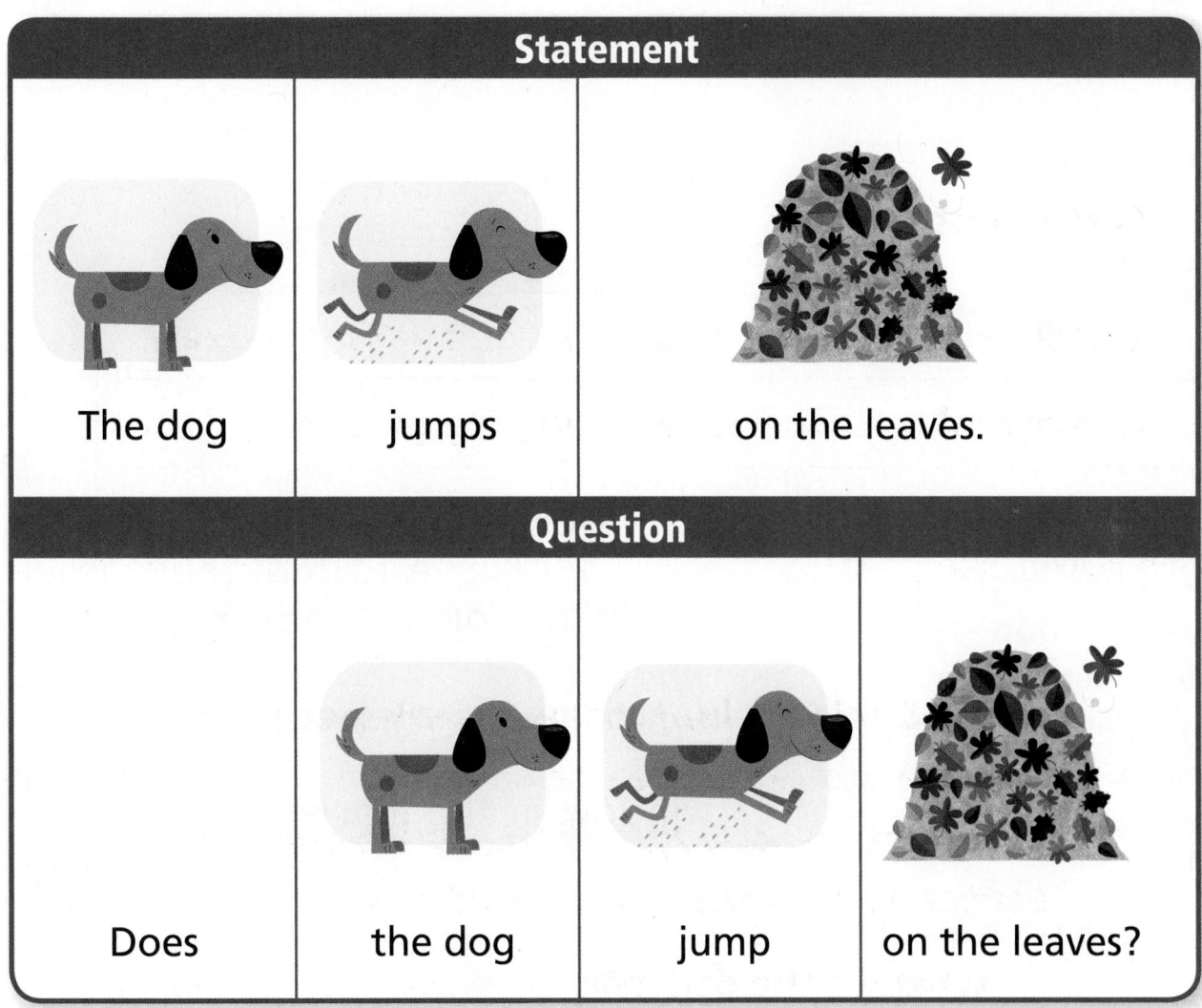

Statement		
The dog	jumps	on the leaves.

Question		
Does	the dog	jump	on the leaves?

Connect Grammar to Writing

When you revise your writing, try using different kinds of sentences to make your writing more interesting.

Narrative Writing

✓ **Elaboration** You can make a **description** more interesting when you use sense words to tell how things look, feel, smell, sound, and taste.

Nadia drafted a paragraph that describes where she lives. Later, she added sense words.

Writing Checklist

✓ **Purpose**
Did I tell about where I live?

✓ **Organization**
Did I tell things in an order that makes sense?

✓ **Elaboration**
Did I use sense words to tell more?

✓ **Conventions**
Did I use different kinds of sentences?

Revised Draft

little green   big blue
I live in a house near a lake.
            ^   ^

I love our house. You can see
                I love to feel the warm
the lake from our porch. ~~The~~
when it
sun comes in my bedroom
      ^

window in the morning.

My House
by Nadia Krimsky

I live in a little green house near a big blue lake. I love our house. You can see the lake from our porch. I love to feel the warm sun when it comes in my bedroom window in the morning. Do you know what wakes me up? The birds start chirping. I smell the pancakes my dad makes. They taste so good that I always ask for more! I want to live in this house for a long time.

Reading as a Writer

Which sense words did Nadia add? What sense words can you add to your writing?

I used sense words to tell the reader more about how things look, feel, smell, taste, and sound.

By Doreen Cronin · Pictures by Harry Bliss

DIARY OF A SPIDER

A SWALLOW AND A SPIDER

🔍 LANGUAGE DETECTIVE

Talk About Words
Work with a partner. Read the sentences on the Context Cards. Choose one of the sentences. Take out the Vocabulary word. Put in a word that means the same or almost the same thing. Tell how the sentences are the same and how they are different.

Vocabulary in Context

▶ **Read each Context Card.**

▶ **Ask a question that uses one of the Vocabulary words.**

1 insects
Ants, flies, and bees are all insects. They all have six legs.

2 dangerous
Be careful! A bee sting can be dangerous. It makes some people sick.

3 scare

Cockroaches will run away if you scare them. They frighten easily.

4 sticky

A spider web is sticky. Bugs get caught, and they can't fly away.

5 rotten

A housefly eats rotten, or spoiled, food.

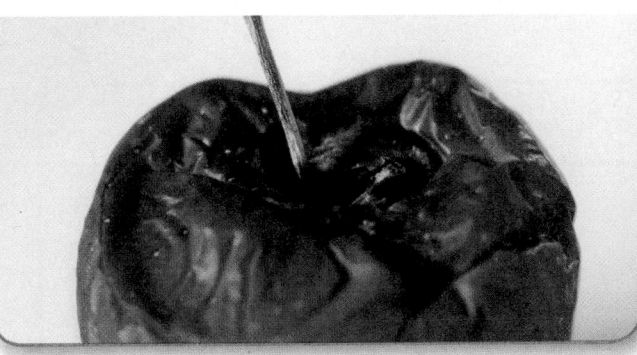

6 screaming

If you see a wasp, walk away quietly. Don't run away screaming.

7 breeze

A ladybug came in when a breeze blew open the window curtains.

8 judge

Look carefully before you judge, or decide, what this picture shows.

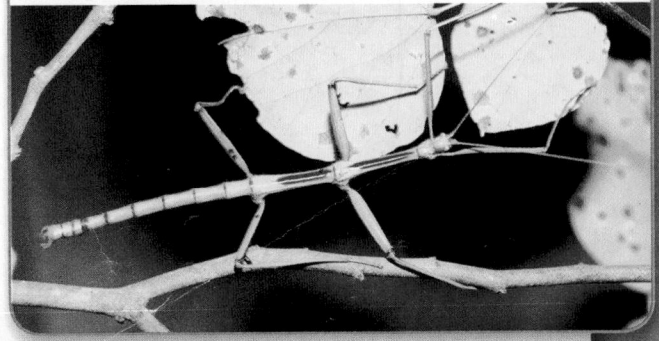

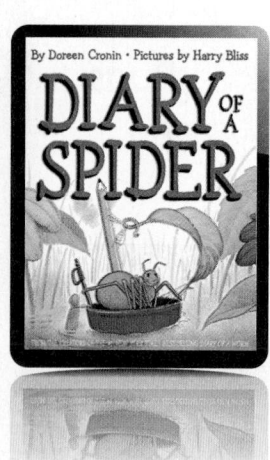

By Doreen Cronin · Pictures by Harry Bliss

DIARY OF A SPIDER

Read and Comprehend

☑ TARGET SKILL

Cause and Effect Some people see a spider and get scared. The two events are linked. Seeing the spider is the **cause**. Becoming scared is the **effect**.

Look at the words and pictures in a story to figure out what happens and why. You can use a chart like the one below to list causes and effects.

Cause	Effect

☑ TARGET STRATEGY

Summarize Stop to tell important events as you read.

ELA RL.2.7, SL.2.1a, SL.2.1c

Getting Along with Others

Diary of a Spider is a made-up story about a spider who is friends with a fly. Think about why it might be hard for a spider and a fly to be friends. For one thing, a fly spends a lot of time in the air, but a spider can't fly. Also, a fly might get caught in a spider's web. Spider and Fly have fun together even though they are different. They learn to work around their differences to get along together.

 Think | Pair | Share

How can friends who like different things have fun together? Talk about your ideas with a partner. Then share with the class.

- ▶ Take turns speaking.
- ▶ Listen carefully to your partner.
- ▶ Stay on topic.
- ▶ Ask and answer questions for understanding.

Lesson 4

ANCHOR TEXT

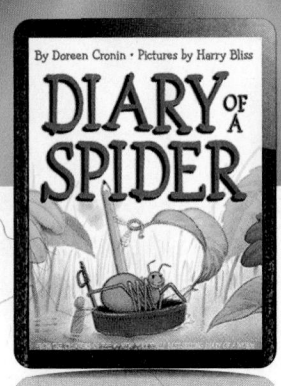

By Doreen Cronin · Pictures by Harry Bliss
DIARY OF A SPIDER

 **GENRE**

Humorous fiction is a story that is written to make the reader laugh. As you read, look for:

▶ characters who do or say funny things

▶ events that would not happen in real life

MEET THE AUTHOR

Doreen Cronin

Two spiders have moved into Doreen Cronin's office, but she says she cannot bring herself to get rid of them. If you like *Diary of a Spider*, check out Ms. Cronin's other books, *Diary of a Worm* and *Diary of a Fly*.

MEET THE ILLUSTRATOR

Harry Bliss

Whenever Harry Bliss visits classrooms, he asks students to scribble on the board. He then turns their scribbles into an animal, a tree, or a cartoon character. This scribble game helps kids use their imagination.

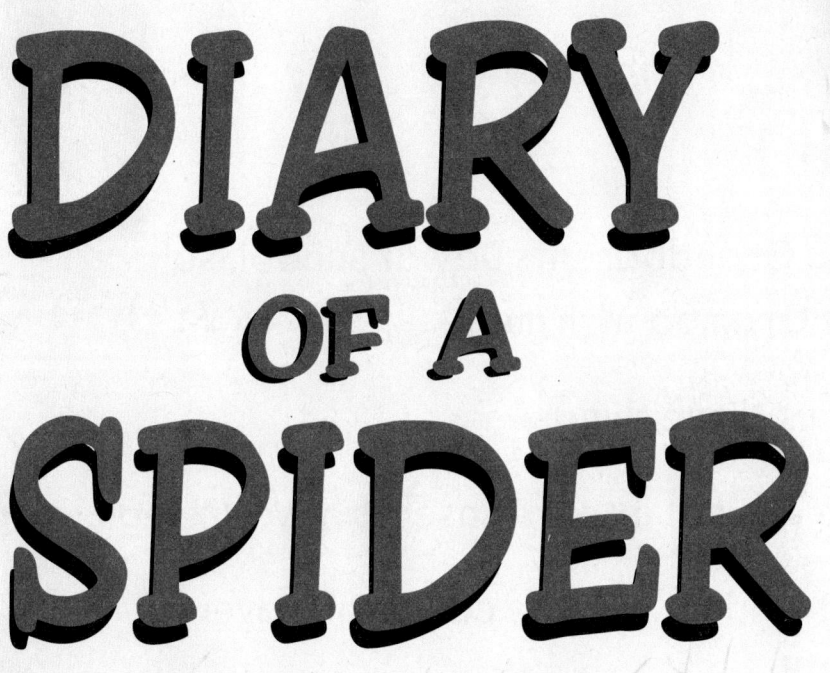

DIARY
OF A
SPIDER

by Doreen Cronin
pictures by Harry Bliss

MARCH 1

Today was Grandparents Day at school, so
I brought Grampa with me.

He taught us three things:

1. Spiders are not insects—insects have six legs.

2. Without spiders, insects could take over
   the world.

3. Butterflies taste better with a little
   barbecue sauce.

MARCH 16

Grampa says that in his day, flies and spiders did not get along.

Things are different now.

MARCH 29

Today in gym class we learned how to catch the wind so we could travel to faraway places.

When I got home, I made up flash cards so I
could practice:

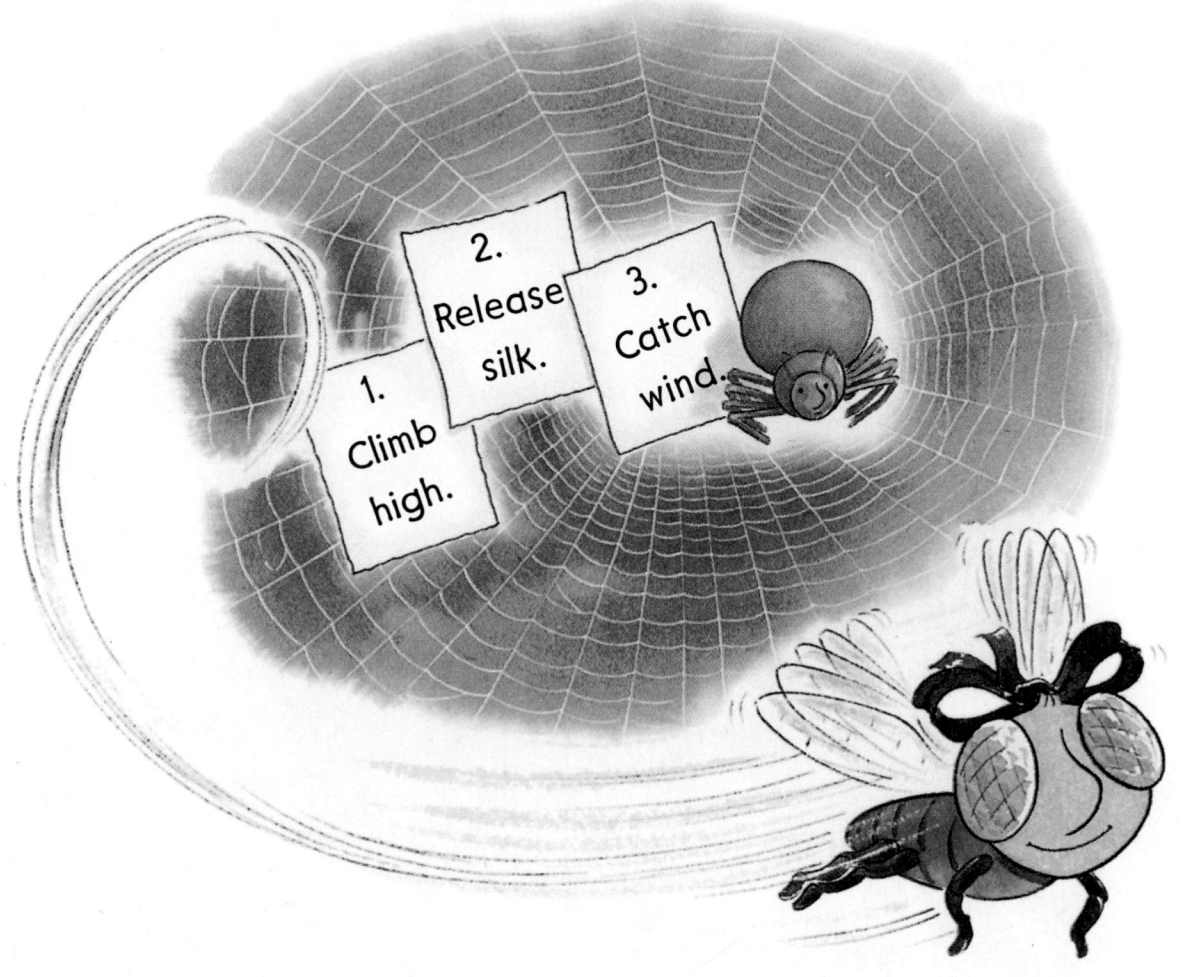

1.
Climb
high.

2.
Release
silk.

3.
Catch
wind.

Fly made up her own flash card:

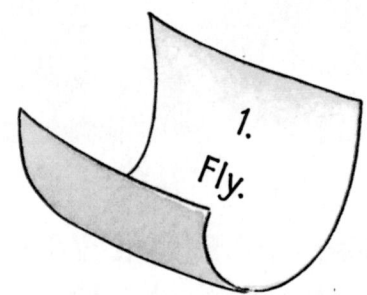

1.
Fly.

I'm starting to see why
Grampa doesn't like her.

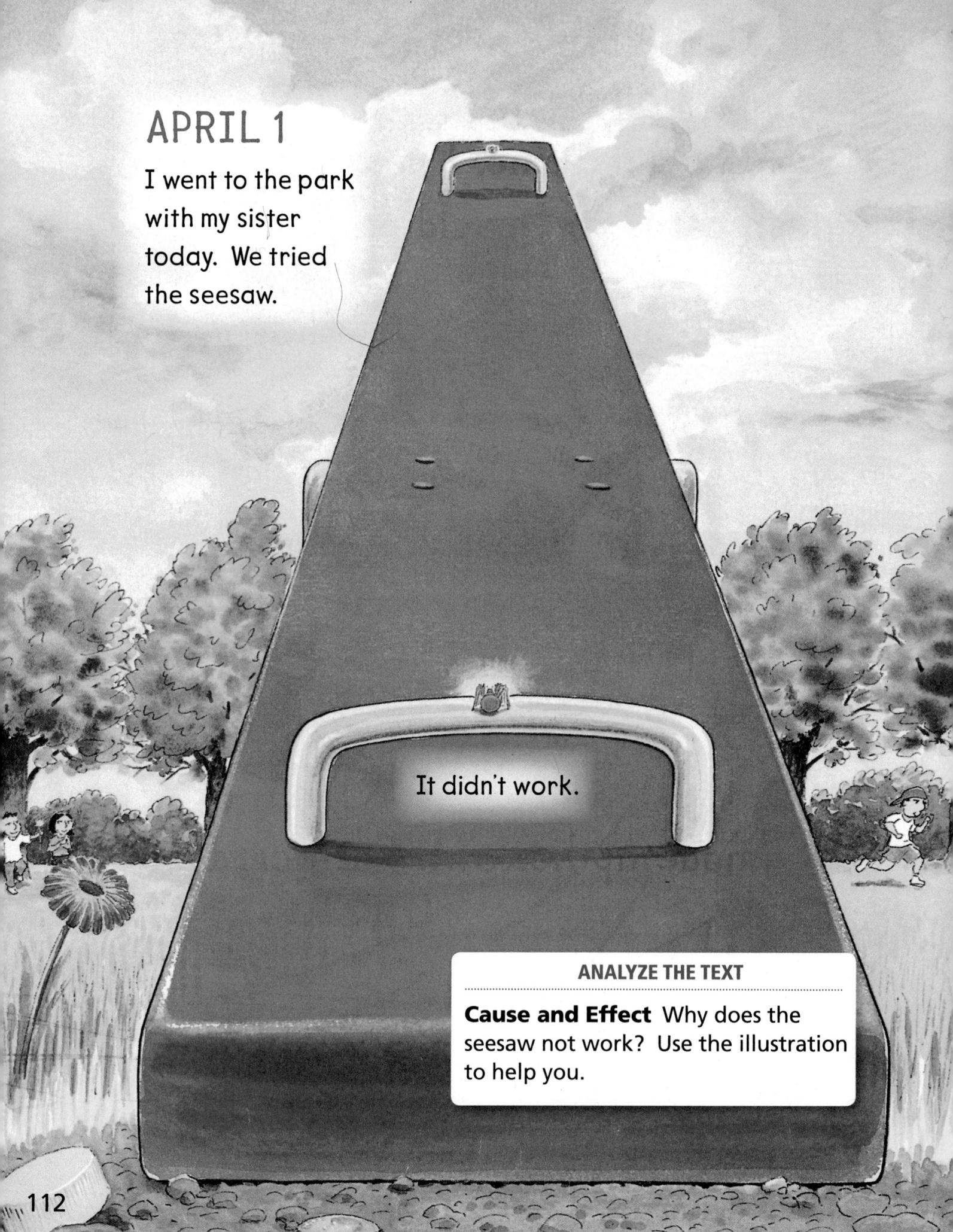

APRIL 1

I went to the park with my sister today. We tried the seesaw.

It didn't work.

ANALYZE THE TEXT

Cause and Effect Why does the seesaw not work? Use the illustration to help you.

We tried the tire swing.

It didn't work.

We spun a huge sticky web on the water fountain.

That worked.

EEEEEEK!

APRIL 12

Today was Safety Day at school. We learned that vacuums eat spiderwebs and are very, very dangerous. If we hear a vacuum, we should Stop, Drop, and Run.

APRIL 13

We had a vacuum drill today.
I stopped what I was doing.

Forgot where I was going.

And ran screaming from the room.

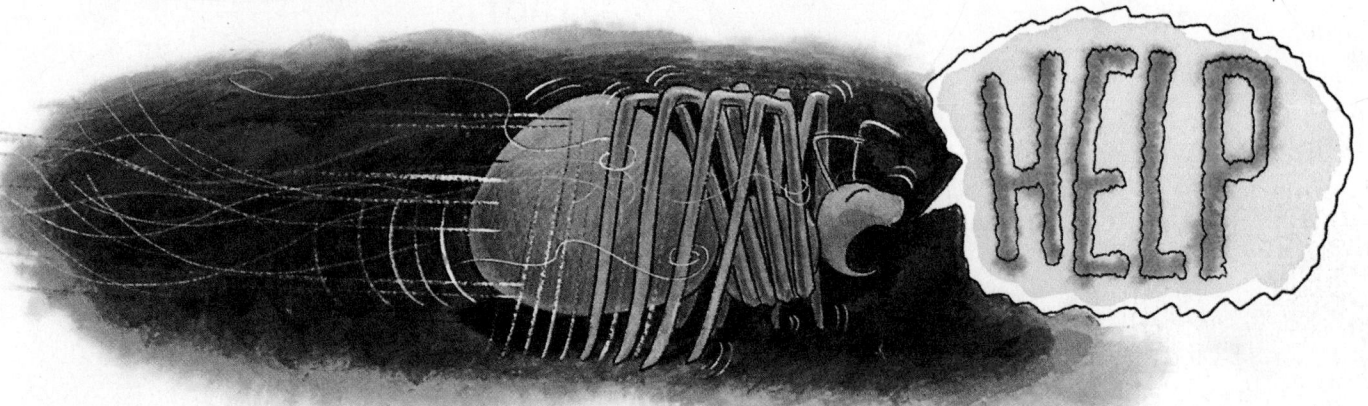

We're having another drill tomorrow.

APRIL 17

I'm sleeping over at Worm's house tonight. I hope they don't have leaves and rotten tomatoes for dinner again.

MAY 7

Mom said I was getting too big for my own skin. So I molted.

MAY 8

Today was show-and-tell. So I brought in my old skin. My teacher called on it to lead the Pledge of Allegiance.

JUNE 5

Daddy Longlegs made fun of Fly because she eats with her feet. Now she won't come out of her tree house.

I'm going to find him and give him a piece of my mind!

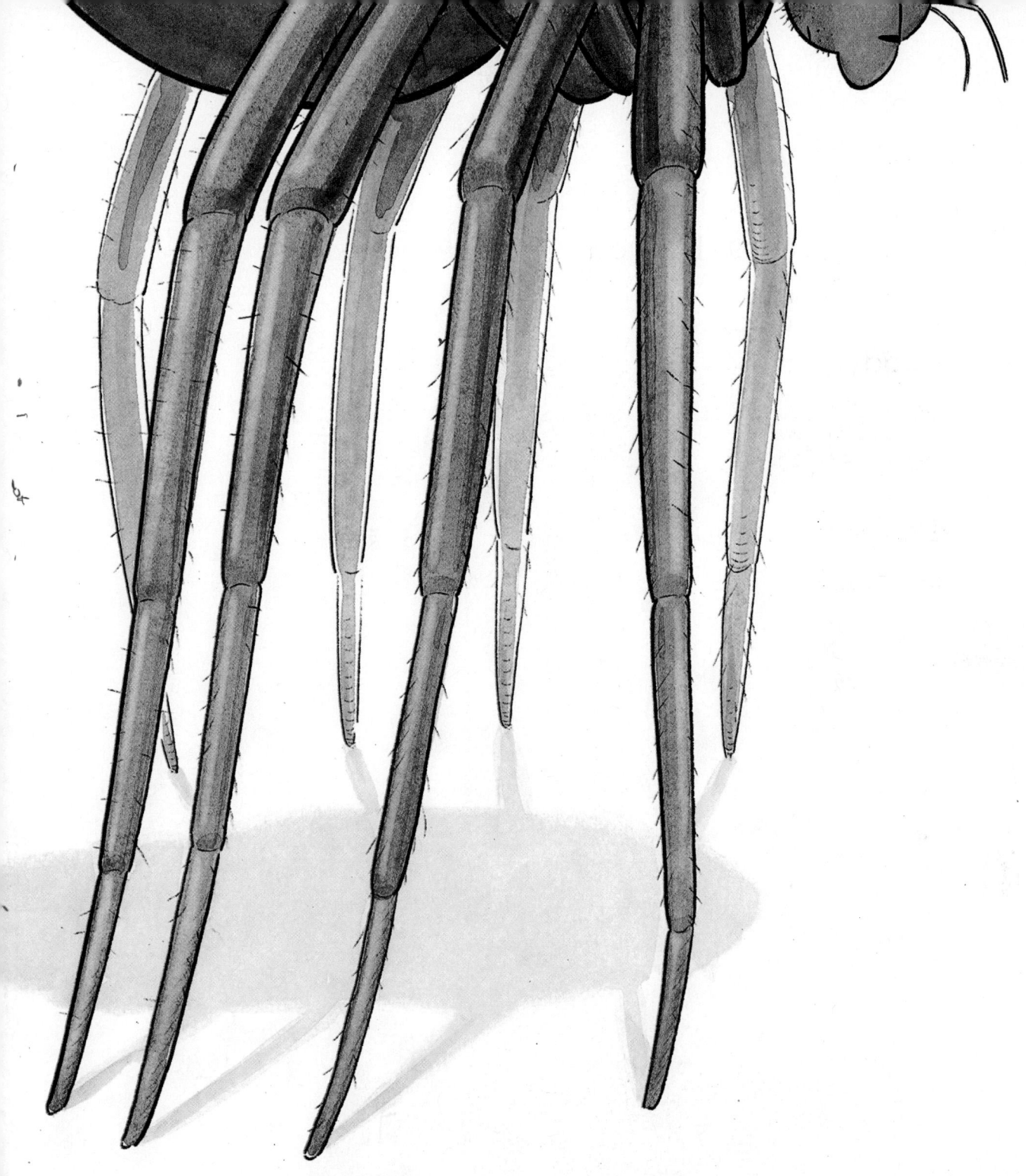

JUNE 6

I found Daddy Longlegs. He's a lot bigger than
I thought he was.

I gave him a piece of my lunch instead.

JUNE 7

Fly's tree house blew away in the wind today.

So did Grampa.

JUNE 18

I got a postcard from Grampa today:

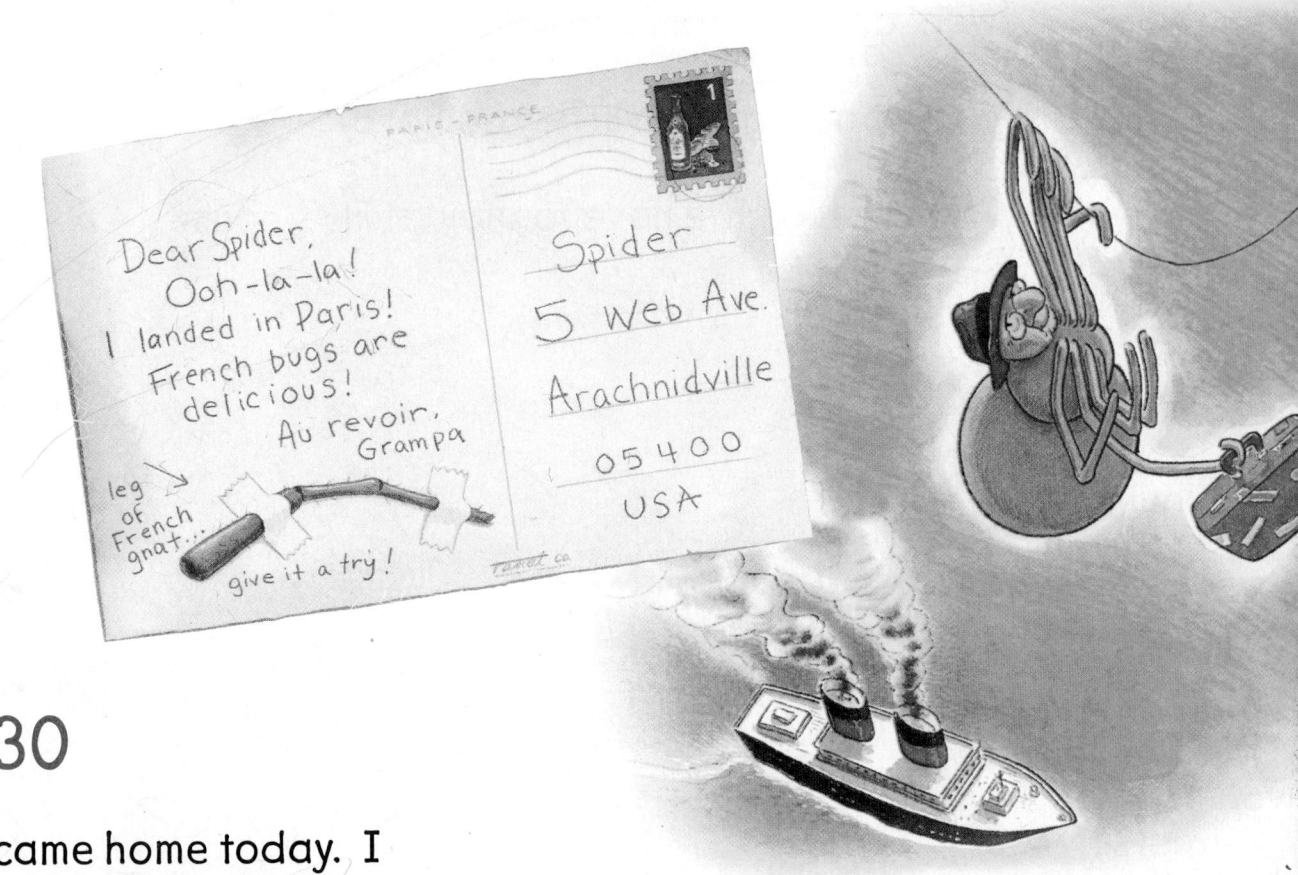

Dear Spider,
Ooh-la-la!
I landed in Paris!
French bugs are delicious!
Au revoir,
Grampa

leg of French gnat...
give it a try!

Spider
5 Web Ave.
Arachnidville
05400
USA

JUNE 30

Grampa came home today. I couldn't wait to hear about how he rode the winds all the way over the ocean!

Turns out, he caught a breeze to the airport and napped in first class.

ANALYZE THE TEXT

Personification What does Grampa do that makes him seem like a person? Use the words and the pictures to help you answer.

121

JULY 2

Fly came over to play today. She got stuck in our web, and her mom had to come get her.

Grampa laughed a little too hard.

From now on, we have to play at Fly's house.

JULY 9

Today was my birthday. Grampa decided I was old enough to know the secret to a long, happy life:

Never fall asleep in a shoe.

JULY 16

Things I scare:

1. Fly's mom

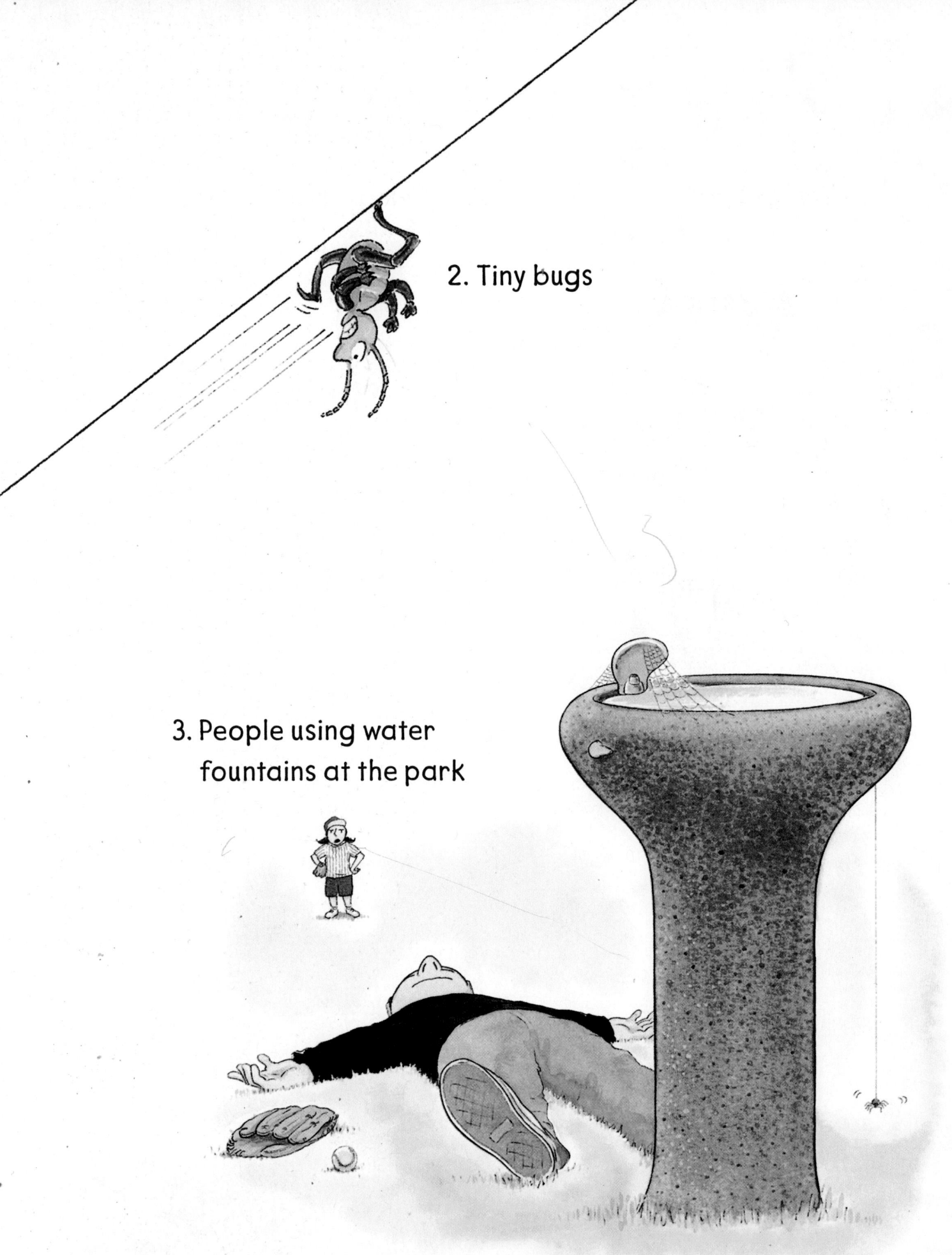

2. Tiny bugs

3. People using water
   fountains at the park

JULY 17

Things that scare me:

1. Daddy Longlegs

2. Vacuums

3. People with big feet

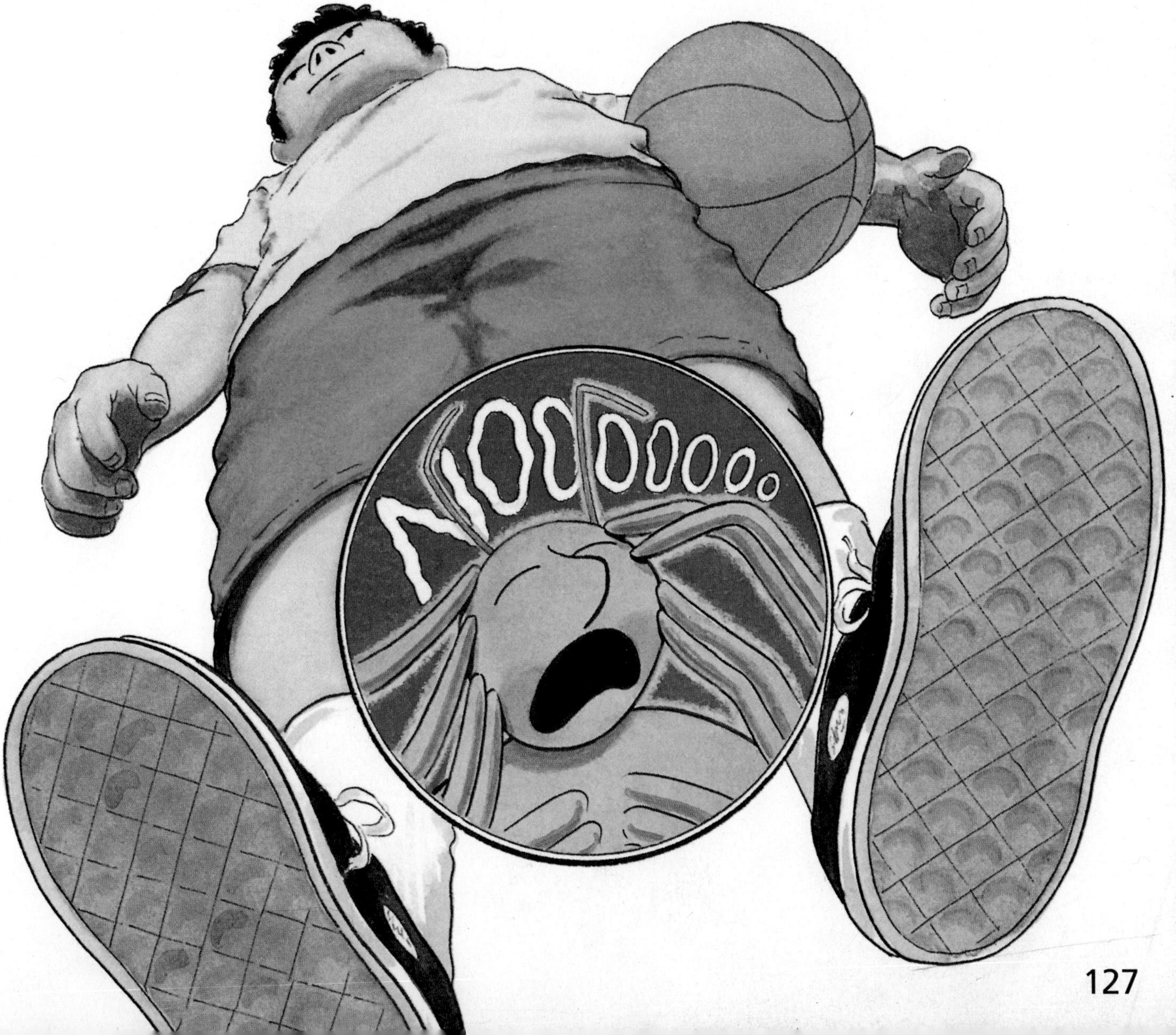

AUGUST 1

I wish that people wouldn't judge all spiders based on the few spiders that bite.

I know if we took the time to get to know each other, we would get along just fine.

Just like me and Fly.

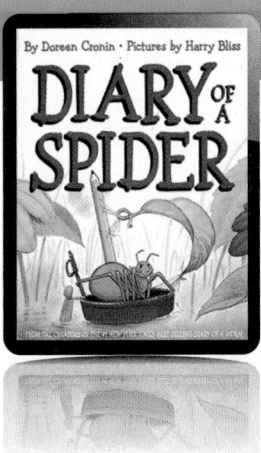

Dig Deeper

Use Clues to Analyze the Text

Use these pages to learn about Cause and Effect and Personification. Then read *Diary of a Spider* again. Use what you learn to understand it better.

Cause and Effect

Diary of a Spider is a funny story about Spider and his friend, Fly. In the story, one event makes another happen. For example, Spider gets too big for his skin, so he sheds it. Spider getting too big is the **cause**. Spider shedding his skin is the **effect**.

When you read, ask questions about the words and pictures to figure out what happens and why. Use a chart to list text evidence of causes and effects.

Cause	Effect

Personification

Sometimes an author will make animals or objects in a story act or speak like people. For example, an animal might wear clothing that a person would wear. This is called **personification**. Look back at page 111. Spider makes flash cards to help him study. Since spiders don't write, this is an example of personification.

Your Turn

How do good friends act?
Find text evidence from the words and pictures in the story. Talk about your ideas with a small group. Let everyone take a turn speaking.

Classroom Conversation

Now talk about these questions with the class.

1. What events in the story cause other events to happen?

2. What problems do Spider and Fly work around in order to be friends?

3. What are some important lessons that Spider learns? Explain your answer with text evidence.

WRITE ABOUT READING

Response By the end of the story, Spider has learned many important things. Write about one important lesson that Spider learns. Give text evidence to tell why you think it is important.

Writing Tip

Use the word *because* to link your reasons to your opinion.

A
SWALLOW
AND A
SPIDER

✓ GENRE

A **fable** is a short story in which a character learns a lesson.

✓ TEXT FOCUS

The **moral** of a fable is the lesson that a character learns. As you read, find the moral of the story.

Readers' Theater

A SWALLOW AND A SPIDER

A FABLE FROM AESOP

retold by Sheila Higginson

Cast of Characters

Narrator   **Spider**   **Swallow**

~~~~~~~~~~~~~~~~~~

Narrator: A spider sat in her sticky web, waiting for dinner.

Spider: I hope some insects will stop by soon.

Narrator: Spider heard the buzz of flies floating in the breeze.

Swallow: Look at those juicy flies!

Narrator: Before the flies could reach her web, they were scooped up in Swallow's beak.

Spider: Swallow is a pest! I will show him what I can do!

Narrator: Spider worked for a whole week. She spun a huge web.

Spider: Swallow doesn't scare me. I may be small, but I am dangerous, too!

Narrator: Spider put some berries in the middle of the web.

Spider: Swallow will smell these berries. Then he will get stuck in my net!

135

Narrator: Spider watched and waited, waited and watched.

Swallow: I smell something delicious. Those berries are just waiting for me!

Spider: Those berries aren't for you! Don't eat them! They are rotten.

Narrator: Swallow scooped up the berries and flew right through spider's web! He didn't even hear spider screaming at him!

Spider: I can judge what I am good at doing. I am good at building webs to catch insects, but I am not a good bird-catcher. I'll go back to my web to wait for a juicy fly.

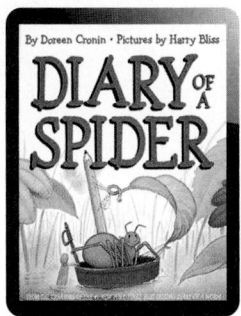

Compare Texts

TEXT TO TEXT

Compare and Contrast Spider and Fly in *Diary of a Spider* are friends. How is this different from how the characters feel about each other in *A Swallow and a Spider*? Share your thoughts with a partner.

TEXT TO SELF

Think About the Moral Think about the moral in *A Swallow and a Spider*. Does this moral apply to your life? Why or why not? Discuss your thoughts and feelings about it with a partner.

TEXT TO WORLD

Connect to Science Make a poster to teach your classmates about real spiders. Talk with a partner about what the spiders are like in *Diary of a Spider* and *A Swallow and a Spider*. Use the stories or science books to help you.

Spider

Grammar

What Is a Noun? A **noun** is a word that names a person, an animal, a place, or a thing.

People	Animals
grandfather girl friend	spider fly bird

Places	Things
home school park	web vacuum tomato

Try This! **Work with a partner. Find the noun in each sentence. Tell whether it is a person, an animal, a place, or a thing.**

❶ Our swing did not move.

❷ The worm sleeps.

❸ My teacher is nice.

❹ The airport is big.

When you write, use exact nouns to paint a picture in your reader's mind. An exact noun gives more information about a person, an animal, a place, or a thing.

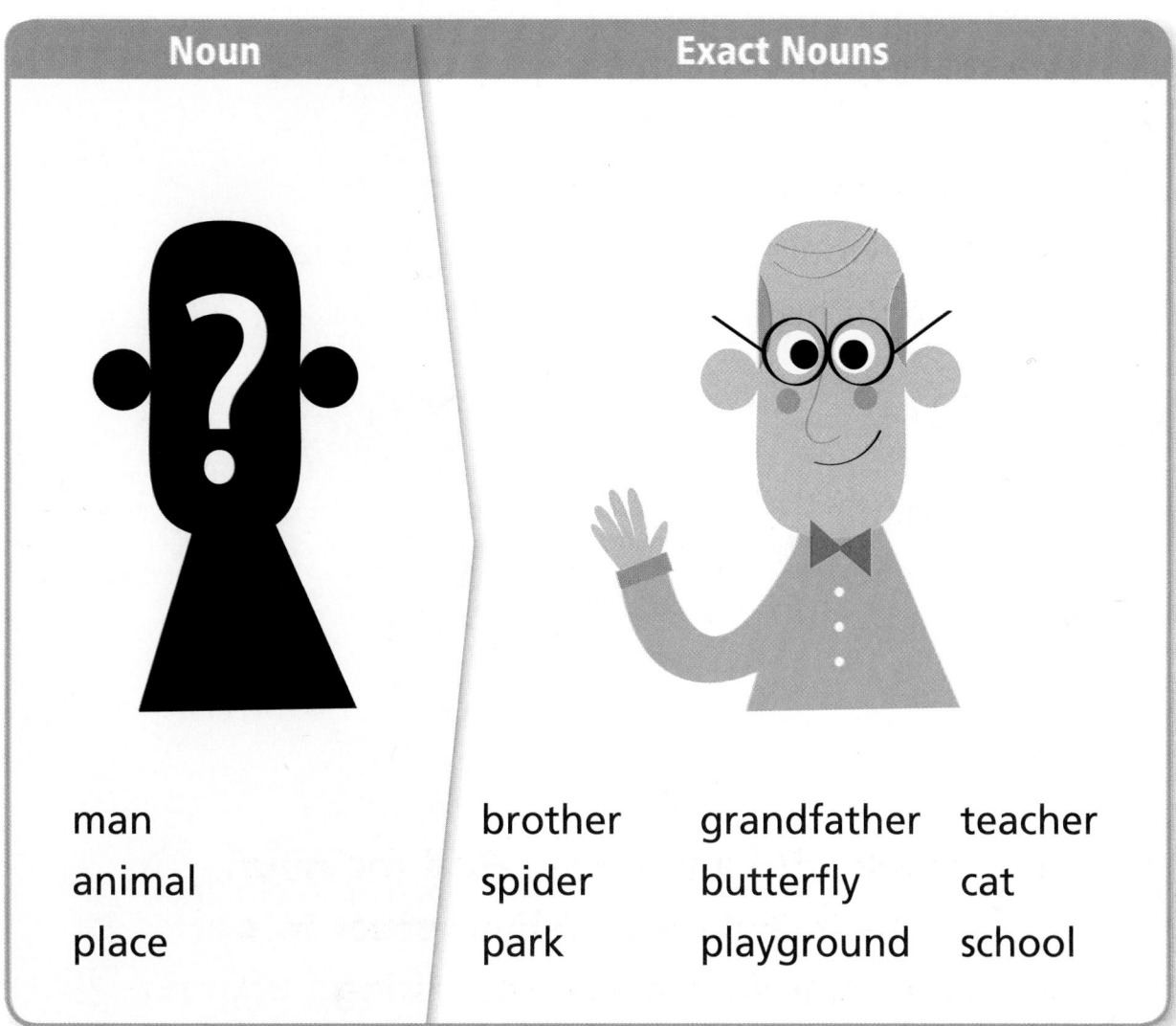

Noun	Exact Nouns		
man	brother	grandfather	teacher
animal	spider	butterfly	cat
place	park	playground	school

Connect Grammar to Writing

As you revise your true story next week, look for nouns you could replace with exact nouns.

Narrative Writing

✔ **Development** The main idea is the most important part of a **true story.** All of the details in your story should connect to the main idea. The details should describe actions, thoughts, and feelings of the characters.

Kevin made a list of ideas for his true story. He decided which idea would make the best story. Then he made an idea web for his true story.

Writing Process Checklist

▶ **Prewrite**

- ✔ What is the most important idea of my story?
- ✔ What details tell about what happened?
- ✔ Do all the parts of the story connect to the main idea?
- ✔ Is there anything that doesn't belong?

Draft

Revise

Edit

Publish and Share

Exploring a Topic

basketball

my sister's cat

video games

⟨ me in the author's chair ⟩

why I don't like to practice

piano

Idea Web

reading my story about Uncle Li and the spider

nervous about reading my story

My Turn in the Author's Chair

practicing in front of my family

class claps for my story

Reading as a Writer

How do Kevin's details in the outer circles connect with the main idea? Which details will you use to connect with your main idea?

I added details to the web that connect to the main idea.

Lesson 5

Teacher's Pets
Dayle Ann Dodds Illustrated by Marylin Hafner

See Westburg by Bus!
BUS

Q LANGUAGE DETECTIVE

Talk About Words
Work with a partner. Choose one of the Context Cards. Add words to the sentences to explain more details about the photo.

Vocabulary in Context

▶ Read each Context Card.

▶ Tell a story about two pictures using the Vocabulary words.

1 wonderful

Pets are wonderful. They make very good friends.

2 noises

Big dogs bark loudly. Small dogs do not make such loud noises.

3 **quiet**

A lizard is a very quiet pet. It does not make a sound.

4 **sprinkled**

The fish food was lightly sprinkled on top of the water.

5 **share**

Take pictures of your pets to share with your friends.

6 **noticed**

This pet rabbit noticed, or looked carefully, at the carrot held for it to eat.

7 **bursting**

Look at this crowded basket. It is bursting with puppies!

8 **suddenly**

A pet parrot might surprise you if it suddenly says a word.

Dayle Ann Dodds   Illustrated by Marylin Hafner

Read and Comprehend

Story Structure The people who are in a story are **characters**. The **setting** of a story is where and when the story takes place. The **plot** is what happens in the story.

As you read *Teacher's Pets,* think about where the story takes place and who is in it. Think about what happens, too. You can use a story map like the one below to tell the main parts of the story.

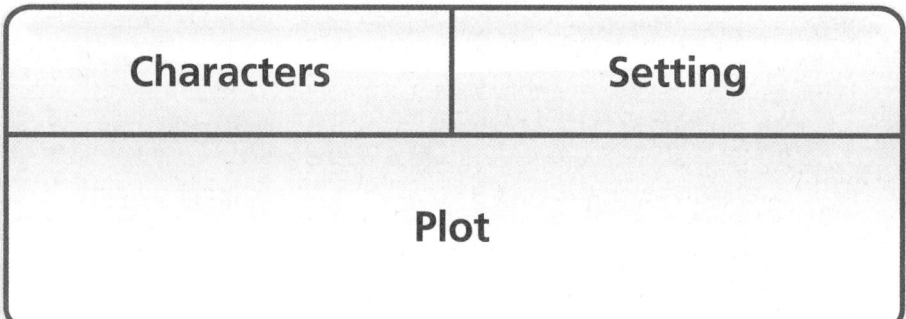

Characters	Setting
Plot	

Visualize Picture what is happening as you read.

Places Around Town

A town is a place where people live and work. Think about a town you have lived in or visited. Each place around town is important for a different reason. A post office helps people keep in touch. Police stations and fire stations help keep people safe. Think about why a school is an important place. You will read about what happens in one town's school in *Teacher's Pets.*

💬 Think | Write | Pair | Share

What are some ways that people work together in a school? Make a list. Then share your answers with a partner. Listen carefully. How are your lists the same and different? Then share your lists with the class.

ANCHOR TEXT

✓ GENRE

Realistic fiction is a story that could really happen. As you read, look for:

▸ characters who act like real people

▸ a setting that could be a real place

▸ story events that could happen to you

MEET THE AUTHOR

Dayle Ann Dodds

Dayle Ann Dodds received a very special honor in 2007. Her book *Teacher's Pets* was read to hundreds of kids on the lawn of the White House during the annual Easter Egg Roll.

MEET THE ILLUSTRATOR

Marylin Hafner

Readers of *Ladybug* magazine know two characters created by Marylin Hafner—Molly and her cat, Emmett. For fun Ms. Hafner designs rubber stamps, usually with kids or animals on them.

Teacher's Pets

by **Dayle Ann Dodds**

illustrated by **Marylin Hafner**

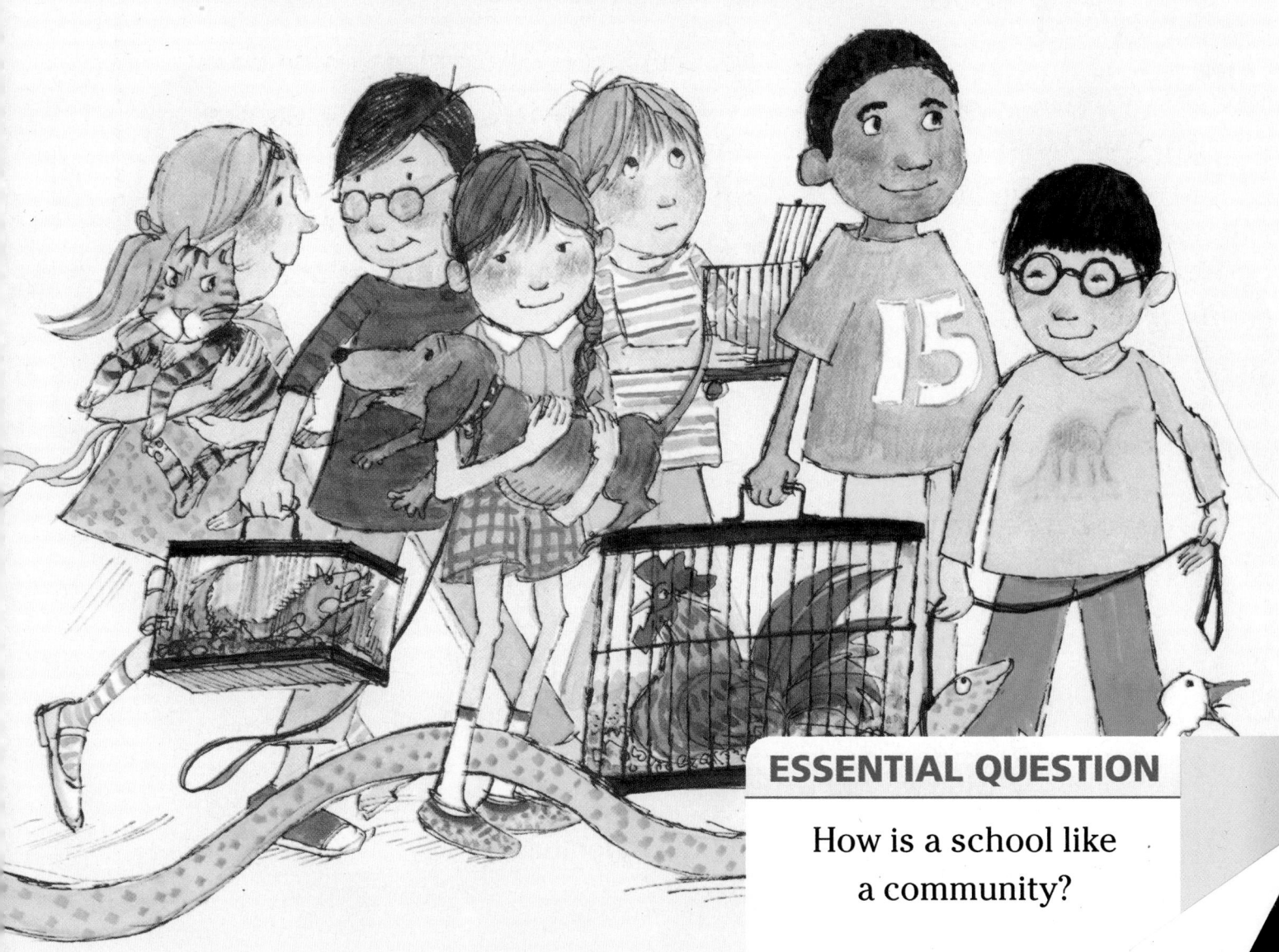

ESSENTIAL QUESTION

How is a school like
a community?

148

Monday was sharing day in Miss Fry's class.

"You may bring something special," said Miss Fry.

"May we share a pet?" Winston asked.

"Yes," said Miss Fry. "But just for the day."

On Monday, Winston brought in his pet rooster.

"I call him Red. He eats corn, and he crows. The neighbors say he crows too much."

"What a wonderful pet," said Miss Fry. "We're happy he can visit us today."

But that afternoon, after all the children had left, there was Red, still sitting on his roost near Miss Fry's desk.

She sprinkled corn in Red's dish, then locked the
door and went home to her quiet little house.

On Tuesday, Winston told Miss Fry, "The neighbors
wonder if Red can stay at school for a while."

"Of course," said Miss Fry. "How lucky for us."

The next Monday was Patrick's turn. "My tarantula's name is Vincent. He likes to eat bugs and hide inside my mother's slippers."

"What a wonderful pet," said Miss Fry. "Don't forget to take Vincent home with you at the end of the day."

But that afternoon, after all the children had left, there was Vincent, still sitting in his jar on Miss Fry's desk. She gave Vincent a big juicy bug, sprinkled corn on Red's dish, then locked the door and went home to her quiet little house.

On Tuesday, Patrick told Miss Fry, "My mother says Vincent likes her slippers too much. We're wondering if he can stay at school for a few days."

"Of course," said Miss Fry. "How lucky for us."

The next week, Roger brought in his cricket.

"His name is Moe," said Roger. "He eats leaves from the garden and sings *chirrup-chirrup* all night long."

"What a wonderful pet," said Miss Fry.

ANALYZE THE TEXT

Author's Word Choice What does Miss Fry say every time a child asks if a pet can stay? What does this tell you about Miss Fry?

154

That afternoon, after all the children had left, Miss Fry noticed Moe sitting in his box on the table. Miss Fry looked at Moe. He almost seemed to smile. "Welcome to our class, Moe."

Right before her eyes, he did a huge somersault—up, up in the air. "Bravo!" said Miss Fry.

She gave fresh green leaves to Moe and a big juicy bug to Vincent, sprinkled corn in Red's dish, then locked the door and went home to her quiet little house.

The next day, Roger said to Miss Fry, "My mother says Moe chirps too much."

"He's welcome to visit as long as he likes," said Miss Fry.

And so it went.

Alia shared her pet goat named Gladys. It said *Baaaaa!* and ate her sister's homework.

Amanda shared her pet dachshund. It liked to chew bones and the pillows on her aunt Judy's new sofa.

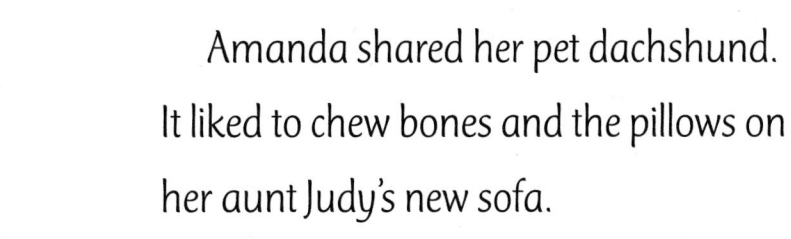

Jerry brought in his pet boa constrictor. It never made a sound. No one knew exactly what it liked to eat, but Jerry said his father's expensive tropical fish had suddenly disappeared one day.

157

There was Megan's cat,

Mitchell's mice,

Daniel's ducks,

and Tom's iguana.

Frankie's frog,

Lily's monkey,

Terrence's turtle . . .

16

and something square and fuzzy that Avery brought in.

"It looks like a kitchen sponge," said Bruce. "A *really old* kitchen sponge."

"It's my pet," said Avery, and that was that.

Before long, Miss Fry's classroom was bursting
with the happy noises of all the children's pets.

On Parents' Night, the mothers and fathers walked around the classroom with great big smiles on their faces.

"Isn't it great," they said, "that Miss Fry loves pets so?"

Only Roger's cricket sat quietly in his box.

"You must miss your garden," Miss Fry said.

Chirrup, said Moe softly. He crawled under one of his shiny green leaves.

On the last day of school, Miss Fry's class had a party with balloons, hats, and ice-cream cups. "Good-bye, children!" Miss Fry sang out. "Have a nice summer . . . *and don't forget to*

take
home
your
pets!"

One by one, the children disappeared,
and with them went their pets.

"No more pets," said Miss Fry.

She looked around the quiet, empty room.

Then Miss Fry noticed a box sitting on her desk.

She peeked inside. A little face looked up at her.

It almost seemed to smile.

A note inside read:

DEAR MISS FRY,
PLEASE TAKE
CARE
OF MOE.
HE LIKES YOU
BEST.

ROGER

"How lucky for me," said Miss Fry.

Moe did a huge somersault—up, up in the air.

Miss Fry carried her new pet to her quiet little house and placed him in the garden, among the rainbow of roses.

That night, Miss Fry opened her window.
She climbed into bed. She turned off the lamp.
By the light of the moon, from outside in the
garden, came a happy noise.
Chirrup-chirrup!

ANALYZE THE TEXT

Story Structure How does the
ending of the story solve the problem
from the beginning of the story?

Dig Deeper

Use Clues to Analyze the Text

Use these pages to learn about Story Structure and Author's Word Choice. Then read *Teacher's Pets* again. Use what you learn to understand it better.

Story Structure

Teacher's Pets is about what happens when Miss Fry lets everyone bring a pet to class. Who are the characters? Where does the story take place?

Think about how the beginning of the story tells the main story problem. Then think about how the problem is solved in the end. A story map can help you describe the **characters**, **setting**, and **plot**.

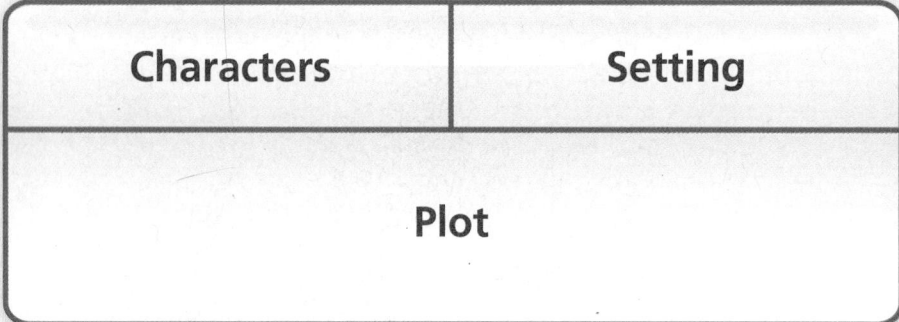

Characters	Setting
Plot	

Author's Word Choice

Sometimes an author repeats words, phrases, or events. This is called **repetition**. Repetition makes a story fun to read and easy to remember.

In *Teacher's Pets*, there is a repeating event. Children keep bringing pets into class. The author also repeats words and phrases. Think about how repeated words and phrases in the story help you understand what happens.

Your Turn

 **How is a school like a community?** Discuss your ideas with a partner. Use text evidence from *Teacher's Pets* to explain. Ask a question if you don't understand your partner's ideas.

Classroom Conversation

Now talk about these questions with the class.

1. What happens at the beginning of the story that gives you a clue about how it will end?

2. Why does Miss Fry let the students keep their pets at school? How do you know?

3. What type of teacher do you think Miss Fry is? Use text evidence from the story to help you.

WRITE ABOUT READING

Response Reread pages 166–167. Why does Miss Fry say that she is lucky after reading Roger's note? Write a few sentences to tell your opinion. Use text evidence from the words and pictures to give reasons for your answer.

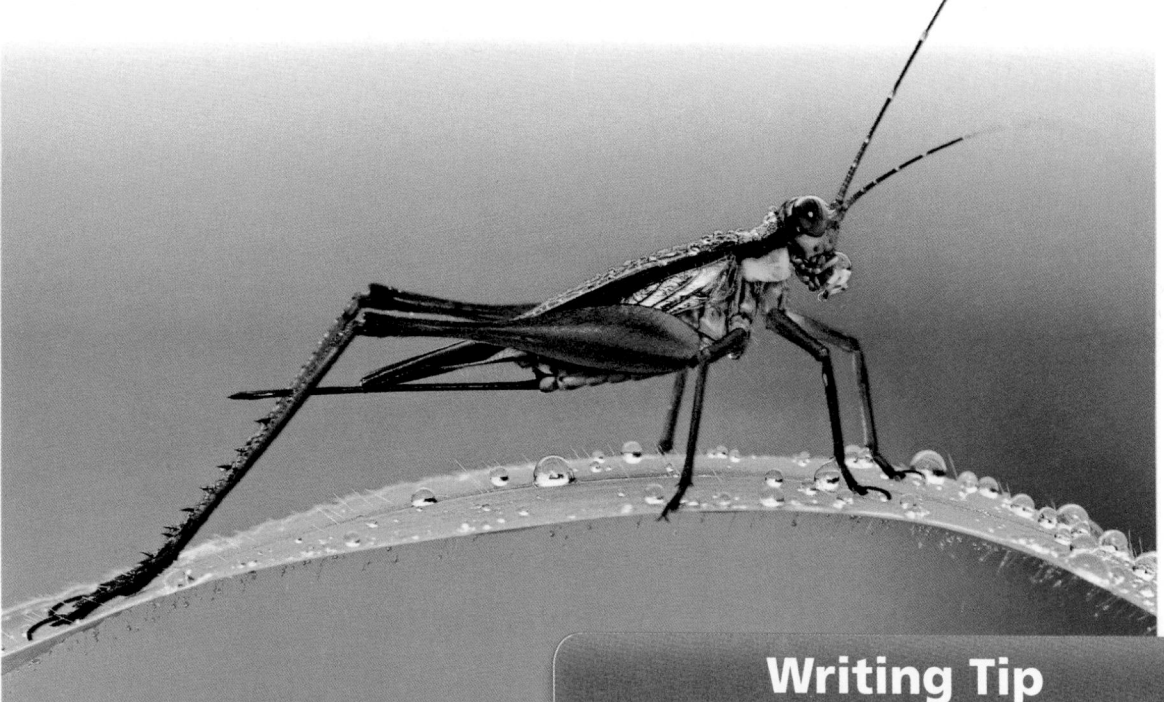

Writing Tip

Make sure that each of your sentences has a subject and a predicate.

INFORMATIONAL TEXT

☑ GENRE

Informational text gives facts about a topic. This is a pamphlet.

☑ TEXT FOCUS

A **map** is a drawing of a town, state, or other place.

See Westburg by Bus!

Welcome to Westburg!

The best way to see our town is on Bus Number 33. Get the bus in front of our Welcome Center. After you get on board, read this pamphlet. Just follow the numbers sprinkled on the map as you go.

We are happy to share our wonderful town with you.

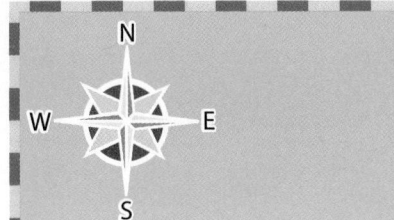

SILVER RIVER

Brown Street

Red Street

② LIBRARY

Blue Avenue

Pine Street

③ Rainbow Park

WELCOME CENTER
①

① Welcome Center

Find the Welcome Center. It is bursting with pamphlets, maps, and books about Westburg.

② Library

The Public Library is on Blue Avenue. The children's room is a great place for books, computer games, and movies.

③ Rainbow Park

Cross Blue Avenue to get to Westburg's largest park. People come here to play, walk, or have some quiet time.

Key

river

bus route ▪ ▬ ▪ ▬ ▪

bridge

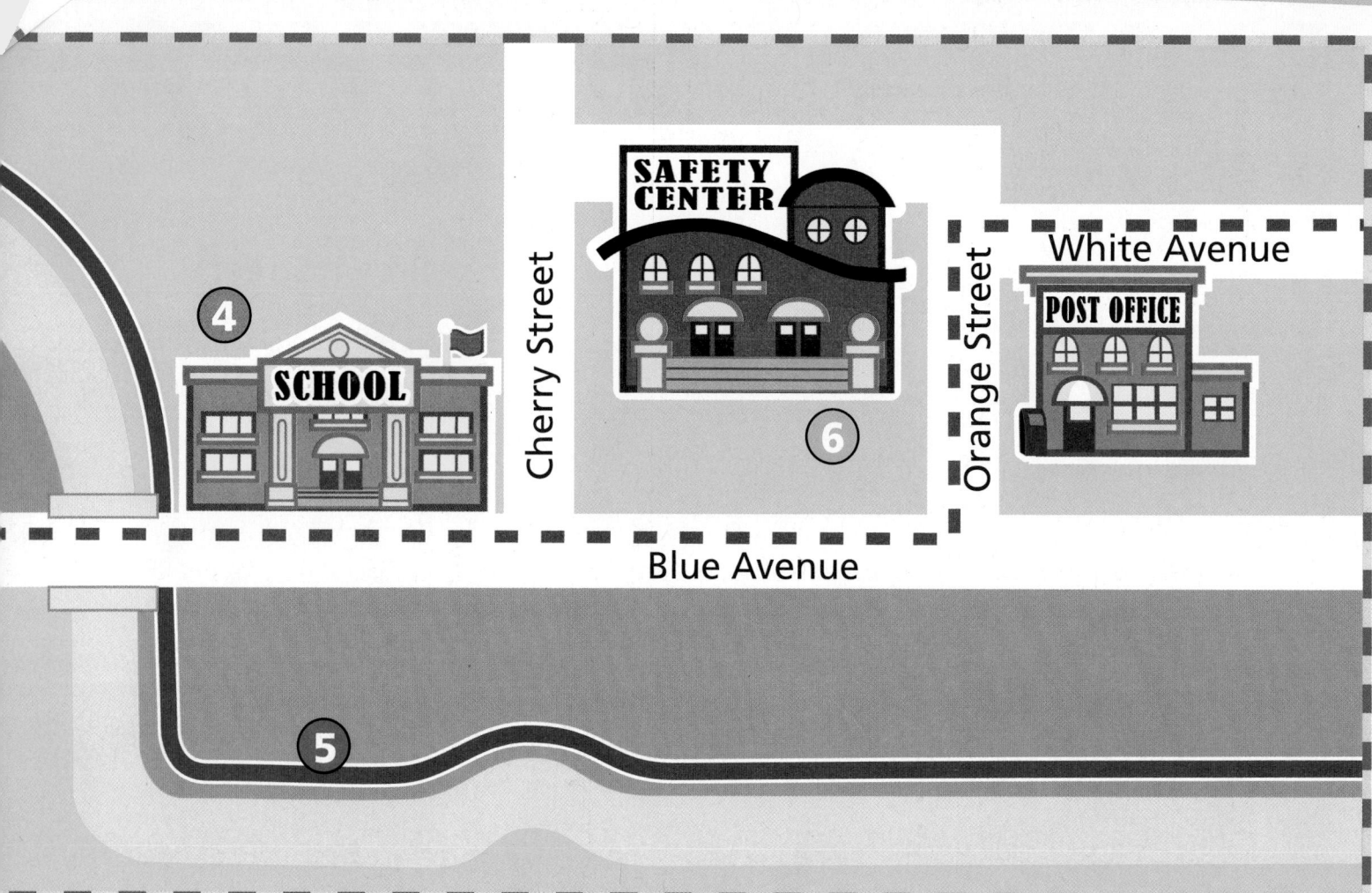

④ School

Take the bridge across the Silver River. When you get on the other side, Cherry Elementary will be on your left.

⑤ Bike Path

Have you noticed how the bike path follows the curves of the Silver River? What a great view!

⑥ Safety Center

If you suddenly hear siren noises as you pass the Safety Center, a fire truck or ambulance may be whizzing by!

Compare Texts

Make Decisions Discuss Miss Fry's classroom and the town of Westburg with a partner. Which place would you rather live if you were a pet? Why? Use the words and illustrations in each selection to help you answer. Speak in complete sentences.

Write About School If you were a student in Miss Fry's class, what pet would you bring to school? Why? Write to explain your answer. Share your ideas with a partner.

Research an Animal Choose a pet from *Teacher's Pets* that you would like to know more about. Research how to care for that type of pet.

ELA RL.2.7, SL.2.6

Grammar

Singular and Plural Nouns A **singular noun** names one person, animal, place, or thing. A **plural noun** names more than one person, animal, place, or thing. Add -*s* to most nouns to name more than one.

Sentences with Singular Nouns	Sentences with Plural Nouns
The teacher talks loudly.	The two teachers talk to their students.
This playground looks big.	All playgrounds are fun.

Try This! **Work with a partner. Read the sentences aloud. Name the singular nouns and plural nouns.**

❶ Two crickets sat in a cage.

❷ My friend has three cats.

❸ Her bird ate some seeds.

❹ Our teacher loves pets!

Edit your writing carefully. Make sure you have used the correct plural form for each noun that names more than one.

Singular Nouns	Plural Nouns
one frog	two frogs
a bug	many bugs

Connect Grammar to Writing

When you edit your true story, be sure to write the correct form of all plural nouns.

Narrative Writing

✔ **Organization** When you write a **true story**, use time-order words and details that describe thoughts, feelings, and actions of the characters.

Kevin drafted a story about the day he read a story to the class. Later, he added details to tell when things happened and how he felt.

Writing Process Checklist

Prewrite

Draft

▶ **Revise**

✔ Does my story have a beginning, middle, and end?

✔ Does the beginning make the reader want to read more?

✔ Did I use time-order words to tell when things happened?

✔ Did I add details?

✔ Does the ending wrap things up?

Edit

Publish and Share

Revised Draft

Last week, it
~~It~~ was my turn for the Author's
∧
Chair. I chose my story about
                        At first,
Uncle Li and the spider. ∧ I was

I thought no one would like my story.
Then,
nervous. ∧ I practiced in front of my
        I felt ready!
family.
      ∧

ELA W.2.3, W.2.5

My Day in the Author's Chair
by Kevin Chen

Last week, it was my turn for the Author's Chair. I chose my story about Uncle Li and the spider. At first, I was nervous. I thought no one would like my story. Then, I practiced in front of my family. I felt ready! Finally, I read the story in class. I read the part about how Uncle Li screamed. The class laughed. I was a big hit!

Reading as a Writer

What time-order words does Kevin use? What details can you add to your story?

I used details to tell about thoughts, feelings, and actions.

Write a Story

TASK Look back at *My Family* and *Dogs*. Think about who makes up a family. Think about what you learned about caring for dogs. Then use what you learned to write a story for your classmates. Your story should be about a family who welcomes a pet family member into its home.

Gather Information Talk with a group of classmates about *My Family* and *Dogs*. How can dogs be a part of a family? What do dogs need?

Use the tools in your eBook to remember facts about *My Family* and *Dogs*.

Then write ideas for your story in a story map.

- Who will be in the family?

- Where will the story take place?

- What is the problem?

- What are the main story events?

- What lesson will the characters learn?

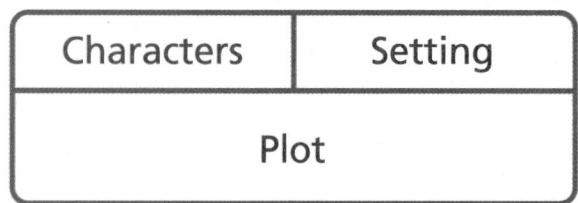

Characters	Setting
Plot	

Write Your Story   Use the information below to help you organize your story.

Write your draft in *my*WriteSmart.

Beginning

Begin your story. Use your story map for ideas. Introduce the characters, the setting, and the problem. Use exact nouns to paint a picture in readers' minds.

Middle

What happens next? Tell what events happen in the story. Use complete sentences to describe what happens.

Ending

Give your story a strong ending. Your story ending should help readers answer these questions:

- How do the characters solve the problem?
- How does everyone feel when the story ends?
- What lesson do they learn?

REVISE

Review Your Draft Read your writing and make it better. Use the Checklist.

Have a partner read your draft. Talk about how you can make it better.

 Is my story about how a family welcomes a new pet?

 Does my story have a beginning, a middle, and an ending?

 Do the characters in my story face a problem?

 Did I use exact nouns?

 Did I use complete sentences?

PRESENT

Share Write or type a copy of your story. Add a picture. Pick a way to share.

- Read your story to your classmates.

- Publish your story into a book for classmates to read.

Pedro's Puppy Problem

UNIT 2

Nature Watch

Stream to Start

"Nature does nothing uselessly."

— Aristotle

Performance Task Preview

At the end of this unit, you will think about two of the texts you have read. Then you will write an informational paragraph comparing information about animals from the texts.

hmhfyi.com

Channel One News®

185

🔍 **LANGUAGE DETECTIVE**

Talk About Words
Nouns are words that name people, places, animals, or things. Work with a partner. Find the Vocabulary words that are nouns. What are your clues? Use the nouns in new sentences.

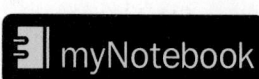

Add new words to **myWordList**. Use them in your speaking and writing.

Vocabulary in Context

▶ **Read each Context Card.**

▶ **Use a Vocabulary word to tell about something you did.**

1
shaped
Have you ever seen a home shaped like this? It is curved like a ball.

2
branches
Tree branches high above the ground are a good home for a sloth.

3 pond

Turtles make their home in a pond, or small lake.

4 beaks

These birds use their beaks to build their home.

5 deepest

The deepest part of the ocean is this eel's home.

6 break

This home won't break! It is made of strong rock.

7 hang

These bats hang upside down in their cave.

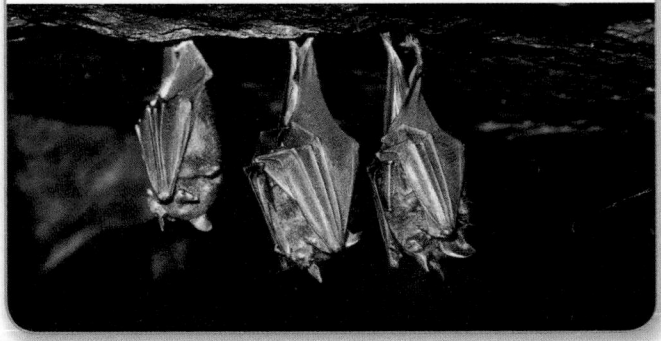

8 winding

Some animal homes have long, winding tunnels that twist and turn.

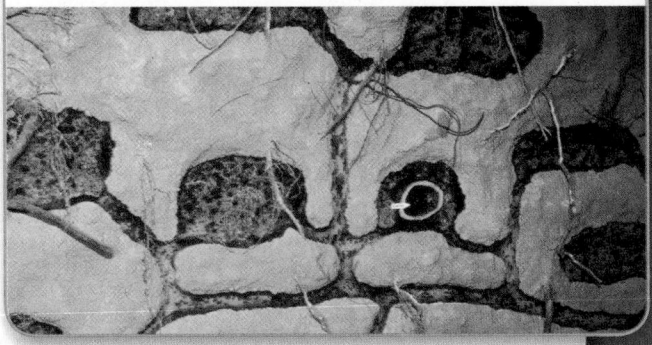

Read and Comprehend

Text and Graphic Features An author sometimes adds special text and graphic features to a text. Some examples of **graphic features** are photos and charts. Some examples of **text features** are headings and words in bold print. These features help you find information quickly. They also help you know what an author thinks is important.

You can use a chart like this to list features you find and tell how they help you.

Text or Graphic Feature	Page Number	Purpose

Question Ask questions about what you are reading. Look for text evidence to answer your questions.

Animal Homes

All animals need homes. Most wild animals find or build homes for themselves. For example, a bear might find a cave to use as its home. A bird builds a nest. Animals' homes help keep the animals safe, warm, and dry.

You will learn more about where animals live in *Animals Building Homes*.

Think | Draw | Pair | Share

Draw a picture of an animal home. Share your picture with a partner. Have your partner ask questions to guess which animal lives there. Listen to the questions and give details in your answers. Then share your pictures with the class.

ANCHOR TEXT

Animals Building Homes

☑ **GENRE**

Informational text gives facts about a topic. As you read, look for:

▶ photos and headings
▶ facts and details about a topic

MEET THE AUTHOR

Wendy Perkins

Can you guess why author Wendy Perkins has been called a "walking animal encyclopedia"? It's because her mind is filled with facts and information about all kinds of animals.

Ms. Perkins has written nonfiction books about animal eyes, ears, feet, feathers, noses, teeth, and tails. She also writes articles for *Highlights for Children* and a magazine put out by the San Diego Zoo called *Zoonooz*.

Animals Building Homes

by Wendy Perkins

ESSENTIAL QUESTION

What are animal homes like?

A Beaver's Home

A beaver is hard at work. It gnaws on a tree trunk. Soon, the tree falls. The beaver floats the log to a pond. There, the beaver builds a **lodge.** The beaver piles up logs. It fills the cracks between the logs with mud and grass. The lodge keeps the beaver safe and warm.

ANALYZE THE TEXT

Using Context What is a lodge? How do the other sentences help you to figure out the meaning?

Safe at Home

Most animals need a home. Homes keep animals safe from **predators**, rain, snow, or the hot sun. Some animals live in their homes for life. Other animals live in their homes long enough to raise their **offspring** or **survive** hot or cold weather.

Building Nests

Many animals live in nests. A hummingbird builds a small cup-shaped nest. The nest is made of moss and bits of spiderweb.

A mouse makes a grass nest in the shape of a ball. The mouse hides its nest in tall grass or in a tunnel under the ground.

Careful Builders

Some animals put a lot of work into building their homes. Weaver birds make nests that hang from tree branches. The birds carefully weave grass and leaves together. Weaver birds use their feet and beaks to tie knots in the grass.

Working Together

Animals can work together to build homes. Termites build **mounds** made out of mud mixed with **saliva**. Other animals cannot easily break through the hard mud.

Polyps are animals that make coral reefs. A polyp builds a **limestone** cup around its body for protection. The cups of the polyps grow together to make a coral reef.

Making a Burrow

Burrows are holes in the ground where some animals live. Gophers use their teeth and paws to dig long, winding tunnels. They make rooms in the deepest parts of the tunnels. The gophers hide their offspring and food in these rooms.

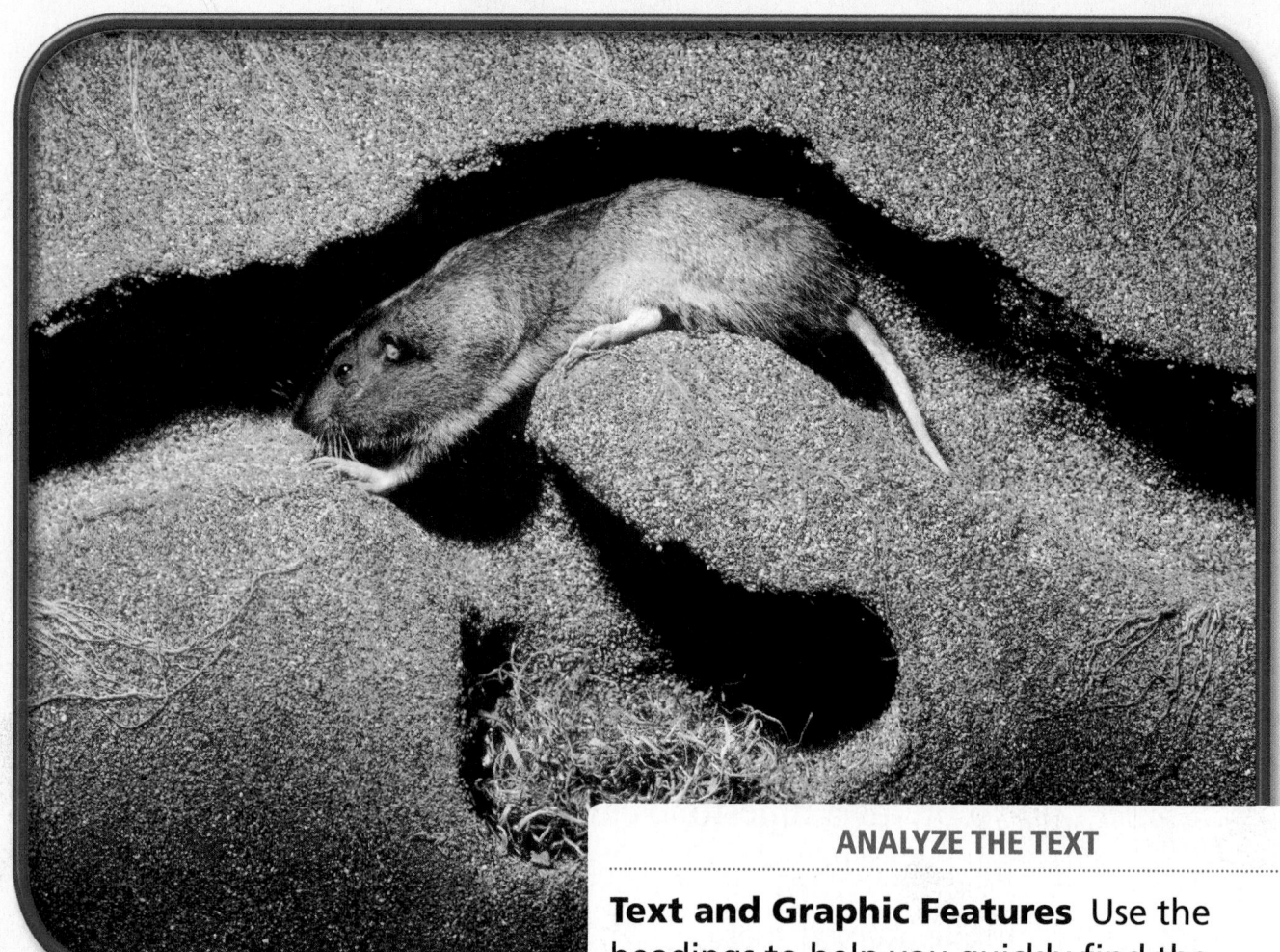

ANALYZE THE TEXT

Text and Graphic Features Use the headings to help you quickly find the information about how a gopher makes a burrow. What is the heading for that page?

Home Improvement

Some animals live in homes made by other animals. Chickadees use tree holes made by woodpeckers. Chickadees bring grass and moss into the hole. They build a nest for their chicks.

Building a Home

Most animals need homes where they can rest and raise their offspring. Homes also keep animals safe from predators. Beavers build lodges. Mice make nests. Gophers dig burrows. How does a polar bear make its **den**?

Dig Deeper

Use Clues to Analyze the Text

Use these pages to learn about Text and Graphic Features and Using Context. Then read *Animals Building Homes* again. Use what you learn to understand it better.

Text and Graphic Features

The author of *Animals Building Homes* uses text and graphic features to make her ideas clear. For example, the headings help you know what you will read about in each section. They help you find information quickly. Use a chart like this to list text and graphic features and how you use them.

Text or Graphic Feature	Page Number	Purpose

Using Context

Authors sometimes use special words about a topic that may be new to you. You can use other words in the sentence to help figure out what a new word means. Looking at the photos may also help you. Using a sentence or a photo to understand a new word is called **using context**.

Your Turn

 **What are animal homes like?** Share your ideas with a partner. Use the text features and photos from the selection to help you. Point to text evidence to explain your answer to the question.

Classroom Conversation

Now talk about these questions with the class.

1. How can you use the headings to find information in the selection?

2. How are homes that people build the same as and different from the homes that animals build?

3. Why does the author put some words in bold print?

WRITE ABOUT READING

Response Write two facts that you learned about animal homes. Use text evidence such as words and pictures from the selection to help you.

Writing Tip

Remember that a statement tells something. It ends with a period.

INFORMATIONAL TEXT

✅ GENRE

Informational text gives facts about a topic.

✅ TEXT FOCUS

A **subheading** gives more information about a selection. **Bold print** text shows which words, sentences, or phrases are most important.

Whose Home Is This?

by Joli K. Stevens

Why Do Animals Need Homes?

Animals need homes just like we do to stay safe and warm. Look at the pictures of animal homes on the next few pages. Can you guess what kind of animal might live in each home?

This nest looks like a pile of dead leaves and branches. It is an animal's home!

Many animals make their nests in trees. These nests are made from things the animals can find close by. Things such as leaves, twigs, moss, or feathers are used in nests.

Who lives here?

211

Some squirrels live in trees.

Squirrels have large, strong claws that help them climb and jump.

Birds are not the only animals that live in tree nests. A large cluster, or bunch, of leaves and twigs high in a tree might be a squirrel's nest. Baby squirrels can stay in the nest for up to ten weeks. A squirrel might use a nest for a few months or even a few years. Sometimes squirrels will build more than one nest and use them all!

These insects are building their home.

There are thousands of small insects that live and work together in this tree. This insect is often called busy because it is always working!

Who lives here?

Bees work together in a hive.

A beehive is a very busy place.

A beehive is made up of parts called combs. Bees make the combs out of wax from their own bodies. The cells, or small spaces, near the edge of the comb hold honey. The cells in the middle are where the queen bee lays the eggs. Some bees look after the hive. Other bees collect nectar from flowers to make their food, or honey.

This Home Can Move from Place to Place...

There are many kinds of animals that live in or near the ocean. Can you guess what kind of animal might live in a shell?

Who lives here?

An empty shell like this one was once home for an animal.

215

Hermit crabs carry their homes with them.

The hermit crabs along the shore can be very shy around people.

A hermit crab does not have a hard shell. It uses another animal's shell for cover. When an animal gives up its shell, a hermit crab may use it for its own. When a crab grows too large for its shell, it will molt, or cast off the old shell. Then it will get a new one. Would you like to live in a shell?

Compare Texts

Alike and Different Think about the most important ideas about animal homes in each selection. What did you learn from each that is the same? What is different? To answer, look for text evidence with a small group.

Share Experiences Think about the animal homes in *Animals Building Homes*. Which have you seen before? Share your ideas with a partner.

Classify Animals With a small group, sort the animals in each selection by the type of home they build, such as a hole or a nest. Research other animals that live in those types of homes. Make a chart to share with the class.

ELA RI.2.9, W.2.7

Grammar

Special Kinds of Nouns Special nouns that end with *s*, *x*, *ch*, or *sh* get a different ending when they tell about more than one. Add *-es* to these nouns to make them **plural.** Other special nouns change spelling to name more than one. A **collective noun** names a group of things.

Plural Nouns	Collective Nouns
two foxes	the team
many classes	a class
some finches	my family
three dishes	an army
four children	the herd

Try This! **Read each sentence. Tell if each underlined word is a plural noun or a collective noun.**

❶ The <u>herd</u> of deer ran away quickly!

❷ The <u>bushes</u> hide animal homes.

❸ The three <u>mice</u> ate the cheese.

❹ Where did the <u>flock</u> go?

When you write, check that all special nouns are spelled correctly when talking about more than one.

Special Nouns About One

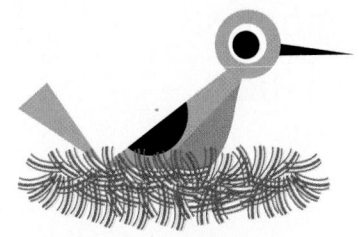

A finch makes a nest.

A mouse makes a nest.

Special Nouns About More Than One

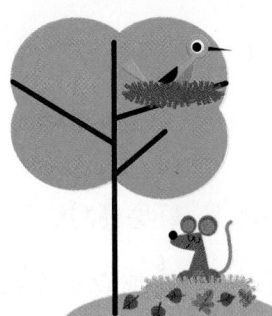

Finches and mice make nests.

Connect Grammar to Writing

When you revise your writing, find special nouns that tell about more than one. Be sure the nouns follow the rules you have learned.

Informative Writing

☑ **Purpose** When you write, always keep your reason for writing in mind. When you write an **informational paragraph,** you want readers to learn something about a topic. You should include details that tell about the main idea.

Sean drafted a paragraph about beaver homes. Later, he added more details about his main idea.

Revised Draft

They use parts of trees to build their homes there. Beavers live on ponds. ∧A beaver can use its teeth to gnaw on a tree.∧ Then the tree falls.

Beaver Lodges
by Sean McDonald

Beavers live on ponds. They use parts of trees to build their homes there. A beaver can use its teeth to gnaw on a tree. Then the tree falls. Beavers float logs to a place to build a lodge. The beaver uses mud and grass to fill cracks. That helps keep the lodge warm.

Reading as a Writer

Which details did Sean add to tell more about his main idea? Where can you add details to your own paragraph?

My purpose for writing was to share facts about beavers' homes.

221

Lesson
7

The Ugly Vegetables
by Grace Lin

They Really Are GIANT!

🔍 LANGUAGE DETECTIVE

Talk About Words
Work with a partner. Take turns asking and answering questions about the photos. Use the Vocabulary words in your questions and answers.

Vocabulary in Context

▶ **Read each Context Card.**

▶ **Make up a new sentence that uses a Vocabulary word.**

1 **blooming**
Sunflowers are blooming in the field. They face the sun as their flowers grow.

2 **shovels**
These children use shovels to help plant a tree.

ELA L.2.6

3 scent

Roses have a scent, or smell, that is as sweet as perfume.

4 tough

A pumpkin has a tough outer skin that is hard to break.

5 wrinkled

A raisin is a dried, wrinkled grape, but it is still sweet.

6 plain

The plant on the left is plain. The plant on the right is fancy.

7 muscles

It takes strong muscles to use a loaded wheelbarrow.

8 nodded

The girl nodded her head up and down to show that she would help in the garden.

Read and Comprehend

Conclusions As you read *The Ugly Vegetables,* use story clues, or text evidence, to figure out more about the events and characters. Use the clues to draw **conclusions,** or make smart guesses, about what the author does not say. You can find clues in the words and pictures. You can write the clues and a conclusion in a chart like this.

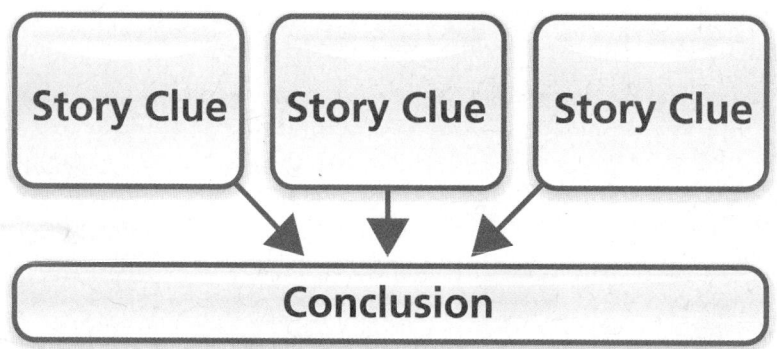

✓ **TARGET STRATEGY**

Analyze/Evaluate To **analyze** as you read, think about the author's words and story events. Then **evaluate,** or decide, how the words and events help you know what is important in the story.

Agriculture

Farmers work hard to grow fruits and vegetables all year long. You do not have to be a farmer to grow your own vegetables and fruits. Some people have a garden in their yard. Others plant fruits or vegetables in containers in their kitchen. In *The Ugly Vegetables,* you will learn about how one girl and her mother grow vegetables in their garden at home.

💬 **Think** | **Write** | **Pair** | **Share**

How do you grow a garden? Write your answer. Then share your ideas with a partner. Listen carefully to your partner. Ask questions if you do not understand your partner's ideas. Then share your ideas with the class.

ANCHOR TEXT

Realistic fiction is a story that could really happen. As you read, look for:

- ▸ characters who act like real people
- ▸ a problem that a real person might have

MEET THE AUTHOR AND ILLUSTRATOR

Grace Lin

The Ugly Vegetables tells the true story of something that happened to Grace Lin when she was little. The book caused a big problem in her family because she didn't include her two sisters in it.

They made her promise to put them in her other books, which she has done. *Dim Sum for Everyone* and *Kite Flying* are about a family with three girls, just like the Lin family.

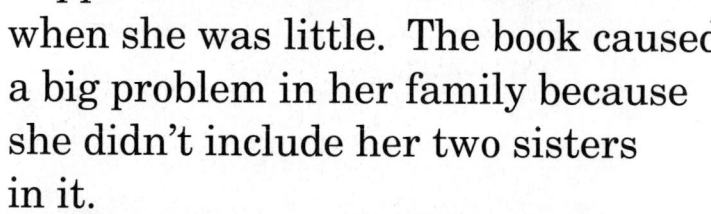

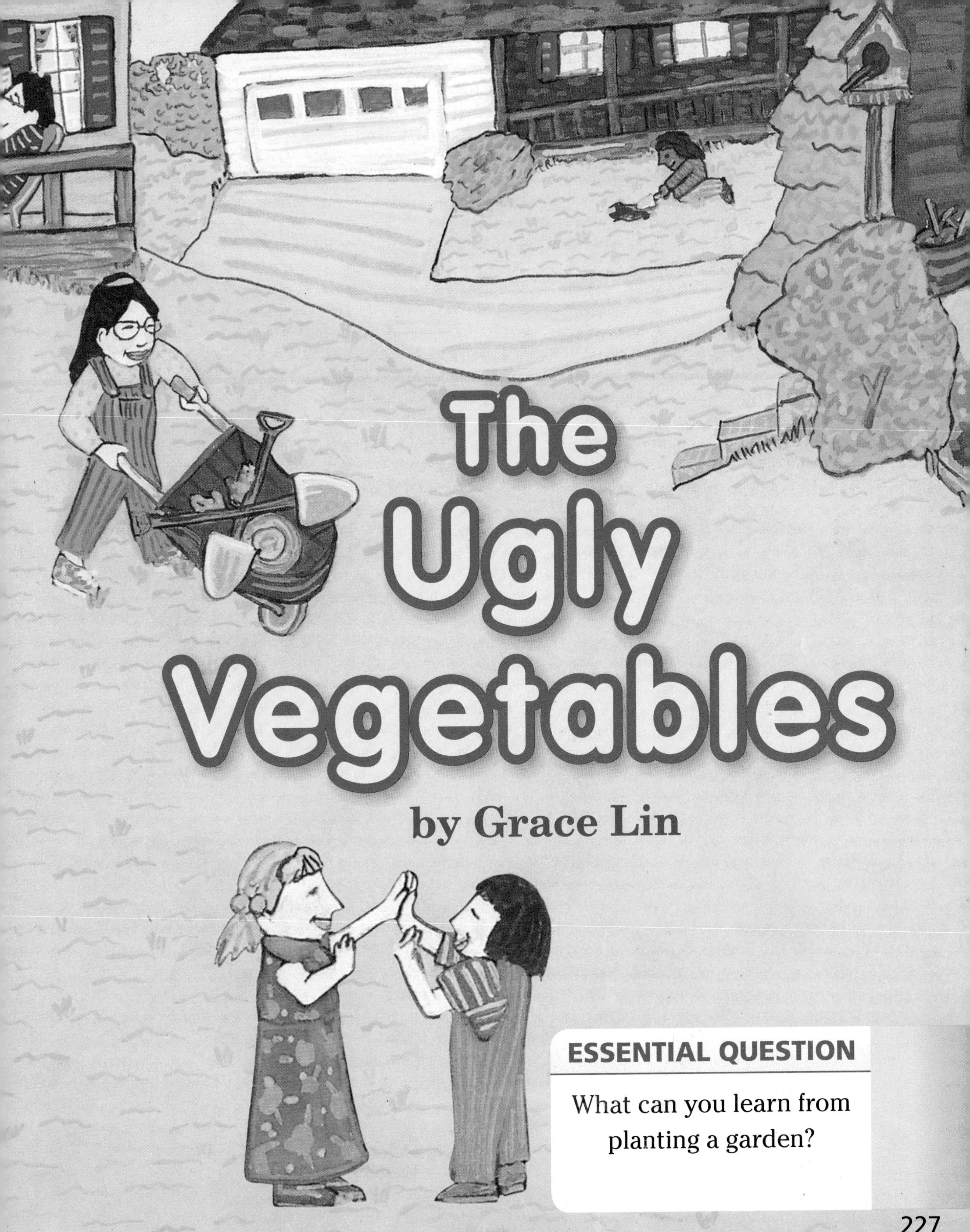

The Ugly Vegetables

by Grace Lin

ESSENTIAL QUESTION

What can you learn from planting a garden?

In the spring I helped my mother start our garden.
We used tall shovels to turn the grass upside down, and
I saw pink worms wriggle around. It was hard work.
When we stopped to rest, we saw that the neighbors were
starting their gardens too.

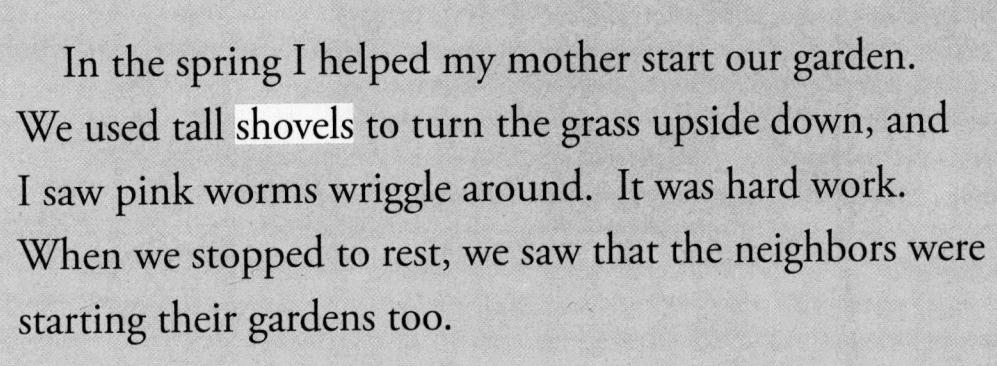

"Hello, Irma!" my mother called to Mrs. Crumerine.
Mrs. Crumerine was digging too. She was using a small
shovel, one that fit in her hand.

"Mommy," I asked, "why are we using such big
shovels? Mrs. Crumerine has a small one."

"Because our garden needs more digging," she said.

I helped my mother plant the seeds, and we dragged the hose to the garden.

"Hi, Linda! Hi, Mickey!" I called to the Fitzgeralds. They were sprinkling water on their garden with green watering cans.

"Mommy," I asked, "why are we using a hose? Linda and Mickey use watering cans."

"Because our garden needs more water," she said.

ANALYZE THE TEXT

Conclusions What can you tell about the people in this neighborhood? Explain your answer.

Then my mother drew funny pictures on pieces of paper, and I stuck them into the garden.

"Hello, Roseanne!" my mother called across the street to Mrs. Angelhowe.

"Mommy," I asked, "why are we sticking these papers in the garden? Mrs. Angelhowe has seed packages in her garden."

"Because our garden is going to grow Chinese vegetables," she told me. "These are the names of the vegetables in Chinese, so I can tell which plants are growing where."

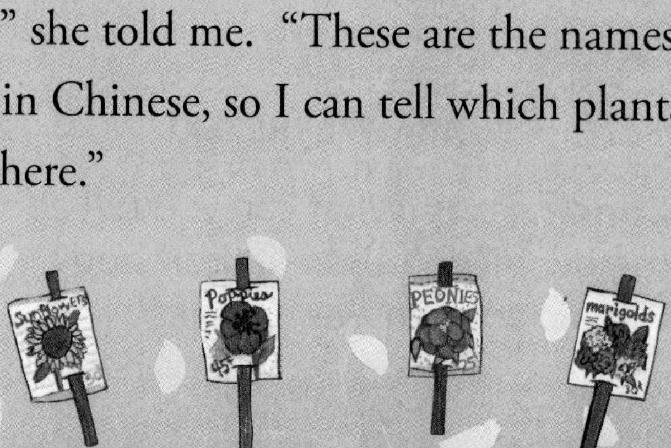

One day I saw our garden growing. Little green stems that looked like grass had popped out from the ground.

"Our garden's growing!" I yelled. "Our garden's growing!"

I rushed over to the neighbors' gardens to see if theirs had grown. Their plants looked like little leaves.

"Mommy," I asked, "why do our plants look like grass? The neighbors' plants look different."

"Because they are growing flowers," she said.

"Why can't we grow flowers?" I asked.

"These are better than flowers," she said.

Soon all the neighbors' gardens were blooming. Up
and down the street grew rainbows of flowers.

The wind always smelled sweet, and butterflies and bees flew everywhere. Everyone's garden was beautiful, except for ours.

Ours was all dark green and ugly.

"Why didn't we grow flowers?" I asked again.

"These are better than flowers," Mommy said again.

I looked, but saw only black-purple-green vines, fuzzy wrinkled leaves, prickly stems, and a few little yellow flowers.

"I don't think so," I said.

"You wait and see," Mommy said.

Before long, our vegetables grew. Some were big and lumpy. Some were thin and green and covered with bumps. Some were just plain icky yellow. They were ugly vegetables.

Sometimes I would go over to the neighbors' and look at their pretty gardens. They would show the poppies and peonies and petunias to me, and I would feel sad that our garden wasn't as nice.

One day my mother and I picked the vegetables from
the garden. We filled a whole wheelbarrow full of them.
We wheeled them to the kitchen. My mother washed
them and took a big knife and started to chop them.

"Aie-yow!" she said when she cut them. She had to
use all her muscles. The vegetables were hard and tough.

"This is sheau hwang gua (show hwang gwa),"
Mommy said, handing me a bumpy, curled vegetable. She
pointed at the other vegetables. "This is shiann tsay
(shen zai). That's a torng hau (tung how)."

I went outside to play. While I was playing catch
with Mickey, a magical aroma filled the air. I saw the
neighbors standing on their porches with their eyes closed,
smelling the sky. They took deep breaths of air, like they
were trying to eat the smell.

The wind carried it up and down the street. Even
the bees and the butterflies seemed to smell the scent
in the breeze.

I smelled it too. It made me hungry, and it was coming from my house!

When I followed it to my house, my mother was putting a big bowl of soup on the table. The soup was yellow and red and green and pink.

"This is a special soup," Mommy said, and she smiled.

She gave me a small bowl full of it and I tasted it. It was so good! The flavors of the soup seemed to dance in my mouth and laugh all the way down to my stomach. I smiled.

"Do you like it?" Mommy asked me.

I nodded and held out my bowl for some more.

"It's made from our vegetables," she told me.

Then the doorbell rang, and we ran to open the door.
All our neighbors were standing at the door holding
flowers.

"We noticed you were cooking." Mr. Fitzgerald
laughed as he held out his flowers. "And we thought
maybe you might be interested in a trade!"

We laughed too, and my mother gave them each their own bowl of her special soup.

My mother told them what each vegetable was and how she grew it. She gave them the soup recipe and put some soup into jars for them to take home. I ate five bowls of soup.

It was the best dinner ever.

The next spring, when my mother was starting her garden, we planted some flowers next to the Chinese vegetables. Mrs. Crumerine, the Fitzgeralds, and the Angelhowes planted some Chinese vegetables next to their flowers.

Soon the whole neighborhood was growing Chinese vegetables in their gardens. Up and down the street, little green plants poked out of the ground. Some looked like leaves and some looked like grass, and when the flowers started blooming, you could smell soup in the air.

ANALYZE THE TEXT

Story Structure How is the neighborhood different at the end of the story than at the beginning of the story?

Dig Deeper

Use Clues to Analyze the Text

Use these pages to learn about Conclusions and Story Structure. Then read *The Ugly Vegetables* again. Use what you learn to understand it better.

Conclusions

The Ugly Vegetables is a story about a girl and her garden. The author does not tell when and where the story takes place. You must find clues in the story and pictures to draw **conclusions** about the setting. When you draw conclusions, you make smart guesses about what the author does not say.

The words and pictures in a story are text evidence that can help you draw conclusions. Use a chart like this.

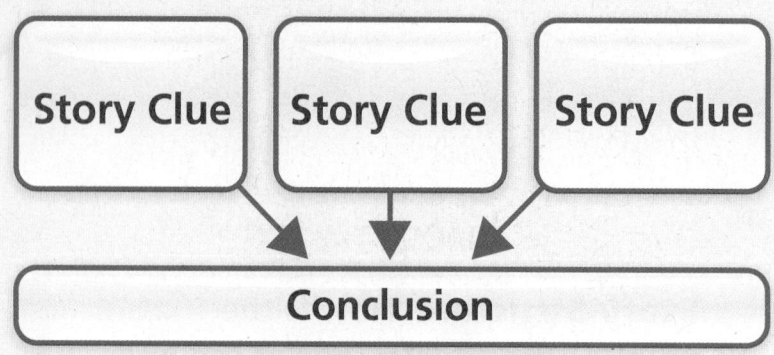

Story Structure

Characters are the people in a story. The **setting** is where and when the story takes place. The **plot** is what happens in the story. The beginning explains who the characters are, when and where the story takes place, and what the main problem is. The ending tells how the problem is solved. All of the story parts make up the **story structure**.

Your Turn

 **What can you learn from planting a garden?** Use evidence from the story to help you talk about your ideas with a partner. Take turns speaking and listening. Remember to speak in complete sentences.

Classroom Conversation

Now talk about these questions with the class.

1. What text evidence does the author give to help you figure out the setting?

2. How do you think Mommy learned to make the soup?

3. Why did the author write this story? Use text evidence from the story to explain.

Performance Task

WRITE ABOUT READING

myWriteSmart

Response Write sentences to tell how the girl's garden is different from the neighbors' gardens. Then draw a picture of each garden. Use the words and pictures from the story to help you.

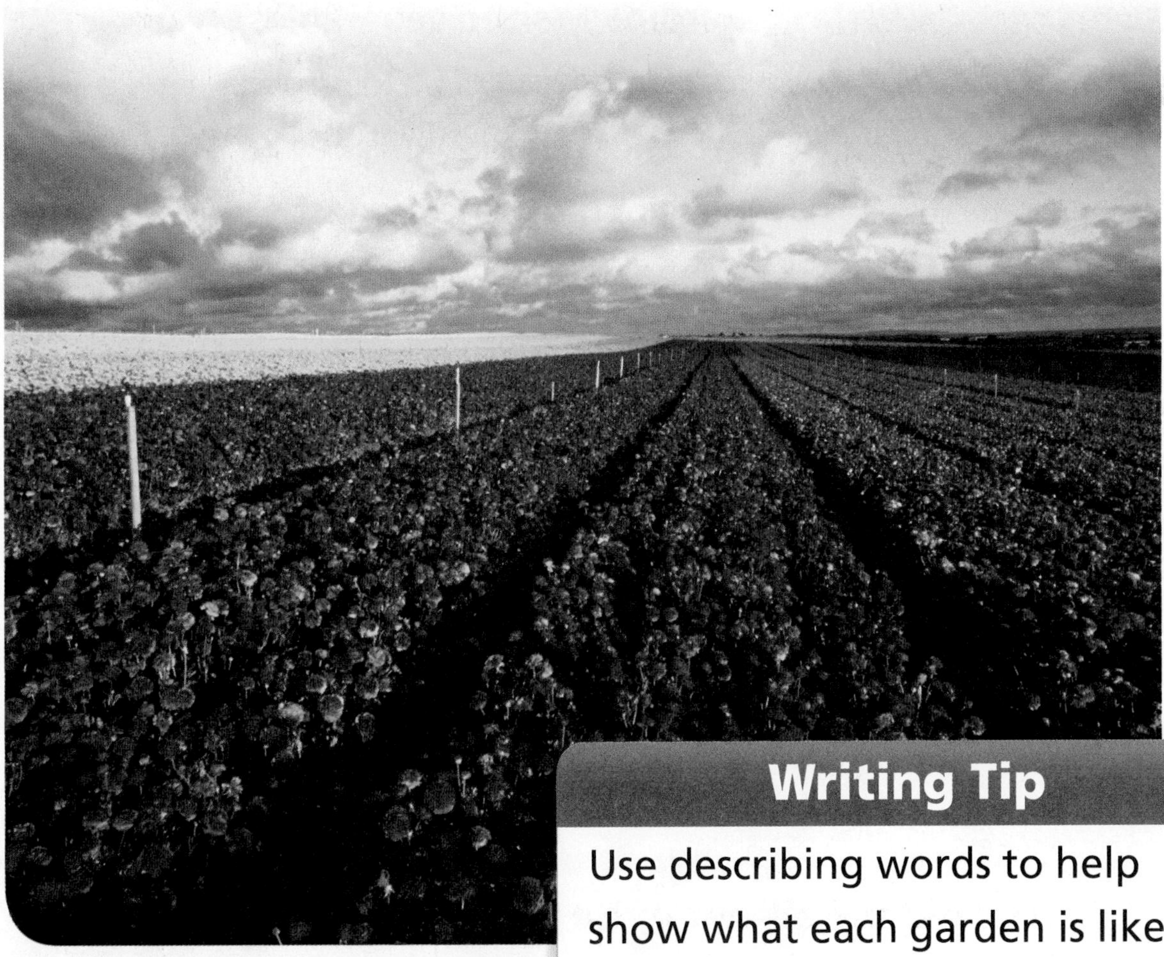

Writing Tip

Use describing words to help show what each garden is like.

Lesson 7

INFORMATIONAL TEXT

GENRE

Informational text gives facts about a topic. This is a magazine article.

TEXT FOCUS

A **bar graph** is a drawing that uses bars to compare numbers.

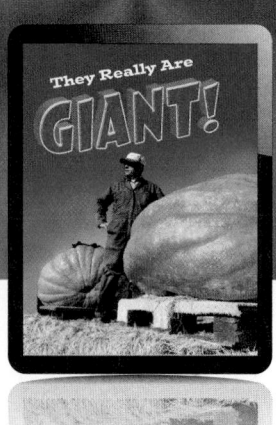

They Really Are GIANT!

by Judy Williams

To some farmers, plain, ordinary-sized vegetables seem boring. These farmers think big. They like to grow the biggest vegetables ever.

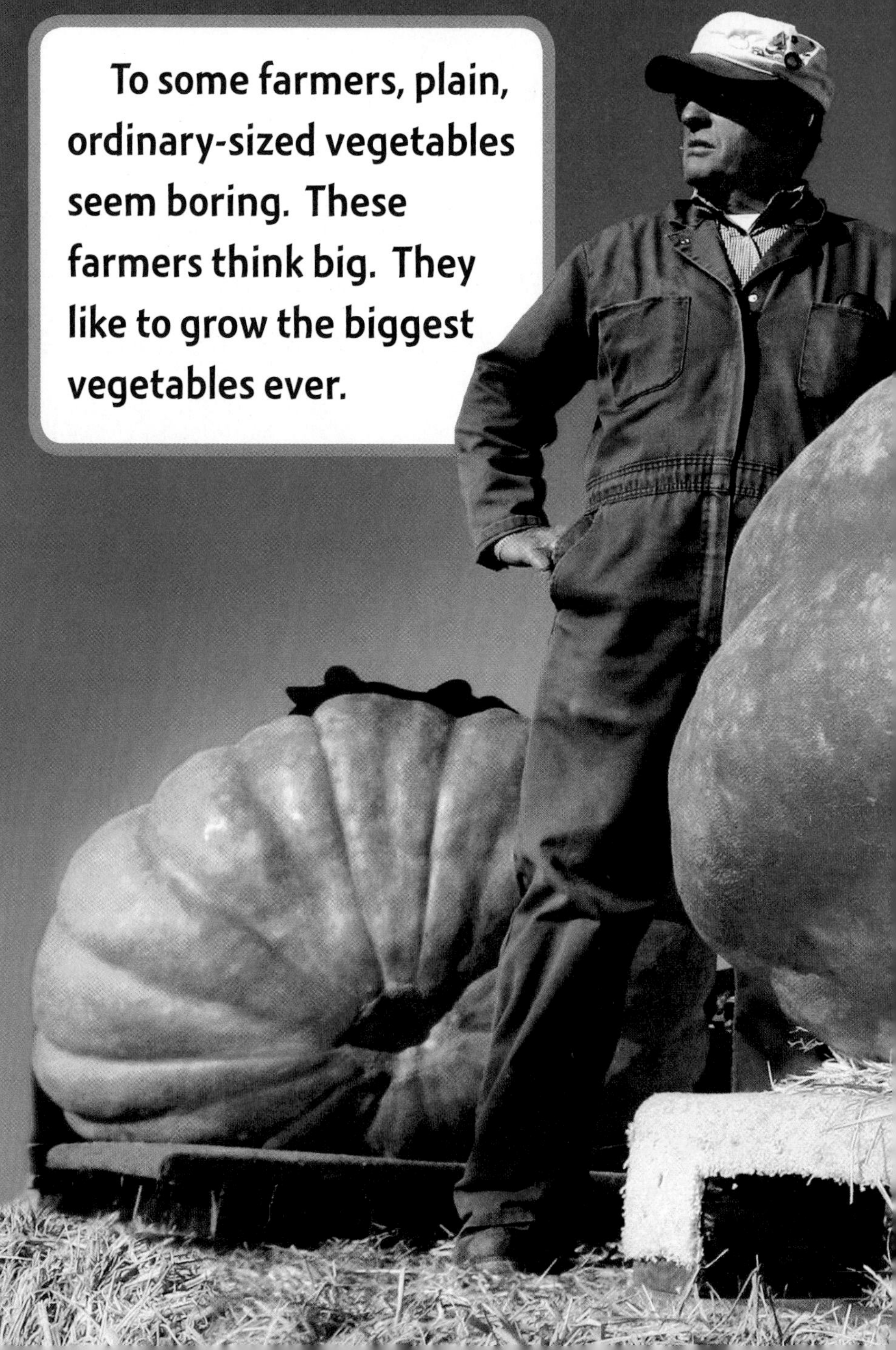

World Record Breakers

Plants are always blooming in California. The scent of rich soil fills the air. Every year in Half Moon Bay, the town holds the World Championship Pumpkin Weigh-Off. The judges all nodded yes when they saw the 2007 winner. It weighed 1,524 pounds, more than a big horse!

Pumpkins aren't the only giant veggies though. Some farmers use their muscles and heavy shovels to dig up 30-pound beets and turnips. Although these giants look tough, they are tender and delicious to eat.

Thadd Starr won first prize at the Half Moon Bay contest for his super-sized pumpkin.

Home of the Giants

Alaska might be the home of giant veggies. More giant vegetables seem to grow there than any other place in the world. Long summer days and good soil make veggies grow and grow. You can see 98-pound cabbages at the Alaska State Fair in Palmer.

Seven-year-old Brenna Dinkel from Wasilla, Alaska, looks small next to this giant wrinkled leaf cabbage!

How Big Are They?

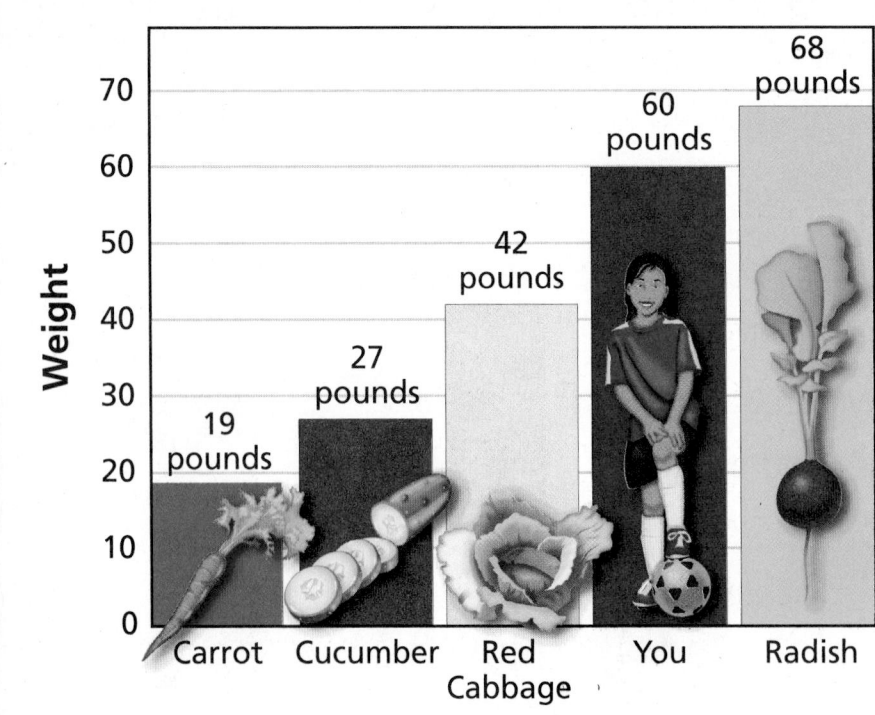

Bar graph titled "How Big Are They?" showing Weight:
- Carrot: 19 pounds
- Cucumber: 27 pounds
- Red Cabbage: 42 pounds
- You: 60 pounds
- Radish: 68 pounds

Compare Texts

TEXT TO TEXT

Compare and Contrast Compare what you learned about the different types of plants in the two selections. Discuss your ideas with a partner. Be sure to speak in complete sentences.

TEXT TO SELF

Share Experiences List the steps that the characters take to plant and care for their vegetables in *The Ugly Vegetables*. Which step do you think is the most important? Why?

TEXT TO WORLD

Connect to Social Studies In *The Ugly Vegetables*, Mommy says she is growing Chinese vegetables. Find China on a map or globe. Talk with a partner about what you found.

ELA RI.2.9, SL.2.6

Grammar

Proper Nouns **Proper nouns** are the special names of people, animals, places, or things. Proper nouns begin with **capital letters**.

Nouns	Proper Nouns
neighbor	Carissa Smith
pet	Fluffy
road	Main Street
drink	So Fruity Punch
state	Florida
country	China

Try This! **Write each sentence correctly. Remember to begin each proper noun with a capital letter.**

❶ There are many gardens in centerville.

❷ My friend molly bowen picked apples.

❸ mei's favorite toy is called action king.

A proper noun names a special person, animal, place, or thing. A proper noun is one kind of exact noun. Use exact nouns in your writing to paint a picture in your reader's mind.

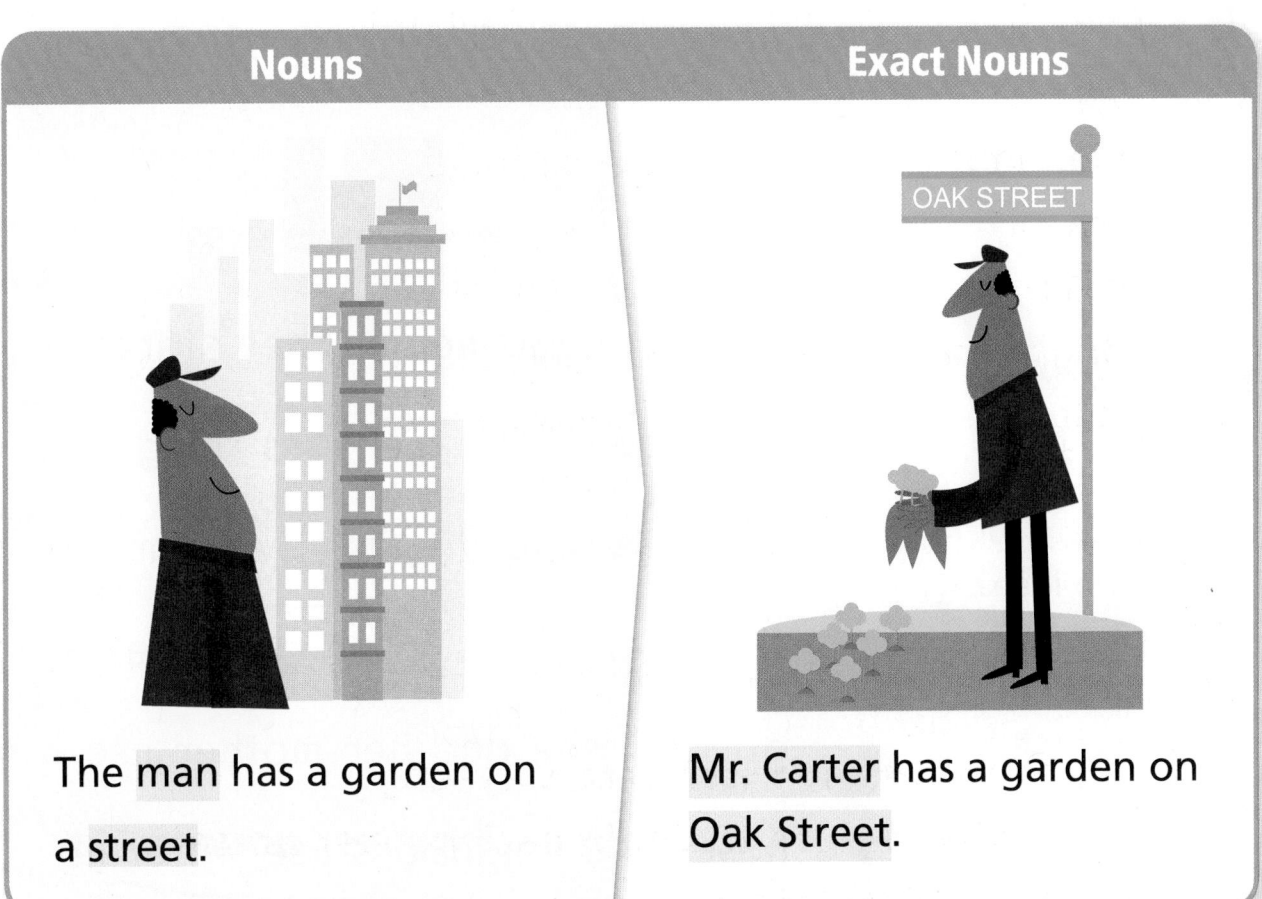

Nouns	Exact Nouns
The man has a garden on a street.	Mr. Carter has a garden on Oak Street.

Connect Grammar to Writing

When you revise your summary paragraph, look for nouns you can change to exact nouns. Be sure to begin each proper noun with a capital letter.

Informative Writing

✔ **Organization**   A **summary** tells what happens in a story by putting the events in the same order as they happened.

Kayla drafted a summary of the first part of *The Ugly Vegetables*. Later, she put the events in the right order.

Writing Checklist

✔ **Purpose**
Did my sentences all tie to the main idea?

✔ **Organization**
Did I tell things in the order in which they happened?

✔ **Evidence**
Did I use only the most important story events in my summary?

✔ **Conventions**
Did I capitalize and punctuate my sentences correctly?

Revised Draft

A girl helps her mother start a garden. The girl sees things they're doing differently from their neighbors. To water the garden, she and her mother use a hose. The neighbors use watering cans. The neighbors use smaller shovels.

My Summary

by Kayla Higgs

A girl helps her mother start a garden. The girl sees things they're doing differently from their neighbors. The neighbors use smaller shovels. To water the garden, she and her mother use a hose. The neighbors use watering cans.

The girl asks why their garden is different from the neighbors' gardens. Her mother says the vegetables they are growing are better than flowers. The girl doesn't believe her until the end of the story!

Reading as a Writer

Why did Kayla move sentences? What can you move in your writing to put events in the right order?

I moved sentences around to tell things in the order in which they happened.

SUPER STORMS

Weather Poems

Q LANGUAGE DETECTIVE

Talk About Words
Work with a partner. Choose one of the Context Cards. Add words to the sentence to explain details about the photo that tell when, where, or why.

Vocabulary in Context

▶ Read each Context Card.

▶ Talk about a picture. Use a different Vocabulary word from the one on the card.

1 **beware**
Beware of dangerous weather when a storm siren sounds its warning.

2 **damage**
Hail and strong winds can do a lot of harm. They can damage crops.

3 bend

High winds have caused the trunks of these trees to bend, or curve.

4 flash

The flash of lightning bolts lit up the dark night sky.

5 pounding

Pounding waves hit the beach hard in a storm.

6 prevent

Heavy snow may prevent, or stop, cars and trucks from traveling.

7 reach

In a flood, water can reach, or go as high as, rooftops.

8 equal

The height of the snow is equal to three feet.

SUPER STORMS

Read and Comprehend

Main Idea and Details The **topic** of an informational text is what the text is about. **Main ideas** are the most important ideas about the topic. **Details** tell more about each main idea. Use a chart like this to list main ideas and details.

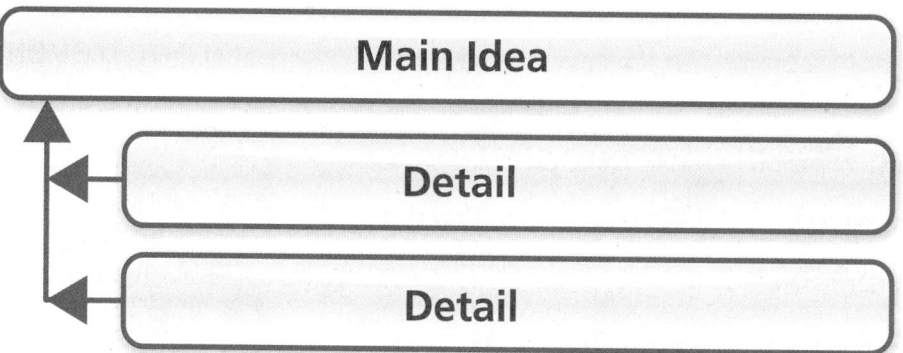

Main Idea

Detail

Detail

✓ TARGET STRATEGY

Visualize As you read, picture what is happening to help you understand and remember important ideas and details.

Weather

Do you ever wonder about the weather? Most people like when the weather is sunny. Sometimes, though, the weather can cause problems. When it rains or snows, you may have to stay inside. Some weather can even be dangerous. Tornadoes and hurricanes are two kinds of dangerous storms.

You will read about some types of dangerous weather in *Super Storms*.

💬 Talk About It

Think about how people find out about the weather. Why is it important to know when a storm is coming? Talk about your ideas with a group.

▸ Take turns speaking.

▸ Listen carefully to your partner. Add to his or her ideas.

▸ Stay on topic.

ANCHOR TEXT

SUPER STORMS

GENRE

Informational text gives facts about a topic. As you read, look for:

▶ photos
▶ facts and details about a topic
▶ maps or charts that help explain the topic

MEET THE AUTHOR

SEYMOUR SIMON

As a former science teacher, Seymour Simon loves to visit classrooms and talk with students. Those visits sometimes help him decide what to write about next.

Mr. Simon has written about everything from bats, bears, and bugs to snakes, sharks, and spiders. Of the more than 200 books he has written, *The Paper Airplane Book* is one of his favorites.

SUPER STORMS

by Seymour Simon

ESSENTIAL QUESTION

How can some storms
be dangerous?

The air around us is always moving and changing. We call these changes weather. Storms are sudden, violent changes in weather.

Every second, hundreds of thunderstorms are born around the world. Thunderstorms are heavy rain showers. They can drop millions of gallons of water in just one minute.

During a thunderstorm, lightning bolts can shoot between clouds and the ground. Lightning can destroy a tree or a small house. It can also start fires in forests and grasslands.

Thunder is the sound lightning makes as it suddenly heats the air. You can tell how far away lightning is. Count the seconds between the flash of light and the sound of thunder. Five seconds equal one mile.

ANALYZE THE TEXT

Cause and Effect What is the cause-and-effect connection between thunder and lightning?

Hailstones are chunks of ice that are tossed up and down by the winds of some thunderstorms. Hail can be the size of a marble or larger than a baseball. Nearly 5,000 hailstorms strike the United States every year. They can destroy crops and damage buildings and cars.

Thunderstorms sometimes give birth to tornadoes. Inside a storm, a funnel-shaped cloud reaches downward. Winds inside a tornado can spin faster than 300 miles per hour. These winds can lift cars off the ground and rip houses apart.

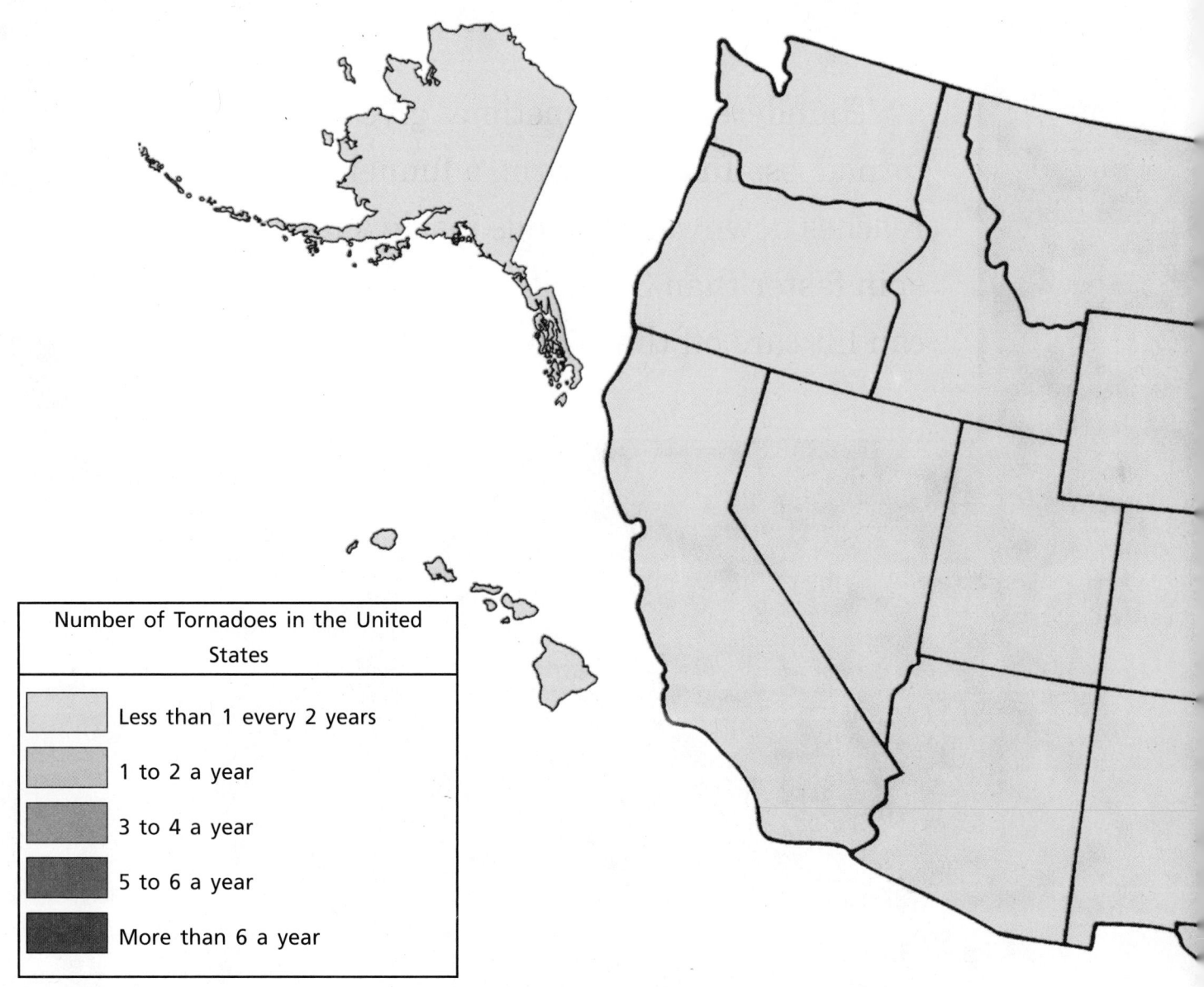

Number of Tornadoes in the United States

- Less than 1 every 2 years
- 1 to 2 a year
- 3 to 4 a year
- 5 to 6 a year
- More than 6 a year

More than 1,000 tornadoes strike the United States each year. Most of them form during spring and summer.

Television and radio stations often give early alerts. A tornado watch means that one may strike during the next few hours. A warning means a tornado has been seen by people or on radar. During a tornado warning you should find shelter in a basement or closet.

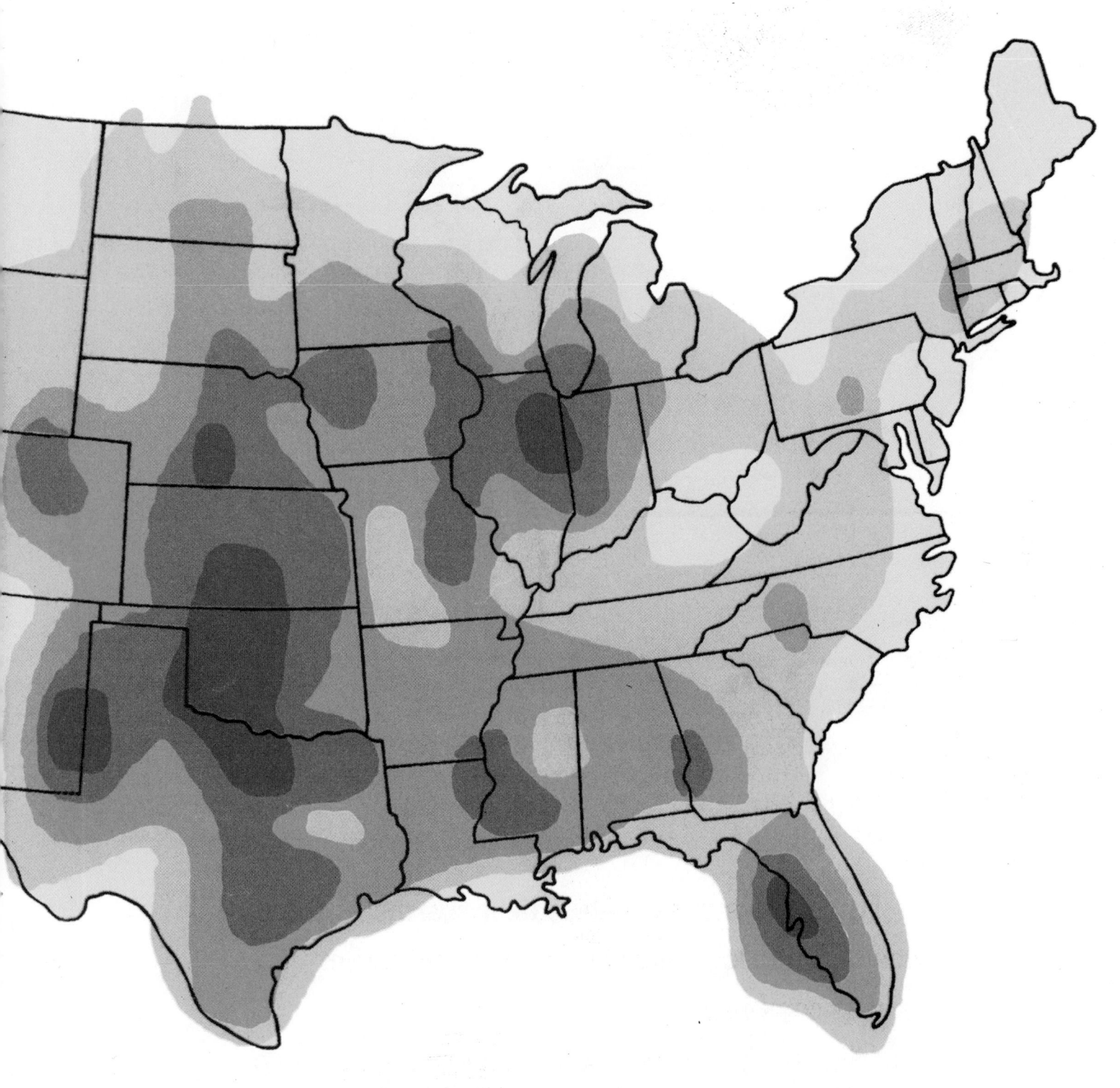

Hurricanes are the deadliest storms in the world. They kill more people than all other storms combined. Hurricanes stretch for hundreds of miles. They have winds of between 74 and 200 miles per hour.

The eye of a hurricane is the quiet center of the storm. Inside the eye, the wind stops blowing, the sun shines, and the sky is blue. But beware, the storm is not over yet.

Hurricanes are born over warm ocean waters from early summer to mid-fall. When they finally reach land, their pounding waves wash away beaches, boats, and houses. Their howling winds bend and uproot trees and telephone poles. Their heavy rains cause floods.

Blizzards are huge snowstorms. They have winds of at least 35 miles per hour. Usually at least two inches of snow falls per hour. Temperatures are at 20 degrees or lower. Falling and blowing snow make it hard to see in a blizzard.

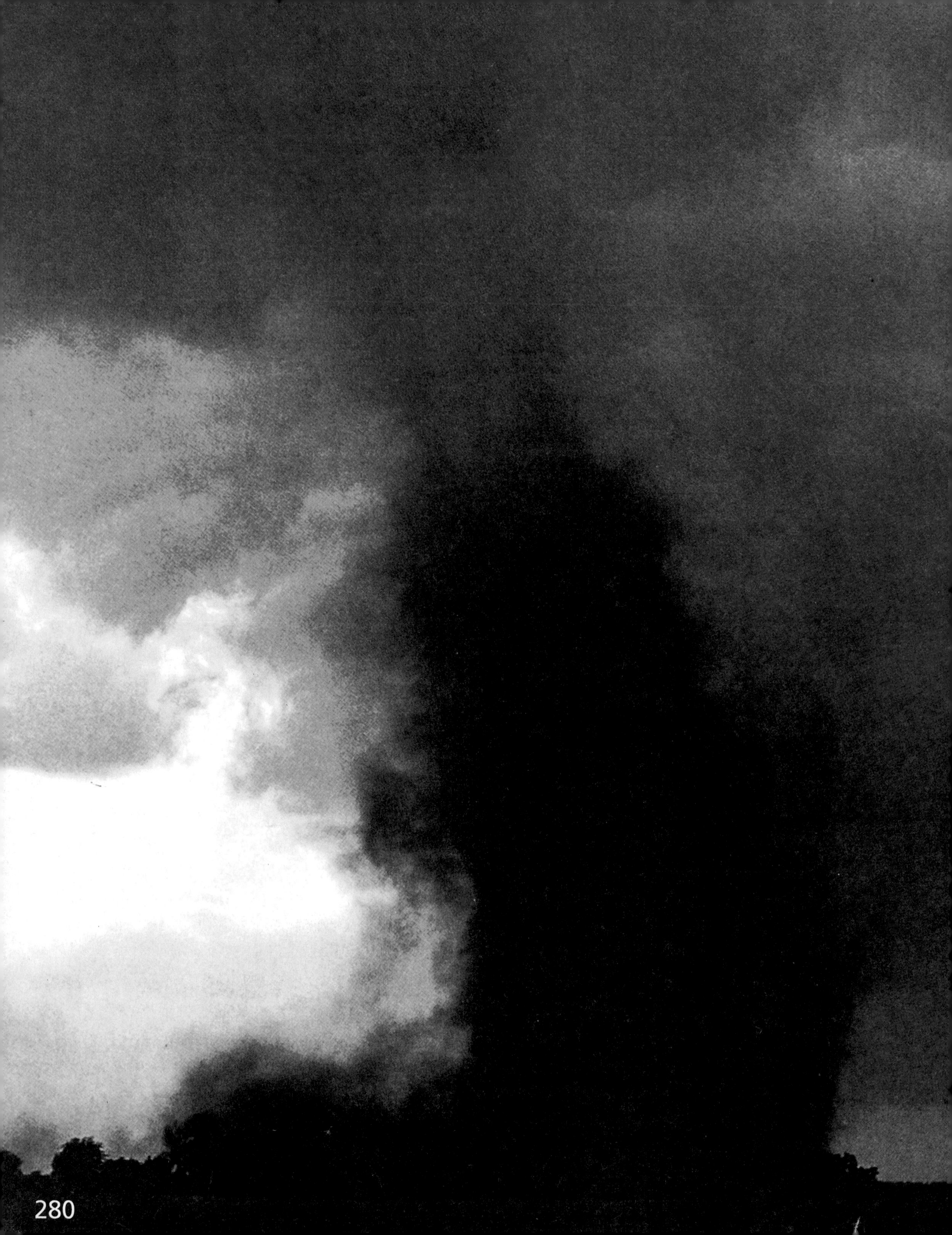

No one can prevent storms. But weather reports can predict and warn us when a storm may hit. The more prepared we are, the safer we will be when the next one strikes.

Dig Deeper

Use Clues to Analyze the Text

Use these pages to learn about Main Idea and Details and Cause and Effect. Then read *Super Storms* again. Use what you learn to understand it better.

Main Idea and Details

The author of *Super Storms* wrote about one main topic. He included a main idea and details in each section that explain the topic. The **main idea** is the most important idea in each section. **Details** tell you more information about the main idea. As you reread, use a chart like the one below. Record each main idea and the details that tell more about it.

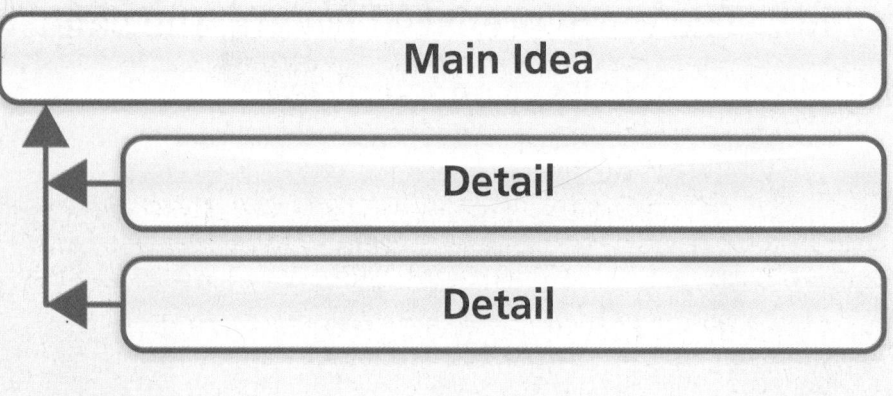

Cause and Effect

When one thing makes another happen, it is called cause and effect. For example, the wind of a tornado can make trees fall over. The tornado is the **cause**. Trees falling over is the **effect**. When you read, ask yourself what happens and why. This can help you understand how ideas are connected.

Your Turn

How can some storms be dangerous?
Use text evidence from *Super Storms* in your answer. Share your ideas with a partner. Remember to use respectful ways to take your turn speaking.

Classroom Conversation

Now talk about these questions with the class.

1 Which details in the selection help you figure out the topic and main idea?

2 How do the photos help you understand more about each storm?

3 Look back at page 279. What is the main idea of this section? What details tell more about it?

ELA RI.2.2, W.2.1, SL.2.1a, L.2.1f

WRITE ABOUT READING

Response Which type of weather do you think is the scariest? Write a few sentences to tell why. Use text evidence to help explain your opinion.

Writing Tip

Join two sentences that have the same predicate. Remember to use *and* between the two subjects.

POETRY

Weather Poems

☑ GENRE

Poetry uses the sound of words to show pictures and feelings.

☑ TEXT FOCUS

Repetition is when the same words are used more than once.

Many poets write poems about the weather. They might write about a flash of lightning or the way wind bends flowers.

The three poems you will read next are about the weather. Listen to the words that repeat in the poem "Night Drumming for Rain." Does it remind you of pounding raindrops?

Night Drumming for Rain

hi-iya nai-ho-o
earth rumbling
earth rumbling
our basket drum sounding
earth rumbling
everywhere humming
everywhere raining

Pima

Who Has Seen the Wind?

Who has seen the wind?
  Neither I nor you.
But when the leaves hang trembling,
  The wind is passing through.
Who has seen the wind?
  Neither you nor I.
But when the trees bow down their heads,
  The wind is passing by.

by Christina G. Rossetti

Weather

Dot a dot dot   dot a dot dot
Spotting the windowpane.
Spack a spack speck   flick a flack fleck
Freckling the windowpane.

A spatter a scatter   a wet cat a clatter
A splatter a rumble outside.
Umbrella umbrella umbrella umbrella
Bumbershoot barrel of rain.

Slosh a galosh   slosh a galosh
Slither and slather and glide
A puddle a jump a puddle a jump
A puddle a jump puddle splosh
A juddle a pump aluddle a dump a
Puddmuddle jump in and slide!

by Eve Merriam

Write a Weather Poem

Write your own weather poem. Include words that repeat more than once. You might describe a hot summer day. You might write about how you feel when it rains. You might even write a funny poem about getting caught in a storm!

Compare Texts

TEXT TO TEXT

Understand Poems Read the poems in *Weather Poems* again with a partner. Which poems use repeated words to help the reader understand what the author wants to say? Which ones use rhythm? Do any of them rhyme? Take turns speaking and listening.

TEXT TO SELF

Make a Plan Choose one type of storm from *Super Storms*. With the class, talk about what you would do to stay safe during that kind of weather. Speak only when it is your turn.

TEXT TO WORLD

Observe Local Weather What types of weather from *Super Storms* or *Weather Poems* do you get where you live? List each type. Compare your list with a partner's.

ELA RL.2.4, SL.2.1a

Grammar

What Is a Verb? A **verb** names an action that someone or something does or did. A verb is found in the action part, or **predicate,** of a sentence.

Verbs in Sentences

Rain falls.

Strong winds blow.

The storm destroyed homes.

The tornado bent many trees.

 **Work with a partner. Read the sentences aloud. Name the verb in each sentence.**

1. I learned about storms.

2. We stay indoors.

3. Tornadoes form in summer.

4. The thunder scared my cat.

When you write, use exact verbs. They make your sentences come alive and tell your reader exactly what is happening.

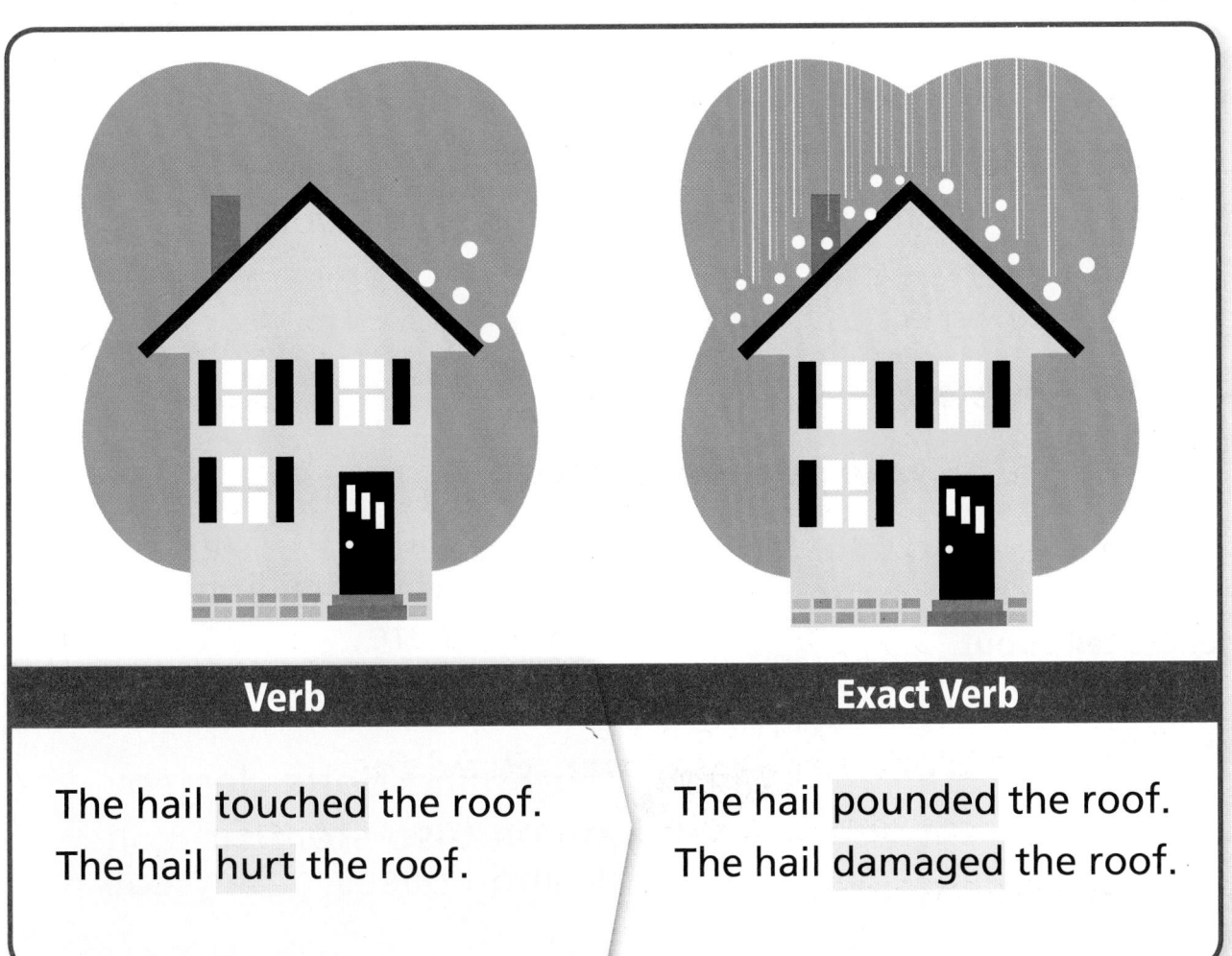

Verb	Exact Verb
The hail touched the roof.	The hail pounded the roof.
The hail hurt the roof.	The hail damaged the roof.

Connect Grammar to Writing

When you revise your writing, look for verbs that you can change to more exact verbs.

Informative Writing

☑ **Evidence** When you write an **informational paragraph,** think about the facts you want to include. Then put the facts in your own words. Use facts and definitions instead of opinions.

    Greg drafted a paragraph about thunderstorms. He used facts and definitions from *Super Storms.* Then he revised some sentences to be in his own words.

Writing Checklist

☑ **Purpose**
Do all of my sentences tell about the main idea?

☑ **Organization**
Does my topic sentence tell the main idea?

☑ **Evidence**
Did I use facts and definitions instead of opinions?

☑ **Conventions**
Did I write neatly and leave margins?

Revised Draft

Thunderstorms bring lots of
Millions of gallons of rain can
rain. ∧ ~~They can drop millions~~
fall in one minute.
~~of gallons of water in just one~~

~~minute.~~ Lightning bolts destroy
Lightning can also start fires in
buildings and houses. ∧ ~~They can~~
trees or grass!
~~also start fires in forests and~~
Thunder is the sound made when
~~grasslands. Thunder is the sound~~
lightning heats the air quickly.
~~lightning makes as it suddenly~~

~~heats the air.~~

ELA W.2.2, W.2.5

Thunderstorms
by Greg Popov

Thunderstorms bring lots of rain. Millions of gallons of rain can fall in one minute. Lightning bolts destroy buildings and houses. Lightning can also start fires in trees or grass! Thunder is the sound made when lightning heats the air quickly. People can tell how close lightning is by counting the seconds between lightning and the sound of thunder. For every five seconds you count, the lightning is one mile away. Try this the next time you see lightning!

Reading as a Writer

How did Greg tell facts in his own words? Where did he use definitions? Where can you use definitions in your writing?

I made sure I used my own words to tell facts.

How Chipmunk Got His Stripes
Joseph Bruchac & James Bruchac
Pictures by Jose Aruego
& Ariane Dewey

Why Rabbits Have Short Tails

🔍 **LANGUAGE DETECTIVE**

Talk About Words
Work with a partner. Choose two Vocabulary words. Use them together in a sentence. Share your sentence with the class.

Vocabulary in Context

▶ Read each Context Card.

▶ Ask a question that uses one of the Vocabulary words.

1 tunnel
A chipmunk knows how to dig a tunnel, which is a passage underground.

2 curled
This fox is curled up around its warm, bushy tail.

3 height

An eagle builds its nest at an amazing height. It is at the top of a tall tree.

4 direction

An owl can turn its head in any direction. It can look all around.

5 toward

These bear cubs run toward their mother so she can protect them.

6 healed

This pangolin will go back to the forest when it is well, or healed.

7 brag

These antlers are something to brag about! They are huge.

8 tease

Never tease, or bother, wild animals. Always respect them.

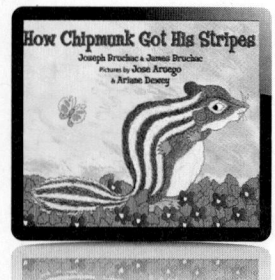

Read and Comprehend

Understanding Characters In *How Chipmunk Got His Stripes,* the characters Bear and Brown Squirrel speak and act like people. Think about what they say, think, and do when something happens to them in the story. Paying attention to this text evidence can help you understand what each character is like.

Use a chart to list the characters and your ideas.

Character	Event	Words, Thoughts, Actions

☑ **TARGET STRATEGY**

Summarize Stop to tell important events as you read.

Traditional Tales

Traditional tales are stories that people have been telling for many years. Some traditional tales are made-up stories about how or why something is the way it is.

Characters in traditional tales usually learn a lesson. This lesson is called the moral of the story. When you read *How Chipmunk Got His Stripes,* think about what Bear and Brown Squirrel learn and what the story explains.

💬 Think | Pair | Share

How are traditional tales different from other stories you have read? Discuss with your partner some details about stories you have read. Be sure to listen carefully and speak in complete sentences. Then share your ideas with the class.

ANCHOR TEXT

Joseph Bruchac and James Bruchac

As a boy, Joseph Bruchac listened to his grandfather tell stories of their Native American heritage. Joseph passed these stories down to his son, James. Now this father-and-son team writes books together, such as *Raccoon's Last Race*.

☑ GENRE

A **folktale** is a kind of traditional tale. As you read, look for:

▶ a simple plot that teaches a lesson

▶ animal characters who talk and act like people

MEET THE ILLUSTRATORS

Jose Aruego and Ariane Dewey

These two artists make a great team. When they are working on a book, Jose Aruego first draws the lines for the characters, using pen and ink. Then Ariane Dewey paints the colors. In this way, they have illustrated more than 60 books.

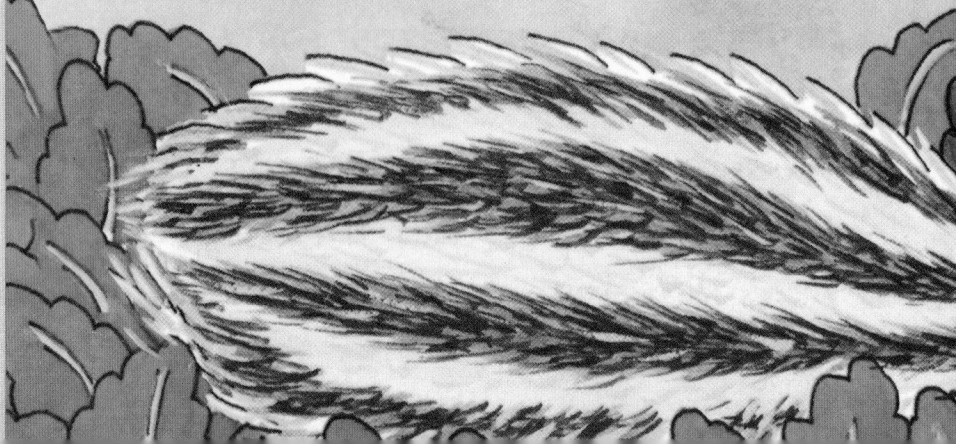

How Chipmunk Got His Stripes

by Joseph Bruchac and James Bruchac
pictures by Jose Aruego and Ariane Dewey

ESSENTIAL QUESTION

How can stories help
you learn a lesson?

One autumn day long ago, Bear was out walking.
As he walked, he began to brag:

"I am Bear. I am the biggest
of all the animals. Yes, I am!
I am Bear. I am the strongest
of all the animals. Yes, I am!
I am Bear. I am the loudest
of all the animals. Yes, I am!
I am Bear, I am Bear.
I can do anything. Yes, I can!"

As soon as Bear said those words, a little voice spoke up from the ground.

"Can you really do anything?"

Bear looked down. He saw a little brown squirrel, standing on his hind legs.

"Can you really do anything?" Brown Squirrel asked again.

Bear stood up very tall. "I am Bear. I can do anything. Yes, I can!"

"Can you tell the sun not to rise tomorrow morning?" Brown Squirrel asked.

"I have never tried that before. But I am Bear. I can do that. Yes, I can!"

ANALYZE THE TEXT

Understanding Characters What does Bear say and do? What does this tell you about him?

Bear turned west to face the sun. It was the time
when the sun always goes down. Bear stood up to his
full height and spoke in a loud voice.

"SUN, DO NOT COME UP TOMORROW."

At his words, the sun began to disappear behind
the hills.

"You see?" Bear said. "Sun is afraid of me.
He is running away."

"But will the sun come up tomorrow?"
Brown Squirrel asked.

"No," Bear answered. "The sun will not come up!"

Then Bear turned to face east, the direction where the sun always used to come up. He sat down. Little Brown Squirrel sat down beside him. All that night, they did not sleep. All that night, Bear kept saying these words:

"The sun will not come up, hummph!
The sun will not come up, hummph!"

But as the night went on, little Brown Squirrel began to say something, too. He said these words:

"The sun is going to rise, oooh!
The sun is going to rise, oooh!"

All through the night, they sat there. One by one, other animals gathered around them. Fox and Wolf, Deer and Moose, Rabbit and Porcupine, Hawk and Owl, Otter and Beaver, Frog and Turtle, and even the little mice came. They wanted to see who would be right, Bear or Brown Squirrel. This is what the other animals heard:

"The sun will not come up, hummph!"
"The sun is going to rise, oooh!"
"The sun will not come up, hummph!"
"The sun is going to rise, oooh!"

ANALYZE THE TEXT

Author's Word Choice Why does the author keep repeating Bear's sentence and little Brown Squirrel's sentence?

Finally, it was just before dawn, the time when the sun always used to come up.

"Look," said Turtle, "a little bit of red is starting to show."

"Yes," said Owl. "I believe the sun will rise today."

Bear only chanted louder:

"The sun will not come up, hummph!"

But right next to him, little Brown Squirrel piped up:

"The sun is going to rise, oooh!"

305

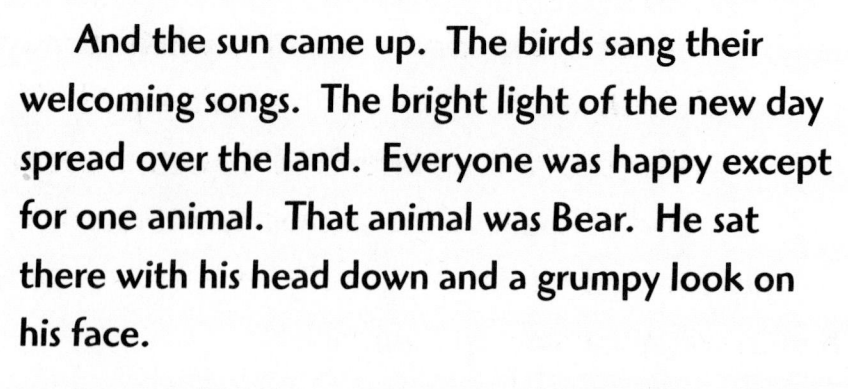

And the sun came up. The birds sang their welcoming songs. The bright light of the new day spread over the land. Everyone was happy except for one animal. That animal was Bear. He sat there with his head down and a grumpy look on his face.

The happiest animal of all was little Brown Squirrel. "The sun came up," he chirped. "The sun came up, the sun came up, the sun came up."

Brown Squirrel was so happy, he forgot what his wise old grandmother had told him when he was very young.

"Brown Squirrel," his grandmother had said, "it is good to be right about something. But when someone else is wrong, it is not a good idea to tease him."

Now little Brown Squirrel began to tease Bear.

"Bear is foolish, the sun came up.
Bear is silly, the sun came up.
Bear is stupid, the sun—"

WHOMP!

Bear's big paw came down on little Brown Squirrel, pinning him to the ground. Bear leaned over and opened his huge mouth.

"Yes," Bear growled. "The sun did come up. Yes, I do look foolish. But you will not live to see another sunrise. You will not ever tease anyone else again, because I, Bear, am going to eat you."

Brown Squirrel thought fast. "You are right to eat me," he said. "I was wrong to tease you. I would like to say I am sorry before you eat me. But you are pressing down on me so hard that I cannot say anything. I cannot say anything at all. I cannot even breathe. If you would lift up your paw just a little bit, then I could take a deep breath and apologize before you eat me."

"That is a good idea," Bear said. "I would like to hear you apologize before I eat you."

So Bear lifted up his paw. But instead of apologizing, Brown Squirrel ran. He ran as fast as he could toward the pile of stones where he had his home. He had a tunnel under those stones and a nice warm burrow underground. Little Brown Squirrel's grandmother stood there in the door waiting for him.

"Hurry, Brown Squirrel," she called. "Hurry, hurry!"

Little Brown Squirrel dove for the door to his home. But Bear was faster than he looked. He grabbed for little Brown Squirrel with his big paw. Bear's long, sharp claws scratched Brown Squirrel's back from the top of his head to the tip of his tail.

But Brown Squirrel got away. Deep down in his burrow, where Bear couldn't get him, Brown Squirrel curled up next to his grandmother and slept all winter while those scratches on his back healed.

When spring came again, little Brown Squirrel came out of his hole and looked at himself. There were long pale stripes all the way down his back where Bear had scratched him. He was Brown Squirrel no longer. He was now Chipmunk, the striped one.

That is how Chipmunk got his stripes. Ever since then, Chipmunk has been the first animal to get up every morning. As the sun rises, he scoots to the top of the tallest tree to sing his song:

"The sun came up,
the sun came up,
the sun came up,
the sun came up!"

And ever since then, Bear has been the last animal to get up. He doesn't like to hear Chipmunk's song. It reminds him—as it reminds us all—that no one, not even Bear, can do everything.

Dig Deeper

Use Clues to Analyze the Text

Use these pages to learn about Understanding Characters and Author's Word Choice. Then read *How Chipmunk Got His Stripes* again. Use what you learn to understand it better.

Understanding Characters

How Chipmunk Got His Stripes tells why chipmunks look the way they do. In this story, the characters deal with some problems. For example, Brown Squirrel tells Bear that he can't keep the sun from coming up.

Think about what the characters do and say when they have a problem. List text evidence in a chart like the one below.

Character	Event	Words, Thoughts, Actions

Author's Word Choice

Authors sometimes repeat words or phrases. This is called **repetition**. Repetition sometimes makes the words you read have a rhythm, or beat. Repetition also helps you understand important parts of the story. On page 300, Bear repeats, "Yes, I am!" This helps you understand that Bear brags a lot.

Your Turn

 Turn and Talk

How can stories help you learn a lesson? Talk with a partner. Use the lesson in the story as an example. Ask for more information if you do not understand your partner's ideas.

💬 Classroom Conversation

Now talk about these questions with the class.

1. What do Bear and Brown Squirrel do when they have a problem?

2. What can you tell about each character from how they act when they have a problem?

3. How could Bear and Brown Squirrel each have handled his problem differently?

WRITE ABOUT READING ·······················

Response What did you learn from Brown Squirrel about teasing? Write a note to him telling how you feel about teasing. Give text evidence that tells why. Make sure you use complete sentences.

Dear Brown Squirrel,

Writing Tip

When you write a note, include a greeting and a closing. Be sure to add a comma to each.

Why Rabbits
Have Short Tails

✅ GENRE

Traditional tales are stories that have been told for many years.

✅ TEXT FOCUS

The **moral** is the lesson a character learns in a story.

Why Rabbits Have Short Tails

adapted by Gina Sabella

Once Rabbit had a long, beautiful tail. It curled over his back like a furry fan. Rabbit was taking his family on a trip.

"We have to travel in the direction of the stream," Rabbit said. "When we see the hill with the tallest height, we should head toward it."

When they spotted the tallest hill, Rabbit saw that they would have to swim across the stream.

Rabbit liked to brag. He told everyone how clever he was. He did not tell anyone that he could not swim. He did not want anyone to tease him.

Rabbit saw a turtle crawling out of a tunnel. Ten tiny turtles followed behind.

"You have a large family," Rabbit said.

"Yes," Turtle replied. "My family is the biggest in the woods."

"I'm not sure," Rabbit answered. "My family might be bigger."

"Line up your children across the stream," Rabbit said. "Then I can see who has a bigger family." Soon the turtles were lined up. Rabbit and his family jumped on their backs and skipped across the stream.

Turtle was not happy. He tried to grab Rabbit by the tail. But Rabbit's tail snapped off and he hopped away.

Even after it healed, Rabbit's tail never grew long and beautiful again.

Compare Texts

TEXT TO TEXT

Write an Ending Review the moral taught in each of the stories you read. Write a few sentences about which moral you feel is the most important to learn. Explain why.

TEXT TO SELF

Act Out a Lesson The characters in the stories you just read all learn a lesson. Act out for a partner a lesson you have learned. Have your partner guess what you learned.

TEXT TO WORLD

Think About Lessons Think about the lessons taught in each selection. How would things be different in our world if no one learned these lessons? Discuss your ideas with a partner. Build on each other's ideas.

Grammar

▶ Multimedia
Grammar Glossary

Verbs in the Present A **verb** in the **present** names an action that is happening now. Add *-s* or *-es* to this kind of verb when it tells about a singular noun. Do not add *-s* or *-es* when the verb tells about a plural noun.

Verbs After Singular Nouns	Verbs After Plural Nouns
The bear sleeps.	Two bears sleep.
The animal runs.	Many animals run.
The chipmunk rushes.	Some chipmunks rush.

Try This! **Choose the correct verb to complete each sentence. Then write the sentence correctly.**

❶ The squirrel (learn, learns) a lesson.

❷ Bears (scratch, scratches)!

❸ The animal (hide, hides) in a hole.

❹ Days (pass, passes) before the animal comes out.

To make your writing smoother, join two short sentences with the same subject. Write *and* between the two predicates to make one longer sentence. Be sure to use the correct verb forms.

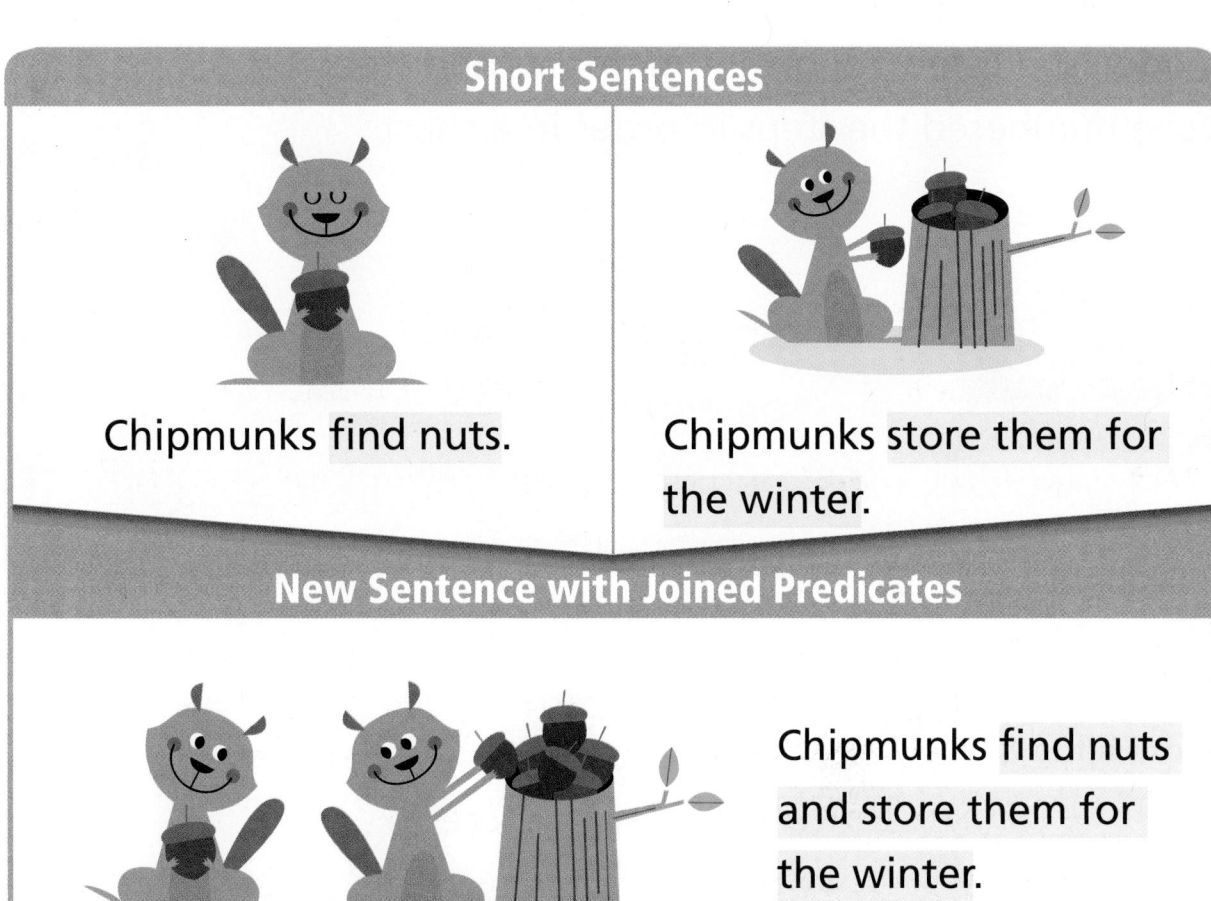

Short Sentences

Chipmunks find nuts.

Chipmunks store them for the winter.

New Sentence with Joined Predicates

Chipmunks find nuts and store them for the winter.

Connect Grammar to Writing

When you revise your instructions next week, try joining two sentences that have the same subject.

Informative Writing

> ✔ **Purpose** Before you write **instructions**, think about what you want readers to do. What does your reader need to know to do this project?

When Alexa planned instructions for making a birdfeeder, she listed important materials and steps. Then she numbered the steps in order in a chart.

Writing Process Checklist

▶ **Prewrite**

✔ Did I think about my audience and purpose?

✔ Did I choose a topic I know well?

✔ Did I include all the important steps?

✔ Are my steps in the correct order?

Draft

Revise

Edit

Publish and Share

Exploring a Topic

Things You Need

pinecone

peanut butter

birdseed

spoon

∧paper plate

∧string

Steps

2 spread peanut butter on pinecone

4 hang on tree

3 roll in birdseed

1 tie string to pinecone

Step Chart

1. Tie a piece of string to a pinecone.

↓

2. Cover the pinecone with peanut butter.

↓

3. Roll the pinecone in birdseed.

↓

4. Hang the birdfeeder in a tree.

Reading as a Writer

What helpful step did Alexa add to her chart? Where can you add important or helpful steps to your own chart?

When I wrote my instructions, I made sure all the important steps were included.

331

Lesson 10

THE LIFE OF JELLYFISH
Twig C. George

Splash
Photography

🔍 LANGUAGE DETECTIVE

Talk About Words
Work with a partner. Think about times when you might use each Vocabulary word in speaking or writing. Do you and your partner have similar ideas or different ideas?

Vocabulary in Context

▶ Read each Context Card.

▶ Tell a story about two pictures, using the Vocabulary words.

1 millions
It looks like this shark has millions of teeth, but it really only has a few dozen.

2 choices
Visitors at the aquarium have many choices of things to see.

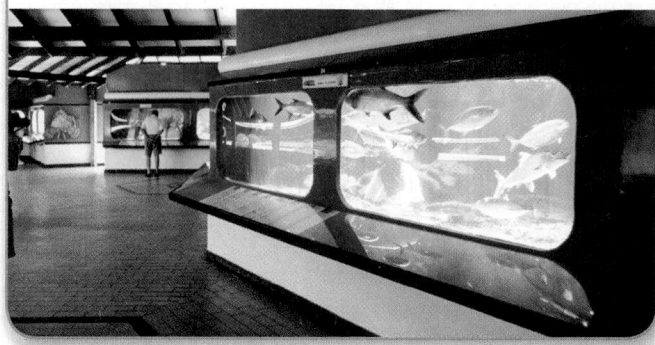

332 **ELA** L.2.5a, L.2.6

3 drift

This clever otter will not drift, or float, away.

4 simple

Dolphins make jumping out of the ocean look simple and easy.

5 weaker

One of these crab claws is weaker than the other. It is not very strong.

6 wrapped

The octopus wrapped its strong tentacles around its prey.

7 disgusting

Yuck! The litter around the trash can smells disgusting!

8 decide

Is this a starfish or a crab? You decide.

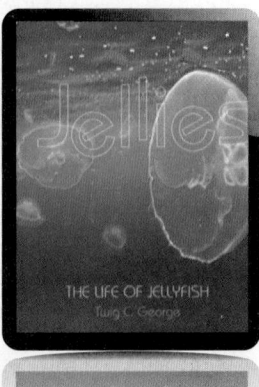

THE LIFE OF JELLYFISH
Twig C. George

Read and Comprehend

✓ TARGET SKILL

Fact and Opinion A **fact** is something that can be proved true. An **opinion** is a belief or feeling. Authors often include facts and opinions when they write. They also give reasons to support their facts or opinions. The reasons may be in the words or photos of a text.

You can use a chart like this to list facts and opinions.

Fact	Opinion

✓ TARGET STRATEGY

Monitor/Clarify Stop and think when you don't understand something. Find text evidence to help you figure out what doesn't make sense.

Ocean Life

Many kinds of animals live in the ocean. Some are large, such as a whale. Some are small, such as a seahorse. Every animal in the ocean needs to eat. Some eat ocean plants, and some eat smaller fish. Most sea animals have ways to keep themselves safe from danger. Life under the sea is very interesting.

Jellies is about jellyfish. You will read more about how jellyfish live in the ocean.

Talk About It

How are animals that live in the sea different from animals that live on land? Talk about it with a group. Use describing words to tell how the animals are different. Add your ideas to your classmates' ideas.

ANCHOR TEXT

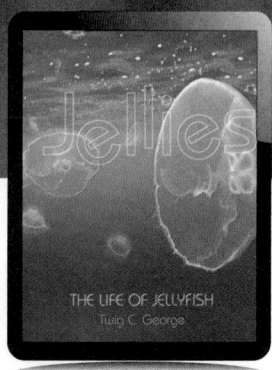

 GENRE

Informational text
gives facts about a topic.
As you read, look for:

▸ photos and captions
▸ facts and details
  about a topic

MEET THE AUTHOR

Twig C. George

Twig C. George's love of nature began while she was growing up around her mom, writer Jean Craighead George. The George household had many unusual pets, including tarantulas, sea gulls, crows, and a screech owl that liked to take showers. Twig George raises her own children around nature, too.

Jellies
THE LIFE OF JELLYFISH

by Twig C. George

ESSENTIAL QUESTION

What is special about
animals that live in
the ocean?

If you were a jellyfish you would have two choices—to go up or to go down. That's it. Two. You would not have a brain, so you could not decide what to have for breakfast or where to go for lunch.

Mangrove jellyfish

The ocean currents would carry you along from place to place. In this way you could travel hundreds of miles. Food might pass by you and get caught in your tentacles. Or not.

Sea turtles, dolphins, and whale sharks would try to eat you.

You wouldn't worry about it because you couldn't.

You would just float on.

Rhizostone jellyfish

Comb jellyfish

You would protect yourself with millions of tiny, mechanical cells that, when touched by another animal, release a chemical and sting. Like a bow and arrow. You would not know if you were stinging a friend or an enemy. You would not even know what a friend or an enemy was!

Jellyfish sting for protection and to catch food.
That's all. They don't hunt and they can't chase.
They just bump and sting. Bump and sting.

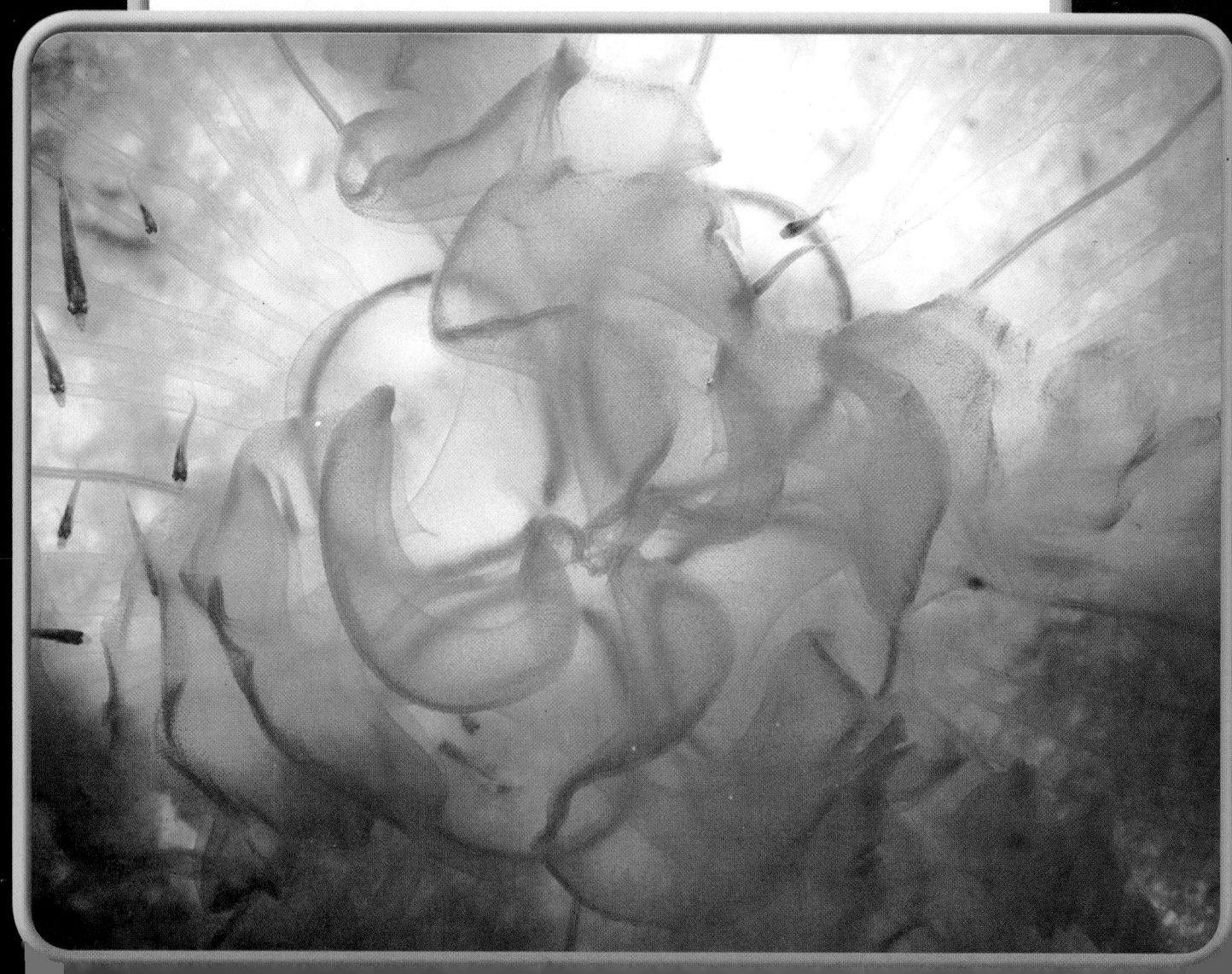

Some jellyfish sting gently. Some jellyfish have a sting so powerful that they are more dangerous than a cobra. These are the Australian box jellies.

Australian
box jellyfish

Thimble jellyfish

Jellyfish are so simple that they look like plastic trash floating in the sea. When an animal eats a jellyfish it stays healthy and strong. When an animal eats plastic it gets weaker and weaker and eventually dies.

Upside-down jellyfish

Some jellyfish lie on the shallow bottom in clear, warm seas and grow their own food. These are called upside-down jellyfish. Once they have eaten small bits of algae, just once, they can grow more inside their bodies by sitting in the sun. They are their own greenhouses and grocery stores all wrapped up in one.

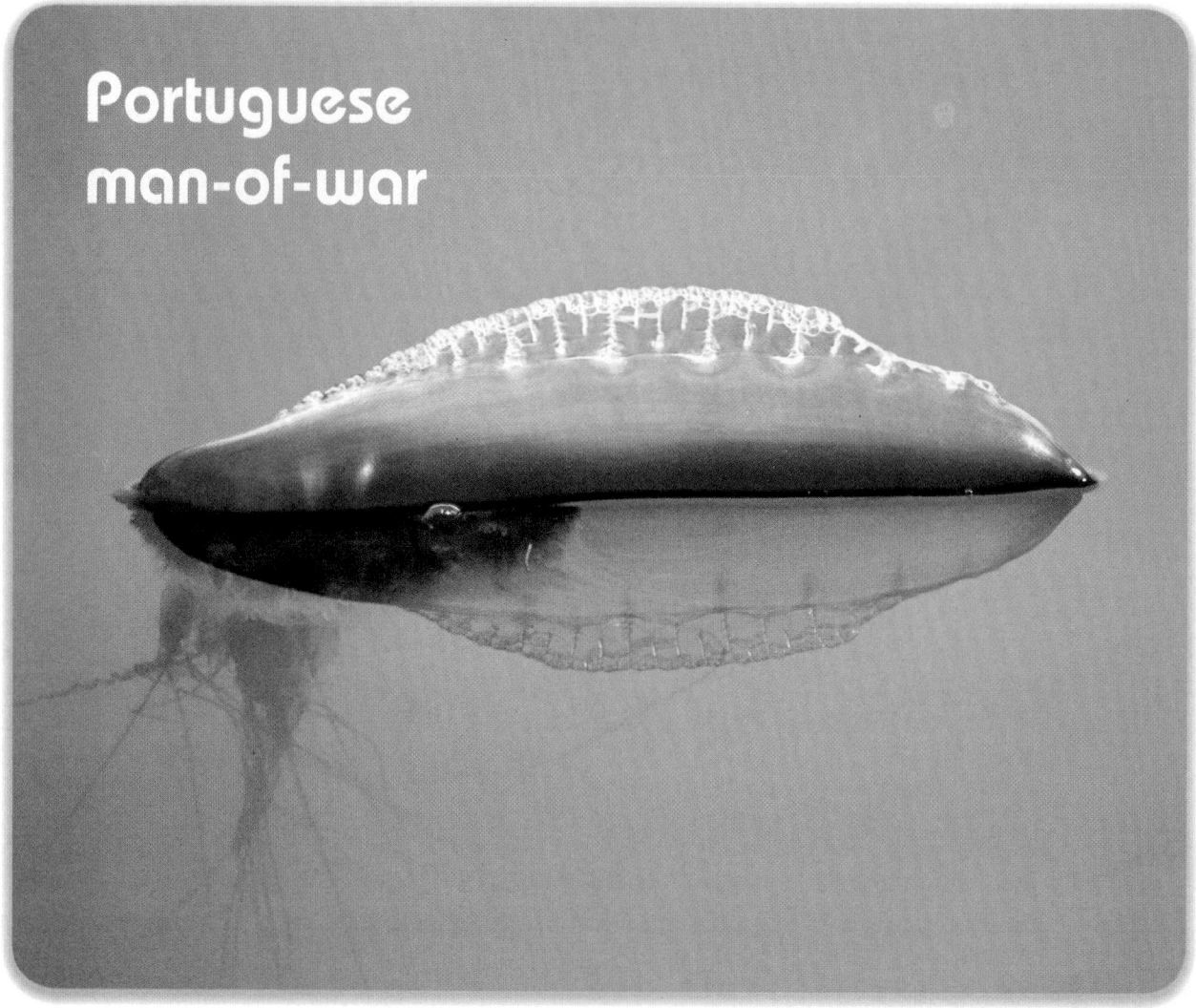

Portuguese man-of-war

To be a jellyfish you need to be shaped like a bell, with at least one mouth, and tentacles. Many animals called jellyfish are really something else. The Portuguese man-of-war is not a real jellyfish. It has an air-filled bubble instead of a water-filled bell.

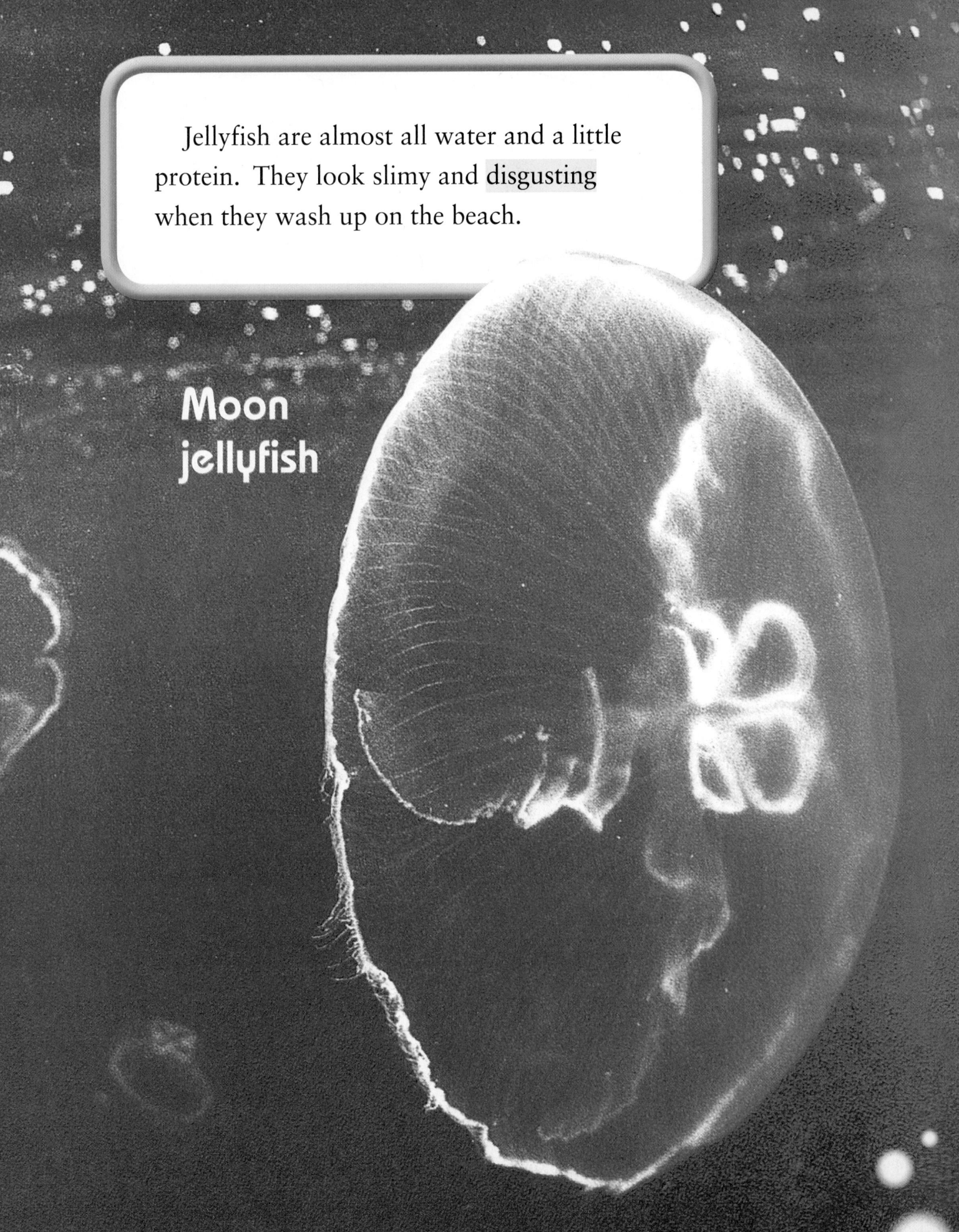

Jellyfish are almost all water and a little protein. They look slimy and disgusting when they wash up on the beach.

Moon jellyfish

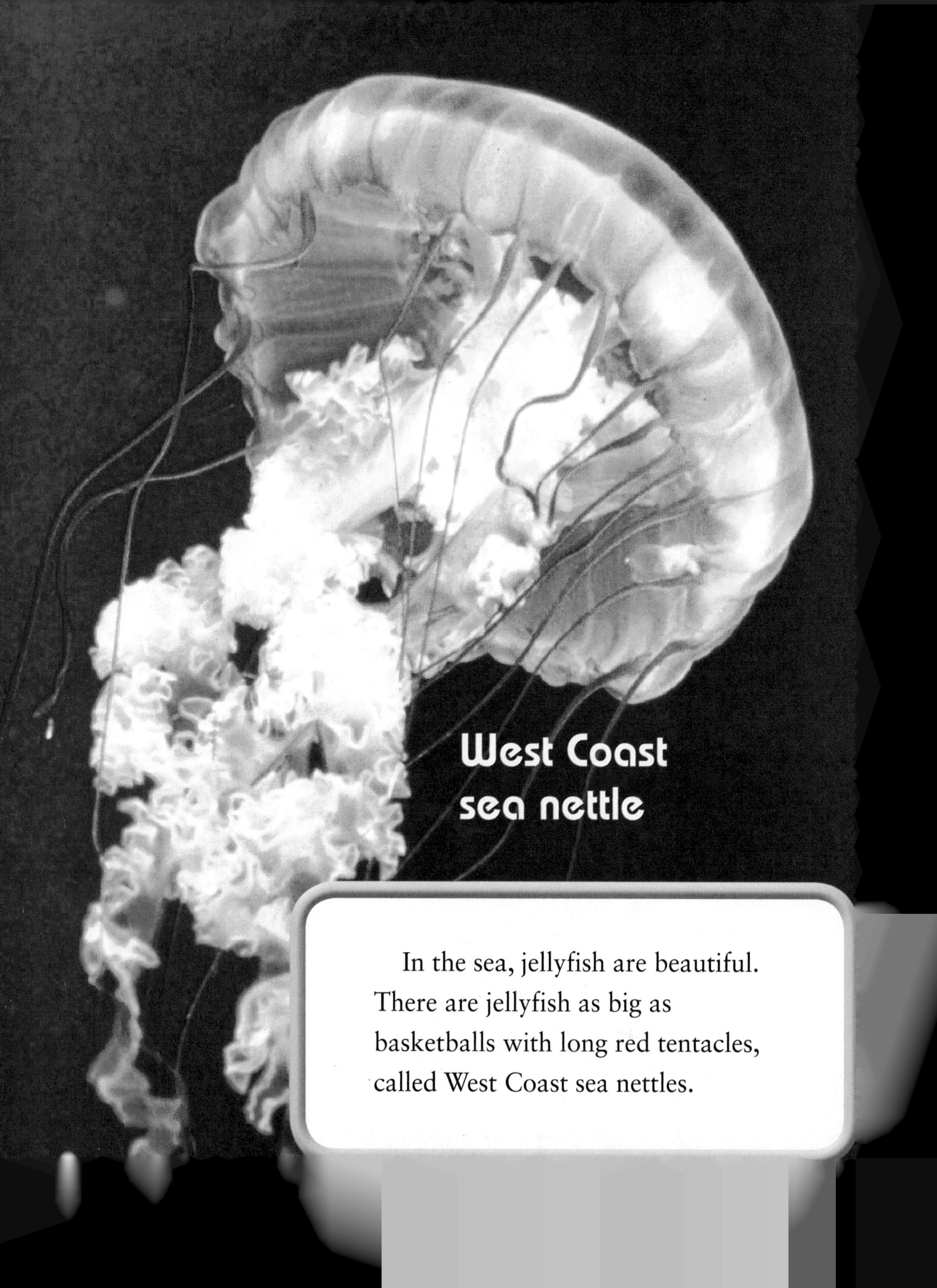

West Coast sea nettle

In the sea, jellyfish are beautiful. There are jellyfish as big as basketballs with long red tentacles, called West Coast sea nettles.

There are tiny, elegant jellyfish that look like a blizzard of snowflakes.

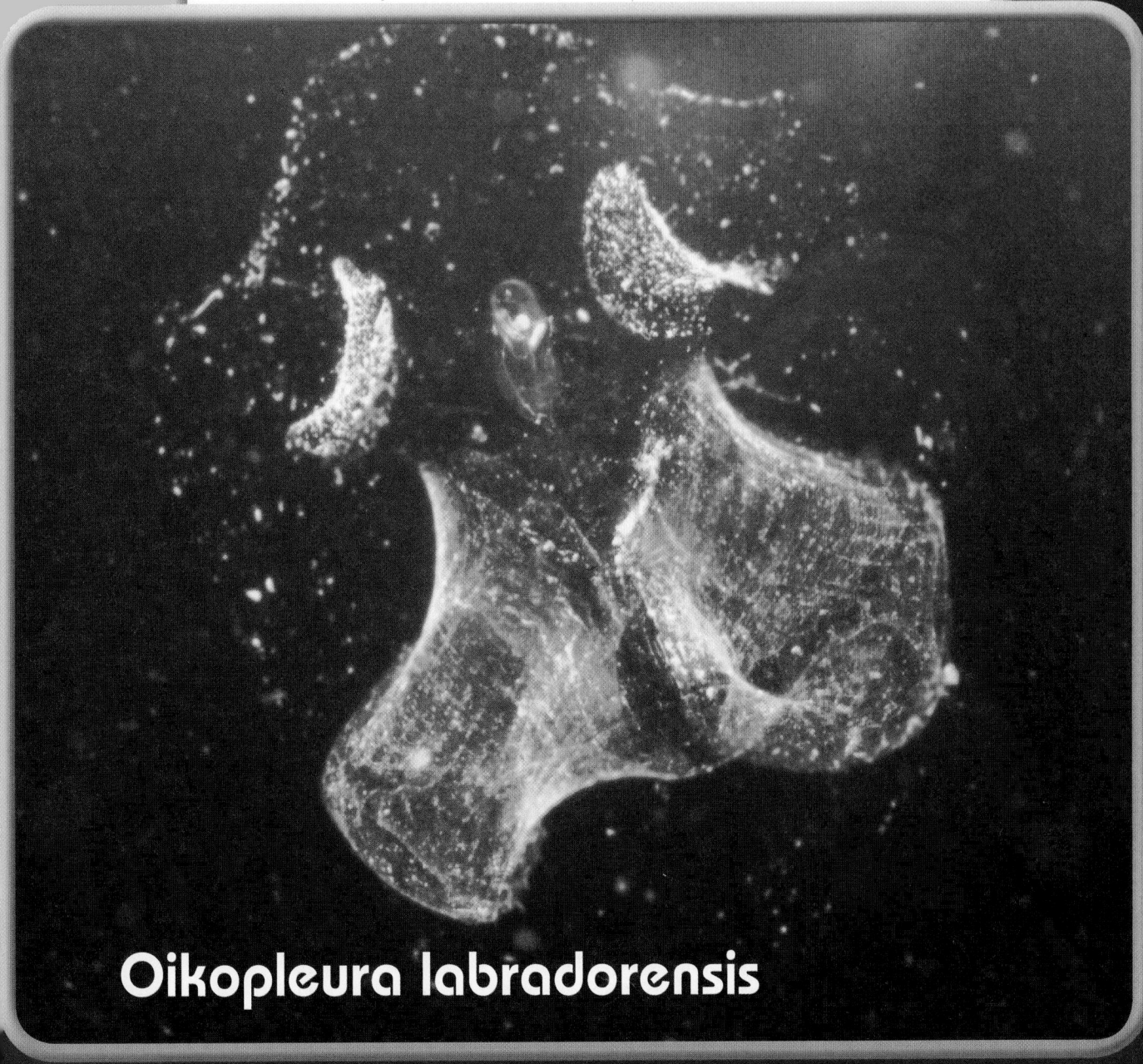

Oikopleura labradorensis

ANALYZE THE TEXT

Fact and Opinion What opinions does the author give? How does the author support those opinions?

Arctic lion's mane jellyfish

There are jellyfish that grow so big that they are as long as a blue whale. They are called Arctic lion's mane jellyfish. They pulse and drift. They eat and reproduce. They live and die. All without a brain or a heart.

Golden Mastigias
jellyfish

Someday you might be very lucky and see an ocean full of jellyfish. And, since you have a brain and a heart, you would know you were seeing something unforgettable.

ANALYZE THE TEXT

Author's Purpose What is the author's purpose for writing *Jellies*? How do you know?

THE LIFE OF JELLYFISH
Twig C. George

Dig Deeper

Use Clues to Analyze the Text

Use these pages to learn about Fact and Opinion and Author's Purpose. Then read *Jellies* again. Use what you learn to understand it better.

Fact and Opinion

In *Jellies*, you read facts and opinions about different kinds of jellyfish. A **fact** is something that is true. You can prove a fact. An **opinion** is the way someone feels about something. You cannot prove an opinion. Authors often give reasons to support their facts and opinions.

As you reread, look for facts and opinions. Then find text evidence that supports what the author says. Use a chart to help you keep track of facts and opinions.

Fact	Opinion

Author's Purpose

The reason an author writes a selection is called the **author's purpose.** An author might write to help you learn a lesson. An author might also write to tell facts or to explain an idea. As you reread *Jellies*, think about why the author wrote it.

Your Turn

Turn and Talk **What is special about animals that live in the ocean?** Think about what text evidence the author gives to show that jellyfish are special. Share your ideas with a small group. Ask a question if you don't understand a group member's ideas.

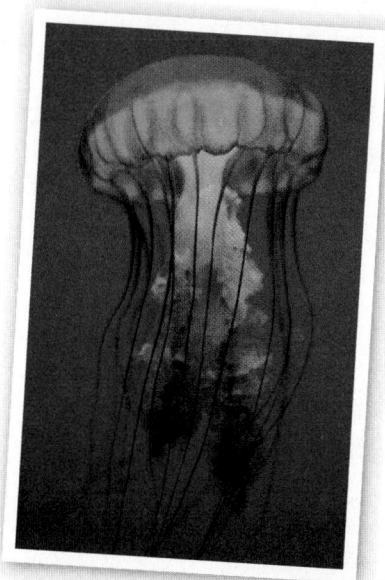

💬 Classroom Conversation

Now talk about these questions with the class.

1 What is the author's opinion about jellyfish? What evidence does she give to back it up?

2 How do the photos and captions help you understand more about jellyfish?

3 Using what you learned from the selection, explain what it would be like to be a jellyfish.

WRITE ABOUT READING ....

Response What do you think about jellyfish?
Think about what you learned about jellyfish
in *Jellies*. Use text evidence from *Jellies* to
give reasons for your opinion. Write a few
sentences to tell what you think and why.

Writing Tip

Write your opinion first. Then
write two or more reasons for
your opinion.

INFORMATIONAL TEXT

Splash
Photography

☑ GENRE

Informational text gives facts about a topic.

☑ TEXT FOCUS

A **diagram** shows how something works. **Labels** point out important parts of a diagram.

Splash
Photography

Smile!

How could you take a picture of a fish swimming under water? You would have to use special equipment, or tools.

People use underwater photography, or taking pictures, for different reasons. A scientist might want to learn more about sharks. Some people like it just because they think it is fun!

Underwater Dress

To take pictures in deep water, a photographer uses a scuba tank, or air tank, to breathe. An underwater photographer also must take lessons to use a scuba tank.

An underwater photographer also wears a mask and swim fins. It is a good idea to wear a rubber suit called a wetsuit. These suits help to keep a person warm and safe from stinging animals.

Using the Right Tools

An underwater photographer uses a special camera to take pictures. The camera is made to keep out water. There are other helpful tools, too. Some tools can be used to light up a dark place. Other tools help to get a closer look at a fish swimming by.

CAMERA
A special camera is used underwater.

SCUBA TANK
This tank holds the air for breathing underwater.

WETSUIT
This suit keeps a photographer safe and warm.

SWIM FINS
A photographer wears fins to swim better.

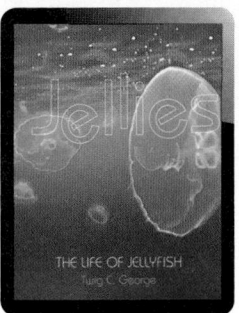

THE LIFE OF JELLYFISH
Twig C. George

Splash Photography

Compare Texts

TEXT TO TEXT

Compare and Contrast Both selections you read are about the ocean. Think about what you learned in each selection. How are the selections the same? How are they different? Discuss your ideas with a partner.

TEXT TO SELF

Think About Jobs Would you rather write about ocean animals or take pictures of them? Tell why using examples from both selections.

TEXT TO WORLD

Connect to Science Choose an ocean animal that you read about or saw in *Jellies* or *Splash Photography*. Use one or two sources to look up information about the animal. Share your facts with a partner.

Facts About Sharks

ELA RI.2.9, W.2.7, W.2.8

Grammar

Verbs in the Present, Past, and Future Some **verbs** name actions that are happening now, or in the **present.** Some verbs name actions that happened before, or in the **past.** Other verbs name actions that will happen later, or in the **future.**

Present	Past	Future
The jellies float.	The jellies floated.	The jellies will float.
We watch them.	We watched them.	We will watch them.

Try This! **Work with a partner. Read the sentences aloud. Tell whether the action is happening in the present, in the past, or in the future.**

1. I like ocean animals.

2. Shelley enjoyed the waves.

3. The jellies swim all around.

4. We will visit the zoo tomorrow.

When you write, make sure your verbs tell about the same time. Your writing will be easier to understand.

Incorrect	Correct
We play at the beach yesterday.	We played at the beach yesterday.
We will jump in the waves yesterday.	We jumped in the waves yesterday.

Connect Grammar to Writing

When you revise your instructions, be sure all your verbs tell about the same time.

Informative Writing

☑ **Elaboration** It is easier for readers to follow **instructions** if the steps are clear. Choose words that tell your readers exactly what to do.

Alexa wrote instructions for how to make a birdfeeder. Later, Alexa revised her instructions and added exact words.

Writing Process Checklist

Prewrite

Draft

▶ **Revise**

☑ Are my steps in order?

☑ Did I use time-order words, such as *first*, *next*, and *finally*?

☑ Did I use exact words to make my steps clearer?

☑ Did I tell my readers what to do with what they made?

Edit

Publish and Share

Revised Draft

You can make an easy birdfeeder.
You will need a pinecone,
∧

peanut butter, birdseed, a spoon
~~utensil~~, a plate, and string.
∧

T
First, tie one end of the
∧
the top
string to ~~part~~ of the pinecone.
∧
C
Cut a long piece of string.

How to Make a Birdfeeder

by Alexa Saperstein

You can make an easy birdfeeder. You will need a pinecone, peanut butter, birdseed, a spoon, a plate, and string.

First, cut a long piece of string. Tie one end of the string to the top of the pinecone. Next, scoop some peanut butter with the spoon, and spread it all over the pinecone. Then, pour some birdseed on the plate. Roll the pinecone in the birdseed. Finally, hang your birdfeeder outside!

Reading as a Writer

Which exact words did Alexa add to make her steps clearer? Where can you add exact words to your own instructions?

I added exact words to make my instructions clearer.

Write an Informational Paragraph

TASK Look back at *Animals Building Homes* and *Jellies*. Read about coral polyps and jellyfish. Use the text and the pictures to help you think about how these animals are alike and how they are different. Then write an informational paragraph for young scientists. Explain how the animals are alike and how they are different.

PLAN ·· 〠 myNotebook

Use the tools in your eBook to remember facts about coral polyps and jellyfish.

Gather Information Talk with a group of classmates about *Animals Building Homes* and *Jellies*. What are coral polyps and jellyfish like? How do they survive?

Then list facts in a Venn diagram.

- Where do coral polyps and jellyfish live?

- How do coral polyps and jellyfish protect themselves?

- Do coral polyps look like any of the jellyfish in *Jellies*? In what ways do they look the same or different?

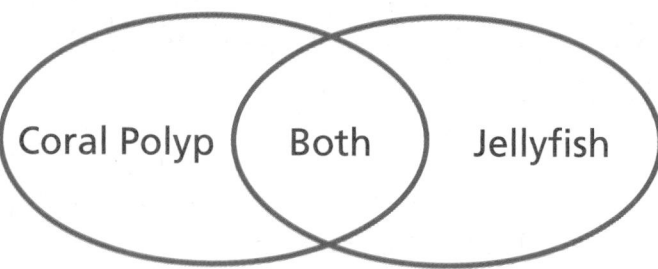

Write your draft in *my*WriteSmart.

Write Your Paragraph Use the information in this chart to help you organize your paragraph.

Main Idea Sentence

Start with a strong topic sentence that tells what your paragraph will be about. The sentence should get the reader's attention.

Details

Write about how coral polyps and jellyfish are alike. Then write about how they are different. Look at your Venn diagram for ideas. Use facts from *Animals Building Homes* and *Jellies*. Use nouns that tell about more than one correctly.

Conclusion

Give your paragraph a strong conclusion sentence. Your conclusion sentence should end the paragraph by saying the important ideas again.

my WriteSmart

Have a partner read your draft. Talk about how you can make it better.

Review Your Draft Read your writing and make it better. Use the Checklist.

☑ Does my paragraph have a main idea sentence?

☑ Do all of my details support the main idea?

☑ Did I write about how coral polyps and jellyfish are alike and how they are different?

☑ Did I use plural nouns correctly?

☑ Did I use complete sentences?

PRESENT

Share Write or type a copy of your paragraph. Pick a way to share.

- Read your paragraph to your classmates.

- Publish your paragraph into a book for classmates to read.

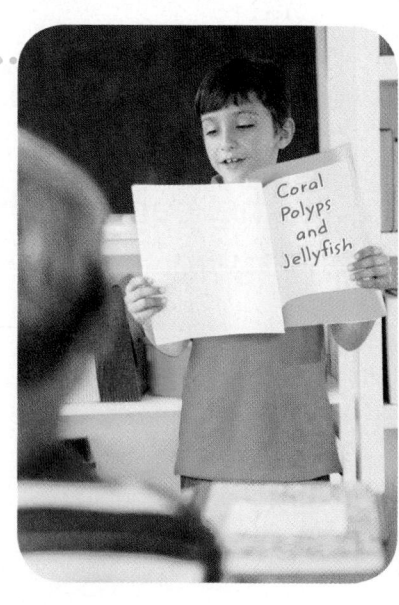

Tell Me About It!

Stream to Start

66 Always walk through life as if you have something new to learn and you will. 99

— Vernon Howard

Performance Task Preview

At the end of this unit, you will think about two of the texts you have read. Then you will use information in the texts to write an opinion essay about learning music in school.

hmhfyi.com

Channel One News®

CLICK, CLACK, MOO
Cows That Type
by Doreen Cronin · pictures by Betsy Lewin

Talk
About
Smart
Animals!

🔍 LANGUAGE DETECTIVE

Talk About Words
Verbs are words that name actions. Work with a partner. Find the Vocabulary words that are verbs. What are your clues? Use the verbs in new sentences.

▤ myNotebook

Add new words to **myWordList**. Use them in your speaking and writing.

Vocabulary in Context

▶ **Read each Context Card.**

▶ **Use a Vocabulary word to tell about something you did.**

1 **understand**
These children talk to each other with their hands. They understand sign language.

2 **gathered**
The students gathered around the computer in order to see the screen.

3 impatient

This girl looks **impatient**. She is tired of waiting so long.

4 impossible

It is **impossible** to hear when there is so much noise.

5 believe

People clap if they **believe**, or feel, someone has done a good job.

6 problem

Raise your hand if you have a **problem** or need help.

7 demand

These lights and sirens **demand** that everyone get out of the way.

8 furious

Babies cry when they are angry. This baby is **furious**!

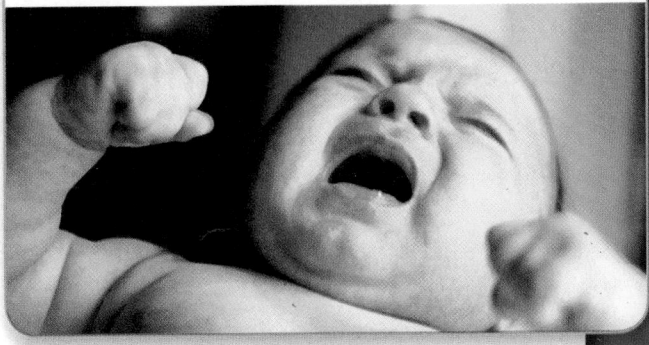

Read and Comprehend

Conclusions In *Click, Clack, Moo: Cows That Type*, the author does not tell you everything she wants you to know. You must use story clues from the words and pictures to figure out what the author does not say. This is called **drawing conclusions.** A chart like the one below can be used to list story clues that help you draw conclusions.

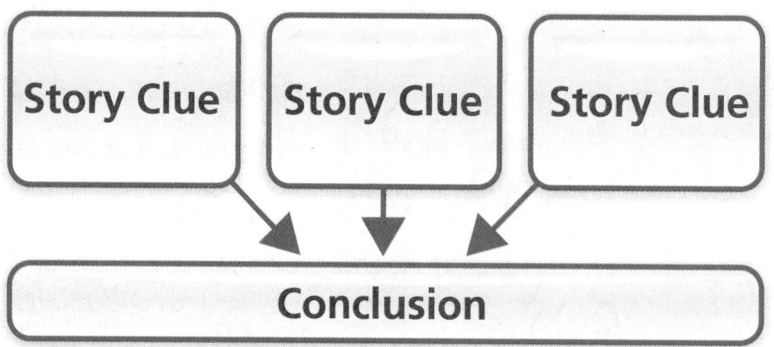

☑ **TARGET STRATEGY**

Infer/Predict Use clues, or text evidence, to figure out more about story parts.

PREVIEW THE TOPIC

Animal and Human Interactions

Animals help people do things every day. Some animals are trained to help people do their jobs. Farm animals help by providing things that some people eat and drink. Even pets at home are helpers. They help their owners by keeping them company. *Click, Clack, Moo: Cows That Type* is a story about some farm animals that will not help their farmer.

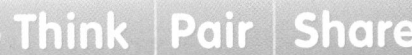

Think | Pair | Share

How can animals show people what they are feeling? Talk about it with a partner. Be sure to take turns speaking and listening. Act out for your classmates what the animals do.

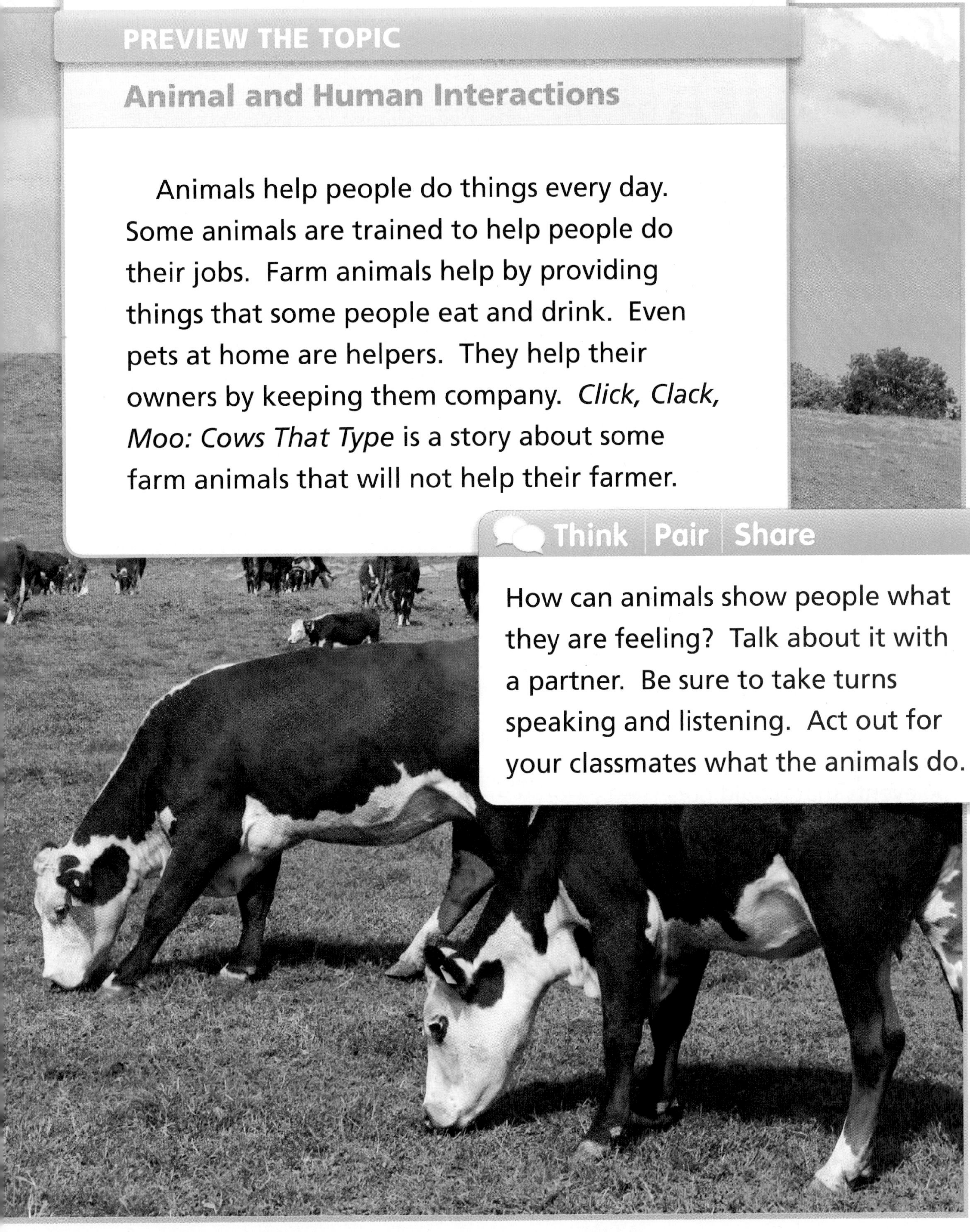

ANCHOR TEXT

CLICK, CLACK, MOO
Cows That Type
by Doreen Cronin pictures by Betsy Lewin

 GENRE

Humorous fiction is a story that is written to make the reader laugh. As you read, look for:

▸ characters who do or say funny things
▸ events that would not happen in real life

MEET THE AUTHOR

Doreen Cronin

Doreen Cronin's father used to tell her funny stories. Years later, she wrote *Click, Clack, Moo.* Her own story made her laugh, just like her father's had long ago!

MEET THE ILLUSTRATOR

Betsy Lewin

Betsy Lewin's pictures are in many books. She lives in New York with her husband and two cats. She says her cats don't type.

CLICK, CLACK, MOO
Cows That Type

by Doreen Cronin   pictures by Betsy Lewin

ESSENTIAL QUESTION

How can people and animals help each other?

Farmer Brown has a problem.

His cows like to type.

All day long he hears

Click, clack, **moo.**
 Click, clack, **moo.**
Clickety, clack, **moo.**

At first, he couldn't believe his ears.

Cows that type?

Impossible!

Click, clack, **moo.**

Click, clack, **moo.**

Clickety, clack, **moo.**

Then, he couldn't believe his eyes.

Dear Farmer Brown,
The barn is very cold at night.
We'd like some electric blankets.
Sincerely,
The Cows

It was bad enough the cows had found the old typewriter in the barn, now they wanted electric blankets! "No way," said Farmer Brown. "No electric blankets."

So the cows went on strike. They left a note on the barn door.

Sorry.
We're closed.
No milk today.

"No milk today!" cried Farmer Brown.
In the background, he heard the cows
busy at work:

Click, clack, **moo.**
  Click, clack, **moo.**
Clickety, clack, **moo.**

The next day, he got another note:

Dear Farmer Brown,
The hens are cold too.
They'd like electric blankets.
Sincerely,
The Cows

The cows were growing impatient
with the farmer. They left a new
note on the barn door.

"No eggs!" cried Farmer Brown.
In the background he heard them.

Click, clack, **moo.**
Click, clack, **moo.**
Clickety, clack, **moo.**

Closed.
No milk.
No eggs.

"Cows that type. Hens on strike! Whoever heard of such a thing? How can I run a farm with no milk and no eggs!" Farmer Brown was furious.

ANALYZE THE TEXT

Author's Word Choice "Moo" sounds like the noise a cow makes. What other sound words does the author repeat?

Farmer Brown got out his own typewriter.

Dear Cows and Hens:
There will be no electric blankets.
You are cows and hens.
I demand milk and eggs.
Sincerely,
Farmer Brown

Duck was a neutral
party, so he brought the
ultimatum to the cows.

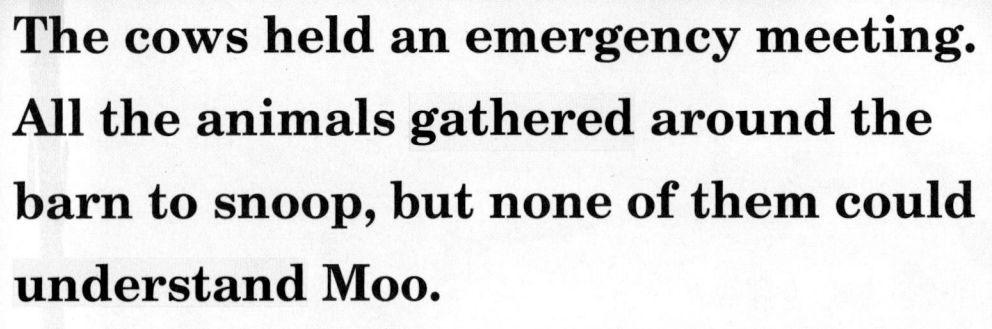

The cows held an emergency meeting.
All the animals gathered around the
barn to snoop, but none of them could
understand Moo.

All night long, Farmer Brown waited
for an answer.

Duck knocked on the door early
the next morning. He handed
Farmer Brown a note:

Dear Farmer Brown,
We will exchange our typewriter
for electric blankets.
Leave them outside the barn door
and we will send Duck over with
the typewriter.
Sincerely,
The Cows

Farmer Brown decided this was a good deal. He left the blankets next to the barn door and waited for Duck to come with the typewriter.

The next morning, he got a note:

Dear Farmer Brown,
The pond is quite boring.
We'd like a diving board.
Sincerely,
The Ducks

Click, clack, **quack.**
  Click, clack, **quack.**
Clickety, clack, **quack.**

Dig Deeper

Use Clues to Analyze the Text

Use these pages to learn about Conclusions and Author's Word Choice. Then read *Click, Clack, Moo: Cows That Type* again. Use what you learn to understand it better.

Conclusions

Click, Clack, Moo is a funny story about cows that type. When you read, you need to **draw conclusions** about what the author does not say. For example, on page 376, the author does not tell you the story's setting. You can draw a conclusion from the picture that the story happens on a farm.

Find clues in the words and pictures to help you draw conclusions about the story. Use a chart like the one below.

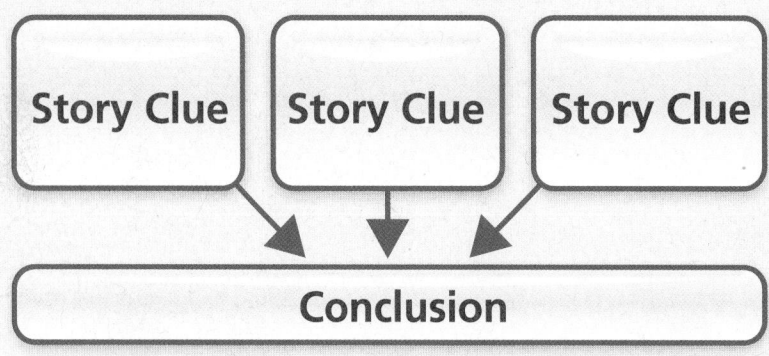

ELA RL.2.4, RL.2.7

Author's Word Choice

Sometimes authors use words that sound like real noises. For example, the cows in *Click, Clack, Moo* use a typewriter. The author writes "Click, clack, moo" to tell what the farmer hears as the cows type. Using words that sound like noises helps the reader imagine what is happening. It makes the story seem more real.

The author repeats these sound words more than once. This **repetition** gives the words in the story a rhythm, or beat.

Your Turn

Turn and Talk **How can people and animals help each other?** Look for text evidence in *Click, Clack, Moo.* Discuss your ideas with a partner. Take turns speaking and listening.

Classroom Conversation

Now talk about these questions with the class.

1 What do the words and illustrations in the story tell you about the characters?

2 Read the last page of the story again. Why doesn't Duck return the typewriter?

3 What do you think other animals on the farm might want from Farmer Brown?

Performance Task

WRITE ABOUT READING ··························

Response How do you think Farmer Brown feels when he gets the note from the ducks? Think about how he responds. Write a few sentences to explain your opinion.

Writing Tip

Remember to use complete sentences when you write your answer. A complete sentence has a subject and a predicate.

Talk About Smart Animals!

by Donald Logan

You may think only animals in storybooks or movies do things that seem impossible. You would be wrong!

Meet Rio and Alex. They are real-life animals. Rio is a sea lion. Alex is a parrot. These animals can do things that most people would never believe animals like them could do.

This Sea Lion Can Match

Rio is not like any other sea lion. She can solve a simple problem and tell the answer to her trainers!

Rio has learned to look at three pictures and decide which two are most alike. First, Rio's trainers show her one picture. Rio studies it. Then her trainers add two more pictures. Rio points her nose at the picture that goes best with the first one she saw. When Rio is right, she gets a tasty treat.

Rio is not impatient. She takes her time before she answers.

Rio is deciding which two of these pictures are most alike.

Not Bad for a Bird Brain!

Alex was an African grey parrot. Grey parrots in the wild are often seen gathered together in large groups. In the wild, parrots communicate using bird calls and other sounds. Alex was special because he had learned to talk. He knew over one hundred words!

Alex's owner had also taught Alex to tell colors apart and to count. Alex could even understand questions and answer them.

Sometimes Alex would get tired. He would become furious and would demand a treat. After a break, he would go right back to solving problems.

"Want a nut!"

Compare Texts

Compare Stories Doreen Cronin wrote *Click, Clack, Moo* and *Diary of a Spider* (Lesson 4). With a small group, discuss how the settings and the events of these stories are the same and different.

Write a Letter Think about the letters that the cows wrote. Write your own letter asking an adult family member for something. Be sure to include commas in your greeting and closing.

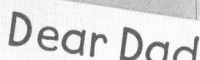

Dear Dad,

Connect to Science With a partner, make a list of things from *Click, Clack, Moo* that the animals in *Talk About Smart Animals!* probably cannot do. Ask and answer questions to make sure you understand what your partner is saying.

ELA RL.2.1, SL.2.3, L.2.2b

401

Grammar

Compound Sentences A **compound sentence** is made up of two shorter sentences. The shorter sentences are connected by words such as *and, but,* and *or*. Use a comma before the connecting word.

Short Sentences	Compound Sentences
She loves cows. She does not like milking them.	She loves cows, **but** she does not like milking them.
I poured the milk. I finished all of it.	I poured the milk, **and** I finished all of it.
Can you find the farm? Should we ask for directions?	Can you find the farm, **or** should we ask for directions?

Try This! **Write each pair of sentences as a compound sentence. Use a comma and a connecting word.**

❶ The hens lay eggs. We collect them.

❷ Will you eat corn? Do you want potatoes?

❸ I drank milk. Carmen drank juice.

Compound sentences can make your writing less choppy and more interesting. Try joining shorter sentences into compound sentences when you write. This will make your writing smoother.

Short, Choppy Sentences	Compound Sentence
I spent the summer on a farm. I had a great time.	I spent the summer on a farm, and I had a great time.

Connect Grammar to Writing

When you revise your persuasive letter, try joining shorter sentences into compound sentences.

403

Opinion Writing

✔ **Purpose** When you write a letter to persuade, be sure your opinion and goal are clear to your reader. Give reasons to explain your opinion using linking words such as *because* and *also*.

Kurt drafted a **persuasive letter.** Later, he revised it to clearly say his reason for writing. Use the Writing Checklist to revise your writing.

Writing Checklist

✔ **Purpose**
Did I state my goal clearly?

✔ **Organization**
Did I use the parts of a letter? Did I use linking words to connect my reasons to my opinion?

✔ **Evidence**
Did I give reasons to support my opinions?

✔ **Conventions**
Did I use commas correctly in the letter?

Revised Draft

Dear Auntie Lorrie,

I'm writing to ask you ~~for~~ to send me some of your old children's books. ~~something.~~ It's for a really

good cause because some

of the books in our classroom

are falling apart.

 ELA W.2.1, W.2.5, L.2.2b

Kurt Atchley
244 Austin St.
Ojai, CA 93023
January 24, 2019

Dear Auntie Lorrie,

I'm writing to ask you to send me some of your old children's books. It's for a really good cause because some of the books in our classroom are falling apart. Also, we have no money for new books. Can you help us? I hope so.

Love,
Kurt

Reading as a Writer

What did Kurt do to make his goal clearer? What reasons and linking words did he use? How can you make your goal clearer?

I made sure my goal was stated clearly.

Ah, Music!

Written and Illustrated by Aliki

THERE'S A HOLE AT THE **Bottom** OF THE **Sea**

🔍 **LANGUAGE DETECTIVE**

Talk About Words
Work with a partner. Take turns asking and answering questions about the photos. Use the Vocabulary words in your questions and answers.

Vocabulary in Context

▶ **Read each Context Card.**

▶ **Make up a new sentence that uses a Vocabulary word.**

---

1 **vibration**

The drummer feels the vibration of the drums and cymbals when he hits them.

---

2 **tune**

He played the same tune over and over again as he learned the new song.

3 volume

The girl didn't hear her mom because the volume of the music was too loud.

4 expression

The voices of the singers were so powerful and had so much expression!

5 creative

Our music teacher told us to be creative, so we made up a new song to play.

6 performance

The musicians played their best during the performance on the stage.

7 concentrate

The girl is focusing on the music. She has to concentrate to learn it.

8 relieved

The conductor was relieved that the musicians played the music correctly.

Read and Comprehend

Text and Graphic Features Authors sometimes include special features when they write. These are called **text and graphic features.** Pictures, headings, and captions are examples of text and graphic features. These can help you understand the text. They can also help you find information in the text.

Use this chart to list text and graphic features and tell how they help you.

Text or Graphic Feature	Page Number	Purpose

✓ **TARGET STRATEGY**

Question Ask questions about what you are reading. Answer using text evidence.

Music can be made in many ways. You can play an instrument, such as a piano or a flute. You can make your own instruments, too. For example, you can hit a can with a spoon to make a drum. Your voice can even be an instrument. You can whistle, hum, or sing to make music. You can make music almost anywhere. You will read more about music in *Ah, Music!*

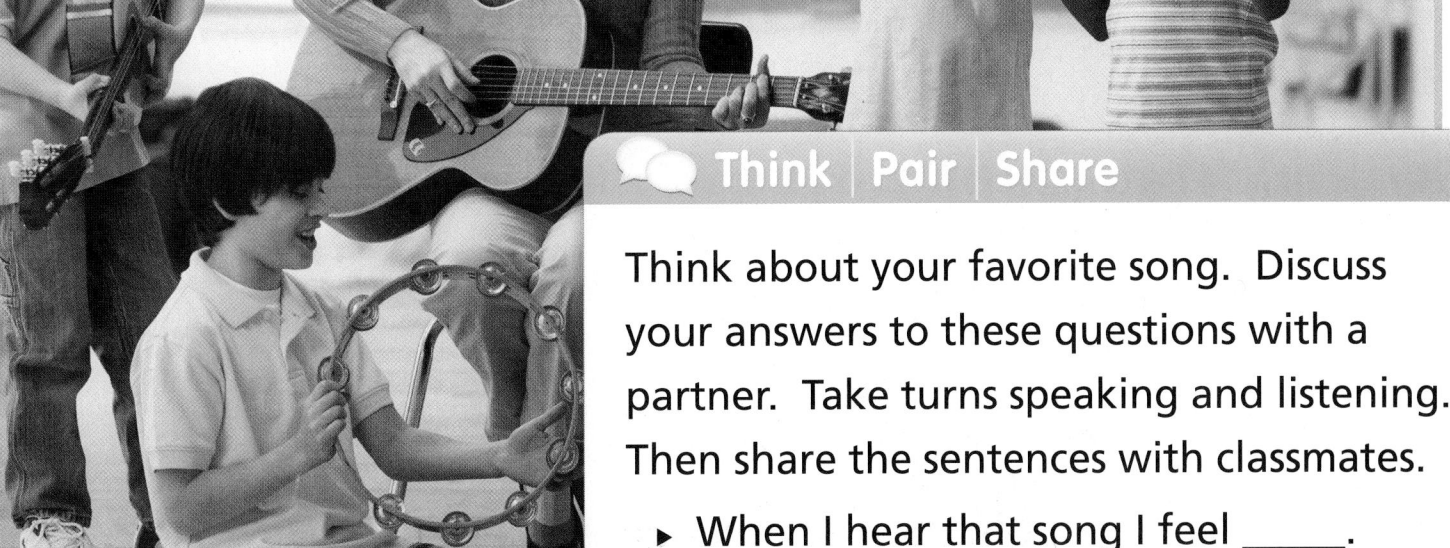

💬 Think | Pair | Share

Think about your favorite song. Discuss your answers to these questions with a partner. Take turns speaking and listening. Then share the sentences with classmates.

► When I hear that song I feel _____.
► I like to _____ when I hear my favorite song.

✅ **GENRE**

Informational text gives facts about a topic. As you read, look for:

▸ pictures and captions
▸ information about the real world

MEET THE AUTHOR AND ILLUSTRATOR

Aliki

Ever since she was a young girl, Aliki has been writing down her feelings. She thinks that doing this was good practice for when she became an author. *Ah, Music!* took over three years for Aliki to write and draw. She had to do a lot of studying to find out about music and what different instruments looked like.

Ah, Music!

written and illustrated by Aliki

What are different ways
to enjoy music?

Music Is Sound

If you hum a tune,

play an instrument,

or clap out a rhythm,

you are making music.
You are listening to it, too.

Music Is Rhythm

That is the beat I can clap.

Rhythm is a marching-band beat, a puffing-train beat,

a beating-the-eggs beat, a heart beat.
Some rhythm beats are stronger than others.
You can count the accents.

A person who cannot hear
can feel the vibration of the beat.

Music Is Melody

That is the tune I can hum,

or the song that is sung
if words are set to music.
Often the words are poetry.

Music Is Volume

That is the loudness or the softness of the sound.

Shhh.

ANALYZE THE TEXT

Text and Graphic Features What is the heading on this page? How do the illustrations help you understand the heading and the text?

415

Music Is Feeling

It sets a mood.

Music speaks not with words, as in a song.

It speaks with expression.

Everyone can understand music, because everyone has feelings.

Music can make you feel happy or sad or scared.

It can make you want to dance, to march, to sing,

or to be quiet, to listen, and to dream.

Ah, music!

Shakespeare said that.

*Here will we sit
and let the sounds of music
creep in our ears.*

I listen to music,
and I can see pictures
in my head.

I imagine I hear
twittering birds.

I hear a cool waterfall.

I see a brilliant sunrise.

I see a scary dark forest.

I hear a noisy city.

Music Is a Creative Art

Just as a writer uses words,

or an artist uses paint,

a composer uses music
to create images and feelings.
He or she writes it down in notes, symbols,
and numbers on lines and spaces.
The notations describe the rhythm, tone, pitch,
feeling, and even the silences of the piece.

Practice Makes Perfect

We make music.
Making music is hard fun.
It takes lots of practice to learn to
play an instrument.

But when you do, it is forever.

That's the hard part.

Here's the fun part.

As you practice and learn,
you begin to make
beautiful sounds.
Practice becomes fun.

You learn new pieces to play.
You feel proud.
Your music teacher says
you will play in a recital.
You will play for an audience.

A metronome helps keep time.

ANALYZE THE TEXT

Fact and Opinion What is the author's opinion about practicing music? What reasons support the author's opinion?

The Performance

At your recital it is your turn to play.
Everyone is looking at you.

You concentrate.
You do the best you can.

When you finish, everyone claps.
It sounds like waves breaking.
It feels good. You take a bow.
You feel relieved and very proud.

You celebrate.
Everyone says you did well.
Next time it will be even
better, because you are
learning more every day.
Practice makes perfect.

420

Music Is for Everybody

Dig Deeper

Use Clues to Analyze the Text

Use these pages to learn about Text and Graphic Features and Fact and Opinion. Then read *Ah, Music!* again. Use what you learn to understand it better.

Text and Graphic Features

In *Ah, Music!*, you read about music. The headings, pictures, and other **text and graphic features** help you understand more about what you read. Headings tell you what each section is about. Pictures give you more information about the text.

Use a chart like the one below to list the text and graphic features. Also list each feature's purpose, or how it helps you.

Text or Graphic Feature	Page Number	Purpose

 ELA RI.2.5, RI.2.7, RI.2.8

Fact and Opinion

Authors of informational texts often give both facts and opinions. A **fact** is something that can be proved true or false. An **opinion** is what someone believes or feels. When you read a selection, look for facts and opinions. Also look for the reasons the author gives to support a fact or an opinion.

Your Turn

 What are different ways to enjoy music? Talk with a partner about your ideas. Use text evidence, such as the headings and pictures in *Ah, Music!*, to help you answer.

Classroom Conversation

Now talk about these questions with the class.

1 What words does the author use to describe and tell about rhythm? Use the headings to help you find this information.

2 Why is it important to practice when learning to play an instrument?

3 Why did the author write this selection?

Performance Task

Response Look back at page 416. How does the author say that music can make you feel? Do you agree? Write a few sentences to tell why or why not. Use the pictures and words that the author uses to help you.

Writing Tip

Break sentences that are too long into two shorter sentences.

425

SONG

✅ GENRE

A **song** is words and music that are sung together.

✅ TEXT FOCUS

Rhythm is a pattern of beats. The music notes, the words, and the phrases in a song can make up rhythm. Rhythm can give meaning to a song.

THERE'S A HOLE AT THE Bottom OF THE Sea

A song is like a poem that is set to music. A song has a rhythm, or a beat. Some songs also rhyme and have repeated words, just like some poems do.

Each section of a song is called a verse. The song you will read has several verses. Each verse has repeated words from the earlier verses. After you read the words, try singing the song!

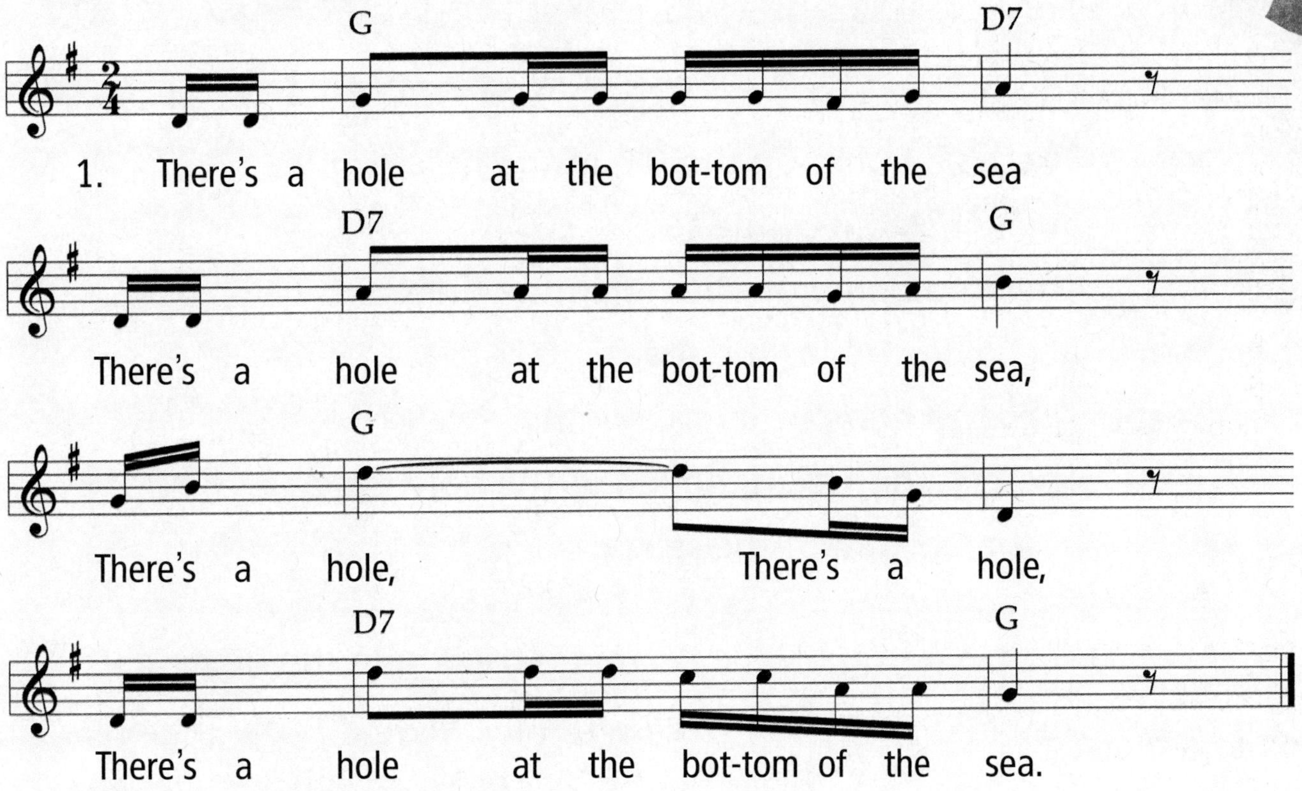

1. There's a hole at the bot-tom of the sea

   There's a hole at the bot-tom of the sea,

   There's a hole,   There's a hole,

   There's a hole at the bot-tom of the sea.

2. There's a log in the hole at the bottom of the sea,

   There's a log in the hole at the bottom of the sea,

   There's a log, there's a log,

   There's a log in the hole at the bottom of the sea.

427

3. There's a bump on the log in the hole
   at the bottom of the sea,
   There's a bump on the log in the hole
   at the bottom of the sea,
   There's a bump, there's a bump
   There's a bump on the log in the hole
   at the bottom of the sea.

4. There's a frog on the bump on the log in the hole
   at the bottom of the sea…

5. There's a tail on the frog on the bump on the log
   in the hole at the bottom of the sea…

6. There's a speck on the tail on the frog on the bump
   on the log in the hole at the bottom of the sea…

Compare Texts

Compare Rhythm How are *Ah, Music!* and *There's a Hole at the Bottom of the Sea* alike? How are they different? Think about how the authors use words and rhythm in each selection.

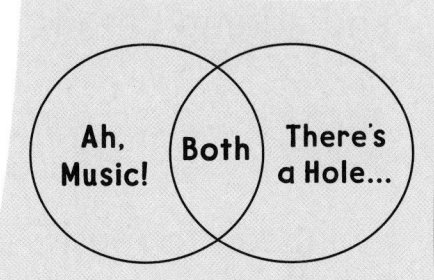

Describe an Instrument What instrument would you like to play at a recital? Why? Share your ideas with a partner.

Using Text Features What features in *Ah, Music!* can you also find in other informational books? How do those features help you find and understand information easily?

ELA RL.2.4, RI.2.5

Grammar

Compound Sentences A **compound sentence** is two **simple sentences** joined by a comma and the word *and, but,* or *or.* You can make **compound sentences** more interesting by moving words around and adding details.

Compound Sentence	Improved Compound Sentence
I listen to music, and I see pictures in my head.	I listen to music, and I see beautiful pictures in my head.
Writers use words, but composers use notes.	Words are used by writers, but composers use musical notes.

Try This! **Move words around or add details to make each compound sentence more interesting.**

① I listen to music, and I feel happy.

② People use music for fun, and music can help people relax.

③ The violin is hard to play, but I like playing the piano.

When you write, you can join short, choppy sentences to make one longer sentence. You can also move words around and add details. This makes your writing more interesting.

Short, Choppy Sentences

Lupe plays the tuba.

Her brother Jaime plays the flute.

Longer, More Interesting Sentence

Lupe plays the tuba very well, and her brother Jaime is a good flute player.

Connect Grammar to Writing

When you revise your opinion paragraph, look for short sentences that you can combine. Combine them with a comma and the word *and, but,* or *or.*

Opinion Writing

☑ **Organization** When you write to persuade, share your opinion in the introduction sentence. Use linking words such as *and, because,* and *also* to connect opinions and reasons. Tell your opinion again in the closing sentence.

Han wrote an **opinion paragraph** about music. Later, he added linking words to connect ideas about how he feels.

Writing Checklist

☑ **Purpose**
Did I state my opinion and give reasons for it?

☑ **Organization**
Did I use linking words to connect opinions and reasons?

☑ **Elaboration**
Does my writing show how I feel about my subject?

☑ **Conventions**
Did I vary the length of my sentences?

Revised Draft

I ~~like~~ music. Music has something
love
 , and people all over the world
for everyone. enjoy music

Music is powerful. ~~It~~ can make
       also   because it

you feel happy, sad, or even

scared.

Music for Everyone
by Han Choi

I love music. Music has something for everyone, and people all over the world enjoy music. Music is also powerful because it can make you feel happy, sad, or even scared. There are many ways to enjoy music. You can sing, dance, play an instrument, or just listen. All children should have a chance to make music.

Reading as a Writer

What did Han add to let you know how he feels about his subject? What can you add to your writing to let your reader know how you feel?

I added sentences to show how I feel about my subject.

433

Q **LANGUAGE DETECTIVE**

Talk About Words
Work with a partner.
Choose two Vocabulary
words. Use them
together in a sentence.
Share your sentence
with the class.

Vocabulary in Context

▶ Read each Context Card.

▶ Talk about a picture. Use a different Vocabulary word from the one on the card.

① **culture**
Culture is the traditions and beliefs of a group of people.

② **community**
A community is a group of people who live together in a certain area.

3 languages

People use different languages to write and to speak to one another.

4 transportation

People use transportation to get from one place to another.

5 subjects

Science is one of the subjects taught in school.

6 lessons

This teacher gives lessons to his students. The students learn from each lesson.

7 special

These students go to a special school for music. They play music every day.

8 wear

These two students wear uniforms at school.

Read and Comprehend

☑ **TARGET SKILL**

Main Idea and Details The **topic** of an informational text is what the selection is about. The **main idea** is the most important idea about the topic. **Details** tell more about the main idea. You can show a main idea on a chart like this. List the details that make the main idea clearer.

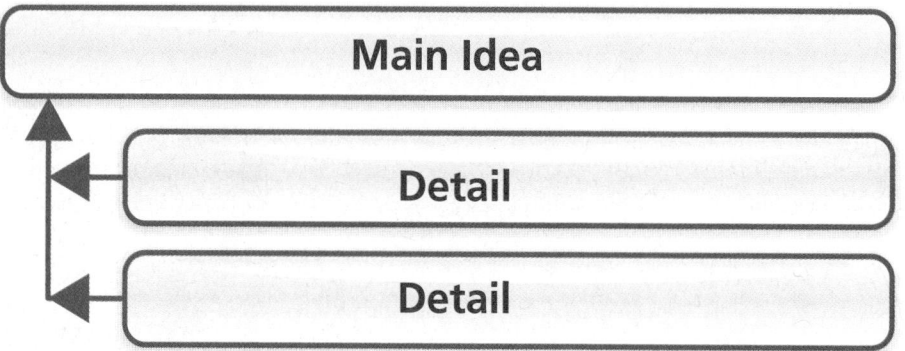

Main Idea

Detail

Detail

☑ **TARGET STRATEGY**

Analyze/Evaluate To **analyze** as you read, think about the author's words and the photos. Then **evaluate**, or decide, how the words and photos help you know what is important in the selection.

School Differences

Not all schools are the same. At some schools, students wear uniforms. Some have special ways to help students get to school, like school buses. Others allow students to take their lessons using a computer. Most schools teach several subjects, such as social studies and math. All schools are places where students learn.

You will read about different kinds of schools in *Schools Around the World*.

💬 Talk About It

What are some questions you would like to ask someone who goes to a different school? Talk about it with a group. Explain what you would like to know about different kinds of schools. Take turns speaking and listening.

437

ANCHOR TEXT

MEET THE AUTHOR

Margaret C. Hall

Margaret C. Hall has written many nonfiction books for children. Her books include topics ranging from national parks to mallard ducks. *Schools Around the World* is part of a series of books she wrote. Other books in the series include *Homes Around the World* and *Games Around the World*.

 **GENRE**

Informational text gives facts about a topic. As you read, look for:

▸ photos and captions
▸ facts and details about a topic

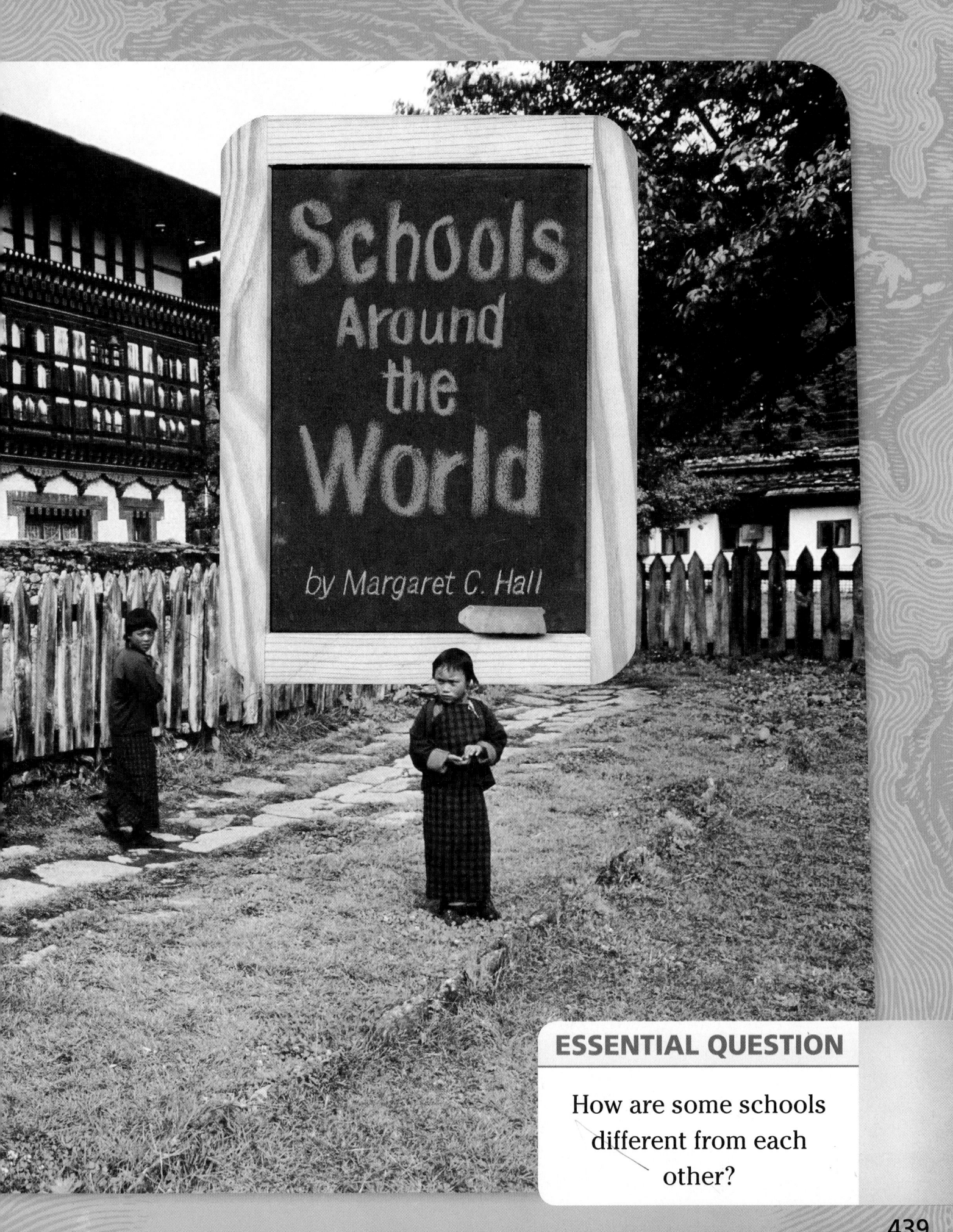

Schools
Around
the
World

by Margaret C. Hall

ESSENTIAL QUESTION

How are some schools different from each other?

439

Schools Around the World

All around the world, children go to school.
Some children spend most of their day at school.
Others spend only a few hours there.

Some school buildings in Asia are tall, like this one.

These students in an American classroom start their day by saying the Pledge of Allegiance.

Schools are different in different parts of the world. But they are all the same in one way. Schools are where children go to learn.

AMAZING SCHOOL FACTS

A long time ago, a German man started a new kind of school. He thought that small children should grow like flowers in a garden. He called his school kindergarten. The word means "children's garden" in German.

These students in Tibet, China, are about to start their morning classes.

School Buildings

The kind of school buildings children have depends on where they live. It depends on the climate and the resources of their community.

School buildings can be large or small. They can be made from many different materials. Some children even go to school outside or in buildings with no walls.

AMAZING SCHOOL FACTS

Schools have been around for thousands of years. The first schools were started to teach children about their culture.

Getting to School

Children travel to school in many different ways. The kind of transportation they use depends on where they live. It also depends on how far they have to go.

Many children walk or ride bicycles to school. Others ride in cars, on buses, or on a train. Some children go to school by boat.

AMAZING SCHOOL FACTS

In some places, children live too far away from their school to go there. Teachers give lessons over the radio or by using computers that are hooked up to the school.

School Clothing

Children around the world wear different kinds of clothing to school. What they wear often depends on the climate where they live. It also depends on what season it is.

In some schools, the students all dress alike. They wear uniforms. Students from different schools have different uniforms.

▲ Students at this girls' school in Panama wear blue skirts and sweaters as part of their uniforms.

*These students in Germany are learning science on a
class trip with their teachers.*

The School Day

All around the world, teachers help students
learn new things. Children do some schoolwork in
groups. They do other schoolwork on their own.
Most children eat lunch or a snack at school.
They may also have time to play. At many schools,
children take class trips, too.

This teacher answers a question for his student at a school in Cuba.

Learning to Read and Write

One important job for teachers is to help children learn to read and write. Students learn to read and write in many different languages. The language children use at school depends on where they live. Some children study their own language and another language, too.

ANALYZE THE TEXT

Text and Graphic Features How do the photos and captions help you understand more about the schools?

At an American school overseas, students study a map of Europe.

Other Lessons

Children learn many things at school. All around the world, they study math and science. They learn about their own country and other countries, too.

Many children around the world study art and music in school. They may also learn how to use a computer.

These students in Great Britain practice playing music at school.

In this school in Japan, students help serve lunch.

School Chores

Most children have chores to do at school. They help to keep the classroom neat and clean. They may even help to set up the classroom every day.

In some places, children work to keep the schoolyard neat and clean. Some children may serve lunch to one another.

This teacher gives extra help to students after school.

After School

Some children go to school even after the school day is over. They may have a tutor to help them with the subjects that are harder for them.

Some children have other lessons after school. They study things they cannot learn in school. They may learn about dance, music, or their own culture.

These boys in Israel learn about their culture.

Students at this boarding school eat, study, and live together.

Special Schools

Some children live at their schools. These schools are called boarding schools. The children go home for visits and on holidays.

This girl cannot see. She goes to a school where she can learn to read and write in a special way. People who are blind read with their fingers. They use a system of raised dots called Braille.

Home Schooling

A home can also be a school. Some parents teach their children at home. They want to decide exactly what their children will learn.

People at schools will often help parents plan home lessons for their children. Many children who study at home go to a school for gym or art classes.

This mother is teaching her daughter at home.

451

School and Work

Some children work as performers. They spend part of their day practicing the work that they do. They spend the rest of the day studying regular school subjects.

The students below perform a traditional Russian dance.

One of the subjects that was taught in ancient Greece was gymnastics. The ancient Greeks thought gymnastics was just as important to learn as math or reading!

This boy is learning gymnastics.

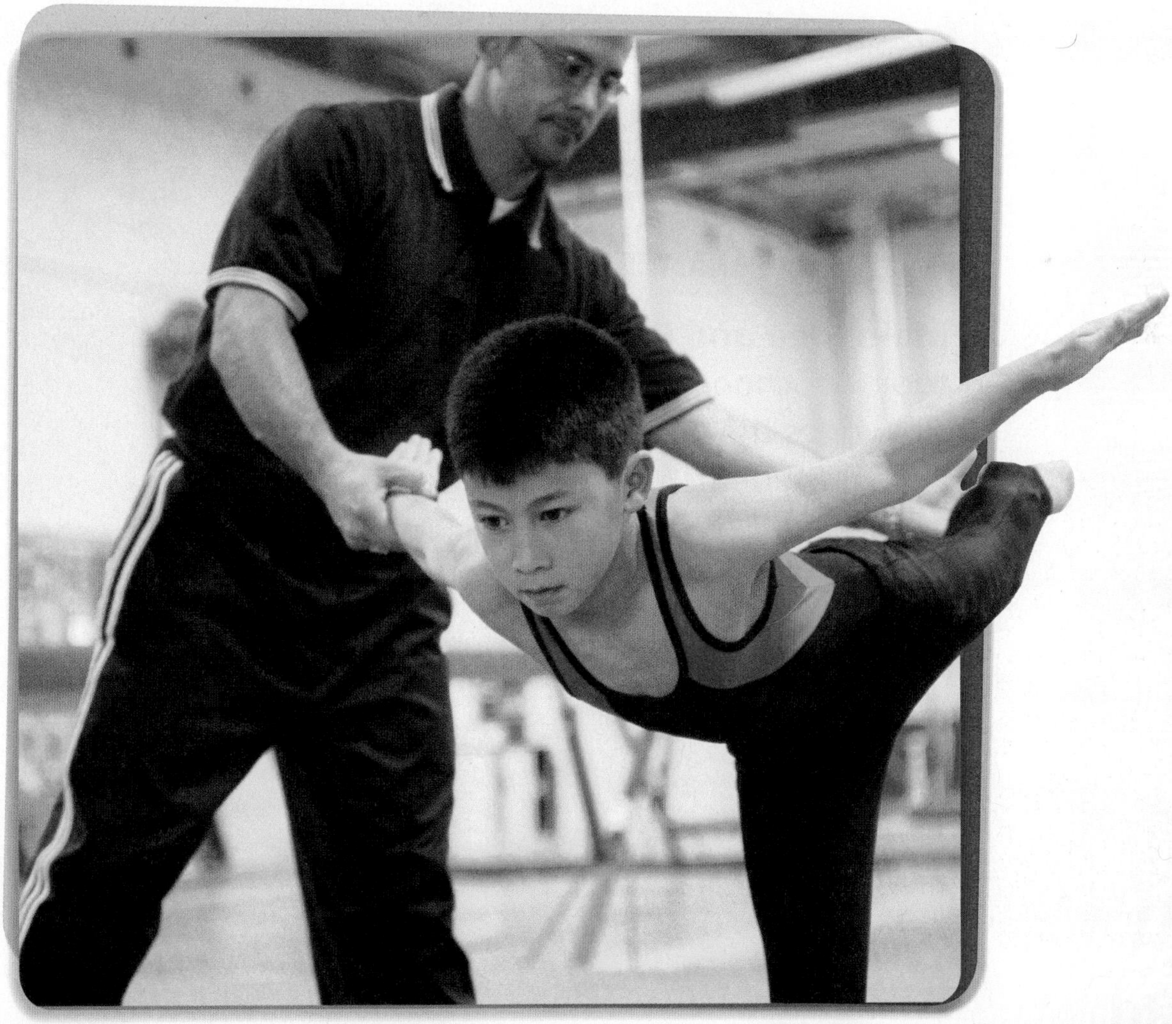

Older Students

Many people go to school even after they are adults. They may go to college. Or, they may go to a trade school to learn how to do a certain job.

Adults also take classes for fun. They study different languages and learn how to do things. No matter how old students are, they go to school to learn.

ANALYZE THE TEXT

Main Idea and Details What is the topic of *Schools Around the World*? How does the main idea of the section "Older Students" fit with the topic?

These women in India go to school at night.

Dig Deeper

Use Clues to Analyze the Text

Use these pages to learn about Main Idea and Details and Text and Graphic Features. Then read *Schools Around the World* again. Use what you learn to understand it better.

Main Idea and Details

The author of *Schools Around the World* wrote about how schools in different places are the same and how they are different. She included a main idea and details for each section. A **main idea** is the most important idea in the section. The **details** tell more about the main idea.

As you read, think about the main idea and details of each section. Use this chart to record a main idea and the details that tell about it.

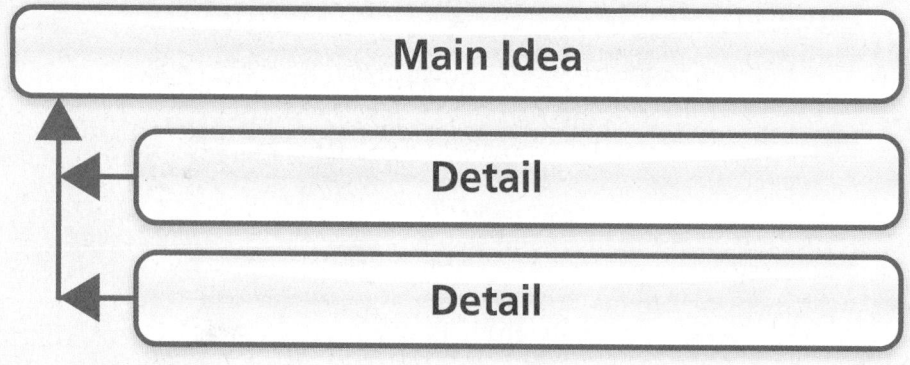

Main Idea
Detail
Detail

Text and Graphic Features

Authors often use **text and graphic features** to help make their writing clear. Headings, captions, and photos are some text and graphic features in *Schools Around the World*.

Text and graphic features can help you understand the text. They can also help you find information quickly. For example, headings tell what each section is about. As you read, think about and use the text and graphic features.

Your Turn

 **How are some schools different from each other?** Use text evidence from *Schools Around the World* to help you answer. Discuss your ideas with a partner. Take turns talking.

💬 Classroom Conversation

Now talk about these questions with the class.

1 How do the headings help you figure out the main idea of each section?

2 Why do you think the author wrote *Schools Around the World*? How do you know?

3 How do some children get to school? Use the headings to look back and find the answer.

Performance Task

WRITE ABOUT READING

Response Look back through *Schools Around the World*. Find facts that are interesting to you. Then write sentences that tell two ways that schools are alike and two ways that schools are different. Draw pictures to go with your sentences.

All schools help people learn.

Writing Tip

Make sure that each statement ends with a period.

INFORMATIONAL TEXT

An American School

Informational text gives facts about a topic.

An **interview** is one person asking another person questions and recording the answers.

Hi, my name is Lily. I go to Washington Elementary School. Aki is my pen pal from Japan. She came for a visit. She wants to ask me some questions about my school.

Aki

Lily

Aki: How did your school get its name?

Lily: My school is named after George Washington who was the first president of the United States. The president is the main leader of our country. The president represents our nation around the world. Our president lives and works in a special home called the White House in Washington, D.C.

Aki: How do you start your day at school?

Lily: We start our day with a pledge to our flag. This is how we honor, or respect, our country and its people. Our flag is red, white, and blue and has stars and stripes. There are fifty stars, and each one stands for one of the fifty states in the United States.

Aki: What subjects do you learn about in school?

Lily: We learn about math and science. We also read a lot of books and learn new words. My favorite subject is social studies.

Aki: What are you learning about in social studies?

Lily: This week we are learning about symbols of the United States, like our flag. Our teacher said that the bald eagle is another symbol. It represents a strong and free country. The Statue of Liberty is also a symbol. When people see it, they think of hope and freedom.

Aki: What are some fun things you do at school?

Lily: I like our music class because we get to sing our favorite songs and play musical instruments. This week we played drums and bells. I also like going to check out books at our school library!

Compare Texts

Write Interview Questions What questions would you ask a school principal? Think about *Schools Around the World* and *An American School*. Use both selections to help you think of questions. Make a list of what you would ask.

Draw and Label What type of school from *Schools Around the World* would you like to go to? Draw what the school might look like. Write labels to tell about your picture.

Schools in Germany

Germany

Connect to Social Studies With a small group, choose one of the countries you read about in *Schools Around the World*. Use books and other sources to read about schools in that country. Make a poster that shows what you learned.

ELA RI.2.1, RI.2.9, W.2.7

Grammar

Digital Resources

▶ **Multimedia Grammar Glossary**

Quotation Marks When you write, show what someone says by putting **quotation marks** (" ") at the beginning and end of the speaker's exact words.

Rules for Using Quotation Marks

Put a **comma** after words such as *said* and *asked.*
> The teacher said, "Take out your math books."

Begin the first word inside the quotation marks with a **capital letter**.
> Mike said, "We are having a quiz today."

Put the **end mark** inside the quotation marks.
> Liza asked, "Who is the class leader?"

Try This! **Write each sentence correctly. Include quotation marks to show the exact words someone said or asked.**

1. The bus driver said stay in your seats.

2. Jack asked how long is the trip?

3. The teacher said it will take an hour.

You have read stories in which people talk to each other. This makes a story more interesting. Make your own writing more interesting by showing the words people speak.

Quotation Marks

Nita asked, "What is your favorite subject in school?"
Raj said, "My favorite subject is science."

Connect Grammar to Writing

When you edit your persuasive paragraph, be sure to use commas, capital letters, and end marks correctly.

Opinion Writing

✔️ **Elaboration** When you write to persuade, use exact words to make your writing more interesting.

Rachel wrote a **persuasive paragraph** asking her teacher to take her class to a museum. Later, she revised her writing to use more exact words. Use exact words when you revise your paragraph.

Writing Checklist

✔️ **Organization**
Did I state my opinion at the beginning?

✔️ **Evidence**
Did I choose reasons that are important to my audience?

✔️ **Elaboration**
Did I use exact words to make my writing interesting?

✔️ **Conventions**
Did I begin my sentences in different ways?

Revised Draft

Our class should go to the Children's Museum.

The Children's Museum has many wonderful ~~lots of nice~~ displays, such as one that shows important people from the past. That's a great display because we're learning about that in social studies right now.

ELA W.2.1, W.2.5, L.2.5b

Let's Take a Trip!

by Rachel Wollmer

Our class should go to the Children's Museum. The Children's Museum has many wonderful displays, such as one that shows important people from the past. That's a great display because we're learning about that in social studies right now. Also, we could write a research paper about what we learn at the museum. Everyone would have a fun day together at the Children's Museum!

Reading as a Writer

Which exact words did Rachel add? What words can you add to make your writing more interesting?

I used exact words to make my writing interesting to my readers.

Helen Keller

Talking TOOLS

🔍 LANGUAGE DETECTIVE

Talk About Words
Work with a partner. Choose one of the Context Cards. Add words to the sentence to explain more details about the photo. Give details that tell when or where.

Vocabulary in Context

▶ Read each **Context Card**.

▶ Ask a partner a question that uses one of the Vocabulary words.

1 knowledge

Knowledge, or information, can come from books and many other places.

2 curious

You can search the Internet if you are curious, or want to learn, about sea animals.

3 motion

A hand held up is a motion to stop!

4 silence

The rule in the library is "Silence! Please don't speak."

5 illness

This child has an illness, but she won't be sick for long.

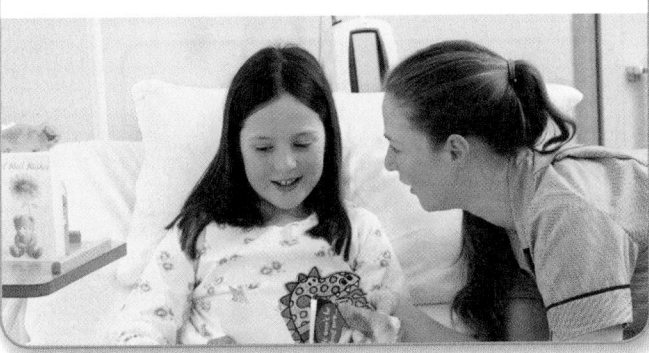

6 imitated

This girl imitated, or copied, her teacher to learn sign language.

7 darkness

Flashlights help people see better in darkness.

8 behavior

Taking a telephone message is good behavior. It is a polite way to act.

Read and Comprehend

Author's Purpose Authors write for many reasons. The reason an author writes something is called the **author's purpose.** You can look for text evidence as you read to help you figure out if the author wrote to make you smile, to tell you facts, or to explain ideas. You can list the text evidence on a chart like this one.

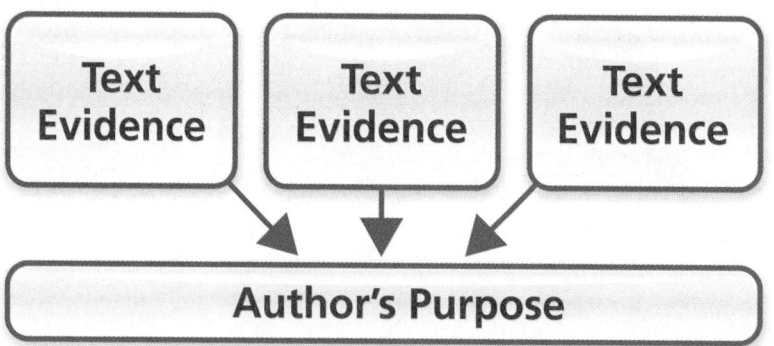

✓ **TARGET STRATEGY**

Summarize As you read, stop to tell important ideas in your own words.

Special Ways to Communicate

People share their thoughts and ideas in different ways. Many people share ideas through talking or writing. Tools such as phones and computers can help people communicate.

People who cannot hear or see have special ways to communicate. In *Helen Keller*, you will read about a girl who cannot see, hear, or talk. She must learn to communicate in other ways.

💬 Talk About It

Do you think using a computer is a good way to communicate? Why or why not? Talk about your ideas with a group.

- ▸ Take turns speaking.
- ▸ Ask questions if you don't understand.
- ▸ Answer questions your partner asks.

ANCHOR TEXT

Helen Keller

 GENRE

A **biography** tells about events in a person's life. As you read, look for:

▸ information about why a person is important

▸ events in time order

MEET THE AUTHOR

Jane Sutcliffe

The library was Jane Sutcliffe's favorite place to visit when she was a child. She says she loved reading biographies "just to get a peek at how other people lived day to day, in different times and places." Now she writes biographies.

MEET THE ILLUSTRATOR

Robert Papp

Most of Robert Papp's clothes are covered in oil paint. That's because he's extremely messy when he paints. Mr. Papp lives in Pennsylvania with his wife, Lisa, who is also an artist. She's not quite as messy as he is, though.

Helen could not see her family's milking cow. But she liked touching it. Helen Keller had been blind and deaf for most of her life. The only way she knew the world was by touch, taste, and smell.

Helen was born in 1880 in Tuscumbia, Alabama. When she was just a baby, she became very sick. The illness took away her sight and hearing. Helen could not hear her brothers' laughter or her mother's voice. She could not see her father's smile or the pretty flowers outside her window. For Helen, there was only silence and gray darkness.

To learn to speak, children need to hear words. But Helen could not hear anything. So she could not speak. Instead, she made motions. When she wanted her mother, she put her hand against her face. When she wanted her father, she made the motion of putting on a pair of glasses. When she was hungry, she pretended to slice and butter bread.

Helen Keller

Helen knew she was different from the rest
of her family. They moved their lips when they
wanted things. Sometimes Helen stood between
two people as they talked. She held her hands to
their lips. Then she tried moving her own lips.
But still no one understood her.

That made Helen angry. Sometimes she screamed and cried and kicked for hours. She threw things and hit people. But it didn't change anything. She was still alone in silence and darkness.

Helen was hard to control. Her parents didn't know how to help her. They took her to doctors. None of the doctors could help Helen see or hear again. When Helen was six, a doctor suggested the Kellers visit Alexander Graham Bell. Dr. Bell was famous for inventing the telephone. He also taught deaf people.

Alexander Graham Bell

Dr. Bell told the Kellers to write to Michael Anagnos in Boston. Mr. Anagnos was the head of the Perkins Institution for the Blind. He believed Helen could learn how to let out the thoughts locked inside her. Mr. Anagnos promised to send Helen a teacher.

Michael Anagnos

Helen and Teacher
March 1887

Helen's teacher came to live with the Kellers that spring. Her name was Annie Sullivan. Annie had studied at the Perkins School. She was nearly blind herself. Annie needed to control Helen's wild behavior so she could teach her. But Helen did not understand that Annie wanted to help her. For two weeks, Helen fought with Annie. She hit Annie and knocked out one of her front teeth. She even locked Annie in an upstairs room. Mr. Keller had to get a ladder and let Annie out through a window.

Annie Sullivan

Still, Annie did not give up. Little by little, Helen learned to trust her new teacher. Annie began to teach Helen about words. She spelled words using her fingers. Her hand formed a different shape for each letter. She pressed each shape into Helen's hand. When she gave Helen some cake, she spelled C-A-K-E into Helen's palm. When Helen held her doll, Annie spelled D-O-L-L for Helen. Helen imitated the shapes. She thought it was a game. She didn't know that the shapes spelled words.

After a month, Helen could spell whatever Annie spelled. But Helen still did not know that she was naming the things she touched.

Annie finger spelling into Helen's hand

One day Helen and Annie walked to the well house. Someone was pumping water. Annie pushed Helen's hand into the rushing water. Helen felt the cool water on one hand. She felt her teacher's fingers spelling W-A-T-E-R into her other hand. Over and over, Annie spelled the word. Suddenly Helen stood very still. All at once she understood! The liquid flowing over her hand had a name. It was W-A-T-E-R!

ANALYZE THE TEXT

Genre: Biography How is learning that all things have a name an important event in Helen's life?

Everything had a name! Helen wanted to learn them all. She ran from one thing to another. Annie spelled the name of everything Helen touched. Then Helen turned and pointed to Annie. T-E-A-C-H-E-R, spelled Annie. From then on, Helen's name for Annie was "Teacher." That summer, Helen learned a lot of new words. She stopped using her old motions. Her fingers gave her all the words she needed.

Annie did not teach Helen words one at a time. She talked to her in full sentences. That way, Helen learned more than just new words. She learned new ideas. Helen and Annie took long walks through the woods and along the river. Annie gave Helen lessons on the walks. She showed Helen how seeds sprout and plants grow. She made mountains out of mud and taught Helen about volcanoes. Sometimes they climbed a tree and had a lesson there.

Helen and Annie having a lesson

Reading a book in Braille

Helen was hungry for knowledge. She wanted to learn everything Annie could teach her. Soon Annie started teaching Helen how to read. The words were printed in raised letters for a blind person.

Helen felt the words with her fingers. She liked to hunt for words she knew. When she learned to read better, she read her books over and over. Her curious fingers wore down the raised letters.

ANALYZE THE TEXT

Author's Purpose What is the author's purpose for writing about Helen Keller? Use text evidence to support your answer.

488

Helen also learned to write. She wrote letters to her family and Dr. Bell. She wrote many letters to Mr. Anagnos in Boston. Mr. Anagnos was amazed by how much Helen had learned. He published some of Helen's letters. Reporters began to write about Helen. Soon she was famous. People all over the world wanted to know about the miracle girl. And Helen wanted to know all about the world.

Dig Deeper

Use Clues to Analyze the Text

Use these pages to learn about Author's Purpose and Biographies. Then read *Helen Keller* again. Use what you learn to understand it better.

Author's Purpose

In *Helen Keller*, you read about real events that happened to a girl who was deaf and blind. The author had a reason for writing about Helen. An author's reason for writing is the **author's purpose.**

You can use details as text evidence to figure out why the author wrote *Helen Keller*. Use a chart like the one below to help you.

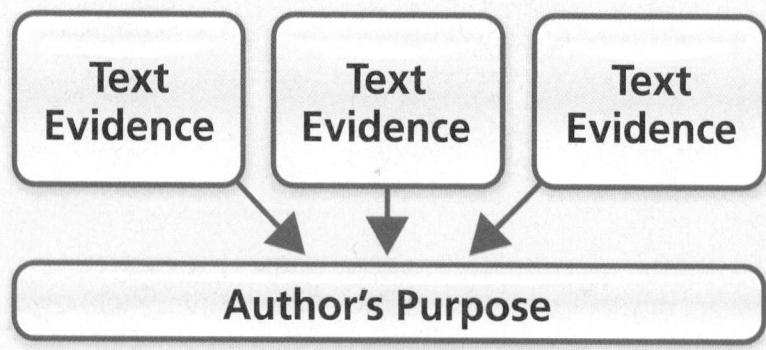

Genre: Biography

Helen Keller is a **biography**. It tells about events in an important person's life. When you read a biography, think about how the events are connected. For example, Helen put her hands to people's lips as they spoke and then moved her lips. This helps you understand that Helen wanted to be able to communicate.

Your Turn

 **How can you communicate in different ways?** Look for text evidence in *Helen Keller* to help you answer. Talk about your ideas with a partner. Listen carefully and take turns speaking. Add your own ideas to what your partner says.

💬 Classroom Conversation

Now talk about these questions with the class.

1. Why did Annie Sullivan keep working with Helen even though it was so difficult?

2. What makes Helen Keller an important person?

3. How are Annie Sullivan and Helen Keller alike? How are they different?

WRITE ABOUT READING ....

Response Who was a bigger hero, Helen or her teacher? Write a paragraph to tell your opinion. Use text evidence to explain your choice.

Writing Tip

Use end marks when you write. Remember that a statement ends with a period.

INFORMATIONAL TEXT

☑ GENRE

Informational text gives facts about a topic. This is a science text.

☑ TEXT FOCUS

Photographs can be used to show ideas in a text. **Captions** tell more information about the photos.

Talking TOOLS

Helen Keller lived in darkness, but she was curious about the world. Braille helped Keller gain knowledge. Today people who cannot see still use Braille to help them read.

Many ATMs (Automated Teller Machines) have Braille labels, for example. That way, blind people can use them to do their banking.

Some ATMs even talk! With just one quick motion, users plug headphones into the ATM. Then the ATM tells them what to do.

A Braille notetaker is a computer that helps people who cannot see. They type their notes on it, using a Braille keyboard. The notes are saved in Braille. Later they can use their fingers to read the notes in silence on the notepad. The machine can also read the notes aloud!

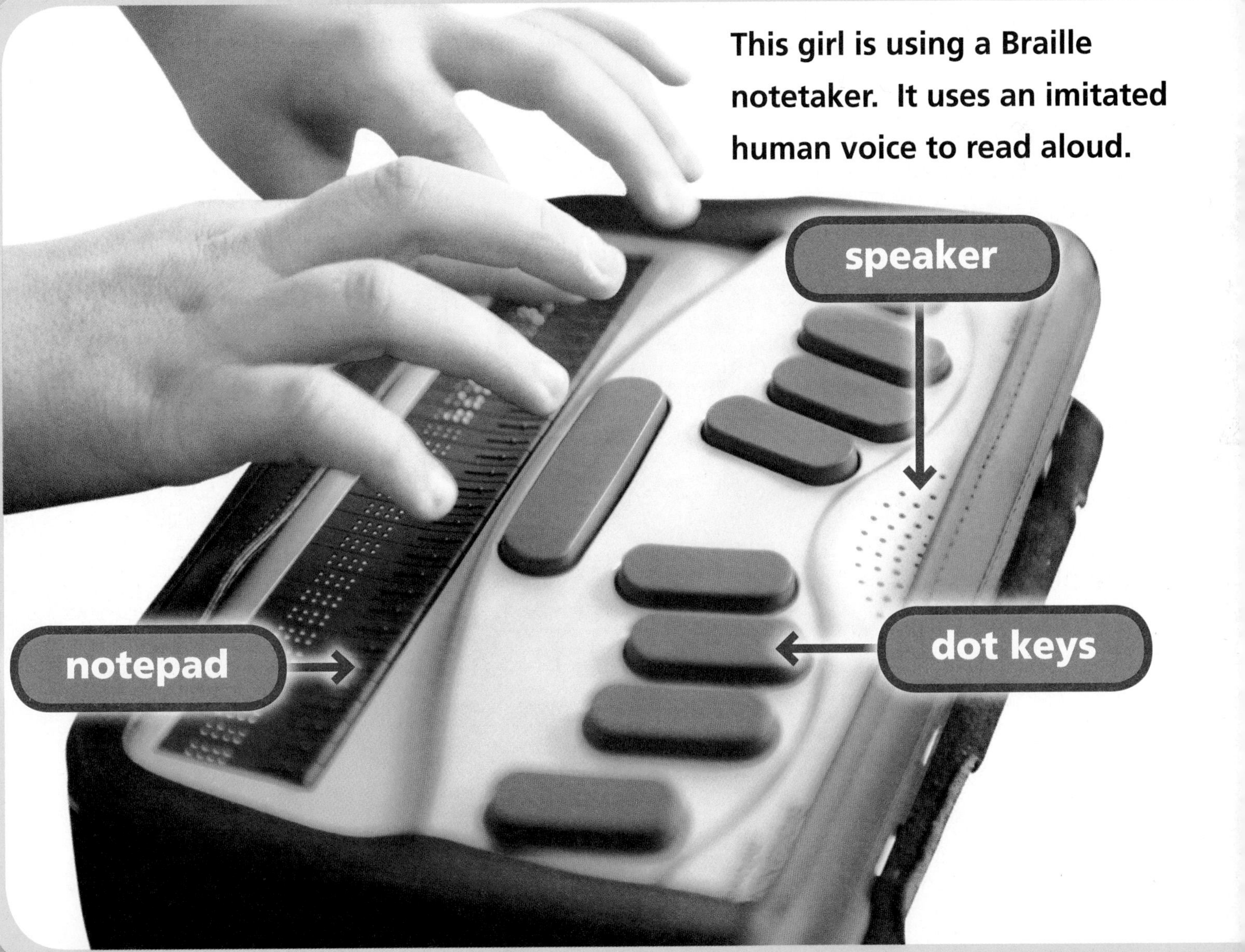

This girl is using a Braille notetaker. It uses an imitated human voice to read aloud.

speaker

notepad

dot keys

What if someone who cannot see has an illness and needs to take a temperature? Use a talking thermometer! There are talking clocks and watches as well. These watches often have Braille faces, too.

If Helen Keller were alive today, she'd be happy to learn of the many ways technology can help people with vision disabilities.

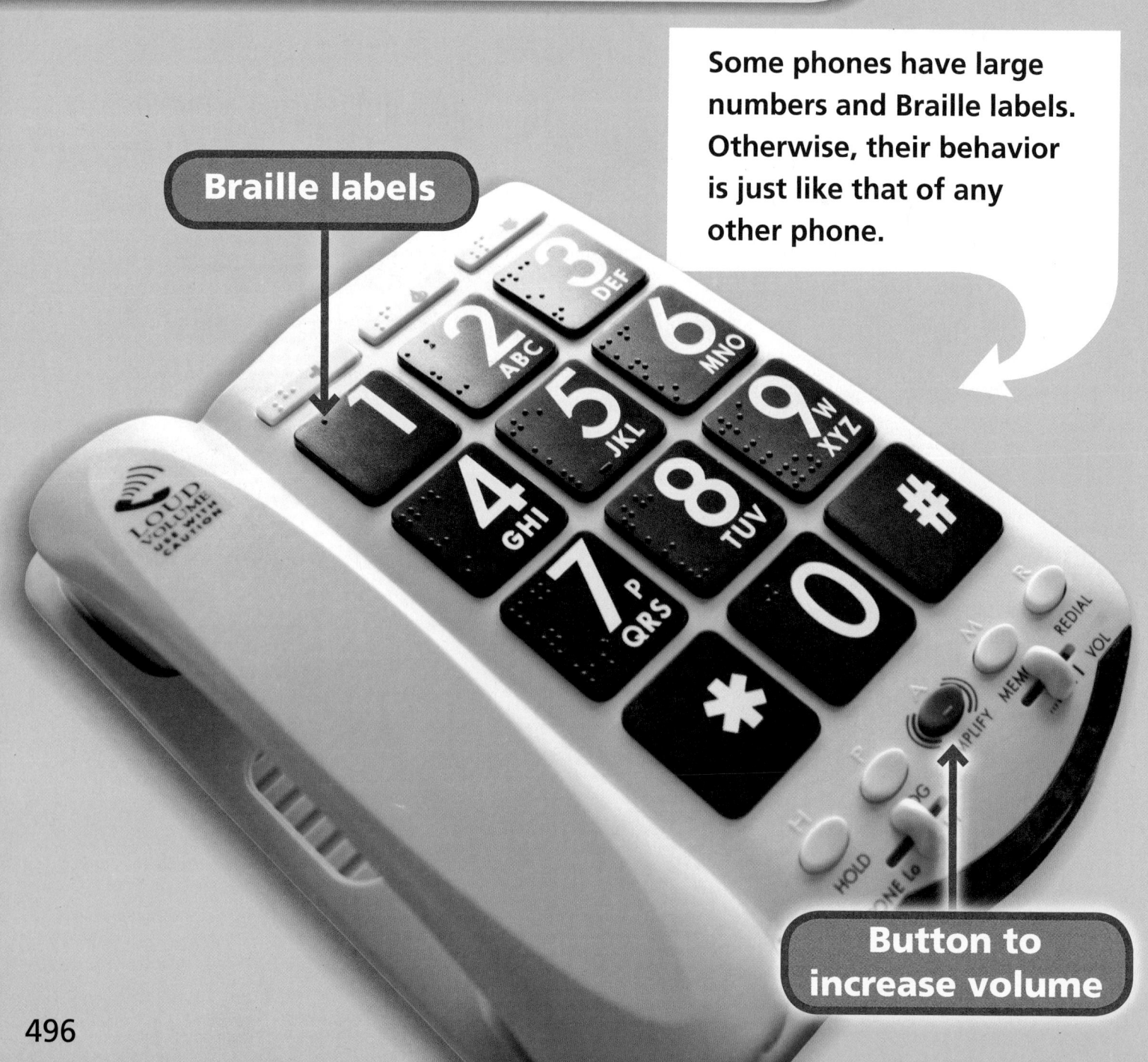

Braille labels

Some phones have large numbers and Braille labels. Otherwise, their behavior is just like that of any other phone.

Button to increase volume

Compare Texts

ELA RI.2.1, RI.2.7, RI.2.9, SL.2.1a

TEXT TO TEXT

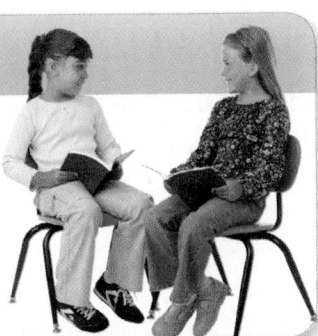

Discuss Tools Could Helen Keller have used any of the tools from *Talking Tools?* Why or why not? Discuss your ideas with a partner.

TEXT TO SELF

Share Experiences Think of some things that Annie Sullivan taught Helen Keller. Talk with a group about the way you learned these same lessons and how that is different from the way Helen learned them. Take turns listening and speaking. Ask a question if you do not understand your classmates' ideas.

TEXT TO WORLD

Making Changes Compare the Braille book on page 487 with the Braille tools in *Talking Tools*. What changes have we made to machines so that people who cannot see can also use them?

Grammar

Using Proper Nouns Names for **days** of the week and **months** of the year begin with capital letters. Each important word in the name of a **holiday** begins with a capital letter, too.

Days	Months	Holidays
Monday	March	New Year's Day
Friday	July	Thanksgiving Day
Saturday	September	Fourth of July

Try This! **Write each sentence correctly.**

1. Is labor day in september?

2. valentine's day is in february.

3. This monday is earth day.

4. I gave my mother flowers on mother's day.

In your writing, use days, holidays, and dates to tell your reader more about when things happen. Remember to begin the names of days, months, and holidays with a capital letter.

Without Words That Tell When	With Words That Tell When

I read books to a neighbor. She lost her sight.	Every Sunday I read books to a neighbor. She lost her sight on May 25, 2007.

Connect Grammar to Writing

As you revise your persuasive essay next week, think about ways to tell your reader more. Add words that tell when.

Opinion Writing

✔ **Purpose** When you write to persuade, clearly state your goal. Then give your readers reasons to support your opinion and goal.

Farah made a web to plan her **persuasive essay**. She had two reasons. Later, she added details and facts to make her reasons stronger.

Writing Process Checklist

▶ **Prewrite**

☑ **Did I choose a goal I care about?**

☑ **Did I give reasons that support my opinion and goal?**

☑ **Did I include details and facts to make my reasons convincing to my audience?**

Draft

Revise

Edit

Publish and Share

Exploring a Topic

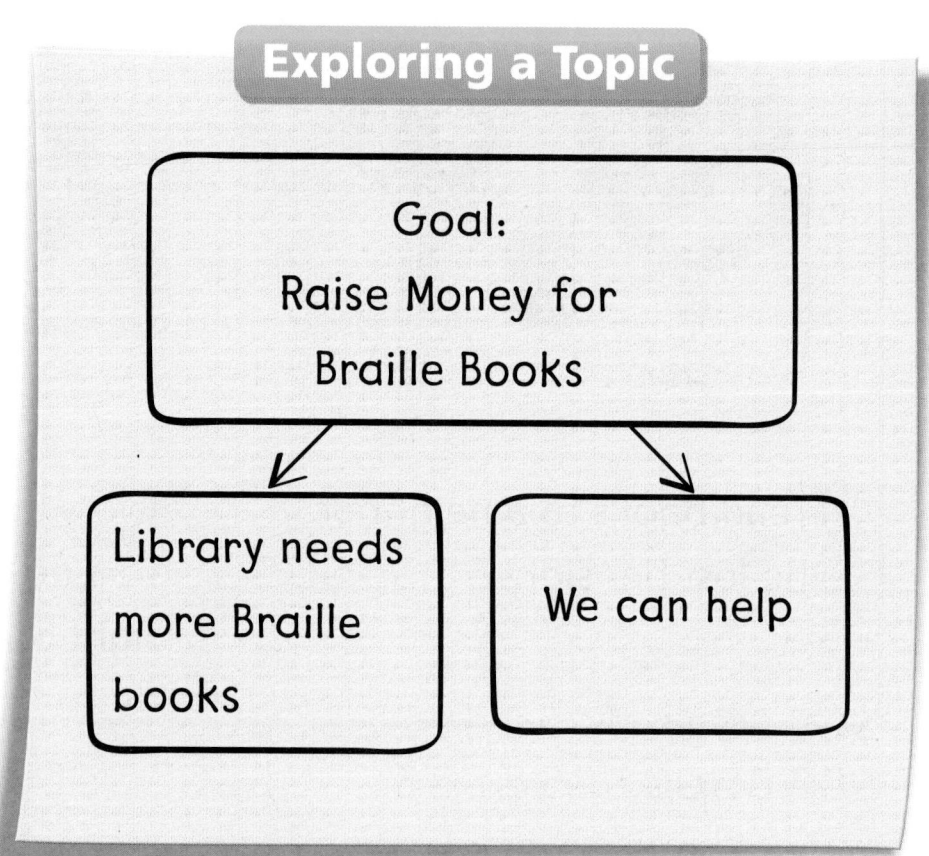

Goal:
Raise Money for
Braille Books

Library needs more Braille books

We can help

```
                    Goal: Raise Money
                     for Braille Books


        Library needs more              We can help
          Braille books


    Many          Library       Our school        We can
   people         has only      wants a           do a
   in town       20 Braille     community       read-a-thon
    read           books         project
   Braille
```

Lesson

15

LANGUAGE DETECTIVE

Talk About Words
Work with a partner. Choose one of the sentences. Take out the Vocabulary word. Put in a word that means the same or almost the same thing. Tell how the sentences are the same and how they are different.

Vocabulary in Context

▶ **Read each Context Card.**

▶ **Tell a story about two pictures using the Vocabulary words.**

1 **obeys**
A careful driver always obeys traffic rules. This driver stops at a stop sign.

2 **safety**
The firefighter talks about fire safety. He teaches about staying out of danger.

3 attention

Before crossing the street, stand at attention and look both ways.

4 buddy

Never swim alone. Always swim with a buddy, or friend.

5 station

A police station is a safe place to go if you need help.

6 speech

His job is to give a short speech. He will talk about airplane safety.

7 shocked

She is shocked at how hot it is outside. She needs to get out of the sun soon!

8 enormous

Only the workers can go inside the fence on this enormous work site.

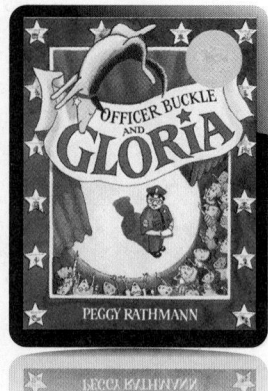

Read and Comprehend

☑ **TARGET SKILL**

Cause and Effect In *Officer Buckle and Gloria*, one event makes another event happen. The first event is the **cause**. The event that happens because of the cause is the **effect**.

As you read a story, ask yourself what happens and why. Find answers by looking at the words and pictures in the story. You can use a chart like this to show how the events connect.

Cause	Effect

☑ **TARGET STRATEGY**

Monitor/Clarify If you don't understand why something is happening, stop and think. Find text evidence to figure out what doesn't make sense.

Personal Safety

It is important to stay safe. You should wear a helmet when you ride your bike. You also should look both ways before crossing a street. These are just two things to do to be safe. Parents, teachers, and police officers can help you learn more about safety.

Officer Buckle is a police officer who loves sharing safety tips. You will read about Officer Buckle and his helpful dog in *Officer Buckle and Gloria*.

Think | Write | Pair | Share

If you could make up a new rule for your home or classroom, what would it be? Write your answer. Then talk about it with a partner. Be sure to take turns speaking and listening. Then explain to classmates why you think this rule would be helpful.

ANCHOR TEXT

☑ GENRE

Humorous fiction is a story that is written to make the reader laugh. As you read, look for:

▸ characters who do or say funny things

▸ events that would not happen in real life

MEET THE AUTHOR AND ILLUSTRATOR

PEGGY RATHMANN

Peggy Rathmann's family had a dog named Skippy. One holiday they were gathered for breakfast. A family member was filming them. It wasn't until later when they were watching the home movie that they caught Skippy in the background, licking the poached eggs on the serving table. No one had seen it happen. Skippy was the model for the dog in *Officer Buckle and Gloria*.

OFFICER BUCKLE
AND
GLORIA

written and illustrated by
PEGGY RATHMANN

ESSENTIAL QUESTION

Why is it important to follow safety rules?

Officer Buckle knew more safety tips than anyone else in Napville.

Every time he thought of a new one, he thumbtacked it to his bulletin board.

Safety Tip #77
NEVER stand on a SWIVEL CHAIR.

Officer Buckle shared his safety tips with the students at Napville School.

Nobody ever listened.

Sometimes, there was snoring.

Afterward, it was business as usual.

Mrs. Toppel, the principal, took down the welcome banner.

"NEVER stand on a SWIVEL CHAIR," said Officer Buckle, but Mrs. Toppel didn't hear him.

Then one day, Napville's police department bought a police dog named Gloria.

When it was time for Officer Buckle to give the safety speech at the school, Gloria went along.

"Children, this is Gloria," announced Officer Buckle. "Gloria obeys my commands. Gloria, SIT!" And Gloria sat.

Officer Buckle gave Safety Tip Number One:
"KEEP your SHOELACES tied!"
The children sat up and stared.

Officer Buckle checked to see if Gloria was
sitting at attention. She was.

"Safety Tip Number Two," said Officer Buckle. "ALWAYS wipe up spills BEFORE someone SLIPS AND FALLS!"

The children's eyes popped.

Officer Buckle checked on Gloria again.

"Good dog," he said.

Officer Buckle thought of a safety tip he had discovered that morning.

"NEVER leave a THUMBTACK where you
might SIT on it!"
The audience roared.

Officer Buckle grinned. He said the rest of the tips with *plenty* of expression.

The children clapped their hands and cheered. Some of them laughed until they cried.

Officer Buckle was surprised. He had never noticed how funny safety tips could be.

After *this* safety speech, there wasn't a single accident.

ANALYZE THE TEXT

Cause and Effect What do the children do when Gloria acts out Officer Buckle's safety tips?

515

The next day, an enormous envelope arrived
at the police station. It was stuffed with thank-you
letters from the students at Napville School.

Every letter had a drawing of Gloria on it.

Officer Buckle thought the drawings showed a
lot of imagination.

His favorite letter was written on a star-shaped piece of paper. It said:

You and Gloria make a good team.

Your friend,
Claire

P.S. I always wear a crash helmet. (Safety Tip #7)

Officer Buckle was thumbtacking Claire's letter to his bulletin board when the phones started ringing. Grade schools, high schools, and day-care centers were calling about the safety speech.

"Officer Buckle," they said, "our students want to hear your safety tips! And please, bring along that police dog."

Officer Buckle told his safety tips to 313 schools. Everywhere he and Gloria went, children sat up and listened.

After every speech, Officer Buckle took Gloria out for ice cream.

Officer Buckle loved having a buddy.

Then one day, a television news team videotaped Officer Buckle in the state-college auditorium.

When he finished Safety Tip Number Ninety-nine, DO NOT GO SWIMMING DURING ELECTRICAL STORMS!, the students jumped to their feet and applauded.

"Bravo! Bravo!" they cheered. Officer
Buckle bowed again and again.

That night, Officer Buckle watched himself on the 10 o'clock news.

The next day, the principal of Napville School telephoned the police station.

"Good morning, Officer Buckle! It's time for our safety speech!"

Officer Buckle frowned.

"I'm not giving any more speeches! Nobody looks at me, anyway!"

"Oh," said Mrs. Toppel. "Well! How about Gloria? Could she come?"

Someone else from the police station gave Gloria a ride to the school.

Gloria sat onstage looking lonely. Then she fell asleep. So did the audience.

After Gloria left, Napville School had its biggest accident ever . . .

It started with a puddle of banana pudding. . . .
SPLAT! SPLATTER! SPLOOSH!

Everyone slid smack into Mrs. Toppel, who screamed
and let go of her hammer.

ANALYZE THE TEXT

Humor What happens when the people don't follow Officer Buckle's tips? How does the author make what happens seem funny?

The next morning, a pile of letters arrived at the police station.

Every letter had a drawing of the accident.

Officer Buckle was shocked.

At the bottom of the pile was a note written on a paper star.

Officer Buckle smiled. The note said:

Gloria missed you yesterday!
Your friend,
Claire

P.S. Don't worry, I was wearing my helmet!
(Safety Tip #7)

Gloria gave Officer Buckle a big kiss on the nose.

Officer Buckle gave Gloria a nice pat on the back.

Then, Officer Buckle thought of his best safety tip yet . . .

Safety Tip #101
"ALWAYS STICK WITH YOUR BUDDY!"

Dig Deeper

Use Clues to Analyze the Text

Use these pages to learn about Cause and Effect and Humor. Then read *Officer Buckle and Gloria* again. Use what you learn to understand it better.

Cause and Effect

Officer Buckle and Gloria is a funny story about a police officer and his dog, Gloria. In this story, one event makes another happen. For example, Gloria does tricks behind Officer Buckle. As a result, the audience laughs. Gloria's tricks are the **cause**. The audience's laughter is the **effect**.

As you read, think about what happens and why. Use a chart like the one below to show causes and effects.

Cause	Effect

ELA RL.2.1, RL.2.3, RL.2.7

Humor

The author of a **humorous fiction** story wants to make the reader laugh. The author may have a character do or say something that is funny. The pictures may also show something funny.

In *Officer Buckle and Gloria*, the safety tips that Officer Buckle gives are serious. Gloria acts out the tips in a funny way. As you read, ask yourself questions about the words and pictures to figure out if the author is trying to be funny or not.

Your Turn

 **Why is it important to follow safety rules?** Look for ideas in the words and pictures in *Officer Buckle and Gloria*. Share your ideas with a small group. Take turns adding your own ideas to what others say.

Classroom Conversation

Now talk about these questions with the class.

1. What events in the story cause other events to happen?

2. How is Gloria different from real police dogs?

3. How might the children at the schools change after Officer Buckle and Gloria visit? Tell why you think so.

WRITE ABOUT READING

Response Do you think that the story is funny? Why or why not? Write a paragraph to explain your opinion. Use story words and pictures as evidence to help explain your ideas.

Writing Tip

Remember to start the name of each person and each proper noun with a capital letter.

READERS' THEATER

Safety at Home

by Margaret Sweeny

Cast of Characters

Dad

Alexa

Jake

☑ **GENRE**

Readers' Theater is a text that has been written for readers to read aloud.

☑ **TEXT FOCUS**

Dialogue is the talk between characters in a play. Dialogue helps readers get to know the characters through their own words.

Dad: What did you do on your class trip?

Alexa: We visited an enormous fire station.

Jake: The fire chief gave a speech about fire safety.

Dad: I hope you were paying attention.

Alexa: We were. Later, we worked with a buddy to make a safety poster. I worked with Jake.

Jake: Look at our poster.

STOP, DROP, AND ROLL

1. If your clothes catch on fire, don't run.
2. STOP where you are.
3. DROP to the ground. Cover your face with your hands.
4. ROLL over and over to put out the fire.

Dad: I'm shocked! You know more about fire safety than I do.

Alexa: Everyone in our school obeys fire safety rules.

Jake: Guess what **get low and go** means?

Alexa: If the house is smoky, get low.

Jake: That's because smoke rises. Get low to stay below the smoke.

Alexa: Crawl to the nearest way out.

Jake: Then go to a safe meeting place to wait for your family.

Dad: Let's pick a meeting place right now!

Compare Texts

TEXT TO TEXT

Compare and Contrast How is the message in *Officer Buckle and Gloria* like the message in *Safety at Home?* How are they different?

TEXT TO SELF

Write a Caption Officer Buckle's safety tips are based on his own life. Think of a safety tip you know. Draw a picture of what Gloria might do to act out that tip. Then write a caption for your picture.

TEXT TO WORLD

Connect to Social Studies Gloria acted out safety tips, and Alexa and Jake made a fire safety poster. Make a poster of classroom safety tips or act them out for your class.

ELA RL.2.2

Grammar

Abbreviations The names of days, months, and places are proper nouns that can be shortened. An **abbreviation** is a short way to write a word by taking out some of the letters and writing a period at the end. Abbreviations for proper nouns begin with a capital letter.

Proper Nouns	Abbreviations
Monday	Mon.
March	Mar.
Main Street	Main St.

 **Write the proper noun for each abbreviation.**

1. Nov.   4. Canton St.

2. Tues.   5. Jan.

3. Elm Rd.   6. Fri.

Write abbreviations correctly. Remember to use a period at the end of an abbreviation. Capitalize the abbreviation for a proper noun.

Incorrect	Correct
mr Wang says the police officer will visit our class on sept 4.	Mr. Wang says the police officer will visit our class on Sept. 4.

Connect Grammar to Writing

When you edit your persuasive essay, make sure you have used capital letters and end marks correctly.

Opinion Writing

☑ **Organization**   When you write a **persuasive essay**, each reason can start a new paragraph.

Farah wrote a draft of her essay. Later, she moved things around so each reason started a new paragraph. She also added more linking words, such as *so, also,* and *because,* to link her opinions to her reasons.

Writing Process Checklist

Prewrite

Draft

▶ **Revise**

☑ **Did I tell my goal in a clear way?**

☑ **Did I give reasons for my goal?**

☑ **Did I include facts and examples for each reason?**

☑ **Did I sum up my reasons?**

Edit

Publish and Share

Revised Draft

Our town library has a problem that we must fix. ¶ The town library does not have enough Braille books for people who need them.

It needs money for Braille books.

There are thirty-four people in our town who read Braille. The library has only twenty Braille books. , so it needs more books.

Help Our Library!

by Farah Jamali

Our town library has a problem that we must fix. It needs money for Braille books.

The town library does not have enough Braille books for the people who need them. There are thirty-four people in our town who read Braille. The library has only twenty Braille books, so it needs more.

Our school should help the library by having a read-a-thon. Each student can fill out a pledge sheet. The money we raise could buy the Braille books our community needs.

Reading as a Writer

How did Farah organize her essay to make her reasons clearer? How can you organize your reasons and details?

I started a new paragraph for each reason.

Write an Opinion Essay

TASK Look back at *Ah, Music!* and *Schools Around the World*. Do you think it is important to learn about music in school? Why or why not? Write an essay to the principal of your school to explain your opinion and your reasons. Use information from the texts to support your opinion and reasons.

PLAN

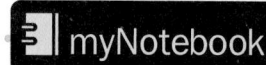 myNotebook

Gather Information Talk with a partner about *Ah, Music!* and *Schools Around the World*. Look for information in the texts to answer these questions:

- What are some reasons that teaching music in school is a good idea?

- What are some reasons that teaching music in school might be a bad idea?

Then list your ideas in a chart. Decide which opinion you will support.

Good Idea	Bad Idea
•	•
•	•
•	•

Use the tools in your eBook to remember details from *Ah, Music!* and *Schools Around the World*.

Write Your Essay Use the information below to help you organize your essay.

Opinion

Start with an opening sentence that tells what your opinion is. This is what you want readers to believe.

Reasons

Write strong reasons that support your opinion. Use the chart you made and evidence from the texts to help you. Use words such as *because*, *and*, or *also* to link your reasons to your opinion. Write simple sentences and compound sentences to make your essay more interesting for the reader.

Conclusion

Give your essay a conclusion that repeats your opinion in a different way.

Have a partner read your draft. Talk about how you can make it better.

Review Your Draft Read your writing and make it better. Use the Checklist.

 Does my essay state my opinion?

 Did I connect my reasons to my opinion with words such as *because*, *and*, or *also*?

 Did I use text evidence to explain my reasons?

 Did I use both simple and compound sentences?

 Did I use capital letters and punctuation correctly?

Share Write or type a copy of your paragraph. Add pictures. Pick a way to share.

- Read your essay to your classmates.
- Make a poster or other visual aid to display in the classroom.

Glossary

This glossary can help you find the meanings of some of the words in this book. The meanings given are the meanings of the words as they are used in the book. Sometimes a second meaning is also given.

A

attend
To look carefully at or take care of: *We try to **attend** to the work we are asked to do.*

attention
A form of **attend:** *They stood at **attention** to show they were listening.*

B

beak
A bill, or the hard mouth parts of a bird: *The baby birds opened their **beaks** wide, waiting for their food.*

behave
To act in a certain way: *We always tried to **behave** well when visitors were in the room.*

behavior
A form of **behave:** *His **behavior** in school was better than it was at home.*

believe
To accept as true or real: *I **believe** that you have the hat.*

bend
To become curved or not straight: *The tree branches **bend** down in the heavy snow.*

beak

beware

To be careful or look out for a problem: *The sign told us to **beware** of falling rocks.*

bloom

To blossom or grow into flower: *Some plants **bloom** in the spring, while others are just starting to grow.*

bloom

blooming

A form of **bloom:** *Butterflies come to the garden when that bush is **blooming**.*

brag

To boast, or speak with too much pride: *She tries not to **brag** about winning, but she wants us to know.*

branch

A part that grows out from a trunk of a tree: *All the **branches** of the tree had yellow leaves.*

break

To separate into pieces or tear apart: *We had to **break** the ground up with different garden tools.*

breeze

A light wind: *The puppy smelled smoke when she sniffed the **breeze**.*

buddy

A pal or close friend: *He became my **buddy** during our first summer in camp.*

burst

To be full to the point of breaking open: *She tried hard not to **burst** out laughing when she saw the silly hat.*

bursting

A form of **burst:** *The milkweed pod was **bursting** with silky seeds.*

bursting

C

canned

Something that was put in a can to help it stay fresh: *We eat **canned** fruit when we do not have any fresh fruit.*

chew

To grind or crush with teeth: ***Chew** your food carefully before you swallow.*

chews

A form of **chew:** *He **chews** gum a lot.*

choice

The act of choosing or the chance to choose: *We had many **choices** about what to see in the city.*

clipped

To be attached with a clip: *The two pieces of paper were **clipped** together so they would not get lost.*

coat

The fur or hair of an animal: *The dog's **coat** was wet after he went outside in the rain.*

collar

A leather, cloth, or metal band for an animal's neck: *Both of our dogs wear red **collars** around their necks.*

community

A group of people who live together in the same area: *Our **community** is filled with friendly neighbors.*

concentrate

To put all of your attention on one thing: *It was hard to **concentrate** on my homework because my brother was talking to me.*

cousin

A child of one's aunt or uncle: *My **cousin** stayed with us for two days.*

creative

To be good at making new things or having new ideas: *My teacher said that my art project was very different and **creative**.*

crown

A head covering that a queen, king, or other ruler might wear: *She used paper, glue, and glitter to make a **crown** for her costume.*

crown

culture

The traditions, arts, and beliefs of a certain group of people: *In his Native American **culture**, the fall harvest is a time for celebration.*

curious

Eager to find out or learn about something: *He was **curious** about many kinds of sea animals, so he loved the aquarium.*

curl

To make a rounded shape: *He showed us how to* **curl** *slices of carrot in cold water.*

curled

A form of **curl**: *The kitten* **curled** *up in his lap and purred happily.*

curly

A form of **curl**: *My brother's hair is so thick and* **curly** *he can hardly comb it.*

D

damage

To harm or injure: *The flood might* **damage** *the bridge so that it must be closed for repair.*

danger

The chance of harm, or something that may cause harm: *We had good reasons to worry about* **danger** *deep in the dark cave.*

dangerous

A form of **danger**: *The little rabbit knew it was a* **dangerous** *place, but she hopped closer.*

dark

Without light or with very little light: *With no moon, the night was* **dark**.

darkness

A form of **dark**: *In the* **darkness**, *he couldn't tell what kind of animal was outside.*

decide

To make up one's mind: *Tomorrow I will* **decide** *what to do about the party.*

deep

Located far below the surface or far from an opening: *They buried the treasure* **deep** *in the ground near a pine tree.*

deepest

A form of **deep**: *In the* **deepest** *part of the ocean, it is very dark.*

demand

To ask firmly or to require: *The teachers in that school* **demand** *hard work from their students.*

direction

The place or line along which someone or something goes: *Walk in the* **direction** *of the town.*

direction

disgust

To cause a sick or bad feeling: *If those movies* **disgust** *you, please stop watching them.*

disgusting

A form of **disgust:** *When she sniffed at the garbage pail, it smelled* **disgusting**.

drift

To float along or be carried along on water or air: *Our raft will* **drift** *if we do not paddle.*

drool

To let saliva drip from the mouth: *My baby sister* **drools** *on my arm and makes my sleeve wet.*

drooled

A form of **drool:** *He* **drooled** *when he looked at all the delicious food.*

E

enormous

Huge, or very large in size: *Hank was an **enormous** dog, almost the size of a cow.*

enormous

equal

To be the same as: *Seven days **equal** one week, and twenty-four hours equal one day.*

expression

A certain mood or feeling that something has: *My sister's voice had a lot of **expression** as she read the funny poem.*

F

flash

To give out a sudden bright light: *The fireworks **flash** in the night sky, and people cheer.*

flash

flop

To drop or hang heavily: *When I'm really tired, I **flop** onto the couch for a nap.*

floppy

A form of **flop**: *Some rabbits have **floppy** ears that droop around their face.*

G7

furious

Full of great anger, or raging: *She was so furious that she threw a pillow across the room.*

G

gather

To bring or come together in one place: *We will gather for the meeting at noon today.*

gathered

A form of **gather:** *After the whole group gathered on stage, they began to sing.*

H

hairy

Having a lot of hair: *It takes a long time to brush my dog because she is so hairy.*

hang

To be attached at the upper end: *Many colorful paintings hang on the walls of the museum.*

heal

To get better or become well: *Most cuts heal quickly if you take care of them.*

healed

A form of **heal:** *When the deer's leg healed, she ran as fast as ever.*

height

The distance from bottom to top: *The height of the mountain is about a mile above sea level.*

height

I

ill

Sick or not healthy: *They have been ill with the flu.*

illness

A form of **ill:** *After an **illness**, people may feel tired for a few days.*

imitate

To copy the actions, looks, or sounds of: *Little children **imitate** their parents or older children in their family.*

imitated

A form of **imitate:** *After I **imitated** the steps many times, I learned to do the dance.*

impatient

Not able or willing to wait: *She walked because she was too **impatient** to wait for the bus.*

impossible

Not possible or not able to happen: *It will be **impossible** to finish on time unless you start now.*

inform

To tell about something: *The guide **informs** people about animals on the nature trail.*

insect

A bug that has six legs, a body with three main parts, and, usually, wings: *She liked to watch **insects** at the pond.*

insect

J

judge

To listen or look at in order to decide about: *At the fair, it was fun to **judge** which pie should win the first prize.*

K

know

To understand or have the facts about: *Do you **know** what causes thunder?*

knowledge

Facts and ideas, or information: *Their teacher had **knowledge** about many subjects, such as weather and history.*

L

language

A system of words, expressions, signs, or symbols shared by a group of people: *At our house we speak two **languages**: Spanish and English.*

lesson

Something to be learned or taught: *After a few more **lessons**, I'll be able to skate like an Olympic athlete!*

litter

More than one animal born at the same time to the same mother: *My cat had a **litter** of four kittens.*

M

mammal

A warm-blooded animal with a backbone and hair: *Many animals, such as dogs and cats, are **mammals**.*

millions

A very large number, or more than a thousand thousands: *There are **millions** of fish in the sea.*

motion

Movement, gesture, or the act of moving: *The **motion** of the boat on the waves made him feel sleepy.*

muscle

Body tissue that helps many different parts of the body move and work: *Her **muscles** will get stronger from exercise.*

N

nod

To move the head down and up in a quick motion that may mean "okay": *You will be out of the game if you move before I nod my head.*

nodded

A form of **nod:** *I was glad when my father nodded to let us know we could go.*

noise

A sound that may be loud or unpleasant: *You could tell from the noises that there were many animals in the barn.*

noise

notice

To pay attention to or make note of: *I sat in the back and hoped that nobody would notice me.*

noticed

A form of **notice:** *The first thing he noticed was how fast the clouds moved across the sky.*

O

obey

To do what is asked: *After training, the horse obeys the rider.*

P

performance

A song, dance, or act that is given in front of an audience: *The singers were nervous before their first performance for the judges.*

piano

A musical instrument with a keyboard: *She could play tunes on the **piano**.*

piano

plain

Not fancy or pretty: *The plants look **plain** before they bloom.*

pond

A small body of water in the shape of a lake or pool: *Frogs sat at the edge of the **pond**.*

porch

A structure with a roof that is attached to the outside of a house: *They kept two chairs and a low table on the **porch**.*

pound

To hammer or hit hard again and again: *When you **pound** on the drum, I want to leave the room.*

pounding

A form of **pound**: *The **pounding** rain on the tent kept her from falling asleep.*

prevent

To stop or keep from happening: *You can **prevent** fires by being careful.*

problem

Something that is difficult to deal with or understand: *The group tried to solve the **problem** by talking together.*

quiet

Silent, calm, or with hardly any sound: *The house was finally **quiet** after all the children were asleep.*

R

reach

To get to or go as far as: *When all the boats **reach** the shore, I will feel better.*

relieved

To no longer be worried about something or someone: *She was **relieved** that she did not miss the bus even though she was late.*

remember

To think of again or bring back in the mind: *I **remember** the first word I learned to read.*

remembered

A form of **remember:** *He always **remembered** his grandpa's stories.*

rotten

Decayed or spoiled: *Some insects eat **rotten** fruit that people throw away.*

row

In a line or in sequence, one after another: *I got an A on two tests in a **row**, which is a new record for me!*

S

safe

Free from danger or harm: *The mother bird saw that her babies were **safe** in the nest.*

safe

safety

A form of **safe:** *Most playground rules were made for your **safety**.*

scare

To frighten or make afraid: *This dragon mask might **scare** some little children.*

scent

A special smell that comes from something: *The **scent** of roses reminded her of her grandmother's yard in the spring.*

scent

scream

To make a long, loud, high-pitched cry: *When my little sister **screams**, I hold my ears.*

screaming

A form of **scream:** *When the game got close, many people started **screaming** for their team to win.*

shape

To give a certain form or shape to: *I **shape** the clay to look like woodland animals.*

shaped

A form of **shape:** *The sign at the farm stand was large and **shaped** like a pumpkin.*

share

To divide with others or take part in: *He wanted to **share** his story with us.*

shock

To surprise or greatly upset: *The news will **shock** you, so please sit down.*

shocked

A form of **shock:** *I was **shocked** when I found that the jewels were missing.*

shovel

A tool with a long handle and a flattened scoop: *We use shovels to get rid of the snow.*

shovel

silence

A form of **silent**: *The silence in the library helps people enjoy their reading.*

silent

Quiet, making or having no sound: *The room was silent, so she thought everyone had gone.*

simple

Easy, or not complicated: *The directions on the box looked simple, and she followed them carefully.*

special

Different from what is common or usual: *Birthdays are special occasions.*

speech

The act of speaking, or a talk: *She practiced at home before she gave the speech in class.*

spend

To cause or allow time to pass: *We will spend the day at the beach.*

sprinkle

To scatter in drops or small pieces: *We always sprinkle salt into the water before it boils.*

sprinkled

A form of **sprinkle**: *The children sprinkled fish food*

stand

To be a certain height: *Medium-size dogs usually* **stand** *between two and three feet tall.*

station

A place where a special service is provided: *We got our tickets and waited at the train* **station**.

station

stay

To live with or visit for an amount of time: *Please* **stay** *at my house after school.*

stayed

A form of **stay**: *We* **stayed** *at my friend's party for two hours.*

stick

To attach or to keep in one place: *We* **stick** *a stamp on each card before we mail it.*

sticky

Holding together as with glue or hard to pull apart: *After eating the honey, they licked their* **sticky** *fingers.*

stood

A form of **stand**: *Last year my sister* **stood** *three feet tall, but now she's almost four feet.*

straight

Not curving, curling, or bending: *My hair is* **straight** *and never gets wavy.*

stuck

A form of **stick**: *The truck got* **stuck** *in the heavy snow.*

subject

Course of study: *Science and social studies are his favorite* **subjects** *in school.*

sudden

Happening or coming without warning: *On the hike, we were caught in a **sudden** storm.*

suddenly

A form of **sudden:** *The birds flew away as **suddenly** as they had landed in the yard.*

T

tease

To make fun of or try to bother: *My friends used to **tease** me about my hair.*

tough

Strong and not likely to break or wear out: *The hiking boots were warm and **tough**, so he could walk outdoors in any weather.*

toward

In the direction of: *We walked **toward** the tower and watched for a light.*

transportation

Means of getting from one place to another: *Trains are my favorite kind of **transportation**.*

tune

A group of musical notes that are put together: *We had fun making up a new **tune** to play on the piano.*

tunnel

A passage underground or underwater: *The train passed through the **tunnel** to the other side of the mountain.*

tunnel

U

understand

To get the meaning of:
*I **understand** the meaning of a few Spanish words.*

V

vibration

A quick movement back and forth: *I could see the **vibration** of the cymbals as the musician hit them together.*

visit

To go or come to see: *We will **visit** our friends in the city.*

volume

An amount of sound: *You should speak in a quiet **volume** when in the library.*

W

weak

Having little or no power, strength, or energy: *The battery was so **weak** that our flashlight didn't help much.*

weaker

A form of **weak**: *She was **weaker** after being sick, but then she grew stronger.*

wear

To have on the body: *In cold places, people **wear** two or three layers of clothes.*

weigh

Find out the weight or heaviness of: *The doctor will **weigh** you on a scale before your checkup.*

weighed

A form of **weigh**: *I **weighed** my dog three times to make sure she was really that heavy!*

wind

To move along with twists and turns: *We **wind** the string around the stick to bring the kite back in.*

winding

A form of **wind:** *They followed a **winding** path higher and higher up the mountain.*

winding

wonder

A marvel or something amazing: *Their tricks on the high wire were a **wonder** to everyone who watched.*

wonderful

A form of **wonder:** *Their day at the beach was **wonderful** from beginning to end.*

wrap

To cover by winding or folding: ***Wrap** a scarf around your neck before you go out in the cold wind.*

wrapped

A form of **wrap:** *We **wrapped** our sandwiches in foil for the picnic.*

wrapped

wrinkle

To form small, uneven lines or creases: *This cloth will **wrinkle** after you wash it, so you will need an iron.*

wrinkled

A form of **wrinkle:** *The shirt was **wrinkled**, so she tried to smooth it out.*

Acknowledgments

Main Literature Selections

"Abuelita's Lap" from *Confetti: Poems for Children*, by Pat Mora. Text copyright ©1996 by Pat Mora. Reprinted by permission of Lee & Low Books, Inc.

Excerpt from *Ah, Music!* by Aliki. Copyright ©2003 by Aliki Brandenberg. Reprinted by permission of HarperCollins Publishers.

Animals Building Homes by Wendy Perkins. Copyright ©2004 by Capstone Press. All rights reserved. Reprinted by permission of Capstone Press Publishers.

Click, Clack, Moo: Cows That Type by Doreen Cronin, illustrated by Betsy Lewin. Text copyright ©2000 by Doreen Cronin. Illustrations copyright ©2000 by Betsy Lewin. Reprinted by permission of Simon & Schuster's Books for Young Readers, an Imprint of Simon & Schuster's Children's Publishing Division. All rights reserved.

Diary of a Spider by Doreen Cronin, illustrated by Harry Bliss. Text copyright ©2005 by Doreen Cronin. Illustrations copyright ©2005 by Harry Bliss. Reprinted by permission of HarperCollins Children's Books, a division of HarperCollins Publishers, and Pippin Properties, Inc.

Dogs by Jennifer Blizin Gillis. Text copyright ©2004. Reprinted by permission of Heinemann Library.

"Everybody Says" from *Everything and Anything* by Dorothy Aldis, copyright ©1925-1927, renewed 1953-1955 by Dorothy Aldis. Reprinted by permission of G.P. Putnam's Sons, A Division of Penguin Young Readers Group, A Member of Penguin Group (USA) Inc. All rights reserved.

"Grandpa's Stories" by Langston Hughes from *The Collected Poems of Langston Hughes* by Arnold Rampersal with David Roessel, Associate Editor. Copyright ©1994 by The Estate of Langston Hughes. Reprinted by permission of Alfred A. Knopf, a division of Random House, Inc. and Harold Ober Associates Incorporated.

Helen Keller by Jane Sutcliffe, illustrated by Elaine Verstraete. Text copyright ©2002 by Jane Sutcliffe. Illustrations copyright © 2002 by Elaine Verstraete. All rights reserved. Reprinted by permission of Carolrhoda Books Inc., a division of Lerner Publishing Group, Inc.

Henry and Mudge: The First Book by Cynthia Rylant, illustrated by Suçie Stevenson. Text copyright ©1987 by Cynthia Rylant. Illustrations copyright ©1997 by Suçie Stevenson. Reprinted by permission of Simon & Schuster's Books for Young Readers, an imprint of Simon & Schuster Children's Publishing Division. All rights reserved.

How Chipmunk Got His Stripes by Joseph and James Bruchac, illustrated by José Aruego & Ariane Dewey. Text copyright ©2001 by Joseph Bruchac and James Bruchac. Illustrations copyright ©2001 by José Aruego and Ariane Dewey. All rights reserved. Published by permission of Dial Books for Young Readers, a member of Penguin Books for Young Readers, a division of Penguin Group (USA) Inc.

Jellies: The Life of Jellyfish by Twig C. George. Text copyright ©2000 by Twig C. George. All rights reserved. Reprinted by permission of Millbrook Press, a division of Lerner Publishing Group, and Curtis Brown, Ltd.

Mi Familia/My Family by George Ancona, children's drawings by Camila Carballo, photographs by George Ancona. Text copyright ©2004 by George Ancona. Children's drawings copyright ©2004 by Camila Carballo. Photographs copyright ©2004 by George Ancona. All rights reserved. Reprinted by permission of Children's Press, an imprint of Scholastic Library Publishing, Inc.

Officer Buckle and Gloria written and illustrated by Peggy Rathmann. Text and illustrations copyright ©1995 by Peggy Rathmann. All rights reserved. Reprinted by permission of G. P. Putnam's Sons, a division of Penguin Putnam Books for Young Readers, a division of Penguin Group (USA) Inc., and Sheldon Fogelman Agency, Inc.

Cover illustration from *Poppleton in Winter* by Cynthia Rylant. Illustrations by Mark Teague. Illustration copyright ©2001 by Mark Teague. Reprinted by permission of Scholastic Inc. SCHOLASTIC'S Material shall not be published, retransmitted, broadcast, downloaded, modified or adapted (rewritten), manipulated, reproduced or otherwise distributed and/or exploited in any way without the prior written authorization of Scholastic Inc.

Schools Around the World by Margaret C. Hall. Originally published as Schools. Text copyright

Credits

Placement Key: (r) right, (l) left, (c) center, (t) top, (b) bottom, (bg) background

2 (cl) Tony Taylor / San Antonio Zoo; **2** (cl) ©George Ancona; **2** (bl) Digital Vision/Alamy; **3** (tc) ©George Doyle/Getty Images; **3** (tl) Don Farrall/ Getty Images; **4** (tc) ©Robert McGouey/All Canada Photos/Getty Images; **4** (tl) ©INTERFOTO/Alamy Images; **4** (tl) ©Jim Zipp/Photo Researchers, Inc.; **4** (tl) ©SuperStock/Alamy Images; **4** (tl) ©Juniors Bildarchiv/Alamy Images; **4** (cl) ©Justin Sullivan/ Staff/Getty Images; **4** (bc) Kul Bhatia/Photo Researchers, Inc.; **4** (bl) ©Terry Vine/Getty Images; **5** (cl) Comstock Images / Getty Images; **5** (cl) ©Poelzer Wolfgang/Alamy Images; **6** (tl) The Alex Foundation; **6** (bl) ©Joshua Hodge Photography/Getty Images; **6** (bl) © David Buffington/Photodisc/Getty Images; **6** (bl) © Getty Images/Digital Vision; **6** (tl) Najlah Feanny/Corbis; **8** ©Julien Tromeur/Shutterstock; **9** ©13/Tony Anderson/Ocean/Corbis; **10** (b) Jerry Shulman/ Superstock; **10** (t) Arco Images GmbH/Alamy; **10** (tr) Tony Taylor / San Antonio Zoo; **11** (cl) Blickwinkel/Alamy; **11** (tr) Dave Stamboulis/

Alamy; **11** (br) ©Alamy Images; **11** (tl) Getty Images; **11** (bl) David Burton/Alamy; **12** ©Big Cheese Photo LLC/Alamy; **27** (t) ©Stockdisc/Getty Images; **28** (b) Artville / Getty Images; **30** (b) Tony Taylor / San Antonio Zoo; **30** (tl) Tony Taylor / San Antonio Zoo; **31** (tl) Scott Doll/San Antonio Zoo; **31** (cr) Gandee Vasan/Getty Images; **31** (br) GK Hart/Vikki Hart/Photodisc/Getty Images; **32** San Antonio Zoo; **32** (b) GK Hart/Vikki Hart/Getty Images; **33** (t) ©Photodisc/Getty Images; **33** (b) Tony Taylor / San Antonio Zoo; **33** (tr) Tony Taylor/ San Antonio Zoo; **37** (br) Exactostock / SuperStock; **38** (t) Edgardo Contreras/Getty; **38** (b) MoMo Productions/Getty; **38** (tc) Digital Vision/ Alamy; **38** (tl) ©George Ancona; **39** (tr) ©Kwame Zikomo/Purestock/Getty Images; **39** (tl) Exactostock/Superstock; **39** (cl) Tom Stewart/ Corbis; **39** (cr) ©Floresco Productions/OJO Images/Getty Images; **39** (bl) Ronnie Kaufman/Age Fotostock America, Inc.; **39** (br) Masterfile; **40** ©George Ancona; **41** ©Stockbroker/Alamy Images; **42** ©George Ancona; **42** (tl) ©George Ancona; **43** ©George Ancona; **44** (t) ©George Ancona; **44** (cl) ©George Ancona; **45** (t) ©George Ancona; **46** (bl) ©George Ancona; **46** (r) ©George Ancona; **47** (t) ©George Ancona; **49** ©George Ancona; **50** (tl) ©George Ancona; **50** (r) ©George Ancona; **50** (cl) ©George Ancona; **51** (b) ©George Ancona; **51** (t) ©George Ancona; **52** ©George Ancona; **53** (l) ©George Ancona; **53** (r) ©George Ancona; **55** ©George Ancona; **56** ©George Ancona; **58** ©George Ancona; **59** ©BananaStock/ Getty Images; **61** (b) BananaStock / Jupiterimages; **61** (tl) ©George Ancona; **62** (b) Stockbyte/Alamy; **62** (tl) Digital Vision/Alamy; **63** (tr) ©Jack Hollingsworth/Photodisc/Getty Images; **64** (b) Digital Vision/Alamy; **64** (br) Digital Vision/Alamy; **65** (t) ©Image Source/Getty Images; **65** (cr) ©Exactostock/Superstock; **65** (tr) Digital Vision/Alamy; **70** (tr) ©Artville/Getty Images; **70** (br) ©JupiterImages/i2i/Alamy Images; **70** (tc) Don Farrall/Getty Images; **70** (tl) ©George Doyle/Getty Images; **71** (cl) ©Glow Wellness/Getty Images; **71** (cr) ©Lightly Salted/ Alamy Images; **71** (br) ©HMH; **72** (tl) ©George Doyle/Getty Images; **73** ©Life on white/Alamy Images; **74** (tl) ©George Doyle/Getty Images; **75** ©George Doyle/Getty Images; **76** (tl) Getty Images/Photodisc; **76** (bl) ©Ingram Publishing/

G25

HANDMADE
IN
AMERICA

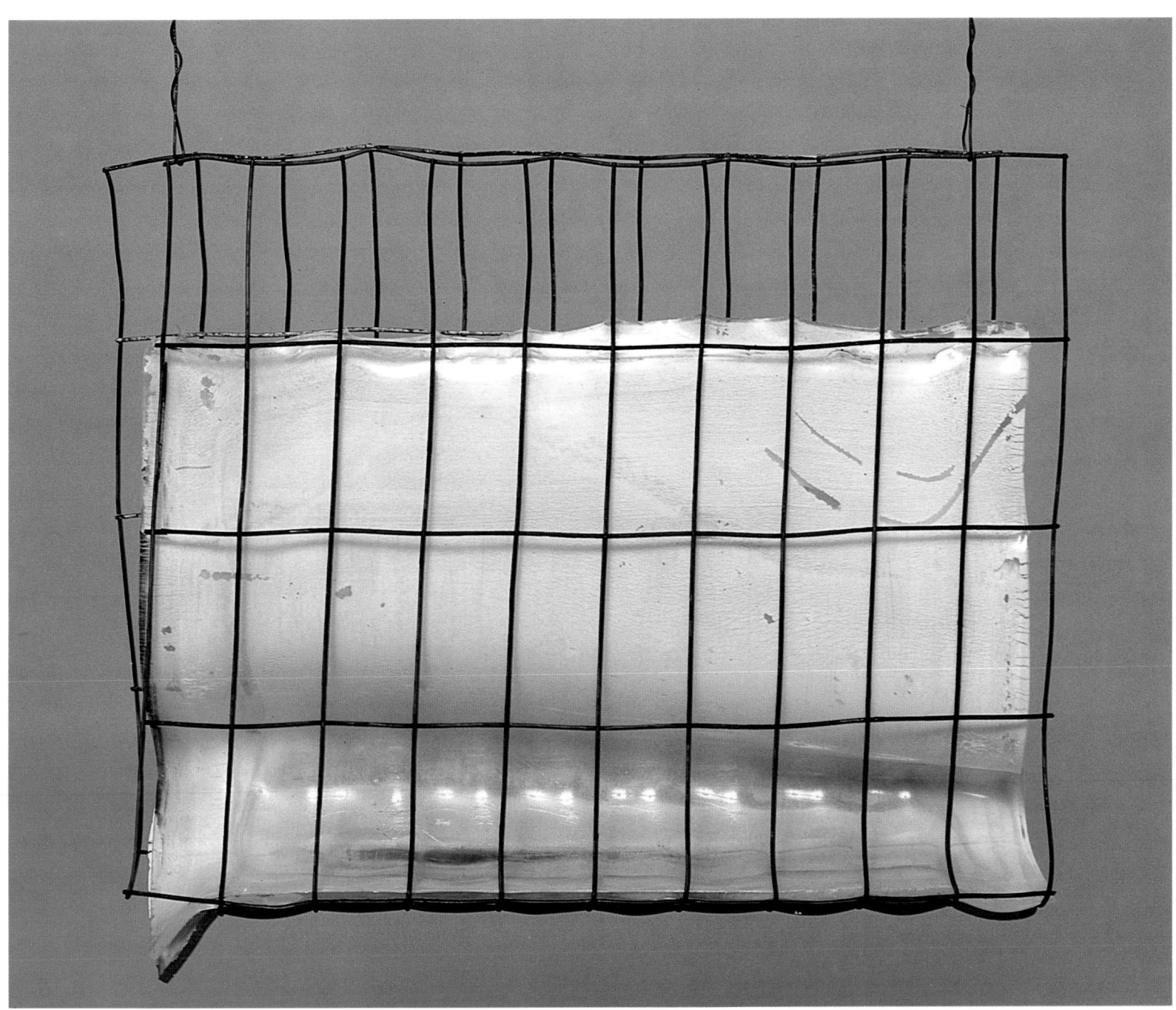

Endpapers: Lia Cook. *Lattice Conversed* (detail). 1980.
Woven, pressed, painted rayon. 48 × 44″

Previous page: Albert Paley. *Garden Gate*. 1976. Mild steel,
forged and fabricated. 115¾ × 102½ × 14½″

Above: Mary Shaffer. *Ode*. 1979. Glass and wire. 14 × 20″

Right: Jack Lenor Larsen. *Magnum*. 1970. Embroidery on Mylar

John McQueen. *Untitled Basket*. 1977. Malaluka and Spanish moss.
10 × 7 × 8″. Collection Robert Pfennebecker

Above: Sam Maloof. *Rocking Chair.* Walnut. 45 × 28 × 46″.
Museum of Fine Arts, Boston

Following pages: Wayne Higby. *White Canyon Landscape Container*
(4 boxes). 1973. Earthenware, raku technique. 12 × 22 × 11″

HANDMADE

Conversations with Fourteen Craftmasters

Harry N. Abrams, Inc.,

IN AMERICA

by Barbaralee Diamonstein

Publishers, New York

For Carl Spielvogel

Project Manager: Margaret L. Kaplan
Project Editor: Joan E. Fisher
Designer: Darilyn Lowe

Library of Congress Cataloging in Publication Data
Diamonstein, Barbaralee.
    Handmade in America.

    1. Handicraft — United States.   2. Artisans — United
States — Interviews.   I. Title.
TT23.D5   1983   745′.092′2 [B]   82-13941
ISBN 0-8109-1083-7

Printed and bound in Japan

Contents

Introduction

by Barbaralee Diamonstein

For a people supposedly obsessed with machines and technology, Americans have become increasingly enthralled with things made by hand. Furniture and fiber arts, ceramics and jewelry, ironwork and glass — all are seen not just as useful objects but as works of art as well. For those who buy crafts — and it is a rapidly expanding public — there is a genuine esthetic interest in the vanishing "handmade," as well as a desire to make a personal statement, to display individuality by means of collecting. For those who create the crafts, the pursuit involves more than simply making things or making a living; it is a way of life.

In the course of the series of conversations that grew into this book, it has become clear to me that for the fourteen craftsmakers with whom I spoke, and no doubt for other craftsmakers with similar skills and enthusiasms, what you make is what you are.

In many ways, the conversations we had were, for the craftsmakers, a joyous affirmation of creativity and life. For these wonderfully talented people are finally and deservedly coming fully into their own. Unlike painting and sculpture, whose primary purpose has been to appeal to the esthetic sense, crafts have traditionally been valued for their utility and practical service. But today the spectrum of crafts ranges from the purely decorative to works that combine decoration and function. Put another way, many of the objects that are coming out of the country workshops or city apartments and lofts of today's best craftsmakers are functional in purpose but also beautiful in form.

The emergence of American crafts is central to an understanding of America's self-image, and of how our culture, commerce, and history evolved. From colonial times, there was a tradition of people who came to this country to become furniture makers and blacksmiths, potters and weavers. Crafts crossed the Atlantic with the early settlers and were vital to their existence here. Prior to 1850, there had been complete accord and mutual respect between artist and craftsmaker. The result: harmonious interiors that were considered of equal importance to the building itself. These interiors were created with patience and care by artisans guided by love of the beautiful. By the mid-nineteenth century the Industrial Revolution was weakening and nearly destroying this tradition. By making products faster and more cheaply than was previously possible, machines were usurping the role of the craftsmaker. Paradoxically, as contemporary America was being born, crafts were dying.

There were, of course, exceptions. In the last years of the nineteenth century, furniture maker Gustav Stickley was inspired by the great English designer-philosopher of the crafts, William Morris, who conducted a lifelong crusade against the superfluity of the machine-made gadgets with which people cluttered their lives. Morris's popular arts and crafts movement stimu-

lated a conscious focus on crafts in the United States and a gradual upsurge of interest in the revival of craftsmanship. As the movement matured and spread from the East coast to the West, it became identified with a style — the craftsman style — marked by simplicity, severity, and a regard for natural materials. The style was aimed at linking furniture to architecture rather than at achieving lasting recognition among the traditional fine arts of painting and sculpture. But, ultimately, it did help significantly in raising the level of artistic worth in the decorative and applied arts within an anti-industrial ethic.

Thus the four-square, massive mission furniture designed by Stickley, suitable to what were referred to as "craftsman homes," enjoyed a considerable vogue in the early years of this century and served as inspiration to such people as designer Louis Comfort Tiffany and architect Frank Lloyd Wright. There was an abundance of other signs that craftsmakers were becoming professionals as artists and guild people. Regional arts and crafts organizations sprouted in principal cities. In 1901 the first school of clay work was founded at Alfred University in Alfred, New York, and other programs like it soon followed. From 1901 to 1916 *The Craftsman* magazine gave the movement a voice. Despite this activity, however, there were still few craftsmakers, and the machine and industrial society continued to hold sway. Crafts, no longer seen as necessary to supply the essentials of life, were freed to become more expressive of human creativity, but also to become superfluous embellishments of life, somewhat charming but nonetheless eccentric and useless.

A real and most significant change came just after World War II. By the end of the war, two striking events had taken place in the United States to enhance this change. One was the immigration of Europe's dislocated intelligentsia, artists, architects, craftsmakers, and writers, some of whom were eager to found new careers in the American educational system. The other was the return from wartime service of a generation of mature Americans who were more practical, perhaps more object-oriented than previous generations had been, and who had a whole new set of expectations from the schools that they attended in unprecedented numbers, thanks to the G.I. Bill. These two groups shared an awareness of the shoddiness of mass production and the vast expense of the best machine-made products. This awareness in turn led to a yeasty climate of dissatisfaction with the industrial process — a fertile environment for the growth of interest in the handmade and for the creation of a new market that could absorb the work of the next generation of crafts artists. University art departments began incorporating crafts into their programs to satisfy the interest of returning G.I.'s. Technical innovations and development rapidly followed.

For nearly forty years the primary catalyst in the crafts movement has been the American Craft Council. This national organization, whose goal has been to focus attention on the work of American craftsmakers, was founded in 1943 by Aileen Osborn Webb, a woman with a cause who coupled breadth of vision with the taste, intelligence, funds, and resolution to breathe life into that cause. Mrs. Webb, herself a potter, began her support and patronage of the arts in the 1930's. Determined to develop marketing opportunities for craftsmakers, she helped organize the American Craftsmen's Cooperative Council in 1938; the founding of America House, a retail program and public "showroom" for crafts, followed in 1940. With her keen awareness of the need for visibility, and her even keener sense of where to find it, she managed to obtain space for this crucial facility at Fifty-second Street and Madison Avenue in New York City. Eventually the council grew to include the American Craft Museum, *American Craft* magazine, and the World Craft Council.

The museum grew logically from America House. It opened in September, 1956, as the Museum of Contemporary Crafts (it was renamed the American Craft Mu-

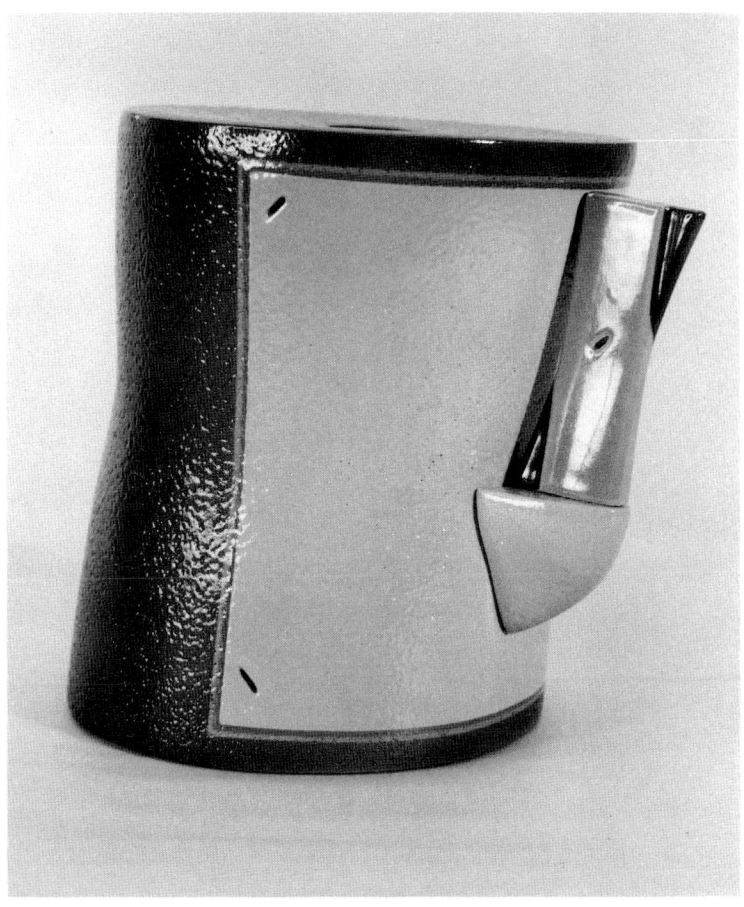

Ron Nagle. *Untitled.* 1975. Fired earthenware. Height: 7″

12

Mary Shaffer. *Three fourths*. 1981. Glass and aluminum

seum in 1979), situated at 29 West 53rd Street, several buildings down the street from the already world-renowned Museum of Modern Art. The timing was auspicious: the visual arts were emerging as a significant area of popular interest in our culture and American artists were beginning to achieve international prominence. When the museum opened, it had a professional director at its helm, Herwin Schaefer, a clear sign that it intended to become a serious, major institution. It was the first public institution devoted solely to exhibiting, researching, cataloguing, documenting, and commissioning contemporary crafts. Until that point, crafts had been shown in a few museums on an occasional or sporadic basis. No serious effort was being made any-

where in the country to "promote" in an ongoing way the very best crafts, nor were any attempts underway to establish or reinforce standards. From its inception, the museum performed a central role in formulating and communicating esthetic and technical standards, in galvanizing the new crafts movements by showing the work of the masters while simultaneously exposing new talent, and in offering a showplace for the work of those who were rarely invited to display their work alongside that of "fine" artists in galleries and museums.

No person has played a more critical role in the renaissance and reassessment of crafts than Paul Smith, director of the American Craft Museum, both by virtue of his individual influence and the forum he created.

Smith first joined the American Craft Council in 1957 and, in the beginning, was not directly involved with the museum. He was hired to assemble a traveling exhibition and create other special projects for the council. His training had been in retailing as a department store display director; the store was sold, leaving him jobless but with experience that was valuable to the council. In the early years he helped the museum with installations and soon became assistant director. In 1963, after the death of David Campbell, the museum's third di-

Robert Arneson. *Nasal Flat*. 1981. Glazed ceramic. 37¼ × 36½ × 18″

rector, Smith was named to succeed him.

Despite the innovative efforts of people like Paul Smith to upgrade the field, the age-old debate over arts vs. crafts is still raging. In my conversations with craftsmakers, that theme kept recurring. A marked schism exists in the self-image of many contemporary craftsmakers. There are those who consider themselves to be artists, not only as a fitting description of what they do but as a guideline to how their work should be exhibited; others are happy — some even defiantly so — to be identified as "craftsmakers."

This conflict is not simply semantic. It seems to exist for two reasons. One relates to the quality of, and review space allotted to, the critical assessment of crafts, contrasted with that received by art. The other reason is a very practical one: art is still more highly prized; there is greater monetary value assigned to work shown in an art gallery than to work shown in a crafts gallery. A number of craftsmakers see sizable differences in price and critical reception. Says ceramist Ron Nagle: "Canvas is king. Western art is painting-oriented, particularly in this country. Here, painting is considered the highest art form, whereas in Japan there was never any question that a tea bowl was the highest level of art."

In our conversations, individual craftsmakers used a wide variety of terms to identify themselves. Take Lia Cook, who first creates the textile (in a sense, her canvas), and then distorts it by painting on it. "In some ways my work is different from that of a painter, and in some it is similar," she says. "There are all kinds of approaches to painting as there are all kinds of approaches to textiles. As a weaver, I'm involved with using fibers to build up a structure. I most likely would call myself an artist who works with woven structure." Dale Chihuly tells us, in contrast, that he doesn't really like calling himself an artist: "I like to think of myself as creative but because I don't do a lot of the physical work now [since a serious automobile accident] I can't think of myself so much as a craftsman; I'm now delegating the craftsmanship to younger, really extraordinary craftsmen. I consider myself a glassmaker or a glassworker." Says the acknowledged mother of the slump glass movement, Mary Shaffer: "I consider myself an artist but I don't think it really matters. Making art is a combination of the two. Crafts is how, art is what." Quilter Sandi Fox would dispute the similarity. "An artist need only be concerned with making something beautiful," she says. "A craftsman must make it beautiful and functional. I take great pride in calling myself a craftsman, and the work should be undertaken without apology." Of all those asked to participate in this project, Robert Arneson and Ken Price were the only ones who declined. Arneson and Price identify themselves solely as "artists," and show their work in galleries traditionally devoted to the fine

arts. Their position underscores, and can be seen as a central metaphor for, the debate now raging within the crafts movement.

There are, however, critics as well as craftsmakers who consider the whole issue a red herring. Penelope Hunter-Stiebel, a knowledgeable evaluator who, though she is the curator for twentieth-century decorative arts at The Metropolitan Museum of Art in New York City, does not hesitate to take independent positions. She says, "I think it's an irrelevant issue. The point is doing the best work one can. Future generations will decide whether to consider these works major esthetic expressions of our time. It just doesn't matter what the label of the person is."

The primary areas nurturing the crafts movement are the university campuses, where the chances for exploration and training in art are not limited to painting and sculpture. The very first small craft center was, of course, Black Mountain College in North Carolina, where Josef and Anni Albers were faculty members. But there have since been many: Haystack in Maine; Penland School of Crafts in North Carolina; the School for American Craftsmen that is now part of the Rochester Institute of Technology in New York; Rhode Island School of Design in Providence; Cranbrook Academy of Art in Bloomfield Hills, Michigan; Tyler School of Art in Philadelphia. At such centers, the torch is passed from generation to generation, with the importance of each center depending on who was teaching there and in what year. As the universities became a kind of teacher-producing industry, there was a growing demand for every crop of graduates to become teachers. At the same time, there was an expanding demand for educational programs. This created a group of artists who had two main concerns: teaching and making art. But this all took place within the confines of their own worlds, sometimes with little connection to the world outside. A gnawing problem for this new generation of teacher-artists was simply making ends meet. Teaching opportunities began to reach their saturation point, thus encouraging a broader spectrum of artistic activity.

This new spectrum was enriched by the country's exploration of alternative ways of living in the 1960's, which included a fascination with making by hand the objects used in everyday life. Alternative materials for esthetic expression became possible, too. After all, not until the late 1950's was ordinary wood considered an appropriate medium for sculpture (Louise Nevelson); neon light (Dan Flavin) was not used in this way until the next decade. Says Mary Shaffer of her initial experimentation with slump glass: "For me, in the early seventies, it was an untapped field; no technical information and no images to work from. It was like skiing down a virgin slope of snow. Every possibility was open

to me. And I tried just about everything." Glass and fiber arts are now beginning to be considered a logical and legitimate extension of that expanded "acceptable" esthetic vocabulary.

Like Shaffer, other experimenters were busy trying "just about everything." In 1962, at a seminar in Wisconsin, Harvey Littleton became the father of the studio glass movement when he introduced methods by which hot glass could be worked at lower temperatures. He and Dominick Labino, a scientist, developed a studio furnace using commercial marbles for glass. Labino found the esthetic potential of glass so compelling that, in 1965, he gave up his position in the glass industry to become a full-time glass artist, creating luminous color effects in delicate forms. As a result of the efforts of Littleton and Labino, individual glassmakers were for the first time able to work outside industry, and more safely. The studio movement symbolized direct involvement of the artist.

Another craft pioneer, Peter Voulkos, broke away from the rigid vessel tradition and helped give rise to a generation of sculptural ceramists. The acknowledged initiator of the revisionist approach to ceramic work, he proposed and encouraged two innovative concepts: that how a vessel was used should no longer determine its

Peter Voulkos. *Untitled Plate*. 1981. Stoneware. Diameter: 21″

validity, and that ceramic material could be used to create classic and innovative art forms. It has been noted that ceramics, of all the crafts disciplines, was perhaps the ideal medium for change at that time, as it was the oldest and the strictest in terms of technique and traditions. Voulkos is said to be one of the greatest influences on clay in the twentieth century. His exuberant influence spread through the country to such artists as Robert Arneson, who became involved with craft imagery within the pop movement. Another student, Ken Price, was a ceramist innovator as well, with his use of low fire to produce an unusual glossy glaze, a technique that has since been widely adopted.

In fiber, Lenore Tawney introduced three-dimensional woven forms. Her poetic departure from conventional structures and methods led the way for the creative explorations of thousands of weavers who were concerned with an expression beyond that typical of clothing or furnishing textiles. In the late 1960's and early 1970's she, Claire Zeisler, and Sheila Hicks executed large, robust forms that celebrated the intrinsic character and texture of the materials themselves.

Back in the 1950's younger craftsmakers embraced the "truth-to-materials" doctrine and the leaders of the movement, encouraged by university support, expanded the technical and esthetic boundaries of each discipline. That set the stage for a more broadly based group, the new craftspersons movement. A particularly interesting phenomenon unique to this movement is the emphasis on collective production of fine crafts objects. While past generations tended to work individually and develop an individual oeuvre within each discipline, we now see teams of highly skilled craftsmakers collaborating in the creation of larger or more extensive work — work that could not be produced by a single artist. As furniture maker Wendell Castle notes, some pieces simply "can't be made by one person. It's impossible. The level of craftsmanship is too high, so a division of labor is essential. And this goes back to another thing: the damage done by William Morris and John Ruskin in the making of fine furniture. They destroyed specialization; they thought it took away from the dignity a craftsman should have, and from his pride in his own creation. John Ruskin felt that any worker left to his own devices would produce wonderful things. Well that, of course, isn't true. I don't question the need for dignity in craftsmen's lives. This philosophy destroyed the highest level of craftsmanship because it takes several different people to do one piece." Evidence of a new, collaborative spirit can be found as well in the studios and workshops of Dale Chihuly, Albert Paley, and Jack Lenor Larsen.

Throughout our history, there have been periods when interest in the handmade was high. This interest grew out of our national genius for improvisation combined with the still-pervasive frontier spirit and the desire to put a stamp of personal identity on things. The present explosion in crafts, beyond the post-World War II surge, is rooted in the turmoil and change of the 1960's — a time that affected the old as well as the young. But the young were the prime movers — it was their time — and few came away untouched. For some, it meant a new direction to their lives, an era of new assessment, discovery, and reevaluation. For many, at the time, it meant a rejection of "gross materialism" — the making of a simpler life with more fulfilling work. It is this generation that has made an enormous contribution to the healthy flowering of the professional crafts movement today.

Much crafts activity concerns the amateur or hobby craftsmaker. According to a recent poll, one out of every two American households is involved in crafts, either professionally or through hobbies and leisure-time activities. Ceramics has always been the most popular and widespread of the craft media. Woodworking is attracting growing numbers; the specialty magazine *Fine Woodworking*, founded in 1975, already has nearly two hundred thousand professional and hobbyist subscribers. The current plethora of craft courses in educational institutions and new approaches to selling wares, even on street corners, has brought not only a wider audience for crafts but also an increase in talented amateurs who have begun to regard their hobby as a career option.

Among longtime professionals, a new entrepreneurial attitude is evident. Large department stores have even begun to market limited editions of their work. Some observers attribute the change primarily to the shift in social values. While the teaching route was very much the sole direction for the craftsmaker in the 1940's and 1950's, when people created mostly personal, one-of-a-kind objects, we are now witnessing a steadily emerging preoccupation with the marketplace. Their work has become not only a business, but also a lifestyle. Says woodworker Wendell Castle: "I don't see anything wrong with influencing industrial design or working for production. It's just that my vocabulary was not suitable. It's actually more suitable now. But the quality would again be the problem. It wouldn't be the forms." Peripatetic Sheila Hicks, the New York and Paris-based textile designer and fiber artist acclaimed for her commissioned installations throughout the world, exemplifies the kind of university-trained artist who today is more than willing to design for contract production. "I will play with anyone's string, in any situation," she says, "as a challenge to try and invent something new."

This notion is confirmed by the experience of

Sheila Hicks. *Soft Sculpture of Nurses' Blouses*. 1979. 26 × 43'

Harvey Littleton. *Paired Yellow-Descending Forms.*
1982. Glass. 11½ × 10 × 4″; 11½ × 11 × 4″

Ken Price. *Tail Piece.* 1980. Glazed, fired clay.
6¼ × 8 × 5½″

metalsmith and jeweller Mary Ann Scherr, chairman of
the Crafts Department of the Parsons School of Design,
a recently created program with the finest facility in the
New York area today. Today's student, she observes, "is
competitive, enjoys personal authority, and demands an
education that will culminate with being prepared to
move into the marketplace, equipped and informed. The
sensitivity gained from working with materials lends
credibility and knowledge to the crafts artist. This artist
is a product designer, capable of solving problems and
aiding in the production of the product through firsthand knowledge of processes."

The importance of university training has not been
forgotten by the new entrepreneurs, it is simply being put
to new uses. Education and the technology involved in
one's craft are as precious to this generation of
craftsmakers as they have always been. Weaver Lia
Cook's newest endeavor concerns resuscitating the use of
the jacquard loom. A large, industrial machine with the
capacity to mass-produce apparel, upholstery, towels,
and other functional fabrics, the jacquard was rarely, if
ever, used by artists. Its use by Cook and other fiber artists is an indication of the innovation with which she
approaches the technology of her craft.

A commitment to technical expertise has yielded
new methods that have changed the nature of more than
one discipline; for example, to satisfy his self-imposed
requirement of technical perfection, Wendell Castle
developed the original technique known as "stack lamination." Then there is the workshop of violin restorer
Jacques Francais. To be a craftsman there requires advanced technical expertise; years of training at specialized schools are needed to become a fine restorer or
maker of stringed instruments. "At Mièrecourt, in
France, the place we were trained for skill and speed,"
says Francais, "unless you were gifted, talented, and had
the ability to handle your tools in a very special way,
they would not teach you. In my years there, when I was
eighteen years old, I had to build two violins a week in
the white — meaning without varnish. They demanded
perfection." Sandi Fox is another craftsmaker who sees a
technical, and even historical, understanding of one's
craft as critical to its esthetic. "As with all creative processes," she says, "one must have a grasp of technique
before one can translate design into reality. I think it is
important, if we are in a renaissance of American quiltmaking, to understand and use nineteenth century techniques so that a hundred years from now the quilts that
were made during *this* renaissance will still be intact."

It is clear that what has not changed but has only
been strengthened since the turn of the century is the
importance of quality in each craft. Says weaver-
entrepreneur Jack Lenor Larsen: "Quality is more impor-

tant than anything else, and mass culture is our common enemy. We must avoid becoming one great supermarket." Albert Paley reinforces this notion when he talks about the influence of his formative years on his present life and work. "I ask myself why I'm motivated," he says. "It's a hell of a lot of hard work — exhausting. When I was young, my family fulfilled the American dream by moving to suburbia. And I think probably all I am doing now is trying to wash the plastic out of my system." This quest for quality can, for these craftsmakers, be satisfied by the handmade. "What I've strived for most," says Larsen, "is a craft quality ... at best, how to give the viewer some knowledge, some experience, of how those fibers were twisted together and interlaced — the pleasure of experiencing the marriage of thirsty cloth and liquid dye."

Where are we headed today? Certainly toward increased focus on excellence. Each discipline is sure to be increasingly discussed, displayed, collected, and made part of the economic process that raises the price of art objects to unheard-of levels. Today's craftsmaker hopes that his creations will one day be known as classics.

Many observers have noted that the recognition of the master craft artist — the individual personality — and the establishment of each reputation will increase the acceptance of crafts as a whole. But there are still major problems to surmount. Other than the American Craft Museum, which has high ideals and ambitions but little staff and few resources in terms of space and money, it is still true that very few museums systematically or comprehensively collect, display, or promote twentieth-century crafts. Most institutions show an amazing indifference to crafts. "There is," says Hunter-Stiebel, "a very strong core conservative market. Adventurous, novel designs will always have a few people interested, but basically people feel they have to make a big commitment to their furniture; they want to be really comfortable when they sit down. The primary concern is not esthetics. They might flirt with something that looks attractive, but often they'll settle for something that looks like the wing chair they remember cuddling in at grandmother's house."

It is clear that, at this point in our history, crafts in America merit serious attention. That was the idea behind this series of interviews, which involved travel over great and contrasting distances to gather the material: from Seattle to Rochester, from New York to Alta Loma, from Queens to Berkeley, from Santa Fe to San Francisco, from Alfred to San Ildefonso. But one problem was selecting craftsmakers. Obviously, it would have been impossible to speak with all those deserving special consideration both for their esthetic contributions and their knowledge. So a serious effort was made to select a representative, if not definitive, group by discipline and, only incidentally, geography.

While the craftsmakers included in this book are all special people leading special lives, few generalizations can be made to explain their interest in the crafts. Some were trained in the so-called fine arts; some were influenced by childhood experiences; some were guided by a remarkable teacher or mentor. All, however, seem continually inspired and nurtured by the aspect of their medium that initially attracted them to it — the material itself. "I don't know of anyone I would consider a real master who doesn't have a deep feeling for materials," says Wayne Higby. "Even for those people who use commercial glazes, because of the way they use them, an intensive understanding of materials is critical. That takes a long time. I think it probably takes longer for a ceramic artist to mature than for any other kind because of the tremendous amount of technical information that you have to assimilate. I've been working with the same glazes for ten years."

The wood that Sam Maloof uses is itself unending nourishment. Says Maloof of the widely imitated exposed joinery technique he invented years ago: "When I first started I thought, 'What a shame to cover something so beautiful.' I just didn't feel that joinery should be covered; it should be there for people to see. After all the hard work of making beautiful joints, to then cover them over took something away." For glassmaker Dale Chihuly, "The material itself is a continuing source of inspiration. The heat and the gravity continually inspire new ideas. I usually have an idea and begin to work on a concept that might be intellectual, but then it is taken over to a large extent by the process itself." For metalworker and former painter Mary Ann Scherr, "The blank canvas is a frightening wall, but a foot square of metal is another kind of canvas, loaded and exploding with ideas and solutions. I feel as though I've used miles of metal and still feel a rich source of inspiration just below the surface."

Of all the groups of "artists" (including visual, performing, architecture, and design arts) I have ever interviewed, it would be fair to say that these craftsmakers are the least celebrated. "When I started," says Sam Maloof, "I never once thought about recognition because I thought, 'How wonderful it is to be able to earn a living working with my hands — to make things that I enjoy making and other people would enjoy having.' So recognition never entered my head at all. I didn't even know what a designer-craftsman was until years later when somebody said to me, 'You know, you're a designer-craftsman.' And I said, 'Ohhh.'"

Certainly, these craftsmakers do not benefit from the economic rewards available to a number of first-rate

Lia Cook. *Impressions*. 1978. Woven, dyed rayon; polyurethane foam. 5 × 5′

artists today. "I'm not one of these guys who's gonna live in a cave and dig clay out of a wall and make it with my hands and shove it off to some guy who's gonna ship it to a gallery in New York," says Ron Nagle. "That's not my style. I think working is the most important thing. It's the only thing that ultimately will keep my sanity together. But then I look at Cole Porter's penthouse and Cole Porter's food, and I dig that, man. I dig the good life." Though many express this half-whimsical desire to earn a good or even extravagant livelihood, as a group they seem less concerned about the benefits of the material world than any other I have known. For many of them, a modest way of life and a willingness to make do with fewer tangible rewards is a reasonable exchange for the spiritual and intellectual nourishment they receive and for the chance to live as they want. Albert Paley might be speaking for many of his colleagues when he says: "The work itself is a vehicle for my own perception and education, really. And I just develop that the best that I can. The museum exhibitions and publicity, that type of thing, are just byproducts of the endeavor. I feel good about the response but that isn't the motivation behind it. In my own life, the pursuit of art lends me a sanity that is important."

Many craftsmakers lack renown not only because of the historical anonymity of the craft artist in America but, I have come to think, also because of a reluctance on the part of many to enter fully into the mainstream of American culture. Are their values and objectives different from those of most people today? "Certainly," says Penelope Hunter-Stiebel, "they have the desire to express themselves in ways they find most satisfying and not to conform to established rules." It has been said that however ambitious many craftsmakers may be today they are not in competition with anyone but themselves and they approach their work and the environment with a special understanding, a personal vision of the human condition. Each seems to have carved out a very special milieu in which to work and live. Most pursue unusually creative, fulfilling, and interesting lives — lives that are absorbed by many hours of exhausting work.

To lead the kind of ordered, integrated life that seems essential to excelling at a craft, the craftsmaker must first know himself. The notion of self-perception is extremely important, especially because the craftsmaker's position in the art world has traditionally been uncertain and his relationship with American culture ambivalent. There are numerous reasons for this unusually clear sense of self. One might be that the work is so immensely time-consuming. "I work anywhere from sixty to eighty hours a week, and a lot of this includes drawings, so I'm in the shop a lot of the time," says Sam Maloof. It is no wonder, considering the time element involved, that the idea of process is so fundamental to

John McQueen. *Untitled Basket.* 1977. White pine bark. 18 × 8″

these artists and that, as a rule, they are very thoughtful about their own work. Ideas must, by virtue of the lengthy process, come much faster than the works can be created. As Lia Cook says of her weaving process: "It is very time-consuming, and there are thousands of threads, but you just work in a very systematic way. It's sort of like meditation. It has a rhythm to it and it's very soothing."

The work is often repetitive — especially for a basketmaker like John McQueen. "If you think about how many 'overs and unders' there are in a square inch of cloth, it would be thousands and thousands," says McQueen. "My head is always way ahead of my hands. It's a constant kind of anxiety, I guess. I always want to finish and get on to the next thing I'm thinking about. The actual physical 'overs and unders' are very tedious work." Ultimately, however, no craftsmaker is bored by the repetitive nature of his work; it gives him time to think and also is capable of inducing a special state of mind. "I work all the time," says Sheila Hicks. "I don't consider it work. I suppose I'm fooling around all the time with thread. I work on the plane while I travel, in a size I can manage, which is why sometimes the work is so tiny. Once off the plane, when I'm in someone's office and they're showing me walls or plans, I can invent on a bigger scale."

To Sandi Fox, "Time is the least of considerations because I make quilts for personal pleasure, really, as much as anything else. I never think of the time that's gone into it, other than the length of pleasure I'm getting from working on it." The repetition that is essential to the craftsmaker's process allows time to clarify, focus, design; it also leads to the kind of detachment necessary to the lonely pursuit of a possibly elusive goal. According to ceramist Wayne Higby, he utilizes the bowl form to communicate "a sense of humanity, of man's needs and intellect, the way he relates to his environment and makes something out of that environment, takes care of his needs."

"Making art," says John McQueen, "is a verb. It's *making* art, it's not *finished-object* art. From the artist's point of view, the satisfying part is the physical activity of it. After it's done, it's done. And I'm into the next thing." It can no longer be said that the craftsmaker is a mere producer of objects, while the artist is primarily concerned with ideas. The maker of crafts objects can be just as "conceptual," and sometimes more so, than the artist. "At the beginning, work with textiles seemed gratifying and beautiful," says Sheila Hicks. "They had dimensions that were pleasurable. In working with them more and more, I haven't changed that idea but I have found that textiles can also carry a message. One can say things with textiles of a very profound nature."

It was clear to me that in visiting the studios and homes of each of the craftsmakers — from the cozy, collectibles-filled house of Sandi Fox that appears countrylike yet is right in the midst of Los Angeles, to the pastoral, idyllic, upstate New York ranch-studio of Wayne Higby — many have evolved a singular, almost seamless way of life. Perhaps more than any other group of artists, they make no real separation between work and play. They avoid the schizophrenia that characterizes most people's work experience and seek a life in which all aspects mesh together. What you make *is* what you are: their work, like any artist's, is singular and intricately intertwined in their lives. Practically all live in quarters that adjoin their studios. Since each one's craft is central to his or her life, the life nourishes and informs the craft at every stage. Those at Dale Chihuly's glassmaking community, Pilchuck, know this to be true: mealtimes are as important to them for exchanging ideas and forging a collective that is essential to the glassmaking process as they are for nutritive value. "We actually have one person here who does only the cooking because the food is so important to their state of mind," says Chihuly. "One person wants steak and eggs in the morning, somebody else wants cereal, somebody drinks tea, or coffee, or wine, or soda water — all these things are part of the process. One of the Italian masters that we brought over will not work in the shop unless he can see the pasta water boiling! It's that important to him to be thinking about the food, as well." Sam Maloof, whose work and life are especially unified (he built his entire rambling house and all its furnishings by hand over the last thirty years or so), cannot stop himself from making new additions to the house, even though, he says, his wife hopes he doesn't add anything else.

Even for Jack Lenor Larsen, whose craft has blossomed into a huge and complex industry, his apartment home, where he can weave on a large wooden loom or a small hand one, is the nucleus of his life and his art: "The space where I live in town is an amalgam of all my interests. I weave there, I write books there, I dine with friends there. And I dream and think there. The collections of things that I like, the sense of structure in materials and how they're put together is important to me. The plants and the light and the reflections on the water in the pool are all part of it."

Working with one's hands offers not only a living, but a way of life. These contemporary craftsmakers are intent on creating a wholeness that it would be wise for us to note. They are important for what they make, and ultimately, for what they *are*. Their work signifies the renewed importance in today's throwaway world of the handmade; their lives enhance that appeal and that need. Their voices, it is to be hoped, amplify, clarify, and

enrich our understanding of both the work and the way of life of crafts artists in America today.

This book could not have been possible without their generosity. I hope all of the craftsmakers involved, who permitted me to share their work and thought, derived some special satisfaction from the enterprise that may compensate for how generously they gave of their talent, energy, and ideas. It is, after all, their book, as well as a tribute to other American craftsmakers and what they represent. These conversations, I believe, validate the theory that animated this project: that the handmade is once more enjoying the prominence in our culture that it so richly deserves — as a symbol and expression of our most enduring American values, skills, and dreams.

Mary Ann Scherr. *Electronic Air Monitor Necklace*. 1971. Sterling silver and amber. 10 × 4″. American Craft Museum, New York City

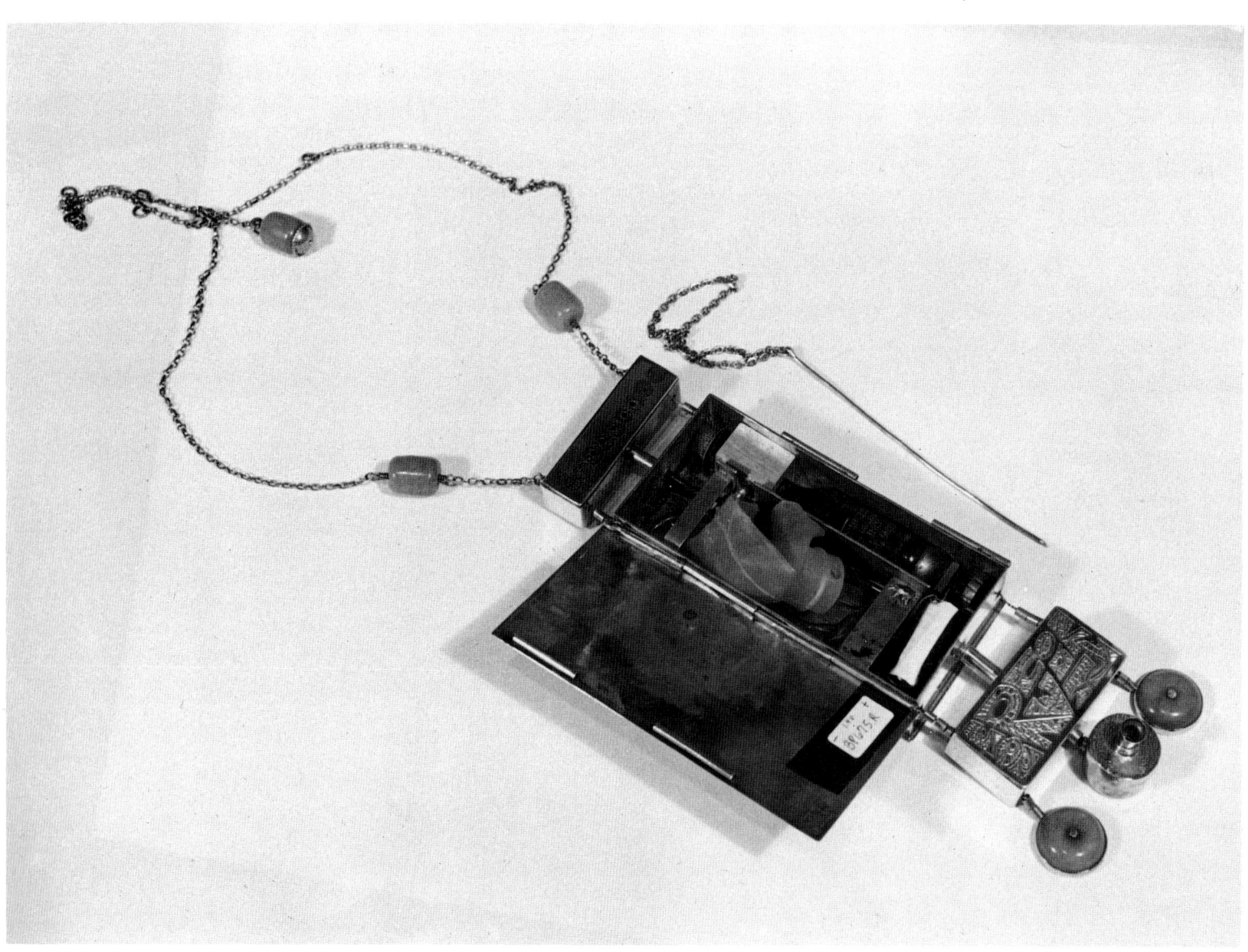

23

Wendell Castle

has been a wood sculptor and furniture maker for twenty years. He introduced a working method called "stack lamination" that opened the door to a new world of form possibilities in wood. Castle has developed an organic style that has become the most widely imitated esthetic in American woodworking. Trained as a sculptor, he has sought to fuse the demands of functional furniture with formal sculptural concerns.

BLDD: Your esthetic sensibility as a sculptor did not leave you when you turned to woodworking. How did you begin and happen to channel that energy into furniture?

WC: The furniture began to happen just at the end of my graduate work in sculpture at the University of Kansas. I didn't really intend to become involved in furniture, but I constructed some wooden objects that ended up with horizontal surfaces that could hold objects or people. I then thought of them as tables or seats. This direction interested me more and more. The pieces became more like furniture and more practically built so that they could withstand use. After graduating with a master's degree in sculpture and spending a short time in New York City just making sculpture, I needed to find a job. Interestingly enough, I was offered a job teaching furniture design in Rochester, New York, at the School for American Craftsmen, although I had made very few pieces of furniture. They felt their furniture program had become stagnant and decided the way to put some new life into it was to hire a sculptor. And I was certainly well qualified, with my sculpture background and interest in furniture. But once I took the job, I became less interested in sculpture and more interested in making furniture. As it worked out, I didn't return to sculpture for fifteen years, although in many cases the furniture was not too different from sculpture in its design. Then, in about 1975, I became a little tired of doing what I was doing. I felt I had so many imitators that in some cases I

even found it difficult to tell my own work from theirs! So I decided not to do any more of that kind of work. I decided that I would let everybody else have that vocabulary. I wanted to write the definitive book on the subject and then just let everybody else have the lamination process. So that's what I did. I wrote *The Wendell Castle Book of Lamination*. It was published in 1980.

BLDD: Your early education, in addition to that master's of fine arts degree in sculpture, includes a bachelor's degree in industrial design. It's easy to understand the influence of sculpture on you and your work. But how did your education in industrial design influence you, and did that experience also help establish any goals or priorities?

WC: I don't know about any goals or priorities, but it definitely was helpful. The background in industrial design included a lot of rather academic drawing and learning to visualize three-dimensionally, and learning to put things down on paper quickly. That was very helpful. I can draw pretty well. I spend a lot of time doing both life drawing and imagined drawing. Industrial design drawing is imagined — you think it up in your head and draw it — as opposed to observed drawing.

BLDD: Your wife, Nancy Jurs, is an accomplished potter. Does she ever assist in your own work in any way?

WC: Not usually. In one piece of the new furniture, she ended up helping us drive in the pegs. Everybody helped drive in those eighty-five hundred pegs!

BLDD: Let's go back to your own beginning. You were

teaching at the School for American Craftsmen. That school — its genesis, its origin — has had a unique effect on the crafts movement. It's little wonder that so many master craftspeople live in the Rochester area, considering the impact of the school. By now, I guess, you're up to the second generation of master craftspeople. How was the school founded?

WC: Well, actually, it's up to the third generation. The school was founded by Mrs. Vanderbilt Webb as part of the American Craft Council. It started out at Dartmouth University in Hanover, New Hampshire, in the mid-forties, but it didn't seem to fit in very well there, so it moved to Alfred, New York. Conflicts developed at Alfred University because Alfred already had a ceramics department, so it was somewhat separate and didn't fit in too well there, either. Then it found its permanent home in 1950 at the Rochester Institute of Technology. It was part of the American Craft Council until the early sixties, but it no longer has any association with them. The first faculty that was brought into Rochester was a fairly distinguished faculty of mostly foreign craftsmen: Tage Frid, Franz Wildenhain, Fred Meyer, Ronald Pearson, Hans Christensen are some of them. Hans Christensen is the only one still teaching in the school. Such a distinguished group was bound to influence the American crafts movement.

BLDD: When did you teach there?

WC: From 1962 to 1970. I taught at the State University of New York at Brockport from 1970 to 1980.

BLDD: So you've been as influential as a teacher as you have been as a furniture maker.

WC: Teaching and producing art fit well together. Two days a week is the most I've taught. Teaching left a pretty good block of time to enable me to do my own work and to experiment and also gave me some security so the work didn't have to pay. In the beginning, it was important for me that the work be experimental. I did not have to be as concerned all the time about being successful and having to sell. Those kinds of requirements can very definitely have an influence on the work and cause it to be more conservative.

BLDD: You recently left your teaching post at Brockport. However, teaching is a commitment that is so long-term, so deep-seated with you, that you decided to found your own school, the Wendell Castle Workshop. What gave you the idea to start your own school, who attends, and how are the students and faculty chosen?

WC: Well, to start at the beginning, I left teaching furniture making in 1970 for the same reasons that I left lamination: I felt my work had too great an influence on people. I saw students turned out who were just copying my work and, not feeling that it was in my power to change the program the way I wanted to, I decided to leave it. I felt that a good way to remain involved in a

teaching situation without those kinds of problems would be to teach sculpture. This was partly true; it really did keep my influence from being so dominant. It kept my own work out of the program. But I missed the furniture part, and I realized that my work still influenced people. I also thought at that time that I'd just sort of keep quiet — not give lectures or seminars or anything. Then I realized that didn't really help anybody either. So I thought what I'd do is make a big effort to help everybody with lamination and then move on to something else. I didn't know at that point that I would create a school. But I've always had it in my mind that it would be nice to have total control over a program. Deciding that the economics could more or less work, I set about doing it. We established our first class of twelve students in the fall of 1980 in an existing space that had been our house. The second year we put on an addition large enough to accommodate eighteen to twenty students.

BLDD: What qualifies someone for acceptance?

WC: Well, we leave the qualifications fairly open. We look at samples of an applicant's work. If the person seems to have intelligence and drive and impresses us in other ways, we might overlook the fact that he hasn't done very much furniture. We start everybody at zero anyway. Even if they've had a lot of experience, they start at the beginning.

BLDD: What is stack lamination and how did you devise it?

WC: It's a technique that frees you from traditional aspects of furniture making in that you can greatly enlarge the size of wood that you can get. In the past, a woodworker would carve one solid piece of wood. But because of the hydroscopic nature of wood — taking in and giving off moisture — very large pieces of wood are likely to crack in the drying process. I wanted the size, and I wanted a more refined surface to work with, so I developed the technique of laminating together thin layers — ones that are easily dried — and in this way I could control a larger mass, one that would not crack. You can make a laminated mass hollow and extend the dimension any way you want by adding on more wood. It was a new vocabulary, a really free vocabulary. I didn't invent the technique; I was only the first to use it in furniture.

BLDD: How was it used in the past?

WC: Some model airplanes in the forties were made by lamination. And, of course, plywood is a form of lamination. Hockey sticks are laminated, and so are various other things. But to actually construct an entire piece of furniture had not been done previously.

BLDD: What gave you the idea?

WC: I wanted a more sculptured approach, and stack lamination gave me three-dimensional freedom. I needed the technique in order to get the form I wanted.

BLDD: Let's talk about the shift in direction of your

Music Stand. 1979. Ebonized oak,
brass. 54 × 24 × 18″

work. How and when did that come about?

WC: To back up for a minute, there is an interim group
of work that came after 1975. Actually, we're still doing a
little of it. It came about when I decided I would do some
carving of a realistic nature. As a sculptor I'd done figures and various other things that were more abstract in
nature. But then I decided to do sculpture that would be
a trompe l'oeil sort of thing associated with furniture.
The idea would be to render soft objects in a hard material that would appear soft, as a sort of challenge. It
turned out not to be any challenge at all; it's very easy to
fool people. You don't even have to be a good carver to
fool people, though of course we are good carvers. And
we still do some pieces, trying for an image in which an
ordinary object is placed on a piece of furniture in a
casual way — like a hat and a briefcase on a table. Then
we carve the objects to make people think that it is a real
hat and a real briefcase.

I realized very early on that I certainly couldn't use my
typical organic furniture in these pieces. That would already set people to looking at them in a different way.
What I wanted to do was surprise them, so I used objects
and styles of furniture they're familiar with. I got out history books and went through them and just picked
things that I thought were nice, and made them. It
turned out to be rather interesting to make them, and I
became more and more interested in them as I researched them, trying to find things I liked to put coats
and hats and umbrellas and all kinds of things on.

The furniture became more important, and the carving part less important. I wasn't interested in reproducing pieces of antique furniture but the craft of antique
furniture entered into it in a much bigger way. It became
obvious to me that workmanship on an extraordinarily
high level could become an art in itself, once you got
into these more complex pieces. The workmanship was
just as important a part of the whole as anything else.
And, always being one who takes things to an extreme, I
decided to make furniture that would be extreme in nature — take it all away, no stops. Very fancy! And another factor enters into it here that had been going
through my mind for ten years, a problem always discussed among art historians: Is it art or is it craft? It's a
very confusing issue.

BLDD: What is the obsession with that terminology? Is it
esthetic or economic?

WC: As far as I'm concerned it's economic. It's economic because a craft work is a useful thing, like a piece
of furniture, and it draws furniture prices. It might draw
slightly higher-than-ordinary prices for furniture but it's
in the range of furniture, whereas sculpture of an equal
size can draw an enormously high price. Twenty years ago
I believed that one of the best economic plusses for me in
this whole field would be that my work would be thought

27

Umbrella Stand. 1980. Mahogany. 36½ × 13".
Collection Charles Rand Penny

Table with Cloth. 1980. Mahogany. 34 × 23 × 20½"

of as sculpture. But that never really quite worked. And I think it caused a lot of confusion, especially among art historians who weren't willing to accept that furniture can be sculpture. They thought that what I made was furniture *masquerading* as sculpture. So with my latest work, I decided to draw a clear distinction. What I made would clearly be furniture, but furniture with an extraordinary quality and extreme kind of form.

BLDD: Let's talk a bit more about your trompe l'oeil period, when you sculpted gloves and coats and books and bags. How did you first come up with the idea of putting the objects in the pieces?

WC: I do a lot of drawing, and if I see something sitting there, sometimes I'll just draw it. Once during a teaching session, between classes or something, when I didn't have anything to do, I had thrown my coat over a chair and just drew it. I rendered it in such a way that I did not try to make any real differences in the appearance of the texture of the chair and the texture of the coat. I'd just done a sketch, and, looking at it, it appeared to be all the same material. I thought, "This is a neat idea. A coat and chair all made out of wood, all fused together permanently." And that was the first one.

BLDD: Let's come back to furniture you're creating now — what you describe as furniture with "extraordinary quality and an extreme kind of form."

WC: Many history books on furniture will suggest that Jacques Ruhlmann was the last of the great cabinetmakers. And I thought, "He hasn't done anything that we can't do." But in getting a chance to look at a lot of Ruhlmann pieces close up — looking at the backs and bottoms and pulling out all the drawers — I saw that they were pretty damn good. In the history of furniture, almost every period had blind spots. There are certain things in furniture that the cabinetmakers don't bother to finish. For example, Louis XV furniture has very beautiful mounts — that is, gilt bronze parts — but they're put on with ordinary old screws, and the makers weren't even careful lining the screw heads up or anything. It doesn't seem to bother anybody. Usually, the back of a piece of furniture is not considered very important. The bottom's not very important. In my newest pieces I give attention to absolutely everything, including backs and bottoms. The chairs are double upholstered. There's another cushion — just like the one on the top — on the bottom, inset upside down. It's not soft but it looks the same. And there isn't any part that you can find on the furniture that isn't just as finished as any other part. Pull out the drawers and look at the back or the bottom and they're just as nice.

BLDD: And as a result, how much does that chair cost?

WC: Well, it's part of a set; a desk and two chairs sell for seventy-five thousand dollars. It sold within two weeks.

28

BLDD: How many hours did it take to create the two chairs and desk?

WC: About four to five hundred.

BLDD: Europeans have described various kinds of work as the American style of woodworking. Obviously, what you're doing now is *not* what one usually thinks of as the American style of woodworking. Before this present direction in your work, did you consider your work as particularly American?

WC: No. I was surprised to find that English publications refer to stack lamination as the American style of woodworking.

BLDD: Two other words often used to describe the organic forms you used to make were "integrated" and "honest." What is it about the organic, as opposed to the geometric or the hard edged, that makes it especially interesting to you?

WC: You can handle it like sculpture. You can laminate up a form and then just start carving and keep working until you feel happy with it. You can make changes and work with it in a modeling kind of way. My recent kind of work can't be done that way; it has to be preplanned very accurately.

BLDD: How does your work process begin . . . with a sketch, or do you do models or mock-ups?

WC: All those things, but more drawing than anything else. I think the key to being able to make the three-dimensional form the way you want is to understand it. And so you draw it and draw it until you understand it. And if you don't understand it, you make a model so you can. You have to know it from every angle.

BLDD: How much is determined in advance in any of these pieces? Is there any room for spontaneity — the happy accident that occurs when you start working with something? Or is the material too precious and the design so carefully conceived that you really can't work spontaneously?

WC: In the organic work, there's some room left for discovering the form along the way, although I don't like to rely on that. I like to have it all worked out. But you certainly keep your eyes open all the way through to see if something is suggested to you that you should pay attention to.

BLDD: Do you find inspiration from everyday objects, like your jacket on the back of a chair, or from the wood itself, from nature?

WC: Drapery folds have been a subject of interest in sculpture for thousands of years. That's what a coat has going for it — it folds and drapes nicely.

BLDD: But, in general, from where do you draw your nourishment, your inspiration?

WC: In the organic pieces, from organic things like shells and bones and plants.

Tail Coat on a French Chair. 1980. Mahogany. 30 × 17 × 17″

Triangle Desk. 1975. Walnut and curly maple. 29 × 41 × 62″

Lady's Writing Desk and Chairs. 1981. Curly English sycamore, purpleheart, ebony inlay.
40 × 41¼ × 22¼". Collection Eric Syz

Game Table and Zephyr Chairs. 1974. Walnut. Table: 29 × 34 × 34". Chair: 17 (seat height) × 28 × 22"

Above: *Coat Rack with Navy Pea Coat* (detail). 1980. Ebonized mahogany.
74 × 22 × 22″

Left: *Coat Rack with Navy Pea Coat*. 1980. Ebonized mahogany. 74 × 22 × 22″

31

Table with Gloves and Keys. 1979. Mahogany. 33 × 40¾ × 16″

Above: *Chopping Table*. 1968.
Cherry. 36 × 25"

Left: *Chair with Sport Coat*.
1978. Maple. 36 × 16 × 20"

BLDD: How many pieces do you produce a year?

WC: Until we started doing the recent work, over a hundred a year. Now it will probably be cut down to approximately twenty.

BLDD: In the past, did you use different kinds of wood?

WC: Yes, I'm using fancier woods now. The cabinet that was on exhibit at the American Craft Museum is Swiss pear and Gabon ebony. The one that was in Alexander Milliken's gallery in New York City is sycamore with ebony. One in progress is a fine English walnut.

BLDD: Where do you get these woods? I assume they are not readily available.

WC: I get quite a lot from a wood dealer in Hamilton, Ontario, near Toronto. It's almost all imported wood. He makes a buying trip to England every year. You can get much better fancy wood in England than you can here. There are also a couple of places in New York City.

BLDD: I assume you can't order this wood over the telephone. Even if it is Swiss pear, don't you need to see the particular piece of wood?

WC: You can't do that, though, unless you want to run and look at it. I usually have them send a sample that I'm sort of stuck with if I don't like it. But if I do, I'll take the rest.

BLDD: Have you often been "stuck" that way?

WC: Well, I got a board of French walnut last week that I wasn't too thrilled about. It *is* French walnut, but it's bland looking. I won't bother with the rest of them; I'll keep the one board and make some little thing out of it.

BLDD: It seems that there is an enormous increase in the number of woodworkers in this country. How do you explain the burgeoning interest?

WC: It's happened in all the crafts; it isn't any more so in furniture than it is in pottery or glass. Now there are places that teach woodworking. The School for American Craftsmen, founded in 1950, was the first. Now there are lots of schools. And there's a magazine devoted to it called *Fine Woodworking*. Galleries are showing it. So it attracts attention now and people see it and say, "I wouldn't mind doing that."

BLDD: When you started, more than twenty years ago, the "truth-to-materials" doctrine prevalent among craftspeople must have made a great impression on you, as it did on most every other craftsperson at the time. What does that doctrine mean to you currently?

WC: In school it was certainly what was talked about; that was the attitude that was accepted. But in my own work, I never really paid much attention to it. The whole lamination process really can't be thought of as a truth-to-materials process. I got accused of the exact opposite, of being untrue to wood. And it didn't really bother me. Of course it's the same now — even more so. My work is not necessarily true to the material; I might paint it or gold-leaf it; I might use metal or dye or other things. It depends on the presence that I want the piece to have. I don't pay any attention to the truth-to-materials doctrine at all.

BLDD: At that time as well, the popularity of Danish modern furniture was widespread. Your work was obviously a rejection of that minimalism. I assume you felt that stand was a necessary one.

WC: I wasn't interested in that approach. That, of course, is more suitable for production pieces. I felt from the beginning that if you were going to make furniture by hand, it clearly ought to make some kind of statement about being made by hand and not look like something that might have been turned out at the furniture factory.

BLDD: At the twenty-fifth anniversary celebration of the American Craft Council, there was a benefit auction, which included work of yours.

WC: It was a table of mine, and it brought an extraordinarily high price. The table was made two years ago. It was a trompe l'oeil piece with just a little "tablecloth" draped over it. It brought twice the reserve.

BLDD: What was the reserve?

WC: Six thousand. It sold for fifteen thousand five hundred dollars. So I felt good about that.

Table with Hat and Briefcase. 1977. Mahogany.
38½ × 38 × 20½"

Lady's Writing Desk and Chairs. 1981. Curly English sycamore, purpleheart, ebony inlay. 40 × 41½ × 22¼″. Collection Eric Syz

BLDD: Every medium has unique possibilities and limitations. What is it about wood that has been so compelling for you for so long?

WC: It's a material you can manipulate. You can move it where you want to move it and make it do what you want it to do. And it's not terribly expensive; it's very reasonable to work with. But it does have a lot of limitations. And you discover those.

BLDD: Have you ever been frustrated by the limitations, or sufficiently so to invent a way to overcome them?

WC: I did that with the lamination process from the beginning. I was frustrated at times by the weight of pieces when I wanted to make something large and I was trying to find ways to put things together. I guess what has sustained me to devote my life to wood, in addition to what I've already said, is that it's beautiful. I like it. And I've always had a reasonable enough response in the marketplace to keep me going.

BLDD: What is it that wood allows you to do that you couldn't do in any other material?

WC: Wood is the most suitable material for furniture. I don't think any other material can compete with it. It's partly a matter of the history of furniture that makes you feel comfortable with those kinds of forms. Wood is light enough so that you can make boxlike, drawerlike things to which other materials don't lend themselves. Wood comes in a variety of colors; it lends itself to lots of different finishes. It has an enormous range of possibilities in the ways it might appear.

BLDD: Another innovative aspect of your work has been the combination of elements — table and chair, for example — into one form. What was your reason for developing that approach? And have you ever been tempted to approach industry with that design?

WC: No, I never have approached industry. I got interested in it because it offered a chance for an unusual form. It seemed clear to me that in an interior quite often the table might be near a chair; there might also be a lamp nearby and an ottoman near the chair. All these various things go together so why not just make them together? And doing this would increase your vocabulary of forms.

BLDD: But it also limits the choice of the user — all those fixed elements. . . .

WC: Yes, it does that. It fixes the elements from the sculptural standpoint. You can arrange them with the relationship that you think is the best, and then nobody can move them.

BLDD: Have you ever been tempted to design anything for mass production?

WC: I designed a whole line of fiberglass furniture in the late sixties. I had been approached a number of times by furniture companies to design something. And the organic nature of wood just wasn't very suitable to being mass-produced. You had to make so many changes in it to make it suitable that it lost everything.

BLDD: How was your furniture accepted by the trade?

WC: It wasn't very well accepted. It was a bit too peculiar looking. In the late sixties I expected that plastic as plastic would be accepted. That never really happened. Only certain items with plastic ever got into the big time, stacking chairs for instance, and a few other things like that.

BLDD: Your colleague Sam Maloof has also been asked to design for industry on numerous occasions, and he says he always refuses. Do you think that craftspeople should remain solitary as craftspeople, or should they at-

Right and opposite:
Collector's Cabinet.
1981. Pearwood
and ebony.
63½ × 17½ × 17½"

36

tempt to influence industrial design and wider numbers of people?

WC: I don't see anything wrong with influencing industrial design or working for production. It's just that my vocabulary was not suitable. It's actually more suitable now. But the quality would again be the problem. It wouldn't be the forms.

BLDD: The scale of your work ranges from jewelry boxes to music stands to the twenty-five-foot-high spiral staircase at the headquarters of Gannett Newspapers in Rochester, New York, to entire suites of offices. What's your favorite scale in which to work?

WC: Right now it's smaller — not tiny, but in the scale of furniture-sized pieces because you can devote more attention to them. Really large pieces would be incompatible with what we're trying to put into it right now.

BLDD: What's your favorite piece to design or craft?

WC: Well, that changes. But I think, overall, probably tables.

BLDD: Why? What's so satisfying about a table?

WC: It has fewer limitations than a cabinet or a chair. A chair has a lot of limitations because it has to fit the human body and there are just so many things you can do with it without destroying the function. A table can be almost anything. It can be twelve inches high, it can be forty inches high, twelve inches square; it can be enormous; it can be at two levels; it can be at three levels. Tables have no limitations and an enormous amount of possibilities.

BLDD: What piece do you consider to be the best work you've ever done?

WC: It's hard to say. You know, you always like the last ones best. My lady's writing desk is pretty good. The cabinet for the American Craft Council is pretty good. But I think the walnut cabinet we're working on right now will be the best.

BLDD: Do you plan to use other precious materials, like metals and stones?

WC: Yes. And jade and ivory, too. I've gotten a tusk, so I'm ready for some ivory.

BLDD: How important are your assistants to this new work?

WC: Very. More so now than ever. In the organic furniture what they did was increase my output because we could get more made. What they do now is an entirely different thing — each person brings a separate expertise to the job. This is furniture that can't be made by one person. The level of craftsmanship is too high, so a division of labor is essential. And this goes back to another thing: that is the damage done by William Morris and John Ruskin in the making of fine furniture. They destroyed specialization; they thought that it took away from the dignity a craftsman should have, his pride in his own creation. John Ruskin felt that any worker left to his own devices would produce wonderful things. Well, that, of course, isn't true. I don't question the need for dignity in craftsmen's lives. What I mean is that this philosophy destroyed the highest level of craftsmanship because it takes several different people to do one piece. There's no hierarchy, though.

BLDD: How do you manage not to have a hierarchy?

WC: We don't consider any of the activities to be higher forms of art than any of the others. They're all the same. And we have enough overlap so that nobody does just one thing. But we do have our specialties. I am the designer and I do the carving. And I think there'll be more of that coming in the future in my work.

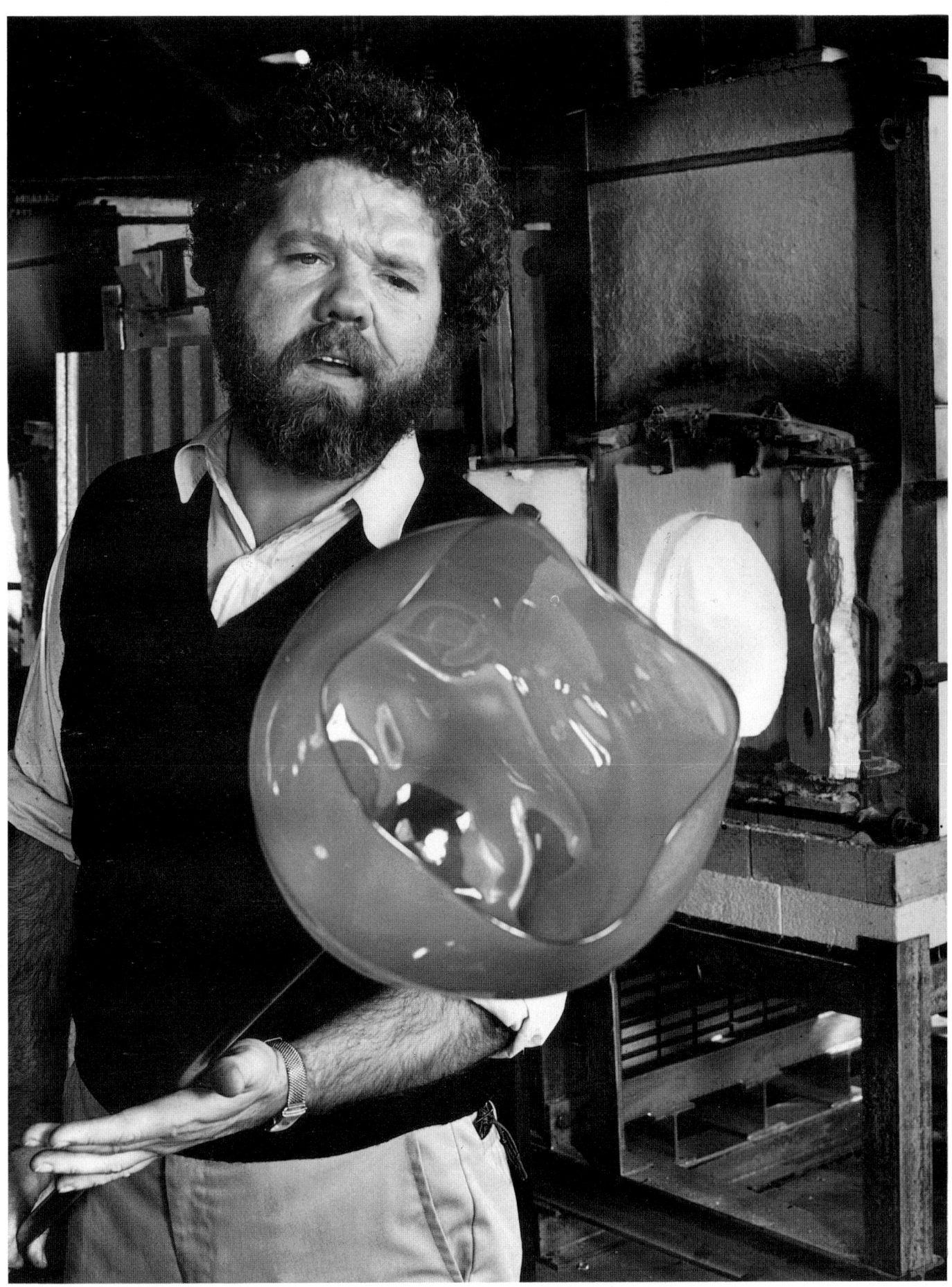

Dale Chihuly, *an influential teacher of many young glass artists, and co-*

founder of the Pilchuck Glass Center in Stanwood, Washington, is a man who really loves glass. Twenty years ago there was no such thing as a glass artist in America. There were those who designed glass objects for industry, but those designers did not execute the work themselves. Today America boasts of the most prolific, the most creative glass movement in the world. The courage to take chances, along with the concern to pass on knowledge of one's craft to later generations of artists, are the polished skills of a master craftsman. Chihuly creates glass with incredible speed — as many as thirty original pieces in one day. In order to accomplish this, he works with teams of highly skilled assistants. Collaboration is an idea he has pioneered.

BLDD: Glass has been treasured for four thousand years for its ability to capture and reflect light and for the enormous variety of shapes and colors that it can be given. I've heard you mention the importance of glass-blowers in Venice around A.D. 1000. Why were they so needed or cherished?

DC: Venice was kind of the wizard of the sea, and also, I guess, the wizard of commerce, and it was there that glass developed into a commodity. Blowing glass started with the Romans but the Venetians are the ones who really developed it to an extreme art and technique. One of the strongest points of Venetian trade was its blown glass, and so on an island outside Venice called Murano they built a couple of hundred factories, and there the glass-blowers were kept. In fact, so valued was their knowledge that if they tried to escape they were executed or if they got away their families were executed — and if they got to England they were knighted.

BLDD: In addition to its colorful history, glassblowing has a unique and colorful language of its own. For example, I've heard glassmakers refer to "punty marks" and "glory holes." One of the important signs of the master craftsman is a very neat punty mark, for which you are particularly celebrated. What do those words mean anyhow?

DC: The glory hole is a term for the volcano of heat in which glass is reheated and formed during the glassmaking process. When a piece is blown on a blowpipe, the bottom of the piece is formed first, and then it has to be taken off the blowpipe and transferred with a punty rod.

The top of the piece is opened up, and the punty is the tenuous little bit of glass that connects the piece to the pipe itself. It's sort of like an umbilical cord, as if the piece stems from this mark.

BLDD: What first inspired you to experiment with glass?

DC: I'd taken a degree at the University of Washington in interior design and I was encouraged by a wonderful lady, Doris Brockway, who was teaching me weaving at the time, to consider incorporating other materials in the weaving. I was very interested in transparency and wall hangings, and so I had this idea of putting glass in a tapestry or in a wall hanging. I started very crudely by putting little bits of glass in tapestries, then I got some kilns to melt the little pieces of glass and infuse copper wires, and eventually the wall hangings became almost exclusively glass. One night I melted some glass in one of the kilns and found a little gas pipe; I rolled it up in there and actually blew a little bubble. Then I inquired about where I could learn how to blow glass.

BLDD: When you graduated from the University of Washington in 1965, the studio glass movement was in its infancy. What made you decide to head for Wisconsin and study glass with Harvey Littleton?

DC: There was a great teacher around Seattle, named Russell Day, who was very interested in glass, and was advising me at the time. I don't think I'd ever seen glass-blowing before I tried it myself. I decided that it seemed like an interesting technique, and that I'd like to pursue it. But first I went to work for John Graham, an architect at the largest architectural firm in Seattle who was doing

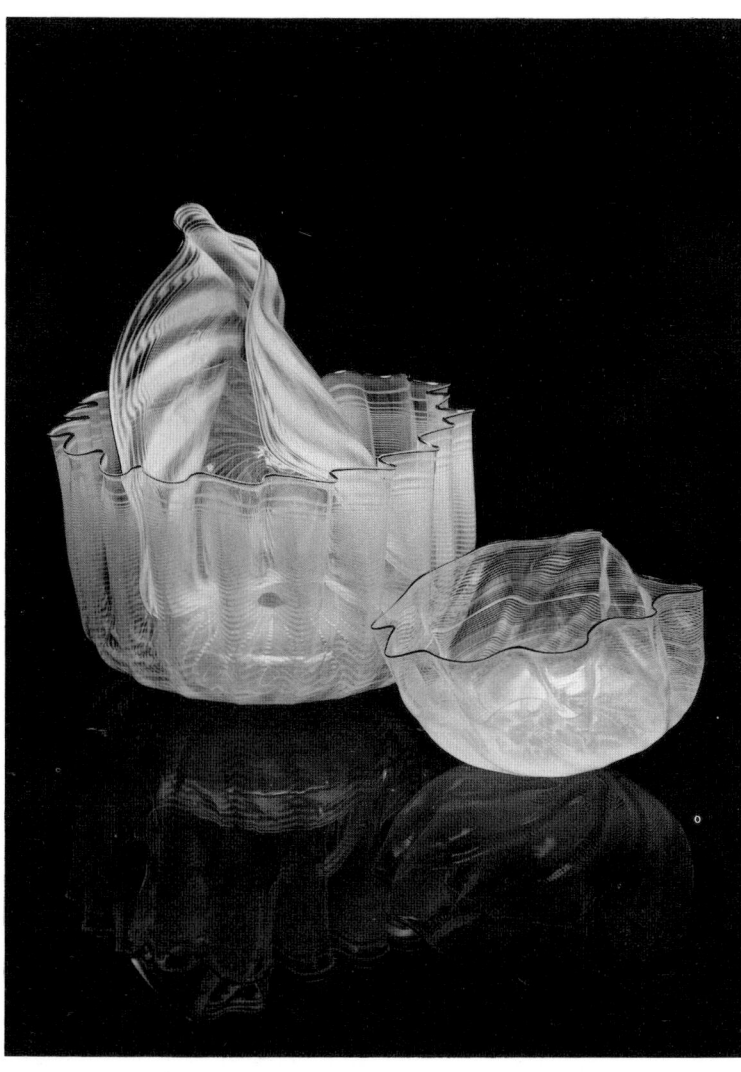

Large Forms. 1981. Hand-blown glass

interiors and design work. I applied to graduate school and ended up going to University of Wisconsin because that's where the studio glass movement started and there they had the best students and the best-known teacher. Harvey Littleton is considered the father of the studio glass movement. It was in 1966 that I began blowing glass, and about four years before that Harvey had started the first glassblowing school in the United States. Now there are reputed to be something like fifty or seventy-five schools that teach glassblowing.

BLDD: There was a lot of excitement about what was going on in glass at that time, but there also was little or no tradition to follow when you first started. Did that free you to experiment or did those circumstances also make you feel a bit unsure of where to go?

DC: I was a bit unsure where to go anyway because not having been trained as an artist or as a craftsman, and having a degree in interior design, the whole thing was very fresh and new to me. Shortly after I started blowing glass, I lost interest in the vessel form and started making sculptures, and I didn't really worry about it. What tradition there was didn't inhibit me because the tradition was always one within the industry. There were designers working for factories, but unlike ceramics, which has a great history in terms of artists working with the material, artists never really had a chance to work with glass because of all the secrecy built up from the Venetian tradition. The glassblowers couldn't leave and couldn't tell the formulas. It was just impossible for any creative people to get into the factories. So when this studio movement started, there was an opportunity to develop a whole new repertoire of forms and ideas.

BLDD: In that period when glass was beginning to come into its own as an art form in America, where did you manage to get your ideas or your inspiration?

DC: Inspiration always changes, of course, but one thing that doesn't change is that the material itself is a continuing source of inspiration. The heat and the gravity continually inspire new ideas. I usually have an idea and begin to work on a concept that might be intellectual, or comes from something I've seen or read, but then it's taken over to a large extent by the process itself. I take advantage of the fact that the material has this unusual ability to move.

BLDD: You've said there are three aspects of working with glass that are particularly important to you: gravity, timing, and spontaneity. What do you mean by that, and how important is the spontaneous in the making of glass?

DC: I think spontaneity is important to virtually every art form, and I think of the things I like as being spontaneous. It's especially apparent in working with glass because decisions have to be made almost instantly. When you work with molten material that's constantly moving, all the important decisions have to be made in

the last fifteen or twenty seconds of the making of the piece. After that, in the case of my work, there's really nothing else to do. I don't do any cutting or engraving so it may take twenty minutes to blow a piece of glass, but most of the decisions are made in the last half-a-minute. It's very spontaneous in terms of approach and it's very spontaneous in terms of material.

BLDD: Isn't that an unusually short time to create something as lovely as what you do? How do you manage to do it so quickly?

DC: Some people spend as long as a day making a piece of glass, but traditionally glass has always been a fast material. I found that the faster we can make the work, the more likely it is that I'm going to like it.

BLDD: Why don't we take a moment and try to find out how Pilchuck ever came about? Was it really necessary to start yet another school?

DC: At the time, I had taught at the Rhode Island School of Design for four or five years, and in the summers I was teaching at a wonderful school called Haystack, in Maine. There was something about Haystack — the idea of being in the woods and the community spirit — and there was something about the Rhode Island School of Design and its professionalism that caused me to feel that the two types of institutions should be merged. First, I got a small grant for two thousand dollars, and I looked for a place in the Northwest. My friend Jack Lenor Larsen got in touch with Anne and John Hauberg and suggested that they consider that I start this little project on their property north of Seattle. They were, in fact, at that time, interested in creating a school, and, of course, were patrons of the arts. We started Pilchuck with a couple of thousand dollars and sixteen students and some friends of mine. I met with John and Anne after the first summer and we decided that Pilchuck should be continued. They've been supporting the school ever since.

BLDD: Does Pilchuck reflect a particular philosophy of glass or education?

DC: The idea has evolved over the last ten years, but from the beginning I wanted a place where artists could produce work and where students could learn from this, sort of like apprentices in an atelier. It's different from an academic situation in which you have artists who act as teachers in the classroom. I feel that it's very difficult to teach art and one of the only ways to learn about art is by being around artists that are active. I mean, the best way to learn about technique is to watch a master. The emphasis has never been on technique at Pilchuck, and we hope it never will be because the technique comes naturally. We bring in master craftsmen from Europe — the best possible craftsmen we can get — but we emphasize esthetics and that's what the discussions center around. The school is about the ideas, the concepts, and the

Large Forms. 1981. Hand-blown glass. Diameter: 18″

esthetics of the work, and the techniques seem to take care of themselves.

BLDD: How does Pilchuck compare to other schools?

DC: Pilchuck is the only school in the country devoted completely to glass. For that matter, it's really unique in the world because though there are two or three other glass schools in the world — one in Czechoslovakia, one in Germany, and another in England — they're primarily trade schools where technique is the primary emphasis. Most of the instructors in these trade schools are master craftsmen but the tradition of the master craftsman in the factory situation is different from what we think of as the master craftsman in this country.

BLDD: In the ten years Pilchuck has existed, how many students have been trained there?

DC: It's now something like two hundred a summer, so certainly over a thousand people have worked at Pilchuck. A couple hundred of those were beginners.

BLDD: Earlier we talked about the spontaneity of the process and the immediacy of the materials. Are those the qualities that make glass so special for you?

DC: I get easily bored in spite of the fact that I'm prolific and make a lot of work. There's no way that I could ever begin to make the same piece over and over for production. Glass offers a never-ending variety of forms and shapes. I'll design something for my crew to work on, just a rough idea. I tell them we're going to work a certain shape, a shell-like, boatlike form, for example, and I'll make some drawings. We'll work on this shape for a couple of days and see what happens. Of course, the pieces all come out different, so I must make the decisions as to which pieces are important. The element of never knowing what's going to happen is exciting.

BLDD: Besides Pilchuck, you've worked and studied and taught at various crafts centers throughout the world, including Haystack in Maine, Penland in North Carolina, the Lobmyer Glass Factory in Vienna, the Royal College of Art in London, the Rhode Island School of Design, and a number of others. Is it particularly useful, or beneficial, or important for you to move about so much, or is it a question of necessity?

DC: I work with at least three assistants, sometimes as many as six or seven, and normally we work intensely for two or three weeks and then, every day, we stop and photograph and analyze the work. We may not work for another month. I've found that by changing locations and reconvening in, say, Vienna, or Tucson, or Maine, there's a new shop and a new experience and a new excitement. All the people that work for me are artists or craftsmen in their own right, primarily interested in their own work. They work for me for a number of reasons: one probably is that they just love to work with glass and it gives them an opportunity to work with glass throughout the year. But in order to keep these people involved with the work here, the change in location seems to add another element of excitement. And, naturally, location and all the different equipment that we are exposed to are going to influence the work to some degree.

BLDD: Not only do you have the benefit of assistants to help you in the process of heating and shaping the glass, but this teamwork seems to be the very basis of the process. Is that unusual?

DC: It's unusual in this country. Of course, the idea of collaboration is unusual in most artistic situations. Traditionally the process of blowing glass was done in a team of three to ten people. It's more efficient to work with a team. I like the community spirit, the idea of one person helping somebody else. The work develops better. When an artist works, there are up periods and down periods, and when you're collaborating, whoever's sort of up is carrying it and will keep the energy going.

BLDD: What about the whole notion of the artist creating in solitude?

DC: I think it's extremely important that the artist have solitude to develop ideas — not necessarily for long periods, but every creative person has to spend time alone. The idea of *working* alone I don't like. That's why artists live in New York or in London; because you need this community spirit in order to learn, to create. I remember a story somebody told me about Picasso. Picasso was supposed to be painting and his servant came in and said, "Pablo, it's time for dinner." And he said, "Oh, the paintings are terrible. I have done nothing today." And the servant said, "Well, why don't you keep working, and make a couple more pictures and maybe you'll make a good one." Picasso said, "No, I must come eat; the ideas come from the people."

BLDD: Well, you must have believed that for a long while because you were one of the first artists back in the late 1960's to collaborate with another glass artist.

DC: I'd only recently started teaching. It was 1969, and I had a bright young student named Jamie Carpenter, a sophomore who came to me with an idea of wanting to make some glass flowers. He was a botanical illustrator. He wasn't necessarily interested in the technique; he wanted to make the object. We actually worked together for about five years and collaborated both esthetically and technically. During that period, I also worked with Italo Scanga and Seaver Leslie and a number of other artists, and I found it very stimulating. I know it's very unusual for creative people to collaborate, and I've always wondered why it's so rare. It wasn't difficult when I worked at Rhode Island and it hasn't been difficult at Pilchuck. Now I see a lot of the people who have worked with me in the past collaborating together on their own ideas.

BLDD: One of your recent series is referred to as the Pilchuck baskets. Where did that idea originate?

Pilchuck Basket Series (detail). 1979. Hand-blown glass

DC: In 1977 I had finished one series of work which I called the "blanket cylinders," and I really felt that the idea had been completed. I was in one of those periods where I didn't feel very creative and I was hoping for a change in my work. I was at the Tacoma Historical Society in my hometown and I saw some Northwest Coast Indian baskets stacked up one on top of the other, collapsing under the weight of each other. I saw those wrinkled forms, the weight of them making the sides bend, and I thought that the only way I could do that in glass would be to make it very thin. I'd been making thick cylinders that weighed up to twenty pounds apiece. So I thought I'd try and work with very thin glass to see if I could make it move like that. It's evolved from that into something now that I don't feel is very basketlike, but that's where the idea came from. I feel personally more strongly about this series than about the cylinders. But I usually like what I'm doing at the time more than what I've done in the past.

BLDD: You referred to this basket series earlier as having shell-like shapes. For me they have many marine or sea life aspects about them, not only in form but in color and texture. Is that a deliberate effect?

DC: You know, I love the ocean — Ireland's my favorite country, and I've been to many islands. And on and off I live on Block Island off the coast of Rhode Island. I was a commercial salmon fisherman before I went to graduate school. Somebody pointed out to me about a year ago the shapes were sealike. But one nice description that somebody used for this work, which I liked, is that it displays mutual buoyancy. Some of the forms *do* look as if they are moving underwater, and there's something about the glass being so thin that makes them almost float. I guess I knew subconsciously that they were looking kind of aquatic, but it wasn't a deliberate effect. My real interest was form. I guess the forms I became interested in looked like they came from the sea. It's always enlightening for me to read what somebody else has to say about my work. Then I learn about what some of my ideas are!

Untitled. 1980–81. Hand-blown glass

Untitled. Macchia series. 1981. Hand-blown glass. Approx. 9″

BLDD: You made reference to your earlier work, entitled "The Navajo Blanket Series," cylinders that you embellished with threads of colored glass and very delicate patterns. How were they fabricated? Did you weave the little bits of glass together the way one might weave a fabric?

DC: Yes, that definitely did come from my interest in textiles. It was a spontaneous glass technique in which we fabricated literally thousands of bits and threads of glass with a hand torch. Then we'd make little drawings, take the molten glass, put it on the drawing, and pick it up. The processs itself contributed to the work looking like fabric, along with my interest in Navajo blankets. You know the Pilchuck baskets reflected an interest in form, and the cylinders were an interest in surface.

BLDD: What's the most difficult color glass to create?

DC: None of them is too difficult for us because we don't actually formulate our own glass. Originally we melted it from sand and other elements. Then we discovered that we could melt recycled glass with certain other materials, which was much easier. And then we discovered that there were a couple of small factories in Germany that manufactured special colors, almost like a palette for a painting. Now we have a couple hundred colors that we can order, and then we can take them and blend them together. The most difficult colors to melt are often in the red range. Some of the reds use gold and it's hard to get gold to work right. It's just a color that's very sensitive.

BLDD: Is there any particular reason why so many soft drinks have been bottled in that pale green glass?

DC: Sand is the basic element of glass and colors are made from different metal oxides. Green is made from iron and it just so happens that a lot of sand has a high iron content, so when the sand melts it has a green color. If the glass was supposed to be very clear, the sand would have to come from some special mountain that was iron free.

BLDD: A number of times I've heard the expression "end-of-day" glass. What does that actually mean and what is its origin?

DC: In the factory there'd be half-a-dozen furnaces, each with a different color glass in it. At the end of the day when there are a lot of scraps left over on the floor and in the garbage can, they'd throw it all back into one of the furnaces, it would melt, and they would get all these different colors gathered on the blowpipe. It just so happens that I'm working on a new series of work which involves a multicolored surface, so we are doing something like that, in a way.

BLDD: What do you call that series?

DC: I have an extremely difficult time naming any of my glass. None of the individual pieces are titled. I call it the "Ugly Series," affectionately named by my mother

just because the glass gets so refined and so beautiful that I feel like working with a different palette. I'm also calling it "Macchia," an Italian word that means spotted.

BLDD: Do you need highly developed facial muscles or any other particular physical ability in order to be a good glassblower?

DC: In the beginning when you're first learning and you don't know how to gauge the temperature of the glass, sometimes you have to blow real hard, but it's actually an effortless process in terms of wind power. When the pieces get large it takes a lot of strength, but it doesn't necessarily have to be a big person doing it. In the factories you often see some little thin guy handle tremendous quantities of glass. It takes balance and understanding of the materials.

BLDD: Are the scientific aspects of the process of interest to you too?

DC: Technically, I guess not really. All I want is to have molten glass to work with. The Venetians are still the best glassblowers. This flair that the Italians have for working with glass is extraordinary, and they have glass formulated in exactly the right way to make it blow in the way I like to work, so, technically, we work on fabricating our glass so that it works in the Venetian manner.

BLDD: What historical period of glassmaking do you think most influenced your own sensibility?

DC: The Venetian tradition — and the fact that Venice is on the water and that I lived there for a year after graduating from the University of Wisconsin — had a tremendous influence on me. I'm also quite influenced by two Czechs, Libenský and Brychtová, a husband and wife team who are still doing extraordinary things in glass. There were also a couple of other Czechs who did some extraordinary glass flowers that are in the Peabody Museum at Harvard.

BLDD: Did you spend that year in Venice studying with a glassblower?

DC: I spent my year there studying and working in a factory called Venini on the island of Murano. It's considered to be the greatest Italian glass factory. And I didn't really study under a master but under the director who was an architect. I did some designing; actually, I designed a large sculpture for Venini. I didn't do much glassblowing when I was in Venice but I was influenced by the Italian methods.

BLDD: Did you invent any of the tools that you use here yourself?

DC: No, neither myself nor anyone else in this new studio glass movement designed many tools. You need so few tools to blow glass that they were all really invented by the Romans. The Venetians hardly invented anything. The tools in glassblowing remain very similar to

what they were when the process was developed around B.C. 50. The blowpipe is almost identical with the exception of the plastic mouthpiece we've developed for it. We also now make the pipes out of stainless steel so they're less corrosive. The wooden block that forms the molten material is almost identical. It's sort of cup shaped to help cool and form the glass, and it's made of fruitwood so that it doesn't leave a mark on the glass and is more durable. The paddles are also made of fruitwood, and they're charred, which leaves a nice surface on the glass and doesn't mark it. The large tong shapes, called "jacks," are primarily used to make the neck so that the piece will separate when put onto the punty. And we have the tweezers, and the punty rod, of course, and we have a wad of wet newspaper that you'll see us use a lot. That's actually a Swedish technique.

BLDD: How are the newspapers used? Doesn't the hot glass burn them?

DC: You can wad up some newspaper and if you wet it you can put it right on the hot glass and it won't burn; that's the closest you can come to touching it. Although lately some of the gaffers working for me are getting into actually touching the hot glass while they're making it. You develop a callus over your hands so that if the glass is very hot, say fifteen hundred degrees, you can touch it and your hands sort of slide off it.

BLDD: How do you relay to your assistants what you want them to do? What's your role in the process?

DC: There are different ways I communicate with them. I'm a glassblower myself so I can take a blowpipe with a punty rod and make the piece. Or I can draw the piece on a piece of paper and put it up on the wall or on the floor. We start to work and then we might take off on an idea that we'd done last time or start with some of the sketches. The real communication takes place the next morning when the work comes out of the lears because the glass has to be cooled overnight, very slowly. Then we'll look at the work and I'll say, "Now this is getting closer to what I want." Until the last year or so, before I started using a lot of assistants, I would take the piece after it went onto the punty, which is the more critical part of the process. Then I decided to try to get off the punty and have other people do the finishing as well as the starting for me. I felt I would be in a better position to have an overall feeling for the work if I could remove myself and watch the process because, actually, the glassblower, when he's on the punty, is about five feet away from the piece and on the opposite end. You're really looking at the bottom of the piece, so you don't see it very well.

BLDD: Do you miss that hands-on part of the work?

DC: I do miss it but I feel that I can develop the work in a better way without having my hands on. Another

thing is that if I'm working as the master gaffer and if something goes wrong it's very upsetting and it reverberates through the entire crew. You see, this is the factory as well. By removing myself and being able to watch the operation, if Billy does something wrong or Ben does something wrong I can sort of pacify them and get them back on track. Being off the punty has a certain advantage for me for that reason.

BLDD: Was there a particular event or experience that caused you to decide to do that?

DC: Yes, there was one in particular. I had a bad automobile accident six years ago and when I recovered from that I went back to the punty and continued to work the best that I could without depth perception. But two years ago I dislocated my right shoulder in the surf down in California and I really could not blow glass for six months. At that point I was working with Billy and I said, "Billy, you're going to have to take over and do the punty work because I want to finish this series." That's when I realized that, in fact, I could give up doing those final gestures and the work would still develop.

BLDD: Does it happen very often that you lose the piece?

DC: In spite of the fact that we're quite prolific and it's a fast process, we have days when everything goes wrong — days when we're developing the ideas and we expect it to go wrong, when we're being overly experimental to the point of pushing it to its not working. Sometimes we lose almost the entire production of the whole period through experimentation. Other times, if I have a form that I really like and I'm trying to develop it, I save one after another because I've perfected that way of working. When everything is right — the weather's right and everybody feels good — I forget about the broken pieces. At the time, though, it's very painful, especially if it's a really good piece. Some of the more radical pieces are the most difficult to keep on the punty and so some of the more interesting pieces are destroyed. But you have to forget about that in order to go on.

BLDD: Did you develop the plastic mouthpiece after someone broke a tooth?

DC: Oh no, we have very few accidents. I can't remember anyone working for me ever having a serious accident, and that includes any of the students. There have been some burns, but I can't remember anybody getting a serious burn.

BLDD: I would think the real hazard of working around so much glass would be getting cut.

DC: No, that doesn't happen very often either, unless you're working with a lot of machinery, which I don't. It's a bit of a problem when you're working with diamond saws and cutting glass. But I don't know, maybe we've been especially fortunate. . . .

BLDD: To what do you attribute that?

DC: A lot of concentration and attention. Watching the crews working, it always amazes me to see so many people moving through our shop without running into each other. You really can't break your concentration for a minute or somebody will run into you or you'll run into somebody else. One critic talked a lot about the physical aspects of glassblowing, about it probably being the most constantly physical of all art forms, almost like a ballet. In fact, it is the breath of the artist that creates the form of the piece. But I've never been fascinated with the physical aspects of it the way many people are. I'm primarily interested in the end product.

BLDD: What about the process itself?

DC: I'm not as interested in the process as most people are. It's amazing but it's true. I don't even like heat, and glassblowing is one of the hottest things you can do. I was head of the RISD sculpture department, and I've been to so many thousands of lectures by artists and craftsmen, and so often people talk about only the material — you know, potters talk about mud, clay, and earth. It doesn't matter what the process is; what's important is what we end up with.

BLDD: How is the work itself affected by all the animated conversation that goes on here? It's such a contrast to the very private acts of solitude that most of us imagine to be the hallmark of artists. Does it get translated into the work that is created?

DC: When we're working, very little is needed to be said in order for everybody to understand what their job is. It could probably all be done rather silently, but actually they enjoy talking to each other. When Billy is telling Rob to blow more or blow less, he could really do it with his head if he wanted to, with sign language, but there's a desire for verbal communication; there's a group spirit. They like to listen to music as they work, have a glass of wine, or eat whatever they want to. We actually have one person who does only the cooking because the food is so important to their state of mind. One person wants steak and eggs in the morning, somebody else wants cereal, somebody drinks tea or coffee or wine or soda water — all these things are part of the process. Most of the crew has lived in Italy, and food is very important to the Italians. Leno, one of the Italian masters we brought over, will not work in the shop unless he can see the pasta water boiling. It's that important to him to be thinking about the food as well.

BLDD: You've said that you don't feel the work is really finished until it's photographed. Why is this kind of documentation so critical to your art? Why is it important to fix the moment so literally? It seems such a contrast to the kind of liquid-in-motion process that you're involved in.

DC: For one thing, I'm not a collector and I don't really collect any of my own work. Once I've put a piece together and I like it, I want to have it photographed because it's the only record I have. Occasionally I might keep a sort of a seminal piece. It's partly because I'm nomadic, I think. First of all, I don't even know where I'd collect it. I wouldn't even understand the collector's mentality, I don't think, if it weren't for the fact that ever since I was little I've liked cars and been frustrated by the idea of seeing a beautiful car and not being able to own it. I always feel, though, that instead of collecting art I could go to the museum and look at it.

BLDD: I've heard you call yourself glassblower, educator, craftsman, artist — which term do you prefer to describe what it is that you do?

DC: I don't really like calling myself an artist. I mean, I like to think of myself as creative but because I don't do a lot of the work now, I can't think of myself so much as a craftsman; I'm now delegating the craftsmanship to younger, really extraordinary craftsmen. I consider myself a glassmaker or a glassworker.

BLDD: If you had the time or the assistance or the funds necessary, is there an ideal project you haven't yet done that you would like to do?

DC: With my degree in interior design and my interest in architecture, I've made attempts in the last ten years at doing large architectural projects. I am very interested in architecture. I can see the possibility of a project where this type of work would become something like a large wall of glass in a public space. There's a real need for more intimate objects that the public can look at closely in large spaces. It doesn't have to be a fifty-foot painting or a huge piece of sculpture in order to have monumental significance.

BLDD: In the forty years of your life history there has been a lot of innovation, a lot of new ideas. What are you planning to do next?

DC: I'm just going to keep traveling and keep working with glass and keep bringing people to Pilchuck. You know, Pilchuck started off with those ideas of community and collaboration and artists and students, but now it's really developed into an international glass center to which people come from all over the world to exchange ideas and to communicate about glass and its potential. Through four thousand years of glass history, there's been a tradition of factories without artists. All of a sudden, in the last twenty years, artists have had an opportunity to see what they could do with this material . . . it's the first time the design or the object didn't have to be produced for commerce or for the church. Undoubtedly, there's going to be lots of innovation and lots of new ideas in the next twenty years.

Above: *Untitled*. Macchia series. 1981. Hand-blown glass

Above right and right: *Untitled*. 1981. Hand-blown glass

Untitled. 1981. Hand-blown glass

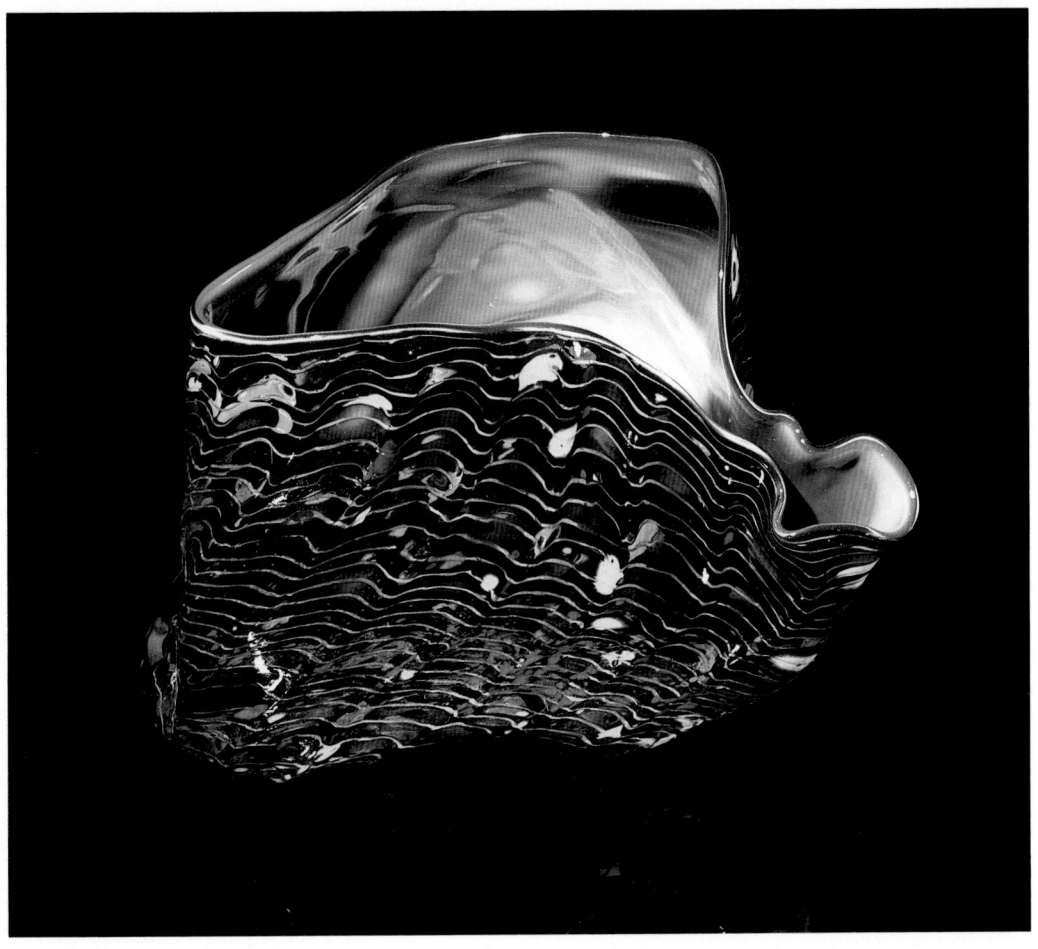

Untitled. Macchia series. 1982.
Hand-blown glass

Untitled. Macchia series. 1981.
Hand-blown glass

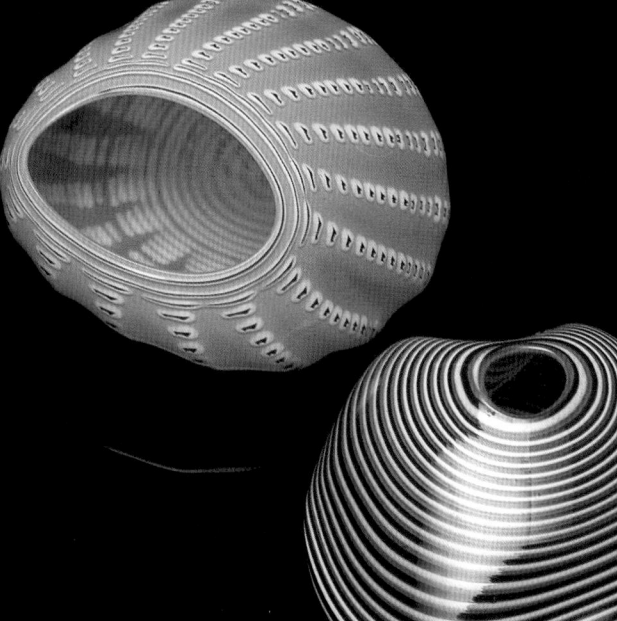

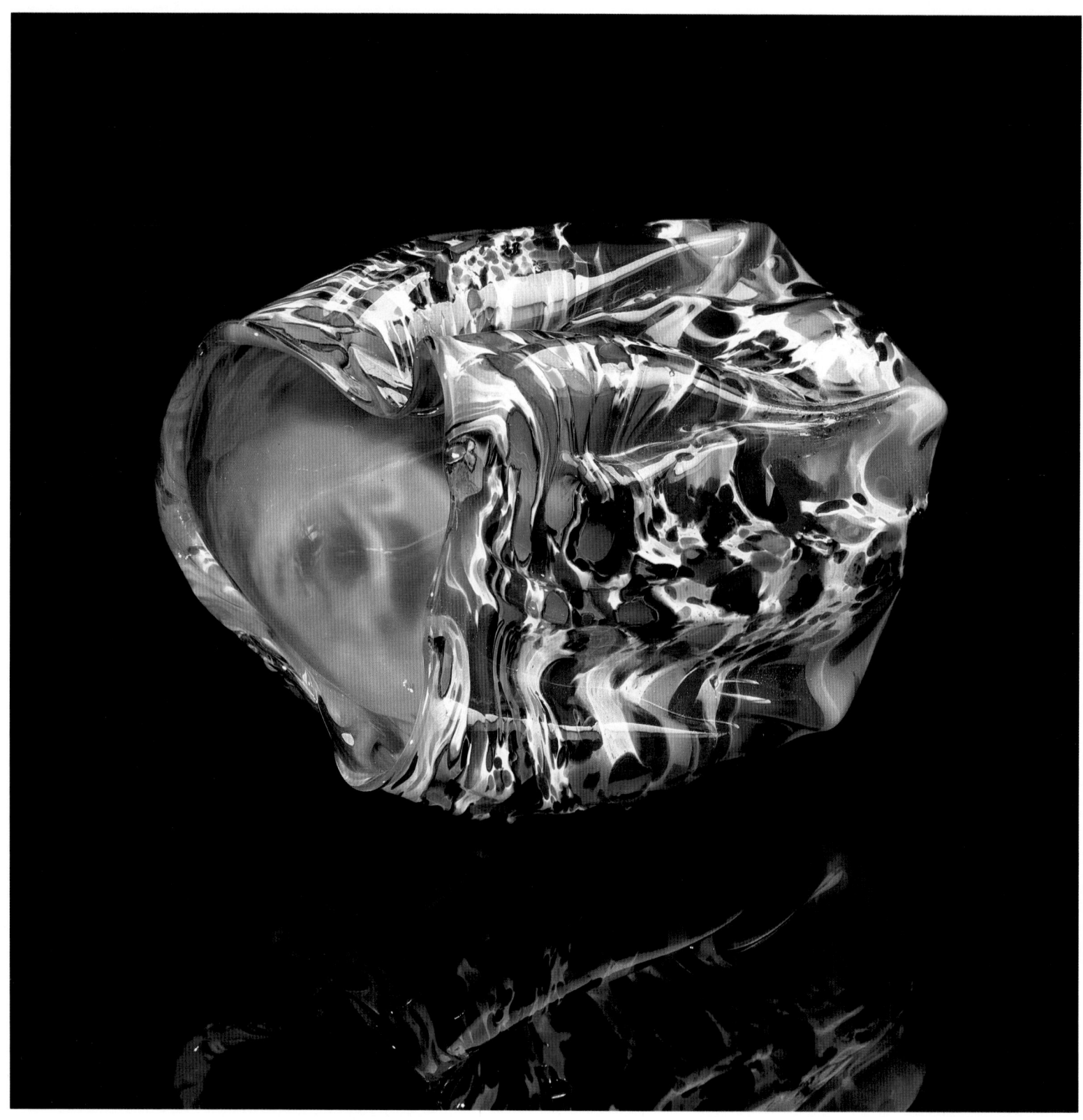

Above: *Untitled*. Macchia series. 1982. Hand-blown glass

Left: *Untitled*. 1981. Hand-blown glass

Lia Cook

stepped into the center of the fiber arts world in the early seventies with huge, undulating tapestries that were hypnotically rhythmical. Cook created a sensuous fiber art that was rare in its optical and illusionistic effect. Her textiles are made by an intricate technique that requires great patience and skill. You'd imagine they must and should be handled delicately. Yet their fate in Lia Cook's creative hands is first to be woven, then pressed by heavy rollers, and finally pounded by hammers. Only then are they ready for her to carefully paint their surfaces. Ideas are as important to Lia as their execution, and she manages both with a sense of scale and invention that is quite remarkable.

BLDD: When most of us hear the term "tapestry," we think of those heavy medieval hangings that were used to insulate and decorate chilly cathedrals and castles. What's the relationship of the works that you create to those of long ago, and what was the evolution of this woven form?

LC: Tapestries were used to cover castle walls and to create warmth in buildings, and they also told stories. Earlier on, tapestries used religious themes, and then they began to tell stories of everyday life that went on in the castles. Some of my work has also been used in very large spaces, and adds warmth to the buildings.

BLDD: Maybe those monumental interior spaces in hotels for which you've designed wall hangings can be likened to contemporary castles. What led to your involvement with weaving originally?

LC: I'm the kind of person who likes to experiment and do a lot of different kinds of things. Being a woman, I had worked with textiles, had known how to sew and all of that, when I was younger. When I picked up fibers and weaving, it just felt right. So I did it. I first started to weave in 1967. I spent a year in Sweden and studied weaving. I knew when I went there that that's what I wanted to do, and I got a pretty good technical background.

BLDD: Your earlier work looked very much like landscape painting. Considering the fact that you studied art, that's not surprising. Was that your intention?

LC: Some of the earlier work *is* like a landscape. It's a textile landscape, though, rather than a conventional landscape — as though a sheet of fabric were laid over a woven structure creating the indentations of a landscape.

BLDD: As you describe it, your work begins with a fundamental structure. Grids, patterns, and even paint are essential. How do you think that your approach to creating art is different from that of a painter?

LC: I think there are all kinds of approaches to painting, as there are all kinds of approaches to textiles. As a weaver I'm involved in using fibers to build up a structure. I would probably call myself an artist who works with woven and painted surfaces. In that way I'm more like an architect or a builder. Sometimes I work with systems in my painting on the weaving. The draft, which is the drawing notation for weaving, is often systematic and mathematical. Then I paint on my work, as a painter would, in a very spontaneous way, working with the underlying systems and structure of the weave, and sometimes also working intuitively with the surface.

BLDD: Let's talk a bit more about the way that you work. You use very traditional techniques to execute even your most innovative ideas. How does the idea for one of your woven patterns develop?

LC: I start by doing a draft on graph paper and I build up an image that I want to use. The draft is something that represents the order in which the threads cross each other; it's what a weaver uses as a drawing. And I see them as drawings in themselves. Filling in a square represents a particular thread combination. So although it may look like a bunch of squares on a piece of paper, I

Interweave Two. 1975. Woven, dyed cotton; photosensitized surface. 6 × 4′

have a vision of how that will look structurally. There are always surprises because when it's translated, when it's beaten and compressed, things are going to collapse. You have a sense about it that you only really get from having done it. I love it; I get very involved in the details. It's building the image up square by square. I'm trying to develop a particular kind of imagery with the draft. Then it is woven thread by thread into a structure. I weave a white piece of fabric that's like a canvas with a repeating image.

BLDD: What happens after you've established the designs?

LC: The surface is woven, white on white. First, of course, the loom has to be threaded up. Then the threads are lifted in a systematic way to create a repetitive pattern.

BLDD: How did you devise the special loom that you use now?

LC: Most of my processes involve distorting the rules. In this case, I'm distorting the tension of the weaving. If I go too far, the weaving will fall apart. I'm always playing on that edge to see how far I can take it, using the distortion for my own purposes. The loom I use is designed to be very, very strong so that I can make the tension extremely tight and distort it as much as possible. It is a heavy-duty loom built for that purpose.

BLDD: Have you ever worked on a less mechanized loom?

LC: Yes, I've worked on fairly simple looms. The one I'm discussing is not terribly mechanized. Weaving itself is structurally very simple. The other loom that I worked on, the dobby loom, is a little more mechanized. You program the weave by putting little pegs into slats, which are called lags. That way you get a more complex weave, and it's easier to weave, too.

BLDD: How large is this loom anyway?

LC: It's about ten feet wide. You can purchase looms of this size, but this one was specially built for the large pieces that I make on it.

BLDD: How complex and time-consuming a process is it to thread the loom?

LC: It's very time consuming and there are thousands of threads, but you just work in a systematic way. It's sort of like meditation. It has a rhythm to it and it's very soothing.

BLDD: How important is the contact and exchange with your assistants while you're at the loom?

LC: Especially when they're beginning, it's important to communicate with them. The kind of weaving I do is not something you can do from a design. You put one thing down, and the next thing is to build on that, and then build on that, and build on that. It's a decision-making

Space-Dyed Photographic Weaving. 1975. Woven, dyed cotton; photosensitized surface. 8 × 12 × 1½′ (depth)

process all the way along. In order to work independently on it you really have to understand what the process is, and you pretty much have to be involved all the way along.

BLDD: After the weaving is done, what's the next step?

LC: After the piece is woven on the loom, it's taken off and washed. The yarn shrinks, which distorts the original woven surface. And it softens the threads. The piece reacts very much like paper — it becomes pliable when it's washed. The piece is then run through a large press that flattens the surface and further distorts the threads. It sometimes takes on the appearance of metal — metal that has been pressed. Then the weaving is shaped and molded by pounding directly on the surface with various kinds of hammers.

BLDD: How important is running it through that press?

LC: I use the press for flattening out the surface of the weave and compressing the fibers. This makes a flat, shiny surface to paint on. So it's definitely a weaving and

yet it isn't a weaving because it's distorted or changed in some way.

BLDD: How long does it take to complete a piece?

LC: That's really hard to tell because it's a long process from beginning to end. It takes perhaps three months. And I often work on several pieces at once, so the pieces are in different stages of the process. I can have an assistant helping me with the weaving part while I'm painting on another part.

BLDD: What are some of the tools you use when you pound on that woven textile?

LC: There are small sledgehammers, hammers for shoes, an assortment of hammers I've collected that create different kinds of impressions.

BLDD: What is it about the hammered surface that is so essential to the overall design that you have in mind?

LC: Not all the pieces are hammered, but in the ones that are, the function of the hammering is similar to that of the painting. The hammering changes the level of the surface and makes the light react differently on it. So you see different faces within the same piece as you look at it. The hammering is an important part of seeing different parts of the surface at once, in different ways. It's all there in the structure but it is brought out by the hammering, by the shaping, and by the painting.

BLDD: Do you derive any of your patterns from old textiles?

LC: Looking at historic textiles is most important. I don't take specific patterns from old textiles, but I look at them for ideas because my imagery is involved with the imagery of textiles.

BLDD: Just what kind of fiber do you use? Is it unusual?

LC: It is a rayon fiber used in making automobile tires and I've had it plied into a heavy size especially for my purpose. I like this material because it's pliable; when it's washed it shrinks, and it can be pounded and formed. Also, it's very shiny and gives a light-reflective quality.

BLDD: How did you ever arrive at using that particular fiber?

LC: Just by experimenting with it. I am interested in the reflective quality of rayon, in its relationship to silk and textiles. If you walk by a damask tablecloth or look at it folded up, you see many images within it; it changes with the light. That's because a weaving is a dimensional structure — it's not flat. I like to work with a material for a long period of time. Before this, I worked with a particular wool that was quite strong. One thing I'm interested in is strength because I have a very physical relationship with the work. And since I do things to it, like hammering the surface, it has to be very strong. Because I could form it and make an imprint on it, the rayon became a good material for me. I like the fact that it is white and absorbent to color. If you use dyes with it, it just absorbs them like watercolor paper. It is a material

that allows me to express the things I want to. Many people experiment with all different kinds of materials, but I set myself certain limits.

BLDD: When I think of Berkeley, where we are now, two things immediately come to mind: one is political involvement, and the other is that Berkeley is a long-term, vital center for American crafts activities. You were a student at Berkeley in the mid-sixties and early seventies, when there was a great deal of student activism. Do you think that activism influenced you or the direction of your work?

LC: I wasn't directly involved in any political activism although it was definitely here. I think I've always been the kind of person who doesn't like to do what I'm told, doesn't like to follow the rules, and likes to find new ways to approach a problem. That spirit probably has something to do with the times. While I was studying political science, my major, I studied countries in Africa and South America, most of which have a rich textile tradition. At the time, though, I wasn't involved in textiles.

Detail of pressed rayon weaving

58

BLDD: You've recently acquired an antique jacquard loom. How and where did you get it, and what do you intend for its use?

LC: I recently purchased a jacquard in Lyons, France, which was the center of the old silk textile industry from the Middle Ages on. I'm interested in using this piece of machinery and adapting it to my work. The jacquard was a precursor of the computer. There are cards onto which you punch out your design. With a jacquard, every thread can be operated separately so it's possible to create any kind of image you want. It will permit me more flexibility in the imagery. I can choose any kind of image that I want to put into my canvas before I paint on the surface.

BLDD: How will you program this "computerized" loom? How does the draft relate to the fabric?

LC: The jacquard isn't actually a loom — it's the mechanism that goes on top of the loom and operates the threads. Each square on the draft is filled in separately, and that tells the threads what to do. Then a card is punched for each line on the graph paper. The punched

cards are put onto the jacquard mechanism, which operates a series of locks, which in turn raises or lowers the threads to create the specific pattern. My plans are to incorporate this into my work, using the white on white and creating a much more elaborate image within the structure of the canvas.

BLDD: The physical connection with the material is very important to your work. Is it considered unusual, and perhaps even a bit disrespectful, to take a textile off the loom — and wash it and hammer it and pound it and then, finally, paint it?

LC: Yes, I think so. I kind of like that idea! Especially for a weaving, which seems to be so precious. And I like the idea that while I'm interested in the structure of the weaving it's only part of the process for me. I always end up doing something with it that is very physical, very direct. Sometimes, for example, I use hammers right on the weaving to mold the surface. It could be disrespectful, in a way, to the material, but I also feel that it is more important to get my ideas across. I want to use any material or any process that will help me communicate those ideas.

BLDD: How do you go about selecting color? Is there such a thing as a weaver's palette?

LC: I work with color rather intuitively. The color of a weaving is always made of blended particles because the threads all cross one another. The particles build up a field of color. In my painting I draw from this, especially in the pieces in which I paint individual threads.

BLDD: What happens when you're painting those individual threads and you decide you'd like to change some part of the color on the fabric? Is that possible on the textile itself?

LC: When I'm working I always like to have a certain kind of structure and a certain area in which I'm spontaneous. So I always have areas in which I can change my mind about the work and change my direction if I want to. Painting the surface allows me to do that. The painting is much more intuitive and emotional and direct.

BLDD: What kind of paint do you use?

LC: I use dyes, which allow the reflectiveness of the material to come through. I also sometimes use acrylic or pigments. I use whatever is necessary to do what I want to do.

BLDD: Your work explores the optical effects of woven structures. If you look at the finished tapestry you can see the depressions and the multiple layers that relate to the underlying structure, and the surface image itself seems to create an illusion. Is that what you have in mind?

LC: I do use illusion in my work but I don't think that's the primary point. When you look at a textile moving in space and how light is hitting it in different ways, you see

Pressed X (detail). 1979. Woven, pressed rayon. 20 × 14″

Below: *Black Craze*. 1981. Woven, pressed, painted rayon. 47 × 40″

Right: *Laminae* (detail). 1980. Woven, pressed, painted rayon. 4 × 4′

Far right: *Lattice Conversed* (detail). 1981. Woven, pressed, painted rayon. 45 × 40″

what I call different faces of that image surface. So even though it's the same image, you see different aspects of it, depending on the way you experience it. That's what I'm trying to capture within the work. Some of it is illusion, and yet it's real. It's based very substantially within the textile.

BLDD: What's your "space dyeing" technique? Is this process one that you've invented yourself?

LC: No, it isn't. "Space dyeing" is the term for a yarn that has been dyed various colors on the same strand of the yarn. In my case a skein of yarn has been dipped into several different-color dyes. It's dyed first and then woven, which is different from those pieces that are painted afterward.

BLDD: One of the distinctive features of your earlier work is the raised sections. What did you use to create those woven ribs?

LC: For that earlier technique I used two-inch strips of polyurethane foam that had been spray-painted the color

of the thread that was woven over it. It's cut and shaped with scissors and then used as weft and pounded down by hand with a forklike tool. When it's taken off the loom, the foam expands and holds its place. That series of pieces had to do with fabric landscape or what fabric is like over a surface. Some of these were actual dimensional structures and some of them were illusionary. I worked with an airbrush on a ribbed fabric for several years and also with a photographic process on the surface. My imagery became more and more involved with the structure of the weaving, as though you had laid a piece of fabric over a woven surface so there would be the impression of a woven understructure.

BLDD: Do you decide in advance what size to cut the strip or are those kinds of decisions spontaneous?

LC: You have to know what you've done before, and you make a new decision each time about how long something's going to be in relation to the one before it. Everything is built up line by line. It's not like making a print,

in which you can work a drawing all over the page. In weaving you have to build it up structurally as if you're constructing a building from the bottom up, one brick at a time. A decision must be made each time, as you go along, to determine exactly the direction and how far and how much.

BLDD: How many pieces have you made this year, and how do you know when a piece is finished?

LC: I would say ten to fifteen. I look at my work in terms of a continuum so I don't necessarily feel that there's one point at which it's finished. I get it to the point where I feel that it could go on, but I could also say that it was finished.

BLDD: The process of weaving itself is so complicated that I wonder if you've ever felt constrained by it — or have you ever found those very limitations could stimulate your ideas?

LC: I do construct a number of limits. I work with the loom and I work with a specific material. I like certain

61

limits. They give me more freedom to explore. I like the structure of weaving, the way that the image is *in* the structure rather than on the surface. It's built into the weaving itself. But I need time to work spontaneously and immediately with the surface. That aspect, of course, involves the painting and the pounding. I like the balance of both aspects: a lot of control and structure, and then a lot of freedom.

BLDD: Obviously you can't make everything that you draw. How often are you able to translate your ideas into a reality?

LC: Of course, I think of a lot more ideas than I can possibly do. This probably is true of any artist. My work is very time-consuming, and that's one thing I'm concerned about because I want to produce as many ideas as I can. I'm constrained by the time, and yet time is a most important element in doing these weavings.

BLDD: Do you work every day?

LC: Yes. I'm also involved in teaching and a lot of other things. But I often work at night, and I'll work day and night for a while. I work most all the time.

BLDD: Does your five-year-old son, Kalle, often play in the studio while you're at work?

LC: Yes, he seems to be able to concentrate and focus on what he's doing.

BLDD: Have you ever been interested in painting directly on canvas, utilizing the fiber quality of the canvas?

LC: I think that's what I do now — I'm weaving my own canvas, with an image within the canvas. And then I paint on that. So it's as though you had a canvas and you were painting on the canvas, bringing the structure of the canvas through.

BLDD: After the linear landscapes you began creating something called "pressed-weave" surfaces. Would you tell us what they are and how you arrived at them?

LC: The pressed-weave surfaces are made from a rayon material with a small repeated image in the canvas. I call them pressed weaves because the material is washed and then run through a press. Although the fibers still have their over/under structure, in being flattened their identity is slightly changed. They look somewhat like metal.

BLDD: Your work's sense of physicality seems even more apparent in the recent pressed weaves.

LC: Physicality is involved in all my work, but perhaps it's more visible on the surface of the pressed weaves. Everything I do is well constructed and solid and has a sense of physicality.

BLDD: You weave, wash, press, and with these pressed weaves, hammer, and finally apply paint to the surface. Is there any particular way that you build a design when you paint on the woven surface?

LC: The color is built up thread by thread, according to the pattern structure of the weave. The color design also has to do with how you see it in different light, so as you

Spatial Ikat. 1974. Woven wool, cotton, polyurethane foam. 10 × 7′

Forays. 1980. Woven, pressed, painted rayon. 48 × 44″

62

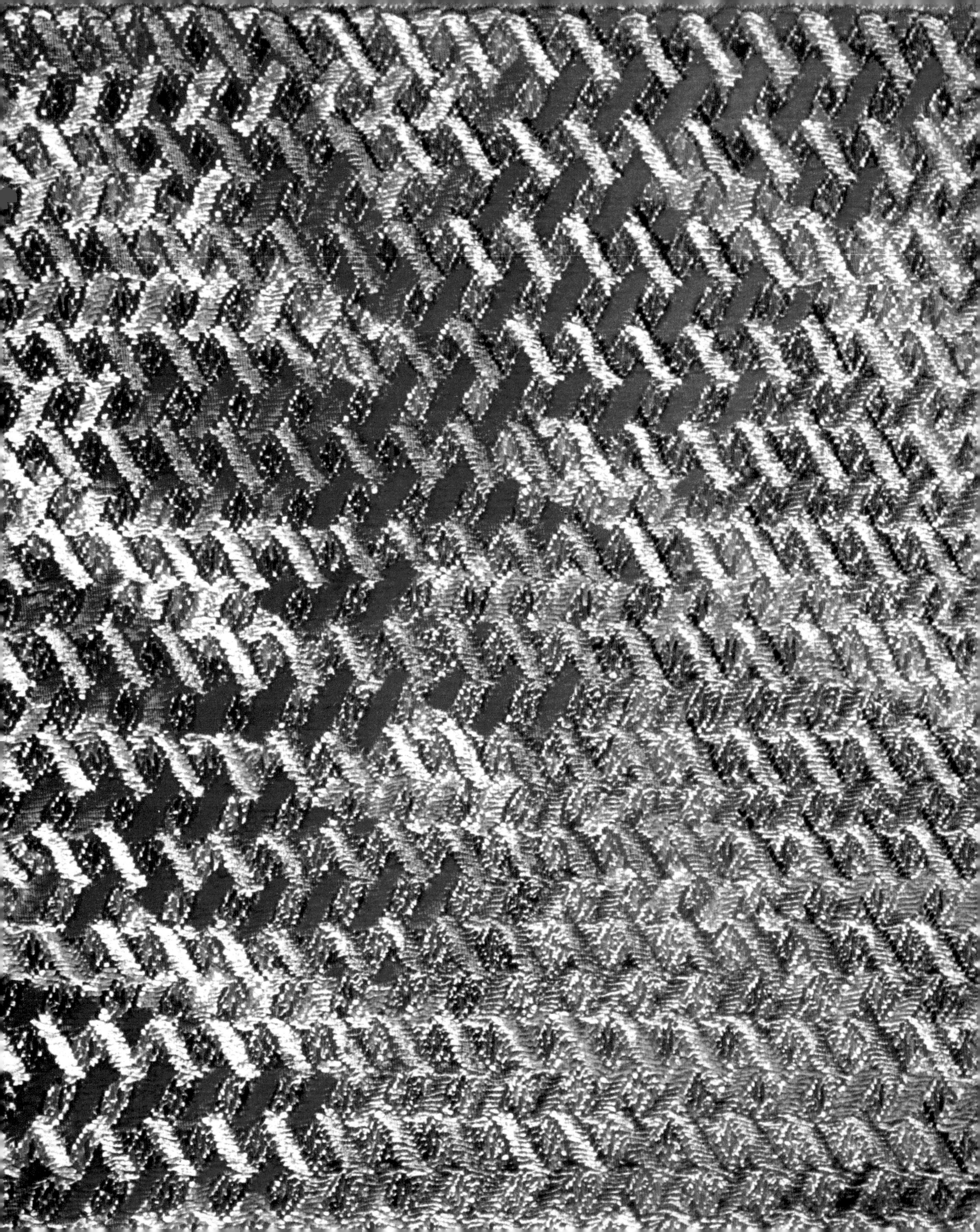

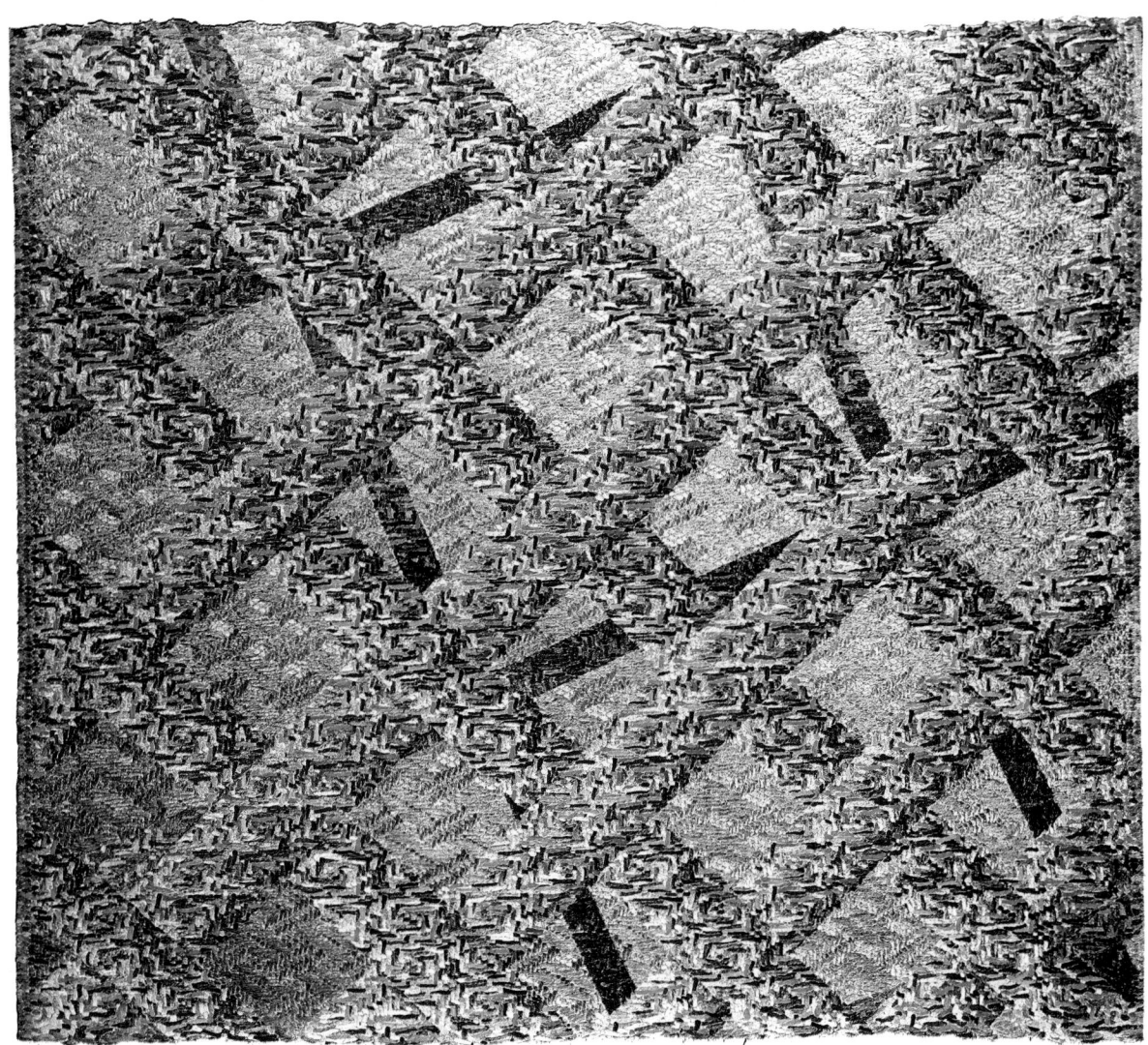

Two Point Four. 1980.
Woven, pressed, painted
rayon. 48 × 43″

move across the image or the pattern structure the color changes. But each thread is often painted separately and the color is built up particle by particle.

BLDD: Do you see it as an overall design, or do you see it block by block as you work on it?

LC: I see it as an overall piece, even though I'm working on sections at a time.

BLDD: Do you use a scale model or a diagram to put the paint on the surface, or is that done spontaneously when you're in front of the canvas you've made?

LC: It's done spontaneously but it's also done according to a certain system. What I find fascinating about this part of the painting process is that the image that I'm building up, though it does become illusion on the surface, has come out of the structure of the weave, out of the systematic crossing of the threads. The dots on the threads in the weaving are not randomly painted; they're painted systematically according to the structure of the weave. If you look closely, it is a patterned structure

emerging from the structure of the weave and creating an image that in some cases is illusionary.

BLDD: How much of the final product do you craft yourself?

LC: I have people working for me from time to time in the studio. I don't like a large number of people working for me but I generally have one or two. They do parts of the process but usually I'm involved pretty much from beginning to end in some way. In my work I have an intimate connection with the process. I think that if there are areas that can be mechanized in a way that doesn't affect the primary relationship you have with the work, it's acceptable. If you have somebody else working on your work, you always lose something. But someone still has to work the loom and weave the surface so it's still very much a hand process. I don't have any investment in keeping it completely a hand process, just for the sake of it, when it isn't necessary. It's important to be personally involved in what I'm doing, and as you become a

manager and more separated from it the work does become different. But if someone can thread a loom according to what I want, there's no reason why that person shouldn't do it. I have nothing invested in the fact that I put the threads on the loom myself. If it relates to the mixture of color, or the real substance of the piece, then my personal involvement becomes important.

BLDD: Can you envision creating a textile that would influence wide numbers of people because it was created for mass production?

LC: I think working with industry, for mass distribution, would be an interesting problem. At this point in my life, I'm involved in developing a more personal style. But I might try to do that sometime.

BLDD: In addition to your studio work, you teach at the California College of Arts and Crafts. You've also taught at other schools and universities. What about the teaching experience continues to engage you? Is there something of real consequence that you gain, that nurtures you, from that exchange with students?

LC: This is always a difficult problem, because I always want more time to do my work, and teaching is a large commitment. I do get a lot from teaching. Mostly it has to do with the contacts with individual students who are excited about what they're doing and the friendships that develop out of this over time. So I think the most important thing about teaching is that contact with emerging artists in the field and a close personal interaction. It's interesting because it's also a generational thing so you make contact not only with your own peer group.

BLDD: Recently you've been looking at textile collections from museums in England and France. How important is research to your own work process, and how important is the history of textiles to what you now create?

LC: I think the history of textiles is important to textiles as art, just as art history is important to contemporary painting and sculpture. In school you study art history but generally not textile history. But it's an important resource because textiles have, of course, been done through the ages. And for most of that time, textiles and art were together. There wasn't the current separation between textile history and art history.

BLDD: Have foreign cultures had a very great influence on textiles, particularly the various Japanese techniques and structures? In what way have they affected your own work?

LC: I think that Japanese textiles and techniques have been quite influential in the contemporary textile movement. The Japanese have a great sensitivity toward textiles and long traditions of dyeing and painting on textiles. The Japanese influence is especially prevalent on the West Coast.

BLDD: When did the contemporary textile movement

come to be known as fiber art? What does that term actually mean?

LC: I don't know exactly when it got its title as fiber art. The term seems to include all people who work with fibers in the traditional and nontraditional senses. The fiber can be plastic; the product can be a basket — the definition of textiles today is very broad.

BLDD: The whole idea of decorative art declined in popularity in recent years. But obviously it's being revitalized and reassessed today. How do you explain that?

LC: I think it's part of a broader thing that's happening in art. What had been in the past, narrow, formal kinds of rules about what is acceptable or good art are barriers that are being broken down. I think that the words "decorative" and "pattern" were negative terms in art. And I think that that has been overturned, due to artists like Joyce Kozloff and various others. Decorative is not considered a negative aspect. The art world encompasses decorative, too. Of course my work relates to decorative and pattern painting. I don't come out of that political persuasion — I'm not making a statement about decorative. I assume that there are decorative qualities to the piece, and these are valuable and important parts of the artwork. So I don't see myself as a pattern painter but I realize that my work involves patterns and involves painting.

BLDD: What do you see as the future direction of what you're doing and of the field of fiber arts in general?

LC: I'm excited about what's happening. A lot of different media are intermixing. Fiber is being combined with plastic, with paper, with ceramics, and eventually the barriers will become less and less significant. What I would hope for in the field is that people working in textiles step out into the world and show their work with confidence — and show it in all kinds of ways. There's a strong support group among fiber artists, but I think they do need to step out. They often complain about not being accepted by the art world, but now they can exhibit their work in galleries. They can continue to educate people around them about textiles as art. There are prejudices. But prejudices are based on lack of knowledge. I think it's an educative process.

BLDD: How would you describe your work now?

LC: Well, the process is different because there's more immediacy in the final painting part of it. And I think the graphic imagery is softer, subtler, more personal. I think I'm moving toward providing a more intimate experience with the materials and with the textiles and I want people to see textiles in an intimate way. If I see a textile, I immediately begin to look at the structure and the personal qualities of it. So there has been a gradual transition from the stronger graphic to a subtler kind of imagery, which I find really interesting.

Sandi Fox, *who lives in Los Angeles, has an unusual combination of talents. The maker of dazzling quilts, she also organizes museum exhibitions of nineteenth-century quilts. Quilts have not always been thought of as precious heirlooms. Old quilts were long used to perform humble functions: to catch dripping oil beneath cars, to wrap around moist pipes, sometimes to protect furniture during moving. In recent years we've come to reassess quilts as fine and valuable art as well as craft, as collectors' items, even as historical records. Sandi Fox hopes to further awaken the country's appreciation of quilts and the people who are making them today by bringing both out of attics and workrooms and before the public.*

BLDD: Every aspect of quilts — their history, their design, their creation, their exhibition — seems to fascinate you. Whatever engaged your interest in the first place?

SF: My interest, which has really been over a thirty-year period, *has* covered every aspect from function to history to sociological interpretations of the quilt. It began when I was a child in Nebraska sleeping under those often rather nondescript quilts of the 1930's and 40's. Then, when I was a freshman in high school in California, at age fifteen, I was bicycling along the beach and I saw, wrapped around a refrigerator that was being moved, an absolutely incredible piece of textile art. I followed the truck. When they stopped and unloaded the refrigerator, I bought, for twenty-five cents, my first nineteenth-century quilt.

BLDD: Is it really possible that many of your early quilts cost twenty or thirty cents?

SF: Yes, of course, but that was twenty or thirty years ago when quilts were looked upon only in a functional sense. Nineteenth-century quilts were barely looked at at all, and certainly not in terms of collectible items.

BLDD: Why did people make quilts in the first place? Was it for practical purposes only or for esthetic reasons as well?

SF: It was for functional reasons. A quilt is, in fact, an object made to keep a body warm. The esthetics came simply because, even in functional items, women have always sought to express the beautiful.

BLDD: Are there quilts that are considered uniquely American?

SF: The pieced quilt is uniquely American in that the geometric repetition of a block pattern across a quilt was an innovation in terms of design used by American women almost exclusively.

BLDD: Where do most antique quilts come from in America? Is there any particular region in the country where the majority were made?

SF: No. It is fair to say that almost every woman in America — unless she happened to have a maiden aunt who would make the quilts for the whole family — would at some time during her life make at least one quilt. It was something that women did both out of necessity and for pleasure. It was something that for a long time bound together women of all classes and all sociological levels across the United States.

BLDD: Could you determine just by looking at a quilt where it was made? Are there regional differences in colors and styles or patterns?

SF: There are, in fact. You generally cannot decide with only a brief look at a quilt when and where it was made, but Pennsylvania quilts are generally easy to identify. Until the time of western expansion there were a number of identifiable distinctions in regional quilts. These, of course, merged together as quiltmakers joined in the opening of the western frontier.

BLDD: I wonder if you could re-create the kind of special environment in which early American quilters did their work. Was it always a group effort?

SF: This is one of the myths that has grown in the current renaissance in American quilts. We tend to think exclusively of a number of women grouped around a

Patience Corners. 1979. Cotton crib quilt. 46 × 44″. Collection Timmy Burton

frame at a quilting bee. Although quilts were often made in groups, the masterpiece quilts, as with almost any craft or art form, generally were individual efforts done in solitude and contemplation.

BLDD: What can we learn about historical and economic developments in this country by looking at nineteenth-century quilts? How much does a quilt also tell about the life of its maker?

SF: It tells us a great deal. Sometimes, of course, we are lucky enough to have a quilt that's signed and dated. At other times, letters or diaries are passed down with the quilt. But by simply looking at a quilt, establishing the fabrics in it, we can also often establish the social class of the woman who made it by whether it's a beautiful silk or a rather humble cotton. We can look at the pattern she chose, such as Whig Rose, Fifty-four Forty or Fight, or Mrs. Cleveland's Choice.

BLDD: What *was* Mrs. Cleveland's choice?

SF: Mrs. Cleveland's choice, whether she knew it or not, was a rather elaborate version of another pattern called "Jack-in-the-Pulpit." We are able to read in the political names that women assigned their quilt patterns

John's Vest. 1978. Wool lined with silk and faced with men's tie labels. 20 × 29″

of the political preferences they were not allowed to express in the voting booth.

BLDD: What's the earliest-known surviving quilt?

SF: If we are talking strictly about quilts — that is; a top, a batting, a backing, held together with a quilting stitch — the earliest-known European work to survive is a series of three quilts from the early fifteenth century known as the Sicilian quilts. Their quilted design is the story of Tristan and Isolde. The earliest-known surviving pieced quilt in America that we can trace was probably made around 1704 in Massachusetts. It has descended

through the family of Leverett Saltonstall and therefore goes by the name of the Saltonstall quilt.

BLDD: Of all the tens of thousands of quilts that you have seen or read about, do you have a favorite pattern or variety?

SF: I have always preferred the pieced quilt. To me it indicates a greater use of material at hand, a greater technical challenge. The woman who was making a quilt had a number of directions in which she could go. She could either appliqué a piece of fabric to get a very literal interpretation of a leaf or flower or figure, or she could cut

small pieces of fabric and work them into something that didn't look like anything but evoked something very meaningful in her life. For example, an Ocean Wave or Flying Geese would be a very simple geometric pattern but would be recognized instantly by quiltmakers across the country.

BLDD: The pineapple is a long-term symbol of hospitality that recurs in many quilts. What are some of the favorite symbols that you use and like?

SF: The two quilt designs that most appeal to me are variations of Flying Geese or the Log Cabin quilt. I like to remember that when the early American quiltmaker was developing her geometric patterns she drew inspiration from what she saw around her. We are not talking about someone with a design background, so when we see a row of flying geese — which is simply a row of triangular shaped pieces of fabric — we are seeing in abstract form what the quiltmaker saw as she looked up into those New England skies: rows of ducks and geese flying clear across them. Her quilt was her interpretation of what she saw.

BLDD: What are contemporary quiltmakers to do? Will they have 747's instead of flying geese? How do you reflect the computer age in a traditional art form?

SF: There are already a number of quilts being made which do exactly that, usually pictorial in design. But, of course, they are drawing on a tradition of pictorial quilts in the nineteenth century. They might be figures, forms, political or family events. They were then, and are now, vignettes of what was happening at the time. I think the most beautiful quilts will always go back to the geometric designs, just as we go back in all craft traditions to simpler shapes, whether the simplicity of wood or the fine curve on a piece of ceramic. I think there will always be a place for simple geometric design in all American quilts.

BLDD: How can you tell how old a quilt really is?

SF: I always like to say that you go to the standard things which means that to establish the age of the fabric you consider the batting that was used, the pattern name, the quality of the workmanship. You research the provenance of the quilt, insofar as it is possible to do so. From that point on I rely on an intuitive sense. I think there has been nothing more valuable to me, in terms of quilts I date and define for exhibition, than simply having had so many quilts passing through my hands. I often get a sense about a quilt of both its age and its story. Ninety-five percent of it is often nothing more than instinct based on fairly solid knowledge about the subject.

BLDD: Is there a kind of hierarchy to quiltmaking? Can you tell by looking at a quilt that its maker was perhaps more aristocratic or fashionable than the maker of another quilt?

SF: Generally you can judge that through the use of fabric. By the end of the Victorian period, for example, we were seeing wonderful creations in silks and velvets. Many of them are called "crazy quilts," although Log Cabin was also being done then in silks and velvets. What we see in those pieces is the opulence of the era reflected in a quilt that in essence has lost its function. You can't wash it. You can only look at it and admire the stitching and the richness of the fabric: it became something to show off rather than to use. The woman who had more humble fabrics in her rag bag would generally do a simpler type of quilt, using calicos and prints. Those quilts remain my favorites, however.

BLDD: You mentioned that they washed those elaborate and beautiful cotton quilts. Can we wash an old quilt? What's the proper way to care for a quilt?

SF: For general care of quilts, the proper thing to remember is to use but don't abuse. And for a nineteenth-century quilt, in terms of its cleaning, its preservation, its conservation, its hanging, its general usage — when in doubt, do nothing. The beauty of cotton is the patina that it attains when it is used, so I don't like to see things folded away, always in drawers. If you don't have space in which to store them on long rollers, most can be loosely rolled with acid-free tissue paper and stored in 100 percent cotton pillowcases. They should be aired regularly because textiles need to breathe. Yes, many quilts can be washed; the cotton ones always have been, but any work on an antique quilt should be done under the supervision or direction of a trained conservationist. They should certainly not be washed in machines. One should never take a nineteenth-century quilt to a drycleaner. If you have a quilt that is valuable to you, either in fact or in sentimentality, go to someone who is trained in textile conservation.

BLDD: What makes a quilt valuable to *you*, either in fact or in sentimentality?

SF: It's now beyond my financial means — as with many craftsmen — to collect the beautiful quilts that I might otherwise acquire. The good thing is that I have always been drawn to quilts for a sentimental reason. I do not like a quilt in mint condition, which is what many collectors and dealers prefer. I don't mind a few frayed edges. I like to know that the quilt was used to keep bodies warm, that it was passed from one generation to another, that it was in fact a functional item, and that the quilt carries a message about the circumstances of a woman's life. I make quilts for the same reason. I want a portion of myself to carry forward into another generation. That sentimentality, fortunately, comes at a slightly less dear price than a quilt in mint condition whose value is based solely on esthetic considerations.

BLDD: You have often said that you thought of yourself as a nineteenth-century woman. Do you still hold that to be true, and what do you really mean when you say that?

SF: Certainly, in terms of cultural and historical preferences, nineteenth century I am. I was very much influenced by what was happening creatively in the nineteenth century, for example, in literature. I was an English Literature major at Pomona College and continue to hold Nathaniel Hawthorne in high esteem. Artistically, American women in the early to mid-nineteenth century were making these incredible quilts, developing abstraction in textiles long before European artists conceived the idea. Then by the middle of the nineteenth century, we have the whole American West opening up, and the strong part that women played in the establishment of the frontier. It was a time when people had control of their lives and it is that control, that strength, that sentimentality, that regard for things you can do with your own hands that draws me more and more closely toward the American quilt.

BLDD: Quiltmakers often intentionally include an error in the design. What was the reason for that?

SF: The practice is a universal one; it goes by a number of names, but is generally called a religious error. The religious error in a quilt may only be a simple deliberate misplacement of one piece of fabric. It is there for the same reason an Oriental embroiderer will deliberately misconstruct a stitch, or an East or West Indian weaver will always make some slight error in the weaving. It can be thought of as the mark of humility — only God can make something that is absolutely perfect. We find it in all media. I think it's particularly exciting when we find them in American quilts.

BLDD: Do men make quilts? Have there ever been, or are there currently, men who are prominent as quiltmakers?

SF: There are indeed. In 1976 I did an exhibition of forty quilts, one of which was made by a gentleman named Robert Toup, of Maysfield, Kentucky, who was a harness maker. He had some sort of an accident, and during the year he spent recuperating he pieced and quilted for himself one of the most magnificent red, white, and blue Blazing Stars I have ever seen. Men are now becoming

Baskets with Pyramid Border. 1981. Cotton crib quilt. 35 × 35″

increasingly aware of the artistic possibilities of quilts, of what can be done with textiles.

BLDD: Why don't we talk for a moment about the quilts that you create? To begin with, how do you choose and store the fabric? Do you shop around until you find the perfect material, or do you save scraps like your great-great-grandmother did? Do you have your own rag bag?

SF: I have a rather neat rag bag. I almost never buy particular fabrics for a particular quilt. I work in the opposite direction. I see a fabric whose pattern, whose color, whose feel draws me, and buy a couple of yards. I draw inspiration from fabrics that are in front of me just begging to be sewn together.

BLDD: How many hours does it take to make the kinds of quilts that you create?

SF: I'm always working on a number of projects and time is really the least of the considerations because I make quilts for personal pleasure, really, as much as anything else. I never think of the time that's gone into it other than the length of pleasure I'm getting from working on it a particular evening.

BLDD: After having spent so much time with the quilt in your lap, in your hands, or at your table, do you often find it difficult to part with it after it's completed?

SF: I did not allow any of my quilts to be sold until my first one-woman exhibition about five or six years ago. At first I could not part with any of them. Then I saw the pleasure that people got from handling them, from looking at them. It is that same sense I mentioned before: to know that as the quilt goes by airplane across the country, to other parts of the United States or abroad, a little bit of Sandi Fox is being carried along and appreciated. I'm very selective about who gets a quilt of mine.

BLDD: You place them?

SF: As much as I can. They're almost like children so I want to know where they go. I delight in hearing about the pleasure that people get from them.

BLDD: How many quilts do you make a year?

SF: Depending on whether or not I am in the middle of mounting a major exhibition for a museum, anywhere from five to ten.

BLDD: What are you working on at present?

SF: I am doing a number of small pieces, and I am doing one of the few commissions that I accept. I had a very exciting offer from the Performing Arts Council of the Music Center, here in Los Angeles, to do a quilt for their annual fundraising. David Hockney did a painting for their posters and their publicity last year. Saul Bass, the illustrator, did one the year before. The ladies are having their turn this year! I suggested doing a typical nineteenth-century autograph quilt. It will be a pieced quilt with a bit of appliqué but, more important, it will bear the signatures of one hundred twenty of the most

prominent performing artists, writers, directors, that have worked at the Music Center over the past ten years.

BLDD: For what purpose was the autograph quilt used in the nineteenth century?

SF: Often for exactly the same purpose. They intend to auction it off early next year. The same thing only in much more meager terms was done in the nineteenth century. My favorite one is a quilt that was done for the Women's Christian Temperance Union of Colorado Springs in 1896. For fifteen or twenty-five cents a donor could have his or her name inscribed on the quilt as a mark of good moral standing. Money was often raised in that fashion. This is my favorite fund-raising quilt because, as I said, it was done for the WCTU, and the pattern that they chose was Drunkard's Path, which seemed particularly appropriate for the occasion.

BLDD: Why are you so reluctant to work on commission? Is it too "twentieth century" for you?

SF: A little bit. But remember that in the nineteenth century we had women who made quilts for a living. In Baltimore, for example, a master quiltmaker in the mid-nineteenth century made a series of remarkable quilts, possibly for trousseaux. When you accept a commission, it becomes more a job of work than something that is presented as a finished product. I've been looking forward to this one and am enjoying working on it.

BLDD: Following that nineteenth-century model you've established for yourself, do you keep a diary, too?

SF: I do. I keep a working journal. I'm a little more fortunate than the nineteenth-century ladies because I am a great clipper and I make sure that during the period of time I am working on a particular quilt I'm clipping articles out of *Time* or *Newsweek* or the *Los Angeles Times*, along with personal letters that I receive during that period of time. A hundred years from now, when people are trying to read my quilts, they will have to do a little less digging and detective work than I frequently do on the antique quilts I use in exhibitions.

BLDD: What do you suppose your quilts will reflect to future generations? When they read that quilt, what will they know about this point in time?

SF: I hope they will know that there were still people who cared about things made by hand — that there was still a place for something that took a while to do, was done in a manner to last, was meant to be kept and cherished and passed on. I think that's the most important thing. And to know that I cared about it.

BLDD: Obviously, a quilt won't speak of anything in the future unless it's preserved properly. And I know you've been disappointed at times to find a once-beautiful quilt in disrepair or falling apart. How do you handle a quilt to really protect it? Is there anything that we should know that would preserve its life?

Log Cabin, Straight Furrow Variation. Cotton cradle quilt. 1980

SF: Keep it away from those things that harm it most. For example, if you are using a quilt on a wall make sure it is properly hung and rotated frequently. Never "repair" a quilt. It is essential to preserve that craftsman's original statement rather than try to put a piece of 1920 fabric over something that has deteriorated. The unavoidable deterioration is part of the beauty of the American quilt. I am concerned by the often incredibly destructive methods sometimes used to present eighteenth- and nineteenth-century American quilts to the public. We have to begin displaying quilts with the same care we would use if we were hanging prints or paintings or tapestries. We have to respect them for what they are — a valid artistic statement. There is a proper way to hang a quilt on a wall and it does not include staples and thumbtacks or bright lights. Those antique quilts not fully mounted can be hung with Velcro, which is the safest method one can use. It bears the weight of the quilt and does not cause it to deteriorate. We have to educate the people who are showing quilts to the public that these precious heirlooms will be preserved only if we take particular care and interest.

BLDD: Have you ever thought of yourself as a kind of preservationist? Are you really trying to preserve an ancient craft or are you trying to kindle a new one, or a bit of both?

SF: All of those things. As with all creative processes, you must have a grasp of technique before you can trans-

Pineapple. 1980. Cotton crib quilt. 40 × 40″

Baskets. 1978. Cotton crib quilt. 33¼ × 33¼″. Collection Mr. and Mrs. Trent Lowe

late design into reality. Those techniques must be kept alive and available. I love working with natural fibers . . . these fingers never touch polyester. I try to restrain myself from getting hysterical when I see a quilt thumbtacked to the wall. But I will certainly point out that if they don't take it down, I will probably make some sort of horrible scene. I think it is important for people to realize that if we are in a renaissance of American quiltmaking we must understand and use nineteenth-century techniques so that a hundred years from now the quilts that were made during *this* renaissance will still be intact. Many of them will not.

BLDD: Do you think that quiltmaking is an art or a craft, or does it matter how it's described?

SF: It does matter to me personally. I describe myself as a craftsman. Unfortunately, that term offends those who would prefer I say "craftsperson" or "craftswoman," and also offends craftsmen who wish to be primarily considered artists. An artist need only be concerned with making something beautiful. A craftsman must make it beautiful and functional. I take great pride in calling myself a craftsman. And I'm fortunate that I am now in a period in which one can say the word craftsman and not have to fall back on saying, "I'm an artist so pay attention to my work." There is increasingly recognized validity in craftsmanship, and it should be undertaken without apology.

BLDD: You've said that more people than ever are turn-

T's with Sawtooth Inner Border and Le Moyne Star Outer Border. 1980. Cotton crib quilt. 40 × 40″

ing now to a love of items that bear the imprint of some-one's hand. To what do you attribute this resurgence of interest?

SF: As you can see by the things in my home, these are things that were used by people. I have a wonderful little tin tobacco box and in it is a message that reads in very ornate Spencerian script, "Dear Alice, this is our darling mother's beads and the box she kept them in. It is all I have to send you now." Particular objects meant things to people. If we allow children to grow up having around them only those things that can be replaced when they break, we're going to have a generation of people that don't understand the beauty of things handmade.

BLDD: You have surrounded yourself with a number of beautiful objects from your favorite period. Tell us something about the range and variety of things that you collect.

SF: We collected from early on, at swap meets and flea markets. My husband has a very extensive collection of early cameras bought when you could still pick them up for fifty cents. We also collect tins, American advertising, Edgeworth Tobacco boxes. My all-time favorite is probably the old rosewood grand piano which I found covered with black paint on its side in a garage about a hundred miles from here.

BLDD: Since you believe in the functional, I assume that you play that piano.

SF: Yes, I do. And after twenty years, I find that no mat-

Pine Tree Medallion with Sawtooth Inner Border and Le Moyne Star Corner Blocks.
1981. Cotton crib quilt. 31½ × 31½"

Ocean Waves. 1980. Cotton crib quilt. 31¾ × 32".
Collection Lois Sutter

Wild Goose Medallion with Flying Geese Border. 1980.
Cotton crib quilt. 34½ × 34½"

ter how badly out of tune it is, I don't really want it sounding like a beautiful Steinway. I want it to sound as I've grown to love it.

BLDD: Do you collect the work of any other craftspersons or artists as well?

SF: We collect Indian rugs and pottery and contemporary ceramics. My husband is a picture framer and, especially during the very early years of our marriage, we would usually barter. John would frame someone's exhibition in exchange for a print from the show. So mostly we have graphics, as opposed to oils. We also collect the work of anonymous craftsmen, not just from the nineteenth but the twentieth century.

BLDD: If you had the time or the funds or the assistance necessary, is there any particular project, a secret dream, that you would like to undertake?

SF: Yes. At this point in my life I would want to think in terms of time. I would love to do a national indexing of nineteenth-century American quilts. Extensive research could be fed into computers, bringing together provenance, patterns, fabrics, and current location of the quilts. Very few museums have a textile curator, let alone the necessary time and funds to put this kind of information together in a scholarly and meaningful manner.

That would be a very exciting and challenging project. I don't know that I would get more pleasure out of it than I do simply sitting and sewing, but it would be a nice thing to leave as a legacy.

BLDD: What patterns do you make most frequently?

SF: I love the Log Cabin. The log cabin itself was really what opened the American West. A man by himself, just one man with an ax, could go out from the eastern seaboard into the piney woods and could put up a log cabin for his family quick enough to provide immediate, necessary shelter yet sturdy enough to last for generations. And at the same time the cabins were being built, the American quiltmaker was developing what is to me the classic American quilt pattern, a log cabin. Its geometric form is based on the same principle: simple strips of logs, but in this case, textiles. And of course there are endless variations, from straight furrow, to barn raising, to zigzag. Visually it's one of the most exciting patterns and, simply because of the connection with the opening of the frontiers, one of the most historically meaningful.

BLDD: You have some older textiles that are sitting here between us. Can you tell us what this is?

SF: Paper. It's in fact an English method of piecing in

Roman Stripe Variation. 1980. Cotton crib quilt. 32 × 32″

and then translating it into cloth is almost like painting by numbers. That's not the way I like to work.

BLDD: Why don't you take us through the steps that you use to make a quilt?

SF: I generally begin with the fabric, or a particular pattern to which that fabric recommends itself. I want my quilts to have the naiveté or spontaneity that to me is a hallmark of nineteenth-century quilts. I begin by cutting out squares, rectangles, or whatever shapes are contained in that geometric pattern. I then sew one block together. Sometimes I work only with a large area, almost a central medallion, which is really a form from quilts of the eighteenth century. Once the central area is done, I begin sewing the more or less intricate bordering. When I decide that's done I put on an initial binding. I then put down a cotton back, add a cotton batting, add the quilt top, stand back and give it a loving look, baste it, and then begin quilting. Quilting is really the most overlooked part of twentieth-century quilts. Quiltmakers today often look upon quilting as something that's simply going to get the whole thing together. In fact, the act of quilting, that step of holding back, bat, and top together, is the frosting on the cake. It adds dimension to the quilt, and a whole new linear element.

BLDD: Are there any colors that you prefer to use?

SF: I work mostly in earth tones. I like the blues, the browns, the colors that would have been obtainable for a nineteenth-century woman had she been dyeing her own fabrics.

BLDD: You're known as a lap quilter. Does that mean you can work anyplace, anytime that you'd like to?

SF: Yes, and I do. I generally work throughout the house, which is where nineteenth-century quiltmakers worked. I do not have quilting bees. I do all the work by myself and I don't use a sewing machine. I don't even mention those words! I work when and where the spirit moves me, which is at least one or two hours a day.

BLDD: Can you tell us how you live in Los Angeles?

SF: We live on a hill above a lake in an area of Los Angeles originally called Angeleno Heights. It used to be very fashionable and still contains some of the best examples of the Victorian architecture in the city. Our home is somewhat unusual in Los Angeles in that it is completely surrounded by trees. One really doesn't get the sense of being in the city. The house is very small, made smaller by the fact that we collect practically everything under the sun. It is a home that I hope presents a picture of a couple — three, when our daughter is home from college — who is interested in a number of things, good books, good music, beautiful textiles, warm things that tell something about us.

which the hexagons were sewn around paper shapes, instead of simply sewn one to another as we usually piece. I brought this one out to show you because paper, of course, was very precious in those days. The woman would take a young child's composition papers or old letters and she would cut them into her hexagon patterns. The wonderful thing about this one is the writing that you can see on each; sometimes it is just a letter of the alphabet written over and over. But on one of them there is the word life, and on another there is the word death. That's one of those unanswered questions you think about in the dead of night.

BLDD: What is your method of designing and making a quilt? How do you begin?

SF: Differently, I must say, from most twentieth-century quiltmakers. My background is — blessedly, I think — not in art and design. I design intuitively, as did the early quiltmakers. And I work from the center out. I do not, in most cases, draft the design on graph paper. I do that only rarely, when I want to get some sense of dimension. I do absolutely nothing but manipulate pieces of fabric until I have centered on a particular block. When that's done, I see what looks good for a border. I simply work my way out. To me, putting the pattern on graph paper

Jacques Francais *owns a studio and workshop where one can witness the remarkable restoration and eventual transformation of wood and strings into objects of visual excellence and instruments of musical splendor. A violin is considered a work of art by most serious musicians. For listeners, the sound this fragile instrument makes is almost mystical. If a stringed instrument is damaged by neglect, accident, or simply age, it takes the patience and precision of a surgeon to mend it. For Jacques Francais, restoring damaged instruments to their former acoustic and visual beauty is a labor of love, as well as a business. His repair shop is the nation's most important for stringed instruments. Jacques Francais and Rene Morel, the master craftsman who runs the repair shop, are known as the men on whom many of the world's most demanding musicians rely to ensure their fullest musical expression.*

BLDD: Players of stringed instruments are said to be unique among musicians because of their attachment to their instruments. Is that true?

JF: I believe that all players are very involved with their instruments. And a string player may be even more so because he has more physical contact with the instrument. It's the only instrument for which the right hand and the left hand are not doing the same thing. And the potential for modeling and tracing colors in the sound is much more developed. Nevertheless, a pianist like Arthur Rubinstein travels with his own piano.

BLDD: Those who play the instruments are obviously not the only ones who cherish them. What is it about the restoration of stringed instruments that first attracted you and that continues to sustain your interest?

JF: I take enormous satisfaction in discovering an instrument in a terrible state of disrepair, which has been mistreated over the years by poor judgment in restoration, or by the player, and in completely rehabilitating the instrument to its former beauty, in both physical appearance and sound. Sometimes she might come without a scroll; sometimes the scroll has been replaced over the years. And it's also a challenge to find a scroll from the same maker on another instrument, and to reunite the two.

BLDD: You've just referred to the musical instrument as "she." Is that usual?

JF: No, not necessarily. It depends on the fiddle. Sometimes I think of a violin in a feminine way and sometimes in a masculine way.

BLDD: Is that judgment on the basis of its shape?

JF: Exactly. I would say this is a more feminine-looking fiddle, or this one is very masculine. The masculine type is usually created in the later part of the life of the violin maker, when the hands become heavier and the character of his trademark becomes heavier.

BLDD: When and where did instrument making begin? I always think of famous violins coming from Italy.

JF: Well, nobody really knows. There has been lots of research and discussion on the subject. I believe personally that the stringed instrument was created in the Middle Ages, in Europe.

BLDD: What evidence do you have toward that end?

JF: Because we have very old instruments in the Middle Ages of all kinds of rustic forms with one or two strings, for example, like the rebec, which was already an instrument with the string being worked by a bow. And at about the same period of time, the gigue, similar to an instrument called the ravanastrone, developed, which is also similar to the rebec. But I think nobody is going to find out much more unless research is done. The first violin that we know of came out of Italy in the sixteenth century. And most likely the first that we have is probably by a maker named Andrea Amati, who was the founder of the Cremonese school. A maker in Germany came much later on, in the seventeenth century. The other Italian maker of the same period was Gaspar da Salo, who was a Brescian maker. I imagine that the Brescian school and the Cremonese school came about at the same time.

BLDD: The names that are familiar to most of us are Stradivari and Guarnieri. Who were they, and where did they work?

JF: They both worked in the beginning of the eighteenth century, and both became famous during their lifetimes, especially Stradivari. Guarnieri became famous later, in the nineteenth century, when a very famous and sparkling violinist by the name of Niccolò Paganini started to play a Guarnerius del Gesù. Before that, Stradivari was the most well known, together with a German maker by the name of Jacobus Stainer, who was making violins at the same period as Nicolò Amati. Nicolò Amati was the teacher of Antonio Stradivari.

BLDD: Over how long a period were violins produced in their workshops?

JF: It depends on the lifetime of each maker, naturally, which varies a great deal. For example, Stradivari died at the rather old age of ninety-four.

BLDD: Is there any evidence of how many violins Stradivari produced?

JF: It's very hard to tell. If we study the life of Stradivari, or the compilation of the volumes made by Herbert Goodkind, it turns out that at least eight hundred violins were made. Some years, like 1706, for example, only five or six violins were made.

BLDD: What happened then?

JF: We feel there was a great plague in Italy. And either everyone must have had to leave Cremona to escape the plague, or Stradivari was sick himself or went away for other reasons. But you do find periods when there was practically no production.

BLDD: And of the eight hundred violins that you know were produced there, how many still exist?

JF: Well, those eight hundred are what's left. He must have had a much larger production than that, because a lot of them have disappeared in wars, revolutions, and airplane crashes. This number of violins is what we know today is in existence. For example, Jacques Thibaud died in an airplane accident, together with his violin. So did Jeanette Neveu. Some violins have been stolen and have never reappeared.

BLDD: How is it possible for an instrument that is so old to produce such remarkably perfect sound?

JF: That is the key question. The sound of the Italian school of the eighteenth century is recognized as being the most important, the most interesting, and the most beautiful. That's why all the great soloists play either a Stradivarius or a Guarnerius on the stage.

BLDD: With all that we know today about technology, why can't we reproduce that same sound?

JF: We can duplicate a Stradivarius to a tenth of a millimeter. We can choose very old pieces of wood. We can do everything that those makers did, exactly the way

they did it, with the same tools. The only thing we cannot duplicate is the filler that goes in the wood. This has been oxidized over the years, and scientists and chemists have been trying to find out the secret of the Italian varnish of the eighteenth century. The filler is liquid which is applied to the violin before varnishing and sinks into the grain of the wood. I believe it must have been a very simple product that was bought at the corner drugstore, since everybody in Italy in the eighteenth century knew about that filler. You can see it on any kind of eighteenth-century violin — that golden reflection in the wood. It disappeared at the end of the nineteenth

Three views of the Greffuhle,
an inlaid and highly decorated
violin made by Antonio Stradivarius,
dated 1709

century, most likely because modern technology came
with quick-drying varnish. I assume that special filler
took months to dry. If you look at the correspondence
between Stradivari and the people who were buying from
him, you see that when the varnish was finished, he still
would not be able to deliver for another six or eight
months because the varnish had to dry.

BLDD: Do you use the same procedure when you restore
instruments here?

JF: Well, we really can't, because we don't have the secret. We would love to have the secret.

BLDD: Are you working on the secret?

JF: Of course. Everybody is trying all his lifetime to find
the secret. Sometime, someday, I hope somebody will
come up with it!

BLDD: Do you have any formula of your own with which
you experiment?

JF: Naturally, everybody does.

BLDD: Any success?

JF: Might be. . . .

BLDD: What today is so valued about a Stradivarius or
a Guarnerius as an instrument? Is it its age, its tone, or
its color?

JF: Well, the violin is primarily an object which is

meant to be used. The main reason why Stradivariuses are so much in demand is because they're extraordinarily good-sounding instruments. The esthetic aspect of the violin is something different.

BLDD: What about your own career? Do you come from a family of musicians or restorers of musical instruments?

JF: In my family, we've been violin makers from father to son for about two hundred years. We come from a small village in France named Mièrecourt, which is called the "cradle of violin making," in France. It is the equivalent of Mittenwald, a village in Germany. Practically all violin makers come from those two sources. Cremona was a center in the eighteenth century, but is no longer. In the seventeenth century, the Duke of Lorraine brought to the city of Mièrecourt a number of makers from outside and created a school that still exists today. A new school was created about ten years ago, and the pupils have become violin makers of great talent.

BLDD: In this two-hundred-year tradition in your family, was there a violin maker or restorer in every generation?

JF: There was another industry in town: lacework. My great-grandfather had a lacework factory in Mièrecourt. But his father was a violin maker as were my grandfather and my father. At the end of the nineteenth century the family moved to Paris, where they eventually took over the most famous shop founded by Nicolas Lupot in 1788. Since I wasn't ready to go back to France, the old place had to be closed last summer.

BLDD: Did you ever question which direction your own work would take — that you would be the member of your generation to be a violin maker or restorer?

JF: I would say that from the age of eight, there was no question as to what I was going to become. And I like to say that I was a violin maker before I was born, due to the long tradition in the family. We are only two boys in the family, and my brother became a diplomat; he is now an ambassador. So, of course, I had to become the violin maker. There was very little choice left for me. If you want to be a craftsman — and I think every violin dealer should learn the tradition and the making of violins from the beginning — it's very important that you start young, I would say at around twelve, which is when I did. On my days off, I worked in my father's office.

BLDD: Is it also very important for every violin maker to be a violin player as well?

JF: To some extent, yes. You don't have to be a professional violinist, but it certainly helps to understand the production of sound to be able to play the violin.

BLDD: Are you a musician yourself?

JF: I play cello very badly.

BLDD: Playing them on any sustained basis is probably the only relationship that you don't have with stringed instruments. You are an appraiser, a businessman, a

craftsman, and a dealer. You spend a great deal of your time traveling around the world hunting down rare instruments. How much of your time do you spend on each of these specialties?

JF: Well, I worked at the bench for my first twenty years in New York. And because the pressure of the business became so strong, and since Rene Morel came with me, he took over the repair shop. I abandoned my craft at the bench, and I concentrated on doing the appraisal, the buying, and the selling.

BLDD: Rene Morel, how did you become a restorer of violins and stringed instruments?

RM: I first began as a violin maker — as all my ancestors were since 1780 — to please my family. But I always overheard talk about the famous violinists who owned those great violins, and about the great violin makers and restorers who were in contact with those artists. That fascinated me . . . I really wanted to be in the ac-

Carved scroll of a violin made by Jean Joseph Honoré Derazey (1794–1883), copied from a violin by Duiffopruggar, a 16th-century maker

84

tion with the stars. So I decided that if I wanted to do that, I had to go where the great instruments were, here in America. So I came to this country, and was able to get employment in a shop where a great man was, by the name of Sacconi, who really opened my eyes to those famous instruments. My education from France as a violin maker plus the exposure to restoration with Mr. Sacconi caused me to decide to stay with restoration, and that's where I am today.

BLDD: Is it necessary to be a fine musician yourself in order to be able to restore instruments?

RM: I don't believe so, because I am not a musician. . . . The only instrument I play is to ring the bell for lunch! I don't play any instrument at all.

BLDD: How do you explain your incredible, unerring appreciation of sound? People come from all over the world to have you adjust a string here, a sound post there. . . .

RM: Sound is the same thing as developing an eye for painting, or a taste for food, or drink, or whatever. And if you study the right way and work on that sense, you will automatically develop it.

BLDD: Have you ever discovered something very special as a result of an appraisal of a violin?

JF: In thirty years of appraising, I have never discovered a Stradivarius that was not yet known. Not one. Nor has my father, and he's eighty years of age, nor my grandfather, who died at eighty-three. So far none of us have discovered an unknown Stradivarius.

BLDD: So as for the violin in the attic, should we abandon hope that it is a Stradivarius?

JF: It could be the violin with the Stradivarius label that was produced commercially by the thousands in the 1920's. People find them and their hopes rise because they think they have found the treasure.

BLDD: In traveling the world in search of violins, the trick is not to sell them, but to find them. How do you go about tracking down the violins that are the rarest and the most precious? Can you tell us some of your secrets?

JF: It's not a secret. Most of them have gone through my hands or the hands of someone in my family in the past. And violin makers keep a special relationship with their customers and their violins.

BLDD: And their customers' families?

JF: Exactly. We visit each other; we talk to each other. I usually know where most of my fiddles are. And sooner or later they come back to me.

BLDD: Where in your travels around the world do you discover the rare and precious instruments?

JF: In Italy, you still, amazingly enough, find violins in their pure condition. Violins that have stayed in one family for two hundred years.

BLDD: Has that happened to you recently?

JF: The last time it happened to me was in Argentina. I found an old Italian family who had been there about a hundred years. And they had a violin in its absolutely pure condition, with its original neck: "Besse Berre." I have now loaned the violin to the Metropolitan Museum of Art in New York City. I don't want to touch it; I want to leave it as is.

BLDD: Besides the maker of violins, like Stradivari or Guarnieri, are there other factors that determine the value of the instrument?

JF: Usually you start with the country of origin, the period in which it was made, the name of the maker, the condition of the instrument, its sound capability, and its visual beauty. When you have put all those answers together, then you can put a price on a violin.

BLDD: And when all of those factors come into play, what is the approximate value of a rare instrument nowadays?

JF: It varies greatly. Eighteenth-century Italian violins are now between twenty thousand and five hundred thousand dollars. One Stradivarius was sold recently for more than a million dollars. It was a very special Stradivarius.

BLDD: Where is the number-one violin in the world today?

JF: The number-one violin, nicknamed "The Messiah," is now in the Ashmolean Museum at Oxford. It's an amusing story. There was an Italian peddler of violins who used to travel from Cremona to Paris in the middle of the nineteenth century. He would sell his instruments to the most important dealers of Paris. And he was always talking about a fantastic violin that was absolutely like new, with a fantastic varnish, with beautiful choice of wood. For twenty years he talked to the Paris dealers about this violin. And he never brought it. So they finally said that this violin must be The Messiah. And when he died, one of the dealers, whose name was Vuillaume, went to Italy, greeted the family, and opening a drawer, found in his bedroom — The Messiah!

BLDD: Are there any contemporary masters who are making instruments of comparable quality to those in the past?

JF: Yes, there are some very important violin makers today who will be recognized or who are already recognized as masters. One great violin maker, Carl Becker in Chicago, in my opinion is comparable to one of the most important French makers of the nineteenth century. Another maker, who used to work in our shop, Luiz Bellini, decided to start making copies of Guarnerius del Gesù and has been extremely successful.

BLDD: What is the cost of the work of a contemporary master?

JF: The violin of a master today sells for around thirty-

Setting a groove for a silver ring on the side of
a frog with hand-bowed drill

Arching a cello being pressed into a corrective mold

five hundred to ten thousand dollars.

BLDD: What is the difference between restoration and repair?

RM: The repair of an instrument can have various stages of work progress. Repair, to me, is an instrument which has had an accident and a crack develops on one of the plates, top or back, or the neck comes loose. And you just put these parts back together and reinforce them with studs or a patch. Very skilled repair demands as much skill as restoration. Restoration is when an instrument has been totally repaired by different and various men who qualify themselves as repairmen. The result is that after one hundred years or so of various kinds of damage, the corners of an instrument are worn out; the arching sometimes loses its shape; the repair has been done unskillfully; the varnish is retouched in an ugly manner. So restoration will be to undo all of these poor repairs, reopen all those cracks, and put them back together to restore the original shape of the instrument. Then comes the varnish retouching.

BLDD: I've heard that sometimes it takes up to three years for an instrument to be restored from start to finish. Why so long?

RM: There is more than one profession in the skill of restoration. One is the wood cut, or the wood carving, fitting a new edge. Then you have varnish restoration.

BLDD: There are many stories, and I can understand why, about your ability to detect the source of an instrument's problem. What was your most unusual or most successful discovery?

RM: Discovery is not really the objective, I would say. But an instrument from a famous maker was known to be in Italy in a shop for many, many years. The instrument had been built as an extremely large one. Different craftsmen, repairmen, or restorers through the years attempted to put it in a normal shape. That instrument was a real mess, and no one wanted to get involved with it any longer to make it playable, with normal proportions. It took me over 530 hours of work, and I consider myself a fast worker. It was one of the most difficult restorations I did in my lifetime. But the pleasure is that that instrument, which was "left for dead," is now enjoyed by a great artist and also by the public who listens to his playing.

BLDD: Have you ever made a violin yourself?

RM: Oh yes, many violins. At Mièrecourt, in France,

Shaping a new bass bar on a violin

Shaping a new neck on a violin with a file

we were trained for skill and speed. And unless you were gifted and had the ability to handle your tools in a very special way they would not teach you. You would be given a trial period. And after that period, you have to be good, or else you wouldn't be advised to study violin making. When I was eighteen years old there, I had to build two violins a week, in the white, meaning without varnish. They demanded perfection.

BLDD: Do you consider what you do a craft, or an art, or both?

RM: It is a craft up to a certain limit. And then it becomes an art, according to the steps you take to pursue the highest skill in your craft.

BLDD: Is there a secret dream that you harbor? Is there anything you'd really like to do?

RM: I would like to be able to reproduce the ingredients that go inside the wood of the old Italian instruments, which give them that special Italian voice. Like everyone else in my field I am experimenting now. I don't think I will ever be satisfied in my lifetime.

BLDD: What's the most important skill for an expert restorer to possess?

RM: We mean by the word "restoration" that we want to

put the instrument back to the original shape, as the maker himself constructed it. The restorer must be able to see first what is the maker's sense of craft. Next, the restorer is supposed to be able to put it back as that maker originally desired.

BLDD: What makes your restoration techniques different from others'? Are there any things that you do here that are unique?

RM: Any colleagues who come in this shop can ask me anything. I have no secrets. As a youngster I was very, very hurt trying to get some advice from the violin shop in my own country. I said, "Someday if I reach my goal, I will not let anybody down if he asks me about anything."

BLDD: Jacques Francais, what kind of wood do you use or buy?

JF: Well, the eighteenth-century makers used all kinds of wood, whatever they could get, to make violins. The top is always spruce or pine. Today the back is always made of maple as it was in the eighteenth century. But when they couldn't find maple, they would also use pearwood, poplar, or willow.

BLDD: Where does the wood come from?

JF: The wood comes today mostly from Austria and

from Yugoslavia. In the eighteenth century the wood also came from Yugoslavia, just across from Venice. The local Italian maple was not good for sound.

BLDD: How do you acquire your wood?

JF: The wood we have today has been in the family for years. Thank God for that! My grandfather kept on buying woods over the years for the use of his children. We do buy wood, but we're not going to use it for ten or twenty years.

BLDD: What country is the center of violin making today?

JF: It's a good question. It has changed. The commercial violins, as well as some of the master violins, are made in Germany and France. But interestingly enough, the Japanese have started making commercial violins and are now competing with German violin making. And so have the Chinese. They needed a lot of violins in a

hurry, and they went to Italy and started to make their own violins. Some of them are quite good.

BLDD: It's frequently been commented on that, during the last fifty years, the leading violinists in the world have been of Russian-Jewish background. Is there any particular explanation?

RM: I must say that many of my customers, big stars, are of Jewish background. In the last decade, many violinists, cellists, and viola players have run away from Russia and come to the free world. They feel they have more liberty to perform whatever they want to. I think it has to do with the parents who induced the love of playing in a child at a very young age. And also, the ability of the parents to get that child to work, and give up all of the other amusements which are available to children these days. And if we have a great deal of Jewish violinists today, that is because they put in the effort to go through with it, and the result is not only talent, but it is lots of work, perseverance, willpower, and you name it — it's all there. . . .

BLDD: It seems to me that there is a resurgence of interest in the craft of making and restoring musical instruments in this country. Is that accurate, and how do you explain this renaissance?

JF: Ten or fifteen years ago, the kids who were eighteen to twenty-five returned to the desire to create with their own hands, along with the desire to grow things on their own. Some of those kids decided to learn to make violins. There was a great need for new instruments; there were not enough eighteenth-, nineteenth-, or twentieth-century instruments to satisfy the needs of the world. So today there is a renaissance in violin making, which is marvelous because we have all kinds of young makers. For example, in our shop we have four makers from American schools in Chicago and in Salt Lake City. They're very talented, very dedicated. And very anxious to learn. It's the first group of American makers born in this country.

BLDD: How many schools of violin making are there in this country?

JF: There are two, one in Salt Lake City and one in Chicago. Outside of this country, there is one in England, one in France, one in Germany, three in Switzerland, one in Italy, and one in Mexico.

BLDD: Rene Morel, is it true that this shop is different from most in that every craftsman knows how to do every part of the process?

RM: Yes. The fact is that we know every part. In order to accomplish full knowledge of restoration, it takes ten to fifteen years after apprenticeship of violin making, which is three to four years. You cannot train everyone who chooses to be a restorer. Some will end up being good repairmen, but never a restorer.

Rene Morel, head of the workshop, adjusting the sound post of a violin

The Greffuhle, after having been restored in the Francais shop by removing a coat of accumulated, dried-out rosin and polish

Workshop at Jacques Rare Violins, Inc.

Working on the inside of a violin's belly

BLDD: Mr. Francais, how does the shop operate?

JF: The shop operates strictly under the guidance of Mr. Morel. He will examine the instrument, judge what has to be done, take it to the shop, supervise the work, and distribute the work to whomever is able best to do that particular work. When it's an instrument that I own we discuss together what kind of repair the instrument will take and what should be done.

BLDD: Rene Morel is the vice-president of your company and the master of the repair shop. How did your collaboration begin?

JF: Well, when Rene came to this country, he went to work with one of the most important violin makers and restorers of all time, whose name was Fernando Sacconi. He was an Italian who was trained in Cremona and in Berlin, and was a genius at developing new techniques and new methods of restoration. Rene was fortunate enough to work with him for ten to fifteen years at the Wurlitzer shop. I spent two years at the Wurlitzer shop but not at that time, unfortunately. I wish I could have spent time with Sacconi. When he died, Rene decided to join forces with me and came to take over the workshop here. He developed his own school, to be another Sacconi. The kids come from all the schools to apply here in order to work under his guidance and learn not only what he has learned from Sacconi, but also techniques that he has developed on his own.

BLDD: Is there any one legendary instrument that you dream of finding some day?

JF: The one violin I've always wanted is the violin that was in my father's private collection and which I inherited by a game of chance. My mother died recently, and we separated the instruments in the collection and drew lots, and that one violin that I've wanted all my life came to me. It's a violin made by Blestrier. He's not one of the most important makers, but it's the most beautiful specimen I've ever seen, full of character, full of varnish, with spectacular choice of wood. It's a fiddle I've fallen in love with.

BLDD: And what is the most important or exciting discovery that you feel you've ever made?

JF: The greatest pleasure I've had was to have found a violin for Yehudi Menuhin. I found a Guarnerius del Gesù called the "Wilton," which is one of the most important violins made by Guarnieri. We are friends from childhood, and he's always said, "Jacques, when you find a Guarnerius del Gesù, please let me know." And I had the great pleasure three years ago of finding the violin and having Yehudi acquire it. That was exciting!

Main reception room of the Francais shop

Nuage (detail). 1981. Cotton wall hanging. 40 × 20′

Sheila Hicks, *fiber artist and textile designer, does works that range in scale from the miniature to the monumental and include such unpredictable materials as institutional linen and sweepings from the studio floor. Her work proclaims the enduring beauty of cloth in whatever humble form she uses. Since 1980, she has been the editor and publisher of the bible of the world textile industry,* American Fabrics and Fashions *in New York City.*

BLDD: To begin with, how do you define "fiber arts" and what different media does the label refer to? How long has the term been in use and what does it mean to you?

SH: I think that one can easily say that working with fiber is probably as ancient as any human activity. Recognizing things made out of fiber as "art" rather than as purely functional or merely decorative is a relatively recent occurrence and has happened within my lifetime. As for myself, I can trace my interest in fiber arts to my discovery of anthropological collections. The origin of museums stems from cabinets or curiosities beginning in the sixteenth century, more interestingly called *Kunstkammern* in German, that included collections of artifacts brought back by explorers, conquerors, and travelers. Many of the items were made of fiber and have been reclassified from curiosities to art. We continue to make and use textiles. Although utilitarian, they have also come to be thought of as fiber art. So you see, "fiber arts" is a term that encompasses a lot of things. Art in public spaces is one example. Large fiber sculpture, something that might be thought of as "soft sculpture," can also be called "fiber art." A thread bas-relief would also be called simply a bas-relief without qualifying it as soft or thread. Examples are the two large walls that I made in the Ford Foundation building and the floor-to-ceiling surface I covered in the walk-in lobby of the Galleria on Fifty-seventh Street, both in New York City.

BLDD: When did you first start to create fiber art on such a scale? What's your earliest large commissioned public piece?

SH: A wall hanging for the ground floor of CBS on Fifty-third Street. It happened at one of those luncheons where people discuss what might be brought into their already existing space. As I remember, the interior architect considered his job finished, but the client, the president or a director of CBS, felt something was lacking. After lunch a consultant from the Museum of Modern Art walked across the street to the museum and returned with something on her back like a big shaggy dog — it was an enormous, white wool wall hanging I had made in a rug workshop in Wuppertal, Germany. She lugged it over to them and said, "For instance?" When the interior architect saw the wall hanging, he agreed that on the massive granite walls it might be worthwhile. That was the winter of 1964. This small version weighed about sixty pounds and was about seven or eight feet high. They ordered one more than twice that size. It is still hanging today. It didn't cost very much at that time. I made it in an industrial workshop and didn't consider it a work of art.

BLDD: That took place soon after you were a student.

SH: I began at Yale in 1954, received my Bachelor of Fine Arts degree, then left for Chile on a Fulbright Scholarship to paint and to study pre-Columbian textiles.

BLDD: What influence did Yale, in general, and specifically your professor Josef Albers, have on you?

SH: Color and clarity. Articulateness, reverence, room to create. I think Albers's poetic dimension influenced me. His view of the world was visual. People have ac-

St. Gobain (detail). 1978. Linen and silk. 6 × 13′

Baby Time Again (detail). 1980. 9½ × 15′

Le Démêlior. 1977. 8 tons of washed laundry placed in front of stitched linen hanging. 20 × 31′

Soft Sculpture of Nurses' Blouses. 1979. 24½ × 42½'

cused him of having a reduced vision and of being auto-cratic, and yet he opened up vast horizons for all his students. We were all bedeviled by Albers. He poked us all the time with a prickly pear. I know it worked for a lot of students. A few may have gone under, but I doubt it.

BLDD: Was there anything else that was happening in the art world at the time that was influential or impressive for you?

SH: Negatively, yes: the big macho abstract expressionist routine and the painters being shown in New York galleries in those days.

BLDD: Is that what prompted you to move to Mexico?

SH: I might have gone to teach in an art school. Unlike today, there were a lot of teaching opportunities then. Or I could have come to New York, facing up to the shock of trying to work in this city. Or, as a third idea, I could have dug back into indigenous cultures, which was

my inclination. I thought I could learn from practical experience, in an unfamiliar rural culture away from the theories of the schools and the roughness of the cities. That notion still persists.

BLDD: Whatever gave you the idea to go to Yale in the first place?

SH: A fellow student at Syracuse University in 1953. We were doing well but we didn't feel challenged. We felt we could come up against bigger and greater and harder tasks. And she came up with the idea that we should go to Yale. She applied and talked me into applying. She went for her interview and I didn't even go because I was sure we wouldn't make it. She was sure we would, and she got us both accepted. But then she committed suicide — gassed herself. I had to decide whether to go or not. I couldn't go back to Syracuse in the fall after that. She had shoved me into the tunnel so I went the

96

Strip Tease. 1981. Textile volume of ripped cotton. 13 × 3½'

whole way. There weren't very many girls at Yale at the time, but Albers was extremely helpful because he was a big paternalistic figure.

BLDD: Was Anni Albers influential as well?

SH: She was not on the scene. You really had to scrape around to find out where she was and what happened to her. She wasn't teaching and she didn't lecture. We just knew about her. We knew that she had been active at the Bauhaus and that her field was textiles. Actually, I met her because of a course on pre-Columbian art that I took with George Kubler. He showed us Peruvian textiles and I decided to do a term paper on them. He advised me to seek out Anni Albers as an advisor for the term paper. Her husband took me home to tea one day so that we could meet and I could show her the paper. It soon became apparent, with her guidance over the next three or four months, that the exciting thing about the

Peruvian textiles was to decipher how they were made. She was as articulate as her husband and inspired those who were in contact with her to work hard in a disciplined and focused way. I later developed the paper into my MFA thesis, and she and Junius Bird helped me with that. I more or less lost contact until I visited her just two weeks ago. Her question to me that I thought was the most indicative of her present outlook was, "Sheila, how can you continue to work with that perishable medium?" She herself gave away all her looms and put her threads in exile in 1970. She thought she had been taken seriously as a teacher and an educator, but not as an artist. She may not realize how important an artist we have always considered her.

BLDD: When did you first begin to discover the singular properties of textiles and fiber?

SH: At Yale we did a lot of experimental work with

View of studio with miniatures

wood, plexiglass, drawing, color, photography, and printmaking, but when I found weaving and thread and textiles, I had found myself. And I have never left it. Nor will I ever — unless I renounce myself! But that doesn't mean I haven't done other things, too.

BLDD: Today when someone refers to a tapestry, is it a hanging wall mural that is designed by one person and created by another? What does the term mean exactly?

SH: Large workshops here and abroad work that way. Others have renounced that as a method and are lobbying very strongly for the do-it-yourself approach: you think it up and you do it. I used to be a grand militant for thinking it up and doing it myself. But I must admit that I have found it rewarding to work in textile factories with industry and even in tapestry workshops, thinking up

ideas within the discipline and examining the range of each production possibility.

BLDD: What caused you to change your view? Was it a particular circumstance or experience, or the fact that you could no longer fabricate on the scale that you wanted to?

SH: In the beginning, as an art student graduating from an art academy, I sought to gain a particular identity. I wanted to develop my own personal language, to be identified with it and to be known for it. Later on it was enough simply to be doing things. I will play with anyone's string, in any situation, as a challenge to try and invent something new. For example, in an industrial complex for cotton-jersey knits in Israel, I went to see how they were cutting out T-shirts. I tried to invent

Back from the Front. 1980. Soldiers' uniforms attached by knotting.
26 × 23'

forms with discarded fabric on the cutting tables. I sculpted with electric saws, almost the way you see it done in
marble quarries in Italy — the way they saw out hunks of
marble. I tried to saw thick layers of cotton-jersey textiles
into shapes, and also to respect the shapes of the T-shirt
patterns. Of course, that doesn't have anything to do
with the purpose of the factory itself. What it did was
help the people in the factory to look at what they were
doing and to think about the shapes, including the
throwaway shapes, and to think about what we call art. I
took something out of commonplace, everyday life. The
result was later shown in the Israel Museum in Jerusalem
with thoughtful lighting and in juxtaposition with hard
materials. It was quite fascinating to see a transformation
into textile art, or fiber art.

BLDD: How do you select the scale for an idea? Your
work ranges from the miniature to the monumental. Is it
in reaction to a commission or do you initiate the idea
yourself?

SH: It's simpler than that. It's not even prethought. What
happens is that I work all the time. I don't consider
it work. I suppose I'm fooling around all the time with
thread. I work on the plane while I travel in whatever
size I can manage, which is why it sometimes is so tiny.
Once off the plane, if I'm in someone's office and they're
showing me walls or plans, I can invent on a bigger scale
and I start imagining a bigger thing — such as the project
I just finished this month for the Embarcadero Center in
San Francisco. John Portman, the architect, asked me to
make things for two concrete walls, each thirty-five feet
high. There I built up two linen cascades.

BLDD: Do you sew?

SH: I darn a lot. Socks. Simple clothes. Functional
darning to reinforce something and also just darning to
play with the darning stitch on a flat surface. It's quite
beautiful.

BLDD: How did you ever learn the stitches?

SH: I'm self-taught. I've never studied in a textile
school. I've never gone to a technical training school.

BLDD: Did you ever feel that was a limitation or did it
liberate you to experiment?

SH: I think it was liberating. I can compare it with
something I'm doing right now. I didn't know much
about publishing, but for the last eighteen months I've
been editing and publishing a magazine. Weaving textiles and textile art are very much the same thing. I've
never studied it formally but I've looked for ways to find
out about it as problems occurred. I've looked for ways to
fight my way out of a paper bag whenever I found myself
in one.

BLDD: The magazine that you're referring to was called
American Fabrics when it was started in 1946. When you
were a student at Yale it was not very old, but at that
time it was already considered the bible of the worldwide
textile industry. Is that accurate?

SH: That's the way people have been referring to it, in
the sense of its origins and history.

BLDD: Now you are the editor and publisher of it. The
magazine is now called *American Fibers and Fashions.*
How did you first become involved?

SH: Back to Yale again. We would escape from New
Haven during the weekend and come to New York to see
exhibitions and explore, and as we were coming to the
end of our schooling, we'd take drawings and photographs and slides of our work and show people in New
York, hoping someone might express interest. One of the
places I visited was *American Fabrics* magazine. It was a

magazine I had seen in the Yale library. I had noted the names of magazines that interested me, but when I came to see them in New York, I never got past the secretary's desk, except at *American Fabrics*. There they were quite cordial, and the editor and publisher took the time to look at my work. That was William C. Segal, who founded the magazine at the end of World War II. He had published several magazines, among them, *Gentry*, *Women's Reporter*, and *Men's Reporter*, all related to fashion and mostly trade magazines. Segal was an artist and still is. We remained in contact through the years. I was a free-lance stringer for the magazine, sending a photo-reportage once in a while, knowing that it would be looked at instead of merely filed or trashed. And our relationship grew over the years. Recently there has been an explosion of interest in textile art, and *AFF* started regularly publishing a lot about it. Then Mr. Segal decided to retire and invited me to step in.

BLDD: Why did you take on such a responsibility, particularly when you have so much work to do of your own?

SH: I didn't know what I was getting into! I'm learning about designing and layout, production, printing, photography, typography, communication, and textiles. It's really a handmade magazine, and it has subscribers in seventy countries.

BLDD: I guess it wasn't until about 1850 that man-made fibers were produced at all; now over 75 percent of all fibers that are used by American mills for textiles and for industrial products are man-made. What are the advantages of man-made fibers?

SH: We don't compare them any longer. People used to think in terms of either/or. Then we started working with all kinds of textures of fibers, and all kinds of mixed yarns. The mixing and the spinning of the textures is where all the fun is today; it's giving the people who work with textiles many more possibilities to invent new worlds.

BLDD: Textures and surface values have interested you for a very long while. You were one of the first to wrap what I would call fiber elements into a spiral form that made a sort of undulating landscape.

SH: I created a handwoven cotton textile in India in 1965. One of the designs, Badagara, is still on the market today and is considered an unusual fabric. The weft is stuffed with irregularly placed short, pea-pod-size bags of loose cotton. I got the idea from collecting thread sweepings after a day's work on a loom. The finished fabric is a half-inch thick in places. The stuffing is embedded into place by subsequent weft shots. This fabric has been used extensively for wall covering, place mats, upholstery, and outer apparel.

BLDD: Besides India, I know you've worked extensively

in other countries. What kind of commissions have you tackled?

SH: Probably my major commissions and best work have not been within the United States' borders but in Mexico, France, West Germany, Morocco, Holland, Sweden, Israel, Togo, and Saudi Arabia.

BLDD: Certainly in many of those places there is a great tradition of well-woven textiles. Why don't we talk about some of the specific things that you've done — for example, in Montreuil, where a particular site determined the kind of work that you created.

SH: It's a suburb right outside of Paris, except you can't tell where Paris ends and Montreuil begins when you get off the Metro. I worked for four months for the municipal government on a project concerning thread that did not have the finality of being a permanent installation or an exhibition. The project was to work with thread within their communities, within the established social structure — for example, in senior-citizen centers, nursery schools, day-care centers, school art departments, an adult night school. I worked alongside the educators and instructors and just planted the idea of working with thread. We not only made things with thread, we collected existing things made with thread. We'd looked through the supermarket, through the popular street markets, through the individual homes and attics and basements for things made of thread that had some meaning to the individuals in the community. They brought to meetings things that they liked made of thread and we looked at them together and thought about them. The community photographed, documented, and brainstormed the subject of thread. You might say it's an ethnological approach to becoming conscious of thread in the community. And then we made a presentation in the community center, which is usually devoted to automobile shows or conventions or political meetings. It became a wonderful, ritualistic gathering on the subject of thread.

BLDD: You use so many terms that relate to anthropology: structuralist, ethnological, ritualistic. . . .

SH: I don't pretend to understand all that anthropologists are doing, but I am fascinated. I go to Claude Lévi-Strauss's lectures on Tuesday afternoons, whenever I am in Paris. A lot of anthropologists are interested in the textiles and weaving of indigenous cultures. I've been to meetings of the American Anthropological Association and found them very interesting because the discipline involved in anthropology is different from that involved in art. The kind of methodical research that anthropologists do is very structured and "objective." The methods artists use are subjective. I'm functioning for the most part as an artist. But I find that attempting to gain access to this labyrinth and maze

Uxmal Pockets. 1981. Cotton wall hanging. 10 × 6′

of other disciplines and other professions helps me extend my own limited subjective view of things and to think in different ways. The scholars observe, record, and interpret, whereas I react and emote: I can clamber around on their scaffolding. So I parachute into ethnological gatherings and listen to how people talk about culture. For better or worse, it makes me more self-conscious. I realize that I'm living and working in the last quarter of the twentieth century.

BLDD: One of the problems with many commissions is that often clients want a repetition of your last work. And your whole approach to things is the next project. How do you deal with that issue?

SH: My work sometimes seems repetitious because I keep working on two or three central ideas. One is corrupting weaving — taking the simple structures of weaving and eccentrically playing with them. Another is taking the established patterns and methods of constructing textiles, once you've studied them historically, and then doing something hysterically with them. There aren't many possibilities, after all, with thread. Add many together, find a way to hold them together, or once held together find a way to splay them open and let them drop apart. These themes are very limited: held together, broken loose, flat, three-dimensional. Then you start outlining them and diagraming them, and try to find things that you have not yet discovered. And once you've discovered something, or think you have, look at it and realize that it has already been done by some tribe in Africa or Indonesia. One investigates how they did it, and then returns to the idea, working it again, and then realizes that the new idea has already been done in Japan or in India. There are really only a few ideas that one keeps working on continuously.

BLDD: What's your third central idea?

SH: To work with thread elegantly. I try to avoid sensationalism and theatricality. My own secret desire is to give the work a classic timelessness, defying the observer to pigeonhole it in time or space. One of the most important things is to respect the material that is your vehicle. Elegance can be expressed very simply.

I'm making an exhibition in a small gallery on the Kaisergracht in Amsterdam right now. I have a lot of washed hospital linen that I got for an exhibition in Sweden. In the past I've piled it up and made volumes almost like carved ice blocks, but this time I sewed it together; for one piece I cut up the material and shredded it into long strips. The sound was frightening! Then I dyed the shreds in my kitchen washing machine so that they were all different tones of rose and terra-cotta and I also left some white. They started unraveling and dethreading, which made them very lively. Then I hung them from the second-story balcony in the small gallery,

in a long, tall totem shape. When I came back a week later, the gallery owner told me an incredible story. A man had come to the gallery twice and was sitting on the steps at the entrance. He told her that he found this piece — he didn't know what to call it — that was quite gay. He said he'd like to have it. He identified himself as the warden or administrator of the Amsterdam prison. In a way this story reveals what I am most touched by and interested in these days: the concept, the idea, the surprise — imagine taking materials that have already seen action, that have been checked out of the stocks of a hospital and were about to go to the rag dealer, and recycling them into art for a magic moment, and then having someone want them. For a prison!

BLDD: How much of the character of the pieces that you create are determined by the site itself?

SH: Mostly I carry ideas around in my head, things I want to make or do, and, like a bloodhound, I scout out and stay alert to situations in which I can realize those ideas. Sometimes someone will actually ask me to walk into a space and think about doing something for it. Recently the authorities of a government building contacted me about doing a large piece for their public space. I asked them if they wanted decoration, a theatrical presence, or some shocking reality. I wondered what they thought of as a work of art when they commissioned one for their building; it could be all of those things or none of them. It then occurred to me that I should investigate the peculiarities of the region to try to make something that's not only my preconceived idea but also would reflect the experience of discovering that special place at that time. So my idea was not just to go back to my Paris studio, make something for the building, and ship it to the site, but to attempt to live and work for a time with the local residents and to find appropriate local materials and invent with them.

BLDD: What experience are you trying to create for the audience who views the environment?

SH: An emotional response of one kind or another — a connection, which is not necessarily pleasant, but it must be meaningful.

BLDD: And what experience are you trying to create for yourself when you create an environment?

SH: Just that I must feel that each work is a step further along and in a new direction. That I can learn from it in order to continue.

BLDD: What is the next thing you are going to make?

SH: Three shows mounted in three weeks in the museums of Perth, Sydney, and Adelaide, in Australia. All the materials used will be local materials.

BLDD: What are they?

SH: In Adelaide it will be textile water bags people tie to their car radiators when they drive into the bush. They

will be used water bags: a notice is being put in the newspaper asking everyone who would like to lend their water bags to participate in the exhibition in this way. We did this once in Lund, Sweden, where people lent their sheets.

BLDD: Do you feel more connected to material after it's been created and used by others?

SH: I'm quite fascinated by these things already used. I like to see the traces of life. I like old people very much. I've always had friends who are "senior citizens," the wise old ones.

BLDD: And what effect does that have on your work?

SH: I like materials that have been used because you imagine all the different things they have gone through, and because they have survived. Survivors are important. In fact I've started doing some articles on the survivors I know, on some of the wonderful people who are in their eighties and very much "with it." I really go for old people who've seen a lot of action, and I go for cloth that's seen a lot of action, too. I think I may have described to you the sculpture I made in Israel of khaki pants and shirts that were borrowed from the army warehouse. They had been to war.

BLDD: What is the first work of that kind that you did?

SH: Darning socks. I think I can trace this interest back to a day in the Carmelite Convent in Boulogne [Billancourt], near Paris. I was working with the nuns there, making a tapestry for an Air France airplane. None of them had ever been in a plane, and we thought of the work as if we were decorating Jonah's space in the whale's belly. As we looked at it someone said, "This really looks like darning." We were skipping spaces and sewing irregularly, and it was almost a darning stitch. Then someone went to the cupboard and took out some socks and said, "If you like darning, look at these." She showed me beautiful, repaired socks that had been worn out on the bottom, on the sole instead of at the heel or the toe, because the nuns wear clogs. When I looked at them I saw them as footprints, darned, worn, repaired; they were lovely. Then she pulled out fragments of sheets —fine wool sheets that had been darned for reinforcement with white stitching on white wool cloth in long striations, crisscrossing back and forth. I held one up to the light and it looked like an embossed or engraved cloth. I showed them to my friend who directs the Museum of Decorative Arts in Paris, François Mathey, and he put them in an exhibition of things made by craftsmen without the intention of being art and which are nevertheless worth looking at.

The Carmelite darned panels were strange mutations, and we didn't know how to consider them. They were among the most provocative pieces in the exhibition. From then on I began looking more and more at con-

ditioned cloths that had been used and had been cherished by someone enough to take the trouble to give them greater longevity. I started becoming very tenderly disposed toward all repaired cloth — cloth that seemed as though it had had many lives.

BLDD: Do you keep a daily sketch book?

SH: I have ever since I can remember. I have kept notebooks for thirty-five years. But sometimes I don't write anything for four or five days.

BLDD: With such a highly structured and mobile existence, how can your life be spontaneous?

SH: Spontaneity can be enjoyed by those who have the will to structure their time so that they have free time.

BLDD: In addition to being a weaver, you're a publisher and editor. Did you ever expect your life to evolve the way it has?

SH: No.

BLDD: What did you have in mind?

SH: Probably teaching at some outpost or border town.

BLDD: Is there any project that you have yet to do that you'd care to do?

SH: I'd like to plan a presentation of textiles that have had former lives. I'd like to show the exhibition in New York. The New York art public is rather tired and cynical, and the general New York public isn't interested in art at all. I'd almost like to do it anonymously and be able to get around the personality cult. Recently Vine DeLoria said that the only sacred thing that's left in our society is *People* magazine. So I ask myself, can people do things anonymously and can other people perceive them as something significant? I think that we have lost the ability to look beyond labels and to find meaning in works. This might provoke enough controversy even to attract the general public and break down the boundaries that isolate art.

BLDD: Why do you think more people are now interested in the handmade?

SH: I think it's an interest that people have in themselves. In being interested in themselves, people try to find out what they are by comparing themselves to the person closest to them whom they might admire or be attracted to. They look at the similarities and the differences. I think the interest comes from a simple new awareness of oneself and one's differences and one's similarities, and results in questions like: What do they do? What do they make? How do they live? What do I do? How do I live? Is it any different from them? And people, I think, seem to be learning that they can make things and get pleasure from this.

BLDD: What is the genesis of this renaissance?

SH: A combination of leisure time and panic, but maybe that's a question for the sociologists and the anthropologists.

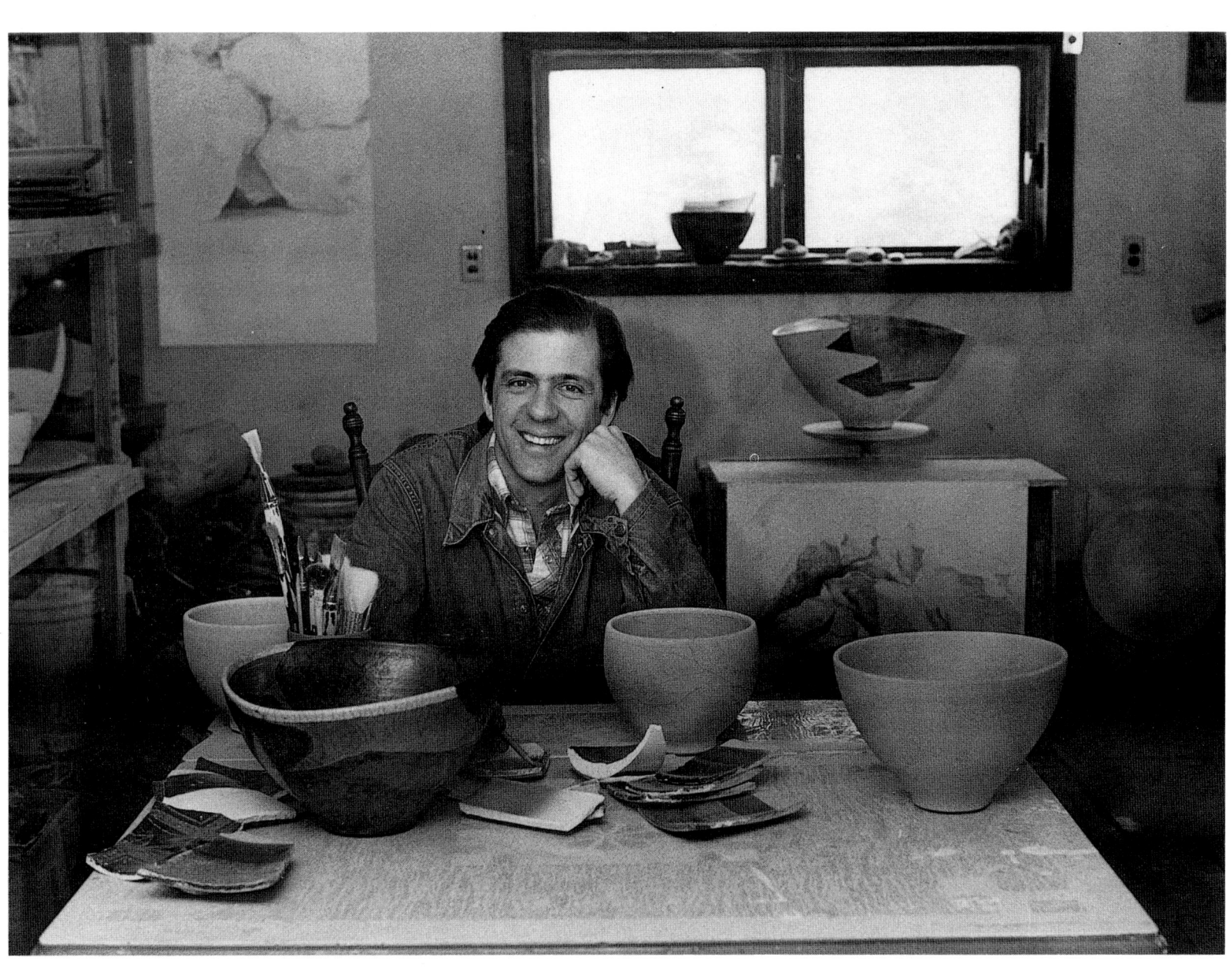

Wayne Higby *is a major force in contemporary clay, and has been since his mid-twenties. He began by revitalizing functional ceramics, bowls, cylinder jars, and storage jars with landscape imagery. These carefully composed, stylized landscapes wedded pictorial imagery and vessel forms in a new way. As his landscapes became more abstract, he chose large, oval-shaped bowls to be the vehicles for his increasingly sophisticated painting. These breathtaking vistas challenge our perception of space and once again prove Higby to be one of the most innovative of vessel makers.*

BLDD: The ceramic vessel tradition is essential to your ideas and your work. What historical ceramics are particularly meaningful to you, and how do you see your work fitting into a historic tradition?

WH: Well, my work is low fire. I work with earthenware clay and glaze fire at temperatures below 1,060° Centigrade. I've always liked earthenware because of the visual feeling of softness in the final product. In contrast, porcelain seems hard even before you touch it. There is a quality of jewellike hardness in fired porcelain. Earthenware is warmer, more human, less scientific.

I first became interested in ceramics during a trip around the world in 1963. I'll never forget the power and beauty of the Minoan pots that I saw on the island of Crete. Those pots were so exciting that the experience of seeing them changed the way I thought about art. Even the small ones were monumental in feeling with lots of volume and magnificent surface patterns. I've been involved in one way or another with those pots ever since.

BLDD: Where did you study?

WH: At the University of Colorado. I'm from Colorado Springs.

BLDD: And how did you wend your way east?

WH: I just took a job wherever there was one. I went to graduate school at the University of Michigan. I had a wife and two children so when I left I had to have some kind of job. I was interested in teaching and took a job at the University of Nebraska, in Omaha, and then was offered a job at the Rhode Island School of Design. I was

there for three years. And then I was asked to come here, to teach at the New York State College of Ceramics.

BLDD: The earliest dairy barn in this county serves as your studio. There is also a stable there. It appears that your boyhood in Colorado serves you in northern New York State, in Alfred, as well. There are a number of horses there, too. Do you ride or show them?

WH: I ride and train them. I'm a 4-H leader, and my daughter belongs to the 4-H Club. We show all over the state of New York, primarily in 4-H competitions. When I was a kid I rode and exhibited horses. I had fourteen horses at one time.

BLDD: You are, among other things, a performer. You are also the choreographer for the high school. And word is out about the Terra Cotta Tappers. What is that all about?

WH: It was a group of tap-dancing graduate students and undergraduates at the College of Ceramics. We performed all around this area. I was working under the theory that if the students' major professor could make an ass out of himself and enjoy their company, then later the communication during critiques would be easier and more direct.

BLDD: Is your style Ray Bolger, a little Fred Astaire, Gene Kelly — which one?

WH: Very eclectic! A little of everything. We did two different numbers, and one of them was to a song by Tony Orlando and Dawn, and the other one was to "That's Entertainment." We all took a class from a

woman who lives in Hornell, the neighboring town. We did that for almost four years but then most of the kids got into other things.

BLDD: You have a very busy schedule. How and when do you have time to do the work for which you're best known, ceramics?

WH: I do that most of the time.

BLDD: How much time do you spend in your studio?

WH: I teach three days a week and I try to spend the rest of the time in my studio. I usually save Sundays for family things. But it's like being a juggler. I'll teach real heavy for a while, and then for a while I'll teach very little. It usually goes in cycles, particularly if I'm working on a show. Then I might be working up to it, and be over at school very seldom. But at least my teaching situation is pretty flexible.

BLDD: Your work involves a unique glazing and firing process that is known as raku. Perhaps you would explain for us what that process is and how one does it. When did it originate?

WH: It is basically a Japanese process but its origin is probably Korean. People were fooling around with it in this country in the fifties. Paul Soldner was one of the people who really started working on it. I got involved in using raku because when I was in graduate school there were ten undergraduates and it was just impossible to deal with all the people when using the kiln. So I built my own small raku kiln.

BLDD: Is there anything about it that particularly suits the kind of work that you do?

WH: I feel that there is; that's why I've become more involved in it. I'm interested in the quality of the fire which is represented in the piece — the feeling of the fire that is left in the object. I'm not only interested in having a color melted on the surface but also in the sense of the fire and the sense of transformation. The fire also gives a quality of light to the piece, in the way that I do it, by taking the piece out of the kiln, putting it in damp straw, and getting the smoke to pass over the surface. A great deal of modulation develops in the glaze that way.

Glen Canyon Dream Landscape Bowl. 1979. Earthenware, raku technique. 11½ × 18 × 14″

That sense of modulation and the sense of light is important to me in terms of the imagery. The softness that the firing gives to the piece is also important.

BLDD: Your work is widely known for its development to the point where the rim barely delineates between the inside and the outside of the container. Instead, there is a continuous surface image.

WH: To experience the image, you have to move all the way around the bowl and into it, so you have to experience the whole object before you get a complete sense of the image. I'm not interested in just presenting a kind of picture but in giving the viewer some feelings of moving through time and space.

BLDD: I can envision these continuous landscapes on a flat surface as well; they seem very related to painting as well as to sculptural forms. Have you ever considered translating those images onto canvas?

WH: I'm not interested in the flat surface — well, I'm actually interested in practically everything, so that's not a very accurate statement! But in terms of my specific approach, I'm interested in the three-dimensional aspects of the object, in that sense of the presence of the object, which is a one-on-one kind of situation. People have asked me why I don't put images of people in the landscape. Well, for me the bowl is a personification. I could go so far as to describe the bowl as a personification of myself.

BLDD: If the bowl is you, what do you hope to communicate?

WH: A sense of humanity, of man's needs and intellect, the way he relates to his environment and makes something out of that environment, the way he structures something that has logic and takes care of his needs. The bowl, to me, represents those things.

BLDD: Well, you have made the interior and exterior of the bowls almost transparent. Could you also anthropomorphize that idea?

WH: One probably could. You could take this as far as you want to. I've thought about it a lot. There are certain basic philosophical positions that I have. Then

Black Granite Quarry Landscape Bowl. 1975. Earthenware, raku technique. 10½ × 11 × 11"

there's a certain point at which I feel the art winds up being more what you say about it than what you see. I'm more interested in the visual phenomena. I'm not interested in presenting you with a very minimal experience and telling you how wonderful it is! But I do have strong metaphysical concerns. I'm interested in the reality beyond what we're experiencing, the things that underlie things. And the transition from the reality of the bowl to the illusion and spatial concept, to present space that is not really there, but in another sense is really there. I am interested in something that transports you through an emotional, visual experience involving beauty and drama — those kinds of qualities rather than something that transports you intellectually.

BLDD: The works on the shelves and walls of your own studio range from a contemporary Mark Rothko to classical Japanese ceremonial bowls. Are there the works of any particular artist, fine or decorative, past or present, to which you particularly respond?

WH: I'm very interested in Japanese decorative art, especially screen paintings. That's an interest which I discovered through some things I found myself doing. I then began to explore it. When I first started doing these landscape boxes that fit together I thought they looked a lot like folded screens.

BLDD: You're interested in so very many things that I was wondering, what is it about clay, this particular medium, that has continued to engage you for so long?

WH: Clay is like a collaboration. It's like doing choreography for the high school musical. You have to talk to it, and it has to talk back. It's like working with another person. Clay is a very responsive material and tells you what you can do and what you can't. I respect that. That's exciting for me!

BLDD: Do you build a bowl in the traditional coiled method?

WH: No, I throw them on a wheel and they're perfectly round. And now they're ovals.

BLDD: How does that happen?

WH: I throw them and then I trim them to get the exact shape of the foot, the base. That particular shape is very important; it relates to those early Minoan vessels. After I've thrown and trimmed it, then I get it wet again and I squish it into this oval shape. When I first made the bowls I sent them to a gallery person I know who has a tendency to be very intellectual, and she wrote me a typewritten paper about the oval versus the sphere and the dynamics of the circle.

BLDD: Did it relate to what your intent had been?

WH: Well, in a way, and in a way not. It was very analytical. But, then, she hadn't made the bowl; she was talking about it. So I wrote back and said I thought those things were probably true. But the fact of the matter was

that the door of my kiln is only seventeen inches wide, and before you squish it the bowl is twenty-four inches across! I go back and forth, you know. It's important to have some kind of basic understanding of what you're doing, and it's also important to respond to the moment. Those two things are implicit in my work. The drawing on the bowl might take six or eight hours, and then it is given over to the fire. During the firing process a split second or an intuitive minute can make the difference. So there's give and take. I think another reason I like clay and fire is because I don't feel that, as an artist, I have all the answers. I think some of the answers are in the fire and the material and in the glazes. I'm collaborating again, I'm asking for the answers. I make the final judgment, but I'm exploring possibilities.

BLDD: The use of molds is another technique that you favor. What is the press mold and how do you use it to create a form?

WH: I make a form and then I take a plaster cast of it. I can then press clay into the plaster cast and duplicate the original form many times. It's a very primitive way of getting idiosyncratic shapes over and over again.

BLDD: Some of your works incorporate multiple units that can be arranged in a variety of configurations. What gave you the initial idea and the inspiration to create a series of forms?

WH: Well, I started by responding to those Minoan pots. When I first started working in graduate school, in 1966, I was making vessels that were not meant to be used but to be looked at. They were reactions to the history of ceramics. And when I started getting interested in the imagery I wanted to make forms which responded more directly to the imagery and did not begin automatically with the historic pot form. So I tried to create volumes and situations which were potterylike and spoke of containers but which were derived from the imagery. That's how the multiple units began: as a way to give a sense of the movement in the landscape, a sense of expanse, but also to create a sense of the containment of pottery.

I did that for a long time, and then I got interested in trying to bring that imagery back into another kind of simpler pottery form. I also wanted to relax the box forms that I was making, which were becoming very angular. This may have been the result of spending all day looking out my studio window — I have a magnificent view, but the landscape's very soft. The light makes it soft, too. In Colorado things are much more angular. I wanted to bring more of this kind of fluidity to my work. And I decided I could do that by throwing some bowls. That, really, is where the oval comes in, to give the shape a sense of becoming, of transition, a sense of movement. I felt that the circle was much too rigid and

Carolina Winter Landscape Plate. 1973. Earthenware, raku technique. 16 × 18 × 4″

stable, and I wanted that movement. I also wanted to reinvestigate the pottery statement in the work, so the bowl form was a logical choice.

BLDD: You have managed to bring in from the outdoors the earth tones of terra-cottas and roses and greens and blues, as well. Yet you've implied that your intention is not simply to depict nature accurately, but to create a sort of a mood.

WH: Yes. I never think of trying to do it accurately. It's accurate in that it is the layout and the way I respond to it at that time. The images come from my own sense of the places that I've experienced. I'm not so interested in accuracy, except in terms of the way I feel and see.

BLDD: Have you or would you ever use colors of a different, less natural tone?

WH: I probably would. I've done a lot of different kinds of things — a lot of things which I'm not known for because nobody's ever seen them. I've done a lot of functional work. And I've used bright colors. I've also done some china painting. I don't respond to the harshness that comes from industrial glazes; natural colors for me are rich and contemplative. Those are qualities that I want in my pots.

BLDD: How heavily influenced do you think you are by your Colorado boyhood?

WH: Oh, probably a lot. And I took that trip around the world when I was in my second year of college. I didn't start in ceramics until I was a senior.

BLDD: What were you studying before that?

WH: Painting and sculpture.

BLDD: What gave you the idea to pursue that course of study?

WH: My father was a lawyer. I went to college to become a lawyer; I was in pre-law. I went to the law building one day for a mock trial, walked into the library, and — this is the absolute truth — I changed my mind. There were no pictures in any of the books and I thought, "I will never survive this. I just can't do this." If the law books had been full of pictures, I might have. I don't know. And so I went to the main library and said, "Well, there must be some books with pictures." Of course, most of the pictures were in art books. At that point I had fourteen horses so I sold all but two, took the money, and went on a trip around the world. I figured, "Okay, if I'm going to be interested in art, I've got to see some." But it wasn't until I hit Crete and saw the pots that it really clicked. They were absolutely incredible.

BLDD: Did you ever think you could make them?

WH: Well, probably. I have a healthy ego. I don't suppose I thought I could make those Minoan pots, but different things happen to different people in terms of what changes them. I saw the Taj Mahal — I saw whatever you were supposed to see — but it was the Minoan pots that

Orange Grass Marsh Landscape Box. 1976. Earthenware, raku technique. 8½ × 9 × 9″

changed how I thought about things.

BLDD: I asked you about your Colorado boyhood because when I look at the colorations and volumes of these pots, I often see a natural drama of canyons and skies and wide open spaces.

WH: Sure. I mean, I was an only child; I had horses and rode all the time. I was on a horse constantly. We lived in the country, in an area called Austin Bluffs where there were big rocks and cuts through rocks and not too much vegetation. I rode almost every day from the age of four until I went to college. I usually rode by myself: just my horse and me and those great bluffs. So there's a sense of solitude in my work, I think; a quietness, a certain amount of emptiness, even though that emptiness is not negative. I think of it as a positive quality. I think all of that comes from those experiences. I haven't tried to avoid them; I've tried to use them.

BLDD: I understand the natural grandeur reflected in your work — but I wonder if those rocklike forms de-

picted on the bowls are a re-creation of the bluffs you knew so well.

WH: I don't think anything's that literal. I mean, everybody works from his own experience. To a large extent, I trust those experiences; that's all I had so I've used them.

BLDD: You started to work with those traditional inlaid coil pots and then hand-built slab boxes until you began the current work, which is wheel-thrown and corrected bowls. What caused the change in direction? Is your intent to continually refine the vessel form?

WH: No. I think you go through different stages and attitudes in your thinking. I'd made lots and lots of bowls but a return to it came from living in my present environment. I wanted to do something that was more relaxed, in a sense, without giving up the high drama of the color. You know, when I look out my window, the sun is setting and the clouds are coming over. And it's like Cecil B. DeMille, but it's not even trying, you see. It's just doing it. And I thought, I've got to get back, I've got to bring all of that to the viewer, but it has to be easy and there has to be a quiet presence about it. And the bowl — because it's thrown, because it's oval, because it's a shape that you're familiar with, brings an ease to the completed piece. If I presented it in another way, there would be an intensity and questions that would have to be confronted before moving into the landscape space. The bowl seemed to be a wonderful way of presenting that space in a very familiar way; to get you to flow into it almost before you know you're doing it. That kind of ease is important. And then, of course, there is an important moment of reflection on the meaning of the bowl in relation to the landscape imagery.

BLDD: How do you begin to paint the bowl? Do you start with a sketch?

WH: No. First I spend some time with the bowl. Usually, if I'm not trying to draw on it, if I just look at it, the drawing will appear on it. Because all the drawings are in me. The drawing must relate to the form of the bowl. And then I'll start playing around with it, putting the drawings on the bowl in pencil. The trick is that it has to work inside and outside, all the way around. Sometimes there's a lot of maneuvering, trying to get the lines to make relationships that will cause the image to pass inside and out. After I draw on it I just put the glazes on, usually the blue first. The blue is usually the smallest area; I use an airbrush to spray it on evenly. If I spray it on afterward, it's blue over all the other places. It's like a coloring book — once you have the drawing on, you just paint in between the lines. It takes probably six to eight hours to paint it in. I have to let it dry well. Then I put it in the kiln. When the glaze is melted, I grab it out of the kiln and bury it in a pit of straw just outside my window.

BLDD: What happens when it's in that pit of straw, which looks like a giant hole in the ground, a bird's nest?

WH: The smoking process alters the colors. It softens them; it creates that modulation that I've been talking about, that sense of light and atmosphere. A tremendous amount of color variation occurs according to how hot the pot is before you do that and what the weather is like outside — if it's twenty degrees below or sixty degrees — and how fast you do it. I can change the quality of the color by playing around with it for the first few moments after I take it out of the kiln.

BLDD: I noticed that you use a scale and plastic containers, a spoon, and what appears to be a recipe book. Does each ceramist create his or her own formula for glazes?

WH: Usually. Most accomplished ceramists have reached a point in their work where they're really doing all of that intuitively. I think a lot of people, when they start, use whatever is available, buy their glazes or use the formulas that are given in books. But I don't know of anyone I would consider a real master who doesn't have a deep feeling for materials. Even for those people who use commercial glazes, an intensive understanding of materials is critical. That takes a long time. I think it probably takes longer for a ceramic artist to mature than it does for any other kind of artist. There's a tremendous amount of technical information that you have to assimilate. I've been working with the same glazes for ten years.

BLDD: Do you think a painter has to endure the same process in order to create a surface?

WH: No, I really don't. It's different. Ultimately the end product isn't necessarily good just because you know a lot of glaze technology. But to come to a palette that responds technically, in terms of the firing, and will give you the kind of color you want in relation to your imagery, takes a tremendous amount of time. I have a theory that this is why younger ceramists frequently do not glaze. They simply don't take the time to develop the essential skill.

BLDD: Who would you consider to be among the major ceramic artists of our time?

WH: Henry Varnum Poor. I always felt his ceramics were exceptional. There's a relationship there to my own interests. On the other hand, there are a number of ceramists who have made an effort to place their work within a contemporary painting context.

BLDD: Are you referring to those ceramic artists who do not like to be identified as craftspersons and prefer to be referred to as artists?

WH: I'm working on a theory for a lecture that has to do with defining great ceramic art. In my definition a number of current heroes are not included. Not because they are not good artists but because their clay and glaze

work is not definitive in terms of the tradition and evolution of ceramic art.

Ron Nagel, Peter Voulkos, and Ken Price (with the exception of his most recent work) are good examples of my point. These three have made a concerted effort to adapt contemporary painting to ceramics. In that sense it is painting that leads the way and the result is work which is primarily a ceramic response to the familiar painting styles of the last forty years. It is my opinion that there are other artists working in the ceramic medium whose work is more important in terms of *ceramic* art. Betty Woodman is one of those other artists. She is not making abstract expressionist ceramics.

BLDD: What plans do you now have to experiment with raku and with form?

WH: I'm working on some things which will take the imagery off the bowl and present it in the end in a three-dimensional context.

BLDD: Are you saying that, in lieu of the canvas, you'll have a ceramic that's a flat surface?

WH: No, it won't be flat but it won't be a container. I have never been interested in refinement. So when I think I have really digested a situation, then I ask myself, "Well, where is this going?" Rather than saying, "I guess I'll make another bowl and it'll get a little better," I'm saying to myself, "I really understand this space now. I enjoy making these bowls but I need more than just the making." So I'm interested in trying to find other ways to push through that bowl or out of that bowl.

BLDD: You once characterized today's clay movement as being comprised chiefly of two kinds of ceramists: there are, on one hand, potters who keep clay in the kitchen as some kind of humble functional pot, and, on the other hand, the artists who either make painting and sculpture. What are the philosophical contradictions between these two types of ceramists and in which direction do you see yourself moving? Is there room for many kinds of ceramic art?

WH: Oh, sure. I've never known where I fit. I just work, and my work is very personal to me. I probably fit in a little more, now that imagery has come back to painting. So when people look at my work they don't say, "Oh god, he's working with landscape — how mundane." Now they're saying, "Oh! Imagery!" I was always interested in imagery. Actually, one reason I went into ceramics was because I used to go to my painting class and was told there were things you did and things you did not do. Simple. You did not paint imagery; you made color field paintings. Most of the teachers were spin-offs of abstract expressionism. You certainly did not work with pattern. The ceramics department didn't care what you made. You could go there and express whatever your feelings were. That was comfortable. I don't know where

I fit. I just have certain very strong personal beliefs that I work with. Sometimes they're sort of in, sometimes they're out.

BLDD: Over the years, your work has grown increasingly abstract, while other ceramic artists seem to be moving in the opposite direction toward more realism. Do you think you are growing more abstract, and why do you think so many others are becoming realists?

WH: Well, I think most visual art followed painting. And ceramics is typical of that. If you are concerned about whether or not you're making art, then you're responding to what the assumptions are about that art. The formula used to be that if you made it out of clay, you found out what the painting movement was, and applied it.

BLDD: You once told a workshop audience that art is a balance between materials and concepts, and then you asked them: "Are you making anything that is worth making?" You asked them to discover basic truths. What are the basic truths that *you* are working to discover, and how do you know when you are making something worth making?

WH: Each one of us houses the basic truth. And somehow, beyond our personalities, more toward the inner workings, we all share some common bonds, regardless of who we are — male, female, white, black. Those kinds of truths and the ability to share them are very important to me in terms of the value of the work. Superficial truths are found in responding to the moment, and what seems to be the immediate thing to do. There are so many different pressures. I work with students a lot. And one of the biggest pressures for graduate students, of course, is to get a job, and to get out there and get a show. Because of that, they have such a hard time finding what I refer to as "basic truth" — just finding the things that are real to them, that are honest and open and straight and real. Those are the most difficult things. For the ones who can do that, their work is always stronger, and people respond more to it. It's true of art in general.

BLDD: Of all the crafts, am I correct in assuming that there are more ceramists, both professional and amateur, than in any other craft form?

WH: Oh, I'm sure. There are more ceramists than anything. According to some poll, something like three out of five Americans have some kind of craft hobby. A lot of people paint. But the funny thing is that when we speak about paintings, we do not enter into a kind of situation where velvet paintings come immediately to mind. We immediately make the assumption we're dealing with Pollock or Matisse or Cézanne. And when you talk about crafts, the reverse is true. Immediately what comes to mind is some kind of terrible macramé.

112

Partly Cloudy Landscape Box. 1970. Earthenware, raku technique. 13 × 13½ × 5½"

Canyon View Landscape Jar. 1973.
Earthenware, raku technique. 13 × 13 × 11″

Firewall Terrace Landscape Container (4 boxes). 1981. Earthenware, raku technique. 13½ × 28 × 9″

Floating Rocks Beach Landscape Bowl. 1980. Earthenware, raku technique. 12 × 20 × 16½″

Marble Dome Landscape Bowl. 1977. Earthenware, raku technique. 13 × 22 × 13½″

Josiah Canyon Winter. 1979. Earthenware, raku technique. 11 × 21 × 16″

Above and below: *Painted Rocks Canyon Landscape Container* (5 boxes). 1981.
Earthenware, raku technique. 14 × 20½ × 19″

White Mesa Landscape Jar. 1975. Earthenware, raku technique. 13 × 13 × 11″

Blackwall Canyon. 1975. Earthenware, raku technique. Each 9½ × 9½″

Jack Lenor Larsen, *weaver, manufacturer, and collector, is*

that rare individual whose life bridges art and commerce. His luxurious patterned and colored textiles look as if they are handwoven. The fact is, these fabrics are designed by him, and then machine woven, and eventually sold in his thirty showrooms in as many countries throughout the world. His thirty-year career as an innovator in textiles has taken him all over the world in search of fresh ideas and techniques. The result is designs that are both elegant and original — designs that enrich our private lives as well as our public spaces.

BLDD: You were raised in Seattle, Washington, the son of Norse-Canadian parents. Was there anything in your home or geographic environment that influenced you to study first architecture and then weaving?

JL: My father was a builder and would have been an architect if he could have been. So I spent my youth constructing all manner of cabins, boats, and underground shelters. And somehow, in the process, I also did a lot of work in handcrafts at camp and whenever else I could. From that to architecture and from architecture to being a craftsman was sort of an evolution.

BLDD: When and how and why did your commitment shift from architecture to crafts, specifically to weaving?

JL: I knew that I wanted to be a landscape architect or an interior architect. But in my second year of school we had a primary materials study course, and I wove for a week. I liked that a lot. The immediacy possible in working with real materials and constructing something on the spot is what began my fascination. It also seemed to be as much fun as arts and crafts were at Boy Scout camp. I left behind the abstraction of drawing something on tracing paper — architecture that would never be built — in order to become a weaver.

BLDD: It's been said that you could have become a painter or an architect or a poet but you decided to be a weaver, and, in choosing to focus on textile design, you are now all three at once. What do you think of that appraisal, and why of all the arts did you choose weaving?

JL: I fell into it like a pit trap! I had no choice whatsoever. I liked architecture a lot; I worked on it till four o'clock every morning as a student. But weaving was a total commitment. I was hooked — always have been. In doing our print designs and jacquard patterns, the role of a colorist gets added to the woven structure, and I like that a lot. It's dessert. I also write a lot. Because we weavers and gardeners have a great deal of private time to think out ideas, I'm now working on my sixth book. It's called *Interlace* and it's on plaiting — the first study that will relate basketry and weaving and plaited hair and bread and all of the other kinds of interlacing from the beginning of time.

BLDD: You were the first person at your college to receive a bachelor's degree in weaving. How did that come about?

JL: When I decided to weave as a profession I went to study in Los Angeles and was disowned by my parents for going to what they called the garbage can of the nation and for abandoning architecture for weaving. I was cut off without any money; they thought that would bring me to my senses.

BLDD: Did it?

JL: It did not. But they finally said I had some money from my grandfather, who had been in real estate. They said they would release that money to me while I was still a minor if I'd only leave Los Angeles and go back to Seattle. And the same people who had been involved in my first weaving were enthusiastic for me to continue. When I finally went back to the University of Washington, I wanted to major in fabric design and creative textiles, but there was no such major. My professor

Architecture, J. P. Stevens towel. 1965. Cotton terry

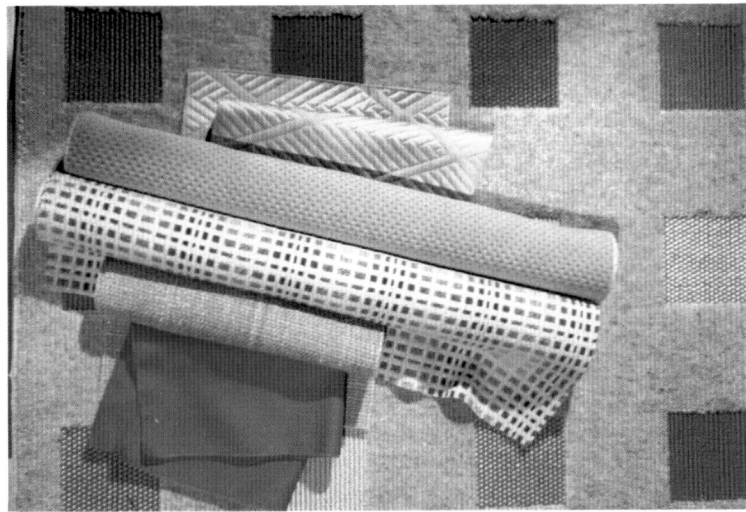

Color coordination, fabrics and carpet. Quadrangle carpet, *Taboret, Intaglio, Hoffman, Boyaca, Marathon*

New Brilliance. 1980. Silks and wool

was finishing a translation of a famous French textile book on pre-Columbian fabrics. I was told if I would work with her on the classification and the textile part of the translation, I could earn credit and therefore get a degree.

BLDD: Who encouraged you in those early days?

JL: That professor, Grace Denny, and the other people involved in handweaving who thought I was a genius simply because I did things they'd never seen before. I was translating weaving technology with an architectural esthetic. No one had taught me fabric design. So it was a new approach to weaving.

BLDD: One of your most influential teachers when you were a student more than thirty years ago was Ed Rossbach. What was your relationship with Rossbach and how is your work influenced by his teaching?

JL: Ed is a fantastically creative American artist-craftsman. At Washington I served as his graduate assistant in my first teaching assignment. And his open approach to exploring every avenue influenced me. He was also enthusiastic about my work, and he literally pushed me to Cranbrook Academy of Art in Michigan. He also helped with a scholarship. He knew more about avant-garde design than anyone else in the Northwest, and about creativity translated into fabric. He's a person who has never tried to sell anything, never put anything on the market. So several times when people asked him for a commission, or the Seattle Art Museum asked if he would teach a course there, he said "No, but Jack will." And I did, at age twenty.

BLDD: Why was he so reluctant, and what lessons did you learn from him?

JL: He was a pure academic and he didn't want to do anything commercial. Even in his own work, as soon as he sees where it's going and what it might eventually be if he stuck with it, he turns around and goes in another direction.

BLDD: After studying and teaching, you moved to what was already the design center of the country, where you still live. Can you describe what your early work was like and what was going on when you first arrived in New York City?

JL: I came here unaware that, of course, if you were a fashion designer or fabric designer, this was the only place to be. I had been here before and I liked it, so I moved here. Then I found out how important New York City is. I hoped to be a consulting designer, but everyone who wanted anything I did at all wanted produced yardage or rugs. They didn't want "designs." They were all architects and furniture designers. So, slowly, I became involved in production.

BLDD: When you first opened your studio what were the options for a young weaver in fabric designing?

JL: At that time there were more possibilities for

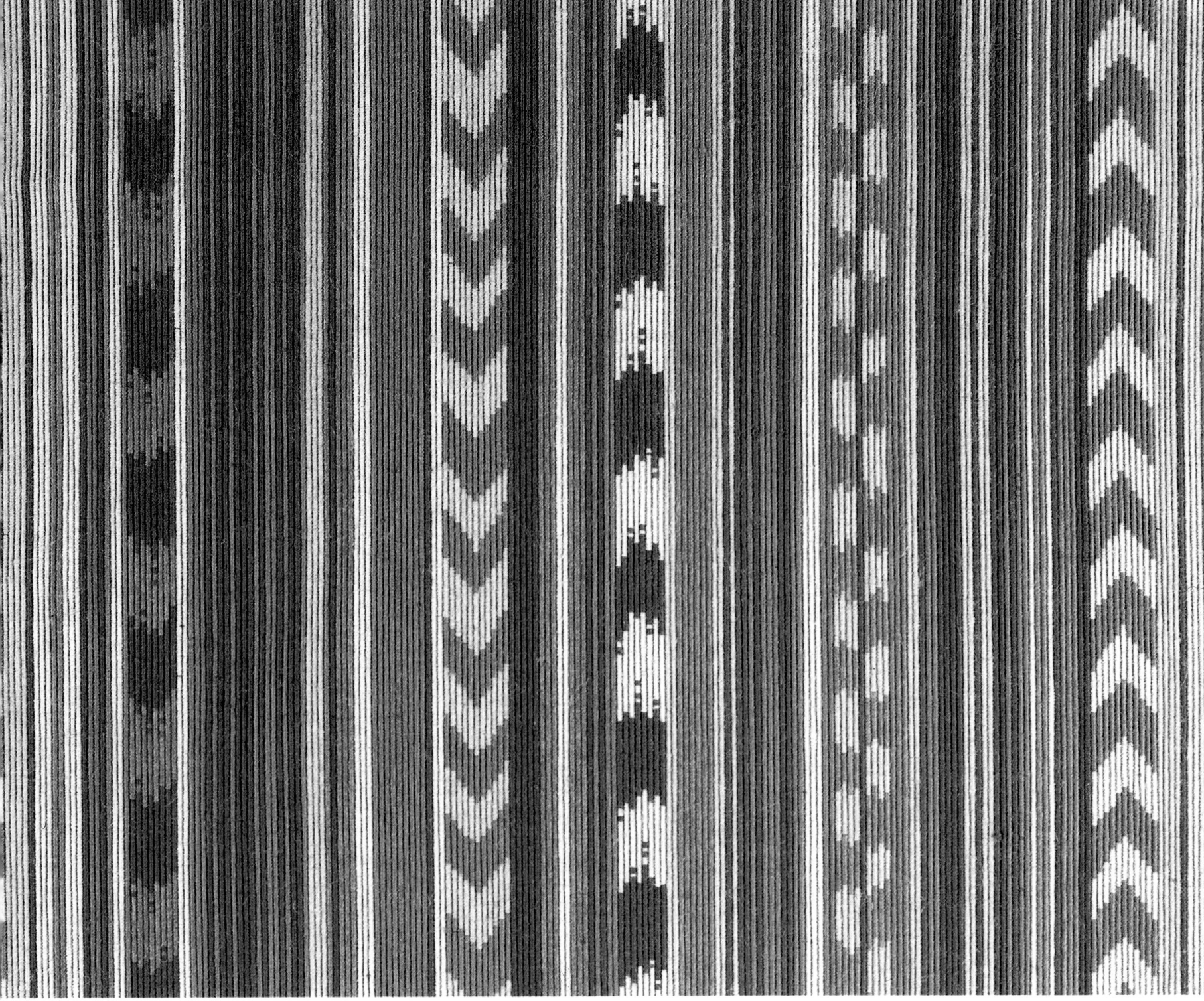

Turkoman. 1979. 100% wool face; 60% wool, 40% cotton

custom-woven fabric. For people who built a new modern house and wanted to furnish it appropriately, having the fabrics and carpets custom made was still rather common. That began to change rather quickly; imports or production fabrics already in inventory became more readily available. Our little firm sort of led the way in that tradition.

BLDD: How did you manage to go into business for yourself in the first place?

JL: Because I didn't know any better! "Fools rush in," and I was one of them. I had no money and no experience, but I just started, and I wove orders and then I got assistance, and we did more. I did other kinds of things — lecturing and various other things — to help subsidize it. And it grew! Then we started working abroad, and then on power looms, and finally with printing. It all expanded very quickly.

BLDD: Thirty years ago when you first came to New York, what did your work look like? What kind of equipment were you using?

JL: I had a very difficult Swedish-type production loom, much too complicated to be as useful as it could have

been, and some other designing looms. And the work spoke of the out-of-doors; it was deliberately rustic. I was most impressed with trying to weave birchbark or sand or grasses. Getting that kind of organic rhythm into fabric, I felt then and still do, compensates best for the monotony of contemporary building materials like glass and aluminum, and could be affordable to a broad range of people. The color ranged from very rich light neutrals to heavy, brilliant, intense color.

BLDD: During the late 1940's and early 1950's, I suspect that design was thought of as a political as well as an esthetic expression. What were your own goals then as a young designer?

JL: I was one of the revolutionaries. And it was a *cause* that we were fighting. It was perhaps more social than political. But we were against all kinds of refinement — elegant furs and cut stones and polished marble and servants; all those things were "over," we thought. We wanted to create a new kind of environment and we thought that people would be happier and more moral in it. I was working as part of a cause, certainly not for money. I was thirty-four, I guess, when we paid our first dividend. I realized then that we were "in business." And as I come to think of it, I worked harder than anybody I knew, but it never occurred to me that it was "work," or

that there was any commercial aspect to it.

BLDD: What events made that period such an exciting chapter in American design history?

JL: First of all, we were the world's leaders. And whatever designers were left in Europe, mostly in Sweden and Switzerland, who had not been in the war, came over here. We had ten great furniture designers, among them Charles Eames, Eero Saarinen, Ed Wormley, T. H. Robsjohn-Gibbings, and Paul McCobb. By the mid-fifties, all of those revolutionary designers were very busy. The emphasis was on *quantity*. You began to hear about a fifty-story building or a $50 million project. And we revolutionaries stupidly thought that we were winning over the establishment. Suddenly banks *had* to be modern. And actually we were being absorbed *into* the establishment. We didn't know it at the time.

BLDD: What happened to that revolution and its promise?

JL: I think we were encouraged when elements of the establishment began to take up not our creed, but our design. This is true in both architecture and design. It took us a very long time to realize that we'd been bought off and captured, rather than having conquered them.

BLDD: Can you describe what that period of experimentation was like?

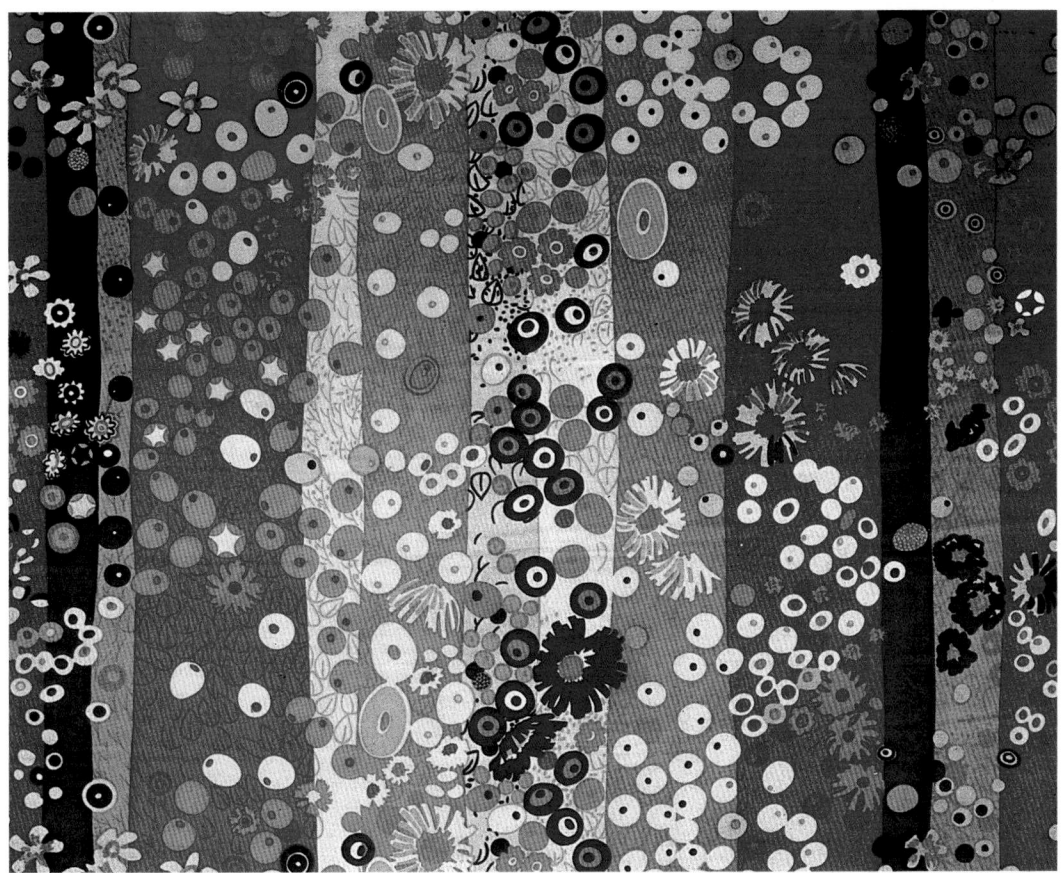

Primavera. 1959.
Printed cotton velvet

Right: *Chan-Chan.* 1966.
Fold-dyed cotton

JL: It was good in that there was a great deal of camaraderie. Designers and architects were not over-committed and not very busy. We had time to talk with each other because we were few in number. Within five or ten years we were all very busy and were going off in different directions, and didn't have as much time for maintaining this cohesive rapport.

BLDD: It sounds like a very exciting chapter in American design history. How do you evaluate what has happened, and how the idealism of that period has evolved? Were your own goals and dreams realized?

JL: In some cases, and much more so. What we've gained in the current slow-down period of the last ten to fifteen years in which there's been less revolution is a wider appreciation, I think. It's not a narrow, tunnel vision of a cutting edge of modern architecture or design but a broader appreciation of all styles. And I think our feeling as a group is that quality is now more important than anything else, and that mass culture is our common enemy. We must avoid becoming one great supermarket.

BLDD: If you consider the high point of American design to be that "design revolution," what would you consider the low point, and where are we today?

JL: The low point is a generalized indifference and not caring. New York, when I came to it, contrasted to the West Coast, was already progressive in that they had invented strip development and neon jungles. Boston and Philadelphia were quiet old city-towns. Whatever they were had been done mostly a long time ago and seemed safe from the gross aspects of further commercialism. And then we see all of these white brick and aluminum buildings loom up, that you cannot ignore. They demand a focus and attention and overstimulation and too much racket, both aural and visual. The sixties seem pretty low from my perspective — the total abandonment, the glorification of sloth. But I think that some good things came out of the social revolution. Certainly, listening to Lena Horne talk about being a black thirty or forty years ago, it's better today than it was then.

BLDD: Did anything come out that applied to environment, the way we work and live and play?

JL: Freedom. I think in the design revolution we were saying, "Let's stop talking about whether the Louis chair is authentic or not. We're not interested in objects." That inventory of objects went out in the sixties. We realize that the important part is how we feel and relate in a space . . . is it a *personal* space? And that was very good; I think there's some durability in that.

BLDD: How did you make design decisions at the very beginning of your career? Was it based on observation,

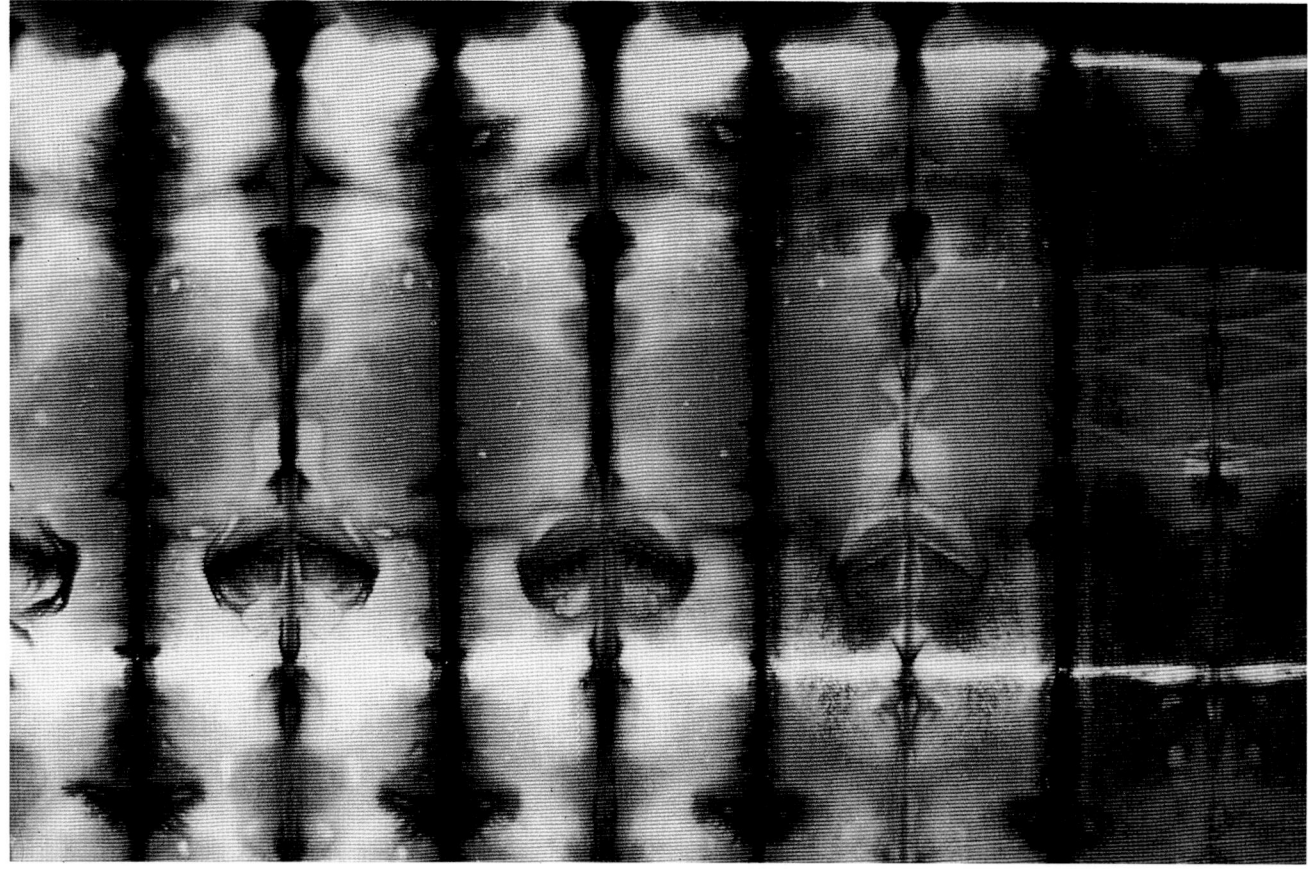

Seascape, wall and window fabric. 1978. Wall: 54% linen,
46% cotton. Window: devore of 65% polyester, 35% cotton

research, your own taste, your own preference?

JL: All of those things. A device I found very useful was not to edit as I was trying to create. Instead I would explore the list of possible solutions to a set of limitations and then tack them up or somehow evaluate them. My feeling as a teacher was that if you have six things lined up any fool could decide which one's the best. But it helps to get it off the loom or the drawing board in order to do that. Take it to another light or another place and sleep on it, and then it's easy to say which is the right one.

BLDD: Who were the leading forces in promoting good design in those days?

JL: One was my good friend Edgar Kaufmann, Jr., who was curator of the Good Design exhibition that was held at the Museum of Modern Art each year. He was relentless in his push for good design. Also his friend Edward Wormley.

BLDD: Who were some of the mentors that had such a strong effect in supporting you, and on the direction of your work?

JL: Georg Jensen was anchorman in the design movement, and George Nelson, Charles Eames, Alexander Girard, and Dorothy Leibes, and I guess most especially, Edgar Kaufmann and Edward Wormley, and another designer, Edward Benesch, have all guided me and have been close-enough friends to say, "Jack, this time you're

wrong." They have evaluated me and sometimes commissioned my work. They've been mentors that I've grown up to be friends with. And that's been very rewarding.

BLDD: Who first involved you in the crafts movement?

JL: Mrs. Vanderbilt Webb, the grand old lady who founded the American Craft Council. I first became involved as a "Young American" — the name of exhibitions they held. And then I juried that kind of show and, eventually, I was on the first board of directors. Now I'm president of the council and the oldest living member. And I was once the fair-haired boy!

BLDD: Your firm was one of the first to produce contract textiles. How and when did you decide to direct your energy in that way, and just what are contract textiles?

JL: One of my first commissions was draperies for the Lever House lobby, an important building in New York City. I worked with Frank Lloyd Wright on fabrics for Taliesin very early on, and with Edward Barnes and Louis Kahn. "Contract" simply means nonresidential. There are specialists in executive office interiors and banks and board rooms, and to them "executive" means no price tag, no budget limitation. There are people working on prisons and subways and those kinds of institutions in which infinite durability, minute cost, and low or no maintenance are the requisites. Hotel suites and country clubs are also contract, but their character is residential.

BLDD: Why don't we talk for a moment about the genesis and evolution of a new design in your studio?

JL: Generally, a new design starts with a new set of limitations. When one of the producers we work with can do something they couldn't have done before, that means that we in turn can do something new. We decide what kind of pattern or weave is appropriate for production in this far-off country and what the limitations are. What are the things that this particular production group or machine or craft *cannot* do well? Once we know the limitations of a challenge, a design evolves. To me, the particular pattern is of the least importance.

BLDD: What is of the greatest importance?

JL: What I've strived for most, I think, is a craft quality — at best, giving the viewer some knowledge of how those fibers were twisted together and interlaced — the pleasure of experiencing the marriage of thirsty cloth and liquid dye. I like those kinds of qualities more than anything else.

BLDD: What about the collaborative process? How and with whom does it work here in your studio?

JL: Collaboration is something I learned late. In the early days I felt I had to give my co-workers a finished description of my vision: how it would be made, what it would look like, and the coloring. Now I come in and say, "I have an idea to share with you," or, "We have a

problem and I need your input as we resolve it." That is collaboration. We like working together in that way. They do and I do.

BLDD: Do you make a small model *before* executing the actual design?

JL: The favorite tool in the studio is the opaque projector, which allows us to work very small and quickly. We can blow up designs in progress to any scale. Sometimes we don't even know which scale feels right until we try a number of different ones. It's a wonderful device. There are no holds barred on how we achieve our maquette. Sometimes we print, sometimes we paint, sometimes we weave. When we're creating something like terry toweling or pile carpeting, we often have to improvise something to give us an idea of how these yarns are going to combine in a structure.

BLDD: How are we, the consumers, to know how to use your designs and fabrics together in an entire room? How do you coordinate all the colors? Do you present a range of fabrics?

JL: The feeling today is that we design collections, not individual designs or colorings, but carpets and fabrics and silks and draperies that work together as a group. Modern shoebox interiors need the specialness of seeming to grow out of components that were designed for that space and that person. I'm trying to build whole groups of furniture, carpets, fabrics, silks, that will go together in that way and have that custom look.

BLDD: What is the most important aspect for you of your enormously complex and, I daresay, phenomenally successful business?

JL: Working as a team. I have a fantasy sometimes of being an infant king who is both looked after and obeyed. And in this family, I have a very central position. When I first started, I envied artists who could work alone and who weren't dependent on assistants and suppliers and deliverymen, and so on. Finally, I decided that perhaps one of the reasons for creating this organization is to be with a group of people with whom I'm secure. I'm very much at home with these people; I like them a great deal.

BLDD: Have a number of them been with you for a long time?

JL: Since the beginning. It's like a larger family. Every once in a while we'll have an enormous party to which we'll all bring our families and eat together and dance together. And that's fun, too.

BLDD: Why do you think it is that good design at affordable prices is still the exception rather than the rule in mass-produced furnishings?

JL: Producers do better in some areas than others. In soft goods, like towels, there are beautiful towels in every store, and people buy them. People take more risks — if they make a mistake they can afford to leave them in the

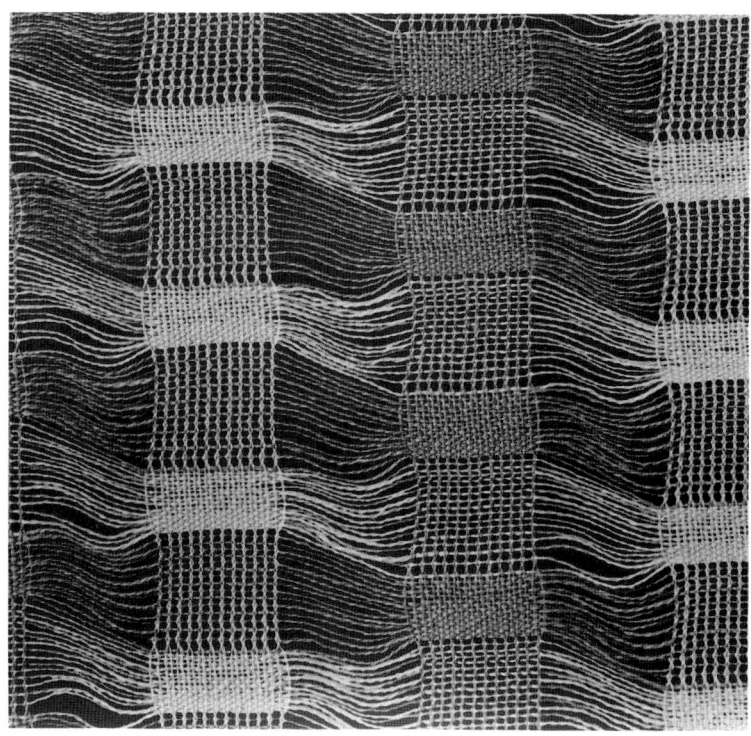

Gossamer. 1973. Wool

closet. With furnishings, however, there's a great deal of fear about making so permanent a commitment as living-room furniture. In America we still have two distribution systems, which I think is a big deterrent. Even people who could afford it do not see our best design, which is in showrooms open to the trade only. There is the retail shop — furniture store or department store; then, on the other hand, there are showrooms that sell only to interior designers and architects.

BLDD: Perhaps your most remarkable achievement has been to merge what we usually think of as art with industry. In the end, is this really possible or desirable on any scale — let alone on as broad a scale as you've attempted to do it?

JL: I think so. In America there is some transition in soft goods, with small firms like ours, between the individual craftsman and industry. Because of this, fabric design is better than our glass industry, for instance: glasses that Americans want to drink from are imported.

BLDD: How do you explain that difference?

JL: In the glass and ceramic industries there's almost no transition between big industry and individual craftsmen. There, very few craftsmen work within industry, and the industry seems blind to what's going on within the crafts movement.

BLDD: You have almost a unique role of being involved in various aspects of the crafts movement, and being, it

would be fair to say, a catalyst in the founding of the only art glass school in the entire country — The Pilchuck School in your home state of Washington. Considering your deep involvement with glass, why haven't you tried to bring the two together?

JL: I think that is a full-time commitment. Maybe it'll begin to come about. It's interesting — for instance, with all the support that Corning Glass Works has given to the American art glass movement, that they're just now coming out with some very beautiful undecorated cooking implements.

BLDD: It took a lot to get those blue snowflakes off those white pots!

JL: Yes. And the wood-grain vinyl covers and so on. But there is beginning to be a very nice transition. As a supporter-patron, Corning is sponsoring some fine designs. I think we're going to learn that there's an even larger market for good, clean design than imports can supply. Some of the stores, such as Crate and Barrel, Pottery Barn, and even Bloomingdale's, will begin to insist on American manufacturers filling that slot. In furnishings what *should* happen is that we need to establish a democratic base of okayness. If you have fifty dollars and are naked, you can buy sneakers, jeans, a T-shirt, and a sweatshirt, and be as good as anybody. In furnishings, you really can't. In appliances, whether it's audio equipment or refrigerators, you can get pretty good value, and the difference between Harlem and Park Avenue is very slight. Nylon stockings are fabulously democratic. Everybody can have the best; there's very little difference between the discount store and Bergdorf's. That use of mass production of man-made fibers in new technology really works. In chairs and sofas and carpets and furnishing fabrics, it's not working nearly as well. We're still using old-fashioned manufacturing processes in many cases. But we should have broader ranges available to most of us.

BLDD: In planning for your exhibition at the Musée des Arts Décoratifs, in Paris, do you have any designs that you would prefer *not* to show to the public today?

JL: Oh, a lot. And it was interesting how crass and aggressive some of our designs and colorings were fifteen or twenty years ago.

BLDD: How do you define crass and aggressive coloring?

JL: As demanding attention. And I think that furnishings shouldn't do that at all. Almost twenty years ago when I went to Europe with our first showroom, people wondered where I got those wild colors that no civilized person could possibly use. But I wanted to make a strong statement and with as much vigor as I could. Some I still like. And even very bright flowers or birds, for instance, are not vulgar. But I've done some vulgar colorings and even they were popular.

BLDD: What are vulgar colorings?

Braniff 747 upholstery. 1969–70. 100% worsted wool, jacquard woven

JL: Ones that are jarring. Very often there's a dark–light contrast and also a color change. In another ten years, they might again seem rather refreshing!

BLDD: Is there any color or color combination that you would no longer use, or never use?

JL: Not anymore. There used to be a great many. I knew I would never use maroon. Or forest green. They're popular now and I find them very interesting. But I use several maroons together, and that seems better. There are cycles that we all go though and it helps make life fun.

BLDD: Are there any colors you avoid because you find them least interesting or appealing?

JL: The purples, unless they're very gray, are used in small amounts. We've never been successful in selling purples. Because furnishings are rather permanent, people who might buy a purple shirt occasionally will not buy a purple room. A little bit of earth violet mixed with browns and olives — that I like a lot. I don't use washed-out colors as much, at least those that seem insipid and thin.

BLDD: What is an insipid color?

JL: One that is terribly pale or feminine. And yet in Persian miniatures you sometimes see those same colors and they're exquisite.

BLDD: What are the colors that are the most popular and salable?

JL: About fifteen years ago we invented lacquer reds, which deepened and became hennas. And it seemed until very recently that we would be stuck with them the

rest of our lives. Fortunately, steely, powdery blues have replaced those as our best-sellers. And I'm pushing a very broad range of greens right behind them. I think that we'll be seeing green as the new color.

BLDD: Is the beige decade over yet?

JL: I think it's over as a fashion, although I feel neutral colors, particularly natural materials — natural wood and cane and wicker and basketry and all of those things that are easy to maintain — are very practical. The horror of a whole generation going through white cotton upholsteries with children and dogs! That wasn't such a good idea, as popular as it was.

BLDD: What neutrals, if any, do you foresee taking the place of classic tones such as beige?

JL: We're finding two things: one, that dyed neutrals, grays, café au laits, bisques, and shades of that sort are more practical and seem newer than simply undyed fiber. And we're also enjoying, and so are our clients, some colors that are between neutral and color — very grayed-out roses, soft celadon greens, sages, steely blues, pearl grays that are very rich in color, taupe, and fawn. Something between color and neutral, but not demanding.

BLDD: How do you decide — in fact, who *does* decide and how much in advance — what color palette to offer to the public?

JL: I sit on the Color Association Board in which we try to forecast environmental color three years in advance to help manufacturers and retailers. And I'm amazed that a group of six or eight of us — some representing such very large segments of the market as Pittsburgh Paint, with

Mary McFadden and me representing more rarefied strata — can come into agreement as to what we think will happen.

BLDD: Well, why don't you give us a fearless forecast? What colors do we have in store for us?

JL: As an antidote to the beige decade, there will be more clear, brilliant color accents — like bringing a bowl of begonias or gladiolus into a beige room — that are not aggressive, hard colors, but ones that are clean and clear. I've been trying to bring those colors into fabric. And I like some of the results, even using polychromes, like the Egyptians and Greeks, of clear, light yellows, oranges and red-oranges, and pale sky-blues. All light colors. My own clients haven't followed me there yet. What I'm most excited about at the moment, and I think could be a major trend, would be using complementary colors together: greens with reds — almost the same value and certainly not Christmas colors, but very grayed greens with off shades of red — ambers with wisteria, pale blues with saffron, and pale green celadons with rose . . . combinations of that sort, which happened in the 1920's and thirties — quite often.

BLDD: I've read that a line in a book of poetry by Paul Eluard influenced you in your selection of palette during the late 1950's and the early 1960's. Will you repeat that phrase and describe how you attempted to capture its meaning in your own work?

JL: At the end of a poem dedicated to his friend Pablo Picasso, he said: "If you love the intense cloud, pour into every image its warm summer blood." I love that cloud and everything under that cloud, the nature that I grew up in, the textures of pine needles and things like that. And it wasn't only color but the amalgam of the craftsmanship, of textile techniques and structure and architecture. I've always been interested in how I could infuse a space, a cloth, a print, with as much richness as reality, with a tactile quality, with a sense of the materials and the process that put it together, how it was connected. In our culture I miss the sense of connection. We seem to be cemented together, and our architecture is too often dry walls and empty shoebox spaces.

BLDD: Why does fabric, of all man-made materials, offer the best potential for, as you put it, "the multitudinous profusion of color"?

JL: Fabric breaks up color in a way similar to the broken color of nature. When you look at a field of grasses, the sun refracts light in a hundred different ways. Grains of sand are not sand colored — sand is twenty colors all reacting to each other. More than anything else that man makes, fabric has this potential both in color breakup and surface interest, highlight and shadow, to give indoors environments in cities the kind of feeling we have out of doors.

BLDD: Part of what makes your work special is its refer-

Jezebel. 1971. Printed cotton velvet

131

ence to so many different cultures. How did you first begin to travel, and how important an influence has that been on your life and work?

JL: A very great one. I've never had the luxury of traveling for inspiration. I was first invited to Haiti in 1952 to help with the first handspun, handwoven fabrics there, and we've been working there ever since. There I first learned to respect handspun yarns. And then we traveled to the Far East. Working with the simplest people in the most remote countries taught me other points of view.

BLDD: How have textiles and crafts of other cultures influenced you the most?

JL: In color, certainly, and in appreciation of the idea that if one has really beautiful yarns, one doesn't need to do anything but retain this beauty in the woven fabric. It shouldn't be upstaged in any way by a complex weave or a combination with other things. In art school, there was a carving in the college gallery saying, "The most perfect art is the most anonymous." As a student I did not want to be anonymous; I was trying to fight my way *out of* anonymity. Now, maybe partly from working with these simple craftsmen, I'm quite content to make designs that are anonymous and seemingly timeless.

BLDD: Is there a Jack Lenor Larsen signature? Can one look at a textile and know it must be a Jack Lenor Larsen design?

JL: I think that's true of a number of them, yes.

BLDD: And how would you characterize your textiles?

JL: Maybe as having vigor. I've long felt that Americans had no business being courtly or trying to imitate courtly traditions. We're too red-blooded. If we have any quality that's good, that's what it is. We say what we mean, what we experience, and what we feel. We're not overly refined. And I feel that our environment should not be either. It's sad to see red-blooded people in eighteenth-century surroundings that impede them and make their natural actions seem coarse.

BLDD: Why do you suppose it is that at this point we've become a nation of collectors?

JL: I think it's a response to our being a mass-production, mass-culture country. Having something that is special, that is uniquely ours, is important. I have less enthusiasm for the people collecting production-ware plates. Even so, if they have enough of them, I guess it makes them feel better. But I think wanting something of value is exactly where we're at. And I appreciate that.

BLDD: How long have you been a collector?

JL: All my life. As a child I collected everything in nature, and when I was in school I started collecting objects. The first were Indian baskets, which in Puget Sound were affordable. I had a professor who said, "As you grow up buy one beautiful thing every year. You'll be surprised how quickly you have some nice things to live

with." And I thought, "But if you did it every week it would go faster."

BLDD: You *are* a passionate, and perhaps, even an incurable collector. What is it that you collect?

JL: I collect almost everything. I'm not a major collector of fine arts, but in art and craft media and ethnographic crafts media I buy passionately, and with great pleasure. Some of it, like the fabrics, is immediately put into storage. Other things I live with and learn from. In fabrics there are now almost four thousand pieces, mostly rolled up and stored in our warehouse. In ceramics, there are several hundred pieces, and in glass, fewer. I have more rapport with art and craft media than I do with painting and sculpture. It's also more affordable, and therefore I have more of it.

BLDD: Why don't you describe the way that you live and your New York City apartment?

JL: The space I live in in town is an amalgam of all my interests: I weave there, I write books there, I dine with friends there, and I dream and think there. The collections of things that I like, the sense of structure in materials and how they're put together, are important to me. The plants, and the light, the reflections of the water in the pool, are all part of it.

BLDD: You say that you weave at home. What is that process like and how much time do you spend weaving?

JL: Weaving is slow. I think one learns patience, and it's as close as I get to meditation, I guess. It's a mechanical process of drawing yarn through treadles or pushing the shuttle through the webs and watching something grow in front of you. I weave at home less now than I used to, but I weave on our small looms in the studio more. Weaving has side benefits that are therapeutic. Watching something grow before my eyes . . . I get some of the same encouragement and refortification in my gardening, and even in some aspects of the books that I write.

BLDD: Many of your own treasures can also be found in East Hampton in Long Island, where you built a unique and wonderful example of an African round house. Whatever gave you the idea to create that kind of environment?

JL: When I was a little boy there was a documentary film of Princess Elizabeth traveling through the West African colonies. What caught my eye were all the kinds of houses behind her. Some were mud and some were stone and some were grass and some were wood. And they had fantastic beehive and pagoda shapes! And I said, "When I grow up, I'm going to go look for those houses. I did, and I liked them enormously. One of the things I liked about them was that although most of them weren't vast, they were as complex and interesting as a Victorian castle. The spaces between them were all part of it, and they were not simple like a small American house. By the time I got to Zululand and saw a people who had

Pastorale, wall and window fabric. 1975. Wall: 54% linen, 46% cotton. Window: devore of 65% polyester, 35% cotton

built a round house with a horseshoe of smaller rooms halfway around it, that seemed even better. I decided I was going to do that. I started making paper models while I was still in camp in Zululand, and came back and set to work staking it out. Before there were plans, it was staked out on the ground for sight. And it's worked wonderfully.

BLDD: With all your achievements, is there anything you haven't done yet that you'd care to?

JL: Oh, yes. I like best doing the things I've never done before. And there are a great many of those. I would like to design for mass production, perhaps not in the fabric area. I've dreamed of coloring the Volkswagen cars.

BLDD: Did you ever expect your life to unfold the way it has?

JL: No! I had no hopes for so much excitement and richness. Having friends in a hundred cities is a richness. Having two beautiful houses is a richness. I like that.

BLDD: If you had it to do over again, what would you do otherwise?

JL: Oh, I wouldn't have made as many mistakes as often. I would have been wiser earlier. But one never knows whether that will happen or not. I think the saying that we never learn anything by our successes, that we need the follies and the mistakes in order to learn, is probably true.

Sam Maloof

, a woodworker for thirty-five years, is a man whose beautifully designed and executed furniture has rarely been matched for its classic form and finish. Sam is probably America's number-one craftsman in wood. In Alta Loma, California, he lives in a splendid, sprawling house which he designed and built, step by step, himself. Sam Maloof has not had a day's formal training as a woodworker in his entire life.

BLDD: By now you've produced more than three thousand pieces of furniture. What's the most difficult piece for you to make?

SM: Well, I think the chair is. I've made so many of them that I don't find it too difficult, but I think for most people the chair would be the most difficult.

BLDD: Why would making a chair be more difficult than making a table?

SM: The joinery. There's an awful lot of joinery in a chair. Then, too, a chair can be beautifully constructed and beautiful to look at, but if it doesn't sit well it isn't a good chair. You have to take this into consideration, too.

BLDD: What's your favorite piece of furniture to design?

SM: The pieces that I'm working on at the time, really. All of them are my favorites, no matter how many times I've made that particular piece before.

BLDD: Well, it's obvious from the results that you achieve, the kind of care that goes into the work that you do. You started to work with wood when you were seven or eight years old. What did you create at that age?

SM: Like most young boys I used to love to make guns and swords and that type of thing. I used to make trucks. I remember, as I progressed, making springs out of tin cans and all. They were really quite nice. My father was a merchant, and no one else in my family had worked with their hands as such.

BLDD: What made you decide to devote yourself to working with wood?

SM: I can't recall a time when I didn't work with my hands. I graduated from high school during the depres-

sion, and, fortunately, I got a job working as a graphic artist, but I still liked to work in the third dimension. I made furniture for my parents' home — that my sister's still using — and I made furniture for a little apartment that I had. Then, after four years in the army, I came back to Los Angeles and didn't like the furniture in our little apartment, so I went to night school and used their equipment to make my own furniture. A teacher at Chouinard (Loren Barton) was a friend of mine. She saw what I did and casually mentioned that I should make it to sell, and that was really the catalyst.

BLDD: Did you ever study woodworking with anyone?

SM: No, I'm self-taught. I worked for an industrial designer, and learned how to work with tools. I then worked with an artist, Millard Sheets, as his assistant. Even then I was working in wood, but it wasn't till I got married that my wife got tired of hearing how I wanted to be a woodworker and she said, "Well, just do it." So, with her faith and hope and backing, I did.

BLDD: Has this lack of formal training been a limitation to you, or has it freed you to experiment?

SM: I think it's been great. I'm very orthodox, I think, in the way I work. Formal training is good for some people; learning the way I did was right for me at the time. I had to learn how to work with hand tools because I couldn't afford power equipment, and that was very good. For my first job, I used hand tools just about exclusively and would say 75 to 80 percent of what goes into making a piece still is handwork, although my power tools make things go much faster.

BLDD: You mentioned the support of your wife in the early part of your career. Does she still assist you?

SM: Oh, yes. I don't think I ever would have stayed at it if it hadn't been for my wife, really. I give her 100 percent credit. Freda has backed me just 100 percent. I don't think I could have done it without her. She's always kept the books and, unbeknownst to me, from the very beginning she kept a record of every piece that I've ever done, who I did it for, the materials, the price. That's something like three thousand pieces — chairs, tables, cabinets, all kinds of furniture. I've done churches and offices but mostly household furniture.

BLDD: With my rough arithmetic, that comes out to approximately one hundred pieces a year: two pieces made by hand, every week over a thirty-five-year period. How do you manage to sustain that level of work?

SM: When I worked alone, my pieces weren't quite as complicated. If you look at a chair I did thirty-five years ago, and then at a current chair, you can see how that chair has developed. I make very subtle changes on all my pieces, and so I think that I have improved the pieces as I work. When I worked alone I used to get up at 7:00 A.M. and get out to the shop and work till one, two, or three o'clock in the morning, six days a week. Now I work five and a half, six days, but I don't go up to the shop until 8:00 A.M. at least. I work anywhere from sixty to eighty hours a week, and a lot of this includes making drawings, because I do have to make drawings for people who don't live in the area. I'm in the shop a lot of time, but then I work in the lemon grove and in my yard. Although I don't feel older, my wife says I should slow down, but I still find it very stimulating and exciting.

BLDD: What causes you to initiate a new design?

SM: Unfortunately, I've sold a lot of the prototypes that I made. I wish I had them, but I'm afraid they'd fill the house. But one idea begets another, and as I sit here I have hundreds of ideas for different things I want to make. I hope I live long enough to be able to do them all.

BLDD: Your work has been described as being influenced by the Shakers, or by the Gothic, or sometimes by the Western. How would *you* characterize your work?

SM: Many years ago, when I first exhibited my work in New York City, the editor of *House Beautiful* called me and said, "I think they're the most exciting things I've seen in twenty-five years." And she asked if I were Egyptian or if I'd been in Egypt or had studied Egyptian art, and I said, "No, why do you ask?" She said, "They have sort of an Egyptian feeling to them." Well, it wasn't till years later that I happened to be in Cairo, and then I saw the King Tut exhibit, and I could see how she saw an Egyptian influence. But there isn't anything new in furniture. I developed my designs just from myself, really. I didn't have any furniture books. I didn't know anyone

Chairs and Pedestal Table with Four Drawers. Walnut

who was working with furniture. It just evolved.

BLDD: What's the process that you use in working? Do you start with a sketch, or a model, a prototype?

SM: When I first started, somebody had seen my furniture and asked if I would do a commission, a dining table and chairs and all, and on the strength of that I quit my job. It was sort of scary, but I did. First of all, I made drawings, a prototype, just nailing the piece together. After I got an okay on the chairs, I climbed up on the roof of the little one-car garage where I was working and dropped the piece to see if the thing would hold together. Well, it held together, except for one broken leg. I worked that way for a while until I decided it was an awful waste of time and started making the actual piece from the beginning. I have a picture in my head of what I

that I make is sold before I start. If it's eight chairs, I cut out all the parts for eight chairs at once. And I do jump from one piece of furniture to another.

BLDD: Have you always worked only by commission?

SM: From the very beginning. I don't think I could work any other way. If I didn't have so much work, I would probably have an inventory for people to come and buy. But that's the reason I don't have any prototypes. People have come in and bought them!

BLDD: Rather than an inventory, I think you have a backlog of orders. Just how extensive is that?

SM: Oh, I should say . . . really, it frightens me! Right now I have about one hundred fifty orders. So far no one has canceled on me. I used to worry about it an awful lot and then I felt that was taking all the fun out of it, and the reason I went into this was that I didn't want to have a systematic sort of working schedule. I'm very loose in my work.

BLDD: I've heard it said that nothing's ever left your shop that you're not proud of. That's a very enviable record. To what do you attribute that consistently high level of quality over such a long period of time?

SM: My daughter-in-law says it's because I'm an Aquarius, but I think I'm a perfectionist. For anything to go out of my shop that I didn't feel was right — I just wouldn't let it happen. I know that some people say that every piece that leaves my shop is of museum quality. But museums or not, I wouldn't let it go out. I think a person should have a sense of pride in what he or she does and if you don't have this feeling about what you make, then you should go into something else. That is one of the problems with products today. The person who's working on them doesn't have that sense of pride in the quality of the work he does. When I started, I never once thought about recognition because I thought, "How wonderful it is to be able to earn a living working with my hands — to make things that I enjoy making and that other people would enjoy having." I didn't even know what a de-signer-craftsman was until years later when somebody said to me, "You know you're a designer-craftsman." And I said, "Ohhh."

BLDD: I know that people can look at a piece and recog-nize it as the work of Sam Maloof. Do you sign your pieces as well?

SM: I've always signed them. When I first started I had little metal letters that I hammered in, and then I had a stamp, and now I just sign them with a burner. I start at the first of the year. For example, no matter what it is, the first piece would be number 1, 1981, and then number 2, 1981. I also keep a ledger of every piece that I've made in addition to what Freda does in the office.

BLDD: This house is really quite remarkable. Can you tell us how you came to live here in the first place and how it all evolved?

want to do and I just start making it. Now that's the way I do all my work. If it's a piece of case goods or a dining table that I'm making for someone, say, back East, I do drawings because I don't want to forget the measure-ments. I don't have a set standard. In other words, if somebody wants a table that is 48 or 52 inches in diame-ter, I don't have jigs, so I can make it whatever size I want. Or if a big person wants a rocking chair an inch deeper, I can very well do it.

BLDD: What's your method of working? Do you go back and forth from piece to piece — say, a chair in the morn-ing, a table in the afternoon? And how many pieces do you work on at any one time?

SM: Well, goodness, I work on a lot of them. In the shop now I must have ten or twelve pieces. Everything

Leather Woven Bench. 1948. Walnut and rawhide.
16½ × 16 × 30″

SM: We lived in a little tract house in Ontario, California, for about a year, and I worked in a single-car garage. I kept talking about moving out to the country. Of course, we couldn't afford that, no way, but Freda finally said very bluntly, "Well, why don't we look in the paper? Maybe you'll find a place and quit talking about it." I picked up the paper and there was an acre for sale. I came to see it, we traded equity, and then I was able to acquire property on either side. There was a little shack that we lived in and, as I was able to, I laid a cement slab and made a room. Then when I saved enough money I would build another room. So the whole house was built room by room. I had help on the cement work. I also had the plumbing done, and then I had help with the electrical work. But just about everything else I've done myself. I was going to remodel the old house but my wife didn't think that it was feasible, so I started with just the one room and then from there it expanded. But the house still sits right in the middle of a seven-acre lemon grove. We also have orange trees, avocado trees — you name it.

BLDD: How long has it taken you?

SM: About twenty-five years.

BLDD: And what will you build next?

SM: Well, Freda hopes I don't build anything! She complains that I'm always adding on. But I've been thinking about building a little room between the guest house and the shop, where I can have one or two pieces of furniture. I tell Freda that she and I can use it to just go in and read and be by ourselves for a while. She said I'd go crazy if I didn't have visitors to talk to. So, I don't know. . . .

BLDD: You and Freda have been lifelong collectors. Each room in this splendid house is another part of your mutual autobiography!

SM: I collected some things before I was married. Freda had been director of Arts and Crafts at the Santa Fe Indian School and had acquired a few Indian objects. Then when we were married I became very interested in Indian art. When I was working for Millard Sheets, he gave us some paintings and drawings; I used to do graphics for Hatfield Galleries in Los Angeles on my own and in turn they would give me paintings. Millard Sheets was responsible for opening up a whole new world in the arts to me.

BLDD: When you've bought lumber for your work do you then decide on the basis of the individual piece of wood what will be created from it?

SM: Often people talk about letting the wood dictate what they're going to do, but I don't do that. I find that I go into my woodpile, and if I find a piece of wood that has extraordinary grain, I set it aside until I find enough pieces so that I can make a tabletop or whatever. I buy all my wood in random widths and random lengths, and go from there. And I use common number-two lumber mostly because it's the most figured and I think the most beautiful. "Figured" means it has more knots in it than common number one.

BLDD: Where does the wood that you use come from?

SM: The walnut that I use comes from the Midwest, mostly from Indiana, Ohio, Illinois, down to the Ozarks.

BLDD: How do you select the wood for a particular piece?

SM: If I'm making a tabletop, I try to use a piece that has a lot of figuration in it, but then I ask the people I'm working for how they feel about sapwood, or if they want quarter-sawn wood. Most of the time they just leave it up to me. Then on my chairs, of course, I use wood that has a straight grain in the legs so they don't break or crack.

BLDD: Where do you keep the wood?

SM: I have four storage sheds. When I first started I could only afford to buy enough wood for whatever piece I was going to make at the time. Then, as I went on, if I had enough for one table, I'd buy enough to make two tables, and I built up an inventory of that kind. Now I have maybe twenty thousand board feet of English brown oak and some rosewood, but mostly walnut.

BLDD: What makes one piece of wood better than another?

SM: The solidity of the wood is important. I prefer the dense pieces of wood, and I prefer the very figured, also. It depends on what I'm using the wood for. I've just finished a tabletop that has three or four great big knotholes in it but it's absolutely beautiful. Sometimes I leave knotholes open, sometimes I'll fill them with epoxy and sawdust. A beautiful chair seat that has a knot in it doesn't bother me at all.

BLDD: How does the potential owner feel about that?

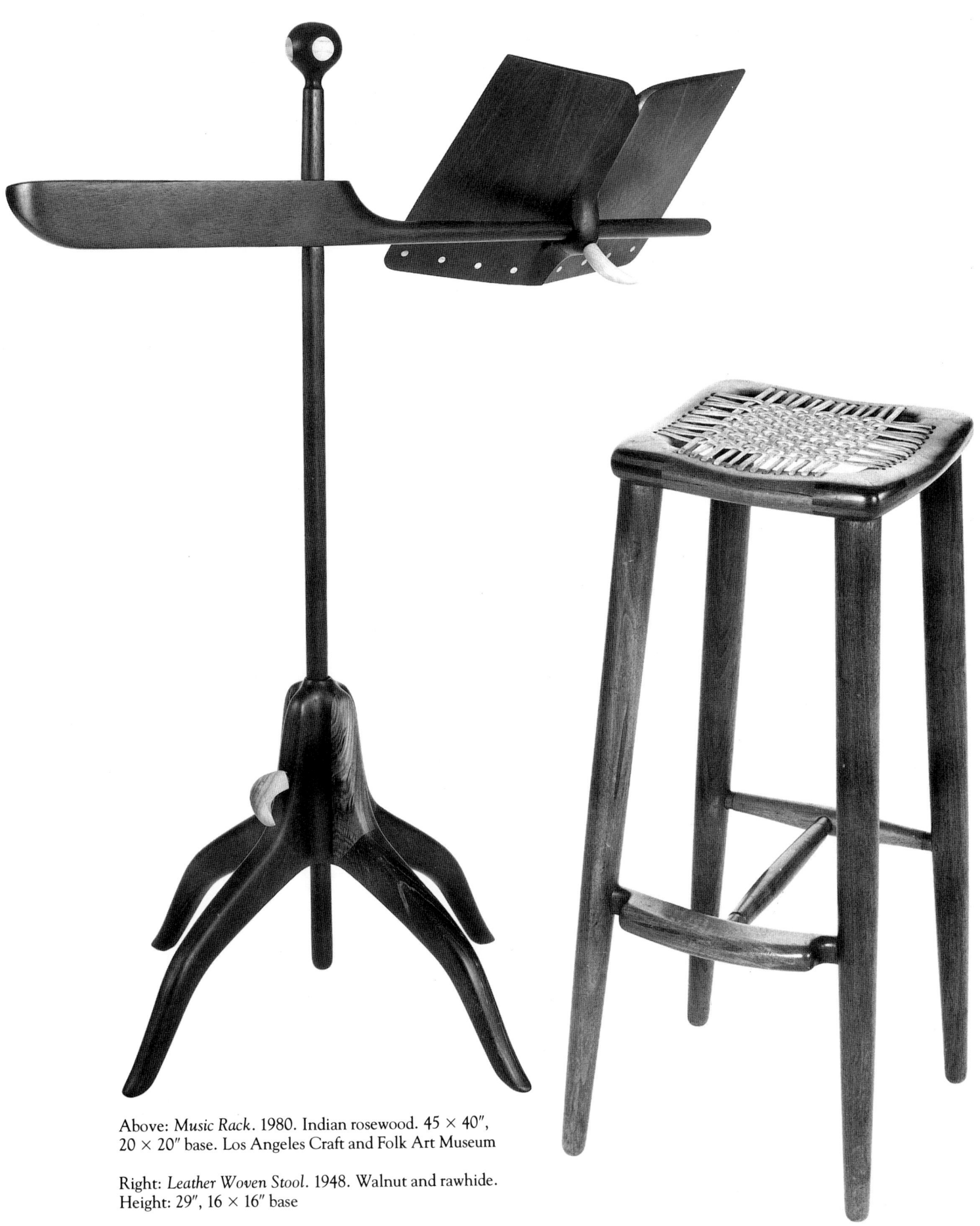

Above: *Music Rack*. 1980. Indian rosewood. 45 × 40″,
20 × 20″ base. Los Angeles Craft and Folk Art Museum

Right: *Leather Woven Stool*. 1948. Walnut and rawhide.
Height: 29″, 16 × 16″ base

Chest. 1979. Walnut. 36 × 38 × 20″. Collection Dr. and Mrs. Marvin Teitelbaum

SM: Well, truthfully, I've never had a rejection. One time I made a tabletop that had an eight-inch area filled with bird shot. Another time, they must have used a walnut tree for target practice and of course the person just raised Cain about it. Then when I told him what it was, and that probably Daniel Boone had been shooting into it two hundred years ago, why, he thought it was great and it became a conversation piece.

BLDD: How do you find the apprentices who work with you?

SM: I get many letters from people all over the country, and from foreign countries too, wanting to work with me as apprentices. I feel very strongly about training young people to work in wood — it would be selfish not to help young people. I remember reading something that Leonardo da Vinci wrote and I quote: "A student who

does not surpass the master fails the master." I used to sort of paraphrase it and say, "The student who does not surpass the master not only fails the master but fails himself."

BLDD: In the approximately sixty to one hundred pieces that you make each year, how much of the actual physical process are you involved in and how much of a contribution do those assistants make?

SM: My shop is a little different from some of the shops I know of. Everything that is made in my shop I design myself. I do all the cutout. I do all the joinery. I do all the rough shaping. If it's a new piece I'll go ahead and finish it up completely. I don't sand it . . . I may do a little bit of sanding but the two young men who work for me are able to carry on from the rough shaping I've done to a finished piece, using a prototype as a guide. Actu-

ally, the most time-consuming part of the work on a chair is the sanding. While they are sanding and rubbing down furniture, I can be making other pieces.

BLDD: One of your best-known and widely imitated inventions is the use of exposed joinery. How did that idea come about?

SM: When I first started, I thought, "What a shame to cover something that is so beautiful." I just felt that joinery should be there for people to see. After all the hard work of making beautiful joints to then cover them over took something away.

BLDD: While you're giving away your secrets won't you tell us how you make your rockers rock?

SM: Every rocker that I make rocks differently because the wood in the seat or the back may be denser than the previous ones. I use the same rocker on all of them, and I have a form that I laminate the wood on, and by moving the rocker back and forth and then just tapping it I see if it rocks perpetually. Then it's fine. I don't have a formula. I just use myself for a model. I'm not that tall, but it seems that no matter how tall a person is, or how short or fat or thin, my chairs seem to fit anyone. Several people have asked me to explain that and I just don't know how. I make the spindles by hand, and I can make a half-inch spindle at the bottom and three-eighths-inch spindle at the top, without even using the calipers; I use my thumb and my forefinger for measuring. And I don't think there is more than a sixty-fourth-of-an-inch difference when I make them that way.

BLDD: You have a wide variety of tools. Can you describe what they are and how you use them?

SM: At the very beginning I had just a few hand tools, and then I acquired power tools as I was able to pay for them. Sometimes years would pass before I could buy a tool, but now I have a very well-equipped shop. I have an oscillating spindle sander, a disc sander, two table saws, a cutoff saw, a thickness planer, a six-inch joiner, an eight-inch joiner, a twenty-inch band saw, a fourteen-inch band saw, three lathes, a drill press, a shaper, an overhead router, and others. I also have a lot of electric hand tools, like electric drills, sanders, and a lot of air tools. The air tools run much cooler and have fewer parts to break down. I prefer the air tools to the electric tools.

BLDD: Where do you keep and store your patterns in the workshop?

SM: The patterns are hanging on the walls, and those are mostly for shaping because I'm not rigid in what I make. In other words, if somebody wants a rocking chair an inch deeper than the ones that I usually make I go ahead and do it as long as it doesn't take away from the design. I make the different patterns out of plywood and I save them and put the person's name on. So if some-body orders a piece that I've already made I just go by the name of the original chair or table.

BLDD: How many steps are there in making a rocking chair?

SM: I'd say twenty-five to thirty steps. When I get through with them they all rock pretty much the same, but they have their own characteristics, their own personalities, really.

BLDD: And how long does it take to make a rocker?

SM: I work awfully fast. If I started in the morning, from scratch — and, of course, you have to consider the drying time and all that — I think that I could put a rocking chair together completely in two days. But that does not include the shaping, the sanding, and the oiling. The sanding takes a long time. So all together, I would figure about two or three weeks for a rocking chair.

BLDD: Your work is well known for its very beautiful finish. Do you stain the wood? Is it oiled? What formula have you created for this wonderful finish?

SM: First of all, I never use stains on any of my furniture . . . the natural wood itself is so beautiful. When I first started working, I saw how beautiful the contrast was between the light- and dark-colored wood, and, besides, wood was expensive and I couldn't do anything with wood that had already been stained for a particular piece. I've used many different kinds of finishes, but for the past twenty years I've used a mixture of linseed oil and beeswax. On my tabletops I use a mixture that is one-third varnish, one-third tung oil and one-third linseed oil. To finish up I use half tung oil, half linseed oil, and then I throw two big handfuls of grated beeswax in a double boiler. I happen to have very big hands, I think, and so a person with small hands has to put in three handfuls of beeswax. It's an old formula.

BLDD: I've heard that you often give finished pieces an extra coating and oiling.

SM: Oh, yes. For example, I have a job now that's going to Seattle — there are eight chairs, a dining table, and a buffet that have been finished for about two to three weeks, with six rubbings. We'll give it another rubbing Monday just before we ship it and then I'll go up to Seattle because I'm doing some other work up there and I'll give it another rubbing after it's installed. Chairs, by being sat in and touched so often, take care of themselves. As for tabletops, the ones that we have here in the house I don't think I've gone over more than once a year, but they do need rubbing down. I always recommend taking a sponge with just a little bit of soapy water and washing off the table first.

BLDD: One of your chairs just recently brought a record price at an auction for the American Craft Museum. What did that chair cost, say, ten years ago, and what did it fetch several days ago?

Cradle Hutch. 1966. Walnut. 84 × 36 × 18″. American Craft Museum, New York City.
Gift of Johnson Wax Company

SM: I think ten years ago I was making these for five or six hundred dollars, and that one brought eight thousand dollars. It surprised me. That's an awful lot of money. My problem's always been in pricing, really. It hasn't been until recently that I've gotten a little nerve. But, in some ways, I think it's obscene to charge these horrible high prices. It means that young people who would want to buy a piece of art work are just not able to afford it. I feel that if a person wants one of my pieces that badly I don't have to have that much money for it. With this horrible inflation now, the cost of wood has skyrocketed. You can't even buy Brazilian rosewood anymore, and I have six orders for rosewood rockers. I happen to have enough to make them, but the price that I'm getting for them wouldn't even buy the wood alone today.

BLDD: What's your favorite wood to work in?

SM: Walnut. It's a very warm wood. I myself could live with walnut, whereas with some of the other woods, I couldn't. It works and wears beautifully. It has a good feeling to the hands. It's a sensuous wood. It's a mellow wood. It's a livable wood.

BLDD: What's the most challenging commission that you've ever worked on?

SM: I did a synagogue once and I had to work with a whole committee, and that was an awful lot of fun. Then I did a Presbyterian church. Those jobs were much bigger than I usually take. I find that every job I do is a challenge, really. Right now, I've been asked to talk to a group in Santa Monica about doing furniture for a big Episcopalian church. I don't know if it'll go through or not, but that would be a lot of fun. In talking about commissions and all, you never have the job until you have a signed confirmation, so I never count on anything till it really happens.

BLDD: If you had the time, the assistance, or the funds, is there any job you haven't done that you'd like to?

SM: I've always wanted to make an instrument, like a guitar or a fiddle or a lute. I think it would be very challenging.

BLDD: Since you're so interested not only in creating furniture but also in making certain that it has a happy home, and you're so concerned about younger persons being able to afford the work you make, have you ever considered designing for mass production?

SM: Not really. I have been asked to many times, especially when I was much younger. Henry Dreyfuss, the industrial designer for whom I did much work, was very concerned about my getting sick and what would happen then. So he wrote to about eight large furniture manufacturers that he knew and they all wrote to me. They were well-known furniture people, but I wrote back and said that I wasn't really interested.

BLDD: Why?

Desk Hutch. 1970. Walnut. 72 × 44 × 22"

143

SM: When I started in the army, I thought, "Never again do I want to be regimented." I guess I followed a different drummer. I wanted to work the way I wanted to work and not be told what I had to do, what would sell, what would not sell, how it was to be marketed, and all. I was never interested in the material side of it as long as my family and I could be happy in what I was doing. I think that if one seeks the spiritual side of what life is all about, then the other falls in place. It is true, I've been told that I was selfish for not designing for more people to use my things.

BLDD: For your own house not only have you designed the buildings and furniture, you've created very beautiful doors and latches to enter and exit from both the outside and inside, and from one room to another. Is there any overall design or plan?

SM: Well, I don't like hardware; I don't use it on my furniture. You don't see any hinges, you don't see any metal at all because there is none. I think the only hardware I use is in my wooden hinges, where I have a brass rod going through. But then they're capped with ebony or rosewood.

BLDD: In addition to your own tremendous productivity you are a great participant and organizer in the country's craft movement. Are there any specific goals that you have in this area?

SM: I've never taught in the universities, but I've given workshops and lectures. I've had friends ask me why I do it when I don't have to. And I feel that it's part of being a woodworker, part of being what I am. If they ask me to share with them, I enjoy it. If you don't share with people you lose so very much. I think you just dry up. And I think I receive as much from them as they perhaps receive from me.

BLDD: What would you like to be doing ten or fifteen years from now?

SM: Making furniture. Not long ago, I had to go to Social Security for my Medicare. The girl asked me, "When are you retiring?" And I said, "Well, I'm not." She says, "You're not? When you do, you're going to get a substantial sum of money." It was more than I ever expected. And I said, "I'm sorry, but I'm not retiring." She said, "Could you give me a date when you'd consider retiring?" And I said, "When I die, and I hope that isn't too soon!"

BLDD: Did you ever expect your life to unfold the way it has?

SM: It's strange — I've always worked with my hands, but I've never anticipated anything. I never expected things to be the way they are. I've asked young people who have come to my shop what direction they're going in. And I'm amazed how many of these people say they want recognition. How can you get recognition when

Chair. 1976. Walnut. 42 × 21 × 22″. Museum of Fine Arts, Boston

you haven't done anything? You've got to work first and produce. I've never sought the little recognition I've gotten — I really haven't. I've never advertised my work; I don't have business cards or brochures. I've never solicited exhibits or write-ups. It has just happened, and I think I've been lucky. I think I've been very fortunate, and I'm thankful for it. I was invited to give a talk at a crafts and religion seminar at the Vatican Museum. The gist of what I said was that I felt that there has to be a communion between the object maker and the material that he is working with. And then, beyond that, a tri-union between the object maker, the material, and the person he is working for, really. So often, as people who work with our hands and make things, we say, "I created this or that. It's all *me*." But I feel it transcends into something much greater than that. God, the master craftsman who creates all things, uses our hands as his instruments to make these beautiful objects. I feel that very strongly.

Above: *Cradle*. 1976. Walnut. 48 × 30 × 36″.
Collection Mr. and Mrs. Maynard Orme

Right: *Dining Chair*. 1974. Walnut. 30 × 22 × 24″.
Museum of Fine Arts, Boston

Left and right:
Interior of Maloof home

Left and below: Door latches

Interior of Maloof home

Left and above: Exterior of Maloof home

Below: *Untitled Basket*. 1981. Red osier and willow.
10 × 10 × 25″

John McQueen, *a basketmaker, walks in the woods for more than just exercise. Among the basswood and the pines, the fields and the streams thick with cattails and reeds, he gathers the natural materials, as well as the inspiration, for his craft. For many centuries and in many civilizations, baskets have been admired and collected as utilitarian objects and sculptural forms. But it was not until about ten years ago that American artists sought to revitalize this so-called humble art. In Alfred, New York, John McQueen — naturalist, sculptor, and craftsman — uses traditional techniques and materials to make distinctly contemporary baskets that are more than beautiful containers. They are the work of an artist whose creative integrity is as evident and timeless as his superior craftsmanship.*

BLDD: Your baskets come in a variety of shapes. In fact, they defy conventional notions of what a basket is. Some are even closed! How do *you* define a basket?

JM: I think a basket, by definition, has to be a container. If it's closed off completely it's not a basket, it's a piece of sculpture. To be a basket, it has to have an inside and an outside. Those baskets of mine that are closed still have an opening somewhere.

BLDD: What *is* the difference between a basket and a piece of sculpture?

JM: They are similar in that they're both objects. The greatest difference is that the basket comes from a different tradition.

BLDD: I've heard you describe the basket as the first man-made object.

JM: There's a theory — and I don't know if it's the truth — that when we still lived in caves, when we were picking berries and swinging from tree to tree, sooner or later we could only hold so many berries in our hands or in our mouths. Someone took a leaf, folded it, put the berries in the leaf, and carried it back — that was the first man-made container. That was the first basket.

BLDD: There are few utilitarian objects, it seems to me, that have evolved less from their original form than the basket. How do you explain the fact that the basket has endured for so long?

JM: It's a very basic, simple form — a container that serves a functional purpose. It's something that you put something in. That's a tight definition, and it's difficult to move outside that definition and still call it a basket. And the container is a universal kind of form. I mean,

our thoughts can be well contained, we're contained on this earth, and this atmosphere contains us.

BLDD: You grew up in Fort Lauderdale, Florida, in the 1950's, before it was a world of high-rises and condominiums. Did anything in that experience introduce you to the naturalism that you practice today?

JM: You could hear the alligators at night during the mating season — it was the time that you never messed with the alligators! So from that you can be sure I didn't live in a high rise. We lived on the west side of Fort Lauderdale, near the Everglades, and I played there in the normal kinds of ways. There was a certain naturalness that I can see in hindsight. I think the basket direction comes more out of other things in my personal development.

BLDD: Your background was as a sculptor. Perhaps you'll tell us where you studied and how that education led to your interests in basketry.

JM: I did undergraduate work in sculpture at the University of South Florida in Tampa. I was out of school for a while and then I went back to the Tyler School of Art, in Philadelphia, where I got a master's degree in weaving. When I was out of school, I started making baskets, and then I went back to school again and learned how to do the "over/under."

BLDD: How did you start on that very first basket? What was the distinction between sculpture, weaving, and basketry?

JM: I was living in New Mexico and Jessie Shefrin, my wife, was going to school at the University of New Mexico. I saw the first baskets that really excited me at

Untitled Basket. 1977.
Elm bark and ash splints.
14 × 13 × 13″.
Philadelphia Museum of Art

the state fair — huge architectural baskets that the Indians had made. It was when I saw those Southwest Indian baskets that I said, "Eureka!" I really started at that point. I'd been working with natural materials like adobe in my sculpture so from that point to the baskets seemed a very small step.

BLDD: Have you devoted a great deal of time to research?

JM: No, I'm not a basket scholar. I learned a lot by looking at baskets because when I make one I naturally see how it's put together. I'm not good at following directions or reading instructions.

BLDD: How do you draw the distinction between those last pieces of sculpture that were done with adobe and grasses and sticks, and the baskets that you then began to experiment with?

JM: I never drew a distinction. At the time it happened naturally. It's like the difference between growing up and growing old; you take certain steps. I never made a definite decision to become a basketmaker, I just became a basketmaker, and that evolved to the point it's at now. It was just a natural progression.

BLDD: What do you see as the difference between sculptured forms and the baskets?

JM: In baskets, there's nothing new — it goes back as far as we do. The difference is in the tradition. Baskets have the special metaphor of being a container so they are different from sculpture because sculpture can be all different kinds of things. But basically they are the same: you work with your hands, making an object that has some kind of meaning to you and other people. Of course, you can only make so many baskets. After a while you try to

154

Untitled Basket. 1981.
Spruce bark and ash. Height: 8″

push that definition; you want to find out what a basket is and what it isn't. In my work I try to push that definition, but they still seem to be baskets — even if they resemble traps or whatever. They still seem to be within the tradition, which I think is important.

BLDD: Your baskets come in a variety of shapes and forms. Have you ever considered making baskets out of materials that are more typical of sculpture, for example, clay or metal?

JM: No. I think baskets, by definition, are made of fiber. A basket has what I call a "mechanical connection"; that is, something that sticks up, a spoke that holds it up. That is an integral part of baskets; they have to be that way. That's the way I see it. If you made a basket out of clay it wouldn't be a basket; it would be a pot or a clay object that looked like a basket. A basket is so

close to the way it was when what it's made from was growing; you see all the marks and scratches that insects made on it. You don't lose that sense as you do in clay. Clay comes from the ground and it goes through so many transformations that you don't really think about that when you look at a pot. Or metal — how did it get to be that shiny slick stuff? But with basket materials, it's right there. I think baskets *are* baskets because they're made out of material in its natural state.

BLDD: How did you come to choose the basket as the expression of your art?

JM: Purely by accident. Some things just happen. Something about the way I am and the way baskets are went together.

BLDD: How do you begin making a basket?

JM: There are lots of ways of beginning. The idea, of

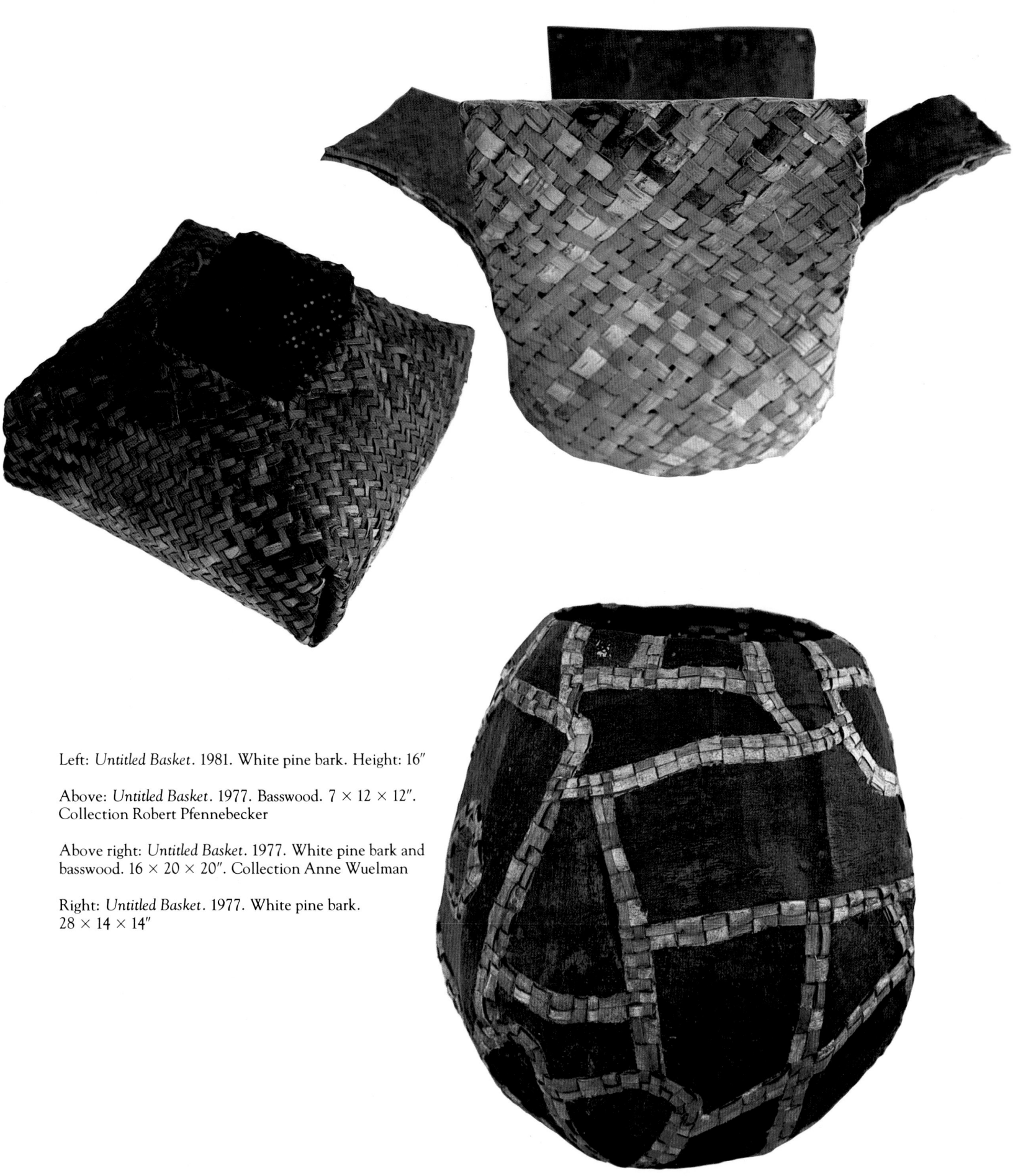

Left: *Untitled Basket*. 1981. White pine bark. Height: 16″

Above: *Untitled Basket*. 1977. Basswood. 7 × 12 × 12″.
Collection Robert Pfennebecker

Above right: *Untitled Basket*. 1977. White pine bark and
basswood. 16 × 20 × 20″. Collection Anne Wuelman

Right: *Untitled Basket*. 1977. White pine bark.
28 × 14 × 14″

Untitled Basket. 1981. Ash. Height: 17"

course, is the first thing. And that idea can come from anywhere — from many, many different places.

BLDD: Do you often make sketches of your work before you begin?

JM: I've always kept sketchbooks with some sketches and a lot of writing — a journal would probably be a good way to describe it.

BLDD: How closely do the baskets relate to the sketches?

JM: Some of them relate directly. You can see where I was thinking about putting words around the top of a basket and I just wrote "words" in the sketch, but then when I made the basket I worked out the words separately. But the idea, the visual image, is direct.

BLDD: There is one drawing that looks very much like a basket with undulating sides.

JM: Right. The idea there was the difference between drawing with a hard pencil, when you have a very stiff, very hard line, and using watercolors, which would be very soft. In this case I wanted to make soft lines, so it's a kind of undulating line.

BLDD: How much of the pattern for a basket is spontaneous?

JM: I try to keep as much spontaneity in basketmaking as I can. But because of my own personality, and also because of the slowness of the technique, it takes a long time to make a basket. So I want to know what's going to happen after I work a long time on a basket.

BLDD: Do you always make a sketch of the basket before you begin?

JM: Oh, yes. It may be done on the kitchen table but there's always some kind of sketch.

BLDD: And how closely does the finished object resemble that initial sketch?

JM: It can be miles from it. I work in a certain direction, of course, but it never happens exactly the way I planned. The natural materials I use are alive when I pick them; then they dry. Something happens to them, and I rewet them; something happens to them and then I weave them together; something happens to them and then they dry again. So the basket never comes out the way I originally saw it, but there's some part of the idea that carries through.

BLDD: Does the sketch evolve as well as the basket?

JM: No, the sketch doesn't get redrawn. The drawing just makes the idea more concrete in my head.

BLDD: You've said that you're not very good at following directions. How do you manage to adhere to what appear to be very complex basket patterns?

JM: They're not complex. There are a lot of elements repeated a lot of times. One sees a very complex surface of texture, but the pattern is really just over and under and over and under. The structure might seem complicated, but the actual weaving is very simple.

BLDD: You begin with a premise that the basket is a container, but the works are never created to contain anything. What is it that interests you particularly in making these nonfunctional baskets?

JM: They always do hold something, even if it's only air. My point is that the basket, to be a basket, has to be functional, and I leave it at that. It is functional. I've never made a basket to hold a particular object; it's more that in making it I know it's going to be a basket, which is inherently functional.

BLDD: One of the remarkable things about your work is that it allows us to see a well-established form from a fresh viewpoint. Do you also make three-dimensional models?

JM: Yes, but the model is no different from the sketch. Drawing is two-dimensional; it's illusionary; it's illustrative in terms of lead on paper. And I'm working with three-dimensional objects. To me, making a model is just another way of drawing — it is a three-dimensional drawing. The basket looks very different when you can walk

Untitled Basket. 1981. White pine bark and ash. 6 × 25″

all the way around it and then when you look at it flat on the page. The model is a tool.

BLDD: Are they scale models?

JM: Usually they're the same size as the basket. Whenever I have an idea for a basket I see it in a particular size as well as shape. The shape and the size go together.

BLDD: In recent times you seem to have a preoccupation with the word and have incorporated it into much of your work. How do you explain that interest with language?

JM: I've always been interested in words as images. I came back from Japan about six months ago and while I was there I realized how important speech is. I always thought that as long as I could put it down visually I had it, but when you can't speak the language and you don't know how to ask for a glass of water you realize that although thought patterns are more than words, words are a very important part of a particular thought pattern. So I've become very interested in the idea of words as physical objects. Because I work with physical objects, I've

tried to find ways of incorporating that physicalness into my baskets. The basket goes all the way around. If you had a sentence and it went around and met its own end, no one would know where to start that sentence, so it would be cyclical. I asked myself, "What kinds of sentences are cyclical?" Sentences that start with the same word and end with the same word, maybe. There is a close connection between what one sees and what one thinks, and I was trying to figure out a way of exploring that with three-dimensional objects. So the word is physically there and, at the same time, you read it as a word. It becomes a double image.

BLDD: Have you reached any conclusions?

JM: No, I've just started! I like the physicalness of words. I've thought about how words begin and end sentences. A sentence is a linear thing with a beginning that's capitalized and a period at the end. What happens if those words, those letters are all mixed up?

BLDD: The image of the word doesn't always look like a word. Sometimes it looks more like a hieroglyph. The

basket that you completed most recently has what appear to be words or images sculpted in a spiral all around it.

JM: The idea for this basket was to make words that would be raised off the surface. When one sees a word on a page, it is really the change of color from the white page to the black ink. So I was interested in how I could make a mark without making a mark. One way of doing that is to physically put the mark there. If I cut a word out of paper and laid it on top of another piece of paper, I would have an image, but it would be a more physical image than if I simply wrote the word there. In this case, the words are actually woven on the surface.

BLDD: What material is the basket woven from?

JM: This is white pine bark, which is kind of a nice idea because white pine bark is actually black.

BLDD: How essential are natural materials to your idea of what a basket is?

JM: Baskets can be made out of anything flexible, and some of the most flexible things are natural materials. Anything I can wrap around my finger is flexible enough to make a basket of. I made a conscious choice to make baskets out of natural materials. That's the way it's been done throughout history, so it's very important to me. I find buying material a rather strange shortcut. It doesn't make sense to me; it's incongruent. But a danger is that basketmaking can easily get sucked in by the materials, because they're very seductive. It's easy to find really beautiful material and then try to make the idea fit that material.

BLDD: How often do you do that?

Untitled Basket. 1981. White pine bark and spruce root. Height: 18″

JM: Well, I cheat a lot but I want it to be the other way. The idea should come first and then I have a vocabulary of materials that I can go to.

BLDD: What are some of those materials, and how do you find them?

JM: I walk in the woods and collect them. There are very few ways of reading about things like that; you have to gather from experience. Some of the different kinds of materials I use are red osier or pine or daylily stalks. Day-lilies grow in front of the house so after the flowers are gone I collect the stalks. And the farmers around all have ponds for their cattle, and cattails have a tendency to fill in ponds, which the farmers don't like. So I have a whole list of farmers who are only too happy to have me clean out their ponds. I have enough cattails or reeds to last forever.

BLDD: If natural materials are so vital to your idea of making baskets, how practical an art form is basketmaking for people who live in urban environments?

JM: Oh, it's quite easy to gather material in an urban environment. When I went to school in Philadelphia I gathered plenty of material along train tracks and in school yards.

BLDD: How much of your time do you spend gathering the materials?

JM: I gather at different times of the year. I'm gathering all the time — it gives me an excuse to walk in the woods. Whenever I go out, I always carry a knife or something to cut with. About half the time of making a basket is spent collecting the materials. So I spend as much time in the woods as I do in my studio. It's more fun walking in the woods than waiting in line in a store.

BLDD: Do you ever find that you're short of a material you need for a certain kind of basket? What do you do then? Do you substitute one material for another, or do you pick up another basket until the material is available?

JM: Probably all those things. I have waited for material, if it's a very particular case. It's a long process so it's not a big deal to finish it the next season. There are plenty of other things I can be working on if I've shelved an idea! But it usually doesn't happen that way.

BLDD: How long does it take for you to create a basket?

JM: The actual weaving time is not so long, but it takes as long to collect the material and get it ready — cutting it into strips or whatever — and then there's another long time that has to be set aside for the material to dry.

BLDD: And how many baskets can you manage to create during the course of a year?

JM: I do ten to twelve a year, about one a month. I work on more than one at a time, so it's hard to say exactly how many.

Untitled Basket. 1981. Cedar bark and red osier. Height: 22″

BLDD: How much of your time do you spend in the studio?

JM: Well, that's my full-time occupation. I go there in the morning and leave in the evening. I try to be as disciplined about it as I can. It's a disciplining kind of activity anyway — you have to spend a lot of time actually doing the overs and unders.

BLDD: Your wife Jessie is a printmaker. Have the two of you ever collaborated on any project?

JM: Yes, we have done a few baskets together. A funny thing is that they have nothing to do with words. Our individual works have words in them but the ones that we made together seem to be much more abstract, and are without words.

BLDD: The baskets you create are so carefully planned and so meticulously executed that I wonder if that is a reflection of the work process itself.

JM: I don't see them as meticulous! I have a hard time with things that are loose, what I feel is not quite together, fringe and things like that. The idea is usually a kind of conciseness. It's a container form. The basket form in itself, with its beginning, middle, and end, implies the finishing of something, a kind of closure. So I want that to be apparent in the work, too.

BLDD: What material have you found is the best to work with?

JM: I have a few favorites. The hill behind our house is called Pine Hill, so I have a lot of pine baskets. And red osier, a kind of dogwood that grows here, has a very bright red bark which I like a lot. And the farmers' cattails. It's usually the materials that are readily available, and there so many! If you go into the store, there may be ten items of the same thing that you want, and you think you have a large selection. But when you go into the woods, there're thousands of possibilities.

BLDD: But those possibilities don't exist in every single season, so how is your life adapted to the seasons?

JM: I collect different materials at certain times — it's a part of my life. I have to collect barks, say, in what I call "maple syrup season." In spring, when the sap starts to rise, everybody else gets maple syrup, and I know that's the time I can start to collect bark. Cattails would be collected after the first frost, which starts the drying process.

BLDD: There are basketmakers who use all sorts of man-made or synthetic materials to create baskets that are different from yours in spirit and in execution. Do you consider those to be authentic baskets?

JM: Yes. I can recognize beauty anywhere but that doesn't mean that I have to make them that way. It's a conflict for me. I want my baskets to look like they were made in the twentieth century. And that's sort of what those basketmakers do by using man-made materials. I

take the other extreme — I use natural materials and try to have a twentieth-century concept. I have a problem with archeological art objects. A lot of contemporary art is made to look like it was dug up. With basketmaking, because it's such an old medium and tradition and discipline, you automatically have an archeological object. I work against that. I want my baskets to have that traditional quality that baskets always have. At the same time, I'm living in the twentieth century — I watch television and do all those other things. And I'm not making old objects, I'm making objects that have to do with ideas I'm coming up with right at the moment.

BLDD: Part of the esthetic of the twentieth century is gargantuanism and hyperbole, yet your baskets are made in the most traditional scale. Why do you choose to do that?

JM: Well, scale's been a real problem. I've thought about what a big basket would be, and I've tried it a couple of times. What usually happens is they become too much like houses. They look like woven buildings made by aboriginal people. I don't have anything against woven houses, but making a large basket is a real problem to overcome. I'm working on it. But it's important that baskets are something you can put something in and pick up. The definition of basket is an object that carries things. That's one reason why they're usually a pick-upable size.

BLDD: You make round baskets and square baskets and even some that are both at once. What is it that you're trying to express with the shapes that you create?

JM: It's a lot of things. I draw from all different shapes, and that includes round, square, whatever. Square baskets are considered strange for basket shapes, but all cardboard boxes — which is the twentieth-century answer to the basket — are square. So it's a similar thing for me to make a square basket.

BLDD: Whatever gave you the idea to put baskets together in a series?

JM: In the first series I did, there was a red line on a tan basket, and you could turn the basket and change the line. It was a way of getting past making an object that was very static. This set of four you could look at in a certain way, and then you could turn those baskets and make that line move. It was a way of changing the basket after it's finished.

BLDD: There is a great deal of repetition involved in creating any single basket. You've referred to "overs and unders." Just how many overs and unders *does* it take to create baskets?

JM: I've never sat there and counted — it would be too depressing — but if you know how many spokes there are and how many stitches in an inch, you can guess at the numbers. Of course, the closer they are woven together

Untitled Basket. 1981. Red osier twigs. Height: 27″

the greater the numbers are. It can go up to thirty or forty thousand.

BLDD: You're doing it by hand! How do you manage to sustain yourself during all those repetitions?

JM: My head is always way ahead of my hands. It's a constant kind of anxiety, I guess. I always want to finish and get on to the next thing I'm thinking about. The actual physical overs and unders are very tedious work. There's also a good side to it: the fact that everything in the structure of the basket is also the image, so everything you see is what holds it together. There's nothing that hides the structure. All those overs and unders are like a skeletal membrane. A "wall hanging" *is* what it sounds like — it hangs with gravity. And a basket is constructed of rather delicate twigs and stems that defy gravity by the way they interlock. They hold themselves up. They overwhelm gravity by numbers.

BLDD: What's the most satisfying part of the process?

JM: Once it's finished, it's not that satisfying to me. Making art — back to words — is a verb. It's *making* art, it's not *finished object* art. From the artist's point of view, the satisfying part is the physical activity of it. After it's done, it's done. And I'm into the next thing.

BLDD: How would you like a viewer to react to your work?

JM: If I'm serious about it, I would appreciate that same seriousness from a viewer.

BLDD: Do you work on commission?

JM: No, I never have. I think it's a strange kind of concept for somebody to commission a basket. Baskets have a funny place in society. Everybody has baskets. But if you notice, baskets traditionally have always been found in the kitchen. Now baskets are coming out into the living room more and more, which is nice.

BLDD: Where do you expect, or want, your baskets to be used?

JM: Oh, anywhere. Once it's finished, the person who owns it should make that decision.

BLDD: Do you keep many of your baskets for yourself?

JM: I don't keep any of them. Once they're finished, I'm done with them.

BLDD: Considering the length of the process and the nature of the materials used, it seems to me it requires a very strong commitment and a very special kind of person to devote one's life and one's art to the making of baskets. How would you describe that kind of person?

JM: To me, basketmaking is a discipline that happened, but I had no control over it and made no conscious decision. A basket is a metaphor for many things and you can take that in different directions. I like that metaphor. And I feel at ease with making baskets.

BLDD: Can we explore that idea of metaphor for a moment? It's obvious that a basket has a kind of roundness

Untitled Basket. 1981. White pine bark, ash, walnut bark. Height: 12″. Diameter: 18″

and singularity and wholeness — those seem to be the obvious definitions. But what are some of the more subtle ones that engage you?

JM: There are a lot. Each basket has a slight, subtle difference in metaphor. But one that comes to mind is the container itself. We are containers. We have outsides and insides. It can be carried to any extreme. I put words that kept getting worse on one basket: it started with something like "cage" and then went to "darkness" and then to "closeness." Another direction could be the metaphor of concise thought. And one hopes a concise thought is better than a rambling thought, or maybe not, so you can take that either way.

BLDD: I still wonder how practical an art form basketry might be for those who live in urban environments.

JM: The earth has certain organic characteristics, and I don't like to think that, as a civilization, we can't find

the naturalness of earth. Even though it'd be more difficult than it is for me here, there is natural growth even in the urban areas. I'm sure you can make baskets out of materials from Central Park — it might be a little tricky, but you could do it!

BLDD: How do you explain the interest in the last ten years in revitalizing baskets as an art form, especially since they were always thought of as a rather humble art?

JM: Humble was one of the better characteristics — there were even worse ways of thinking about baskets! The new interest in baskets came with the crafts movement, as it did also with fiber and weaving. Pottery was breaking through certain boundaries, and then along came fiber. The basket is now looked upon as more than an object. It can be looked at as an idea, which is exciting for me.

BLDD: Considering the fact that you studied originally

as a fine artist, have you ever considered decorating or painting the surface of any of the baskets that you create, using them as a different kind of canvas?

JM: Never in a separate way. I try to make only marks or applied material on as much of the structure itself as possible, like the three-dimensional words. This new group of baskets with words on them will be the first time I've attempted to deal with decoration in a conscious sense. Traditionally, baskets had images on them, and that was a kind of decoration. So now I'm trying to put words on them — another kind of decoration. Before, it was possible to collect materials with so many different textures and colors that I figured I didn't need additional decoration. It was all there; all I had to do was use it. I didn't need to consciously paint it.

BLDD: In some of your most recent work, you are creating letters from twigs, and then you apply yet another layer on top of a finished layer of words made from twigs. What is the idea behind that work?

JM: Again, it's working with the word idea. In that particular case I'm trying to physically make the basket out of words, instead of making a basket and putting words on it. I want the words themselves to be the structure. If you wrote out words in a sentence, you'd notice that the letters don't touch each other. All I've done is added another layer of words so that I end up with enough structure to hold it together. That's the physicalness of it. The idea has to do with the building up of ideas or thoughts: you never have an isolated thought, there's another thought on top of it or underneath it if you think of it in the physical sense. There are a lot of important ideas that build up on top of each other, and that's the way that basket is — the wall consists of two or three layers of words.

BLDD: Here you are, one of the most admired basketmakers in the country, and you choose not to teach. Is there a particular reason for that?

JM: I don't choose to teach because I am a maker. I make the object and I think it's very important that there's somebody physically doing it as well as other people talking about how it's done. But the most obvious reason is that there is no place you can go to study basketmaking. There's no department of art that includes basketmaking as one of its courses. In the fiber classes there are basketry techniques, but there's no place where you can major in basketmaking. Jessie teaches in the art department at Alfred University. That is why we came here, and the reason we choose to stay here is because we really like this part of the country.

BLDD: You like it enough to build a house here. Can you tell us something about that?

JM: Well, that's the biggest basket I ever made! It's a container for sure. We've started building a stone house, so it goes very slowly. One stone at a time. It's a very direct kind of activity. Now we're up to the ground, which is a funny concept in itself. But from now on everything will show, so we're reached that point, after two summers.

BLDD: What is next for you in your own work?

JM: I can never say what will happen next. I might know the next two or three baskets I'm going to do, but I don't have a direction in a linear sense.

BLDD: What are the next two or three like?

JM: They'll have words on them. I haven't gotten the words down yet, so I can't tell you exactly what they'll be. I'm interested in words that, in the dictionary, are called oxymorons: two words opposite in meaning that are used together, like "upside-down."

BLDD: Is it the irony and the juxtaposition that you're interested in?

JM: Right.

BLDD: Which oxymoronic words are you engaged by, now?

JM: "Forced choice" is one, "stable changes" another.

BLDD: Did you ever expect your life to unfold the way it has?

JM: Of course not. But then, I never questioned it either. I believe what will happen, happens. When you're making a basket, you can't say this is going to be a good basket and this is going to be a bad basket, or you'll only make the good ones. So it's all accidental. And I think that's how life is: sort of accidental. What happens happens.

BLDD: I'm struck by your modesty, both as a person and as an artist; the modesty with which you approach your craft.

JM: You've got to watch those that are the most modest — they're trying to hide something! I don't know. I think my personality has a lot to do with why I make baskets. I have no idea what it is exactly. But when I found my basketmaking I found a very quiet, sort of inward activity. I hate to use the word meditation because it's so overused. It's the kind of activity that that kind of quietness grows out of. And I think that fits me well.

BLDD: Is there any secret dream that you harbor — any way or shape or form that you'd like your work or your life to take?

JM: If there is, it's very secret because I haven't found it yet, either. I hope to just keep working and take it in the direction that it's going, whatever direction that is. So there's no real secret; it's just moving along one step at a time. I guess that comes from all these "overs and unders!"

Untitled. 1981. Fired earthenware. Height: 10″

Ron Nagle

is an artist's artist. The San Francisco—based ceramist is also an accomplished songwriter and record producer. He has created what some consider the very essence of the cup form. His simple shapes with hand-built walls, spattered paint, thickly layered glazes, and vestigial handles, after being fired sometimes up to thirty times, are the height of soul, as well as of elegance and technique.

BLDD: The ceramic artist seems to have had a long-term struggle for esthetic and intellectual recognition. In fact, at one point, you even said that canvas was king. Do you think that's still true?

RN: Oh, sure it's still true. Canvas *is* king. Western art is painting oriented, particularly in this country. Here, painting is the highest art form, whereas in Japan there was never any question that a tea bowl wasn't the highest level of art. It was always accepted as such, and it still is accepted as such in the Japanese national treasury. In this country, clay has had a tradition of being a cheap or somehow illegitimate material.

BLDD: Why is it that clay has been the victim of so much prejudice?

RN: Because so much crap has been done in clay. Let's get that straight. I'm supported and appreciated by the clay community, if we can call it that, and when it's advantageous to me or I think I can get something of value, I will participate in that community. I'd rather be thought of as an artist and not as a ceramic artist.

BLDD: Why?

RN: As I've said before, there's this real schizophrenia. When we were first starting to get mixed up in clay, there were the people who followed Peter Voulkos — the second-generation ceramic people, including myself — and there were the "straight" pottery people, like Tony Prieto or Carlton Ball — the traditionalists who did what I call a quasi-Greek look or the Scandinavian three-spouter. Voulkos came along, and the several branches out from Pete, namely Mike Frimkus and Ken Price, who

to this day I think are great. We had to fight all those straight pottery people because they thought what we were doing destroyed form and ruined pottery. So we weren't getting any support from those people and the mainstream art people thought we were working with this stuff that wasn't legit. And what happened is that most people eventually wound up doing "modern" clay.

I became interested in pottery and still am very much in love with certain kinds of it, particularly Japanese Momoyama and Bizen — you know, that soulful stuff that just to look at it takes you somewhere else. It's not that I'm not interested in pottery — it's just that particular kind of wheel-throwing mentality that is a craft-skill. I don't feel that I'm part of any "craft" movement. A lot of times I'm referred to as highly technical, and I'm pleased by that, but that's not what I consider my contribution to be.

BLDD: Every movement seems to have a catalyst and it's generally agreed upon that the central figure in the modern ceramic movement was Peter Voulkos. How would you assess his achievement and influence? How might contemporary ceramics have developed — or would it have developed at all — without his contribution?

RN: Well, you're got to take the guy as a complete embodiment of talent — somebody who is capable, due to his charisma as well as his talent and his energy, of attracting this wide spectrum of crazy guys in a conservative environment like the Los Angeles County Museum of Art. These were the founding fathers of ceramics: Mike Frimkus, John Mason, Ken Price, and Billy Al

Tahoe Cup. 1968–69. Multifired earthenware. Height: 6″

Bengston, and then, later, other people. Pete set an example just being a heavy guy.

BLDD: You worked with Voulkos for a while. How did that come about?

RN: Yeah, I worked with him for about twelve years. I always admired his work. The other important thing in the early days was the kind of exposure you got. I became attracted to what people had told me about Peter Voulkos, and then I took a summer school course with one of his students, Henry Takemoto. By that time Pete had moved up to San Francisco and he came by and told Henry that if I wanted to work to come on over. I tried to get into graduate school, couldn't get in — through some screw-up which turned out not to be grades. Anyhow, Pete gave me a place to work and I started working there. He was such a heavy role model that everybody tried to emulate everything that he did, including his cigars and brand of Scotch and Beatle boots.

BLDD: Including you?

RN: To a degree, yeah.

BLDD: And who hangs out with you, now?

RN: I don't hang out too much. I write and produce music with a partner — we're close on a personal and professional level, but he leads his own life. He lives two doors down the street. And I hang out with my family, Cindy and my kid. I shmooze with my students and talk to them about their work.

BLDD: One of the reasons I ask is because it has been said very often that the relationships among peers in the ceramic movement have been vital to the movement's development in the last few decades.

RN: There is a bit of camaraderie, if that's what you mean.

BLDD: Could you describe this special camaraderie, this special milieu, and how important it's been for you in your own work?

RN: On two levels: first of all, I don't share that camaraderie, I see it from the outside. There are these NCECA [National Council on Education for the Ceramic Arts] conferences, or Supermud, which is like a plumber's convention for ceramic people, basically. And there is this closeness because it's like the NAACP or something; you're sort of battling it from both sides and trying to gain legitimacy so you might as well hang out together. I think it's one of the things that's helped to screw up ceramics. Ceramics is a very incestuous art form, and the reason it's slow to develop is because it draws too much only from itself. I think those of us who have contributed something have drawn from many other sources besides ceramics — painting and music and so on. When you have this kind of close camaraderie, I suppose I'm a little against these conventions — which I'm skeptical of and, at the time, participate in to get in my own two bits. It's like all these people going to the beach and having a marshmallow roast and making raku pots. I'm not into any of this "good fellowship" that happens when people get their hands in mud together. All this has nothing to do with making high-quality art. I'm not knocking the friendship and the fellowship and the support, believe me. If I didn't get that support from those people out there . . . I mean, I thank them very much for it and I'm not laughing at them, and I'm even participating in NCECA this year. But the only ceramic people who I consider soul mates are people like Ken Price, and that's not because my work has been influenced by what he's done.

BLDD: Why don't you describe your relationship with Ken Price? How did his work in the early 1960's affect your idea about what you want to do?

RN: Well, everybody started working and started to deviate from simply taking from a pottery wheel and stacking it and calling it sculpture. I went through this phase as well as everyone else. I mean, I made big walls. I was

168

going to San Francisco State but still hanging out and making pilgrimages to Los Angeles because in my mind that's where the real art was. I'd seen Kenny's stuff in slides and I suddenly realized that, in this realm of abstract expressionism and macho art and big canvases and wide brushes, here was a guy making boxes with cups in them with lace and stuff. And it blew my mind. I don't make cups anymore, you know. I call them "wares." Now I make forms that grew out of the cup form. Anyway, Kenny influenced my work with the cup format, certainly, and also with the color chain.

BLDD: The teacup is a format that you've returned to again and again. Why this form? Do you think its possibilities can ever be exhausted?

RN: One of the reasons I go back to the cup format is that there are enough elements: there's the handle, the foot, the middle — certain things that you can play off against one another. The parameters are varied. Also, the fact that it's asymmetrical appeals to me. In fact, I go nuts if I see one of my pieces and it's flipped around.

BLDD: How about the ceremonial and the historical roles of the cup form?

RN: All those things come into play, although I never consciously chose the cup for that reason. I just thought there was more in that format. Other ones appeal to me. The hardest one is probably a plate. Pete Voulkos is doing a good job with that! I don't know why I chose the cup, to tell you the truth. It just appealed to me and I started going off on it. Then I sort of drifted away from it. Now I'll probably do it again.

BLDD: What is it about small-scale work that has always fascinated you?

RN: I'm drawn to it — that intimate thing, that parlor art stuff, everybody from Joseph Cornell to H. C. Westermann.

BLDD: What can small forms evoke that larger ones cannot?

RN: Presence, I guess. There are certain kinds of subtlety and presence that I found when I looked at Japanese bowls. I compare what I'm doing to that — I think that's the heaviest, you know — and if I get that good, thank you very much! That's the standard. This sounds pretentious but there's a profundity there, a certain kind of humility, a certain kind of soul, of unassuming grace and magic. I'm trying to make some bigger stuff. I don't know if it's going to work. It could just be a parody of my own work.

BLDD: What was your first introduction to clay?

RN: My mother, of course. She did china painting. China painting is a technique in which you use an oil base overglaze material and you paint it on. Traditionally you see rosebuds or little cherubs or birds on the top of the porcelain. She had a club that used to meet in our basement. At the time I thought it was completely bor-

Aquayama. 1978. Multifired earthenware. 4 × 5″.
San Francisco Art Institute

ing. She was doing Santa Claus mugs and ballerinas with skirts. But I stored away all of those hobby techniques, and they became part of the new ceramic tradition.

BLDD: You mentioned earlier that you associated more with the Los Angeles than the Bay area art mentality.

RN: Well, San Francisco is incredibly provincial. During the time I was going down to Los Angeles, I was the outsider looking in. This was in the early 1960's. But there was a great deal of camaraderie between Billy Al Bengston, Ken Price, Larry Bell, Ed Ruscha, Ed Kienholz, and John Altoon. I mean, there were guys who were all trying to be heavy. It was very competitive, but there was this real spirit, a real art scene.

BLDD: You were born and raised in San Francisco, yet never identified with the esthetic scene there. What caused you to remain?

RN: I don't know. Home is home is home. It's very weird. Maybe I'm another provincial guy, too. I hope not. I like it here. Various events in my life caused me to

Untitled. 1980. Fired earthenware.
Height: 6″. Philadelphia Museum
of Art

stay here. I have an eighteen-year-old son. I'm divorced from his mother, but I wanted to stick around for that reason. Also, my job.

BLDD: Certainly, both technically and esthetically, your work has had considerable influence on artists who now work with low-fire clay. To begin with, what is low-fire clay and how did you discover its sculptural properties?

RN: Well, it's not only the sculptural properties. At the time that ceramics was starting to take a turn for the better through Voulkos and several other people, everything was geared to stoneware, which is a high-fire rugged look. It's the material that Pete works in to this day. The esthetic of low-fire means, really, more than anything, color. I was really influenced by painting. I'm not gonna say "I'm doing painting on clay." I shy away from all that

stuff, but it's this color possibility, this variety, directness, immediacy that I prefer for the way I work.

BLDD: When did you first encounter the early Japanese works that left such an impression on you?

RN: Henry Takemoto showed a lot of it. And then I went out and looked for books, and I remember going over to Pete's studio because he used to get them. Kenny was into it, too. All my friends are into the raku tea bowl. I'm really big on just about anything Japanese: I love the architecture and dig the way the food's presented. There's an esthetic that I think is lacking here. Everything is very well considered. It was early, when I was twenty or so, when I saw it. You can't see many of the real ones because they're in the Japanese National Treasury, so I look at the pictures.

BLDD: Have you ever been to Japan?

RN: No, I want to go sometime. I've never even been to Cleveland!

BLDD: You've always said that you wanted your work to have the tough and tender look that Japanese wares have. What makes for visual toughness, or tenderness, in their work?

RN: I don't know. They call it "wabi-sabi" or something — you know, it's yin and yang, just the right balance of the top and bottom end of things. A tea bowl has a kind of grace, but still a clumsiness, an awkwardness.

BLDD: In addition to being intensely involved as an artist-ceramist, you have also written songs and are a producer of records. How did that come about?

RN: I've always had a love of music, since the time I was a kid. I play piano adequately enough to write and lay down basic tracks. I don't consider myself a great piano player. Some other art guys and I had a band in the 1960's. I became interested in writing. We were one of the first bands in the city, called "The Mystery Trend." Nobody could really play, but it didn't matter. It sort of developed over the years. Then I had a house and I built a recording studio in there. And I kept wanting to make records. I made a solo album twelve years ago which I'm not nuts about, but which the critics seem to like, called "Bad Rice," on Warner Brothers. My partner and I made another record that we like, which didn't sell, but also got good acclaim — the "Durocs" record.

BLDD: What about the songs you've written for other people?

RN: We had success with The Tubes' "Don't Touch Me There," which was sort of an underground hit. Then Barbra Streisand did two of our songs on the "Superman" album: "Cabin Fever," which is about a housewife who feels trapped in a suburban situation, and another one which was called "Don't Believe What You Read."

BLDD: What is similar in your experiences of writing songs and making sculpture? Do the two of them nurture each other?

RN: Well, sometimes I kid and say I keep my lyrics in the same bag I keep color chips in. Which is about as close as it gets. The experience is two different things and I think that's why I do both. That's why I have to do both.

BLDD: What else do you think you're good at?

RN: Teaching. Even though I hate academia — I'm not a team player as far as art departments and art politics go — I think I can teach well. I like making videos. I like acting . . . I'm a complete ham, and I'm terrible, but I like doing it. It's fun. I enjoy humor.

BLDD: Are you more interested in producing records or creating ceramics?

RN: It changes. It's both. It's really got to be both. I al-

Untitled. 1980. Fired earthenware. Height: 5"

171

Untitled. 1981. Fired earthenware. Height: 10″. Collection Rick Dillingham

Untitled. 1981. Fired earthenware. Height: 10″

ways tell people, just to scare them, "Oh, I'm stopping, retiring from the ceramic business." And all of a sudden it would get back to me, "Oh, I heard you quit." It would be a joke. I'd tell people that once we got our recording studio finished, I was never coming out and never going to make anything in clay again. And then things started happening — all of a sudden there was an interest in my work. Sometimes I'm serious and I get pissed off at the art scene, although I haven't had that feeling in quite a while. It's starting to happen for me, but I don't know for how long. Things are just beginning right now for our music, too, and for everything we're doing. Our studio's just about completed.

BLDD: If every songwriter dreams of writing the Great American Hit Single, what about every ceramic artist? What are your aspirations there?

RN: I guess just to have some sort of artistic and financial success, artistic credibility, and self-respect for what I'm doing. I try to make the stuff as good as I can — that's the bottom line. And, through the quality of the work, I want to receive the recognition. And I think every artist would like to be independently wealthy — I certainly love money and think it's the greatest.

BLDD: Why do you suppose it is that people in the art community, particularly in the early sixties, didn't approve of your musical involvement, while the music people encouraged your work and efforts in art?

RN: I got shit for the music from a lot of people in the beginning. I don't know if they didn't approve of it or if it just adversely affected my activity in the art scene. Certainly I had some support from the art people, but they'd say, "Well, he's not making enough art so he must

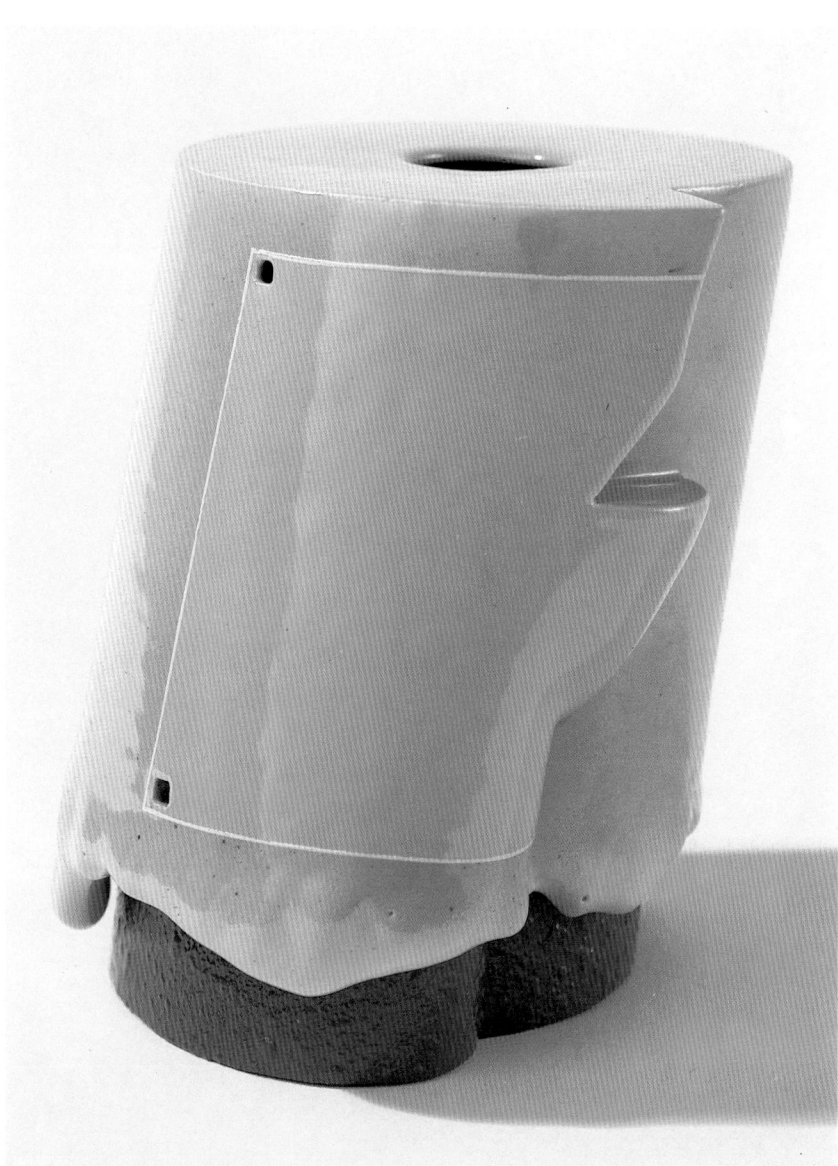

Untitled. 1980. Fired earthenware.
Height: 4½″. Collection Levi Strauss

174

be a musician." And people would give me shit about playing rock and roll.

BLDD: How is your time divided? Is it divided equally between music and art?

RN: It's a real juggling act, I must say. But I have a very hard time relaxing and I have a short attention span, so it's working out because I can juggle it around. I get up in the morning and work on ceramic stuff, and then I put it in the kiln and fire it, and Cindy comes and does something, and I come back later on in the day. But in between those times I might be in the music studio recording.

BLDD: What does Cindy come and do?

RN: I do all the glazing and surface stuff but I depend very much on her for casting and all the technical stuff.

BLDD: For how long has she been doing that?

RN: Just for the last year or so. And it's worked out real good. It's hyped up my production. We actually have a schedule now. My life was scattered; I didn't know what the hell I was doing for a long time. So this is as close to organization as I've gotten.

BLDD: What occurred that caused you to be so much more focused in everything you do?

RN: The writing on the walls said it was time to quit wasting time. Get your act together. I'm not saying I don't get messed up once in a while — I do. I was drinking a lot. Six or seven years ago I was on a bad dive and had to turn it around and get positive. I am pretty disposed to being bummed out and sometimes just don't feel like working. You say, "Why, nobody's interested in what I'm doing anyway," and all this negative crap. I can't say that things don't disappoint me periodically. If some rec-

Untitled. 1981. Fired earthenware.
Height: 6″. San Francisco Museum of Art

Untitled. 1981. Fired earthenware. Height: 9″.
Collection Daniel Jacobs

Untitled. 1981. Fired earthenware. Height: 7″

ord company says, "No, I don't like this song," it still hurts a little bit. But you keep doing it because you love it. That's what you have to do; that's what you are.

BLDD: What is the most fun in what you do of all your work?

RN: Writing songs with my partner. When you come up with a one-liner or some stupid pun or some obscure reference, you just go, "Yeah!"

BLDD: Do you ever get that same reaction in ceramics?

RN: No, I don't, and that's one of the reasons I'm involved in music, where you can just fall out. You're on the floor laughing. Or when you can come up with a sound, and you say, "Okay, let's try that, and let's put that with that, and hook this up to that," and you play it, and you go, "Yeah, wow, man!" I mean, I get that in art too, but I think the funny, ha-ha stuff is in the music.

BLDD: How important is humor in your ceramic work?

RN: Humor's important, but not on an overt level. The thing that attracted me about Price's work is that humor. That quirkiness, that goofiness has always attracted me

to Frimkus. Frimkus was the first guy in modern ceramics to put humor into clay. Unquestionably. He did that without even knowing that he was doing it.

BLDD: You said that now that you have Cindy to help you, your production has increased; to what?

RN: Probably about three or four pieces a month. I don't like to feel like I'm cranking them out. I'm not saying that if I made more, I would be cranking them out. It's a matter of how many kilns I've got in proportion to how many pieces I have going, and things like that. The studio is relatively new. I've only had my own ceramic studio for the last two years, thanks to the National Endowment for the Arts. I used to work in the basement, on the kitchen table, anything.

BLDD: You've always alternated between writing music and working in clay. Can you foresee a time when you might decide to select one medium or the other?

RN: I hope not! That would be like splitting a baby in half. I know I have to do both.

BLDD: At present, you're teaching at Mills College in

Untitled. 1980. Fired earthenware. Height: 3″

Oakland, but you've taught at several other colleges and universities. How does your teaching experience relate to or influence your own creative work?

RN: It doesn't at all except for one important factor. If you're going to be a good teacher, you have to be first and foremost a good professional artist. That's what I learned from Voulkos. In your own personal development and your own work, you have to be a good example. You can't be authoritative unless you're doing something.

BLDD: What's your method of working like? Do you begin with drawings?

RN: Actually, I'm a terrible drawer. You wouldn't even believe these sketches I do. I draw little minisketches on a two-and-a-half-by-three-inch piece of paper, while I'm watching TV or looking out the window or something.

BLDD: Do you draw them in color?

RN: No! They're terrible. The lines are cockeyed. And I'll just keep drawing them until I get them the way I want them. I mean, I cannot draw. But I'll give them to

Cindy and I'll say, "I want it this big, and here's the way we're gonna go," and she'll blow it up and start making the model. We make the models out of Styrofoam.

BLDD: Do you think that your really important innovation and contribution has been the extraordinary glaze? How do you build those layers of color?

RN: Yeah, I would say this is something that I'm basically credited for developing. Spraying china paints and overglazing. For a very long time, ceramics had this kind of classroom mentality where you had to get the project done before the bell rang. We're still dealing with this phenomenon to this day. I'm not saying that a great painting can't be done in one day, but if you're to make a great painting, you know you have to spend time on it.

BLDD: How many layers of color do you generally use?

RN: They go in and out of the kiln, I'd say, thirty times. There might be twenty layers. It's just like painting.

BLDD: You said you begin with color, and then you kill it. How does that actually work?

RN: Well, I don't do that with every piece. What I mean by "killing it" is if you take orange and then spray green on top of it and you'll get a weird gray that you couldn't get by mixing black and white. And you get a kind of sharkskin iridescence, too, picked up on that pebbly surface.

BLDD: How did you know how to apply so many layers of glaze at the beginning? What you were doing then was really unprecedented. Where did you get the technical knowledge?

RN: I just figured it out myself. I took whatever was known about traditional china painting, which I'd seen my mother doing — mixing oil and pigments together. If you want to spray it, you have to thin it out. Then I just started working with different solvents and different combinations and I started building a newer approach. And I also had a lot of experience when I was a kid doing hot rods.

BLDD: You've called your most recent work the "new wares." What are the new wares and how have they evolved? And why did you invent that word to describe the work?

RN: For one thing so that people wouldn't try to read things in them that relate to the cups that are not there. As I say, the format has evolved. The "ware" idea I got from Kenny. It was almost a humorous phrase, instead of calling it "pottery." When you use the label, it's like, what do you call somebody you've lived with for fourteen years who is not your wife? It's the same thing. [He and Cindy married on February 14, 1982.] I don't want to have difficulty, so why don't we call them "wares?" I don't want to be pretentious and call them sculpture. That's for somebody else to say. Somehow sculpture is supposed to legitimize what is basically a vessel format.

BLDD: Why do so many ceramic artists resent or refuse to be identified with the word "crafts" and insist on being called artists? I think there's more of that dichotomy in crafts than any of the other disciplines.

RN: Because of the discrimination. As Robert Arneson once said, they had one hundred sculpture people involved in a show and he felt he was number one hundred. I know exactly what he was talking about. You get it from both sides. Just say I'm an artist. I mean, am I an artist or a musician? I don't know. Any label seems pretentious, so I'll just say, "Ask that guy, he'll tell you what to call me."

BLDD: *Rolling Stone* called you "a Renaissance man." How comfortable do you feel about that?

RN: It's flattering, I guess. But somebody else would say, "He's not a Renaissance man, he's a dilettante. He's a smattering of this and a smattering of that."

BLDD: How would you describe your life and your work?

RN: I don't know. My life is pretty hectic. I refer to myself as a sedated hysteric.

BLDD: You've also called yourself a "diehard romantic."

What does that mean?

RN: Looking out my window with some soft music playing, with my girl friend, sipping champagne. Things like that appeal to me. Things that touch one emotionally, I guess.

BLDD: Do you mean living well *is* the best revenge?

RN: Yeah, exactly. I dig the good life. I think working is the most important thing. That's the only thing that's ultimately going to keep my sanity together. Take a look at Cole Porter's penthouse and Cole Porter's food. I'm saying I dig that, man. That's how I want to live. I'm not digging garret life one iota. That's why we built the studio up here. I never have to leave the house. We've got the ceramics; we've got the art. It's more than I could ever hope for. And I'm grateful as hell that I have that and that I have people that I can work with. It's taken so long.

BLDD: You once mentioned that you learned more from watching Peter Voulkos light a cigar than from watching him throw clay. What did you learn from Voulkos?

RN: A couple of things. For one thing, I meant that metaphorically. What I meant is that the guy has style. That's the bottom line. I'm very proccupied with style.

BLDD: What does style mean?

RN: It has nothing to do with fashion. It has to do with quality, the quality of being, and it has to do with presence. Either you've got it or you don't. He has it. He could walk into a room and completely stink the place up. I don't mean that with a cigar. Figuratively, his presence would be there. His greatness would be there. And that carried right through from the cigar to the potter's wheel. That was a total thing. And nobody knew what an artist was. Nobody had long hair like Pete. There was this whole stylistic element that carried over into the work, I think.

BLDD: You are considered, I guess, to be an artist's artist, and you have described your work as being of the "precious asshole" school. It seems clear that there's a contradiction within your work between those two distinct idioms — on one hand, fine art; on the other, low-down pop music.

RN: Yeah, I guess you could analyze it that way. My humor, I guess, is sometimes too self-effacing, but that's basically what I mean. I say "precious asshole" because there's a certain elitist over-ring to that, too. If you were to break down the various kinds of clay, they're fairly limited: from macho to yuk-yuk to trompe l'oeil to precious asshole. Myself, Ken, and a few others would be of that latter school. I mean that not at all derogatorily; it's more self-effacing humor, I guess.

BLDD: You've said that you reject the "mud-fire into immortality" attitude in favor of the "dimestore cheap preciousness" of low-fire earthenware. Please describe, if you will, a little more fully the history and esthetic of each of those schools.

Cup. 1975.
Fired earthenware.
Height: 4″

RN: The mud immortality does *not* refer to something like what Voulkos is doing. That's transcendent. But there is a stoneware mentality in much of the craft movement — the raku party and the rest. It is basically a quasi-spiritual idea — I say "quasi" because I do believe in spiritual aspects of pottery and ceramics — that man digs the earth, then fires it into clay, and it's a stone, and all this other crap. It's a lot of what in music we call "wanking," which means masturbatory. It's just going nowhere. And I use the "dimestore cheap" reference because that's the closest thing people could see that related to low fire, when that started happening — the bright colors and other business.

BLDD: Have you ever made anything that you now wish had blown up in the kiln, before anybody had ever seen it?

RN: Actually, when I first started working, I broke a lot of pieces which I wish now I had saved — which is the opposite of that.

BLDD: Why did you do that?

RN: Because I was so self-critical at the time. I didn't think they were original enough. I threw the pieces away because I didn't think they were good enough.

BLDD: How do you expect or how would you like your work to evolve?

RN: I can't say. That's the fun of doing it — not knowing where it's going to go.

BLDD: Is there any secret dream or project you harbor that you wish you could do?

RN: Sure! For my partner and me to have a number-one hit single three times a year. To have artistic acceptance on a level other than big-time ceramics. I could tell you basic dreams: to have my house paid off and a lot of money so I could do what I wanted to at my own leisure; to have artistic credibility, as far as having another artist know what I'm doing and digging it; to have peace of mind — constant, continual peace of mind, something everybody's striving for; and to have health, even though I do things to abuse mine. You know, the good life. No sadness, no problems, no troubles. I want the same thing as the next guy. Don't we all want that?

179

Albert Paley

is the leading metalsmith in the United States today. To forge monumental metalworks takes extraordinary talent. It also takes physical stamina and mental discipline to create curving, swirling gates, fences, and furnishings. It's rare for a single individual to spark a new movement, and yet little more than a decade ago Albert Paley did exactly that. At the time, he was making elegant sculptured jewelry until he shifted his purpose and his materials to a grand scale. As the decade of the seventies began, he turned the world of metalsmithing upside down by reviving the almost forgotten art of blacksmithing — forging steel gates, fences, and other architectural elements. Blacksmithing was reborn, metalsmithing was freed of its small-scale involvements, and the National Organization of Blacksmiths was founded in 1970. Albert Paley has managed to weld ancient craft with contemporary sensibilities, and in the process has given us both new meaning and new beauty.

BLDD: Metal is an extremely difficult material with which to work. Why did you choose this unwieldy medium?

AP: Metal is an extremely versatile medium. You can do very intricate work in jewelry with gold, platinum, and diamonds, or large-scale work with bronze or steel achieving architectural scale. It's the flexibility with a material that is unrestrictive that allows this diversity of exploration.

BLDD: While you were at the Tyler School of Art in Philadelphia you studied with Stanley Lechtzin. Can you tell us who he is and describe the influence he had on you and your work?

AP: An incredible influence. This was in the early sixties, an era of social revolution and cultural questioning. The art school environment seemed to epitomize that time. The establishment of professionalism in the arts was quite apparent. In retrospect, Lechtzin's greatest influence on me was fostering a foundation in professionalism, emphasizing innovation and research. The significance of this involvement was not postured toward financial success, but using the working process as a means to develop perception. How do you perceive form, what are the limits and parameters? For me, this form of questioning has resulted in a dialogue with metal. It is a continual evolution and a pushing for form manifestation, resolution, and clarity. Everybody has his own internal sense of order, his own sense of balance emotionally and physically. If design concepts are drawn

from what this foundation is about, the dialogue thus reflects personal awareness and honesty manifested in the work. However, the problem is that the material has a nature and you have a nature, and tools and technology get in between. Discipline is necessary and a lot of years have to pass before you become so well versed in technique and process that that becomes second nature.

BLDD: Was there anything having to do with metalwork in your home environment while you were growing up?

AP: No, not really. Actually, all it comes down to is motivation. I always ask myself why I'm motivated; it's a hell of a lot of hard, exhausting work. When I was young, my family fulfilled the American dream by moving to suburbia. And I think probably all I am doing now is trying to wash the plastic out of my system. The vitality of being alive, of breathing and touching and feeling is taken away from people because they have to do it in a given style or consume a certain thing.

BLDD: How did your interest in art and in craft first begin?

AP: I arrived at the Tyler School of Art of Temple University, where I received a B.F.A. and an M.F.A. I was twenty when I went to school. When I became involved with art, sensibilities were presented to me that I hadn't found previously in the business or the social environment. There was a humanism and a directness professed through the arts that was very rich and rewarding. This touched a lot of very private needs. After several years of training in the various media, I felt that my personality

Bannister (detail). 1981.
Mild steel, forged and
fabricated. Length: 20'.
Private commission,
Rochester, New York

and self-discipline were more in tune to metalworking practices. I just felt that I could express myself much better in the metal vocabulary.

BLDD: Does the work of any other metalsmith or artist inspire the work that you do now?

AP: Well, abstract expressionism gives a lot of credence to the work because it dealt with movement, proportions, and that kind of thinking. Philosophically, I feel I'm more aligned with the decorative art tradition, stemming from the philosophy of William Morris and John Ruskin and the arts and crafts movement, through Art Nouveau and Art Deco.

BLDD: When did you first set up shop, and what was your studio like in those early days?

AP: I started out as a goldsmith, doing one-of-a-kind pieces of jewelry, working out of an apartment. It's only been in the last ten years that I've had an industrial space for the architectural metalwork we're now doing.

BLDD: When you were a goldsmith, some of those pieces of jewelry started out on a small scale and then got larger and larger — almost, in fact, like breastplates. Was there something about the human body and its proportions or gestures that determined the scale and form of the jewelry you created?

AP: Considering that I was disciplined in the art tradition and not as a fashion designer, the jewelry relates to the same criteria of evaluation as any artwork and never was addressed as a fashion accessory. I was concerned mainly with jewelry as a three-dimensional form relating to human form, to the proportions and the movement of the human body. So the environment of the jewelry and its identity was found in human contour gesture rather than the dictates of the garment industry. At this point I feel that architectural ornamentation can make a more significant statement.

BLDD: What was happening in blacksmithing when you first became involved, and when was that?

AP: I became involved in the late sixties. Part of my work as a goldsmith had involved investigating materials and processes with platinum, gold, silver, and copper. Iron was a natural extension of that kind of investigation. In the sixties, plasticity was kind of a key word. Everything was very plastic and very fluid. Contemporary glassmaking had just started; plasticity, the changeability, of the material was very, very exciting. I found myself in that kind of emotional environment working with gold and silver, which have inherently plastic characteristics but are also very resistant. In forging practices,

Bannister. 1981. Mild steel, forged and fabricated. Length: 20′.
Private commission, Rochester, New York

the steel is worked in a heated state,
and at that point the metal is quite plastic;
it bends to pressures and yields. Those types of plastic
responses founded in alterability and changeability
solicit emotional responses. That's still quite intriguing.

All my work has been one of a kind in nature. I've
never dealt with editions. And each individual piece has
been a problem-solving situation, dealing with a specific
mechanism, technique, or design construct. Therefore,
one piece would lead to another in that kind of progression. I've always worked quite intensely; I work continually. In retrospect, it looks like quite a dramatic change
from the jewelry to the ironwork, but it was a natural
evolution. The sympathy is now to the architectural
space rather than to human form. I would say that emotionally, for me, the challenge and the discipline have
always been the same; only technique differs. Working
with the iron is very similar to the way a glassblower
works: you create an environment in which you are a
participant. The iron has a certain vocabulary, certain
dimensions. A dialogue takes place. I'm dealing with
material, human gesture, rhythms, movements, gravity
— all these seemingly invisible things ultimately manifest themselves in form development.

BLDD: You've written that your work is not based on a system of design principles but rather on what you call a manifested perception of order. Can you describe what that means?

AP: What I was trying to say is that many times people develop a philosophy and then from a philosophy a system of order is developed. And that becomes your design construct. Even though I, too, have that kind of rationale, I feel that the only condition that one truly possesses is emotion — not my political beliefs, not my religious beliefs, but my emotion. It's what constitutes my stability. It's more an intuitive approach to design than order. The work makes that visible to me, makes that clear. Usually in an artist's retrospective exhibition this consistency is apparent. The artist is usually so close to the work that he never sees it at the time of creation, only in retrospect. Then, all of a sudden, you go back and you say, "Oh, yeah, I was very confused at that time and the work is very fragmented." Or if there's a lot of

stability, then the drawings or the paintings have the stability and sense of order and continuity.

For me, the object itself is a byproduct. It is only the residue of a thought process. I take photographs of it; it's sold; it gives me money. But the object to me isn't important. Most important is my perception of order and the sensitivity to that order. The work itself and engaging in the work is my own learning process. It creates situations that force me to see relationships, to develop sensibilities that normally would not occur. And in that way, the studio is a very artificial reality.

BLDD: Why is the studio artificial?

AP: Right now, there is no other studio that is working in iron with the scale or the involvement we have. Most of the iron that's done is very historical in nature, not just in this country, but internationally. If it were a natural cultural evolution, a foundation familiar for a lot of people, there would be more of it happening. But it isn't. So out of my own will I have created a situation that

Glass-Topped Dining Table. 1979. Mild steel, forged and fabricated; glass. 30 × 60 × 48"

184

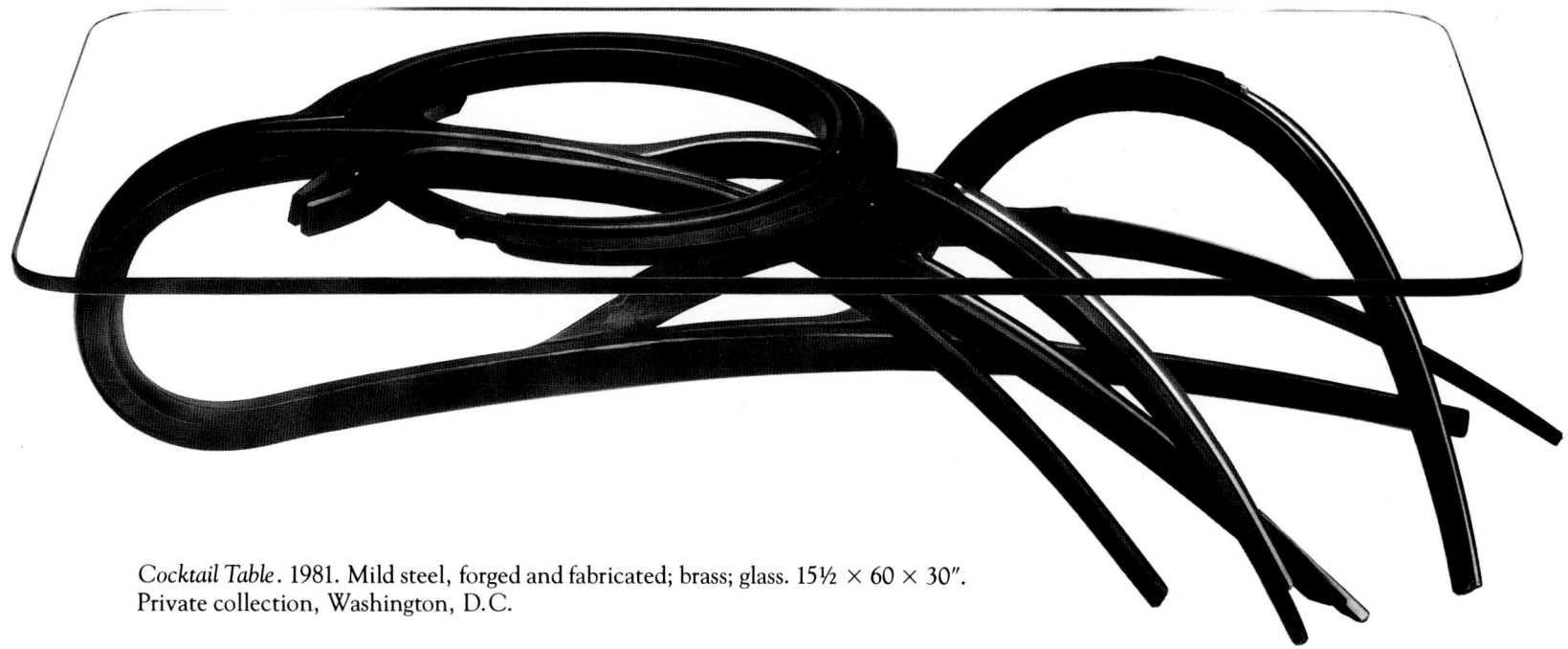

Cocktail Table. 1981. Mild steel, forged and fabricated; brass; glass. 15½ × 60 × 30″.
Private collection, Washington, D.C.

makes certain things possible, by building the machinery, training people.

BLDD: The time when you became involved with your large-scale work, the end of the 1960's, was just about the time that you moved to Rochester, New York. Was there any particular individual or circumstance that prompted that relocation?

AP: I accepted a position at the School for American Craftsmen at the Rochester Institute of Technology, teaching goldsmithing. And, morally, I'm very concerned about education. I'm now a professor at Brockport College, part of the New York State University system, teaching jewelry, sculpture, and design theory.

BLDD: Are your basic concerns the same now as they were when you worked on smaller-scale work?

AP: The formal problems change drastically, obviously, if you're designing a ring or designing a door for a building. I think the basis of the work is personal awareness. The metal is a vehicle to explain and explore personal feelings, and working with this material allows the flexibility to do that. I don't think one's basic nature really changes. You just learn skills to express yourself better.

BLDD: What are some of the personal feelings that you are trying to explore?

AP: It's very abstract. Mainly, what you are seeing in the work is an expression of balance, of harmony, of opposites, of various rhythms that are hopefully unified into a singular statement.

BLDD: What especially attracts you to the work? Is there anything about the physical and spontaneous nature of the metalwork process that's especially important?

AP: One thing about the activity here is that it makes one function in a total way — the physical demands, the mental demands, simply the logistics of doing large-scale projects. Just sitting at a drawing board, designing, there are so many capacities that one never is able to experience.

BLDD: Watching you work, the importance of collaboration is immediately apparent. The coordinated movements of you and your assistants are almost like a choreographed dance; they are rapid and graceful and done with such economy of motion and gesture. How many people work with you and how important is the collaborative nature of this enterprise?

AP: We have five people now. The shop exists in order to execute my designs. The contour, the shape, and the complexity of the work are totally dictated by the design. In order to do this it was necessary to train people to the tolerances that I feel are important. So it is a direct expression through unified effort.

BLDD: Is that collaborative aspect of your work very satisfying to you, or in the end would you really rather be able to do it alone? It's very different from working on jewelry, where you alone control every aspect of the material.

AP: No one person is ever in control of everything. It's not really a matter of compromise; it's just a given condition. The pace of the shop has a lot to do with the material itself. When the steel's heated, you have a certain amount of working time so, therefore, efficiency is very important. The operation is quite an anachronistic en-

deavor. You're drawing on all of the individuals' perceptions and skills in the development of each piece. It's a very human interchange. And on that level it's incredibly satisfying.

BLDD: What is your favorite material to work with currently?

AP: My main concern now is with forged and fabricated steel. The vocabulary that I've developed is one of metal forms, and, technically, right now I'm involved with steel as a material.

BLDD: I imagine that it must be important to be in excellent physical condition to be a metalworker. How physically demanding is the work?

AP: Basically, the question every time I walk in the shop is: what am I capable of doing? And that's physical and mental, sensitizing and desensitizing. I mean, if you're a raw nerve every time you're working, no matter how good your physical condition is you can't make a decision and you can't keep a concept together. You have to go through a lot of emotional adjustment every time.

BLDD: How much of the technique that you use is a result of your invention and how much is based on traditional methods of metalsmithing?

AP: It's not technically revolutionary at all. The blacksmithing disciplines we utilize are very basic. However, improvisation occurs quite often.

BLDD: How did you learn the basic techniques?

AP: I read books and went to museums.

BLDD: Were you never apprenticed to a blacksmith?

AP: No. Most blacksmiths function in industry, whereas my work is a continuation of the decorative arts tradition. Decorative ironwork died out in this century.

BLDD: Where do you begin? Do you start with an image in mind, do you start with drawings on graph paper, or do you construct models?

AP: None of the jewelry or the earlier ironwork was drawn at all. I would create an environment of one element next to another that then established basic relationships. The piece was an evolutionary process moving to its own conclusion. It wasn't that I had a preconceived idea or image and then made it. The working process and the perceiving process, and the mechanics involved, became synonymous. My present involvements with architects and large commissions are established on presentation drawings, so I've had to develop these skills as a means to relate my ideas and concepts to committees or architects. Exhibition pieces are different, however. I start with a basic idea, a basic structure. It is an emotional base, and the form manifests itself from that base. In the beginning, I have no idea of detail or finish or even application, but the piece develops as one would compose a song, with certain rhythms, counterpoints, and accents. At times when I intend to do an edition, I start out with a basic format to have all the objects iden-

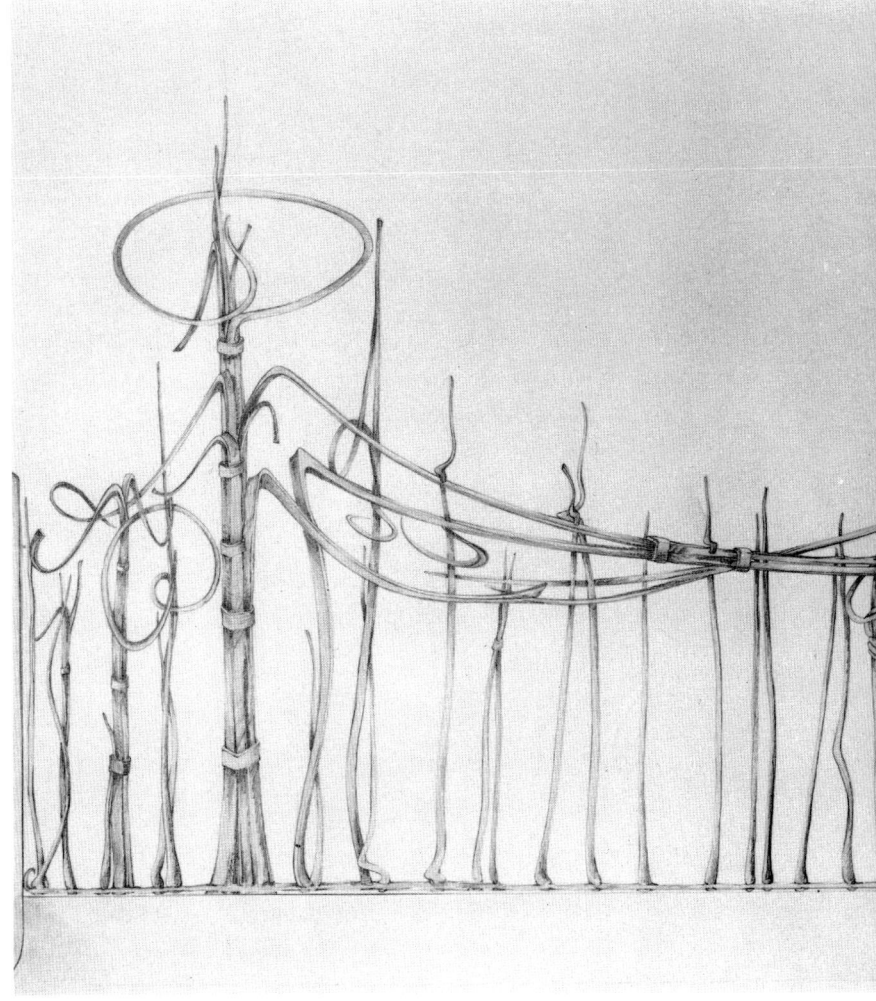

Wrought-Iron Fence, Section #2. 1974. Pencil and red ink on paper. 17¼ × 33″. Hunter Museum of Art, Chattanooga, Tennessee

tical, but they just never end up that way. It becomes a series instead.

BLDD: So the design changes during the actual making of a piece?

AP: Oh yeah, sure. Unless it's predetermined by contract.

BLDD: How closely does the finished piece usually resemble your preliminary sketch?

AP: The work in the studio has a tendency to be quite intuitive. The initial designs or drawings rarely represent the final piece. Throughout the working process, decision making is entertained, which changes the definition and the character of the work. The drawing is a design concept, not necessarily meant to represent the final work.

BLDD: What's the most important part of the process for you?

AP: The entire process is important to me. I try not to

make hierarchical judgments about it. The discipline of getting here, of working, of seeing the metal evolve, the finishing — it's all part of the process, and I really don't segment it into categories.

BLDD: How much time do you spend on a work? As I recall, you've described yourself as a compulsive worker.

AP: Well, I don't see myself as a metal manufacturer. If I did, I could say I worked from eight to five, or whatever. What I'm concerned with, though, is how one perceives one's own reality. If you're alive and aware, the work goes on twenty-four hours a day. So many people work and then have leisure time and play or whatever. This does not seem to be the pattern for me.

BLDD: What do you do when you play?

AP: To me, it's all the same thing. The excitement and the release and the experimentation and the newness and the freshness and regeneration and everything — all that happens in the work, in the vision. Sitting down or

going out I just find terribly boring. I mean, I do it for social balance, but it doesn't have much value for me.

BLDD: Physically, how much time do you spend at the foundry?

AP: We usually put in a ten-hour day.

BLDD: And before you ever get there, I know you spend considerable time drafting at your wonderful new carriage house.

AP: There's a lot of design time, layout work, structural concerns, and research that has to be done with materials. We don't use anything rare or exotic. It's all readily available. We just deal with it in different ways.

BLDD: Why don't you describe your foundry in an industrial park.

AP: My studio is set up basically as a metalworking operation. We deal primarily with one-of-a-kind metal objects for architects and also for private commissions. It's approached as art form, working primarily with forged and fabricated steel.

BLDD: How do you begin? How is the metal formed?

AP: The steel is heated first in a coal forge. An air blast is used that increases the temperature of the steel to a yellow color. This temperature is most sympathetic to the various forging and forming processes. The power hammer is a machine primarily used for preforming of stock before the actual forming is done on a given piece. Repetitive blows delineate the softened steel, establishing cross-section, plane, line, and direction. After the primary elements are delineated through the forging process, they are then applied to a given structure. The forming is usually done directly upon a forming jig, which is a preexisting structure. The steel is heated for the second time, then clamped and bent and held in place on this structure, allowing for various expansion and contraction factors.

BLDD: Tell us about the welding process.

AP: After the preliminary elements have been formed and fitted, they have to be joined. Many times, riveting or collaring or wrapping is used. However, in many applications, we use a welding process. Molten metal is fused to the parent metal, and then is finished by grinding. Each individual element in a piece goes through these various forming processes. In some instances, the hammer or tool marks are left as a reference to the form's own development. However, there are situations in which greater refinement is appropriate, and the piece must go through a finishing stage. This is done with the use of air-driven grinders. A rough wheel is used, and then we go to finer and finer emery paper. Final finishing is done with sandblasting. And then either a painted surface or a chemically blackened surface is used as a final application.

BLDD: How often do you use a painted surface?

AP: Usually for exterior work. So when you produce

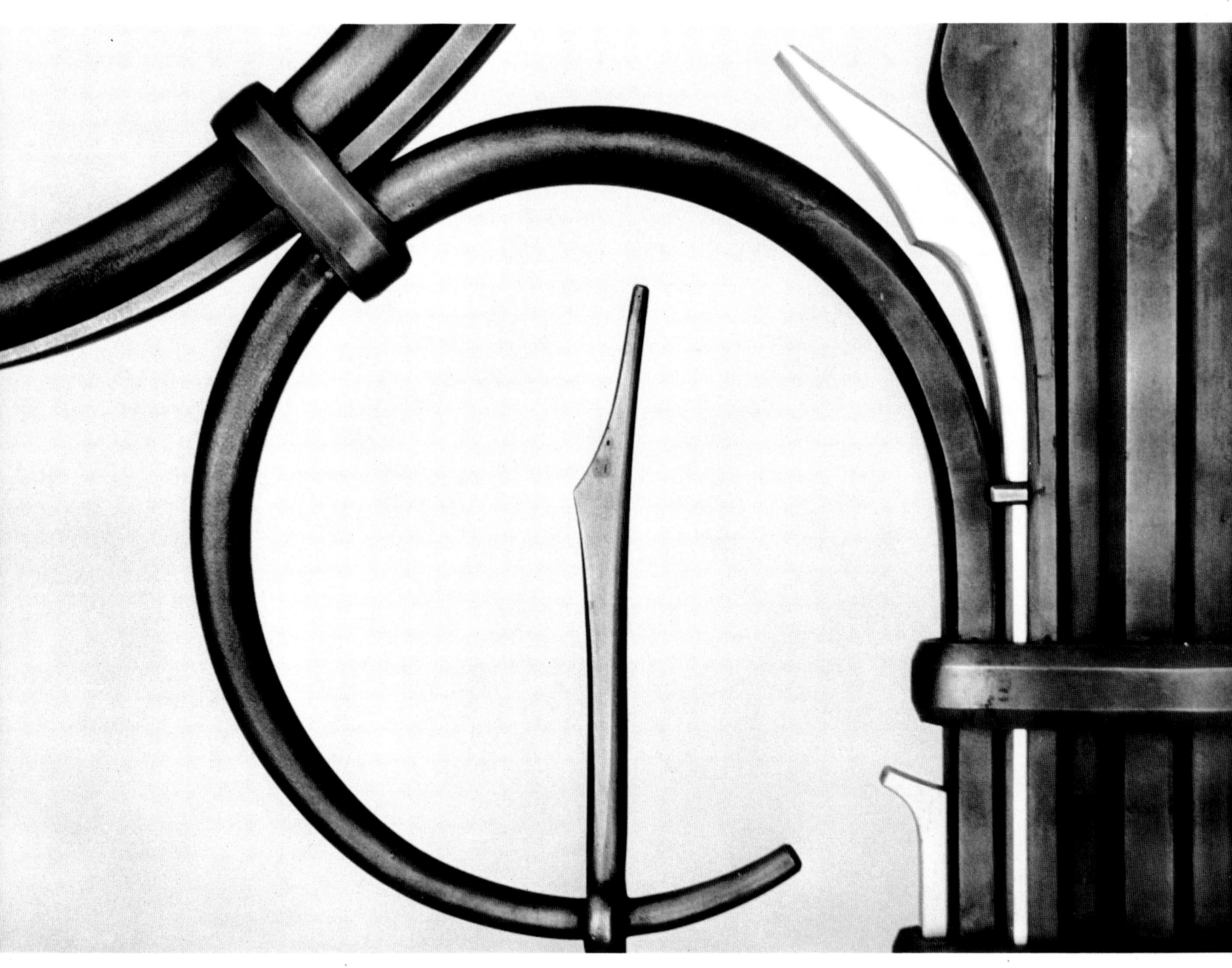

New York State Senate Chamber Gates (detail). 1980. Mild steel, forged and fabricated; brass; bronze. 13½ × 9'

fences or gates which are going to be outdoors, it's necessary to use something like a zinc chromate or zinc oxide base that is rust inhibitive.

BLDD: What sort of tools do you use?

AP: The majority of tools in the studio relate to traditional blacksmithing disciplines: the forge, the anvil, the mandril, and the various hand hammers. I've accumulated an antique collection of hammers and tongs over the years. However, there are several contemporary pieces of equipment — such as the plasma arc, the stick welder, the metal inert gas or mig unit, the carbon arc gouger, and various power hammers and grinders — to augment this basic metalworking vocabulary.

BLDD: How safe is it to work in a foundry? Are there many hazards? And what have you done to protect yourselves against them?

AP: Our approach to metalworking is fairly hazardous. Eye protection is always necessary because of the grinding and cutting that goes on. Many times special glasses have to be worn because of oxidizing flame and the coal fire. Ear protection is necessary because of the power hammers and the high pitch of the air grinders. And safety shoes are worn because of the heavy bars of steel all around. That's about the only way you can protect yourself against the hazards. Most important, I guess, is an individual's awareness.

BLDD: Do you work only on commission?

AP: Probably about 85 percent of the work is commissioned. It's primarily word of mouth and publicity. One thing just begets the other. Now we're involved in finishing up some objects for an exhibition at the Fendrick Gallery in Washington, D.C. The largest piece in the exhibition is a one-and-a-half-ton king-size bed that's forged in fabricated steel, brass, and bronze. The bed functions more as an environment than it does as a conventional bed structure. There'll also be several dining-room tables, coffee tables, plant stands, and sculpture. Most of the objects are concerned with functionalism, one way or another, emphasizing the forged esthetic. We are involved in doing a commission for The Strong Museum in Rochester, New York, a fourteen-foot-high Cor-ten welded steel sculpture.

BLDD: A sculpture rather than a gate or a portal? Is that the first time you've gone to that form?

AP: No. There have been some others. As far as pure sculptural statement, though, this is the largest. Also, right now I'm coming to the end of a project in Washington, D.C., in which we've made park benches and tree grates for Pennsylvania Avenue from the Treasury Department to the Capitol Building. There are approximately a thousand units being installed now. They're being cast in Wisconsin.

BLDD: Since working in forged metal, you've done a number of large commissions around the country. I guess the best known, until this point, is the state capitol building in Albany. In fact, you've said that those two double gates are the best things you've ever done. Do you still feel that way?

AP: Well, I think that the endeavor was the most demanding and the most taxing. Part of the challenge of the work is to exceed one's own dimensions. The first large architectural commission I did was two portal gates for the Renwick Gallery in Washington, D.C. And on that basis I was commissioned to do the ones for Albany. There were approximately thirty-six thousand man hours in the construction. The thing that's really incredible about the work, in this day and age, is that 99 percent of it is handwork, requiring manual skills and the discipline which normally do not exist. It's a unique endeavor in that respect.

BLDD: Between the cost of the metal itself, those thirty-six thousand man hours, and what we all know are the amounts generally connected with public commissions — modest at best — how do you manage to sustain yourself economically?

AP: We broke even. But I always break even. That's a good place to be — even. Especially considering so much of the involvement is concerned with exploration. If I wanted to make money, I probably would have gone to school and studied business administration. My concerns have to do with a given statement and the relevance of that contribution.

BLDD: However, you are no longer just a craftsman in your studio. Architectural commissions, as you know, require a great deal of coordination with architects, clients, the community groups, and environment. You are now, among other things, a business administrator. How did you learn to deal with all of that?

AP: It's a learning process. And I think that the work itself, initially, sets up challenges. You draw a line on a piece of paper and look at that line; that line begets another line. The complexity grows and one expands. It's part of the discipline, that's all.

BLDD: Your jewelry as well as your larger-scale ironwork appears to be heavily influenced by Art Nouveau. Is that a fair or an accurate reference?

AP: Yes and no. One of the things that Art Nouveau tried to do was to break with historicism and to deal with new forms. When the Art Nouveau actually developed philosophically, it was the new art: it was going to scrap hundreds of years of historic synthesizing. If anything characterizes the work, it is its organic nature. And, as a designer, I'm dealing with organic logic, cause and effect, resolution of and the acceptance of opposites. Stylisti-

cally, the only aspect of my work that relates to Art Nouveau is the concern for line.

BLDD: Was there anything in your background that made you particularly attracted to the handcrafted? You spent a small part of your early life living in your grandparents' immigrant community when your father was off to World War II.

AP: To me, the work is a balancing act in which there are certain things that I feel very deeply and certain things that I perceive very deeply. When I'm in an environment where those things do not exist, I try to make it whole again. The work is a healing agent. For instance, in that immigrant background, those things that were based in humanism and were very rich and, I feel, fundamental to the human condition. . . I did not see them in the pasteurizing nature and the conformity of the fif-

ties, where individuality was lost and conformity was the mode. The decade of the fifties was so stagnant that everything that happened in the sixties was a break away from that. I'm part of all that.

BLDD: You talked about Art Nouveau but, as I see it, your designs are also influenced by the arts and crafts movement of the nineteenth century and by living in this part of the country. Can you describe what else you are interested in, and influenced by, from the past?

AP: The arts and crafts movement was actually the precursor of Art Nouveau — the seeds of Art Nouveau are based in the arts and crafts movement. The English, as staunch as they are, germinated Parisian development. But that's all the same. Those sensibilities were inherent in nineteenth-century perceptions and are not modern. However, that is where my attachment lies.

Above and right: Heating and forming of steel bars in the studio

BLDD: So it turns out that the self-described child of the sixties is really a nineteenth-century man?

AP: If there's anything that epitomized that decade, it was idealism. The development of the modern world, manifesting conformity and institutionalization, was the opposite of that. The pendulum is returning, I assume. Right now we might be going through a latent period. The students now are very, very pragmatic. I guess that's important for survival. Being an artist and involved in these kinds of pursuits isn't economically feasible. It doesn't make any sense to the culture at large. It's a very awkward, anxious, uncomfortable position. And most people don't find reassurance in that.

BLDD: It's been said that, to some extent, contemporary crafts are caught between pure invention that is independent of tradition and a reinvention of the past. Would you agree with this idea and is it ever in conflict with the way you work?

AP: When you talk about contemporary crafts, it's a catch-all word for everything that isn't fine arts. Our identity as Americans was founded in the Industrial Revolution. We never had a crafts tradition. I think rather than looking at the crafts today as a craft revolution, you should think of folk art, and the position folk art has always had in our culture. The current craft movement is more related to a folk art tradition, possibly a new peasant revolt.

I've been lucky that I've been functioning and developing in a cultural fabric that has made certain things possible for me. And I've been able to develop my own ideas and perceptions. Timing is important: I think I was fortunate in terms of timing. You can have people that

191

are very perceptive and talented but are caught in a time warp and never have a chance to manifest their perceptions. Yeah, that gives me a lot of satisfaction. But that's not the reason that I work. The work itself is a vehicle for my own perception and my own education, really. And I just developed that the best I could. The museum exhibitions and the publicity and that type of thing, they're just byproducts of the endeavor. I feel good about that kind of response. But that isn't the motivation behind it. In my own life, the pursuit of art lends me a sanity that is important.

BLDD: Do you think of yourself as an artist, a craftsman, a folk artist, all three, or none of the above?

AP: It's very awkward, because labels imply separation. Each one is so loaded with stereotyping that it really doesn't apply. The work is unique unto itself, and it functions that way. I think if this craft involvement is viewed in the scheme of what folk art is, you'd find more answers than people seem to be getting now.

BLDD: How would you describe your work?

AP: I think it's a personal vocabulary of form and design sense. And it so happens that other people respond to it, which is reassuring. An artist always takes that gamble. If you're making a personal statement and no one's able to hear what you say, it's a lost effort.

BLDD: Do you dream of working larger and larger?

AP: We're becoming drawn more and more closely into the problems that architects usually address. We're investigating the possibility of designing interiors for elevator cars, and lobbies for hotels, and gazebos, etc. And, also the studio involvement is engaged in larger corporate projects, such as the castings for Pennsylvania Avenue.

BLDD: Did you ever expect your life to unfold the way it has? Here you are, thirty-eight years old, the leading metalsmith in the country, perhaps the world. What's next?

AP: Just continuance, I guess. It's all right here all the time. And that doesn't change. So many people feel they go through various stages and plateaus and perceptions and so on and so forth. I think my basic feelings and my nature have been the same for as long as I can remember. And all I'm doing is exercising that nature through my work.

New York State Senate Chamber Gates. 1980. Mild steel, forged and fabricated; brass; bronze. 13½ × 9'

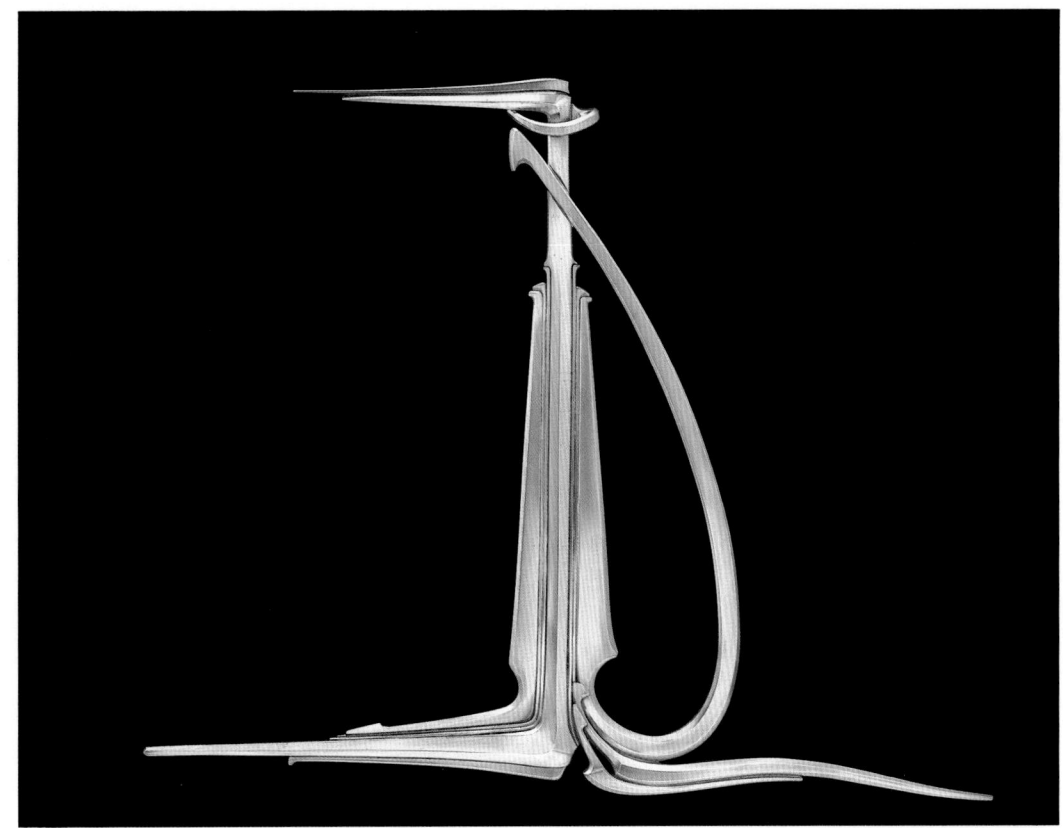

Bronze Revolving Door Push Plate.
Commissioned by Clyde's of
Tyson's Corner, Virginia. 1979.
Cast bronze. 27 × 32 × 4″
The Metropolitan Museum of Art,
New York City

Bed. 1981. Mild steel, forged
and fabricated; brass; bronze.
87 × 79 × 115″

194

Wrought-Iron Fence (detail). 1975. Mild steel, forged and fabricated. 6–12 × 85′. Hunter Museum of Art, Chattanooga, Tennessee

Fireplace Hood. 1977. Mild steel, forged and fabricated. 10 × 6′

Mary Ann Scherr, *metalsmith, jeweler, and educator, has designed everything from toys and children's books to automobiles and stationery. A pioneer in the use of stainless steel and other exotic metals, she is presently chairman of the crafts department at Parsons School of Design in New York City. Her extensive research and development of groundbreaking "body monitoring" devices in jewelry has earned praise from the medical establishment as well as the art community.*

BLDD: When did you first begin to work with metal?

MAS: As my son once said, "She started making jewelry because she was bored being pregnant." And that's just about the way it was. From an active professional design career, I was home six weeks from the hospital with this new infant and a drawing board stacked with projects, and I decided that I had to do something different. That was in 1949. I started taking a course in jewelry, a subject I had not studied in art school. I had never worked in metal before and discovered that I felt very comfortable with the material. I was designing cookie jars at the time my son was born. So between the cookie jars and the metal, I chose to become a metalsmith. From what I'm beginning to understand about metal, there's no end to the techniques that have come through civilizations and cultures. So as long as there is more to learn, I guess I'll be a metalsmith.

BLDD: How does one begin? How do you become a metalsmith? The technology and the equipment are alien to most of us.

MAS: Not if you're a painter; I started out being a painter and an illustrator. The blank canvas is a still, frightening wall, but a foot square of metal is another kind of canvas loaded and exploding with ideas and solutions. I feel as though I've used miles of metal and still feel a rich source of inspiration just under the surface. I've rarely felt at a loss or empty or saturated. Each generation investigates an old technique. The rediscovery

starts to make a personal comment that updates the influence and expresses yet another contemporary image. My work is highly influenced by historical roots. I am both criticized and applauded for this. My work reflects everything. It isn't just this moment, and it isn't only historically related.

BLDD: Does the work or technique of any particular culture particularly inform your own work?

MAS: I seem to care about sources: all of African art, the Byzantine era. I move in and out of themes after effecting an influence in a few pieces. I am restless and have to move on. It's a little like needing to change a record replaying a melody.

BLDD: What is it about body ornament that especially intrigues you?

MAS: All my life I have loved clothes, fabrics, textures, leather, and have designed much of my wardrobe. In high school, as a lark, I made spaghetti and cork jewelry. A local store bought fifty of them and ordered more. That was a beginning and an end. Fortunately. I have sixty running feet of closet loaded with things I cannot part with — the unique, the handmade, the ethnic — all clothing parts that I've put together, that have, in a way, become classics of my own.

BLDD: Did you ever consider designing clothing, as you have jewelry, for a wider audience?

MAS: Being at Parsons means constant exposure to the fashion design department. The knowledge necessary

Trach Cover. 1981. Sterling silver, gold finish on brass. 9 × 7″

Ovals and Lines. 1981. Titanium.
12 × 9″

Necklace, Bracelet, Earrings. 1981.
Titanium with "painted" surface

Bracelet with Smokey Quartz Crystal. 1980.
Black chrome on brass. 4 × 3″

Man's Trach Neckpiece. 1980. Sterling silver,
ebony, ivory; Han dynasty brass artifact.
Diameter: 7″. Smithsonian Institution,
Washington, D.C.

Sterling Silver Bib. 1979. 20 × 20″

199

Elements-in-Series. 1976. Walrus tusk, black
coral, jade, gold, silver, opals. Diameter: 10″

Right: *Dragon Necklace*. 1981. Titanium overlay, riveted sections. Diameter: 8″. Collection Channel 13

Below: *Dragon Belt*. 1980. Sterling silver on brass; engraved. 8 × 27″

these days to be a well-qualified fashion designer would require another entire education. I know that inspiration is not enough. A designer in any field, to survive this period, must be a serious and trained competitor.

BLDD: When did people begin adorning themselves with various metals and gems?

MAS: While I have no proof of the origins of adornment, the first evidence of objects shaped for personal use was found in caves. Claws, shells, stones appeared to be the earliest expression of human reaction to colorful objects — or was evidence for the need for magical symbols. The early amulets that controlled evil spirits or cast spells evolved into such religious objects as the Christian cross, the Egyptian eye, or the Hebrew star, and were worn as symbols of associations. Early jewelry forms described authority, position, or rank in battle dress. The ring became a sign of personal importance. Organizations continue to use symbols that describe a fraternity or club. Wedding rings still symbolize the relationship between a man and a woman. The amazing abilities of the primitive artist who made the tools that shaped the stone images and accomplished techniques continue to be used by contemporary metalsmiths. Early Scythians and Egyptian jewelers made gold a common word with techniques such as repoussé, chasing, and stone setting. The early Greek jewelers used granulation, filigree, and enamels, although adornment became less regarded around the sixteenth century B.C.

The brooch was essential to the medieval robes, and religious objects became a natural effect within the Catholic church. The craft guilds that formed in the thirteenth century A.D. created some of the first jewelry industries, and the Crusades fostered the use of gems and cameos. With the Renaissance, jewelry became a symbol of status and wealth, resulting in a form of investment. The eighteenth-century style expressed nobility and wealth. Rich ornamentation was copied for the emerging middle class through multiple production techniques that simulated the precious stones and metals worn by the richer classes.

The nineteenth century realized a changing society somewhat confused in esthetic decision. The metalwork encouraged inferior alloying. Mass-production techniques often obscured historical adaptation. The amazing work of Carl Fabergé came into historical significance during this period, followed by the art of the then "modern movement" — Art Nouveau and Art Deco. Both continued to seed contemporary jewelry thought, the revival of enameling, and the ongoing use of semiprecious stones.

Today's jewelry designer reflects all ages, cultures, and experience. There appears to be no specific theme requirement; this may be a significant sign describing the selective power of the person wearing jewelry as a personal expression. While fashion continues to dictate the scale and amount of jewelry tolerated in trends and dress mode, the jewelry designer is forming a critical link between style and treasure.

BLDD: How has the purpose and function of jewelry changed and evolved through the ages? You started to say that man adorns himself for various reasons. Is the function of jewelry esthetic, social, economic?

MAS: Unfortunately, the pure esthetic of jewelry as an art form is often obscured by the associative powers assigned to conventional practices — the wedding ring, amulets, badges, the cross, the star, the crown — as well as investment considerations. Ideally, when selected for the qualities inherent in the appearance and worn as an expression of the personality of the individual, jewelry will then achieve the artistic importance it deserves.

BLDD: How are your concerns as a jeweler different or similar to jewelers in the past?

MAS: The past stays with us. The really fine foreign goldsmiths that come to this country, with their amazing awareness of craftsmanship — skills with gold and precious stones — have incredible training, especially as technicians. I know that I will never be that skillful technically. Designing is probably where I am most comfortable. What matters most is that I can design, and that I can educate capable hands to assist in some of the making.

BLDD: Does that mean that you work largely in association, in collaboration, or with assistance?

MAS: With assistance, not really collaboration, although I have worked that way. I am responsible for my own work. As a designer I am responsible for concept. My studio functions with this law. I've had many people working for me over the last fifteen years. I've discovered that the satisfaction I feel comes from being able to express all of the ideas. My concepts never include techniques or effects I am unable to demonstrate. There is always a project on the board ready to be made. Where there is one, there are twenty-one, and if I were to use the precious little time to file away on a piece that I know I can file well, I would be fracturing time. If a capable assistant can reflect my own intention, I then am satisfied and go on to design another piece. I have my hands on everything. Every piece has some sense of what I am or the way I work. There's no decision or part of a piece that is not some part of me.

BLDD: Would you describe yourself as a craftsperson, an artist, both, or does the term really matter?

MAS: I've always labeled myself an artist. For me, art lies in the creative act. Whether the performance occurs with a brush or stone or paint or steel, it is not the tool that identifies the maker. All other issues, while related, do not form the internal force that causes a painting, a book, or a song. I am sometimes a designer, a craftsman, and I am conscious of the eternal conflict between the major and minor arts. I will relieve you of that burden-

some discussion by telling you that titles really don't matter because I know my capabilities. In the best sense of the word, all artists who *make* anything are craftsmen, skilled and unskilled, at least on one level of the presentation. In working with metal I realized for the first time that I felt free to do whatever I wanted without the infringement of requirements and specifications. This new, edgeless freedom contributed to my desire to be an independent artist. I first called myself an artist-designer; for a while I called myself a designer-craftsman, and now full circle back to artist.

BLDD: And what is that transmogrification all about?

MAS: This is a very interesting human period to observe. When I was teaching at Kent State in Ohio in 1970 the students and other young people were concerned with remaining independent of authority and creating a world in which they felt comfortable. The *Whole Earth Catalog*, describing ways to survive with less mechanical assistance, became the how-to bible, and life returned to hand tools for building houses and making objects. The term "crafts" became important, generating educational programs that accommodated those needs. The student in 1980 has a very different outlook. The parents of these students are concerned with the futures of their children, the cost of education, and their career potential. Today's student is competitive, enjoys personal authority, and demands an education that will culminate with being prepared to move from education into the marketplace, equipped and informed. This artist is a product designer, capable of solving problems and aiding in the production of the product through firsthand knowledge of processes. The change from "craft" to "product design" as a departmental effort will bring art and technology together through a curriculum that will give the student alternatives and choices within the industry and the independent art intention.

BLDD: How many schools have as elaborate crafts programs as Parsons?

MAS: My department at Parsons/New School covers clay, fiber, glass, and metal; there are a B.F.A. degree program, continuing education, certificate programs, and adult education. We have approximately seventy-five part-time faculty members, and eight hundred students at different stages of instruction. The schedule offers a really diverse and challenging educational potential. Perhaps the program is not larger or more elaborate than other universities', but the methods and subject matter are different because the needs for most students in New York City are different.

BLDD: In what way?

MAS: The metals student in New York City does not share the same concerns that affect the student elsewhere. In moving from the Midwest, I offered my knowledge and quickly discovered the student demanded a different standard. Not interested in teaching, or posterity, this student wants information that guides the accumulated knowledge into a professional level of achievement challenging industry, as well as having the desire for artistic recognition. As an independent artist or as a production technician with skilled competence, the student is a strong competitor, supporting an intense educational schedule of day and night studies.

BLDD: Do you think that your work professionally, both as a maker of jewelry and as a director of what is probably the largest crafts program in the country, reflects a new direction in crafts; that is, the craftsperson-artist as entrepreneur?

MAS: I feel that we're coming to a point in the development of artists and skills and people and designers when the better artist will have to be skilled in both directions.

BLDD: How important was your own schooling to the evolution of your work?

MAS: Self-realization started really early with my mother. She made any artistic act seem important. She played classical piano and before her marriage was a dress designer. While never pressuring, she made me want to draw, just to hear her exclaim. We had very little money, and with a three-penny allowance I bought bakery wrapping paper to draw on. After a while, I increased the purchase to five cents, which apparently was the first sign of a lifetime desire. The Cleveland Art Institute awarded me several continuing scholarships. This important training covered all art forms (except an advanced course in metals) and prepared the way for any direction I may have chosen. And I chose many. My first résumé read like a telephone book; the experiences with toy sculpture, furniture design, fashion illustration, greeting card design, advertising agency/studio art, dress design, and a bit with show business and coloring books all contributed toward being prepared to make the larger decision concerning a life study, whatever that will be.

BLDD: You have also taught at various schools, including the Penland School of Crafts in North Carolina, Haystack in Maine, as well as your current position at Parsons in New York. How has your own work been influenced by your teaching?

MAS: A great deal. Students ask for answers to questions that set me in motion. If I work with fifteen students, I solve fifteen problems differently than I might have independently.

BLDD: You are known for making pieces that are meant to be used as well as looked at. What do you think the role of jewelry should be? Does it have to be functional as well as esthetic?

MAS: No. First, it should be attractive; it should enhance the wearer; it should express the character of its owner. Every person who selects jewelry is making a statement about the way they feel about themselves. It is

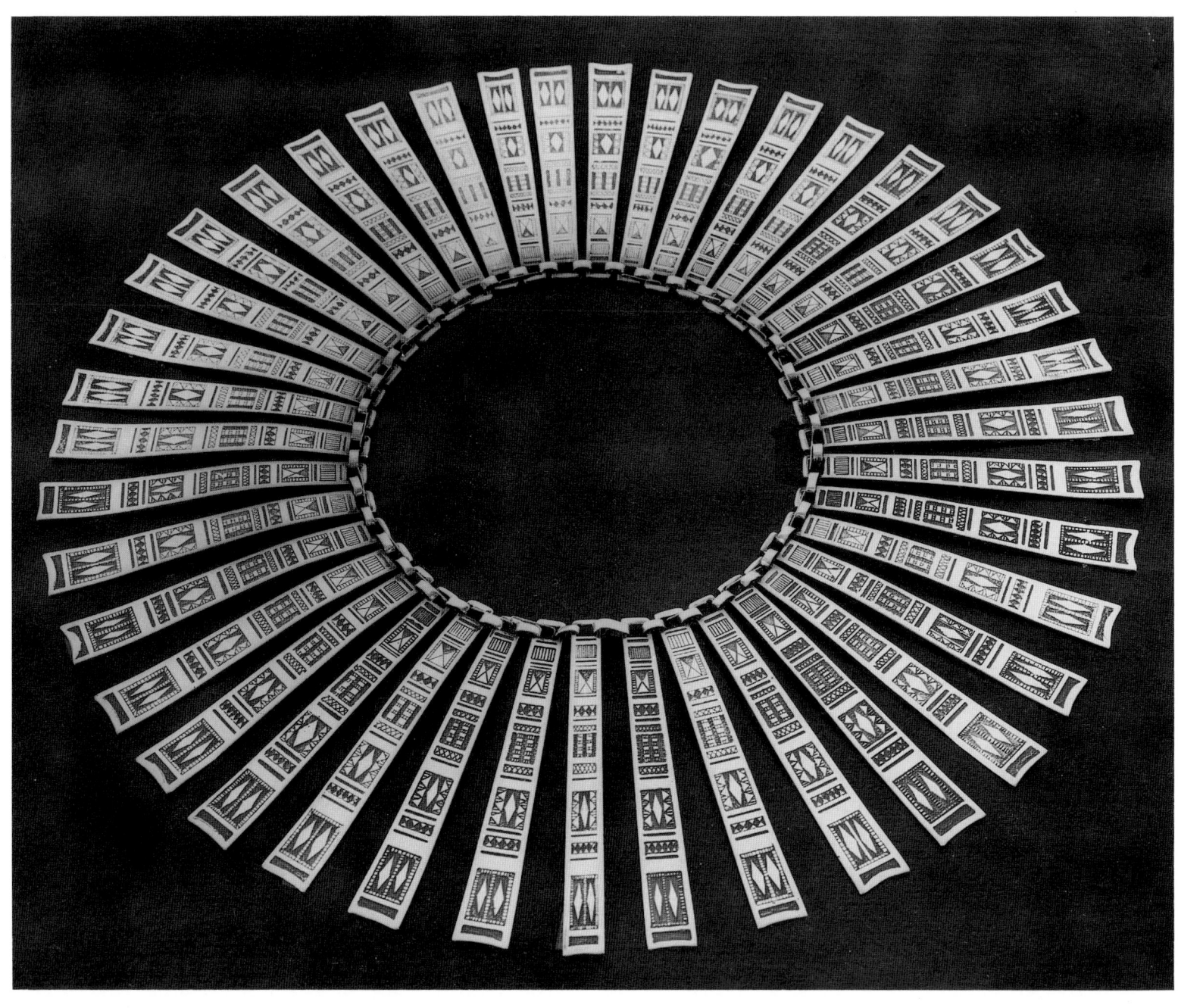

Easterling Collar. 1957. Etched sterling silver. Diameter: 15"

by accident that I am into "functional" jewelry, but I love the accident because it allows me to continue research. If I were to make a choice of what to be in the jewelry field, I would prefer doing research.

BLDD: You are a pioneer in the use of stainless steel in jewelry. Why do you think stainless steel has not been more popular?

MAS: Fortunately, the recent use and acceptance of titanium has forced everyone to look twice at gold, which now costs too much for artists to experiment with.

BLDD: What is titanium?

MAS: It's a rare earth metal and its qualities have been known by engineers for the past twenty years. It's one of those tricky metals that is going to be popular because of its color and because it is different. I think that the time is right to investigate aluminum and other metals in the same eager way.

BLDD: Does "tricky" mean that it's a fad?

MAS: It is a fad and it is fun to play with. There are many rare earth metals that have inherent value. The main quality of titanium as we work it is its color. I'm not that excited about the material because the integrity is not really there in it. My work with it was merely an experimentation. With stainless steel, I remain enchanted with this wonder metal. The pieces that I have in my collection, which I probably will have all my life, are pieces that look the same ten years after being made. The integrity is there as part of the working process. As I began to understand it, and once I converted my full studio to include heavy-duty power equipment, the metal began to respond. The handsaw cuts stainless instead of wood, and suddenly the process is tamed and works for a design.

BLDD: You reinforced my notion that new metals such as titanium may be a fad, a thing of the moment. Do you think we'll be seeing more of these rare, "exotic" metals in use?

MAS: Once people get over the notion that gold and silver are the only materials in the world, copper, brass, and iron become natural substitutes. Japanese, German, and Finnish designers have all worked with different metals: pewters; white, yellow, and black metals. Now we have iron jewelry and public acceptance of the right to work with all the metals. I'm pleased to see this because I love the color and quality of all the metals.

BLDD: Have you incorporated any of those materials in your own work? Does anything and everything go for you?

MAS: When I conceptualize a design, there is an ongoing mental image. These images carry color, texture, contour, and gestures that give the perceptions form and life. If unique patterns are a part of the illusion, I search for a material that fulfills the effect. The James A.

Bracelet with Rotating Discs. 1978. 14k gold, sterling silver. 4 × 4″. The Metropolitan Museum of Art, New York City

Michener commemorative sculpture at Kent State is mostly plastic — an edge-lit maze and a core of pierced metal lace holding a brilliant, faceted crystal. Another piece holds fur, crystal, and feathers. I have a profusion of materials such as grass, gravel, wood, silk, wool, and anything that blends in the mix.

BLDD: I wonder if you feel that there is a close relationship between the design of jewelry and the political, economic, or philosophical climate of any age? And, if you do, what would be the most careful expression of jewelry in this age? *Are* diamonds forever?

MAS: Diamonds and precious stones, pearls, and precious jewelry rarely reflect current fashion trends. Changing the mounting or adding a stone allows diamonds and precious jewelry to live in a separate and perfect comfort. We're in the "large jewelry" period. Magnificent, bold, and brightly colored belts, bracelets, and massive neckpieces fill the magazines and stores.

BLDD: Is more and more jewelry being designed for men? Has it gotten beyond gold chains or one earring?

MAS: Yes. Wide bracelets, really big bracelets, and large

Neckpiece. 1970. Sterling silver. 4 × 7"

belt buckles are very much in demand.

BLDD: How often do you work on a commission?

MAS: There is always a commission in process. Often I am asked to incorporate antiques, family heirlooms, or collected treasures into jewelry. I enjoy these projects; the results are unusual and unique, and they often force design considerations that never would have occurred through natural channels. A Picasso ceramic medallion, rare and precious shells, a doubloon, an African mask of ivory, and a second-century bronze coin describe some of the commissioned work.

BLDD: What has been your most unusual commission to date?

MAS: I admit to being impressed by a few significant personalities, such as the Duke of Windsor, when we were working with the ring sizer and discussing his numerology. But there was a moment of disbelief, relief, and uncontrolled joy when one of the body monitors, against all odds, began to function. The device is a medical "first": the heartbeat is shown in a full-color, bull's-eye pattern, liquid-crystal display. We connected the electrodes to

the body, touched the switch, and to our amazement the color pattern radiated with the heart action. That moment will forever continue in my mind.

BLDD: Let's talk for a moment about your medically oriented designs. What idea or experience first encouraged you to design jewelry that would monitor as well as embellish the body?

MAS: Two things happened: I was teaching and a woman who is a sculptor walked toward me. Her scarf fell away from her neck to reveal some ugly equipment lodged in her throat. The scene paralyzed me, and I asked her if I could cover it up with something that would cause the device to appear less menacing. I made a necklace that caused a remarkable change. She felt amazingly different about herself. She didn't feel "ugly" — her comment. That was a first cosmetic cover-up. Then the mayor of Cleveland asked if I would design a costume for Miss Ohio in the Miss Universe contest. Practically all the first men in space were from Ohio, so that seemed like a logical design theme. While I was working on the belt with all the devices that monitored body functions, I was also watching a television screen monitoring the heartbeat of an astronaut moving toward the moon; a mental connection, of course, occurred. I finished that costume in 1969 and I started searching for miniature devices that could monitor human functions. There was then very little around small enough to be portable. I had to make most of the parts and managed to find some very important engineers who were also aware that it was a worthwhile project. Harry Hosterman and I worked together and patented the first piece, a pulse monitor. Another was the oxygen mask pendant.

BLDD: How did you know how to create body monitors?

MAS: I didn't — it's like "Fools rush in." We have probably put just under $100,000 into this project. That's a lot of money in these past ten years. We are now capable of producing a body monitor in Detroit. Maybe it will start to recoup some of the investment. My next most important piece right now is a smoke detector that we've been working on for twelve years. This one is sort of fun, because it detects cigarette smoke and plays "Smoke Gets in Your Eyes." It nags the smoker and suggests that the cigarette be snuffed out in a very gentle way. And for the smoker who may have fallen asleep smoking, it is a music alert, too.

BLDD: Do many objects that you now produce monitor various body functions or protect our bodies?

MAS: Yes. Mostly I'm working on tracheotomy necklaces where there's a need for cosmetic coverage. All of the pieces that are so-called life-saving devices have to go through rigid Federal Drug scrutiny and I am really not interested or qualified to take them further. My interest remains in the concept and in a functioning model.

Niello Necklace. 1975. Niello alloy, sterling silver and feathers. Height: 15″

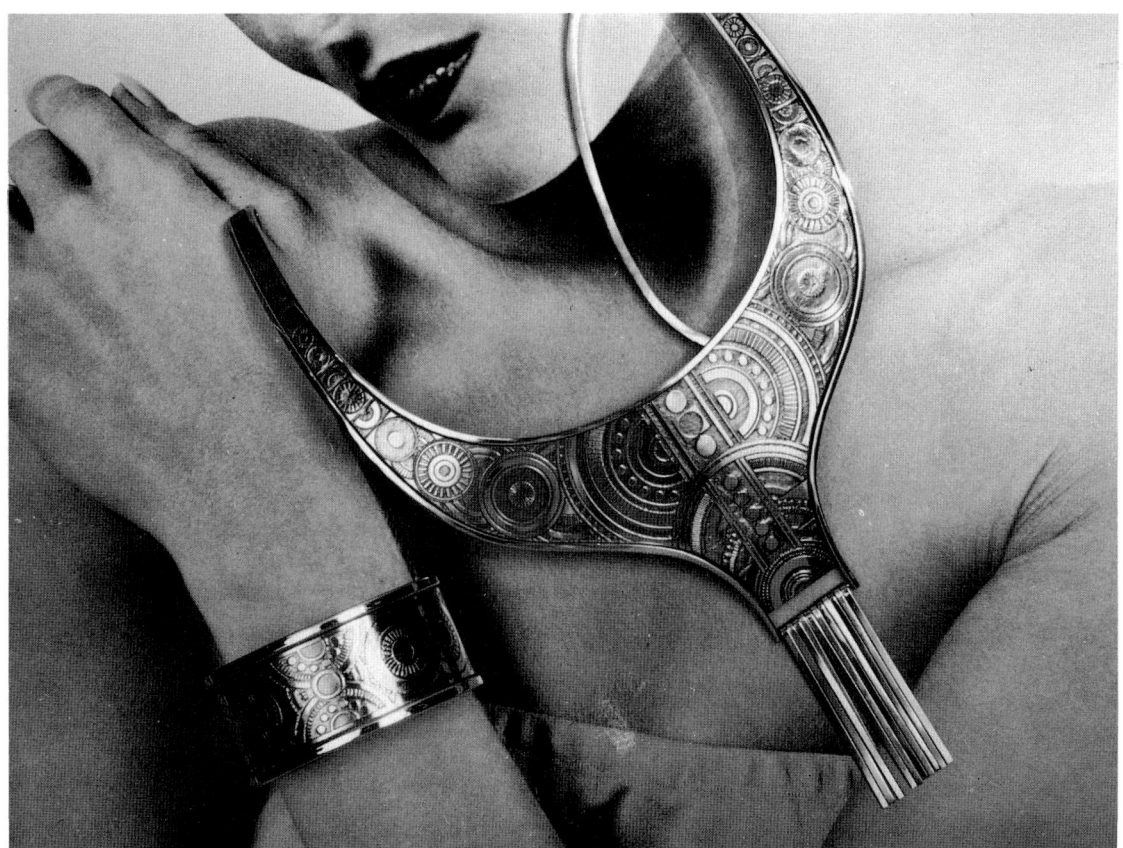

Photo-chemical Inlay (necklace). 1977. 18k gold inlay on sterling silver. 14 × 8″. Collection Reed and Barton, Taunton, Massachusetts

There are several: the belt monitor, a posture monitor, and a sleeping monitor for driving or studying — all these are very interesting thoughts. It is my concern that I have the thought; to carry them through the manufacturing is another level of action.

BLDD: What are some of the most successful monitoring devices that you *have* devised — would it be the "trach" device?

MAS: The trach, I think, probably does the most for humanity. I'm working with Dr. Steven Kanor on a concept that relates to his work with cerebral palsied children who never know where their heads are. Their heads can fall everywhere. With this device they keep moving until the buzzer stops. Then they know they're sitting up. There isn't enough attention being paid to these needs. A number of people have come to me with such problems as large holes in their throats and holes in their arms. They want to live normally. With the jewelry, I'm able to design products that allow them to function without being stared at. The "ugly" equipment magically becomes a necklace.

BLDD: Your medically oriented designs include a pulse-monitoring bracelet, a pendant that holds a ten-minute supply of oxygen, and silver ornaments to replace lost fingers. What plans do you have for future designs?

MAS: Many directions have been supplied by people with real problems. I've been working with migraine headaches, epileptic seizures, bee serum syringes, to name a few. A breath monitor to determine "breath quality" is a current collaborative effort with Dr. George Malindzak. I've also been working with colostomy bags, and many other ways of allowing people with problems to be more comfortable with themselves. I know when I badly slashed my thumb I experienced a handicap, physically and visually. It was a remarkable insult to look at my hand. So I covered it up with one of the "thumbles" that I designed. The moment it was covered, I was less embarrassed to use my hand normally. I'm now designing a "thumble" for a lady who cut off her thumb in a boating accident. I made her a self-portrait with the same little diamond earrings that she always wears. Now in viewing her hand she sees herself, not an injury.

BLDD: What factors are most important for you to take into consideration in designing jewelry? How do you start?

MAS: I start by being away from everything familiar to the actual process, and by thinking. I think the whole image eventually comes to pass like an apparent flash.

This happens after, say, three months of mentally considering and designing it. I actually design the total piece somewhere in my mind, like closed-eye thinking. The work is an image on a screen in my head, and a pencil is an instrument that merely records an illusion. I like to think that I'm designing with a completely unconscious intuitive response. One example was the design of a breastplate that seemed beyond jewelry. One problem that I have in New York is not having chunks of private time. While at Kent State University, I had two hours to drive to and from work, and could design anything in that drive, in almost a subconscious state. Every facet of that breastplate was solved in my mind, even including the clasp, while I was driving. All I needed to do with the pencil was the refinement. For me, this is the best way to design. I advise students to keep a pencil out of reach, to be somewhere alone and without interruption, to be totally removed. I design on planes and before I sleep.

BLDD: Other craftspersons have not been willing, or as willing, to produce their work on such a broad scale as a prototype, or even a limited edition. Why did you choose that path, and how do you explain others' reluctance?

MAS: I believe physical location may contribute to this condition. Exposure to the creative challenge of the fashion industry as well as the demands for information concerning the fashion marketplace by students eager to join this field have caused a profound change in my professional direction and time allocation. There is, at the foundation of this involvement, a very private need for continuity of development, integrity, and response. My first broad venture into the jewelry industry began with Reed & Barton Silversmiths in Taunton, Massachusetts. They selected five artists in the United States to act as consultant jewelry designers. We were shown the production facility and were given simple production guidelines. With no other limitation imposed, we were set free to create. The products we submitted were produced with few changes. The experience was extraordinary. My work was selected because it is bold. I have continued to work with jewelry manufacturers. Systems and techniques for the multiple object have become a very real mechanical science. Educating the student to accommodate this requirement is as much a challenge as teaching

any other technique. The current career goal — to be self-supporting and perhaps industry oriented — demands that the student must be broadly informed on all levels of design, from concept to consumer, regardless of the level on which this market occurs.

BLDD: What is it about the medium of metal that continues to fascinate you?

MAS: The distinctive factor that forces me to remain with metal is *discovery*. I am not unique in this desire to understand — this phenomenon affects nearly all metalsmiths and accounts for the amazing growth in the metalsmithing community over the past fifteen years.

BLDD: Did you ever think that your life would turn out the way it has?

MAS: There is a mental exercise that asks, "When was your last surprise?" I find my answer always seems the same: "A few moments ago." My life is packed with unique moments. I've accepted most challenges, responded to all changes, and attempted nearly all interesting adventures. Luck and timing have always been my allies, and I married a person whose imagination allowed both of us to investigate a wide variety of experiences. We shared three children in the development of a professional life that included invitations to participate in a world conference on "Art & Technology" hosted by Russia through UNESCO; surveying the jewelry industry in Guyana, South America; initiating a design center in Korea; government invitations to Japan, South America, India, Afghanistan, England, and Canada to participate in programs. We were prepared to manage living a full daily schedule wherein the work day was and is a part of the creative development. These and many other experiences have added dimension to an already full living intention.

I am sometimes convinced that being there in a beginning phase of industrial growth allowed us to be selected as active participants. In addition, being selected for permanent collection status is one of the most important experiences an artist may realize. That the museums are great and respected elevates the spirit even more. The Metropolitan Museum of Art and the Vatican are very special for me, like a Pulitzer. . . . When considering the continuous flow of great opportunities, I think of "luck-timing-and-location" and also realize that being prepared is an important factor.

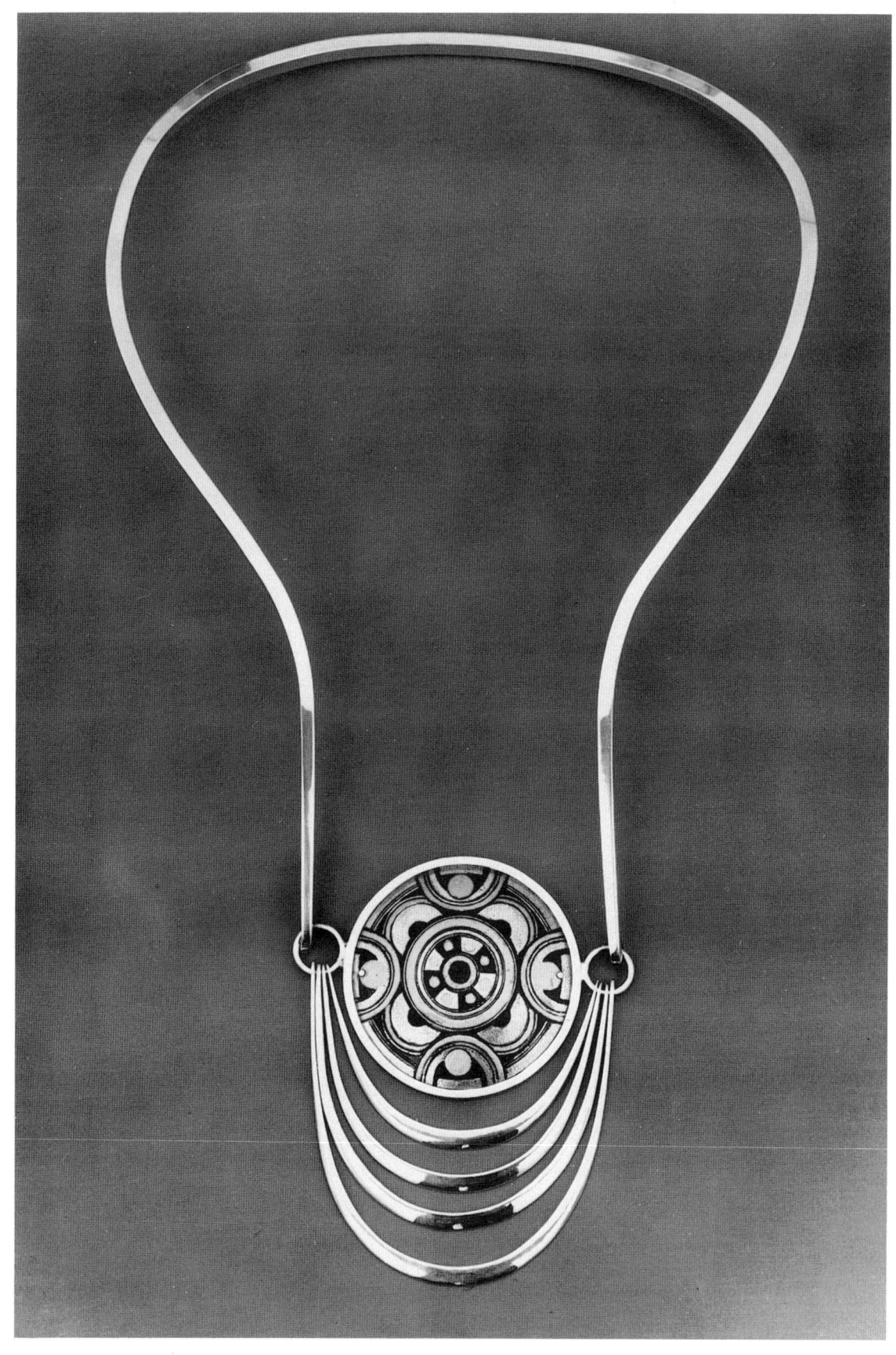

Damascene Inlay. 1977. Nickel, copper, brass on silver. 14 × 8″. Collection Reed and Barton,
Taunton, Massachusetts

Mary Shaffer

takes an ordinary substance — plate glass — and transforms it into a sensuous composition that sags and stretches, cracks and shatters. It is daring art that takes chances, just as Shaffer is a daring artist who takes risks with her medium. Mary Shaffer is unusual among glass artists. Not content to use the medium in traditional ways, she has explored its properties and potentialities to the limit, and beyond. She shows us its brilliance, its transparency, its malleability when hot, and its brittleness when cold. Gravity and heat are her means, and a unique form of glass sculpture is the result.

BLDD: You were a painter long before you began working in glass. I assume the two mediums are very different. Can you tell us how you moved from painting to becoming a glass artist, and how your goals as a painter permitted you to allow to transfer all that creative energy to glass?

MS: There was a three-year period in my life when I couldn't paint. I was working for the Labor Department as a director of a medical manpower program, a forty-hour week, and at the same time had two babies in diapers. Painting takes an enormous amount of time sitting in front of the canvas because you can't paint in your mind and you can't paint while you are away from the canvas. You can have marvelous ideas, but the actual application takes hours and hours. In my office I kept a file of ideas of what I would do if I painted again. During this time my thoughts about my work split in two directions. One was a continuation of the visual concerns in a painting — window and light. This led into working directly with the materials that made up the images — window shades, cloth, controlled light, and glass. The other direction could be called "conceptual" in the sense that the work was an idea first, not tied to any specific material.

I loved the reflections in the edges of walls and buildings when the sun went through glass and showed heat rising. The image moved. I loved that. I wanted to share this love of glass reflection and the visibility of heat rising. That was the first work I tried to do with glass. I discovered heat reflections could only be done with sun-light; you couldn't just use an ordinary bulb — you had to project parallel light. You also had to have a heat source. The heat rod was about twelve hundred degrees Fahrenheit; I attached this heat element to the glass; it shattered of course. But there were pieces of glass stuck to it that were absolutely hot on one side and touching the cold basement walls on the other. I thought, "What an amazing material!" I thought glass was so fragile, and here it was so strong.

I noticed that glass broke differently if it was shattered by heat or by impact. Impact leaves a lot of parallel lines, while heat causes a curvy, wild kind of line, and it also springs apart. I made a number of pieces called "Don't Break the Glass," which I sent to some friends who didn't understand and threw the stuff away because they thought it was broken.

BLDD: Was that how you started working with glass?

MS: Not exactly. I was friends with a lot of glass artists, like Fritz Drysbach and Dale Chihuly. I was living in Providence, where Dale ran the glass department at the Rhode Island School of Design. While Dale was on sabbatical, Fritz ran the shop. He needed a place to live and we invited him to live in our guest room but instead he wanted to live in our driveway — in his truck with his dog. When winter came, Fritz moved into our basement. I was using the basement as a studio. I was trying to paint the undulating, moving light you found in closed curtains and was building different wooden models for the stretchers I would need. Fritz said, "Why don't you use glass? Slump it; it's a lot faster." ["Slumping": process

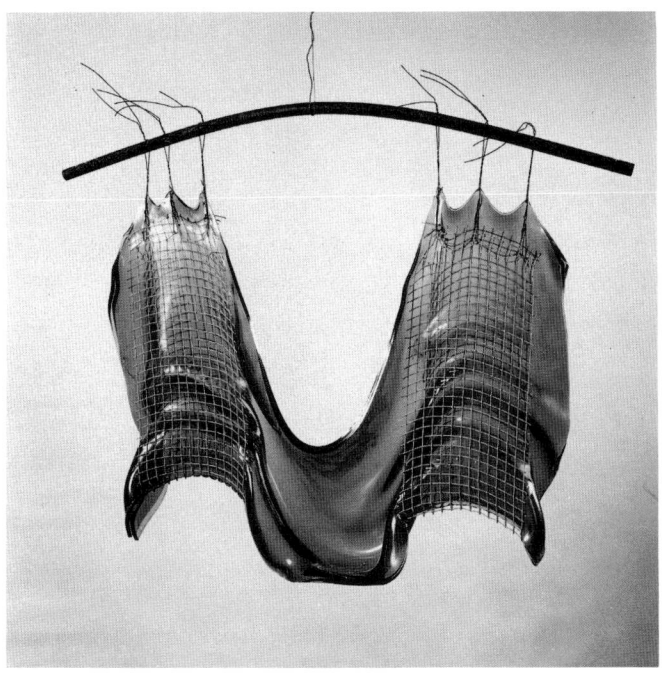

Hanging Series #36. 1978. Glass and metal. 24 × 40 × 4".
Zimmerman collection

through which plate glass, exposed to extreme heat,
takes on new forms as it melts.] That meant I would
paint on glass instead of canvas. Kandinsky is one of my
favorite painters; he has a series of religious paintings on
glass which I knew from the Lenbachhaus in Munich.
"Well how do you slump glass?" He said, "I don't know.
It's an industrial process. I think it takes twelve hours."

I then started working that way. That was in 1972.
One of Dale's students, Toots Zynsky, was babysitting for
me regularly. She helped me regulate the ovens — there
is a lot of tending the ovens in slumping. She started putting her own work in the ovens as well, and that got me
back into exhibiting.

BLDD: What interests and excites you most about the
material?

MS: Once you start working with it, you see what an incredible material it is. You want to do more. If you ask
your students to paint the most difficult thing in the
world, nine times out of ten they will come up with a
glass of water. A glass of water is beautiful. It's difficult to
paint transparency, and it's wonderful to look at. There
are also other qualities — of danger, of getting cut, of
breaking it. There's a duality, too. Here we are, skinning
our buildings with glass and we think nothing about it.
An eighth of our cars appears to be made of glass. We
don't worry about that. We have glass all over the house.
We drink from it! But as soon as people see glass art or
when they are around sheets or panes of glass they get
afraid.

BLDD: How dangerous is it to work with glass?

MS: When you're working with big sheets, it's dangerous. You have to be very careful. I wear gloves. I was fuss-
ing at one of the people in the factory who was carrying a
large piece of glass. I said, "Why don't you put on a pair
of gloves?" He said, "Mary, it's going to cut the glove
too." And he was right. If it's going to cut your hand, it'll
cut the glove too, then go through your hand. You just
have to be very careful.

BLDD: How did you discover the glass slumping process
as your own personal direction?

MS: As soon as I saw the first piece come from the ovens
at the Rhode Island School of Design, I was intrigued.
The transparency of glass and its ability to reflect and
carry light corresponded to my other work. I was making
constructions then that dealt directly with windows. I
used curtains, wind, window shades, acetate, and different light sources. I would take light and disperse it —
pull it, contain it, use it reflected off other materials.
The first slump glass forms were identical to the acetate shapes I was making, an undulating surface that
stretched light. The glass was solid, not flimsy, and could
do all the magic with light that I was trying to get from
other materials.

BLDD: The slumping process is an industrial method.
Can you describe what takes place?

MS: I take plate glass — straight window-pane glass —
heat it, and put it into a structure that holds the glass but
also allows it some free movement. The structure can be
made of brick, metal, wire, a plaster mixture, anything
that can withstand the heat. I prefer not to use a mold. I
like the glass to help form itself, mid-air. I like that living
aspect of the glass. I found that the slumping process was
totally compatible with my ideas. It was a funny period.
My other work was dealing with cyclical time, with
building and destruction — every point in time was equal
to any other point. The slumping process was also cyclical. You start with a piece of plate glass. It moves into a
form; then if you overheat it it could hit the oven floor
and become a puddle of flat glass similar to its original
shape.

I also liked very much that the slumping process allowed the nature of the glass to come out; set up a particular way, the glass could help determine its own form.
Working with the material in that way was a dialogue.
Many artists I admired at the time were involved with
earth works, ideas of displacement, or conceptual art.
No one was seriously making objects.

BLDD: How did your own knowledge about this industrial method of altering the shape of glass evolve? Did
you visit factories or plants?

MS: No, it was intuitive. I found out with that first experience that glass can withstand enormous heat, enor-

mous abuse. Fritz Drysbach said slumping takes twelve hours, but that isn't necessarily true; it can go much faster. Through observation, I developed all my technical knowledge and discovered a lot of misinformation in published documents. Studio art glass came out of the ceramic shops, and a lot of the technical information that ceramists had was passed on to us using their experience.

BLDD: The studio glass movement is not very old. I believe it started with Harvey Littleton in 1962, when he added glassmaking to the art department of the University of Wisconsin, where he was then teaching.

MS: Yes, very true. Littleton's friendship with Erwin Eisch is also interesting. They had a lot in common. Lit-

tleton's father was a physicist with Corning Glass Works and the Eisch family owned a glass factory in Bavaria. Both were interested in art. Littleton studied ceramics, and Eisch, painting. When Littleton finally got a glass shop going at Wisconsin he invited Eisch over to work with him. Their friendship was significant. They thought of glass as art, right away. Littleton didn't spend much time trying to make vessels. He did work from a blowpipe. But instead of blowing out the forms he pulled them into long rods he looped, and twisted them in upon themselves. His work is characterized by its clarity of glass and brilliance of color. He also did slumped glass in 1974, but for some reason, slumping never caught on. I simply started with it because I was trying to find a sur-

Waterfall. 1981. Glass. 9 × 9 × 6′

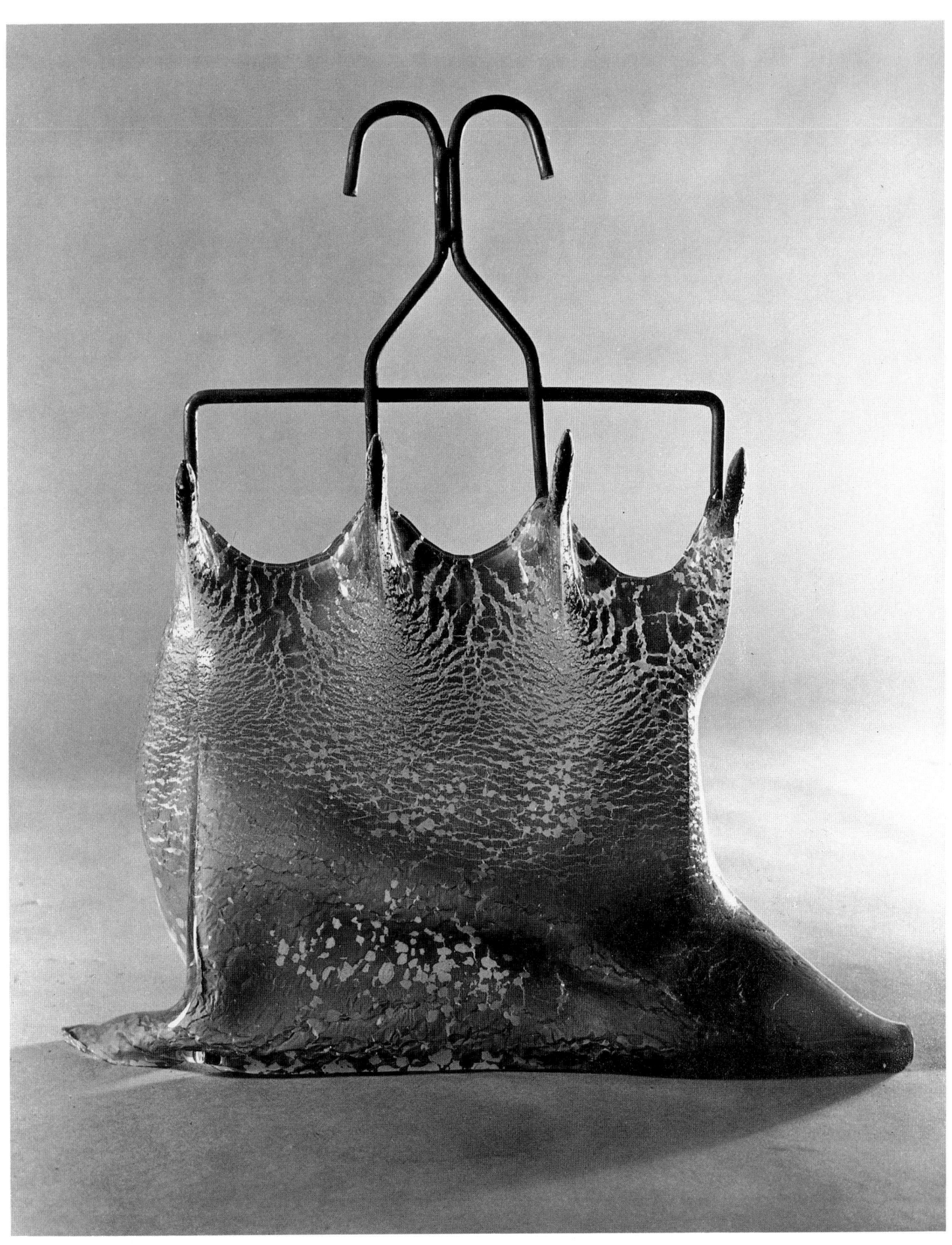

Hook and Glass. 1973. Glass and metal. 12 × 11 × 5″

face for my paintings. It was like skiing down a virgin slope of snow. Every possibility was open to me. And I tried just about everything. I used wires, brick, metal, pullies, rods, metal tools — which were actually the influence of the sculptor Italo Scanga. He was pouring hot, liquid glass on rakes and things. I used the tools as a support for the glass.

BLDD: There don't seem to be many women glass artists. Does the fact that you're a woman isolate you? Is being a female glass artist different from being a male glass artist?

MS: There are a lot of women glass artists. However, the glass shops tend to be very macho, as does the Glass Arts Society, which seems to be run on the buddy system. They tend to exclude the participation of women on a professional level. A glassblower needs assistants and a fairly elaborate shop. I work alone as a painter would. My isolation does also come from being a woman; two children keep you at home.

BLDD: It seems many other glass artists do like working together; they don't like working in isolation. They seem to enjoy the camaraderie of gaffers, the assistants, the colleagues.

MS: Well, this probably begins to touch on a basic difference between the art world and the craft world. The craft world is based on imitation, on learning a trade from a master — in other words, preserving the culture. Maria Martinez makes a beautiful bowl and that's then continued by her daughter, and her granddaughter Barbara Gonzalez. It's tradition. The same thing has been true in glass shops. The master determines the form and the assistants carry out the work. Imitation of the teacher's work in crafts is not looked down on. In art, assistants are not used in the same manner. Artists are expected to find their own vision, not imitate the master. Brancusi is said to have told Rodin, who had asked him to work with him: "Nothing grows in the shade of great trees."

BLDD: Do you consider yourself an artist, a craftsperson, both, or does it really matter?

MS: I have very strong opinions on crafts and art. I consider myself an artist, but I don't think it really matters. Making art is a combination of the two. Crafts is how; art is what. In crafts, one is generally taught how to work with a material. My approach was different. I'm self-taught and my approach to working with glass was totally experimental. From the age of nine I wanted to be a painter.

BLDD: Do you continue to cherish that notion?

MS: I do, as a matter of fact. But more than anything I want to work. The craft world has a chip on its shoulder. Craftsmen feel that they're not accepted by the art world and many want to be. Crafts deal specifically with material. Art deals primarily with ideas through the use of

materials, and because of this basic difference they often end up as different kinds of work. I view objects as one: if you produce an object, it can be produced through the craft tradition or through an art tradition. It doesn't really matter. I think art deals first with a concept. Art does not even have to be an object. Craft will never divorce itself from material objects. That's the crucial difference. I started out showing in fine art galleries. Now I show at O. K. Harris. Once craft galleries started inviting me to show, I said, "Yes, why not?" A lot of craftspeople said, "Mary, don't do that, don't get into the craft world, it's a dangerous place to be. They will limit you and lower your prices." I am not prejudiced against the crafts. It's a friendly world and an easier marketplace. There is no mystery to applied arts and many artists have found real support there. Lucio Fontana made ceramic fireplaces; Picasso painted plates; Sonia Delaunay designed everything.

BLDD: It seems to matter to a number of persons who work in ceramics or in glass whether they are called artists or craftsmen. I wonder if the matter is not only because of the perceived, more serious, critical evaluation of the work that takes place, but also because people are often more willing to pay a higher price for a work of art than for a work of craft.

MS: It's a question of the uniqueness of the works. Craftsmen may produce twenty a day or hundreds a year — pieces that are not all that different from each other. Crafts generally use the material in a traditional way that seeks to be pleasing to the viewer. It's also a question of the marketplace. Vessels tend to be priced so that every household can own many. The average artwork is priced much higher. However, a $300 vessel may be a lot higher priced than a $10,000 work of art. If a craftsman can make even ten vessels a day he will take home a lot more money than the artist who may take months to make one work. The artist's work tends to be unique; each piece, even of the same series, will be very different from another.

The craftsman is primarily concerned with how he is doing something. The artist questions not only how, but why? That may be a self-important notion, but it led to the manifestoes of the early twentieth century. Artists promote their thinking, as well as the product. For instance, when painter Judy Chicago used ceramics in *The Dinner Party*, she expended enormous amounts of energy explaining the purpose of her work. Many artists who work with ceramics and glass and who work with the vessel as form do not want to be associated with crafts. I like the fact that crafts reach a large number of people. I like having *some* of my work shown there at craft galleries. All galleries are marketplaces, which is why most of my installations that aren't salable have been done at uni-

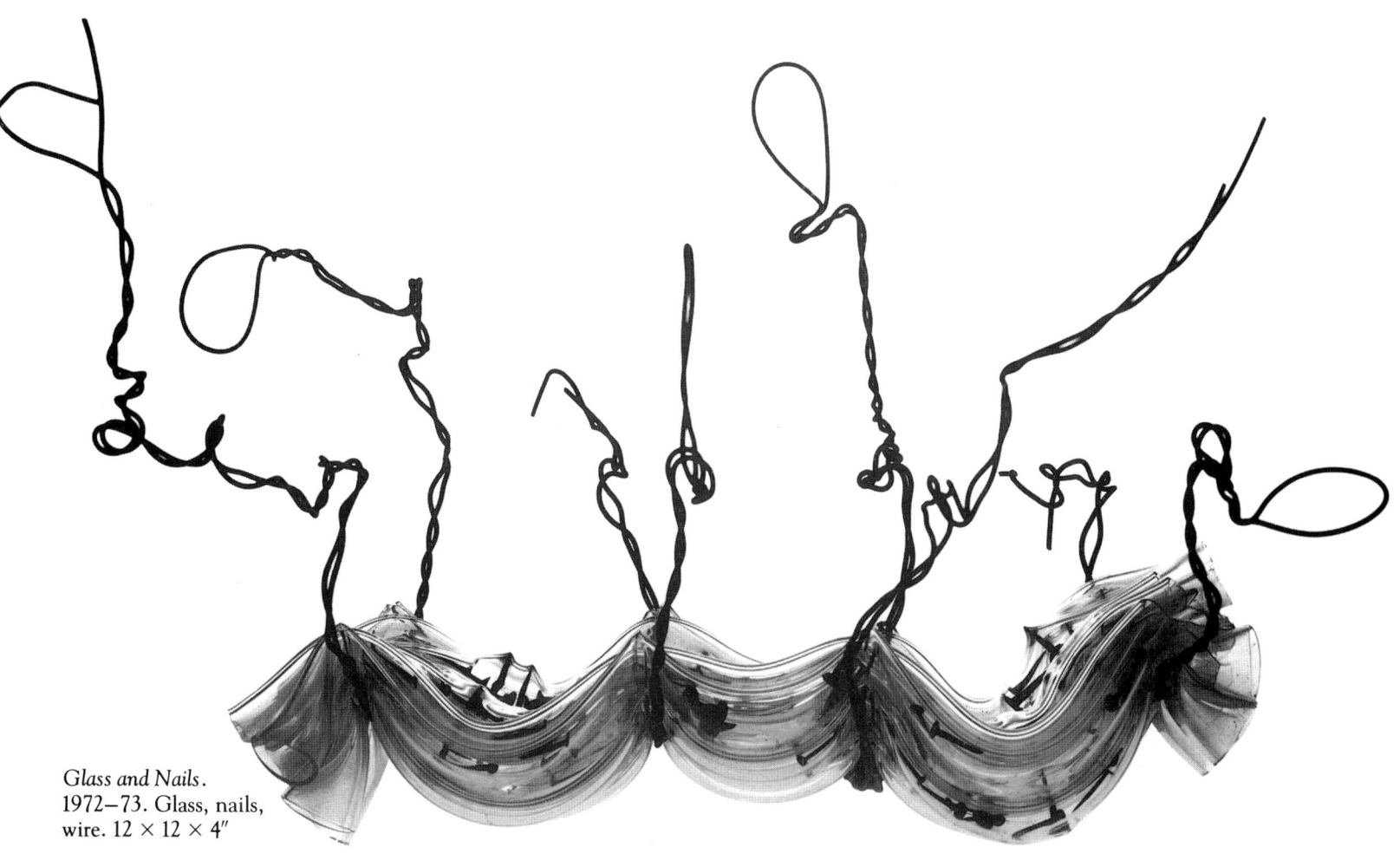

Glass and Nails.
1972–73. Glass, nails,
wire. 12 × 12 × 4″

versities. You can't be a self-supporting artist without selling. That's why crafts have traditionally been a support system for artists. Crafts reach a wider audience with less money to spend.

BLDD: What do you think of the contemporary glass movement — is there a movement?

MS: Well, there's definitely a movement. The studio glass movement is commanding so much attention partly because it's so accessible to a great number of people — people who would never go into a gallery, who would be terrified. But they're not scared to walk into a shop and pick up a blown vessel and say, "Isn't that pretty, the way the light goes through here?" Or, "I like seeing that tree." It's important to share that kind of looking.

BLDD: To the work of which glass artists do you most respond?

MS: That's a crucial question, because my affinity is not with the tradition of glassmaking, of vessels, or with the tradition of craft. The work that has most influenced me has been Goya's painting of the execution, Dubuffet's crazy wild drawings of figures, or the linear shapes and spaces you see in Giacometti. The tradition of fine arts is what I respond to. I love glass as a material, and there are many, many people working in glass whose work I respond to because I love the material, but I don't look to any as a guide. I did travel to Czechoslovakia to find out

who the masters were. They turned out to be the husband-wife team of Stanislav Libenský and Jaroslava Brychtová, René Roubíček, Václav Cigler. There are many good glass artists in America — Joel Myers, Henry Halem, Dale Chihuly, and younger artists like Carla Trinkley and Toots Zynsky, who takes hot glass and wraps it around vessels. The glass splinters into sharp little pieces and catches the light beautifully, yet if you tried to pick it up you could get cut. So there is repulsion and seduction in those particular pieces of hers.

BLDD: There is some violence in your earlier works in which you used not only wires, but nails, chains, hooks, and even barbed wire. What was your reason for doing that?

MS: I think that art often deals with issues of life and death, violence, fear, sorrow, and rejection, strong human emotions.

BLDD: Is that what you're trying to express with your glass?

MS: No, I'm not trying to express that directly with my glass work. I try to express that through my installations where I'll use any material — such as sound, smell, wind, fire — to get a specific idea across to the viewer. The viewer understands the work through his or her emotional response to the work. These works can reach a larger number of people because I think it's more difficult

216

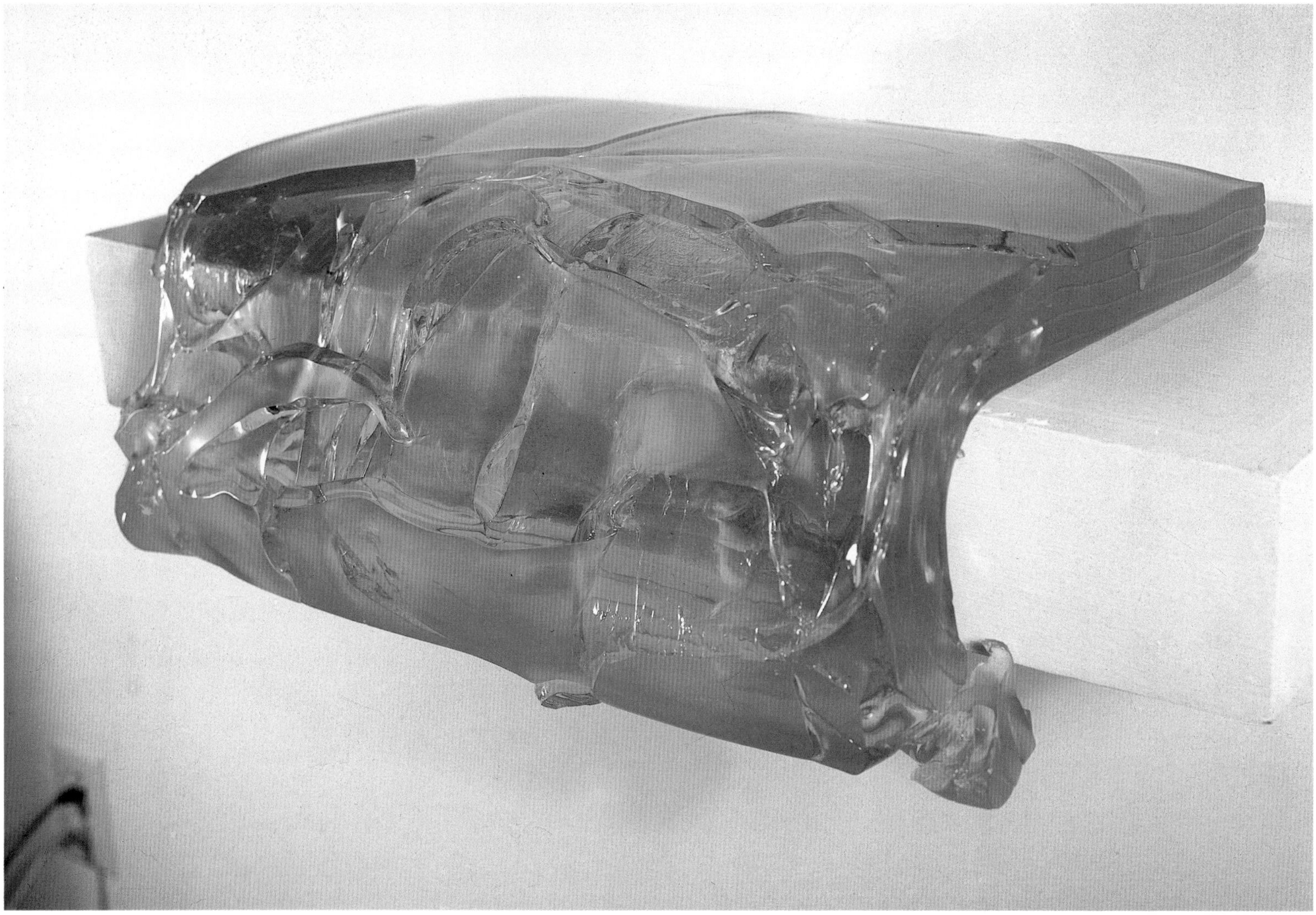

Above: *Bens*. 1980. Fused and slumped glass. 9 × 13 × 10″

Right: *On Edge*. 1980. Glass. 12 × 11 × 5″

217

Pick Up Series. 1980. Fused glass threads on Vitrolite. 24 × 110 × 3″

to understand a message in stationary objects. It is true that the glass work corresponds to strong emotions, however.

BLDD: In the evolution of your work there seems to be at least one recurring theme, and that is the window grid structure. What is it about that structure and the use of wire that continues to be meaningful to you?

MS: It's that contrast between a rigid idea and a flowing idea. In our society, we have rigid rules, or structure, and then we have a fluid, wild, crazy nature. Or we have unreason and reason. I think it's the contrast of those two things.

BLDD: Did the idea of working in any other medium ever appeal to you?

MS: Yes, and I still do work with many other materials — I still draw.

BLDD: How did you come to have a studio in an industrial plant, in what otherwise appears to be a residential neighborhood in Queens, creating these unique and bold

and daring works in this seemingly conservative neighborhood? And what is your relationship to this factory and the people who work within it?

MS: Well, in one word — Ben Mildwoff. He is the owner of the factory and an art collector himself. He saw my work at the O. K. Harris Gallery and said, "Hey, that looks like the kind of glass I have several crates of. She could probably use it." That was three or four years ago. He showed me the whole factory. During that visit, I thought, "I have found a colleague." He slumps glass and so do I. He bends glass; so do I. It takes the form of lighting fixtures for ceilings. In fact, almost everyone has Ben's glass in their house: in the bathrooms, surrounding the neon or fluorescent lights, or on ceiling lamps. They also sometimes have ashtrays or a bent-glass tabletop or coffee table.

BLDD: What, in your experience with your patrons, made him such a likely colleague for you?

MS: Well, the fact that we could talk shop, and also the

218

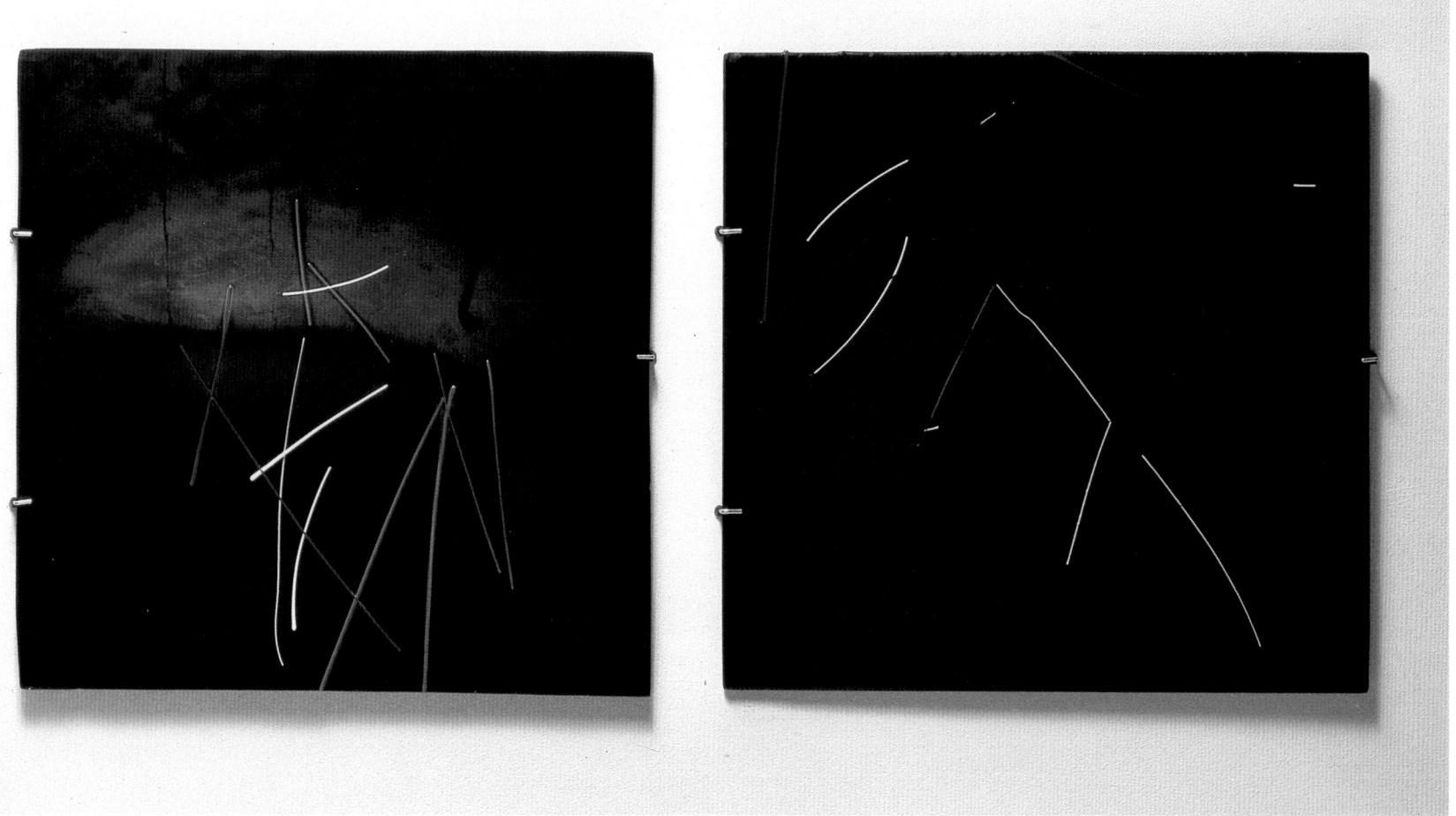

fact that Ben loves art. He has an intuitive feel for glass. He discovered you could bend glass in thirteen minutes when every other factory was taking all day.

BLDD: And where does your intuition lead you these days?

MS: Now I'm working on large outdoor commissions and larger commissions for public places. I've always liked the affinity glass has with ice or with water. What I'm working on now is a series of glass waterfalls, showing the fluid nature of glass rather than just its breaking and its shattering.

BLDD: Has the idea of creating functional glass objects ever interested you?

MS: Never, not at all.

BLDD: You're so interested in your work being made available to wider numbers of people that the thought that production would make it even more accessible. . . .

MS: I'm not interested in making something that people put a flower in. I want people to reflect on something vital, on a vital human emotion, either terrifying or pleasant. And you simply can't do that, in my thinking, through a goblet.

BLDD: On one hand you do think of yourself as an artist, on the other hand you are the chairman of the crafts program at New York University. How do you compromise the two?

MS: I had taught painting at Wellesley College and sculpture at the University of Rhode Island, jobs I enjoyed very much. I had planned to stop teaching but then the job in New York opened up — I knew there would be bad economic times ahead and I liked the attitude toward crafts at New York University — it was similar to my own. Also, they wanted someone who was involved with both the art world and the craft world and someone who would really revitalize their crafts program. I am not very interested in teaching straight technique classes but I am interested in building a program and a

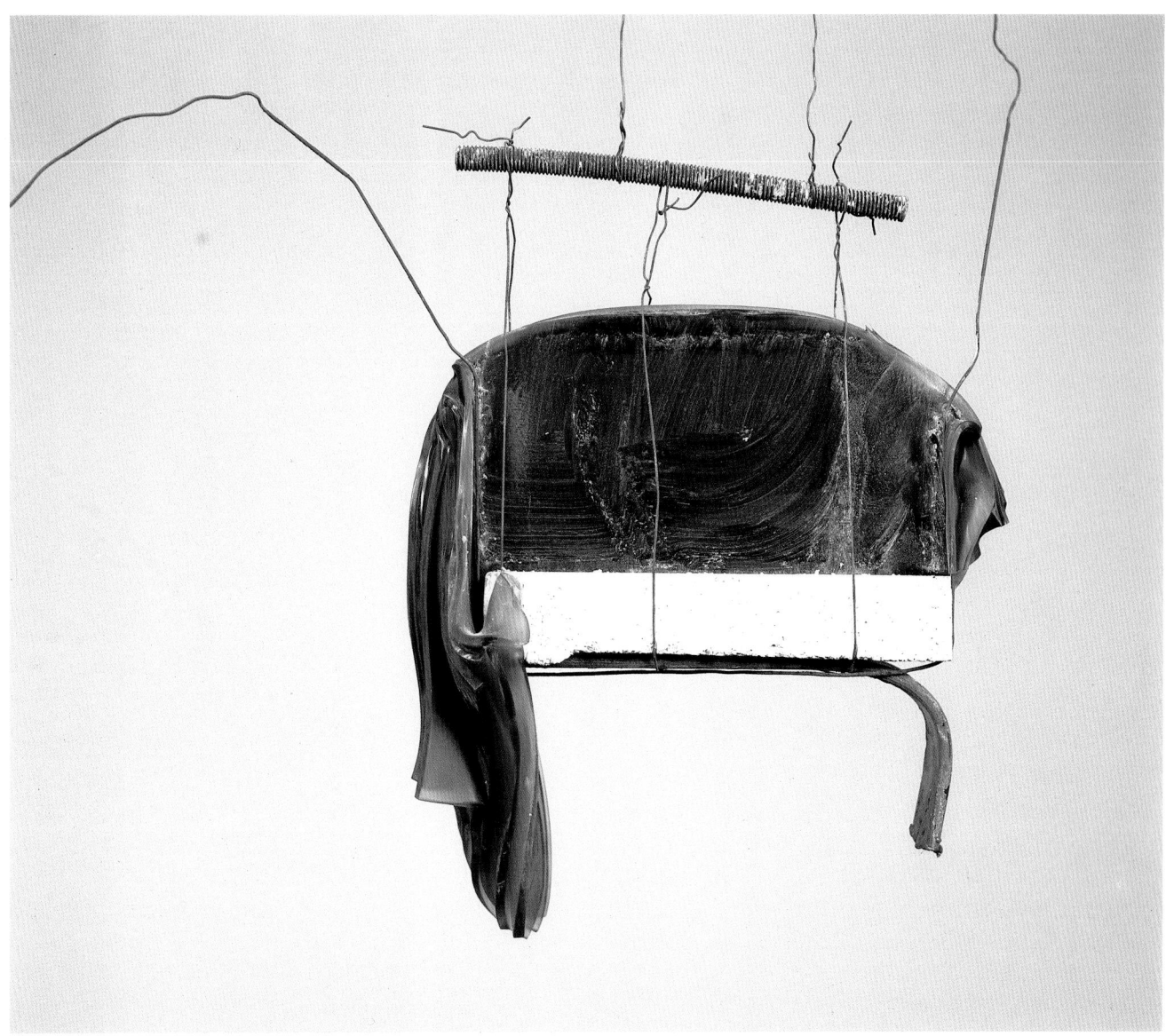

Aaron Likes It. 1978. Glass, brick, metal. 13 × 12 × 5″

course structure that allows students to learn the many different skills they need in order to achieve their personal goals. For instance, many craftsmen want to know how and where to sell their work. We offer a course in the business side of arts. Our emphasis on scholarship is not only historical; students learn a critical awareness of contemporary art and craft. We also believe in practical experience; our apprenticeship program places students in museums, galleries, with craftsmen, artists, and business. It's a good program. Running it has been hard work. The first year at NYU I was so busy I couldn't get out to the factory. But last summer I started constructing my own equipment.

BLDD: What is the work method you use?

MS: There are a lot of different phases. When I start working with a material, I say that I'm not going to limit myself. In other words, I don't have one particular method. Sometimes the idea of the finished piece is totally clear in my mind, and then I figure out how to make it. Sometimes I simply say, "I wonder what would happen if I put glass in this situation?" And I make a lot of little test pieces without specific consideration or thought. I refer to them as drawings, as notes for larger pieces. I have enough now to last me five lifetimes. But primarily I am involved with two kinds of work. One comes from the bundle series, which is plate glass crushed together, and the other is the hanging, suspended series. And the work that I'm doing now, even the architectural work, also follows those two patterns.

BLDD: How often does the accidental happen in your works? Without being frivolous, amidst all this remarkable work, one piece looks a bit "over-slumped," sort of like a failed soufflé.

MS: In Providence, when I was living next to my oven, I

never had a piece I rejected. When I lived fifteen minutes away, there were also very few accidents, maybe two percent. Now I'm working in a new situation and living an hour away from my studio. The timing on some of these pieces involves subtle shifts of oven temperature over a week's period. I'm finding that I get a lot of failed pieces. And I simply have to work out the right system.

BLDD: By the way, do you know how to cook or bake?

MS: Oh, I'm very good. I'm not a good baker but I can cook. I enjoy it.

BLDD: Is there any transference of skills?

MS: Not really, but you always do make that association. I gave a lecture once at the University of California in Santa Cruz. The sculptor Jack Zajac invited me out there. After I had finished talking and answering the questions, one woman said, "You have such a casual manner, it sounds as if you're giving out cake recipes!"

BLDD: Well, there is an element of that. You seem very tough minded and at the same time you are as fragile as your most delicate pieces. That same duality seems to exist in you, as it does in your work. You do make it sound as if blueberry muffins are going to pop out any moment!

MS: I'm not that homey . . . blueberry muffins, no. But it is familiar. You did touch on something, and that is a kind of love and caring that I have for my work. And this relates directly to my children. I like glass as a material because it lives, and because I want it to take part in the creative process and want to be sensitive to it and what it wants to become. When you make a piece, you have a specific idea, which sometimes is not what the glass has in mind at all.

BLDD: What do you think would most help to encourage a greater exchange between the fine arts and crafts?

MS: I think if the crafts world would stop being so worried about its position it would help. I have never heard an artist belittle a craftsman; even the most conceptual artist will speak lovingly about materials and almost cherish his tools. I have often heard prejudice the other way around — craftsmen speaking bitterly about an artist using "their material" for questionable ends.

BLDD: What can you do to bring the two together?

MS: Teach people to be proud of what they make. I think people who have grown up through the crafts should not turn against them.

BLDD: In your early works, at a time when most glass artists were making things that were pretty and pleasing and familiar, you were doing work that was kind of shocking. What was your reason for doing that?

MS: I think the reason is that I wasn't involved in the studio glass movement. I didn't come out of a glass department. I was a painter, and I was continuing to deal with issues that were important to me as a painter. I've never been particularly interested in making "beautiful" objects.

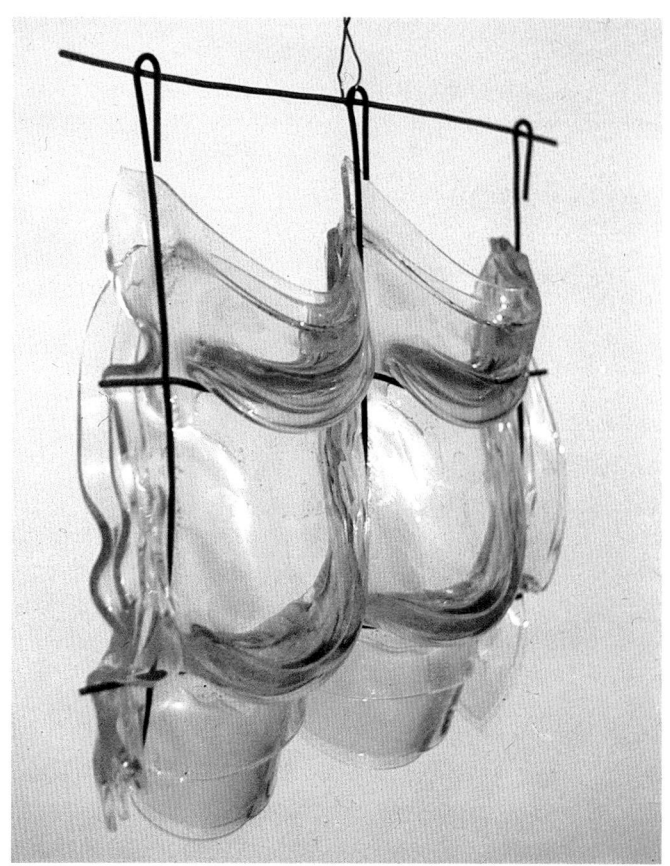

Artemis. 1979. Glass and metal. 20″ square. Collection Ivan and Marilyn Karp

Glass and Hook. 1974. Glass and hook. 24 × 12″

221

BLDD: I would consider it unusual for almost any artist or craftsperson to be interested in such a wide range of materials and attempt to address an audience as diverse as you do. What is the motivation for that, and do you think that you've succeeded in reaching a wide number of persons?

MS: I hope so — I make the work to share it. Because I show the glass work in both craft and fine art galleries, it reaches a lot of people. Women usually respond more strongly to my glass work. And the buyers are museums. Most people don't dare to purchase at this point.

BLDD: Why are they resisting?

MS: Perhaps because they're unfamiliar with the material. Or the fact that a lot of my work is ugly. The forms are unfamiliar, too.

BLDD: I think of your work as being assertive rather than ugly. And the later work, particularly the gray and the yellow pieces, have a great calming elegance.

MS: Even the most brutal pieces, they've always had a kind of elegance, an intrinsic elegance, which I can't define.

BLDD: You are so in love with the medium that it is a bit of a surprise to see you use color, thereby taking away one of the very important qualities of glass, its transparency. Why did you do that?

MS: I like the way the glass absorbs the color, like water absorbing dye. I don't find any other material that can do that. I thought for a while that I wanted to combine glass with ceramic tile, but I find that I have to make the tile out of glass in order to get the kind of depth that I want. That probably goes back to painting in the sense that you can get colors that you can never paint, but you can get them through glass, through overlapping and layering the color.

BLDD: In spite of the fact that you're accustomed to working in isolation, there is some interchange with the people in this factory.

MS: No direct interchange — in terms of influencing the work. I like working in a factory because, as an artist, one often endures a lot of hardship. Poverty is probably number one, and also a kind of prejudice that your family, first of all, has toward art, because you're not earning enough.

BLDD: In New York City alone, there are said to be thirty thousand artmakers. Isn't it a respectable bourgeois occupation now?

MS: I think that most people romanticize it. They say, "Isn't it wonderful that you're doing what you want to do?" But they still think making art is odd. One thing I like about working in the factory is that you look around here and see factory workers who are really working under hardship. They're doing the same thing over and over again — the working conditions, the lighting conditions are mind-numbing. And there you are, struggling with something that you really want to do, and something that you want to say.

BLDD: Is it worth it to you?

MS: Yes, absolutely. I understand the language.

BLDD: I guess it was less than twenty years ago that the studio glass movement was nonexistent. It all happened very quickly. What do you see as unfolding in the next twenty years?

MS: I see that glass will become as acceptable a material for making sculpture as stone, bronze, and marble have always been in Western art — and wood has become. What glass can do as a material is astounding: it's strong, can bend into all sorts of shapes, can create new forms never seen or made before. It catches light, reflects it, alters it, and can absorb color. Because of the glass movement glass departments have sprung up all over the country. The next twenty years will see glass in schools the way a foundry is, or metal and wood shops are. We'll see more artists using glass with other materials, and see more of it in public places.

BLDD: And what do you see as the future direction of your own work?

MS: I'm not as interested now in the dream-discovery, unconscious kind of work, nor in materials exploration — what can glass do? I've learned what it can do. Now I want to use a similar kind of thinking that has gone into my installation work concerning form making. In the most recent work, "Waterfall" and "Path" — which looks like a wave — the references to water, fluid shapes, liquid crystal are important. Strong geometrical shapes, something nature made that looks gentle but suggests danger. In "Path" one instinctively wants to walk the narrow space between the two rows of glass. If one did, it would be very difficult to get out. It's a trap. In "Waterfall" the danger is also imagined; the piece looks as if it could fall down, slip. I'm working on commissions and would like to do more large outdoor pieces so more people could see the work. I would like the work to be seen and understood for its inherent logic . . . but I want that logic to lead to a puzzle.

Once when I was a child my class went to the aquarium in San Francisco. While my classmates were upstairs I wandered into the basement and found a locked glass door. On the glass was a brilliant shape, one could barely make out the huge machine that appeared to be in the room. It seemed able to change form instantaneously, small in one moment and possessing long, crystallike tendrils the next. The noise I made brought a man who impatiently unlocked the door. The mystery was sunlight, a star.

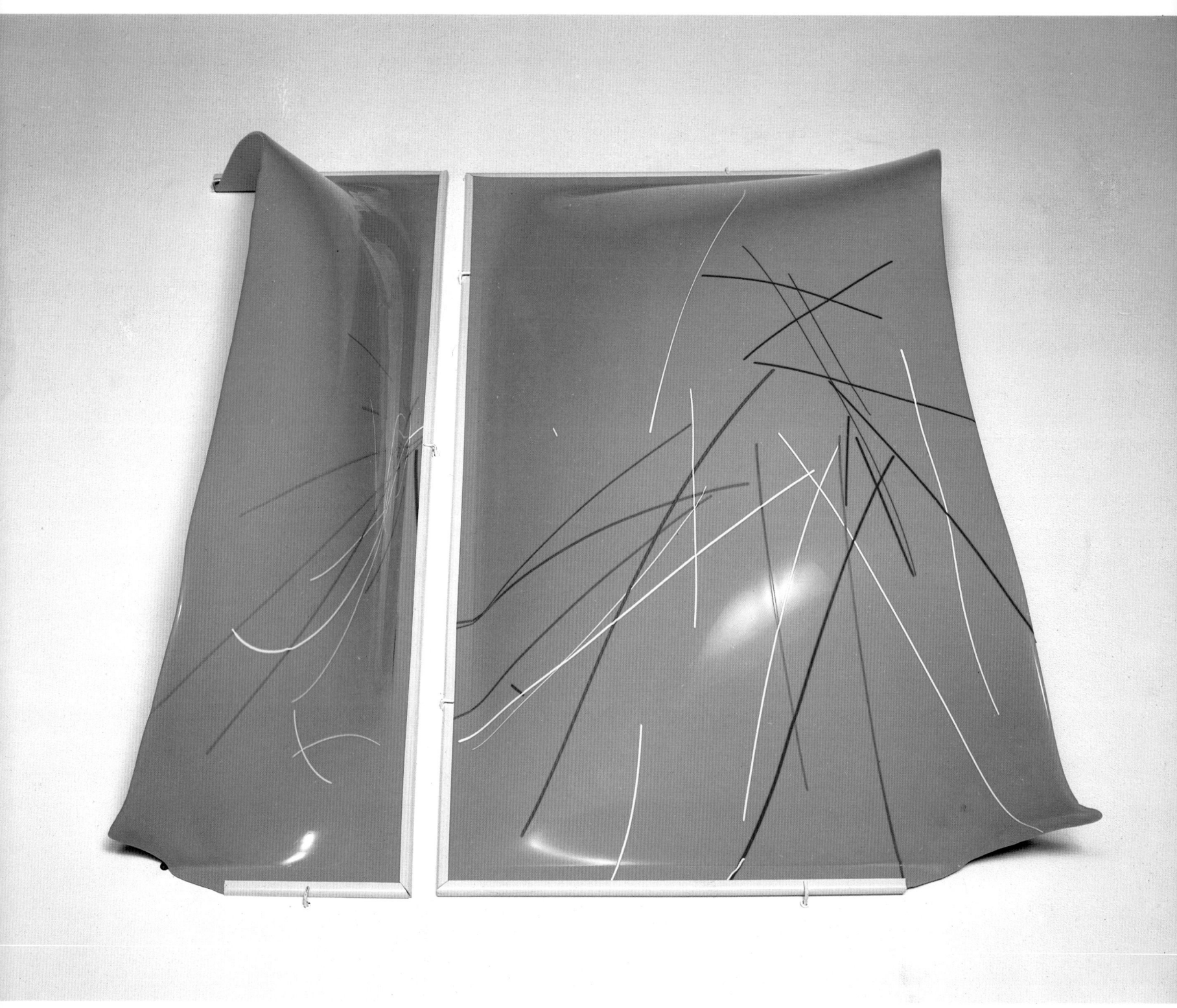

Opposite Blue. 1980. Slumped Vitrolite with fused glass threads. 56 × 40 × 9″

Photograph Credits

My special thanks go to my able assistants, Jean Zimmerman and Jill Shaffer, to whom I owe so much for their part in bringing this book into being, and for their enthusiasm and intelligence from the beginning of the project. And thanks, too, to those who were so helpful at the American Craft Museum, for their pioneering efforts, as well as their willingness to share their abundant resources.

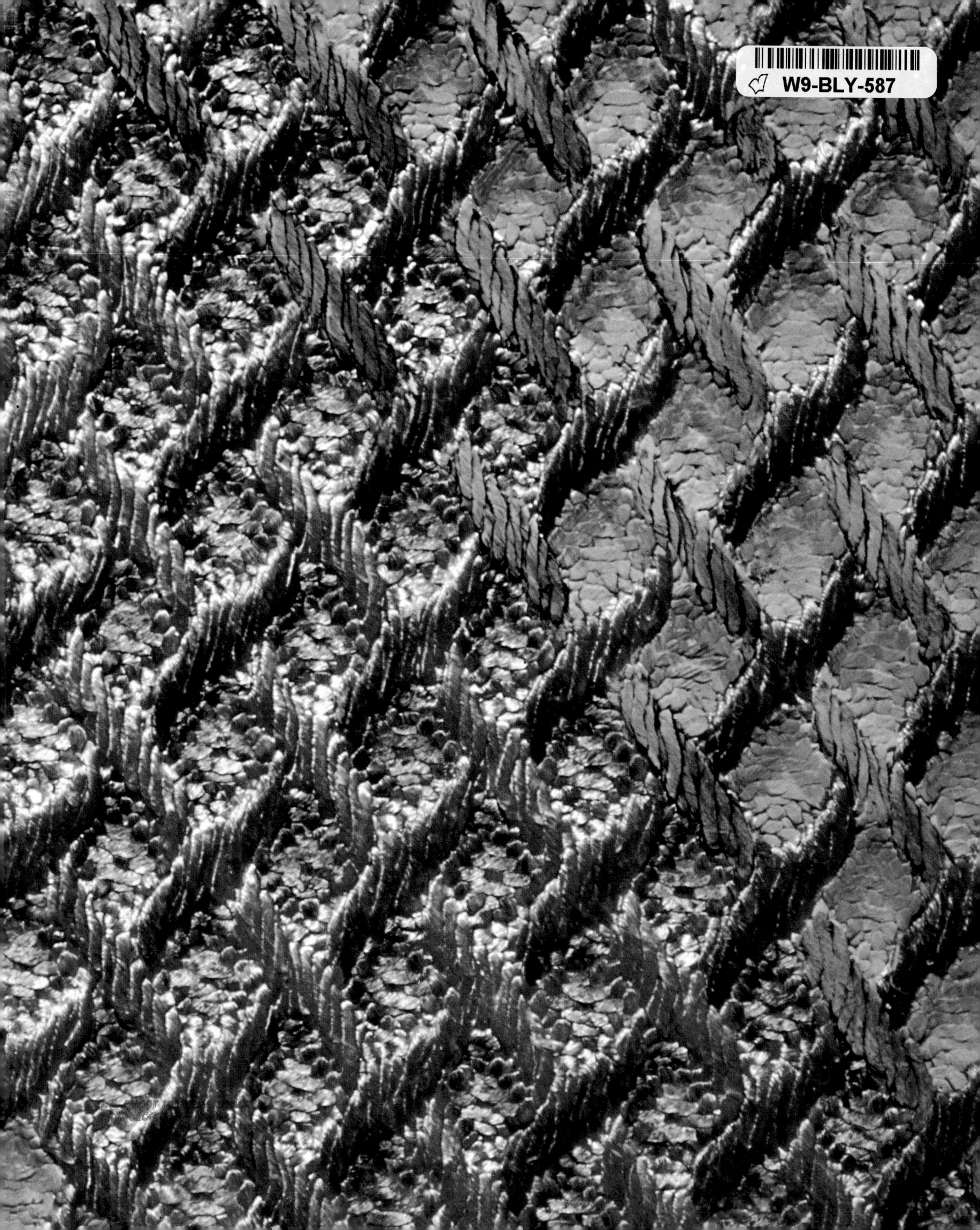

Degas

Degas
A Dialogue of Difference

Werner Hofmann

With 244 illustrations, 184 in color

Thames & Hudson

Contents

Chapter 1

A Man Apart

'It seems to me today that if one wishes to create art seriously and find
an original corner for oneself or at least keep one's personality as pure as possible,
one must immerse oneself in solitude. There is too much idle gossip. One would think that
paintings are made like stockmarket deals, by the scuffling of people desperate for gain…
All this business saps your mind and twists your judgment.' – Degas, 1856

Degas was not an Impressionist, and never thought of himself as an Impressionist. Those who admired him saw him as an outsider. In 1872, Edmond Duranty in his novel *Le Peintre Louis Martin* describes him as 'an artist of rare intelligence, preoccupied with ideas – which seems odd to most of his colleagues.' And then Duranty names the 'invention' – it would be more precise to say the 'discovery' – to which the painter owes these ideas: 'profiting from the fact that he had no method and no transitions in his ever-active brain, always working at fever pitch, he was known as the inventor of social chiaroscuro.' This term, *social chiaroscuro*, coined by Duranty himself, is the key to Degas's world. It separates him from the Impressionists, even though he regularly contributed to their group exhibitions. In 1879, Duranty lavished praise on him for the work shown at the 4th exhibition: 'The extraordinary artist named Degas is at this exhibition; with all his spirit, all his caprices, all his caustic wit and acuity, a man apart who is beginning to be appreciated and who, in a few years' time, will have earned a singular reputation.' He enjoyed the same respect among his fellow artists, who were themselves following different and less complex paths. On 9 May 1883, Pissarro wrote in a letter to his son Lucien: 'Degas is most probably the greatest artist of our time.'

The social chiaroscuro in which Degas made his vital discoveries was distinct from the clear realities of the Impressionists. These remained rooted in the tradition established by Leon Battista Alberti in his 15th-century treatise *De pictura*, in which he called painting an 'open window'. Zola used the same image when he wrote of Monet's work as 'an open window onto Nature'. Degas was not satisfied with straightforward, superficial realism. He preferred to open several windows onto several views at a time, to look both outside and inside, penetrating into those areas of double meaning that provided the settings for the tensions of social

1
Self-Portrait in a Soft Hat
(detail of ill. 2)

chiaroscuro. This problematical zone marks his contribution to 'Realism' and its overcoming – a subject that was much discussed during the mid-19th century. It was Diderot who first launched the debate on Realism, although only Duranty was aware of it, since he used Diderot's criteria to justify the originality of Degas's work.

In March 1874, a few weeks after the opening of the first Impressionist 'group exhibition' in the former studio of the photographer Nadar, Degas wrote a letter to his painter friend James Tissot (ill. 65), advocating a new form of Realism: 'The Realist movement no longer needs to fight against other movements. It is, it exists, and it should show itself independently. There needs to be a Realist Salon.' He follows this with a hefty dig: 'Manet doesn't understand this – I have to say, I believe his vanity far outweighs his intelligence.' Manet, in his own way, actually defined himself as a man 'apart' by not participating in any of the Impressionist exhibitions. His aspirations were vainly directed towards the official Salon and its great annual exhibition.

The openness of the terrain in the final third of the 19th century left the way clear for several options, of which Impressionism was just one. This arose out of a desire for realities that could be experienced spontaneously and filled with effects of light and colour, along with contemporary subjects and immediate truth-to-life. Herein lay the credo of the Realists too, though of course it was more complex and comprehensive than this, for it did not subject reality to the physiological processes of perception as conveyed through analysis of the seven colours of the spectrum, but extended its data to include the conflicts of social chiaroscuro. Within this field, there was no chromatic '*harmonie générale*' to reconcile all the differences. Essential components of the programmatic realism embraced by Courbet and the critic Jules Champfleury around 1850 were the city suburbs and their inhabitants, and this was the perspective that guided the avant-garde in the second half of the century. Degas's contribution to this revolutionary breakthrough involved both form *and* content – a fact which even today has not gained the attention it deserves, and which will form a central theme in this study.

The Realists tended to look in either one of two directions. In his novel *Chien-Caillou* (1847), Champfleury summed these up very vividly. In the midst of this tale of the etcher Rudolphe Bresdin, the author digresses for a moment and postulates two kinds of realism: one poetic and one prosaic. He uses the metaphor of the attic in which Chien-Caillou ekes out his miserable existence, in order to compare two types of garret. He shows this typographically through a perpendicular line which divides one page of the book into two halves. The left half represents the poetic idea of the attic, and the right half the 'real' one. On the left, the sunlight brings warmth and a gently awakening *joie de vivre*. Below the window, a small garden – Nature's haven amid the bustle of the city – plays its own little part in the idyll. In contrast to this poetic serenity stands the desolate reality of the other garret. Its atmosphere is grey and

2

Self-Portrait in a Soft Hat
1857–58
Oil on paper on canvas
26 x 19 cm (10 1/4 x 7 1/2 in.)
Williamstown, The Sterling and
Francine Clark Art Institute

3
Dancers Resting
1881–85
Pastel
49.8 x 58.4 cm
(19 5/8 x 23 in.)
Boston, Museum of Fine Arts

forlorn, and beyond the window lies a grim cityscape of roofs and chimneys. One's eye falls on the ragged figures of the poor. Here is '*la vérité vraie*' (Théophile Gautier) – the real truth of urban misery.

Champfleury's contrasting attics – and he kept quiet about this, or possibly hid it even from himself (and it has remained hidden ever since) – go back to a simple idea put forward by Diderot in his *Essay on Painting* (1765), in which he encapsulated the clash between poetry and prose right at the start of the debate on Realism. His starting point was the Republican conviction that all subjects are equal. In order to demonstrate this, he did away with the hierarchical superiority of history painting over bourgeois genre painting. For him, Greuze's *Father of the Family*, the *Ungrateful Son* and the *Engaged Couple*, and Vernet's paintings of the seashore with their many different incidents, were just as much history paintings as Poussin's *Seven Sacraments*, Le Brun's *Family of Darius*, and Van Loo's *Susannah*.

Diderot was advocating a paradigm shift, but it took more than a century for this to happen in the Parisian art world. When Duranty published his treatise on *La nouvelle peinture* in 1876, he used Eugène Fromentin's conservative criteria to distinguish the new prosaic aspirations from those of tradition. Fromentin restricted the doctrine of Realism to a 'better' observation of colours and their laws. As a result of this, he felt that the diffuse *plein air* and the 'real sun' took on an importance they did not deserve. He complained that everything springing from subjective imagination was now decried as artificial. The public only wanted an art that was an exact mirror of its own customs and appearances. History painting might guide such trends, but did history painting still exist? Even within this genre, which as far as Fromentin was concerned was the loftiest of all forms of art, there had been a change of emphasis. Once again, his criterion was the new colouring: dark became light, black became white, depths became surfaces, softness hardened, gloss turned matt, and from *clair-obscur* right through to Japanese

4
Ludovic Halévy Backstage
c. 1880
Monotype with chalk
16 x 11.9 cm
(6 1/4 x 4 3/4 in.)
Private collection

wallpaper, we learn that the whole environment was changing – the studio was turning towards the daylight.

All of this is true, but it says nothing about the new subject matter, or about the 'heroism of modern life' described by Baudelaire in his *Salon* (1845), personified by the anonymous bourgeois in his cravat and polished boots. When Manet painted his *Music in the Tuileries* (1862), he gave his bourgeois subjects a nonchalant anonymity, and with his *Old Musician* (1862), he made a stalwart fringe figure into a worthy subject for a painting, in the manner of Velázquez. Now the painter turns his gaze on the milieu and the dress, on the work and leisure activities of the urban dweller. Duranty comments on this change of perspective, and speaks up for the individuality of each character, each period of life, focusing on the significant detail – the hands that express the merchant or the official. Human beings are no longer abstractions based on aesthetic ideals – they live and they work in a social environment. And so the painter departs from the uniform anatomy which treats people as decorations with the fine curves of a perfectly formed vase.

Duranty has borrowed these criteria from Diderot, who discussed them in his *Salon of 1765* and then in his *Essay on Painting*. In the name of Nature, which admits nothing 'incorrect', he favoured the portrayal of everyday events, in which people act according to their own nature. Diderot's concept of naturalness finds its fulfilment when the subjects in a painting do not have even the slightest air of posing, but instead behave as if nobody is watching them. This is of course the goal that Degas was aiming for in his later work: the women occupied with their own bodies (see Chapter 11) do not seem to expect observers. Their nakedness speaks of what Diderot acknowledged as natural body construction: all parts – even those lacking in harmony – form a unified whole. If you cover the body of a hunchback, you will see that even his legs will betray his deformity. Duranty quotes this and other points from the *Essay* and comes to the following conclusion: Diderot stands at the threshold of everything that the 19th century has sought to put into practice. He expands the ideas of his great predecessor by also incorporating the coincidental, the partial, the fragmentary among the constituent parts of the picture. He defends off-centre composition, which may disconcert us with its empty centre, and he argues in favour of asymmetry and the shock of proximity turning into distance. All of these new factors should burst upon us with the suddenness of the unexpected, undermining our habits of perception and jolting us off the rails on which we are used to travelling.

Duranty found all these artistic devices in Degas's work. They made him godfather to the rule-breaking with which the Parisian avant-garde drew attention to itself, although no one could match Degas for risk-taking and sheer audacity. His abbreviated forms are aphorisms, pieces in shorthand, even though they are far from being the spontaneous sketches they seem

5
Gustave Courbet (1819–77)
The Painter's Studio: A Real Allegory Determining a Period of Seven Years of My Artistic and Moral Life
1854–55
Oil on canvas
361 x 598 cm (142 x 235 in.)
Paris, Musée d'Orsay

to be. In this respect Degas, who learned his superb draughtsmanship from Ingres, ignored one ideal that was as important for Diderot as it was for the Impressionists: the *harmonie générale* of colour. His compositions are calculated dissonances, and this ultimately is what sets his 'Realism' apart from that of Duranty, who saw what he wanted to see – a unified whole whose parts were brought together by *feeling*. For Degas, reality defied the harmonization which Duranty had praised twenty years before *La nouvelle peinture*: 'Everything seemed to me to be arranged as if the world had been made uniquely for the pleasure of painters, for the pleasure of their eyes.'

At the time when Duranty wrote those words, the *plein air* painting of the Impressionists had not yet begun; in its place, Courbet had produced a gigantic composition in which he

6
Self-Portrait
c. 1855
Oil on canvas
81 x 64.5 cm (31 7/8 x 25 3/8 in.)
Paris, Musée d'Orsay

invented a reality of multiple meanings: *The Painter's Studio* (ill. 5), which he exhibited at the Paris Universal Exhibition in 1855, alongside works by Ingres and Delacroix (who both represented France in the official exhibition), in a pavilion which he called 'Le Réalisme'. This painting announced the establishment of a third perspective. Its subtitle, however, made it clear that the painter was not satisfied with merely reproducing facts. In a challenge to the very essence of the genre, he called it an *allégorie réelle* – 'a real allegory determining a period of seven years in my artistic and moral life'. The painting reflects the contradiction inherent in its subtitle. It is a mixture that breaks the bounds of all conventional categories. Courbet borrows elements from genre painting, presents a gallery of portraits, and makes the isolated landscape on the easel into a message that will go out from the darkness of the assembled society into a world that is seemingly free of conflict, where it is not only the painter who will enjoy the pleasures of the eyes described by Duranty.

As an ambitious outsider casting an eye on Ingres and Delacroix, Courbet invented a new genre of painting – the anti-history painting, which nevertheless set out to do no less than reproduce the 'morals and customs of my era'. Never before had any artist undertaken such a programme. Like Degas after him, the 'Realist' Courbet was full of ideas. His *Studio* heralded a new iconography and a new subject matter, and yet it still stood within a traditional context. He was in fact returning to a form of painting which from the Middle Ages right through to Rubens represented a convenient means of conveying ideas through narrative: the triptych. Courbet's canvas, measuring nearly 6 metres in width and 3.6 metres in height, is composed of three sections. The painter in the middle is working on a landscape – which is imaginary. Clearly, then, painting for him is a 'cosa mentale' (Leonardo). The people in the two side sections translate Champfleury's attic metaphor into contrasting social classes, with Diderot's linguistic levels of prose and poetry also playing their part. In other words, the misery painted on the left corresponds to the prose of proletarian realism, while the people on the right stand for the poetry of bourgeois realism. Courbet expressed this slightly differently: 'I am in the centre, painting. On the right are all the shareholders, that is to say friends, workers and lovers of the art world. On the left is the other world of trivial life, the people, poverty, wealth, the exploited, the exploiters, all those who live on death.'

Courbet deliberately chose to give his painting a contradictory subtitle. The oxymoron points to something that has still not been fully appreciated: the productive artistic conflicts that marked the 19th century. Courbet was giving expression to one of the consequences of the clash – first pointed out by Diderot, but even a century later still not resolved – between poetry and prose, and between the ideal and the real. This makes his composition (which is a virtual deconstruction of five centuries of European art) into the key work of this whole epoch. It heralds Realism but at the same time disrupts it dialectically, and a purely factual record is given multiple layers of mood and meaning by way of dissonance and fragmentation. It is this multilayered Realism that Degas develops through the mystifying defamiliarization that runs through his life's work. His characters, especially the women, are exposed to ill treatment, whether real or imaginary, which makes them into puppets – artificial creatures whose actions are purely mechanical. They have become disposable objects bearing all the stigmata of objectification until, in the later works (see Chapter 11), they gain a new freedom through their nakedness. Then, in their communion with themselves, their bodies become an image for rebirth.

Chapter 2

Before the Change of Course

'In the choir the heads of Franciscans – I go down – I weep, oh!
those people felt life, life, they never renounced it – Le Sueur was surely
one of them. If I become a personality fixed and convinced enough to make
paintings that are worthy of sermons – at least, if I am not a religious painter,
then let me feel how they felt.' – Degas, on a visit to Assisi, 1858

By the time the young Degas had finished his academic education, he was already secretly preoccupied with the problematic area of bourgeois genre painting so superbly developed by Courbet. Of course any direct link with Courbet can only be a matter of speculation, though we can be quite certain that in 1855 Degas not only studied the two beacons of the age, Ingres and Delacroix – even making detailed copies of some Ingres paintings – but also attended the rival exhibition that Courbet mounted at the same time in his pavilion of Realism. However, there are no direct references to be found in any of Degas's notes or letters.

From the very beginning, he worked in a variety of fields – including history, genre and portrait painting. Between 1857 and 1868, he tested himself in the most prestigious of all the genres by painting five history paintings, but at the same time he satisfied his own latent talent for observation of reality, as can be seen from the prosaic objectivity of his portraits. These range from old Italian women to self-portraits as well as pictures of his family and friends. If we compile a chronological table of these two separate fields, it looks like the box overleaf.

These three fields – history, genre and portrait – cover the public and the private Degas. The histories, which he wished to exhibit, were for the public, whereas the portraits remained in his studio, many of them until his death. The only history pictures that he could have displayed in the Salon were the last two – *Scene of War in the Middle Ages* in 1865, and *Mlle Fiocre* three years later. Of the two 'Family Portraits' mentioned in the 1867 Salon catalogue, one may have been *The Bellelli Family* and the other *M. and Mme Morbilli*. There are no clear details in the reviews.

7
At the Races in the Countryside
(detail of ill. 18)

Table of Degas's subjects, 1857–68

	Past	**Present**
1857–58		Roman Beggar Woman (ill. 25)
		The Old Italian Woman
		Self-Portrait in a Soft Hat (ill. 2)
1859		Study for The Bellelli Family
		(ills. 34 and 35)
1860–62	Young Spartans Exercising (ill. 17)	Marguerite de Gas, etching (ill. 26)
	Semiramis Building Babylon (ill. 11)	
1861–64	The Daughter of Jephthah (ill. 10)	
1865	Scene of War in the Middle Ages (ill. 12)	The Bellelli Family (finished 1867) (ill. 16)
1866–68		M. and Mme Morbilli (ill. 27)
	Mlle Fiocre in the Ballet 'La Source' (ill. 13)	The Collector of Prints (ill. 53)
		Racehorses Before the Stands (ill. 102)
1868		James-Jacques-Joseph Tissot (ill. 55)

In spring 1855, after he had studied law for a few years, Degas was accepted at the École des Beaux-Arts to study under Louis Lamothe. He declined to take part in the competition for the much coveted Prix de Rome. Of far more influence than the Ingres imitator Lamothe was the great event of the year, the clash between Ingres and Delacroix at the Paris Universal Exhibition. His own inclination was towards Ingres, the virtuoso of the sensuous, calligraphic line, whose *Valpinçon Bather* he copied. He had already familiarized himself with the old masters of this formal language at the Louvre, where he had obtained a copying permit in 1853. He copied heads painted by the Italian masters as well as by Rogier van der Weyden (ill. 14) and Hans Holbein, and these had a major influence on his own portraits, with their detachment,

8
The Bellelli Family
1858–67
Oil on canvas
200 x 250 cm (78 3/4 x 98 3/8 in.)
Paris, Musée d'Orsay

10
The Daughter of Jephthah
1861–64
Oil on canvas
195.5 x 293.5 cm
(77 x 117 1/2 in.)
Northampton, MA,
Smith College Art Museum

Previous pages:
9
Scene of War in the Middle Ages
(detail of ill. 12)

elegance and fine detail. During a two-month stay in Lyons during 1855, he got to know the archaisms of Hippolyte Flandrin, a pupil of Ingres who, with the aid of Lamothe, was then decorating a church in Lyons.

The dedication with which Degas worked on this broad spectrum of artistic experience is clear from the notebooks and sketchpads that accompanied him from 1853 onwards. The copies he made in Paris show just how painstakingly he studied the originals. The first book opens with grotesque heads copied from Leonardo. Between 1856 and 1860, he journeyed every year to Italy, and the swift sketches from this period often betray the time pressures of travel, although they also provide us with a diary-like record of the rich experiences, both artistic and personal, that arose from these sometimes quite arduous excursions. The range of copies extends from early Italian (Giotto, the Campo Santo in Pisa, Mantegna, della Robbia, Gozzoli, Bellini and Botticelli) to the classics (Raphael, Michelangelo, Domenichino). The North is represented by Dürer and Rembrandt. In one and the same book, we find David's *The Death of Bara* (from Avignon) and a series of drawings based on Hogarth's *The Rake's Progress*. Mingled in with these copies are fragmentary details: he drew his left leg seen, foreshortened,

from above, and his left hand holding a pencil (ill. 237). He sketched ideas for pictures to which he frequently returned: John the Baptist with the Angel, Christ with Mary and Martha, Candaules's wife (ill. 229), Tasso in prison, a contemporary music salon with a woman sitting on a man's lap and facing the observer (ill. 220), like Raphael's *Fornarina* and the lady who is *Sulking* (ill. 37). Genre-style snapshots caricature a dancing couple, a butcher's shop, and Sorrento women with picturesque headgear. This broad miscellany also includes forms that will recur in future compositions. One such forerunner is a group of five interwoven men (ill. 75), anticipating *Six Friends at Dieppe* (ill. 76). Some complicated drapes and the study of a pansy look like the flowery hats that Degas would depict in later years. But the copyist also allowed himself to indulge in alienating effects, such as the confrontation of two groups to create a sort of dialogue: on the right, Dante and Virgil on the bank of the Cocytus, and on the left a group of soldiers who have turned to face them.

When Degas set out on the first of his Italian journeys in July 1856, it was an important step in his quest for his own identity. His father, to whom he sent some of his new pieces, congratulated him in a letter of 11 November 1858 on having left behind 'that flabby, trivial drawing in

11
Semiramis Building Babylon
1860–62
Oil on canvas
151 x 258 cm
(59 1/2 x 101 5/8 in.)
Paris, Musée d'Orsay

12
Scene of War in the Middle Ages
1861–65
Oil on canvas
85 x 147 cm
(33 1/2 x 57 7/8 in.)
Paris, Musée d'Orsay

the style of Lamothe and Flandrin', and advised him to concentrate more on portrait painting. Degas did not exactly ignore this advice, but continued to fix his sights on the principal goal of all ambitious painters in Paris: the official Salon. There one could only hope to gain attention by becoming a convincing history painter. He evidently decided to meet this challenge through three pictures on which he began work almost simultaneously in 1860–61: *Young Spartans Exercising*, *Semiramis Building Babylon*, and *The Daughter of Jephthah*. We do not know why he eventually decided not to submit these paintings to the Salon.

The Parisian 'Salon', which was the name given to the annual Fine Arts Exhibition, had a long history which oscillated between affirmation and confrontation according to the political and aesthetic strategies in operation at the time. In 1663, Louis XIV granted his Académie Royale – which he had founded in 1648 – the right to hold exhibitions, and thus institutionalized the dependence (coupled with protection) of the arts on the ruling powers. This pact was to go on into the 20th century. Right from the start, the Salon was the launching pad for competition and for debate on the direction that art was to take. It was named after the '*Salon carré*' [square salon] in the Louvre, where the first meetings took place. The preservation of academic, i.e. conservative norms was the task of a very strict jury. The Salon of 1848, which was held without a jury, proved to be an exception that died a quick death. After various changes of venue, the Salon moved in 1856 to the Palais de l'Industrie on the Champs-Elysées, which had been built specially for the Universal Exhibition.

13
***Mlle Fiocre in the
Ballet 'La Source'***
1866–68
Oil on canvas
130 x 145 cm (51 1/2 x 57 1/8 in.)
New York, Brooklyn Museum

As the institution responsible for setting and stabilizing matters of taste, the Salon held fast to the hierarchy of subjects which Diderot had fought so hard to eliminate in favour of equality. His arguments found no support in a jury of academics. They all insisted on a scale of importance which, until the mid-19th century, placed all the so-called imitative forms (genre, landscape, portrait and still life) below history painting, which was crowned champion through the power of its imagination. This critical hierarchical structure found expression through the prizes, grants and awards that gave material impetus to the competition. The official standing of this was what fired individual ambitions, but it also obliged the competitors to treat the prescribed rules and regulations with the utmost respect. Anyone who dared to stand up for himself and, like Courbet, to risk causing a scandal was summarily cast out into the artistic wilderness.

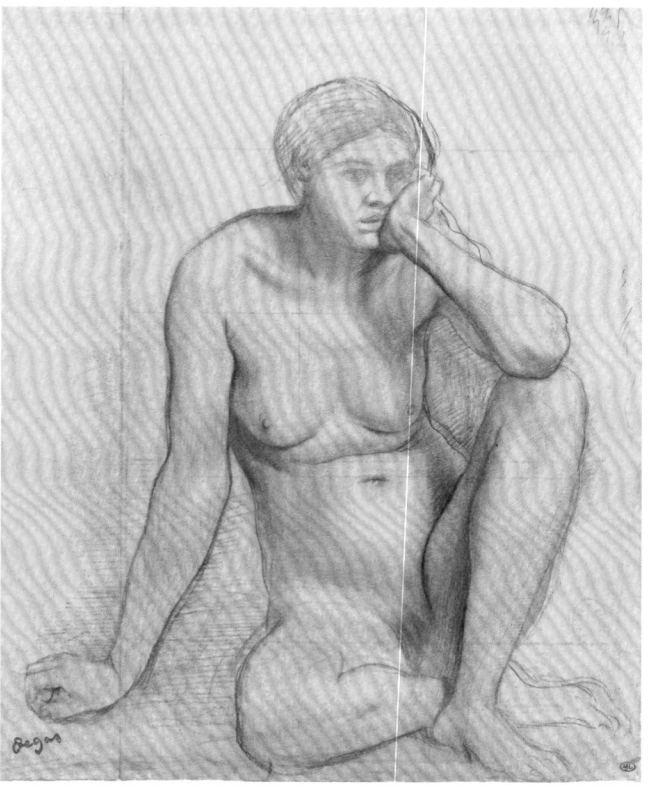

Clearly, then, the major snag with this competition for a place among the gods was the rigidity of the academic conventions that underlay a system which allowed for no innovation or even compromise. The advantage of the Salon was that it offered an albeit limited democratic platform, which enabled the public to discuss matters of judgment and to expand the range of art criticism by allowing freedom of expression to voices other than those supporting the normative status quo. The institution of the Salon certainly made an important contribution to the fact that the arts were put on exhibition and became the subject of passionate public debates both for and against, with room for serious argument, as well as for humour and satire.

Before Degas helped to undermine the monopoly of the Salon through the Impressionist exhibitions, he had made up his mind to get down to the current rules of the game. In his five history paintings, he did this as an artist with a humanist education and a 19th-century background. All five pictures deal with women. The sacrificial death of *The Daughter of Jephthah* (ill. 10) is a parable on the domination of women by men (in this case the father). Degas playfully reverses this domination with the *Young Spartans Exercising* (ill. 17), in which the girls are shown throwing down a challenge to the boys. *Scene of War in the Middle Ages* (ill. 12) shows the violent, sadistic treatment of female victims by their male conquerors, whereas *Semiramis* (ill. 11) stands serenely looking over her creation, the city of Babylon, the apotheosis of matriarchy but also of the *femme fatale*. *Mlle Fiocre in the Ballet 'La Source'* (ill. 13) is a cross between stylized pseudo-history and a review of a Parisian ballet.

With these five pictures, Degas set himself up in competition with the great masters of contemporary French art, but gave a new slant to their teachings. With the *Young Spartans Exercising* he corrected the dogmatic classicism of David by parodying, neutralizing and humanizing him. But behind the playful acrobatics of these figures lies the cruelty of Spartan customs: 'You know,' he apparently told some friends, indicating the background of his painting, 'that the Spartans used to hurl from the top of this cliff any newborn babies that were

deformed or unlikely to survive. With this terrible custom, they spared them a lifetime of suffering and shame.' The foreground of this scene emphasizes equality, with both sexes displaying themselves in preparation for a free choice of partner.

Semiramis is gazing on her city from a distance, in a manner reminiscent of a mural by Puvis de Chavannes (whose famous *St Genevieve*, gazing at a sleeping Paris, was painted some decades later). The legendary ruler of the Assyrian Empire seems here to belie her reputation as a murderous *femme fatale*; instead we see the foundress of a vast community whose dimensions are hinted at by the massive architecture that forms the background. The critical mind of the artist may well have been focusing on the present here, drawing a parallel between the Babylonian scene and Haussmann's brutal redesigning of Paris. The picture is dominated by women. Semiramis's attendants have no individual identity of their own, apart from the girl kneeling beside the bunch of flowers. Apparently the humblest of all the servants, she recalls the theme of reflective self-awareness (see Chapter 11). By comparison, Semiramis seems like a lifeless model. This is an important indication of Degas's reversal of the social hierarchy between mistress and servant, in keeping with the increased attention and importance that the Realists gave to their marginal figures. The plain sobriety of the whole composition can be read as his response to the oriental splendours of Rossini's *Semiramis*, which had graced the Paris Opéra in and after 1860.

In *The Daughter of Jephthah*, Degas set out to emulate Delacroix. In this, the largest of his canvases (195.5 x 293.5 cm), the theme of the female victim takes on an Old Testament flavour. The story is taken from Judges, chapter 11: Jephthah, son of a harlot, is asked to lead Israel against the 'children of Ammon'. He vows that if he returns home

17
Young Spartans Exercising
c. 1860–62
Oil on canvas
109.2 x 154.3 cm
(42 7/8 x 60 3/4 in)
London, The National Gallery

Page 28 top
14
Copy after a Madonna by Rogier van der Weyden
from Degas's Notebooks
(NB. 18, p. 209)

Page 28 bottom
15
Seated Woman
Study for 'Scene of War in the Middle Ages'
1861–65
Pencil on card
31.3 x 27.6 cm (12 1/2 x 10 7/8 in.)
Paris, Musée du Louvre

Page 29
16
Nude Study for Mlle Fiocre in the Ballet 'La Source'
1866–68
Oil on canvas
81 x 65 cm (31 7/8 x 25 5/8 in.)
New York, Brooklyn Museum

18
At the Races in the Countryside
c. 1869
Oil on canvas
36.5 x 55.9 cm (14 3/8 x 22 in.)
Boston, Museum of Fine Arts

victorious, he will sacrifice to the Lord the first creature or person to come out of his house to greet him. When this person turns out to be his only daughter (the Bible does not even provide us with her name), he tears his clothes in despair, but she asks only for two months in which she can go with her friends into the mountains to 'bewail' her virginity. She then faithfully returns to her father, who fulfils his promise to the Lord. In Degas's composition, we cannot see any of this narrative at first glance, as the female protagonist is tucked away in the margins at the top of the picture. It is the male component – the fulfilment of the vow – that occupies the whole width of the foreground. The colours and movements are all profoundly influenced by Delacroix – to be more precise, by the frescoes that he completed in 1861 for Saint-Sulpice. In the 14th notebook (1859–60), we find several lively copies of Delacroix's Apollo Gallery in the Louvre. (In the same period and in the same style, Degas also made a copy of Dürer's *Man in Despair*.)

Scene of War in the Middle Ages (ill. 12) deals with the traditional roles of the sexes against a background of Christian distaste for the naked body. It is as if the women are being punished by the archers for the exposure that has been inflicted on them. The vicious cruelty is compounded by their utter humiliation. As discarded objects, these bodies are evidently not even attractive enough for sexual conquest. Degas sets the eight women in poses that he will later re-use for the part that women play in the 'heroism of modern life'. There, however, the focus is no longer on male brutality but on the unselfconsciousness, quite oblivious to shame and to shamelessness, of the woman in the bath or at her toilet (see Chapter 11). With hindsight, it is clear that the naked bodies in the *Scene of War* already herald this subject matter, so that the historical genre disappears almost imperceptibly behind the timeless sensitivity.

An exception to this is a study of a seated woman (ill. 15) whose expression is full of terror, as if she were remembering some dreadful moment of suffering. It is this that separates her from the mere physical exhaustion of her companions. Degas must have sensed this, which is why he did not incorporate this monumental, Michelangelo-like metaphor of Fate into the composition – its intensity would have destroyed the focus of the narrative. This woman shares the knowledge of the fallen Eve, and she anticipates Gauguin's Tahitian women but also, and even more significantly, she embodies the collective martyrdom to be inflicted on the helpless by the perverse wars, persecutions and extermination camps of the 20th century. Perhaps it is no coincidence that in 1863, the year of her creation, Degas acquired Goya's *Desastres de la Guerra*.

Mlle Fiocre in the Ballet 'La Source' (ill. 13) refers directly to a ballet by Léo Delibes and Ludwig Minkus which had its premiere on 12 November 1866. Eugénie Fiocre, whose beauty somewhat exceeded her talents as a dancer, was one of those female public figures who, in the words of Heine's *Lutetia*, kept people guessing as to 'where the actress and the courtesan trade places'. Degas admired her, which is no doubt why he portrays her – in a scene evidently more Degas than Delibes – in a pose of pale, enchanting reverie. Behind this picture, however, lies a decisive change of direction in Degas's work – the switch from poetry to prose. For this diaphanous figure and her seated maidservant, he first did a preliminary study in oils, using models, and these tell a different, far more prosaic story (ill. 16). Deliberately chosen and posed by the painter, the two nude models present a direct contrast to the imaginary, fairytale world of the final picture; they sit there in completely prosaic artlessness.

In this preliminary painting, we can see Degas's scepticism at the pale flawlessness of the countless nudes that fascinated the Salon public. Zola spoke disparagingly of the 'boudoir paintings' that contained *'rien de vivant'* [nothing alive]. He felt that this detachment from real life was caused by misguided ambitions: 'Our artists are poets…Look at the Salon: nothing

19

The Rehearsal of the Ballet On Stage

1874

Oil on canvas

65 x 81 cm (25 5/8 x 31 7/8 in.)

Paris, Musée d'Orsay

but stanzas and madrigals. This one pens an ode to Poland, that one an ode to Cleopatra....' When Zola ended his 1866 critique of the Salon with this dismissal, Degas was in the act of bidding farewell to his *Semiramis*, his *Young Spartans*, and also his *Daughter of Jephthah*. In the victims of the archers, however, there are already the beginnings of those worn-out, almost animal bodies that were to fascinate him for the rest of his life.

Degas made up for this departure from history by a kind of dual vision, which enabled him to move around the same flexible territory in different ways. The process is much like that described by Nietzsche, who observed that 'one can conceive...of Flaubert's being well able to transform all his heroines into Scandinavian or Carthaginian women, and then to offer them

to Wagner in this mythologized form as a libretto.' For Nietzsche, the focus was on 'all very modern problems, all problems which are at home in big cities.'

Degas's creations also seem to be waiting for a change of role that will enable them to escape from their historical, mythological detachment and take their place in the here and now. Eugénie Fiocre and Semiramis's maidservant already belong to those contemplative Parisian women whom he selected from among his friends and models. The defenceless victims in the war scene are his contemporaries, and the archers are forerunners of the jockeys, those nimble, perfectly tuned riders whose bodies become one with those of the animals they ride. It was in the early 1860s that Degas painted his first racing scenes.

20
The Rehearsal of the Ballet On Stage
c. 1874
Pastel
52.1 x 70.8 cm
(20 1/2 x 28 7/8 in.)
New York, The Metropolitan Museum of Art

In 1874, at the first Impressionist exhibition, Degas himself made an indelible impression. He invented new metaphors for the 'heroism of modern life'. His ten exhibits were all related to Nietzsche's modern, big-city problems, with ballet rehearsals, women ironing, racing scenes, a woman after her bath. Some of the canvases can be identified (ills. 7, 131, 19). Of the critics, only Jules Castagnary sensed the true nature of these works, although even his positive review omitted to mention the contemporary slant of such slices of life. Castagnary felt that Degas stretched the unusual to the point of the bizarre, but he nevertheless praised the accuracy of the draughtsmanship and the excellent use of colour, both of which were qualities ignored by other critics.

The exhibition, which opened on 15 April 1874, was held in the former studio of the photographer Nadar, on the Boulevard des Capucines, and it marked the first collective attempt to break the monopoly of the official Salon. The latter had already suffered a loss of prestige in 1863 when, as a result of the jury's over-zealous rejection of more than 3000 paintings, Napoleon III felt obliged to establish a 'Salon des Refusés'. Manet's *Déjeuner sur l'herbe* was the sensation of this showpiece of the outcasts. Along with this spokesman for the avant-garde, Cézanne, Fantin-Latour, Pissarro and Whistler also exhibited their work, and although this jury-less break with tradition remained an exception and the Salon continued to defend its position, from then on it had to contend with rival attractions. The 1874 exhibition in Nadar's studio was one of these. In the years leading up to it, Degas and his friends had sought recognition from the Salon, though secretly they despised it and wanted to reform it. Manet, despite many rejections, was the most persistent in his quest for official approval, and no doubt that was what held him back from participating in the group exhibitions of the Impressionists.

The 1874 exhibition, however, was not quite as radical as one might think, for under the businesslike title of '*Société anonyme*' it extended its liberal tastes to thirty artists, of whom half have now been forgotten. Apart from Degas, the contributors who were later to be dubbed 'Impressionists' included Monet (12 works), Morisot (9), Renoir (7), Sisley (5), Pissarro (5) and Cézanne (3). These were the painters who made up the artistic bulk of the exhibition, but they did not present themselves as a group, and there was no specific, revolutionary programme underlying the choice of exhibits. It was only thanks to an ironic remark by a journalist that Monet's *Impression: Sunrise* (ill. 22) gave rise to the label – initially applied as a joke – for a new aesthetic which many regarded as an aberration of taste. Very few people imagined then that this exhibition had opened a new chapter in the history of French and indeed world painting. The subsequent and lasting triumph of Impressionism became a celebration of middle-class life. As a result, the innovative element of *plein air* painting disappeared, along with other less spectacular ruptures which from the present point of view have proved more important. They are of special significance in the work of Degas.

Chapter 3

Contemplation, Alienation
and Self-Awareness

'The women here are almost all beautiful, and many even have in their charms
that touch of ugliness without which there is no salvation.' – Degas in a letter
to Henri Rouart from New Orleans, 5 December 1872

If we take Courbet's *Studio* as our frame of reference, with its social divisions, we can see that it contains a collection of prototypes for working-class and middle-class realism, the latter to the right and the former to the left of the painter. The old beggar woman (ill. 25) that Degas painted in 1857 during a trip to Rome might well have come from Courbet's group of poor people (with some of their exploiters). The woman – who is clearly a model – does not, however, make a great display of her poverty; on the contrary, she seems to be at ease with her simple way of life. Like *The Old Italian Woman* (Metropolitan Museum), as Loyrette has indicated, she fulfils the pedagogical aim – attributed to Victor Schnetz, director of the Académie de France in Rome – of raising the genre to the level of history painting. Whether Degas himself had this hierarchy in mind we do not know. His familiarity with the tradition of painting, however, may have led him to place these two Roman models in particular traditions: the serious, thoughtful Italian woman in the yellow shawl is descended from Michelangelo's biblical sibyls, while the beggar woman, with her eyes turned upward in an expression almost of worship, might be Spanish. There is no concrete evidence for such an assumption, as Degas could not have known Velázquez's early genre paintings, but in the 11th notebook, which he used in Rome and Florence in 1857–58, there is a series of sketches for a *Homage to Velázquez* (now in the Neue Pinakothek in Munich). The composition of this small canvas goes back to the Spanish painter's *Las Meninas*, a copy of which Degas must have seen. As for the beggar woman, one's attention is drawn to the warm brown material of the dress and the headscarf. This woman is not wearing rags, and there is nothing shabby about her; she looks after herself, and is a person in her own right, not a picturesque symbol of poverty. *'Elle est peuple'* [she is people], as Degas remarked later in another context, adding: 'It is in the common that we find grace.' He was not referring here to social class, for the comment was made about a lady whom

23
Sulking
(detail of ill. 37)

24 *(see also ill. 230)*
Actresses in their Dressing Rooms
1879–80
Engraving and aquatint
22.5 x 31 cm (8 3/4 x 12 1/4 in.)
Washington DC, National Gallery of Art, Rosenwald Collection

he and his friends were discussing over an evening meal. Before focusing his early portrait realism on a middle-class milieu, Degas was already aiming with this artlessly dignified beggar woman to convey a femininity whose grace had nothing to do with class.

During this period of study and travel, *The Roman Beggar Woman* (ill. 25) represents a kind of digression for Degas, and there was no follow-up. The series of portraits that he undertook at this time was exclusively middle-class – drawn from the right-hand wing of Courbet's studio. The elegant couple in the foreground are the prototype for Degas's posing couples, but the more straightforward Courbet had no eye for the subtle breaks that hint at alienation. The masklike faces of his friends and relatives set Degas off in search of some characteristic feature specific to the bourgeois idler, and it is this that he discreetly draws forth from their class-consciousness: he discovered the *contemplative self-awareness* of the class from which he came. He sublimates the retreat of the bourgeoisie from their worldly preoccupations, from their ceaseless quest for efficiency, productivity and profit, which has driven them 'all over the globe', as the *Communist Manifesto* put it – not without a tinge of admiration. With melancholy resignation, these men and women withdraw to a private dream world, renouncing their material ambitions in favour of some inner experience that will come through their meditations.

Bourgeois contemplation is not the only psychological constant that Degas incorporates into his portraits. For this characteristic level of consciousness he creates various dissonances that disturb the *spatial composition* of his pictures. These strategies, which in the 20th century led to significant changes of focus, require detailed analysis. The heterogeneous spaces which the classically trained Degas devises have no direct predecessors or even analogies in high art, and so we need to look elsewhere for influences. It is my belief that the answer is to be found in the commonplace popular artforms of the 19th century. In these 'peripheral' fields there are certain artistic devices that help to express the disparateness and transience of connections; Degas introduced these into the syntax of high art, radicalized them and – most important of all – legitimized them by applying them to the subject of deteriorating human relationships.

An example, if we may take a leap forward into the 1870s, will show just how far Degas's alienation effects took him. The etching *Actresses in their Dressing Rooms* (ills. 24, 230), of which there are at least five versions, shows the confusingly fragmented three-dimensionality of one or several interiors. It is as if space is being subtracted from space, and we are looking into a cabinet of mirrors. The interior is cut up into four perpendicular, unconnected strips with a freedom of technique that was first applied not in high art but in those forms of art associated with mere diversion.

In 1825, Paris saw the publication of a *Componium Pittoresque* – a 'collection of several thousand landscapes in different genres' (ill. 28). It consisted of 56 watercoloured etchings,

25
Roman Beggar Woman
1857
Oil on canvas
100.3 x 75.2 cm
(39 1/2 x 29 5/8 in.)
Birmingham Museum
and Art Gallery

each of which contained a section of a landscape in vertical format. The challenge was to combine these different sections to form a vast variety of new scenes that would be mixed and yet also convincingly consistent. The game was based on a simple artistic device: the backgrounds and the foregrounds were related in such a way that there was always a continuous line to link them. This automatically cancelled out the arbitrary nature of the combinations.

This is yet another case of the Zeitgeist splitting its ideas. The French trick was echoed in remarkable fashion by a similar principle of composition by which Goethe felt tempted. In his youth, Goethe might have been familiar with games like the *Componium*, because he actually mentions the idea that lay behind them: playing cards and their different combinations. In a letter he wrote to Schiller on 23 October 1799, he describes his recent reading. Inspired by Humboldt, he is reading the works of French dramatists, among whom the elder Crébillon seems to him 'remarkable in a special way': 'He treats the passions like playing cards, which one shuffles and deals, and can shuffle and deal again without them ever undergoing the slightest change.' It is a simple procedure, though he notes an obvious deficiency in it: one cannot produce any chemical affinities. Ambiguous relationships are also beyond the playing-card method, and so Goethe relegates it to a minor role: 'Certainly by taking this route he [Crébillon] produces situations that would be impossible in any other way. But this method would be absolutely unbearable for us; only I wonder whether one could or should use it for subordinate compositions, operas, romances and conjuring tricks.'

Goethe could not have known that in the 20th century, playing cards would legitimize important methods used in modern art: the collage and montage techniques of the Cubists, for instance, and the *cadavre exquis* drawings of the Surrealists. Chance and its random combinations have been one of the surprise strategies used by the avant-garde since the beginning of the 20th century, or even earlier.

Long before these games of consequences became common practice, Degas added to the playing-card technique that of the fragment – a dimension that was not yet known to the

26
Marguerite de Gas
1860–62
Etching and drypoint
12.5 x 11 cm (4 7/8 x 4 1/4 in.)
Boston, Museum of Fine Arts

Opposite:
27
M. and Mme Morbilli
c. 1867
Oil on canvas
116.5 x 88.3 cm
(45 7/8 x 34 3/4 in.)
Boston, Museum of Fine Arts

Componium. In *Actresses in their Dressing Rooms*, he did away with the cohesion of the third dimension, and with the divided interior also placed its human content under the banner of flexibility – i.e. of randomness. These disparate relationships run counter to the traditional rules of aesthetics. They deal with the alienation of partners, and lead to the paradox of what we might call 'distant proximity'.

Before he embarked on his penetrating analysis of the breakdown of an upper-class marriage, in his portrait of the Bellellis (ill. 8), Degas produced a series of self-portraits. In one of these (ill. 6), his 'first real painting', comparisons with the 24-year-old Ingres's self-portrait of 1804 (ill. 30) are unavoidable, but one can already see signs of Degas establishing his own artistic identity. It is in the form of his questioning uncertainty. The figure is more central in the picture than that of the young Ingres, but this symmetry is subtly undermined by the tension evident in the features of the face. The expression is a mixture of aloofness and surprise – not shrinking so much as disapproving – but of what, of whom? Perhaps of himself, for the model has exposed himself to the analytical gaze of his other self – the painter. This 'double' self belongs to someone who sets high standards.

The vertical form that marks this portrait is no longer dominant in the small-format self-portrait of 1857–58 (ill. 2). The additional tag '*in a Soft Hat*' denotes a change from the coolness of the first portrait to a warmer, gentler approach. The three-quarter view of the face is the same, but now Degas allows himself to come much closer, which not only softens the aloofness of the face, but also provides it with a breath of human warmth. There is a dim light falling even on those parts of the face that are in shadow. The brush limits itself to a few sketchy strokes to indicate the clothing, and the curved brim of the hat provides an elegant finishing touch to the composition. It is the face of a man whose journeys to the South have imbued him with the nonchalance of the seasoned traveller. But this young man has not forgotten the emotive elements that underlie classical portrait-painting. This is evident from the portrait of his grandfather Hilaire de Gas, which he painted in 1857 in Naples (ill. 31). The self-confident pose of the 77-year-old head of the family combines the calm authority of the man of the world with the dignity of the patriarch. The rectangular shapes that form the background are an early indication of Degas's artistic trick of turning a room into an arrangement of screens.

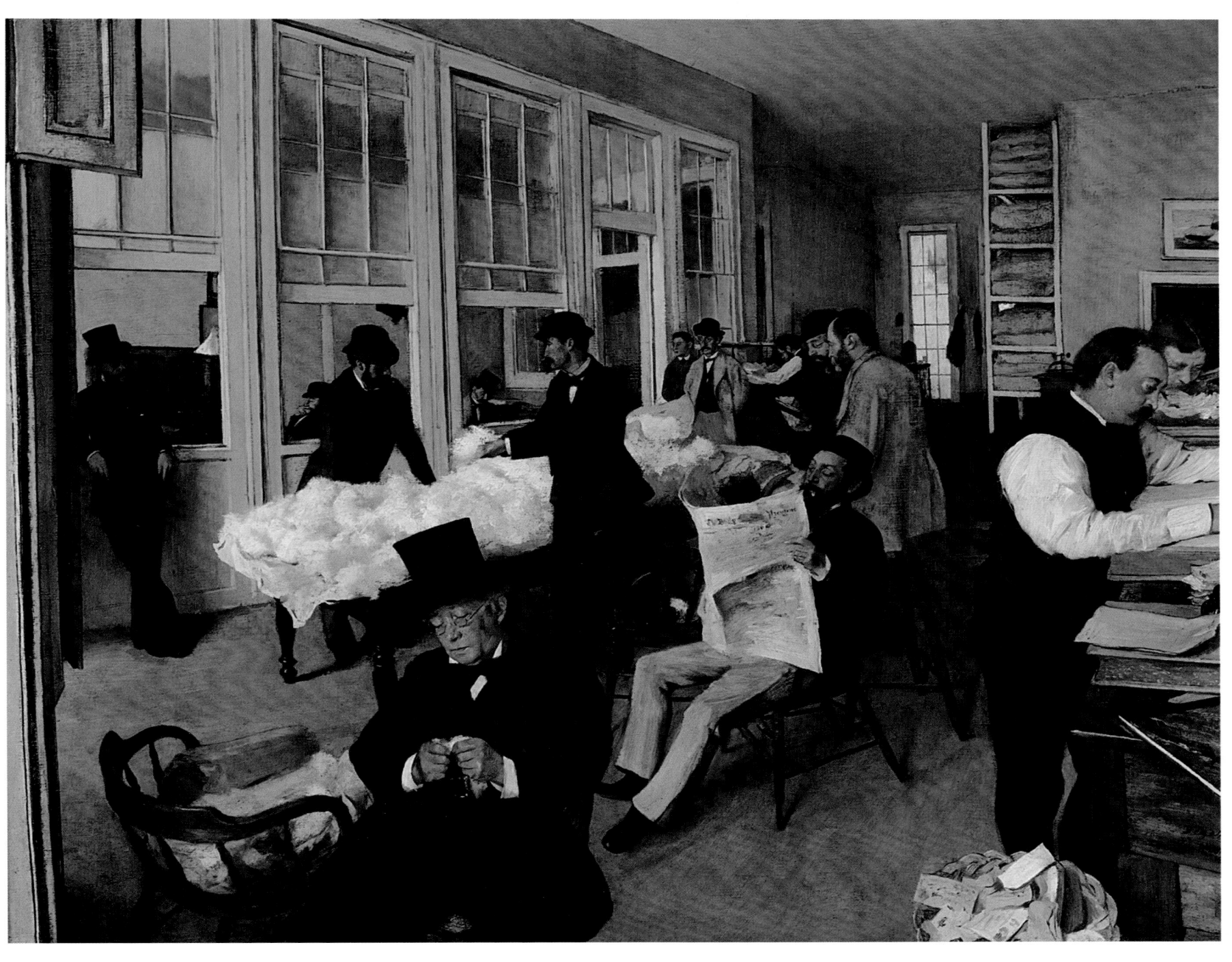

30
Jean-Auguste-Dominique Ingres
(1780–67)
Self-Portrait
1804
Oil on canvas
77 x 61 cm (30 1/4 x 24 in.)
Chantilly, Musée Condé

For his trademark expression of questioning uncertainty, Degas uses a new and rather touching gesture in the etching of his sister Marguerite (ill. 26), which appears once again in the later portrait of his sister Thérèse as Mme Morbilli (ill. 38). The same pose, with hand held hesitantly to chin, recurs in another self-portrait, reinforcing the impression of insecurity and indecisiveness. The same image reversed also finds its way into the double portrait Degas painted of himself with his artist friend Evariste de Valernes (ill. 32).

In this picture, Degas gives the foreground to his partner, but at the same time uses him as a *repoussoir* (a person placed in the foreground in order to direct the observer's eye deeper into the picture, rather in the manner of one actor upstaging another). It is believed that he got the idea for this pairing from a Raphael in the Louvre, in which two people are brought together but at the same time kept apart: in the foreground an unknown man, and behind him at the side of the picture, Raphael himself, gazing directly at the observer. He acts as he paints. Degas gives himself a similar role. His friend Valernes is allowed to occupy the foreground and the whole width of the picture. The jauntily placed top hat and the crossed legs denote his desire to convey an impression of worldliness, and the blankness of the face reinforces this. One feels that there are no thoughts lying behind the mask.

By contrast, the facial expression and gesture of Degas denote self-questioning, although he still keeps his distance from the observer. The directness of the gaze is veiled and even darkened by its uncertainty. Degas is in fact the main character in this picture, and there is as little dialogue in it as in the Raphael. A picture of friendship, even if the friends disagree, would not normally look like this.

In 1863, Hans von Marées painted the volatile relationship between himself and his artist friend Lenbach (ill. 33). Here too the painter withdraws into the background and gives prominence to the inscrutable physiognomy of his friend. In Degas's picture, the staggered proximity of the two men is set against a background that suggests Rome but also has the emptiness of a *terrain vague*, while the room itself has no identifiable features to indicate that anyone lives there.

After this double portrait, Degas the painter lost interest in his own features, although in old age he discovered new dimensions of self-portraiture and ironic role play through photography (see Chapter 12).

As well as having many friends, the young Degas was a family man. His family was very much in the mould of the liberal French bourgeoisie, with a flexible but coherent network of relationships. The pursuit of wealth was carried out in a considered fashion, but also with an instinctive liberal-mindedness. The strategies of commerce demanded some risk-taking, and this led not only to a degree of internationalism but also to a quest for social betterment, with the aim of rising from the middle class to the aristo-cracy. The founder of the 'dynasty' was more or less forced into this ambition by political circumstances: René-Hilaire de Gas (1770–1858) was compelled to leave Paris in 1793 by the purges of the *Terreur*. Via Marseilles, he travelled to Naples. A corn merchant by trade, he entered the banking business of a distinguished Genoan family named Freppa. In 1804, he married Aurora Freppa, who bore him four sons and three daughters. Auguste de Gas, the painter's father, was the firstborn, and he became director of the Parisian branch of the family bank. In 1832, at the age of twenty-four, he married Céles-tine Musson, a Frenchwoman of Creole descent who was seven years younger than him and whose family ran a flourishing

cotton business in New Orleans. Two of Degas's brothers, Achille and René, entered this family firm, and in 1866 they opened an import-export company called 'De Gas Brothers, Cottonbuyers'.

Thus the main Franco-Italian line – the sons regarded themselves as French and the daughters as Italian – was supplemented by a secondary Franco-American branch of the family. Edgar Degas was born in Paris on 19 July 1834, the eldest of five children. As an artist

and as a member of the clan, he was fascinated by this cosmopolitan network. In
1857–58, he went to Naples to visit his
grandfather (ill. 31) shortly before the latter
died, and so he got to know his uncles, aunts
and cousins. In 1872–73, he went to New
Orleans, and met the equally extensive
Musson side of the family.

In the 1870s, however, disaster struck, and
the family lost its fortune. The Parisian bank
had been keeping its head above water only
thanks to its creditors, and when Degas's
father died in 1874, the situation became
hopeless. Two years later, it went into liquidation. Meanwhile, in New Orleans Achille
and René had got involved in some bad deals

33
Hans von Marées (1837–87)
Portrait of the Artist (left)
with Franz von Lenbach
1863
Oil on canvas
54.3 x 62 cm (21 3/8 x 24 3/8 in.)
Munich, Neue Pinakothek

and in any case had proved to be poor businessmen. The brothers and sisters had to assume
liability for the debts of the unprincipled René, and drastically alter their lifestyle. Edgar, who
suffered a great deal from this family disgrace, had to sell some of his art collection in order to
pay off his brother's debts.

Degas painted two large-format pictures that gave vivid expression to the lifestyles of the
two lineages. *The Bellelli Family* (ill. 8) and *The Cotton Exchange in New Orleans* (ill. 29) are
group portraits staged as genre paintings and depicting two very different modes of conduct.
Of course a comparison between such completely dissimilar milieux is rather like comparing
apples to pears: the one is a private scene specially posed for (or by) the painter, and the other
is a snapshot of semi-public business life, even if it was also arranged by the painter to suit his
purposes. But the common denominator between these two glimpses of middle-class society is
the fact that all the protagonists are caught doing their own thing. In this respect, they provide
us with exemplary insight into the manners and conduct of the bourgeoisie, the two poles of
which are European formality, which shows the four members of the Bellelli family in all their
social dignity, and the shirt-sleeved anonymity of the New World, where everybody follows his
own bent and nobody takes any notice of anybody else. Here we have a measured class consciousness opposed to a democratic free-for-all. The Bellellis pose within rigid rectangular
coordinates, whereas the axes of the cotton exchange are livelier, with a number of criss-crossing diagonals. Similarly, the people themselves occupy their own spaces, between which there

Opposite:
32
Degas and Valernes
1865
Oil on canvas
116 x 89 cm (45 5/8 x 35 in.)
Paris, Musée d'Orsay

is no continuity. The Bellellis are as stiff as the system that hides their isolation behind their middle-class solidity and yet at the same time exposes it. By contrast, the cotton exchange is like a passing show, such as we will see again in the pictures of ballet rehearsals. About a dozen man are scattered round the room, bent over their books or studying samples of cotton on the table. Right at the front sits Degas's uncle, Michel Musson, who is closely examining a hank of cotton. Contrasted with this man at work are the painter's two brothers: René is buried in a local newspaper, and Achille is leaning against a window on the left. The nonchalance of the two men brings a touch of Parisian idleness into the business world of the bourgeoisie, though without disturbing it.

All these shifts of emphasis indicate the development of Degas's art during the period between the two paintings. The first sketches for the *Bellelli Family* date from 1857, but the painting was not finished until ten years later; *The Cotton Exchange in New Orleans* was painted in 1873. What divides the two compositions technically is their spatial structure. In the later picture, the room and the people in it are given no fixed frame of reference to create a central perspective; this would draw all the elements together within a system of axes that would focus our attention on a single vanishing point. Instead, Degas devises centrifugal forces that destabilize the composition. It is this very destabilization that captures human relations and endows them with the uncertainty of experimentation. Here we have the leitmotiv that was to fascinate Degas throughout his life: human alienation. In the family portrait this alienation is depicted through rigid formality, whereas in the cotton exchange it is in the form of relaxed disunity. The tensions that Degas conveys from behind the upper-class façade of his first group portrait are subtly reproduced in the portrait of *M. and Mme Morbilli* (ill. 27). Once again they arise from the smouldering dissonances of a conventional marriage.

36
Giulia Bellelli
1859–60
Oil on board
36 x 25 cm (14 1/8 x 9 7/8 in.)
Washington DC, Dumbarton Oaks
Research Library

The Bellelli painting may have been one of the two family portraits that Degas exhibited in the 1867 Salon – without gaining any critical recognition. The composition itself certainly belongs to the genre of group or family portraits, but it also subtly prepares the way for the subversion of these two categories. It depicts the parents and the two daughters, Giovanna and Giulia. Degas's Aunt Laura – a sister of his father's – had married Baron Gennaro Bellelli in 1842; he was a liberal politician who was condemned to death following the unsuccessful revolution of 1848, fled to Sicily, and subsequently lived in exile in Florence. The painting had a long gestation period, the beginning of which appears to have been a planned double portrait

37
Sulking
c. 1870
Oil on canvas
32.4 x 46.4 cm
(12 3/4 x 18 1/4 in)
New York, The Metropolitan
Museum of Art

of the sisters (ill. 34). Then Degas posed the two girls together at more or less the same eye level, with their mother standing front on between them, dominating the trio (ill. 35). However, to this pyramid structure he added a subtle variation in the form of a gap: while Giovanna stands directly under the protection of her mother, the younger sister Giulia has turned away from the steep-sided triangle towards where, in the final version, the father will be sitting. In the final version, Giulia's wilfully independent pose – for which Degas did a swift preliminary sketch in oils (ill. 36) – takes on the function of a hinge that separates the halves and yet at the same time provides a link. To this little girl, who has freed herself from her mother and sister and has turned towards her father – although she is looking into empty space rather than directly at him – Degas has assigned a position of pivotal importance. She occupies the exact centre of the picture, and the rectangular corner of the table behind her accentuates her autonomy. But she belongs to both halves of the composition. She is linked to her mother and sister, though now separated from them, by her black dress and, perhaps even more, by the greyish white of her pinafore, and the leg jutting out at an angle emphasizes the lively, independent nature of this seven-year-old. Her pinafore is not as neat as her sister's.

Giulia's pose is fairly relaxed, like that of the baron, who seems to be taking no notice at all of the painter. Both heads are symmetrically turned, but father and daughter are gazing past each other, just as the glassy stare of the baroness completely ignores her husband. Between the mother's half of the room – with its cold blue wallpaper containing nothing but a portrait of the grandfather, Hilaire – and Gennaro's half, with the mirror and various objects on the mantelpiece, one can discern a coded dividing line. It runs perpendicularly from the frame of the mirror down the edge of the fireplace, and through the leg of the table to the chair on which Giulia is sitting.

Concerning the consonances, assonances and dissonances that arise out of this structure, Emil Maurer offers the most complete analysis. All of them are variations on the main theme of alienation between man and wife. By splitting the composition in two, the 24-year-old Degas – a mere beginner – has captured the relationships within this bourgeois-cum-aristocratic family perfectly, with Laura acting the part of the aristocrat through her dignified posture. The married couple have drawn apart from each other. The baroness is rigid with cold rejection, and her husband is the marginal figure, the loser buckling under his political defeat. (In 1861, however, he was rehabilitated and appointed senator under the new monarchy).

The whole scene is set in the cool bright light of day – not yet shadowed by the 'social chiaroscuro' with which Degas would later depict such situations of conflict. There is an ingenious coda to this painting – an oil sketch of the hands of the baroness (ill. 40). One is hanging

38
Madame Morbilli
c. 1869
Pastel on board
51 x 34 cm (20 1/8 x 13 3/8 in.)
Private collection

loosely while the other rests on the top of the table. The rest is pure painting, done with a brush that has no other object to consider. It is a *capriccio*, or what Schiller might have called a 'dark total idea'. Perhaps with this sketch Degas was fulfilling one of Flaubert's dreams: '...a book about nothing, a book with no outer attachment, that would stand on its own through the internal strength of its style.' Or perhaps this 'idea', which was certainly painted after the commencement of the portrait, was meant to be a recapitulation and also a correction to the frozen rigidity of the baroness, softening it into a more relaxed attitude, wrapped in a whirl of dark and warmly shining colours.

During the same period that he was working on the Bellelli portrait, Degas was painting another non-couple: M. *and Mme Morbilli* (ill. 27). His sister Thérèse married their cousin Edmondo de Morbilli, a young Neapolitan, in 1863. The union had been made possible by a papal dispensation. In an earlier double portrait (National Gallery of Art, Washington), we can see signs of the young woman's pregnancy. The child died, however, soon after it was born. When Degas painted his sister and brother-in-law for the second time, both of them must still have been very conscious of this loss. Once again, he uses the technique of bringing two figures together, one behind the other (cf. the portrait of Degas and Valernes, ill. 32). Thérèse may appear to be overshadowed and marginalized by her husband, but in fact she is the dominant personality here. Edmondo has all the casual ease of a man well aware of his own imposing presence, but Thérèse is far from being merely the supportive wife; she is a character in her own right. The questioning look and the half-open mouth give expression to her insecurity, in much the same way as the picture of her brother with Valernes. Through that portrait we are already familiar with the gesture of the chin resting on the hand, which is not part of the rhetoric of a formal portrait. In addition to self-doubt, it creates a feeling of inner fragility and, at the same time, a degree of detachment. This is enhanced by the dark intensity of her eyes, whose shy but penetrating gaze was evidently a family trait. In 1860–62, Degas did an etching of his other sister, Marguerite (ill. 26), whose round, childlike eyes have a similar expression. Here too the hand is raised to the cheek, lending support.

40
Study of Hands
c. 1860
Oil on canvas
38 x 46 cm
Paris, Musée d'Orsay

Previous pages:
39
Interior (The Rape)
(detail of ill. 41)

When Degas painted *Madame Morbilli* on her own in 1869 (ill. 38), she was a different woman. This time he did not use any of the soft, pastel nuances of the earlier painting. The prosperous, middle-class ambiance remains intact, but the lady herself is only outwardly part of it. She maintains her composure, but now her expression is one of cold mistrust, enhanced by her tight-fitting outdoor garb. Here she is suppressing every emotion, even the questioning vulnerability that we saw four years previously when she sat in the shadow of her husband. Her searching gaze no longer has the gloom of an Egyptian mummy portrait, and perhaps that was precisely how the brother saw the face of his unhappy favourite sister – frozen into a mask.

At this point in his analysis of people's conduct, Degas appears to have become conscious of the fact that his work was indiscreetly wounding in its forthrightness. He hit upon the idea of compressing the battle of the sexes into a metaphor in the form of two genre paintings: *Sulking* (ill. 37) and *Interior (The Rape)* (ills. 39, 41). In this way, he was able to neutralize the sensitive subject matter and to escape the suspicion of voyeurism that might have been attached to him as nephew and brother, but at the same time he could record objectively the social misery which, in the end, came down to the violent nature of men.

It seems perfectly reasonable to trace a line, as Reff has done, between *Madame Morbilli* and *Sulking*, and although the latter is in a smaller format, it offers a new view of the same large theme: a man and woman together at a moment when their relationship has broken down. The place is the office of a bookmaker. The English colour print on the wall, partially hidden by both the man and the woman, establishes a kind of formal link between them. Their separateness is a mixture of turning towards and turning away, for although the two figures fail to make any contact, Degas relates them to each other in such a way that they form a kind of arc. This separated togetherness, however, is too artificial to convey a real feeling of breakdown. The confrontation seems more formal than emotional, which may well be due to the fact that Degas was not dealing here with the alienation of an actual couple (as with the Morbillis). These were two friends whom he had engaged to pose for him: the woman was Emma Dobigny, and the man was the critic Duranty.

When Courbet was trying to explain the *Studio* to a friend, he cunningly resorted to a description that freed him from any interpretation and left the observer to find his own solutions: 'It is rather mysterious. Let him who can, guess!' The programmatic harbinger of Realism was pointing out that in every reality there are several realities: perceptions, memories, dreams and more. Degas's realities are also multilayered, particular in the case of a canvas which he himself called 'my genre painting' (ills. 39, 41). It has two conflicting but also complementary titles: *The Rape* and *Interior*. 'Interior' is misleadingly matter-of-fact, as befits the linguistic reserve of an artist whose use of understatement extended to calling his works 'my

41
Interior (The Rape)
c. 1870
Oil on canvas
81 x 116 cm (32 x 45 in.)
Philadelphia, The Philadelphia
Museum of Fine Arts

articles'. The neutrality of this title is so obviously disproportionate to the mysterious, even sinister connection between the two figures that no one can possibly miss its irony. The harmless bourgeois genre of the interior is merely a euphemism – a meaningless tag to give a veneer of propriety to what is really happening (or not happening) here. The other title leaves no doubt as to the subject matter. But if we interpret it literally, this too fails to resolve the mystery behind the painting, because it names an act of violence that is not taking place, although even without the title we can sense the imminent confrontation between the perpetrator and his victim. A similar composition appears in the illustrations for *Physiologie de la femme honnête* (ill. 42), although this version lacks the element of masculine threat.

The fact that the bed has not been touched suggests that the man has not yet done the deed, although rape does not necessarily depend on this particular piece of equipment. The manner in which the young woman, dressed only in her underwear, is slumped with her back to the man indicates that she knows she is at his mercy; she seems almost to be waiting for him to pounce, whereas he stands at the door, apparently enjoying his victim's terror of physical abuse. Perhaps there is no point in our speculating about whether it has happened or is about to happen. Degas did not in fact give the picture its melodramatic title *The Rape*, which he dismissed as a critic's bad idea, but he tolerated it; such a title lured the observer onto a false track and aroused voyeuristic expectations which the actual content of the painting quickly dispelled. In other words, it is the non-event that constitutes the real action here. The abuse, which cannot be seen in terms of a real-life incident, expands to embrace the human condition itself as applied to bourgeois society's treatment of the 'weaker sex'. The woman suffers two different kinds of rape in this picture: the one physical in terms of a violent action, and the other psychological in terms of the role she is permanently forced to play. Degas was more concerned with the latter than with the former.

In the light of the above, there seems little point in searching for a literary source for this episode, but some critics have done so, and have pointed to Zola as the most likely. Jean Adhémar traces it to a scene from *Madeleine Férat* (1868), while Theodore Reff thinks it refers to an episode in *Thérèse Raquin*, which began to appear in serialized form in 1867, under the ironic title *A Marriage of Love*. A year after they have murdered Monsieur Raquin, Thérèse and her lover Laurent meet to celebrate their wedding night.

It seems to me that although these literary scenes may tie in with the contemporary atmosphere conveyed by the picture, such details themselves do not help us to solve the mystery that Degas painted. There are a few preliminary studies he made of the room, of the man at the door and of the young woman. One sketch shows the man standing next to a veiled woman dressed for outdoors. The pairing is completely neutral – neither meeting nor seduction. In *Interior*, the man looks thoroughly menacing, in a pose that will recur a few years later in *Painter and Mannequin* (ill. 74), where once again the woman falls prey to the man.

There is another mystery in the form of an envelope, with writing on both sides, giving advice concerning the colours and lighting of the objects in the *Interior*. Written in a hurry, this advice suggests that the author was also a painter – possibly Tissot (ill. 65). It relates to the syntax of the painting and not to any literary model. What matters here in any case is the visual impact of the picture. Unlike the novelist, who has to depict the battle of the sexes through dialogue and narrative, Degas does not even hint at any verbal communication. He sets the whole clash within a zone of complete silence, even intensifying the silence to muteness from which there can be no escape.

Probably without even knowing it, Degas was putting into practice Lessing's precepts outlined in *Laocoon*, whereby poetry narrates actions and painting is concerned with bodies in a

42
Anonymous
'A Subjugated Woman'
From: Physiologie de la femme honnête, p. 34

Overleaf:
43
Lorenzo Pagans and
Auguste de Gas
c. 1871–72
Oil on canvas
54.5 x 40 cm (21 3/4 x 15 3/4 in.)
Paris, Musée d'Orsay

44
Henri Rouart with
His Son Alexis
1895
Oil on canvas
92 x 73 cm (36 1/4 x 28 3/4 in.)
Munich, Neue Pinakothek

45
**Louis Rouart with
His Wife Christine**
c. 1904
Pastel
152 x 115 cm (59 7/8 x 45 1/4 in.)
Private collection

Opposite:
46
**Madame Rouart
with Her Children**
c. 1905
Pastel and charcoal on paper
160 x 141.5 cm (63 x 55 3/4 in.)
Paris, Musée du Petit-Palais

room. The painter has nothing but what Diderot called the *seul point de vue*. But this is fertile when it allows completely free rein to the imagination, which is precisely the case here: *Interior* forces us to extend the painted moment into both the past and the future.

Bodies in a room: the gap between the man and the girl could not be any greater. The space between the two motionless figures, however, is foreshortened like a path cutting through the depths, and we are sucked into it, so that the non-event takes on an aura of inescapability. On

47
The Duchessa di Montejasi
with Her Daughters
1876
Oil on canvas
66 x 98 cm (26 x 38 5/8 in.)
Private collection

the little round table, our attention is caught by an eloquent symbol that Henri Loyrette has interpreted for us: he compares the dark, open box lined in salmon-pink to a famous metaphor signifying lost innocence – Greuze's broken jug.

In the context of Degas's development, the *Interior* marks a transition between the early works and those of his maturity. The link is supplied by the girl. It has long been recognized that the prototype for this figure is the rear view of the naked woman in the far left of the *Scene of War in the Middle Ages* (ill. 12). This figure, which in turn refers back to Eve's expulsion from Eden that began the whole sorry saga, was the formal matrix that returned to the artist's mind when he painted *Interior*. The empty centre is another link between the 'genre painting' and the history painting. This space, devoid of people and action, produces a tension-filled vacuum that we feel to be menacing. The setting has changed, but the subject matter is the same. Abuse in the Middle Ages remains a component of everyday life in the 19th century, and even if it gives rise to a different set of circumstances, the message contained within the picture denotes an unbroken continuity of thought.

On the other hand, the figure of the young woman also prefigures the anonymous creatures that Degas would later call upon during the two most productive decades of his artistic career, between 1870 and 1890. Her contemporary successors were the bending bathers, the women ironing, the dancers, the singers at the café-concerts, and the prostitutes in the brothels.

Of the various levels of consciousness which, in the processes of reflection, can result in certain transient combinations, the breakdown in the relationships of the Bellellis and the Morbillis represents an extreme example. There are, however, areas of thoughtfulness that entail lasting tensions without leading to an irrevocable breakdown. Degas also recorded these areas among his relatives. He shows how they protect their fragile psyches with gestures of self-defence. The device that he uses here is a confrontation between two different characters, two different age groups, or two different social classes. Out of this confrontation arises the 'game of consonances and dissonances' (Emil Maurer) that separates the parties and yet at the same time creates a dialogue between them.

Degas was not the inventor of this game. In 1859, Fantin-Latour painted a portrait of his two sisters (Saint Louis Art Museum): Marie appears to be absorbed in her book, while Nathalie is looking up from her embroidery – neither knowingly nor questioningly. In this juxtaposition of the two young women, there is no trace of any sisterly relationship: Degas used the same device in his portrait of the two Bellelli girls (ill. 8). Ten years later, Fantin-Latour painted his *Double Portrait of the Dubourg Sisters* (Museu Calouste Gulbenkian, Lisbon), which could easily be cut in two right down the middle. Charlotte is facing the painter, and clearly wishes to be seen. Victoria is reading, and seems to be totally self-sufficient. She would later become Madame Fantin-Latour, and Degas had painted a portrait of her the year before (Toledo Museum of Art), showing her in all her domesticity.

Degas takes these antitheses even further. The Spanish guitarist *Lorenzo Pagans* (ill. 43) appears to be improvising a song as he plays his instrument. He seems to be doing this purely for himself, just as the elderly gentleman in the background – Auguste de Gas, the painter's father – appears to be alone with his thoughts and memories.

In the double portrait of *Henri de Gas and his Niece Lucie* (ill. 48), it is the difference in age that both links and divides the two figures. Neither Pagans nor Auguste de Gas had taken the slightest notice of the painter, but here both uncle and niece are looking straight at the man by the easel, fully aware of their own part in the scene. The elderly uncle has looked up from his newspaper, but does not seem in any way disturbed. His niece, with the shining eyes so typical of the family, is as sweet and fresh as only a well-brought-up, middle-class young lady can be. But despite the tangible informality of the scene, there is no contact between them, and they remain at a distance, one behind the other.

There is an even clearer example of this detachment in the portrait of the *Duchessa di Montejasi with Her Daughters* (ill. 47). The canvas is almost like a diptych of two playing cards waiting to be cut down the centre. Such an operation would give the 'helpless grief' of the unhappy widow that isolation which is natural to anyone who knows that they are alone in their despair. But it would also deprive this dignified lady – who is looking not at us but into empty space – of the counterbalance provided by the painter's two cousins, each of whom is also lost in her own world. Something similar occurs in the double portrait of the sisters from the late 1860s, in which one has turned towards the other, and one has turned away.

In his later years, Degas again laid bare the fragile tissues of bourgeois society. As his own family had by then scattered far and wide, and could therefore no longer serve as models, he looked for the dissonances among his friends the Rouarts. He compressed his findings into three episodes, which together amount to a paraphrase of the middle-class 'sham' existence so ruthlessly exposed by the plays of his contemporary Henrik Ibsen. The double portrait of the collector *Henri Rouart with His Son Alexis* (ill. 44), painted in 1895, sharpens the contrast between generations into a brusque illustration of 'to each his own'. Alexis dominates the composition only physically, for he is no match for the seated patriarch. The latter has the fixed stare of old age, and the red hollows of his eyes are almost like a festering wound. The tentative, indistinct brushwork gives the impression that the head is in the process of fading away. Degas painted his own old age into this picture.

The two large pastels of 1904 and 1905 were painted in defiance of the eye disease that eventually blinded him. Both of them extend the father–son contrast into an imaginary triptych of the ages of life. Louis, another son, poses with his wife Christine for a double portrait (ill. 45) illustrating the decline and fall of the bourgeois conversation piece. If the first glance takes in the formal harmony established by the two bodies, this impression is quickly dispelled by the decisive manner in which they have turned away. They take no notice at all of one another. This is the ultimate stage of alienation, which we have already seen in M. *and Mme Morbilli* (ill. 27). Louis and Christine Rouart were an unhappy couple. The second large pastel, from 1905 (ill. 46), shows Alexis's wife, Valentine, together with her two daughters Madeleine (born 1896) and Hélène (born 1901). Evidently there is a conflict here too, which has proved too much for the mother. Helplessly she seeks support from little Hélène against Madeleine, who has turned away from them, her almost animal intensity – note the receding brow – exuding the fascination of evil. Contemplation, alienation, self-awareness are drawn together in these three episodes of middle-class family life in an atmosphere of bitter resignation.

48
**Henri de Gas and
His Niece Lucie**
c. 1876
Oil on canvas
96 x 113 cm (39 1/4 x 47 1/4 in.)
Chicago, The Art Institute

Chapter 4

Women and Their
Daydreams

*'If only I could find a nice little wife, simple, quiet, who understood the
follies of my mind, and with whom I could spend a modest working life!
Isn't that a lovely dream?'* – Degas, Italian journals, 1858

This chapter should be regarded as an entr'acte. It is meant to give you some relief from the battle of the sexes and to prepare you for the painter's great theme: women. At this point, let us once and for all do away with the myth that Degas was a misogynist. He was quite the opposite. No 19th-century artist looked at women with such discernment or – without seeking to create any sort of synthesis – so vividly captured the total essence of femininity. He explored the female being in all its disguises and with all its self-revelations. Among the disguises were those of the middle-class ladies whose outward show of self-confidence rarely even hinted at the wounds of alienation that lay beneath. Their thoughts ran free and produced daydreams in which the bourgeois mask could at last be discarded, suppressed desires could be fulfilled, and forbidden fruits could be savoured.

In the hands of painters and writers, people can assume various, even interchangeable identities. Degas painted Emma Dobigny, his favourite model, as herself (private collection, Switzerland), as a woman ironing (ill. 86), and as a young woman turning away from her ill-tempered partner and beginning a calculated flirtation with the observer (ill. 37). Madame Schlésinger, the 'only passion' of Flaubert's life, was the model for his *Salammbô*, but was also the mysterious Madame Arnoux with whom Frédéric, in *L'Education Sentimentale*, exchanged the silent looks that heralded an adulterous relationship. Sexual promiscuity was rife among all levels of Parisian society: 'The women of the so-called better classes can dance the cancan, the dance of whores; they know the cocottes and their nicknames, and they fight with them over their lovers.' (Viel-Castel).

The ladies we see daydreaming may also be leading double lives of this kind. They appear cool and reserved like the men, but in attitude and gesture, as befits the grace of their sex, they are freer and more spontaneous. This is thanks to the manner in which Degas posed his

49
**Madame Jeantaud
at the Mirror**
(detail of ill. 59)

Woman Seated Beside
a Vase of Flowers
1865
Oil on canvas
73.7 x 92.7 cm (29 x 36 1/2 in.)
New York, Metropolitan Museum

models, including the non-professionals. Their states of mind range from the questioning insecurity of self-reflection to an escape into daydreams, the content of which we should not inquire into.

This range is already hinted at in *Woman Seated Beside a Vase of Flowers* (1865; ill. 50). The gigantic bouquet, which almost seems to have taken over the room, was initially the only subject of the painting. It is generally agreed that Degas later added the woman on the right to his still life, quite literally as a marginal figure, but he also fragmented this figure. The imbalance of the composition, accentuated by the fact that she is turning away half in and half out of the picture, violates all the traditional rules of unity and indeed of decorum.

And yet despite her marginalization, the woman – assumed to be Madame Hertl – still makes her presence felt. Her alert gaze suggests a sharp intelligence that is well able to stand up for itself. One should not read too much into this juxtaposition of woman and Nature, but

once again we see the motif of contrast that was apparent in the double portraits, in which Degas captured the different qualities of his subjects through their detached togetherness.

We can see more clearly the contrast inherent in the pairing of woman and flowers if we compare this picture with Courbet's *The Trellis*, painted in 1863. Here the flowers form what seems almost like a burgeoning landscape – a piece of Nature that Hélène Toussaint's sharp eyes have identified as a cross-section of three different seasons. The active movements of the young girl in the painting make her part of this organic life, whereas the flowers have no link with Madame Hertl, and have none of the vitality of Courbet's. What Degas painted was, in the literal sense, a *nature morte* (the French term for still life), for here Nature is indeed in the process of fading. And the fading of the flowers lends to the face of the woman – despite the dullness of her clothes and the stillness of her pose – a contrasting quality of life that is still in full bloom.

51
Hortense Valpinçon
c. 1869–71
Oil on canvas
75 x 114 cm (29 3/4 x 44 3/4 in.)
Minneapolis, The Minneapolis Institute of Arts

52
Madame Camus
1869–70
Oil on canvas
72.7 x 92.1 cm
(28 5/8 x 36 1/4 in.)
Washington DC, National Gallery
of Art, Chester Dale Collection

Even more self-assured (though not at all contemplative) is *Hortense Valpinçon* (ill. 51), born in 1862, the daughter of a childhood friend. Degas painted her at their country home some time between 1869 and 1871. Once again the balance of the composition is off-centre. We are given no information about the interior, as everything is in close-up. The girl is leaning on the edge of a chest of drawers that is covered with a flower-patterned cloth, which if not exactly Japanese certainly looks quite exotic. This in turn is covered with a piece of embroidery that has a different pattern. The whole of the background consists of faded wallpaper, again with a flower pattern and somewhat reminiscent of the huge bunch of flowers beside Madame Hertl. The wallpaper functions like a screen, denying the room any depth and reducing the picture itself to a refined interplay between its two-dimensional components. The vague yet intimate nature of this picture – an extract from the three-dimensional real world – suggests something almost fictional that anticipates many features of the interiors painted by Bonnard and Vuillard. One also thinks of Matisse, and especially his *Still Life with Geraniums* in Munich, painted in 1910.

In the midst of these various floral materials stands Hortense, quite uninhibited, with a half-eaten apple in her hand. She is no Eve, but all the same there is an inviting look in her eye, which is given an added coquettishness by the fashionable hat on her head. She is neither

53
Rose Caron
c. 1885–90
Oil on canvas
76.2 x 82.5 cm (30 x 32 1/2 in.)
Buffalo, Albright-Knox Art Gallery

detached from the décor nor restricted by it, and she represents one of those delicate balancing acts that no one could perform better than Degas.

The decorative surroundings in which *Madame Camus* (ill. 52) finds herself also offer a complex, atmospheric web of assonances. The background is provided by a range of warm reds against which the repertoire of objects delivers a number of variations: part of a rococo frame at the top of the picture, the statuette of a black man, the curve on the left which begins vertically, goes over into the arm of the chair, joins up with the back of the woman, rises to the silhouette-like head, and then gradually fades into the dress. This *glissando* rhythm is taken up again by the Japanese fan, which seems almost emblematic, and by the mistress of the salon herself, who sits in the midst of the beautifully staged harmony, knowing that she is an integral part of it. This 1870 portrait was Degas's last submission to the Salon. From then on, he withdrew from the parade ground of official taste.

54
Madame Théodore Gobillard
1869
Oil on canvas
55.2 x 65.1 cm
(21 3/4 x 25 5/8 in.)
New York, The Metropolitan Museum of Art

55
*Melancholy
(Young Woman on
a Chaise Longue)*
c. 1874
Oil on canvas on wood
19 x 24.7 cm (7 1/2 x 9 3/4 in.)
Washington DC, Phillips Collection

This did not stop him, however, from continuing his artistic pursuit of elegant ladies. With the soprano *Rose Caron* (ill. 53), the expansive colours take on a dynamic life of their own, which swamps the dimensions of the room. The model seems totally absorbed in communion with her own body, and ignores the painter, who is in the process of enhancing the generous décolleté even further by merging the colour of the skin with that of the barely perceptible glove. Elisabeth Bronfen, to whom we owe this observation, saw Rose Caron as playing the role of someone who has withdrawn from the public and is now quite lost in thought.

Degas was rather more circumspect with his artist friend *Mary Cassatt* (ill. 60), who sits contemplatively in an indeterminate setting (more likely exterior than interior), holding three playing cards in her hands. It was, however, precisely these attributes to which her bourgeois, puritanical mentality took exception, and she complained that her family would be upset. She saw herself being portrayed as someone 'repulsive', and she did not like the fact that Degas had made her into some kind of fortune-teller and, as such, associated her with a disreputable activity. (The playing card as a metaphor for a new formal language had not yet

come into vogue.) It is only recently that a female critic has interpreted the bright area around Mary Cassatt's head as a modern, abstract halo.

When Degas painted his figures in vaguely sketched settings, he often worked with reflections. He placed Madame Jeantaud (ill. 59) in front of a full-length mirror, so that the observer is compensated for the loss of profile by a reflected frontal view. The shaded reflection contrasts with the three-dimensional, brightly lit head. As she looks out of the picture, the lady's self-perception also contains the outsider's perception by the painter and the observer. Once again, Degas separates and joins the two halves of his picture. The vertical division that runs between these two halves is masked at one point by the muff, giving rise to a parabola divided equally between the two views. The physiognomical bipolarity makes the model more interesting than in the somewhat conventional portrait in Karlsruhe, in which Degas makes up for the lady's diffidence with a free flow of paint that extends into her surroundings.

The question of how beautiful or attractive his bourgeois models are does not seem to concern Degas when, for instance, he paints a *Woman at a Bright Window* (ill. 57) and has her conducting a light and dark dialogue with surroundings that are barely perceptible. The profile does, though, contain one tiny detail that arouses our curiosity: the little button nose.

Sometimes the rooms are completely expunged, or they appear with no character of their own, merely as a background or organic 'wrapping' for the person or persons portrayed, as in *The Invalid* (ill. 58). The idea is akin to one of Courbet's diaphanous female figures, the 14-year-old *Gabrielle Boreau*, who gazes dreamily into a distant land which perhaps lies within herself. The resting hand has turned the head to one side as she waits in expectation.

With Degas's sick woman, everything droops listlessly. Her nightdress flows over her limp body, and her headscarf and shawl bring no life to the exhausted figure. Out of this amorphous void rises the head resting on the hand, and the eyes looking sideways and downwards emit the only tentative signs of life – though even this interpretation depends on whether we can believe the second title of the painting: *The Convalescent*. The almost glutinous masses of paint slide over the figure in an apotheosis of contrasting light and dark. One can scarcely imagine a gentler, more empathetic metaphor to depict the borderline between sickness and health, between fading away and returning to life.

Degas approaches the intimate world of the daydream with sensitivity and complete freedom from voyeurism, although he still gives his model her own identity without, as it were, putting her on show. A prime example of this is a small canvas he painted in around 1874, to which Lemoisne gave the title *Melancholy* (ill. 55). The young woman in a housecoat occupies the complete width of the landscape format. She seems lost in thought, but the outline of the figure allows for two possible interpretations. On the one hand, the brown

59
**Madame Jeantaud
at the Mirror**
c. 1875
Oil on canvas
70 x 84 cm (27 5/8 x 33 1/8 in.)
Paris, Musée d'Orsay

chaise longue cups her body like a hollow shell or bowl – suggesting a kind of secure privacy that makes her seem untouchable. On the other hand, there is something dangerously unbalanced, even insecure, in the horizontal angle of her body as she leans out over the edge. One is reminded of a figurehead. The expression on her face indicates that maybe she is listening for something; there is a certain tender vulnerability about her which justifies Lemoisne's title. This little painting is a rare instance in Degas's work where the different layers of meaning do not diverge but actually come together with an almost Venetian warmth of colour.

The 'spatial coat' worn by the melancholy daydreamer lies at one end of Degas's three-dimensional spectrum. The other is the room, which takes its structure from the windows in such a manner that the rectangular coordinates form a framing background beyond which the out-of-perspective distant world is simply a blur. The portrait of *Madame Olivier Villette* (1872)

Opposite:
58
The Invalid
1872–73
Oil on canvas
65 x 47 cm (25 5/8 x 18 1/2 in.)
Private collection

is another that uses this technique. A subtler though even more rigorous example of Degas's use of frames and spaces working with and against each other is the somewhat austere *Madame Théodore Gobillard* (ill. 54), a sister of Berthe Morisot. She is seated in a dominant central position against the various elements of the background. The frames create an effect of improvisation, in the sense that the rigid rectangular shapes open up into a kind of stage set, with movable scenery. In no other work of the 1860s is Degas's theme more clearly articulated: rooms become screens.

For an art historian, the two portraits indicate two contrasting concepts of space. The view behind Madame Villette stands for mastery of depth as demanded by Alberti in 1435, when in establishing the concept of central perspective he defined painting as an 'open window'. On the other hand, the portrait of Madame Gobillard illustrates a retreat from endlessness and a return to what Maurice Denis calls the 'surface plane', which at the end of the 19th century enabled the second dimension to profit from a new syntax of its own. The renunciation of spatial depth probably goes back to Poussin's self-portrait in the Louvre, with paintings concealing the third dimension rather like partition walls. Both Poussin and Degas treated the room not as a fixed measurement but as a variable product of compositions that the painter was free to adjust according to his own requirements.

60
Mary Cassatt
c. 1880–84
Oil on canvas
73.3 x 60 cm (28 7/8 x 23 5/8 in.)
Washington DC, National Portrait Gallery, Smithsonian Institution

Chapter 5

Rooms Become Screens

'Study a face or an object from all angles, whatever it is.
One can use a mirror for this without moving one's place.
The mirror is only lowered or tilted; one moves around it.'
– Degas, 1877–83

Degas's handling of the third dimension gives us some insight into the experimental impetus behind his art. Ultimately, the room for him is not an organizing factor but a cause of tension, disturbing the geometry of the picture and throwing it out of balance. The beginnings of this syntax are to be found in the problem areas dealt with by Courbet in his *Studio* (ill. 5), where he strips the room of its clarity and by doing so endows it with several layers of meaning. This gigantic, unfinished spatial conglomeration corresponds to the human conglomeration to which it serves as a background. It is not a cube-shaped box but a shadowy stage set of indeterminate depth and movable sections.

We stand before veils and painted curtains and dirty backcloths, all of which – especially in the left half of the picture – seem to belong to some colossal, fragmented mural. When Delacroix visited the exhibition, he praised the 'uniqueness' of this painting, but noted one ambiguity: the sky in the picture in front of which the artist is sitting seems not to be painted but real. Delacroix did not, however, register the spatial ambivalences and obscurities of the background.

It is clear to us today that this is precisely where the forward-looking formal potential of these great screens lies – in their suggestion of in-between worlds of two and three dimensions, of interior and exterior, such as only the imagination can explore. Is this the work of a dedicated 'Realist'? Or of someone who forgets his 'declaration of war on the imagination' (Klaus Herding) the moment he picks up his brush?

Degas developed new procedures for transforming rooms into walls and screens. He used the playing card as a metaphor for spatial fragmentation and destabilization. In order to illustrate this, I shall look at portraits of contemporaries that could have come from the right-hand side of Courbet's *Studio* – portraits of collectors, artists and critics.

61
Manet and His Wife
(detail of ill. 69)

The context within which Degas carried out his spatial experiments can be seen in *The Collector of Prints* (ill. 63) from 1866. Earlier, Daumier had painted an art collector in the midst of his treasures (ill. 62). With the air of an expert, the elderly gentleman is gazing at a statuette of the Venus de Milo. Judging by the artworks that cover the walls of his gallery, the collection consists entirely of variations on the classical canon of beauty. It is a closed and homogeneous world with which Daumier evidently identifies himself, since this great revealer of social dissonances appears to find not a single dissonant element here. Inside this sanctuary, nobody would boldly declare (like Hussonet in Flaubert's *L'Education Sentimentale*) that a *lorette* is more amusing than the Venus de Milo.

Degas's *Collector of Prints* does not seem to be bound to one particular set of values. His art world has evidently been influenced by the liberality of taste characteristic of that period, in which the main criterion was what one liked. If we look at the pieces in the frame on the wall, they would seem to point in the direction of the provocative antithesis propounded in the *Alchimie du Verbe* (1873) by Arthur Rimbaud, in opposition to current norms, when he knocked off their pedestal what he regarded as the ridiculous 'celebrities of modern art and poetry': 'I loved absurd pictures, fanlights, stage scenery, mountebanks' backcloths, inn-signs, cheap coloured prints....' One is reminded of the art dealer in *L'Education Sentimentale* who seeks the emancipation of the arts and high art at low prices. One can imagine Degas's collector, who seems to be weighing us up rather than inviting us in, strolling with amused curiosity through the 'Salon des Incohérents' which in the early 1880s was for a short time the talk of the town among Parisians. The main target of the 'Incohérents' was the official Salon and its intellectual inflexibility, but they also made fun of the Impressionists.

The liberality of taste suggested by the *Collector of Prints*, however, points elsewhere, and since this signifies an important switch of direction, it is worth a digression. The motley collection stuck in the frame behind the collector proclaims the anti-norm with which Degas will attack the established canon of taste. The things that have been randomly assembled

63
The Collector of Prints
1866
Oil on canvas
53 x 40 cm (20 7/8 x 15 3/4 in.)
*New York, The Metropolitan
Museum of Art*

within this frame constitute a picture within a picture, but they also show the raw material with which half a century later the avant-garde would produce their collages and assemblages. It comes as no surprise, in the light of this striking background motif, that Degas later had an idea that would develop still further the deconstruction of composition he was embarking on here. He suggested to Zola's publisher Charpentier that he should bring out a deluxe edition of *Au Bonheur des Dames*, using pasted-in pieces of fabric as illustrations. The publisher, whose wife had just been painted by Renoir in the pose of a *grande dame*, evidently did not think much of the suggestion. We do not know how Zola himself reacted. In his novel, though, there is mention of a shop catalogue containing pasted-in samples. It is, of course, a far cry from a fictional advertisement to a deluxe edition, but there is a passage in this novel – published in 1882 – which certainly touches on Degas's aesthetics of deconstruction.

In 1870, Degas made a few suggestions to members of the Salon jury concerning reforms to the design of their exhibitions. He insisted that works should not be displayed symmetrically on the walls and in the rooms, as symmetry 'has nothing to do with an exhibition'. Needless to say this advice, which he was already following in his own compositions, was ignored, since symmetry was the very backbone of all academic aesthetics – indeed it was the principal stabilizing factor which prevented visitors to the exhibition from becoming confused. But Mouret, the main character in Zola's novel and owner of the department store mentioned above, actually sets out to 'confuse the senses', as he seeks to expand his business and to find new ways to advertise it. One day, he wanders through the tastefully organized stacks of wares in one of his shops, finds it all tedious, and spontaneously sets about destroying the immaculate symmetry of all the displays. He throws things everywhere, as if Chaos had taken over the store, and then says to his bewildered colleague Hutin: 'Why do you want to spare the eye [of the ladies]?' He prefers to dazzle those eyes with colour, to stage a firework display of goods, so that they will all go home with eye-ache. As far as Hutin is concerned, this wild orgy is sheer nonsense.

But at the very moment when Mouret the tycoon has reached the zenith of his power as a commercial seducer of women, he returns to the orderly, symmetrical display of his goods. Zola compares it to art galleries and the nave of a cathedral, by which he means that symmetry is the guiding principle. At the same time, Degas was capturing in his milliners and their wares the extravagant wealth of materials that provided the customers with a whole world of artificial beauty (ill. 64). The veritable cloudburst of colour is calculated to shock the eye, and is not the product of chance. But one can well imagine conservative critics turning their backs on this 'chaos' as an injurious offence to the eye. This was not Degas's intention. But he was determined not to paint things that would flatter the eye of the observer, and in this he was at one with Mouret's strategy of confusion. Neither was willing to 'spare' the eye; instead they demanded a discerning gaze, which would be ready to decipher complex combinations of forms and colours.

The frame behind the collector is not the only focus for this discerning look. The observer should also see that the collector himself is sitting in a house of cards, the various parts of which – the prints and samples scattered over three areas – 'shuffle' the room. All of these prints etc. are miniature screens, small fragments of wall which are situated in front of the actual room and each of which forms a separate zone in itself. This room within a room has no stabilizing coordinates (or symmetry), but it is a product of chance, a changeable improvisation. The 'screens' could all be arranged differently.

With this disruptive syntax, Degas has for the first time embarked on the playing-card method which for painters of his century led to a renunciation of precise spatial dimensions

65
James Jacques Joseph Tissot
c. 1867–68
Oil on canvas
151.4 x 111.8 cm (59 5/8 x 44 in.)
New York, The Metropolitan
Museum of Art, Rogers Fund

and physical shapes. The journalist Albert Wolff is said to have heard Courbet comment on Manet's *Olympia*: 'It is flat, it has no depth…a Queen of Spades from a deck of cards, just out of the bath.' This criticism anticipates Degas's disparaging comment many years later on Manet's *Bar at the Folies Bergère*, that it was a 'playing card with no depth'. And yet he was himself working with this same playing-card aesthetic even if, typically, he was doing so entirely in his own way. When Manet, in his portrait of Zola (ill. 66), opted for a flattened surface, he used a frame-like 'assemblage' which brought stability but also a certain stiffness to the composition of the picture. On the left is the fragment of a screen, and in the top right-hand corner – with one piece telescoped into another – is the 'assemblage' of a Japanese woodcut, an engraving of Velázquez's drinkers, and a reproduction of Manet's own *Olympia*. Degas, however, in his *Collector of Prints* – which Zola knew – improvised a house of cards whose components, while also dispensing with spatial depth, form not a rectangular but a diago-

66
Édouard Manet (*1832–83*)
Émile Zola
1868
Oil on canvas
146 x 114 cm
(57 1/2 x 44 7/8 in.)
Paris, Musée d'Orsay

nal system of coordinates. This is achieved mainly through the items in the frame and the portfolio of prints. This system of coordinates is carried through to the informal posture of the man, which suggests that the seat itself is at an angle. With this subtle element of randomness, Degas is taking the first steps in the direction of what might be called the formula of 'rooms become (mobile) screens'.

In the portrait of his artist friend James Tissot (ill. 65), Degas again works along the lines of playing card/screen/canvas. All connections in this painting are determined by the common denominator of balanced detachment. In contrast to the *Collector of Prints*, in which the man and his attributes are depicted amid a criss-cross of diagonals, the composition here (with Tissot appearing to be just a visitor) is dominated by intersecting vertical and horizontal coordinates, the rectangular frame being echoed by variations all through the picture. Although the arrangement of the objects in the studio still seems a little haphazard, it all seems generally quite tidy. Cranach's portrait of Frederick III, the Wise, stands iconically right in the middle – a stable element against which the painter's angled figure appears out of balance. The unsteadiness of his posture entails an almost unnatural turn which one would hardly make unless asked to do so. Degas may well have persuaded his friend to adopt this pose, but on the other hand it has commonly been said that he most enjoyed portraying people who themselves were *poseurs*.

Almost the entire width of the wall is taken up by the bottom of a painting which sets an art historian straight into detective mode. Is this picture based on a Japanese model, or is it simply a pastiche of that style? Whichever it may be, it is a pointer to an historic moment that took place in 1867. At the Universal Exhibition in Paris that year, for the first time there were works of art from Japan – the catalogue lists no less than 1,308 of them – and this unleashed a tidal wave of taste which, under the label of '*Japonisme*', was to have a lasting influence on the West European avant-garde throughout the last third of the century. What fascinated Parisian artists, collectors and critics can be attributed to elements of playing-card aesthetics: a flattening of space, renunciation of central perspective foreshortening, reduction of body-modelling, homogeneous fields of colour, and precise (calligraphic) outlines. In the *Collector of Prints* there is a subtle analogy to all this, as has been pointed out by Theodore Reff. He compares the pseudo-collage in the frame to a Japanese embroidery, over which are scattered – with a deliberately random effect – cards containing poems, with portraits of the poets. In this 'card game', one has to find words and pictures that go together. Since the *Collector of Prints* was painted in 1866, it cannot be said to show a direct influence so much as an innate affinity with the language of Far Eastern art. It cannot, however, be excluded that these miniature screens were indeed based on Japanese models.

There was another import from the Orient that he does not seem to have known about at all – the screen as a means of transforming rooms. Whistler used this device for some of his cleverest effects. In *Pink and Silver: The Princess from the Land of Porcelain* (1864), a five-part screen (actually owned by Whistler) conceals the depth of the room. Together with the carpet and the kimono, it helps to give the 'Princess' (who was Jo, Courbet's Irish model) an exotic aura. Thus a room becomes the product of a screen, which gives it independent and variable dimensions. The most striking example of Whistler's 'rooms becoming screens' is *Caprice in Purple and Gold: The Golden Screen* (ill. 68). The screen again conceals the depth of the room, and its two-dimensional verticality is itself communicated to the carpet on which the kimono-clad lady sits looking at her scattered Japanese prints. Together with her surroundings, she becomes a picture within a picture, and the whole becomes a montage of playing cards.

Degas may well have seen these pictures at Whistler's home, but even if he did, one should not assume that he was influenced by them. It is true that, as Reff points out, Whistler in the early 1860s was more innovative than Degas, as is evident from the two screen pictures, but his concept of the room does not by any means conform to the ideas that were slowly forming in the head of his Parisian friend. Their decorative balance suggests an overall harmony, and this could scarcely have inspired Degas, who was in search of dissonance – unless the inspiration was to do things differently from Whistler. Much closer to Degas's approach was an idea like that of the *Music Room* (ill. 67), in which the room is distorted and fragmented by reflections which give it a mysterious complexity.

The implication of all this is that Degas had a somewhat detached attitude towards *Japonisme*. As a collector, he prized his Japanese prints – the catalogue for the auction of his estate listed 117 works (without giving the year of acquisition) – but as a painter, he went his own way. Some critics have linked the *Bathers of Kiyonaga*, which hung in his bedroom, with his pictures of women at their toilet, but there are very basic differences. The passive, seemingly boneless rubber-like bodies of the naked Japanese women are quite the opposite of Degas's powerfully built ladies, who always seem to perform wilful acts with their bodies.

In terms of the line I am pursuing, these questions of influence are of minor importance, since Degas's transformation of rooms into screens has a very different slant from that of Whistler and the Japanese. He avoids all the strategies of decoration and harmonization, and instead makes disturbing and damaging inroads into the homogeneity of the illusory room. For this purpose he uses not only diagonal axes that break it up (as in *The Rape*, ills. 39, 41), but also rectangular frames that run into one another and obscure the third dimension, creating an uncertainty that transfers itself from the objects to the person, as in the portrait of Madame Gobillard (ill. 54). The room is full of question marks, just like the woman sitting in it.

67
James Abbott McNeill Whistler
(*1834–1903*)
Harmony in Green and Rose:
The Music Room
1861, Oil on canvas
92 x 68 cm (36 1/4 x 26 3/4 in.)
Washington DC, Freer Gallery of
Art and Arthur M. Sackler Gallery,
Smithsonian Institution

68
James Abbott McNeill Whistler
(*1834–1903*)
Caprice in Purple and Gold:
The Golden Screen
1864, Oil on wood panel
50.1 x 68.5 cm (19 5/8 x 27 in.)
Washington DC, Freer Gallery of
Art and Arthur M. Sackler Gallery,
Smithsonian Institution

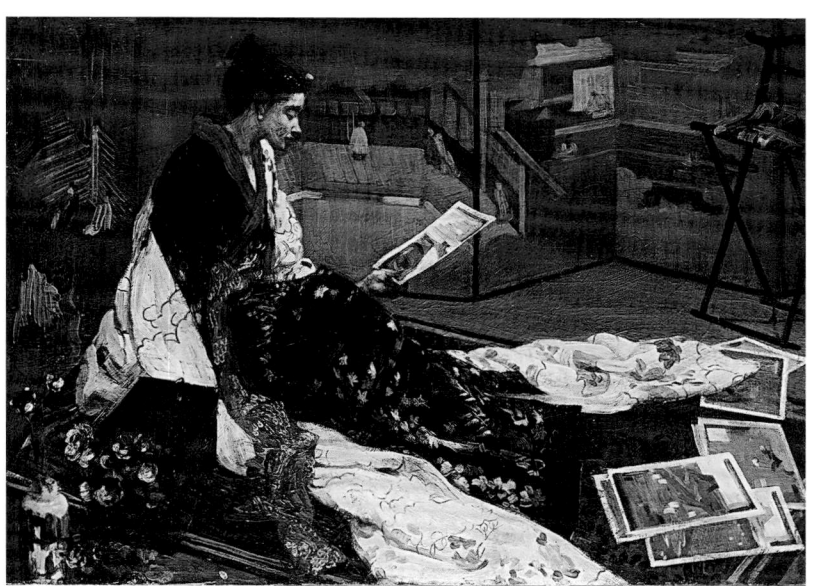

69

Manet and His Wife
1868–69
Oil on canvas
65.2 x 71.1 cm (25 3/4 x 28 in.)
Kitakyushu, Municipal Museum
of Art

The spur for this excision of the third dimension came not from Japanese screens but – in my estimation – from a different, far more prosaic experience that had nothing to do with the priorities of art history, and everything to do with human relations in the form of a sudden conflict. This was an incident that caused a rift between Degas and Manet.

The two artists had known one another since 1862, when they met in the Louvre while Degas – who was two years younger – was copying the old masters. At the time, Degas was preoccupied with history painting (see Chapter 2) and had not yet discovered the contemporary scene. This meeting led to a somewhat volatile friendship, the first fruits of which were Degas's etchings of Manet from between 1861 and 1864–65. In these he applied his technique of criss-crossing oblique axes and sharp angles, but in one important area these etchings differ from the paintings of the *Collector of Prints* and *Tissot*: there is no setting, and there are no

tools of the trade. Manet is not portrayed as a painter. In one etching he sits turned to the left, with his hat in his hand, as if he were just one of many people in a waiting room (ill. 71). The four lines that Degas has drawn across the discarded copper plates follow the diagonal rhythm that permeates the figure of Manet himself: they form an abstract echo, almost a subtext. In the other etching, Manet is looking the opposite way (ill. 70). The back of a large canvas suggests that this gentleman – perhaps a visitor or collector – is with an artist or dealer. There is no sign here of a Bohemian painter – Manet has disappeared into the role of the anonymous middle-class citizen. The bare neutrality of the room is so strikingly empty that it demands an explanation. Why this total void surrounding his friend? Perhaps Degas was overcome by a mixture of respect and embarrassment, as might well be the case in the presence of the painter who, with his *Déjeuner sur l'herbe* and *Olympia*, had set new standards for modern art. If he had

74
**Painter and Mannequin
(Portrait of Henri Michel-Lévy)**
c. 1878
Oil on canvas
40 x 28 cm (15 3/4 x 11 in.)
Lisbon, Museu Calouste
Gulbenkian

Previous pages:
72
Edmond Duranty
1879
Tempera, watercolour and
pastel on cloth
100.9 x 100.9 cm
Glasgow, The Burrell Collection

73
Diego Martelli
1879
Oil on canvas
110.4 x 99.8 cm
(43 3/8 x 38 7/8 in.)
Edinburgh, National Gallery
of Scotland

placed Manet in a particular ambiance, as he did Tissot, he would have made the portrait into a story rather than just a likeness. Manet never produced any portraits of Degas.

When in 1869 Manet began to collect a regular circle of artists and critics around him, he and Degas soon established themselves as the main spokesmen, and their sharp tongues were both admired and feared. Even if they tended to talk on the same wavelength, they used a very different syntax in their work. Manet was less brusque and radical than Degas, who was developing a method that was intended to create an irritating effect: he worked with vertical dividers that split the social chiaroscuro into grids and parallels. It is my contention that these alienating divisions may well have arisen partly out of a quarrel that took place in the late 1860s. Degas painted a kind of genre portrait of *Manet and His Wife* (ill. 69), with Suzanne seated at the piano and her husband lounging behind her on the sofa. They do not seem to be particularly well suited. Manet did not like this double portrait, and decided to take drastic action by mutilating it, with a view to getting back at Degas and possibly at Suzanne as well. He made a vertical cut in the figure of the pianist, reducing her to the side view of her back and removing the face altogether. The right-hand side of the canvas therefore ends with Suzanne's back. Degas's reaction to this assault was very creative. He assumed that the insult was directed at him, took his painting back, and turned loss into profit by adding a strip of blank, light brown canvas which restored the picture to its original proportions. He also put his signature on this band, and thus laid claim to the addition as a composite part of the picture. This whole concept was totally new, accentuating the emptiness and giving it equal value to that of the painted surface. We can see here an important departure from the combinations Degas might have seen in the *Componium* (ill. 28). The strips of landscape included in this game allowed for an almost infinite combination of scenes, but they never allowed for any empty space. Against the principle of continuity, Degas inserts the break, the space, the absence of paint.

Degas applies his ideas to different settings in which the people he portrays function almost as the third dimension of the room. The latter is deprived of its 'objective' neutrality (as normally established by a central perspective) and is no longer an obvious cube, and instead it becomes an expressive background for human conduct and character. Degas has his subjects 'wear' the room like an article of clothing, and it is as much a part of them as their own gestures. This subjective coding of the spatial dimensions is at its most convincing in his portraits of friends, whose relationship to their rooms conveys their creative temperament like a signature. We can see this clearly in his portraits of Diego Martelli and Duranty, as well as in the *Painter and Mannequin*.

In his portrait of the critic Diego Martelli (ill. 73), Degas abandoned the vain or modelled poses of previous portraits and painted what can only be described as an anti-pose. The rather

corpulent Martelli has turned away from the table. He sits with folded arms and legs – a compact figure whose rounded contours echo and rephrase the curves of the sofa (which merges into the table). Once again Degas has, so to speak, taken the room off its hinges, and changed the third dimension into a circle viewed from above. This 'aerial' view dispenses with the usual box-shaped room. The jumble of books and brochures confronts us with the sitter's materials, just as we saw in the frame on the wall behind the *Collector of Prints*, but this time the chaos has arisen from a collection of ideas and their concrete manifestations. There seems to be no apparent system of order applied here to the writer or to his surroundings. Martelli perches precariously on a folding chair, such as he would use when studying a portfolio of prints, and this reinforces the uncertain ambiance of the room. The back wall is barely hinted at. To the left is a doorframe, and next to it a white frame which seems to contain a coloured circle. The abstract regimentation of this colour diagram, the source of which has yet not been found in the work of any contemporary theorist, contrasts starkly with the mess on the critic's table. The framed circle also echoes the gentle curve of the green sofa. In other words, the chaos is linked to the thought process, while the coloured circle is associated with abstract order. In another version of this portrait (in Buenos Aires), a large-scale landscape has replaced the circle.

Edmond Duranty criticized the foreshortened legs of the Martelli portrait. This is somewhat surprising, coming from a critic who identified what was new in *La nouvelle peinture* (1876) as being the natural 'slice of life' element, and was actually referring – though not by name – to Degas and his artistic strategies. Degas painted Duranty sitting in his study (ill. 72), and in the portrait he seems to be pondering on the function of portraiture in the 'New Painting'. In his treatise, he expressed quite definite views: 'We shall no longer separate the person from the background of the apartment or from the background of the street. In real life, he never appears before us against neutral, empty or vague backgrounds.'

Degas captures Duranty's milieu, but he condenses it into a collection of fragments which again function like screens: the slanting bookcase and the desk full of catalogues, books, folders and manuscripts. Around the middle of the picture, the objects on the desk accumulate to form an angle that frames the subject and sharpens our focus on him. This abstract, purely two-dimensional paper world screens him from the concrete, three-dimensional world outside, though his sharp gaze seems to be directed outwards, its reflectiveness reinforced by the 'thinker's' gesture of fingers held to temple. Thus the portrait conveys the impression of a solid, independently-minded intellectual, ceaselessly writing and observing, and perhaps wearing himself out in the process. Duranty died in 1880 at the age of 47. We do not know what he thought of the portrait.

In *Painter and Mannequin* (ill. 74), once again Degas uses the screen as a metaphor for protection and for spatial vagueness. This time it is paintings that act as screens, along the lines of his playing card aesthetic, making rooms into screens whose provisional layout allows at least two different interpretations: the break-up of three-dimensional continuity, or the very opposite – a first tentative effort to establish such continuity. Whatever message comes across here contains the seeds of its own invalidation. Degas has devised a paradoxical combination of elements whose fragmentary nature ultimately excludes the possibility of any unifying connection. One fragment is the woman on the ground, another the open box of paints with the palette, and another the two canvases on the left and right behind the standing figure of the painter. The sketchiness of all these is the equivalent of the seemingly improvised

76
Six Friends at Dieppe
1885
Pastel
115 x 71 cm (45 1/4 x 28 in.)
Providence, Museum of Art,
Rhode Island School of Design

room. The thoughtful-looking man – identified by Theodore Reff as the painter Henri Michel-Lévy – stands solidly before us, but he is isolated from the rest of the picture. He is both the maker and the prisoner of his works.

The course of events here remains open, but there are two plausible possibilities. The painter is having a break, and is hesitating between the two canvases – one in portrait format, one in landscape; the left one contains a figure which may have been based on the slumped mannequin. Alternatively, he may be rejecting what he has painted and unsure of what to do next, and so thinking of starting all over again. An Italian critic has aptly spoken of the '*dramma della pittura*'. Degas has latched onto this vacillation and brought it into focus by painting a dilemma which seeks out the borderline between reality and painted illusion and makes it doubly uncertain. The world of facts dissolves into pictures, but at the same time it is condensed into the mannequin – a lifeless artefact which belongs in both worlds. The painter stands there as if a deed has been done, like the man in *The Rape* (ills. 39, 41), coolly gazing at his female prey. The contemplative Michel-Lévy has also taken possession of a female figure, used and abused her, and another artist – Degas – has given this lifeless creature the illusory life of art. The materiality with which shortly afterwards Degas was to endow his bronze figure of the *Little Dancer Aged Fourteen* (ill. 143) is already hinted at here in this transitional figure. The drama of painting is represented as a contest between fiction and fact, and Degas concludes that it is a paradoxical combination of both, devising an independent, in-between world where reality – the mannequin – is reconstructed as a fiction, beyond imitation, idealization or *trompe-l'oeil*.

With this particular piece, Degas seems to be alluding to the contemporary fascination with waxworks. These were displayed at fairgrounds and cabinets of curiosities, where they attracted bored voyeurs as well as writers and painters in search of new sensations. The most disturbing record we have of this particular vogue is a short story by Champfleury, *L'Homme aux figures de cire* (The Man with the Waxworks), which appeared in 1855 in a volume entitled *Les Excentriques*. The plot concerns a trip with Courbet through the murky world of waxwork shows. The figures are sometimes seductive, sometimes macabre, and their ambivalence can give rise to all kinds of transformations and distortions. A smiling face can turn into a skull. These creatures are variations on Pygmalion's desire to bring a work of art to life so that he can possess it sexually. Degas, however, ignores this desire, and is equally unaffected by the shock of the painter in Poe's tale *The Oval Portrait*, in which the artist paints a woman's portrait, and as he does so gradually takes away her life. She dies with the last brushstroke. Degas resolves such conflicts through ambivalence: his mannequin is both a model *and* a portrait, injured and damaged both as creature and as creation. She is the living dead and the dead brought to life.

With the discarded doll-like figure, Degas epitomizes the role of women as defined by male despotism, bringing it to an extreme of physical abuse and mental incapacitation. In order to achieve this, he had to devise an ambivalent man-made being, and to place the artist in the role of the abuser. No genre scene, and not even the coldly observed *The Rape* (ills. 39, 41), could so oppressively and vividly convey the metaphorical dimensions of the brutal callousness underlying the discarding of the mannequin. And yet this scene also conveys the *dramma della pittura*, or rather the innermost core of that drama: the moment when artistic mastery of the model turns into rape.

The pastel *Six Friends* (ill. 76) finds Degas's artist friends not in the studio but out in the open air, on the beach at Dieppe. This 'de-composition' probably goes back to Fantin-Latour, who had undertaken to restore the harmony of the group portrait which Courbet had undermined in his *Studio*. Fantin-Latour did this mainly through three paintings: *Homage to Delacroix* (1864), a strictly symmetrical act of respect paid by ten artists and critics to the great painter who had died the year before, and whose framed portrait dominates the composition like an icon; *A Studio at Batignolles* (1870), a group of friends paying homage to Manet; and the prosaic *Around the Table* (ill. 78), an ambivalent digression on the subject of isolation within a group. Degas's *Six Friends*, however, sharpens the subversion begun by Courbet's *Studio* and launches a double attack – on the group portrait and on the illusion of three-dimensional space. What friends are these? Five of them, of different ages, constitute at best the heterogeneous material of a bourgeois pyramid of life which is composed with deliberate randomness and carefully planned improvisation. The result is anything but a snapshot of life on the beach. On the other hand, when we compare it with a drawing from the second notebook (ill. 75), we see that this human pyramid goes back to a very early *prima idea*.

Half a dozen artists and friends of art are depicted in the anonymous garb of the bourgeoisie. Top right is Ludovic Halévy with his son Daniel; bottom right is Albert Boulanger-Cavé; they are joined by two painters who were then the darlings of Parisian society: Henri Gervex

78
Henri Fantin-Latour
(*1836–1904*)
Around the Table
(*from left: Paul Verlaine, Arthur Rimbaud, Elzéar Bonnier, Léon Valade, Emile Blémont, Jean Aicard, Ernest d'Hervilly and Camille Pelletan*)
1872
Oil on canvas
160 x 225 cm (63 x 88 5/8 in.)
Paris, Musée d'Orsay

(seated behind Cavé) and Jacques-Émile Blanche, whose large figure partially conceals the Halévys. The third painter, Walter Sickert, is separated from this tightly packed quintet. He is so ostentatiously an outsider that one cannot help recalling the macabre rumour concerning this Englishman of German origin – namely, that he was the notorious Jack the Ripper.

These men are telescoped together as if captured by a zoom lens, and yet there is no contact between them. Space is suspended. This uneven pile of bodies has been compared to a totem pole, but I see it rather as a mixture of more or less randomly shuffled playing cards.

Chapter 6

A Painted Parable

'If one now considers the person, whether in a room or in the street,
he is not always to be found situated on a straight line at an equal distance from
two parallel objects; he is more confined on one side than on the other by space.
In short, he is never in the centre of the canvas, in the centre of the setting.
He is not always seen as a whole: sometimes he appears cut off at mid-leg,
half-length, or longitudinally.' – Edmond Duranty, 1876

'For the perfect flâneur, for the passionate spectator, it is a huge pleasure
to find a home amid the crowd, amid the ebb and flow, amid the movement, amid the
fugitive and the infinite. To be away from one's home and yet to feel at home everywhere;
to see the world, be at the centre of the world, and yet remain hidden from the world....
The spectator is a prince who rejoices in his anonymity everywhere.'
– Charles Baudelaire, 'The Painter of Modern Life', 1860

Brusque separation and isolation can, as in the pastel *Six Friends* (ill. 76), break up a seemingly tightly-knit community in which there is a virtual absence of space. But isolation really occurs only when a centrifugal impulse arises from static, related elements and opens the way to creating centrifugal forces that empty the space and destabilize the people in it. This is what happens in another painting that negates the conventional group portrait. It has two titles: *Viscount Lepic and His Daughters: Place de la Concorde* (ill. 81). The first suggests a family gathering, and the second the topographical reproduction of a famous square in Paris. Both titles arouse expectations which are not fulfilled by the picture.

With the four persons, Degas goes against everything that constitutes a group portrait – the links that bind several people together – and at the same time he omits the relevant topographical information by concealing an urban landmark within an anonymous setting that could be anywhere. These two omissions are what give the content of the picture its decisive direction, and through them he creates a new form of composition. Instead of the conventional patterns of order he establishes something that at first sight appears chaotic. From this emerges the basic message of the work: the breakdown of relationships.

79
Viscount Lepic and His Daughters: Place de la Concorde
(detail of ill. 81)

What, then, is happening on this canvas? A gentleman is walking to the right. We cannot follow his progress precisely because his legs are cut off, but there are clues to be gained from the angle of his body – echoed and complemented by the slant of the umbrella – points to the right. But is he really walking? He is flanked by two girls whose dresses, hats and facial features suggest a certain strange maturity. Dressed up like little ladies, they could almost be dwarfs. Both children are looking vaguely to the left, but in different directions. The girl on the right with the rather insolent-looking face is just about to bump into the man, who is taking no notice of her. It is the sort of thing that happens when puppeteers lose control of their puppets.

A dog echoes the girls – his muzzle forming the left corner of the constellation, which an art historian will immediately recognize as a triangle whose apex has slipped off its central axis, which is why the two legs of the triangle are of unequal length. If we look to the left, we see a thin, marginal figure stuck to and cut off by the frame – another top-hatted gentleman who occupies the full height of the canvas. The perpendicular cane emphasizes the motionlessness of this spectator, who is looking to the right with such indifference that he scarcely seems to notice the man with the umbrella and the two girls. The slenderness of his figure allows room for a sketchy background scene at chest height, where we catch the only glimpse of what might count as traffic. A rider is heading right, and merging with him is a coach that is heading left. Clearly Degas needed a completely empty square – but why?

The area that we assume to be the square is nothing but a gigantic empty space apart from the items lined up at the top. There we see a horizontal row of houses, streetlamps, a sketchy statue with a wall and trees behind it – just the bare minimum of features to enable anyone who knows the area to reconstruct the corner where the Rue de Rivoli joins the Place de la Concorde. This frieze-like scene lies *behind* the square, and its component parts are cut off by the top of the picture, so that we can see neither the sky nor the horizon. Thus space has been robbed of a crucial dimension: its opening out into the distance. Parallel to this amputation is another applied to the figures in the foreground: Degas has cut off their legs and feet. A recent analysis of the canvas has revealed that he even added another fragmentation to the original painting by folding back a strip of canvas 7 cm wide. With no ground beneath them, this left the man and the girl hanging in mid-air. They were neither standing nor walking, but hovering, pulled around by unseen forces. As the 'frieze' containing the cityscape is *behind* the empty square, the three figures themselves are not *on* it, but *in front of* it.

Since there are no perspective axes to separate foreground from background and thus establish some kind of continuity for the observer, the square – almost in anticipation of de Chirico – becomes a kind of no-man's-land before which Degas's characters act out their cha-

rades of disconnectedness. The strategy behind this decomposed structure is clear: people and things are deprived of space, and nothing is left to play on but the empty board of the 'square'. The complex, three-dimensional system of references determined by central perspective and so crucial to post-medieval painting no longer provides a context for an experience, but instead acts merely as a background, in front of which these disconnected people act out their isolation in frozen mime. Once again, as we have seen in Courbet's *Studio* (ill. 5), one thinks of sleepwalkers living and acting within a world of their own.

Degas's device of making rooms into walls or screens also helps to create apparently perpendicular levels out of horizontal surfaces – in the picture under discussion, screens and not

81
**Viscount Lepic and His
Daughters: Place de la
Concorde**
c. 1875
Oil on canvas
78.4 x 117.5 cm (31 x 46 1/4 in.)
Berlin, Gerstenberg Collection
(currently St Petersburg, Hermitage)

walls. The space which is no longer a space, and of which the human subject has been deprived, creates an area of tension which increases his or her isolation to the point of alienation. Shut out and marginalized, such characters seem to be suspended in a kind of intermediate world, which makes the metaphor of puppet theatre a very apt one. The Place de la Concorde does not exactly become a place of discord, but it does turn into a place of solitary individuals who are not in search of concord.

The 18th century, which delighted perhaps more than any other in the exchange of ideas, emotions and insults, had not yet heard the voice of the lone outsider – until J.-J. Rousseau's *Promeneur solitaire* found himself 'on this earth as if on a strange planet'. He used the loneliness of the man in the crowd as a basis for analysing the collective sham life of society, and revealed the wounds to the self which were then further explored by Poe and Baudelaire. Initially in the late 18th and early 19th century, isolation and its companion, alienation, were still the preserve of the rebellious or hypersensitive elite. The self-portraits of Carstens, Friedrich and Barry bear this hallmark. Isolation was the proud price that the creative artist paid for his autonomy. Thus Delacroix saw himself as Michelangelo, as Hamlet and as Tasso, mocked by his gaolers. His opposite number, Ingres, however, did not recognize the artist as a man of grief. His portraits are placed in their natural milieu, in their familiar domestic settings; they encapsulate respectability and bear no hint of the temptations of self-questioning.

Meanwhile, the Realists democratized the emotional formulas of isolation that had hitherto had an aristocratic touch. When Champfleury comments with gentle forbearance on the commonplace faces of the mourners in Courbet's *Burial in Ornans* that 'many bourgeois citizens look like that', he also points to exceptions. He finds that in their grief the mourning women are as beautiful as all the Antigones of ancient times, and in their midst he is struck by the 'fine and delicate' features of a young girl. This beautiful creature, isolated within the group, stands out from the 'conventional types' (Champfleury is thinking of Thomas Couture and his pupils) and from the collective grief around her. Courbet endows her with a loneliness amid the crowd which is no longer the privilege of the elite.

Does the man in the *Place de la Concorde* have an ordinary face? No more and no less than the top-hatted gentlemen who meet in Manet's *Music in the Tuileries* (1862) or who crowd the *Masked Ball at the Opéra* (1873–74). These public places form the stage on which the heroes and the supernumeraries parade and satisfy their love of self-display. In Janus-headed 'character masks' (Heine), the fluctuations of social ambitions and their settings take on concrete form. A new species has arrived on the scene: the *flâneur* [idler]. As one who crosses social borders, he is both a catalyst and a mediator, independent of class barriers and hierarchies, but without any firm identity of his own. The *flâneur* may be a middle-class businessman or an

82
Giovanni Bellini
(1425/30–1516)
Sacred Allegory
1460
Oil on wood
73 x 119 cm
(28 3/4 x 46 7/8 in.)
Florence, Uffizi

aristocrat, a rake or a stockbroker, an artist or an intellectual, or simply a drop-out. He is at home everywhere and nowhere.

Who, then, is the gentleman in the picture? He is Viscount Ludovic-Napoléon Lepic (1839–90). He took Law before going to study under Charles Gleyre and Alexandre Cabanel at the École des Beaux-Arts. Well versed in all techniques of art, from etching to sculpture, he was also an amateur archaeologist, bred dogs, and in 1872 founded the municipal museum in Aix-les-Bains. The naval ministry, the facade of which Degas has sketched in the background, employed him as a draughtsman. As a dilettante, he wandered from one camp to another: in 1874 he exhibited at the official Salon, and at the same time contributed two seascapes – which were virtually ignored – to the first Impressionist exhibition. A few years earlier, around 1871, Degas portrayed the viscount and his young daughters in a modest setting that was apparently characteristic of his home life (ill. 80). Here the family is very much together – there is no sign of alienation. But the viscount in the Place de la Concorde painting is a different man, a typical *flâneur*, which would seem to confirm the general assumption that Degas painted this picture, unlike the first portrait, for himself and not for Lepic. This is not the portrait of an individual but, rather, a parable on a particular manifestation of the human condition – the *flâneur* as a metaphor.

This many-sided 'man for all seasons', the nowhere man of everywhere, is a matrix for the whole concept of man in a condition of non-commitment – a condition that should not be seen as a stigma or a deficiency. Non-commitment allows the *flâneur* the freedom to test himself out, first in one role, then in another. In this respect, Lepic used his freedom for self-determination – a privilege available only to the elite, since most people are subject to determining factors outside themselves. The ubiquity of the viscount ties in with the social utopias of the early 19th century (one thinks of Charles Fourier) as well as with ideals such as Karl Marx developed in *The German Ideology* (1845–46). His polemic against fixed employ-ment allows itself a euphoric excursion into dreamland as he conjures up a vision of future man, free to 'to do one thing today and another tomorrow, to hunt in the morning, fish in the afternoon, rear cattle in the evening, criticize after dinner, just as I have a mind, without ever becoming hunter, fisherman, herdsman or critic.' This paean of praise to dilettantism also embraces the *flâneur*. Since property ownership and conditions of production make universal self-determination impossible – hence Marx's call for revolutionary change – the privileged, as embodied by Lepic, wander alone through the city, surrounded by an anonymous mass which acts out its role halfway between acceptance and subversion. These are the different levels of interrelationships which Degas deals with in his art. Even though the prostitutes in the brothels and the singers in the street cafés are dictated to by economic pressures, never-theless they make up for their subjugation by exercising their right to demonstrate subversively their own particular, lower-class way of life. In this they have Degas's full support.

The scene on the Place de la Concorde does not show these discrepancies and 'discords' between the social levels. We do not even know whether Degas actually thought about the contrast between self-determination and determination by outside forces. What we do know, however, is that this is what he painted. No one who has studied his life's work could fail to see it. As a middle-class painter, Degas was no longer financially so secure once the family busi-ness had collapsed, and he depended not so much on commissions as on regular sales of his works. As the observer of the social chiaroscuro in which different classes came together, he was a privileged figure who continually explored those zones of the city where people were forced to sell themselves and their labour.

Degas realized that bourgeois society's techniques of exploitation were applied especially to women. Whether as skivvies or as courtesans, women as a species were subjugated to men's

needs. In relation to the *flâneur*'s repertoire of self-presentation, women's availability was translated into terms of prostitution, the range of which embraced the pleasure industry as well as those professions in which sexual favours were expected. The latter category included laundresses and milliners.

Baudelaire summed up the partnership as succinctly as anyone: 'What is art? Prostitution.' But this entails a two-way relationship. As far as Degas is concerned, it also raises a question which will be discussed in the chapters that follow: did this solitary outsider, who seldom made public pronouncements but preferred to keep his opinions to himself, this man who scorned the economic contract between producer and consumer – did he see in the members of the city's 'pleasure' industry, in the chorus girls, the café singers, the milliners and the washerwomen, the prostitutes on the street and in the brothels, the tragically grotesque counterparts (or even extensions) of the role of negation which he as an artist could afford to play?

An answer to this question may be found in his works, which during the 1870s took on unmistakable forms. Viscount Lepic in the Place de la Concorde is the male introduction, like a master of ceremonies announcing the start of the *comédie humaine*, whose actresses will from now on be Degas's main subject, almost to the point of obsession. Lepic is his first archetypal *flâneur*, though there will not be many more. All of them wear the same uniform: coat and tails and top hat. As against these few isolated figures, whom Degas follows down in the corridors of the Opéra or around the stock exchange (ills. 154, 155), there are countless women from the world of what Götz Adriani refers to euphemistically as the sex service industry. These women and the *flâneurs* are interdependent, but it is worth observing that the feminine form of the latter – the *flâneuse* – even though it exists in the dictionary, is a linguistic rarity.

Degas was not the discoverer or inventor of this world, but he was the first to lift it out of the sphere of trivial, journalistic social history and make it the subject of serious art. His ten submissions to the first exhibition of those who were later to be known as the Impressionists already covered the range of his urban themes: two laundresses, three racing scenes, four rehearsals at the Opéra, and one drawing entitled *After the Bath*.

To these subjects, Degas applied the transforming qualities of his art, which extracted some revelatory moment out of everyday events, and brought the poetry of ambiguity out of the prose of facts. This is what distinguishes Degas from the series of encyclopedic records that included *Physiologies* (1840 onwards) and *Les Français peints par eux-mêmes* (1840–42), which registered every type of city-dweller: rag-and-bone man and prostitute, writer and soldier, student and housewife, provincial and concierge. The series on 'The French Painted by Themselves' (ills. 56, 84, 87, 114, 132) is a veritable 'sociography' – a complete and exemplary record of democratic equality. Every social class and every profession was given a full-page illustration and an essay with a title vignette. Among the authors of the texts were Balzac and Gautier, and the illustrators included Daumier and Gavarni. The figures covered every type that the Realists began to tackle just ten years later. The range extended from the social Establishment to the dark edges of society, where there resided *The Man Without a Name* and *The Woman Without a Name*. But the slippery social slope was gently glossed over by the illustrated realism of the costumes. There were no critical or even satirical allusions. Only the last of the five volumes bore a reminder of the monarchical constitution of the State. After a profusion of statistical tables, quantifying the citizens under every conceivable category, homage was paid to the 'citizen king' (Louis-Philippe) and his army, and the social hierarchy was reinforced both by word and by image.

The little books of the *Physiologies* series supplemented the systematic grandiosity of the *Français peint par eux-mêmes* with the unsubtle observations of journalists, who lay in wait for the unsuspecting city-dweller. The inquisitiveness of the reporters, both writers and sketch-artists, reached deep into the different layers of the petty bourgeoisie. They delved with equal relish into the lives of outsiders and the anonymous man-in-the-street. They recorded the *ennui* of an evening 'do', the monotony of a day at the office, and the before and after of a marital spat. They captured the laundress at her washing (ill. 125) and the concierge at her

84
Anonymous
The Flâneur
From: *Les Français peints par eux-mêmes, vol. III*

Opposite:
83
Viscount Lepic and His Daughters: Place de la Concorde
(detail of ill. 81)

door (ill. 85). These were all subjects that would later be taken over by the high art of painting, and Degas played a major role in elevating Parisian everyday life to this level. What we do not know, however, is whether he actually knew of these publications. My own feeling, although I can prove nothing, is that he did. Degas was not an epic recorder of moral history as Zola was, and he never pretended to be objective. He used the people of the metropolis to build up an ironic balance sheet of gains and losses that emerged from this never-ending spectacle. The price of contemporary freedom from all social conventions and moral taboos was the brutal commercialization of the body – now nothing more than an object – in the service of the pleasure industry.

With his daydreamers, Degas had already taken the romantic 'skin' (Nietzsche) off the bourgeois worlds of dreams and retreats and deposited them in the sober, prosaic ambiance of everyday facts. He also became the constant witness to the expectations of pleasure experienced by the middle-class citizen seeking to lose his identity in the social chiaroscuro of those twilight worlds that offered him cheap refuge. Degas haunted the opera stage and the ballet rehearsal rooms, the private places where women attended to their toilet, the café-concerts on the boulevards, and the brothels. He also went to the workplaces of the ironers and milliners, and indeed to wherever women extended their availability by dominating and yet at the same time subjecting themselves to the male *flâneurs* who exploited them.

With his entrance into the darker regions of the metropolis, the middle-class Degas left the right half of Courbet's *Studio* (ill. 5) and began to explore its left side, in which the '*excentriques*', the marginal figures of society, eked out their existence. Conventions and the rules of decorum had no place in this promiscuous world, where – rather like Champfleury's visit to the limbo land of the waxworks – dangerous temptations lured the eager new arrival into a labyrinth from which there was no escape.

The *Place de la Concorde* stands right on the threshold of the journey which Degas – a Dante without the comfort of an accompanying Virgil – undertook during the following decades into the *clair-obscur social*. Here he laid bare the various forms of emotional and physical self-debasement, but also the innocence of vice, though he did not stress antitheses as Courbet did in the *Studio*. With a degree of critical detachment, he sympathizes with these marginal figures without becoming their ideological accomplice or their judge. It is a detachment rather like that of Flaubert, who persistently refused to draw any sort of conclusion from his tales from history. Despite this scepticism, Flaubert praised St Julian the Hospitaller for acting according to the Christian empathy with the sick and the leprous. Degas did not go so far, but he took the first crucial steps across the social borders that would lead ultimately to Toulouse-Lautrec's demonstrative participation in the everyday life of the brothel. The artist

openly consorts with the prostitute in the dingy liberties of social exclusion that go together with this artificial paradise of ill repute.

This theme of human alienation finds a precedent in the mysterious *Sacred Allegory* (ill. 82) by Giovanni Bellini, which the 27-year-old Degas had copied in the Uffizi during one of his trips to Italy. This was Bellini's equivalent of the *Place de la Concorde*. Here too the observer stands before the canvas and knows that something is happening and yet nothing is happening. Although this scene has a religious aura, since it involves the Virgin Mary and several saints, of whom some can be identified, what these dignified and in some cases deeply thoughtful men and women are doing has remained a mystery even to modern iconographers and iconologists. Even if someone were to succeed in finding a theological, philosophical or literary source, it would still not explain the sheer disconnectedness that characterizes the visual impact of this picture. It would remain in direct contrast to the coherence of Bellini's favourite genre of painting, the *sacra conversazione*. Perhaps with this *capriccio*, Bellini was trying to depict a group of leading Christian figures without linking them together through any identifiable biblical message. If so, this would relate the act of worship to meditative isolation – a revolutionary idea many years before Luther! This may explain the otherwise puzzling scene: Bellini dispenses with the traditional composition based on hierarchical convergence, does away with the whole idea of an all-encompassing context, and renounces the *sacra conversazione*. He does this by breaking the picture down into a series of non-connections from which connections could be extrapolated. Looked at in this light, the *Allegory* can be seen as a direct antecedent of *Place de la Concorde*.

The loss of contact which strips this picture if any factual, episodic or narrative coherence is a discovery made by a painter who had observed two kinds of isolation in the people of his time. One was that of the elite (hence the parallel between Hamlet and Delacroix) and was reserved for those nonconformist intellectuals and artists who did not wish to identify themselves with the aesthetic and moral *idées reçues*. The other was the isolation of the downtrodden, the nameless dregs of bourgeois society. Both forms – and an art historian cannot help but return to this thesis – can be derived from Courbet's *Studio* (ill. 5). Baudelaire reading and Champfleury sitting on his own embody the elite misfits, while the milling crowd in the left half of the painting represent the underclass, all together in a potential madhouse, for it is my belief that Courbet had seen Kaulbach's *Madhouse* (1838) – a drawing which had been circulated in France at the time in the form of a print.

If art is prostitution, prostitution may also be seen as a form of art. Artists and prostitutes are outsiders, know that they have been excluded from the social network, and yet are still subject to its economic rules. Thus they end up dependent on yet critical of social conformity, benefiting from it, but at the same time despising it. It is a system of mutual dependence and complicity. Whenever painters and authors of the 19th century make prostitutes their subject matter, it is themselves that they are representing, albeit in coded fashion. Middle-class norms are revealed to be permeable, wide open to the temptations of the light and dark worlds that lie beyond.

It was Engels who wondered how many of London's street girls lived off the virtuous bourgeoisie. Forty years later, Paul Lafargue in his treatise on *The Right To Be Lazy*, pointed out that the expensive dresses displayed by the ladies of high society at their charity balls had been made by seamstresses 'working themselves to death'. To mark the one-hundredth performance of the stage adaptation of Zola's *L'Assommoir*, a ball was planned at which the society gentlemen dressed up as labourers and the ladies as washerwomen (Joris-Karl Huysmans).

The middle classes organize, watch and take an active role in the urban human comedy. It is for their sake that the horses race, the dancers dance, and the chorus girls wait backstage after the show. And it is for their sake that museums and galleries are opened, and the Salon puts on its yearly exhibition. It is the bourgeoisie that produces outsiders in the form of the dandy and the *flâneur* as partners of the underclasses that depend on them – or rather, as accomplices since these poor creatures work for the rich, expose themselves to the rich, and sell themselves to the rich.

87
Anonymous
Flâneurs
From 'Les Français peints par eux-mêmes', vol. III

Chapter 7

The Bourgeois in His World:
The Discovery of Leisure

'To do a hundred laborious trifles that demand a constant good mood
(the good mood needed to even tackle sad subjects), a strange excitement
that needs shows, crowds, music, even street lamps, that's what I wanted to do!
I'm only up to sixty and I can't go any further. I need that proverbial
bathing in the multitude whose impropriety so rightly shocked you.'
– Baudelaire to Saint-Beuve, 4 May 1865

After industrialization, the world of organized labour brought forth the man of leisure. His wealth allowed him to escape from the pressure to succeed, to switch off the mechanisms of economics, and to detach his private life from all the distortions and alienations that followed on from the '*Zerstückelung*' [dismemberment] of the work process. It was Schiller who used this term when, long before Marx, he lamented the consequences of industrialization: 'Enjoyment was separated from labour, the means from the end, the effort from the reward.' Thus people found themselves cut off from the 'spirit of business' and became a 'fragment of the whole', 'a mere imprint of the business', all bound like Ixion to his wheel. Such was the level of alienation that in the 19th century, wage-earners would do their twelve hours of daily drudgery and then turn principally to two sources of relaxation: debauchery in drinking and sex (Engels).

The middle classes enjoyed a greater variety of activities. Right from the start, leisure took on the form of busy idleness. Roles were devised that had nothing to do with what since the Middle Ages had counted as one of the seven deadly sins – namely, sloth. This was not the sloth associated with lands of milk and honey, for this was a socially acceptable form of consumerism, linking relaxation with a succession of new delights to stimulate, flatter and satisfy the desire for 'show'. The range extended from pure entertainment to the most refined of tastes, from seedy nightclubs to museum visits. Onto the scene now stepped a new kind of figure: the observer, the viewer, the spectator. Degas watched this bourgeois species at the

88
Woman with Opera Glasses
(detail)
c. 1877
Oil on cardboard
48 x 32 cm
Dresden, Gemäldegalerie

Opéra, the museum, the races, and adjusted his own artistic device of 'dismemberment' accordingly. The world of the middle classes opened up the visual age, experiencing itself in optical terms: anyone who wanted to see a lot also had to be seen a lot. And this required sensations and illusions such as emanated from the stage of the Opéra, the café-concert, the Folies Bergère.

In his portraits of the orchestra at the Paris Opéra, Degas unites the two levels: swift absorption of the action on stage, and the self-display of leisure. This series begins with a picture painted in 1870 (ill. 89), showing the orchestra pit at the Opéra and representing a group portrait in disguise – friends making music together. At the centre is the bassoonist Désiré Dihau,

89
The Orchestra of the Opéra
c. 1868–69
Oil on canvas
56.5 x 46.2 cm
(22 1/4 x 18 1/8 in.)
Paris, Musée d'Orsay

Opposite:
90
The Ballet from
'Robert le Diable'
1871–72
Oil on canvas
66 x 54.3 cm (26 x 21 3/8 in.)
New York, The Metropolitan
Museum of Art

THE BOURGEOIS IN HIS WORLD: THE DISCOVERY OF LEISURE 121

a friend of Degas. The musicians occupy about three-quarters of the painting, and although they know they are being observed by the painter, there is no sense of their posing for him. Their professional concentration is such that they are not even concerned with what is happening on stage. The hazy coloured frieze is more reminiscent of a chaotic ballet rehearsal than a choreographed scene, and the scroll of the double bass intrudes on this floating image like the head of some strange sea creature.

In the Städel Museum version that was completed soon afterwards (ill. 92), Degas gets even closer to the musicians, but he also offers us more information about the action on stage. A prima ballerina is acknowledging the applause of the audience, while the corps de ballet remain respectfully in the background.

Degas painted two versions of the ballet scene from Giacomo Meyerbeer's *Robert le Diable*. In both, Degas brings the observer into direct contact with the musicians and shows the sharp division between the stage and the auditorium, with Degas's disillusioning perception making the most of the discrepancy between the two artificial worlds. On both sides a game is being played, but the two forms of 'appearance' take place in spheres that are irreconcilable. In the brightly coloured area of the stage, we see nuns dancing like wild seductresses, but the frantic extravagance of their movements seems to leave the audience absolutely cold. The taste of the regular customers from the higher échelons of Parisian society is embodied in the second version at the Metropolitan Museum (ill. 90) by a gentleman with opera glasses looking to the left of the picture. He is the collector Albert Hecht, who obviously regards the magic of the stage as secondary to the other ambivalent show put on by the ladies in the boxes.

Degas paints the Opéra as one of the settings for the game of partner-seeking. But ultimately, there is a wide gap between these two sources of pleasure (on stage and in the auditorium). The horizontal division of the composition reflects not only the gulf between theatrical illusion and the need for social validation and for a partner – for which the ballet serves merely as a pretext – but also the tension between man and woman. We can see here the more or less explicit sexual mechanisms of a society in which women are disposable objects made available to men. The dancers exhaust themselves in an orgy-like display, while in the audience, the dignified gentlemen conceal their lust behind the undemonstrative facade of their dinner suits.

Around 1891, Degas painted a sequel to this series: the single ballet dancer now at the Hamburg Kunsthalle (ill. 93). This small-scale picture is a witty aphorism and at the same time a concentrate of the conventional elements which here are given a new slant. Integrated into the colouring, the gigantic necks of two double basses attract our attention. (The painter takes the position of one of the bass-players.) Anyone who is not familiar with this instrument

93
Ballet Dancer
1891
Oil on mahogany
22 x 15.8 cm (8 5/8 x 6 in.)
Hamburg, Kunsthalle

will be puzzled, because the section shown has been chosen deliberately to create an alienating effect. Behind them is a dancer, and the set is a brownish cliff overlooking the sea. The gap between the orchestra pit and the stage is so cleverly disguised that the two areas form a transitory inbetween-world with fictional properties. The musical instruments, apparently not being held by anybody, are transformed into mysterious figureheads, of which the magic world of the stage appears simply to be an extension. Degas's 'dual vision' is no longer focused on the

Opposite:
92
Musicians of the Orchestra
1872
Oil on canvas
69 x 49 cm (27 5/8 x 19 1/4 in.)
Frankfurt, Städel Museum

94

Visit to a Museum

c. 1885

Oil on canvas

91.8 x 68 cm

(36 1/8 x 26 3/4 in.)

Boston, Museum of Fine Arts

95
Mary Cassatt at the Louvre
c. 1879
Pastel on paper
71 x 54 cm (28 x 21 1/4 in.)
Private collection

Above left: 96
Mary Cassatt at the Louvre
1879–80, Aquatint and electro-
engraving, no. 2 of 6 states
26.7 x 23.2 cm
(10 1/2 x 9 1/8 in.)
Chicago, The Art Institute

Above right: 97
Mary Cassatt at the Louvre
1879–80, Aquatint and electro-
engraving, no. 6 of 6 states
26.7 x 23.2 cm
(10 1/2 x 9 1/8 in.)
Berlin, Kupferstichkabinett

Above left: 98
At the Louvre
1879–80
Aquatint, electro-engraving and
drypoint, no.3 of 20 states
30 x 12.5 cm (11 3/4 x 5 in.)
Chicago, The Art Institute

Above right: 99
Portraits in a Frieze
c. 1879
Tempera and pastel
50 x 65 cm (19 5/8 x 25 5/8 in.)
Private collection

exposure of conflicts, but instead offers us a synthesis of the illusory worlds of the Opéra: the setting and the music.

Museums and art exhibitions are public places for private people, whose individual taste can have its say without them being under any obligation to buy. One can make a selection, and then one can change one's mind. That works well for the leisured classes of both sexes: they can compare and choose, evaluate and reject.

Degas's device of 'dismembering' pictures so that the solid space-cube gives way to a flexible space is also applied to the world of exhibitions. Walls become screens which allow for different combinations, and this illusory world encompasses characters whose nature and conduct is equally changeable. They are like posing puppets who could be transferred from the art gallery to the antiques department and not be out of place. Degas illustrates the point – as if he were on an economy drive – by using one and the same model in different contexts. He has Mary Cassatt, his American painter friend, pose for him as a visitor to the Louvre. He begins with various studies of her, and finishes up on a metaphorical level in which two forms of artificiality meet up with each other: paintings form a background against which the public – in the form of women dressed in the latest fashion – can test its attitudes towards civilization (ills. 96, 97).

A frieze of pastel portraits (ill. 99) offers us three such attitudes: the model for the frontal figure may have been Ellen Andrée, the seated woman is Mary Cassatt, and the third may be her sister. For another pastel, Degas composed a condensed version (*Mary Cassatt at the Louvre*, ill. 95), this time with two figures. The composition consists of seven strips of paper stuck together after a process of careful separation and joining together again. Loyrette has described all the phases. Initially, the two women were placed next to each other at the same height, again in a kind of frieze. Then they were separated, with the dividing line running precisely and visibly through the present central axis. With this separation, Degas began his search for a new relationship between the standing woman and the seated woman. He found it in the diagonal, by putting the seated woman lower down. This new, slanting link is echoed by the umbrella – like the needle on a scale – and the composition emphasizes but at the same time justifies the physical imbalance between the two figures. The new juxtaposition brings with it a precarious, dynamic tension, and the change of emphasis is made all the more effective by the principle of rooms being changed into walls. The axes rising on the left not only enhance the difference between the horizontal parquet floor and the vertical wall of pictures, but they also create a strange transformation through dissolution. The red bench on which the lady with the catalogue is seated suddenly disappears and is continued as the floor. Like the beam of a scale, a light-coloured floorboard emphasizes the diagonal link between the two figures. Degas was so preoccupied with these refinements of space and surface that he was prepared to sacrifice the faces and individuality of the women themselves. His mastery of the nonchalant pose can be seen in a painting now in Boston (*Visit to a Museum*, ill. 94). Here Mary Cassatt and her companion (they may have come together by chance) represent the prototypes of the bourgeois 'museum visitor' playing the requisite social role. They are as anonymous as the pictures on the walls.

In an etching (ill. 96), the two ladies have turned sideways, and initially there is no spatial link between them. In a second version, they are in the Etruscan section of the Louvre (ill. 97). The whole room is filled with a jumbled blur emanating from the panes of glass and the cabinets on the walls. It was precisely such impressions that caused Paul Valéry to complain in 1923 that the 'problem with museums' was the 'cold confusion' that he found in all the rooms: 'I am amid a tumult of frozen creatures, each of one of which vainly demands the non-existence of all the others.' Out of these glass 'rooms within a room' come bewildering reflections, and the past which is interred within them – we recognize the famous sarcophagus with reclining couple from Cerveteri – is profanely put on show at the same time. Thus the *Visit to a Museum* takes on a metaphorical dimension.

In another etching (ill. 98), Degas devises a physical amalgamation for his two ubiquitous visitors. He encloses them within a single outline which seamlessly moves from the standing to the sitting woman. This perpendicular double body is squeezed between two sections of wall. The left third of the picture is taken up by a vertical band which is obviously a marble pillar. Its surface is full of spots and specks, as if the etcher had used it as a practice board. But exactly the same amorphous scratches are also to be seen on the two paintings, obscuring whatever might have been their subject matter. The parquet flooring is transformed into three equally scratchy bands. One might be tempted to see this regression into amorphousness as a first step to 'informality', but that can hardly be the case. The marble pillar, the paintings and the floor form 'screens' between which the two visitors are hemmed in, rather like the painter Henri Michel-Lévy surrounded by his paintings and his mannequin (ill. 74). There is something forced and yet also randomly casual in this relation between observer and artwork. The paintings are available for viewing, and observers may look wherever they wish, but they are also imprisoned in a straitjacket of artificiality, just like the paintings, in this golden cage called a museum.

The greatest degree of liberty is that enjoyed by the spectators at a racecourse. They are not enclosed in a room, like the visitors to the museum, and can watch the races or the preliminary proceedings (the equivalent of going backstage), but can also wander around unhindered, chatting and moving from one vantage point to another. A kind of prelude to this urban social

Overleaf:
100
Racehorses before the Stands
(detail of ill. 102)

ritual is to be seen in a small painting in which Degas depicted all the participants in the racing scene at a private racecourse that had not yet come under public control. When *At the Races in the Countryside* (ill. 18) was exhibited at the first Impressionist exhibition, the highly regarded critic Ernest Chesneau praised it with a string of clichés that included 'exquisite colouring, draughtsmanship, lifelike poses, and overall finesse'. Some forty years later, however, Lemoisne thought he detected in the work a trace of the typical Degas confusion (*désarroi*) of the time, expressed in the lack of attention to perspective and in the cropped composition, which he felt to be an affectation. Lemoisne's vision was more acute than Chesneau's, but from a modern standpoint his judgment was wrong.

The scene is a landscape that is neither cultivated nor wild. If the term were not so heavy with other associations, one might almost call it a no-man's-land. A uniformly green area stretches all the way across the canvas, rather like the *Place de la Concorde* (ill. 81). A few trees and low-roofed houses (possibly tents) break up the background, but there is little else. The setting does not stand for any sort of space fading through linear or aerial perspective into the distance. The green is simply a background sparsely occupied by people and horses. There is a minimum of contact between them. Two galloping riders are having a practice run, but no one is watching them, and the rest of the riders seem to be there by chance. On the extreme left we see the rear view of a cart, and the horse that is harnessed to it would appear to have only two legs. The staffage scenes in the background are too small in relation to the foreground figures. An elegant Tilbury occupies two thirds of the foreground, and its occupants are taking no notice whatsoever of what is going on behind them. A nanny is feeding a baby, and the mother is holding up a parasol, though this seems to be more for the sake of privacy than protection, since the dull, diffuse light is not enough to dazzle anyone. A bulldog is keeping watch over this domestic scene, and the gentleman on the coachbox – Monsieur Valpinçon, whose daughter we have already met (ill. 51) – is looking at the ladies, not so much an active participant as an interested observer, gazing from the lofty heights of male supremacy down at the cosy nest of female privacy.

Is this two pictures in one? Or a single picture with two complementary messages? I would suggest the latter. This close-up genre scene is certainly not a family portrait, for the nanny is playing the mother's role, and the father is the coachman, while the riders on the field are not taking part in a race but are simply training. There are no judges or crowds, and there are no

obvious competitors. Degas both conceals and accentuates these gaps by depriving both the background and the carriage of any real action and making both zones of the picture into a kind of still life.

At the exhibition on the Boulevard des Capucines, this subtly decomposed composition was different from anything that had hitherto surprised the public as *plein air* painting. When Chesneau expressly singled out Monet's view of the *Boulevard des Capucines* for praise, he showed himself to be in accord with the intentions of the painter: a moment is captured in all its shimmering transience of light and shade, people and carriages. Even though Degas's *At the Races in the Countryside* has none of the vibrancy of Monet's brushwork, nevertheless Chesneau simply accepts the absence of Monet's snapshot spontaneity with no further comment.

102
Racehorses Before the Stands
c. 1866–68
Oil on paper on canvas
61 x 46 cm (18 1/8 x 24 in.)
Paris, Musée d'Orsay

In his preliminary remarks, he laments the fact that the innovators (later known as the Impressionists) have failed to separate themselves from their fellow travellers, and have not put all their eggs in one basket. Clearly he did not see in 1874 that there were already two distinct modes of what would soon be called Impressionism: one was embodied by Monet's *Boulevard*, and the other by Degas's *Races*.

This dichotomy becomes even clearer if we compare an earlier racing scene by Degas – the *Racehorses Before the Stands* (ill. 102) – with Manet's *Racing at Longchamps*, which exists as both a painted version (c. 1867, in Chicago) and an undated lithograph (ill. 101).

In both the painting and the lithograph, Manet chose for himself and the observer an exposed standpoint that could only be adopted in one's imagination: we find ourselves as fictitious spectators right in the middle of the racecourse. At full gallop, the riders come racing towards us, whereas the real spectators are safely tucked away behind the barriers. In the painting, they form an amorphous mass, whereas in the lithograph the crowd is like a tidal wave, surging with the headlong, unstoppable approach of the riders. The artist has removed the distinction between the passivity of the barricaded spectators and the dynamic movement of the jockeys, for here the energy flows both ways. Such a radical equation of mass and energy has no parallel in 19th-century art. Even the swift, concise brushwork of the Impressionists lags behind these almost abstract figures. And yet Manet also managed, as Françoise Cachin points out, to capture an impression of spatial depth, springing from a distant vanishing point, and to convey it two-dimensionally, thereby avoiding the 'hole-in-the-wall' effect.

Such unison, in which everything seems to flow from a single outpouring, was not what Degas was after. His focus was on isolation. Behind this lay an eye that was ever on the lookout for alternatives. That was why he had the Bellelli sisters pose facing in different directions (ill. 8), as was also the case with the daughters of the Duchessa di Montejasi (ill. 47). We should remind ourselves that dissociation was the characteristic element of the social portraits (ill. 43), families (ills. 44, 45, 46), friendships (Valernes, ill. 32), public life (Lepic, ill. 80) and the workplace (New Orleans, ill. 29).

In *Racehorses Before the Stands* (ill. 102), isolation extends to both fields of action. The people in and outside the stands look tiny by comparison with the riders. The space is divided into two zones. The spectators are a collection of individual figures, and are not dissolved into a coloured mass, as in Monet and Manet. Degas made careful preliminary studies which were then not used in the paintings. His sharp eye once more reveals its parsimonious side: he has a single model staging the languid poses of a dozen different ladies (ill. 103). His eye seizes on

104
**Amateur Jockeys
near a Carriage**
1876–87
Oil on canvas
66 x 81 cm (26 x 31 7/8 in.)
Paris, Musée d'Orsay

105
The Fallen Jockey
1866–67
Oil on canvas
180 x 151 cm (70 7/8 x 59 1/2 in.)
Basel, Kunstmuseum

every nuance of movement, which gives rise to a random combination of attention and indifference. Some of the women are thoughtful, others gaze into space, and just like the jockeys, they practise their roles, each one for herself. But the idea of transmuting these individuals into a seething, hydra-like crowd evidently did not interest Degas or, possibly, was beyond his scope. His people are simply busy doing nothing. This paradox was more important to him than the collective body geared to a specific expectation. Spectators, when he does integrate them into his racing scenes, are generally no more than a band of bright colours in the distance. This is the case with his *Amateur Jockeys near a Carriage* (ill. 104), where one is struck by the calculated disorder so typical of Degas. The left half of the picture is practically empty. The horse galloping through it draws our gaze to the right, where jockeys, horses, spectators and a carriage merge together in a single mass, further confused by a bright-coloured hat whose wearer we can only guess at. On the carriage, the hubs of the wheels are not central, and the spokes look defective. The gentleman in the top hat, whose cane also looks like a spoke, is a remarkably disinterested spectator whom one might perhaps describe as looking thoughtful. He functions as a vertical barrier holding up the crowd of amateur jockeys and stabilizing the scene from the side.

In the background is the relaxed to-and-fro motion which marks the jockeys' warm-up – the word should recall the ballet rehearsal scenes – and which was already anticipated in the *Scene of War in the Middle Ages* (ill. 12). This painting has long been regarded as an important introduction to two of Degas's favourite themes: riders and abandoned women. The jockeys, who ignore one another in all of his pictures, do not interest him as a single collective unit, or as coordinated participants in a contest. His focus lies on the confused juxtaposition of individuals, each trying to make his own mark in the event that is about to happen. Degas's eye frequently falls on isolated incidents, where something goes wrong and the scene is disrupted: a false start or a fall (ill. 105) – extreme instances of isolation leading to dissonance.

The Fallen Jockey in fact falls out of the setting that Degas provides for the three dozen or so jockey pictures he painted during the 1860s and 70s. Some of them are close-up snapshots (ill. 107), though most are in extended, frieze-like landscape format, whose wide angles encompass groups of what might be described as mounted *flâneurs*. Once again we are confronted by the paradox which is inherent in Degas's compositions and which he used more daringly than any of his contemporaries: he emphasizes the provisional, chaotic, unorganized elements of these practice rides, endows them with a formal finality, and yet secretly also allows for the possibility of correction, or of retraction, since – as we are soon made to realize – they are all simply variations on a single theme. The idea is to get oneself and the horses into form and ready for competition. Thus there is an analogy between the painter and the jockeys,

106
Amateur Jockeys before the Start
1862 (reworked 1882)
Oil on canvas
48 x 61 cm (18 7/8 x 24 in.)
Paris, Musée d'Orsay

for the painter is a secret participant in these practice rides; he too is seeking a final resolution, and discovers that there is not one but several. No form – and this is his quarrel with the academic world – is final.

The Fallen Jockey (ill. 105) has a complicated history, which Loyrette has traced back to the 1860s, when Degas painted a steeplechase scene which today forms part of the Paul Mellon Collection at Yale. Of four horses that fill this canvas, two have thrown their jockeys, but Degas has painted only one of the fallen riders. Two of the competitors are racing past the

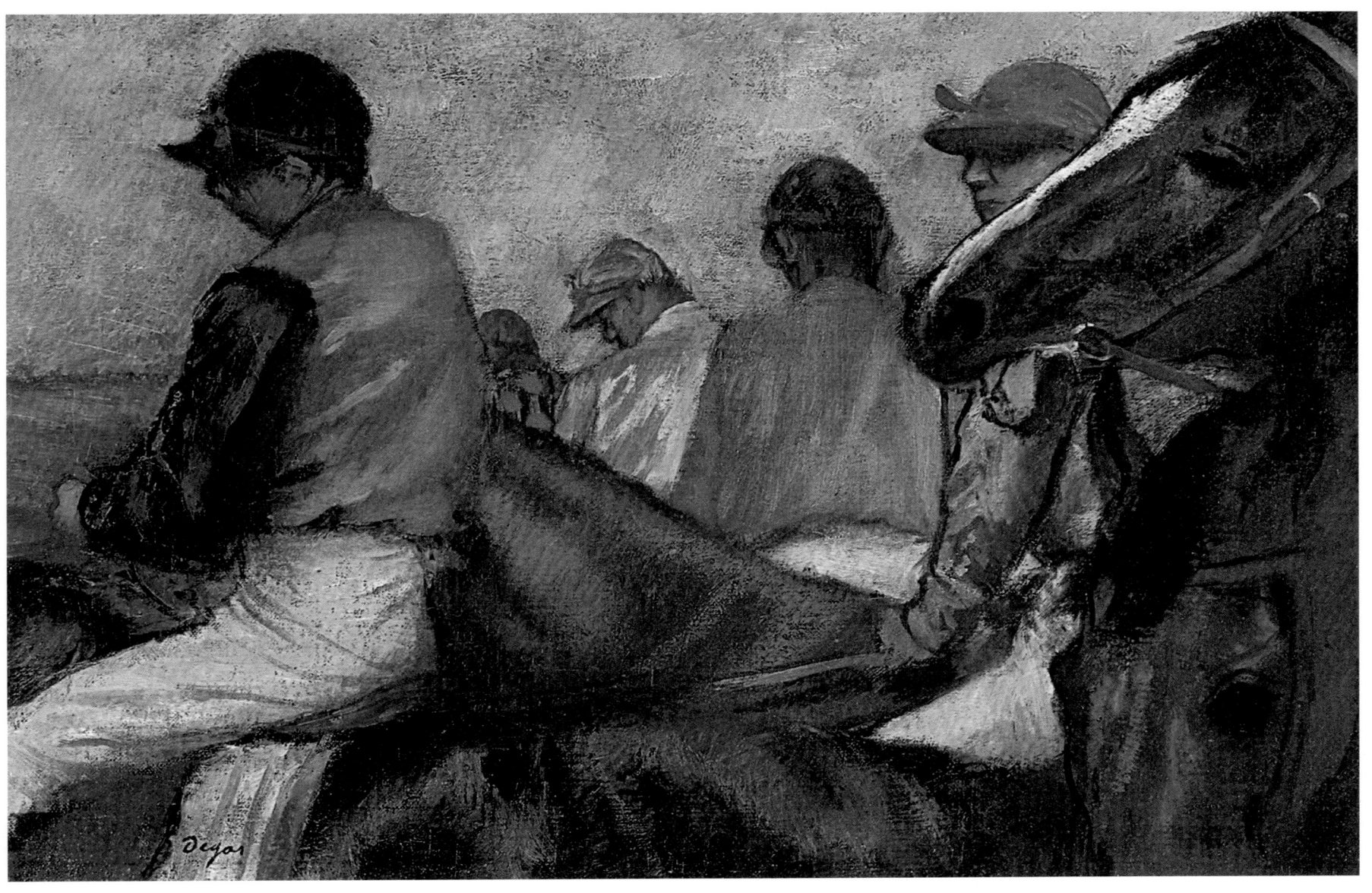

accident. Around 1896, Degas extracted the central theme from this episode: a riderless horse gallops across the canvas, the rich green of which does not suggest depth, but rather a compact, vertical wall, with just a narrow sunlit strip giving any hint of distance. In the foreground, where the fallen man is lying, everything is in shade. Gary Tinterow sees the painting as an attempt to raise a scene of contemporary life to the level of myth.

I would not go so far, although I do think that the scene represents more than the record of a single moment. This is apparent as soon as one analyses the form, which shows that Degas

107
Jockeys
1881–85
Oil on canvas on board
24.6 x 39.9 cm (9 3/4 x 15 3/4 in.)
New Haven, Yale University
Art Gallery

deliberately ignored one of the basic rules of illusionism, which is the empirically demonstrable link between cause and effect; this always entails a compressed sequence in time. Degas sees no causal connection in the accident. If the horse had been involved, it would not now be galloping over or behind the prostrate man, but would already be out of the picture. Degas is postulating a totally disconnected simultaneity between horse and fallen rider, which has nothing to do with the accident. The horse, then, is not the cause but simply an emblem.

Degas's refusal to pursue the process of cause and effect has a formal antecedent in Parmigianino's *Conversion of St Paul*, the *Urszene* of the mental reversal in which man turns from the false to the true faith. But Degas is not concerned with any such revelation. His fallen man might be in a state of rigor mortis, and his outstretched arms have no counterpart in heaven or anywhere else in the great beyond. Nevertheless, the idea behind this painting is an example of the later works where a strict simplification of form corresponds with content becoming enigmatic. Horse and rider come together as a memento or even a parable of failure.

108
Laundresses and Two Horses
1902–4
Pastel and charcoal on paper
84 x 107 cm (33 1/8 x 42 1/8 in.)
Lausanne, Musée des Beaux-Arts

The last time we see horses is in a large work that probably dates from around 1902–4 (ill. 108). Once again, Degas dispenses with cause and effect; here we have two horses and two women put together for no apparent reason and turning the material for two pictures into one. The women hark back to the *Laundresses* (ill. 123). We only get a partial view of the horses – the rear of one, and part of the head, the neck and one front leg of the other. It is the confusion of formal structures and relationships that gives rise to the ambiguity of the meaning. Forty years after the *Scene of War in the Middle Ages* (ill. 12), we again find woman and horse facing one another, but this time linked to separate ideas. The horses are not performing any service, whereas the women are bound to their work. Since there is no explanatory background to the action, the close-up technique chosen by the artist creates areas of uncertainty. One of the women, for instance, seems unaware that the horse is right behind her, as if it is about to trap her between its legs, while the other is making a gesture of grooming, though apparently not actually touching the horse's skin. As fragments, the animals seem unapproachable and almost statuesque – as if they are part of a dream – while the women are hard-working, and very much part of the real world.

What, then, is the key to this pictorial puzzle? When a person is hard-working, we sometimes refer to him or her as a workhorse, and perhaps it is just this expression that provides us with a link between the two animal natures: the horses have been relieved of their burden, and the women have to take it on, thus being reduced to the level of animals – a theme not uncommon in Degas. But it could be something quite different. The two *Laundresses* (ill. 123) may have resurfaced in the memory of the old artist – after all, memory plays an important part in the combination of forms – and since they represent one of his most striking, indeed monumental concepts, this would scarcely be surprising. The painting would then constitute a witty combination of the washerwoman theme with another of Degas's obsessive images: the horse and its animal nature. He would thus be projecting the one into the other. But, as Courbet said of his *Studio*, 'Let him who can, guess!'

Chapter 8

Bodies Adorned and Used

'Yesterday I spent the whole day in the studio of a strange painter called Degas.
After a great many attempts in all directions, he has fallen in love with modern life,
and from modern life he has thrown his gaze upon washerwomen and ballet dancers…
He places before our eyes, with their various poses and their graceful foreshortening,
washerwomen and still more washerwomen, speaking their own language and explaining
the technical details of the motions of pressing and ironing… An original fellow, this Degas,
sickly, neurotic, and afraid of losing his sight; but for this very reason extremely sensitive and
receptive to the character of things. Of those I have met so far, he is the man who has best been able,
in representing modern life, to capture its soul. But will he ever produce anything complete?
I doubt it. His mind is too restless.' – Edmond de Goncourt, 13 February 1874

The female body was a lifelong obsession for Degas. He observed it in all the stages of transformation and deformation that life could inflict on it, and he observed it in the plural. Whether the many bodies that he studied centred around a single prototype, and whether they represented something like a counter to the ideal of beauty that still haunted the academic dream, will become apparent in the course of our analysis. We shall be looking at the complete range of Degas's work in this field: bodies dressed, bodies adorned, bodies marketed, and bodies set free simply to be themselves.

We shall begin with a basic idea derived from a dialectical simplification – a model concept which is another indication of the continuity that marks French thinking, where theory and practice are constantly interchanging. Once more, we turn to Diderot. We have already seen how his distinction between prose and poetry was applied to Champfleury's two contrasting types of attic, and soon afterwards to the complementary wings of Courbet's *Studio*, which in turn led to Degas's two modes of Realism: the bourgeois and the proletarian. It is to Diderot that we also owe another dichotomy which arose from the different social classes of the Industrial Age: that between natural and artificial man. In his supplement to *Bougainville's World Tour* (published in 1777), he compares *l'homme naturel* and *l'homme artificiel*, linking the latter to the old age of Europe and all its misery. He contrasts this *misère* with the childhood of

109
At the Mirror
(detail of ill. 119)

mankind, which he believes still exists in Tahiti. The question of what has caused this European sickness is the subject of a dialogue between A and B. Once, says B, there was a natural man, into whom an artificial man was transplanted; within him there then took place a conflict that lasted all his life. At one moment, the natural man was the stronger, and the next moment he was struck down by the moral, artificial man.

Both prototypes are to be found in Courbet's *Studio* (ill. 5). The 'elegant couple' represent the artificial, particularly the woman, whose costly shawl is a striking contrast to the simple white drapery – the colour of innocence – which almost unintentionally conceals part of the

III
At the Milliner's
c. 1882
Pastel on paper
70.2 x 70.5 cm
(27 5/8 x 27 3/4 in.)
New York, The Museum
of Modern Art

body of the 'Naked Truth'. The latter stands as model and muse behind the painter at his easel – the embodiment of the natural being, just like the breast-feeding mother at the artist's feet, the two boys, and the mixed-race Jeanne Duval standing behind her lover Baudelaire – though she is reduced to a mere smudge because, at the behest of the poet who feared a scandal, Courbet painted her over at the last minute.

Baudelaire is absorbed in a book and seems unaware of both his mistress and the elegant lady; he does not yet know that he is confronted by the classic dilemma of the traveller faced with two paths. Baudelaire was, in his own words, a '*homo duplex*' (see his essay on 'The Double

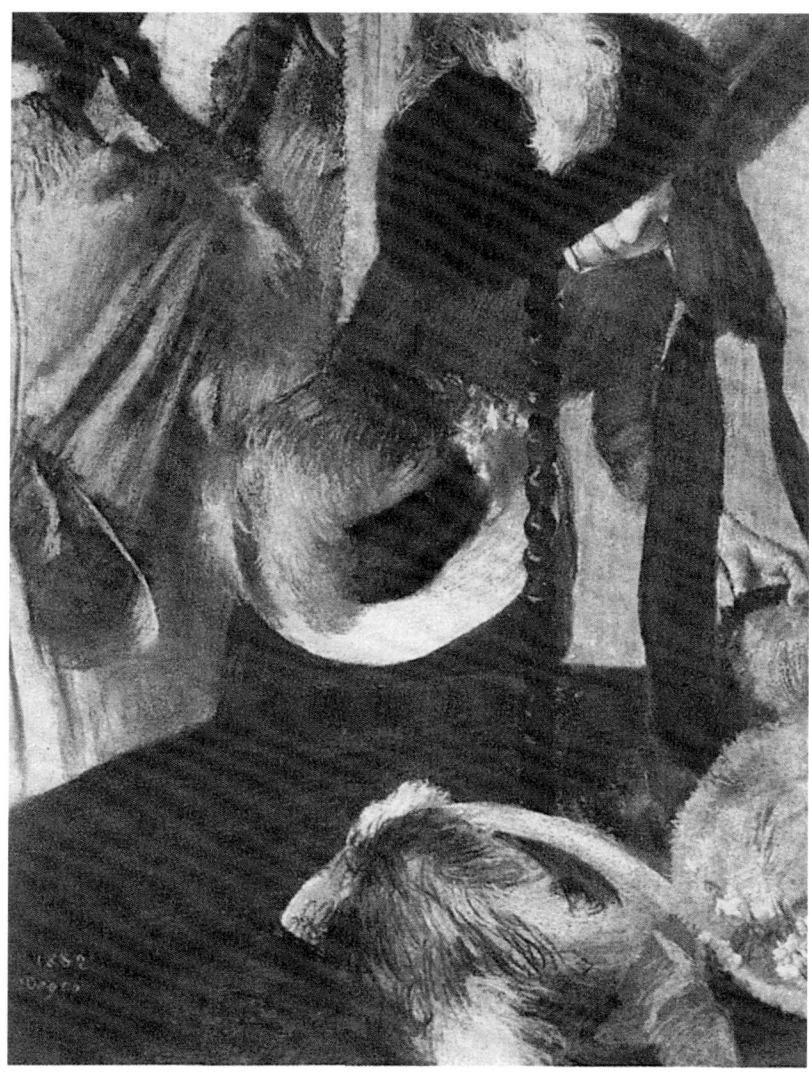

Life of Charles Asselineau'). With his pen he acknowledged the two types of woman that could be derived from Diderot's classifications: the artificial woman, living by dressing and disguise, and the natural woman, living by undressing. In the early 1860s he made the devastating comment: '*La femme est naturelle, c'est-à-dire abominable*' [woman is natural, that is to say, abominable], in a note which was never meant for publication and in which he stripped his heart bare (*mon coeur mis à nu*). Shortly before that, in his essay on Constantin Guys (1860), which was published in *L'Illustration* under the title 'The Painter of Modern Life', he had recognized additional 'dimensions'. Taking up Joseph de Maistre's terms, he identified the '*bel animal*' [beautiful animal] that served man as a '*femelle*' [female], but he also admired the refined harmony in which the body merged with its clothes in a '*totalité indivisible*'.

Baudelaire's two concepts of woman neatly corresponded with those that Degas developed in his works, ranging from the fashionable mannequin to the unadorned, naked creature. Let us first consider one of the attributes of the artificial woman – namely, her hat. We shall be looking at works in which the painter places this requisite of female display back in the hands of the anonymous creatures who have produced it. Degas is not interested in the dressmakers, but in the milliners who make hats into works of art.

The milliner was one of the indispensable satellites of the middle-class world whose fringes she inhabited. It was to her that the fashion-conscious Parisian woman owed the crowning glory of her appearance, in the context of Baudelaire's 'indivisible totality' of physical and decorative attributes. Degas was as fascinated by this show as he would later be by the natural woman at her toilet – both of these being threads that run through his life's work – and he

depicted the trying on of hats as still lifes and genre scenes. There are three characters in these little dramas: the milliner, the customer and the hat, which stands between the other two as both a barrier and a connection. What absorbed Degas was the fact that the hat made the human into an object among objects, even freezing her into a puppet available for the use of others. In one pastel, he uses a particularly cunning device to show that this dehumanizing effect applies more to the role of the milliner than to that of the client. *At the Milliner's* (ill. 110) presents an eye-catching view of a lady standing in front of a mirror – Mary Cassatt acknowledged that she was the model for this. But what the eye alights on next is a barrier, the brown mirror which cuts the room in two like a solid beam, but also '*dismembers*' the body of the milliner, making her totally unrecognizable. This was the term used by Schiller in his

113
Two Milliners
1882
Pastel
48 x 70 cm (18 7/8 x 27 5/8 in.)
Private collection

analysis of how people are fragmented by the modern business world. The fragment here, frozen almost literally into a 'helping hand', stands behind the mirror, and is used but not perceived by the client. One of the two hats that the milliner is offering seems almost to be hovering in the air, an amorphous smudge of colour. The customer has a decisive air about her – she knows what she wants. The subservient milliner has no identity of her own, and is merely one of Degas's generic puppets.

From the observer's point of view, the client is easy to decipher. The real action staged here by Degas takes place independently of her, between the mirror and the milliner. We are presented with a paradoxical puzzle. The vertical room divider fragments the picture *and* the milliner, and the double break in continuity is a disturbing factor. What initially seems like a spontaneous snapshot – one critic called it an *instantané* – turns into a motionless metaphor of detachment, illustrating the social gulf between the two women.

In another pastel at the Museum of Modern Art (ill. 111), the milliner has brought her goods to the client and is standing behind her, offering her two hats. Both milliner and client are like 'artificial' strangers, between whom the only contact is the hat as a hybrid *objet d'art*. Once again, the subserviently bowed body is fragmented, almost shoved out of the way in the top corner of the picture. Thus people and objects are squeezed onto an imaginary vertical plane which excludes the openness of the third dimension. A similar confusion reigns in the pastel with the succinct double title *Hats: Still Life* (ill. 112). Ignored by this title, the milliner is hidden, like part of a picture puzzle, between hats and hat stands. We finally discover her, once again dismembered, behind the curve of the table. Another packed picture is that of the two friends in the hat 'salon' (ill. 64). They have sent the salesgirl away and are now playing the game of 'busy doing nothing'. Sometimes Degas leaves his milliners with their bodies intact. Then he makes them anonymous artists in their own right, absorbed in their work and not overshadowed by its splendour. For such pictures he creates an almost frieze-like sequence, rhythmically alternating between hats and their makers (ill. 113). The horizontal composition is punctuated by verticals, so that it can be seen as a rise-and-fall pattern. The effect of weightlessness – the two women have no surface to stand on – prepares the way for a metamorphosis such as Grandville devised in *Another World* (1844), in which a flower in a vase turns into a flower on a hat. The Realist Degas does not go to such lengths; for him the empirical world is ambivalent enough. Although his repertoire of hats may be reminiscent of Respighi's ballet *La Boutique fantasque*, he does not even venture into the realms of fantasy. Nor do his analogous forms follow on from one another, as in Grandville – they co-exist. The artificial flower is already in the hat, and vice versa. The hat is a hybrid, half derived from nature and half from artistic inspiration. Several hats together form a motif that makes a loose arabesque

116
The Milliner
c. 1882
Pastel and charcoal on paper
47.6 x 62.2 cm
(18 3/4 x 24 1/2 in.)
New York, The Metropolitan
Museum of Art

round the room (ill. 115). At the same time as we see this ensemble, we also witness the work process, the concentration on balancing the elements that will go to make up the composition of the hat. Degas's interest in this almost artistic job brings out the sympathy of an artist who preferred artificial flowers to natural ones.

To the degree in which the hat conceals its wearer, it makes her into an object. Degas emphasizes this transformation by looking down diagonally from above at his models. This gives the hats a formal autonomy which they lose when we see them perched on someone's head (see ill. 64). Three women in an interior (ill. 117), each leaning on her elbows and bent over horizontally – not a pose appreciated by the academic camp – are hiding under their hats. Can this disconnected juxtaposition really denote a conversation, as the title suggests? If so, at best it is the hats that are talking to one another. The concealed women might as well be dolls.

We seldom find partners of equal rank engaged in conversation. In one pastel, a clever device is used to counter the frozen rigidity of the artificial: a milliner is entertaining herself with her own creation (ill. 116). Through this flirtatious girl we can see an analogy between hat-making and the artistic process: it lies in improvisation, in the playful but sensual mastery of the material. The alienation that is caused by the work process has been completely eliminated by this (perhaps stolen) moment of pleasure as she takes her little break. As with the Hamburg dancer (ill. 93), the painter's dual vision enables him to resolve the clash between person and object. Also in Hamburg (ill. 119) is another lady, trying on an expensive hat in front of a mirror, but she has forgotten her reflection, so that the dialogue with the object of disguise has turned into an inner monologue, a meditation in which the bare shoulders play an important part, for they belong to a different person – the natural woman.

117
Women in Conversation at the Milliner's
c. 1884
Pastel
63 x 84 cm (24 3/4 x 33 1/8 in.)
Berlin, Alte Nationalgalerie

Degas's last milliner is a kind of homage to the affinity between this profession and art. The large pastel *At the Milliner's* (ill. 120) dates from around 1898. While Grandville depicted flower, hat and wearer in an accumulative sequence which the eye could easily grasp, Degas chooses a subtler method of conveying objects and their transformation – a method that is far more difficult for the observer to decipher. The vertical composition of this large-scale expanse of form and colour contains three phases that merge into one another. On the worktable are samples of materials which seem like amorphous splashes of colour. From this formless mass the milliner selects what she needs. Her hands seem to be lifting the embryonic form of a hat out of the tangle of colours, almost like a midwife gently delivering a baby. The central section, dominated by the milliner, is followed by a finished hat on a stand, the vertical line of which is linked to the woman's elbow, giving rise to a sort of hat-plant. The massive hat is so close to the woman's head that it seems like an extension of it. Thus the three phases capture the transformation of the raw material into a work of art – or, to be more precise, the milliner herself is a work of art who combines both the beginning and the completion of the artistic process.

120
At the Milliner's
Pastel
c. 1898
91 x 75 cm (35 7/8 x 29 1/2 in.)
Paris, Musée du Louvre

Honoré Daumier (1808–79)
The Laundress
c. 1860
Oil on canvas
49 x 33 cm (19 1/4 x 13 in.)
Paris, Musée du Louvre

This transubstantiation is executed with exquisite delicacy by a Degas who by now was almost blind and yet was still clearly a master of large-scale composition. What gives this pastel the stamp of a late work is the marginal figure of the assistant, who is passing a blue feather. The pairing of the two women is reminiscent of the washerwomen with the two horses (ill. 108). The assistant also reminds us of the maidservants combing their mistresses' hair after they have finished their toilet. Here the fact that the milliner has an assistant suggests

122
A Woman Ironing
1873
Oil on canvas
54.3 x 39.4 cm
(21 3/8 x 15 1/2 in.)
New York, The Metropolitan
Museum of Art

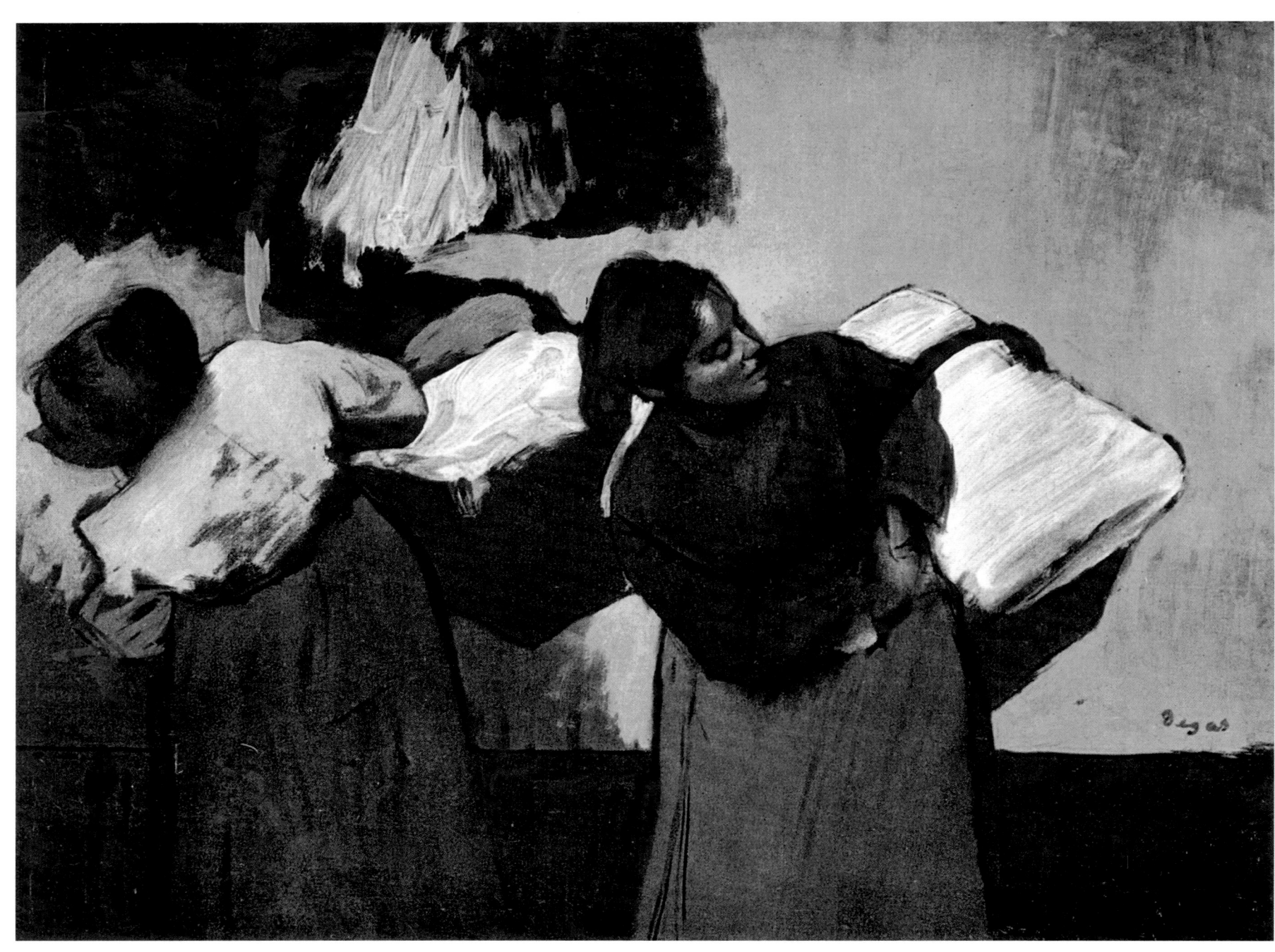

123
Two Laundresses
1876–78
Oil on canvas
46 x 61 cm (18 1/8 x 24 in.)
New York, Howard J. Sachs
Collection

that she is the proprietor of the establishment. She is certainly higher-ranking, as we can see from her closeness to the hat on the stand – it belongs to her and not to a customer. In earlier pictures, the milliners were fragmented or 'dismembered'. Now this vulnerable status has been passed to the helper, though the milliner herself is still totally engrossed by her products. She does not pose (as her clients do), but is simply herself, absorbed in the work she is doing. This gives the whole composition the aura of a gentle apotheosis.

In Degas's panorama of the Parisian woman, the laundress stands for the exhausted body, worn out with hard work. But not even these creatures are spared the curious gaze of the voyeur.

124
The Laundress
1876–84
Oil on canvas
65 x 66.5 cm (25 1/2 x 26 1/4 in.)
Reading, PA, Reading Public
Museum

To satisfy the latter, in December 1860 the *Variétés* put on a revue entitled *Oh! Là! Là! Qu'c'est bête tout ça!* ['Oh la la! How stupid it all is!'], which offered a through-the-keyhole glimpse of the everyday life not only of prostitutes but also, just as spicily, of washerwomen. The actresses had to bend so low over the washing that their breasts hung out. The director who staged the show was the holder of a distinguished order, as the Goncourts noted – without comment – in their journal entry for 31 December. A few months later, a counterpart to this offering was exhibited in the official Salon of 1861: a *Laundress* by Daumier (ill. 121). This now famous little painting would have attracted far less attention at the time than the vulgar revue.

Degas followed on from Daumier, whom he admired and whose lithographs he collected. He had three hundred of these, fifty of them *avant la lettre* prints. The Daumier–Degas legacy is a convincing one if we consider the formal similarities between them, but it does throw up a small puzzle. Why was it that when Degas saw the *Laundress* in the Salon (as I presume he did), it took him so long – until around 1869 – to take up the subject himself? Perhaps the real impetus came from another version of the painting which he may have seen (though one wonders when) at Nadar's studio, and which Théodore de Banville described in 1878 as 'the tender, desolate image of wretchedness'. This comment would have applied equally well to the laundresses and ironing women as seen by Degas – though not initially. His first two ironing women are more like portraits of the role than of the class of woman. Once again his model was Emma Dobigny. In one pastel, which was exhibited at the 1874 exhibition, she is turned to the right (Musée d'Orsay), whereas the painting in the Neue Pinakothek in Munich (ill. 86) shows her front on to the observer. She has interrupted her task for the painter, but the alternating positions of the arms suggest the repetitive movements of ironing. In unconscious anticipation of kinetic techniques, Degas evidently enjoyed telescoping two conflicting phases. The blank expression of the young woman shows no sign of tiredness or boredom, but there is no critical self-awareness either. Nor is there any attempt to gloss over the realities: the woman is framed by the washing on the line and the dress on the ironing board, completely surrounded by the materials which she must clean in order to live. This is her world, and she knows no other. The white garments are studies in themselves – painting at its most basic, like self-expression through handwriting. A strange transformation has taken place here: the subject of the laundress abandons the social chiaroscuro of the fringe people as soon as the painter ceases to depict the milieu neutrally and instead makes it the pretext for colour variations that are almost devoid of objects. This creates a symbiotic relationship between the ironing woman and the painter.

Degas does, however, return to this chiaroscuro with an ironing woman begun in 1882 and not completed until 1886 (ill. 124). His tried-and-tested device of turning rooms into screens

127
The Laundresses
c. 1884–86
Oil on canvas
76 x 81 cm (29 7/8 x 32 1/8 in.)
Paris, Musée d'Orsay

enables him to obscure the room completely. The third dimension has only a virtual exist-ence, comprising fragments of background. Like hovering screens, the suspended items of laundry gather round the woman, supplemented below by the worktable, so that there is just a narrow gap in which the fragmented woman appears. Her bent head has no features. Her arms are arranging an indefinable garment which spreads across the surface of the table almost as if it were on a conveyor belt and the woman had to iron it all in one go – the task of a Sisyphus! And yet the warmth of the colours, reminiscent of Daumier, creates a feeling of intimacy and security. The worker and the work are absorbed in and by each other, and in terms of pure form, they create a balance of perpendiculars and diagonals that suggest an almost abstract pattern.

Very much in the Daumier spirit of silhouettes with substance – a calculated contradiction in terms! – Degas depicts another ironing woman with backlighting, which fills her workplace with a pale light that is just enough to conceal the solid, three-dimensionality of the room (ill. 122). The woman, whose iron is just visible, has a measured, gentle grace as she goes about her work. Her conscientiousness is brought out even more in a later version (ill. 126) that is pro-vided with more detail in the convention of genre painting. The ambiance is very precise, with a pile of shirts in the foreground, already ironed, to show the quality of the work – just as the artist would hope to achieve with *his* work.

In the mid 1870s, Degas extended his subject by depicting two women ironing. Of the dif-ferent versions, the one in the Musée d'Orsay is the best known (ill. 127). The almost square painting is already striking for its gentle, pastel-like colouring, which is so delicate that at times the coarse grains of the canvas show through. The result is a soft and hazy atmosphere of cosy domesticity into which Degas deliberately sets his two women in contrasting positions. One is using all her strength to press the iron onto the shirt, while the other is yawning with all the intensity of Bruegel's Dutch yawners, and at the same time she is grasping a bottle. One is reminded of Luke's parable (10: 38–42) concerning the hard-working Martha and her sister Mary, though in this case there is no wise guest to teach them a lesson, and the yawning woman is reaching for a different kind of distraction. The biting humour with which Degas seasons the pictures of prostitutes (ills. 174–77) painted at the same time also helps to dampen the social pathos of this slice of working life.

Degas's idea of making several versions of one subject – already announced during his stay in New Orleans – sometimes leads him to paint several versions of one figure in a single picture, e.g. in the woman combing her hair (Phillips Collection, ill. 180).

From the same period we have *Two Laundresses* (ill. 123), in which we can make out two versions of a single woman. Their complementary movements are totally in accord, so that

128
The Laundresses
c. 1879
Etching and aquatint
11.8 x 16 cm (4 5/8 x 6 1/4 in.)
Washington DC, National Gallery
of Art, Rosenwald Collection

one could blend into the other. The very fact that here we have two forms in unison indicates just why this duo has such a fascinating effect: it comes not least from the harmony of the colours. The warm, dark brown (again reminiscent of Daumier) contrasts with the honey yellow of the background, which like the gold backgrounds of medieval paintings makes for a two- and not a three-dimensional effect. The loose-hanging, ragged clothes create the necessary intrusion of colour, but in realistic terms they are as untrue to life as the yellow background. In a similar manner, Degas paints an ice-green 'wall' in the picture with the two milliners (ill. 118). The two women are so self-assured that the white loads they are carrying in their baskets seem like an extension of themselves. The painter's formal composition suggests that this burden is easily borne.

The monumental harmony of this rhapsody in brown, white and yellow was not, however, Degas's last word on the subject. In an etching of around 1879 (ill. 128), he created a black and white contrast to the rich colours of the *Laundresses*. The idea is now extended to cover the workroom of the washerwomen – though this is not depicted in any detail. We see three laundresses in a dark interior, which is divided vertically by two posts on the left. The dimensions of this partitioned area are obscured by reflections, like those in Degas's street cafés (ill. 159) and dressing rooms (ill. 230). This inner room seems to lead to an equally diffuse outer room. Two women are working at the ironing table, while a third – front left – has sunk into a contemplative pose. She could be sitting in some cheap nightclub lamenting her fate. We have met her before: Degas sketched her prototype for his *Scene of War in the Middle Ages*, where she was gazing despairingly into space (ill. 15). This pose, not used in the painting, had clearly been saved in the painter's memory of forms, and here in the etching he uses it again. But the woman in the war scene is now a laundress, drawn to express the monotony of an unchanging routine. Even the most powerful of the coloured versions of the laundresses and ironers do not come close to conveying the bitterness of this metaphor. We can understand why Degas called black and white his passion. A remark handed down to us by Antoine Terrasse goes even further: 'If I could live my life over again, I would only work in black and white.' Art history would have lost far more than it would have gained by such a decision. It is true that Degas's excursions into social chiaroscuro would have taken on a sharper contrast, and his photographic bent would have flourished even more, but the overall history of 19th-century art would have been a great deal poorer without the greatest and most inventive of all its experimental painters.

Chapter 9

Dancers:
Flying High and Falling Low

'The same limbs constructing, deconstructing and reconstructing shapes,
or movements responding to equal or harmonic intervals, form an ornament of duration,
just as the repetition of motifs in space, or their symmetry, forms the ornament of extent.'
– Paul Valéry, 'Degas Danse Dessin', 1938

Milliners, laundresses and ironers all worked to enhance the appearance of their prosperous clients. The milliners invented creations that enabled the artificial woman to take on the aura of an artwork, which was also of benefit to the hat-maker herself who, in the late pastel *At the Milliner's* (ill. 120), symbiotically turns into her own work of art. The proletarian washerwomen and ironers also contribute to the spectacle, but they belong to a category whose job has no prestige. Unlike the milliners, who play a role in the trying on of hats, they remain entirely in the background, and even the result of their work – good clean laundry – is of secondary importance. And so for Degas they remain anonymous workhorses. The clothes that they themselves wear are loose, shapeless coverings that will not hinder them in their work. Their smocks and blouses are as worn as the bodies they have to cover.

Milliners and ironers represent the two ends of the spectrum that reaches from the artificial to the natural woman. It was this contrast that Degas made into one of his greatest themes when in 1870 he discovered the profession that united both ends of the spectrum in a single figure: the dancer. The same creature that could enchant her audience with the illusion of weightlessness could also wilt with exhaustion. In the perfection of her artificiality were concealed all the deficiencies of the natural woman. Since Diderot had pointed out the equal rank of poetry and prose, hierarchies had disappeared, and for Degas this revaluation opened up areas of humanity which were far more interesting to him than the canonized beauty that ballet-lovers held in highest esteem. In the ambivalent world of the stage (and behind it) he could see the natural being hidden by the footlights, and he discovered movements that had

129
Dance Class
(detail of ill. 130)

130
Dance Class
c. 1873
Oil on canvas
47.6 x 62.2 cm
(18 3/4 x 24 1/2 in.)
Washington DC, Corcoran
Gallery of Art

not been rehearsed, and creatures that disciplined their bodies or let their bodies go loose in a moment of quiet relaxation. He witnessed exhaustion from which suddenly the damaged creature would emerge in all her self-awareness. He discovered people who sold their bodies for the art of beautiful appearances, and then received them back again worn out and good for nothing. Of more than 200 works dealing with the ballet, only just over a fifth depict events on stage. The majority of these paintings and pastels take us behind the scenes to observe rehearsals, or to go into the changing rooms, where the dancers are not yet under orders and are still in command of what is left of their individual, physical selves.

This peripheral world, hidden from the public gaze, was from the start the focal point of Degas's attention. The very first painting, *The Dancing Class* (ill. 134) contains his programme, with tentative movements gradually leading to perfection. This little painting was exhibited in 1874 at the exhibition in Nadar's studio, and the critics were enthusiastic. Degas was introduced to the world of opera-ballet by friends like Viscount Lepic, Albert Hecht and Ludovic Halévy, who as regular guests enjoyed the privilege of going backstage during performances and in the intervals. One had to have a permit to do this, and it was not until 15 years later that Degas finally obtained one. Initially, he had to be content with visits to empty rehearsal

131
The Foyer de la Danse at the Opéra on the Rue Le Peletier
Oil on canvas
1872
32 x 46 cm
(12 5/8 x 18 1/8 in.)
Paris, Musée d'Orsay

rooms during the day, and with inviting the dancers to pose for him in his studio. At first sight, these conditions are not obvious in the pictures themselves. They are like snapshots taken by a hidden observer, but in fact they are very carefully composed. Degas would keep juxtaposing things in his mind until they gave him the tensions and contrasts that he needed for his dissonant structures: continuity and discontinuity, composition and decomposition. These contrasts become evident as soon as we succeed in finding the hinges on which they turn. In *The Dancing Class*, it is the mirror that fulfils this function. It breaks the continuity of pause and movement with a reflection that belongs to another reality, which is extended in the background into a complex zone of more fragmented reflections that reach right to the top of the picture. In this manner, the room unexpectedly turns into a network of false walls. The confusion is compounded by a simple device in the foreground: the violin case. This points us in the direction Degas wants us to look. Our perception in fact follows a 'wedge' that begins with the crowd of people around the piano and moves towards the right. The arc of the mirror creates a break but it also acts as a bridge that holds the two unevenly balanced halves of the picture together. Over and above this function, the mirror contains a concentrated version of the rehearsal – a picture within a picture.

Degas plays off density against emptiness: the left-hand side is packed with figures, but by the time we reach the extreme right, there is only one, seen from the rear and turned towards the wall, separated from the others by a perpendicular crack of light. The bare, virtually empty dance floor is being used by just one dancer, whose performance is watched by some and ignored by others.

As this idea found approval among collectors and public, Degas made it the starting point for many variations. For his second dancing class, he chose a larger format (ill. 131). The scene takes place in a rehearsal room at the old Opéra in the Rue Le Peletier (which burned down in 1873). Here, the room is a large hall, which has none of the intimacy of the earlier studio. Two male figures of authority, the ballet master and the violinist, give the beat. Once again, though, Degas brings different roles together. The dancer on the left is the only one who is actually performing, but at least some of her fellow dancers are watching. The rest are preoccupied with themselves, practising at the barre, reading the notice board, or looking out of the window. Despite the apparent naturalness of the scene, we can follow a calculated movement that starts from the dancer on the left and leads across the room, following the red line of the barre, all the way to the dancer sitting on the right with her left leg outstretched to round off the gentle curve of the whole composition. The empty chair provides a central, stabilizing weight while at the same time giving vertical closure to the arc. This axis is the equivalent of the link between the violin case and the mirror in *The Dancing Class* (ill. 134). Like the mirror,

134
The Dancing Class
c. 1871
Oil on wood panel
19.7 x 27 cm (7 3/4 x 10 5/8 in.)
*New York, The Metropolitan
Museum of Art*

the classical archway acts as a break and a bridge between the two halves of the picture. The empty chair creates a profane but complementary contrast to the noble poetry of the arch. In the 'curve' of the dancers we find the beginnings of those frieze-like series of figures which Degas would later incorporate into his variations (ill. 140).

The two dance studios have a formal counterpart in the grouping of *The Cotton Exchange in New Orleans* (ill. 29), the large-scale genre painting that captures the atmosphere of everyday life in the De Gas Brothers' business in New Orleans. In this, Degas shows a man's world in much the same way as he depicts the woman's world of ballet lessons: the juxtaposition of the different figures bears the stamp of randomness. The only link between them is the rule of laissez-faire. There is no one giving orders, and no one is in anyone else's way. The same applies to the dancers, who during these classes are still in control of themselves. The essence of liberal capitalism, the freedom to choose, applies to the world of business as to the world of the rehearsal room.

If randomness is left entirely to itself, it comes close to chaos, but Degas subtly orchestrates the confusion, partly by veiling the rehearsal room (ill. 130) in a warm and dusky half-light.

There is no dazzling white here to draw attention to itself, and the tutus are muffled by a diffuse, leather-brown shade with just the occasional highlight: the pink of a flashing dancing shoe, the stitching on a dress, the red of a sash. The ballerinas, left to their own devices, like schoolchildren without a teacher, are passing the time practising movements, watching or talking. Although groups and dialogues are only hinted at, there is a fluctuating sense of togetherness, which can be ascribed to the painter and his art of composition. Even if this peep behind the scenes might seem to shatter the illusions so carefully created on stage, it should not be taken as an intrusion by an indiscreet voyeur. On the contrary, Degas provides a background to the finished, choreographed creation, reminding us that behind the dancing puppets are real live people. The down-to-earth ballet workshop with its cast-iron spiral staircase becomes the setting for a variety of exercises that do not aim at any finality but are to a performance what preliminary sketches are to an oil painting. Degas's artistic aim was to maintain the spontaneity of such earlier sketches in the paintings themselves, and so in his studies he took great pains to capture the prosaic attitudes of the individual dancers before incorporating them into the composition.

135
The Dancing Lesson
c. 1880
Oil on canvas
39.4 x 88.4 cm
(15 1/2 x 34 5/8 in.)
Williamstown, MA,
The Sterling and Francine
Clark Art Institute

In this way he made them into his own creations, and gave them back the identity that they had to suppress in perfecting their own art. This was his way of expressing his sympathy with their gestures of physical insecurity, as can be seen from the flexing of the limbs, the massaging of the joints, the adjustment of the costumes. In recording these intimate moments, he endowed them with the same primality that he sought to convey with his own drawings and sketches. Sympathy becomes symbiosis, and the artist recognizes himself in his models.

Among these studies are some in which the dancer literally removes her dancer's guise and in her nakedness seems to be thinking about her role (ill. 21). The pencil then gives to the body a firm solidity that transcends its physical tiredness but still conveys a sense of self-doubt, the intensity of which only Rodin, among Degas's contemporaries, was able to match. One thinks of his *Eve* gazing into the abyss (1881). In other words, this contemplative nude is like the feminine counterpart to Rodin's *Thinker* (1880), although the correspondence should not be taken as a sign of influence.

136
The Dancing Lesson
c. 1873–76
Oil on canvas
95 x 75 cm
(37 3/8 x 29 1/2 in.)
Paris, Musée d'Orsay

137
Waiting
1880–82
Pastel on paper
48.2 x 61 cm (19 x 24 in.)
Pasadena, Norton Simon Museum/
The J. Paul Getty Museum

138
Dancer Stretching
c. 1882–85
Pastel on paper
46.7 x 29.7 cm
(18 3/8 x 11 3/4 in.)
Fort Worth, Texas,
Kimbell Art Museum

Sympathy can also turn into empathy, as when Degas's imagination isolates a figure from the rest of the crowd, showing a self-awareness that has not yet been suppressed by the rules of the dance (ill. 136). The ballet master, the famous choreographer Jules Perrot, stands magisterially, like a lion tamer, in this 'arena' of women. Degas has separated one figure, who is not passively watching like most of the others but is clearly critical. This woman is no mere novice – she knows her métier. Her pose has something monumentally calm but also severe about it, something final. It seems to me that Degas was identifying with this woman. She embodies a balanced detachment, which he himself as an imaginary observer would have adopted towards the scene. Her proud stance contrasts with the casual pose of her neighbour, who is sitting on the piano looking bored and scratching her back with her left hand.

We meet this creature more than once. She has a central position in *The Rehearsal of the Ballet on Stage* (ill. 19), which was exhibited in 1874 at Nadar's studio. In this monochrome picture, whose sepia shades recall those of old photographs, Degas works with lighting effects that give the dancers a pallor like that of lifeless wax figures, while the empty room has a ghostly aura. In this, and in two other variations on a subject which obviously found favour with the public, Degas has smuggled in a discordant note in the shape of a girl yawning. This goes totally against the grain of decorum, which is rigidly adhered to by most of her colleagues. Ten years later, there is an even more drastic case: an ironing woman who yawns (ill. 127). But from the same period, there is a drawing (ill. 138) in which Degas turns this facial distortion into an expression of suffering that again reminds us of Rodin, whose *Youth in Despair* (1882) elevates the suppressed groans of Degas's dancer into a veritable howl of rebellion.

The rehearsal with the critical observer also contains an idea which the swiftly ageing Degas drew from the generation gap and applied to the world of ballet. When youth and age are coupled together, each throws the other into relief. The old Perrot cuts a powerful figure among the young girls, but as a creative choreographer he had long since had his day. In the confused activity of the scene, his obsolescence is not so obvious, but the past becomes a memento when an older man turns his back on the girls for whom he is performing, as if he were playing the violin only for himself (ill. 139). It is the same when older women – ex-dancers, perhaps – are fitting the girls with their costumes or acting as chaperones (ill. 142). In

139
The Dance Lesson
c. 1879
Pastel and black chalk
64.5 x 56.2 cm
(5 3/8 x 22 1/8 in.)
New York, The Metropolitan
Mueum of Art

140
Frieze of Dancers
c. 1895
Oil on canvas
70 x 200.5 cm (27 5/8 x 79 in.)
Cleveland, Museum of Art

Waiting (ill. 137) – the title alone tells us a lot – young and old sit next to one another. In the woman with the umbrella we see again the thoughtful attitude that we noticed in the middle-class ladies who had been left to themselves (see Chapter 4), but this time the young girl seems to give some substance to the thoughts: the fleetingness of our existence, a subject that Daumier had already tackled (ill. 141). Where the dancer is now may correspond to where her companion was in her youth. The young girl waits to make her entrance, and her companion waits for her exit. The tip of the umbrella points to the inevitable course of events.

At the turn of the century, a poet also turned to the dancer as a metaphor for Fate. Rilke too saw her as a debased and helpless creature trapped in a world of suffering. In 1898 he wrote in a review of a Berlin exhibition for the *Wiener Rundschau*: '…many pictures of ballerinas full

of sequinned rubbish and stage lighting. They surprise us with their hopeless ugliness, these girls, whose whole life gradually descends into their legs, so that on their low, twilight brows nothing remains except a dull, dumb memory of things never known, and even that will soon be lost in the acquired smile. For the most part they stand around in groups on the barren dance floor and tie up their shoes or adjust their cloudy dresses; as sad as birds who on the verge of an evolution have lost their wings but not yet learned to use their legs.' Rilke's Degas experience would later find expression in the *Duino Elegies* and the *Sonnets to Orpheus*.

The admiring glances cast on these dancers by Max Klinger (1857–1920) were those of a graphic artist: 'He [Degas] has chosen a specialized field for his pictures: ballet and theatre. Thus he has produced a series of sylphs flying around the stage, indefinably lit by lights from

the stage and the soffits, seen from the side, high up in one of the boxes. The legs shoot forth from dresses of bilious green gauze – real ballet legs, thin and muscular. The unpleasant colour of their leotards, and the made-up faces with their breathless smiles, are set mask-like against the harsh bright green of the dresses and the dull, dark background of the stage boards; behind them is the corps de ballet in bright red, waiting in a delightfully theatrical pose for the signal to dance. How all this is made, drawn! With the minimum of means, what an effect is achieved!' The admiration of this German contemporary is also directed at Degas's courage in depicting ugliness: '…the end of a ballet apotheosis. At the front, the orchestra; the curtain falls, and in the narrow gap left open we can still see the exhausted dancers in their prescribed curtain-call poses. Their breathlessness opens a wide gap between their sharp collarbones and their corsets – a space which the footlights sympathetically conceal in darkness.'

141
Honoré Daumier (1808–1879)
'To think… in my day, I was a great dancer too…'
1857
Lithograph
26.2 x 33.1 cm (10 1/4 x 13 in.)
San Francisco, The Museum of Fine Arts

Even when inventing parables, the experimenter Degas never lost sight of the two levels he always worked on: poetry and prose. While he gave his public the ethereal figures – the weightless, wingless angels that seem to hover down from another world – which even today still delight bourgeois taste (ill. 148), he did not forget to balance that beauty with the earthly material from which the dreams are made. He provides his *Little Dancer Aged Fourteen* (ill. 143) with a bodice, a real gauze tutu and dancing shoes. In 1881, after much hesitation, he sent the little wax figure to the sixth Impressionist exhibition, where the reactions of critics and the public were mixed. The sculpture caused a major stir for several reasons. It upset the purists, who liked the human body to be portrayed in all its marble perfection and timelessness. But on the other hand, this was precisely why critics who admired truthfulness and prosaic reality greeted it as liberating. Charles Ephrussi praised it as a new attempt to bring realism to sculpture, and for Joris-Karl Huysmans it represented the only modern advance in sculpture. At the same time, he also justified the bold use of real materials by pointing out that there had been similar practices in the past, for instance in 17th-century Spain. Judgment was less favourable when it came to the face of the girl and her pose. Paul Mantz and others saw a 'bestial insolence' and viciousness in the features, and the low forehead that Rilke was later to attribute to all dancers signified a criminal bent. Degas seems to have chosen this feature deliberately. As if to reinforce the negative reactions of the public, he portrayed the accused in

The Ballet Class
c. 1880
Oil on canvas
82.2 x 76.8 cm
(32 3/8 x 30 1/4 in.)
Philadelphia, The Philadelphia
Museum of Art

143
Little Dancer Aged Fourteen
1880–81
Painted bronze with muslin and silk
Height: 81 cm
Zürich, Sammlung Bührle

Opposite, above:
144
Heads of Criminals
1881
Pastel
48 x 76 cm (18 7/8 x 29 7/8 in.)
Private collection

Opposite, below:
145
Four Studies of a Dancer
c. 1878–79
Pencil and charcoal on paper
49 x 32.1 cm (19 1/4 x 12 5/8 in.)
Paris, Musée du Louvre

court during a murder trial with receding foreheads, which both public opinion and science regarded as evidence of their guilt (ill. 144). This pastel was also displayed at the Impressionist exhibition.

Today, the *Little Dancer* would count as one of the figures that Zola dug up (or invented) from the dregs of Parisian society, which indeed was where the model actually came from. Little Marie van Goethem was the daughter of a Belgian washerwoman. After Degas's death, on instructions from his heirs, the single wax figure was cast and made into more than twenty copies.

Huysmans hit on the right formula for the subtle balance of expression when he described the girl as 'both sophisticated and barbarian'. There is indeed a stimulating mixture here of insolence and innocence. But Degas does not just break the spell of the adored, coquettish little 'ballet rats' (as Halévy called them in his *Cardinal Family*); he also supplements his own insights into the exhausting routine of dance rehearsals with a creature that is mysteriously used but unused; we do not see her as 'broken' (*brisée*) – to use Huysmans's term – but as stepping out with a confidence that poses a challenge to the observer. Degas moderates the insolence of her appearance by removing the portrait-like close-up of her features that he had worked on in his preliminary studies. Less than lifesize, the graceful figure is, after all, a work of art, and we find ourselves confronted by someone who might almost be

sleepwalking, groping her way with her eyes closed. The strict stylization prevents any *trompe l'oeil* effect, and one might compare her to the stepping poses found in Egyptian statues.

The *Little Dancer* clearly shows the 'dual vision', changing between poetry and prose, that Degas employed even more frequently in his ballet scenes than in his other subjects. The tension between high and low, light and dark, also found its way into his choice of formats. For his prima ballerinas in their bright colours he chose the portrait format, but the anonymous corps de ballet were compressed into landscape format, with their low, badly lit rooms (ill. 135). In these we have all the uncertainty of the workshop, and here too we have the deceptive, confusing compositions that seem to begin with symmetry but then immediately break it up. At the centre of *The Dancing Lesson* stands a ballerina whose head is held in a position like that of the *Little Dancer*. This central axis is given two flanking accompaniments, so that everything including the symmetry is thrown out of balance. On the one hand, the standing dancer's crossed feet link her to the two seated dancers in the foreground, but on the other, her upper body protrudes into the loose frieze of the four girls close to the window. In this way she both separates and combines the different elements. But when Degas uses a post as a room divider – for example, in *Ballet Rehearsal*, in the Yale University Art Gallery – the emphasis clearly lies on the separation, with the picture being split into two parts whose dimensions come close to the golden section. In one picture (ill. 151), he draws a dividing line in the form of a bench diagonally across the canvas, and places two dancers in isolated spaces, where they meditate alone. The way that a diagonal can cut across space and divide it into two distinct zones can be seen in *Dancers Practising at the Bar* (ill. 147). The bare austerity of the room in which they are rehearsing is reflected in their stances: exhausted bodies pushed to the limit and held up only by the bar. The prose of this scene is sliced diagonally, dividing the image into dark and light. Although the emptiness of the wooden floor constrasts with the pale wall, the two oblique areas create a kind of dissonant similarity. The watering can is a crucial accent, halting the falling diagonal and echoing the position of the dancers' feet on the floor. Degas originally wanted to remove the can; fortunately, Henri Rouart dissuaded him. How could the radiance of a prima ballerina emerge from the starkness of such a room? This is where the dual vision comes into action.

In the famous pastel *The Star* (ill. 146), Degas takes the dance out of its physical context and sets it in a sphere of weightless immateriality. But even here, the observer cannot avoid getting a glimpse behind the scenes. Waiting there is a profane destroyer of the dream: a gentleman on the lookout for the goods which he is used to picking up at this spot. The black silhouette indicates the prose – i.e. the promiscuity of everyday life from which the sylph has come and to which she is about to return.

146
The Star
Pastel
c. 1876–77
58 x 42 cm (23 5/8 x 17 5/8 in.)
Paris, Musée du Louvre

It is not just this form of disillusionment that is inscribed into the illusion of dancing stardom. The following remarks are based on an observation that came to me by chance. I suddenly discovered one day that, without realizing it, I had stuck a postcard of *The Star* upside down on a pinboard. But even when the picture was standing on its head, it still made sense. The upward flight now became a downward plunge from endless space into a fissured formation of rocks. Once again, the composition was just right! If my assumption is correct that the illusion of weightlessness carries within it the change to exhaustion, then the fall is already contained within the flight. Rilke, in the last lines of his tenth Elegy, seems to have been thinking along the same lines – possibly even guided by remembrance of Degas's work:

'And we, who think of happiness
rising, would feel the emotion
that almost shakes our souls
when happiness falls.'

Opposite
148
**Swaying Dancer
(Dancer in Green),**
1877–79
Pastel and gouache on paper
64 x 36 cm (25 1/4 x 14 1/8 in.)
Museo Thyssen-Bornemisza,
Madrid

147
Dancers Practising at the Bar
1877
Mixed media on canvas
75.6 x 81.3 cm
(29 3/4 x 32 in.)
New York, The Metropolitan
Museum of Art

A 'satyr play' on the conduct of dancers onstage and backstage was Ludovic Halévy's *Cardinal Family*, a cycle of eight tales which he began in 1870 and which was published in book form. In 1873, the 'Grand Dictionnaire' of Larousse, an institution charged with safeguarding the reputation of France, reacted with moral indignation. Works such as this, they cried, belonged to the domain of the 'unhealthy' (*malsaine*) literature that had earned France such a bad reputation abroad. We do not know what gave Degas the idea of devoting a series of monotypes to the Cardinal family, but we do know that his friend Halévy did not think very highly of them and preferred to illustrate the book with mediocre, unadventurous pictures that lagged behind the ironic humour of his prose. Even the editors of Larousse could raise no objections to the efforts of Messrs Morin, Maigrot and Mas (ill. 156).

Unlike them, Degas did not follow the various episodes of the stories, but condensed the action by

Above left: 149
Mme Cardinal with an Admirer
c. 1880, Monotype
21 x 16 cm (8 1/4 x 6 1/4 in.)
Private collection

Above right: 150
**Dancers Coming from the
Dressing Rooms on to the Stage**
c. 1880, Monotype
Measurements unknown
Private collection

disregarding the scenic descriptions and concentrating on the characters: Madame Cardinal, her two daughters and their admirers – a mixture of rakes and fops. At no time did he ever consider his ideas as illustrations. There are several grounds for this assumption. Firstly, the three dozen or so monotypes that have survived only cover the first three tales. Secondly, the monotype is anything but suitable as a technique for book illustration. In relation to the printing process, it presents a dilemma, because unlike woodcuts, copperplate etchings and lithographs it does not duplicate an original in a series of prints but allows for only one copy, hence the name monotype. This unique copy is made by pressing a sheet of paper onto a painted glass or copper plate before the paint has dried. The single print can then be worked

on further, and a few more copies can be made, but they will come out fainter. Degas created both 'pure' and reworked monotypes, using pastel or gouache on the latter, but most of the Cardinal pictures remained pure, which gives them a provocatively sketchy spontaneity – a feature that was not attractive to the sellers of illustrated books in those days. Such reservations may also explain why Degas showed his pure monotypes only to a few friends. Not until after his death did they emerge 'not even catalogued' and bundled up in boxes.

Pauline and Virginie, Monsieur and Madame Cardinal's two young daughters, are among the 'ballet rats' whom the regular customers lie in wait for backstage. The two sisters are like livestock – the capital which the parents 'invest' for their own benefit, not only on stage, but

Above left: 151
In the Green Room
c. 1880, Monotype
Measurements unknown
Whereabouts unknown

Above right: 152
Dancers Coming from the Dressing Rooms
c. 1880, Monotype
Measurements unknown
Whereabouts unknown

153
Meeting Mme Cardinal Backstage
c. 1880
Monotype
27.3 x 30.7 cm (10 3/4 x 12 in.)
Private collection

Opposite:
154
Friends Backstage
c. 1878
Pastel
79 x 55 cm
(31 1/8 x 21 5/8 in.)
Paris, Musée du Louvre

also and far more profitably offstage. The footlights offer the two girls and their rivals the radiant, seductive showcase in which is played the prelude to the show that will take place later behind the scenes in the dark corridors and dressing rooms. This is where the rakes come to the fore – or rather, to the point. The mother knows just how to establish lucrative contacts, presenting her two 'products' and selling them with beautifully acted modesty when she grants a top-hatted gentleman the chance to glimpse her little girls rehearsing on stage (ill. 153). The maternal matchmaker and the future pot of gold negotiate backstage, while the objects of the deal take practically no notice of the haggling that is going on in their name. The formal model for this situation is a lithograph by Daumier from 1857 (ill. 141). An old woman, as lined as the crumbling stage set, is deep in thought as she looks at the young dancer,

for she remembers that once upon a time she herself possessed the same supple grace. Degas was sensitive to the motif of *vanitas*, but that was not what interested him in these stories. His sole concern was the business being done in the shadows behind the stage, and the contrast between the respectable gentlemen and the puppets tripping over stairs (ill. 152), scurrying along corridors, or huddling together like animals in a cage (ill. 151). Some of the men are sure of themselves, and others stiff and awkward (ill. 139). While one climbs the steps, another stands in the cold corridor rubbing his neck in embarrassment, and a flash of tutu disappears on the right (ill. 4), and you might think these are evil-doers committing dastardly deeds or even planning heinous crimes. The hunt for female flesh can be frozen in a stark confrontation, as when a voluptuous bosom is paraded before a gentleman who seems to be hesitating between his lust and his class-conscious respectability (ill. 149). This near collision between the two parties is conveyed with heavy brushstrokes which are suggestive of the violence that underlies the struggle between desire and inhibition.

The carousel of lust turns in such narrow circles that there is no room for the dimensions we talked of earlier: no flights and falls, no exhaustion or self-doubt. None of this is to be observed in the flirting and fluttering, for all that is required is sex for pleasure, which is the stuff of caricature. This applies particularly to the men, whose social rank in these intimate situations gives rise to a comedy of helplessness. In addition but exempted from this gallery of masked lechery, Degas paints his friend Halévy, the creator of the Cardinal family. When he visits the dressing room in which Madame Cardinal, surrounded by junk, is reading her newspaper, he remains the figure of the inscrutable dandy, coolly playing the role of the mere observer (ill. 157).

We have already noted a connection between the bustle of the dancing classes and rehearsals and the leisurely activities in the office of the New Orleans cotton firm (ill. 29). In both places, the attitude is one of laissez-faire. There is also, however, a link between the backstage flirting and the business world. Those gentlemen who have some dignity, unlike the comical roués, maintain it even when confronted by the temptations of the tutus. Ludovic Halévy chats with his friend Cavé (ill. 154) backstage at the Opéra just as earnestly as his friends and fellow bourgeois discuss tactics at the stock exchange (ill. 155). Whether he is selling shares or hunting girls, a gentleman keeps his lust and his strategies under tight control. The central figure in Degas's stock exchange scene, Ernest May, also had a foot in the art world. This rich financier collected pictures ranging from the 18th century right through to the Impressionists, and also tried his hand at publishing, with the journal *Le Jour et la Nuit*. He was an entrepreneur who, as Degas wrote in a letter to Felix Bracquemond, 'throws himself into the arts'. Degas accompanied these gentlemen of high society, who had both desires and the means to

156
Copperplate print by J. Massard after E. Mas
Book illustration for 'The Cardinal Family' by Ludovic Halévy, 1883

Opposite:
155
At the Stock Exchange
Oil on canvas
c. 1878–79
100 x 82 cm
(39 3/8 x 32 1/4 in.)
Paris, Musée d'Orsay

157
Ludovic Halévy and
Mme Cardinal
c. 1880
Pastel over monotype
21.3 x 16 cm (8 3/8 x 6 1/4 in.)
Stuttgart, Staatsgalerie

fulfil them, to the various places where gentlemen of high society liked to be seen: the stage (and its attendant areas), the stock exchange, and dealers in modern art. A little later, he would also observe members of this species during their visits to brothels.

From the standpoint of those whose toes were trodden on, the *Cardinal Family* monotypes were indiscretions on a par with the photos shot nowadays by the all-intrusive paparazzi. This was sheer prose, comparable to the scandalmongering of the popular press. Degas, however, was no voyeur, and he was not out to expose individuals but, if anything at all, their sociologically conditioned role-playing. What he found even more fascinating, though, was the ambivalent context in which the art of ballet flourished during the peak period of capitalism. There were the wildly acclaimed stars – Maria Taglioni, Fanny Elssler, Carlotta Grisi – surrounded by the corps de ballet, who were merely dancers. Both categories, the stars and the 'foot soldiers', provided the services – on different levels – that the male portion of their public expected of them.

Although Degas once paid homage to a star in the person of *Mlle Fiocre* (ill. 13), he was later far more concerned with ballet's loss of aura, whereby human dignity was cast aside and the art of the dance was relegated to the economic grey area of male gratification. Bit by bit, the artistic rituals were vulgarized and ultimately bastardized, made synonymous with the pantomime of commercialized sex. In this manner, the ballet satisfied the male need for illusion in two complementary ways: on the stage, and behind it. The theme of 'The Bourgeois in his World' thus takes on its characteristic feature of the fractured mind, which was one of the great discoveries of bourgeois art in the 18th and 19th centuries. Ballet had now become ambivalent, representing both the beautiful appearance and disillusionment through its ready availability for sex. In the next chapter, we shall be dealing with this again as we consider the commercialized liberties of the metropolis.

Chapter 10

Liberties
Bought and Sold

'She gazed in a stupor at the strange poses of her comrades, showy and vulgar beauties,
screeching gossips, mannish women and scrawny girls, some stretched on their bellies,
head in their hands, some crouching like bitches on a stool,
some perching like butterflies on the corners of couches....'
– Joris-Karl Huysmans, Marthe, Histoire d'une fille, 1876

Woman is an object for the use of man. Among the middle and lower classes of the 19th century, that was the patriarchal and economic basis of relations between the sexes. It was backed by the law, and it provided the public and private rules for their conduct. In such a structured society, prostitution played a major role, because it linked the different layers of society together in sexual complicity. The Goncourt brothers found a pithily cynical way of putting it: 'The revenge of the poor man on the rich: his daughters.' Prostitution was ubiquitous: 'Our bourgeois, not content with having wives and daughters of the proletarians at their disposal, not to speak of common prostitutes, take the greatest pleasure in seducing each other's wives.' (Marx and Engels, *Manifesto of the Communist Party*). Thus at every social rank, woman became an object for sale, at the mercy of man's will.

To flourish in the age of capitalist competition, saleable love relied on advertising, and that was taken care of by various kinds of exhibition. I shall deal with just two, which covered public and private 'consumption'. First of all, there was the entertainment business; the café-concerts, covered walkways, bars at music halls – places where you could find a partner and where, according to the handbook *Paris-Parisien* (1897), you would meet a 'very mixed public'. Was that a warning or an advertisement? Other 'shows' took place away from the public eye, in the brothels. Degas visited both spheres of sexual offerings.

He not only knew how to split pictures up and 'splice' them by inserting divisive elements, which compressed their message but at the same time made things more difficult for the observer's processes of perception, but he also extracted from some of his ideas the seeds for several pictures. These would be his starting points, which he would then work on, tighten up,

158
Women on the Terrace of a Café
(detail of ill. 162)

159
Women in a Café
1876–77
Monotype
11.2 x 16.1 cm
(4 1/2 x 6 1/4 in.)
Whereabouts unknown

Opposite
160
In a Café (Absinthe)
1875–76
Oil on canvas
92 x 68 cm
(36 1/4 x 26 3/4 in.)
Paris, Musée d'Orsay

and bring to the critical point. One of his earliest monotypes, *Women in a Café* (ill. 159), shows two young women coolly waiting for company. While one of them is quite at ease doing nothing, the other is looking expectantly to the left, from where a man is approaching – possibly a customer. This genre scene suggests the prelude to a gallant encounter, but we do not see it. Degas wipes out this starting point, splits up the scene, and from it creates two passive moments of disillusionment: one is the famous painting *In a Café (Absinthe)* (ill. 160), and the other *Women on the Terrace of a Café* (ill. 162).

The two people in *Absinthe* are linked by what divides them: their vacant expressions and their frozen lack of contact. As in *Sulking* (ill. 37), the middle-class prologue to this scene, Degas took both models from his own circle of friends. The woman who posed for him was the actress Ellen Andrée, who was well-known in the art world, and the man was Marcellin Desboutin. Many years later, Ellen Andrée recalled: 'I'm sitting in front of a glass of absinthe, and Desboutin in front of a perfectly innocent drink – the world on its head! – and we look like a couple of fools.' If there were signs of smouldering conflict and resentment in *Sulking*, what we have here is the final stage of alienation. The woman's gaze is vacant. The 'customer' – so an

interpreter remembering the monotype might conclude – has arrived, but has nothing to offer except the drinks, which obviously neither of them is in the mood for. But this was not the kind of episode that Degas had in mind. It is not a chance meeting, such as the *flâneur* might be hoping for, but the pair are a couple whose silent togetherness has become a thing of custom. Although they are sitting at the same table, Degas contrives to emphasize the gap between this and the other table (with the bottle) in such a way that it becomes a metaphor for insurmountable separation. Just like the tables, the two people are cut off from each other. Furthermore, Degas uses the geometry of the tables – as he uses the worktop of one of his ironing women (ill. 124) – to divide the room. He switches the formula of 'rooms becoming screens' from the perpendicular of the screen to the horizontal, so that ultimately all three (fragmented) tables form the dismembered elements of a smooth, cold barrier creating a no-go area all around the man and woman. This device underlines the finality of their united detachment. The relaxed informality of the monotype *Women in the Café* has here given way to something irrevocable. Both sets of figures are trapped within the boundaries of their respective 'playing' fields, but here there is no longer any way out. *Rien ne va plus*.

Opposite:
161
The Café-Concert des Ambassadeurs
1876–77
Pastel on paper
37 x 27 cm (14 5/8 x 10 5/8 in.)
Lyons, Musée des Beaux-Arts

162
Women on the Terrace of a Café
1877
Pastel
54.5 x 71.5 cm
(21 1/2 x 28 1/4 in.)
Paris, Musée du Louvre

163
Cabaret
1876–77
Pastel over monotype on
paper and board
24,2 x 44,5 cm (9 1/4 x 17 in.)
Washington, Corcoran Gallery of
Art, William A. Clark Collection

The pastel *Women on the Terrace of a Café* (ill. 162) offers a different kind of disappointment: the futility of public self-advertisement. The scene is a boulevard along which an amorphous crowd of people are taking an evening stroll. The brightly lit shop windows on the opposite side of the street represent a single, continuous attraction, the disillusioned reverse of which is embodied by the four women in the foreground. The terrace that opens out onto the street – a gigantic display case – is divided by three sharply defined pillars. These pale coloured bands – we do not know what they are made of – produce the syncopated rhythm of a 'de-composition'. Asymmetrically positioned, with two on the left and one on the right, they form a counterpoint to the woman in light blue who sits in the centre, undermining any suggestion of balance.

The women are among the goods being offered on this urban promenade. They barely take notice of one another, and seem equally indifferent to the attentions of the passers-by. One has put her thumb to her top lip, which one expert has interpreted as a dismissive reaction to a stingy client. The very existence of these anonymous women is made marginal by the vertical bands, beyond which the strollers in the brightly lit street are strutting their way. The scene is made up of these dismembered fragments, even to the extent that the woman second from left is in two halves that do not quite fit together. Though stabilized by the pillars, the showcase 'terrace' has no spatial dimensions of its own – it is a single opening, although it seems like an exclusive area. Degas has orchestrated this with typical ambivalence: the women, unheeded, are alone in it, but at the same time they are trapped in the cage of the permanent peepshow, waiting for their cue, which is the summoning eye of the customer. The vertical barrier, like the horizontal one in *Absinthe*, is Degas's metaphor for social bondage – as we can also see in the analogous room division of the etching with the ironing women. There he places the women in a room which, as in the boulevard café, is split up by two posts.

Degas wanted *Absinthe* and the *Terrace* to be shown at the second Impressionist exhibition in 1876, along with three other pictures. But he could not complete *Absinthe* in time, and so he sent the canvas to London, where it was snapped up by a private collector who lent it to the third exhibition the following year. Both in London and Paris, the subject aroused hostility verging on outrage.

In *Mlle Bécat at the Café des Ambassadeurs* (ill. 166), cleverly inserted vertical bands are once again used to create a screen effect. The performance of the celebrated Mlle Bécat is punctuated by asymmetrically intersecting axes, of which the dominant perpendicular one is left of centre, reinforced by another further to the left. The perpendicular overlaps a garland of gaslights, the line of which is continued in the outstretched arms of the singer. She herself might be a puppet on a string. She is gesticulating out into the darkness, where right at the front we can see a few fragmentary top hats, whose wearers do not appear to be interested in the performance. While Degas more or less dismisses the apathetic audience, he makes us the addressees

164
At the Café des Ambassadeurs
1877
Etching, aquatint and drypoint
26.6 x 19.6 cm (10 1/2 x 7 3/4 in.)
Washington DC, National Gallery of Art, Rosenwald Collection

of what is probably a fairly suggestive song. Our perception changes the mood entirely: the singer, who is wasting her talents on these indifferent spectators, in our eyes becomes a messenger from the gods, illuminated by magical lighting effects. The sparkling, shimmering brightness of the scene transmits a strange sensation that is concentrated on the graceful figure of the singer. Her all-embracing gesture becomes that of a sorceress who seeks to seduce us into a fairytale world that is completely artificial. This ecstasy negates the three-dimensional depths of the interior and its accessibility, and everything becomes hazy. What was once a room is now a screen, a curtain, behind which the sober facts of reality will disappear in a land of dreams.

Degas gives us a very different view of the *Café des Ambassadeurs* (ill. 164) in an etching where illusion turns into confused disillusionment. Once more exercising his gift for dual vision, he changes the observer's standpoint and takes us behind the scenes. This place is like a dingy booth – more shed or tent than architecture – where the singers and the posing hostesses go through their puppet-like routine, as if there were no audience at all. In the foreground, a barrier conceals the floor they are standing on. On the right, two crooked poles reach all the way up to the top of the picture, and behind them is a crooked canvas. These three elements function as screens and prevent the formation of any accessible depth. In other words, the space has no perceivable dimensions, but is simply an improvised combination of tent roof, poles and barrier. Not only the observer but also the performers, who are acting in the dark, find themselves in an area of uncertainty, as do the spectators, who we can only assume are also sitting there in the darkness. Degas was fascinated by the nocturnal side of the pleasure industry, but not exclusively so. A few years later, he revised the lithograph of Mlle Bécat and the etching, using pastel crayons, which enrich and soften the coldness of the black and white. The background of the lithograph now contains a veritable firework display of delicate light blue, ice-green and violet, but the three ladies in the foreground undergo a somewhat less pleasing change: they not only block the spectators' view, but now they also dominate the composition. There is a lessening of tension in the etching too, which was revised with pastels. Perhaps these changes were concessions to public taste.

Just occasionally, Degas averts his analytical, disillusioned gaze and makes himself comfortable amid the boisterous crowds at the café-concert (ill. 163). The detached observer then joins in the collective festivities, to which people on both sides of the footlights make their contribution – the singers, hostesses, musicians and guests. The ladies in the audience and the ladies on stage could easily change places. And like the girls in the limelight, the good-humoured artist does his best to get his own audience in the appropriately merry mood. But it still remains open as to whether the effusive gestures of the star in the red dress will eventually gain the attention of an audience mainly preoccupied with itself. If not, it would not be a disaster, as it would be at the opera (ill. 90), because here events on the stage depend for their success on the colourfulness of the spectators. This is where the artful hats that Degas has already made us admire come into their own.

On the stage of the pastel in the Corcoran Gallery we see some of those shameless physiognomies that awaken the masochistic expectations of men. Degas had a penchant for them too, as he showed when depicting the famous Thérésa belting out *The Song of the Dog* (ill. 165) with appropriate gestures and screeching voice (according to contemporary witnesses). The low forehead, already familiar to us from the *Little Dancer,* once again points to the working-class origin. Seen in close-up and from the front, this type of street-market vulgarity takes on a shrill suggestiveness that is accentuated by the footlights, which seem to endow the facial features with the accompaniment of a mighty voice (ill. 167). It is a voice crying out what the silently yawning ironing woman is suppressing (ill. 127). The admiring Degas, however, actually had a different impression of Thérésa: 'She opens her great mouth, and out comes the roughest, finest, most wittily tender voice there could ever be. The soul, the taste – where could one find anything better? Admirable!' A few years later (1884), he paid tribute to her in a pastel – 'tribute' perhaps being the operative word, since he

165
The Song of the Dog
1875–77
Gouache and pastel on paper
51.8 x 42.6 cm
(20 1/4 x 16 3/4 in.)
Private collection

166
Mlle Bécat at the Café des Ambassadeurs
c. 1877
Lithograph
20.5 x 19.3 cm (8 x 7 5/8 in.)
Paris, Bibliothèque Nationale

Opposite:
167
Singer with a Glove
c. 1878, Pastel on canvas
52.9 x 41.1 cm
(20 7/8 x 16 1/8 in.)
Cambridge, MA, Fogg Art Museum,
Harvard University Art Museums

was flattering a star whose best years and seductively slim figure were long gone.

Related to this discreetly adjusted retrospective is another rather nostalgic pastel study of a singer in two poses – or possibly two different women (ill. 170). There is a tone here that we have not seen before in Degas's robustly vulgar singers. He does not hesitate to reproduce the hand-wringing emotion that was part of the contemporary repertoire, but he also conveys the lyrical tenderness of a lament which gives us a glimpse of the person behind the role.

Another variation on the theme of women on public display, this time in the arena of mass entertainment, is *Mlle Lala at the Cirque Fernando* (ill. 168). This circus artiste fits in with none of the groups of stars and walk-on parts that Degas selected from the Paris entertainment industry. She is neither a ballet dancer nor a music hall act, but a species entirely apart. Research has revealed that Lala was of mixed race, and for a time it was believed that her real name was Lola. We do not know if Degas was an admirer of hers, as he was of Mlle Fiocre and Thérésa. There are no stories, and no clues. His reporter's-eye view of the circus ring suggests that he actually saw the act from this angle. He reproduces all the details of the architecture, and so striking are the ribs and arches and coloured decorations that they distract our attention from Lala herself. This is no doubt intentional, as the structure of the dome merges almost symbiotically with

the acrobat, providing both a prelude and an epilogue to her effortlessly graceful performance.

Many years ago, Sigfried Giedion compared one of Degas's ballerinas to the base of a three-pinned arch from Ferdinand Dutert and Victor Contamin's Hall of Machines, which was used in 1889 together with the Eiffel Tower to demonstrate the possibilities of construction with iron. I do not find this comparison particularly convincing, and would like to offer another. A constructional drawing by Viollet-le-Duc (ill. 169) contains elements for which there are no precedents in the architectural repertoire: on the walls and ceilings are supplementary structures bearing a dome. By comparison with the walls themselves, these supports seem almost alien. Lala embodies a similar kind of eye-catching matter-of-factness. She is the contrapuntal addition to the circus dome, correcting the cheap illusionism with the solid reality of her endangered body, and becoming a partner to the structure surrounding her. With his precise eye for detail, Degas has painted her against a vertical which begins at the bottom of the picture with a brownish-red column, and then changes into an embedded shaft from which (behind Lala's body) there protrudes an iron construction reminiscent of a flying buttress.

Degas does not, however, make Lala into a pseudo-caryatid. She is drawn up into the dome on a rope, the end of which is hooked into her mouth. The snapshot from below and the thin rope dangling down into the arena emphasize the danger of this bravura performance and integrate it into the composition.

Degas made several preliminary studies, one of which even shows the metal hook on which everything quite literally depends. This was a detail that interested him, even though neither the public nor the painter would have been able to see it during the act. As she hangs in mid-air, Lala stretches her arms out wide in a gesture that makes her seem almost to be hovering. Once again, there is parallel in the architecture, which is also meant to create an impression of ethereal weightlessness. By holding out her arms, Lala is showing that there is no trickery involved and that she is placing her trust entirely in the strength of her teeth and jaws. With her masterly control over her own body, she seems to have overcome the role that Degas had identified in his *Scene of War in the Middle Ages* (ill. 12) as the fate of women in a male society – to be objects of sexual lust and the discarded victims of abuse.

Lala's unique situation raises her – at least momentarily – above the net of the sexual service industry. She seems untouchable. Male desire stays down below on the benches and must be content with the role of distant spectator. At this moment, the woman is the object of

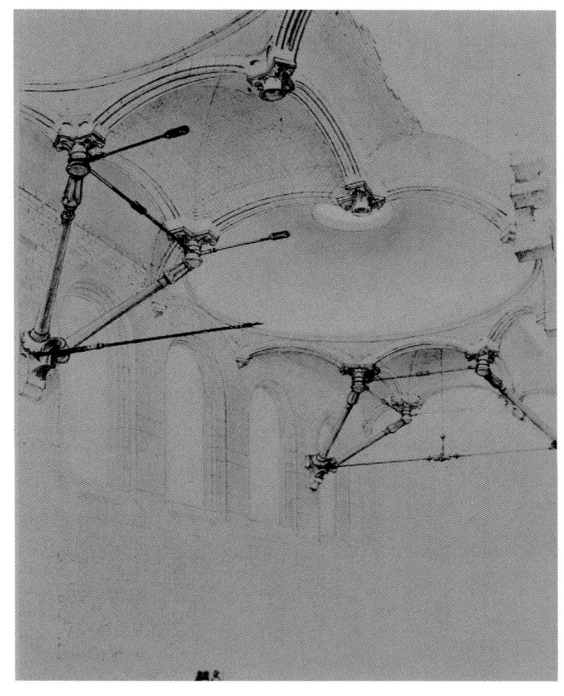

169
Eugène Viollet-le-Duc *(1814–79)*
Architectural drawing from 'Cours de l'Architecture', 1864

Opposite:
168
Miss Lala at the Cirque Fernando
1879
Oil on canvas
117.2 x 77.5 cm
(46 1/4 x 30 3/8 in.)
London, National Gallery

no man, and is not even displaying her 'wares'. And yet there is no denying the fact that what she is doing, and indeed what she is paid for, *is* on show. But with her head turned away from the audience, and looking upwards towards the heavens, she is far from the razzle-dazzle of the circus and its sensationalist atmosphere. Like the *Fallen Jockey* (ill. 105), who is now out of the race, she seems to have been set free. He too has his arms outstretched, which might signify a Damascus-style vision, but there is nothing holy about Lala, his female counterpart. She is neither saint nor martyr. Her earthly pathos lies in the human ability to suffer – which the Christian religion made into a worthy subject for art. A concrete example of this is the two thieves, one of whom defiantly and rebelliously throws back his head. As they hang on their crosses, one feels that they too might hover, and they too might overcome their suffering. When the young Degas was studying the old masters in the Louvre, he copied Mantegna's crucifixion – although admittedly this did not contain a thief throwing his head back. But bearing in mind Degas's prolific memory for forms, it is conceivable that with alterations of his own, he was projecting his memory of Mantegna's crucifixion onto his depiction of Mlle Lala.

171
Three Prostitutes on a Sofa
c. 1879
Pastel over monotype
in grey on paper
16 x 21.5 cm (6 1/4 x 8 1/2 in.)
Amsterdam, Rijksmuseum,
Rijksprentenkabinet

In 1858, he also copied Giovanni Bellini's *Sacred Allegory* in the Uffizi (ill. 82). As with his *Place de la Concorde*, the observer is left puzzled, because something is happening here, and yet at the same time nothing is happening. Lala's connection with Bellini's painting is different, though. Among the characters in the *Allegory* who once figured in a *sacra conversazione*, or are about to do so, is a St Sebastian who, with an arrow in his breast, is calmly strolling across the stage. This walking monument appears to have shaken off his martyr's death – the vulnerable proving to be invulnerable. Lala is in a similarly ambivalent situation: she does not seem to feel the strain on her body, as her self-control triumphs over the challenge which she has imposed on herself. But the role which the public expects her to play cannot make up for the danger to which her body is exposed.

In this respect, Lala is more like the weightless dancers, of whom we noted that their flight implied the possibility of a fall. But what was merely hinted at *in effigie* with the ballet stars – a simple fall – in the circus arena becomes a mortal risk. To the degree in which Lala diverges from the passive role of the woman in the shop window, she transcends the classic theme of

exhibition and transforms it into a kind of apotheosis. The test of her strength and courage has nothing to do with the dancer's bravura or the routine availability of the café singers. Her solo performance stands outside all aesthetic conventions, as an *acte pur*, but at the same time as the iconic compression of a transient event. Degas's concept here reaches into the dimension of meaning that Baudelaire was referring to when he wished for a painter who would 'extract the epic side from the present moment... It is society's outsiders who most clearly demonstrate these sides: street entertainers, dandys, prostitutes and criminals.'

Perhaps at the back of Degas's mind was a parable, comparable to Daumier's *Man on a Rope* (c. 1860, Boston, Museum of Fine Arts), in which the artist – according to Klaus Herding's interpretation – makes painting his theme. For him, the man in the air is the epitome of 'nomadism', and he places him among the street entertainers. Such people 'know no security; they act in an intermediate zone without support, and they move from one place to another; they are constantly taking risks. Daumier's art lies in making this risk a subject of *art*, and elevating it to a reflection on painting.'

Degas, however, treats painting in a different way. It seems to me that with Lala he has created an image of the desire for form, by which he himself was possessed and driven – that concentration, raised to the point of obsession, which is determined to tread its own path. He had the courage of single-mindedness, of omission, and of 'unlearning'. The lone-wolf side of Degas is reflected in Lala's resolute isolation as she performs her *acte pur*. With this self-determination, even though she hangs by a single thread, Lala has nothing in common with a marionnette like the one slumped at the feet of the painter in the Museu Calouste Gulbenkian (ill. 74), who has no will of her own, seems more dead than alive, has been sucked dry and discarded – as a woman and as a mannequin, an image for the *dramma della pittura*.

172
Jean-Auguste-Dominique Ingres
(*1780–1867*)
The Turkish Bath
1862
Oil on canvas on wood
Diameter: 108 cm (42 1/2 in.)
Paris, Musée du Louvre

If we consider the whole of Degas's oeuvre, Lala represents a change of direction. Hitherto, his women had always borne the stamp of men's lust; they were the trademarked product of male fantasy, duty bound to provide sexual services. Lala proclaims liberation from this dependence, a self-containment which he extended in a number of variations to women bathing, combing their hair and performing other acts of personal hygiene. His eye had now alighted on the body attending to itself. (See Chapter 11.)

Lala transcends showmanship, because she seems to be taking no notice of the gaping crowd down below. This gives her verticality an almost aristocratic air. In direct contrast to this isolation are the anonymous crowds (horizontal) of women in the brothels. Relegated to the lowest level of the sexual show (total surrender), they embody the prostitute, in whom the

173
**The Brothel-Keeper's
Name-Day**
1876–77
Pastel on paper
27 x 30 cm (10 5/8 x 11 3/4 in.)
Paris, Musée National Picasso

174
Waiting
Monotype
1879
21.6 x 16.4 cm (8 3/4 x 6 5/8 in.)
Paris, Musée National Picasso

product of men's imagination has turned to waste. This aspect becomes clear from the bodies which Degas observed on his visits to the *maisons closes*. More than forty monotypes bear witness to his research. What initially seems like a series of snapshots is the work of a highly imaginative eyewitness, for whom the data supplied by perception were merely the raw material for his inventions, though he executed these with all the spontaneity of a sketch done on the spot. Each episode seems totally authentic, apparently following the dull routine of the prostitute, whereas in fact what we are looking at are distillations that condense the long day into the briefest of vulgar aphorisms. Here too, Degas practises the art of omission, of 'unlearning'. The painter, who learned how to draw from Ingres, who devised oblique perspectives and sophisticated interlocking rooms and a syntax of sharply pointed succinctness, here uses a diction that seems to verge on the slipshod. And it corresponds perfectly to the cynical jargon of the prostitutes. The shabby waiting rooms, with their mirrored walls, do not inspire him to variations on a screen, for all that he is interested in are the naked or half-naked items for sale. Under his brush, the worn-out bodies of the whores become boneless inflated balloons to be grasped, used, and discarded. Apathy has killed off the animal instinct that normally lies in wait for the male prey. But the customers paying for these bloated bodies are also like emotionless puppets. Surrounded by the

swirling tide of naked flesh, the men too have lost the fire of lust. As if without a will of their own, they follow the outstretched hand that summons them to the place of execution – caricatures of male clumsiness.

When they are not subjecting themselves to the service of their clients, the 'inmates' play childish games: they sprawl on the divans and carpets (ill. 175), or guilelessly spread their legs and stretch (ill. 174) – like young animals in a zoo. When they celebrate the brothel-keeper's name day (ill. 173), there is no life in their expressionless eyes or warmth in their gestures of congratulation, so that if anything the effect is one of unintentional, parodic comedy. We

175
In the Salon
1879
Monotype
16.4 x 21.5 cm (6 5/8 x 8 3/4 in.)
Paris, Musée National Picasso

rarely come across a face that could be a portrait. Just once, in *Three Prostitutes on a Sofa* (ill. 171), there is an expression in which deadened passivity gives way to human feeling. The woman in the centre, though staring, is fully alert, whereas one of her neighbours simply takes things as they come, and the other is looking down in resignation. The exposed upper bodies merge into a mass of blubbery flesh.

The brothel monotypes date from the second half of the 1870s. Perhaps some of the less shocking prints were among those that Degas exhibited in 1877 at the third Impressionist show – incidentally, another justifiable reason for some critics to question the extent to which his art is Impressionist. Once more, he takes up the position of the neutral observer, and refuses to indulge in dark metaphors – such as Baudelaire's: 'Like pensive cattle stretched out on the sands' – in order to endow these 'damned women' with significance. But he also avoids the downbeat emotions of alienation, for which in that same period he found a metaphor in *Absinthe* (ill. 160) that was to remain unsurpassed. There is no sign either of the social criticism inherent in the novels of Joris-Karl Huysmans (*Marthe, Histoire d'une fille*, 1876), Edmond de Goncourt (*La fille Elisa*, 1877), and Zola (*Nana*, 1880), which at the time were both disturbing and secretly fascinating to the bourgeois reading public. Degas does not depict the highs and lows, or the dark psychological depths of the whore's life; all we see is the stultifying emptiness, the monotony that paralyses this world apart and all its inhabitants. To this collective waiting room, Godot never comes.

Degas set out to depict what Gautier termed '*la verité vraie*', or in other words, to call a spade a spade. The literary gallant's 'grotto of love', or Courbet's primeval *Origin of the World* (ill. 227), was for him a tuft of dark hair between a woman's legs. When he sets a naked woman in front of a giant mirror in which we can also vaguely see the back of a client (ill. 177) – before or after? – he is parodying Manet's *Olympia*; for the confrontation with the observer sought by this street-girl he substitutes a sideways glance that betrays the lack of interest of someone completely detached from her own job. Her obvious disdain for her work is a feature that distinguishes Degas's prostitutes from those of his Parisian contemporaries. But his approach is not only a satire on the myth in which his colleagues cloaked prostitution; his irony also protects the girls against the role of the outcast which, in order to arouse the social sympathy of the bourgeois art-loving public, painters liked to represent as a model of misery personified.

Degas's own insights into the world of the brothel were soberly objective. Without burdening himself with theories of social criticism or with visions of utopia, he simply used these 'good-time girls' to point out one of the contradictions of bourgeois-capitalist society. Excluded from the disciplined world of industrial production, which cynically exploited people's 'right to work', the girls are living caricatures of the *Right To Be Lazy*, as Paul Lafargue (a son-in-law of Karl Marx) proclaimed in a treatise of 1883. His argument took a global stance: 'When once we begin to consume European products at home instead of sending them to the devil, it will be necessary that the sailors, dock handlers and the draymen sit down and learn to twirl their thumbs. The happy Polynesians may then practise "free love" as they like without fearing the civilized Venus and the sermons of European moralists.' We do not know whether Gauguin heard this siren call of anti-civilization when in 1891 he turned away from the 'civilized Venus' and fled to the South Seas, only to fall into the hands of those self-same preachers.

Degas depicted the Parisian brothels as paradoxical places where heteronomy was in conflict with self-determination. In his caricatures of Lafargue's utopia, the girls do indeed enjoy the right to be idle, but their bodies must always be available for exploitation. Their existence has two sides: they vegetate heteronomously, but they do not have to serve any illusory codes of beauty, decency or decorum. Degas, for whom the academic code of beauty was a mere cliché, grants them the right to be ugly, which does not entail any exaggerated expressiveness, as would be the case later with the Expressionists, but is purely and simply a matter of physical or physiognomical defects, a violation of the norm. The ugliness of the commonplace is also part of *la vérité vraie*.

This approach was, in my view, what underlay Degas's critical view of Ingres's *Turkish Bath* (ill. 172), which he saw in 1867, along with Courbet's lesbians (euphemistically called *Sleep*) at a private exhibition held in his house by the collector Khalil Bey, a former Turkish diplomat. The Goncourts' journal contains a devastating commentary on this event, which is all the more surprising for the fact that it lumps Ingres and Courbet together: 'At the two extremes of art we see the two popular idiots tackling the female nude. There we have two lesbians – two dirty, earth-coloured bodies knotted together in the most repulsive, most disgusting movements you can imagine arising from the lust of a woman in bed…Here, in this ancient bathhouse, a tangle of bodies like stiff mannequins, so badly proportioned as to be almost cartoon-like, a gathering of wild women from Tierra del Fuego…. Oh my God, the Venus of the Capitol. And even the female forms of Boucher.'

The objective Degas did not condemn either of the two 'idiots', but by comparison his eroticism is more sharply spiced. The entanglements of Courbet's lesbians seem involuntary and also pointless, a state for which the second title, *The Dream*, offers a convenient, euphemistic excuse. Degas sees the entwining of bodies differently – as the lustful seizure by an active body of an indifferently passive one (ill. 204). Set against Degas's coarse prose, Courbet's women are like the poetry of the boudoir.

Compared to the Ingres, Degas's *In the Salon* (ill. 175) takes away the devilry of this carefully staged show of modest and immodest flesh, this apotheosis of the right to be lazy which the admired master offered to any man who wished to peep through the keyhole. As against this calculatedly detached proximity, Degas's *Salon* offers us a collection of bodies sprawling and lounging all over the place. The one stretched out in the foreground is only partially visible, but she is the epitome of the collective sloth. She is in fact a secret hermaphrodite, because Degas himself is in her body. Where the woman's top half is missing from the picture, you will find the artist (in the position of the observer). He is looking at the scene through the eyes of the prostrate woman, as if drawing her body into his own. There is an interchange in this symbiosis: just as Degas absorbs the body of the prostitute, she also absorbs his. The observer of the monotype is thus given the chance to experience this reciprocal penetration.

With automatic professionalism, the prostrate woman has opened her legs to greet the incoming gentleman in the top hat, but he overlooks the invitation because at this precise moment he is being welcomed by the brothel-keeper. With such scenes, Degas disregards the rules of aesthetic decorum which, since antiquity, had been epitomized by the 'civilized Venus' – feminine nakedness with the sterile motionlessness of an idol. Next to the ornamental availability of Ingres's lifeless dolls, the anarchy that reigns in Degas's 'harem' is that of a ghetto of uninhibited, self-determined, utterly prosaic whores. The artist uses the slouching, lounging shapelessness of these bodies as a paradigm sharpened into a protest against Ingres's 'civilized Venus'. But this amorphous freedom is only granted to the idling women so long as they are waiting for a client. Once they have been chosen, they must use all the tried and trusted tricks of their trade to satisfy the male craving for illusion, As an artist, Degas had no interest in this form of prostitution, and only once do we see a whore satisfying a passive male customer. He does, however, depict a lesbian embrace, which brings together an indifferent partner and an active one whose features look distinctly masculine (ill. 204).

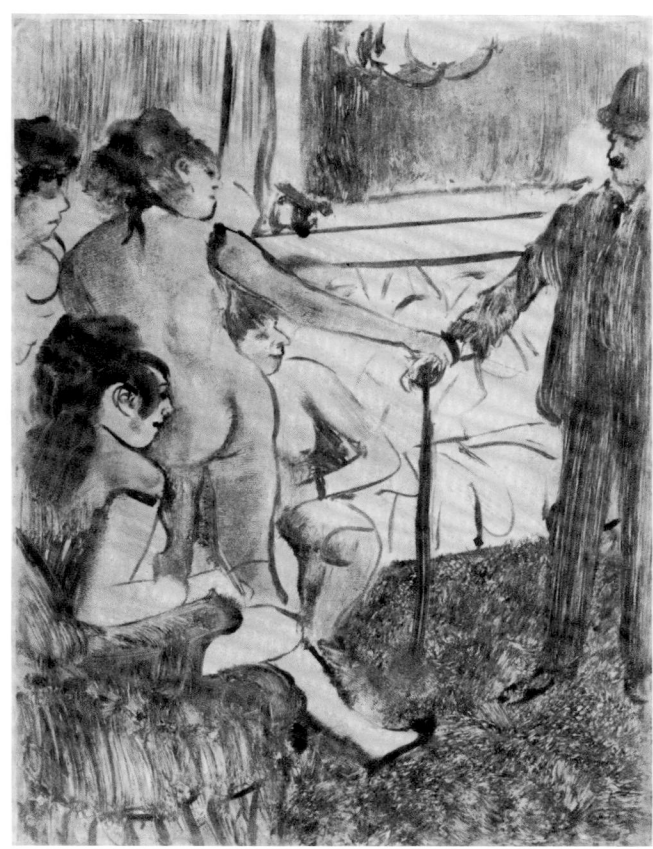 

Chapter 11

The Body
Attending to Itself

'...it is said that they are obscene! Oh, if ever works were not,
if ever works were, without tricks or clever tactics, fully and definitively chaste,
it is these! They even glorify the disdain for the flesh, as no artist since
the Middle Ages has dared to do!' – Joris-Karl Huysmans, 1889

When civilized man uses his leisure to go out into nature, he takes his rituals and his disguises with him. He remains the 'artificial man', though admittedly in a somewhat vulnerable state that may affect his self-confidence. Hence the contretemps hidden in the scenes of the seaside (ill. 181). The man, lady and dog in the background are obviously new to this resort. The group on the left seem to be shivering in their bathing costumes and are about to leave for a more congenial environment. These are all marginal figures, but they help the main scene in the foreground to unfold its own gentle tale. A young girl has just finished bathing; her swimming costume is drying in the sand, crudely spread out like the mannequin at the feet of the painter Henri Michel-Lévy (ill. 74). The child has already donned the trappings of civilization again. Her expression is something between apathy and tiredness. A parasol is protecting her from the sea breeze, and she is lying in the care of the maid, who is carefully combing the hair of her young charge. This nanny, quite a powerfully built young woman, is the only person on the beach who is not taking it easy. For her, life on the beach is the same as life in the city.

All his life, Degas was so fascinated by the smooth texture of women's hair that he remembered certain shades and consistencies – sleekness, lightness, wiriness – and called them to mind when he was painting. He shared this obsession with the Pre-Raphaelites, and also with Courbet, who framed the features of his friend Jo in a shining sea of colour. Above all, though, it was Baudelaire who, in *La Chevelure* (from *Les Fleurs du Mal*, XXIII) allowed himself to be seduced by the hair-filled dreams of exotic worlds. Degas, however, did not suffuse women's hair with romantic longings; he simply left it to flow freely, as a metaphor for woman in her

178
Woman Having Her Hair Combed
c. 1886–88
Pastel on paper
74 x 60.6 cm (29 1/8 x 23 7/8 in.)
New York, The Metropolitan Museum of Art

uninhibited naturalness. It may be that these were the thoughts in his mind when he was painting his *Beach Scene*, and they may have also been his inspiration when he painted three women combing their hair, all of them being the same model (ill. 180). The figures, dressed in their chemises, form a triad that creates a continuous sequence out of the disparate studies, almost like a film. In short, this is a scene in three phases which we can observe from left to right or vice versa. It is conceivable that with this 'triptych' Degas was actually going against the modern grain, and was reverting to the classical tradition of portrait painting, or to be more precise, to those portraits which on *one* canvas showed a head from the front, with two profiles. These would also give sculptors additional information. Such speculations, however, are of minor importance when we consider the formal compression and intensity with which Degas endowed these three phases in the private life of a young woman. Concerned only with herself, she radiates a spontaneity which is certainly not based on any classical model, but

179
Peasant Girls Bathing in the Sea
1875–76
Oil on canvas
65 x 81 cm (25 5/8 x 31 7/8 in.)
New York, Private collection

which nevertheless captures the spirit of antiquity in its earthy, independent naturalness. Her gentle, pleasurable movements are so slow that she seems to be almost motionless.

Only rarely did Degas seek out the natural person (in the form of a woman) where the city-dweller believed herself to be at her most natural, i.e. in the country. One example of such an excursion is that of *Peasant Girls Bathing in the Sea* (ill. 179). Only two of the girls are taking part in the lively dance, as the third has gone off on her own. Behind her we can see three more companions, who are doing what all Degas's bathers do, showing their nakedness or getting ready to do so. One is sitting stripped to the waist and meditating alone, one is in the process of taking off (or perhaps putting on) her blouse, and the third is naked and seeing to her hair. Their quiet seclusion contrasts with the animated dance in the foreground. These

180
Women Combing Their Hair
1875–76
Oil on canvas
31 x 45 cm (12 1/4 x 17 3/4 in.)
Washington DC, Phillips Collection

Previous pages:
181
Beach Scene
1869–70
Oil on paper
47.5 x 82.9 cm
(18 3/4 x 31 5/8 in.)
London, National Gallery

creatures do not know about the cult of hair care, and their tanned naturalness creates the same harmony of veiling and unveiling that we saw in the woman combing her hair in triplicate. This is why the composition – a constant source of surprise for those seeking to interpret it – is something unique in Degas's work. Years before Gauguin, he seems just for a moment to have stumbled across another Eden. But of course it meant sacrificing the tensions that were inherent in all his ambivalent pictorial thinking. Normally, he could not stand natural flowers, which is why he had the artificial flowers of the milliners burst into bloom, and so the naked woman in paradisiac surroundings ultimately could not provide an erotic stimulus to his sharp perception, because the dingy scenery of the urban interior was missing; it was in such surroundings that in future years his women at their toilet would restore the worn-out but still elemental nakedness that was the hallmark of Degas's women.

Count Harry Kessler quotes in his diary something that was said in June 1907, during supper at the home of Ambroise Vollard. It confirms the supposition that exposed, naked flesh provided Degas with neither sexual nor artistic inspiration. He had walked out of a naked dance at the Cercle Hoche in disgust: 'I left in order to excite myself with women who were clothed.' Not the coolly dispassionate observer, then? In everything Degas sought the unclear. Sexual excitement was assuaged when he picked up his brush or crayon. And then he would work with his model – even setting up the rudiments of a bathroom in his studio – proceeding with many variations in which the imagination would reshape the recollections of perception. Thus *in effigie* he would constantly produce new ways of depicting man's appropriation of the female body.

In all these scenes, we see the tensions of a conflict that is as old as the subject itself. When the young Dürer drew his *Women Bathing* in 1496, he gave a new, totally profane slant to the contemporary nude, showing women in nothing but their animal naturalness. He offered two different approaches to this nakedness. The six bathing women are not posing for a Paris-style judgment; they represent 'the widest possible age range, from young and pretty through composed and majestic to old and ugly.' Four of the six seem to be totally preoccupied with themselves and take no notice of the artist; only two are happy to be observed: they are looking straight at us, almost flirtatiously. Already we can see the two approaches to the subject of women attending to their bodies: one is conscious display, and the other is self-absorption, unconcerned with others who might be watching, and secretly giving pleasure only to themselves. In his brothel pictures, Degas has already opted for the second of these, which comes to full fruition in the toilet scenes. This fits in with the chastity of his own vision. Might he have known Charles Ephrussi's *Les Bains de Femmes d'Albert Durer* (Nuremberg, 1881)? Among the copies of Dürer in his 14th notebook is the head of one of the *Four Women*

of 1497 (ill. 182), and we know from George Moore that Degas felt himself to be in competition with Dürer throughout his life.

For the toilet scenes, Degas switched between different levels, ranging from sheer vulgarity to Arcadian idylls. The so-called *Baker's Wife* (ill. 183), showing a woman who has just got out of bed, shocked the public in a manner that was by no means as complimentary as George Moore's admiring quotation from Baudelaire, that it was a *'frisson nouveau'* – a new thrill. The main cause of this was the fat, fleshy hands resting vulgarly on the buttocks. In a preliminary drawing, Degas had placed them at hip level, but obviously he felt that was not provocative enough.

Not long after, there is a similar pose in a large pastel (ill. 178), but here the body is turned towards the light and is more frontal, while the woman's forefinger makes a hollow in her flesh. She is having her hair combed. For some critics, the pose suggests comparison with Rembrandt's *Bathsheba* in the Louvre, but I find this unconvincing. The voluptuous body of the lady who has caught King David's eye is framed by both arms, but she is not holding her

183
The Baker's Wife
c. 1885
Pastel
67 x 52.1 cm (26 3/8 x 20 1/2 in.)
New York, The Henry and Rose
Pearlman Foundation

own flesh, and furthermore her pensiveness – related to the letter she has just received from David – has no equivalent in Degas.

The Rembrandt–Degas comparison does, however, possess a broader base, because they both had concepts of beauty that were in conflict with contemporary norms. Bathsheba and Degas's bathers have the beauty of *la vérité vraie*. As the Dutch poet Adries Pels wrote in 1681, in a poetic treatise: Rembrandt does not take 'a Greek Venus as his model, but a washerwoman...; he paints sagging breasts, shapeless hands, and even the weals made by the bodice and by the garters on the legs have to be made visible if Nature is to be given full rein. This is *his* Nature. It knows no rules or proportions of the human body.'

As the 'rules' of good taste abhorred this new, uncompromising view which Degas also espoused, a body like that of the *Baker's Wife* inevitably caused outrage. If her bulging flesh showed every sign of sexual exploitation and exhaustion, she could have been a prostitute in a hotel room. For Degas, the boundaries between milieux were interchangeable. The critic Felix Fénéon used the disparaging term '*maritorne*', the name given in *Don Quixote* to a repulsively filthy servant girl. But does all this really apply to the *Baker's Wife*? Her attitude, which is not meant to be seen by anyone else, is that of someone who has just got up and is trying to bring life back into her limbs and to ensure that everything is working properly. She is not posing (which does not exclude the possibility that Degas got a model to pose), but is behaving spontaneously and instinctively, just like the *Little Dancer Aged Fourteen* (ill. 143), although with the latter there was also the resolve to take her first bold step in public, which would have been less effective if she had allowed her arms to rise from her body. That is why Degas has her place her arms behind her back. But later in life, when the child's body is all used up and run to fat, maybe her hands like those of the baker's wife will also land on her buttocks. This weighty, coarse physicality was to undergo another alteration, in Maillol's *Action in Chains* (1905). In 1925, in his *Ile-de-France*, Maillol also referred back to the *Little Dancer*.

The claim that the *Baker's Wife* reveals a woman in control of her own life requires further consideration. It is only true in so far as this nude does present an example of a woman totally preoccupied with herself in a completely private situation. However, implicit in this picture is the presence of a man – the artist himself. Her posture, slimmed down, was obviously a familiar one to Degas, because we see it in an etched portrait that his friend Desboutin made of him in 1876 (ill. 184). With his chest thrust out, he is looking around, with his hands placed so firmly on his hips that the latter take on a feminine curve. But could we imagine this gentleman in a state of undress, forming a counterpart to the *Baker's Wife*? Scarcely. His posture has nothing unrestrained or natural

184
Marcellin Desboutin
(1823–1902)
Degas, Standing
1876
Drypoint
Paris, Bibliothèque Nationale

185
The Tub
1886
Pastel
60 x 83 cm
(23 5/8 x 32 5/8 in.)
Paris, Musée du Louvre

about it. This suggests that the woman owes her naturalness to the wishful thinking of the man who has put her in the role – as a product of his fantasy and as a secret image of himself. This is his way of compensating for what he sees as a deficiency in himself – his relationship, thwarted by self-consciousness, with Nature and with what Nature means as a metaphor: the inexhaustible abundance of life. Degas comes closest to this dream as the detached observer that Desboutin saw in him. And so it would be wrong to construct any congenital contrast between man and woman, because ultimately we are talking here about modes of behaviour which the process of civilization imposes on *both* sexes. Women are, however, particularly caught up in

this context. We have seen them appearing in the showplaces of artificiality, forced to satisfy men's desires. We have also seen them wanting to be rid of this role and to return to paradisiac naturalness, but here too they serve to fulfil the fantasies of men. This is apparent from the various scenes discussed in this chapter, where – under strict guidance from Degas – women relate to their own bodies as if they were alone. I shall not present my case chronologically but following an imaginary thread through the many variations on the theme of women at their toilet, which leads from the narrow confines of the city into the questionably 'idyllic' freedom of Nature.

186
The Tub
1886
Pastel
70 x 70 cm
(27 1/2 x 27 1/2 in.)
Farmington, CT,
Hill-Stead Museum

Degas begins the gestural monologues of his women in modest rooms. A bather who can only just fit her body into the shallow tub has to adapt her movements to the circumstances. She illustrates the constrictions people have to face when they cannot afford anything better. But these poor surroundings also have a symbolic dimension. The oval tub is in the shape of an egg, from which comes life. And so the female body that has inserted itself into this 'egg' has something embryonic about it.

Seen from above, the narrow room is very compressed (ill. 185). A small section shows a woman in a portable tub that has obviously been put in a gap because otherwise she would not be so close to the dressing table, which divides the room vertically and considerably restricts her freedom of movement. This room, possibly a servant's room, is the very converse of liberty. In the other pastel (ill. 186) the woman seen from above seems to be falling. The verticality of the thin body could not be more bent and the movements more fragile. There seems almost to be a crack in her pelvis, as if it were broken. The roundness of the tub again forms an oval which keeps out the disorder of the room and holds her in vulnerable isolation.

The sharp downward bend has a history that begins with a *Pathosformel* of emotion (to use Warburg's term) developed in the late Middle Ages in relation to the Last Judgment. In paintings by Jan van Eyck, Stefan Lochner, Rogier van der Weyden and Hans Memling, the faithlessness of the damned ends with their plunge into the jaws of hell. The medieval imagination saw them as being beyond hope of salvation and consequently in a quasi-secular no-man's-land. Their disobedience is depicted by the painters through vivid gestures of despair and of rebellion – innovations that are kept away from the Chosen Few. For example, in Rogier van der Weyden's *Last Judgment* in Beaune (ill. 188), there is the singular figure of a condemned woman whose hair, which a condemned man has reached up to grasp, could not have been more luxuriantly painted by Degas himself. He reinvents this exposed, defenceless nakedness in his *Woman Bathing* (Hill-Stead Museum, Farmington).

Rogier's condemned women inspired Panofsky to make a comment that is highly relevant to our context: 'Natural feeling attaches a positive significance to height, and a negative one to lowness.' This applies as much to those who have been damned by the Lord as to those who have failed in the social struggle for life which preoccupied the artists and writers of the 19th century. In their works, they reversed the traditional order: the low were revalued and, as *la vérité vraie*, were set above the so-called high. The capitalist meritocracy, however, ignored the revaluation of the marginal people proclaimed by Champfleury, Flaubert, Zola, Courbet and others. It banished the 'low' to those areas that in earlier times were associated with hell and purgatory. In secularized bourgeois society, the metaphysical punishment inflicted by the Last Judgment was replaced by social discrimination in the here and now. Some of Degas's bathers are a reference to this situation.

Even in the petty bourgeoisie, lack of space can be a problem. This is vividly illustrated by an etching from the late 1870s, *Leaving the Bath* (ill. 187). A lady whose voluminous body rivals that of the *Baker's Wife* is climbing out of a narrow tub which must have had difficulty accommodating her ample frame. Once again, Degas plays the game of 'rooms become screens'. The room, unclear in perspective, is a kind of salon which serves as a temporary bathroom. It is full of bits and pieces that crowd in on the naked woman from all sides. In the foreground is the back of an armchair, which leads to the patterned carpet; on the right is a

188
Rogier van der Weyden
(*1399/1400–64*)
Female figure from
'The Last Judgment' (*detail*)
between 1443–51
Oil on wood panel
Beaune, Hôtel-Dieu

Opposite:
189
Woman with a Towel
c. 1895–98
Pastel
70 x 70 cm (27 5/8 x 27 5/8 in.)
Paris, Musée du Louvre

Left:
190
Woman with a Towel
1894
Pastel on paper
95.9 x 76.2 cm (37 3/4 x 30 in.)
New York, The Metropolitan
Museum of Art

covered table with a gigantic vase of flowers, and behind that (against the back wall) a sofa; next comes the huge towel held up by the maid, standing on we know not what, the frame of a mirror or picture, a door, and finally the bath. All of this is massed round the two women like a stage set, enclosing them in a claustrophobically narrow space from which there seems to be no escape.

This etching, however, is an exception. Its descriptive detail goes back to the genre painting style of the early toilet scenes, where for instance *The Pedicure* (1873) was depicted with clinical precision. In the etching, the precision gives way to brutal mockery. He must have felt this himself, since he once remarked self-critically: 'Perhaps I saw woman too much as an animal.' This self-reproach ignores the fact that, like a professional cartoonist, Degas set out to unmask hidden truths. Such an approach inevitably gives precedence to living ugliness over the hollow clichés that represent established norms of beauty. There is an aesthetic dimension to this, contained in the cynical pronouncement of the witches in *Macbeth*, that 'fair is foul, foul is fair', anticipating the '*harmonie des contraires*' [harmony of contrasts] advocated by Victor Hugo in the preface to *Cromwell* (1827). As a charitable Christian gazing on ugliness, Van Gogh wrote to his brother about a ball in Antwerp in December 1885: 'There were some very beautiful girls there, and the most beautiful of them all was ugly.' The woman – probably 'an innkeeper's wife' – had an ugly, irregular face, 'but full of life and charm, in the style of Frans Hals'.

Degas, like Van Gogh, was anything but a misogynist, but he had the love of distortion natural to a (perhaps frustrated) caricaturist. Van Gogh had a similar bent which sent him, as it did Degas, in search of models who were potentially already prone to distortion. Degas exaggerates the body rather than the face. Baudelaire applied a comment of Diderot's to Daumier which could also be applied to Degas: 'As the nose, so the forehead, so the eye, so the foot, so the hand…' Degas inverted this observation: to him the face is like the body. The body of the woman climbing out of the bath has been distorted into a bulging sack, and although the head is turned away from us, we can guess that her face will probably match the rest of this nude mountain of flesh.

The refusal to be reined back by good taste is also evident with the women who go about their ablutions with natural grace. Here getting out of the bath entails a kind of metamorphosis, as in the large pastel in the Phillips Collection (ill. 191). If the crowded room in the etching was a factor in the feeling of constriction, here the room suggests the opposite. This appears quite natural, and it is only when we look more closely that we can see the subtlety of the composition, which lies in the interconnected curves and axes. These are arranged in such a way that the centre of the body – the vagina, which is turned away from the observer – is

191
Woman Getting Out of the Bath
1895–98
Pastel
77 x 84 cm (30 1/4 x 33 1/8 in.)
Washington DC, Phillips Collection

192

After the Bath
(Woman Drying Herself)
c. 1896
Pastel on paper
89.5 x 116.8 cm (35 1/4 x 46 in.)
Philadelphia Museum of Art

precisely in the centre of the almost square picture. The cloths, drapes and articles of clothing, and also the soft armchair in the foreground, surround the naked body like an open calyx. The sheer materiality of the tumbling confusion of colour not only sur-rounds the body but also gives it an aura of profanity.

In *Woman with a Towel* (ill. 190), the calyx metaphor is easier to discern. The technical devices that Degas uses here aim to create a symbiosis between the action of the picture and its formal equivalent. The woman wants to go from wet to dry, but instead of repro-ducing the traces of moisture still clinging to the body, Degas takes a wet brush and vigor-ously smudges the right-hand side of the bath towel. He uses a sponge or rag to work on the other side. By employing his own tools to participate in the woman's toilet, and by making them an element of the process of composition, Degas is physically taking care of her body. No misogynist would have allowed himself to enter into such a dialogue, and it is one that he continues with all the women that are drying themselves.

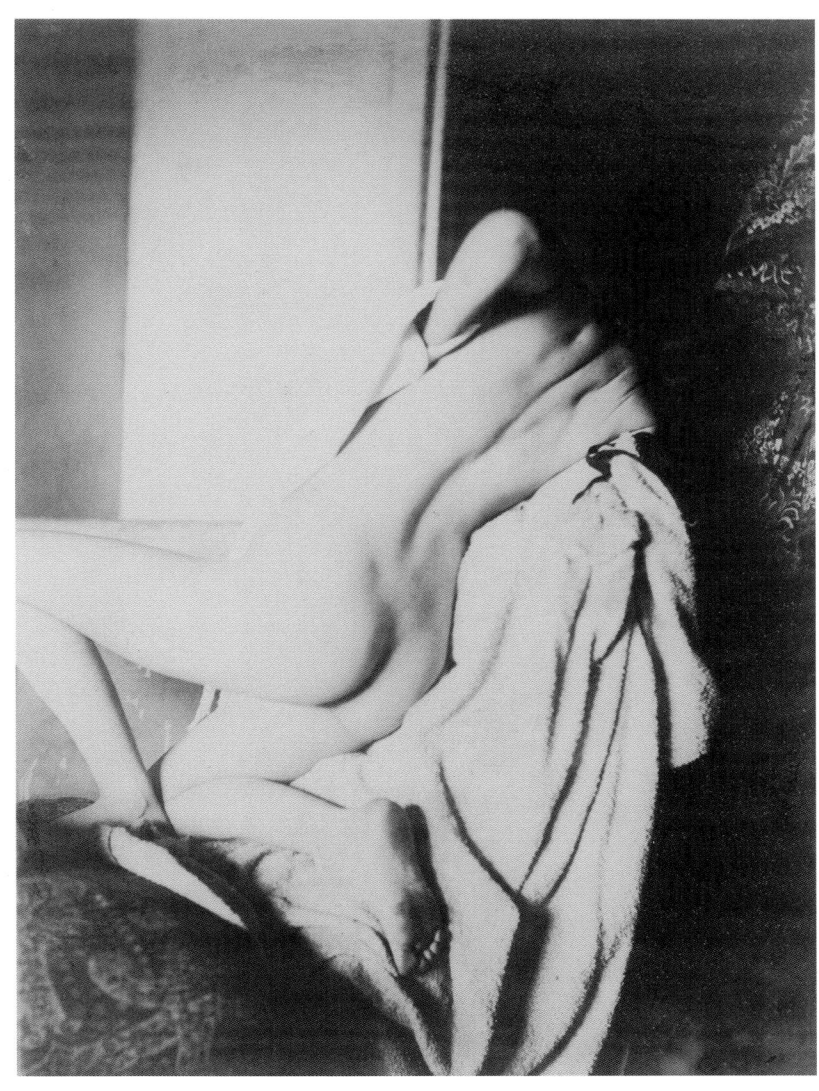

193
**After the Bath
(Woman Drying Her Back)**
*c. 1895
Photograph
Los Angeles,
The J. Paul Getty Museum*

The care that they are taking corresponds to the care that he also takes, as their partner in this intimate act.

In the 1890s, the last decade in which the now almost blind Degas was able to use the pastel crayon with a degree of confidence, he varied his approach. In one picture (ill. 192), his manipulative will bends the model into a tormented deformation that suggests serious injury. One is reminded of the *Scene of War in the Middle Ages* (ill. 12), which was still in his studio at the time, but perhaps he also knew Caravaggio's *Mary Magdalene in Ecstasy*. A photograph which Degas took himself (ill. 193) confirms his predilection for imposing form. The naked woman, pressed into her bath towel, has to submit to several contortions. Her upper body is tilted so far backwards that her head goes out of the lighted area and so appears to have been cut off. Also her legs are trying in vain to help her restore her balance. Helplessly, they are pulled into the eccentric distortions that deform the whole body. Several large-format pastels followed on from this mock execution. The one in Philadelphia (ill. 192) enhances and sublimates the deformation in the photograph. The soaring buttocks lead straight through to the arms, having missed out the shoulders altogether, and the distorted head is reminiscent of *Mlle Lala* (ill. 168), but also of Rembrandt's *Sacrifice of Isaac* in St Petersburg. But thanks to the orchestration of the colours, the overall effect is less overpowering than in the black and white photograph. Nevertheless, there is something like a levitation even in this Mannerist concept. Although the contorted limbs have lost their naturalness, the extraordinary artificiality of the whole construction not only diverts the observer's attention away from the torture inflicted on the model, but also suggests that the physical burden has somehow been overcome thanks to an arabesque that gives the limbs unexpected room to move in.

The relation of the body to its surroundings contributes to this impression. The bather's position within the composition is as out of kilter as the body itself. The latter is over on the right of the central axis, though not completely off-centre, and it has a life of its own that is as detached from the bath tub as it is from the prosaic act of drying. The movement away from the centre is countered by a warm red that permeates the whole picture and integrates everything within it. Thus the jarring dissonance of the composition is balanced by the overall coherence of its component parts. One may even have the impression that the woman and her towels are freeing themselves from the floor and floating weightlessly upwards. And so the initial idea that the body is about to fall turns into the exact opposite – a desire to rise, and to overcome the material constraints and their weight. Once again, Degas's pictorial language leads a double life.

The partnership between painter and model, which is basically one of master and servant, is joined by a third party in the form of the maid combing her mistress's hair (ill. 194). Unlike the milliners, trying on finished hats for their customers, the women with brush and comb are confronted with material that has yet to take shape. Even if their hands touch nothing but the hair, they will be responsible for the whole design. The body will change its tangible essence according to the shape of its crown of hair, and what was flesh and bone then becomes a substance of soft fluidity. This is clear if we follow the process in the other direction, and see the fluidity of the hair moving into the body and seeming to soften it. Between the hair and the dress, with their merging red, the gently yielding head suggests a kind of self-abandon which – with reference to the myth of Danaë – one might describe as readiness to conceive. Will all these natural locks give way to the stylized artificiality we call *coiffure*? We can probably answer

in the negative, for it is the free-flowing hair that Degas saw as liberation from the constrictions of civilization.

Sometimes the situation becomes almost excessive. In a pastel of 1894 (Tate Gallery), the woman doing the combing turns into a fragmented maidservant who is bringing a cup of tea. The hair is wild, and the room is equally unruly – a table with a huge vase, and an amorphous pile of things at the back on the left. The intimate naturalness of the scene is due to the painter's staging of this confusion, which has all the spontaneity of *la vérité vraie*. It was this particular painting that was used to illustrate Walter Sickert's recollections of his friend,

194
La Coiffure
(Combing the Hair)
c. 1896
Oil on canvas
114.3 x 146.7 cm
(45 x 57 3/4 in.)
London, National Gallery

which were published in 1917, shortly after Degas's death, in what was then the most highly regarded arts journal in England, the *Burlington Magazine*.

In the 1890s, though, at the same time as he was painting the above-mentioned pastel, Degas was also abandoning this confusing opulence and inventing his own version of the Arcadian idyll, in which naked women are alone together in the midst of Nature (ills. 195, 196, 198). But this Nature is barren and bare. Unlike his friend Renoir, who set his trio of *Bathers* (1887, Philadelphia) amid luxuriant vegetation, Degas dispensed with all the trappings of the countryside. He also deprived his women of their conventional requisites: they are 'bathers' in the dry – creatures of the studio joined together in a space with the merest hint of a landscape, devoid

195
The Bathers
1890–95
Pastel
Private collection

of plants and trees and – thanks to the view from above – even the horizon. There is no paradise in these pictures. Demonstrating the abstinence imposed on him by his oft-proven detachment from nature, Degas stripped his idylls of all paradisiac enticements and in this respect distanced himself from Renoir, whose equation of humanity with nature poeticized the enchanting sensuality of the three bathers and offered it to the sensuality of his (male) public. Their uncomplicated existence runs parallel to that which Ingres portrayed in his mural of *The Golden Age* (1862), in which he painted 'a crowd of handsome idlers', whom he described in a letter as follows: 'The men of this generation knew nothing of old age. They were long-lived and always beautiful…They were good, just, and loved one another. They had no food other than the fruits of the earth and the water of the springs, milk and nectar.' This permanently sunlit world image was taken up again by Renoir, but Degas had no time for those vegetating in the bosom of nature. Nor did his women – always without male partners! – ever have the ambition to organize themselves into pyramids or other symmetrical compositions. And so, clinging to the poetry of their bodies is the prose of random combinations that can change at any moment. Each one sits or lies down on her own – just like the singers at the cabaret, the dancers in the rehearsal room, and the prostitutes in the brothel and in the café.

Opposite:
196
The Bathers
1885–95
Pastel and charcoal on paper
113.4 x 115.7 cm
(44 5/8 x 45 1/2 in.)
Chicago, Art Institute

197

Woman Combing Her Hair

c. 1879–85

Pencil and black ink

31.5 x 28 cm

(12 3/4 x 11 in.)

Paris, Musée du Louvre

One pastel (ill. 196) brings together a woman kneeling, a woman bending, a woman lying on her side, and a woman sitting down and putting on a stocking (her masculine physique is reminiscent of the boy with the bowl haircut in Seurat's *Bathers* of 1891). Another pastel (ill. 195) is equally heterogeneous: one woman lying on her stomach, another – headless – on her back with legs crossed, and the long legs (but nothing else) of a standing woman in extreme close-up. Only one pastel (ill. 198) has as its central focus a woman with long blonde hair that

198
The Bathers
c. 1890–95
Pastel on paper
108 x 111 cm (56 x 56 3/4 in.)
*Dallas, Museum of Art, The Wendy
and Emery Reves Collection*

covers one of her breasts, like Lady Godiva riding through the streets of Coventry. Behind this half-naked figure (and almost perched on her head) are the round buttocks of a woman bending, while in the foreground we see only the legs and thighs of a woman lying down.

In late Degas, the art of omission – which Duranty regarded as a defining feature of modern heterogeneity – takes on the brusque decisiveness of capricious old age. There is no longer any clear semblance of order, sharply divided conflict is preferred to any kind of convergence, and the unlearning or deliberate violation of the rules is carried out without scruple. The random jumble of bodies makes explicit what was only present as a twisted allusion in the prostitutes;

the right to idleness, and the anarchic right to dispose of one's own body, independently of social clashes and conventions, but in total harmony with the artist's own aspirations to freedom, which he delegates to his women. Herein lies the contact between two partners, each of whom is dependent on the other.

In the monotypes of the 1870s and 1880s, the partnerships are marked by totally unexpected relationships and discoveries, for with this technique the whole process goes in a different direction. It shifts from the imitation of empirical forms to their origin. In the history of artificial signs, Degas is here opening a new chapter.

For centuries, artists were at pains to fulfil the demands of Illusionism by capturing the whole range of the perceivable world – bodies and objects, water and clouds – accepting them as given data and trying to reproduce their formal characteristics. In the course of time, the relation between content and form became ever closer, but then gradually painters began to change their standpoint, and instead of reproducing the solid facts, they started to investigate how things changed under different atmospheric conditions. This shift of emphasis was at the heart of Impressionism, and was the *raison d'être* for a mode of painting that discovered in light and atmosphere the driving forces that truly constituted the appearance of the world as we perceive it. Thus the outside world changed from a state into a series of processes.

From that moment on, nothing was certain, and nothing could be defined by a single determinate shape. Everything took the coded form of a suggestion, with a different appearance and consistency from one minute to the next. Inevitably, this led to the flexibility of the brushwork, with solid precision and detail giving way to fleeting signs, devised to capture rapidly changing appearances without pinning them down to precise forms and outlines. Nevertheless, the principle of imitation remained intact. Only now it conformed to a new criterion: spontaneity. This is what underlies the swift dots and dashes, commas and accents of Impressionist handwriting. The repertoire of signs is a kind of shorthand which is not always easy to decipher. However, not only does it adhere to appearances, but it also aspires to recording the disparate contents of our perception more precisely – because it does so more directly – than is possible with conventional procedures of description, because these do not take into account the physiological processes of perception.

Degas did not take part in the 'unlearning' strategies of his Impressionist friends, and did not contribute to the vocabulary of their shorthand. He was concerned with a deeper level of perception – the genesis of forms created out of nothing. It was in the monotypes that he tracked down these amorphous origins, beginning with women at their toilet. The monotypes contain his revolutionary contribution to the new, elemental representation of humanity in female form, and this in turn leads to a no less innovative interpretation of the landscape.

199
Woman in a Bathtub
c. 1882–85
Monotype
36 x 27 cm (14 1/8 x 10 5/8 in.)
Paris, Musée du Louvre, Cabinet
des Dessins

200
Rembrandt van Rijn (1606–69)
Joseph and Potiphar's Wife
1634
Etching
9 x 11.5 cm (3 1/2 x 4 1/2 in.)
Munich, Staatliche Graphische
Sammlung

Opposite:
201
Sleep
c. 1885
Monotype
27.6 x 37.8 cm
(10 7/8 x 14 7/8 in.)
London, The British Museum

Both themes are interconnected, because in women as in nature Degas opens up dimensions of form and formlessness that none of his contemporaries were aware of (ills. 197, 199, 201, 203).

In the women whose bodies free themselves from the dark interiors, energies are released that seem effectively to wage the age-old war on darkness and at last to bring self-determination. But it would be going too far to suggest that religious or theological messages such as '*fiat lux*' or '*lux et tenebris*' are represented metaphorically in these episodes. Degas is not looking for any bringers of light. The bulky bodies do not throw off the darkness, but continue to bear their origins within themselves – a pregnant darkness, to be identified with the homogeneous ground laid down by the brush. After that, when Degas uses his sponges, rags, brushes and even his fingers to do the equally rapid but also equally thorough work of lightening the dark, gradually human limbs and various objects come into being: a lamp, a cushion etc. Each of these incursions into the original blackness entails a sudden appearance which can easily change into an abrupt extinction. The content arises out of the form, and for Degas's central theme – humanity in social chiaroscuro – this interrelation between light and dark brings out what the Impressionists' aphoristic, daylight-related mode of painting brought out of the colourful atmosphere of a landscape. Degas did not, however, work with the device of the spontaneous sketch, and he did not work with the exposed contours of an Ingres. His forceful linearity, like that of Daumier, always carries the potential of substance.

A bending nude, seen from the rear, has the verticality and solidity of an independent, unalterable substance. She does not come out of the darkness so much as she seems anchored *in* the darkness. A bath tub, painted with a broad brush, does not take on any tangible materiality, but its curves correspond to the curves of the bather's light-coloured back. We seek in vain for facial features: in their place are dark clots, abbreviations which we can only make out through the abundant hair. Degas takes anonymity so far that he omits not only the face but also the whole head. This is especially the case with the nudes that are lying down, and it reminds one of similar omissions in drawings by Ingres, which fill the waxwork sensuality of the women in *The Turkish Bath* with pulsating life (*Sleeping Woman*, ill. 202). Another influence frequently mentioned is Rembrandt's etching of a reclining nude (formerly known as the *Negress*), turned towards the concealing darkness just like Degas's women. Christopher White's apposite formula, 'a study in black', applies even more convincingly to Degas's monotypes. There is another of Rembrandt's etchings that has a different link to Degas (ill. 200).

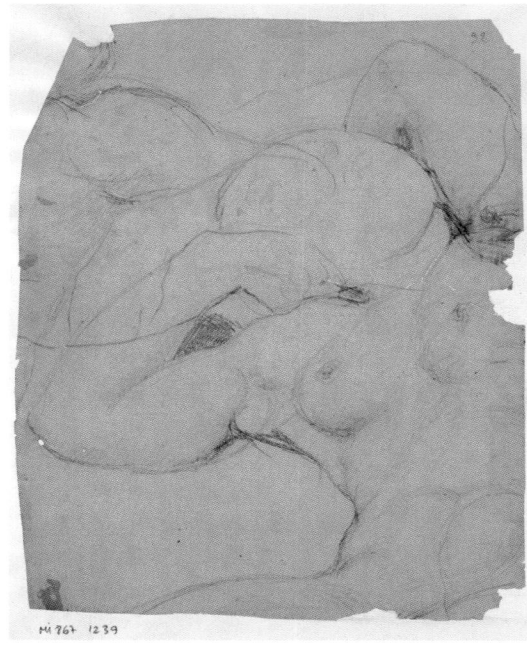

202
Jean-Auguste-Dominique Ingres
(1780–1867)
Sleeping Woman
Pencil on paper
Montauban, Musée Ingres

Potiphar's wife offers her shapelessly repulsive body to Joseph, the man she desires, and in doing so she humiliates herself, just as Degas's *Sleeping Woman*, evidently tossing and turning in the middle of a nightmare, also seems to be suffering. On this self-preoccupied body sits a discarded skull, metaphor for unresisting sexual surrender. And yet there is no sign of violence in the room. The body is nestling in a hollow that might be a bed, so that is seems to be protected by a kind of 'shell'. It is a symbol, later used by Redon for his representations of Venus, that Degas inserts into the poetry of his prose: a resting place becomes a wave of soft, intertwining limbs.

When he charges his *Woman on a Bed* (ill. 203) with erotic energy like this, with the apparent expectation of sexual intercourse, he leaves the moment of fulfilment to the imagination and contents himself simply with the overture. In the sense of an opening, this can be taken quite literally, since the open legs of the woman anticipate the embrace that is left to the observer's fantasy – perhaps from a god in the immaterial form adopted by Jupiter when he entered the beautiful Danaë's bed as a shower of gold. Perhaps this mythological interpretation of the densely conceived forms is more illuminating that the psychoanalytical equation of the lamp with a phallus.

When forms take on multiple contents and meanings, we find ourselves confronted with an inextricable tangle. In the landscape monotype, reworked with pastel, in the Krugier Collection (ill. 228), a reclining nude conceals – or possibly reveals – herself. Degas was probably working from a copy. The anatomical anomalies in this figure as listed in the Paris catalogue of 1988 build a landscape of female hills and hollows. In a nude that has become a landscape, the emphasis shifts from anthropomorphic sensuality to a pervasive, restful calm in which there is no expectation of fulfilment because fulfilment is already inherent in the calm. In this way Degas expands the theme of the body engaged with itself to encompass landscape-like bodies that have not yet been brought to life (ills. 235, 206, 226).

The landscape monotypes were the result of a journey lasting several weeks that Degas and his friend, the sculptor Paul-Albert Bartholomé, made through the region of Burgundy in autumn 1890. They hired a carriage and, as the third member of the party, a white horse which, according to their letters, was a four-legged 'character'. Degas did not work from nature, however, which is why he called these landscapes '*paysages imaginaires*'. But by this he did not mean invented, fantasy worlds; they were compressed memories, although their fleetingness fitted in with what Odilon Redon called a 'sense of mystery', containing 'images within images'. Degas also made a something of a mystery out of these landscapes among his

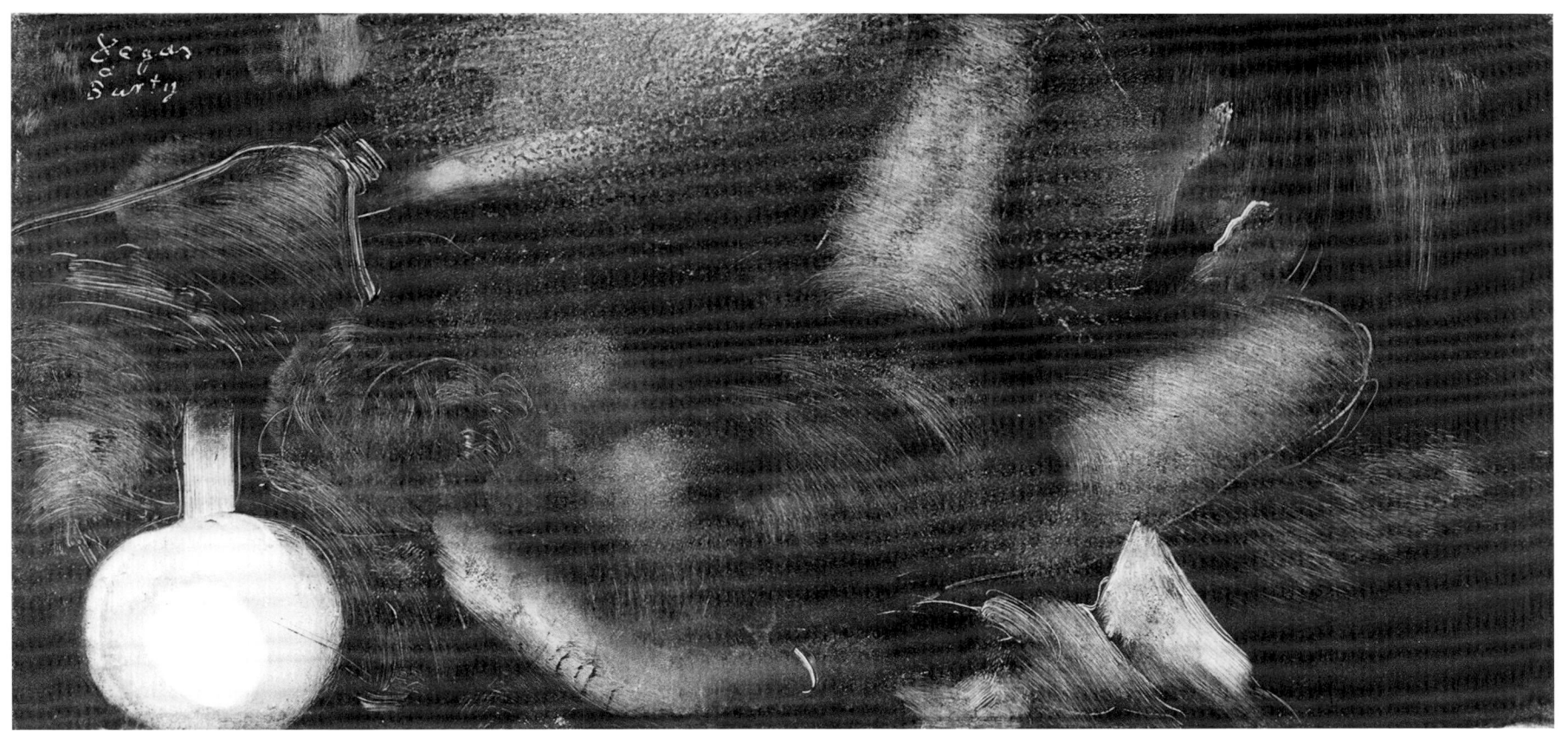

friends. During an evening meal with the Halévys, he surprised them by alluding to his current finances: 'I can pay for them. I have twenty-one landscapes.' General surprise, and Halévy wanted to know more: 'Very vague things? States of the soul?' He was thinking of Henri-Frédéric Amiel's description of landscapes as an '*état d'âme*'. Degas replied dismissively, 'States of the eye. We do not speak such a pretentious language.' He was giving himself an excuse, playing down the increasing deterioration in his eyesight, but at the same time making it responsible for the vagueness of his landscapes.

We should not ignore this understatement. When Paul Durand-Ruel exhibited these landscapes in his gallery in October 1892, the public response was poor. The prints did not fulfil expectations aroused by his dancers. Only the critic Arsène Alexandre spoke of the experience that lay behind the fleeting rhythms of the colours: '…to *find* this theme, one must have meditated a great deal in the heart of nature.' This judgment had a great deal to do with the temporal concept of slowness, which did not exist for the Impressionists because their kind of

203
Woman on a Bed
c. 1885
Monotype
20 x 41.7 cm (7 7/8 x 16 3/8 in.)
Chicago, The Art Institute

perception was satisfied with the single moment. Degas, however, based these works on the slower processes of contemplation and memory. This brought him – even if involuntarily – close to the artistic aspirations that the Symbolists advocated in their programme at around the same time.

How did this come about? In October 1892, Daniel Halévy noted that Degas was keeping himself apart, obviously wishing to isolate himself and conceal from his friends the melancholy that he had always had to struggle against. This withdrawal from society was clearly not due just to the physical problems that had set in – particularly the deterioration in his eyesight and hearing. Over and above these, at around the age of sixty he felt that he was on his own as an artist, cut off from his natural environment. It appears that this led him to compensate for his losses by defiantly risking new beginnings that would alienate him still further from his fellow artists. The circle of the Impressionists, which had always been a loose association of friends and colleagues, cliques and rivals, had finally broken up after the sixth exhibition in 1886. This last show, staged with much difficulty, presented a confused image that in itself heralded dissolution. As neither Monet nor Renoir took part in it, the nucleus was reduced to Degas and Pissarro. They were joined by newcomers such as Gauguin, Redon, and particularly Seurat, whose monumental *Grande Jatte* caused a sensation. The overall picture, then, was one of several transitions, from the first generation to new approaches and ideas. The critics did not know what to make of it. No one could come up with any sort of general analysis of events which – from a present standpoint –made the year 1886 an historical turning point. For quite apart from it being the last Impressionist exhibition (though this label was not specified in the title), spring saw the publication of Zola's latest novel *L'Oeuvre*, and in September *Figaro littéraire* published Jean Moréas's Symbolist manifesto.

Zola's novel caused consternation among the Impressionists. The tragic figure of the painter whose powers lag behind his ambitions continued the line that he had already adopted in 1880 in his criticism of Naturalism in the Salon. Although he did find words of praise to say about Degas's series of laundresses, dancers and bathers, he also found their '*vérité pleine de finesse*' [truth full of subtleties] too specialized and insular, His final verdict was devastating: 'The real disaster is the fact that not one of the artists in this group has been able to give potent and definitive expression to the formula to which they all adhere and which is scattered throughout their works. The formula is there, divided ad infinitum, but nowhere and in none of them does one find it applied by a master. They are all precursors, but the man of genius has not been born. One can see very well what they are after, and one can agree with them; but in vain do we search for the masterpiece that will set the formula and make all heads bow down. That is why the struggle of the Impressionists has not yet finished: they remain inferior to the work that they are attempting – they are stammering without being able to find the words.'

Zola's novel gives this judgment a gripping narrative development. The painter, Claude Lantier – in whom Zola's childhood friend Cézanne may well have recognized himself – fails with a multi-layered concept, a kind of *allegorie réelle* of Paris. This huge canvas is meant to encompass two groups of themes, with the Seine flowing between them: on the left is the city of work, and on the right the city of pleasure. The reference to Courbet's *Studio* is obvious, especially as Zola's Symbolist imagination devoted the centre of the painting to a municipal goddess dressed up as an idol – which also makes one think of Moreau. Claude's creative powers cannot cope with this figure, and he hangs himself. (In passing, the *femme artificielle* – the goddess – conquers the *femme naturelle* – Christine, the painter's wife.)

The fact that Degas's landscapes brought him into the Symbolist field of forms and multiple meanings, but that the Symbolists themselves did not realize this, can be taken as an illustration of how proximity and contemporaneity may be accompanied by blindness. This

205
Landscape
1892
Monotype in oils, with pastel
highlights
25.4 x 34 cm (10 x 13 3/8 in.)
New York, The Metropolitan
Museum of Art

applied to Mallarmé, who was always looking for the '*occulte*' in everything, to Gauguin, who sought to make ideas visible through forms, to Redon, who labelled the admired Degas a Realist, and to Moréas, who wanted the Symbolists to adopt an 'archetypical, complex style'. None of them noticed that Degas, the outsider, had already quietly arrived at the place where they wanted to go. Similarly, Zola failed to spot that Seurat's *Sunday Afternoon on the Island of La Grande Jatte* offered at least part of the synthesis that he believed was missing from the work of the Impressionists.

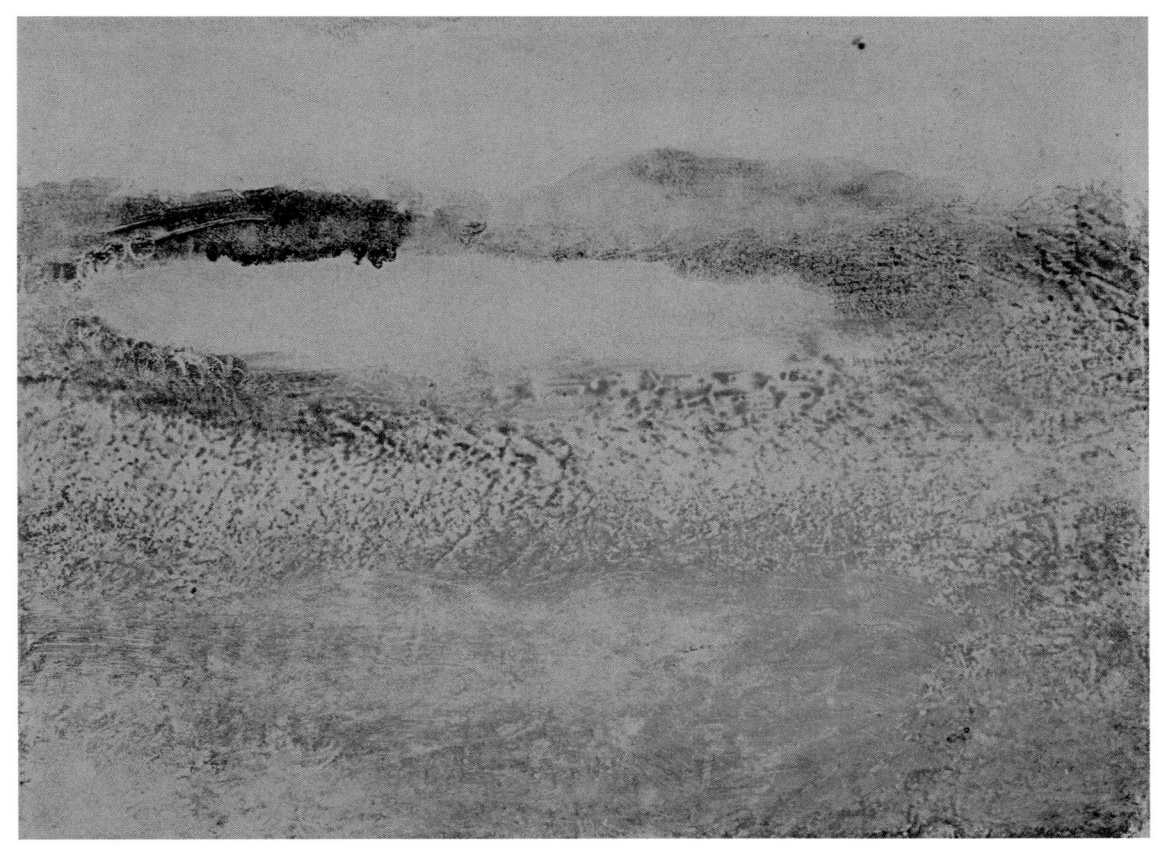

206
Lake in the Pyrenees
c. 1890
Colour monotype
29.8 x 39 cm
(11 5/8 x 15 3/8 in.)
London, The British Museum

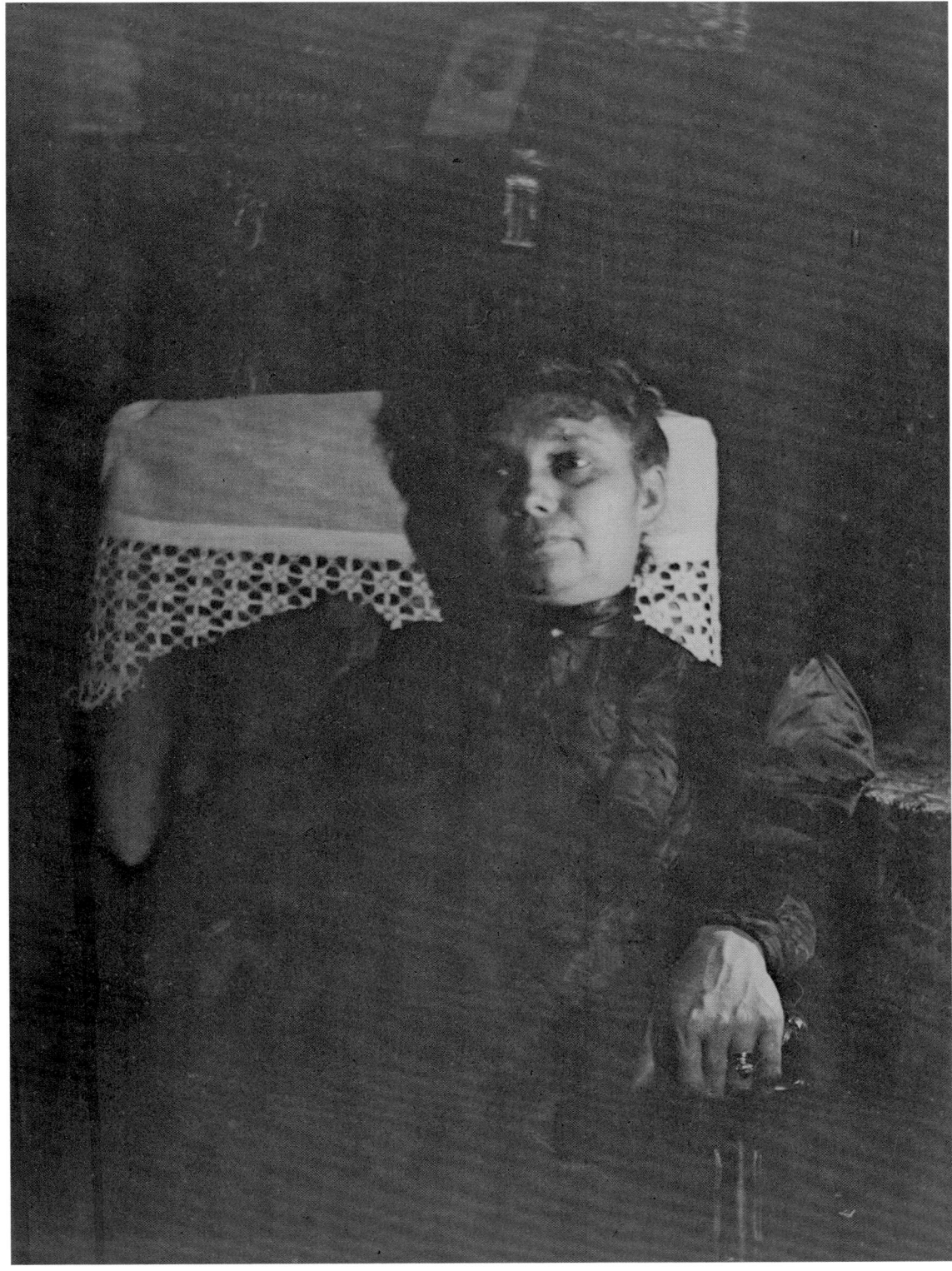

212
Louise Halévy
c. 1895
Photograph
Los Angeles,
The J. Paul Getty Museum

result is group photographs in which the unity of the group is dissolved, and a social gathering is transformed into an accumulative juxtaposition of individuals who we know must have been forced to stand for minutes on end, frozen in the poses and contortions imposed on them by the photographer. The double portrait of Renoir and Mallarmé (ill. 210) is known to have entailed a sitting that lasted a quarter of an hour. Daniel Halévy and Paul Valéry have both left accounts of how painstakingly Degas set about his task.

Surprisingly Degas, who had not painted or drawn any self-portraits for many years, suddenly took to giving himself a prominent role – although not without his usual insistence on emotional detachment, capturing himself frozen in the midst of interior monologues. He was probably influenced by the authenticity of the new technology – that *vérité vraie* which the fragile painter could no longer demand of his failing eyes and his uncoordinated hand.

The self-portrait with his housekeeper (ill. 211) is a moving human document of alienation in proximity, simultaneously dividing and uniting two people. In Zoë Closier, the bachelor Degas had an assistant who provided him with all his everyday needs. She received visitors and looked after the models, cooked for him (though not particularly well), and did his washing. There were, however, certain restrictions placed on her within the household. She was 'only allowed to make the fire and occasionally clean the worktable, the stove and the passage leading to the front door.' The gruff tone of voice that Degas was famous for must have been reinforced by Zoë's own rural taciturnity. The closeness of their relationship is evident from the fact that he took this self-portrait with her, so that posterity would also have a picture of her. The 61-year-old artist occupies the foreground, and she stands close behind him. This arrangement is reminiscent of the classic double portrait in which the man is seated in front of the standing woman who acts as his companion and his muse. Zoë's position is not that of a mere servant. Some critics have suggested that the model for this is Ingres's *Luigi Cherubini and the Muse of Lyric Poetry*. But this allegorical portrait is a later and more elevated version of a painting which initially showed the composer on his own. Zoë is no afterthought, but was incorporated into the composition right from the start.

Degas's head rests on his hand – the pose of the visionary – and gazes beyond us, whereas Zoë's gaze is directed straight at the camera. It is she and not the artist who seems at home in this atmosphere. Her fleshy but striking features are marked with lines, and her rather wistful expression is that of someone who has had to put up with a great deal – including the torture of having her photograph taken. Degas appears to have liked this long-suffering but basically robust kind of woman, as she is very similar to Louise, his friend Ludovic Halévy's wife, who according to contemporaries was like a sister to him. As blindness approached, he would get Zoë to read the newspaper to him, and Louise to read the post.

Zoë Closier and Louise Halévy: the difference in social class disappears when one compares the photographs of these two women's faces (ills. 211, 212). Female coquetry would have been utterly alien to them both. Louise has a trace of thoughtful melancholy, typical of the expressions of bourgeois ladies painted by Degas when his eyesight was still good. Zoë had no illusions about the role she played – it was another relationship of distant proximity, forged by years of being and not being together. Just as he belonged to her, so she was ruled by him, in a partnership that was far from simple but was nevertheless dependable.

Madame Halévy aroused the interest of Degas the artist: 'Louise,' he said one day, 'I would like to do a portrait of you – you are very finely drawn.' Evidently he saw in her his concept of natural, undemanding femininity, and in due course he was able to fulfil his wish through the medium of photography. Similarly, Zoë must have fitted in with the image of woman that he once mentioned during an evening meal: '*Elle est peuple!*' [She is people]. And then he added: 'It is in the common that we find grace.' The anti-bourgeois sentiment is unmistakable. Even in his youth, his notebooks proclaim the inversion of the aesthetic hierarchy, and he quotes Barbey d'Aurevilly as follows: 'There is sometimes a certain ease in awkwardness which, if I am not mistaken, is more graceful than grace itself.' The 'grace' that the Parisian roués expected of the ladies at their disposal is not to be seen in the housekeeper or the middle-class wife of a friend, but they have a spiritual presence of which the physical frame suggests both strength and stability of character.

Sometimes, as with the Lerolle sisters (ill. 214), the wait helped to create dissonance between the lifeless pair of figures. One of the women is seen front on, and radiates self-assured unapproachability, while the other has turned away in self-absorption, apparently lost in her daydreams. It is evident that the stage director Degas, having them at his manipulative mercy, has forced them into poses that they would scarcely have adopted of their own accord. We have seen the same disparities in earlier portraits of sisters: the Bellellis (ills. 34, 213) and the Montejasi ladies (ill. 47). In this photograph, Degas has withdrawn from the private world (which in fact he is negating) into the darkness at the side, but it is this very position on the fringes that exposes the sisters to the discreet and indiscreet gaze of the man who appears not to be there. This makes them subject to his concepts and yet at the same time leaves them alone. It is not a portrait of three, but a threefold violation of the rules of conduct that govern urban society. With his insistence on the isolation of both sisters, he also goes against the customary procedure of creating a coherent group picture from several combined negatives. This was the trick that enabled Oskar Gustave Rejlander and Henry Peach Robinson to produce their allegorical, symbolic compositions, which imitated those of academic painting. As painter and as photographer, Degas always rebelled against the demand for consensus.

Of course the paradoxical comparisons, additions and groupings of dissonant figures did not always establish the intended order. Renoir and Mallarmé are united in discord (ill. 210), as Degas once again gives different emphasis to two figures, just as he did in his self-portrait with Valernes (ill. 32), where he avoided any semblance of balance in the composition. The poet is standing and looking down on the painter with half-closed eyes; he has the serene calm that eludes Renoir. The latter is clearly ill at ease. Leaning back on a sofa, he has raised his left leg so that he is sitting uncomfortably, with the air of someone following the photographer's instructions with haughty reluctance. Degas obviously wanted to include himself as the third member of the group, but the mirror shows only the camera, as the photographer is swallowed up in the dazzling light of nine paraffin lamps. The room disappears in an endless succession of mirrors reflecting mirrors. Here the technical range of photography had reached its limits, unless we count as a success the fact that we are shown exactly how the scene was staged.

Some of these interiors consist of two superimposed negatives printed at the same time (ill. 207). Whether this happened deliberately or accidentally we do not know, but what is important to us is that these 'images within images' have been kept and collected. The scenes interweave two axes: the normal view is joined by a second if we turn the photo 90 degrees to the left. Then any contact that there might have been between the subjects is lost, but in their place are new connections. The wall, covered with small pictures, forms a coordinating grid – more a screen than a firm room divider – against which the superimposed subjects have been placed almost like the pieces of a board game. If one interprets this confused mixture of two competing pictures as integrated subversion, the whole thing takes on the status of a precursor to the spatial anarchy of 20th-century art. Here we have the abnegation of the perspective rules that had held sway for centuries, with painters adopting a single viewpoint – Diderot's 'seul point de vue' – in order to reproduce the outside world. The mystifying superimposition of two camera angles offers an experience on two different levels: an incoherent, simultaneous 'double exposure', together with the new and ambivalent autonomy of the two-dimensional composition.

These photographs are more than mere curiosities. In them, Degas lays bare what we have called the 'distant proximity' in which his friends were placed, as if under a spell. The blending of two perspectives results in the coexistence of contradictory statements, and in the confusion the observer finds himself caught between two fragmented islands between which there is no bridge. It is impossible to decide on any one combination, because each person is caught up in his own 'interior monologue'. The same mystifying technique of multiple focuses, in this case applied to narrative prose, was used by Édouard Dujardin in his novel *Les lauriers sont coupés* (1888). But perhaps the modern primogenitor of this mixture of association and

Dancer from the Corps de Ballet

c. 1895

Photograph

Paris, Bibliothèque Nationale

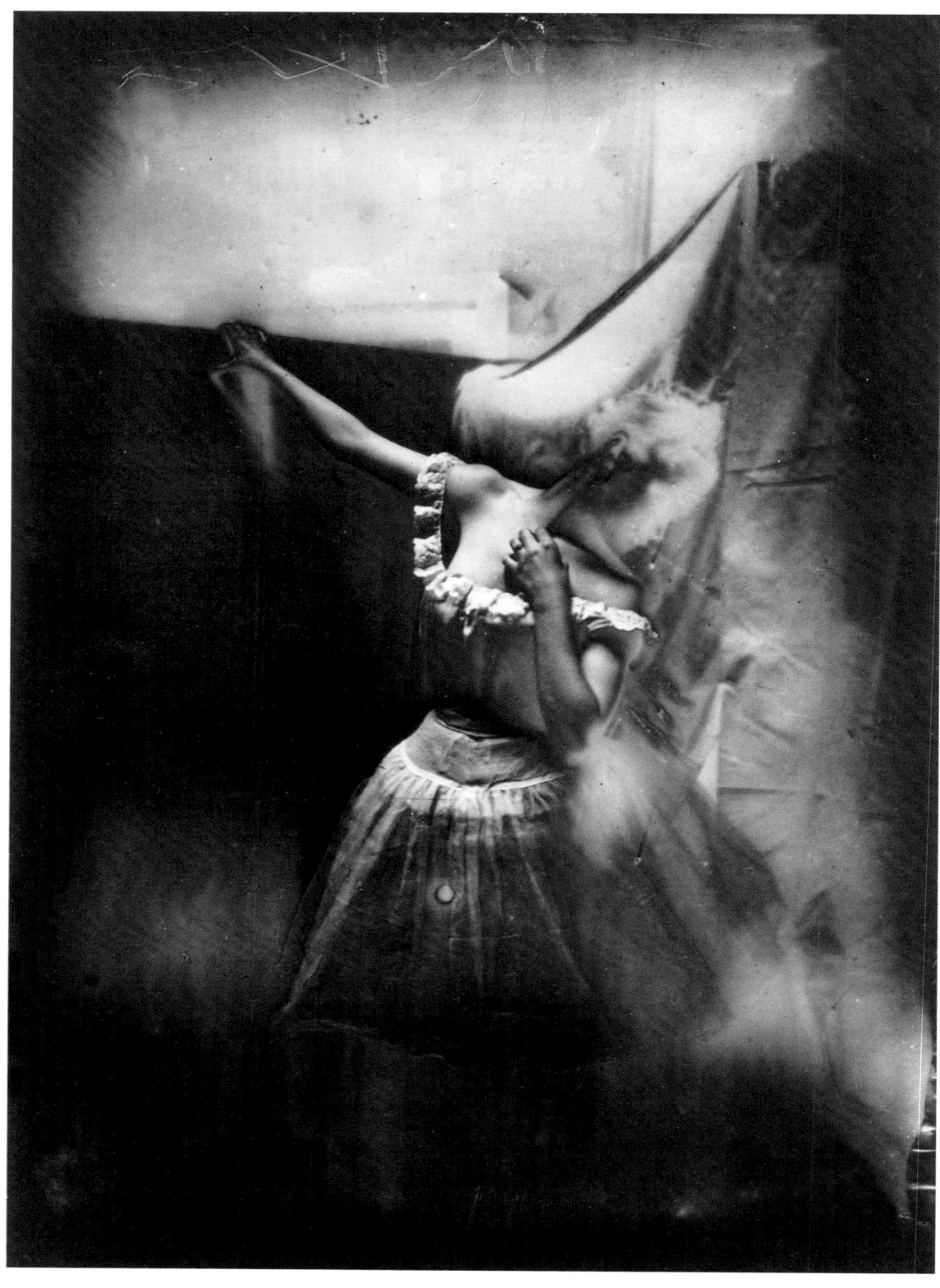

disassociation is to be found in chapter 8 of *Madame Bovary*, where Flaubert interweaves the private conversations between Emma and her lover Rodolphe with the platitudinous public pronouncements of an official praising the virtues of the agricultural fair (*comices agricoles*).

With his photographic superimpositions, Degas created a new form of mystery. The very beginnings of the process had a touch of magic about them. The process invented by Niepce and Daguerre initially produced a latent image which was made durable by the developing process. But for this unique positive image to be perceived, certain conditions had to be fulfilled: 'It could be seen only in certain lights; in direct rays of the sun it became a shiny sheet of metal.' In the photographs of dancers (ill. 215), Degas seems to have been experimenting with precisely this inconsistency – i.e. the appearance and disappearance of images – assuming that the prints discovered in his studio were indeed made by him. These experiments put one of the characteristic features of photography, its documentary precision, in a fascinating new twilight zone that recalls Redon: 'The sense of mystery lies in constant equivocation, in double or triple views, hints of views (images within images), forms that are about to exist, or that may come into existence depending on the observer's state of mind. All these things are more than suggestions, because they actually appear.'

The photograph *The Apotheosis of Degas* (ill. 218) has multiple meanings of a different sort. This is a document to which the artist entrusted the most eloquent of his 'interior monologues'. He once again staged a group portrait, but did not take it himself. It seems to me that this self-portrait 'against the grain' reveals a great deal about the artistic nature of Degas as anti-hero, and it therefore provides an excellent starting point for our final chapter on Degas and his century.

Chapter 13

Degas in His Century

*'There is a sort of shame in being known mainly
by people who do not understand you.'* – Degas, 1877–83

'To desire without ardour, to hope without worry, to possess without upheaval.'
– Saint-Evremond, paraphrased by Degas

Degas painted against the grain of his century. People were at the centre of his art, and not the conflict-free landscapes in which his era sought refuge. This statement, however, requires qualification, because we have seen in Chapter 11 that his late monotypes contained a new and revolutionary view of Nature. Nevertheless, it is true to say that people formed the backbone of his life's work. When he took humankind off the poetic stage of the history paint-ing and transplanted it into the prose of the everyday world, which Baudelaire had characterized as the 'heroism of modern life', he discovered his very own terrain, that of 'social chiaroscuro'. In this mixture of light and dark, he met the artificial and the natural human being, in all phases of his or her contradictions and transitions – a bipolarity that had already made its presence felt in his five history paintings, which were not merely the labours of an ambitious beginner. They stand in the context of the conflict that had polarized French paint-ing since David, between man as a timeless ideal and man as a contemporary. It is necessary to look back over this problem area if we are to appreciate that Degas the history painter, with *The Daughter of Jephthah* (ill. 10), *Young Spartans Exercising* (ill. 17), *Semiramis Building Babylon* (ill. 11), *Scene of War in the Middle Ages* (ill. 12) and *Mlle Fiocre* (ill. 13), was already marking out intuitively the focal points of his future work. This was the basis on which he was to produce his dissection of the city-dweller's alienation and privation. He never lost sight of the tensions between the artificial and the natural being. They guided his artistic double life, and this should also prevent us from trying to reduce his work to a single common denominator. Twice he blazed a trail into totally new territory: once when he displayed humanity in the artificial cage of alienation – the prime example being his etching *Actresses in their Dressing*

216
Walter Barnes (*1844–1911*)
The Apotheosis of Degas
(*detail of ill. 218*)

217
Jean-Auguste-Dominique Ingres
(1780–1867)
The Apotheosis of Homer
1827
Oil on canvas
386 x 512 cm
(152 x 201 1/2 in.)
Paris, Musée du Louvre

Rooms (ill. 230) – and again when he transformed it into a natural event with *Landscape Woman* (ill. 228). Between these two poles, he laid bare all the cracks and ruptures and refuges of modern man.

The bearded gentleman who, at the age of sixty, already looked like an old man knew that the people in his circle compared his features to those of Homer, to whom Ingres had devoted a huge *Apotheosis* for a ceiling in the Louvre (ill. 217). Another, though less godlike, comparison might have been more apt: the self-portrait of an ageing Tintoretto in the Louvre, of which incidentally the young Manet painted a copy in 1854. Degas was not averse to the comparison with Homer, but at the same time the sceptic in him was led to question his own role as an admirer of Ingres as well as the latter's position in 19th-century art. In 1885, he composed a *tableau vivant* that parodied *The Apotheosis of Homer* and asked the American photographer Walter Barnes to take a picture of it. *The Apotheosis of Degas* (ill. 218) is a joke with several layers of meaning which were long overlooked because Degas hid them behind his ostensible admiration for Ingres. It was Theodore Reff who noted this piece of subterfuge:

the more Degas's work diverged from that of Ingres, the more enthusiastically he praised the old master's art.

With this self-mockery, Degas opened up a new dimension for photography which had previously been touched on just once by Hippolyte Bayard. Annoyed by the lack of interest shown by the public in his photographs, Bayard posed in 1840 for a self-portrait as a half-naked suicide. Having just been invented as an instrument of unadulterated factual reproduction, in the twinkling of an eye the photograph became a new means of deception and, provided with Bayard's caption, a cunning mode of self-advertisement. But apart from this clever variation – which no one bothered to follow up – the great and the good only wanted to be photographed in their deep-thinking, monumental glory. No photographer performed this task more impressively than Nadar, with his portraits of famous contemporaries. When Charles Hugo photographed his father Victor looking at himself on a medallion, the snapshot of the present was linked up with sculpted immortalization. At the turn of the century, Edward J. Steichen was to endow the artist-thinker Rodin with the dimensions of a Titan, while the

Right and opposite:
219
Daniel Nikolaus Chodowiecki
(1726–1801)
**Natural and Affected Actions
in Life**
1780
Etchings
8.2 x 4.7 cm (3 1/4 x 1 7/8 in.)
From the Göttinger Pocket Calendar
for the year 1780
Hamburg, Kunsthalle

Natur

exact opposite to this homage was Toulouse-Lautrec's double self-portrait by Maurice Guilbert, which showed him both drawing himself and posing as a model.

Degas's homage to himself anticipated the ironic double exposure. In this way he placed photography iconographically alongside the satires that sharp-witted caricaturists produced for the popular press to mock the major works – both praised and condemned – on show during the exhibition season. But the real innovation was Degas's courage in parodying himself (the way having been paved by Bayard).

Everything in this artistically unartistic composition is shifted into the half-light of uncertainty because of the irony. This is aimed simultaneously at two artists: Ingres and Degas himself, but with an additional sideswipe at Homer and his lasting fame. First of all, he knocks down the artist-idol of the 19th century, the godlike genius. The bourgeois Degas suffers visibly during this ritual, in which he makes himself the central figure. He acts the part of the helpless doubter who does not understand what is happening to him. Next the irony is turned on those delivering the ovation. The three ladies (the Lemoinne sisters) and the two male worshippers (sons of the Halévys) perform with applied earnestness the traditional rites of homage. Their adoration is rather like laying someone in state while he is still alive.

Finally, the irony casts doubt on the enormous energy and skill that Ingres invested in his 'apotheosis'. This is the irony of an artist who called his own works his 'articles' and emphatically rejected the pseudoreligious aura applied to the artist. He quotes a formula that he despises and avoids, that of hierarchical symmetry, and has himself framed by it, like a lifeless puppet, and helplessly delivered into the hands of his admirers. But the questions and doubts that Degas raised with this photograph are not limited to the role of the artist in the age of bourgeois capitalism. They are also directed at one of the central problems of the century –

that of credibility, the very *raison d'être* of an 'apotheosis' which in the name of Homer embraced the whole cultural heritage of the West, made it untouchable, and played it off against the present day. What had these ancient norms in fact become? The direct answer to this question lies in the three ladies of the coronation: their bodies are stiff, and tightly stuffed into their corsets. This anomaly illustrates the gap that Degas sensed between his present and the ideal of the past (as a form of life) – an ideal which, if we look closely enough, had already become an empty formula in the shape of Ingres's goddess of victory. There is exactly the same lack of credibility in the fancy-dress ball which the painter arranges at the feet of Homer: nothing but famous character masks, all ready for permanent sittings at the Académie Française.

Afectation

Lumbered with this pantheon of famous law-givers and upholders of tradition, the anti-hero Degas seems to be asking: 'Is the *Iliad* possible at all when the printing press and even printing machines exist?' This doubt concludes a famous list of questions with which a German contemporary of Ingres and Degas encapsulated the problem: 'What is Vulcan compared with Roberts and Co., Jupiter compared with the lightning conductor, and Hermes compared with the Credit Mobilier? …What becomes of Fama side by side with Printing House Square?' These were the questions asked by Karl Marx in his introduction to *A Contribution to the Critique of Political Economy* (1857). He answered them as an educated member of the middle classes for whom the works of Antiquity are still 'in certain respects regarded as a standard and unattainable ideal.' And in Paris too, that was precisely the conviction, raised to the level of dogma, held by the conservative camp which governed the public taste in art.

The canonization of antiquity was a provocation to those who wished to champion the present. In his diary entry of 9 April 1856, Delacroix referred to the authority of Voltaire, who had an Indian from the Huron tribe say: 'Greek tragedies are good for the Greeks.' Delacroix also warns that it would be wrong in our times to swim against the tide and 'invent' archaisms. The philosopher Proudhon made his position clear in *Du principe de l'art* (1865): 'The artist, like the writer, must belong to his time.' As George Boas has shown, this war cry – which Daumier was fond of quoting – goes back to Emile Deschamps's *Préface des études françaises et étrangères* (1828).

Where did Degas stand in this controversy? He brought to it a kind of reciprocity that was typical of his 'dual vision'. In his 22nd notebook (1867–74), he turned to Giotto as the mediator between past and present: 'Ah! Giotto, let me see Paris, and Paris, let me see Giotto!' The precondition for this desirable dialogue is that both parties should stick to their own standpoints. Degas sees Paris as the present and Giotto as the past. What he is looking to foster is an exchange of energies between two equally valid forces – bringing those of the past into the present, and focusing those of the present on creating an equivalent timelessness. He does not want to devalue either era, but on the contrary to revalue both of them. This distinguishes him from Nietzsche (the discoverer of *Doppelblick* or 'dual vision'), who disparagingly sought to downgrade Wagner: 'Would you believe it that the Wagnerian heroines, each and all, when one has only stripped them of their heroic trappings, are like counterparts of Madame Bovary!' (*The Case of Wagner*, 1888).

Degas once said that he painted ballet dancers because he saw in them the movements of the Greeks. In another age, he would have painted Susannah and the Elders, but today he contented himself with Parisian women bathing. Behind such statements was his bifocal mentality, which saved him from the conflict which Flaubert – three years his senior – was going through at the time. Sick of the banalities of the bourgeois world which had obsessed him in *Madame Bovary,* he sought refuge in mythical Carthage and embarked on the '*grande machine*' of his *Salammbô*. But he still kept his feet firmly on the ground of prosaic objectivity, and as he stressed in a letter to Sainte-Beuve, wanted to 'be simple', using the same method as in a modern novel – i.e. by casting off the ballast of rhetoric. He succeeded to the degree that the Carthaginian princess reminded Sainte-Beuve of Emma Bovary. The decision to keep things simple is one of the strategies connected with the process of '*désapprendre*' [unlearning]. This began in France when the complicated artifices of Rococo were rejected by the new, middle-class demand for truth. For Diderot, Boucher the painter was Boucher the liar: 'This man has everything, except the truth' (1761). Four years later, he pointed out the consequences of these aesthetic falsehoods. Wherever one went, he argued, the degradation of taste was followed by the corruption of morals.

In Germany too, Herder blamed the frivolity of modern taste for the loss of truth and realism: 'Nature has left us and hidden herself. Art and status, machinery and patchwork are

all there: but it seems to me that they are not to be formed in clay or in wax.' The three ladies in *The Apotheosis of Degas* continue this masquerade in the 19th century. Herder goes on to ask the question that also concerned Degas in his *Young Spartans Exercising* (ill. 17): 'Greek games, Greek dances...Youth and joy, where are they, where can they be?' With this lament in his essay *Plastik* (*Sculpture*, published 1778) – which could have come from the lips of a sculptor – Herder laid down his marker in the discussion begun by Diderot when, in the supplement to *Bougainville's World Tour*, he drew the contrast between the '*homme naturel*' of the South Seas and the '*homme artificiel*' of Europe. Copies of the text were circulated until it appeared in print in 1796. In keeping with Diderot's argument, Chodowiecki set 'natural and affected actions' against one another (ill. 219) in the '*Göttinger Taschenkalender*' of 1780, with commentaries by Lichtenberg. He contrasts the 'fashionable couple' with another, whose near nakedness embodies 'Nature' in all its innocence. Herein lie the origins of the dream which, a hundred years later, would lure the world-weary Gauguin to Polynesia.

Herder, Chodowiecki and Lichtenberg captured the superficial deceitfulness of their age, but in the European context their views were marginal by comparison with events in the place

211
Théodore Géricault (1791–1824)
Have Pity on a Poor Old Man
1821
Lithograph
37.5 x 52.8 cm
(14 1/2 x 20 3/4 in.)
Paris, Bibliothèque Nationale

where such criticism mobilized public awareness and was one of the factors that led to the Revolution of 1789. Antiquity was regarded as the model for republican renewal in all areas of private and public life. In May 1790, the decision was made in Paris that there should be a monumental painting of the *Tennis-Court Oath*, not only to record an event of the moment, but also to endow that historic event with the symbolic status of a secular altarpiece. Charged with this squaring of the circle, Jacques-Louis David made every effort to combine the two levels of expression – the prose of reportage and the poetry of the forthcoming new 'millennium'. In one of his preliminary drawings, some of the deputies hastening to the royal tennis court are shown naked, while others are already dressed in the bourgeois accoutrements of the time. David's grand concept of a Republican Antiquity established 'from below' was to collapse in the political turbulence of the following years, and the picture was never painted. From now on, the history painter David abandoned the bipolarity of the two different levels, and opted instead for the moral and aesthetic model of an archaeologically accurate Antiquity 'from above', peopled by positive heroes whose flawless bodies predestined them to be conquerors. Thus the all-powerful artist of the moment sacrificed the ideal of truth to that of a new, sentimental artificiality. David's doctrines, derived from a strict ethic of reform, were eventually themselves in need of reform. It was Adolphe Thiers who articulated this need in 1824, and the response was not long in coming. In that same year, Delacroix exhibited his *Massacre at Chios* in the Salon – siding with the Greeks in their fight for freedom against the Turks, and at the same time laying a new emphasis on the human element of such events. This turning point had to a degree been anticipated by Géricault with his *Raft of the Medusa* (1819). A new anti-hero had now arrived on the scene: the anonymous, wounded or humiliated creature at the mercy of oppressors or disasters. Later, looking back on the immaculate world of Ingres, the philosopher Pierre-Joseph Proudhon saw the contemporaneity of Géricault's *Raft* (which depicted a shipwreck of 1816 caused by negligence) as negating all the Madonnas, odalisques, apotheoses and St Symphorians.

Géricault was not only interested in the epic scale of a major disaster. When he visited London in 1821, he discovered the heroism of everyday modern life in its anonymous territory: a paralysed woman in a wheelchair, a bagpiper, three condemned

222
Hecuba
From Degas's notebooks
(NB.12, p. 95)

men beneath the gallows. His aged beggar lying outside a baker's shop (ill. 221) is another Job, reminiscent of the dead Christ of Rubens's *Mourning* (in Antwerp), to which a decade later Daumier's dual vision would add a proletarian postscript: the worker shot in the Rue Transnonain. We are confronted with precisely such victims in the left half of Courbet's *Studio*, and from now on they are ennobled to the level of great art.

When Degas began his *Young Spartans Exercising* (ill. 17), the first of his five history paintings, in 1860, the protagonists in the dispute over what constituted art had already firmly established their positions. Ingres stood for history painting, and drew the criteria for his love of calligraphic line from Antiquity in academic attire. Delacroix was the champion of richly coloured, emotionally charged compositions conveniently called 'Romantic'. Courbet advocated a realism that drew its strength from ordinary people. The ever-questing Degas took account of these internal French disputes, but set his sights on wider horizons. His years of travelling (and learning) in Italy opened up to him the relics of Antiquity and the traditions of painting from the Middle Ages right through to modern times. Added to this knowledge were the landscapes of Italy and everyday life in town and country. The fruits of his open-minded perceptions, collected in his notebooks, already contain early signs of his determination to go his own way. An evening get-together of young people (ill. 220) is far from the cliché of the bourgeois social gathering. Here everything is seen as improvisation – the musical contributions, the conversation, and the intimate, totally natural contact between the participants. It might be possible to derive some overall consensus from this scene, but the artist leaves it as something ephemeral. He himself had withdrawn to a marginal position behind his easel, but eventually he felt that even this was superfluous and scraped himself out with a knife – an action which I feel is not without significance. Degas lays no claim to having any place in this gathering. He does not belong here.

A drawing in the 12th notebook (ill. 222) shows Hecuba, the mother of Hector, beside a wall and perhaps lamenting the prophecy she has received in a dream: she will give birth to a burning torch, the fire of which will devour the city of Troy. The choice of this rare subject is an indication of Degas's detailed knowledge of ancient myth, but the drawing also contains – in the person of the naked, cowering queen – an extraordinary foretaste of a figure from which later he would derive countless variations. The cruelly exposed Hecuba, whose body is racked with grief – one is reminded of the woman at the feet of Delacroix's *Sardanapalus* – leads to the animal nakedness of his women attending to their toilet. The abundant head of hair is already shown in the early sketch, as is the worn-out body, from which one can extrapolate no norm of idealism. The pencil of the draughtsman had a spontaneity which the painter's brush had yet to master.

Meanwhile, the history painter was still trying to find a language of his own in which to compose his picture. His choice of subject was already original: the men who made history were not what fascinated him. In all five paintings, what interests him is women and their fate – his theme of the future. The *Young Spartans* correct the dry Classicism of David by neutralizing it with an Antiquity seen 'from below'. This gives the scene an everyday touch, which is reminiscent of the words of Winckelmann: 'In Sparta, even young girls practised wrestling naked or in an almost complete state of undress.'

In *Semiramis* (ill. 11), Degas avoids the normal focus of the court on its ruler. What holds these women together is not a rigid hierarchy but a private, almost archaic motionlessness. The whole composition is imbued with a contemplative stillness that we shall soon see again in the daydreaming women of Paris (Chapter 4). Semiramis's attendants resemble the women who try to support Jephthah's daughter as she prepares herself to be sacrificed (ill. 10). For this latter group, Degas referred to a detail in Mantegna's *Crucifixion*, which he had just been copying: the crowd of barely distinguishable women at the foot of the cross. There is far more animation in the gestures of those entrusted with the sacrifice. The masculine movements of the father and his retinue fill the scene in the foreground and make it into a homage to Delacroix. This expansive composition is set at the moment between what is and what is about to be. The manly display of heroism, which Degas will later renounce altogether, still speaks in a strong voice, whereas the women are confined to gestures of silent devotion.

In the preliminary drawings for the *Scene of War in the Middle Ages* (ill. 12), Degas revealed a wealth of invention, though he could only incorporate a selection of these devices in the final painting. He had now found a theme that would occupy him for the rest of his life – female nakedness in all its exposed naturalness. The other side of feminine self-experience, contemplation and daydreaming, comes to the fore in the last of his history paintings, *Mlle Fiocre in the Ballet 'La Source'* (ill. 13).

Apart from the theme of women, the five history paintings have another, secret common denominator. This lies in the reaction of the young painter to the classicist pedants' dogma of formal perfection. Degas renounced this norm. The evidence lies not only in the breadth of his interests as a copyist, but also in the unorthodoxy of his own means of expression. He had no time for the antique model of 'noble simplicity and quiet grandeur' – a formula which, incidentally, Winckelmann drew from a French source – but used the past in order to experiment with modes that had not yet been exhausted or categorized. What was to develop into a change of paradigm is announced with precision but also with subtlety in a preliminary oil sketch of Mlle Fiocre and her attendant (ill. 16). There are no class distinctions between them, and in their sturdy nakedness they speak a common, prosaic language which is lost in

the poetry of the finished painting. Since it is, however, clear in the preliminary study, it takes on the exemplary status of an initial idea. Degas dressed his heroine and her maid in stage cos-tumes – just as David had his deputies cover their nakedness with their bourgeois suits – but in future works he would distance himself from this artificial poetry, and settle for prosaic cloth-ing or complete nudity.

With this change of direction, Degas freed himself from the pedantic perfectionism of David and his successors. Ingres's admirer crossed over – and not only as a copyist – into the camp of Delacroix, whose lifelong principles were encapsulated early on in a diary entry: 'Do not chase after vain perfection. There are certain defects in the common view that often bring things to life.' New territory, such as was shunned by good taste, would open up to those who dared to 'unlearn'. From this concept emerged the most significant advances of art over the last two hundred years. 'Unlearning' produced a new and challenging vitality, which gave Courbet and Manet in the 1860s an advantage over the ostentatious ease and fluency of a Baudry, a Cabanel or a Bouguereau. Delacroix may well have been referring to such violations of the norm when on 7 September 1854 he once again opposed perfect beauty and insisted that disproportion also contained an element of beauty.

The first to stand up against the hollow rhetoric of the Salon was Courbet. Even the highly critical Baudelaire with hindsight gave him credit, when he said in 1862: 'Only recently a neat and tidy form of painting still reigned undisputed – pretty, silly, muddled, pretentious daubs… all of that is sufficient to explain the enormous success that Courbet's pictures had right from the start.' Then Baudelaire sums up by saying: 'One must in all fairness grant that Courbet has contributed more than a little to re-establishing a sense of simplicity and honesty, and a self-less and absolute love of painting.'

Let us leave the selflessness to one side. As I see it, Courbet's *Studio* (ill. 5) turns 'unlearning' into a monumental 'vulgarity'. In the subtitle, he promises to summarize 'Seven Years of My Artistic and Moral Life'. The idea behind the picture, however, contains something else: the prototypes of two contrasting levels of society, with the painter in the middle, sitting at his easel, completely preoccupied with a landscape which he sees entirely in his mind's eye. Between the middle and the two outer 'wings', in contrast to the traditional triptych, there is no formal or narrative connection. In 'unlearning' the syntax of the history painting, Courbet reveals his polemical purpose. He is setting out to unmask coherence and harmony, those images of a sound, unharmed world, as deceptions carried out by the idealizing painter. And so the self-proclaimed Realist sets the painter and the two social collectives within the topography of a separate togetherness in which we can easily distinguish what Duranty so aptly termed the '*clair-obscur social*' [social chiaroscuro]. And this all took place years before Degas (re-)discovered it.

With this dissonance and disconnection between heroes and 'foot soldiers', Courbet turns his epic into static prose. The figures are no longer linked by a common action, and he does not use the atmospheric factor of common thought. In this flock of sleepwalkers, everyone is on his own. Even the painter's intended homage does not take place overtly, as it does in Ingres's *Homer* (ill. 217), but in a kind of code amid all the confusion emanating from the people and the room, filled as it is with non-connections and screens randomly shoved together. Courbet did not paint a three-dimensional continuum, but a diffuse storeroom containing nothing but human dummies and the gaps between them.

The characters in Degas's human comedy come straight from the *Studio*. Unlike Courbet, who created two groups and set them opposite one another – on the left the have-nots and the degraded, on the right the well-to-to and the spokesmen for the Zeitgeist – Degas concentrated his attentions on the exposed loner. Courbet abandoned individuality to the anonymity of a passive and seemingly paralysed crowd, while Degas's edgy approach isolates them from

224
Adolph Menzel (*1815–1905*)
Head of a Workman
1875
Pencil
Private collection

Opposite:
225
Gustave Courbet (*1819–77*)
The Painter's Studio
(*detail of ill. 5*)

the collective ambiance. His speciality, man as a significant alienated individual, made him, as Duranty correctly pointed out, a master of omission – an operation that Courbet would have had no idea how to perform.

At this point, I should like to embark on a little digression, to consider the relationship between Degas and Adolph Menzel. Like Courbet, Menzel was so overwhelmed by the materiality of the empirical world that he found it difficult to leave things out. What drove him on – and once again it was his Parisian admirer Duranty who found the right formula – was '*La névrose du vrai*' [the neurosis of truth]. Although he was deeply sensitive to the fleeting impressions made by '*ondulations et vibrations lumineuses*', he did not use reality to translate these into paint, but mastered them with his intellect. This is what Duranty was referring to in the last sentence of his fine appraisal of Menzel, which was published in the *Gazette des Beaux-Arts* shortly before his death in 1880: 'He has not only been an artist, but also a great intellect.' Duranty could equally have been thinking of Degas. The two painters had been introduced to each other in 1867 or 1868 by Alfred Stevens. Later they met frequently – Menzel's Paris address is in the 24th notebook – and they even played the role of rivals, as when Degas painted from memory a variation on Menzel's *The Supper at the Ball* (ill. 223), which he had seen at Goupil's in 1879. Menzel turns his ironic gaze on the Vanity Fair of the Berlin court, and loses himself in a labyrinth of details. But this garish confusion contains no conflicts – simply people thrown together higgledy-piggledy, like the coloured patterns in a kaleidoscope. Nowhere in this babel of babble could Degas find a break into which he could insert some telling point. As it went against his own dashing approach to try and imitate, let alone compete with Menzel's great agglomeration of detail, he decided to transform the monotonous randomness of all these intermingling figures into a painting that would use the subject matter simply as a pretext for coloured *ondulations*. In other words, since he could not distinguish any social chiaroscuro in the hollow splendours of palace decorum, he blurred and softened all the participants into a seething mass of colour.

Degas probably admired Menzel the draughtsman even more than Menzel the 'neurotic' painter, because the graphic compression revealed his swift but precise grasp of even the tiniest splinter of reality, while at the same time he had the courage to abbreviate and omit. In 1881, a pencil portrait of a workman (ill. 224) which Menzel had given to Duranty as a present was left to Degas as part of Duranty's estate.

I should now like to return to Courbet and Degas. There is no evidence that there was ever any direct connection between them, for example in anything Degas might have said about the older master. Nevertheless, there is a rather charming *indirect* way of establishing a spiritual bond between them. There is one document in words and pictures that holds the key to a view that both of them shared: a sympathy for the simple, anonymous man – *l'homme naturel.*

The intermediary is Champfleury, spokesman for Realism, who sits in the right-hand half of the *Studio,* a kind of figurehead for the shareholding, art-loving class. His intellectual authority is clear from a letter he wrote in 1855 to the highly respected George Sand. In it he argued that painting did not recognize highs and lows, and so an old peasant woman was as beautiful as all the Antigones of Antiquity. The idea was not new. George Sand's sympathy for country life did not need such a spur since in her novel *The Devil's Pool* (1852), she had compared the young peasant Germain's earnest and touching meeting with 'little Marie' to Jacob's first sight of Rachel at the well of her father Laban. 'Little Marie' also reminded Sand of Holbein's brides of Henry VIII.

Around 1860, when Degas was painting the *Young Spartans,* he made a collage of text and pictures which explained in its own way the theme of equality between the high and the low. As an enthusiastic reader of Sand's novel, Degas wrote out a long passage describing Marie's headdress, and he pasted it in his 18th notebook under a copy after Rogier van der Weyden, which he had made in the Cabinet des Dessins at the Louvre (ill. 14). The delicate head of this young woman fitted in perfectly with the style of George Sand. Meant as a representation of the Madonna, the head could just as well have been that of

226
Rocky Coast
c. 1890–92
Pastel on monotype
33 x 42 cm (13 x 16 1/2 in.)
Vienna, Österreichische Galerie

a young country girl – another '*petite Marie*' – whom Rogier had used as a model. The passage Degas chose from the novel forms the link between his admiration for a 'primitive master' and the grace of the young peasant girl. Sand was sorry that this fashion had disappeared, and it seems that Degas too felt that the feminine charm he had captured in his copy was missing from the present – in the words of the novelist: 'the old chastity and modesty – naive majesty – the shyness of adolescence.' All these feminine qualities are embodied in the Italian peasant girls, with their beautifully simple headdresses, whom the Parisian art student drew in a sketchbook.

In quoting the novelist, Degas was taking refuge in old-fashioned ideals, using someone else's words, just as he borrowed the image of timeless grace from Rogier. Perhaps it all added up to the 'noble simplicity and quiet grandeur' that Winckelmann nostalgically projected onto Antiquity. The personal confessions that the young Degas confided to his notebook also speak of an ideal of untouched purity, which carries more weight than the many words he spoke or is said to have spoken about women. What he is talking about there is the chaste and modest woman who resists male domination.

This is the focal point of an subject that Degas treated several times in the 6th notebook (1856) but never developed into a painting: the wife of King Candaules. The king was so proud of his wife's beauty that he forced her to reveal herself to the eyes of a hidden observer. Her feminine honour having been thus besmirched, Nyssia demanded that Gyges, the peeping Tom, should avenge her by killing the king. This is the story as told by Théophile Gautier in 1844, and he based it on Plato and Herodotus (Degas's source). The studies show the beautiful

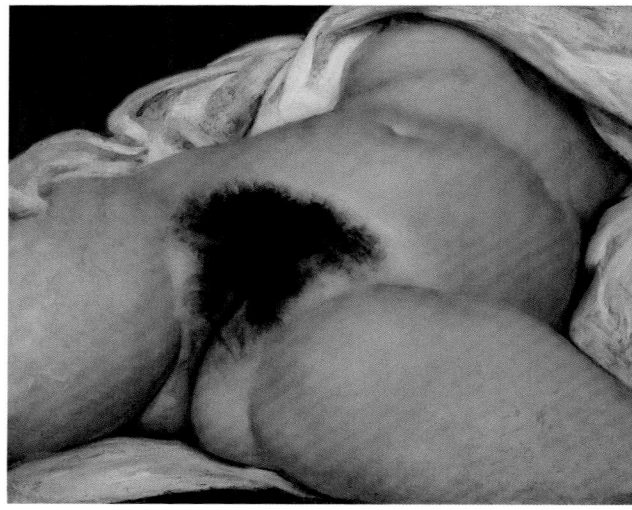

227
Gustave Courbet (1819–77)
The Origin of the World
1866
Oil on canvas
46 x 55 cm (18 1/8 x 21 5/8 in.)
Paris, Musée d'Orsay

bare back of the queen, who is about to get into bed (ill. 229). Degas made a note of what interested him: 'The whole body should be simple and tranquil, and only the eye should burn with shame and the desire for revenge.' In the anatomy of the woman are echoes of Ingres's *Valpinçon Bather*, which Degas had copied at the 1855 International Exhibition. The two male characters do not interest him, although it is their conduct that has sparked off the whole idea. The conspiratorial interplay between them, however, holds the key to one of Degas's most important themes: the woman in the bath and at her toilet. The manner of these women as they attend to their bodies – again they are mainly seen from the rear – is a prose equivalent

228
Steep Coast
('Landscape Woman')
c. 1892
Pastel on monotype
42 x 55 cm (16 1/2 x 21 5/8 in.)
Geneva, Galerie Jan Krugier

of the naked queen. Just like Nyssia, these anonymous Parisian women wish to avoid putting themselves on show to the prying eyes of men – or that at least is the message delivered by the anti-pose Degas has placed them in.

Male curiosity, fanned by the proud king, is now directed by the artist towards a third party – the person looking at the painting. Candaules turns into the painter who deliberately parades his possession in front of Gyges, who is the forerunner of the art-loving public. The step Degas takes from the archaeological antiquity of an Ingres – as seen in *Antiochus and Stratonice*, another tricky triangular situation – to the present of women in their bath tubs fits in with the change of emphasis that the Candaules theme was also undergoing at that time in literature. Gautier turned the king into an art-loving aesthete, and Hofmannsthal (1903) described him as representing 'the artistic existence, which even in love gains enjoyment only from observation and detachment.' This distance, which Degas was aware of in himself, was what he made into a central theme with his women, while trying to bridge it through the process of artistic formulation and appropriation.

Chastity for him meant restraint and renunciation, as we can see from the laconic account of an incident recorded in his 30th notebook (1877–83): 'One evening, I put my hand on her shoulder, in an embarrassed manner. I didn't know what I was doing. As I did so, I felt her cheek, which she had rested on her shoulder and which now suddenly touched my hand.' To represent such a moment in a picture, and therefore make it public, would probably have seemed to Degas painfully indiscreet. Manet was scathing about the shyness of his fellow artist: 'He lacks naturalness; he is not capable of loving a woman, or even telling her so.'

The naturalness that Manet found lacking was for Degas the dimension that gave his painting its alchemy. The price he had to pay – his own shyness of women – made him into their observer. The same detachment may also have given him the eye that could transform the female body into a hilly landscape. An incident reported by Halévy points in the direction from which this metamorphosis came. When once again Degas arrived for lunch with the Halévys, he brought with him one of the cobblestones that were used to pave the Parisian roads. As his hand slid over the surface, he cried out enthusiastically, 'What a line – as lovely as a shoulder!' obviously thinking of a woman's shoulder – petrified beauty, inviolable to man. He wanted to paint it as a sea of rocks: 'A cape, and I know what sailors call such places: the Cape of Fine Shoulder.' The metaphor stood for the distant proximity that characterized all Degas's dealings with women.

This brings us to the theme of the century: the landscape. On its triumphant march, landscape painting gradually drove all the other genres out of public expectation. The reasons are obvious. Unburdened by any intellectual or literary message, landscapes offered city-dwellers

229
**Study for the Wife
of King Candaules**
*From Degas's notebooks
(NB. 6, p. 62)
Paris, Bibliothèque Nationale*

the chance to experience Nature for themselves. The Impressionists directed this point of view onto urbanized space, restricting it to excerpts and moments, focusing on places of bourgeois sociability where there were no apparent class differences and no conflicts between work and play.

Once again, however, the outsider Degas went his own way. He had no time for domesticated Nature. Initially, in the early sixties, he painted deserted beaches, too miserable for people to stroll along – desolate scenes for painters who turned their backs on civilization, like Courbet in Whistler's famous painting of the beach at Trouville (1865). Later, he kept away from the idyllic, privatized Nature of gardens and parks, and from the Sunday stroll along the banks of the Seine. He did not paint the cityscapes of the boulevards, but simply extracted the raw material from which they were made: a bare cobblestone. The 'pars pro toto' gaze of the outsider invested this anonymous *objet trouvé* with the boundless expanse of a remote Nature far beyond the genre of the landscape painting. Degas refused to reduce Nature to a series of extracts, and in the technique of the monotype he discovered bodiless, formless images of it *in statu nascendi* – a morphology of coloured deconstructions and liquefactions that transcended the struggle between man and Nature, but also transcended loneliness and others 'states of soul' (Amiel).

The reluctance to dream and to idealize fits in with the symbiosis contained in the *Landscape Woman* (ill. 228). Here the nude woman becomes a landscape, but she is not *natura naturata*, a piece of Nature already created; she is an active participant in its formation, *natura naturans*. She is an image of age-old concepts that we shall be discussing in a moment. The Impressionist view of the world had no memory of these, and no means of expressing them. It drew all its colourful transformations from the changing surface of things, and so was limited to the momentary nature of the experience. The protracted process of genetic development, which seems inherent in the monotypes of the Krugier collection, was excluded from the Impressionist repertoire.

Another outsider, however, the 'Realist' Courbet, had an eye that was sensitive to precisely this slow evolution. His work begins with the natural woman, who in bathing rediscovers her naturalness and links it to Nature. The same harmony is the hope of the woman gazing at the landscape painting in the *Studio* (ill. 225). That is where she belongs, but she is still trapped in civilization and in the necessity to cover herself up. Courbet brings about an integration simply by concealing the woman in the feminization of Nature. She dwells in the great cavern from which springs the Loue, the river which after 20 kilometres arrives at Ornans, birthplace of the painter; but she is also to be found in grottoes and fissures and other natural hiding places where Courbet's imagination can incorporate the female body; but he also reverses the procedure, as in the notorious, long lost painting showing a close-up of a woman's pudenda, which he laconically described as *The Origin of the World* (ill. 227).

This elemental femininity has its roots in myth. Courbet's *'regressus ad uterum'* harks back to it, which distinguishes his grotto metaphor from the miracle that befell Bernadette Soubirous in 1858. The setting for that was also a cave and a spring that revealed a mystery, but the experience of little Bernadette was bound to the miraculous appearance of the Virgin Mary, and so it was promptly harnessed to the service of religious propaganda. The statue of Mary in front of the cave, a product of devotional aesthetics, fixes the vision to the one and only message. Courbet, however, keeps his grottoes free from all such connotations. His myth of Nature is totally heathen, and rests on the physical immanence of ceaselessly self-renewing organic life.

Duranty praised Degas for the fact that he dealt with ideas, 'which seldom happens with most of his colleagues'. Degas was, however, anything but a painter of ideas. He devised visual metaphors that were full of polysemy, and he abandoned the empirically provable, topographically guaranteed extract from reality selected by the famous 'view from the window'. His 'landscape woman' comes under two different categories of experience: one archaeological, and the other phenomenological.

We should look first at the mythical dimension, which was not merely confined to Degas's background knowledge. His study of the (literally) torch-bearing Hecuba (ill. 222) shows that he was also interested in potential hybrid creatures and their conflicts. In the monotype of the *Landscape Woman*, he may well have been thinking of Gaia, the Earth-Mother of the Greeks (we still use the term Mother Earth). Hesiod's *Theogony* tells us all about Gaia: 'At first there was Chaos, and after that the full-breasted Gaia, unwavering seat of all the immortals... First Gaia brought forth the starry Uranus, so that he might cover her and be an unwavering seat for the sacred gods. Then she gave birth to the high mountains, lovely and divine dwellings for nymphs that live in rugged caves. And the thriftless ocean that swells and storms she also produced, though without demanding love.'

In so far as the pictorial concepts of Courbet and Degas relate to the Earth-Mother, historically they go back to the notion of matriarchy, rediscovered by Johann Jakob Bachofen around the middle of the century. But as far back as 1724, Joseph-François Lafitau had researched *La Gynéocratie ou Empire des femmes*. It may well be that Flaubert knew this study but apparently he did not use it for his *Temptation of St Anthony* (1874). In this, he journeyed through the dark areas of oriental creation myths, and had their heroes appear in short scenes. One is Oannès, an androgynous Chaldean deity, who has a man's head and a fish's body. He introduces himself as a 'contemporary of the origins', and speaks of his achievements with the pride of an artist:

'I lived in the formless world where hermaphrodite creatures slept…I, the first consciousness of Chaos, arose from the abyss to solidify matter, and to shape the forms….' Oannès was what St Anthony in his last words wished to be: matter. Another who, like Gaia, has the creative power to fashion material is the Phrygian Cybele. A statuette representing this Great Mother is addressed and worshipped by one of the elders (Archi-Galle), as 'Mother of the Mountains'. What Degas articulates in his merging of landscape and female body is coded by Flaubert in his welter of learning, but nevertheless his labyrinthine diversions in and out of the unformed world eventually lead us to the same goal, the Great Mother.

The Austrian writer Adalbert Stifter (1805–68) took the same route when he looked back on his childhood. He wrote a short text, the fragmentary character of which raises images of delving that have an extraordinary immediacy. He gropes for words to describe his phenomenological approach to the primary experiences that precede every pictorial or verbal expression. Such recollections may also have inspired the pictorial thinking of Degas: 'Far back in the empty void there is something like joy and delight that penetrated with a violent hold, almost destructively, deep into my being, and there was nothing like it in my future life. The characteristics that were captured were radiance, chaos, something below. This must have been very early, because it seems to me as if a high, wide darkness of nothingness lay all round the thing. Then there was something else that passed softly and soothingly through my inner being. The characteristic: there were sounds. Then I was swimming in something gently moving, I swam back and forth; it became ever softer and softer inside me, then I was as if intoxicated, then there was nothing more.'

The visual equivalents of these words are the late landscape monotypes, the 'dreaminess' of which has been vividly described by Françoise Cachin: 'Nature seems to Degas to have something elemental and indeterminate, a clash of breadths and spaces, of darknesses and illuminating light; it is oceans before there were ships, hills before there were farmers, paths that are mostly deserted, and the trees have not yet had time to grow; it is landscapes from primeval times – swamps, lichens and mosses, steaming rocks whose somewhat disturbing magic is not sweetened by the relations between the colours and the refined material effects.' (ill. 226).

Along with the mythical twilight of these elemental, plasmatic regions, Degas does not forget the social chiaroscuro that surrounds him in Paris. His artistic intentions lie in both zones, and in both he incorporates visual structures whose revolutionary potential is of equal rank. He constructs barred rooms that offer no way out (ill. 230), or the flowing beginnings of indeterminate spaces. At all times he pursues the same goal: avoidance of the box-shaped room with its central perspective that ties the whole world of appearances to a single point of view, and thus makes it all too easily accessible. Sometimes the room will be entirely devoid of objects and of boundaries, simply a blur of colour; and sometimes it will be narrowed to a cage with labyrinthine bars. The bars and room dividers of these constricted spaces are in fact parodies of the rational axis system of the central perspective. Degas is suspicious of their systematic standardization, which organizes a picture into a rigid stasis. This is because the coordinates set by the frame and its rectangular axes treat the connections between the objects in the room as if they were subservient. People and objects are divided up into horizontal areas, and at the same time fixed orthogonally. Degas rebels against this discipline. In his 30th notebook, he drew the Pantheon from a worm's-eye view, and noted that no one ever reproduced monuments and houses from below, from underneath, as one sees them when passing in the street. He did not exclude people from this rearrangement of perspectives, and wanted to do portraits seen from above (cf. *Diego Martelli*, ill. 73), and 'some seen from below – sitting very close to a woman and looking at her from below, I shall see her head in the chandelier…'

The aesthetics of the unusual perspective are not confined to oblique angles. Degas made provocative inroads into the whole structure of the room. For someone who mocked the *plein air* painters for their adherence to single points of view, the three-dimensional facts of the real world were nothing but raw material with which he could conduct his experiments in alienation. He invited the observer to see things differently by placing a question mark behind the certainties of central perspective, and thus endowed rooms and spaces with multiple meanings that we might term 'polyfocal'. At the heart of this process is the zone where rooms are compartmentalized or split up into screens, and where people are turned into puppets or are frozen in a dialogue of distant proximity.

The *Actresses in their Dressing Rooms* (ill. 230) are perhaps the boldest of all Degas's spatial puzzles. The etching is said to have undergone at least five variations on the concealment of three-dimensional connections. The woman at her dressing table is squeezed to one side and so firmly shut off by a curtain that one could almost take the latter for a wall. Next comes an indefinable blank band that runs roughly through the centre of the composition: it might be some kind of surface, or a glimpse into another room at the back. The limbs of the strange shadow might belong to a doll, and they certainly have nothing to do with the woman. A broad perpendicular break cuts the silhouette into a fragment. Behind it is a second dressing room with similar contents, and this is the only area with clearly recognizable dimensions. The outline of a screen might lead one to the assumption that the projected shadow also comes from a screen. The last of the four vertical bands repeats the pattern of the curtain on the left. Exactly where these bands come to rest on the floor we cannot see, and the same applies to the ceiling. We are expected to view all of this as a vaguely floating pattern, attached to nothing. Thus the observer remains excluded, and can only take in the fragmentary nature of the composition.

At some time, Degas worked on the etching with pastel crayons, endowing it with a colourfulness that was easier on the eye. But of course this gain also results in losses – in particular of the consistency that was part of the austere charm of the etching. The colour softens the harsh contrasts and also weakens the mystery of the disconnectedness, precisely by making the scene more accessible to the eye. The same applies to the shadow in the bright central zone. Although it retains its lifeless, off-centre outline, it no longer falls into a bare gap – raising the question of whether this is a surface or another room – but onto the frame of a half-open door. While the etching was composed of four separate, incomplete bands that might be interchangeable, the pastel presents a clear spatial gradation that causes no confusion at all. The original shock effect gives way to something much more reassuring. This comparison is not meant as a criticism that Degas has taken an easy option, but one cannot help thinking that the pastel version may have been inspired by the desire to make the work more saleable. It may even be that a collector had expressed a particular wish. The two versions relate to each other as a highly disciplined, experimental monologue to a colloquial piece in which the artist speaks directly to the observer.

Concession and/or compromise? The question touches on the ever uncertain identity of the artist in a society that wants to be shocked by him, but also served, challenged and entertained. His multiple role allows for changes of identity, but it also relieves him of the effort that the self-consciously avant-garde must make if they are to be convincing in *their* role. Before Degas's experimental rooms compressed and codified his polyfocal juxtaposition of social alienations, that same multiple focus was inherent in the mental structure of his artistic quest. The critical observer of the Paris scene and its chiaroscuro was preceded by the hunter of multiple forms and meanings. Perhaps part of this quest was his inborn scepticism, which prevented him from seeing any one form as clear and unchangeable. His restless gaze set all forms of the empirical world in a constant state of change, or 'polyfocality'. This endless reshaping is the *basso continuo* that holds everything together. And so the narrow, barred rooms and the spacious landscape woman are opposites that are tied by a common, morphological umbilical cord.

Before Degas extended his aesthetic of the unfamiliar angle to the whole structure of his compositions, his copyist's eye had already fallen on certain unusual details. In 1855, he selected from Ingres's monumental *Martyrdom of St Symphorian* not one of the main figures, but one that was squeezed into a gap – a youth kneeling on the right behind the saint (ill. 233). In the copy, his anatomy seems not just compressed but actually patched together. But Degas

230
Actresses in their
Dressing Rooms
c. 1879–80
Etching and aquatint
22.5 x 31 cm (8 3/4 x 12 1/8 in.)
Washington, National Gallery of
Art, Rosenwald Collection

did not change anything. That is how the original figure looks in Ingres's painting – gnarled and knotted, and pressed into a gap. What could have led him to copy this marginal and indistinct figure? Perhaps it was the awkwardness, which was totally at odds with the normally smooth handiwork of the admired master, or maybe the telescoping, which later he would use himself in his groups of friends and dancers (ills. 76 and 75). A few years later, in the 15th notebook (1859–60), he tackled another Ingres: *Ruggiero Rescuing Angelica* (ill. 232). Again it was a peripheral motif that fascinated him – the fluttering drapery. He treats it like an autonomous form. The elbow of the knight is of little interest to him, but instead he focuses all his attention on the falling folds. He turns Ingres's curves into hard, angular creases, a kind of rocky landscape, the true identity of which we can only decipher very slowly. The young Degas intuitively engaged in the process of the 'complicating form', to which half a century later Viktor Shklovsky devoted a programmatic essay.

The form-changing vision with which Degas was blessed can be demonstrated on different levels. It gave him the licence to make things either clearer or more obscure (ill. 234). He used

231
Factory Smoke
c. 1880–84
Pencil and black ink on paper
11.9 x 16.1 cm (4 3/4 x 6 1/4 in.)
New York, The Metropolitan
Museum of Art

linear foreshortening, like the Carraccis, as a secret key for portrait caricatures or phallic love-birds. Such jokes reveal a vision that could both compress and combine, and this flexibility distinguishes him from the single-minded brushwork of the Impressionists, which from the very beginning was fixed on one particular theme and would not allow any arbitrary diversions from it. For them, the fleeting moment stood in the tradition of the *prima idea* which, since the Renaissance, had guided the process of composition. Degas, however, stands in a different, older tradition. The vision of pictures within pictures goes back to ancient sources that gave rise to random formations which could help painters devise new forms. In this territory, which Leonardo explored in theory and in practice, we also find Shakespeare's Mark Antony: 'Sometimes we see a cloud that's dragonish; / A vapour sometime like a bear or lion' (*Antony and Cleopatra*, IV, 12).

Degas had an imaginative vision similar to Antony's. On page 34 of the 13th notebook, which he used on his Italian journey, there is a pencil drawing whose truncated forms seem like an embryonic landscape from which figures like riders appear to be emerging. The accompanying note confirms this impression and extends it: 'The smoke of the railway engine threw

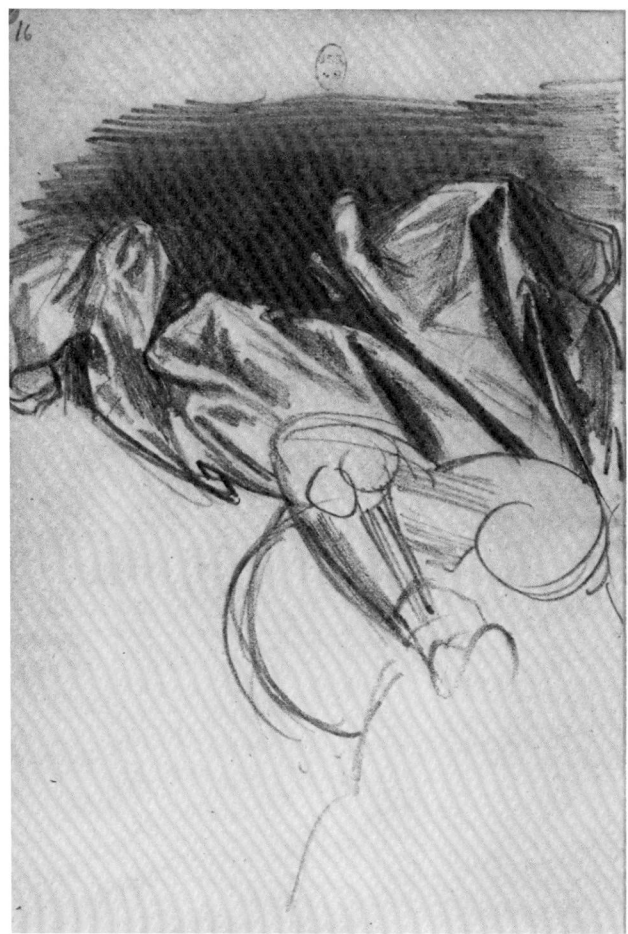

shadows over the countryside, and was like an endless horde galloping over hill and dale.' In the 30th notebook (1877–83), there are notes about formal motifs which he detaches from larger contexts (ill. 231): 'About smoke. Smoke from smokers, pipes, cigarettes, cigars, smoke from railway engines, factory chimneys, steamships etc., smoke trapped under bridges; steam.' In these observations, Degas is not activating his transforming vision so much as investigating the different contexts that can change phenomena. Smoke therefore is a plural concept, in the sense that it is a series of metamorphoses.

In the 22nd notebook (1867–74), he looks into ambivalent forms which allow for different interpretations: 'There is a possibility that one might find as much resemblance between a face and a pebble as between two pebbles... The question of form is not worth raising, since one often finds as much similarity between a pebble and a fish, a mountain and a dog's head, clouds and horses etc...' The uses Degas made of this ambivalence were noted by Valéry: 'It is said that he made his studies of rocks in his room, taking as his subjects pieces of coke borrowed from his stove. He apparently emptied the bucket on the table, and then painstakingly drew the formation that his act had chanced to create….' Long before that, Cennino Cennini had recommended in his *Trattato della Pittura* (c. 1400) that one should take 'a few rough, uncut stones and paint them after Nature.' The result, he said, would resemble mountains that 'look natural'. In 1910, Renoir wrote a preface to the French edition of this treatise, and so the text had by no means been forgotten and may even have provided the material for discussions in various studios. The transformation of the small into the large – which Degas was alluding to when he linked cigarette smoke and railway engines together – also preoccupied Delacroix. On 6 May 1852, he wrote in his diary that on the beach in Tangier he had seen 'little furrows which could have been mistaken for the stripes on the skin of tigers….' Degas may have read this passage in René Piot's first edition of the diary (1893), and it may have reinforced his own very similar observations.

When Degas used bits of coke as a model, he did not do so as a copyist but as an alchemist of paint, dematerializing his subject and transforming it into coloured pigments. We are made to plunge into a premorphic continuum in which everything is simultaneously close to us and yet distant. There are no firm outlines and no tangible bodies. The picture simply falls out of the frame of the 'open window', which for centuries had served as the regulating force by taking a piece of the empirical world, presenting it to the observer through central perspective, but at the same time allowing him a degree of detachment. This distance, which was maintained by the Impressionists, was eliminated by Degas. Nor was he the only one to do so. In far-away Aix-en-Provence, another lone artist was working out his own solution to the problem: Cézanne. Each of them developed their own concepts without any contact with one another, and initially without any response from the art world.

In his first critical evaluation of the Impressionists (1880), Zola missed out both of these painters, who from the beginning were not satisfied with the discovery of *plein air*, and in 1896, in his last piece of art criticism, he deliberately avoided dealing with their later work. Instead he bemoaned the rampancy of mysticism, the *'peinture d'âmes'* [painting of souls], and the *'peinture d'idées'* [painting of ideas]. Still fixated on the 'open window', he closed his mind to the possibility that a glimpse of the open air might contain something other than the illusion of pure facts. This, however, was the area in which Degas and Cézanne were working. They sought a more intense connection between the world and its contents, or in art-historical terms, between three-dimensional space and the volumes distributed inside it. Both of them therefore dispensed with the stability established pictorially through central perspective, which could only legitimize the positioning of bodies next to or behind one another, and they

used the third dimension to create something new: the interweaving of space and body. For the observer, this turned the composition of the picture into something disturbingly vague and uncertain.

Cézanne transformed illusory space into a tissue of autonomous – but not outlined – splashes of colour, which simultaneously denoted depth and surface; in other words, he removed the categorical distinction between space and body. The result is a welter of potential connections, and the picture becomes ambivalent – a hybrid of space and substance. People and objects are no longer separate in space but are woven into the '*stabilité de l'édifice spatial*'. This 'stability', however, also contains dynamic fluctuations, so that it seems constantly on the verge of producing something new. Space is not a given dimension, and so it does not precede its contents; the two are simply interrelated. Together they form a symbiotic unit. Cézanne pursued his concept of composition with a persistence bordering on obsession. His goal was to capture an all-embracing cosmic harmony, a homogeneous whole that would encompass man and so take him out of his isolation.

Degas held back from this ultimate stage, and unlike Cézanne, who studied Nature intensely before committing it to canvas, he preferred to work from memory. When he placed women in natural surroundings (ills. 195, 196, 198), he barely hinted at the presence of vegetation. In *Landscape Woman* (ill. 228), the hills do bear the greenness of organic life, but logically the human element is missing, as that would be – almost literally – a foreign body.

The liquefaction of space in this and in the other monotypes is complemented by the cramped, inaccessibly telescoped rooms that are a prerequisite of civilization (ills. 29, 37, 54, 74, 96, 117, 140, 162). In these nooks and crannies, once again there is no clear distinction between room and object, and the third dimension has no autonomy but results from the interweaving of people and objects. Degas achieves this with his tried and trusted method of transforming solid rooms into movable walls, screens, backdrops and grilles. What this led to in the 20th century can be seen in the works of Beckmann and Bacon – the former with his bulky cages in which strange rituals are performed, and the latter in his arbitrary voids reflecting the distortions of androgynous human figures. These dissonances were already to be seen in Degas's space-body combinations, which are different from Cézanne's interior still lifes, whose dislocated, lop-sided objects contain at least contain the seeds of harmony. Degas's two spatial concepts – the flow of *Landscape Woman* and the constrictions of his *Dressing Rooms* – paradoxically come together, with continuity changing into discontinuity, and vice versa.

The dual vision that gave rise to these two revolutionary concepts made Degas into a unique figure in his era. His experimental restlessness and his ever-wandering, form-changing gaze separate him from the single-minded approach to which Cézanne subscribed almost religiously. And yet the combination of openness and closure that we see in *Bathing Women* (Philadelphia), in which the women and trees merge into an almost cathedral-like structure, and the repeated depictions of Mont-Sainte-Victoire, are not dissimilar to the variations that the sceptical Degas explored through the many stages of his etchings and in the interlinking motifs of his dancers. There is, however, one all-important difference: Cézanne's line of thought always headed towards *convergence*, whereas Degas could never tear himself away from *divergence*. He would not allow himself the sight of any finishing line, or any earthly paradise. His spaces, containing rooms and people, are always the bearers of tensions and conflicts, and can never take on any self-contained and settled form, any homogeneous unity.

235
Cap Hornu
c. 1890
Colour monotype
29.9 x 40 cm (11 3/4 x 15 3/4 in.)
London, The British Museum

The contrast between these two great artists already signals the future bifurcations of the 20th century: on the one hand, the Constructivists, who aimed for harmony and balance that ranged from the unison of everyday routine to the cosmic, metaphysical oneness of the universe; on the other hand, the Dadaists and the Surrealists, who were intent on building disparate, anarchic 'other worlds' and raised the taboo on the darkest sides of the psyche and of human instincts that had first been explored by Degas, in the field of social chiaroscuro. This he did without ever waving the banner of the trail-blazing critic. He subscribed to no doctrine, and his dissatisfaction with the state of society had its psychological roots in a universal dislike of institutionalized and ritualized civilization. While Cézanne would explode when people talked of art professors, Degas reserved his tantrums for the word '*arrivé*' in the sense of someone who had 'made it'. Mallarmé relates how furious Degas was when he cautiously relayed a request from the Director of the Beaux-Arts, asking if he might be willing to donate one of his paintings to the Musée du Luxembourg, which showed the state holdings of modern French art. (It was the same official who refused to give the *légion d'honneur* to

Cézanne.) 'Of course I said no. These people would like me to believe that I've arrived. Arrived – what does that mean? You always arrive, you never arrive. Arrive where? Does it mean hanging on a wall next to one of Bouguereau's women or Toto Girod's slave market? I won't. When everybody is doing his own thing and getting his own little audience, why should the bureaucrats start meddling? I pay my dues, so what have my pictures got to do with them? But no! They have to poke their noses in everywhere! They've got the chessboard of the arts on their table, and we the artists are the pieces…they push this pawn here, and that pawn there…Well, I'm not a pawn, and I don't want to be pushed around.'

When Ludovic Halévy gently tried to intervene, Degas went on: 'You're not seeing the whole picture. The fact is, if I went into the Luxembourg, I'd think I was being taken to the police station! Arrived! So you can't move again! …I don't want to be seized by the fine arts police, or by that police officer who goes by the name of Roujon….'

His defiant hostility towards all officialdom and authority left Degas ideologically free to lead whatever life he chose. Only once did he put a foot badly wrong, and that was over the

Dreyfus affair, which split French society during the 1890s; he sided with the army, and hence with the French establishment, and it led to a break with his best friends, including the Halévys. Perhaps what drove him to it was that notorious contrariness of the outsider who, in this case, thought that the truth was a lie spread by his arch-enemy the Press. In the end, this estrangement from his friends really did turn him into a rootless *flâneur*, who made his social chiaroscuro not only a subject of his art but also a hiding place where he felt at home, in keeping with his expressed desire to be 'famous and unknown'. In a snapshot taken in July 1889 by Giuseppe Primoli when Degas was just leaving a public urinal (ill. 236), he is a completely anonymous figure coming out of the protective darkness of the convenience into the everyday world – a gentleman who has just attended to himself, and whose bearing suggests that he sees everything around him from the perspective of distant proximity.

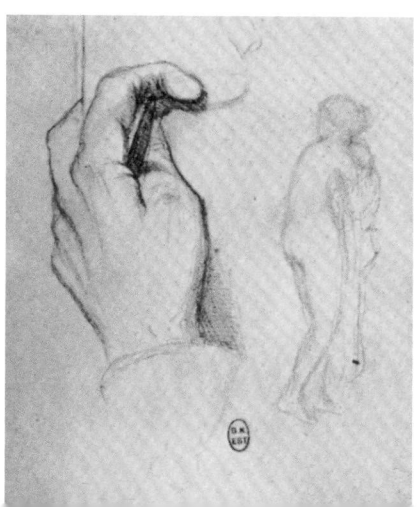

237
Degas's Left Hand
From Degas's notebooks
(NB. 6, p. 56)

Acknowledgments

The author makes no claim to being one of the world's leading experts on Degas. His aim is to try and understand this great but mysterious figure against the overall background of events that took place during his lifetime. Anyone who bemoans the gaps in the selective bibliography – which faithfully reflects my own current knowledge of what is available – should consult Adriani (*Bordell und Boudoir*), Loyrette 1988, and Zurich 1994.

I have found confirmation of my views on Degas and his art in studies by Carol Armstrong, Henri Loyrette, Emil Maurer and Theodore Reff, not to mention Duranty (*La nouvelle peinture*), to whom I am indebted for the key expression '*le clair-obscur social*' (social chiaroscuro).

While I naturally hope that readers will pay close attention to my words, my text also depends on their visual cooperation. For this reason, I am especially grateful to Wolfgang Beck for so graciously acceding to my demands as regards the illustrations. My editors – Stefanie Hölscher, Beate Sander and Alexandra Schumacher – have been models of thoroughness and efficiency. Thanks also to Christa Schauer for combining the text and images so successfully, and to Wolfgang Beck for his ideas.

W. H.

Degas: A Chronology

The most detailed and reliable biographical information is to be found in Loyrette 1988.

1834   Hilaire-Germain-Edgar de Gas is born on 19 July in Paris (8 rue Saint-Georges).

1840   His sister Thérèse is born in Naples.

1842   His sister Marguerite is born in Paris.
             Laura, his father's sister, marries Baron Gennaro Bellelli in Naples.

1845–53 Degas attends the Lycée Louis-le-Grand as a boarder, and makes friends with Ludovic Halévy, Henri Rouart and Paul Valpinçon.

1847   Death of Degas's mother. First visit to a museum.

1853   Awarded his final school diploma (*Bachelier ès lettres*). Acquires a copying permit for the Louvre and the engravings department of the Bibliothèque Nationale.
             November: begins his studies at the Faculty of Law, but soon gives up.

1855   Paul Valpinçon takes him to visit Ingres. On 6 April, registers for a course with Paul Lamothe at the Ecole des Beaux-Arts.
             July–September: travels to the South of France (Arles, Nîmes, Avignon), and stays in Lyons for two months.

1856   17 April: goes to Naples, and then Rome.

1857   Stays in Rome until July, then goes back to his grandfather in Naples. Spends winter of 1857–58 in Rome. Meets Gustave Moreau.

1858   24 July: goes from Rome to Florence, stopping off at Siena.

1859   March: Siena, Pisa. April: back to Paris via Genoa.
             October: moves to an apartment at 13 rue de Laval (now rue Victor Massé).

1860   March: goes to Naples. April: stays with the Bellellis in Florence.

1861   September–October: spends three weeks with the Valpinçons in Normandy.

1862   Chance meeting with Manet while copying in the Louvre.

1864   Visits Ingres in his studio.

1865   *Scene of War in the Middle Ages* (ill. 12) exhibited at the Salon.

1867–68 Meets Adolph Menzel at the home of Alfred Stevens.

1868   *Mlle Fiocre in the Ballet 'La Source'* (ill. 13) exhibited at the Salon. Becomes a regular at the Café Guerbois, where Manet meets his friends (Monet, Renoir, Morisot, Duranty etc.).

1869   Travels to Brussels. July/August: visits Manet in Boulogne-sur-Mer. Landscapes in pastel.

1870   Takes part in a Salon exhibition for the last time (*Madame Camus*, ill. 52). After outbreak of war with Prussia, volunteers to join the National Guard. Assigned to an artillery unit, where he meets his childhood friend Henri Rouart.

1871   First signs of eye trouble. October: travels to London.

1872   January: makes contact with the art dealer Paul Durand-Ruel, who buys three paintings.
Takes part in the summer and autumn exhibition by the Society of French Artists in London.
October: goes to New Orleans.

1873   March: returns to Paris. 27 December: together with Cézanne, Monet, Morisot, Pissarro, Sisley et al., founds the Société Anonyme Coopérative à Capital Variable des Artistes, Peintres, Sculpteurs, Graveurs etc.

1874   February: Degas's father dies. 15 April: first exhibition of the Société Anonyme.

1875   Travels to Naples for the funeral of his uncle Achille. Returns via Florence, Pisa and Genoa.

1876   Contributes 22 works to the second Impressionist exhibition at the Durand-Ruel gallery.
The Paris firm of De Gas goes into liquidation. July: works with monotypes and engravings.
October: moves into a new apartment at 50 rue Lepic.

1877   Third Impressionist exhibition. Degas exhibits paintings, pastels and monotypes.
Complains about deteriorating eyesight.

1878   *The Cotton Exchange in New Orleans* (ill. 29) is exhibited in Pau and bought by the town's 'friends of the arts' for the local museum (first sale to a museum).

1879   March: Degas succeeds in having the 'Impressionists' renamed as 'Peintres Indépendants'. Exhibits 25 works at the fourth exhibition, including five fans.

1880   Fifth group exhibition of the Impressionists. On 9 April, Edmond Duranty dies.
After an interval of six years, Durand-Ruel buys another work by Degas.

1881   A heated discussion between Degas, Caillebotte and Pissarro about whether to extend the circle of contributors to the Impressionist exhibitions. At the sixth exhibition, Degas shows the bronze of the *Little Dancer Aged Fourteen* (ill. 143).

1882   Does not take part in the seventh Impressionist exhibition. Quarrels with Gauguin.
July: Visits the Halévys in Etretat. September: travels to Switzerland (Geneva, Ouchy, Zurich).
Zoë Closier becomes his housekeeper. New apartment at 21 rue Pigalle.

1883   Rejects Durand-Ruel's offer of a one-man exhibition. Dowdeswell and Dowdeswell in London exhibit seven of his works.

1884   Inherits *The Departure of the Folkestone Boat* (Winterthur, Reinhart Collection) from Manet's estate, and expresses his delight.

1885   Acquires Ingres's *Oedipus and the Sphinx*. August–September: meets Sickert and Gauguin at the Halévys' home. Is now among the privileged few allowed to go backstage during performances at the Opéra.

1886   Eighth (and last) group exhibition. Degas contributes ten works, especially women at their toilet. At the Impressionist exhibition that Durand-Ruel organizes in New York, he is represented by 23 works.

1887   The art dealer Theo van Gogh acquires *Woman Seated Beside a Vase of Flowers* (ill. 50) for the Boussod and Valadon Gallery.

1888   Moves to 18 rue de Boulogne (now rue Balla). August: goes to Cauterets via Pau and Lourdes to take a cure. Writes eight sonnets.

1889	Refuses to take part in the art show at the Universal Exhibition. July: thanks Count Primoli for the photograph of him leaving a public lavatory (ill. 236). September: travels to Spain and Morocco (Tangier) with Boldini.
1890	Rents a studio at 3 rue Victor Massé. March: buys Delacroix's portrait of Baron Schwiter (National Gallery, London). September: travels with the sculptor Bartholomé through Burgundy in a horse-drawn carriage. First landscape monotypes.
1891	Encourages Toulouse-Lautrec. Although not a fan of Wagner, admires Rose Caron (ill. 53) as Elsa in *Lohengrin*.
1892	Visits Evariste de Valernes in Carpentras. November: Exhibition of landscape monotypes at Durand-Ruel's gallery.
1893	Visits the Morbillis in Interlaken. Buys Gauguin's *The Moon and the Earth* (Museum of Modern Art, New York).
1894	His anti-Dreyfus stance spoils his friendship with Pissarro. Buys El Greco's *St Ildefonsus* from Millet's estate, and also two of the fragments of Manet's *The Execution of Maximilian*.
1895	Concentrates on photography, and exhibits his work at the picture-framer Tasset and Lhote.
1896	Attends the funeral of his friend Valernes in Carpentras. Buys two of Cézanne's still lifes. After much controversy, the Louvre accepts Caillebotte's legacy, which contains seven works by Degas. Hugo von Tschudi buys the pastel *Women in Conversation at the Milliner's* (ill. 117) for Berlin's Nationalgalerie.
1897	The Dreyfus Affair strains relations with the Halévys.
1899	Tries in vain to prevent his *Cotton Exchange in New Orleans* from being lent out for the centenary show of French art at the Universal Exhibition
1903	Takes part in an exhibition by the Berlin Secession and is represented by six works at the Impressionist exhibition mounted in Vienna by Julius Meier-Graefe. The poet Alfred Walter Heymel donates the pastel of a dancer to the Kunsthalle in Bremen.
1904	Travels to Besançon, Ornans and Nancy.
1905	Shows 35 works in the Impressionist exhibition at the Grafton Galleries in London.
1909	Sees a performance by Diaghilev's Ballets Russes.
1911	Solo exhibition at the Fogg Art Museum, Harvard University.
1912	Because of the demolition of his house in rue Victor Massé, is forced to move to 6 Boulevard de Clichy – with the help of Suzanne Valadon. The Metropolitan Museum of Modern Art in New York buys *Dancers Practising at the Bar* (ill. 147), and the Frankfurt Städel buys *Musicians of the Orchestra* (ill. 92).
1913	Paul Cassirer mounts a 'Degas/Cézanne' double exhibition in Berlin.
1917	Degas dies of a brain haemorrhage on 27 September, and is buried the following day in the family tomb at the Montmartre cemetery. The mourners include many different and even opposing factions from the art world: Bartholomé, Bonnat, Cassatt, Forain, Gervex, Monet, Raffaëlli, Zandomeneghi, as well as friends like Rouart, Vollard and Louise Halévy.

Notes

Chapter 1: A Man Apart (pp. 9–17)

p. 9: *epigraph*: Notebook 6, p. 83.

Duranty: Edmond Duranty, *La nouvelle peinture: À propos du groupe d'artistes qui expose dans les galeries Durand-Ruel*, Paris, 1876; new edition edited by Marcel Guérin, Paris, 1946 (p. 43, note on *Le Peintre Louis Martin*).

Duranty 1879: in *La Chronique des Arts*, 19 April 1879, p. 127 (cited in Loyrette 1988, p. 310).

p. 10: *Tissot*: Cited by Jean Sutherland Boggs, 'Chronologie – Degas als Portraitist', in Zurich 1994, p. 91.

p. 12: *Gautier*: Théophile Gautier, *L'Art moderne*, Paris, 1856, p. 265.

Diderot: Denis Diderot, *Essai sur la peinture*, in *Œuvres*, Ed. de la Pléiade, Paris, 1968, p. 1113. See also Duranty, *La nouvelle peinture*, p. 41.

p. 13: *Fromentin*: Duranty, *La nouvelle peinture*, p. 21. On Fromentin, see also Carol Armstrong, *Odd Man Out: Readings of the Work and Reputation of Edgar Degas*, Chicago and London, 1991, p. 77.

p. 14: *Diderot 1765*: Denis Diderot, *Salons*, eds. Jean Seznec and Jean Adhémar, vol. II, Oxford, 1960, pp. 77, 85, 105.

p. 15: *'Everything seemed to me to be arranged…'*: Duranty cited in the journal *Réalisme* (1856–57); from *La nouvelle peinture*, p. 48.

p. 16: *Courbet*: On the *Studio*, see Alan Bowness and Hélène Toussaint, *Gustave Courbet (1819–1877)*, exhibition catalogue, Paris, 1977, p. 241; and Hélène Toussaint and Lola Faillant-Dumas, *Le dossier de 'L'Atelier' de Courbet*, Paris, 1977.

Chapter 2: Before the Change of Course (pp. 19–37)

p. 19: *epigraph*: Notebook 11, p. 85.

p. 25: *letter from his father*: Lemoisne, vol. I, p. 30. Jean Sutherland Boggs, 'Chronologie – Degas als Portraitist', in Zurich 1994, p. 87.

p. 28: *The Salon*: see Oskar Bätschmann, *The Artist in the Modern World: the Conflict Between Market and Self-Expression*, New Haven, NJ, 1997.

Degas on 'Young Spartans Exercising': Pierre Cabanne, *Edgar Degas*, Paris, 1957, cat. 7 (cited in Georges Jeanniot, 'Souvenirs sur Degas', in *La Revue universelle* 55 [15 October 1933], p. 152.). See Linda Nochlin, 'Degas's *Young Spartans Exercising*', in *Art Bulletin* 68 (1986), p. 486.

p. 33: *Zola*: Émile Zola, *Mon salon* (1866), in *Salons*, eds. F. J. W. Hemmings and Robert J. Niess, Geneva and Paris, 1959, p. 63 (chapter: 'Le Moment artistique').

p. 34: *Nietzsche*: Friedrich Nietzsche, *The Case of Wagner* (1888), in *The Complete Works Of Friedrich Nietzsche*, ed. Oscar Levy, vol. VIII, London, 1911.

p. 36: *Castagnary*: *Le Siècle*, 29 April 1874. Cited in the second edition of Hélène Adhémar (ed.), *Centenaire de l'Impressionnisme*, exhibition catalogue, Paris, 1974, p. 265.

Chapter 3: Contemplation, Alienation and Self-Awareness (pp. 39–67)

p. 39: *epigraph*: Degas, *Lettres*, p. 28.

'Elle est peuple': Cachin in Adhémar/Cachin 1973, p. 21.

p. 42: *Componium*: See Werner Nekes and Bodo von Dewitz (eds.), *Ich sehe was, was Du nicht siehst! Sehmaschinen und Bilderwelten. Die Sammlung Werner Nekes*, exhibition catalogue, Göttingen, 2002, p. 263.

p. 44: *his 'first real painting'*: Felix Baumann, 'Die frühen Selbstbildnisse', in Zurich 1994, p. 164.

p. 49: *Bellelli Family*: See Harald Keller's monograph, *Degas: Die Familie Bellelli*, Stuttgart, 1962; Emil Maurer, 'Vom Bildnis zum Bild. Zu einem Spannungsverhältnis in Degas' Portraitwerk', in Zurich 1994, p. 108; and Tobia Bezzola, 'Die Familienportraits', in Zurich 1994, p. 189.

The Cotton Exchange in New Orleans: See Jean Sutherland Boggs and Gail Feigenbaum (eds.), *Degas and New Orleans: A French Impressionist in America*, exhibition catalogue, New Orleans, 1999.

p. 57: *Reff on 'Mme Morbilli'*: Reff 1976, p. 110.

p. 58: *The Rape*: Reff 1976, p. 200. Recently another (possible) source for the origin of the scene came to light: the 5th plate in the series *Les Lorettes* (1841) by Paul Gavarni (whose work Degas admired and collected): Felix Krämer, *Das unheimliche Heim. Zur Interieurmalerei um 1900*, Cologne, 2007, p. 147. It shows a *lorette* (kept woman) sitting on a rug and dealing cards, while what the cards predict stands in the doorway in the form of a blond man. It is quite possible that Degas knew this scene – while it may be the inspiration, it is also very different, because *The Rape* has nothing to do with common prostitution. The subject of his scene is a *femme honnête*, as featured in the episode of that name from the *Physiologies* series. See the illustration of 'A Subjugated Woman' (ill. 42).

p. 59: *envelope*: Reff 1976, ills. 150, 151.

p. 64: *broken jug*: Loyrette 1988, cat. 84, p. 144.

p. 65: *Victoria is reading*: Loyrette 1988, cat. 83, p. 142.

p. 66: *'helpless grief'*: Tobia Bezzola, 'Die Familienportraits', in Zurich 1994, p. 196.

Chapter 4: Women and Their Daydreams (pp. 69–81)

p. 69: *epigraph*: Notebook 11, p. 94.

'The women of the so-called better classes': Horace de Viel-Castel, *Der Karneval des Zweiten Kaiserreichs. Memoiren aus der Welt der Kaiserin Eugénie*, Dresden, n.d., p. 43 (4 March 1851). See Edmond and Jules de Goncourt, *Journal. Mémoires de la Vie littéraire*, ed. Robert Ricatte, vol. I, Paris 1956, p. 7. (11 March 1860) on the 'masked suppers' at which men dressed as women and women dressed as men.

p. 71: *Toussaint*: Bowness/Toussaint, *Gustave Courbet (1819–1877)*, cat. 70.

p. 75: *Elisabeth Bronfen*: Elisabeth Bronfen, 'Bei Sichtung der Gesichte – Degas' Frauenportraits', in Zurich 1994, p. 240.

Cassatt on her portrait: Loyrette 1988, cat. 268, p. 442.

p. 76: *a female critic*: Marianne Karabelnik, 'Im Kreis der Künstler und Intellektuellen', in Zurich 1994, p. 271.

Melancholy: See Jean Sutherland Boggs, 'Degas als Portraitist', in Zurich 1994, p. 28.

Chapter 5: Rooms Become Screens (pp. 83–103)

p. 83: *epigraph*: Notebook 30, p. 65.

Delacroix: Eugène Delacroix, *Journal*, ed. André Joubin, Paris, 1950, vol. II, p. 363 (3 August 1855).

p. 86: *suggestion to Charpentier*: Berthe Morisot, *Correspondance de Berthe Morisot avec sa famille et ses amis Manet, Puvis de Chavannes, Degas, Monet, Renoir et Mallarmé*, ed. Denis Rouart, Paris 1950, p. 165.

p. 87: *Degas and the Salon jury*: Theodore Reff, 'Some Unpublished Letters of Degas', in *Art Bulletin* 50 (1968), p. 87.

the nave of a cathedral: Thomas W. Gaehtgens, 'Das Kaufhaus als Kathedrale', in *Architectura. Zeitschrift für Geschichte der Architektur* 7 (1977), p. 193.

p. 89: *Albert Wolff*: Cited in Françoise Cachin (ed.), *Manet 1832–1883*, exhibition catalogue, Paris, 1983, p. 182.

Degas on Manet's 'Bar': Degas, *Lettres*, p. 63 (2 May 1882).

p. 90: *'poseurs'*: Marianne Karabelnik, 'Im Kreis der Künstler und Intellektuellen', in Zurich 1994, p. 266. See André Gide, *Journal 1889–1939*, Ed. de la Pléiade, Paris, 1965, p. 876.

Japonisme: Klaus Berger, *Japonisme in Western Painting from Whistler to Matisse*, Cambridge, 1992. See Reff 1976, p. 15. (Chapter: 'The Butterfly and the Ox').

pseudo-collage: Reff 1976, ill. 67.

p. 92: *Degas and Manet*: Victor I. Stoichita, 'Vaporization and/or Centralization. On the (Self) Portraits of Manet and Degas', in *Canadian Art Review* 26 (1999), p. 13.

p. 98: *Duranty criticized*: Letter from Federico Zandomeneghi to Diego Martelli, November 1894, cited in Loyrette 1988, p. 312.

In his treatise: Duranty, *La nouvelle peinture*, p. 45.

p. 99: *'thinker's gesture'*: Jean Sutherland Boggs, 'Degas als Portraitist', in Zurich 1994, p. 47.

p. 100: *Henri Michel-Lévy*: Reff 1976, p. 125.

'dramma della pittura': Fiorella Minervino, *L'Opera completa di Degas*, Milan, 1970, no. 362.

Chapter 6: A Painted Parable (pp. 105–117)

p. 105: *epigraph 1*: Duranty, *La nouvelle peinture*, p. 46.

epigraph 2: Charles Baudelaire, 'Le Peintre de la vie moderne', 1860, in *Œuvres complètes*, Ed. de la Pléiade, ed. Claude Pichois, Paris, 1954, p. 889.

Viscount Lepic and His Daughters: Max Imdahl, 'Die Momentfotografie und "Le Comte Lepic" von Degas' (1970), reprinted in *Zur Kunst der Moderne, Gesammelte Schriften*, vol. I, Frankfurt am Main, 1996, p. 181; Emil Maurer, 'Vom Bildnis zum Bild', in Zurich 1994, p. 111; Albert Kostenevich, *Hidden Treasures Revealed: Impressionist Masterpieces and Other Important French Paintings Preserved by the State Hermitage Museum*, St Petersburg, New York and St Petersburg, 1995, p. 68.

p. 109: *loneliness of the man in the crowd*: Jean-Jacques Rousseau, *La Nouvelle Héloïse*, Ed. de la Pléiade, Paris, 1969, p. 231 (part 2, letter XIV, Saint-Preux to Julie: 'ce vaste désert du monde…'); François René de Chateaubriand, *René*, Ed. de la Pléiade, Paris, 1969, p. 127 ('je me mêlais à la foule: vaste désert d'hommes'); Charles Baudelaire, *Le spleen de Paris*, XII: 'Les Foules' (in which the second stanza begins 'Multitude, solitude'), in *Œuvres complètes*, Ed. de la Pléiade, ed. Claude Pichois, Paris, 1956, p. 295; Edgar Allan Poe, 'The Man of the Crowd', in *Tales of Mystery and Imagination*, London, 1959, p. 101.

Champfleury: 'L'Enterrement à Ornans', in *Le Messager de l'Assemblée*, February 1851. Reprinted in Jules Champfleury, *Le Réalisme*, eds. Geneviève and Jean Lacambre, Paris, 1973, p. 158.

p. 110: *Lepic*: Adhémar, *Centenaire de l'Impressionisme*, p. 239.

p. 112: *laundresses and milliners*: These 'were associated with clandestine prostitution' (Carol Armstrong, *Odd Man Out*, p. 54).

p. 113: *sex service industry*: Götz Adriani coins this expression and expands on it in his exhibition catalogue *Bordell und Boudoir*.

p. 114: *Flaubert and his refusal to draw 'conclusions'*: 'Les gens légers, bornés, les esprits présomptueux et enthousiastes veulent en toute chose une conclusion…' ('Fickle and narrow-minded people, arrogant and effusive minds want everything to have a conclusion…'), letter to Mlle Leroyer de Chantepie, 18 May 1857, reprinted in Gustave Flaubert, *Correspondance*, Ed. de la Pléiade, vol. II, Paris, 1980, p. 718. See Degas's annoyance at the insinuation that he had 'arrived' as an artist, discussed in Chapter 13, p. 308.

p. 116: *Sacred Allegory*: See Anchise Tempestini, *Giovanni Bellini. Catalogo completo*, Florence, 1992, no. 78. The critic who comes closest to my view is Rainer Metzger, 'Fantasia. Zu Giovanni Bellinis "Allegoria sacra"', in *Kunstpresse* 3 (1990) p. 16.

p. 117: *Engels*: Friedrich Engels, *The Condition of the Working-Class in England* (1845), in Marx/Engels, *Collected Works*, vol. 4, Moscow, 1975–2005.

ball for L'Assommoir: mentioned in Joris-Karl Huysmans, *Lettres inédites à Emile Zola*, ed. Pierre Lambert, Geneva, 1953, p. 21.

Chapter 7: The Bourgeois in his World: The Discovery of Leisure (pp. 119–143)

p. 119: *epigraph*: Charles Baudelaire to Sainte-Beuve, 4 May 1865, in *Correspondance*, ed. Claude Pichois, vol. II, Paris, 1973, p. 493.

Schiller: Friedrich Schiller, 'Über die ästhetische Erziehung des Menschen' (1793–94), 6th letter, in *Werke in drei Bänden*, vol. II, ed. Herbert G. Göpfert, Munich, 1984, p. 455.

Middle-class entertainments: Robert L. Herbert, *Impressionism: Art, Leisure and Parisian Society*, New Haven and London, 1988. (On p. 35 Lepic is described as a *flâneur* and the man on the left side of the painting as a *badaud* [onlooker].)

p. 131: *Valéry*: Paul Valéry, *Le Problème des Musées* (1923), in *Œuvres*, Ed. de la Pléiade, ed. Jean Hytier, vol. II, Paris, 1960, p. 1290.

p. 134. *Chesneau*: cited in Adhémar, *Centenaire de l'Impressionisme*, p. 269 ('œuvre exquise de coloration, de dessin, de justesse dans les attitudes et de finesse d'ensemble').

p. 136: *Chesneau's preliminary remarks*: ibid., p. 268. ('S'ils avaient eu jusqu'au bout le courage de leur opinion…ils eussent peut-être pleinement réussi à frapper un grand coup.' ('If they had only had the courage of their convictions, they would perhaps have succeeded in making a great impact.')

'hole-in-the-wall': Françoise Cachin in *Manet 1832–1883*, exhibition catalogue, p. 267. To Zola, who saw the painter as an opener of windows, creating a 'hole in the wall' was the mark of a great talent ('Mon Salon' [1866], in *Salons*, p. 63).

p. 141: *Tinterow*: Loyrette 1988, cat. 351, p. 561.

Chapter 8: Bodies Adorned and Used (pp. 145–167)

p. 145: *epigraph*: Goncourt, *Journal*, vol. II, p. 967.

Diderot, supplement to 'Bougainville's World Tour': Denis Diderot, *Supplément au Voyage de Bougainville ou Dialogue entre A. et B. sur l'Inconvénient d'attacher des Idées morales à certaines Actions physiques qui n'en comportent pas*, in *Œuvres*, Ed. de la Pléiade, Paris, 1962, p. 963.

p. 147: *Baudelaire, traveller faced with two paths*: Charles Baudelaire, 'La double vie de Charles Asselineau', in *Œuvres complètes*, Ed. de la Pléiade, Paris, 1956, p. 1016.

p. 153: *dialogue with the object*: Sergiusz Michalski, 'Degas. Spiegelungen und Doubles', in: Victor I. Stoichita (ed.), *Das Double*, Wiesbaden, 2006, p. 197.

p. 162: *Daumier's Laundress*: Jean Adhémar, *Honoré Daumier*, Paris, 1954, plate 114.

p. 164: *several versions of one subject*: 'J'entasse donc des projets qui me demanderaient dix vies à exécuter.' ('I am amassing projects that would take me ten lifetimes to complete.') Degas, *Lettres*, p. 23 (27 November 1872).

Chapter 9: Dancers: Flying High and Falling Low (pp. 169–199)

p. 169: *epigraph*: Paul Valéry, 'Degas, danse, dessin' (1938), in *Œuvres*, Ed. de la Pléiade, ed. Jean Hytier, vol. II, Paris, 1960, p. 1171.

p. 172: *carefully composed*: Degas believed: 'L'instantané, c'est la photographie et rien de plus.' ('The instantaneous is for photographs and nothing else.') Degas, *Lettres*, p. 23 (Letter to Lorentz Frölich, 27 November 1872).

p. 182: *Rilke, 1898*: Gisela Götte and Jo-Anne Birnie Danzker (eds.), *Rainer Maria Rilke und die bildende Kunst seiner Zeit*, exhibition catalogue, Munich, 1996, p. 41.

p. 183: *Klinger*: Max Klinger, *Malerei und Zeichnung. Tagebuchaufzeichnungen und Briefe*, ed. Anneliese Hübscher, Leipzig, 1985, p. 64 (reference: Richard Hüttel).

p. 184: *Little Dancer Aged Fourteen*: Loyrette 1988, p. 343. (with quotes from contemporary critics).

p. 185: *the accused at a murder trial*: Loyrette 1988, p. 207; (Douglas W. Druick and Peter Zegers) Zurich 1994, cat. 161.

p. 190: *'unhealthy' literature*: Loyrette 1988, p. 280.

p. 192: *monotypes*: Cachin in Adhémar/Cachin 1973, p. 15. See Eugenia Parry Janis, *Degas: Monotypes. Essay, Catalogue and Checklist*, Greenwich, CT, 1968; and Sue Welsh Reed and Barbara Stern Shapiro, *Edgar Degas: The Painter as Printmaker*, Boston, 1984.

p. 197: *Degas on Ernest May*: Degas, *Lettres*, p. 47 (undated letter to Bracquemond). The journal, which Degas had been going to collaborate on, never materialized.

Chapter 10: Liberties Bought and Sold (pp. 201–223)

p. 201: *epigraph:* Joris-Karl Huysmans, *Marthe, Histoire d'une fille* (1876), Paris, 2002, p. 19.

prostitution: See the outstanding account (in both words and pictures) in Götz Adriani, *Bordell und Boudoir* (with bibliography).

the revenge of the poor man: Goncourt, *Journal*, vol. II, p. 176, 8 July 1865: 'La vengeance du pauvre contre les riches, ce sont ses filles.'

'Our bourgeois…': Karl Marx and Friedrich Engels, *Manifesto of the Communist Party* (1848), in Marx/Engels, *Selected Works*, vol. 1, Moscow, 1969, pp. 98–137. To Marx, wage labour was prostitution, and therefore prostitution was also a form of wage labour: 'The factory workers in France call the prostitution of their wives and daughters the nth working hour, which is literally correct.' (Karl Marx, *Economic and Philosophic Manuscripts of 1844*, in Marx/Engels, *Collected Works*, vol. 3, Moscow, 1975–2005.)

Paris-Parisien: Paris, 1897, p. 137: 'public très mêlé'.

p. 202: *Ellen Andrée recalled:* Loyrette 1988, cat. 172, p. 288. ('Je suis devant une absinthe; Desboutin devant un breuvage innocent, le monde renversé, quoi! et nous avons l'air de deux andouilles.')

p. 207: *her thumb to her top lip:* To Georges Rivière this gesture meant 'Pas seulement ça' ('not just that!'); Georges Rivière, 'L'Exposition des impressionnistes', in *L'Impressionniste* (6 April 1877). Cited in Loyrette 1988, cat. 174.

hostility verging on outrage: Douglas Cooper, *The Courtauld Collection: A Catalogue and Introduction*, London, 1954, p. 42.

p. 209: *'She opens her great mouth':* Degas in a letter to Henry Lerolle (Degas, *Lettres*, p. 75, 4 December 1883). Thérésa told a drunken suitor that what she really needed was 'a man with poise' ('un homme posé'): Goncourt, *Journal*, vol. II, p. 163 (11 May 1865).

p. 213: *Giedion:* Sigfried Giedion, *Raum, Zeit, Architektur. Die Entstehung einer neuen Tradition*, Ravensburg, 1965, p. 191.

p. 214: *Mantegna's crucifixion:* Loyrette 1988, cat. 27 (Musée de Tours). See Erica Tietze-Conrat, 'What Degas Learned from Mantegna', in *Gazette des Beaux-Arts* 26 (1944), p. 413.

p. 216: *Baudelaire, 'the epic side…':* 'Salon de 1845', in *Œuvres complètes*, Ed. de la Pléiade, ed. Claude Pichois, Paris, 1956, p. 596.

Herding: Klaus Herding, 'Daumiers "L'Homme à la corde"', in Uwe Fleckner (ed.), *Jenseits der Grenzen. Französische und deutsche Kunst vom Ancien Régime bis zur Gegenwart, Thomas W. Gaehtgens zum 60. Geburtstag*, 3 vols., Cologne, 2000, vol. II, p. 329.

p. 218: *women in brothels:* Cachin in Adhémar/Cachin 1973, cat. 83–123.

p. 219: *Brothel-Keeper's Name Day:* This scene depicts an event that traditionally involved riotous parties (sometimes involving role-swapping). See Goncourt, *Journal*, vol. II, p. 25 (3 March 1864).

p. 221: *'two popular idiots':* Goncourt, *Journal*, vol. II, p. 395 (31 December 1875).

p. 222: *no interest in this form of prostitution:* We know, however, that Degas's family destroyed some prints that they considered 'obscene', including *Fellatio* (Adhémar/Cachin, cat. 123).

Chapter 11: The Body Attending to Itself (pp. 225–259)

p. 225: *epigraph:* Joris-Karl Huysmans, *Certains*, Paris, 1889, p. 226.

p. 230: *Count Harry Kessler:* Harry Kessler, *Das Tagebuch. IV (1906–1914)*, ed. Jörg Schuster, Stuttgart, 2005, p. 294.

Dürer's 'Women Bathing': See the monograph by Anne Röver-Kann, *Albrecht Dürer. Das Frauenbad von 1496. Eine Ausstellung um eine wiedergefundene Zeichnung*, Bremen, 2001.

p. 231: *George Moore:* cited in Loyrette 1988, p. 445 (cat. 270).

Degas and Dürer: George Moore, in Degas, *Lettres*, p. 260.

p. 232: *Andries Pels on Rembrandt:* Andries Pels, *Gebruik én misbruik des tooneels*, Amsterdam, 1681. See Duncan Dull and Dirk Zimmermann (eds.), *Rembrandt – Caravaggio*, exhibition catalogue, Amsterdam, 2006, p. 169.

Felix Fénéon: Loyrette 1988, cat. 270 (p. 445).

p. 237: *Panofsky:* Erwin Panofsky, *Early Netherlandish Painting: Its Origins and Character*, eds. Jochen Sander and Stephan Kemperdick, 2 vols., Cambridge, MA, 1953; vol. I, p. 270.

p. 240: *Degas's self-criticism:* 'J'ai peut-être trop considéré la femme comme un animal'. Degas in conversation with Walter Sickert (Walter Sickert, 'Degas', in *The Burlington Magazine* 31 [1917], p. 185).

Diderot/Baudelaire: Denis Diderot, *Essai sur la peinture*, in *Œuvres*, Ed. de la Pléiade, Paris, 1968, p. 1114; Charles Baudelaire, 'Quelques caricaturistes français', in *Œuvres complètes*, Ed. de la Pléiade, ed. Claude Pichois, Paris, 1956, p. 741.

p. 243: *Caravaggio:* See Jürgen Harten (ed.), *Caravaggio. Originale und Kopien im Spiegel der Forschung*, exhibition catalogue, Ostfildern, 2006, cat. 35 and 36.

p. 246: *'a crowd of handsome idlers':* Ingres in a letter to his friend Gilibert; see Norman Schlenoff, *Jean-Auguste-Dominique Ingres. Ses sources littéraires*, Paris, 1956, p. 257.

p. 254: *Redon:* Odilon Redon, *A soi-même. Journal (1867–1915)*, Paris, 1961, p. 100: 'Le sens du mystère, c'est d'être tout le temps dans l'équivoque, dans les double, triple aspects, des soupçons d'aspect (images dans images)…' (1902).

p. 255: *an evening meal with the Halévys:* Degas, *Lettres*, p. 277.

Durand-Ruel exhibited these landscapes: Loyrette 1988, p. 502 (cat. 298–301). See Janis, *Degas Monotypes*, Checklist 264–321.

Alexandre: Arsène Alexandre, cited in Loyrette 1988, p. 503.

p. 256: *Degas's melancholy:* 'Even when contemplating nature I easily grow bored.' Notebook 11, p. 66, written in 1858 on a trip to Assisi and Perugia ('L'ennui me gagne vite à contempler même la nature'); 'People think me cheerful because I smile stupidly in a resigned fashion.' Letter to Bartholomé, 16 August 1884, in Degas, *Lettres*, p. 78. ('On me trouve gai parce que je souris bêtement, d'une façon résignée.')

p. 257: *Moréas:* Jean Moréas, 'Un manifeste littéraire', in Guy Michaud, *La Doctrine symboliste. Documents*, Paris, 1947, p. 23.

Chapter 12: The Experimenter (pp. 261–273)

p. 261: *epigraph 1:* Cited in Adriani, *Bordell und Boudoir*, p. 99, note 203.

epigraph 2: Paul Valéry, 'Degas, danse, dessin' (1938), in *Œuvres*, Ed. de la Pléiade, ed. Jean Hytier, vol. II, Paris, 1960, p. 1210.

letter to Pissarro: Adhémar/Cachin 1973, p. 54; Degas, *Lettres*, p. 54.

p. 264: *He began sculpting:* John Rewald, *Degas: Works in Sculpture, A Complete Catalogue*, New York and London, 1944.

Daumier: See lithographs D. 2781 (*Hippophages* series) and D. 3048 (*Les plaisanteries que se permettent les chevaux*), in Loys Delteil, *Delacroix: The Graphic Work. A Catalogue Raisonné*, San Francisco, 1997.

Degas and photography: Antoine Terrasse, *Degas et la Photographie*, Paris, 1983; Malcolm Daniel et al. (ed.), *Edgar Degas, Photographer*, exhibition catalogue, New York, 1998.

the studio of a friend: Tassett, the picture-framer. See Beaumont Newhall, 'Degas photographe amateur', in *Gazette des Beaux-Arts* 61 (1963), p. 61.

p. 268: *long portrait sittings:* See Loyrette 1988, cat. 333, 'Renoir und Mallarmé' with quote from Valéry.

Zoë Closier: Alice Michel, 'Degas et son Modèle', in *Mercure de France*, 16 February 1919.

p. 270: *'Louise', he said one day…:* Daniel Halévy, in Degas, *Lettres*, p. 268.

'Elle est peuple': 'She is people'. Cited by Cachin in Adhémar/Cachin, p. 21.

Barbey d'Aurevilly: 'Il y a parfois une certaine aisance dans la maladresse, qui, si je ne me trompe, est plus gracieux que la grâce même.' (Notebook 22, p. 6) In the introduction to the Notebooks, Reff includes the source of the quotation: Barbey d'Aurevilly, 'Quelques bouts d'idées', in *Le Nain jaune*, 7 June 1867, p. 6.

Rejlander and Robinson: see Beaumont Newhall, *The History of Photography from 1839 to the Present Day*, New York, 1949, pp. 73 and 74.

p. 273: *'shiny sheet of metal'*: Peter Pollack, *The Picture History of Photography, From the Earliest Beginnings to the Present Day*, New York, 1958, p. 35.

Chapter 13: Degas in His Century (pp. 275–309)

p. 275: *epigraph 1*: Notebook 30, p. 20.

epigraph 2: Notebook 21, p. 36.

p. 276: *Reff*: Reff 1976, p. 53.

p. 277: *Bayard*: see Beaumont Newhall, *The History of Photography from 1839 to the Present Day*, New York, 1949, p. 54.

p. 279: *Marx*: Karl Marx, *A Contribution to the Critique of Political Economy* (1857), Moscow, 1977.

Delacroix: Eugène Delacroix, *Journal*, ed. André Joubin, Paris, 1950, vol. II, p. 439 (9 April 1856). ('Les tragedies des Grecs sont bonnes pour les Grecs. De là le ridicule de tenter de remonter le courant et de faire de l'archaisme.')

p. 280: *Proudhon*: Pierre-Joseph Proudhon, *Du principe de l'art*, in *Œuvres complètes*, eds. Jules L. Puech, Célestin Charles Alfred and Henri Moysset, vol. XI, Paris, 1939, p. 274.

Boas: George Boas, 'Il faut être de son temps', in: *Journal of Aesthetics and Art Criticism* 1 (1941), p. 52.

Degas once said he painted ballet dancers: Daniel Halévy, *Degas parle*, Paris and Geneva, 1960, p. 159.

Flaubert to Sainte-Beuve: In Gustave Flaubert, *Œuvres*, Ed. de la Pléiade, eds. A. Thibaudet and R. Dumesnil, vol. I, Paris, 1951, p. 1031.

Diderot on Boucher: Denis Diderot, *Salons*, eds. Jean Seznec and Jean Adhémar, vol. I, Oxford, 1957, p. 112, and also vol. II, Oxford, 1960, p. 75.

Herder: Johann Gottfried von Herder, *Plastik* (1778), in *Werke*, ed. Wolfgang Pross, vol. II, Munich, 1987, p. 519.

p. 283: *Thiers*: P. L. Jacob, 'David et son école jugés par M. Thiers', in *Gazette des Beaux-Arts* 1 (1873), p. 295.

p. 285: *'In Sparta even young girls…'*: Johann Joachim Winckelmann, *Die Geschichte der Kunst des Altertums*, Mainz, 2002, p. 255.

Winckelmann's French source: 'Noble simplicité' and 'grandeur sereine' are found in French translation in Jonathan Richardson, *An Essay on the Theory of Painting* (*Traité de la peinture et de la sculpture*, trans. Antoni Rutgers, Amsterdam, 1728). See Elisabeth Decultot, *J. J. Winckelmann. Enquête sur la genèse de l'histoire de l'art*, Paris, 2000, p. 297.

p. 286: *Delacroix, 'Do not chase…'*: Eugène Delacroix, *Journal*, ed. André Joubin, Paris, 1950, vol. I, p. 96 (9 May 1824).

'unlearning': On primitivism in an international context, see Melinda Curtis and Georges Levitine, *Search for Innocence: Primitive and Primitivistic Art of the 19th Century*, exhibition catalogue, College Park, MD, 1975.

p. 287: *Delacroix opposes perfect beauty*: Eugène Delacroix, *Journal*, ed. André Joubin, Paris, 1950, vol. II, p. 257 (7 September 1854): '…la disproportion même est un élément de la beauté.'

Baudelaire on Courbet: Charles Baudelaire, 'Peintres et aquafortistes' (1862), in *Œuvres complètes*, Ed. de la Pléiade, ed. Claude Pichois, Paris, 1956, p. 844.

p. 288: *Duranty*: Edmond Duranty, 'Adolphe Menzel', in *Gazette des Beaux-Arts* 1 (1880), p. 201, and 2 (1880), p. 105. ('Il n'aura pas été seulement un artiste, mais une intelligence.') See Henri Loyrette, 'Menzel in Paris', in Claude Keisch and Marie Ursula Riemann-Reyher (eds.), *Adolph Menzel 1815–1905. Das Labyrinth der Wirklichkeit*, exhibition catalogue, Cologne, 1996, p. 533 (*Head of a Workman* is illustrated on p. 536).

p. 289: *Champfleury to George Sand*: Published under the title 'Du Réalisme' in *L'Artiste*, 2 September 1855. Cited in Herding, *Realismus als Widerspruch*, p. 53.

copy after Rogier van der Weyden: See Reff 1976, ills. 111–112.

p. 292: *Italian peasant girls*: Notebook 7, pp. 4 and 21.

p. 293: *Degas on the wife of King Candaules*: Notebook 6, p. 62. ('Tout le corps doit être simple et tranquille, l'œil seul doit être brûlant de pudeur et de vengeance.')

p. 294: *Hofmannsthal*: Elisabeth Frenzel, *Stoffe der Weltliteratur. Ein Lexikon dichtungsgeschichtlicher Längsschnitte*, revised edition, Stuttgart, 1963, p. 232.

Manet on Degas: Morisot, *Correspondance*, p. 31.

'Cape of Fine Shoulder': Degas, *Lettres*, p. 278.

p. 297: *Lafitau*: Friedrich Meinecke, *Die Entstehung des Historismus* (1936), 2nd ed., Munich, 1946, p. 70.

p. 298: *Stifter*: Fritz Novotny, *Adalbert Stifter als Maler*, 3rd ed., Vienna, 1947, p. 66.

Cachin on the landscape monotypes: Adhémar/Cachin 1973, p. 27.

p. 301: *Shklovsky*: Viktor Shklovsky, 'Art as Device' (1916), in *Theory of Prose*, trans. Benjamin Sher, Ellwood Park, IL, 1990.

p. 302: *'The smoke of the railway engine…'*: 'La fumée de la locomotive portait des ombres sur le giron et paraissait une horde sans fin par mons et vaux.' (Notebook 13, p. 24).

p. 303: *'About smoke…'*: 'Sur la fumée. Fumée des fumeurs, pipes cigarettes, cigare fumée des locomotives des hautes cheminées des fabriques, des bateaux à vapeur etc. écrasement des fumées sous les ponts la vapeur.' (Notebook 30, p. 205).

'There is a possibility…': 'Il y a chance de rencontrer autant de resemblance entre une figure et un caillou qu'entre deux cailloux puisque tout le monde sait qu'on voit encore deux figures…la question de la forme n'est pas à soulever puisqu'on trouve tant de rapport souvent entre un galet et une poisson, une montagne et une tête de chien des nuages et des chevaux etc.' (Notebook 22, p. 3.)

Valéry: Paul Valéry, 'Degas, danse, dessin' (1938), in *Œuvres*, Ed. de la Pléiade, ed. Jean Hytier, vol. II, Paris, 1960, p. 1193.

p. 306: *'stabilité de l'édifice spatial'*: Liliane Brion-Guerry, *Cézanne et l'Expression de l'espace*, Paris, 1966, p. 180. Degas copied two men from the *Bathers Resting* (now in the Barnes Foundation), which he saw in 1877 at the Impressionist salon (Notebook 28, p. 3). He later acquired a total of seven pictures by Cézanne for his collection (see Daniel Halévy, *Degas parle*, Paris and Geneva, 1960, p. 86; also Loyrette 1988, p. 491). See Ann Dumas et al. (eds.), *The Private Collection of Edgar Degas*, exhibition catalogue, New York, 1997.

p. 308: *fury over the word 'arrived'*: Degas, *Lettres*, p. 278.

Bibliography

Works cited

ADHÉMAR/CACHIN: Jean Adhémar and Françoise Cachin, *Edgar Degas. Gravures et monotypes*, Paris, 1973

LEMOISNE: Paul André Lemoisne, *Degas et son œuvre*, 4 vols., Paris, 1946–49; supplement by Philippe Brame and Theodore Reff, New York and London, 1984

LETTRES: *Edgar Degas, Lettres*, ed. Marcel Guérin, Paris, 1945

LOYRETTE 1988: *Degas*, exhibition catalogue, eds. Henri Loyrette, Jean Sutherland Boggs and Gary Tinterow, Paris, 1988

NB.: Theodore Reff, *The Notebooks of Edgar Degas. A Catalogue of the Thirty-Eight Notebooks in the Bibliothèque Nationale and Other Collections*, 2 vols., New York, 1985 (cited by notebook number and page number)

REFF 1976: Theodore Reff, *Degas: The Artist's Mind*, New York, 1976

ZURICH 1994: *Degas. Die Portraits*, exhibition catalogue, eds. Felix Baumann and Marianne Karabelnik, Zurich, 1994

Catalogues raisonnées

Eugenia Parry Janis, *Degas. Monotypes. Essay, Catalogue and Checklist*, exhibition catalogue, Greenwich, CT, 1968

Fiorella Minervino and Franco Rossoli, *L'opera completa di Degas*, Milan, 1970

Anne Pingeot, *Degas. Sculptures*, Paris, 1991

John Rewald, *Degas. Works in Sculpture. A Complete Catalogue*, New York, 1944

Sue Welsh Reed and Barbara Stern Shapiro, *Edgar Degas: The Painter as Printmaker*, exhibition catalogue, Boston, 1984

Further reading

Hélène Adhémar (ed.), *Centenaire de l'impressionnisme*, exhibition catalogue, Paris, 1974

Jean Adhémar et al., *Émile Zola*, exhibition catalogue, Paris 1952

Götz Adriani, *Bordell und Boudoir. Schauplätze der Moderne. Cézanne, Degas, Toulouse-Lautrec, Picasso*, exhibition catalogue, Ostfildern-Ruit, 2005

Carol Armstrong, *Odd Man Out. Readings of the Work and Reputation of Edgar Degas*, Chicago and London, 1991

Klaus Berger, *Japonisme in Western Painting from Whistler to Matisse*, Cambridge, 1992

Jean Sutherland Boggs and Gail Feigenbaum, *Degas and New Orleans: A French Impressionist in America*, exhibition catalogue, New Orleans, 1999

Alan Bowness and Hélène Toussaint, *Gustave Courbet (1819–1877)*, exhibition catalogue, Paris, 1977

Pierre Cabanne, *Edgar Degas*, Paris, 1957

Champfleury (a.k.a. Jules Fleury-Husson), *L'homme aux figures de cire* (1855), Paris, 2004

Champfleury, *Chien-Caillou, Fantaisies d'hiver* (1845), Paris, 1988

Champfleury, *Le chien des musicians* (1859), Paris, 1997

Champfleury, *Le Réalisme*, eds. Geneviève and Jean Lacambre, Paris, 1973

Malcolm Daniel et al. (eds.), *Edgas Degas, Photographer*, exhibition catalogue, New York, 1998

Ann Dumas et al., *The Private Collection of Edgar Degas*, exhibition catalogue, New York, 1997

Ann Dumas et al., *Degas: The Last Landscapes*, exhibition catalogue, London, 2006

Edmond Duranty, *La Nouvelle peinture. A propos du groupe d'artistes qui expose dans les Galeries Durand-Ruel*, Paris, 1876; reissue edited by Marcel Guérin, Paris, 1946

Edmond and Jules de Goncourt, *Manette Salomon* (1867), Paris, 1996

Edmond and Jules de Goncourt, *Journal. Mémoires de la vie littéraire*, ed. Robert Ricatte, 4 vols., Paris, 1956

Robert L. Herbert, *Impressionism. Art, Leisure and Parisian Society*, New Haven and London, 1988

Klaus Herding (ed.), *Realismus als Widerspruch. Die Wirklichkeit in Courbets Malerei*, Frankfurt am Main, 1978

Joris-Karl Huysmans, *L'Art moderne*, Paris, 1883

Joris-Karl Huysmans, *Certains*, Paris, 1889

Max Imdahl, 'Die Momentfotografie und "Le Comte Lepic" von Edgar Degas' (1970), in *Gesammelte Schriften*, vol. 1, ed. Angeli Janhsen-Vukicevic, Frankfurt am Main, 1996

Harald Keller, *Degas: Die Familie Bellelli*, Stuttgart, 1962

Richard Kendall, 'Degas and the Contingence of Vision', in *The Burlington Magazine* 130 (1988), p. 180

Ron Kitaj, 'An Uneasy Participant in the Tragicomedy of Modern Art, Mad about Drawing', in *The Burlington Magazine* 130 (1988), p. 179

Albert Kostenevich, *Hidden Treasures Revealed: Impressionist Masterpieces and Other Important French Paintings Preserved by the State Hermitage Museum, St Petersburg*, New York and St Petersburg, 1995

Henri Loyrette, *Degas: Passion and Intellect*, London, 1993

Henri Loyrette, 'Edouard Manet by Edgar Degas', in *La Revue du Louvre* 1993, p. 89

Emil Maurer, 'Der ganze (der ganze?) Degas', in *Neue Zürcher Zeitung*, 12–13 February 1988; reprinted in *Im Bann der Bilder. Essays zur italienischen und französischen Malerei des 15.–19. Jahrhunderts*, Zurich, 1992, p. 224

Sergiusz Michalski, 'Degas. Spiegelungen und Doubles', in *Das Double*, ed. Victor I. Stoichita, Wiesbaden, 2006, p. 197

George Moore, 'Degas: The Painter of Modern Life', in *Magazine of Art* 8 (1890), p. 416

Berthe Morisot, *Correspondence With Her Family and Friends: Manet, Puvis De Chavannes, Degas, Monet, Renoir, and Mallarmé*, ed. Denis Rouart, Kingston, RI, 1989

Linda Nochlin, 'Degas' Young Spartans Exercising', in *The Art Bulletin* 68 (1986), p. 486

Ronald Pickvance, 'Degas's Dancers, 1872–1876', in *The Burlington Magazine* 105 (1963), p. 256

Camille Pissarro, *Correspondance*, vol. I. 1865–1885, ed. Janine Bailly-Herzberg, Paris, 1980

Theodore Reff, 'Degas's "Tableau de Genre",' in *The Art Bulletin* 54 (1972), p. 316

John Rewald, *The History of Impressionism*, New York, 1946

Wilhelm Schmid (ed.), *Wege zu Degas*, Munich, 1988

Walter Sickert, 'Degas', in *The Burlington Magazine* 31 (1917), p. 183

Susan Sidlauskas, 'Resisting Narrative: The Problem of Edgar Degas's *Interior*', in *The Art Bulletin* 75 (1993) p. 671

Monika Steinhauser, 'Der inszenierte Blick des Flaneurs. Manet und Baudelaire', in: *Im Blickfeld* 1 (1994) p. 9

Victor I. Stoichita, *Ver y no ver. La tematización de la mirada en la pintura impresionista*, Madrid, 2005

Antoine Terrasse, *Degas et la photographie*, Paris, 1983

Richard Thompson, *Edgar Degas: Waiting*, Malibu, CA, 1995

Erika Tietze-Conrat, 'What Degas Learned from Mantegna', in *Gazette des Beaux-Arts* 26 (1944) p. 413

Paul Valéry, *Degas, danse, dessin* (1938), in *Œuvres*, ed. Jean Hytier, vol. II, Paris, 1960, pp. 1163–1240

Lionello Venturi, *Les Archives de l'Impressionnisme*, Paris and New York, 1939

Ambroise Vollard, *Souvenirs d'un marchand de tableaux*, Paris, 1937

Émile Zola, *Salons*, eds. Frederick Williams Hemmings and Robert Judson Niess, Geneva and Paris, 1959

Captions for opening pages:

page 2: *At the Milliner's* (see ill. 64)
page 4: *Painter and Mannequin (Portrait of Henri-Michel Lévy)* (see ill. 74)

page 5: *The Star* (detail of ill. 146)
page 6: *Waiting* (see ill. 137)

Translated from the German *Degas und sein Jahrhundert* by David H. Wilson

First published in the United Kingdom in 2007 by
Thames & Hudson Ltd, 181A High Holborn, London WC1V 7QX

www.thamesandhudson.com

First published in 2007 in hardcover in the United States of America by
Thames & Hudson Inc., 500 Fifth Avenue, New York, New York 10110

thamesandhudsonusa.com

Original edition © 2007 Verlag C. H. Beck oHG, Munich
This edition © 2007 Thames & Hudson Ltd, London

British Library Cataloguing-in-Publication Data
A catalogue record for this book is available from the British Library

Library of Congress Catalog Card Number 2007901211

ISBN: 978-0-500-09341-2

Printed and bound in Germany

PREHISTORIC JAPANESE ARTS
JŌMON
Pottery

by J. Edward Kidder

with contributions by
Teruya Esaka

PUBLISHED BY
KODANSHA INTERNATIONAL LTD.
TOKYO, NEW YORK & SAN FRANCISCO

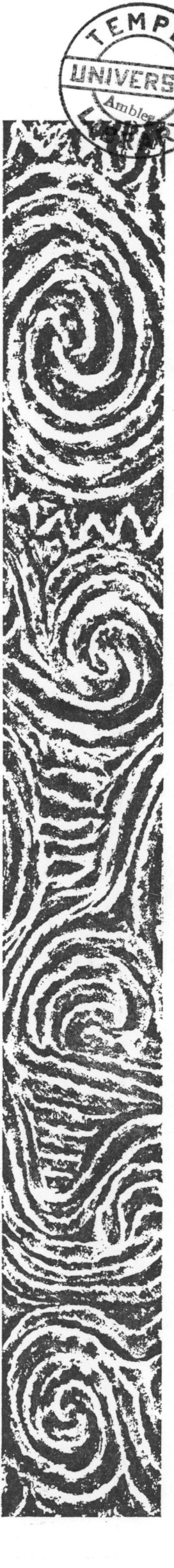

Distributors

UNITED STATES
Kodansha International/USA, Ltd., through Harper & Row, Publishers,
Inc., 10 East 53rd Street, New York, New York 10022

CANADA
Fitzhenry & Whiteside Limited, 150 Lesmill Road, Don Mills, Ontario

UNITED KINGDOM
TABS, 7 Maiden Lane, London WC2

EUROPE
Boxerbooks Inc., Limmatstrasse 111, 8031 Zurich

AUSTRALIA AND NEW ZEALAND
Book Wise (Australia) Pty. Ltd., 104–8 Sussex Street, Sydney

THE FAR EAST
Japan Publications Trading Company, P.O. Box 5030, Tokyo International, Tokyo

*Published by Kodansha International Ltd., 2–12–21 Otowa, Bunkyo-ku,
Tokyo 112 and Kodansha International/USA, Ltd., 10 East 53rd Street,
New York, New York 10022 and 44 Montgomery Street, San Francisco,
California 94104. Copyright in Japan 1968 by Kodansha International
Ltd. All rights reserved. Printed in Japan.*

LCC 68–17458
ISBN 0–87011–095–0
JBC 3070–780739–2361

First edition, 1968
Third printing, 1976

Contents

To Cordelia
Aide, Disputant, Spouse

Preface

An American, Edward Sylvester Morse, was the scholar who initiated studies of Jōmon culture from a purely archaeological point of view. It was Morse who, in 1877, excavated the Ōmori shell-mound in Ōta Ward, Tokyo, and conducted the first academic study of shell-mounds in Japan. In a sense, this event was fortuitous: one day, Morse, en route by train from Yokohama to Tokyo, recognized a shell-mound through the window on the left side of the train as he passed Ōmori Station. His academic studies in the United States had included a study of shell-mounds in Florida for the purpose of comparing ancient and modern shell types.

Morse arrived in Yokohama in June, 1877. He had come to collect and study brachiopods living in the seas around Japan, and established a marine biological station on the island of Enoshima in Kanagawa Prefecture, where he collected the marine animals of Sagami Bay. Learning of the arrival of Morse, the Japanese government invited him to become professor of zoology at Tokyo University. It was on the journey from Yokohama to Tokyo to take up this position that Morse happened to discover the Ōmori shell-mound.

He published a fifty-six page report of his findings on the Ōmori site in 1879 entitled "Shell Mounds of Ōmori." (*Memoirs of the Science Department*, University of Tokio, Vol. 1, Pt. I.) In this report Morse describes the decoration on the vessels, referring to "the lines being cord-marked." These words were translated as "*sono uchi wo sakumon ni shi*" by Ryōkichi Yatabe in the "*Ōmori Kaikyō Kobutsu Hen*" published in December, 1879. In the magazine *Jinrui Gaku Kaihō* (Vol. 3) (forerunner of the present *Jinrui Gaku Zasshi*) published in 1886, Kōtarō Shirai wrote an article entitled "*Sekizoku Kō*" ("A Study of Stone Arrowheads"). In this he translated the term "cord-marked" as "*jōmon*" and used the term "*jōmon doki*" ("Jōmon pottery") for the first time. Thus, almost precisely eighty years have elapsed since the term Jōmon was coined.

The stone implements and pottery of the Jōmon period, however, had been observed by the Japanese for many centuries. In the *Hitachi Fudoki*, compiled during the early part of the eighth century, the Ōkushi shell-mound, which was located in the eastern suburbs of present-day Mito City, Ibaragi Prefecture, was mentioned and linked with a legend concerning giants. In Volume Eight of the *Shoku Nihon Kōki*, compiled around the middle of the ninth century, it is mentioned that a large number of stone arrowheads were discovered after a severe storm on the shores of Nishihama, Yūsa-machi, Yamagata

Prefecture, and that the inhabitants, thinking this discovery to be an omen of natural calamity, prayed to the gods for deliverance from disaster.

Jōmon pottery pieces were objects of interest among connoisseurs from early in the nineteenth century, and pottery exhibits as well as "exchange" meetings were held in old Edo. It was not until quite recently, however, that Jōmon culture was discovered to have a history several times as long as the period since the ascension to the throne by the legendary Emperor Jimmu approximately twenty-five hundred years ago.

The chronological study of Jōmon culture began in 1894 with a joint announcement by Sōzaburō Yagi and Miyokichi Shimomura of a theory concerning the existence of two different types of Jōmon pottery, which they termed simply old and new.

In 1919, Professor Hikoshirō Matsumoto of Tōhoku University excavated a shell-mound in the vicinity of Sendai, Miyagi Prefecture, and conducted a study on the pottery contained in each layer of the mound. This stratigraphical method was continued from 1920 by Kashiwa Ōyama, Isamu Kōno, Sugao Yamanouchi and Ichirō Yawata. The five chronological divisions now in current use—earliest, early, middle, late and latest—are based on the studies of these four scholars.

This book presents a full and representative survey of the latest material and research on Jōmon culture. It is my pleasure to have contributed a discussion of cord-marking techniques and charts of the Jōmon stratigraphic and C_{14} chronology, design types and shape types to this volume, and to have aided in the compilation of the photographs, especially for the Earliest Jōmon period. It is my feeling that it will be many years indeed before a book as complete and comprehensive as this will be attempted again—if it ever will. It is thus with both acknowledgements to the publishers and to my many colleagues in this country that I join Dr. Kidder in hoping students of archaeology and readers throughout the world find meaning and pleasure in the unique Jōmon pottery presented here.

T. ESAKA

Tokyo, 1968

Introduction

ANY ATTEMPT to trace the circuitous path of Jōmon studies invariably leads back to the arrival in Japan of Edward S. Morse (1838–1925) in 1877 and his recognition of a Neolithic stage in Japan's prehistory when he saw railway builders cutting through a kitchen-midden. Morse's discovery of the Ōmori shell-mounds between Yokohama and Tokyo revealed an entirely new dimension in Japanese cultural studies. He set out soon afterwards to dig the mounds, with nothing short of spectacular results. That his locally printed book, *Shell Mounds of Ōmori*,[1] should still retain much value today—to the extent of being reprinted recently—speaks not only for its historical significance but also for the accuracy of its drawings and typesetting, and is in itself a tribute to Morse's scientific discrimination.

Morse's efforts had been preceded by an exhibition of Jōmon objects held at Yushima Seidō in Tokyo in 1872, prior to the opening of the National Museum. Morse, however, inspired the excavation of many more shell-mounds in the Kantō Plain, and reports of these were already appearing before the turn of the century.

During the early decades of the twentieth century, Jōmon studies were dominated by men who today would be called anthropologists—in contrast to archaeologists for later prehistory. Shōgorō Tsuboi (1863–1913) was given a chair at Tokyo University in 1892. His voice, and that of the Society of Anthropology that he led, was the *Jinruigaku Zasshi* ("*Journal of Anthropology*"), the oldest and hardiest of the archaeological periodicals, which did not relinquish its claim on Jōmon studies until after World War II. This journal was joined in the field of general archaeological studies by the *Kōkogakukai Zasshi* ("*Journal of the Society of Archaeology*"), later the *Kōkogaku Zasshi* ("*Journal of Archaeology*"), as archaeological investigations broadened into the later pre-Buddhist periods. The editors of the *Journal of Anthropology*, however, faithfully maintained their special concern with Stone Age studies, thus reflecting a widely held view that "archaeology" dealt more with material and time periods that had a direct bearing on traditional Japanese history, and that the Jōmon period—then thought to be the ancient Ainu culture—need not be considered a basic part of the empire's actual origins.

At that juncture the Yayoi period, which succeeds the Jōmon and spans the last centuries B.C. and the earlier centuries A.D., was almost unknown. The Yayoi period witnessed the establishment of clear links with the continent through the introduction of rice cultivation, metals and new burial practices, including grave goods. The appearance of large tumuli, an event that marks the end of the Yayoi period and heralds the beginning of the Kofun period, is identified with the rise of the Yamato state. These tumuli received restrained attention. Smaller mounds or the more exposed ones were dug, largely under the supervision of excavators from national universities.

Tsuboi's generation had its successors in personalities like Ryūzō Torii (1870–1953), who joined Tokyo University in 1892. Torii's most lasting efforts came at a time when Japan's territorial expansion facilitated anthropological fieldwork abroad. Leading the trend that lasted for several decades, the Department of Anthropology at Tokyo University was chiefly involved in Jōmon studies, while the Department of Archaeology dealt with the metal ages or continental archaeology.

Torii wrote his ethnological monographs shortly after World War I, and influenced a rising generation whose investigations carried the work into the thirties. The inhibitions on intellectual effort preceding World War II did not discourage digging itself. Major strides were made at that time in recovering buried materials. The material and its context were important, while speculation on the cultural aspects of prehistory and chronological significance were exclusively subordinated to the official interpretation of history.

The founding of the Prehistoric Institute by Kashiwa Ōyama marked a major forward step. Its members dug numerous sites in the Kantō Plain, publishing these systematically in the Institute's journal, *Shizengaku Zasshi* ("*Journal of Prehistory*"), appearing in early 1929. Their first actual report was the excavation of the Katsusaka site in Kanagawa Prefecture, embodied in a small booklet in 1927.[2] Until quite recently it could be said that the years 1933–39 witnessed the greatest literary output from all sources on Jōmon archaeology, and were paralleled only by 1951–53.[3] Since that time the volume of publications has settled down to a frightening deluge, seemingly unimpeded by the rising costs of printing.

The Prehistoric Institute was tragically destroyed by bombing toward the close of the war, after which Ōyama retired from archaeological work. Several scholars who made major contributions to Jōmon studies were members of this institution and were influenced by Ōyama's German, theoretical orientation. Basic problems of chronology were constantly being investigated, and it was during these years that shell-mound analyses coupled with typological studies of pottery provided the raw material for determining finer points of Jōmon chronology.[4] A key figure in the pottery studies was Sugao Yamanouchi, whose five divisions for the Jōmon period, organized on the basis of pottery types in the Kantō Plain, became the accepted scheme by all archaeologists working in the field.

Up to this time the extent and depth of the problems had not been fully realized. The Jōmon-equals-Ainu equation was simple and hard to refute. Physical anthropological studies by Kenji Kiyono (1885–1955), for instance[5]—at appropriate times oriented toward "proving" the ancestors of the Japanese were not the Ainu—had yet to be refined to the point where the theories had much relevance, and the approaching Pacific war and the crisis of the war years made it imperative that the Ainu be erased from this lofty position.

The term *jō-mon*, "cord pattern," used for the period itself and applied to all the pottery of this period whether decorated with cord-marking or not, had a rocky road before its acceptance was complete. Morse described the Ōmori pottery as "cord marked." Any cross section of the writings as late as the 1920's will show that there were still quite divergent sentiments on its terminology. Ōyama used *Jōmon-shiki doki* ("Cord-marked style pottery"), Kiyono sometimes employed *Kaizuka doki* ("Shell-mound pottery"), Torii was known to call it *Ainu-ha doki* ("Ainu school pottery"), and Yamanouchi sometimes, and Hasebe almost always, spoke of *Sekki-jidai doki* ("Stone Age pottery"). Even though all but Hasebe were also using Jōmon, differing concepts of cord-marking led them to write the term in one of two ways. To Ōyama, Nakaya and Yamanouchi it was 縄紋, to the others it was 縄文. While the difference may be semantic, the former is intended to include the idea of impressions produced by twisted strands; the latter embodies a wider idea of impressions made from knotted strands.

The two views met head on in 1940 at the national meeting of the Society for Anthropology. The proposal to adopt 縄文 (simple strands) as the official title for the pottery was spearheaded by Kotohito Hasebe and Morichi Gotō. A minority, including Yamanouchi, opposed it. The majority eventually prevailed and the ranks were closed— undoubtedly ultimately aided by the national tendency to simplify the written language.

While arguments were proceeding as to the overall title of the pottery, its subdivisions went through rather similar throes. Torii spoke of *Atsude-shiki* ("Thick style") for Middle Jōmon pottery, and *Usude-shiki* ("Thin style") for Late Jōmon pottery. Sōsaburō Yagi (1866–1942), at the turn of the century, was using *Ōmori-fu* ("Ōmori style"), the first of the types to be named after a site, applying it broadly to Late Jōmon pottery in the Kantō area.[6] In the meantime, Hikojirō Matsumoto was employing terms of a graphic, though unwieldy, character. The applied patterns of Middle Jōmon were *Totsu-kyokusen Jōmon-ki* ("projected curved-line, cord-marked pottery"), and the incised patterns of Late Jōmon were *Ōkyokusen Jōmon-ki* ("depressed curved-line, cord-marked pottery"). Matsumoto's English writing described early Jōmon pottery (now Middle) as "bas-relief decorative pattern of curve and spiral design," and for middle (now Late), "incised decorative pattern of curve and spiral design," for late (now Latest), "decorative pattern of the secondary order of geometrical design."[7] Yagi had used Okadaira-*fu* for middle Jōmon, after a shell-mound by that name.[8]

Many scholars adopted the Torii sequence, which ran from the *Atsude*, through the *Usude* to the Mutsu, the last named after the region of northern Japan where large quantities of very late Jōmon pottery had been found. Yamanouchi revised this scheme, since it was apparent by the mid-1930's that space could not be found in this arrangement for several newly discovered types; he added two more subdivisions. The five subdivisions, based on Kantō Plain developments, took the form of a working system by around 1935 and were immortalized on paper within two years in a short article in *Senshi Kōkogaku* ("*Prehistoric Archaeology*"),[9] a journal that fell victim to an intradisciplinary squabble after only three issues.

These five divisions stand today as devised at that time, although Yamanouchi has proposed an even earlier one to cope with the rock-shelter and other early pottery that seems to have "pre-Jōmon" traits. The five are *Sō-ki*, *Zen-ki*, *Chū-ki*, *Kō-ki* and *Ban-ki*. *Ki* is period, a unit of time; the five might be translated as Early, Prior, Middle, Succeeding, and Evening; these may not appear to follow each other in translation quite as smoothly as dawn follows night and twilight follows day, but they have become the established tradition. English usage has fared less consistently. Gerard Groot in his *Prehistory of Japan* (1951) spoke of the Proto-Jōmon, Early-, Middle-, Later- and Final-Jōmon periods, and within the last, Epi-Jōmon in north Japan.[10] Richard Beardsley, in an article in *The Far Eastern Quarterly* (1955) called them Initial, Early, Middle, Late and Final Jōmon.[11] I discussed the terminology in *The Jōmon Pottery of Japan* (1957), stating that suggestions had included Early, Early-Middle, Middle, Late-Middle, and

Late, a scheme recommended to those with predilections toward simple mathematics, but did not follow the five divisions too zealously there, then as now, being concerned about the organic applicability of the scheme.[12]

By 1959 I had settled on the terminologically smoothest Earliest, Early, Middle, Late and Latest in *Japan Before Buddhism*,[13] succumbing to the overwhelming usefulness of this breakdown as the inevitable alternative to invading the jungle of type names in more general writing—and have employed it since that time when called upon to record the sequence in print.

The new stage before Earliest might well merit formal definition if one is willing to accept the implications of C$_{14}$ dates for its extreme length. Called *Sōsō-ki*, it not only does not lend itself to direct translation (literally "grass origins," it is the grass roots of Jōmon pottery) but defies the imagination to find a term accurately designating a period earlier than Initial or Earliest that is not too artificial. One solution has been to use Incipient Jōmon. Mr. Yamanouchi was not very impressed with this author's suggestion of Sub-earliest.

Once the subdivisions were firmly in place, attention in Jōmon archaeology turned to pottery typology, although no aspects of the culture have been overlooked in recent years. There was the tendency to accept with these divisions the theory that every stage of the Kantō's evolution would be represented elsewhere in the country. While the process of filling out this ideal chronological scheme has proved that there is much truth to this, it falls just short of full accuracy to have become a deterrent in recognizing the actual character of Jōmon cultural developments. Modifications are now working their way into the diagraming of this "unilinear evolution," and doubtless additional ones will come when dating systems provide adequate information deviating from the ladder-like sequence.

There has been unrestrained freedom in naming local types. It results from viewing all types within a local chronological framework. A few writers devote considerable attention to interregional relationships, notably Mr. Esaka, but this is unusual, as it would be anywhere in the world. Local type names, unfortunately, give no clues as to their typological connections, family or time relationships. There is, for instance, no binomial device, as in American archaeology (i.e., Savannah Check Stamped), which quickly narrows down the distribution range and, to anyone with some familiarity with the successive changes in decorative styles, limits the time possibilities very greatly. Such a device would be possible, since Japanese archaeologists have shown obvious genius in standardizing terms. Also, some types have been known by fairly manageable sequences, yet there is pressure to use individual site names (i.e., Moroiso a, b and c become Yagami, Yonmaibata and Jūsanbodai).[14] Scores of type names have been added since I calculated a possible total in the neighborhood of three hundred when finishing my Jōmon pottery book in 1955. Over a decade and thousands of digs later it is safe to estimate that they now number half again as many.

The digging in Japan has been so intensive and so thorough that the results would lend themselves ideally to pottery groupings, involving subtypes, type clusters, and ceramic systems. The word normally used for style—*shiki*—is applied to both Jōmon pottery as a whole (*Jōmon-shiki doki*) and a type itself (Ishiyama-*shiki*). Thus the term must be understood in its context. The English idea should be conveyed as Jōmon style pottery, Ishiyama type. Equivalents might be found to view ceramic manifestations in type clusters (a basic type and its variants), ceramic systems (grouping of type clusters, covering a wide area and occupying one time period) ; ceramic sequence (developmental implications); and ceramic series (geographically limited, unspecified time). Terminology of this kind cuts through time and space and gives weight to both where needed without setting up the partitions of geographical barriers. It might be argued that in a country the size of Japan there is no call for these devices, and they embody in themselves certain encumbrances that are difficult to manage. Whether it be one or another, some locally suggested methods will be useful in redirecting the present drift.

Finding one's way around the bewildering maze of type names often has the result of solidifying the security and comfort of one's local territory and its terminology, and may be accompanied by firm resolutions never to venture far afield again. For those who brave them, like Mr. Esaka, the rewards of the broader view are considerable. The shifting centers of the subcultures come into focus; they may at times show steady progress where the situation was adequate for relatively comfortable living, or at times appear vigorous and dynamic, bolstered by abnormally good economic conditions, or even at other times seem to be weak and receptive, implying that the small, unsettled inhabitants never quite grasped the potential of their resources and were unable to increase their numbers. Many such groups tended to migrate toward areas where the resources could provide better support. Mr. Esaka constantly reassesses these country-wide relationships, adjusting charts and other visual correlation methods to the most recent information.

🖾 FACTORS IN THE MAKING OF POTTERY All Jōmon pottery was handmade, apparently without resort to any kind of turntable or wheel. Without the restriction of tools or devices, which tend to standardize workmanship, it always reflects the personal quality of hand-modeled work, each piece with the potential of infinite variation. The vessels were not only simple utensils for domestic use, but were the primary form of artistic creation—in fact, the only one throughout most of the Jōmon period—giving service daily, inevitably on view and subject to criticism as to function and decoration. The comforts of the home depended on the success with which a vessel was made and fired—whether by the housewife or someone else—and its manageability, durability, porosity, shape and size all had a direct bearing on how much effective service it would afford. Any locally made domestic earthenware of this sort is of such a highly intimate nature (it was probably made by one of the family, often for the use of a special member) that it must represent the family's taste and meet the family's sanctions, under circumstances that may not have required the frequent making of pots and thus did not foster the improvement of skills and techniques. Reliance on these vessels for heavy daily use points up their crucial role in human survival at this time.

Suggestions have been made that small stands may have been used during and after the Middle Jōmon period for supports while building up vessels.[15] A circular table-like object of clay averaging around eighteen centimeters in diameter, often with pairs of holes in its walls, has been found in several Middle Jōmon sites. Only one or at best a small number has come from a site, but these show no sign of wear, and it could be expected that more would be discovered if the practice were very common.

After Middle Jōmon some bases bear marks of mats or of leaves, the mat-marks often so sharply imprinted as to leave little doubt that the imprint could not have occurred by accident. The stacking of pots on mats during drying was a customary explanation, and would account for only one of many bases (the bottom pot of a stack) being marked.[16] This explanation now seems inadequate, since the fairly firm clay needed for the making of this kind of pottery would be unlikely to register such neat imprints without conscious effort on the part of the potter. One also doubts that Jōmon pottery was made in such quantity at any one time as to require "stacking." Far more likely is the building up of a vessel on a mat, first pressed down to hold the vessel well in place. But not every potter did it; perhaps it is a kind of potter's mark, the distinguishing feature of certain potters in a community.

The earliest vessels in Japan are almost exclusively cooking pots and have pointed or rounded bottoms. Different views have been expressed as to how these were constructed: one that they were built upside down, the other that this need not necessarily have been the case.[17] The former is generally accepted; in any event, inverted construction, if it existed, was discontinued when flat bases and wavy rims became fashionable in Early Jōmon. Many Middle and most Late Jōmon pots will break in horizontal bands of roughly equal width. This phenomenon led to the popular belief that these vessels were not built up in the common coiling manner, but in flat, broad ribbons of clay, overlapping each other slightly by a narrow lip. Recent experiments, however, have shown that vessels constructed with coils of local Kantō clay will often break this way, thus reopening the entire question.

Firm clay was required for hand-building, often calling for considerable tempering. The red "Kantō loam" would have been of adequate quality, and to some extent the quantity of production in various regions of the country is as closely related to the availability of good clays as it is to the relative size of the communities.

Short, cut fibers were mixed with the clay in Early Jōmon, in an effort to reinforce the walls. These burned out, leaving highly irregular impressions on rough, uneven surfaces. Sand, grit containing quartz, and mica were being used for tempering by Middle Jōmon, with accelerating progress being made toward pure clay already in the Late Jōmon period. The pottery from one site in Kyushu near Karatsu contains a high percentage of talc, and its surface has a greasy quality.

Most vessels are fairly porous, at least through Middle Jōmon when the clays used were less dense. Porosity has some recognized value for keeping water cool by slow evaporation. Large Middle Jōmon vessels in the Chūbu region are said to lose about ten percent of their contents if filled with water and allowed to stand overnight. The red paint seen on an occasional vessel, and later, lacquering, might conceivably have been efforts to reduce the porosity of a vessel by giving it a lining or veneering. Only in late stages is pottery decorated with designs in red paint, and these examples are so rare as to be looked on as atypical.

Very few Jōmon vessels are lacking in any ornamentation whatsoever, and most bear decoration over a large part of the surface. The coarseness of the decoration is a distinctive feature until Late Jōmon, by which time the pottery takes on a slightly more professional air, perhaps partly because the manufacturing process was repeated more frequently. This coarseness has clear advantages in handling a vessel.

One of the more interesting aspects of Middle Jōmon pottery, notable for its numerous fantastic forms, is where, if at all, the makers drew the line between decoration contributing to and decoration definitely detracting from the usability of a vessel—or, perhaps more to the point, why they seemed unable to make this practical distinction. This utility vs. Middle Jōmon decoration question involves: the likely loss of vital parts like handles because the sculptural ornamentation is overweight for the vessel's size; rims with no unbroken surfaces to drink or pour from; bases too narrow to give adequate stability; and decoration too asymmetrical for good balance. Since any suggestion of a "flower vase" concept before Late Jōmon at the earliest would find little agreement, one is forced to regard this Middle Jōmon trend as a striving for the greatest artistic impact, even to the disadvantage of other factors. The narrow bases could well be styling, but it must always be remembered that the Jōmon people lived right on the ground, their pots were usually on house floors and were normally seen from a higher angle. Holes could easily be dug to hold pots, as must have been necessary when bottoms were pointed or rounded, and the practice of using pots for fireplace centers in Middle Jōmon may have encouraged a tendency to magnify the decoration toward the top of the vessel. Pottery in no way reflects local religious systems before Middle Jōmon (except in the rare appearance of figurines), but does begin to do so at that time, and theories concerning the sets of vessels appearing in Middle Jōmon are now being taken quite seriously;[18] but all things considered, it seems quite unlikely that any pots served a primarily ornamental purpose before Late Jōmon.

Open-firing was customary for Jōmon pottery, with unpredictable results and unquestionably high mortality rates. The temperature may have averaged six hundred degrees centigrade. Fragments will sometimes be found in early Middle Jōmon sites that can hardly be distinguished from the baked clay around the fireplace of a house pit. The vessels must have been propped up with stones, covered with brush and burned for several hours; in many instances the thick walls are not consistently fired throughout, the core of the clay being a different color than its surfaces. Good or bad, anything that made it this far would get some use, with life expectancy depending greatly on the outcome of this last stage in production.

The larger pots of Middle Jōmon suggest a far more venturesome attitude toward losses. Whether potting took place at regular intervals during the year or just as needed will never be known, but despite allowance for firing losses, having adequate containers on hand must have been one of the more serious supply problems to Jōmon people. The cases of holes bored through walls to tie up a crack and add longer service to a vessel are seen from almost the earliest pottery, especially in the early cooking-pot shapes and in the bowls toward the end of the Jōmon period. Very few examples of crack lacing have ever been found for Middle Jōmon. The thicker walls were hard to salvage, and breaks are less neat; many vessels disintegrated from the bottom up as a result of long exposure to heat. Early, bullet-shaped pots had sturdily built bases and tended to crack from the top down. They were worth trying to save, as were the thin-walled Late Jōmon vase shapes.

A major technical advance takes place in the Kantō Plain toward the end of Middle Jōmon. The typical shell-mound pottery of Late Jōmon is thin, rather hard, often with well-smoothed surface, fired evenly, has relatively pure clay with all signs of tempering carefully obscured, and is light to dark brown in color. The shell-mounds are often large and give every indication of fairly settled communities. It may be presumed that more free time was available for more people to be involved in pottery production than was the case in earlier times, and more frequent making of pottery developed and sharpened latent skills. Improvements reflect a far clearer recognition of the limitations of the medium, and somewhat more controlled ambitions. The relative moderation of decoration in Late Jōmon stands in striking contrast to the exaggerations of Middle Jōmon. The latter made rather inefficient cooking pots. The thin walls of Late and Latest Jōmon transmitted the heat far better and may well have given longer service. Certainly they did not present the difficulties of requiring rather large fires and the dangers of confronting the family daily with nothing but stew. It need hardly be said that the number and size of the containers had much to do with the size of the family and the way food was stored, prepared and served, but by Late Jōmon it looks as though it may have been possible to cook different foods in separate pots if so desired, and members of the family may not all have had to share the same bowl. The appearance of cups and pouring vessels and many unusual shapes all point to refinements resulting from ritual needs and greater discrimination in the shape-function relationship. The potential for religious paraphernalia in various pottery forms was constantly being explored, and Late Jōmon sees the addition to the repertory of what must have been its share of religious equipment.

The increase in shapes and number of vessels is quite phenomenal in Latest Jōmon in northern Japan. Just the opposite holds true in the south, where the social situation obviously differed greatly. One gets the impression, in dealing with so many handsomely decorated, often burnished or red-painted little cups, bowls, plates, bottles, incense burners and the like, that the northern society lived in a highly ritualized and perhaps static state, still directing most of its artistic energy toward pottery making. The workmanship is unsurpassed in sheer virtuosity; the neatly decorated, small vessels show the result of much manual dexterity; the walls may be paper-thin, the surface resembling metal. The strength of the traditions were never more evident; the nimbleness of workmanship never more apparent. There is often a modern-day preference for the more rugged, sculpturesque work of Middle Jōmon, but in the field of earthenwares, the Latest Jōmon people of northern Japan were the only ones to master all the technical problems, devoting their attention to the perfection of decorative detail and surface finish.

I am deeply grateful to the following persons for their generous aid and counsel, and to the many unnamed private collectors and the people in universities and museums whose kind permission allowed the reproduction of their valued objects: Mr. Teruya Esaka has been more than willing to provide information and assistance and has greatly enriched this volume with valuable contributions; Mr. Shūzo Koyama, my assistant, has aided in ways almost too numerous to mention, but especially in locating basic research material and in such projects as the Glossary; Miss Chiho Nakamura helped to check place names. My sincere gratitude also goes to Kodansha, Ltd. for making available for use in this book the vast number of photographs taken in the compilation of the Japanese language Jōmon Pottery volume. My wife has continuously been a partner in the work, and I am indebted to her wisdom and advice.

J. Edward Kidder

I.C.U., Tokyo, 1968

Earliest Jōmon

THE GEOGRAPHICAL features of Japan account for many of the local variations in customs, religious practices, folk arts, dialects and, to some extent, physical differences. These local characteristics are still one of the most interesting facets of the Japanese scene; they are only now being threatened by the advent of the automobile, improved highways, television, and the large-scale exodus of the rural populace to the cities in search of salaried positions.

A projection of this fact beyond the imaginary line that divides history from prehistory helps to explain the phenomenal number of local pottery types. Pottery was the primitive artifact most responsive to change and most likely to reflect specific contacts with neighboring communities. The islands of Japan were not only isolated as a whole in the Jōmon period, but the country consists of "islands within islands," boxed-in valleys and relatively small rivers. If the communities were many, rather small and somewhat isolated, a logical consequence is numerous local pottery types. More than this, the infinitesimal number of variants of a type point to just enough contact between localities to suggest a general awareness on the part of prehistoric people of neighboring activities, these contacts being essentially the result of hunting and foraging expeditions.

To Japanese archaeologists the beginning of the Jōmon culture is marked by the first appearance of pottery. This is the sign that man was moving out of savagery and beyond a hand-to-mouth existence; he would be in a position to utilize and manipulate his environment. He would be able to stay long enough in one place to cook his meals in a container, have pots for holding foods he had gathered, and for the overnight storage of water. The devisers of the chronology thought of pottery in terms of artifacts, not as a landmark of cultural change, and it illustrates the regard in which Jōmon pottery has been held by Japanese archaeologists. Even today there is no agreement as to whether its appearance opens the Neolithic phase of existence or not.

In recent years the pursuit of the earliest pottery has led to excavations in caves in widely separated parts of the country, and back into undreamed of antiquity. It is safe to say that most Japanese archaeologists—conditioned as they are over the years to look toward China for the source of all major ancient inventions—would have still believed not much more than a decade and a half ago that pottery-making had been introduced from the continent.[1] The C_{14} dates (see chart, p. 286), each older one a surprise, now fall into a consistent pattern that speaks for itself; they affirm the overall validity of the chronological sequence, although they do snarl local sequences in several places and show many interregional relationships to be hazy and in need of reassessment.[2] Even if for some unknown reason an extended variation of the C_{14} level upset the balance seriously during those millennia and the dates are, hypothetically, two thousand years too old, they still give an incredible antiquity to pottery in Japan. Many Japanese are duly proud of this achievement, but are equally modest in their expectation that such ancient pottery will be found on the continent once the archaeological work is as intense and extensive as it is in Japan and the Chinese establish C_{14} testing centers. When they do, their work is cut out for them—to produce dates older than the Japanese dates.

A survey of caves made by Ōyama's Prehistoric Institute in the 1930's reached the conclusion that there was little substantial evidence to indicate their occupation by Jōmon people.[3] Some of these caves were used as shelters during World War II and their floors were disturbed with fortifications. Uninformed workmen or soldiers must have turned up a lot of Jōmon pottery, but, if so, no one passed on any information of note. The real spark that reopened the whole question of cave occupation in prehistoric times was the revelation of the pre-pottery culture following the 1949 discovery of the Iwajuku site in Gumma Prefecture[4] and the ensuing archaeological events. The digging of scores of pre-pottery sites after that time at first tended to leave the impression of a hiatus between the Palaeolithic and the Jōmon period, but the results of detailed investigations of rock shelters within the last few years have wiped out this gap. Pottery levels succeed pre-pottery levels directly; the pottery is the most primitive found to date and is recovered in very small quantities. All of its features—quality of clay, implied size of pots, simple decoration if any—are features of an incipient stage in pottery making. To sum up, the stratigraphic position of these wares coupled with the early C_{14} dates and the rudimentary traits of the pottery have furnished more than enough information to piece together a tight cultural sequence.

An early reaction to these discoveries was to speak of "pre-Jōmon" pottery.[5] Rock-shelter pottery, however, does include a form of string-impressing, in which twisted fibers were pressed directly on the surface (*ōatsu-jōmon*), probably with pressure from the thumb. It is an embryonic cord-marking, and must somehow be related to the later use of short sticks wound with fibers and the standard cord-marking of several twisted fibers rolled across the clay's damp surface.

A quick glance at the map of the chief sites of this extremely early pottery points up the unexpectedly wide dispersion of types with surprisingly similar traits. For instance, *Pls. 1, 6, 7* pottery with clay ridges—linear relief (*ryūsen-mon*), a little like a corrugation—ranges from Yanagimata in Nagano Prefecture to Fukui cave in Nagasaki, with Kamikuroiwa in Ehime Prefecture between. This widespread occurrence of the same type is more comparable to the dispersion of Palaeolithic tool types than Jōmon pottery types, and, indeed, it does represent more of the former's pattern of subsistence involving far-reaching expeditions for food. The distribution of these sites hardly conforms to any normal historical idea of the Japanese preference in habitats. That preference always made good use of the large plains. Most of these early pottery sites follow mountain chains. Jōmon people did use plains, but chiefly because the rivers flowing across them served their needs and the plains often terminated in gentle coastlines. But plains were often an anathema to early foragers; they were worried by the monotony of their yield, the limitations of shelter, and the flooding of the rivers.

As for the possible sites in between these widely scattered points, a few are probably there, but they will be hard to find. Some will be discovered by accident; they will be deep (below the surface of the loam in the Kantō region), small, contain a handful of little sherds in poor condition, and some cracked stones. In fact, one is already reported from the Kōfukuji Temple site in Kawasaki City, Kanagawa Prefecture.[6]

Since whole pots have not yet been found in the earliest pottery, now believed to come from the Fukui cave in Nagasaki Prefecture, it can only be presumed from the shape of the sherds that the vessels were rather small and rounded at the base. Slabs of clay were joined together, the junctures were reinforced by pressure and squeezed, and finger-pinching produced narrow ridges. The quick discovery that this makes the vessel easier to handle than a fully plain surface and gives it some aesthetic interest may have encouraged the broadening of this technique into pure decoration. Called linear relief, it must be functionally allied to the corrugation found on much very early coil-made pottery throughout the world. The forming process of such pottery naturally results in surface ridges. In all fairness, it should be said that one theory holds that some if not all of these ridges were applied rather than pinched up from the surface.

The ridges average no more than three millimeters (one-eighth inch) in width. Calculations by curve of sherds show pots to have been about fifteen centimeters (six inches) in diameter and approximately the same height. Variations on decoration are combinations of wide and narrow pinched ridges, the wider ridges being perhaps a later development. Extremely fine ridges (*sairyūsen-mon*) ranging between one and two millimeters (one-sixteenth inch) can be seen on pottery excavated at Hibakoiwa, Ishigoya and *Pl. 1* Nittori. Hibakoiwa's latest variant of this, found in Level IV, also bears ハ-shaped indentations along the rim. These are the oldest known surface marks, and may herald the nail-marking (*tsumegata-mon*), which here appears in full form in Level III.

The regional interrelationships based on levels may be diagramed by using selected rock shelters in the way shown below. The stratigraphy of the Hibakoiwa Lower Cave in Yamagata Prefecture is extremely complicated, and has to be pieced together from several excavations. I trust that my simplified version does it no injustice.[7]

FUKUI, NAGASAKI	KAMIKUROIWA, EHIME	HIBAKOIWA LOWER, YAMAGATA
	I Haji	I Disturbed: mixed Jōmon; Yayoi; Sue
	II Late, Latest Jōmon	II Mixed Jōmon, Early; Haji; Sue
	III Early Jōmon, Todoroki type	III Mixed Jōmon: Earliest, Early, Late, Latest
		IV Cord-marked; nail-marked
I Rouletted; string-impressed	IV Rouletted	
	V Sterile	V Nail-marked; linear relief
	VI Plain (8,135±220 B.C.)	
II Nail-marked; linear relief (10,450±350 B.C.)	VII Sterile	VI Fine linear relief; scratched
	VIII Sterile	
IIIa Nail-marked; linear relief	IX Fine linear relief (10,215±660 B.C.)	VII Fine linear relief
		VIII Fine linear relief
IIIb Coarse and fine linear relief (10,750±500 B.C.)	X-XIV Various geological layers	
IV-IX Non-ceramic		
(VII) 11,650±600 B.C.		

EARLIEST JŌMON MAP I

TYPE	SITE
1. Numajiri	Numajiri, Kushiro City, Hokkaido
2. Kojōhama	Kojōhama, Shiraoi-chō, Shiraoi County, Hokkaido
3. Sumiyoshichō	Sumiyoshichō, Hakodate City, Hokkaido
4. Shirahama	Tatehira, Araida, Hachinohe City, Aomori Pref.
5. Daidera II	Takashimizu, Tsukidate-chō, Kurihara County, Miyagi Pref.
6. Tado Lower	Suganda, Nanyō City, Yamagata Pref.
7. Unoki	Unoki, Tsunan-machi, Naka-uonuma County, Niigata Pref.
7a. Hanawadai	Hanawadai shell-mound, Tone-chō, Kitasōma County, Ibaragi Pref.
8. Tado Lower	Tōnodai shell-mound, Omigawa-chō, Katori County, Chiba Pref.
8a. Inaridai	Daimaru, Yokohama City, Kanagawa Pref.
9. Tado Lower	Natsushima shell-mound, Yokosuka City, Kanagawa Pref.
10. Hosokubo	Hosokubo, Suwa City, Nagano Pref.
11. Onoe	Konokuchō, Asai-chō, Higashi-azai County, Shiga Pref.
12. Ōko	Ōko, Yamazoe village, Yamabe County, Nara Pref.
13. Kōzanji	Kōzanji, Tanabe City, Wakayama Pref.
14. Kijima	Kijima shell-mound, Ushimado-chō, Oku County, Okayama Pref.
15. Mawatari 3 Lower	Taishaku-mawatari, Tōjō-chō, Hiba County, Hiroshima Pref.
16. Fudōgaiwaya	Fudōgaiwaya cave, Nishiyama, Sakawa-chō, Takaoka County, Kōchi Pref.
17. Sōzudai	Sōzudai, Hinode-chō, Hayami County, Ōita Pref.
18. Sōzudai	Matsubaseōno shell-mound, Matsubase-chō, Shimomashiki County, Kumamoto Pref.
19. (Iwashita)	Iwashita cave, Matsugase-chō, Sasebo City, Nagasaki Pref.

NOTE: *Height of No. 8, 28 cm; others to scale, except sherds.*

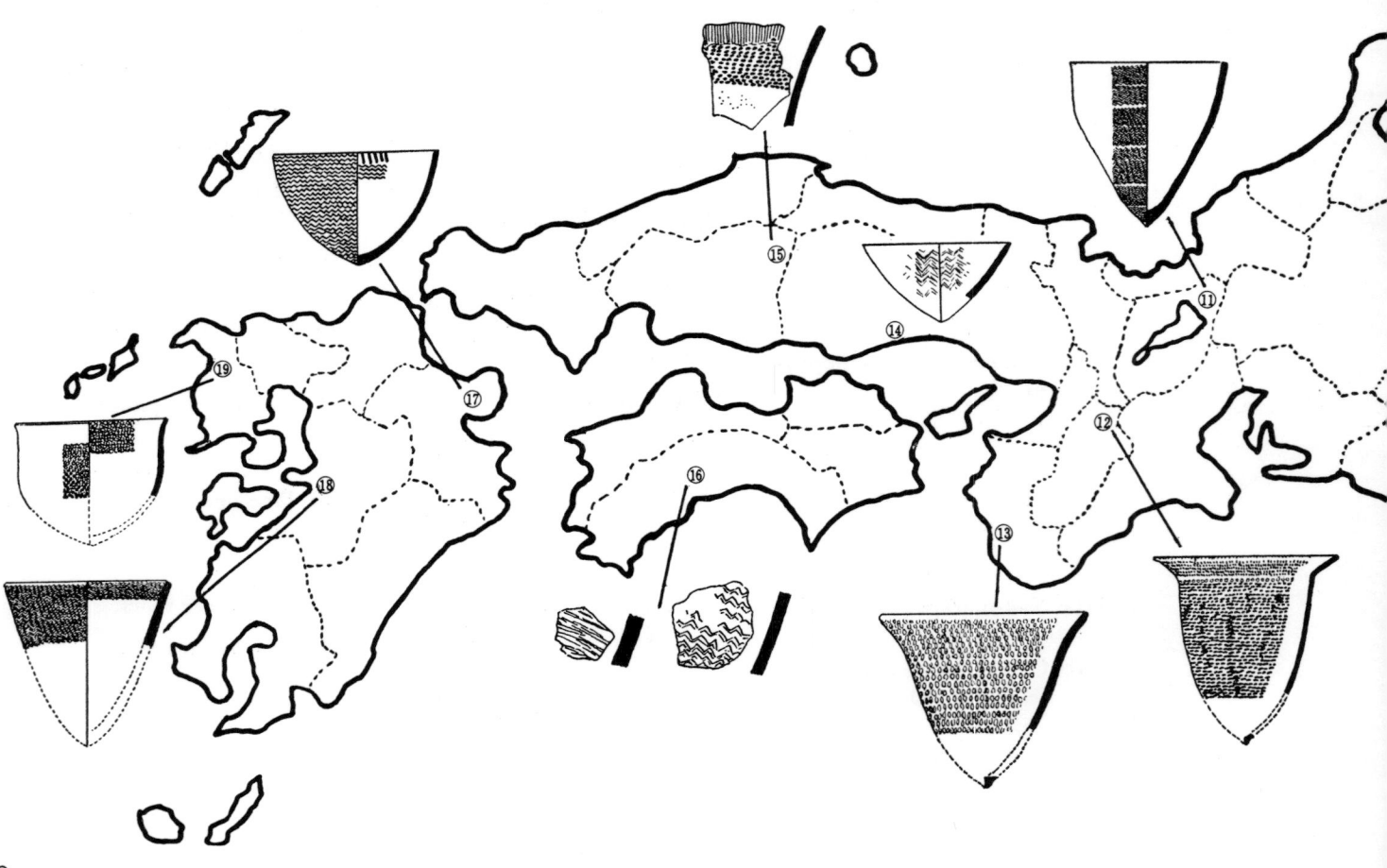

20

The vertical relationships in rock shelters are distinctive enough to point to nail-marking as the next consistent type of decoration. How one works into the other—if it does—or whether entirely new factors should receive credit for the change is not yet clear. The oblique indentations on Hibakoiwa sherds might possibly be the prototype, but nail-marking from some sites is so regular as to suggest other possibilities. An example of this would be the Sone material, recovered long ago from the bottom of Lake Suwa, for which no proper chronological place could be found. The marks are slightly curved, a little deeper toward the middle of the imprint, and are about the right size for an actual thumb or fingernail. This is in contrast to Early Jōmon's "nail-marking," which was apparently done with a split bamboo stick. The variation in direction is considerable at this stage. The decoration is on thin, small sherds, making it likely that the vessels were not large. The bases may have been generally rounded, but there is some indication that these were being elongated, though not yet pointed.

Pl. 9

The oldest forms of cord-marking were always thought to be on the earliest types in the Kantō Plain. The C_{14} dates and rock-shelter stratigraphy have shown these Kantō Plain types were preceded by direct string-pressing. The caves in Takahata-chō yielded the finest examples, showing use of a single-strand vegetable fiber, twisted and pressed against the clay, using the end only. It could have been wrapped around the thumb; it has just enough variation to prove that it was exclusively a manual operation. One can imagine that a little rolling of the thumb, like taking a fingerprint, might be followed by trying ways of improving the technique and lead to the use of a cord-wrapped stick.

One of the earliest ways in which a rolling device was employed is shown by the marks on sherds from Kosegasawa rock shelter Levels III and IV in Niigata, and Ichinosawa in Yamagata.[8] The object used was a squarish stick much like a matchstick and about the same length. It was rolled and pressed continuously. It looks as though almost the entire surface of a pot was perhaps marked this way.

Pl. 8

Full rouletting (*oshigata-mon*), that is, marking the surface with a carved stick by rolling it across the damp clay, has traditionally been recognized as southern Japan's most characteristic early technique. The border was for long the Tone River in the Kantō area, which marked the frontier between the southern rouletted and the northern shell-decorated types. The Kantō area itself contributed string-impressing to the repertory.

Pl. 38

In recent years varieties of this kind of roller-stamping have been showing up in the north. Hokkaido has a very unusual rouletting (*tokushu-oshigata-mon*), a special type, which has not been securely anchored in time, and may be as late as Early Jōmon. A little of this same type, which is based in Hokkaido, has now been found in the Tōhoku region.

Pl. 44

Rouletted pottery is widely scattered throughout Kyushu, the Inland Sea, Kansai, Chūbu and the lower Kantō region. In Kyushu it is not exclusively confined to pointed-bottom vessels, but outlived them to continue being used on flat-bottomed, rather cylindrical pots of Early Jōmon. All other signs point to a strongly entrenched tradition in Kyushu. The simplest form—zigzag rouletting—is the earliest of the widespread types, and is followed by the lattice and elliptical rouletting. Since an occasional vessel will carry more than one type, contemporaneity in some cases is obvious. Rolling was usually done parallel to the rim, but many variations can be seen. Although once thought to have originated perhaps in Kyushu and to have been related to stamped pottery in south Asia, feeling may soon reach a consensus that the rolling process, whether with cords wrapped around sticks or with sticks alone, had its beginnings in central Japan and spread extensively to southwestern regions.[9]

The Kyushu manifestation of rouletting is the most interesting, where it tends to be an inland rather than a seashore pottery. Often called Senbagatani type, after a site in Saga Prefecture, it is heavily concentrated in Kumamoto and north Kagoshima prefectures, and is found in most of the counties of Miyazaki. Zigzags and ellipses are widely seen, but the finest workmanship are the diamonds within diamonds—nothing short of genuine artistry—at the Kuroda site in Kumamoto. Type sites of well-known later pottery, such as Ataka (Middle) and Goryō (Latest), have yielded rouletted pottery, implying much persistence of the type, and a continuing preference for the advantages of the sites.

The clay of rouletted pottery is usually gray-brown to dark brown and quite coarse. The rims are flat, wavy or rippled. The makers of rouletted pottery sometimes pulled the roller across the surface to terminate the decoration along the rim with parallel, vertical grooves. The inner rim is often marked, especially in the Inland Sea region, to a depth of about three millimeters (one inch).

Other regional variations include a pattern much like a fishnet, fairly widely used in the Chūbu region during the early stages of elliptical rouletting. The Kinki district's well-developed style reached its climax toward the end of the rouletting stage. For instance, the flared-rim vessel from the shell-mound in the grounds of the Kōzanji, a *Pl. 38* temple in Tanabe City, Wakayama Prefecture, covered with large, high relief bumps, has the late unevenness that tends to go with the end of the development. It can be compared with the flat surfaces of the bullet-shaped pot from Unoki, Niigata Prefecture, *Pl. 37* on which zigzags and ellipses alternate in horizontal bands. The Unoki variant is earlier.

The oddest form of what appears to be a kind of rouletting is to be seen at Ōko in *Pl. 36* Nara and Jingūji in Osaka. The one restored Ōko vessel is illustrated here. If not rouletted, it was marked with a spatula by an amazingly sure hand.

Stratigraphy again is brought to bear on the relationship of rouletted pottery to other Kantō types. This pottery seems to follow the types normally looked on as the oldest in this region: Igusa, Natsushima and Inaridai. These are all pointed bottomed and string- *Pls. 10–13, 16* impressed. No Igusa pots have been restored, but it is presumed that they were in the typical cone shape and, like the others, served as cooking pots. Natsushima vessels are *Pls. 11–14* fairly standard in size, but are interesting for their variety of string-impressing. Much variety—or lack of standardization—may imply infrequent potting. Whatever the implications, it shows a healthy experimentation with the tools at hand.

The Inaridai vessel illustrated in Plate 16 bears marking with twisted fibers doubled back, the wrapped stick then rolled diagonally to produce vertical indentations. The striking feature about Inaridai decoration is the width of space between indentations. Such decoration was made by rolling the wrapped stick from top to bottom.

Stratigraphically Igusa and Inaridai have the rare distinction of being found in the Kantō loam. Pottery like Inaridai has come from as far away as the Kurokawa Fumonji site, Hishi-chō, Kiryū City, Gumma Prefecture, but this is quite unusual. It was for the Natsushima shell-mound in Yokosuka City that the first of the "old" C_{14} dates were given, which initiated the "long" chronology. These were $7,500\pm400$ B.C. for shell and $7,290\pm500$ B.C. for charcoal, published in 1960.[10]

The penetration of the north by rouletted pottery was sporadic and only incidental. In fact, so much so that it is difficult to fix its temporal relationships satisfactorily. All of the early northern chronology is in a state of flux and under reconsideration. Some arguments have been made for cord-marking as the earliest form of decoration, others for shell-marking.[11] Both arguments can claim the usual early shape of pointed bottoms

EARLIEST JŌMON   MAP II

	TYPE	SITE
1.	Higashikushiro III	Higashikushiro shell-mound, Kushiro City, Hokkaido
2.	Kasugachō	Kasugachō, Hakodate City, Hokkaido
3.	Nozuki	Nozuki, Morikoshi, Nagawa-chō, Sannohe County, Aomori Pref.
4.	Nashigibata	Nashinoki-gakoi shell-mound, Naruse-chō, Monou County, Miyagi Pref.
5.	Sanami	Sanami, Notojima-chō, Kashima County, Ishikawa Pref.
6.	Kayama Upper	Yoshii shell-mound, Yokosuka City, Kanagawa Pref.
7.	Irimi 2	Irimi shell-mound, Higashiura-chō, Chita County, Aichi Pref.
8.	Ishiyama VI	Ishiyama shell-mound, Ōtsu City, Shiga Pref.
9.	Hajima Lower 1	Hajima shell-mound, Kurashiki City, Okayama Pref.
10.	Hishine	Hishine, Taisha-chō, Hinokawa County, Shimane Pref.
11.	Yatokoro	Yatokoro, Takeda City, Ōita Pref.
12.	Atoe II	Atoe, Miyazaki City, Miyazaki Pref.
13.	Todoroki A	Kurokawa cave, Fukiage-chō, Hioki County, Kagoshima Pref.

NOTE: *Height of No. 3, 14 cm; others to scale, except sherds.*

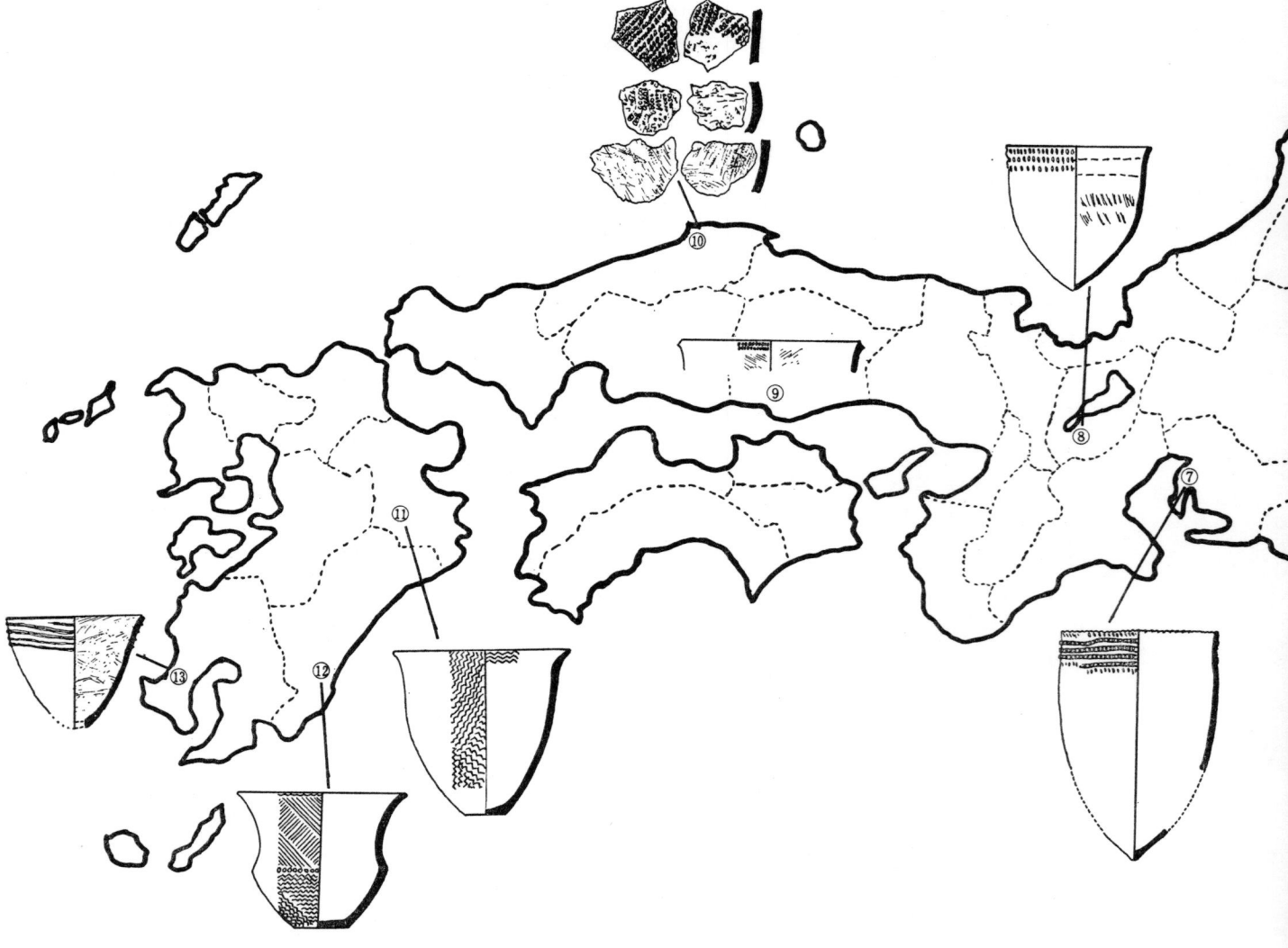

24

Pl. 20 along with certain primitivisms. C$_{14}$ dating seems not yet to have been applied to organic material associated with the earliest pottery, and the oldest dates (for Kojōhama, 5,730±200 and 5,750±200 B.C.) may belong to pottery of about the end of the Earliest Jōmon period.[12] All things considered, the evidence is still lacking to suggest that the upper Tōhoku region and Hokkaido entered the pottery picture as early as central and southern Japan. This may sound a little strange to a generation or more of Jōmon students who always suspected but could not prove that pottery was introduced into Japan from the northeast Asian continent by way of Hokkaido. This attractive view may have to be given up forever, but the chances are above average that more intense investigation in Hokkaido, especially in its caves, will push the date of local pottery back a good deal farther.

Hokkaido, it must be remembered, is a large island unlikely to represent a unified culture. The southern leg and coastal areas are little more than an extension of northern Honshu. The northern maritime provinces maintain connections with northeast Asia, and the central zone draws from both, although it is usually oriented toward the south.

Pl. 28 The Shirahama type is probably northern Tōhoku's oldest type. The best examples come from the Tatehira site in Hachinohe City, Aomori Prefecture. Shell-scraping worked the surfaces down both inside and out on this steep-walled, pointed-base type, and shell-imprinting with the edge of an *Anadara subcrenata* shell (a scallop), accompanied by stick-made punctates, decorates the rim zone. The rim itself is notched.

Other shell-marked types (Kominatotai, Fukkirizawa, Monomidai and Nozuki, etc., and other names used by local scholars) have affinities to the Shirahama type, embodying only minor distinctions. The Kominatotai type, for instance, has a laminated band that served to thicken the rim. The deep, pointed vessels become more bullet-shaped. Fukkirizawa pots pick up undulating rims with projections, and the chronologically later Monomidai type has vessels that break away from the simple traditional shape and have a swelling body, narrowed neck and flared rim. From this time on in the north much attention was given to symmetrical arrangements of four projections on the rim. The first modest effort to make a squared-off base can be seen in the Nozuki type. It has a strangely rugged quality.

Shell-marked types from Hakodate City in southern Hokkaido may be connected with those of later Earliest Jōmon centered in Aomori Prefecture. Many sherds from the *Pl. 42* Sumiyoshichō site bear full-face imprints of a shell. The varied use of a shell to decorate pottery increased considerably in popularity and seems to have moved south by way of the coast. Shell-marking joined with the fiber-tempering of the Kantō during the time pointed bottoms were still in fashion and produced the types known as Mito and Tado. *Pl. 22* Tado Lower, for instance, has the rootlike solid base, the four slight peaks of northern origin, and the first Kantō Plain effort at working haphazard surface grooving into a decorative pattern. The junctures of these grooves are supplemented with single indentations, and additional surface interest is provided through the unevenly spaced pellets of clay. The distribution center of these types is the Miura Peninsula.

Archaeologists like to include a stage of undecorated pottery before the Mito-Tado Lower types just described.[13] This is a difficult category to work with, since many sherds must be plain parts of rouletted and string-impressed pots. Plain sherds have been unearthed in many sites in Tokyo, Chiba and Kanagawa prefectures. These are especially *Pls. 15, 18* well known at the Hanawadai and Hirasaka shell-mounds, where several other types were also found. The reason for including undecorated wares in the chronology is clear *Pl. 15* enough: the Hanawadai pot is perfectly plain. It was smoothed by a blunt instrument.

Additional evidence for some distinction here is the fact that rouletting found with plain sherds seems to differ from rouletting found with string-impressed Inaridai sherds in the Kantō area. In a narrow sense, plain pottery does fit in the chronology of certain sites, but it seems acceptable to me only as a highly localized production—perhaps to the degree of being one or two pots in a site—that is by and large contemporary with rouletting and string-impressing elsewhere in the Plain.

The earliest cord-marking in the north is to be seen on pointed-bottom vessels, where it already assumes the regional characteristic of tightly spaced, rather deep indentations. It displays little evidence of having evolved on local territory, but as late as the Middle Jōmon period the string-impressing techniques of farther south were still alive on Entō type vessels. The likelihood of having borrowed this advanced cord-marking from farther south seems greater in the light of the fiber-tempering of the pottery—a Kantō trait. This would seem to be a good example of borrowing an invention, expanding it and adapting it to where it becomes an inviolable tradition. Examples from the Chō- *Pls. 25, 26* shichiyachi shell-mound in Hachinohe City, Aomori Prefecture, may be cited in regard to early cord-marking on pointed-bottom vessels. One peculiar local technique is a rope-marking (*tsuna-mon*), appearing as though a massive rope were wound around the *Pl. 27* surface and pressed tight. The marks may be as much as two centimeters (three-fourths inch) in width. The heavily fiber-tempered clay walls are about the same thickness (2 cm.), and the vessels must have been quite large. They are rounded at the bottom. Perhaps roughly contemporary is the unusual drag-and-jab technique used on the Todohokke type pot from the village of the same name, Kameda County, Hokkaido, *Pl. 24* near Cape Keizan in the north of the Watajima Peninsula.

The shell-marked Kojōhama vessels, with their finely peaked rims and flat bottoms, *Pl. 20* fit in the Earliest Jōmon in regard to decoration, but the bottoms are typical of Early Jōmon. They must be an intermediary type.

THE CAPTIONS

What may appear to be inconsistencies in terminology are the result of various methods of typing pottery. Generally speaking, roman numerals indicate stratigraphic layers (i.e., Muroya I); arabic numerals and lowercase letters in most cases indicate older typological sequences that may or may not be borne out by modern stratigraphy (i.e., Umataka 1, 2, 3 is not stratigraphic; Entō Lower a, b, c is not stratigraphic; Moroiso a, b, c has proved to be stratigraphic). Uppercase letters are usually used for "spots" dug at a site (i.e., Kasori E, Kasori B; in the Inland Sea material, S, Z, C, K and B are used for Earliest, Early, Middle, Late and Latest respectively). These complexities are compounded by lack of correspondence between pre-stratigraphic and stratigraphic results, and by a mixing of terms (i.e., the Angyō 1a, 1b, 2a, 2b, etc. subtypes are the products of pre-stratigraphic methods, but have been adopted and applied wholesale to the modern stratigraphy).

The systematization of the empirical terminology used to describe this complex Jōmon culture period—a terminology that has tended to grow more fecund over the years—is still held back by tradition and, as in many specialized studies, the physical inertia of sheer mass. It would be an immense job to systematize these terms now, and no work in that direction seems to be pending at this writing. Until such a time as a fuller concept of the society and culture of the Jōmon period allows a sounder theoretical working model for pottery typology, the student is faced with the necessity of mastering and manipulating a profusion of varied terms and (even to the Japanese speaker) strange local place names.

A temporary type name is indicated by (t). The limitations of space have allowed only the site name and prefecture to be included in the captions. Shell-mounds are indicated by an asterisk (Katabira-jinjakami*); the numbers in parentheses ( ) refer to entries on the Map of Archaeological Sites.

1. Linear relief type. This exceedingly early pottery is dark brown, rather coarsely grit-tempered with much mica, and has a hard, smoothed surface. The fine, linear relief is either finger-pinched or stick made, possibly as reinforcing where coils or strips of clay were joined. The lower part (restored) may have been slightly more pointed.
Ishigoya cave, Nagano (105) • *height: 25.0 (9.8 in.)*

2. Muroya I type. The 1961 and 1962 excavations of the Muroya cave shelter in Niigata Prefecture revealed the unexpected relationship of lightly cord-marked pottery with flat bottoms occurring in levels below pointed-bottom vessels. Small patches of cord-marking can be seen on this collared pot. The rim is cord-indented.
Muroya cave, Niigata (98) • *height: 21.0 cm. (8.3 in.)*

3. Muroya I type. The decoration of this rough-surfaced vessel is confined to the rim band, taking the form of a complicated variety of cord-marking and fine punctates around the two widest points. A hole, pressed out from the inside, is probably an overflow vent for liquids.
Muroya cave, Niigata (98) • *height: 14.0 cm. (5.5 in.)*

4. Muroya I type. The decoration is concentrated at the rim, here in diagonal cord-marking. In this case the twisted fibers are of slightly different sizes, and the furrows alternate between shallow and deep. The edge of the rim is indented, perhaps by a cord.
Muroya cave, Niigata (98) • *height: 10.5 cm. (4.1 in.)*

29

5. Muroya I type. This seems to be the typical shape for vessels from the lower levels of Muroya cave. The walls are thin; the rim band projects above a slight constriction, but is not normally thickened. The rim carries most of the decoration, here probably a very primitive string-impressing; the band is outlined by cord-indentations.

Muroya cave, Niigata (98) • height: 19.0 cm. (7.5 in.)

6. Linear relief type. The Kamikuroiwa cave in Ehime Prefecture yielded small pottery sherds dated by C_{14} tests to 10,214±600 B.C., suggesting this may be the second oldest pottery in Japan. Linear relief like a corrugation and a simple string-impressing are identifying features. ▷

Kamikuroiwa cave, Ehime (144)

7. Linear relief type (*left*). The Ichinosawa material is quite similar to the Hibakoiwa and Hinata caves' pottery—all caves being rather closely situated—in its horizontal, linear relief; occasionally the relief runs vertically at the rim. This "corrugation" is a feature often seen on very primitive pottery.

Ichinosawa rock shelter, Yamagata (52)

8. Stick-impressed type. One of the most unique decorative techniques appears at this cave as a kind of stick-marking. A small, squarish stick about the size of a match was rolled and pressed into the surface in narrow rows about a centimeter in width. Japanese terminology describes it as resembling a bamboo screen.

Kosegasawa cave, Niigata (98)

9. Nail-marked sherds. Sherds from the controversial site on the floor of Lake Suwa have a primitive kind of regular nail-marking. The probability of this decoration literally having been done by the fingernail is greater than with the so-called nail-marking (*tsumegata-mon*) of Early Jōmon.

Sone lake-bottom site, Nagano (107)

10. Igusa type. Igusa type pottery has a thickened rim bearing oblique string-impressing, a plain band just below, and a plain or string-impressed body. The string-impressing is sometimes herringbone in pattern. Igusa's distribution center is eastern Saitama Prefecture and Tokyo.

Igusa, Tokyo (85)

11. Natsushima type. A typical cone shape of the Kantō area with slightly thickened rim, the vessel bears string-impressions carried all the way to the foot. The wall is about one centimeter thick. C_{14} dates have given an antiquity of over nine thousand years for this pottery.

Natsushima*, Kanagawa (94) • height: 33.9 cm. (13.4 in.)

12. Natsushima type. Pottery in the Kantō Plain at this stage served hardly any other purpose than for cooking, and size and shape were fairly standardized. This relative consistency may have been due to the constant movement of small groups of people, who became acquainted with their neighbors' utensils.

Natsushima*, Kanagawa (94) • height: 25.1 cm. (9.8 in.)

31

13–14. Natsushima type. The vessel of Plate 14 (*right*) is a historic discovery, coming from Shell Layer 1 in the first excavation of the Natsushima shell-mound carried out in 1950. The replacement of pots was always difficult, hence the effort to save these two from any further breaking by drilling holes and binding or lacing together the cracks.

Natsushima*, *Kanagawa* (*94*) • *13*) *height: 25.0 cm.* (*9.8 in.*)
14) *height: 25.9 cm.* (*10.2 in.*)

15. Hanawadai type. The surface was smoothed with a hard object, leaving smoothing facets still visible, and is otherwise undecorated. The clay is quite fine. Sherds from this shell-mound may be plain, incised, scratched or string-impressed.

Hanawadai*, *Ibaragi* (*61*) • *height: 19.8 cm.* (*7.8 in.*)

17. Ōurayama type. The trademark of this type is rather odd string-impressing, some of which crisscrosses, while much of it runs more or less horizontally.

Jūōdōmen, Kanagawa (*93*)

16. Inaridai type. Probably the thickening of rims was believed to be a way of reducing cracking under the strain of constant use. The lip gave an advantage in picking up the vessel. *Daimaru, Kanagawa (93) • height: 28.2 cm. (11.1 in.)*

18. Hanawadai type. Hanawadai type vessels can be judged from the sherds to have been more or less cone shaped or with rounded base and gentle flare toward the rim. The string-impressed indentations are widely spaced and run diagonally, sometimes reversing the field. *Hanawadai*, Ibaragi (61)*

19. Sumiyoshichō type (*left*). Vessels of the Sumiyoshichō type have uneven surfaces, nipple-shaped bases and slightly everted and thickened rims. The edge of a shell was used both for the impressions near the rim and for smoothing the surface.
Sumiyoshichō, Hokkaido (10) • height: 23.2 cm. (9.2 in.)

20. Kojōhama 1 type (*right*). Kojōhama 1 is now looked on as one of the oldest Earliest Jōmon types in Hokkaido. The clay is sand-tempered, the surfaces hard and the color brown. Varieties of shell-marking and shell-scraping constitute the decoration.
Kojōhama village, Hokkaido (7) • height: 17.6 cm. (6.9 in.)

34

21. Nozuki type. Once inexplicably called the Tateba type, this rather odd vessel has been redesignated after the site name. The body is heavily shell-scraped and the tapered base has been flattened. Rim perforations are rare in early types.
Nozuki, Aomori (20) • height: 14.0 cm. (5.5 in.)

22. Tado Lower type. Tado Lower vessels are incised in broad lines, constituting the earliest decorative patterns in the Kantō area. This pottery is normally a dark reddish-brown color. The rim has four slight peaks, and the narrow, pointed base is solid.
Shironodai*, Chiba (73) • height: 27.0 cm. (10.6 in.)

23. Unnamed type. Much northern workmanship is characterized by dense cord-marking, which, in this case, runs obliquely from the edge of the rim to a point near the base where it changes direction. This pottery has so far avoided the stigma of being typed.
Obuchi, Aomori (13) • height: 27.0 cm. (10.6 in.)

36

◀24. Todohokke type. The Hakodate Municipal Museum received this brown pot along with other objects as part of the Notogawa Collection. It is known that Mr. Notogawa dug it up about 1935, but other details are lacking. It must be a late example of Earliest Jōmon.
Todohokke village, Hokkaido (8) • height: 16.6 cm. (6.5 in.)

25. Akamidō type. Finely pointed, well thinned toward the turned-out lip, this cooking pot of the standard, convenient, small family size was marked by intertwined thick and thin fibers, leaving a groove beside the beaded impressions.
Chōshichiyachi*, Aomori (18) • height: 27.5 cm. (10.8 in.)

26. Akamidō type. Coarsely punched around a thickened, uneven rim, simpler fibers were used to mark this vessel than for the prior example. This pot is impressive for its adherence to primitive features.
Chōshichiyachi*, Aomori (18) • height: 21.5 cm. (8.5 in.)

27. Rope-marked vessel. A thick rope was used to mark this type of vessel, the so-called *tsuna-mon*, resulting in coarse, horizontal depressions. Such vessels are usually found around Funka Bay, Watajima Peninsula, southwest Hokkaido.
Mitsuhashi, Hokkaido (3) • height: 28.5 cm. (11.2 in.)

29. Ōtera type (*bottom left*). Rim-marking only is rather unusual for this type, which has very light-brown surfaces and reveals distinct quartz-, feldspar- and sand-tempering. The two parallel rows of punctates vaguely follow the uneven rim.
Ōtera, Miyagi (37) • height: approx. 26.0 cm. (10.2 in.)

30. Funairijima Lower type (*bottom right*). Typical of this type is the confused body decoration, which apparently consists of both cord-marking and shell-scraping, the two often running at different angles. The thick rim has been impressed with a single-fiber, coarsely twisted string in widely spaced furrows.
Funairijima*, Miyagi (41) • height: 31.9 cm. (12.5 in.)

28. Shirahama type. Tall, slender, cone-shaped vessels, shell-scraped and shell-marked, often deeply indented and marked along the outer edge of the lip, are characteristic of the Tōhoku region type. Other examples have even sharper bases.
Tatehira, Aomori (18) • height: 42.0 cm. (16.5 in.)

31. Tado I type. In both the decoration and sharply pointed base this grooved and excised vessel is very close to the Tado I type of the Kantō Plain, especially of the Miura Peninsula. The surface here is far rougher. Some Tado I pottery bears red paint on the interior. *Muroya cave, Niigata (98)* • *height: 30.5 cm. (12.0 in.)*

32. Nojima type (*top left*). The vessel comes from the shell layer of the south Nojima shell-mound. Comparable to an early stage of the Kayama type, at the midpoint of Earliest Jōmon, the major traits of Nojima pottery include fiber-tempering and waved rims.
Nojima*, Kanagawa (93) • height: 27.0 cm. (10.6 in.)

33. Kayama Upper type (*top right*). Pottery from the upper level of this shell-mound is coarser than pottery from the lower level. Surface scraping is exceptionally prominent and fiber-tempering contributes to the relatively rough effect. The four rim projections are rather unusual.
Kayama*, Kanagawa (94) • height: 38.0 cm. (14.95 in.)

34. Kayama type. The Kayama type is shell-scraped; the clay is coarse and copiously fiber-tempered. The walls are fairly thick, the bases flat or rounded. The slight peaks on the rim are not carefully coordinated with the decoration, which consists of heavy punctates in the zones formed by the incised zigzags and rim-collar line.
Tobinodai*, Chiba (81) • height: 27.0 cm. (10.6 in.)

40

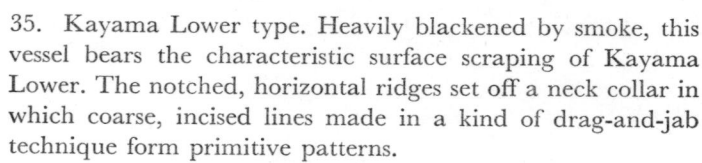

35. Kayama Lower type. Heavily blackened by smoke, this vessel bears the characteristic surface scraping of Kayama Lower. The notched, horizontal ridges set off a neck collar in which coarse, incised lines made in a kind of drag-and-jab technique form primitive patterns.

Kayama*, Kanagawa (94) • height: 47.0 cm. (18.5 in.)

36. Ōko type. This is the only pot that could be restored from the excavations at Ōko, one of the rather few Jōmon sites in Nara Prefecture. The color is reddish brown, the walls rather thin (approx. 5 mm.), and the surface carries a variety of rouletting.

Ōko, Nara (132) • height: 33.0 cm. (13.0 in.)

42

39. Irimi 2 (or Ishiyama IV) type. Excavated primarily from a shell-mound along the bank of the Seta River near the Ishiyama Temple not far from the southeast corner of Lake Biwa, this relatively coarse type is recognized by its square-sectioned, notched ridges and rows of indentations.
Ishiyama*, Shiga (129) • height: 32.0 cm. (12.6 in.)

38. Kōzanji type. Slightly fiber-tempered, a reddish dark brown in color, the walls of the vessel are thicker (approx. 1 cm.) than is usual in pottery with rouletted decoration. The large ovals represent the last stage in the evolution of the rouletted style.
Kōzanji*, Wakayama (138) • height: 28.5 cm. (11.2 in.)

40. Ishiyama V type. The prototype of the Kitashirakawa type, Ishiyama V has a distribution embracing the Chūgoku region. This vessel's profile follows a gentle curve with a very slight rim flare, the color tends to bluish black, and the surface is conspicuously shell-scraped.
Ishiyama*, Shiga (129) • height: 41.0 cm. (16.1 in.)

37. Unoki type. Oval and zigzag rouletted impressions in alternating bands weave an interesting surface pattern on this vessel from western Japan. Most of the pot is a blackish brown, while the fragile lower part is a strong red. Carbonized food still encrusts the interior.
Unoki, Niigata (104) • height: 23.0 cm. (9.1 in.)

41. Shell-marked vessel. The cone shape is found from Hokkaido to Kyushu, but northern pots tend toward straighter walls. This eastern Kyushu vessel bears a shell-imprinted rim band.
Mandokoro, Ōita (156) • *height: 25.0 cm. (9.8 in.)*

42. Sumiyoshichō type. This shell-marked pot, probably imprinted with a scallop shell, has a far more exaggeratedly peaked rim than most pointed-bottom vessels. The walls are fairly straight, and characteristically northern.
Sumiyoshichō, Hokkaido (10)

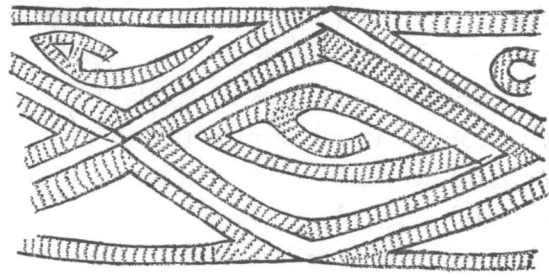

Early Jōmon

COOKING POTS of relatively simple shape almost completely dominate the first stages of Early Jōmon. It is not surprising then that a utilitarian appearance is the pottery's most salient characteristic. The almost total lack of other objects in clay (except for a very small number of figurines) shows how bare the subsistence was and how much effort went into only minor improvements of objects for daily needs. The rituals were not elaborate enough to require non-perishable paraphernalia; or, conversely, there was little time to make equipment for whatever rituals may have existed.

Early Jōmon man was blessed by a warming climate, and the expanding groups of people utilized and exploited the plentiful resources of the sea to the fullest. Climate changes during Early Jōmon and a general rise in temperature since Earliest Jōmon (with the possible exception of Middle Jōmon) can be seen through the incidence of two molluscs, *Anadara granosa* and *Pecten yesoensis*, in shell-mounds on the east coast. The former prefers a warm-water habitat, the latter a cold-water habitat. *Anadara granosa* has been found along the north coast of Japan in early shell-mounds (as far north as the Daigi shell-mound in Miyagi Prefecture in the Early Jōmon period), but it disappeared slowly from northern shell-mounds as it increased in number farther to the south. It is rare even today in the Tokyo area, and is normally seen from Shizuoka Prefecture to south Japan. The cold-water *Pecten yesoensis* is not found in Early Jōmon shell-mounds along the northeast coast—it had not yet made its way that far south, but today is not at all infrequent in Tokyo Bay.

The Early Jōmon shell-mounds of the Kantō Plain, while fairly widely distributed, are nevertheless most numerous along an old bed of the Tama River in east Kanagawa Prefecture, by the Ara River in Saitama and Tokyo, and the Edo River in northwest Chiba Prefecture. Farther inland they naturally tend to contain more fresh-water shells.

The fact that some shell-mounds have lower layers of marine shells and upper layers of riverine shells is related to the recession of the sea and the choice of the inhabitants to remain in the same spot, converting their efforts to gathering the resources most closely at hand. It was a recognition of this phenomenon that aided Ōyama in establishing the chronological system for the Kantō.[1] Within a cluster of mounds, the shell-mounds most distant from the ocean with a preponderance of marine shells would be the oldest; those closest to the ocean with a preponderance of fresh-water shells would be the youngest.

45

After Ōyama's Prehistoric Institute had arrived at a basic chronology using this observation, the details of pottery typology were not difficult to work out.

The pits of houses of Early Jōmon tend to be squarish or oblong in shape, perhaps five meters north-south to four east-west, on an average. They may or may not have a central fireplace, depending on the presence of a center pole. Some are rather irregularly shaped, with six or more postholes. As many as forty-seven were counted for one house. A pit-dwelling at Moroiso in Kanagawa Prefecture contained four fireplaces, indicating considerable use and reuse of the pit,[2] and another elsewhere contained nine. The excavators felt that this latter house had been enlarged at least four times.[3] These details are selected to draw attention to the fact that traditions and experiences had not yet brought on standardized sizes and shapes. Reference is made to the presence of pit-dwellings here to present evidence for a slightly more sedentary existence, producing a population increase, for which the larger size and greater number of shell-mounds than in Earliest Jōmon is ample evidence. The strikingly domestic character of the pottery means only that the basic comforts of life were met. Time was occupied by the acquisition of food, and energies were adequate to meet the daily necessities. The stone tools were little improved over the pebble tools and chipped axes of Earliest Jōmon. But the manpower was a little greater, and warmer weather negated the necessity for digging deep house pits. Much living undoubtedly took place directly on the surface. Personal adornments seem to be exclusively limited to stone earrings that were slipped onto the lobe of the ear. The stone arrowheads were triangular and concave-based or V-shaped, as they had been in the late stage of Earliest Jōmon. A projectile point shaped like a laurel leaf was probably a small spearhead. New, however, is the tanged scraper, beginning to appear in the north. Bone fishhooks, harpoons, needles and other perforators were part of the tool kit. The well-known Kamo canoe, complete with oars, belongs to the Early Jōmon period and requires little imagination to recognize its significance in fishing and coastal travel.[4]

The appearance of flat bottoms on cooking vessels marks the beginning of Early Jōmon in the Kantō Plain. Even if this change came about through the normal development of pottery, it evidences the larger groups of people to be accommodated with pots of greater capacity. It can be said that the first half of this period witnessed the creation of a standard design for a cooking pot, while the second half witnessed the efforts to improve its efficiency and usefulness. The latter is combined with attempts at making it more aesthetically interesting.

Starting with the Kantō Plain and moving outward (without in any way implying that the plain was the sole hub of the Jōmon sphere at this time), the most significant types can be listed chronologically as follows: Hanazumi Lower, Sekiyama, Kurohama, Moroiso and Jūsanbodai. Less important types are frequently inserted by some archaeologists, but they have more limited distributions. From my "multilinear" (see page 12) view, the inclusion of these lesser-known types simply reinforces the concept of an "ideal" unilinear chronology, which is in fact not applicable to any single region.

The early cooking pots were a little over thirty centimeters in height, with walls of rather irregular shape, becoming progressively narrower toward the base with the passage of time until some become distinctly unstable. The rims were usually flared and thickened by a band of clay. Bases were occasionally slightly raised. The problem of sagging walls had yet to be surmounted, and attempts to strengthen them were made by mixing quantities of short vegetable fibers with the clay.

Pls. 46, 64–66   The Hanazumi type's contributions are restricted to cord-marking effects, since its makers seem to have been relatively reserved in their attitude toward new shapes. Herringbone cord-marking became standard practice and was supplemented by shell-imprinting. The Kikuna shell-mound in Yokohama City has yielded the most typical examples. A vessel is covered with imprints produced by the edge of an *Anadara granosa* shell; this decoration can be called pseudo-cord-marking. The last possible impact the shell-marking of Earliest Jōmon of northern Japan could have had on the Kantō area and areas farther south would have been during the Hanazumi stage. This technique falls off after the Hanazumi type, to be replaced by much more extensive cord-marking (from the north?), while part of the slack is taken up by incising and grooving with a stick.

Hanazumi's immediate predecessors can be compared in regard to shell-marking, since their own role as the possible transmitters should not be overlooked. The Shiboguchi type (limited to the Yokohama and Yokosuka City areas) and the Kayama type (rather widely distributed as far as northeast Honshu and into the Chūbu district) were both copiously fiber-tempered and heavily shell-scraped. Kayama has some flat bases, and even oval-shaped rims, as though the vessels were made for easier holding while pouring. The Shiboguchi vessels have the typical Earliest Jōmon pointed bases; Kayama has some rounded, some flattish and some flat bases. Kayama pots may carry shell-grooving worked into very simple patterns of oblique lines running in several directions.

Hanazumi pottery, in other words, kept the shell-marking alive at the same time it was the chief introducer of cord-marking to this region. String-indenting in registers on the necks of the vessels are set apart by obliquely lined ridges of clay. The string indentations curve and loop back in parallel furrows, and the intervening spaces are stick-marked. Perhaps a pair of cords were held together in one hand to do the work. The standard herringbone cord-marking, used even on the neck zone of typical vessels, was produced by taking two strands of fibers twisted to the right, joining them by twisting them together to the left, then rolling the cords horizontally to get a right-oblique series of indentations. For the band directly below, the opposite procedure was followed: two strands, each twisted to the left, were combined by twisting them together to the right. This roller was run across the surface from right to left, thus producing a left-oblique series of indentations.

Throughout the time that fiber-tempering was consistently used in the Kantō area, there seems to have been considerable difficulty in controlling wall shapes. Bulging bodies were directly related to attempts at increasing surface exposure to heat from the cooking fire, but non-symmetrical shapes and uneven wall surfaces tell a tale of rudimentary techniques and inexperienced workmanship.

The fiber-tempered pottery of the Tōhoku, the Entō ("cylindrical") types, are by far *Pls. 48–57* the most successful in regard to wall control. It was in these types that fiber-tempering was used to best advantage in Early Jōmon Japan. Shapes were fairly standardized, flat bases became customary, and credit may be given the potters for holding to conventional shapes of remarkable stability.

The earlier of the Entō subcultures—Entō Lower—is distributed as far north in Hokkaido as Sapporo City; in the Tōhoku region it is especially concentrated in the Kitakami valley and along rivers like the Mabuchi, which flows in toward the Akita-Yamagata prefectural border, and the Yoneshiro River. Most probably the spread of the type and the relative consistency of the shapes may be accounted for by the movements of people along these and other fairly large river valleys and their rather frequent contacts with each other.

EARLY JŌMON MAP I

Type	Site
1. Onnetō	Onnetō, Wasa village, Kushiro City, Hokkaido
2. Todokawa	Todokawa, Esashi-chō, Hiyama County, Hokkaido
3. Entō Lower a	Mushiri, Higashidōri village, Shimokita County, Aomori Pref.
4. Katsurajima	Katsurajima, Shiogama City, Miyagi Pref.
5. Nunome	Nunome, Maki-machi, Nishikambara County, Niigata Pref.
6. Sekiyama	Fujioka shell-mound, Fujioka-chō, Shimotsuga County, Tochigi Pref.
7. Hanazumi Lower	Kikuna shell-mound, Kikuna-chō, Kōhoku Ward, Yokohama, Kanagawa Pref.
8. Kaminoki	Kaminoki, Chino City, Nagano Pref.
9. Kijima	Kijima, Fujikawa-chō, Ihara County, Shizuoka Pref.
10. Kitashirakawa 1b	Torihama, Mikata-chō, Mikata County, Fukui Pref.
11. Hajima Lower 2	Hajíma shell-mound, Kurashiki City, Okayama Pref.
12. Mawatari 2	Taishaku, Tōjō-chō, Hiba County, Hiroshima Pref.
13. Todoroki Lower	Todoroki shell-mound, Uto City, Kumamoto Pref.
14. Yoshida	Ōhara, Yoshida village, Kagoshima County, Kagoshima Pref.
15. Sobata	Nishino-omote Honjō, Tanegashima, Kagoshima Pref.

NOTE: *Height of No. 6, 20.3 cm; others to scale, except sherds.*

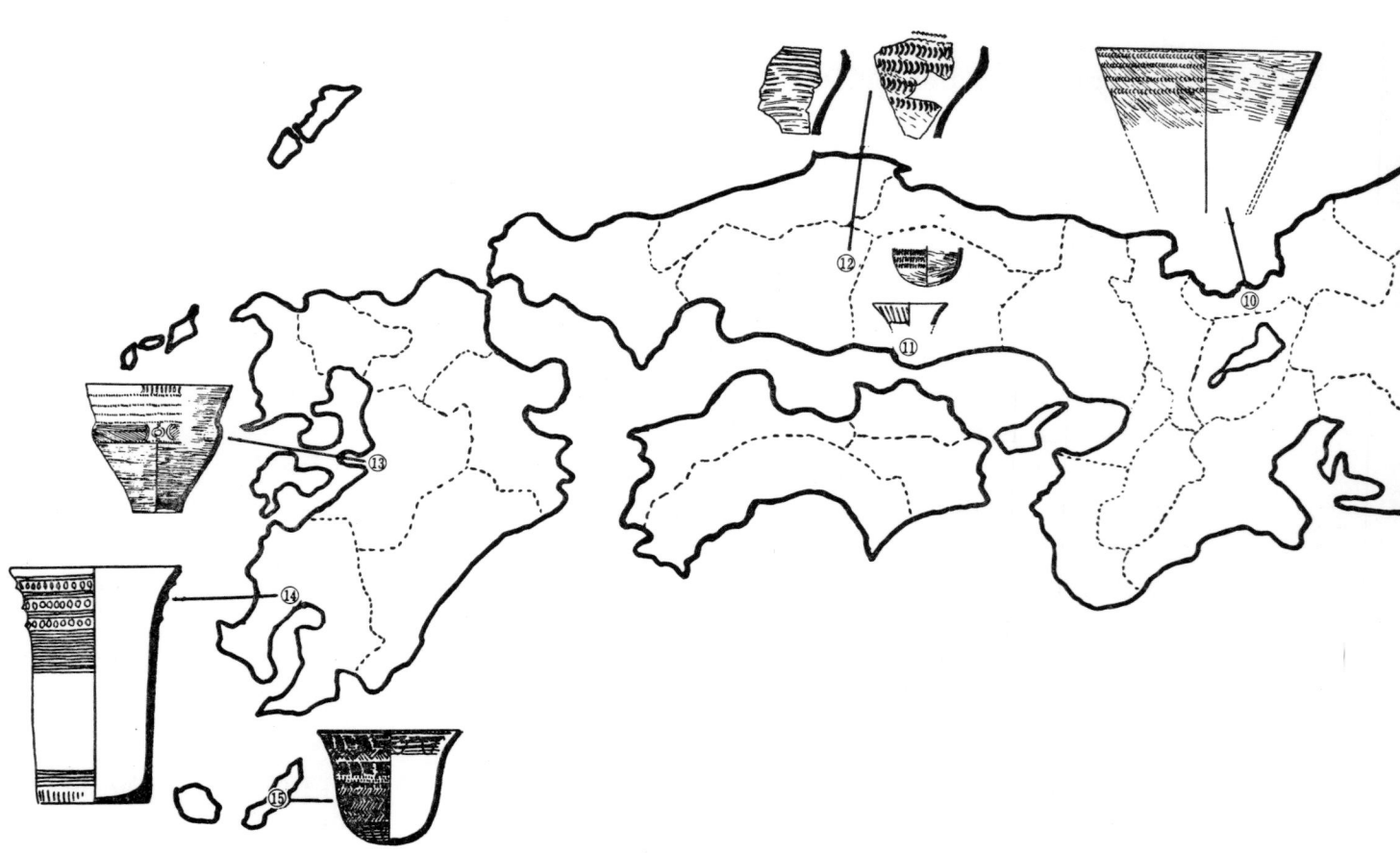

48

49

As a minor insight into the archaeological hierarchy, the Entō types were named many years ago by the venerated Professor Hasebe before the site-type terminology was developed and elaborated upon by his students.[5] The Entō name has remained inviolable—the sole extant symbol of resistance to the proliferation of type names that pervades the field elsewhere.

Entō shapes change rather little and suggest centuries of satisfaction with a simple vessel of fairly large capacity whose walls are virtually straight or taper gently toward the base. The color ranges from dark to occasionally light brown, or from gray to blackish. Large smoked areas indicate considerable contact with fire.

Entō Lower was subtyped as a, b, c and d in 1929 by Yamanouchi.[6] Entō a and b are regarded as earlier than c and d and are normally characterized by full coverage of fairly coarse cord-marking that may run almost vertically or horizontally. String-indenting is sometimes found around the rim, which may have slight peaks.

Entō c and d are far more imaginative, with wider variations in shapes. They may have bulging bodies strongly narrowed toward the foot, greater flare to the rim, a wavy rim, and a heavy, collar-like rim formation. Most of the new ideas appear as variant forms of cord-marking—though Entō c and d show the most variation, Entō pottery as a whole in regard to shape, color and size bordered on the monotonous. Many of the most intricate kinds of cord-marking belong to this area and time period: string-indenting; string-impressing; knotted cord-marking in herringbone or other shapes; combinations of thick and thin strands, and variants like "wheat-patterns." Even bundled, cord-wrapped sticks were used, producing marks that only by sheer accident could be duplicated exactly today. The possibilities in sizes of strands, twisting, knotting, braiding and interlacing are unlimited. One extreme is the "maggot" effect—wormy indentations with no apparent rhyme or reason to their arrangement. By and large, however, it should be said that order and systematic repetition was greatly appreciated in cord-marking, and most vessels display a disciplined effect in respect to this technique.

Pl. 56

Yamanouchi, who excavated in northern Honshu for many years before moving to Tokyo University after World War II, set up a compressed sequence for the lower Tōhoku based on his work at the Daigi shell-mound in Miyagi Prefecture. Daigi is a rather large mound occupying the top of a hill in Shichigahama-machi, outside Shiogama City. Sherds can be picked up on the site that bear a wide variety of cord-marking. The hillside topography does not lend itself to naturally undisturbed stratigraphy, and Yamanouchi's scheme is both stylistic and ideal in its arrangement; it is also drawn up in correlation with Kantō Plain developments.[7] The Yamanouchi typology can be listed chronologically in the following way for the Early Jōmon period:

Type	*Traits*	*Kantō Plain type*
Daigi 1	String-indenting at the rim; herringbone cord-marking; rope-marking; fiber-tempering	Sekiyama
Daigi 2a	String-impressing; herringbone cord-marking	Kurohama
Daigi 2b	Clay strips; some fiber-tempering	
Daigi 3	Stick-marking in parallel lines; punctation; string-impressing; shell-imprinting; sand-tempering	Moroiso a
Daigi 4	Applied strips of clay; oblique, fine cord-marking; shell-marking; punctation; stick-made ridges of clay	
Daigi 5	Applied strips of clay; bamboo-stick-marking; cord-marking	Moroiso b
Daigi 6	String-impressing; herringbone cord-marking; bamboo-stick-marking; clay strips	Moroiso c Jūsanbodai

Cord-marking was adopted on Japan's west side and even in the central mountains—the latter a region that always seems to have had some aversion to cord-marking, as though it were foreign to the inhabitants' tastes. From the Kinki region moving south, cord-marking is negligible and in most areas non-existent. Stick-marking, which emerged as the main decorative technique of the latter half of this period, began to appear in incipient ways. The slightly irregular punctation and grooving in the Inland Sea sites may be taken as evidence of this.

Kyushu is two relatively distinct entities. The high mountain chain that runs almost north and south divides the prefectures of Kumamoto and Miyazaki along its crest. The largest shell-mounds are in west Kumamoto along rivers that flow into Shimabara Bay and, to a lesser extent, Yatsushiro Bay. A number lie along the coastline of Kagoshima Bay. There are many open sites inland, but these are fewer in contrast to central and north Japan. Some pottery types never cross the natural geographical boundaries, one example being the Sobata type; others occasionally do. Nevertheless, Kyushu's topography has set up strong deterrents to the movement of people and the diffusion of pottery types. *Pls. 93, 94*

The sequence of types in Kyushu undoubtedly includes more overlapping than is generally realized, and the real limitations in distributions often seem greater than in most other regions. Oddly enough, the island's types frequently appear to be both unrelated to Honshu types and to what are claimed to be the local preceding types.

The familiar and controversial Todoroki shell-mound in Uto City of Kumamoto Prefecture may perhaps be assigned to this developmental stage as the most distant outpost of shell-marking of northern origin. The Tamukeyama type of northern Kagoshima is rouletted, but the decoration is on vessels of both pointed and flat bases; it is usually viewed as Early Jōmon in time. The Yoshida type, limited in space and time, is the most fantastic of all shell-marked types. Grooving and imprinting is done in tight, methodical rows. These are deeper and more sharply articulated near the rim. The vessels must have been more or less cylindrical with a slight flare toward a thickened lip. The Sainokami type (locally pronounced Senokam) is another Kagoshima type. Its *Pl. 97* vessels have a roughly cylindrical body and sharply flared rim. It is noted for its net-shaped cord-marking. It is, in effect, one of the earliest forms of zoned cord-marking, but it would not be possible to relate it directly to Late Jōmon's extensive use of this kind of decoration.

The best known of the west Kyushu types of Early Jōmon is the already mentioned Sobata type, a familiar name to Jōmonologists since it was reported in 1918.[8] The site is *Pls. 93, 94* in west-central Kumamoto Prefecture. Its distribution embraces parts of northern, western and southern Kyushu, and Tanegashima and Yakushima, two islands to the south. There are many local modifications of the basic short-groove decoration on rounded-bottom pots, and some sherds are shell-scraped on the inner surface. The rather unaccented decoration seems to include some uncommonly pedestrian examples of overall, largely parallel, grooving. Most interesting are the geometric patterns, such as large zigzags or triangles filled with stick-made grooves.

Sobata has been connected with the Kammkeramik of Korea. Its distinctiveness tends to set it apart from other Kyushu types and to indicate that its fundamental affiliations are not within the Japanese sphere.

In the Kantō area, the Sekiyama type cooking pots illustrate the first of the serious *Pls. 67–71* efforts to create sophisticated designs. These are lozenge-like shapes near the rim, marked in ladder fashion, accompanied by circular punctates, or parallel diagonals

EARLY JŌMON MAP II

TYPE	SITE
1. Saibesawa II	Loc. 2, Higashiyama, Furano City, Hokkaido
2. Entō Lower c	Onnadate shell-mound, Mutsu City, Aomori Pref.
3. Daigi 5	Nukazuka shell-mound, Hasama-chō, Tome County, Miyagi Pref.
4. Fukura	Fukura cave, Yusa-chō, Akumi County, Yamagata Pref.
5. Moroiso c	Tōkodai, Kiryū City, Gumma Pref.
6. Okitsu	Okitsu shell-mound, Miho village, Inashiki County, Ibaragi Pref.
7. Nabeyachō	Nabeya, Kakizaki-chō, Nakakubiki County, Niigata Pref.
8. Asahi Lower	Asahi shell-mound, Himi City, Toyama Pref.
9. Moroiso b	Orimoto shell-mound, Yokohama City, Kanagawa Pref.
10. Moroiso a	Yagamiyato shell-mound, Yokohama City, Kanagawa Pref.
11. Shimojima	Shimojima, Chino City, Nagano Pref.
12. Kitashirakawa Lower	Ebiyama, Minokamo City, Gifu Pref.
13. Kitashirakawa Lower	Kitashirakawa, Ogura-chō, Kyoto
14. Kitashirakawa Lower	Kō, Fujiidera City, Osaka
15. Hikozaki 2 II	Hikozaki shell-mound, Nadasaki-chō, Kojima County, Okayama Pref.
16. Isonomori	Isonomori, Kurashiki City, Okayama Pref.
17. Satakōbu	Satakōbu shell-mound, Kashima-chō, Yatsuka County, Shimane Pref.
18. Minamikusaki	Minamikusaki shell-mound, Nio-chō, Mitoyo County, Kagawa Pref.
19. Kariwata	Kariwata, Miyazaki City, Miyazaki Pref.
20. Isoichi	Isoichi, Miyakonojō City, Miyazaki Pref.
21. Senokan	Senokan, Hishikari-chō, Isa County, Kagoshima Pref.

NOTE: *Height of No. 10, 23.5 cm; others to scale, except sherds.*

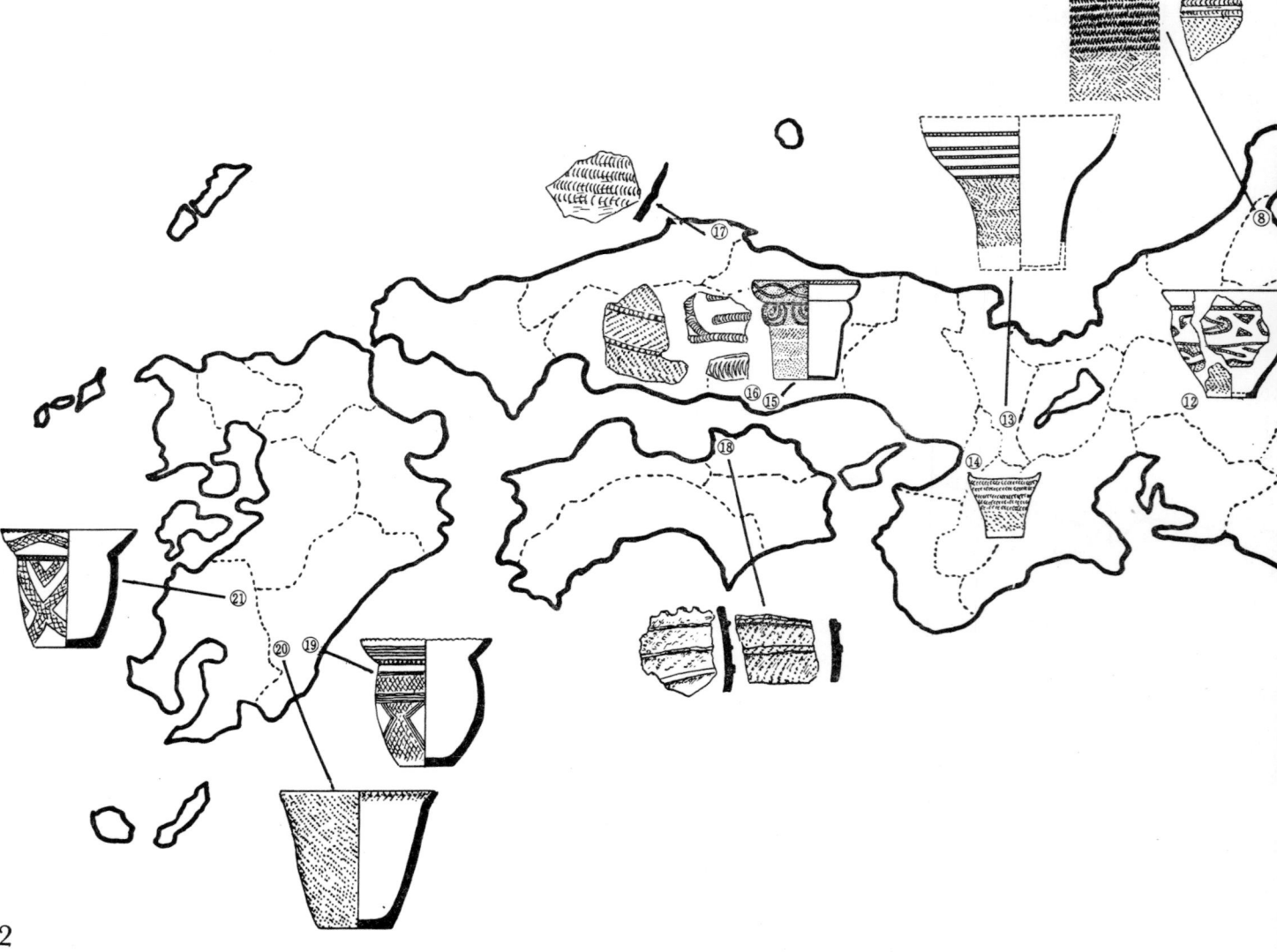

53

adorned with bosses. Bamboo sticks were sometimes used to produce corduroy effects, often over cord-marked surfaces. The typical cord-marking is herringbone, knotted or otherwise, but there are examples in which a loop was made to terminate the cord, which was eye-spliced. Rims may be peaked and notched, but of unusual interest are the lip-spouts and the one known example of a tubular spout, a vessel found at Nishi-yokono in Gumma Prefecture—the oldest in Japan. Two lip-spouted vessels, one from Saitama, the other from Tokyo, have heat-reddened lower parts, the usual sign of constant exposure to a fire. They were not normal storage vessels, unless they were before they were put to use for boiling water or foods, but must have had some special reason for having these spouts. A personal guess here, which takes into consideration both the fairly substantial capacity of these vessels and the presence of so many piles of baked and heat-fractured stones in Early Jōmon houses and nearby, is that they were used for boiling water, which was then poured over hot stones for instant steam heating.

The Kurohama type received its name from a hill overlooking the Motoara River. This hill and several others are the scene of many shell-mounds that have yielded Kuro-hama and other types of pottery. The clay is coarse, extremely fiber-tempered, and the walls are thick. Vessels often look surprisingly crude, have very narrow bases, and their cord-marking may be touched up with short, choppy vertical grooves in the neck zone. Kurohama shapes show some progress toward the cup-shaped rim that later became a common Middle Jōmon feature.

Moroiso is the family name for the major types of the latter half of the Early Jōmon period. As early as 1897 the Moroiso shell-mound in the Miura Peninsula, Kanagawa Prefecture, was investigated by Yagi.[9] He was followed by a procession of diggers in the 1920's and 1930's.[10] The type is of such consequence for this stage, and the term so deeply entrenched and widely employed, that it is a little disheartening to see continuing efforts to exchange Moroiso a, b, and c for site names that have none of the sense of continuity the Moroiso name has contained for at least a generation of archaeologists.

Pl. 79   The Moroiso ceramic types of the Kantō, Chūbu, Kinki and the middle Inland Sea are often virtually indistinguishable, making it apparent that they belong to one and the same pottery subculture. To take examples, the Kitashirakawa material of Kyoto, *Pl. 91*   the pots from Kō in Osaka, or the many sherds from the Asahi shell-mound in Toyama Prefecture, can only be distinguished from each other by minor differences in local clays. The crescent-shaped indentations—nail-marking—are concentrated around a flared rim, and were done in a drag-and-jab manner (unconnected crescents), by pulling the stick across the surface then going back to punch in the crescents (crescents in grooves), or in a rocker motion (zigzag crescents). Most of the technical possibilities are exploited at all the sites.

Nail-marking (*tsumegata-mon*, presumably named by one of the first archaeologists who encountered it with the idea that thumb or fingernails were used) is, like rouletting, a southern Japan manifestation, but it has not been found in extreme southwest Honshu and Kyushu, which by this time had become detached from basic Honshu developments. This pottery is no longer fiber-tempered, the walls are medium to thick (the Kitashira-kawa sherds are rather thin), and the color is usually brown.

Moroiso owes its nail-marking to initial efforts with this technique during the prior Sekiyama stage. The Sekiyama patterns are rather coherent, confined to a limited space near the rim, and often attract immediate attention. Moroiso potters developed consid-erable competence with the lengthwise-split bamboo stick in sites like Kitashirakawa in Kyoto, yet at many sites they seem to have dragged it over an already cord-marked surface quite carelessly, even aimlessly. This same range of quality characterizes the rouletting in southern Japan at an earlier date; the individual skills involved in carving a stick for rouletting may have varied much more than in plaiting fibers for cord-marking.

The Kantō area sequence for Moroiso can be outlined very briefly. The suggested type names do not correspond precisely with a, b and c.[11]

Moroiso	Oblique cord-marking	Mizuko
Moroiso a	Nail-marking; oblique cord-marking; horizontal ridges of clay	Yagami
Moroiso b	Oblique cord-marking; simulated rope in raised ridges	Yonmaibata
Moroiso c	Numerous parallel incisions; clay bosses	Kusabana

Shapes in Moroiso types include not only the standard cooking pot, but variations on small bowls and even a necked, globular jar. Rims may be wavy, and the cup-shaped rim was being even further refined (from the earlier Kurohama type) in Moroiso b. *Pl. 84* The best example of this is the notable pot from the Orimoto shell-mound in Yokohama *Map, p. 52, #9* City. A container of less depth, basically Moroiso b in type, would be represented by the Fukura vessel from northern Yamagata Prefecture. The lower wall narrows rapidly to *Pl. 63* form an S-shaped body curve, while the rim juts out sharply from the constricted neck.

What is called Moroiso c is exemplified in some unusual vessels whose cradle was in the east Nagano-west Tochigi district. Half-moon-shaped strips of clay are alternated with punched bosses around the shoulder and rim. In addition, the rim is provided with *Pl. 82* four concave, shell-shaped clay discs.

The Kasumigaura district, the riverine lakes separating the prefectures of Ibaragi and Chiba, is the northern perimeter of the characteristic south Kantō Plain types of Early Jōmon. Just north of this are the limited distribution zones of the Ukijima and Okitsu *Pls. 75, 76* types. Stick and shell-marking are combined on large deep bowls, the shell-imprinting neatly fitted within zones in a way that resembles a preview of the zoned cord-marking of Late Jōmon.

The type that bridges the Early and Middle Jōmon periods is Jūsanbodai, named *Pls. 87–89* after a site at Nogawa, Kawasaki City, Kanagawa Prefecture. It can be described as a form of Moroiso b, only much more sculptural. The ridges have a beaded effect, resulting from sharp angle-punching with a bamboo stick. The cord-marking is strong and deep. The shapes must be visualized from the sherds; they would not be unlike the Moroiso b shape of bulging body, narrowed neck and cup-like rim. The rims carried projections or gentle peaks.

The Jūsanbodai site is situated along the south bank of the Yagami River on fairly high land. In one part of the site only Jūsanbodai material was found. The stick-marking of this type, in which the stick is pulled across the surface and at regular intervals back-tracked and pressed down hard, had been seen as early as the Sekiyama type. The angle at which it was held resulted in a pattern resembling the overlap of curved roof tiles.

The site is significant for its bearing on the broader aspects of Jōmon chronology, yielding pottery of the Kayama, Moroiso, Jūsanbodai and Horinouchi types. Kayama is now looked on as an Earliest Jōmon type; Moroiso and Jūsanbodai are regarded as consecutive types at the end of Early Jōmon; Horinouchi is Late Jōmon. No Middle Jōmon pottery was found, although the site is located in the kind of riverbank setting often encountered in Middle Jōmon sites. Kayama pottery is not uncommon in or near Middle Jōmon sites. Apparently both its makers and Middle Jōmon people often chose the same sort of terrain. The Kayama and Jūsanbodai types are relatively limited in distribution. The commonly accepted pottery sequence suggests that there is a time gap between Kayama and Moroiso. If so, this site was resettled by the Moroiso people, perhaps because they noticed the earlier debris and recognized that the location had proved itself as a base for hunting and foraging expeditions.

The Middle Jōmon people may have lived at a time when the rivers were running at their highest. Late Jōmon people, when occupying the same location, often elected to live slightly closer to the bank, possibly because the rivers were overflowing less frequently and the convenience of proximity could be enjoyed with less fear for safety of house and possessions. On the basis of C_{14} dates, however, it might be suggested that very little time, if any at all, actually separated the occupation of the site between Early and Late Jōmon. It may have been in almost continuous use from Early Jōmon through the introductory stage of Late Jōmon, the Jūsanbodai type here giving way to the Horinouchi type as a consequence of contacts with developments in other areas. This possibility raises a major question concerning the Jōmon chronology, which will be dealt with briefly later (see chart, p. 171).

43. Higashikushiro III type. In this eastern Hokkaido type, the cord-marking is used in alternating broad and narrow bands. The latter, including the rim band, contain vertical, widely spaced furrows resembling string-impressing. The walls of Hokkaido vessels are usually more massive, and the proportions and decoration less refined than on Honshu.

Higashikushiro*, Hokkaido (4) • height: 15.5 cm. (6.1 in.)

44. Kamui type. From a technical standpoint, the rare rouletting in Hokkaido seems to be the same as that of Honshu, but the accompanying stone industry is quite different, leading one to conclude that the subcultures could not be more than superficially related.

Higashikagura village, Hokkaido (5) • height: 25.0 cm. (9.8 in.)

45. Nunome type. The site lies on a sandbank along the shore of the Kamisekigata (a swamp), and has yielded a single pottery type—named after the site—which is apparently a variant of the Entō types. The dense cord-marking is disposed in narrow registers.

Nunome, Niigata (100) • height: 37.0 cm. (14.6 in.)

46. Hanazumi Lower type. Heavily cord-marked in alternating oblique bands produced by knotting and twisting the cords in the opposite directions, this vessel is much like Early Jōmon pottery of east and north Japan. Its presence above the other types in the cave points to a very prolonged period of occupation.

Muroya cave, Niigata (98) • height: 33.0 cm. (13.0 in.)

47. Kijima type. Kijima pottery is known in the Kantō, Chūbu, Kinki regions and along the Tōkai coastal zone, but this is the only complete pot of the type. Fiber-tempering was not used, despite its presence in the Hanazumi Lower type with which Kijima is often associated in excavations.

Nakahara, Nagano (111) • height: 20.5 cm. (8.1 in.)

48. Entō Lower c type. Entō types are known for their extensive cord-marked surfaces, often displaying string-impressions in simple patterns near the rim. These types, with their dense cord-marking, graphically illustrate the variety of such decoration in contemporary use.
Ichiōji*, Aomori (18) • height: 40.3 cm. (15.8 in.)

49. Entō Lower a type (*bottom left*). Knotted cords produced the rim marking on this vessel, below which holes were bored, the signs of an effort to save a cracking cooking pot. Fiber-tempering has been reported as occurring in the core of the walls, as though sandwiched between sheets of clay.
Mushiri, Aomori (11) • height: 35.6 cm. (14.0 in.)

50. Entō Lower b type (*bottom middle*). Oblique cord-marking on a simple body is a common feature of most Entō Lower variants, in this case on an exceptionally pure cylindrical shape. The decoration on the collar is the result of using knotted cords.
Ichiōji*, Aomori (18) • height: 56.0 cm. (22.0 in.)

51. Entō Lower b type (*bottom right*). This example of the tall, cylindrical subtype has a broad collar band of string-impressing and cord-marking above a row of finger-sized indentations, and the customary slanted, body cord-marking. The fragmented lower wall is the telltale sign of a cooking pot.
Shizumukai, Akita (48) • height: 33.0 cm. (13.0 in.)

52. Entō Lower c type. This piece is somewhat more restored than appearances suggest. The cord-marking was first applied more or less vertically then slightly overlapped with diagonal marking, each furrow sharply imprinted. Most Entō examples are more systematically decorated than this vessel.

Ichiōji*, Aomori (18) • height: 52.3 cm. (20.6 in.)

53. Entō Lower d type. Cylindrical vessels were made in Early and Middle Jōmon around Ninohe and Kokonohe, as far south as Morioka City in Iwate Prefecture. This fiber-tempered vessel is one of the largest of about ten pots found clustered at one site, and is a very fine example of decoration produced by a cord-wrapped stick.

Tashiro, Iwate (27) • height: 43.0 cm. (16.9 in.)

54. Entō Lower d type. The Kanisawa site contained Entō pottery with both wide and narrow collars of cord-marking, the former being found stratigraphically higher. The vessel is low fired, the color a grayish brown. Such horizontal string-impressing near the rim is unusual for Entō Lower d.

Kanisawa, Aomori (18) • height: 33.7 cm. (13.3 in.)

55. Entō Lower d type. This vessel is fiber-tem- ▷ pered and a yellowish-brown color. The herringbone cord-marking is done by knotting the cords and reversing the twist of the fibers. Considerable skill was required to connect the registers of cord-marking so precisely.

Kanisawa, Aomori (18) • height: 23.5 cm. (9.3 in.)

60

61

57. Entō Lower d type. This string-impressed vessel has short, crossing indentations near the foot of each band of marks. These were made by fibers extending beyond the knot, wherever the potter pressed them hard enough.
Kanisawa, Aomori (18) • height: 39.5 cm. (15.5 in.)

56. Entō Lower d type. This vessel is fiber-tempered, reddish brown, and was recovered with the pot of Plate 54. The rim has clustered projections, and the body a shape quite comparable to Daigi 6 vessels from the southern Tōhoku region. Several twisted fibers were used in producing the cord-marking.
Kanisawa, Aomori (18) • height: 24.0 cm. (9.4 in.)

59. Daigi 4 type. Daigi 4 picks up a little of the Kantō Plain's penchant for plastic decor, starting with application of clay strips in a modest way, and here including braidlike patterns. Additional decoration was made by a bamboo stick.
Shimizu*, Iwate (35) • height: 37.0 cm. (14.6 in.)

58. Fukura type. The Fukura type is a northern branch of the Moroiso family, but under Entō Lower and Daigi 6 influences. Much heat-reddened around the lower part, this vessel's shape illustrates one of the best solutions to the problem of designing an efficient boiling pot.
Fukura, Yamagata (51) • height: 28.0 cm. (11.0 in.)

60. Fukura type. A thick layer of carbonized material was removed from the pot after excavation, presumably remnants of food. The rather confused decoration is the consequence of incising with a bamboo stick over a roughly cord-marked surface.
Fukura, Yamagata (51) • height: 23.0 cm. (9.1 in.)

61–62. Daigi 4 type. A few bold efforts and imaginative shapes break the uniformity of the early Daigi types, Daigi 4 representing the first steps in this respect with a modest, geometric "cake decoration" style, especially notable on vessels from this shell-mound. The open projections on the sides complement the peaks forming the boat shape.
Nukazuka*, Miyagi (38) • height: 26.8 cm. (10.5 in.)

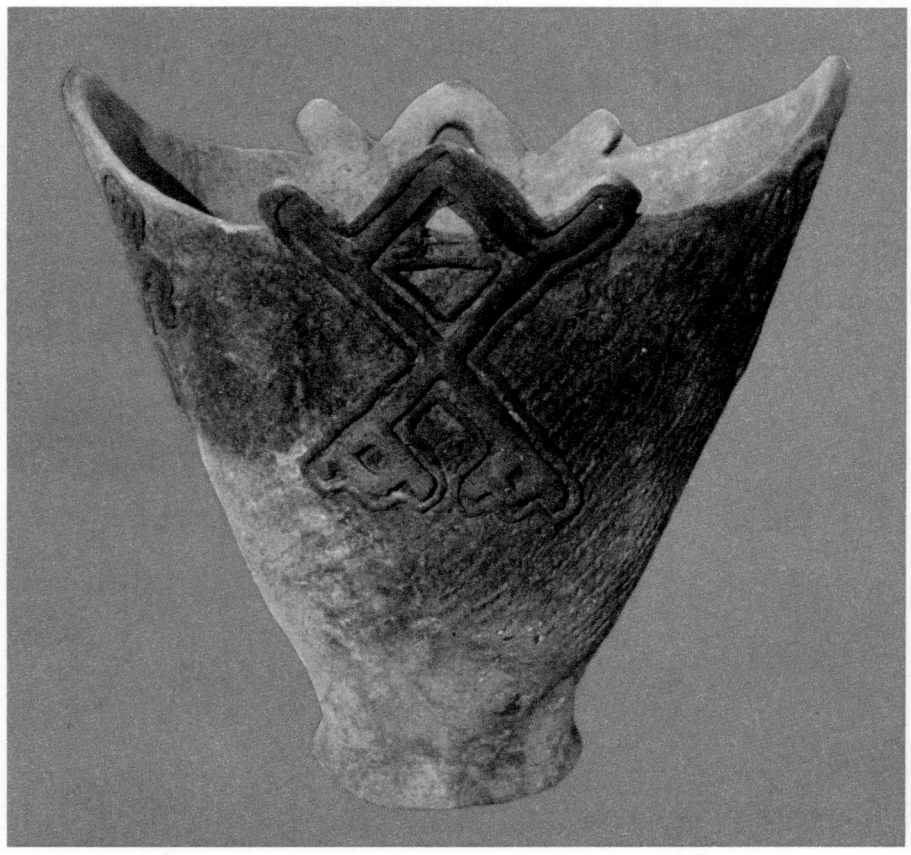

64. Hanazumi Lower type. The walls are relatively thin, with some tendency to sag, but a widened waist goes with efforts toward building a better cooking pot. Hanazumi potters often gave up the choice of varied decoration in favor of overall cord-marking.
Kikuna*, Kanagawa (93) • height: 30.5 cm. (12.0 in.)

63. Fukura type. The thin, closely notched ridge, often occurring in parallel pairs and here resulting in a beaded effect, was widely used in the latest types of Early Jōmon, such as Daigi 6, Jūsanbodai and Otoshiyama, all distant relatives within the Moroiso family. The lower wall of this pot is much heat-reddened.
Fukura, Yamagata (51) • height: 19.7 cm. (7.8 in.)

65. Hanazumi Lower type. Purely domestic ware of the Hanazumi Lower type has uneven walls, extensive cord-marking, and frequently a slightly raised base. The clay is fiber-tempered.
Kikuna*, Kanagawa (93) • *height: 28.3 cm. (11.1 in.)*

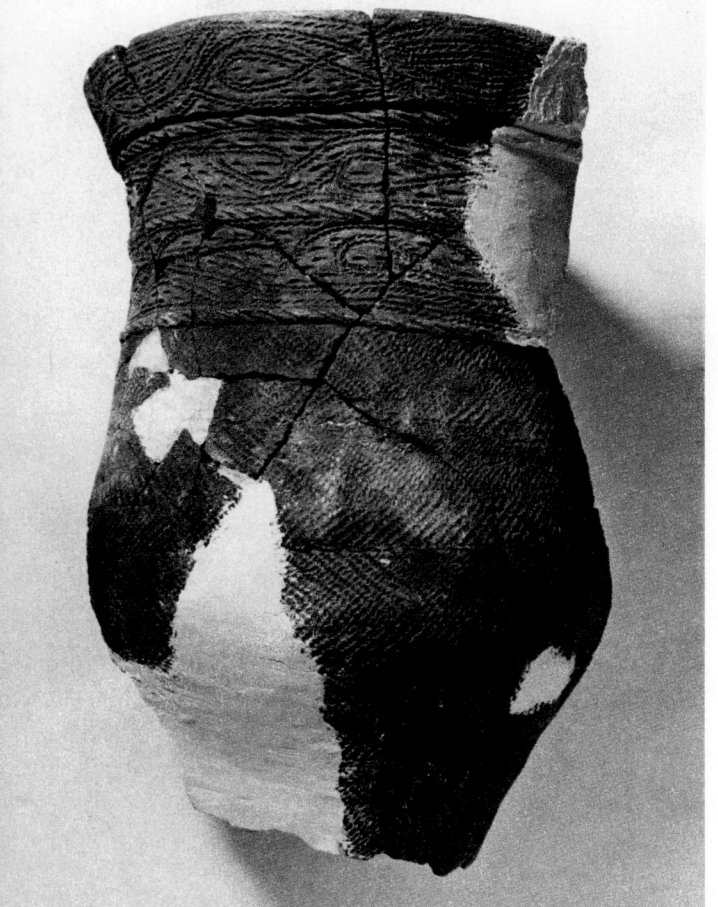

66. Hanazumi Lower type. Once called the Kikuna type, Hanazumi Lower pottery tends to retain the older, rather narrow bases, employing string-impressing for designs. The northern, full-body coverage by cord-marking here appears on a piece from the Kantō Plain.
Kikuna*, Kanagawa (93) • *height: 39.0 cm. (15.3 in.)*

65

67. Sekiyama type. Sekiyama type pottery has a fairly consistent appearance. It occurs chiefly in the prefectures of Tokyo, Saitama and Chiba, and is more abundant than any of its predecessors in the Kantō Plain. First attempts at spouts are to be seen in this stage.
Nishiyokono, Gumma (68) • *height: 14.0 cm. (5.5 in.)*

68. Sekiyama type. Bamboo-stick-marked patterns on the rim collar and herringbone cord-marking characterize this type, as does the bulging body. This was a new shape in the Kantō area and was a practical effort toward functional improvements in the cooking pot.
Futatsugi*, Chiba (79) • *height: 35.0 cm. (13.8 in.)*

66

69. Sekiyama type. Beginning with Tado Lower in the Kantō area, small nodes were used to punctuate the decoration, but the Sekiyama type tends to restrict them to the rim collar, often placing them at the junctures of the geometric patterns. *Shinoyama*, Tochigi (65)* • *height: 20.3 cm. (8.0 in.)*

70. Sekiyama type. From the same shell-mound as the vessel of Plate 68, this fiber-tempered and ruggedly cord-marked cooking pot is restored at the base and is lacking the one additional strip of decoration that would complete the more ornate rim typical of Sekiyama. *Futatsugi*, Chiba (79)* • *height: 30.3 cm. (11.9 in.)*

67

72–73. Kurohama type. The example in Plate 72 (*left*) of the densely fiber-tempered Kurohama type is the usual cooking pot. The type is noted for the introduction of new shapes despite the crudity of most of the potting and decoration. The fiber-tempered vessel in Plate 73 (*right*) is brown with blackened areas. Shaped to increase the amount of surface receiving the heat of a fire, the pot was finely cord-marked on the body and coarsely on the flared rim, then sketchily decorated with a bamboo stick. The Kurohama distribution is rather limited.

72) *Nowata*, Tochigi (66)* • *height: 42.5 cm. (16.7 in.)*
73) *Kaizuka*, Saitama (69)* • *height: 20.0 cm. (7.9 in.)*

74. Kurohama type. This strangely circumscribed type may well have made a major contribution to new shapes in Jōmon pottery, but added nothing to the development of decoration. The potters' disinterest in precision or inability to control the shape may have accounted for this.
Kanoezuka*, Chiba (80) • *height: 15.0 cm. (5.9 in.)*

◁71. Sekiyama type. With lip-spout to facilitate the emptying of the pot, the rim of this vessel has been enhanced by semicircular projections. The curved and diagonal stick-marked patterns on the upper half were superimposed on the oblique cord-marking.
Asukayama Park*, Tokyo (83) • *height: 33.0 cm. (13.0 in.)*

75. Okitsu type. This exceptionally large vessel has been spoken of as a prototype for the big bowls of early Middle Jōmon. Stick-marking and shell-imprinting, here rigidly horizontal, enhance the curves of the vessel and add to its clean-cut, functional appearance. *Okitsu*, Ibaragi (62) • height: 44.5 cm. (17.5 in.)*

76. Okitsu type. The Okitsu type is almost completely limited to the Okitsu shellmound, where widemouthed, deep bowls or squat boiling pots seem to have been preferred. Shellimprinting is used here like cord-marking, giving a foretaste of the zoned cordmarking of Late Jōmon. *Okitsu*, Ibaragi (62) • height: 29.5 cm. (11.6 in.)*

70

78. Moroiso a type. Fortunately, enough was recovered for the upper two-thirds to be reconstructed. The Moroiso type ridges are much heavier than usual, and the arc-shaped parallel lines marked with the end of a split bamboo stick are only one notch above doodling.
Murayama, Gifu (124) • height: 47.5 cm. (18.7 in.)

77. Moroiso a type. A cousin to the next piece, also with oval-shaped rim, the applied work on the piece provides only a thickened rim and minor other decoration. Drag-and-jab patterns are more interesting; lightly done cord-marking appears faintly in a few enclosed areas.
Murayama, Gifu (124) • height: 32.0 cm. (12.6 in.)

79. Moroiso a type. This is a typical Moroiso type bowl, bamboo-stick-marked and obliquely cord-marked. The cardinal Moroiso traits are found from the Kantō area to the Inland Sea, across the central mountains to Niigata, and as far north as Miyagi Prefecture. Variants appear even beyond these limits.
Provenance unknown • height: 32.0 cm. (12.6 in.)

80. Shimojima type. Detail of Color Plate I.

81. Moroiso b (Yonmaibata) type. The large Moroiso family was widespread in the Kantō area and reached well into the Kansai region. In direct continuation of the Sekiyama-Kurohama types, most vessels are obliquely cord-marked, profusely stick-marked and, at times, bear rather interesting, sometimes coherent, patterns.
Orimoto*, Kanagawa (93) • height: 34.5 cm. (13.6 in.)

82. Moroiso c (Kusabana) type. The last Moroiso type reflects a growing interest in the plastic decoration best seen in the Middle Jōmon period. Cord-marking is largely ignored in favor of liberal stick-marking, and fiber-tempering is abandoned in favor of grit-tempering.
Hanatoriyama, Yamanashi (115) • height: 22.4 cm. (8.9 in.)

83. Kaminoki type. Decoratively speaking, this type is the equivalent stage of development as the Sekiyama-Kurohama types of the Kantō area, but it is somewhat retarded as to shape, being only a slight advance—and one of dubious value—over the pointed bottoms of Earliest Jōmon.
Kaminoki, Nagano (108) • height: 54.5 cm. (21.45 in.)

84. Moroiso b (Yonmaibata) type. The practical value of the in-turned rim is not entirely clear. If it is not the result of styling or perhaps of certain methods of coiled construction, it may have been designed to stop liquids from boiling over or in some way to hold a lid.
Hanatoriyama, Yamanashi (115) • height: 28.5 cm. (11.2 in.)

85. Moroiso b (Yonmaibata) type. More Kansai than Kantō in appearance, and probably a Kansai shape, this vessel was once painted and polished, but the present condition does not adequately attest to its original quality. Four small holes are located between the narrow rim ridges. *Hanatoriyama, Yamanashi (115) • height: 11.2 cm. (4.4 in.)*

86. Moroiso b (Yonmaibata) type. The productive Hanatoriyama site yielded many vessels of oddly variable quality. The faint cord-marking looks more like a poorly finished surface, and the simulated ropes are sharply slashed ridges.
Hanatoriyama, Yamanashi (115) • height: 11.4 cm. (4.5 in.)

89. Jūsanbodai type. A shape that sees ▷ some development in the Middle Jōmon period, it has a wide orifice, slightly inturned rim, blunderbuss upper body, and narrow base below a globular lower body. Applied strips sometimes form ladder patterns; heavy strips depending from doubled arcs at the rim are repeated four times.
Provenance unknown • height: 34.5 cm. (13.6 in.)

87. Jūsanbodai type. A rare and strikingly peaked globular vessel displays the Moroiso family's trait of cord-marking with superimposed clay strips. In the Jūsanbodai type the strips are angular in section and deeply indented.
Hanatoriyama, Yamanashi (115) • height: 19.5 cm. (7.7 in.)

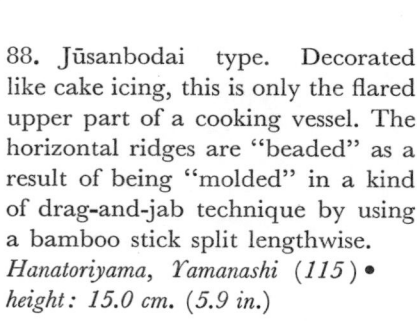

88. Jūsanbodai type. Decorated like cake icing, this is only the flared upper part of a cooking vessel. The horizontal ridges are "beaded" as a result of being "molded" in a kind of drag-and-jab technique by using a bamboo stick split lengthwise.
Hanatoriyama, Yamanashi (115) • height: 15.0 cm. (5.9 in.)

76

77

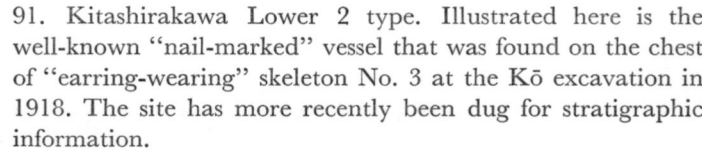

91. Kitashirakawa Lower 2 type. Illustrated here is the well-known "nail-marked" vessel that was found on the chest of "earring-wearing" skeleton No. 3 at the Kō excavation in 1918. The site has more recently been dug for stratigraphic information.

Kō, Osaka (131) • height: 16.0 cm. (6.3 in.)

90. Comparable to the Goryōgadai type. This high-peaked vessel is a grayish brown and well fired. The roughness of its surface is a result of light cord-marking. The lip and the high ridges are all deeply notched, traits that suggest a peripheral Kansai area version of the Goryōgadai type.

Uragaito, Gifu (125) • height: 24.0 cm. (9.4 in.)

92. Kitashirakawa Lower 2 type. Part of the Moroiso family and with the Kitashirakawa site perhaps as its hearth, the type spread into the Inland Sea and into the west side and eastern edge of the Chūbu district. Horizontal bands of cord-marking are sometimes separated by a narrow, smoothed zone.

Kitashirakawa, Kyoto (130) • height: 22.0 cm. (8.7 in.)

93–94. Sobata type. Usually round bottomed, Sobata type pottery is widely scattered in western Kyushu and out into Tanegashima and Yakushima islands. Rather short, straight line grooving is customary.
Sobata*, Kumamoto (151) • 93) *height: 37.0 cm.* (14.6 in.)
94) *height: 12 cm.* (4.7 in.)

95. Maebira type (*left*). Quite unusually shaped, difficult to date—supposedly Early Jōmon—this shell-marked vessel belongs to a type found in a restricted area around Kagoshima.
Nagano, Kagoshima (162) • *height: 26.0 cm.* (10.2 in.)

96. Ishizaka type (*right*). Part of a large vessel from southern Kyushu—probably a very early type of Early Jōmon—neat, oblique shell-marking is the characteristic decoration, with a fine kind of imprinting adorning the sharply flared rim band.
Ōbara, Kagoshima (163) • *height: 27.6 cm.* (10.8 in.)

79

97. Senokam type. The main distribution of this type, noted for its string-impression in netlike zones and neck and rim notching, is southern Kyushu, but it has recentry been discovered in the Shimabara Peninsula of Nagasaki Prefecture.
Nabeya, Kagoshima (159) • *height: 24.2 cm. (9.5 in.)*

I. Shimojima type. Belonging to a lesser-known type of which virtually no complete vessels exist, this piece is heavily sand-tempered, well fired, and has thin walls. Combing and appliqué arcs attached to the shoulder and rim curves dominate the surface. *Shimojima, Nagano (108)* • *height: 35.4 cm. (13.6 in.)*

II. Daigi 9 type. Cord-marking was applied within deep-set zones formed by rounded, red-painted ridges. The surprising state of preservation of the paint on this shell-mound pot suggests that the pigment is the more durable cinnabar rather than red ochre. *Minamisakai*, Miyagi (42)* • *height: 14.0 cm. (5.5 in.)*

III. Katsusaka type. A typical Katsusaka shape, ▷ with inturned mouth and thickened rim, the body slightly flared toward the base then cut back sharply, the pot exhibits a coarse, vertical cord-marking in undefined zones—a relatively rare form of decoration. A single rim head normally faces inward.
Nakahara, Tokyo (91) • *height: 24.8 cm. (9.7 in.)*

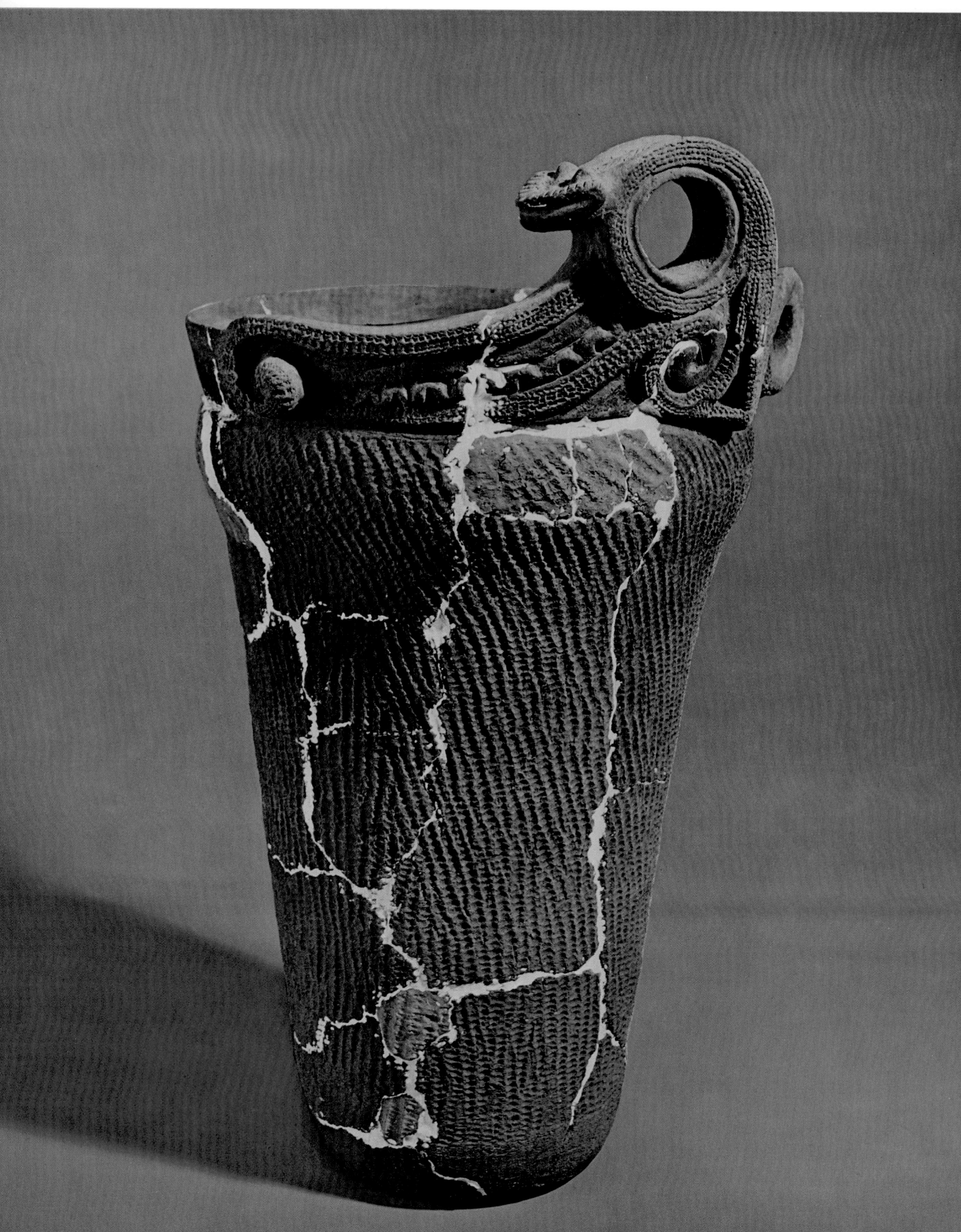

IV. Katsusaka 1 type. The realism of snake motifs increases as the quantity of other decoration on a pot decreases. They also become increasingly realistic as the Katsusaka types move down into Yamanashi Prefecture and Tokyo from the mountains of Nagano Prefecture.
Miyanoshita, Tokyo (91) • height: 39.0 cm. (15.3 in.)

V. Idojiri type. Its massive hollow handles largely intact, this vessel is in an exceptional state of preservation. The body decoration compares well with the general decoration found in the Tokyo area, but the face-like handles are not found outside of Nagano Prefecture. This is equivalent to the Katsusaka 3 type.
Idojiri, Nagano (109) • height: 35.0 cm. (13.8 in.)

85

VI. Tōnai type. The spiral, lined-oval panel and other plastic details are characteristic of Katsusaka family decoration, but the squat shape is less usual, and the extreme angularity of the rim perhaps even less so. The handle has been called a human figure with spread arms and legs.
Sori, Nagano (109) • *height: 27.3 cm. (10.7 in.)*

VII. Tōnai type. An "incense burner" type, this cord-▷ marked vessel has typical Katsusaka decoration in the slashed and notched ridges. Unique, however, are the four figures of the handle and rim, marked in the same way and variously called slugs, frogs and snake heads.
Fudasawa, Nagano (109) • *height: 16.6 cm. (6.5 in.)*

VIII. Kamiyamada type. The simple cylindrical form and cup-shaped rim are obscured by heavy, angular, boldly conceived ridges and slashed knobs, creating the plastically exaggerated surfaces typical of the southern Hokuriku region. The base is missing.
Asahi*, *Toyama* (119) • *height: 37.4 cm. (14.8 in.)*

Middle Jōmon

THE DYNAMIC subculture of Middle Jōmon that evolved in central Honshu has recently attracted much attention in regard to its importance in Jōmon period cultural development. C_{14} dates indicate that it flourished between about 2500 and 3000 B.C. The largest sites are located in southern Nagano Prefecture—along the upper Tenryū River, which flows out of Lake Suwa through Nagano and Shizuoka prefectures to the sea—in Yamanashi Prefecture, western Tokyo, and in the northwestern part of Kanagawa Prefecture. Sites such as Hiraide, Togariishi, Idojiri, Nashikubo, Kumakubo and Takeda, for instance, are situated at an altitude that varies between eight hundred and thirteen hundred meters above sea level, and, where the springs, rivers, plateaus and valleys tend to conform to rather similar topographical configurations, the subsites lie about four kilometers apart.

The ancient communities in this area left as their remains the largest clusters of pit-dwellings of the entire Jōmon period. Dozens of pits have been excavated, and calculations based on the size of the sites have been made for many more.[1] These pits were by no means all in use at any one time, as pottery seriation has shown, but the evidence is for active, cohesive groups of people whose energy contributed to the phenomenal and rapid development of this local culture.

The pit-dwellings are circular, and have evenly spaced posts and a central fireplace; the center post was eliminated. The shape and construction of the house was not only relatively standardized but was built for the best utilization of its space around the family hearth. It is not facetious to suggest that the fundamental unity of the Japanese "family" may be traced to this cultural stage.

Houses may contain figurines and phallic objects. The existence of the latter is often taken to mean the prolonged presence of men in the community and their participation in daily activities, as compared to a purely hunting society. This fact is an additional mark of economic stability. Some pits of houses in Yosukeone, Nagano Prefecture, possessed stone platforms in the northwest (and less used) side of the house. On these stood a tall stone, or were laid stone phalli, figurines or broken pottery. These platforms could rightly be called the oldest household altars in Japan.

The large and richly adorned pot is the hallmark of this subculture. Apart from the many new decorative details and functional changes in pottery use, the most impressive feature of this ceramic industry is its transformation from the almost purely domestic

89

ware of Early Jōmon to a powerfully artistic and ritual ware, now to be displayed and used in special ways.

This cultural stage goes by the name of Katsusaka, after a site in Kanagawa Prefecture dug by Ōyama's Prehistoric Institute in the late 1920's. The relevance of the site to major cultural changes was already suspected by Ōyama when he recognized at Katsusaka an unusually high incidence of sandstone and shale tools. He believed these would have been too dull or too soft to have served as axes, and he assumed that they were ground-working implements.[2]

In recent years serious studies have been made of the likelihood of incipient agricultural practices at this time—perhaps only the manipulation of certain food-producing roots and nut-bearing trees—and the maintenance of "kitchen gardens." The discovery and use of such means of supplementing a normal hunting economy is credited with the rapid rise of this mountain culture. It may be assumed that the climatic conditions were favorable, even invigorating; the rivers and springs were flowing well—many of the same springs are in use today—and exploitation of the environment led to a newfound security. The plateaus made ideal home bases and settlement areas. The distances separating sites located near the edges of these plateaus would have afforded a community a foraging radius of not less than two kilometers and usually much more. At the least, walnuts, chestnuts, horse chestnuts, acorns and lily bulbs were gathered. The discovery in later Jōmon sites in other parts of the country of various fruit seeds is not at all unusual.[3]

Without trying to pinpoint the beginnings of agriculture in Jōmon Japan, research was at first focused on the nature of the community as it might represent the social organization of a settled society, as seen in the presence of female figurines and many digging tools.[4] But the skeptical view did not concede that the complexity of this Middle Jōmon culture could have been the product of mixed economic systems.

Esaka narrowed the entire question down very sharply when he suggested that the beginnings of agriculture in Japan would have occurred in this south Nagano-Yamanashi zone in the earliest stages of the Middle Jōmon period.[5] Foraging parties more than likely collected seedlings of the horse chestnut tree (*Aesculus chinensis*) in the mountains or highlands and brought these down to the lower terraces for planting. Yams (*Dioscorea japonica*) were cultivated, as were the *mizu-imo* (taro), *Yama-imo* (*yama*, contraction for Yamato, i.e. native—a large edible root), in addition to lily bulbs(*yuri*). Starch may have been leached out of these roots in the running water of the ample springs situated along the slopes of the plateaus. Only certain locations meet all of the requirements for this ecology—a fact that helps to explain the topographical similarity of so many of these Middle Jōmon sites.

Until 1960 the evidence was largely circumstantial and had been argued chiefly on theoretical grounds. The search took a more positive turn when Eiichi Fujimori found carbonized "bread" beside a fireplace in pit-dwelling 5 at Sori, one of the many Fujimi-chō sites centered around Idojiri in Nagano Prefecture. It was identified only as made of starch. In pit-dwelling 9 of the Tōnai site, a piece of carbonized "bread" was discovered in association with a large number of chestnuts. Fujimori was led to conclude that vegetable foods seem to have been one of the most important staples at these Idojiri sites.[6]

The bread turned out to be four cakes and one small piece described as *mochi*-shaped (like a rice ball). The cakes average 16.5 × 10 centimeters in size. Fujimori took as the crowning proof of cultivation practices the discovery of a set of vessels: a pot with lid, a deep and well-decorated bowl, and several deep but coarse pots. He reasoned that the vessels' shapes were differentiated according to function; they were, in other words, designed for storage, offerings and boiling foods. Additional evidence in reference to Fujimori's argument might be given for specially deposited pairs of large pots and bowls found together in Loc. 1D of the I.C.U. site in 1964, and to these arguments can be added a number of other new shapes that may have a bearing on the question: "incense burners;" stemmed cups; chalice shapes; barrel-shaped pots; amphora-like vessels; and wide, low bowls. Katsusaka potters were well beyond the stage of preoccupation with the perfection of the shape of a boiling pot; they were experimenters, and it is this element of variation that stimulates so much of the modern interest in this pottery.

Even size and elaborate decoration of pottery gives an impression of a well-settled social system. Many vessels fall into a non-portable category—in terms of household use—and it appears unlikely that so much effort would have been expended on their production only to abandon them shortly afterwards. Their capacity and quantity—and pottery sherd deposits are normally extremely dense in these Middle Jōmon sites—must be relative to the number of people they had to serve.

To evaluate this complex of traits within the Jōmon evolution, the following features should be kept in mind: the appearance of new shapes, many intended to serve specific functions; a sculptural attitude toward decoration, based on appliqué work and a general disregard for the cord-marking tradition; the inclusion of zoomorphic or anthropomorphic motifs; and a rather limited use (to judge by what remains today) of surface painting. All of these traits are alien in varying degrees to the fundamental trends in Jōmon pottery. There is therefore good reason to raise the questions regarding the origins of this local culture.[7]

Connections with Moroiso pottery of the Kantō Plain show up most prominently at Aramichi, Fujimi-chō, Nagano Prefecture, where, for instance, on a goblet-shaped cup *Pl. 119* the horizontal nail-markings are obviously in the direct tradition of the Early Jōmon style, but are in the higher relief of Middle Jōmon. Cord-marking appears on some Aramichi pots. Six vessels were unearthed in pit-dwelling 1 at this site. One is this *Pls. 111, 112* stemmed cup, another is a barrel-shaped vessel, a third is a bowl, and the remaining vessels are the familiar cooking-pot shape.[8] Such a household, in other words, had provided itself with both the usual domestic vessels as well as ritual types. Incidentally, a glance at these vessels will point out certain deficiencies in the typological system. Without a detailed knowledge of the conditions under which they were found there would be no normal way of typing them together.

Local archaeologists give the major types following Aramichi as Tōnai, Idojiri and Sori, names all taken from the many sites in the Fujimi-chō district of Suwa County in Nagano Prefecture. The Nagano types most closely resembling Katsusaka in the Kantō Plain are Tōnai and Idojiri. The connection existed because of the movement of peoples, due either to the expeditions of active hunters or the lengthening of trade routes for materials like obsidian. Such trade routes led down through the Kōfu valley region of Yamanashi Prefecture and into the western Tokyo area. That the connections were close is shown by the fact that vessels from the mountains or the outer fringes of the Kantō Plain are often indistinguishable from vessels found in western Tokyo.

The sculptural surfaces of Katsusaka pottery result from the application of high relief ridges. These are shaped into panels, the most common of which are oblong and horizontally oriented. The ridges are notched or slashed, and the panels marked in parallel lines, three-pointed stars, zigzag lines, contiguous arcs and in other ways; surfaces are

MIDDLE JŌMON MAP I

Type		Site
1.	Saibesawa V	Loc. 1, Higashiyama, Furano City, Hokkaido
2.	Katsuyamadate III	Irie, Abuta-machi, Abuta County, Hokkaido
3.	Entō Upper b	Korekawa, Hachinohe City, Aomori Pref.
4.	Nukazuka	Nukazuka shell-mound, Hasama-chō, Tome County, Miyagi Pref.
5.	Umataka	Umataka, Nagaoka City, Niigata Pref.
6.	Atamadai	Sannendate, Shirakawa City, Fukushima Pref.
7.	Atamadai	Shinmei shell-mound, Omikawa-chō, Katori County, Chiba Pref.
8.	Katsusaka	Kusabana, Akita-chō, Nishitama County, Tokyo
9.	Kamiyamada	Asahi shell-mound, Himi City, Toyama Pref.
10.	Katsusaka	Hiraide, Shiojiri City, Nagano Pref.
11.	Katsusaka	Kaido, Okaya City, Nagano Pref.
12.	Katsusaka	Nagamine, Chino City, Nagano Pref.
13.	Awatsu	Shimohaya, Tanabe City, Wakayama Pref.
14.	Funamoto	Funamoto shell-mound, Kurashiki City, Okayama Pref.
15.	Hashi	Sarugahana cave, Mihonoseki-chō, Yatsuka County, Shimane Pref.
16.	Takezaki	Takezaki shell-mound, Tensui-chō, Tamana County, Kumamoto Pref.
17.	Ataka	Ataka shell-mound, Jōnan-chō, Shimomashiki County, Kumamoto Pref.

NOTE: *Height of No. 11, 49.5 cm.; others to scale.*

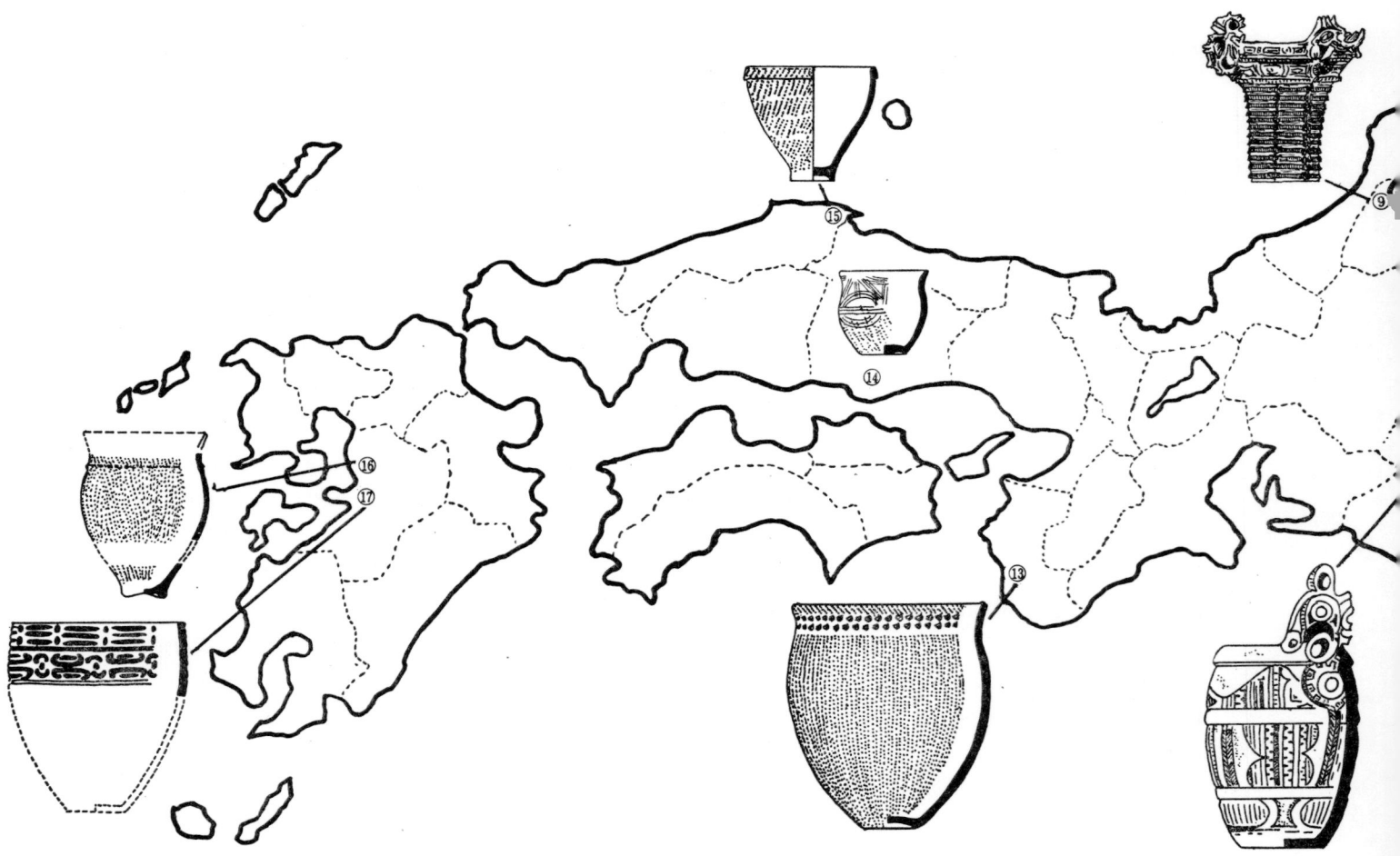

① ② ③ ④ ⑤ ⑥ ⑦ ⑧ ⑩ ⑪ ⑫

93

invariably alive with line and plastic form. In most cases (the barrel-shaped vessels are an obvious exception) they are heavily encrusted with decoration, often in a "horror vacui" manner. Needless to say, there is little room left for cord-marking, even if cord-marking had been desired. Where the Katsusaka types moved into the Kantō Plain, however, they absorbed the traditional practices, and proportionally more cord-marking was used. Exotic rim decorations, whose more dramatic forms characterize the west coast pots, become one of the type's most prominent features. In the mountains and to the east a single, strikingly asymmetrical projection, perhaps looped like a handle, was often preferred. Many Katsusaka motifs are rather suggestive and are worked into the decoration just frequently enough to imply that they probably had some simple symbolic value. Realistically modeled snakes appear first in the Tōnai type and represent the *mamushi*, a pit viper, Japan's only poisonous snake. The snake patterns become increasingly more conventionalized in later types and disappear as recognizable snakes by the latter half of Middle Jōmon.

Pl. 189

Pls. 135, 136

Pls. 128, 129, IV

The presence of snakes on pots is used as evidence to support theories on plant cultivation,[9] and the additional phenomenon of animal-like or subhuman heads set into the decoration of rims of large vessels must have been in some way related. Suggestions have been made that these rim heads are totemistic.[10] They are rarely realistic enough to be indentified by species, and any possible development into full totemistic practices would have been cut short—as most other aspects of this culture were—by the eventual evacuation of the region by most of its inhabitants.

Pls. 138, III

These rim heads are usually limited to one to a vessel and normally face inward. The back of the head merges with the normal rim decoration of such vessels. Rarely more than one of these will be found in a site.

The pottery stands that were mentioned in the Introduction and the barrel-shaped vessels are also extremely few in number. It is not uncommon to find only one to a site. The impression one gets of these "barrels" is of a shape quite foreign to Jōmon pottery. By and large they are made of finer clay, and may bear red paint that had been applied before the pots were fired. The rim carries a series of perforations, either in pairs or equally spaced, directly above an encircling ridge.

Pls. 147–154

The small number of these vessels, especially in a given site, is reason in itself for regarding them as of special significance, but it has even been suggested that they may be in some way directly related to the cradle of the subculture.[11] They have been explained in several ways, notably as drums, the stretched skin perhaps fastened in place by little wooden pegs in the holes;[12] or as jars for fermenting grape wine (which seems rather unlikely);[13] or perhaps as cooking pots—the one from Morioka City is believed to have been suspended over a fire by its holes, since the lower part is badly weakened by heat.[14] If this last is true, the ridge would furnish good protection for the suspension cords against the heat of a fire.

Pl. 154

The Morioka pot is entirely devoid of decoration, but the painted vessels could hardly have been intended to serve in such an ordinary way. The distribution of these vessels is heavily weighted to the west, especially in Toyama Prefecture. From Nagano—where the type most likely had its beginnings—the distribution follows the same trend out of the mountains into western Tokyo, and is carried across into Chiba Prefecture by the end of the Middle Jōmon period. There must be many other sites where the shape goes unnoticed, since its recognition often requires the discovery of just the right rim sherd to be identified.

The single figure, arms and legs akimbo, and the pre-firing painting—almost unique

Pls. 148–151

to Jōmon pottery—remind one of the rare painted skeletonized figures on prehistoric Chinese pottery of the Yang-shao stage. The connections may be tenuous at best, but one can point to the round pit-dwelling of Middle Jōmon (which the Chinese also had), and to these people's knowledge of plant manipulation and the sophisticated ritual practices as impressive changes from the relatively impoverished stage of Early Jōmon. Internal developments would seem to be inadequate to explain these advances. Outside stimuli may have contributed in some way. The Yang-shao-Katsusaka time periods may correspond favorably, and Chinese Painted Pottery is now known to have reached the coast of China. Any conversion of painted motifs to this kind of non-painted pottery style would take the form of sculpturally modeled figures. Oddly enough, the barrel-shape is the only Katsusaka form that has large, undecorated surfaces. They were probably supposed to have been painted in the earliest examples.

Equally interesting are the so-called "incense burners." These are now claimed to be lamps.[15] They are bowl-shaped, with plain walls, and high-arched, bridge-like handles. Such loops must have been intended to aid in suspension of the vessels. Later ones may have erect, tower-like handles. The most unusual carry little frogs or slug-like creatures on the handles, and one from Enzan City in Yamanashi Prefecture has three snub-nosed animals that must be wild boar. The "three-fingered hand" appears on these, as it does in so many other characteristic examples bearing typical Katsusaka decoration.

Pls. 164–171

Pls. 168, 169, VII

The imagination of the Middle Jōmon potter at times seems boundless. On one hand the pottery represents an obvious effort to reproduce certain fairly set motifs, yet on the other hand originality and surprise are fundamental aesthetic principles. The uninhibited, artistic and what might be called non-functional approach was contagious. It was as though potters in a village were intent on outshining their neighbors. In the process they produced a highly personalized style.

Most of the technical factors of Katsusaka pottery are highly variable. It is relatively low fired, often reddish orange to brown, rather strongly grit-tempered, and thick. The clays tend to crumble rather than break after long exposure to heat. Ambitious in size, the pots are often awkward to handle. Whether the potters recognized their unresolved technical problems but were willing to sacrifice practicality for artistic effects, or whether they perhaps unconsciously tended to cover up their technical problems by drawing attention elsewhere, is difficult to say. In any event, they were often driven to produce well beyond the limits of practicability. In any broad perspective of Japanese ceramics, the Middle Jōmon period stands out in remarkable contrast to the prehistoric and historic traditions of simple, functional appearance, with modest decoration subordinated to shape.

A unique relationship appears in the cultural zones occupied by Katsusaka and its contemporary type, Atamadai (Otamadai). The latter is essentially an east coast type; its distribution extends across the country almost directly north of the Katsusaka zone. The center of the Atamadai type may have been in the Kasumigaura lake region, and sites occur in the Tone basin in Ibaragi Prefecture and throughout Chiba Prefecture. From this area it was diffused along the Tone River, through Gumma Prefecture and into the east side of Nagano Prefecture (Kitasaku County) and the eastern edge of Niigata Prefecture. The geographical overlap is most often seen in western Tokyo; it occurs with progressively less frequency westwards. Very little Katsusaka pottery has been found in the most eastern Atamadai sites, for instance, in the Atamadai shell-mounds along the eastern bay district of Tokyo.

The relationship between these zones takes on a resemblance to tribal territorial

MIDDLE JŌMON MAP II

	TYPE	SITE
1.	Tokoro 6	Tokoro shell-mound, Asahi, Tokoro-chō, Tokoro County, Hokkaido
2.	Miharashichō	Miharashichō, Hakodate City, Hokkaido
3.	Daigi 8b	Tsunagi, Shizukuishi-chō, Iwate County, Iwate Pref.
4.	Daigi 8b	Tashirojima, Onagawa-chō, Ojika County, Miyagi Pref.
5.	Daigi 8b	Michiya, Taishin village, Nishishirakawa County, Fukushima Pref.
6.	Tōgasaki	Umataka, Sekihara-chō, Nagaoka City, Niigata Pref.
7.	Kasori E	Yosukeone, Chino City, Nagano Pref.
8.	Kasori E	Kasori shell-mound, Chiba City, Chiba Pref.
9.	Kasori E	Minamizawa, Kurume-chō, Kitatama County, Tokyo
10.	Sori	Sori, Fujimi-chō, Suwa County, Nagano Pref.
11.	Shinzaki	Asahichō, Kanazawa City, Ishikawa Pref.
12.	Kasori E	Nakatsugawa City, Gifu Pref.
13.	Sakihata	Sakihata shell-mound, Minamichita-chō, Chita County, Aichi Pref.
14.	Tenric	Kitashirakawa, Ogura-chō, Kyoto
15.	Hashi	Onsen-chūgaku, Kisuki-chō, Ōhara County, Shimane Pref.
16.	Shidehara	Shidehara, Kubokawa-chō, Takaoka County, Kōchi Pref.
17.	Type uncertain	Harizuri, Chikushino-chō, Chikushi County, Fukuoka Pref.
18.	Iwasaki Lower	Iwasaki, Makurazaki City, Kagoshima Pref.

NOTE: *Height of No. 5, 38.7 cm.; others to scale, except sherds.*

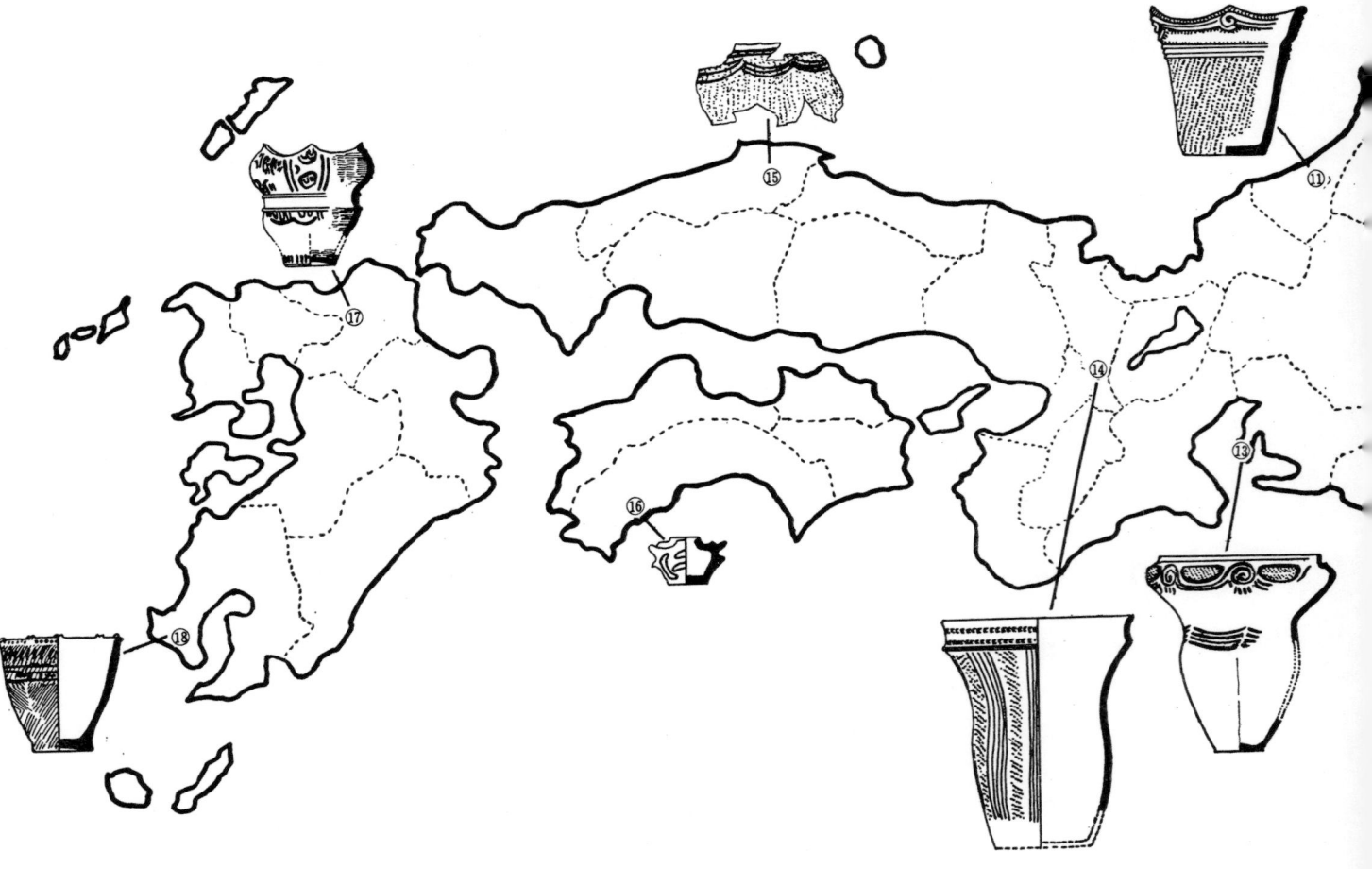

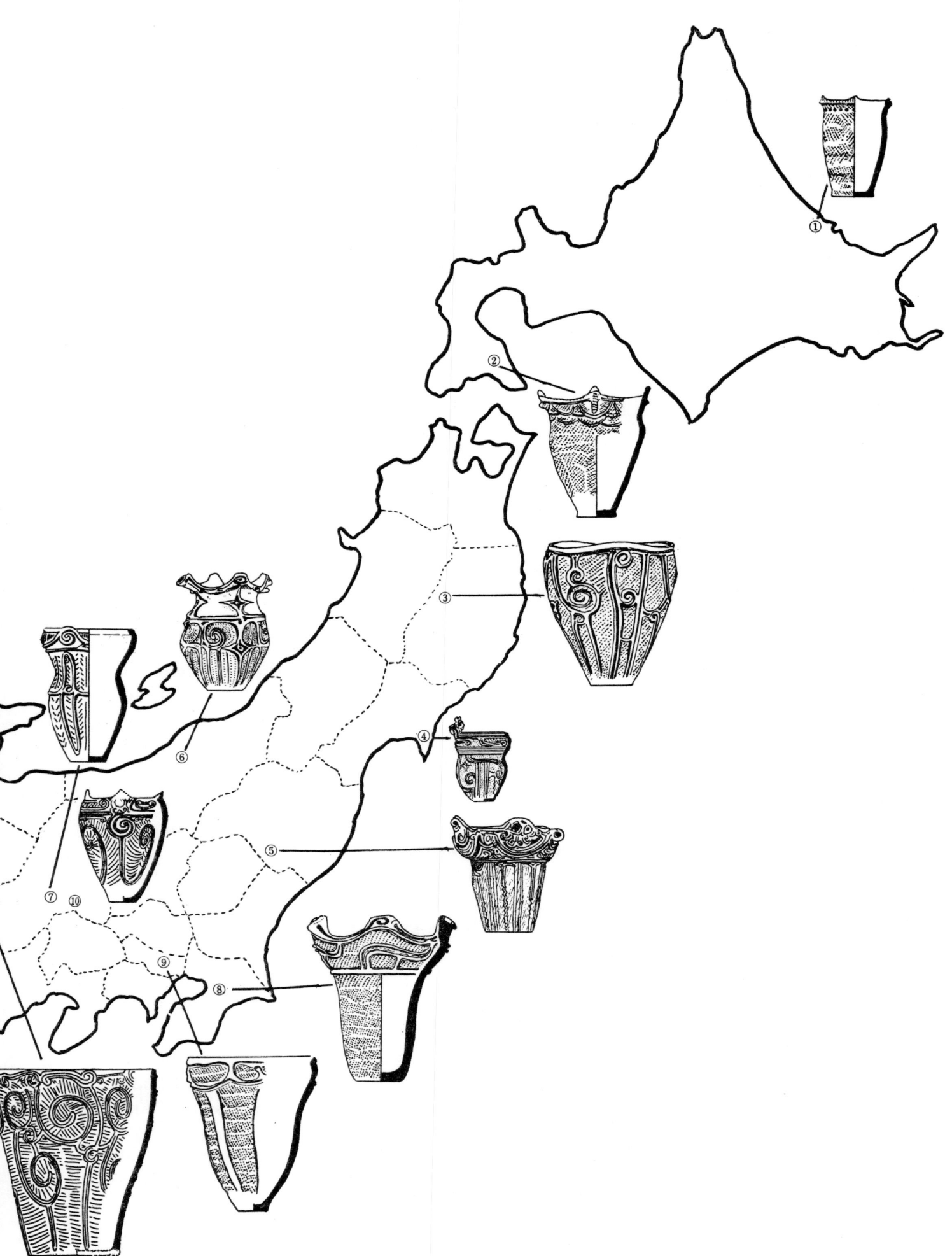

claims: the traits of the two types differ strikingly, yet they draw mutually on each other. Atamadai potters almost always sought out clays with a strong mica content or sandy beds containing mica for material to temper the clay. The pottery surfaces are liberally flecked with mica. Superficially speaking, this is Atamadai's most distinctive trait, but in construction the two types are clearly distinguishable. Atamadai clays are laminated; the layers often pull apart, or sherds show a layered effect. It is probable that the combination of mica-tempered clay and a purer clay lacked a common shrinkage coefficient, resulting in layers separating with the passage of time. Finger-pressing forced the layers together, producing a shingle-like overlap of bands of clay with thumb-size depressions. This overlap and series of depressions is the only form of decoration on some sherds.

Pls. 106–110   Although somewhat more modest in surface working, Atamadai decoration as a whole bears considerable similarity to Katsusaka. Mutual borrowing must have taken place, but Atamadai ridges are pinched up from the surface, have a triangular cross-section, and are set off by stick-made punctates. The Katsusaka ridges are applied and rather squarish. Vessels are sometimes furnished with wide rims that support fantastic, towering castellations, which may outdo the most elaborate Katsusaka examples.

Cases can be cited of an Atamadai pot occurring in a house pit of a Katsusaka community.[16] In rare instances this may happen unexpectedly far outside the normal contact zone of the types. From all appearances, the people of these two subcultural zones maintained tolerable relations with each other, probably through trade. Atamadai bowls
Pl. 109   find their way into Katsusaka pit-dwellings, and it may have been trade in bowls that initiated closer connections. While Atamadai vessels are almost exclusively pots and bowls, the Katsusaka people only eventually made their own bowls—but never used as many—following the Atamadai models fairly closely.

The chief contrasting feature between Katsusaka and Atamadai is the absence of all the rich Katsusaka paraphernalia in Atamadai sites. There are virtually no pits of houses, practically no ceremonial equipment, including figurines, few unusual pottery shapes, and nothing unusual in stone tools. It was doubtless a more traditional cultural area, not involved in incipient agriculture and needing none of the accoutrements that went with it. A personal comment here is that perhaps the "foreignness" of the Katsusaka subculture tended to keep the peoples apart. In any event, no similar situation appears to have existed at any other time during the Jōmon period.

Pottery of Middle Jōmon in the southern Tōkai region and the Kinki district, often
Pl. 227   called the Kitayashiki type, is especially noted for its unusually thin walls. The Daigo type in Shiga Prefecture would represent this. The best known types of the Inland Sea
Pls. 224–226   are Funamoto and Satogi, but discoveries in recent years have enlarged their zones of distribution to include the Kinki. The sites yielding these types seem to be coastal;
Pls. 224, 225   they moved around the Kii Peninsula and into eastern Mie Prefecture. Funamoto is cord-marked, often with ridges carrying angular indentations, and stick- and shell-marked. The face of a small shell was sometimes used to produce a series of imprints immediately below the rim. Connections with Moroiso b are visible, although Funa-
Pl. 226   moto may be later in time. Satogi vessels have slightly more swelling bodies. Fine punctates accompany cord-marking, and the rim may be thickened into a kind of collar. The Early Jōmon ancestry of these types is relatively clear; they could follow only slightly in time, but there is a tendency now to designate them as later, perhaps in order to span the Middle Jōmon time period, which would otherwise look bare indeed.
Pl. 229   Ataka is western Kyushu's chief type. Often said to have been derived from the Sobata type through its grooved decoration, its similarity in distribution would seem to bear

this out. The Aya type in Miyazaki Prefecture is affiliated, but its traits are just different enough to allow the claim that the Ataka type—for which almost no complete pots are known—never crossed the mountains into east Kyushu.[17] Ataka is recognized by its boldly cut-out grooves on neck and upper body. In most classification schemes, eastern Kyushu is generally devoid of Middle Jōmon pottery.

The earlier half of Middle Jōmon in the upper Tōhoku region and Hokkaido represents a direct continuation from the Entō tradition of Early Jōmon. The Entō Upper vessels are larger in size—conforming to the normal Middle Jōmon trend—and are best known for their flared rims and four striking castellations. The decoration is concentrated near the rim and consists of square-sectioned ridges of clay in a variety of patterns, supplemented with string-impressing. Entō Upper was caught up in the current of higher relief decoration, with more of it moving down to the body. Clay colors are dark browns usually; all traces of fiber-tempering have disappeared.

Pls. 98–103

Returning to central Honshu again to pick up at the end of the Katsusaka stage, changing climate such as might have caused the springs to dry up temporarily or, less likely, calamitous disease drained the vigor from the inhabitants. They died or left, and only small pockets of people remained until the Late Jōmon period. By the latter half of Middle Jōmon the last of the Katsusaka types had fused with the older east coast types to form the Kasori E (or Ubayama in most English books) family type. The chief difference is a modification in the applied ridges and a return to grooving and lower relief. Decoration is carefully correlated with the shape in curvilinear, raised lines and sweeping spirals usually located near the rim. Oblique cord-marking is ubiquitous and frequently occurs to the exclusion of all other decoration on the body. Walls may also bear perpendicular grooves or serpentine vertical lines. The clay is rather coarse; the inner surfaces may be rather well smoothed toward the end of the period. The color varies between a light brown and a salmon-colored orange-brown.

Named after the E "spot" dug in the Kasori shell-mound in Chiba City, or the Ubayama shell-mound in Ichikawa City, the types can be said to begin with the "cake decoration" style (Kasori E 1), which filters out of the mountains into the western Tokyo area. They continue with ridges produced through excising. The ridges take the shape of large spirals and curved, outlined panels, which flow easily around the surface; open spaces are usually cord-marked (Kasori E 2). They conclude with modestly decorated patterns, ordinarily flush with the surface, characterized by obliquely cord-marked areas outlined by broad grooves (Kasori E 3). Later Ubayama work is stylish and dignified. The decoration is itself scaled to the fairly large size of the vessels.

Pl. 175

Pls. 177, 178

In the northern Kantō and southern Tōhoku regions and stretching across the island to Niigata, the Daigi types correspond precisely with the Ubayama of southern Kantō. They often bear patterns that resemble birds' heads with curved beaks. These are probably the ultimate stylization of the Katsusaka snake motif. Daigi 8 potters were especially adept at gouging and smoothing surfaces in the process of producing graceful raised curves and spirals set off by area-filling cord-marking.

Pls. 205, 207, 208

The large size of vessels in later Middle Jōmon made it easy to convert some into burial jars. A small number of such burials are known from Early Jōmon, but the practice was rather widely adopted during Middle Jōmon and occasionally employed later. Most jar-burials have been discovered in open sites, in which no skeletons would be preserved. The pots are customarily of substantial proportions (ranging up to about sixty centimeters), found upside down, and either have no base or a small hole bored throught the bottom. Several good examples are illustrated. They come from Nakasugao,

Pl. 175

Pls. 140–141,
179, 205–206
Tokyo; Tōnai, Nagano; Samukaze shell-mound, Chiba; and Tsunagi, Iwate. The typological evolution shows that the practice started as the central Honshu subculture was phasing out, and moved along the diffusion lines both east and north.

At Tsunagi and Kakinokidaira (Morioka City) in Iwate Prefecture, seven and five burial pots respectively were unearthed.[18] At I.C.U., Tokyo, Loc. 27 A, in a rather isolated spot behind the normal Middle Jōmon residential area along a bluff, two inverted pots and a pair of large rims inside each other were found when groundwork was done for the construction of a house. All of these lay within a space measuring about two by one and one-half meters. Elsewhere at I.C.U.—Loc. 21—a large pot was discovered by itself, upside down.

The condition of such burial pots indicates that they all were put to some prior use before serving as bone containers. In fact, it seems clear that no pots were made solely for this purpose, and probably whole vessels were believed to be unsatisfactory. The perforations could not have been water drains—the pots were inverted. Perhaps termination of a pot's use had to be signified; or, more hypothetically, the "spirit" had to be furnished with a means of escape.

98. Entō Upper b type. A pot of impressive proportions, the four large castellations are the hallmark of the Middle Jōmon cylindrical types of the upper Tōhoku region. Fiber-tempering had been dispensed with by this stage and replaced by gritty clay.
Ichiōji*, Aomori (18) • *height: 67.5 cm. (26.6 in.)*

101

99. Entō Upper b type. Applied clay strips are common on the shorter Entō vessels and often ornament the entire upper half. They overlap each other at the junctures and are customarily cord-marked or indented. Wider strips of clay heavily weight the rims of this type.
Ichiōji*, Aomori (18) • height: 22.5 cm. (8.9 in.)

100. Entō Upper c type. Bold castellations, thickened and emphasized by pairs of marshmallow-shaped bosses climax a vessel built up in a manner that emphasizes forceful surfaces over finesse of finish. Later Entō shapes are less cylindrical.
Nagane, Aomori (18) • height: 24.6 cm. (9.6 in.)

102

101. Entō Upper b type. The people who made the early
Entō types quite probably felt that they had arrived at an
all-purpose shape. It changes little for centuries. Applied
strips give a strong two-layer effect to the decoration.
Ichiōji*, Aomori (18) • height: 18.0 cm. (7.1 in.)

102. Entō Upper b type. This is a very remarkable pot of Entō
Upper b type. Its most striking feature is the open, vertical, zigzag
arrangement of clay strips resembling an oyster shell on the heavy
rim collar. String-impressing can be seen in several places.
Sannai, Aomori (14) • height: 24.7 cm. (9.7 in.)

103. Entō Upper b type. With
somewhat less clearly defined
areas of decoration than customary in Entō types, this thick-
walled, brown vessel bears string-
impressing on the neck and rim,
and coarse, shallow cord-marking
on its lower half. The incurved
rim shape perhaps shows slight
influences from central Japan.
*Saibesawa, Hokkaido (9) • height:
12.5 cm. (4.9 in.)*

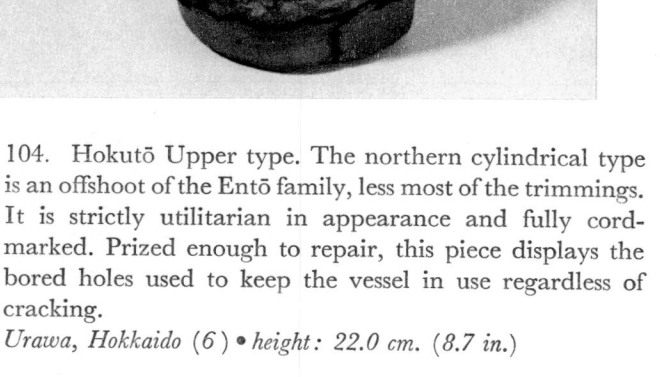

104. Hokutō Upper type. The northern cylindrical type
is an offshoot of the Entō family, less most of the trimmings.
It is strictly utilitarian in appearance and fully cord-
marked. Prized enough to repair, this piece displays the
bored holes used to keep the vessel in use regardless of
cracking.
Urawa, Hokkaido (6) • height: 22.0 cm. (8.7 in.)

103

105. Nashikubo type. Related to such types as Goryōgadai and corresponding in time, the vessel is claimed by Eiichi Miyasaka, the excavator of Togariishi, to bear motifs of a snake and frog in the rim decoration. The concave outline is typically Middle Jōmon.
Nakahara, Nagano (108) • *height: 29.5 cm. (11.6 in.)*

108. Atamadai 3 type. Atamadai's castellated rims ▷ are Jōmon pottery's most extreme. They rise off a large, overhanging rim collar and are so ornate as to bring into question the essential usability of the vessel. The lower part received intense heat from a fireplace, beside which the pot was found.
Tsukayama, Tokyo (85) • *height: 52.0 cm. (20.5 in.)*

107. Atamadai 2 type. Plates 106–110 illustrate Atamadai vessels, but none is from the Kasumigaura district, the center of the Atamadai culture. Although the vessel was found in Nagano Prefecture, the mica-tempering, color and decorative details indicate it must have been carried up from the eastern Kantō area.
Nagamine, Nagano (108) • *height: 44.0 cm. (17.3 in.)*

106. Atamadai 1 type. Cultivation has seriously damaged the Narukamiyama shell-mound, but this vessel was found during a 1951 excavation in a shallow remnant of the shell stratum beside another Atamadai vessel about twice its height. Pinched ridges, laminated walls, and sharply-angled indentations are Atamadai traits.
Narukamiyama*, Chiba (80) • *height: 27.2 cm. (10.7 in.)*

109. Atamadai 3 type (*top*). This bowl was found with the pot of Plate 108 in a pit-dwelling along with other vessels, including some of the Katsusaka type. The Atamadai culture found particular use for large bowls, which are otherwise little known in Jōmon times.
Tsukayama, Tokyo (85) • height: 11.5 cm. (4.5 in.)

110. Atamadai 2 type. Typically Atamadai in laminated ridges, drag-and-jab decoration and clearly visible tempering, this bowl was recovered from a pit with a late Katsusaka type handled vessel, a deep Ubayama type pot, and a painted shallow vessel, probably Katsusaka in type.
Jakuzure, Tokyo (86) • height: 9.5 cm. (3.74 in.)

106

111. Aramichi type. This and two other vessels of this group from pit-dwelling 1 were almost entirely soot blackened from use in cooking. This one has a simple, functional quality, enhanced by relatively restrained decoration. *Aramichi, Nagano (109) • height: 18.7 cm. (7.4 in.)*

113. Shinzaki type. Coarse pottery of this sort, the surface pitted and the ponderous decoration concentrated around the neck, is found in Ishikawa and Toyama prefectures and is associated with early Middle Jōmon. *Asahichō, Ishikawa (121) • height: 16.0 cm. (6.3 in.)*

112. Aramichi type. The earliest products of the Katsusaka family in the region of Lake Suwa are examples of this type, bearing rows of nail-marking and other details surviving from Early Jōmon. This vessel was found in pit-dwelling 1, along with the pots of Plates 111, 119 and others not shown. *Aramichi, Nagano (109) • height: 15.0 cm. (5.9 in.)*

114. Kusudashin type. Some of the late Middle Jōmon pottery of the west coastal region of the southern Hokuriku district is shell-scraped, with punctates done in a drag-and-jab manner. The double band of punctates here passes under the shoulder handles like a trouser belt through its loops. *Kitazukamachi, Ishikawa (121) • height: 10.0 cm. (3.9 in.)*

107

115–116. Kamiyamada type. This surprising vessel has a figure clinging to one side—which one archaeologist has described as a bald-headed child—and decoration composed mainly of tightly spaced punctate work. A hole about one centimeter in diameter perforates the widened base.
Kamiyamada*, Ishikawa (123) • *height: 10.0 cm. (3.9 in.)*

117. Idojiri II type. This astonishing vessel—on which ridges of triangular section were incised obliquely, outlined, then the outlines punched to further emphasize the ridges—shows the Atamadai type's appearance of sewn leather, the ridges resembling loosely hanging ropes.
Tōnai, Nagano (109) • *height: 27.5 cm. (10.8 in.)*

118. Nashikubo type. Early Middle Jōmon frequently depends on extreme contrasts for dramatic effect, in this case a plain surface serves as background for finely stick-marked, rounded ridges, and there is an abnormal ratio of height to diameter. The lower part of the vessel was subjected to much heat.
Karasawa, Nagano (107) • *height: 30.0 cm. (11.8 in.)*

119. Aramichi type. The rare stemmed vessels of Middle Jōmon most likely fulfilled a special ritual function. Eiichi Fujimori believes that vessels of this period are functionally specialized and can be divided into cooking vessels and serving vessels, while the chalice shape may have been a cup for alcoholic beverages.
Aramichi, Nagano (109) • *height: 16.5 cm. (6.5 in.)*

120. Katsusaka 3 type. This hourglass shape, with its narrow base, strongly slanted rim and handle-peaks, is most likely an invention of the lower mountains, carried ultimately into the Kantō Plain. A closely related example comes from Koku-bunji (Pl. 121).

Tsutano, Yamanashi (118) • height: 45.5 cm. (17.9 in.)

121. Katsusaka 3 type. Vertical cord-marking covers the banded body, and four impressive peaks are looped and opened toward the interior of the vessel. Notched ridges, spirals and gashed lugs are exaggerated here in a way that magnifies the dramatic effect.

Takikubo, Tokyo (88) • height: 36.8 cm. (14.5 in.)

110

122. Tōnai type. Although looking much like a brother to the pot of the following plate, this vessel is much larger and hails from a different prefecture. The similarity occurs in other prefectures toward the east. This pot is one of eight found in pit-dwelling 1 at this site.
Iwakubo, Yamanashi (112) • *height: 64.5 cm. (25.4 in.)*

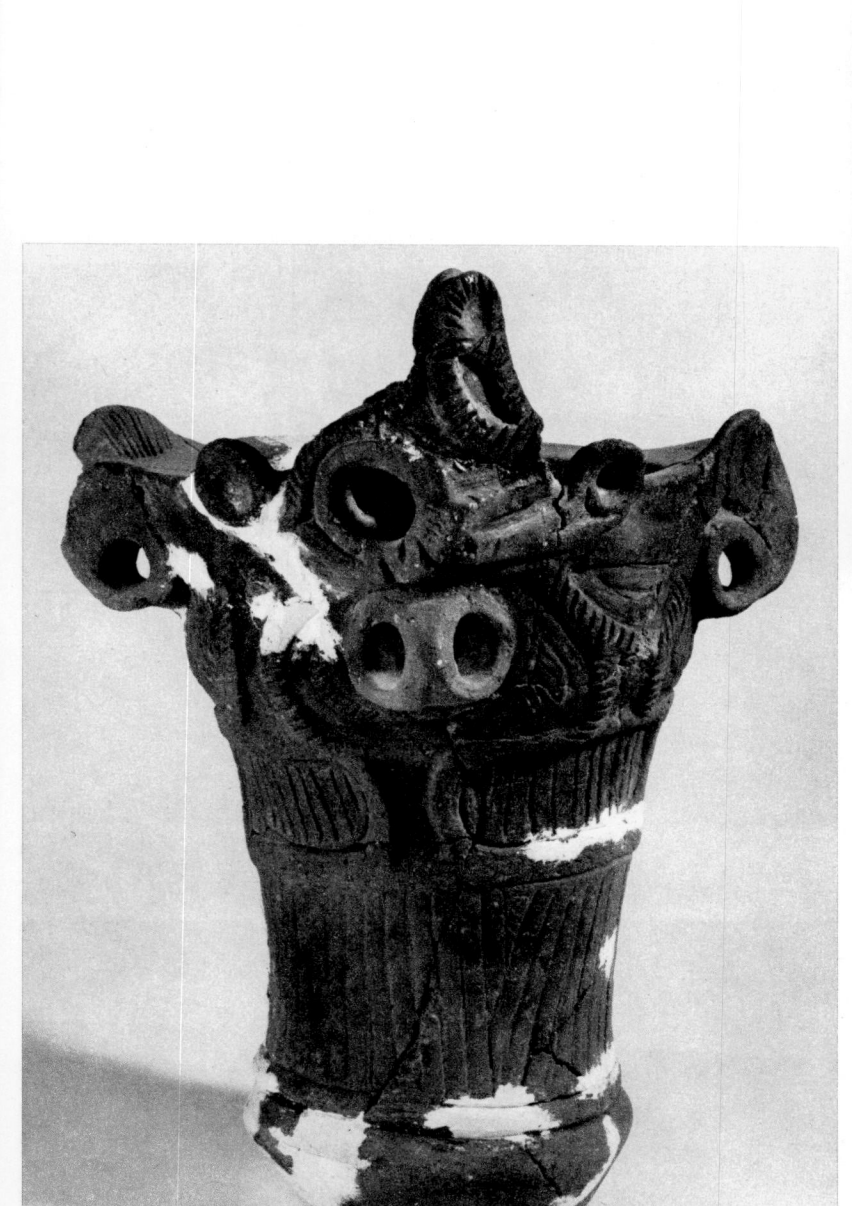

123. Tōnai type. This vessel admirably demonstrates the peculiarities of the Katsusaka style: indented ridges of squarish cross-section; alternately notched band; horizontal, oblong panels; asymmetrical rim projections; gritty clay; and reddish color from low firing.
Tōnai, Nagano (109) • *height: 37.0 cm. (14.6 in.)*

111

124–125. Tōnai type. The curved ridges on either side of the body have been called snakes by a number of archaeologists working with the Middle Jōmon stage. Teruya Esaka has written that it may not be too much to suggest that all Middle Jōmon decoration is snake derived.

Tōnai, Nagano (109) • *height: 37.0 cm. (14.6 in.)*

112

126. Katsusaka type. More cocklike than snakelike, the asymmetrical handle seems to have no other purpose than to give prominence to the motif—it is neither fish nor fowl, neither handle nor spout.
Togariishi, Nagano (108) • diameter: 17.0 cm. (6.7 in.)

127. Katsusaka type. The great Togariishi site has yielded more than the usual share of serpentine motifs—which ride the crests of the rims and handles. A common Katsusaka shape is the trumpet-flared body and widened base; decoration is carried to the top of the base.
Togariishi, Nagano (108) • height: 19.5 cm. (7.7 in.)

113

130. Katsusaka 2 type. Katsusaka vessels are of reddish ▷
clay; the clay often quite gritty, the walls thick. The cup rim
is somewhat obscured here by the steep peaks, two of which
resemble breaking waves. Panels outlined by notched ridges
are the Katsusaka trademark.
Nakahara, Tokyo (91) • *height: 37.2 cm. (14.7 in.)*

128. Katsusaka 1 type. Snake motifs can be found in inverse
proportion to the quantity of other decoration on a pot;
where the other decoration is minimal the snake stands out in
stark realism. They become increasingly realistic as the
Katsusaka types move down into Yamanashi Prefecture and
Tokyo from the mountains of Nagano Prefecture.
Miyanoshita, Tokyo (91) • *height: 39.0 cm. (15.3 in.)*

129. Katsusaka type. This amazing vessel was found with
several others in the 1967 excavation of the Yanagida site in
Enzan City. Somewhat roughly cord-marked, it was the only
vessel bearing a snake. The snake is joined to a widened rim,
then runs down the vessel curve as a flattened circle, its tail
turned up near the foot.
Yanagida, Yamanashi (114) • *height: 41.5 cm. (16.3 in.)*

114

132. Tōnai 2 type. Heavy, piled-up appliqué may be rather extreme, yet in some cases it must have seemed imperative to keep the rim uncluttered. Why this was done is uncertain, but perhaps there were instances of fitted lids. Handles here are eyelike; other examples resemble ears. The horizontal tiers of relief, so common to the Katsusaka family types, with irregular repetition of patterns, attract attention to the decoration but away from the vessel's shape. *Tokuri, Nagano (109) • height: 47.0 cm. (18.5 in.)*

131. Katsusaka 2 type. Sites in west Tokyo, especially between Mitaka and Hachiōji, have yielded magnificent Katsusaka vessels, many virtually indistinguishable from pottery of the central mountains. The heavy appliqué is Chūbu region derived; the cord-marking is more popular on vessels from the Kantō Plain. *Nakahara, Tokyo (91) • height: 35.5 cm. (14.0 in.)*

133. Katsusaka 2 type. Several Katsusaka type designs could pass for reproductive symbols, as might be expected in a culture that made and used the snake motif, female figurines and phallic stones. *Nakahara, Tokyo (91) • height: 27.0 cm. (10.6 in.)*

134. Katsusaka 2 type. One of the trimmer Katsusaka shapes, the silhouette completely unbroken, the wavy (alternately notched) ridges are especially stressed here, and the zones are filled with spirals and the corners by three-pointed stars. *Akitachō, Tokyo (92)* • *height: 25.5 cm. (10.0 in.)*

135. Katsusaka 2 type (*left*). Asymmetrical rim projections, collars of decorated horizontal panels, concave walls that reverse sharply at the foot to form a small base, are all diagnostic Katsusaka 2 traits. Kantō area Katsusaka uses some cord-marking on certain basic types. *Narahara, Tokyo (91)* • *height: 34.5 cm. (13.6 in.)*

136. Katsusaka type (*right*). Numerous pot handles found in large Middle Jōmon sites prove that breakage was commonplace, and the functional use of elaborate handle-like projections had a very short time span. Such functional parts lent themselves too readily to extensive embellishment. *Takikubo, Tokyo (88)* • *height: 37.4 cm. (14.8 in.)*

117

137. Katsusaka type. Katsusaka traits are here displayed at their finest: oval shaped panels within horizontal ridges, spirals, alternately notched ridges of medium to high relief, and a gritty clay that adds its own textural quality to the forcefulness of the decoration.
Takikubo, Tokyo (88)

138. Katsusaka 3 type. More like a human mask than the zoomorphic rim heads of the Chūbu region, this may be a local version produced from a misunderstanding of the prototype. Most rim heads face toward the interior of the pot and are more fully integrated with the decoration. Nine-tenths of the vessel is restored.
Nanyōji, Tokyo (89) • height: approx. 45.0 cm. (17.7 in.)

118

139. Katsusaka 1 type. The rodent-like head, with pointed nose, slanted eyes and slight harelip, is typical of rim heads, but a strange aberration is its presence here on a bowl—in itself an oddly rounded shape for Katsusaka—and on the wall rather than the rim. *Sori, Nagano (109)* • *height: 11.4 cm. (4.5 in.)*

140–141. Tōnai type. Vibrantly alive—evoking an aerial view of interlacing highways and plowed fields—the surface is a maze of half-relief ridges and incised panels masterfully done by an experienced hand. This well-conceived decoration conforms to the unexpectedly plain shape for this stage of Middle Jōmon.
Tōnai, Nagano (109) • *height: 47.6 cm. (18.7 in.)*

142–143. Katsusaka 3 type. Covered by strangely unaccented decoration for Middle Jōmon—perhaps once compensated for when the rim was intact—this elegant vessel was buried upside down and was excavated with the hourglass jar of Plate 120. A small hole in its base measures about 2.5 centimeters in diameter.
Tsutano, Yamanashi (118) • *height: 59.0 cm. (23.2 in.)*

146. Tōnai type. This is a pot of enormous ▷
capacity. The wavy rim is vertically ribbed over
nodes pushed out from the inside with a stone the
size of a tennis ball, displaying an unusual technique for Jōmon Japan. Undulating ridges, panels
and the three-pointed star are typical Katsusaka
features.
Tōnai, Nagano (109) • *height: 60.0 cm. (23.6 in.)*

144. Katsusaka type. This large pot, with restored base,
retains a remarkably unbroken flatness on the surface for this
type and time. Applied strips of clay on the body are bordered
by cut-out ridges; the panels are either crosshatched or marked
in a drag-and-jab manner. Parts of the rim are ruffled.
Narahara, Tokyo (91) • *height: 80.0 cm. (31.5 in.)*

145. Katsusaka 2 type. Extensive split-bamboo-stick-marking
appears with applied strips; the former might have inspired
the latter, or at least the chronological relationship suggests it.
The surface here is flat for this type, and all decoration points
to the fact that these potters concerned themselves chiefly with
plastic form and variety in effect.
Ushinuma, Tokyo (92) • *height: 59.0 cm. (23.2 in.)*

123

147. Idojiri type. The vessel forms of Plates 147–154—barrel shaped, jar shaped or segmented—are found in very small numbers in over forty sites. Arguments over their use revolve around the rim holes, neck ridge and large mouth that they all display.
Idojiri, Nagano (109) • height: 35.0 cm. (13.8 in.)

148. Tōnai type. Special attention was given to the preparation of the clay for these pots. The fine surfaces were apparently polished and painted before firing, a most unusual technique for Jōmon pottery. Red-painted, eyelike motifs on the shoulder bulges give the general appearance of a face.
Nagamine, Nagano (108) • height: 42.0 cm. (16.5 in.)

124

149–150. Tōnai type. Light brown in color, made of purer clay than pottery found with it, and once painted red, this pot is unique within this distinctive class. Interest is heightened by a figure on one side—called a human by Teruya Esaka and Eiichi Fujimori, and a frog by Namio Egami—and the disc on the opposing side, called more imaginatively a sun symbol by Fujimori.
Tōnai, Nagano (109) • height: 51.4 cm. (20.3 in.)

151. Tōnai type. The earliest examples of this type are shaped more like barrels, the later ones more like jars. This one falls between the extremes. The creature, now missing its head, has been termed a frog. If so, it is a greatly anthropomorphized amphibian.
Fudasawa, Nagano (109) • height: 35.2 cm. (13.9 in.)

152. Katsusaka type. This little pot of miniature size seems to be one of the barrel-shaped vessels. It bears four circular discs, two with subhuman faces and two with simple spirals. The clay is coarse, the color reddish with blackened areas. *Sakai, Yamanashi (113) • height: 8.0 cm. (3.15 in.)*

154. Daigi 7 type. The northernmost example of the barrel-shaped vessels with collar ridge and perforations, this one is of the usual large size, but is entirely plain. The excavators believed it was suspended over a fire; the lower part is in a heat-weakened condition. *Hataino, Iwate (32) • height: 43.0 cm. (16.9 in.)*

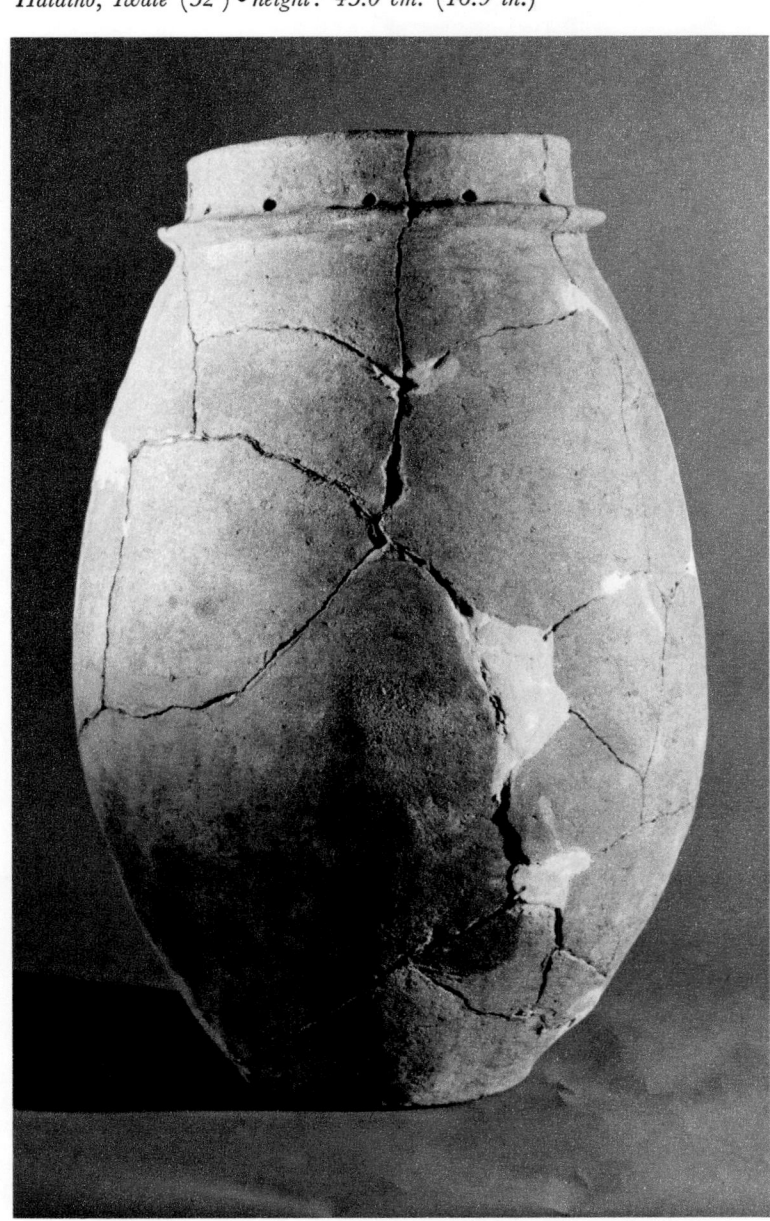

153. Katsusaka 1 type. This is one of the smallest examples of the barrel-shaped vessels. The decoration on the lobes becomes simpler in descending order. The rim is not thickened, but has a wide groove cut into the inner wall. *Nakahara, Tokyo (91) • height: 12.8 cm. (5.0 in.)*

126

155. Katsusaka (?) type. Oddly plain at a time when so much stress was placed on sculptural decoration, and symmetrical when asymmetry was a common aesthetic principle, this deep bowl illustrates the early Middle Jōmon preference for the unexpected and the unusual.
Tōnai, Nagano (109) • height: 8.5 cm. (3.35 in.)

156. Idojiri type. Simple pairs of symmetrical handles connecting the rim with the body were perhaps too ordinary for common Jōmon period use; they are quite rare. This vessel is gray in color and of relatively fine clay. One archaeologist claims the surface is crawling with snakes.
Idojiri, Nagano (109) • height: approx. 27.5 cm. (10.8 in.)

127

157. Katsusaka 1 type. This Siamese-twin vessel, dug up more than thirty years ago, is unfortunately missing its rims, leaving few clues as to how the superstructure looked. Double vases have always been accepted as a part of Late Jōmon's repertory, but Middle Jōmon's prior claim on the shape has gone unrecognized.

Minebata, Nagano (106) • *height: 21.6 cm. (8.5 in.)*

158. Sori type. This pot was recovered with its brother of Plate 160 in pit-dwelling 4 of the Sori site, along with five more reconstructable vessels, all of which resemble each other in color, tempering and nature of firing.

Sori, Nagano (109) • *height: approx. 37.0 cm. (14.6 in.)*

128

159. Katsusaka type. This type should be closely connected with the central mountains, but seems to have diffused into the Tokyo region through Yamanashi Prefecture. The decoration of the vessel here seems incoherent except as it gives ornamental effect to the handles and is used to avoid symmetry.
Nakahara, Tokyo (91) • *height: 36.6 cm. (14.4 in.)*

130

160–163. Sori type. Devoid of the smooth rim collar—and therefore the contrast seen in Plate 158—this reddish-brown vessel stood by the central fireplace; its lower third all but disintegrated in the heat. Grooves, loops, spirals, frets and the resulting effects of light and shade rank the maker as much a sculptor as a potter.

Sori, Nagano (109) • height: approx. 42.7 cm. (16.8 in.)

131

164. Katsusaka (?) type. The "incense burners" or lamps range from the most simple to the most elaborate. It is doubtful, however, that such differences represent a chronological or stylistic development. To some extent the potters were experimenting with both light-diffusing and suspension methods.

165. Katsusaka type. Yamanashi Prefecture's few "lamps" are of the Katsusaka type, like those of Nagano Prefecture, the cradle of this shape. These are flatter and more basket-like, and were apparently quite serviceable.

Kuwakubo, Yamanashi (117) • height: 19.4 cm. (7.7 in.)

166. Idojiri type. Claimed to revolutionize views on Jōmon "incense burners," this handled bowl was lying apart from several other vessels in a pit-dwelling. It has remains of a black wick near the juncture of handle and body and a soot-covered interior, implying that it served as a lamp.

Idojiri, Nagano (109) • height: 24.0 cm. (9.4 in.)

168–169. Tōnai type. Views of Color Plate VII.

167. Kasori E (Ubayama) type. The lamp type moved out of the central mountains and into the Kantō Plain by the latter half of Middle Jōmon, sometimes becoming ungainly and, with wider handles and smaller holes, less able to diffuse the light. *Mukōppara, Tokyo (91)* • *height: 23.0 cm. (9.1 in.)*

133

170. Katsusaka 3 type. This kind of vessel was designed to be suspended. The whole "incense burner" class has been a problem because such vessels have normally not been found with other pottery. One suggestion now is that this is due to the fact that as lamps they were hung on beams, later falling haphazardly. *Sakai, Yamanashi* (*113*) • *height: 21.0 cm.* (*8.3 in.*)

171. Kusudashin (?) type. The relatively simple globular shape of this lamp is entirely overshadowed by the finlike handles, whose shape and deep punctates give it a rugged masculinity. It must be quite late, and has been classified by some archaeologists as Late Jōmon. *Sofuku, Ishikawa* (*120*) • *height: 14.7 cm.* (*5.8 in.*)

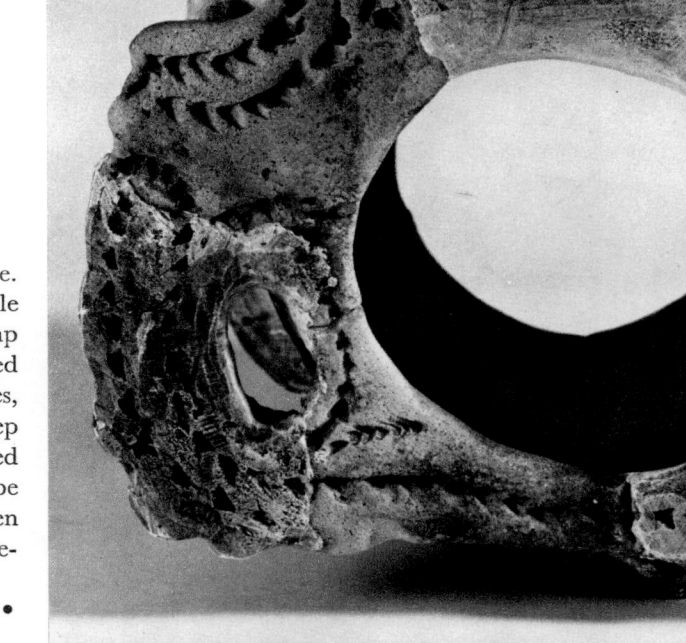

172. Sori type. Reddish brown and rather poorly fired, the vessel comes from pit-dwelling 5, and, according to the chief excavator of the Idojiri sites, the decoration quite likely shows a dragonfly in flight, a snake and other creatures.
Sori, Nagano (109) • height: 29.5 cm. (11.6 in.)

173. Kasori E 1 (Ubayama) type. The cake decoration is a trademark of the transitional type between Katsusaka and Ubayama; this is a crude and provincial version of it. The style probably moved out of the lower mountains and into the Kantō Plain, undergoing refinement in some cases, becoming cruder in others.
Koigakubo, Tokyo (88) • height: 22.3 cm. (8.8 in.)

135

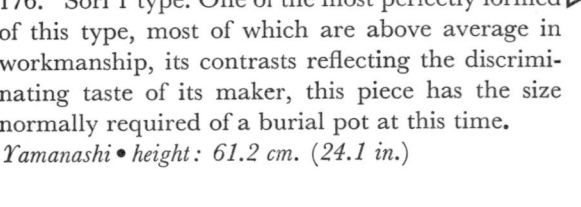

176. Sori 1 type. One of the most perfectly formed ▷
176. Sori 1 type. One of the most perfectly formed ▷ of this type, most of which are above average in workmanship, its contrasts reflecting the discriminating taste of its maker, this piece has the size normally required of a burial pot at this time.
Yamanashi • height: 61.2 cm. (24.1 in.)

174. Sori type. Recovered from the same pit as the pot of Plate 172, almost identical in size and most probably by the same potter, the vessel shows a personal style of real distinction. Five carbonized pieces of starch reported as bread were found alongside the fireplace in this house.
Sori, Nagano (109) • height: 29.0 cm. (11.4 in.)

175. Kasori E 1 (Ubayama) type. A fine example of the cake decoration type, with a plain Katsusaka cuprim, the vessel was located upside down in a small pit in the loam and was found during construction of a road. It must have been a burial jar. Similar pottery comes from the foot of Mt. Fuji and from the Izu Peninsula.
Nakasugao, Tokyo (92) • height: 65.5 cm. (25.8 in.)

136

137

180. Kasori E (Ubayama) type. Huge in capacity, ▷ displaying paired "fins" on the rim and one of the finest rope handles ever seen, this vessel in cake decoration style (rounded, applied strips) has a lively two-layer effect and controlled plastic surface. *Miyanomae, Nagano (110)* • *height: 59.5 cm. (23.4 in.)*

177. Kasori E 2 (Ubayama) type. Vessels of this cake decoration style have a standardized shape with strongly inturned, narrow rim, and bulbous body curving toward a small base. The body is combed, and the strips pressed on and crisscrossed around the rim. The clay is usually fine, the color a light brown. *Hanatoriyama, Yamanashi (115)* • *height: 22.4 cm. (8.9 in.)*

178. Kasori E 2 (Ubayama) type. These vessels, of light-brown, rather pure clay, came out of the mountains, spread through the Kōfu valley and into the Kantō Plain, evolving from relative crudeness to remarkable refinement. *I. C. U., Tokyo (87)* • *height: 25.4 cm. (10.0 in.)*

179. Kasori E (Ubayama) type. This pot with a base so narrow that it obviously restricts the vessel's use is one of the largest Jōmon pots ever found. It is thought to have served as a corpse or bone container. *Samukaze*, Chiba (78)* • *height: 61.5 cm. (24.2 in.)*

139

183. Umataka type. This tour de force of the ▷
Umataka type in its unrestrained intensity of
sculptural decoration represents a style so personalized and so powerful that one imagines a single
pacesetting potter winning the plaudits of the
community and inspiring other potters to greater
fantasies and extravagances.
Tokushōji, Niigata (101)

181. Umataka type. Rims in this type range from almost
flat through a row of sharp points to four large, sweeping peaks
sheered off at the top. The heavy, corduroy-like effect is common to all Umataka type vessels.
Tokushōji, Niigata (101) • height: 20.6 cm. (8.1 in.)

182. Umataka 1 type. The Umataka type seems to begin in a
fairly orderly way, perhaps basing its decoration on the
widespread Moroiso stick-marking style. The shape of both
body and rim are not yet obliterated; inner surfaces are clean
and smooth, yet the sculptural explosion is clearly imminent.
Umataka, Niigata (102) • height: 29.7 cm. (11.7 in.)

141

184. Umataka type. The rim lip and the clay shapes like *magatama* (curved beads) on the rim are variations of orifice decoration of this type. Most typical is the meticulously done ribbed surface and whirlpool configurations near the neck and flared mouth.
Umataka, Niigata (102) • *height: 25.0 cm. (9.8 in.)*

186. Umataka type. Many of these elaborate vessels come from a small number of sites, which were dug many years ago and inadequately published. The information on the field conditions is very sketchy. A number remain in the hands of private collectors.
Tokushōji, Niigata (101) • *height: 24.0 cm. (9.4 in)*

185. Umataka type. Questions arise as to the extent of usefulness of these vessels. It can be said that up to a point much ornamentation on Jōmon pottery enabled the user to get a better grip on the vessel, but beyond that the decoration becomes burdensome and too prone to break. This vessel would seem to represent the maximum extent to which decoration can be carried and not interfere with portability.
Okura, Niigata (97) • *height: 17.8 cm. (7.0 in.)*

142

189. Umataka type. Giving vent to all ▷ artistic impulses, using clay pictorially, the potter fashioned a rich array of handle and rim details, heightening the artistic impact through the intricate play of light and shade.
Tokushōji, Niigata (101) • height: 29.2 cm. (11.5 in.)

187. Umataka 1 type. Less precise and more ambitious than the pot of Plate 182, the typical inturned cup-rim is fully recognizable only when seen from above. It has acquired teeth along the upper edge as well as "breaking waves" leading toward the rim handles—not unlike parts of Niigata's rugged coastline.
Umataka, Niigata (102) • height: 37.5 cm. (14.8 in.)

188. Umataka 2 type. The geographic distribution of early Middle Jōmon, extending in a band across the center of Honshu, is represented at the westernmost end by extremes in elaborate embellishment, and at the easternmost end by surprising moderation. Here the handles and rims are like cocks' heads and combs, and the surface teems with bizarre shapes and forms.
Umataka, Niigata (102) • height: 30.0 cm. (11.8 in.)

190. Kamiyamada type. This peaked bowl represents the early forms of high ridging—found in sites near the west coast—done with a bamboo stick while the clay was relatively damp. Increased experience with this technique led to fantastic decoration as an end in itself before the Middle Jōmon was over.
Kubochō, Ishikawa (121) • height: 19.8 cm. (7.8 in.)

191. Kamiyamada type. Kamiyamada pottery is a west coast relative in the Katsusaka family, and sets the stage locally for the corduroy effect of the Umataka type vessels. Fine slashes on ridges accent the decoration at periodic intervals.
Kamiyamada*, Ishikawa (123) • height: 25.6 cm. (10.0 in.)

192. Umataka type. From the Umataka site, which is known for the products of competitive potters whose painstaking efforts were boundless, this late vessel has the sweeping, truncated peaks of the type, but the surface combing and indented ridges are traits associated with Horinouchi family pottery of Late Jōmon.
Umataka, Niigata (102) • height: 32.5 cm. (12.8 in.)

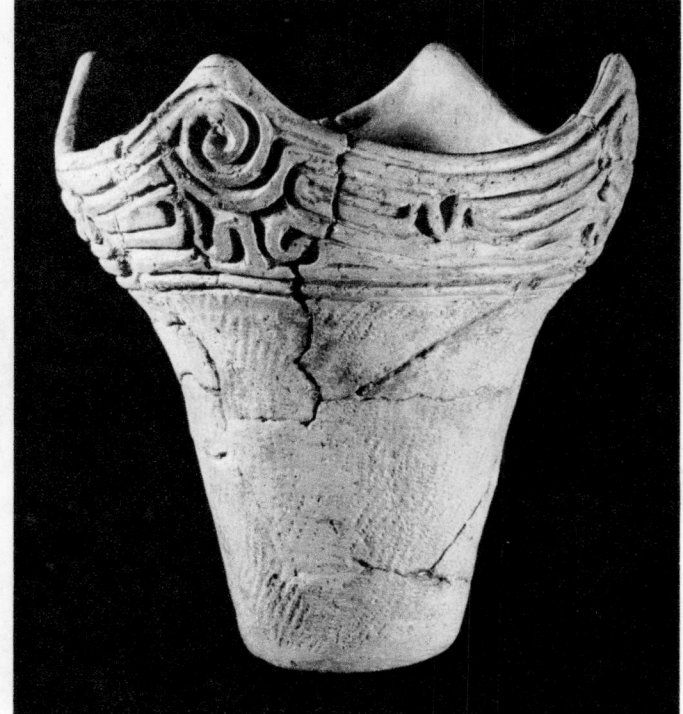

193. Tochikura 2 type. The Tochikura 2
type combines deep grooving for rim decoration and body cord-marking, showing
some return to a discriminating concentration of decoration and appreciation of
textural contrasts.
*Tokushōji, Niigata (101) • height: 23.3 cm.
(9.2 in.)*

194. Umataka 3 type. By the last of the Umataka pots the merger
is almost complete with the Ubayama family. The lower part of
this piece would pass as typical Ubayama in eastern Japan; the wild
and exuberant rim forms now incorporate more modest Ubayama
spirals.
Umataka, Niigata(102) • height: 34.0 cm. (13.4 in.)

147

195. Kamiyamada type. Kamiyamada pots are usually simple predecessors of the Umataka type. This large, wide-mouthed vessel is entirely cord-marked and must have been more useful domestically than the fancifully carved examples.
Kamiyamada*, Ishikawa (123) • height: 28.0 cm. (11.0 in.)

196. Umataka type. The Umataka pottery type shades off from earlier into later Middle Jōmon, an example of the latter being this fine, cord-marked bowl. Excision has produced accented decoration—less a characteristic of earlier examples—concentrated around rim peaks and on the exterior inturned curve of the body.
Umataka, Niigata (102) • height: 11.0 cm. (4.3 in.)

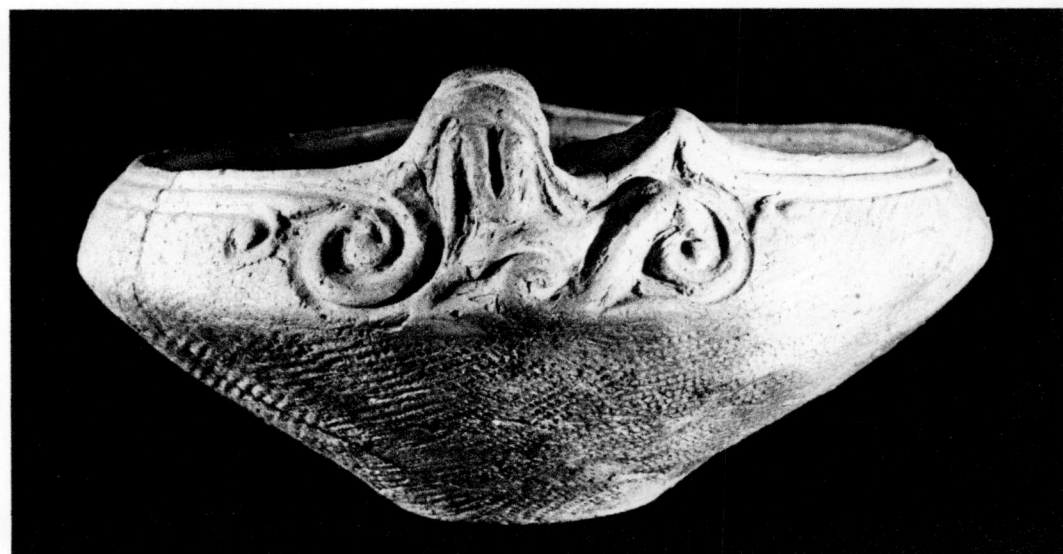

197–198. Daigi 7b type. Fine, rounded ridges are, in some regions, cord-marked along with the entire surface, in the usual oblique, now widely popular manner. Four terminal spots in the decoration and an equal number of intermediate spirals provide the rim with an octagonal shape.
Tochikura, Niigata (99) • height: 10.7 cm. (4.2 in.)

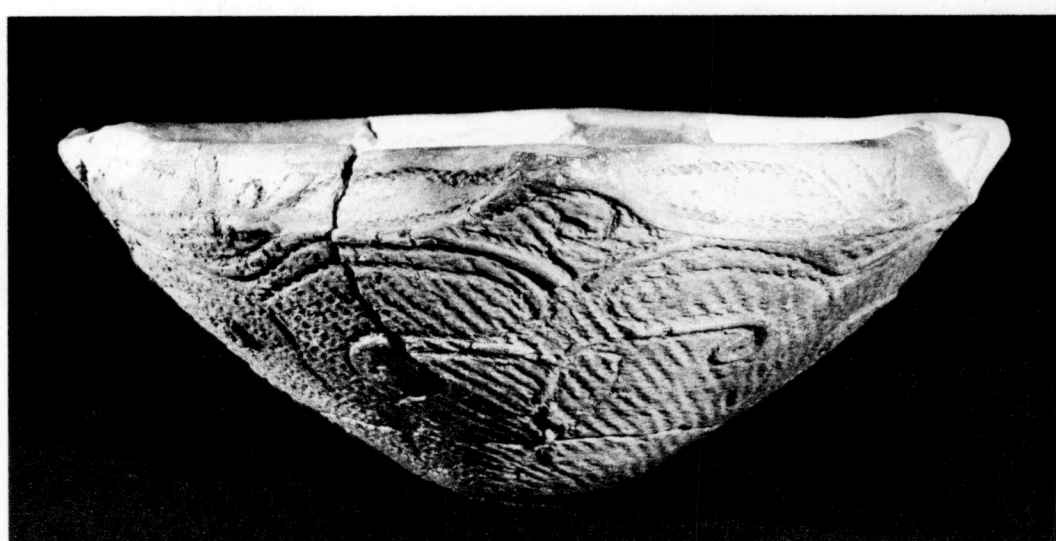

148

199. Umataka 3 type. The rise and fall of the Umataka type—involving finally a return to some semblance of practicality—is an interesting phenomenon, well documented here as a photographer's delight. The piece here displays cuneiform-like punctates and double ridges.
Umataka, Niigata (102) • *height: 32.0 cm. (12.6 in.)*

200. Tochikura 2 type. Middle Jōmon potters in Niigata Prefecture had a flair for the spectacular, while retaining a surprising consistency in vessel size in these types. The design repertory includes the rim lip, spirals uncurling into handles, and hatching in lieu of cord-marking.
Tokushōji, Niigata (101) • *height: 23.2 cm. (9.2 in.)*

149

201. Kasori E 1 type. Strips, added after cord-marking, are shaped into flowing birdlike patterns—presumably a corruption of the earlier snake motif—and are paired and terminated by spirals.
Sakai, Yamanashi (113) • height: 21.0 cm. (8.3 in.)

202. Daigi 9 type. Deep-set ovals filled with cord-marking have produced a kind of zoning across a highly sculptural surface. The coarse clay has resulted in a rough, worn surface. The little legs must have been intended to raise the vessel above a fire.
Shibahashi, Yamagata (55) • height: 14.8 cm. (5.8 in.)

203. Daigi 8b type. The older cup-shaped rim and bulbous pot has here received a massive spout, attached as though the maker was not too familiar with such devices. The handle-like spout makes an ordinary pot into a pitcher.
Shirasuka, Yamagata (53) • height: 14.0 (5.5 in.)

204. Monzen type. This was a cooking pot whose bottom was ruined after considerable use. This type seems to be analogous to Daigi 8b, but it has been connected with Late Jōmon through its gently waved peaks, early form of zoned cord-marking and vertical strips below the rim peaks.
Monzen*, Iwate (36) • height: 26.5 cm. (10.4 in.)

150

205–206. Daigi 8b type. This huge burial jar, found with several others, bears the sharply raised decoration of the Daigi 8b type and has a small, roundish hole in the base. This hole is seen in several examples of burial pots.

Tsunagi, Iwate (33) • height: 50.0 cm. (19.7 in.)

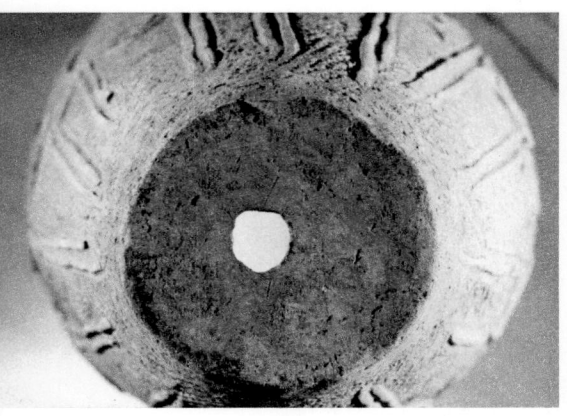

207. Daigi 8b type. Doughnut-shaped vessels were made either to rest horizontally or to stand vertically. This form has been found to allow a maximum retention of heat, perhaps the intention of the makers. There is a thick layer of charred material in the bottom of the vessel.

Oyama, Iwate (32) • height: 7.5 cm. (2.95 in.)

151

208. Daigi 8a type. Daigi 8a is the equivalent of the Ubayama type of the middle Tōhoku region, but with Entō features still visible around the rim. The attention to rim ornamentation is a natural corollary of Entō elements fusing with late Middle Jōmon decoration of the Kantō area.
Ochiai, Yamagata (54) • height: 75.0 cm. (29.5 in.)

209. Daigi 7b (?) type. In another cake decoration style, an interesting feature is the way the decoration is scaled down from very high and thick at the rim to thin and almost flush with the surface at the foot. Oblique cord-marking covered the surface before the clay strips were applied.
Ogonizawa, Yamagata (54) • height: 34.5 cm. (13.6 in.)

152

210. Daigi 8b type (*top left*). Consistent oblique cord-marking usually accompanies parallel incisions marking off the neck of a vessel. Periodic vertical lines are here broken by spurs, and broad, sweeping curves end in brief, tight spirals. The rim groove is continuous.
Daigi*, Miyagi (40) • height: 20.5 cm. (8.1 in.)

211. Daigi 8a type (*top right*). This vessel has an ideal size and a stable shape that would do yeoman service as a cooking pot. It is modestly decorated with an early form of zoned cord-marking and smoothed surfaces. Areas of the brown clay are smoke-blackened.
Daigi*, Miyagi (40) • height: 19.3 cm. (7.6 in.)

212. Kasori E 3 type. An immense vessel, perhaps for storage purposes, it bears the early form of zoned cord-marking, at this stage utilizing relief effects of Middle Jōmon to define the areas. In Late Jōmon the zones run horizontally and are outlined, the ridges no longer being needed for this purpose.
Ōne, Gumma (67) • height: 56.0 cm. (22.0 in.)

213. Daigi 8b type. Heavily finger-worked and sculptured, some of the grooves still preserve a chocolate-colored lacquer, suggesting that the entire surface may have once been covered in this way. Monochrome lacquer painting of the entire vessel is probably unique to Middle Jōmon, although lacquer had already been used by middle Early Jōmon.

Ichiōji*, *Aomori* (*18*) • *height: 21.0 cm. (8.3 in.)*

214. Kasori E 3 (Ubayama) type. In competition for the prize as the largest Jōmon vessel found to date, this one from the central mountains with a trim shape and handles neatly tied into the linear decoration has a kind of pseudo-cord-marking and reptile-like figures on the body.
Nakahara, Nagano (108) • height: 74.0 cm. (29.1 in.)

215. Kasori E 3 (Ubayama) type. Togariishi is the westernmost point from which these large pots are found; Yamanashi Prefecture is their distribution center. Magnificent, sweeping ornamental curves link the handles organically with the body decoration in an integration of functional parts with decoration known in few other types.
Yosukeone, Nagano (108) • height: 53.5 cm. (21.2 in.)

155

216. Kasori E 2 (Ubayama) type. With a smooth rim—particularly simple for Ubayama types—as though designed to hold a lid, and with the macaroni-style decoration unmistakably characteristic of Ubayama, this pot bears surface marking in the less frequently seen form of diagonal incisions. *Nagamine, Nagano (108) • height: 39.0 cm. (15.3 in.)*

217. Comparable to the Kasori E 2 (Ubayama) type. Six vessels were found in a semicircle during road construction. This and one other of the group are kept in the nearby Araki Shrine. The base seems to have been intentionally removed. The color is blackish brown and reddish in the lower part. *Miyaji, Gifu (124) • height: 48.0 cm. (18.9 in.)*

156

218. Kasori E (Ubayama) type. Pinpoint marks seem to serve in lieu of cord-marking on this two-handled vessel. The symmetry of the handles is part of a reaction that leads back toward balanced and modestly decorated pots in the latter half of Middle Jōmon. The continuous patterns seem to have been selected for their curvilinear interest rather than displaying the panel concept of the Katsusaka family pottery.
Togariishi, Nagano (108) • *height: 21.8 cm. (8.6 in.)*

219. Kasori E 3 (Ubayama) type. Postwar construction of a school building resulted in the discovery of this jar. Other material had been found at Ōtsuki City in 1928. The site's location on the Saruhashi lava stream relates to the question of Jōmon man's ability to live near active Mt. Fuji.
Tsuru High School, Yamanashi (116) • *height: 34.0 cm. (13.4 in.)*

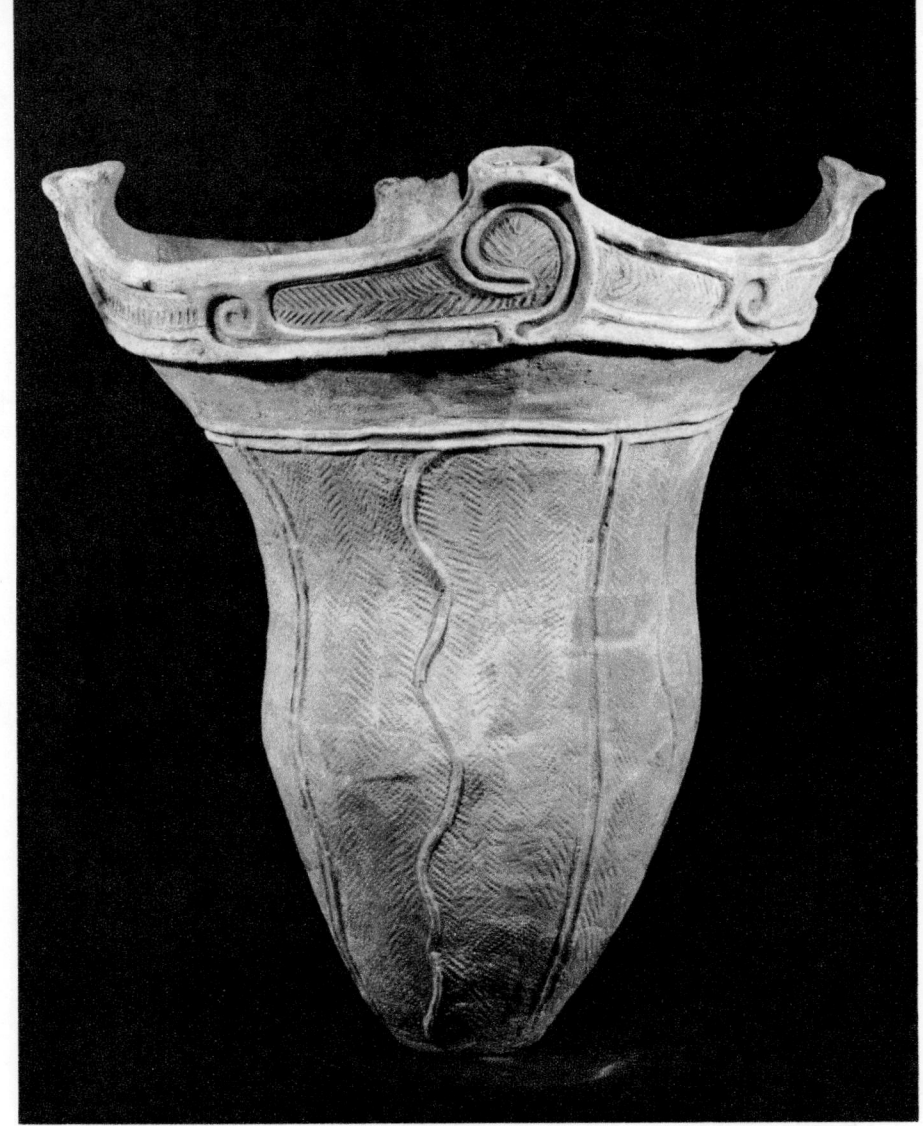

220. Kasori E 1 (Ubayama) type. This and the next vessel are believed to be from the same pit-dwelling, and a third vessel with fan-shaped castellations was unearthed with them. By the latter half of Middle Jōmon the lug-shaped rim projections are an obvious survival of the extravagant earlier Middle Jōmon rims. *Ōne, Gumma (67) • height: 78.0 cm. (30.7 in)*

221. Kasori E 1 (Ubayama) type. Spirals between grooved panels, macaroni-style ridges and smoothed-over tempering all lend a strong but dignified character to Ubayama type vessels, the result of a discriminating relationship between shape and decoration. *Ōne, Gumma (67) • height: 64.0 cm. (25.2 in.)*

222. Kasori E 2 (Ubayama) type. The squat proportions, undue emphasis on the rim, rather nondescript projection, and the handle of this vessel are not fully characteristic of Ubayama pottery and point to tenacious Katsusaka features. Ubayama pottery is normally a buff to salmon-orange color. *Renkōji, Tokyo (90) • height: 23.4 cm. (9.3 in.)*

223. Kasori E 2 (Ubayama) type. The Narahara site yielded great quantities of Katsusaka and Ubayama pottery in the 1930's. The vertical, wavy grooves are limited almost exclusively to the Ubayama type. Overhanging rims and rough surfaces were useful in lifting and carrying pots. *Narahara, Tokyo (91) • height: 25.7 cm. (10.1 in.)*

158

224. Funamoto type. A notched rim, the shell-imprinting popular in the Inland Sea, slashed ridges resembling the straw rope draped before Shintō shrines (*shimenawa*), the body marked by hard, fibrous cords, and double lines of punctates in large zigzags give the pot a rough elegance and a thoroughly grippable surface.
Sea-bottom site, Okayama (141) • height: 18.5 cm. (7.3 in.)

225. Funamoto type. The pot is reddish brown in color and has walls about one centimeter thick. It was fired at a relatively high temperature. Shell-imprinting sets off the rim, while slashed and cord-marked ridges form shapes of pendant triangles and skeleton-like anthropomorphs.
Ōmisaki, Wakayama (139) • height: 39.8 cm. (15.6 in.)

226. Satogi 2 type. The globular shape is characteristic of this region. It is here accompanied by a double-thickness rim with a pair of peaks, cord-marking varying between the vertical and an angle of seventy-five degrees, and simple shapes produced by a sharp punctation technique.
Kamanotaira, Mie (135) • height: 21.7 cm. (8.6 in.)

227. Daigo 2 type. The Daigo site seems to have absorbed ornamental features from both east and west Japan. The site yielded pottery of the Funamoto and Satogi types of the Inland Sea and the Kansai area. The decoration (a string-impressing) and shape of this pot show it to have connections with Ubayama of the Kantō area.
Daigo, Shiga (127) • height: 39.0 cm. (15.3 in.)

229. Ataka type. The Ataka type depends for its ornamental effects on incisions and grooves. This is a rare case of a low bowl with internal incisions and slight finger indentations along the rim.
Okinohara, Kumamoto (153) • height: 22.0 cm. (8.7 in.)

228. Unnamed type. Complete vessels ranging from the rouletted pots of Earliest Jōmon to Latest Jōmon types, excluding Early Jōmon, were found in this site on the bottom of Lake Biwa at a depth of about sixty meters. Blackish brown and with a thick wall, the pot's inner surface has iron encrustation, indicating that it must have been on the lake bottom for a long time.
Lake Biwa, Shiga (128) • height: 23.5 cm. (9.3 in.)

IX. Umataka 1 type. Ōkura is known as a stone circle site, and this kylix-shaped vessel found in the neighborhood of the circle presumably had some ritual use. In remarkable condition, the upper part is much smoke-blackened over the normal light-tan clay of the Umataka type.

Ōkura, Niigata (97) • height: 12.5 cm. (4.9 in.)

161

X. Kusudashin type. This very unusual—and presumably cere-monial—vessel was found alone, buried upright within a three-sided enclosure composed of river rocks each about forty centimeters in length, at a distance of 1.6 meters north of the fireplace of pit-dwelling 3 of this site.
Kitsunezuka, Ishikawa (122) • *height: 15.4 cm. (6.1 in.)*

XI. Kasori B 2 type. This much-restored vessel is shaped like a stemmed display platter, with four rim knobs and smaller intermediate projections. It bears red paint suggestive of broad designs, but the outlines they took, if any, are no longer recognizable. *Fukuda*, Ibaragi (59)* • *height: 11.9 cm. (4.7 in.)*

XII. Kamiyama type (t). Clay copies of natural shapes appear in several forms in Late Jōmon. Here is a simulated deep-sea conch shell known as *kabutobora*, found in the Pacific Ocean off central Honshu. The parallel ridges joined by small bosses were popular during the late stage of Late Jōmon.
Kamiyama, Niigata (96) • *length: 16.6 cm. (6.5 in.)*

XIII. Kasori B 2 type. This vessel of sandy clay, ▷ with thick walls, thickened rim forming six peaks, notched outer edge and shoulder ridge, exhibits an unusual degree of precision workmanship for this Kasori B type. The body was first cord-marked then freely incised.
Yoyama*, Chiba (69) • *height: 21.0 cm. (8.3 in.)*

164

XIV. Ōbora C 1 type. Red paint of iron oxide, lead or cinnabar as well as burnishing are not unusual for pottery of the Kamegaoka family in northern Honshu. This small vessel bears typical cord-marking and is a good example of painted Kamegaoka work. *Kamegaoka, Aomori (22) • height: 9.7 cm. (3.8 in.)*

XVI. Ōbora C 1 type. A red lacquer (iron-▷
oxide pigment) pattern painted on black lacquer
(faintly visible at the extreme left of the shoulder)
is a combination of materials seen only at the
Kamegaoka site; black and red lacquer were
used independently elsewhere.
Kamegaoka, Aomori (22)

XV. Nusamai type. Boat-shaped vessels are not uncommon in the
region of Kushiro in eastern Hokkaido. Elliptical in shape, built up
in two broad bands, with finely notched rim and decorated with
coarse to fine incisions, the vessel was apparently once entirely
covered with red paint.
Nusamai, Hokkaido (4) • *height: 17.1 cm. (6.7 in.)*

Late Jōmon

IT HAS already been suggested that the defining "culture" of the Middle Jōmon period was a regional phenomenon whose rapid rise and growth may have been due to the discovery by mountain inhabitants of efficient ways of managing their economy—namely, an incipient agriculture. The decline of this central Honshu culture coincides with the expansion on the east coast of the shell-mound population and the prosperity of the associated fishing economy. There must be a direct correlation between the two, yet there is also much to indicate that the coastal peoples at this point made new discoveries as to how the resources of the sea could best be tapped. Their application of new fishing techniques gave birth to the major Late Jōmon cultural developments. Their shell-mounds show well-selected locations near the ocean, a bay or along a river, and tools and fishing equipment vary in these sites according to the kind of seafoods most available locally.

The variety of fishing equipment and fish bones in shell-mounds is rather astonishing. The large quantity and increasing size of hooks and sinkers give evidence of how ambitious this activity had become. Canoes and rafts were used for deepsea fishing and coastal travel. The presence of globefish bones leads one to suppose that the people learned how to dispose of the poison and eat the meat. Especially fine needles were made from the tail spike of the stingray. Deer and wild boar bones attest to extensive hunting trips and considerable effort to supplement the seafood diet, and the chances are very good that garden plots were developed.

Marrow was extracted from animal bones and long bones of animals frequently show traces of working and use. These shell-mounds yield rather few stone tools. Some are close to the Middle Jōmon ax or adze, but proportionally more ground and polished or pecked, chisel-shaped stone axes occur than in Middle Jōmon sites, and the same may be said for stone sinkers or weights. The type of arrowhead most peculiar to Late Jōmon is tanged; it is not large, and is made of chert, obsidian and other stone. Arrowheads of bone and sharks' teeth are occasionally found. The laurel-leaf-shaped spearhead is smaller at this stage.

The few Late Jōmon pit-dwellings that have been excavated tend to be squarish or rectangular in shape. Central fireplaces were still used, and floors were often paved with stones. Much living must have taken place directly on the surface and not in pit-dwellings. The Late Jōmon people were certainly residing on a higher stratigraphic level than their Middle Jōmon predecessors, and, at least in the Kantō Plain, where the Middle Jōmon pits penetrate the reddish loam, the Late Jōmon pits are shallower in the ground, chiefly in the black humus layer and far more difficult for the archaeologist to find.

The increase in population is most strikingly seen in the large number of skeletons in shell-mounds, rising sharply toward the end of Latest Jōmon. For instance, the Yoshigo shell-mound in the Atsumi Peninsula of Aichi Prefecture, which was started by Late Jōmon people, was found to contain over 330 skeletons.[1] Shell-mound burial had reached its peak of popularity, and organized concentration of burials in the center of the shell-mound evidences the development of a cemetery concept.

The most interesting evidence provided by the human remains is in respect to ritual practices. The nature of the accoutrements found with skeletons seems to indicate the importance of the individual within the group. The presence of earrings is thought to be the mark of a shaman.[2] Shell-bracelets are more frequent, and may be talismans. Among about twenty human remains in the Late to Latest Jōmon shell-mound of Ikawazu, Aichi Prefecture, one skeleton was accompanied by earrings made of the bones of a monkey, a necklace of blue stones and anklets of the bones of a wild boar.[3]

Various forms of teeth mutilation were practiced, extraction, apparently, involving males a little more frequently than females. Dental mutilation is fairly common along the east coast and the Inland Sea, and never uniform in any one shell-mound. Since no examples of deformation of milk teeth have so far been found, it is assumed that the practice involved puberty rites. The shaman of the Ikawazu shell-mound had forked incisors, filed into a V-shape. The incidence of filing is about the same for males and females.

The significance ritual was assuming in community life is attested to in several other ways. The figurines were gradually humanized. Most come from the large shell-mounds in the east where very specific representations of human pregnancy replace the general obesity of the Middle Jōmon types. The faces are given a mask-like character as a result of the joined raised eyebrows and nose, and the ears are connected by a ridge outlining the face.

The most obvious examples of cooperative efforts and community ritual are the circular formations of stones in northern Japan. More than thirty of these have been found, the best known being the circles at Ōyu in northern Akita Prefecture.[4] These circles are arranged as a pair of concentric groupings of thousands of stones, the larger one measuring about forty-six meters in diameter, its inner circle about fourteen meters; the smaller measuring about forty-one meters, its inner circle about eleven meters. The two large rings lie about seventy-five meters apart. There is little chance that these were not large cemeteries, accommodating several hundred human remains, although no bones have been preserved. Nevertheless, it must be presumed that they served additionally as the scene for the fertility rites of the community. Each pair of concentric circles has a sundial-shaped arrangement of stones with a central menhir, in both cases located in the same relative position between the circles. While I am inclined to regard these as the chiefs' graves, their position must be significant. They would lend a calendrical usefulness to the entire group, which may then have been the stage for ceremonies associated with the cycles of nature.[5] At the least they could have acted as guides for the seasonal changes in food-acquiring habits.

The style and style constituents of Late Jōmon pottery are better understood against the background of the relative chronology now suggested by the C_{14} dates. My feeling is that the Late Jōmon period stems from two traditions: the older one of Early Jōmon along the east coast, and the newer one of Middle Jōmon in the central mountains. The usual manner of listing one type after another on a diagram will miss this fact and over-simplify the complexity of Late Jōmon. A plotted scheme of C_{14} dates, however, sheds more light on the actual cultural interrelationships.[6]

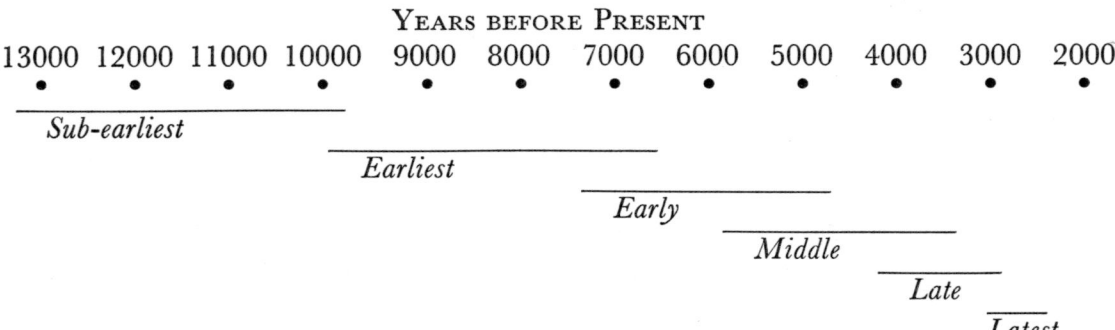

YEARS BEFORE PRESENT

Accelerating developments logically account for the shortening of succeeding periods. On the other hand, the time overlaps vary greatly. Recognition of these overlaps aids in understanding this view of the twin-faceted derivation of Late Jōmon.

Length of period		Time overlap	
Sub-earliest	3000 years	Sub-earliest to Earliest	85 years
Earliest	3240	Earliest to Early	380
Early	2930	Early to Middle	1100
Middle	2260	Middle to Late	710
Late	1280	Late to Latest	780
Latest	1220		

If one includes the extreme deviations of the youngest of the Early Jōmon dates and the oldest of the Late Jōmon dates, only 460 years appear to separate the two (Muko-yama, Ibaragi Pref., 4520±130; and Horinouchi, Chiba Pref., 3780±150). Culturally speaking, there is no need to argue Late Jōmon's debt to Middle Jōmon, but stylisti-cally—from the standpoint of pottery style as a reflection of basic attitudes toward the problems of shape and decoration—the Late Jōmon debt to Middle Jōmon is nominal at best. Fundamentally, on the east coast, shell-mound traditions were stronger; stimula-tion of these traditions by Middle Jōmon people moving into these and adjacent areas added new vigor and energy; the fishing economy was bolstered and the population expanded correspondingly. Hunting was always carried on, but where space and top-ography permitted, simple forms of agriculture were probably practiced.

Pottery production in the Late Jōmon period was facilitated through the standardiza-tion of certain shapes. This is especially true of the pot with slightly flared walls. By making thin walls, thus requiring a shorter firing period, and perhaps by firing in hollowed-out places on slight slopes, there must have been better heat control and more uniform baking of the clay. Early clays of the Late Jōmon period are a light brown. They become dark brown by the end of the period and are often meticulously smoothed and polished. The coarse textures of Middle Jōmon have disappeared.

This same systematization is even more apparent in the decoration. For the first—and only—time one form of decoration is to be seen in all parts of the country during this period: cord-marking within sharply outlined areas. These areas are usually fairly

LATE JŌMON MAP I

	TYPE	SITE
1.	Teine	Sunayama, Teine-chō, Sapporo City, Hokkaido
2.	Horinouchi	Ajigasawachō, Nishitsugaru County, Aomori Pref.
3.	Horinouchi	Kuraishi village, Sannohe County, Aomori Pref.
4.	Ōyu	Ōyu, Towada-chō, Kazuno County, Akita Pref.
5.	Shōmyōji	Minamisakai shell-mound, Inai-chō, Oshika County, Miyagi Pref.
6.	Kasori B	Batōchō, Nasu County, Tochigi Pref.
7.	Horinouchi 2	Horinouchi shell-mound, Ichikawa City, Chiba Pref.
8.	Shōmyōji	Shōmyōji shell-mound, Kanazawa Ward, Yokohama City, Kanagawa Pref.
9.	Shōmyōji	Daianji, Suwa City, Nagano Pref.
10.	Horinouchi	Sakami, Togi-chō, Hagui County, Ishikawa Pref.
11.	Kiya	Kiyatakahata, Unoke-chō, Kahoku County, Ishikawa Pref.
12.	Horinouchi	Hachiōji shell-mound, Nishio City, Aichi Pref.
13.	Hamazume K 2	Kitashirakawa, Ogura-chō, Kyoto
14.	Hamazume K 1	Hamazume, Amino-chō, Takeno County, Kyoto
15.	Nakatsu	Fukuda shell-mound, Kurashiki City, Okayama Pref.
16.	Sarugahana	Sarugahana, Mihonoseki-chō, Yatsuka County, Shimane Pref.
17.	Aya	Otate, Aya-chō, Higashimorogata County, Miyazaki Pref.
18.	Izumi	Kotsunagi, Minamata City, Kumamoto Pref.
19.	Ibusuki	Kasugachō, Kagoshima City, Kagoshima Pref.

NOTE: *Height of No. 8, 52 cm.; others to scale, except sherds.*

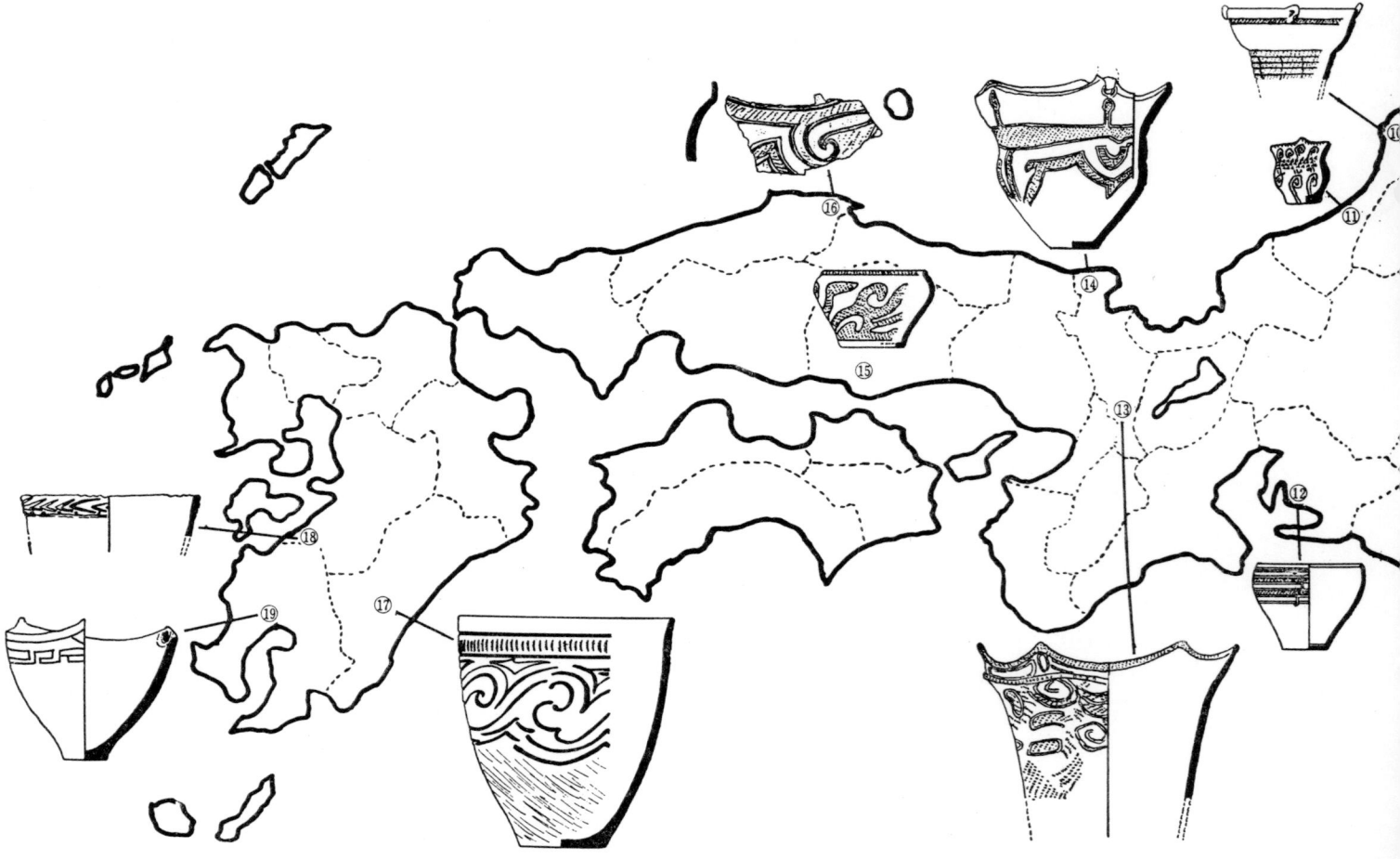

173

narrow bands that tend to move around a vessel toward the right. The technique was one of marking out the zones, applying the cord-marking, and finally smoothing down the surrounding areas; hence the term *surikeshi-jōmon*, "erased cord-marking." It occurs in every possible variation, but is known from Hokkaido to Kyushu before the period is over. Because of the fact that this decoration style permeates the entire country, its sheer quantity and apparent duration allow it to be regarded as the most typical feature among the many decorative traits of Jōmon pottery.

Various reasons may be offered for this phenomenon: enlarged communities that were more frequently in contact with each other; increased production of pottery and a resulting tendency for it to be more uniform; the production of pottery by fewer people within a community, or by a more specialized group that tended to produce for the community—presumably in exchange for equal services. If comparisons can be made with the Middle Jōmon period, the economic situation would lead one to say that more time was available for pottery making, but that the chances are very good that fewer people were actually instrumental in making it and that they were spending less time on each pot.

The impression given of the artistic aspect of this work is one of arrival at a form of decoration that was satisfactory aesthetically, applicable to all shapes regardless of variation, and that at no time interfered with the usefulness of a vessel. As a form of decoration it was used at the beginning of this period on the most traditional of all vessels— the cooking pot. In consequence, zoned cord-marking was probably diffused more rapidly than if it had been stigmatized by association with an esoteric shape that neighboring regions may have had little reason to adopt. It is hard to say whether its wide distribution is related to climatic conditions—favorable or unfavorable as the case may be—the former providing stability and therefore normal trade and peaceful relations, the latter causing instability and therefore wider sweeps and more distant expeditions for food. But if one may judge by the size and number of the shell-mounds on the northeast, north and northwest of Tokyo Bay, stability is the answer. It was a stability gained through accepting some of the practices of the Middle Jōmon people.

Pl. 264

The pottery type that is looked on as transitional between Middle and Late Jōmon is Shōmyōji, named after a shell-mound in Yokohama City. Shōmyōji sites are not large; they were occupied by small groups of people with an almost exclusively fishing economy.[7] Some pots bear high rim peaks that show the type has a clear connection with Middle Jōmon. In this type, however, these peaks form a squarish orifice and emphasize the corners. This squaring of the rim is not uncommon in Late Jōmon, and often appears later in plate-shaped vessels or bowls. The cord-marking is applied within wide zones of large spirals or curves that run more or less vertically, or in obliquely oriented panels. The connections with Middle Jōmon can be seen in the shape of the wide, flaring, peaked rim and narrowed neck.

Pls. 263, 265, 266, ff.

When Horinouchi type pottery dominated the eastern part of the Kantō Plain, the sites were large, especially in the area of Chiba City, and pottery was being made in considerable quantity. Horinouchi is the "classic" ware of Late Jōmon. It was probably getting underway while Shōmyōji was being produced on the southwestern side of Tokyo Bay. Horinouchi is a well-known shell-mound in the precincts of Ichikawa City that has yielded both Late and Latest Jōmon pottery. The kitchen-midden measures about two hundred meters in one direction and 110 in the other. It has been dug many times, and again in 1954 as a joint venture by several institutions to mark the seventieth anniversary of the founding of the Anthropological Society of Japan.[8] So-called Horinouchi 1 type came from lower shell layers in its northern part, where pit-dwellings were also found; scattered around the shell-mound were Kasori B and Angyō 3 pottery types.

Horinouchi 1 is best represented in the vase-like vessels. These tend to be incised only, in four large panels formed by thin ridges, which follow the line of the rim and run vertically to just below the midpoint of the vessel. The ridges are lightly grooved in an angular direction. Both Shōmyōji and Horinouchi, incidentally, owe the general vertical orientation of their designs to their Middle Jōmon connections. In Horinouchi the compositional system is based on the coordination of the rim projections with the body decoration, and systematic repetition. From an artistic viewpoint, it is the first consistent repetition of decorative patterns—in this case the scheme is simple because the symmetry of the castellations provides the guidelines—a symmetry that was a late Middle Jōmon legacy. The appearance of this aesthetic concept and an increasing uniformity in its application is a major characteristic of Late and particularly Latest Jōmon. In the case of the latter, far more complicated schemes were formulated in which individual motifs required detailed planning without any natural guidelines.

Pls. 263, 265, 266, 270, 276

If one were to put any stock in an old view that the Neolithic arts were responsive to the cyclical nature of life of the time, each year an exact repetition of the former in an interminable rhythm, and that repetition of patterns—normally geometric in Neolithic arts—reflect the routine of existence, then it might be said that this artistic device coincides with a settling down to a more restrained but steady development of community life, rich in early agricultural rituals, in contrast to the heady Middle Jōmon.

Once Horinouchi became well established, the morning-glory shapes inherited from Middle Jōmon became fewer and a variety of other shapes made themselves known. There are several kinds of jars, bowls, dishes, pouring vessels and even covers for vessels. The cover, however, is less a lid than a separate bowl in its own right. New and strange shapes increase in number with time in Late Jōmon, especially pedestaled vessels, containers with legs, incense burners, doughnut shapes, double vessels, copies of natural forms (gourds, shells, turtles, etc.), and a few others that defy description.

Pls. 214, 215, 220

Horinouchi 2 sees the change from vertically to horizontally arranged decoration, with magnified emphasis on the typical Late Jōmon linearity. It is not a stage of great refinement; sometimes the surface effects seem to be little more than incising over cord-marking, with little effort made to smooth around the carelessly made zones—if they were intended to be zones at all.

Pls. 268, 269, 278–288

It has been suggested that the spouted vessels may have had their prototype in the Daigi distribution zone of southern Tōhoku in the late Middle Jōmon period.[9] At any rate, in this stage they start off fairly modestly with a relatively short spout strengthened by an attachment to the rim. Later this spout is fully separated and often becomes long as the vessels take on more of the appearance of a modern teapot. The decoration on the pouring vessels in the Kasori B type is almost exclusively linear, restricted to narrow bands of cord-marking or parallel incisions of remarkable precision. Normally a pair of large loop handles aligned on an axis with the spout were designed as holders for a rope handle. Occasionally an ambitious potter actually made a complete handle of clay, but a guess is that no more than middling success with these discouraged further experiments. Some pouring vessels are fully globular; others have a low foot. Later examples tend to be angular in profile and rather squat, more comparable to the typical northern, low ewers. The spouts increase in length until the mid-stages of Late Jōmon and rise off the widest point of the body. Many are drastically shortened by the end of the period. Some are phallic, borrowing a common northern feature.

Pl. 203

Pls. 280, 282, 283, 285, 286

Pls. 280, 282

Pls. 249–251

LATE JŌMON MAP II

	TYPE	SITE
1.	Funadomari Upper	Funadomari, Rebun-chō, Rebun County, Hokkaido
2.	Teine	Sunayama, Teine-chō, Sapporo City, Hokkaido
3.	Gotenyama	Gotenyama, Shizunai-chō, Shizunai County, Hokkaido
4.	Gotenyama	Yokozawa, Shingō village, Sannohe County, Aomori Pref.
5.	Ōyu	Ōyu, Towada-chō, Kazuno County, Akita Pref.
6.	Ōyu	Sodekubo shell-mound, Naruse-chō, Monou County, Miyagi Pref.
7.	Kasori B 3	Ogawa shell-mound, Shinchi village, Sōma County, Fukushima Pref.
8.	Takaragamine	Kamadohara, Aizubange-chō, Kawanuma County, Fukushima Pref.
9.	Sabushō	Sabushō, Kamishioya, Ojiya City, Niigata Pref.
10.	Angyō 2	Ōyaba, Urawa City, Saitama Pref.
11.	Soya	Kamitakatsu shell-mound, Tsuchiura City, Ibaragi Pref.
12.	Kasori B 3	Ubayama shell-mound, Ichikawa City, Chiba Pref.
13.	Kasori B 2	Ōmori shell-mound, Ōta Ward, Tokyo
14.	Kasori B	Nakanosawa, Minamimaki village, Minamisaku County, Nagano Pref.
15.	Kasori B 2	Motai, Mochizuki-chō, Kitasaku County, Nagano Pref.
16.	Sakami	Sakami, Togi-machi, Hagui County, Ishikawa Pref.
17.	Kasori B	Hachiōji shell-mound, Nishio City, Aichi Pref.
18.	Angyō 2	Ikawazu shell-mound, Atsumi-chō, Atsumi County, Aichi Pref.
19.	Miyataki	Miyataki, Yoshino-chō, Yoshino County, Nara Pref.
20.	Motosumiyoshiyama	Sonechō, Owase City, Mie Pref.
21.	Fukuda K 3	Fukuda shell-mound, Kurashiki City, Okayama Pref.
22.	Hirajō	Hirajō shell-mound, Mishō-chō, Minami-uwa County, Ehime Pref.
23.	Mimanda	Mimanda Higashibaru, Shisui-chō, Kikuchi County, Kumamoto Pref.
24.	Kanegasaki	Sobata shell-mound, Uto City, Kumamoto Pref.

NOTE: *Height of No. 8, 11.4 cm.; others to scale, except sherds.*

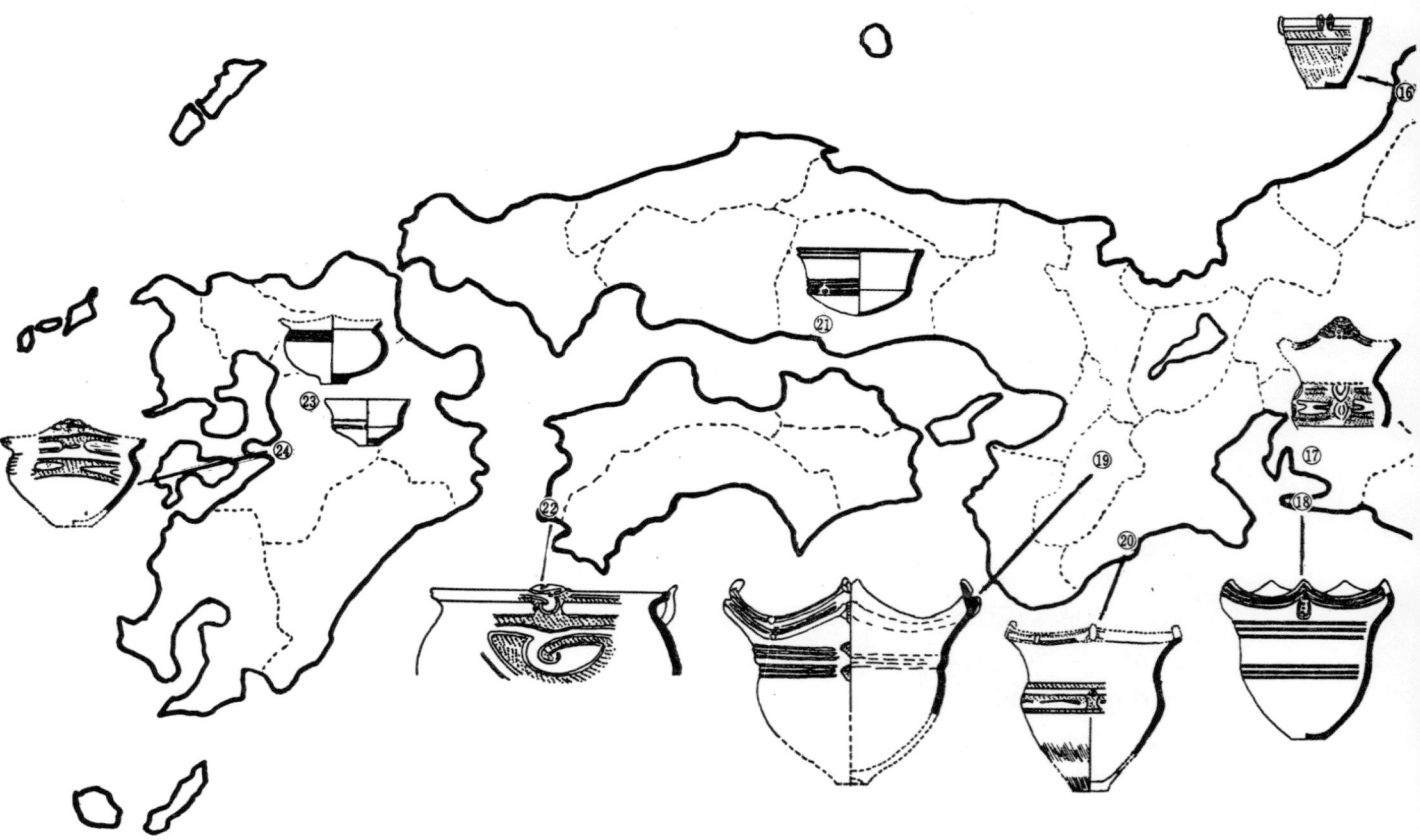

176

It must be no coincidence that small bowls of an ideal size to hold in two hands were made at the same time. For ritual or other purposes—there are not many spouted vessels to a site—some sort of drink was being concocted for which accompanying bowls were needed.

Cord-marking in the earlier stage of Late Jōmon normally followed the Middle Jōmon manner of running obliquely from left to right. This became variable, and by the middle stages (Kasori B type) had become multidirectional, the indentations produced by very short, often fine, cords. This is a logical climax to developments in zoned cord-marking. By and large, by the conclusion of the period (Angyō types)—where cord-marking is *Pl. 312* playing a lesser role—there is some return to more systematically diagonal markings. It should be added that the persistence of this zoned cord-marking was so strong that it is later a prominent feature in Yayoi pottery in the region of the Kantō and farther north.

Equivalent types to Horinouchi are distributed as far south as the Inland Sea *Pls. 323, 324* (Nakatsu type). The zoned cord-marking is probably adopted slightly later in western *Pls. 330, 331* Shikoku and Kyushu (Hirajō, Kanegasaki and Nishibira types respectively), and may be better connected with the Kasori B types of the Kantō area. Inland Sea zoned cord-marking covers large surface areas of the typical dishes and bowls. There is much pseudo-cord-marking done with shells, best exemplified in the Hikozaki K II type in the Inland Sea, although adjacent regions also saw use of the technique.

Iwasaki Upper and Ibusuki may be regarded as southern Kyushu types that fall into the earlier half of Late Jōmon. They appear to belong to a different, here perhaps older, *Pl. 336* tradition. Much of Ibusuki decoration is strictly linear; wall surfaces are obliquely shell-scraped. The vessels may be deep bowls with strongly curved walls and rather narrow bases.

Pls. 337–340 Ichiki pottery is sometimes found in sites that yield Kanegasaki and Nishibira zone-cord-marked types. There is an obvious geographic relationship, but its time relationship is not fully clear. Ichiki has heavy collars; the decoration consists chiefly of shell-marking and shell-scraping. Its distribution is in southwestern Kyushu, where it has sometimes gone by the subdivision names of Izumi and Nampukuji, both shellmounds, the former in Kagoshima, the latter in Kumamoto.[10] It is probably best placed at the end of Late Jōmon.

Returning to the same cultural stage of development as Horinouchi in northern *Pls. 232, 254, 255* Japan, the most unique manifestation can be seen at Ōyu, the site of the great stone circles in Akita Prefecture. Ritual types would be expected here, but hardly the extremely strange shapes that run the gamut from tall-stemmed vessels with lip spouts or wavy rims, through small vessels with long spouts, to rounded bottles. Curvilinear areas are cord-marked; upright and branching-out zones are sometimes treelike in appearance. *Pls. 233, 253, 257, 258* The early Tokoshinai types of northeastern Tōhoku have much in common with standard Horinouchi types as well, although the shapes are in different proportion to the Kantō: jars and bowls occur in considerable number, spouted vessels and bottles come in only with later Tokoshinai types. In Hokkaido, the Irie type, with its linear incision work, can be connected with types at least as far south as Ōyu. Examples in both areas have similar internal incisions and wavy rims.

Pls. 236–243, 245, 261 The Takaragamine and later Tokoshinai types are relatives within the large Kasori B family. The clay is thin and hard, the surface often polished, occasionally burnished, and frequently dark brown to black, or even bluish black. Cord-marking occurs in *Pls. 234, 235* bands, sometimes sweeping around the body. Tokoshinai 3 has notched outlines for its zones, concentrated around a central node. The decoration is moving again in the direction of higher relief, taking the form of low, cord-marked, parallel ridges, accented by clay bosses where the ridges are joined. Kasori B 1 has the narrow, horizontal bands of cord-marking; some vessels are incised only. Kasori B 2 has large, curved, often incomplete zones of cord-marking. Kasori B 3 has rows of arcs above and below parallel lines, the junctures marked by bosses. These patterns have a leaf-like appearance. In Kasori B 3 the repeated motifs are carefully calculated to fit the size of the vessel.

Pls. 267, 275, ff.
Pls. 291, 293, ff.
Pls. 301, 304, 306

Late Jōmon sites contain an increasing number of coarsely made vessels, usually the traditional cooking pot. These were often initially cord-marked and then roughly incised in more or less parallel lines. Certainly by the latter half of Late Jōmon a "domestic" category of vessels had been created, and made much headway. The direction pottery takes in southern Japan is almost exclusively toward domestic types. In the north the domestic wares tend to be isolated from the other wares by a continuing degeneration on the one hand and an intensified finesse of finish on the other.

Pls. 306, 307

Angyō types used to be classified with Latest Jōmon.[11] Now only Angyō 3 is usually included in this period. One reason for this is that it has proved difficult to draw a satisfactory line across a natural development that runs through Kasori B and into Angyō. Another factor that has encouraged this change is the recognition of time differences between the Kantō area and the Tōhoku region, and a resulting effort to push Angyō ahead of the Kamegaoka types, which logically then fill the time span of Latest Jōmon.

Angyō 1 is little different from Kasori B in the use of low, horizontal ridges interspersed at various points with small hemispherical lumps of clay. Angyō 2 is the most impressive of these types. Notched clay ridges envelop a vessel—particularly pouring pots and incense burners—like a supporting net; heavy lugs resemble knots at the junctures. The surface is crowded; the decoration is restricted to a small number of shapes. Probably some attempt was actually being made to reproduce the appearance of supporting nets for pots and baskets. Angyō 3a is in the direct tradition of zoned cord-marking, although the work is roughly done. It is probably a mistake to regard Angyō 2, with its network of ridges, as an intervening type; it is more than likely a local phenomenon that does not break the Angyō 1 to 3 development.

Pls. 308–315, 317–319

Walls of Angyō type pottery are thin and hard. The clay is relatively pure and usually a slightly reddish to dark-brown color. High polishing was more a northern trait and was going out of style after Kasori B in the Kantō Plain.

The most representative type of the later stages of Late Jōmon in the Kinki region is the Miyataki type. It forms a kind of buffer zone between Kantō-influenced areas and regions to the south. Miyataki pottery has a thickened rim with four high, cleft peaks; fine, parallel incisions on the isolated rim "collar"; shell-face impressions; and bands of horizontal incisions encircling the neck and waist of the vessel. Plain surfaces are getting larger and some vessels are entirely undecorated.

Pl. 321

Fukuda K III may correspond with Miyataki in the Inland Sea. Only the rim receives much attention. In this case it is a series of deep grooves that set the orifice off from a high neck. The junction of neck and body on the jars is emphasized by horizontal grooves. Like most late and southern pots, the bases are rather narrow.

The last of the Late Jōmon types in Kyushu is Mimanda, named after a rare site in Kumamoto that yielded several figurines. The clay is dark and hard; the vessels consist of dishes, bowls, and high, wide-necked spouted pots. Feather-shaped hatching follows horizontal lines or appears in zones, and circular punctates may run parallel to the lines of the zones. Most of the decorative work was done with a shell, as had been the case with the Ichiki type.

Pl. 332

The Goryō type has often been included with Mimanda in Late Jōmon. It has a hard, burnished surface in common with Mimanda, but it has here been included in Latest Jōmon partly because this author would like to place this polished type with angular profiles as late as possible in order to make a stronger effort to connect such shapes and techniques with continental crafts in metal and lacquer materials, and by so doing, fill an artificial gap in the type sequence diagrams of some scholars; there is no reason to believe that pottery production ceased in early Latest Jōmon in western Kyushu. Theories of Latest Jōmon Kamegaoka influences from the Tōhoku region reaching Kyushu seem quite inadequate, despite the widespread occurrence of Kamegaoka wares in other parts of the country.

The Mimanda site has appeared only incidentally in publications. Its excavation was the work of a Shintō priest who digs locally. In addition to Mimanda type pottery, he recovered rouletted pottery of Earliest Jōmon, Ataka pottery of Middle Jōmon, and Nishibira and Ueno pottery of Late Jōmon. No stratigraphy has been mentioned in references to the site. Bowls must have been the standard cooking pot during the period of Mimanda production in this region, and the food was probably served in dishes, although the presence of figurines at this site in Kyushu, where figurines are relatively rare—means one should not rule out the possible use of not only the small number of pouring pots but also the numerous dishes in some ritual manner.

230. Nopporo type. Country cousin to the Kantō area's Kasori B type, this vessel shows the local halfhearted adaptation of cord-marking in zones, borrowed—but unexploited— along with the gentle peaks. Hokkaido's colors are usually a dull grayish brown.
Oshōnnai, Hokkaido (*1*) • *height: 20.0 cm.* (*7.9 in.*)

231. Gotenyama type. This little vessel, with impractically narrow base and blatantly symbolic spout, apparently served a ritual purpose, as suggested by its position alongside a pile of stones covering an interment. The simple cord-marking is aligned in one direction at this early stage of Late Jōmon.
Gotenyama, Hokkaido (*6*) • *height: 13.0 cm.* (*5.1 in.*)

181

232. Ōyu type. Vessels from Ōyu display a variety of unconventional shapes, for which ingenious adaptations of ornamentation were required. Parallel incised lines or zoned cord-marking were used extensively; much less common in the Tōhoku region is this sagging globular shape and squared rim.
Nanukaichi, Akita (45) • height: 27.3 cm. (10.7 in.)

233. Tokoshinai 1 type. As a representative of the Tokoshinai type, this vessel is more moderate than examples of the Ōyu type. The surface is light brown with smoke-blackened areas, and was smoothed then incised with the point of a stick.
Sarusawa, Aomori (24) • height: 32.2 cm. (12.7 in.)

182

234. Tokoshinai 3 type. This remarkably finished spouted vessel was found decades ago at Tokoshinai, a site that has been scientifically redug in recent years. The cord-marking is trimly outlined; one projection adorns the base of the arched spout. *Fudōdō, Aomori (16) • height: 21.5 cm. (8.5 in.)*

235. Tokoshinai 3 type. This pourer with polished, hard surface is a bluish-brown color. It is similar to the Kantō Plain's Kasori E type, but has more irregularity in the cord-marking. Small lumps under the spout occur everywhere except Kyushu during this stage. *Yonden, Aomori (19) • height: 19.5 cm. (7.7 in.)*

236. Tokoshinai 4 type. Comparable to Kasori B type in the Kantō area, the sweep of designs here, using single-direction cord-marking framed by the five flared peaks with miniscule split rim lugs, was done with real flourish and sense of style. *Sarusawa, Aomori (24) • height: 26.7 cm. (10.5 in.)*

183

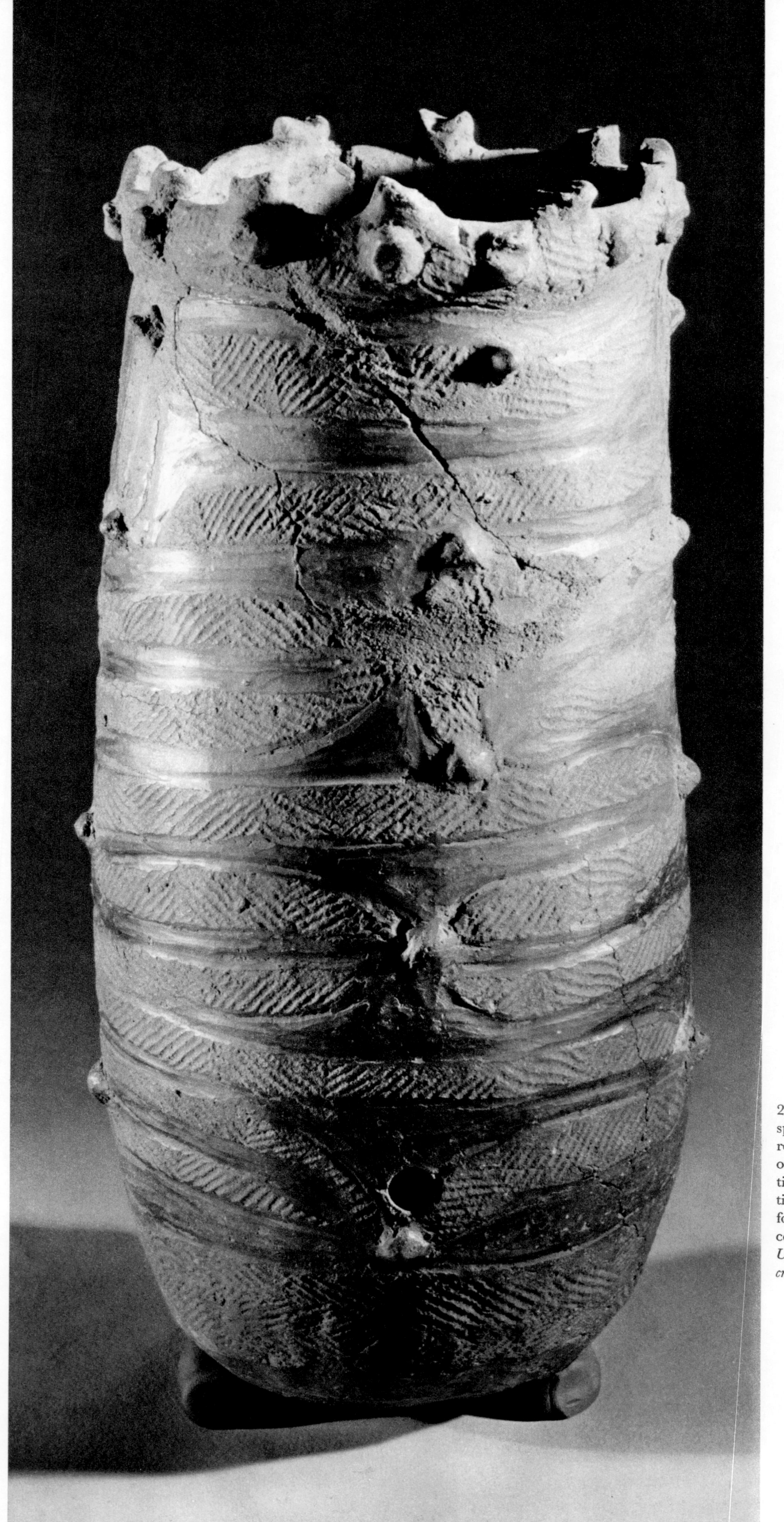

237. Tokoshinai 5 type. Close inspection of this illustration will reveal a rounded hole near the base, one centimeter in diameter. Cultivation brought to light only two additional vessels with holes near the foot, a spouted pot and two tiny containers, perhaps libation vases. *Ushimadate, Iwate (28) ● height: 26.8 cm. (10.5 in.)*

239. Tokoshinai 4 type. Almost interlacing, the zoned cord-marking weaves around the curved surface, enhancing the globular shape of the vessel. The small hole near the bottom may have been for a plug—like a beer barrel.
Ushimadate, Iwate (28) • *height: 11.2 cm. (4.4 in.)*

238. Takaragamine type. This is a reddish blue-brown vase, once painted, with a small hole (on the opposite side) set too low to fit a normal spout. The site yielded two other rather odd vessels, one like Plate 237, and only a few other artifacts. The jars were lined up about fifty meters apart in what must have been a ritual arrangement.

Ōhira, Fukushima (58) • *height: 18.0 cm. (7.1 in.)*

240. Tokoshinai 5 type. The stork's-beak spout and conical top give this vessel a birdlike appearance. Stability was probably no factor since the object must have been held in the hands while in use. (It is too large for one hand.) Parallel lines here replace cord-marking.
Nagakubo, Aomori (15) • *height: 10.9 cm. (4.3 in.)*

241. Tokoshinai 5 type. The spout resembles the neck of a bird, and the open handle is shaped like a spout; both projections look as though they are held on by neck bands. A lumpy orifice gives the vessel an additional opening. Some surface areas are well smoothed.
Yakata, Aomori (16) • *height: 9.0 cm. (3.54 in.)*

185

242. Tokoshinai 5 type. This vase may well be unique in being the only example with full figures on either side. Similar but not identical, they are finely cord-marked in more than one direction, as are the narrow horizontal bands and the loops that serve as their feet. *Tokoshinai, Aomori (24) • height: 22.5 cm. (8.9 in.)*

243. Tokoshinai 5 type. The studding of zones of cord-marking lends greater articulation to a systematically repeated motif. This was the artistic principle of decoration in the latter half of Late Jōmon and in Latest Jōmon, especially in northern Japan. *Tokoshinai, Aomori (24) • height: 23.0 cm. (9.1 in.)*

186

244. Shinchi (t) type. Two almost complete vessels were given a common base—rather like an afterthought—their flared rims and bulging midsections making a creaky marriage. A little decoration remains unfinished near the midriff. The use for such a vessel is unclear.
Sanganji*, Fukushima (56) • *height: 15.5 cm. (6.1 in.)*

245. Tokoshinai 5 type. Showing the rather narrow base characteristic of Late Jōmon in the north, this regularly decorated vessel has the central constriction coordinated with the decoration above the midpart, thus keeping to a minimum the area of decoration that would come into contact with the cooking fire.
Karumai, Iwate (26) • *height: 34.0 cm. (13.4 in.)*

246. Shinchi (t) type. Repeated ellipses, often leaflike in shape, of the latter half of Late Jōmon, are the closest to vegetative patterns ever seen in Jōmon pottery. The split body projections have the appearance of knots holding a horizontal band (perhaps basketwork) together. The stalagmite rim has its modified counterpart in Latest Jōmon in the Tōhoku region.
Sanganji*, Fukushima (56) • *height: 26.5 cm. (10.4 in.)*

187

247. Shinchi (t) type. This is a remarkably fashioned, spouted vessel, meticulously cut down to leave outlined, thread-relief ridges; the surface is smoothed and polished. The pot illustrates a rare piece of quality workmanship in a prefecture better noted for its borrowings.
Sanganji*, Fukushima (56) • height: 11.8 cm. (4.6 in.)

248. Shinchi (t) type. The rounded bottom with segmented shape is Tōhoku in origin, and is less commonly seen in Fukushima Prefecture than farther north. The network of tiny outlined ridges leads one to suspect that the shape and decoration may both have been inspired by basketry or suspension devices. The surface is polished. Firing or later use near a fire produced smoked areas sharply set off from the usual light-brown clay.
Ogawa*, Fukushima (56) • height: 15.0 cm. (5.9 in.)

249. Shinchi (t) type. This is one of the more bizarre creations of Late Jōmon, reminiscent of the Han dynasty "hill censers." The limited number of motifs and accented effects of paired knobs at junctures of cord-marked zones gives the decoration a coherence that did not exist before this time.
Ōhira, Fukushima (58) • height: 10.8 cm. (4.2 in.)

188

250–251. Comparable to the Kongōji type. Apparently these oddities were produced in only a handful of sites in northern Japan. As pouring pots they have bases too small to stand safely, and are characterized by phallic spouts and mammaryesque bulges below the pot mouth that include apertures perhaps for suspending the vessel.
Kanisawa, Yamagata (50) • height: 19.0 cm. (7.5 in.)

252. Horinouchi type. This little cup with perforated base, light-brown color and somewhat smoothed surface is typical of the modest decoration of Late Jōmon and the interest in experimenting with shapes of vessels impractical for daily use. Grooving decoration is focused on the sides and on the slight rim-lip flares at either end.
Hinoto, Iwate (31) • height: 13.4 cm. (5.3 in.)

189

190

253. Tokoshinai 1 type. Rather extreme shapes begin to appear in the Tōhoku region, breaking the monotony of the Entō types of Middle Jōmon. Small sizes, narrow necks, beaklike spouts, and high pedestals are new features and, when combined, make up an interesting collection of vessels. The parallel ridges resemble suspension devices for baskets or even pottery jugs for travelers.
Aomori • height : 9.7 cm. (3.8 in.)

254. Ōyu type. This bottle, a peculiar shape at this stage, with treelike patterns rising off the midriff cord-marking, is just one more of the puzzling vessels from the unusual Ōyu site, where the evidence of habitation is minimal, but all signs point to extensive ritual activity.
Ōyu, Akita (46) • height: 14.6 cm. (5.7 in.)

255. Ōyu type. The Ōyu type, like Tokoshinai, is simply a northern extension of the Horinouchi type. It could hardly even be classified as a variant, but by the vagaries of classification methods it receives a local name. This vessel fits the hand nicely. The long spout would make it easier to pour liquid into a small cup.
Manza, Akita (46) • height: 12.0 cm. (4.7 in.)

191

256. Comparable to the Ōyu type. A cooking pot in shape and size, this vessel with free zoned cord-marking displays a rare type of spout fully attached to the body. The holes near the points of the five peaks are not complete perforations.
Kawame, Iwate (32) • height: 17.5 cm. (6.9 in.)

257. Tokoshinai 1 type. Decoration on the Tokoshinai type is not necessarily ideally controlled, but it moves rapidly across the surface and never prevents the shape from being shown off to best advantage.
Tokoshinai, Aomori (24) • height: 15.5 cm. (6.1 in.)

258. Tokoshinai 1 type. Late Jōmon pottery has a less intimate, personal character—at the same time it shows greater competence in handling of materials. Pots are usually fairly modest in size and rather thin walled. Small bowls are now found in the same sites as pouring vessels.
Tokoshinai, Aomori (24) • height: 12.0 cm. (4.7 in.)

259. Comparable to the Horinouchi 2 type. Nagano Prefecture's Horinouchi type is not a strong manifestation. Very few sites are essentially Late Jōmon, and at a Middle Jōmon site the sherds rarely account for more than one percent of the total. This fine little bowl has almost microscopic cord-marking imprints lying across its globular surface. *Sarukubo, Nagano (109) • height: 9.5 cm. (3.74 in.)*

260. Kiya type. This fine bowl is an interesting case of a potter caught with his alternating zones not fully enclosed; foreground and background melt into each other, leaving unexpected results. *Kiyatakahata, Ishikawa (123) • height: 14.5 cm. (5.7 in.)*

261. Takaragamine type. A well-formed vessel of considerable capacity, this example bears cord-marking in zones that complement the shape ideally. The finely twisted, slender fibers used in making the cord-marking were very short and were rolled over the surface in many directions.
Shiozawa, Fukushima (57) • *height: 36.5 cm. (14.4 in.)*

262. Shinchi (t) type. Potted and combed by a very sure hand, this vessel—twice the size of the average cooking pot—was probably used by a relatively large family. Blackened areas above the foot lead one to suspect that the pot was placed upright in the ground.
Sanganji*, Fukushima (56) • *height: 48.5 cm. (19.1 in.)*

194

263. Horinouchi 1 or Shōmyōji type. This vessel was unearthed at the 1959 excavation of the Soya shell-mound, standing upright about two meters outside a pit-dwelling. It contained bones assumed to be those of a newborn child. The freely incised decoration was laid out in zones but never cord-marked.
Soya*, Chiba (80) • height: 31.0 cm. (12.2 in.)

264. Shōmyōji type (*bottom left*). Perfect symmetry in large vessels was very difficult to achieve for Jōmon potters, as this unstable example from the highly productive Shōmyōji shell-mound shows. There is some ambiguity in the cord-marking of the loosely defined zones.
Shōmyōji*, Kanagawa (93) • height: 52.0 cm. (20.5 in.)

265. Horinouchi 1 type (*bottom right*). Horinouchi 1 type includes rather refined, overall cord-marking over which grouped parallel lines and space-filling spirals are incised. The rim is modest and joined by a vertical, notched ridge.
Kanazawachō, Kanagawa (93) • height: 47.5 cm. (18.7 in.)

195

266. Horinouchi 1 type. This vessel and the following four illustrate popular decorative techniques of early Late Jōmon: cord-marking within zones, incising alone, and incising over cord-marking. The pot came from a deep layer of clamshells and displays the early Horinouchi light-brown color and diagnostic rim groove.
Soya, *Chiba* (*80*) • *height: 27.0 cm.* (*10.6 in.*)

267. Kasori B 1 type. Typically Kasori B in type, the walls thin, the surface perhaps all once polished (see upper rim and handles), the narrow bands of cord-marking on this piece are interrupted by vertical arcs that often resemble figure eights. The base bears mat-marking.
Nishigahara, *Tokyo* (*83*) • *height: 21.5 cm.* (*8.5 in.*)

196

268. Horinouchi 2 type. Technical improvements in Late Jōmon brought progressively thinner walls, accompanied by smaller vessels and narrowed bands of decoration. These are filled with cord-marking or a reasonable facsimile. A groove inside the rim was fashionable.
Ubayama, Chiba (80) • height: 29.0 cm. (11.4 in.)

269. Horinouchi 2 type. During the 1959 excavation the much-worked Soya shell-mound yielded this vessel from a thick shell layer directly over the pit of a house. Finely made, with unusually thin walls, its meticulous cord-marking (almost invisible here) runs mostly in one direction.
Soya, Chiba (80) • height: 25.0 cm. (9.8 in.)

197

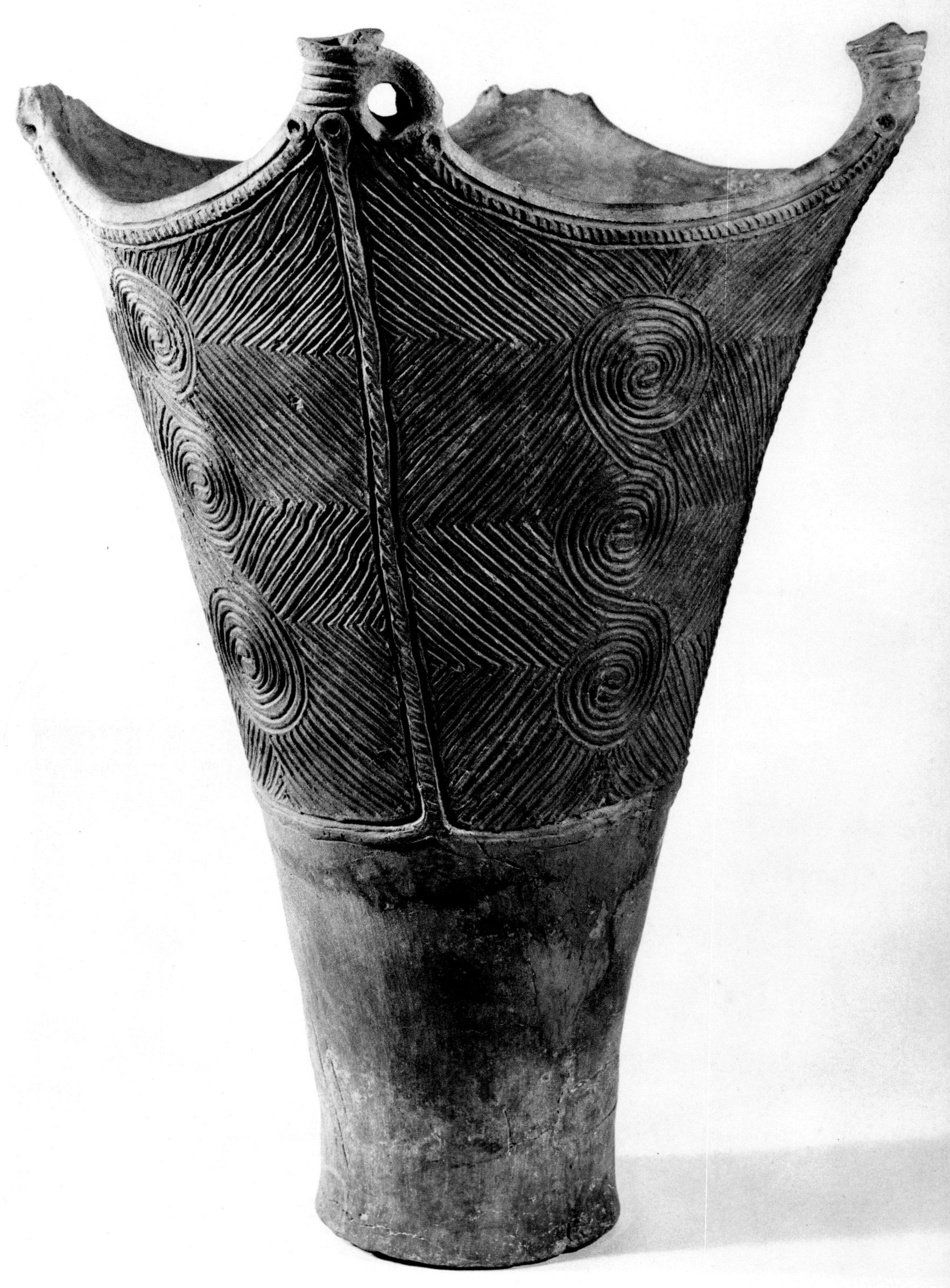

270. Horinouchi 1 type. In classic Horinouchi proportions—gently flared toward the top, the peaks in the shape of spools, the incised decoration framed by outlined and indented ridges— this vessel has all the stock features that make up the type, named after this site. *Horinouchi*, Chiba (80) • height: 50.7 cm. (20.0 in.)*

271. Kasori B type. The Fukuda shell-mound people experimented cautiously, making most of their vessels in rather simple, practical, tried and proven shapes. The size of the hole for the spout suggests that the spout would have been of moderate size. Four points are tied in with the outlines for the cord-marked zones, the cord-marking running in several directions. *Fukuda*, Ibaragi (59) • height: 12.5 cm. (4.9 in.)*

272. Takaragamine type. This unique, cylindrically-shaped vessel, discovered many decades ago, belongs to the group in northern Japan with holes near the foot. It would be interesting to know the original shape of the top. *Ōminatomachi, Aomori (12)*

273. Kasori B type. An attempt to be different ended with surprisingly good results—only one foot does not reach the ground. A well-made and sturdy bowl, the smoothing was done with a hard-surfaced object, and tiny patches of overflow cord-marking went untouched. *Shiizuka*, Ibaragi (60) • height: 10.2 cm. (4.0 in.)*

274. Kasori B type. Well made, with slightly coarse clay, this thick-walled double vessel bears the classic zoned cord-marking of the Kasori B type. The asymmetry is an attractive feature. *Fukuda*, Ibaragi (59) • height: 7.6 cm. (2.95 in.)*

275. Kasori B 1 type. Found around 1882 at one of the earliest sites to be investigated in Japan, this vessel still poses the same problem: what was it made for? One wonders if it may not have been a drinking vessel.
Okadaira*, Ibaragi (62) • height: 18.0 cm. (7.1 in.)

276. Horinouchi 1 type. A curious container with a pair of side loops coordinated with handled lid, this is a peculiar shape for the time and suggests that some thoughtful potter was trying to invent a vessel with a tie-on lid for carrying or storage of foods or liquids.
Kosaku*, Chiba (81) • height: 18.0 cm. (7.1 in.)

277. Horinouchi type. Although the decoration is obviously closely related to the sharp ridges of the Daigi 8 type, the spout is too poorly balanced for later Middle Jōmon. The potter planned ways by which the lid could be secured in place.
Batōchō, Tochigi (64) • height: 12.0 cm. (4.7 in.)

200

278. Kasori B type. A strangely shaped pourer, the spout would have had to be short for the vessel to maintain its balance. Some attempt had been made to clean off the broken area and attach a spout with the aid of pitch. The grooved registers are rough; alternate registers are smooth
Shiizuka*, Ibaragi (60)

279. Horinouchi type. Another of Late Jōmon's curious creations, a human face on an "incense burner" (the opposite side is open), this piece is an interesting departure from the type inherited from the mountainous region during Middle Jōmon. With the addition of the stand, the incense burner or lamp takes on the fundamental form of all later examples.
Kaizuka*, Chiba (73) • height: 16.0 cm. (6.3 in.)

202

280. Kasori B 1 type. This magnificent pouring vessel, an old discovery, has always been looked on as a superb marriage of shape and decoration. Body curves are accented by swaths of incised parallel lines linked by S-shaped motifs. The clay handle is most unusual.
Shiizuka*, Ibaragi (60) • height: 21.8 cm. (8.6 in.)

281. Horinouchi 2 type. A well-smoothed pouring vessel with curved-up spout, this piece exhibits a pair of projections above the loop handles in a position that would interfere with the best use of a removable fiber handle.
Kaizuka*, Chiba (73) • height: 13.0 cm. (5.1 in.)

282. Kasori B 1 type. Better techniques now employed by the potters seem not to have necessarily fostered successful results in the experiments in new shapes for special functions. The results when using this as a pouring vessel should have been very interesting.
Kamiyushizawa, Kanagawa (95) • height: 15.8 cm. (6.2 in.)

283. Kasori B 1 type. The first report on the Fukuda shell-mound, from which this spouted vessel came, was published in 1894 and brought important east Kantō region finds to the early attention of the public. Many vessels are remarkably well preserved. This particular pouring-pot shape calls for an awkwardly long spout if the contents are not to spill out.
Fukuda*, Ibaragi (59) • height: 12.5 cm. (4.9 in.)

284. Horinouchi type. This, like so many of the other pouring vessels, is a well-formed teakettle shape, the decoration done with much restraint. The handles and spout (here missing) were magnified as though to symbolize the vessel's distinctive use.
Katabirajinjakami*, Kanagawa (93) • *height: 19.5 cm. (7.7 in.)*

285. Kasori B type. The perfect body shape is lightly engraved with two, three or four parallel lines in swirling curves, in some places drawn to resemble ropes. The large spout is unnecessarily long, leading one to suppose that its visual effect was intended to compete with its function in importance. The base is mat-marked. The original vessel was lost in a fire.
Provenance unknown • *height: 20.0 cm. (7.9 in.)*

286. Kasori B type. Although the Ubayama shell-mound is best known for its large yield of Middle Jōmon vessels, many remarkable Late Jōmon pieces have also come from this site. This pouring vessel of sharply angular outline, complemented by linear decoration, has a striking pair of high-set handles. The spout is a restoration.
Ubayama*, Chiba (80) • *height: 16.0 cm. (6.3 in.)*

204

287–288. Horinouchi 2 type. This "fruit dish," decorated exclusively on the interior, is a good illustration of the way flaring bowls became natural vehicles for the development of internal incised and sometimes cord-marked designs. Two tiny holes in one lobe are the familiar signs of an ancient effort to stretch the life of the dish.
Shiizuka*, Ibaragi (60) • height: 9.8 cm. (3.8 in.)

289. Kasori B 1 type. This bowl, bearing only interior decoration, was found in the 1962 excavation of the Ubayama shell-mound along with a number of other unusually shaped vessels, including spouted pots. All of these seem to have been deposited like grave goods alongside skeletons.
Ubayama*, Chiba (80) • height: 11.0 cm. (4.3 in.)

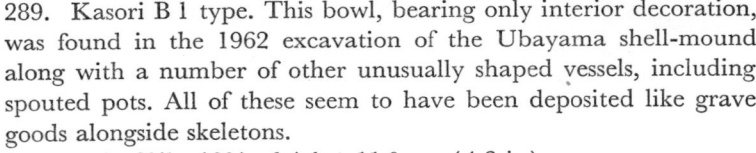

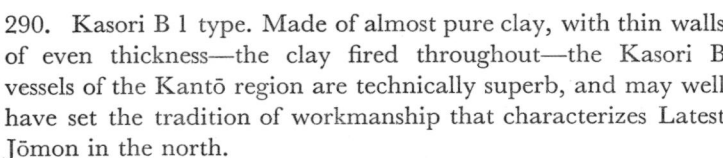

290. Kasori B 1 type. Made of almost pure clay, with thin walls of even thickness—the clay fired throughout—the Kasori B vessels of the Kantō region are technically superb, and may well have set the tradition of workmanship that characterizes Latest Jōmon in the north.
Fukuda*, Ibaragi (59) • height: 15.4 cm. (6.1 in.)

205

291. Kasori B 2 type. Handsomely waved, the narrow bands of minute cord-marking following the curve of the rim and linked together by figure-eight patterns, this fine vessel is one of many astonishing pieces from the Yoyama shell-mound in Chiba Prefecture.
Yoyama*, Chiba (72) • height: 14.6 cm. (5.7 in.)

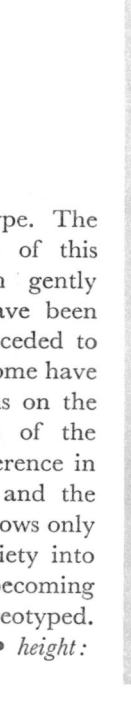

292. Kasori B 1 type. The demand for vessels of this general shape with gently waved rim must have been great. They are conceded to be cooking vessels: some have charred encrustations on the inside—the remains of the daily stew. The difference in shape between this and the following example shows only an effort to put variety into an art that was becoming technically more stereotyped.
Yoyama*, Chiba (72) • height: 21.5 cm. (8.5 in.)

293. Kasori B 2 type. Bowls appear in a variety of shapes. This one with roller-coaster rim has strong oblique incisions as the chief wall decoration, a feature that is especially popular at the Ōmori shell-mound.
Tachigi*, Ibaragi (61) • height: 13.1 cm. (5.1 in.)

294. Kasori B 1 type. In earlier stages of zoned cord-marking much care was usually taken to remove the marking and emphasize the contrasts. When zones were sometimes left open in later stages, less interest seems to have been shown with the contrasts and less concern with the spill-over.
Shiizuka*, Ibaragi (60) • height: 27.7 cm. (10.9 in.)

207

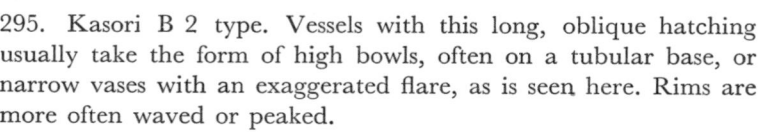

295. Kasori B 2 type. Vessels with this long, oblique hatching usually take the form of high bowls, often on a tubular base, or narrow vases with an exaggerated flare, as is seen here. Rims are more often waved or peaked.

Tōbe*, Chiba (76) • height: 27.5 cm. (10.8 in.)

296. Kasori B 2 type. A series of horizontal ridges furnishes a natural and pleasing set of proportions for this stemmed bowl, encircling the rim shoulder, neck and base of the stand. Regardless of variation in shape, the capacity of the bowls of this stage is remarkably equal.

Yoyama*, Chiba (72) • height: 23.5 cm. (9.3 in.)

297. Kasori B 2 type. Popular parlance calls this a bird-shaped vessel, encouraged by the off-axis, opposing "spouts." The additional advantage this feature would have for pouring or even for use in drinking was undoubtedly very little. Surfaces are well polished and cord-marking runs in many directions.

Fukuda*, Ibaragi (59) • height: 7.3 cm. (2.86 in.)

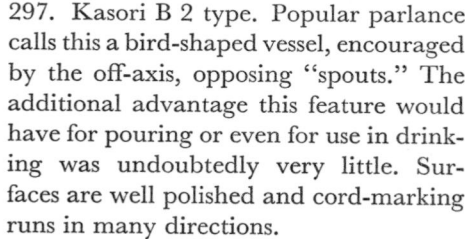

298. Takaragamine type. What practical use a dish on a high base would have had at this stage of cultural development is difficult to say. A plate designed for display of fruit or nuts is a reasonable conjecture— perhaps for a ritual purpose.
Takaragamine, Miyagi (39) • height: 7.2 cm. (2.86 in.)

299–300. Kasori B 2 type. An old find, no details are available on the discovery of this cup. Modeled after an abalone shell and provided with a kind of spout, it has been called both Late and Latest Jōmon. The reproduction of natural objects is not uncommon in Late Jōmon.
Shiizuka*, Ibaragi (60) • height: 6.4 cm. (2.56 in.)

209

301. Kasori B 3 type. This vessel bears characteristic Kasori B 3 traits: unidirectional cord-marking in arcs lying on either side of horizontal, parallel lines, and periodically spaced pellets of clay. The latter are inside rather than at the junctures of the lines.
Hirohata*, Ibaragi (63) • *height: 17.0 cm. (6.7 in.)*

302. Soya type. Simple segmented vessels may have been initially modeled after gourds. They were made in the Kantō area and became common in the Latest Jōmon vessels of the north, evolving into more complicated shapes. The two holes near the rim of the vessel here may have been suspension devices.
Fukuda*, Ibaragi (59) • *height: 23.3 cm. (9.2 in.)*

210

303. Kasori B 2 type. The Shiizuka shell-mound, from which this vessel comes, is recorded as having been first dug around 1893. Many vessels and figurines have since been unearthed there. The incompletely defined zones of cord-marking tend to be late in the development of the zoned cord-marking style.
Shiizuka*, Ibaragi (60) • height: 22.2 cm. (8.8 in.)

304. Kasori B 3 type. Also excavated in Meiji University's 1962 dig in the Ubayama shell-mound, this vessel was retrieved from a pit in the thick shell layer over an abandoned pit-house site on the west side of the mound. The rim decoration is out of character and more like a throwback to Early Jōmon (see Color Plate I and Plate 80).
Ubayama*, Chiba (80) • height: 26.0 cm. (10.2 in.)

305. Soya type. Some archaeologists have separated the Soya type, here represented, from Kasori B. This piece is more stable than most shapes of this time period, and has a straight, flared rim. The broad band of horizontal, alternating arcs filled with cord-marking is the salient trait of the type.
Nishigahara*, Tokyo (83) • height: 32.2 cm. (12.7 in.)

306. Kasori B 3 type. Vessels distinguished by their simple shapes and coarse decoration were obviously made for domestic use. Little time was wasted on their decoration other than for enough surface roughening to facilitate handling. Such purely functional vessels become part of the daily scene in the Late Jōmon period.
Kotehashi*, Chiba (82) • height: 30.8 cm. (12.1 in.)

307. Kasori B 1 type. An all-purpose pot for cooking, storage of foods or water, this simple container has a slightly triangular shape to the rim and bears sketchily applied cord-marking in various oblique directions and more or less vertical, fine-line incising. It retains the rim ridge of Horinouchi type pottery.
Soya*, Chiba (80) • height: 42.5 cm. (16.7 in.)

308. Angyō 2 type. The square-sectioned ridges with fine indentations are the Angyō 2 trademark. Some cord-marking was used, but it is largely obscured by freely incised, oblique lines.
Nado*, Chiba (74) • height: 36.1 cm. (14.2 in.)

212

309. Angyō 1 type. This pretty little vessel can be nicely held in the hands; the decoration aids in the grip. Recent analysts have pushed back the Angyō 1 type into Late Jōmon; it includes slightly raised bands of cord-marking coupled with paired studs. The holes may have been used in hanging the vessel.

Fukuda*, Ibaragi (59) • height: 15.5 cm. (5.9 in.)

310. Angyō 2 type. Reduced decoration toward the base on vessels like this suggests that the lower part had to be sunk in the ground. Rounded, slender ridges and notched protuberances are Angyō 2 features.

Nado*, Chiba (74) • height: 35.5 cm. (14.0 in.)

311. Angyō 1 type. The major centers of the Kantō area's Late and Latest Jōmon are marked by shell-mounds along the coast and rivers of Ibaragi and Chiba prefectures, and to a lesser extent Saitama Prefecture and east Tokyo, evidenced by numerous vessels illustrated here. The incomplete zones of cord-marking are a late development.

Kotehashi*, Chiba (82) • height: 23.8 cm. (9.4 in.)

213

◁312. Angyō 2 type. Richly castellated rims and heavily notched lugs are in keeping with Angyō type ornamentation. Cord-marking—or oblique incising in lieu of it—usually runs only in a single direction. This was a cooking pot, as judged by the charred food remains and the grayish-red lower part.
Ishigami*, Saitama (71) • height: 28.2 cm. (11.1 in.)

313. Angyō 1 type. Bowls on perforated stands are one of the more interesting innovations of the last stages of Late Jōmon. This one probably comes from a large shell-mound in the eastern Kantō Plain. It has low ridges of square section, horizontally slashed, and joined near the holes by clay knobs.
Provenance unknown • height: 14.8 cm. (5.8 in.)

314. Angyō 2 type. The Yoyama shell-mound, where this vessel was found, was formed during Late and Latest Jōmon. Large, knobby rim projections are a borderline characteristic between the two periods and may be the only plastic feature on an entire vessel.
Yoyama*, Chiba (72) • height: 10.9 cm. (4.3 in.)

215

315. Angyō 1 type. So-called incense burners come from sites—mostly shell-mounds—in Chiba, Saitama and Tokyo prefectures. Their actual use is uncertain, but all are rather small. This particular one looks as though it could be inverted and be equally as useful.
Yoyama*, Chiba (72) • height: 16.0 cm. (6.3 in.)

316. Kasori B 2 type. The earliest "incense burners" with side holes and pedestals appear at this time, although the lineage of the class of vessels can possibly be traced back to Middle Jōmon "lamps" in the Chūbu region. The idea seems to move north from the shell-mound sites of the Kantō Plain.
Fukuda*, Ibaragi (59) • height: 16.8 cm. (6.6 in.)

317. Angyō 2 type. Quite small, even for these so-called incense burners, this vessel has the usual wall and base holes. Its decoration is more carefully done than is typical of Angyō pottery types.
Tenjindai, Chiba (77) • height: 12.8 cm. (5.0 in.)

318. Angyō 2 type. Possibly used as lamps, these ▷ vessels are small, have both stand and cup perforations, and tubular handles. Style dictates notched ridges and rather heavy lugs. In some examples these ridges and junctures look like a supporting net with knots.
Shimpukuji*, Saitama (70) • height: 11.0 cm. (4.3 in.)

216

217

319. Angyō 2 type. This pouring vessel has a rugged appearance with its sharply broken rim lines, the arrangement of ridges and knobs resembling a net and knots. The phallic spout is borrowed from the north, but now done in a less specific way.
Fukuda*, Ibaragi (59) • *height: 12.2 cm. (4.8 in.)*

320. Comparable to the Horinouchi type. The vessel exhibits the usual neat cord-marking in zones, but it also bears the unusual feature of red paint on the cord-marking. It was well fired; the clay color is blackish brown. A spout-handle at either end makes the vessel look ingeniously serviceable.
Lake Biwa, Shiga (128) • *height: 12.2 cm. (4.8 in.)*

321. Miyataki type. Miyataki type pottery comes from more than ten sites along the Yoshino River in Nara Prefecture. The shapes are chiefly wide-mouthed jars, bowls and spouted vessels, with angled and shouldered profiles, peaked or flat rims. *Mizonokuchi, Wakayama (136) • height: 19.5 cm. (7.7 in.)*

322. Motosumiyoshiyama type. Cord-marking in zones forms the angled rim and encircles the waist of the vessel in narrow bands. The rim was once adorned by seven points, each marked by a rounded oval of clay. The shape is fairly typical of late cooking pots, but the proportions are rather southern. *Sone, Mie (134) • height: 25.0 cm. (9.8 in.)*

324. Nakatsu type. The decoration on this little bowl shows up an Inland Sea preference for strikingly used cord-marking in zones, running vertically as often as not, much like the beginnings of the zoned decoration system in the Kantō area at the end of Middle Jōmon.
Fukuda*, Okayama (140) • height: 7.5 cm. (2.95 in.)

323. Fukuda K I (Nakatsu) type. The Fukuda shell-mound lends its name to the Late Jōmon types. This vessel's surface is finished rather roughly, and its thickish walls are decorated with panels of the kind that are cord-marked at a slightly later time.
Fukuda*, Okayama (140) • height: 28.6 cm. (11.2 in.)

219

325. Fukuda K II type. Still bearing a little of its original red paint, the bowl's marking is related in general to the Kyushu brand of zoning, although the Fukuda K II type itself is said to extend only as far south as the Neinomaru shell-mound in Yahata City of northern Kyushu.
Fukuda*, Okayama (140) • height: 18.0 cm. (7.1 in.)

326. Fukuda K II type. Four modest but outward-jutting peaks furnish a squarish shape to the mouth and act like a collar—a striking southwestern Japan trait.
Fukuda*, Okayama (140) • height: 14.8 cm. (5.8 in.)

327. Unnamed type. Few complete Jōmon vessels have been found in Shikoku. This low-fired, thick-walled, yellowish-brown pitcher is heavily tempered with quartz, feldspar and other sandy particles. Some red paint still remains on the surface.
Shidehara, Kōchi (145) • height: 10.0 cm. (3.9 in.)

328. Comparable to the Kasori B type. This vessel was recovered from the ocean bed in 1959 by a schoolboy while swimming close to the shore. The scarcity of whole vessels in Shikoku has led to some natural skepticism, but the black to grayish surface is much water-worn. Its details match well with Kantō area pottery.
Sea-bottom site, Ehime (143) • height: 22.5 cm. (8.9 in.)

329. Aya B type. The large Aya site, first dug in 1918 by Kyoto University, is located on the upper tableland of the Ōyado River. Other institutions have dug it since that time. The pottery was initially divided into Aya A and B, and more recently subdivided. This shell-marked pot is Aya B.
Odate, Miyazaki (158) • height: 22.5 cm. (8.9 in.)

330. Nishibira type (*top left*). The Ikada site, from which this vessel comes, is one of Kyushu's more productive sites, known for its burials and dwelling remains. It lies on a hill overlooking the east coast of the Shimabara Peninsula. The pottery is of the Nishibira and Mimanda types.
Ikada, Nagasaki (148) • *height: 28.2 cm. (11.1 in.)*

331. Nishibira type (*top right*). This vessel was discovered in the grounds of a shrine on the outskirts of Yoshii, a shrine well known for its two mounded tombs. Characteristic is the zoned cord-marking in narrow bands, but four rather than three peaks would be more customary for the Nishibira type.
Wakamiya Shrine, Fukuoka (147) • *height: 10.5 cm. (4.1 in.)*

332. Mimanda type (*right*). This spouted vessel is of the Mimanda type—a variant of Nishibira—of the latter half of Late Jōmon in Kyushu. Besides vessels, clay figurines, stone knives and pestles were found at Mimanda itself. The surfaces of such vessels are a deep brown to black, and the decoration is finely engraved.
Mimanda, Kumamoto (150) • *height: 16.8 cm. (6.6 in.)*

333. Comparable to the Mimanda type. The Mimanda type would seem to be the forerunner of the better-known and more widely distributed Goryō type. The shapes are complex in profile; the rfasu ceis brown instead of Goryō's black and is smoothed and marked with miniscule feather-shaped incisions.
Jinnai, Miyazaki (157) • *height: 11.4 cm. (4.5 in.)*

222

334. Comparable to the Kanegasaki type. Complete Jōmon vessels are relatively rare in Kyushu, where they are, of course, proportional to the number of sites and amount of pottery produced. Kanegasaki traits consist of multiple zones, small handles below each rim projection, slightly sandy clay, thin walls and brownish-gray color.
Koikebaru*, Ōita (154) • *height: 36.0 cm. (14.2 in.)*

336. Ibusuki type. The Ibusuki type, found chiefly in southeastern Kyushu, may be this region's answer to the Ataka problem; why Middle Jōmon's Ataka type never went east. By the time it would have, it was superseded by the Ibusuki type. The pottery is reddish brown, lightly sand-tempered, and the walls are shell-scraped.
Kasugachō, Kagoshima (160) • *height: 27.6 cm. (10.8 in.)*

335. Aya type. Miyazaki Prefecture has yielded rather little Jōmon pottery. This Aya type is named after a site in the center of the prefecture. Its decoration is most likely a legacy of the Ataka type of Middle Jōmon, here modified and concentrated nearer the rim.
Odate, Miyazaki (158) • *height: 41.6 cm. (16.3 in.)*

223

337. Ichiki type. The pronounced collar of this type was probably intended to improve the handling of a vessel. Both-sand-with mica-tempering and shell-tempering are sometimes seen; the surface finishing has left fine scratches.
Kusano*, Kagoshima (161) • height: 35.0 cm. (13.8 in.)

338. Ichiki type. The heavy rim collar, powerful grooving, and narrow bands of shell-imprinting are features of the Ichiki type. The type name is taken from a village in which the Kawakami shell-mound is situated; this mound yielded several Late Jōmon types.
Kusano*, Kagoshima (161) • height: 21.2 cm. (8.4 in.)

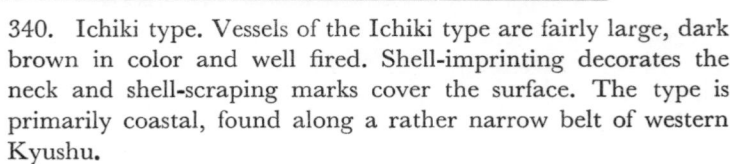

340. Ichiki type. Vessels of the Ichiki type are fairly large, dark brown in color and well fired. Shell-imprinting decorates the neck and shell-scraping marks cover the surface. The type is primarily coastal, found along a rather narrow belt of western Kyushu.
Kusano*, Kagoshima (161) • height: 32.5 cm. (12.8 in.)

339. Ichiki type. Ichiki type pottery is usually accompanied by the Kanegasaki and Nishibira types, which have their centers of distribution farther north. Much emphasis is placed in Ichiki on shell-marked rims accented by four simple peaks.
Kusano*, Kagoshima (161) • height: 9.7 cm. (3.8 in.)

224

Latest Jōmon

ATTENTION HAS been directed to developments along the east coast in the Early Jōmon period, to the central mountains in Middle Jōmon and again to the east coast in Late Jōmon. This approach was not intended to minimize the contributions of other regions to the overall evolution, but only to concentrate on the locus of primary cultural developments during each stage. Attention is now shifted to the Tōhoku region, at this juncture the scene of the greatest production of pottery and the most advanced techniques of the time. The development moves rapidly to about the midpoint of Latest Jōmon, after which some retrogression and degeneration sets in.

All the decorative touches known to potters at the time were used: polishing, burnishing, painting and lacquering. None was entirely new to this period, but all were employed and sometimes in combination. The varied use of such techniques seem to represent efforts to be different, as does the great variety of shapes. However, despite the technical virtuosity, Latest Jōmon pottery might be said to have reached a dead end beyond which development would not have been possible without new techniques. The potter's wheel would have been a major contribution at this point, but its introduction came somewhat later.

Uniformity of quality in the non-domestic class of vessels had reached such a level that pottery-making had apparently become a relatively specialized art, equivalent to the products of craftsmen and apprentices in more advanced societies. The entrenchment in the north of the most traditional elements of the Jōmon culture helped to produce the particular phenomenon known as the Kamegaoka style. In contrast, the southern part of Japan was more vulnerable to external cultural influences, lying as it does opposite the continent of Asia. This southern area—at this point becoming receptive to outside stimuli—presents a completely different situation from that in the north. I do not discount the outside stimuli and a responsiveness to them in the north, as I will try to point out, but the Kamegaoka style can be seen as a culmination of the artistic efforts of the potters in Jōmon Japan, in a sense, the product of the compounded traditions.

This term—Kamegaoka—has long been in use, and derives from a large peat-bog site in Kizukuri-machi, Aomori Prefecture.[1] The very name itself comes from the fact that the hill yielded so much pottery. The site has been incredibly productive, so much so that fine pots flowed from Kamegaoka to all parts of the world in the early twentieth century, and enterprising local people have lined their closets with numerous,

225

remarkable pieces. The wide attention the site has received has worked adversely to the best interests of archaeology and left little to dig scientifically. It would be a difficult site to dig in any event, but lesser sites now lend their names to the typology of the Tōhoku region. Located along the right bank in the Iwaki River valley, about two meters above water level, a peat layer over a sandy bed has yielded all of the Kamegaoka (or Ōbora) types of pottery.

First reports on the site go back to 1623. It was dug in 1896, and many times since. A considerable number of figurines have been found, along with stone plaques, all sorts of beads and stone objects, antler and bone artifacts and lacquer pieces.

Since the 1930's Yamanouchi has been using the results of investigations at the Ōbora (or Ōhora) shell-mounds in the northern corner of Ōfunato Bay, Iwate Prefecture, which Hasebe and he conducted jointly in 1925.[2]

Four more or less connected shell-mounds were designated A, A′, B and C. Fourteen skeletons were found, ten of which were in B and four in C. The last mound contained a very large number of objects made of antler and bone. Different types of pottery occurred in each mound, causing Yamanouchi to designate them first as Ōbora B, C, A and A′. Six types were subsequently separated: Ōbora B, B–C, C 1, C 2, A and A′. Yamanouchi later split up B, B–C and A, and thus made a total of nine types.[3] The situation has been further complicated by other efforts to subdivide Ōbora into five types. The history and application of the scheme points up a less than satisfactory arrangement, partly because of the non-alphabetic sequence. Question marks after type names underscore the problem. One could wish for something more along the order of Kamegaoka 1–6, but it may not be forthcoming. Communication at the present is by means of the most widely used system, so an enumeration of the traits will follow.

Pl. 351 Ōbora B 1. The type illustrates a tendency toward sketchy, zoned cord-marking in incompletely outlined zones, coupled with a refinement of the leaflike motifs of Kasori B. It is the northern version of Angyō 3a, and may be regarded as evidence at this stage that the Angyō type diffused and adopted northern characteristics. Cord-marking is usually oblique; it occurs in elliptical-shaped zones with hooks that attach a zone to another below, all placed within clearly defined horizontal registers. The arcs of Kasori B and Angyō 2 may still be present, but are more elongated. The three-pointed star or a dotted circle marks the junctures of these zones in some examples. Like Angyō, the rims may have a row of cleft peaks.

Pls. 347, 381, 384, 392 Ōbora B 2. The roots of this type are also clearly in the zoned cord-marking of Late Jōmon. The vessels are often spherical, with short necks, thickened rims and decorated collars. The motifs consist of tight curves terminating in truncated spirals. Such motifs form patterns meeting around the midriff of the body, usually repeated four times. The decoration is a flattish relief, set off by grooved outlines and backgrounds excised at a slight angle. Background surfaces are well smoothed; zones are finely cord-marked with some change of direction. Motifs again may be almost floral. Walls are extremely thin, hard and usually a dark brown.

Like B 1, the lower part of the vessel is cord-marked. The three-pointed star occurs rather frequently. The sides of rims may be cord-marked, and the edges may carry rather small projections. A variety of bowls, with or without pedestals, and spouted vessels are typical of the B types.

Pls. 348, 349, ff. Ōbora B–C. The decoration takes on the more customary characteristic of narrow bands of the Kamegaoka types, although not yet with simple repetition. The motifs are not quite fully individualized; like B 2, they tend to be connected, continuous zones. The narrower bands contain interlocked S-like patterns, too small to be cord-marked.

Ōbora C 1. The "cloud-scroll" has materialized as a clear-cut motif by this stage, since the tangled decorative motifs of the B types have finally become isolated. The motifs are the standard S-shaped, simple-to-complex dragonesque forms, usually disconnected, and usually repeated four, five or six times around a vessel. Many are cord-marked, although the same motifs frequently are left unmarked. *Pls. 350, 360–362, ff.*

The motifs move from left to right in horizontal registers, covering the entire surface in the case of most bowls, bottles and certain upright spouted vessels, and covering only the upper part on the higher, pedestaled bowls or cups and the squat pouring pots. These motifs are interlocked in long, S-like curves, and range from simple shapes resembling large bones through stylized birdlike patterns that have "beaks," "crests," and even "wings," to long, animal-like shapes, serpentine or feline in appearance. Systematic repetition is the artistic principle, but each band follows its own rhythm. Sometimes as many as three registers and occasionally even a fourth circumscribe a vessel, each with its independent system. Judged on the basis of relative width, only two at the most could be called primary registers; the others would be secondary. This simple artistic formula is given additional vigor by the independent rhythms of each register. Options in using cord-marking lend variety.

All of this may have come as a natural climax to finishing work, as is generally believed by Japanese archaeologists; but I have the impression that some knowledge of metal surfaces and lacquer products would have inspired this preoccupation with surface finish. Lacquer combs, baskets, and wooden "swords" come from several Latest Jōmon sites in Hokkaido and Aomori and Saitama prefectures. Japan's lacquer was inferior in quality to the lacquer of China; it seems unlikely that the material would have normally been chosen for use unless outside inspiration had spurred it on.[4]

Certain conventions in Jōmon decoration at this stage compare admirably with the stylized treatment of birds and animals on Han dynasty bronzes and lacquers. This is especially the case with the most portable and highly prized Chinese objects, notably the bronze mirrors. The mirrors, in particular the TLV type, examples of which are known in Japan, bear bands of stylized "clouds" derived from animal forms, in which the motif is alternately repeated upright and inverted. A similar compositional device may be seen in the pottery motifs. In fact it is the only time it is consistently used in Jōmon designs. The Han dynasty feline motif representing an animal seen from above but with neck twisted to show the head in profile is far too complex to have been arrived at by accident in Japan. The motif appears in only slightly more abstract form on this pottery.[5]

Most paint used on Jōmon pottery is red iron oxide (Fe_2O_3). Even as early as Tado Lower of Earliest Jōmon, traces of this kind of paint occur, and by later stages of the same period it is found on sherds in the Kinki region. It is doubtful if this red paint is the result of any serious attempt at decorating a surface, but rather represents the use of containers for transporting or storage of materials. Cinnabar (HgS) was occasionally used, but this was primarily by Late Jōmon people in the Kantō Plain. The Kantō people also tried a little more often than others to paint designs on vessels—but even this was relatively infrequent—and chiefly on surfaces like the inside of low bowls (fruit dishes?) where rather large display areas were exposed. In general, however, the practice of *Pl. XI*

LATEST JŌMON MAP I

	TYPE	SITE
1.	Gotenyama	Gotenyama, Shizunai-chō, Shizunai County, Hokkaido
2.	Kaminokuni	Takeuchiyashiki, Kaminokuni-chō, Hiyama County, Hokkaido
3.	Ōbora C 1	Kamegaoka, Kizukuri-chō, Nishitsugaru County, Aomori Pref.
4.	Ōbora C 1	Korekawa, Hachinohe City, Aomori Pref.
5.	Ōbora C 1	Aso, Takanosu-chō, Kita-akita County, Akita Pref.
6.	Ōbora B	Shimoyamadera, Yajima-chō, Yuri County, Akita Pref.
7.	Ōbora B	Daigi-gakoi shell-mound, Miyagi County, Miyagi Pref.
8.	Ōbora C 2	Terawaki shell-mound, Furuminato, Iwaki City, Fukushima Pref.
9.	Angyo 3b	Naraseto, Nara-chō, Ōmiya City, Saitama Pref.
10.	Angyo 3a	Horinouchi shell-mound, Ichikawa City, Chiba Pref.
11.	Angyo 3a	Azusawachō, Itabashi Ward, Tokyo
12.	Nakaya	Nakayachō, Kanazawa City, Ishikawa Pref.
13.	Angyo 3	Tennozan, Shimizu City, Shizuoka Pref.
14.	Angyo 2 or 3	Ikawazu shell-mound, Atsumi-chō, Atsumi County, Aichi Pref.
15.	Shigasato	Shigasatochō, Ōtsu City, Shiga Pref.
16.	Shigasato	Miyataki, Yoshino-chō, Yoshino County, Nara Pref.
17.	Tanji	Tanji, Yoshino-chō, Yoshino County, Nara Pref.
18.	Type uncertain	Tsukumo shell-mound, Nishi-ōshima, Kasaoka City, Okayama Pref.
19.	Yasutomi	Yasutomi, Masuda City, Shimane Pref.
20.	Ōishi	Ōishi, Ogata-chō, Ōno County, Ōita Pref.
21.	Ōishi (?)	Negino, Takeda City, Ōita Pref.
22.	Goryō	Goryō shell-mound, Jōnan-chō, Shimomashiki County, Kumamoto Pref.
23.	Kurokawa (?)	Kureishibaru, Shimabara City, Nagasaki Pref.
24.	Goryō	Jinnai, Takachiho-chō, Nishiusuki County, Miyazaki Pref.

NOTE: *Height of No. 11, 27.3 cm.; others to scale.*

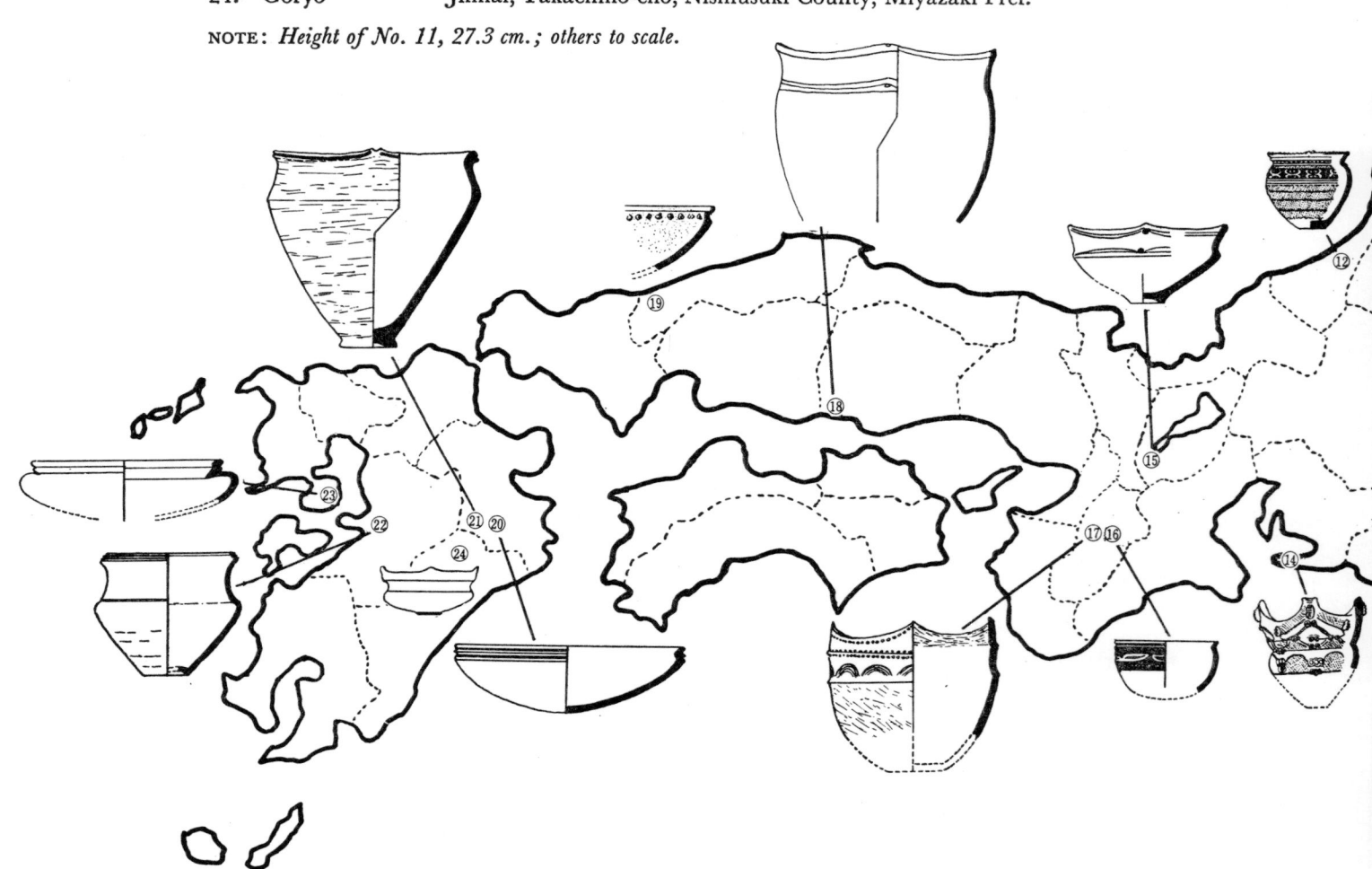

228

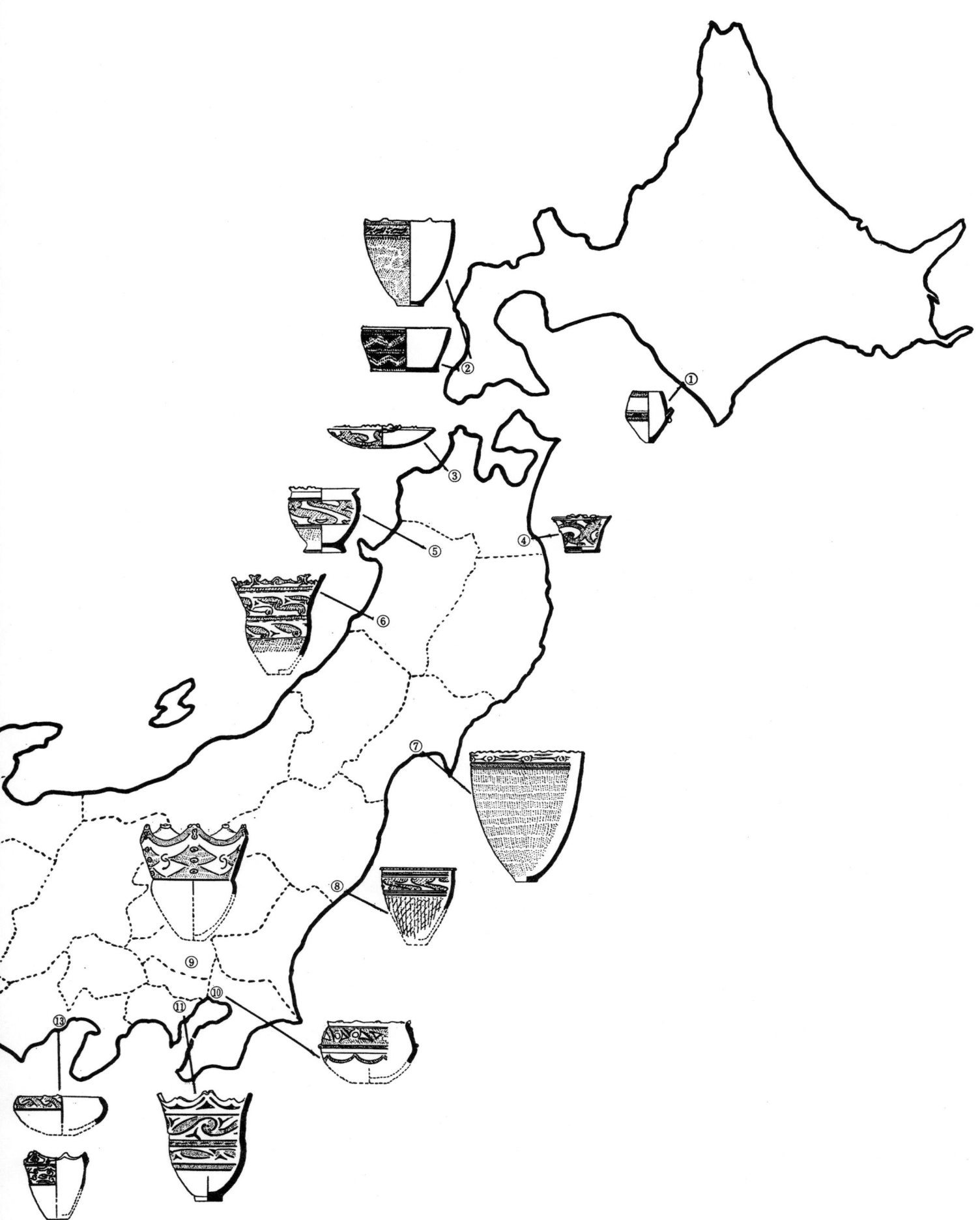

229

painting after firing leaves much to be desired in regard to permanence: the paint washes off easily. Presumably, painted pots could not have been washed very often, and paint was probably applied to vessels for which exposure to water was not intended.

Pl. 148 A different situation would obtain with the large Middle Jōmon barrel-shaped vessels. These are now known to have been painted before firing. The exterior paint is decoration; the interior paint may have been a lining or veneering, designed to reduce the porosity of the vessel. This same technique is not recognized again until the Latest Jōmon period, in lid-shaped bowls from the Nakagawa site in Toyama Prefecture and elsewhere.[6] Under the latter circumstances, the practice may be related in some way to the larger question of painted bones, bone containers, grave goods and other objects connected with the dead.

Pl. XVI A black paint may also have been used, as is implied by the surface of one of the Kamegaoka vessels illustrated—a vessel that also bears red paint. The use of this material could be another effort at reproducing a metallic luster, otherwise normally achieved through burnishing in the middle stages of Kamegaoka work.

The lacquer of the Latest Jōmon period is a resin used as a clear coating over the paint. The conditions of the peat-bog sites (Kamegaoka and Korekawa, both in Aomori Prefecture, for instance), have resulted in a hardening of the surface and corresponding protection of the paint, despite the post-firing application of the pigment.

Pls. 354–356 Ōbora A: This type was established with the view of continuing the line of development as a kind of crystallized version of the convoluted patterns of Ōbora C 1. Closely-spaced, horizontal, raised lines are reversed at intervals and weave back and forth like a maze. It is close to the "flowing water" (*ryūsui*) pattern of middle Yayoi, with which, in fact, it could very well be connected. With all due respect to the viewpoint of an internal evolution, it is hard to see logic in the change from the convoluted decoration to these simple linear shapes. The existence of intermediate examples, or examples that tend to have a little of both, does not in any way alter the possibility that the "flowing water" pattern of Middle Yayoi pottery, bronze bells and wooden objects is reflected in this northern material. There are no C_{14} dates yet to disprove it.[7]

Classifying this linear pattern as Jōmon would mean grafting it to the existing repertory of patterns. Pots could carry a little of both until the later style was well established. The configurations seem to be too complex for normal developments in Jōmon pottery —even in this terminal stage, and the appearance of this pattern is too coincidental to be completely disassociated from Yayoi products; a hypothesis predicating a relationship between Ōbora A and Yayoi "flowing water" designs would seem to lead to more fruitful lines of inquiry than the complete rejection of such a possibility.

Pls. 425–426 Ōbora A': As the conclusion of what this whole development is thought to be, Ōbora A' represents the ultimate crystallization of the style. The same weaving, raised lines, formerly parallel, are connected by oblique lines with those above, the spaces between the outlined shapes now opened up and angular. The neck and body designs or shoulder and body designs, which had been fairly distinctly separated, here merge with each other and lose their individuality. The final result is sometimes sketchily done, large triangular or rectilinear, decorative shapes.

By Ōbora C 2 all known shapes were present in the Tōhoku region. Yet in the A and A' types, spouted vessels were rarely made (there are virtually none for A'), and the bottles and incense burners had disappeared. Bowls of various shapes with angular profiles are most common for A'. The row of six or eight small cleft peaks on the rim so

closely resembles Angyō 3a that it can hardly be a revived trait—it must be in the direct *Pl. 402*
line of descent in some localities.

Kamegaoka was not limited to northern Honshu, but appears in Hokkaido in the same way many of the earlier Tōhoku types are distributed. The workmanship is usually less sure, the quality of surface finish rarely measures up to Tōhoku standards, and the finer shades of development claimed to exist on Honshu cannot be followed in precisely the same way. Nevertheless, Hokkaido is part of the cultural zone in which these types flourished.

Hokkaido also has other types that are one step removed, and can be looked on as the fringe products resulting from the Kamegaoka style.

There is an interesting possibility regarding the diffusion of the Angyō types in the formation of the Kamegaoka style. It looks as though Angyō moves up the east side of Honshu, while Kamegaoka later moves down the west. Kamegaoka pottery occurs in Niigata and Toyama—prefectures along the Japan Sea—and in parts of Nagano. Comparable material extends down to Nara Prefecture, since it can be shown that Kashiwara pottery, for instance, is related. This appears to represent a newly developed *Pl. 411* north-south route; it may be due to the movements of people and trade in that part of the country because of some blocking of the regular eastern, south-north route. In any event, the concentration of pottery types and other cultural evidence now speaks for more formidable tribal groups, who could, as a matter of fact, have been straddling the normal migration routes. There is one view that the Latest Jōmon period in northern Japan is an Ainu cultural stage.[8] Far less than a millennium later the historic records report the presence of battle frontiers in northern Honshu, which correspond not at all unfavorably with the southern limits of this Kamegaoka style in the eastern Tōhoku region.[9] It is entirely possible that this defensive pattern found its beginnings in an increasing tribal territorial control during the Latest Jōmon period.

A significant development is the intrusion of Kamegaoka vessels and figurines into regions where other types existed. These vessels are exceptionally lightweight and readily portable; they must have been highly prized in areas where the quality was inferior to that in the Tōhoku region—which included most of the country. Examples have been found in the Tōkai and Kinki regions, in association with local types; this phenomenon has had the advantage of dating these local types in relation to Tōhoku types.

This same phenomenon can be seen in the appearance of a little Kamegaoka pottery with Angyō 3 types. Less regard for precision of workmanship, quality of clay and finesse of detail occurs at this point. The technique of carving the decoration links these types with the north. Angyō 3a has the interlocked S-patterns and spaces filled with *Pls. 399, 400, 402, 403* three-pointed stars. But this is often drastically reduced on simple cooking pots to exclusively linear designs in the shoulder zone without cord-marking, and smooth rims. Spouted vessels have the shorter spouts of the north and incomplete zones of cord-marking shaped like large, breaking waves. These rims are also usually plain, and follow the Kantō's traditional treatment of rims on such vessels. Angyō 3b has hanging arcs *Pls. 394–396* derived from the Kasori B cord-marked shapes, but most of these arcs are now simply roughly punched. Parallel, incised, loosely connected arcs are most typical of Angyō 3b; the rim peaks of 3a are now lower, usually six in number and normally not notched. High-necked, globular vessels are popular, along with bowls, and cups on high stands. The so-called Sugita 2 type (Yokohama City) is probably contemporary and is best known by its plain bowls with a single line around the rim both inside and out. Other bowls are provided with cord-marked patterns shaped much like broad zigzags.

LATEST JŌMON MAP II

	TYPE	SITE
1.	Midorigaoka	Nusamai, Kushiro City, Hokkaido
2.	Hinohama	Nishimura, Naganuma-chō, Yūbari County, Hokkaido
3.	Hinohama	Hihohama, Shirikishinai-chō, Kameda County, Hokkaido
4.	Sunazawa	Sunazawa, Hirosaki City, Aomori Pref.
5.	Ōbora A′	Korekawa, Hachinohe City, Aomori Pref.
6.	Ōbora A	Nakagami, Hanaizumi-chō, Nishi-iwai County, Iwate Pref.
7.	Ōbora A′	Fujidōzuka, Sōma City, Fukushima Pref.
8.	Fujihashi	Fujihashi, Nagaoka City, Niigata Pref.
9.	Ōbora A	Hitorigo, Kōriyama City, Fukushima Pref.
10.	Kōri	Kōri, Komoro City, Nagano Pref.
11.	Shimono	Shimono, Torigoe village, Ishikawa County, Ishikawa Pref.
12.	Chiami	Arami shell-mound, Narita City, Chiba Pref.
13.	Sugita II, III	Sugita, Isogo Ward, Yokohama City, Kanagawa Pref.
14.	Mamizuka	Mamizuka, Ichinomiya City, Aichi Pref.
15.	Kashiwara	Kashiwara, Kashiwara City, Nara Pref.
16.	Funabashi	Funabashi, Kashiwara City, Osaka
17.	Kurotsuchi B 1	Takashima-kurotsuchi, Kasaoka City, Okayama Pref.
18.	Harayama	Kanjiku, Inukai-chō, Ōno County, Ōita Pref.
19.	Yamanotera	Jinnai, Kumamoto City, Kumamoto Pref.
20.	Yamanotera	Matsuba, Sagara village, Kuma County, Kumamoto Pref.

NOTE: *Height of No. 14, 35 cm.; others to scale, except sherds.*

Pl. 408

Two Kantō types, Chiami, named after a site in Kiryū City, Gumma Prefecture, and Arami, a shell-mound in Chiba Prefecture, could be called local Kamegaoka products, that is, variants of Ōbora A and A′ in the west and east Kantō respectively. Sugita 3 is comparable to Ōbora A, the others to either Ōbora A or A′. This same stage of Ōbora

Pls. 397, 398, 409

A′ or its obvious derivatives is represented by the Fujihashi type in Niigata Prefecture and the Kōri 1 type in Nagano Prefecture. In such areas the vessel shapes are simple, rims rarely carry any projections, and decoration is held down to a low relief.

Preceding Kōri 1 in the Nagano area is the Sano type, named after a site in Yamanouchi-chō, Shimotakai County, which yielded large quantities of sherds. The Sano type actually corresponds with Angyō 3a in some cases and Ōbora A in others. The pottery bears zones of cord-marking shaped in spirals, arcs, small circles, hanging hooks and interlocked and oblique S-shapes. Rows of punctates may replace grooves.

The Kinki types most closely related to the Kamegaoka family are to be found in some of the material at Kashiwara in Nara Prefecture. Here the stylized features of late Kamegaoka are unmistakable. Kashiwara is a large site, or, more properly, sites, in the local public park, recorded as early as 1902.[10] The chief discoveries, however, came during wartime years when leveling was being done on a large playing field. The pottery

Pls. 410–413, 415, 416

is a brown to volcanic gray color, quite coarse and gritty in texture, with a minimum of surface finishing. The decoration, if any, is incised. Local peculiarities at Kashiwara include this incised decoration in strongly angular shapes, and striated borders of designs. Occasionally the designs themselves are striated, evidently as a kind of pseudo-cord-marking. Cord-marking itself is rather rare. The presence of so many figurines and other objects of clay makes Kashiwara an extraordinary site, and seems to suggest that the cultic role the area played in later times had very early origins. One unusual feature about the Kashiwara designs is the repeated leaflike patterns. Moving around a vessel like large zigzags, they are arranged like an Ōbora A′ design. They look as though they may be a further stylization of the Kasori B version of this theme. The time relationship, however, is not clear.

Pl. 414

The Shigasato type, named after a site in Shiga Prefecture near the southwest shore of Lake Biwa, with its largely plain vessels and four simple rim peaks is a modification of the Miyataki type. A neck collar is grooved in long curving lines that follow the shape of the rim or the horizontal outline of the base of the collar. The Kamegaoka-type pottery from Shigasato is well smoothed, and bears cord-marking within incomplete zones. The body decoration is very close to Angyō 3a in the Kantō, but rim projections may be knobbed on top in a way that resembles Angyō 2.

Kurozuchi B I in the Inland Sea region is related to the plainer Shigasato ware. The rims are rather similar in that a kind of collar takes the incised decoration, but the body is heavily scraped. This scraping is found in most of the remaining types in this region

Pl. 418

and farther south. Kurozuchi B II is usually plain except for notched ridges that encircle the rim and shoulder. The effect is usually of a coarse, functional vessel, chiefly the cooking-pot shape, with narrow base. The aesthetic value is minimal. This simplicity and "utilitarian" approach leads toward the standards of Yayoi pottery and makes it difficult to separate the last of the Jōmon pottery in Kyushu from the first of the Yayoi wares. The nature of the site and its contents—reaping knives especially—may provide clues

Pl. 421

to the answers.

The last of the fine surface finishes in the south occurs on Goryō type pottery, an offshoot of the Kanegasaki-Nishibira-Mimanda types, but in particular the Mimanda type. It takes its name from a shell-mound in western Kumamoto Prefecture. Goryō's

shapes are mostly bowls and strongly shouldered jars with rim "collar" and often with a raised foot.[11] The walls are thin, highly polished or burnished and remind one of the high point of Kamegaoka production in the north. Kurokawa is a related type; it is sometimes classified with Yamanotera. *Pl. 420*
Pls. 419, 424

There is some difficulty with the identification of very late types in Kyushu. These types have a shoulder emphasized by a notched ridge and a rim strengthened in the same manner—a device that reaches as far north as the Kinki region. The surfaces are scraped and combed. The deep pot is typical of the time. There are regional variations in the character of the clays, firing and other technical matters, despite a general similarity in external appearance. *Pls. 418, 419,*
427–429

The jagged rim of both jars and bowls are mostly southeastern Kyushu in provenance. Two jagged rims do not combine well for burial jars; some rims of pots actually look as though they were shaped to take a low bowl. The Tamura type in Ōita Prefecture is a good example of this. The largest number of jar-burials of Latest Jōmon found in one site is forty-four in the shell-mound of Yoshigo, Aichi Prefecture. All of these are single jars. They contained the remains of every age group, from infants to adults.[12] The numerous other burials in the same mound are more or less contemporary, showing that burial in a jar was most likely a mark of status at this time. Rank or otherwise, the practice had become fairly common by Latest Jōmon, at least among the shell-mound people. *Pls. 427–428*

The contacts incoming Yayoi pottery had with Jōmon pottery served to produce composite forms with traits of both traditions. This becomes far more apparent in regions where Jōmon pottery had its strongest traditions, i.e., from the Kantō area north. It is already recognizable north of Shizuoka Prefecture, when Yayoi pottery adopts cord-marking. Above the Kantō there is zoned cord-marking of a Yayoi type, used to cover the entire body of a vessel. Where the pottery cannot definitely be shown to be Yayoi (the assemblages are still Jōmon) yet is still believed to follow the Jōmon period, the transitional stage has received the name *Zoku-jōmon*—"continuing" Jōmon, less correctly termed in English Post-Jōmon. This kind of pottery is distributed throughout all of Hokkaido, for instance, where the Yayoi culture failed to penetrate, and in much of the northern Tōhoku region.

There is cord-marking on many Post-Jōmon types; it does not follow the customary oblique direction of normal Jōmon pottery but runs vertically or in all directions. Ōbora A′ influences are frequently apparent on Post-Jōmonware. Many type names are given for this material in both northern Honshu and Hokkaido, but the problems of its relationship to those regions where rice is known to have been cultivated have not yet been ironed out.

The so-called Satsumon types—"rubbed pattern"—a rather old term descriptive of the surface working, is also found throughout Hokkaido. The decoration consists chiefly of incision work, and the pots are usually deep and have rather narrow bases. Found in association with typical Sue and Haji wares of the Tomb period, Satsumon can probably be dated in the seventh and eighth centuries A.D. Other accompanying artifacts belong to the Tomb period or later.

Stone implements decrease in number and are replaced by wood and metal tools after the Satsumon stage in all parts of the island except the northern littoral where the Okhotsk culture arose. Situated along the Okhotsk Sea, this latter is related to the coastal cultures of northern Asia. By and large it succeeds Satsumon, if one may judge on the basis of the small number of Chinese objects found at the Moyoro shell-mound.[13]

Okhotsk pottery is dark in color, decorated with incising, punching, indenting and outlined pictures of animals. It is particularly noted for its strips of clay that were made by forcing liquid clay through a tube and directly onto the surface of the vessel. Grooves appearing under the strips are evidence of the technique. Some Okhotsk cultural objects are rather similar to types used by the modern Ainu. Much trade was going on, through Sakhalin in particular, and during Post-Jōmon and subsequently, Sakhalin and the southern Kuriles shared common cultural features with Hokkaido.

342. Comparable to the Ōbora A type. Lacking the original refinement of the Tōhoku region work, this little jar is clearly an imitation of Kamegaoka pottery in its style of cord-marking and rim lumps and comes from a region where finesse seems not to have been valued. Some surfaces still bear red paint.
Hokkaido • height: 10.9 cm. (4.3 in.)

344. Okitsu type. Estimates on the dating of this vessel range from Late or Latest Jōmon to Post-Jōmon. Cord-marking crosses the vertical ridges and the elliptical-shaped orifice has two full apertures reinforced by clay doughnuts.
Okitsu, Hokkaido (4) • height: 16.5 cm. (6.5 in.)

341. Comparable to the Ōbora A type. Some red paint still remains on the decorated frieze of the upper body. Kamegaoka influences from northern Honshu are so strong in the area around Kushiro as to have elicited the suggestion that this vessel may have been brought to Kushiro from a genuine Kamegaoka center.
Nusamai, Hokkaido (4) • height: 20.5 cm. (8.1 in.)

343. Midorigaoka type. The rim is squarish in shape, the neck incisions and cord-marking quite coarse. The vessel is painted. Examples like this are often found as burial furniture. Perhaps, as funerary objects, there was little concern for quality.
Midorigaoka, Hokkaido (4) • height: 18.2 cm. (7.2 in.)

237

345. Midorigaoka type. The boat shape is not uncommon at the end of the Jōmon period in Hokkaido. Perforations at either end between vertical ridges were used to suspend the vessel. Cord-marking runs from the notched rim to the base, and the incised zone carries traces of red paint.
Midorigaoka, Hokkaido (4) • height: 22.6 cm. (8.9 in.)

346. Nusamai type. This type includes vessels often painted red and found buried alongside the dead. The accompanying pottery is frequently Ōbora C 2, giving the clue for dating. It has been suggested that the designs resemble the *kamushiki*, the "eyes of the god" found on traditional Ainu embroidery.
Ōmagari, Hokkaido (2) • height: 20.3 cm. (8.0 in.)

347. Ōbora B 2 type. Plates 347, 348, 350, 353, ▷ 354 illustrate the evolution of jars of this shape, from Ōbora B 2 through Ōbora B–C, C 1 and A. The basic shape is globular, with narrow base and segmented neck, and low, cup-shaped mouth. This vessel was painted with a kind of reddish-brown lacquer.
Kawahara, Aomori (16) • height: 42.0 cm. (16.5 in.)

238

239

349. Ōbora B–C type. This vessel is a typical shape of north Japan at the opening of Latest Jōmon. The principle of decorating such a shape seems to have changed from full surface coverage to two registers of repeated motifs, each of different size, occasioning a complex rhythmical system.
Nakai, Aomori (18)

348. Ōbora B–C type. Vessels of this shape may have exceedingly thin walls and be brittle and easily broken. Here cord-marking appears around the rim and on alternate, horizontal bands of decoration composed of rhythmically interlocked S–like motifs.
Ishinadate, Akita (49) • height: 27.0 cm. (10.6 in.)

350. Ōbora C 1 type. This vessel has a less attractive shape than its predecessors in this book, and displays a wide, angular excising that sets off the cord-marked, cloudlike patterns. A hole in the shoulder shows the wall to be paper thin. The color ranges from a gray to black.
Takaya, Aomori (16) • height: 45.0 cm. (17.7 in.)

240

351. Ōbora B 1 type. This pot of handsome form, precisely cord-marked and provided with eight cleft peaks, hailing from Honshu's most northern prefecture, in many features resembles a vessel excavated in the metropolis of Tokyo, thus showing a remarkable relationship between these two regions at this time.
Momoishichō, Aomori (17) • height: 18.4 cm. (7.3 in.)

352. Ōbora B type. Vessels from the Ōbora shell-mound tend to be larger on the average than most northern pots at this stage. A cooking pot here illustrates the continuous production of utilitarian containers, a category of vessels overshadowed by the more interesting, elaborately decorated vessels.
Ōbora*, Iwate (35) • height: 38.1 cm. (15.0 in.)

353. Ōbora C 2 type. The "flowing water" design rarely covers the entire body, making this vessel quite unusual. The decoration here is less precise than on most examples of the type.
Botan-batake, Iwate (34) • height: 14.0 cm. (5.5 in.)

354–355. Ōbora A type. This bottomless vessel is said to have been found by itself, buried upside down, without other artifacts in the vicinity. From this it is surmised that it may have served as a burial jar. The highly polished surface is reddish brown.
Matsubara, Aomori (21) • height: 35.0 cm. (13.8 in.)

356. Ōbora A′ type. This decoration represents the most advanced and stylized form of the "flowing water" design, a design normally limited to the upper shoulder of the vessel and measured off to fit the circumference exactly.
Hachigasaki, Aomori (21) • height: 20.0 cm. (7.9 in.)

242

358. Ōbora B–C type. Minor variations on this bottle shape in the three northern prefectures of the Tōhoku district are well known. They remind one of the saké bottle of today, and could well have been used at that time to contain a special drink.
Nakayama, Akita (44) • *height: 17.3 cm. (6.8 in.)*

357. Ōbora B–C type. Red paint covers the inside surface and the outside to the bottom of the neck of this piece. The shape would be ideal for a hanging bottle, a usage for which the thinness of the piece could be considered additional evidence. The size is unusually small for this shape and decoration.
Amataki, Iwate (25) • *height: 12.5 cm. (4.9 in.)*

360. Ōbora C 1 type. Rather peculiar in shape—at a time when the peculiar was becoming commonplace—this piece might perhaps be described as a wide-mouthed vase. The neck is cut back and smoothed, and cord-marking covers the underside.
Ōno, Akita (43) • *height: 11.4 cm. (4.5 in.)*

359. Ōbora C 2 type. Basket-shaped, the outer surface carefully finished and painted, this vessel represents a conscious effort to reproduce the effect of lacquering—a lacquered basket came from the Latest Jōmon site of Korekawa in Aomori Prefecture.
Kamegaoka, Aomori (22)

243

361. Ōbora C 1 type. The cord-marked motif is repeated six times around the body; above, notched, irregular ridges are joined at periodic intervals. On the lower body of the opposite side of this piece is a small hole made after firing, around which can be seen some asphalt, apparently once used as a glue.
Higashizage, Akita (47) • height: 17.0 cm. (6.7 in.)

362. Ōbora C 1 type. Proportionally little scientific investigation has characterized the Kamegaoka site excavation, which yielded this vessel, but in a 1948 dig this one and a smaller, painted vessel of the same shape were found upside down on the reddish sandy layer of an old riverbed, in a presumably ritual arrangement.
Nagamori, Aomori (14) • height: 16.0 cm. (6.3 in.)

244

363. Ōbora B–C type. This is an excellent example of the chief motif repeated in two registers on a fixed scale—reduced on the lower register only enough to conform to the narrowing shape—hence a simple rhythm throughout. Spaces around the shorter "worms" on the lower register are filled by one bump less than in the upper register.

Amataki, Iwate (25) • *diameter: 10.0 cm. (3.9 in.)*

364. Ōbora B–C type. This is another of the small Amataki vessels, named after this site where the excision technique is especially prominent. Long, interlocked S-shapes form the prime motif—to which all other details are strictly supplementary space-fillers.

Amataki, Iwate (25) • *height: 6.3 cm. (2.46 in.)*

245

365–366. Ōbora C 1 type. This attractive bowl, with finely cord-marked "cloud-scroll" pattern on the base and wall in narrow bands, and with the other surfaces highly polished, was sufficiently appreciated during its lifetime of use to have been repaired. Three pairs of holes are visible along the old crack. The fine cord-marking runs mainly in one direction.

Shirayama, Iwate (25) • *height: 6.0 cm. (2.36 in.)*

367. Ōbora B–C 2 type. This very elegantly decorated bowl has a slightly raised base and bears a single birdlike motif repeated four times. The patterns are cord-marked and heavily outlined in a technique comparable to sunk relief.
Amataki, Iwate (25) • diameter: 21.5 cm. (8.5 in.)

368. Ōbora C 1 type. Exquisitely carved, smoothed and polished, with minute indentations of cord-marking running in several directions, the walls have the thinness and brittle ring of lacquer ware. Four convoluted figures are sharply articulated against the rounded-off background.
Kindaichigawa, Iwate (25) • diameter: 20.0 cm. (7.9 in.)

369. Ōbora C 2 type. Bases of bowls in Latest Jōmon in the north are often quite picturesque, frequently bearing a continuation of the main decoration. Four tiny feet terminate the leaflike, incised patterns.
Provenance unknown • height: 7.7 cm. (3.0 in.); diameter: 18.8 cm. (7.4 in.)

247

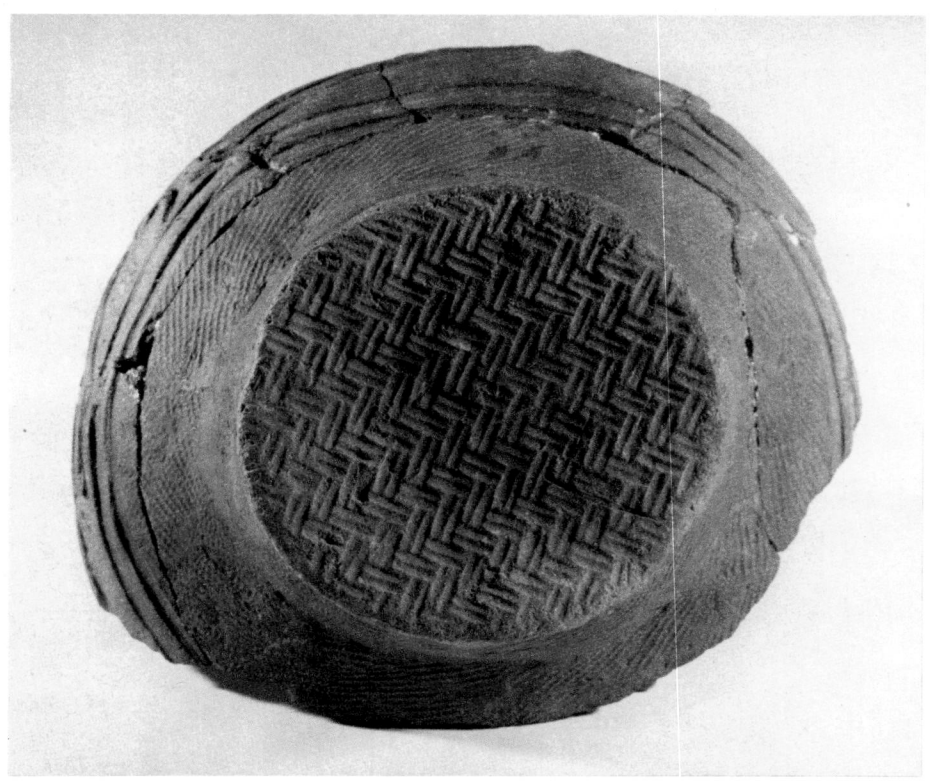

370. Ōbora B–C 2 type. The decoration-covered base of so many bowls in the north leads one to believe that there must have been considerable sedentary appreciation of their beauty—not too unlike the formality of the tea ceremony of later historic times.
Chōjayashiki, Iwate (30) • *height: 5.3 cm. (2.0 in.); diameter: 16.4 cm. (6.5 in.)*

371. Arami type. Marks on bases of vessels show that several different types of mat weaving were in existence since the Middle Jōmon period, but rarely does one find such a perfect impression as this. Special pains were obviously taken to insure precise results.
Arami*, Chiba (75) • *height: 11.7 cm. (4.6 in.); diameter: 23.2 cm. (9.2 in.)*

248

372. Ōbora B–C type. Amataki pottery shows remarkable workmanship, especially in the minute detail. Fine cord-marking is here combined with the carving technique to produce a very attractive bowl.
Amataki, Iwate (25) • height: 6.1 cm. (2.36 in.)

373. Ōbora B–C type. Multidirectional cord-marking on the body's serpentine designs is another example of the fact that the Amataki site has yielded all variations of the current modes of decoration. More than sixty tiny waves decorate the rim.
Amataki, Iwate (25) • height: 7.9 cm. (3.15 in.)

374. Ōbora C 2 type. This vessel comes from the Ōbora (sometimes called Ōhora) shell-mound itself, where digging in several spots enabled Dr. Yamanouchi to work up a chronological scheme for the Kamegaoka family of pottery. Four peaks here are larger; intervening peaks are slightly smaller.
Ōbora*, Iwate (35) • height: 16.8 cm. (6.6 in.)

375. Sunazawa type. This bowl was found on the edge of a pond and typed after the site. Six flared rim projections are aligned with coupled small knobs that mark the junctures of broad diagonal and horizontal line incisions.
Sunazawa, Aomori (24) • height: 10.4 cm. (4.1 in.)

376. Ōbora C 1 type. Uncommonly flat even for the north, this pedestaled low bowl came up with much Ōbora C 1 type pottery at a depth of about 1.5 meters below the surface. The "cloud-scroll" patterns are not cord-marked, leaving less than the customary differentiation between excised design and background.
Hosono, Aomori (23) • height: 10.0 cm. (3.9 in.)

250

377. Ōbora B–C type. If pedestaled, flattish bowls were for ritual use, such as exposition of food, the rituals must have been frequent occurrences indeed, judging from the large number of such pieces. The unusual openwork pedestal of this piece is constructed with a systematic repetition of long, interlocked S-shaped figures. *Higashizage, Akita (47) • height: 11.7 cm. (4.6 in.)*

251

378. Ōbora B–C type. Perched slightly precariously, but nicely shaped, this bowl on a pedestal poses the question asked about so much of Jōmon pottery: how was it used? A broken rim line is far from ideal for drinking. The upper part of the vessel is smoke-blackened, suggesting, because of its size, that it was perhaps used for cooking small or individual portions of food.
Provenance unknown

379. Ōbora C 1 type. One commonly held belief is that Latest Jōmon in the north is a period of declining creativity, socially cramped by its rituals, evidence of which is the great number of peculiar vessels and the obvious tendency to devote an overwhelming amount of attention to the exhibition of pottery skills. This cup on a high base illustrates a full mastery of pottery techniques.
Hiranuma, Aomori (13) • height: 25.0 cm. (9.8 in.)

380. Ōbora C 2 type. A cup on a high base is one of the north's most popular shapes. In this case the decoration is about halfway between the "cloud-scroll" pattern and the incised, elongated zigzags of the last Tōhoku region types. The notched rim and paired projections are well-known features of this type.
Botan-batake, Iwate (34) • height: 12.8 cm. (5.0 in.)

381. Ōbora B 2 type. The pottery from this Terashita site—a site that yielded quantities of pottery, stone and bone implements and other artifacts—has been typed primarily as Ōbora B, B–C and C 1. The top-heavy shape with stubby spout is not particularly uncommon. Examples are well polished.
Terashita, Aomori (20) • height: 12.5 cm. (4.9 in.)

382. Ōbora B–C type. Spouted vessels in the north are usually squat, angular and small in capacity. This one, however, is based on the upright jug shape of the north, to which has been added the northern short, stubby spout.
Makumaetai, Iwate (29) • height: 11.0 cm. (4.3 in.)

383. a) Ōbora B–C type. Much of this vessel has little more than ornamental use, since it cannot be filled much above the rounded base because of the position and length of the spout. The capacity is therefore reduced to the size of a cup, giving rise to the idea that these are actually drinking vessels.
Yokamachi, Aomori (21) • height: 11.7 cm. (4.6 in.)

b) Ōbora B–C type. Spouted vessels like this, which look as though the upper part had been forced down into the lower part, have a truncated appearance as though designed to take a lid. Entirely unbroken rims are a rare phenomenon by this time in the Tōhoku region.
Yawata, Aomori (18) • height: 10.0 cm. (3.9 in.)

384. Ōbora B 2 type. Dated near the beginning of the long development of pouring vessels in the north, this piece shows the more globular southern shape, with proportions and placement of the spout that are more northern. The surface, however, is poorly finished for northern work.
Ōno, Akita (43) • height: 13.4 cm. (5.3 in.)

385. Ōbora C 1 type. Most of these vessels have low-slung proportions, short spouts following closely the rising curve of the body, and rather strongly projected, excised decoration encircling the "waist" at the juncture of the high, rounded base and the concave body.
Tokoshinai, Aomori (24) • height: 9.5 cm. (3.74 in.)

386. Ōbora C 2 type. The decoration on this superb piece is developed toward the spout of the vessel. Such pourers fit the hands perfectly, and lead one to suspect that certain of the fundamental historic traditions of scale in Japanese ceramics were born at this time.
Hachinohe City, Aomori (18) • height: 7.5 cm. (2.95 in.)

387. Bowl with Arami type base. Dug up in Chiba Prefecture, this vessel is included in the selection to illustrate the penetration into the Kantō area of the last of the Kamegaoka types of northern Japan. The color is blackish brown and the base bears a leaf-impression. *Arami*, Chiba (75) • height: 11.5 cm. (4.5 in.)*

388. Sunazawa type. Resembling wicker or rattan work, this bowl points up the strong likelihood that a highly developed woodworking craft was influencing the last stages of the Jōmon ceramic art in the north. The rim is thickened, all surfaces well polished, and the color is grayish brown. *Sunazawa, Aomori (24) • height: 15.0 cm. (5.9 in.)*

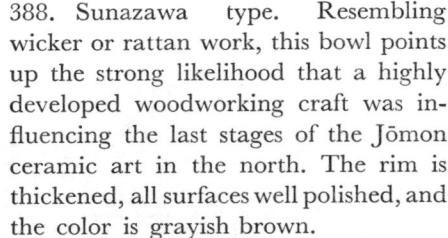

389. Sunazawa type. Reddish brown, well fired, highly polished, and provided with six graceful, divided rim peaks, this elegantly made bowl would in some classifications be called Ōbora A′ type. The centers of the floors of such bowls often have circular punctations. *Sunazawa, Aomori (24) • height: 11.8 cm. (4.6 in.)*

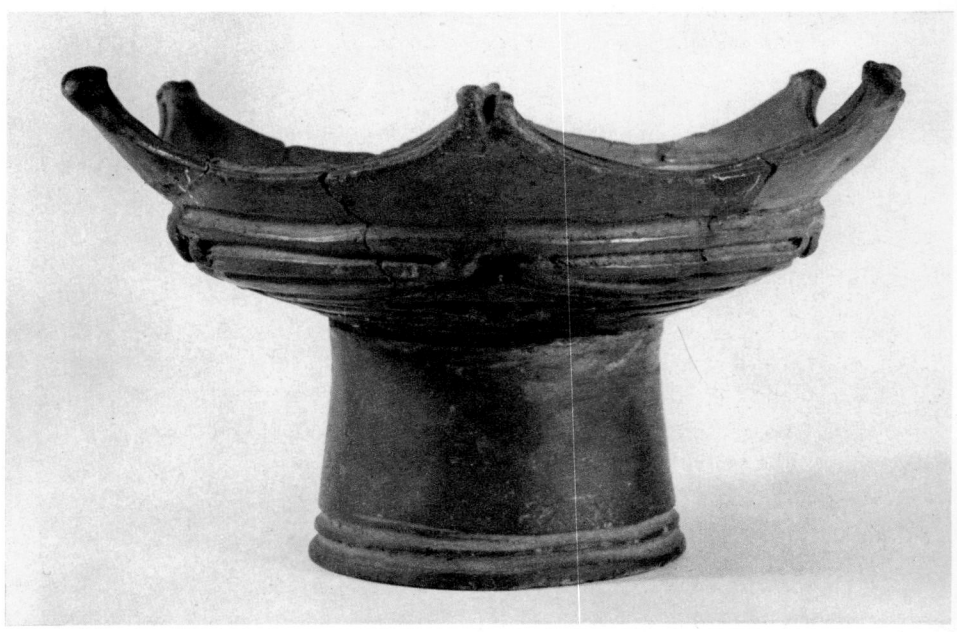

256

390–391. Ōbora B–C type. An odd, lamplike object of fairly large size that can be held easily by the projecting part, this piece bears the dolphin-like motif, rows of squarish projections, the fanciful, broken outline of the rims of northern pottery, and a highly polished surface. It was an exercise in technical virtuosity.
Kamiyashiki, Aomori (21) • height: 9.5 cm. (3.74 in.)

392. Ōbora B 2 type. The so-called incense burners can perhaps be successfully traced back to the Middle Jōmon period, through Kasori B of Late Jōmon (Pl. 316), but this particular type of shape seems to have little connection with previous types, displaying a pair of large holes, other apertures and crownlike terminals—the terminals in this case vaguely resembling bird's heads. The color is orange-brown.
Makumaitai, Iwate (29) • height: 14.5 cm. (5.7 in.)

393. Ōbora B type. The many northern "incense burners" are not fully represented in the illustrations here. They have by this time become standardized as a cup on a pedestal, having a cone-shaped top with a pair of large, oval holes. Most are crowned with rather elaborately sculptured peaks.
Nakayama, Akita (44) • height: 11.8 cm. (4.6 in.)

394. Angyō 3b type. The Shimpukuji shell-mound, from which this vessel hails, was not well published initially, but from it has been reported such unusual finds as gingili, buckwheat and many varieties of wild plants.
Shimpukuji*, Saitama (70) • height: 30.0 cm. (11.8 in.)

395. Angyō 3b (?) type. A precise knowledge of the provenance of this stemmed cup would be useful in pinpointing its type. The rim projections—modest as they are—are Angyō features; other details seem to warrant assignment to the Angyō 3b type.
Ibaragi • height: 24.5 cm. (9.6 in.)

396. Angyō 3b (?) type. As a shape introduced in Late Jōmon in the Kantō Plain, this vessel illustrates the slackened interest in the appearance of a finished product for utilitarian needs in the Latest Jōmon. This level of workmanship is common enough to lead one to believe that it was gaining increasing acceptance by Jōmon people at this stage.
Asahi, Niigata (103) • height: 8.5 cm. (3.35 in.)

397. Fujihashi type. Stylized "flowing water" patterns constitute the decoration of the neck band, here less exact and orderly than is customary in the Tōhoku region. The rim is pinched at regular intervals and slightly grooved on the outer edge between the points (almost invisible here).
Fujihashi, Niigata (102) • height: 18.6 cm. (7.3 in.)

398. Fujihashi type. A good example of the strictly domestic pot of the time, this vessel is almost exactly the same size as the earliest cooking pots in the Kantō Plain made thousands of years before. This pot comes from the type site, Fujihashi.
Fujihashi, Niigata (102) • height: 17.0 cm. (6.7 in.)

399. Angyō 3a type. An old discovery in the Fukuda shell-mound, this unusual pouring pot has a puffy, anthropomorphic face, eyebrows joined to nose, an oval hole in the back of the head, a collar of zoned cord-marking, the familiar three-pointed star, and cord-marking surrounding the now missing spout.
Fukuda*, Ibaragi (59) • height: 17.5 cm. (6.9 in.)

400. Angyō 3a type. Short, stubby spouts, large body spirals, and three-pointed stars on squat vessels are characteristic traits of Angyō 3a. The Shimpukuji shell-mound, from which this vessel comes, yielded many fine examples of this stage.
Shimpukuji*, Saitama (70) • height: 13.7 cm. (5.4 in.)

401. Angyō 2 (?) type. This interesting creation is ostensibly a bowl with handle, but it cannot be used satisfactorily for drinking, nor does it seem very practical for transferring liquids from one container to another. The wormy decoration is almost unique; the rim projections may be the ultimate clue to its type.
Shimpukuji*, Saitama (70) • height: 6.0 cm. (2.36 in.)

402. Angyō 3a type. Angyō 3a is strongly influenced by Kamegaoka, as seen in the rim waves, body decoration and shapes of vessels. This rim has a single asymmetrical projection. Angyō walls are rather thin. *Kotehashi*, Chiba (82) • height: 9.3 cm. (3.64 in.)*

403. Angyō 3a type. Bands of cord-marking, squared rim projections, and the three-pointed star are prominent traits of this type. The color is dark brown; the walls relatively thick; each rim projection is different. Such a bowl shape is quite rare for the Angyō types. Normal preference was for simpler shapes.
Nado*, Chiba (74) • height: 6.0 cm. (2.36 in.)

404. Angyō 3c type. The decorative technique is identical to that of the early stage of Latest Jōmon in the Tōhoku region; it is a technique fairly frequently seen in the Kantō area's Angyō 3a and 3c types. Even the precision of workmanship compares favorably with the north at this time.
Sonnō*, Chiba (82) • height: 9.2 cm. (3.64 in.)

405. Angyō 3c type. The rounded bottom is common among the Angyō types. The rim is thickened, perhaps as a means to reduce the chance of cracking in cooking pots. The three-pointed star has been incorporated directly into the broad-line incision work.
Shimonumabe, *Tokyo* (*84*) • *height: 6.7 cm.* (*2.66 in.*)

406. Angyō 3c type. The 1962 excavation of Loc. B of the Horinouchi shell-mound yielded this complete vessel from the shell layer. The decoration of waved rim and clustered (here paired), small projections, the undulating, broad-line incision—or partial excision—along the collar, and the notched shoulder are typically Angyō 3c.
Horinouchi, *Chiba* (*80*) • *height: 13.4 cm.* (*5.3 in.*)

407. Ōbora C 2 type. This is an exceptionally large bowl for Latest Jōmon. Its light-brown walls are relatively thin for its size. Beneficial Kamegaoka influences often stimulated local production efforts in Latest Jōmon in the Kantō area, as evidenced by this high bowl from Yokohama.
Sugita, *Kanagawa* (*93*) • *height: 19.6 cm.* (*7.7 in.*)

408. Chiami type. More or less typical of northern and western shapes, although a little irregular, this vessel illustrates the perennial preoccupation with rim decoration, tried in every imaginable way. One horizontal band of excision work constitutes the chief ornamentation.
Arami*, Chiba (75) • height: 11.0 cm. (4.3 in.)

409. Fujihashi type. Surfaces tend to be rough on pottery from the basin of the Shinano River in the Echigo region, in all likelihood because of poor firing methods. Despite the most careful treatment of this vessel—according to the report—its red paint has virtually vanished.
Fujihashi, Niigata (102) • height: 10.2 cm. (4.0 in.)

410. Kashiwara type. Kashiwara pottery is mostly dark brown to in grayish color, of rather coarse clay and mediocre artistic workmanship. This particular design—a repeated unit of four leaflike patterns—is the most characteristic and has been called a derivative of Shigasato pottery designs.
Unebichō, Nara (133) • height: 9.5 cm. (3.74 in.)

411. Kashiwara type. Plains with few rivers emptying into the ocean did not attract Jōmon people as much as the lower mountains, accounting for the smaller number of Jōmon sites in the Kansai region and correspondingly less pottery. Most of the Kansai pottery shows considerable dependence on other types. Kashiwara is a rare site in quantity of material; the pottery is usually brown to gray and coarse in texture.
Kashiwara Shrine park, Nara (133) • height: 10.3 cm. (4.0 in.)

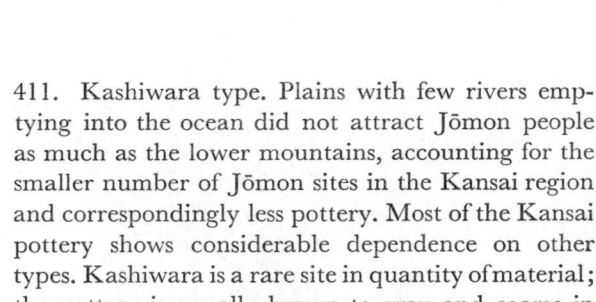

412. Kashiwara type. The work in the Kansai area and south stands in sharp contrast to the northern craftsmanship at this time. There is little interest in finishing the surface and experimenting with shapes. The clays become increasingly coarse; the vessels vary little from basic utilitarian shapes.
Kashiwara Shrine park, Nara (133)

413. Kashiwara type. Kashiwara traits include imprecise shapes, rough surfaces requiring deep punctation to enable the decoration to be adequately seen, and a size that is easily held in the hand. The workmanship is slipshod. The nature of the site leads one to feel that the vessels may have had a votive use.
Kashiwara Shrine park, Nara (133) • height: 11.7 cm. (4.6 in.)

265

414. Shigasato type. Pottery of the Shigasato type has thin walls and may be decorated or plain. Surfaces here are well smoothed but not polished. This piece is a trim, practical, basin shape.
Kashiwara Shrine park, Nara (133) • height: 13.5 cm. (5.3 in.)

415. Kashiwara type. Decoration on vessels from the Kashiwara site ranges from relatively modest to completely plain. This round-bottomed bowl with ornamental rim would certainly not be easy to use.
Kashiwara Shrine park, Nara (133)

416. Kashiwara type. This bowl type, of which large numbers were found at Kashiwara, usually appears in association with plain vessels that are polished or refined, and also coarse bowls. Pottery that shows Kamegaoka characteristics of northern Japan is also found at this site, in a notable display of interregional borrowings.
Unebichō, Nara (133) • height: 14.3 cm. (5.6 in.)

266

417. Comparable to the Ōbora B–C type. Except for its stocky proportions, this vessel could easily be mistaken as a much more northern example of a fairly early Kamegaoka type. The frieze of decoration is smoothed, but the unmarked lower half of the vessel shows the typically rough surface of this latest ware.
Wasa, Wakayama (137) • *height: 17.2 cm. (6.8 in.)*

418. Kurozuchi B II type. From the Kurozuchi site itself—a site helpfully labeled B (*Banki*), Kurozuchi stage II—this pot's heavy, notched ridges and lightly brushed, coarse surface are characteristic of the type.
Kurozuchi, Okayama (142) • *height: 15.2 cm. (6.0 in.)*

419. Yamanotera (?) type. Large vessels of this kind might ultimately have served as containers for children's bones. The wide mouth and collar-like top is common in Kyushu. Here the coarse clay was scraped away horizontally, the rim and juncture of collar and body then lightly notched.
Sakata, Fukuoka (146) • height: 40.0 cm. (15.75 in.)

420. Kurokawa type. Kurokawa is a cave on the peninsula west of Kago-shima City. It seems to represent the last Jōmon type of south Kyushu. The small vessels, made of pure clay, have thin walls, are black and well polished. Decoration is kept to a minimum.
Mimanda, Kumamoto (150) • height: 10.8 cm. (4.2 in.)

421. Goryō type. The angular profile and mouth diameter equal to the widest part of the body are traits of the Goryō type clearly seen in this example. The walls are thin, the pots well fired. Their fragility gives the impression that the larger vessels would have required much care in use if long service were to be had from them.
Takenoato, Kumamoto (149) • height: 33.2 cm. (13.1 in.)

269

422. Jinnai type. From the Jinnai site, this bowl was excavated from a stratum containing Latest Jōmon material. The area was obviously receptive to influences spreading out from the Mimanda type home area; Jinnai is viewed as one of the earliest Latest Jōmon types in Kyushu. The dark-brown surface is highly polished.
Jinnai, Miyazaki (157) • height: 9.8 cm. (3.8 in.)

423. Goryō type. Goryō pottery is made of pure clay and fired at a rather high temperature. The surfaces are smoothed and usually polished. The strong shoulder, concave neck and rim collar are diagnostic traits of the type. The rims sometimes carry incision work.
Goryō*, Kumamoto (152) • height: 17.5 cm. (6.9 in.)

424. Yamanotera (?) type. The efforts to make attributions to this so-called Yamanotera type, named after a site in Nagasaki Prefecture, have not been wholly successful. This plain, brownish piece from the Mimanda site, with wide, angular but simple rim projection, may perhaps be satisfactorily called Yamanotera.
Mimanda, Kumamoto (150) • height: 12.5 cm. (4.9 in.)

425–426. Ōbora A′ type. Small children were often buried in jars set vertically, bowls acting as lids. This example is from the north, whereas Plates 427 and 428 illustrate the same practice in the south. Such bowls were carefully made, and are often found intact. The wide-mouth jars have not held up so well.
Kindaichigawa, Iwate (25) • *total height: 61.0 cm. (24.0 in.); jar height: 52.0 cm. (20.5 in.); bowl height: 21.0 cm. (8.3 in.)*

427–428. Tamura type. The Tamura site is interesting in having Early Jōmon remains in lower layers, Latest in the top layer; there is no Middle reported. Several burial jars were recovered from this top layer. These are similar, coarsely shell-scraped jars with sharply angled shoulders and added bases.
Tamura, Ōita (155) • jar height: 28.0 cm. (11.0 in.); bowl height: 13.0 cm. (5.1 in.)

429. Mamizuka type. Purely utilitarian vessels of Latest Jōmon may often be difficult to distinguish from Yayoi pottery when the color is reddish to light brown. These burial vessels, from the northwest part of Aichi Prefecture, are smoke blackened on the upper half. A collar of horizontal grooving hides the otherwise rough, pitted surface on the lefthand piece.
Mamizuka, Aichi (126) • height of lefthand pot: 35.0 cm. (13.8 in.)

Decoration
Techniques

INEAR RELIEF   No type name has been given the oldest pottery yet found in Japan—the pottery displaying slender clay ridges like a linear relief. Tentatively, type names can be assigned as follows: Fukui I for pottery discovered in northwest Kyushu; Kamikuroiwa I for pottery excavated in the Chūgoku region and in Shikoku; and Yanagimata for pottery found in the Chūbu district. This linear relief pottery is also reported to have been excavated recently in the Kantō area, at the site within the Kofukuji Temple in Ikuta, Kawasaki City, Kanagawa Prefecture.

In making this type of pottery, a lump of clay about four centimeters in diameter was first rolled between the palms of both hands and molded into a ball. It was then flattened by both hands into an oval clay slab. Several of these clay slabs, it seems, were joined together to form a hemispherical bowl with a diameter of from fifteen to twenty centimeters. Only fragments of this type of pottery have been found so far, and it is impossible at present to restore a whole vessel. However, the impression one obtains from the sherds indicates that the bowl was shallow bottomed and generally hemispherical in shape. Plate 6 includes a bottom sherd of this type of pottery. A small coil was attached as a stabilizing "foot" to the bottom of the vessel. A number of coils were also attached parallel to and below the rim, forming small ridges. Sherds in Plate 6 display applied, small ridges running diagonally to the left from the rim, meeting ridges running diagonally to the right and forming a hatched pattern. The firing temperature of this pottery seems to have been low.

The round-bottomed, deep vessel shown in Plate 1 has minute clay ridges around the rim. It is believed that this pottery type may be of a later date than the type represented by the sherds in Plate 6. Unlike the latter type, whose clay ridges have all been pinched with the tips of the fingers to form wavy lines, not all the Ishigoya cave pottery shows this feature. In the Plate 1 example there are two lines of wavy ridges directly below the rim and four lines of ridges somewhat below these. The lower four ridges were pinched between the tips of the thumb and forefinger and pressed into the body of the pot, resulting in extremely thin, welt-like broken lines.

🔳 NAIL-MARKING   The next pottery to appear shows a "nail-marked" pattern made by the thumbnail or the pointed end of a spatula-like instrument. The marks appear in several rows laterally and parallel to the rim.

273

The chronological relation between linear relief and nail-marked pottery has been fairly well established, but the transitional relationship between the two has not been clarified yet. It is conceivable that the two cultures may have been of a completely different character, but a definite conclusion must wait until new researches are conducted in the future.

Only sherds of nail-marked pottery (Plate 7) have been discovered so far; here, also, a full restoration of the original pottery has not yet been possible. Nail-marking appears in various patterns on the pottery—vertically, diagonally to the right and to the left, and laterally. Patterns running diagonally to the right are the most common. The sherds are thin—around five millimeters—so it is presumed that the original pottery was not large.

🕱 STRING- AND CORD-IMPRESSING   In the Osegasawa (also called Kosegasawa) cave in Niigata Prefecture, and the Hinata, Ichinosawa and Hibakoiwa caves in Takahata-chō, Yamagata Prefecture, layers of nail-marked pottery occur above a layer of linear relief pottery. Above this nail-marked material are layers containing various types of pottery with string and cord impressions. At the Hinata and Ichinosawa caves this pottery includes impressions made by pressing the top part of a cord and impressions, measuring about two centimeters, made by winding a string over the top of the thumb and pressing parallel to the rim. Both these types were excavated from the same layer. The upper layer has yielded sherds showing continuous imprints made by knotting the string and pressing the knot on the pottery surface with the thumb, as well as sherds with string-wrapped-stick cord-marking.

These patterns have not been created by rolling a cord over the clay, as is done in orthodox cord-marking. Instead, a cord was pressed into the clay surface with the fingertips. This type of marking appears after the nail-marked pottery.

The bottom layer of the Osegasawa cave has yielded sherds with a pattern presumed to have been made by a piece of stick, probably the size of a square matchstick, which was rolled and pressed on the surface of the pottery (Plate 8). Sherds showing carved stick rouletting have been excavated from the Hibakari site in Hachinohe, Aomori Prefecture. The Hibakari site also yielded pottery with zigzag variant and overlapping diamond rouletting. These patterns were made by a round stick about five centimeters in diameter, carved with the above-mentioned patterns and rolled across the clay surface.

🕱 IGUSA AND NATSUSHIMA TYPES   From layers indicating periods both before and after nail-marked and early rouletted pottery, string-impressed material (Plates 10–14) has been excavated in the southern Kantō area. The oldest is the Igusa type (Plate 10). Large sherds of this type have been excavated at the Igusa site in Tokyo, but not enough of the sherds have been found to make a complete restoration of the original pottery. It is thought that this type did not spread except somewhat to the south of the Kantō area.

Fig. 2, p. 281

Fig. 3

The Natsushima type vessel in Plate 11 shows a pattern made by two left-twisted cords that were doubled, twisted together, and rolled left diagonally from the rim, resulting in vertical cord-marking. The vessel of the same type in Plate 14 shows decoration made by coiling a right-twisted cord around a stick with a diameter of about eight millimeters, which was then rolled from the rim toward the bottom of the pot vertically. The Inaridai type vessel shown in Plate 16, dated later than the Natsushima type, is characterized by decoration made by cords wound at wider intervals on a stick, resulting in more widely spaced marks.

🔲 ŌGO TYPE   The flared-mouth, bomb-shaped and pointed-bottom vessel shown in Plate 36 is a restoration from pottery sherds excavated at the Ōgo (also called Ōko) site. The whole surface of the vessel is covered with a pattern of gouges made by a spatula-like instrument. Some vessels of this type have impressed patterns directly below the mouth and neck at equal intervals of approximately one centimeter. Some vessels display wavy patterns made by a spatula-like instrument.

Pottery with zigzag rouletting has been excavated in small quantities. The decoration was done with a cylindrical stick about eight millimeters in diameter and five centimeters long that was carved in wavy patterns around the stick in about five rings. Other rolled decoration was made by winding sticks with crisscrossed cords, resulting in diamond, square and rectangular lattice-pattern "rouletting." Other material indicates decoration conceivably made with a blank stick that was rolled across the surface of the pottery and strongly pressed by two fingers at equal intervals. This author believes that the Ōgo and Jinguji sites were transitional sites when the impressed decoration shifted to rouletting.

🔲 ROULETTING   Rouletting seems to have appeared after string- and cord-impressing, cord-marking, and cord-wrapped-stick cord-marking. The types of rouletting found at the Osegasawa cave, at the Hibakari site, at the Ōgo site and at the Jinguji site mentioned above must have preceded the types to be discussed below.

In the southern Kantō area, rouletted pottery appears after the Inaridai type, which included numerous patternless vessels. Patterns made by designs spirally carved on a stick appear only in the first half of the period when rouletting flourished. Such spiral carving seems to have disappeared with the advent of elliptical rouletting.

Sherds similar to the Inaridai type have also been excavated from the Ōhara site in Kawaguchi City, Saitama Prefecture, and at the Kurokawa Fumonji site in Hishi-machi, Kiryū City, Gumma Prefecture. Among the types of rouletting found here the zigzag rouletting was made by rolling the stick laterally in parallel with the rim and directly under it to form several lines of decoration on the collar of the pot. Under this, the same rouletting is displaced vertically to the bottom of the vessel. There are also numerous vessels displaying rouletting inside and parallel to the rim, as well as some on which one line of this rouletting appears on the rim lip.

A variation of this zigzag rouletting followed in time. Here, the stick is rolled once or twice around the rim and parallel to it and then vertically to the bottom of the vessel at intervals of two or three centimeters. Undecorated areas were smoothed with a spatula-like instrument.

Elliptical rouletting appears after this. This pattern is made by the following method. Three elliptical depressions are carved around the circumference of a small stick, beneath which another three fill the intervals, and so on for about six bands of ellipses. The result is a continuous pattern of bean-sized, uneven ovals on the surface of the pottery.

Plate 37 shows alternate zigzag and elliptical rouletting, which appears in a later period than the pottery mentioned above. Still later, elliptical rouletting predominates over zigzag, and the direction of the impressions becomes much more irregular, vertical, diagonal and lateral patterns being found on the same vessel.

Aside from zigzag, elliptical and diamond rouletting, small amounts of pottery with fishnet, trapezoid and concentric rouletting have been excavated. Of these, fishnet rouletting is distributed widely in the Chūbu district, appearing after the zigzag and diamond rouletting, but disappears during the period when elliptical rouletting flourished.

 SHELL-MARKING   Plate 28 shows a deep, pointed-bottom vessel of the Shirahama type. The vessel has been shell-scraped, leaving a more or less diagonal pattern of lines from the rim collar to the point. These marks were made with the "top" of the *Anadara subcrenata*. On the rim collar, the edge of the same shell was used to make vertical imprints, below which appear deep punctates made by a spatula-like instrument in a drag-and-jab manner.

The surfaces of the Shirahama type are completely covered with lateral shell-grooving, and below the rim are several horizontal bands of punctates made by the point of a spatula-like instrument. This is the most common pattern, but sometimes shell edge imprints also appear below the rim.

Plate 5 shows an example of a pointed-bottom vessel of the Sumiyoshichō type, and displays patterns that have been made by pressing the top of the "shoulder" of an *Anadara subcrenata* shell on the surface of the piece, as evidenced by the imprints of the back of the shell that can be seen on the upper half of the vessel. Aside from shell-impressing, zigzag grooving and shell-scraping, there are numerous Sumiyoshichō vessels with impressions made by the shoulder of the shell.

Fig. 1   Plate 30 shows a Funairijima Lower type vessel discovered below the shell layer of the Funairijima shell-mound. A single-twist (right twist) was used for the diagonal cord-marking. The interior of the vessel is shell-scraped. The same twisted string that was used to imprint the rim collar was rolled over the vessel body to form the cord-marking. This type of pottery occurred at the end of the Earliest or the beginning of the Early period.

Pottery of the Late Jōmon excavated from districts from the Inland Sea through Kyushu also have shell-impressions made by the shell top of an *Anadara* species or by a small cerithidea. But this shell-marking is visible only as grooves, the vessel surfaces having been smoothed by a spatula-like instrument.

From the end of the Middle through Late and Latest Jōmon, parts of the cord-marking were erased, with the result that the remaining decoration was laid out in zones. This method of erasing some cord-marking to form cord-marked zones spread to the northern half of Kyushu in the Late period. In the Inland Sea area and in the northern half of Kyushu, shell-impressing was treated in a similar manner to form a zoned pseudo-cord-marking.

 CORD-MARKING   The vessel in Plate 64 displays one form of herringbone cord-marking. Two right-twisted cords were left-twisted into one strand and rolled around the rim collar of the vessel to create a right-diagonal pattern. Under this, a left-diagonal pattern was made by rolling a right-twisted strand (composed of two left-twisted cords) across the surface of the piece. These right-and left-diagonal patterns alternate over the entire body of the piece in horizontal registers. Japanese archaeologists call herringbone "bird's-feather" pattern.

The vessels shown in Plates 54 and 55 are Entō Lower d types from the end of Early Jōmon. The "bird's-feather" pattern on this pottery was made by one piece of cord composed of right-and left-twisted cords. In Plate 55, the uppermost band derives from the left-twisted, and the band below that from right-twisted portion of the same cord made in the following manner. A right-twisted strand and a left-twisted strand were crossed at the middle and interlooped, the two ends of each strand being caught together. The two left-twisted ends were then left-twisted together, and the two right-twisted ends were twisted together correspondingly to the right. The single cord resulting, which changes direction at the middle, was then rolled laterally with the palm of the hand to create the "bird's-feather" cord-marking.

Fig. 4

Herringbone or "bird's-feather" cord-marking on Hanawadai type vessels (Plate 18) of Earliest Jōmon in the Kantō area differs from the types mentioned above in that a right-twisted cord was rolled laterally and then vertically to form the pattern distinctive of these vessels.

On the rim collars of Kikuna 2 type vessels are various types of impressed patterns made by pressing a single twisted string or strings into the surface of the pottery. Kikuna 2 also displays circular impressions made by the end of a small bamboo stick in the center of a string-impressed coil often resembling the fiddlehead of a fern. There are also vessels with slashes or punctates filling the spaces between the string-impressions.

Plate 71 shows a Sekiyama type vessel with a single rim spout. The cord-markings appear to be of the ordinary variety, but actually are not. Two cords were crossed in the middle and the four strand ends crossed over each other in a clockwise order (left strand first) like the braiding of a four-strand lanyard. A considerable quantity of Sekiyama type vessels display this type of cord-marking. The vessel in Plate 71 also has a stick-marked pattern of arcs and spirals superimposed on the cord-marking, which was made by the end of a bamboo stick split in two lengthwise. A split bamboo stick of this kind results in parallel line designs. This type of decoration was widespread in the Kantō area after the period of the Sekiyama type and up to the end of Early Jōmon.

Plate 83 shows a vessel of the Kaminoki type, found chiefly in the southern part of Nagano Prefecture. The cord-marking on this vessel shows one thick and two slender alternating impressions. At a glance it seems that the cord-marking was made by two slender cords and one thick cord twisted together, but this is not the case: the cord that produced the marking is quite complex. Two right-twisted strings (A) were left-twisted into a single strand (A'). Two left-twisted strings (B) were right-twisted into a single strand (B'). These two were then combined and left-twisted into a single thick cord (A'B'). The marking effect of two slender impressions and one thick impression was produced by the fact that the final left-twisting resulted in the right-twisted double strand (B')—that was originally two left-twisted strings (B)—unwinding and remaining as two parallel strings wound around the left-twisted double strand and thus creating the two slender impressions. The left-twisted double strand (A') made the thick impression. This type of cord-marking is found in large quantity among middle Early Jōmon pottery of eastern Japan, particularly the Sekiyama type. It also occurs rarely in pottery of the end of Earliest Jōmon, and after Middle Jōmon. Another Early Jōmon cord-marking variant was produced by right-twisting two pairs of left-twisted strands (thus making two cords) and left-twisting these into one cord.

Fig. 5

Fig. 6

The cord-marking seen on the Sekiyama vessels in Plates 68–70 was made by the following method. A piece of twisted string was folded in two, twisted together and a small loop left at the end where it was folded. This loop was then rolled across the surface of the vessel to form question-mark-like impressions. Plate 70 shows a vessel on which the impressions of the loop cover the body in lateral bands. Vessels with this type of pattern have been discovered in large quantities from the period when the Sekiyama type of the Kantō area and the Daigi 1 type of the southern Tōhoku region flourished.

Fig. 2

Among other cord-marking variants of eastern Japan in Early Jōmon is a lace-like pattern made by threading a twisted string through a strand of several twisted strings and winding it around the strand in a spiral.

🔖 CORD-WRAPPED-STICK CORD-MARKING The decoration on the vessel shown in Plate 53 is the so-called wood-grain pattern produced by string-wrapped-stick marking. It has an obvious resemblance to the grain of a vertically cut tree trunk. This pattern was most popular during the Entō Lower d type period at the end of Early Jōmon in the Tōhoku region. This pattern imprinted laterally can be found on the Daigi 2b type of middle Early Jōmon, also in the northern Tōhoku region. Vertically imprinted patterns, as shown in Plate 53, are found on pottery of the Daigi 7b type of the beginning of Middle Jōmon, as well as on vessels of the same period in the Hokuriku district. The wood-grain pattern was made by the following method. A slender piece of bamboo about eight centimeters in diameter was split slightly at one point, the middle of a twisted string was stuck inside this split, and both ends of the string were coiled right and left, respectively, around the bamboo, which was then rolled across the vessel surface (see Fig. 8).

The chain-like pattern seen on the body of the vessel in Plate 48 was made by the following method. A string was laid along the axis of a bamboo stick, then another string was wound once around the stick and tied to the first, wound once around again and tied to the first, and so on for the length of the stick. The result would be one of a cylinder tied closely with package-wrapping knots in a straight line. This type of rare impression is seen only on pottery excavated from the Tōhoku region in middle Early Jōmon.

Fig. 9 Fishnet-like patterns are made by the following method. Twisted string was wrapped around a slender bamboo stick at even intervals right diagonally; then another piece of twisted string was wrapped left diagonally, crisscrossing the right-diagonally wrapped string, and the resulting cord-wrapped stick rolled across the surface of the vessel. A small number of Hanazumi Lower type vessels with such patterns have been discovered in eastern Japan of Early Jōmon. Vessels with this type of decoration excavated from the southern Tōhoku region and northern Kantō area of Late and Latest Jōmon have been found in quantity. The cord-wrapped-stick rollers of the Late and Latest Jōmon, however, apparently used fiber bundles rather than bamboo sticks as the shafts upon which to wrap the cords.

Thus, during Early Jōmon, various types of complex cords were used to impress the surface of pottery. Several of such cord types existed from Early through Latest Jōmon. It is not known why the cord-marking of the beginning of Earliest Jōmon disappeared in western Japan during the latter half of the same period.

🔖 FROM EARLY TO MIDDLE JŌMON Jōmon culture saw an extraordinary development from the end of the Early period to the beginning of the Middle. This was due probably to great changes in the living environment of the Japanese people. A drastic change was also seen in pottery-making techniques during this period, and some of the pottery produced at this time defies comparison with anything produced elsewhere in the world. Several factors can be cited as reasons for the notable improvement in pottery making. The first is that an abundance of food caused an expansion in the size of the primitive communities, and the people were able to lead a more sedentary life. The second was that this abundance made it possible for the people to cultivate plants and vegetables, thus freeing them from a completely hunting and fishing existence. What type of plants and vegetables they cultivated at that time is a problem that must be solved by future study.

The method of making various types of patterns on pottery by splitting a piece of bamboo in two vertically and using the end of such a split stick to draw two parallel lines was seen in the Kantō area from the middle of Early Jōmon. This technique saw great improvement at the end of the Early period. Examples are shown in Plates 81, 82, 84 and Color Plate I. The "grass-and-flower" decoration shown in Plate 82 and Color Plate I has parallel lines laid out in rectilinear forms made by a split bamboo stick, over which button-like clay lumps and wafers have been applied to create a three-dimensional effect. Plate 105 shows an advanced type of this pottery made during the beginning of Middle Jōmon.

On entering the Middle period, a major culture sphere occurred in an area composed of the southern part of Nagano Prefecture, the upper reaches of the Tenryū River to Yamanashi Prefecture, down through the western part of Tokyo and the northwestern part of Kanagawa Prefecture. In recent years Eiichi Fujimori and others have conducted an extensive study of sites of this culture in the southern foothills of Mt. Yatsugatake in Nagano Prefecture. The first noteworthy report on this Middle Jōmon pottery culture was made by Dr. Kashiwa Ōyama in 1927 concerning the Katsusaka site in Sagamihara City, Kanagawa Prefecture. In the chronology of Kantō area Jōmon material, the Katsusaka type name has been used since the publication of Ōyama's report to denote a pottery of the first half of the Middle period. This author also uses this type name to denote this entire culture sphere.

As a result of the studies carried out at Mt. Yatsugatake, the first half of Middle Jōmon (the Katsusaka type pottery culture) is divided into seven types. The oldest is the Aramichi type pottery shown in Plates 111, 112, and 119. These vessels are restorations of three out of six pots excavated from the No. 1 pit-dwelling at the Aramichi site. Plate 119 shows a "nail-marking" pattern, made by continuous punching with the end of a split bamboo stick, which is a holdover of the decoration widespread at the end of Early Jōmon. The three-dimensional, ridged surfaces, which also began to appear at the end of Early Jōmon, saw a great development in the first half of the Middle period.

There is much ridged decoration during Middle Jōmon that is considered to have been patterned after the body of a snake. The vessels shown in Plates 128 and 129 correspond to the period when the Tōnai type was made. The ringlike handles are realistic depictions of a *mamushi* (a pit viper). The tops of two handles of the vessel shown in Plate 121 are believed to represent serpent heads. The Tōnai 1 vessel in Plates 124–125 also has decoration representing a snake. Realistic patterns are found in quantity during the time of the Tōnai type, but these subsequently become more stylized.

Some Middle Jōmon vessels display a human face inside the rim handle (Color Plate V). Also, Plates 138, 147, and 149–151 are examples of vessels that show strange figures in relief with three fingers, which may be taken either as human or as frogs. The unusual vessel in Plates 115–116 is a product of the first half of Middle Jōmon. Although it belongs to a different culture sphere, the relief decoration seems to resemble the three-fingered anthropomorphic figures.

In districts of eastern Japan the ridged decoration developed in the Middle period, but in western Japan it underwent a different type of development. (Plates 224–228).

On entering Late Jōmon, ridged decoration almost disappears. Shown in Plates 263 and 266 are vessels of the beginning of the Late period in the Kantō area. Vestiges of the ridged decoration of Middle Jōmon are visible on the rim handles, but the decoration on the body of the vessels has changed to grooving. During Earliest and Early Jōmon, there were many rectilinear geometric patterns, but the grooving of Late Jōmon contains more curved than straight lines.

Whereas twisted cords were used to create diagonal cord-marking in Early Jōmon by rolling the cord laterally, in the Middle period the cord was placed parallel to the rim of the pot and rolled vertically. This type of cord-marking was popular from the southern Tōhoku region to the eastern Kinki district.

Some cord-marking of Middle Jōmon was made by rolling the twisted cord diagonally over the surface of the pot to form vertical patterns. This type of pattern is particularly numerous in the Katsusaka pottery culture sphere. But in Late Jōmon most of the cord-marking reverts to diagonal patterns created by rolling the cord laterally on the vessel surface.

Fig. 10 An interesting cord-making pattern produced by a knotted cord is found on vessels of early Middle Jōmon in the eastern Kantō area and on middle Late Jōmon pieces of the southern Tōhoku region.

In the northern Tōhoku region in the last half of Late Jōmon, pottery with beautiful curvilinear grooving was produced. During the same period, jar-shaped vessels like those shown in Plates 232 and 233 came into vogue. During middle Late Jōmon, vessels like those shown in Plates 236 and 237 with beautiful, zoned cord-marking were produced.

The color of the vessels of the first half of Late Jōmon was an orange-brown, whereas the color of most of the zone cord-marked vessels of the middle and last half of the Late period was generally a lustrous blue-black. In the Kantō area numerous vessels exhibit this blue-black color in Late Jōmon. Shown in Plates 267–270 are flared vessels representative of the Kantō area in the last half of Late Jōmon. The decoration is an intricate combination of straight and curved grooving. Of the pottery of this period, there are zone cord-marked vessels and vessels without any cord-marking, as shown in Plates 275, 280, 283, 287–288, and 297. Bowl shapes of the middle Late Jōmon (Plates 287–289) show decoration on the inside of the rim.

The end of Late Jōmon sees two types of common decoration: one is bands of zoned cord-marking on the rim collar, and the other has hatching on the entire vessel surface, like that on the upper half of the vessel shown in Plate 311.

During the middle of Late Jōmon, zoned cord-marking was produced profusely from Hokkaido in the north to Kyushu in the south. However, in the southern part of Kyushu, in the Kagoshima district, only grooving was in vogue and there was hardly any cord-marking.

TERUYA ESAKA

Cord-marking Samples

1. *Musetsu:* simple linear; single-strand cord.

2. *Tansetsu:* simple beaded; double strand cord.

3. *Dai-isshu iwayuru yoriitomon:* beaded curtain; single-strand cord-wrapped stick.

4. *Ujō jōmon kessoku dai-isshu:* herringbone; double-direction-braided cord.

5. *Ijō shajōmon:* seersucker; 4-strand-braided, double-strand-untwisted cord.

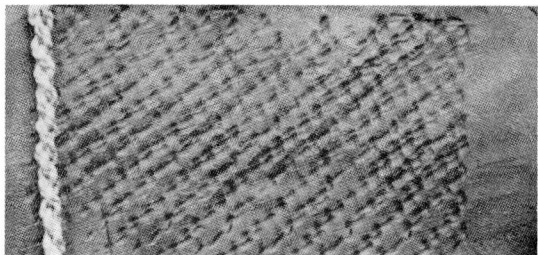

6. *Fukusetsu:* gunnysack; 4-strand-braided cord.

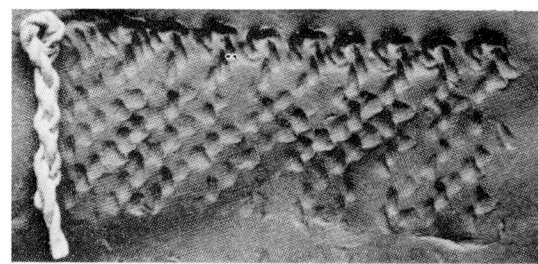

7. *Jōmon gentai no mattan no henka:* floret; **cord** loop.

8. *Iwayuru mokumejō yoriitomon:* wood grain; double-direction cord-wrapped stick.

9. *Iwayuru amijō yoriitomon:* fishnet; crisscross cord-wrapped stick.

10. *Kessetsu no kaiten:* coil; simple-knotted **double-**strand cord.

	DESIGN → TYPE ↓	LINEAR RELIEF	NAIL-MARKING	SHELL-SCRAPING	SHELL-IMPRESSING	SHELL-IMPRINTING	PUNCTATION	GROOVING	STRING- AND CORD-IMPRESSING
Latest	ARAMI							A	
	ANGYŌ 3c							A	
	ANGYŌ 3b							A	
	ANGYŌ 3a							C	
Late	ANGYŌ (2)							C	
	IWAI							C	
	SOYA							A	
	KASORI B 3							A	
	KASORI B 2							A	
	KASORI B 1							A	
	HORINOUCHI 2							A	
	HORINOUCHI 1							A	
	SHŌMYŌJI							C	
Middle	KASORI E 3							C	
	KASORI E 2							C	
	KASORI E 1							F	
	KATSUSAKA 3							F	
	KATSUSAKA 2							F	
	KATSUSAKA 1							F	
	GORYŌGADAI							F	
Early	KUSABANA							R	
	YONMAIBATA			F				R	
	YAGAMI			F	R	F		R	
	MIZUKO				R	F		R	
	KUROHAMA				R	F		F	
	SEKIYAMA				R			F	
	FUTATSUGI				R			F	
	NONAKA				R	F		F	
	SHIMOGUMI				F	F		F	
	KIKUNA 2		F		F	F		F	
	KIKUNA 1		A		C	F		F	
Earliest	KAYAMA UPPER		A				C	F	
	KAYAMA LOWER	C	A				C	F	
	NOJIMA	C	A				C	F	
	SHIBOKUCHI	F	A		F	F		F	
	TADO UPPER		F			F	C	C	
	TADO LOWER		F	F		F	C	A	
	MITO		C	F				A	
	HANAWADAI 2							R	
	HANAWADAI 1								
	INARIDAI								
	NATSUSHIMA								
	IGUSA								
	SAISHIKADA		A						
	HASHIDATE	A							
Southern Tōhoku	DAIGI 10								
	DAIGI 9								
	DAIGI 8b								
	DAIGI 8a								
	DAIGI 7b								
	DAIGI 7a								
	DAIGI 6								
	DAIGI 5								
	DAIGI 4								
	DAIGI 3								
	DAIGI 2b								
	DAIGI 2a								
	DAIGI 1								
	ZAŌ VII (HIBAKARI)								
	ICHINOSAWA 4								
	ICHINOSAWA 3								
	ICHINOSAWA 2		A						A
	ICHINOSAWA 1	A							
Northern Tōhoku	ENTŌ LOWER d1								
	ENTŌ LOWER c								
	ENTŌ LOWER b2								
	ENTŌ LOWER b1								

List of Collections

The Plate numbers of the objects in the respective collections are listed in parentheses; private collections are not included in this list. Local collections are usually found in proximity to the archaeological site of the object(s) included here.

Abashiri Regional Museum (346)
Araki Shrine (217)

Beppu University (41, 330, 427, 428)
Bihoro City Hall (27)

Chidō Museum (58, 60, 63)

Dōshisha University (36)

Gosen Municipal Education Committee (185, IX)

Hachinohe Commercial High School (100)
Hachinohe Municipal Education Committee (349, 383a, 386)
Hakodate Municipal Museum (24)
Heian School (39, 40)
Hirosaki Municipal Education Committee (233, 236, 243, 257, 258)
Hokkaido University (19, 20, 103, 230)
Hokugō Middle School (328)

Ichinomiya Municipal Education Committee (429)
Idojiri Archaeology Museum (117, 123–125, 128, 139–141, 146, 147, 149, 150, 155, 156, 158, 160–164, 166, 172, 174, frontispiece, V, VI)
International Christian University (178, 211)
Iwate University (53, 252, 256)

Kagoshima Prefectural Historical Research Society (95–97, 336–340)
Kansai University (91)
Keiō University (26, 28, 49, 54, 93, 94, 109, 222, 239, 249, 254, 282)
Kizukuri Municipal Education Commission (359)
Kōchi Prefectural Education Committee (327)
Kōfu Regional Museum (190)
Kokubunji Cultural Properties Commission (121, 136, 137)
Kokugakuin University (51, 79, 82, 84–87, 89, 177, 267, 296, 305, 360, 361, 377, 384, 395)
Kumamoto Municipal Museum (423)
Kunitachi First Middle School (138)
Kushiro Municipal Regional Museum (43, 341, 343–345, XV)
Kyoto Educational College (227, 228)
Kyōto University (38, 72, 92)
Kyushu University (419)

Matsumoto City Museum (157)
Meiji University (11–14, 23, 32, 42, 69, 74, 106, 255, 263, 266, 268, 269, 289, 295, 304, 307, 357, 363, 364, 372, 373, 375, 378, 388, 389, 402, 404, 406, 407)
Misaka East Middle School (120, 142, 143)
Miyazaki Prefectural Museum (329, 333, 422)

Morioka Regional Museum (154, 204, 207)
Murayama Agricultural High School (208)
Murayama City Hall (209)
Musashino Regional Museum (71, 108, 159, 264, 301, 405)

Nagaoka Municipal Science Museum (2–5, 31, 37, 46, 182, 184, 187–189, 194, 196, 199, 396, 409)
Nakui Agricultural High School (21)
Nanzan University (15, 68, 70, 286)
Nie City Hall (229)

Ōbunsha Publishing Company (88, 285)
Odajima City Hall (250, 251)
Osaka Municipal Art Museum (274, 280, 287, 288, 291, 292, 294, 299, 300, 302, 303, 309)

Sakai Remains Museum (152, 170, 201)
Seisui Temple (99, 213)
Shell-mound Preservation Society (279, 281)
Shizunai High School (104)
Shizunai Municipal Education Committee (231)
Sōma High School (247)
Sone Elementary School (322)
Suwa Archaeology Institute (80, 111, 112, 118, 119, I)

Takayama Regional Museum (77, 78)
Takizawa Grade School (350)
Tochio Municipal Education Committee (197, 198)
Togariishi Archaeology Museum (83, 105, 107, 126, 127, 132, 148, 214–216, 218)
Tōhoku University (29, 30)
Tokyo National Museum (52, 144, 145, 180, 232, 242, 265, 311, 315, 348, 367–369, 379, 394)
Tokyo Second Commercial High School (130, 131, 133, 153, 167, III)
Tokyo University (34, 48, 50, 98, 165, 210, 244, 246, 248, 262, 271–273, 275, 276, 278, 283, 290, 293, 306, 313, 314, 316, 318, 319, 342, 352, 358, 374, 393, 400, 401, VIII, XIX)
Towada City Hall (241)
Tsunagi Middle School (205, 206)
Tsuru High School (219)

Wakamiya Hachiman Shrine (331)
Wakayama Prefectural Education Committee (225)
Waseda University (55–57, 75, 76, 179, 308, 310, 353, 371, 376, 380, 387, 403, 408)

Yamagata University (202)
Yamashika High School (332, 420, 424)
Yamato History Hall (410–416)
Yoita Municipal Education Committee (181, 183, 186, 193, 200)
Yokosuka Municipal Museum (33, 35)

	IMPRESSING VARIANTS	ZIGZAG ROULETTING	LATTICE ROULETTING	ELLIPTICAL ROULETTING	DIAGONAL CORD-MARKING	COMPLEX TWISTED CORD-MARKING	HERRINGBONE CORD-MARKING	KNOTTED-CORD-MARKING	OBLIQUE VARIANT CORD-MARKING
				C —					
				C —					
				C —					
				C —					
				C —					
				C —					
				C —					
				C —		F I			
				C —	C II				
				A =	F I				
				A I					
				C /					
				C /					
				C /					
				C I					
				F —		C —			
				A =		A =	A =		
				A ≡		A ≡≡≡	C =	C —	F —
				A ≡		A ≡≡≡			
				A =		A =			
				F —					
	F	F	F	R —					
	C	C	F	R —					
	F	F		R —					
	R			A II =	A I				
				F /	C —				
				A //					
				A //					
				C I	C I				
				C I					
				C C A / — II					
				C A — II					
				C II					
				C III					
				C —					
					C				
A									
						C A I =			
				A —					
				A —					

This page is a chronological chart of Jōmon pottery types and their surface-treatment (design) techniques.

"WHEAT" PATTERN	KNOTLESS CORD-MARKING	CORD-WRAPPED STICK CORD-MARKING	WOOD-GRAIN PATTERN CORD-MARKING	NET-SHAPED CORD-MARKING	ZONED CORD-MARKING	BAMBOO-STICK-MARKING	INCISING	TYPE	(Period)
								ARAMI	Latest
								ANGYŌ 3c	
								ANGYŌ 3b	
						C		ANGYŌ 3a	
				C		C		ANGYŌ (2)	Late
				C		C		IWAI	
				C		C		SOYA	
				C		C		KASORI B 3	
				A		C		KASORI B 2	
				A		F		KASORI B 1	
				A		F		HORINOUCHI 2	
				A				HORINOUCHI 1	
				C				SHŌMYŌJI	
				C		C		KASORI E 3	Middle
				F		C		KASORI E 2	
						F		KASORI E 1	
								KATSUSAKA 3	
								KATSUSAKA 2	
					F			KATSUSAKA 1	
		R	I		C			GORYŌGADAI	
					A			KUSABANA	Early
R	I			R	A			YONMAIBATA	
R	I			R	A			YAGAMI	
R	I				A			MIZUKO	
F	I				C			KUROHAMA	
					C			SEKIYAMA	
					F			FUTATSUGI	
					R			NONAKA	
				R	R			SHIMOGUMI	
R	I				R			KIKUNA 2	
								KIKUNA 1	
						F		KAYAMA UPPER	Earliest
								KAYAMA LOWER	
								NOJIMA	
								SHIBOKUCHI	
						F		TADO UPPER	
						C		TADO LOWER	
								MITO	
								HANAWADAI 2	
								HANAWADAI 1	
								INARIDAI	
								NATSUSHIMA	
								IGUSA	
								SAISHIKADA	
								HASHIDATE	
				C				DAIGI 10	Southern Tōhoku
				C				DAIGI 9	
				F				DAIGI 8b	
						F		DAIGI 8a	
								DAIGI 7b	
		F	I					DAIGI 7a	
					A			DAIGI 6	
								DAIGI 5	
								DAIGI 4	
								DAIGI 3	
		F	I					DAIGI 2b	
								DAIGI 2a	
								DAIGI 1	
								ZAŌ VII (HIBAKARI)	
								ICHINOSAWA 4	
								ICHINOSAWA 3	
								ICHINOSAWA 2	
								ICHINOSAWA 1	
	C I	A II						ENTŌ LOWER d1	Northern Tōhoku
	R I	A R I						ENTŌ LOWER c	
								ENTŌ LOWER b2	
								ENTŌ LOWER b1	

DESIGN / TYPE

Incidence of Principal Jōmon Design Types in the Southern Kantō Area (including the southern and northern Tōhoku district)

KEY: A: abundant   C: common   F: few   R: rare

DIRECTION OF ROLLING OF CORD OR CORD-WRAPPED STICK			
	Vertical	Horizontal	Diagonal
Abundant	II	=	◇
Few	I	—	╱

Carbon$_{14}$-Dated Sites

Site and Location	Period and Associated Tools or Pottery	C$_{14}$-Laboratory
Yasumiba, Ashitaka, Kanaoka Numazu City, Shizuoka Pref.	Paleolithic; microblades	Gak-604
Fukui cave, VII, Yoshii-chō, Kitamatsuura County, Nagasaki Pref.	Paleolithic; microblades	Gak-951
Fukui cave, III, Yoshii-chō, Kitamatsuura County, Nagasaki Pref.	Earliest; linear relief	Gak-950
Fukui cave, II, Yoshii-chō, Kitamatsuura County, Nagasaki Pref.	Earliest; nail-marked	Gak-949
Kamikuroiwa rock-shelter, IX, Mikawa village, Kami-ukena County, Ehime Pref.	Earliest; linear relief	I-944
Kamikuroiwa rock-shelter, IV, Mikawa village, Kami-ukena County, Ehime Pref.	Earliest; nail-marked	I-943
Saishikada, Kasagake village, Nitta County, Gumma Pref.	Earliest; nail-marked	Gak-311
Natsushima shell-mound, Natsu-shima-chō, Yokosuka City, Kanagawa Pref.	Earliest; Natsushima type	M-770
Tochihara rock-shelter, Kita-aki village, Minamisaku County, Nagano Pref.	Earliest; rouletted	Gak-1056
Kijima shell-mound, Ushimado-machi, Oku County, Okayama	Earliest; Kijima type (rouletted)	M-237
Kojōhama, Ponayono, Shiraoi-chō, Shiraoi County, Hokkaido	end of Earliest (?)	I-551
Ōmagari cave, Abashiri City, Hokkaido	beginning of Early (?) (shell-marked)	GX-281
Ta shell-mound, 424 Jūwa, Yawara village, Tsukuba County, Ibaragi Pref.	Early; Sekiyama type	N-191-1
Kamo, Maruyama-chō, Awa County, Chiba Pref.	Early; Kurohama or Mizuko type	N-386

Site and Location	Period and Associated Tools or Pottery	C$_{14}$-Laboratory
Sobata shell-mound, Udo City, Kumamoto Pref.	Early; Sobata type	N-268
Ishigami, Tokomai, Morita village, Nishitsugaru County, Aomori Pref.	Early; Entō Lower d (?) type	N-242
I.C.U., Ōsawa, Mitaka City, Tokyo	Middle; Katsusaka and Atamadai types	UCLA-279
Ōmiyama, Kawakami village, Minamisaku County, Nagano Pref.	Middle; Katsusaka (?) type	SI-93
Todoroki shell-mound, Udo City, Kumamoto Pref.	Middle; Ataka type	N-317
Horinouchi shell-mound, Kokubu-chō, Ichikawa City, Chiba Pref.	Late; Horinouchi 1 type	N-59
Ōyu, Nakadōri, Ōyu, Towada-chō, Kazuno County, Akita Pref.	Late; Ōyu type	N-114
Sobata shell-mound, Udo City, Kumamoto Pref.	Late; Kanegasaki type	N-269
Takayagawa (right riverbank site), Yatsudai, Yokoshiba-machi, Sanbu County, Chiba Pref.	Late; Kasori B type	N-37
Ishigami shell-mound, Nishi-machi, Ishigami, Kawaguchi City, Saitama Pref.	Late; Angyō type	N-94
Yahatazaki, Onoue-chō, Minami-tsugaru County, Aomori Pref.	Latest; Ōhora B-C type	N-110
Shimpukuji peat layer, Iwatsuki City, Saitama Pref.	Latest	N-117-2
Nishippara, Owasu, Nasu-machi, Nasu County, Tochigi Pref.	Latest; Ōhora C 2 type	N-53
Arami shell-mound, Narita City, Chiba Pref.	Latest; Arami type	N-166-2
Tongsandong shell-mound, Zetsuei Island, Pusan, Kyongsangnamdo, Korea		GX-379

Gak: *Gakushuin University, Tokyo*
GX: *Geochron Laboratories, Cambridge, Mass., U.S.A.*
I: *Isotopes, Inc., Westwood, N.J., U.S.A.*

Abbreviations for C$_{14}$ Testing Laboratories

M: *University of Michigan, Ann Arbor, Michigan, U.S.A.*
N: *Riken: Institute of Physical and Chemical Research, Tokyo*
SI: *Smithsonian Institute, Washington D.C., U.S.A.*
UCLA: *University of California at Los Angeles, Calif., U.S.A.*

UPPER PALEOLITHIC　　　　　　　　　　**EARLIEST**

Chronological correlation chart (site names arranged in vertical columns; read left → right within each horizontal band). C₍₁₄₎ dates shown in **bold**.

Band	Sites (left → right)
1	Tachikawa · Todohokke · Kojōhama **B.C. 5750±200** · Ōmagari **B.C. 4845±150** · Sumiyoshichō 2 · Sumiyoshichō 1
2	Monomidai · Saibana · Hibakari · Shirahama · Kominatotai · Shimomatsu · Fukirizawa · Monomidai · Nōzuki · Akamido · Mushiri B 2 · Ruike · Fugōda · Kamikawana 2 · Shimogumi · Katsurajima · Nonaka · Murohama · Futatsugi
3	Ecchūyama · Ichinosawa 1 · Ichinosawa 2 · Ichinosawa 3 · Ichinosawa 4 · Ichinosawa 5 · Ichinosawa 6 · Zaō VII · Zaō VI · Soyama Lower · Daidera · Tsukinoki 2 · Zaō V · Soyama Upper · Kamikawana 1 · Funairijima Lower · Kikuna 2 · Kikuna 1 · Kayama Upper · Kayama Lower
4	Moro · Takei · Nemokami · Hashidate 1 · Saishikada **B.C. 8700±250** · Igusa · Natsushima **B.C. 7290±500** · Inaridai · Hanawadai · Mito · Tado Lower · Tado Upper · Shibokuchi · Nojima · Kasubata · Uenoyama · Irimi · Kijima
5	Yasumiba **B.C. 12,350±700** · Yanagimata B · Ishigoya VIII · Sone · Ishigoya VII · Tatsuno · Tochihara **B.C. 6650±180**
6	Ōgo · Kōzanji · Ishiyama I · Ishiyama { II · III · IV } · Ishiyama V · Ishiyama VI · (Azuchi Upper) · Kitashirakawa Lower 1
7	Miyatayama · Ishima 2 · Ishima 1 · Kishima **B.C. 6450±350** · Hajima Lower 1 · Hajima Lower 2
8	Kamikuroiwa IX **B.C. 10,215±600** · Kamikuroiwa VI **B.C. 8135±220** · Kamikuroiwa III · Kamikuroiwa II · Iwashita VII
9	Fukui VII **B.C. 11,750±600** · Fukui III **B.C. 10,750±500** · Fukui II **B.C. 10,450±350** · Iwashita VI · Iwashita V · Iwashita IV Lower · Todoroki Lower { 1 · 2 · 3 }

In the chart above, brackets [ ] indicate a C_{14} dated site that is not a type site; (+) designates an unnamed type; parentheses ( ) indicate temporary site names; all C_{14} dates are in **bold face.** Further information on the C_{14} dated sites appears on page 285.

LATEST	HOKKAIDO	NORTHERN TŌHOKU	SOUTHERN TŌHOKU	KANTŌ	CHŪBU	KINKI	SANYŌ	SHIKOKU	KYUSHU	OKINAWA AND Korea
	(+)	Kenyoshi	Ōhora A′	Arami **B.C. 340±120**	Kōri 2					*Susokri* **B.C. 390±120**
	(+)	Kuzusawa	Ōhora A		Kōri 1					
	Hinohama	Okamachi	Ōhora C 2	Nishippara (Ōhora C 2) **B.C. 750±170**	Sano 2	Karako 1	Takao	Nishikentō	Itatsuke 2	Gusukudake
	Menasawa	Taira	Ōhora C 1	Angyō 3c	Sano 1	Funabashi	Kurotsuchi B 2	Irita	Itatsuke 1	
	Kaminokuni	Yahatazaki **B.C. 870±130** / Korekawa / 6	Ōhora B-C	Shimpukuji **B.C. 990±130**		Kashiwara	Hara Lower	Nakamura 2 / Nakamura 1	Yusu	
			Ōhora B	Angyō 3b		(Tanji)			Yamanotera	
	Terugishi	Miyato 4	(Angyō 2) Angyō	Angyō 3a		Shiganosato	Kurotsuchi B 1	Hattantsubo	Kurokawa	
				Ishigami **B.C. 1140±120**				Arioka K		

YAYOI CULTURE

Jōmon Chronology

EARLY	MIDDLE	LATE

EARLY

Hokkaido Entō Lower
(+) (+) (+) (+) (+)

Entō Lower — Ishigami B.C. 2920 ±130
a2 b1 b2 c d1 d2

Daigi 1	Daigi 2a		Daigi 6 / 5 / 4 / 3 / 2b	Nukazuka	Daigi 7a
Ta B.C. 3690 ±130	Sekiyama / Kurohama	Minamiōhara	Kano B.C. 3340 ±140 (Moro-iso / Yonnai-bata / Yagami / Mizuko)	Goryōgadai	
Kaminoki	Ario		Uwappara / Shimojima / Harugamine / Kusa-bana	Kyūbei-One 1 / 2	Mujinazawa / Aramichi
Kitashirakawa Lower 2			Kitashirakawa Lower 3 / Ōtoshiyama	(Awazu)	
	Hajima Lower 3	Isonomori Lower	Isonomori	Hikozaki Early 1 / 2	Tai
			Minamikusagi	Funamoto	
	Karatsu	Sobata B.C. 3240 ±130		Sukumo Lower	
			Misari (?)	Amsari (?)	Tongsandong B.C. 2995

MIDDLE

Hokkaido Entō Upper
(+) (+) (+)

Saibana (Daigi 9) Entō Upper
a1 a2 b c d

Fudachi (+)

Daigi 7b	Daigi 8a	Daigi 8b	Daigi 9	Daigi 10	Monzen	Miyato 1 B.C. 1830 ±150
Atamadai or Katsusaka 1 / 2 / 3		Kasori E 1 / 2 / 3		Shōnyōji	Horinouchi 1 / 2	
Tōnai 3 / 2 / 1	Idojiri 3 / 2 / 1	Sori 3 / 2 / 1 / 4-5	Una-taka 3 / 2 / 1	Daianji		
I.C.U. Mitaka B.C. 2620 ±150	Omiyama B.C. 2630 ±60					
		Daigo 2	Daigo 3 / Bannome	Tenri K		
		Satogi 2	Fukuda C	Nakatsu		
			Shidehara	Shimomasuno		
			Ataka	Nanpukuji / Kitakuneyama		
		Todoroki (Ataka 2) B.C. 2130 ±180		Iha-Ogido		

LATE

Wakimoto | Irie | Teine | Ōyu B.C. 1730 ±130 | Toko-shinai
1 2 3 4 5

Nishinohama	(Angyō 1)
Miyato 2	Soya
Kasori B 1 / 2 / 3	Takayagawa B.C. 1120 ±120
U'enodan	Ichijōji K 1 / Kitashirakawa Upper
	Motosumi-yoshiyama 1 / 2 / Miyataki
Hikozaki K 1	Hikozaki K 2 / (Namikata) / Umatori / Fukuda K 3
Fukuda K 2	Sukumo / Mitarai B / Mitarai A
Hirose Upper	Kanegasaki / Kadena
Nishibira / Sobata B.C. 1350 ±125	Mimanda / Goryō
Attabaru B.C. 1420 ±80	Ōyama 1 / Chiyarubaru / Kayauchibanta

		BASE						RIM			
SHAPE / TYPE		ROUNDED	POINTED	GLOBULAR	RAISED	FLAT	FOOTED	FLAT	PEAKED	HANDLED	RIM HEAD
LATEST	ARAMI							C	C	F	
LATEST	ANGYŌ 3c					A		C	C	F	
LATEST	ANGYŌ 3a					A	F	C	C	F	
LATE	ANGYŌ 2					A	F	C	C	F	R
LATE	ANGYŌ 1					A	F	C	C	C	
LATE	SOYA					A	F	C	C	C	R
LATE	KASORI B					A	F	C	C	C	R
LATE	HORINOUCHI					A	F	C	C	C	
MIDDLE	KASORI E					A	F	C	C	C	
MIDDLE	KATSUSAKA					A	F	C	C	C	F
MIDDLE	ATAMADAI					A		C	C	C	R
MIDDLE	GORYŌGADAI					A		C	C	C	R
EARLY	KUSABANA					A		C	C	F	
EARLY	YOMAIBATA					A		C	C	C	F
EARLY	YAGAMI					A		C	C	F	
EARLY	MIZUKO					A		C	C		
EARLY	KUROHAMA					A		C	C		
EARLY	SEKIYAMA				F	A		C	C		
EARLY	FUTATSUGI				F	A		C	C		
EARLY	NONAKA				C	C		C	C		
EARLY	SHIMOGUMI				C			C	C		
EARLY	KIKUNA 2			C	C			C	C		
EARLY	KIKUNA 1	C		C	C			C	C		
EARLIEST	KAYAMA UPPER			C	C	C		C	C		
EARLIEST	KAYAMA LOWER	C		C				C	C	R	
EARLIEST	NOJIMA	A						C	C		
EARLIEST	SHIBOKUCHI	A	F					C	C	R	
EARLIEST	TADO UPPER	A	F			F		C	C	F	
EARLIEST	TADO LOWER	A						C	C		
EARLIEST	MITO	A						A			
EARLIEST	HANAWADAI 2	C	C			F		A			
EARLIEST	HANAWADAI 1	C	C			F		A			
EARLIEST	INARIDAI	C	C			F		A			
EARLIEST	NATSUSHIMA	C	C					A			
EARLIEST	IGUSA	C	C					A			

NAIL-MARKING C A*

LINEAR RELIEF C A**

OT"	SINGLE LIP-SPOUT	FOOTED CUP	FOOTED BOWL	"COMPOTE"	"INCENSE BURNER"	RED PAINT	LACQUER	TYPE	
						F	R	ARAMI	LATEST
			F	F		F	R	ANGYŌ 3c	LATEST
						F	R	ANGYŌ 3a	LATEST
		R	F	F	R	F	R	ANGYŌ 2	LATE
		R	F	F	R	F	R	ANGYŌ 1	LATE
		R	F	F	R	F	R	SOYA	LATE
	R	R	F	F	R	F	R	KASORI B	LATE
R						F	R	HORINOUCHI	LATE
						F	R	KASORI E	MIDDLE
	R					F	R	KATSUSAKA	MIDDLE
						F		ATAMADAI	MIDDLE
						F	R	GORYŌGADAI	MIDDLE
						F	R	KUSABANA	EARLY
						F		YOMAIBATA	EARLY
								YAGAMI	EARLY
								MIZUKO	EARLY
								KUROHAMA	EARLY
	F							SEKIYAMA	EARLY
								FUTATSUGI	EARLY
								NONAKA	EARLY
								SHIMOGUMI	EARLY
								KIKUNA 2	EARLY
								KIKUNA 1	EARLY
								KAYAMA UPPER	EARLIEST
								KAYAMA LOWER	EARLIEST
								NOJIMA	EARLIEST
								SHIBOKUCHI	EARLIEST
								TADO UPPER	EARLIEST
								TADO LOWER	EARLIEST
								MITO	EARLIEST
								HANAWADAI 2	EARLIEST
								HANAWADAI 1	EARLIEST
								INARIDAI	EARLIEST
								NATSUSHIMA	EARLIEST
								IGUSA	EARLIEST

APPLIED PIGMENT
SHAPE / TYPE

Shape Incidence Among Southern
Kantō Area Pottery Types

							BODY				
SNAKE	GLOBULAR-BOTTOMED POT	HEMISPHER-ICAL BOWL	CONICAL POT	BULLET-SHAPED POT	CYLINDRICAL POT	FLARED POT	COOKING POT	SHOULDERED JAR	NARROW-BASED BOWL	PLATE	"T
							C	F	C		
							C	F	C		
							C				
				C			C				
				C		C	C	F	C	C	
						C	C	F	C	C	
					C	C	C	F	C	C	
					C	C	C	F	C		
F					C	C	C	F	C		
F					C	C	C		C		
					C	C	C		C		
					C	C	C		C		
					C	C	C		C		
					C	C	C		C		
					C	F	C		C		
					C	F	C		F		
					C	F	C		F		
					C	F	C				
					C	F	C				
					C	F	C				
					C		C				
					C		C				
					A		C				
				F			C				
				C							
				A							
				A							
				A							
			A	C							
				C							
			F	A							
			F	A							
				C							

A*

A**

JŌMON SITE MAP

PREFECTURES (*encircled numbers on map*)

1. Aomori	16. Yamanashi	31. Okayama
2. Iwate	17. Toyama	32. Shimane
3. Miyagi	18. Shizuoka	33. Hiroshima
4. Akita	19. Ishikawa	34. Yamaguchi
5. Yamagata	20. Fukui	35. Kagawa
6. Fukushima	21. Gifu	36. Tokushima
7. Ibaragi	22. Aichi	37. Ehime
8. Tochigi	23. Shiga	38. Kōchi
9. Gumma	24. Kyoto	39. Fukuoka
10. Saitama	25. Nara	40. Saga
11. Chiba	26. Mie	41. Nagasaki
12. Tokyo	27. Wakayama	42. Kumamoto
13. Kanagawa	28. Osaka	43. Ōita
14. Niigata	29. Hyōgo	44. Miyazaki
15. Nagano	30. Tottori	45. Kagoshima

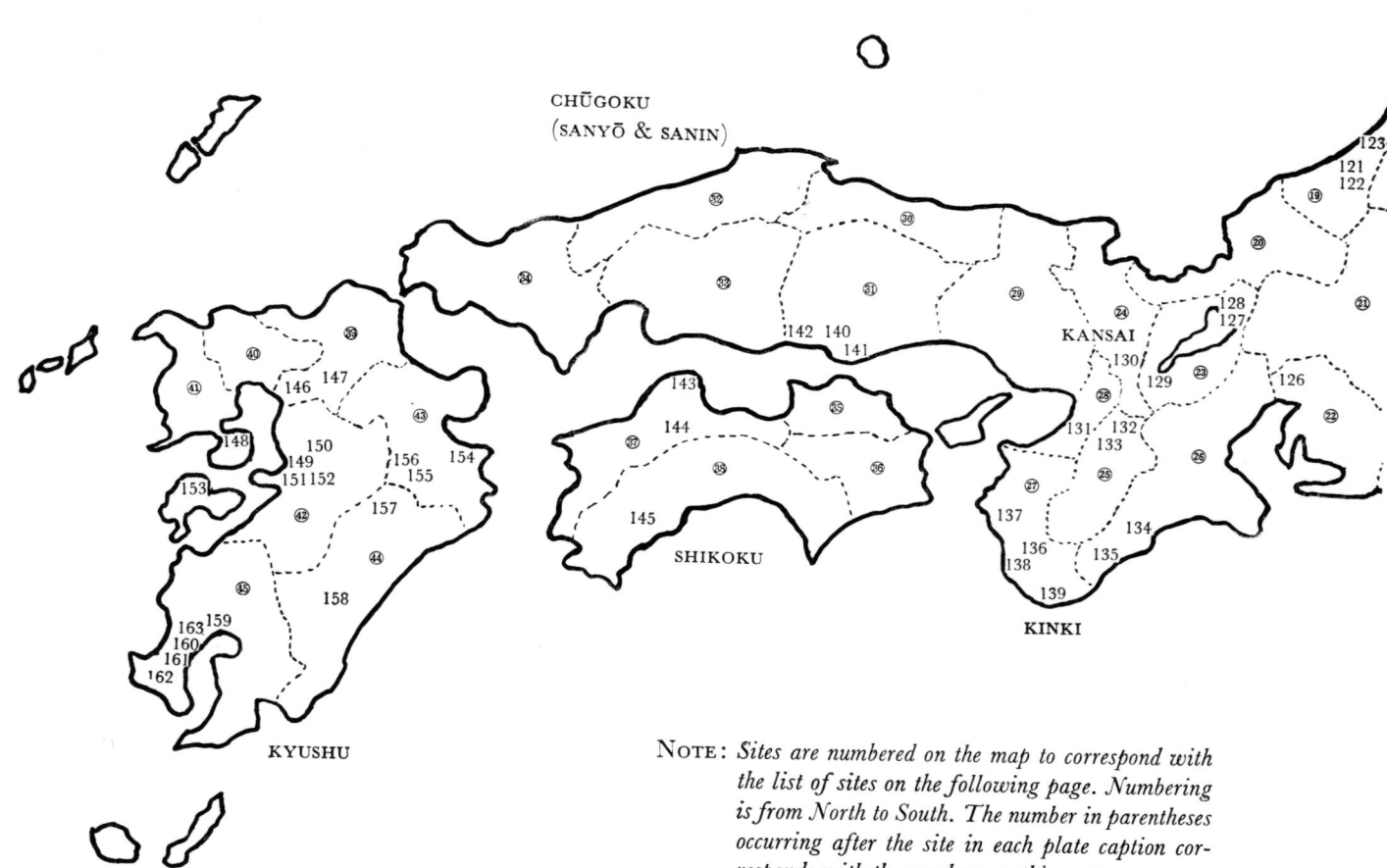

NOTE: *Sites are numbered on the map to correspond with the list of sites on the following page. Numbering is from North to South. The number in parentheses occurring after the site in each plate caption corresponds with the numbers on this map.*

Archaeological Site List

Parentheses ( ) enclose Plate numbers; an asterisk* indicates a shell-mound; hyphenization of administrative subdivisions is eliminated in the site names (i.e., Akitachō, Nishitama County; Nakasugao, Akita-chō, Nishitama County). The Hokuriku district includes Fukui, Ishikawa, Toyama and Niigata prefectures; the Tōkai coastal area includes Shizuoka, Aichi, Mie and sometimes part of Gifu prefectures.

HOKKAIDO

1. Oshōnnai, Funadomari (Rebun Island), Rebun village, Rebun County (230)
2. Ōmagari, Abashiri City (346)
3. Mitsuhashi, Bihoro-chō (27)
4. Midorigaoka, Kushiro City (343, 345)
   Okitsu, Kushiro City (344)
   Nusamai, Kushiro City (341, XV)
   Higashikushiro*, Kushiro City (43)
5. Higashikagura, Asahikawa City (44)
6. Urawa, Shizunai-chō, Shizunai County (104)
   Gotenyama, Shizunai-chō, Shizunai County (231)
7. Kojōhama, Shiraoi-chō, Shiraoi County (20)
8. Todohokke village, Kameda County (24)
9. Saibesawa, Nishikikyō, Kikyō, Kameda-chō, Kameda County (103)
10. Sumiyoshichō, Hakodate City (19, 42)

TŌHOKU   AOMORI PREFECTURE

11. Mushiri, Shiriya, Higashidōri village, Shimokita County (49)
12. Ōminatomachi, Mutsu City (272)
13. Obuchi, Rokkashō village, Kamikita County (23)
    Hiranuma, Rokkasho village, Kamikita County (379)
14. Sannai, Aomori City (102)
    Nagamori, Miyata, Aomori City (362)
15. Nagakubo, Shichinohe-chō, Kamikita County (240)
16. Takaya, Takizawa, Towada City (350)
    Yakata, Towada City (241)
    Fudōdō, Towada City (234)
    Kawahara, Takizawa, Towada City (347)
17. Momoishichō, Kamikita County (351)
18. Chōshichiyachi*, Araida, Hachinohe City (25, 26)
    Tatehira, Hachinohe City (28)
    Kanisawa, Hachinohe City (54—57)
    Ichiōji*, Korekawa, Hachinohe City (48, 50, 52, 98, 99, 101, 213)
    Nagane, Tōka-machi, Hachinohe City (100)
    Nakai, Korekawa, Hachinohe City (349)
    Yawata, Hachinohe City (383)
    Hachinohe City (386)
19. Yonden, Kanayamazawa, Hashikami village, Sannohe County (235)
20. Terashita, Nagawa-chō, Sannohe County (381)
    Nozuki, Morikoshi, Nagawa-chō, Sannohe County (21)
21. Matsubara, Umenai, Sannohe-chō, Sannohe County (354-355)
    Hachigasaki, Sannohe-chō (356)
    Yōkamachi, Sannohe-chō, Sannohe County (383a)
    Kamiyashiki, Sannohe-chō, Sannohe County (390-391)
22. Kamegaoka, Kizukuri-chō, Nishitsugaru County (359, XIV, XVI)
23. Hosono, Namioka-chō, Minamitsugaru County (376)
24. Sarusawa, Tokoshinai, Hirosaki City (233, 236)
    Tokoshinai, Hirosaki City (242, 243, 257, 258, 385)
    Sunazawa, Hirosaki City (375, 388, 389)

IWATE PREFECTURE

25. Amataki, Kindaichi village, Ninohe County (357, 363, 364, 367, 372, 373)
    Shirayama, Shitazaki, Kindaichi village, Ninohe County (365-366)
    Kindaichigawa, Kindaichi village, Ninohe County (368, 425-426)
26. Karumai, Karumai-chō, (245)
27. Tashiro, Kunohe village, Kunohe County (53)
28. Ushimadate, Shimotomai, Fukuoka-chō, Ninohe County (237, 239)
29. Makumaitai, Ichinohe-chō, Ninohe County (382, 392)
30. Chōjayashiki, Matsuo village, Iwate County (370)
31. Hinoto, Tamayama village, Iwate County (252)
32. Hataino, Morioka City (154)
    Oyama, Higashinakano, Morioka City (207)
    Kawame, Morioka City (256)
33. Tsunagi, Shizukuishi-chō (205-206)
34. Botan-batake, Kitakami City (353, 380)
35. Shimizu*, Ōfunato City (59)
    Ōbora*, Ōfunato City (352, 374)
36. Nonzen*, Otomo-machi, Rikuzen-takata City (204)

MIYAGI PREFECTURE

37. Ōtera, Takashimizu, Tsukidate-chō, Kurihara County (29)
38. Nukazuka*, Hasama-chō, Tome County (61-62)
39. Takaragamine, Kanan-chō, (298)
40. Daigi-gakoi*, Shichigahama-machi, Miyagi County (210, 211)
41. Funairijima*, Urato, Shiogama City (30)
42. Minamisakai*, Ishinomaki City (II)

AKITA PREFECTURE

43. Ōno, Niyawata, Noshiro City (360, 384)
44. Nakayama, Gojōme-chō, Minamiakita County (358, 393)
45. Nanukaichi, Takanosu-chō, Kita-akita County (232)
46. Ōyu, Towada-chō, Kazuno County (254)
    Manza, Ōyu, Towada-chō (255)
47. Higashizage, Osarizawa, Osarizawa-chō, Kazuno County (361, 377)
48. Shizumukai, Hachimantai village, Kazuno County (51)
49. Ishinadate, Rokugo-machi, Senboku County (348)

YAMAGATA PREFECTURE

50. Kanisawa, Higashine City (250-251)
51. Fukura, Yusa-chō, Akumi County (58, 60, 63)
52. Ichinosawa rock-shelter, Takahata-chō, Higashi-okitama County (7)
53. Shirasuka, Ōkura village, Mogami County (203)
54. Ochiai, Murayama City (208)
    Ogonizawa, Shiratori, Murayama City (209)
55. Shibahashi, Sagae City (202)

FUKUSHIMA PREFECTURE

56. Sanganji*, Shinchi village, Sōma County (244, 246, 247, 262)
    Ogawa*, Shinchi village, Sōma County (248)
57. Shiozawa, Nihonmatsu City (261)
58. Ōhira, Shimo-okeuri, Kawamae, Iwaki City (238, 249)

KANTŌ   IBARAGI PREFECTURE

59. Fukuda*, Higashi village, Inashiki County (271, 274, 283, 290, 297, 302, 309, 316, 319, 399, XI)
60. Shiizuka*, Edozaki-chō, Inashiki County (273, 278, 280, 287-288, 294, 299, 300, 303)
61. Hanawadai*, Hayao, Tone-chō, Kita-sōma County (15, 18)
    Tachigi*, Tone-chō, Kita-sōma County (293)
62. Okitsu*, Miho village, Inashiki County (75, 76)
    Okadaira*, Miho village, Inashiki County (275)
63. Hirohata*, Sakuragawa village, Inashiki County (301)

TOCHIGI PREFECTURE

64. Batōchō, Nasu County (277)
65. Shinoyama*, Fujioka, Fujioka-chō, Shimotsuga County (69)
66. Nowata*, Nogi village, Shimotsuga County (72)

GUMMA PREFECTURE

67. Ōne, Nitta-chō, Nitta County (212, 220, 221)
68. Nishiyokono, Matsuida-chō, Usui County (67)

SAITAMA PREFECTURE

69. Kaizuka*, Kurohama, Hasuda-chō, Minami-saitama County (73)
70. Shimpukuji*, shell-mound, Iwatsuki City (318, 394, 400, 401)
71. Ishigami*, Kawaguchi City (312)

CHIBA PREFECTURE

72. Yoyama*, Chōshi City (291, 292, 296, 314, 315, XIII)
73. Shironodai*, Omigawa-chō, Katori County (22)
    Kaizuka*, Omigawa-chō, Katori County (279, 281)
74. Nado*, Daiei-chō, Katori County (308, 310, 403)
75. Arami*, Neda, Narita City (371, 387, 408)
76. Tobe*, Sakura City, Inba County (295)
77. Tenjindai, Inzai-chō, Inba County (317)
78. Samukaze*, Kashiwa City (179)
79. Futatsugi*, Kogane-chō, Matsudo City (68, 70)
80. Kanoezuka*, Ichikawa City (74)
    Narukamiyama*, Ichikawa City (106)
    Soya*, Ichikawa City (263, 266, 269, 307)
    Ubayama*, Ichikawa City (268, 286, 289, 304)
    Horinouchi*, Ichikawa City (270, 406)
81. Tobinodai*, Kaijin-chō, Funabashi City (34)

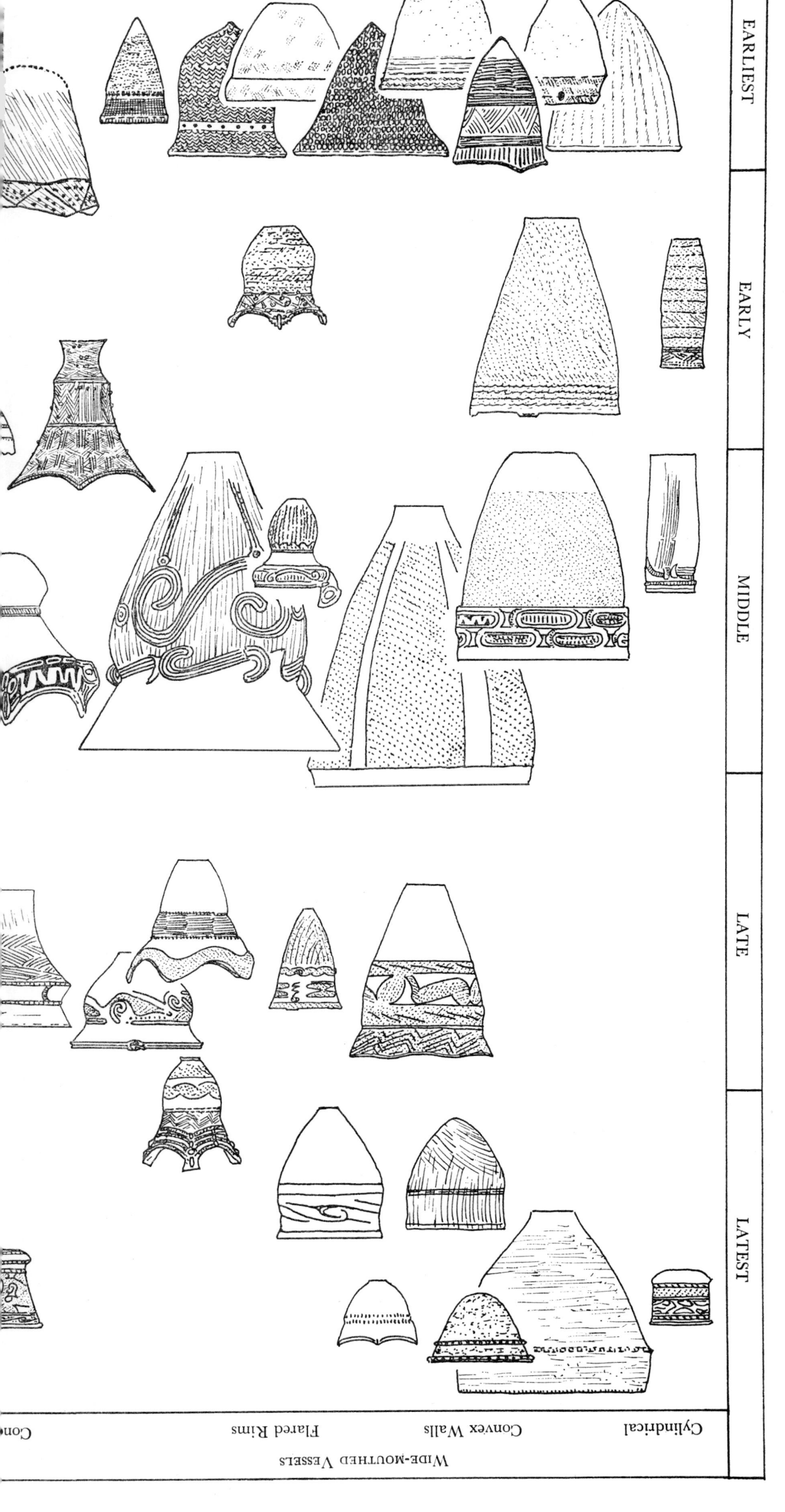

Con

Flared Rims

Convex Walls

Cylindrical

WIDE-MOUTHED VESSELS

Shape Development Chart

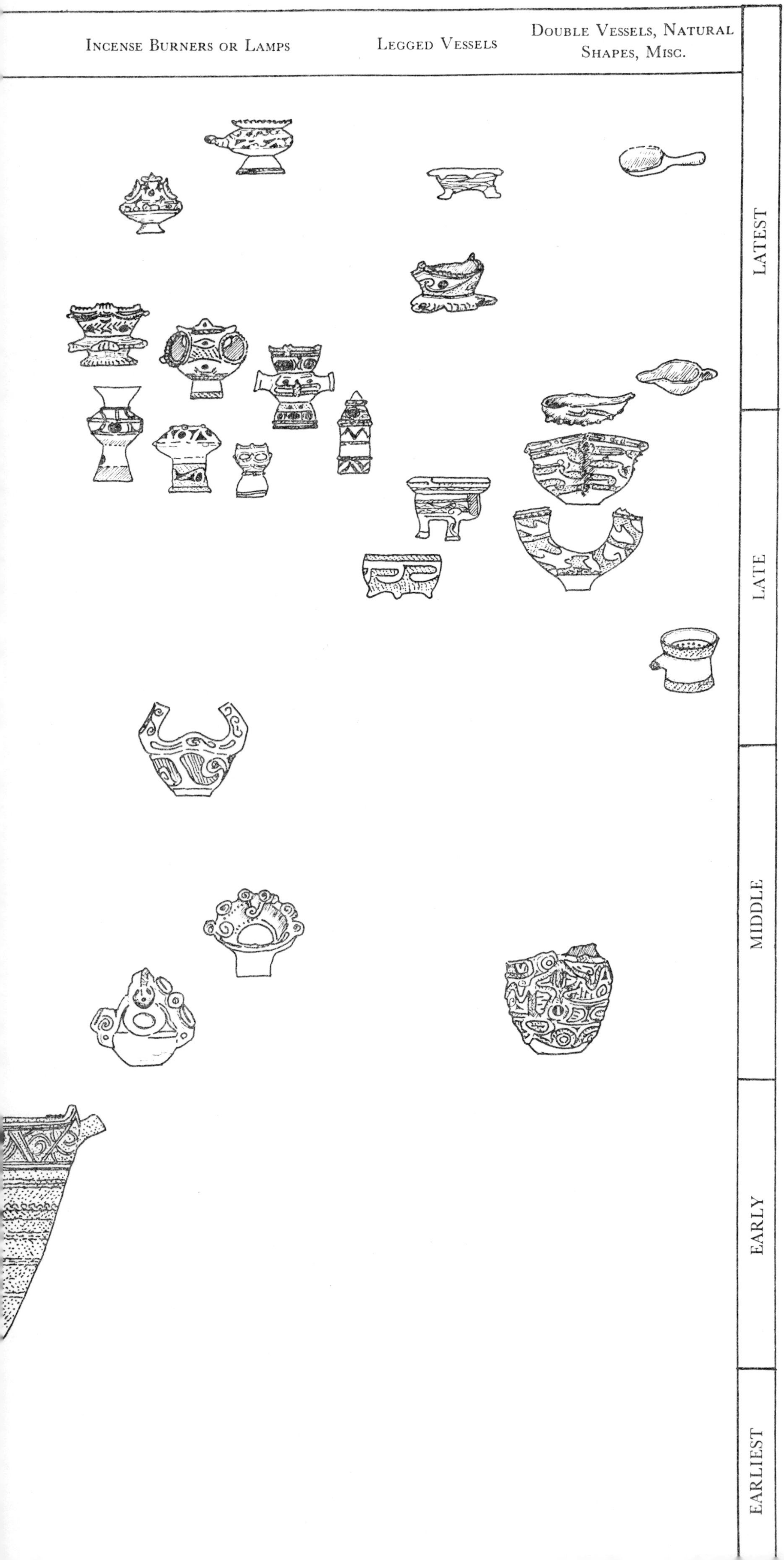

Incense Burners or Lamps
Legged Vessels
Double Vessels, Natural Shapes, Misc.
LATEST
LATE
MIDDLE
EARLY
EARLIEST

Pedestaled Vessels | Bottles | Spouted Vessels

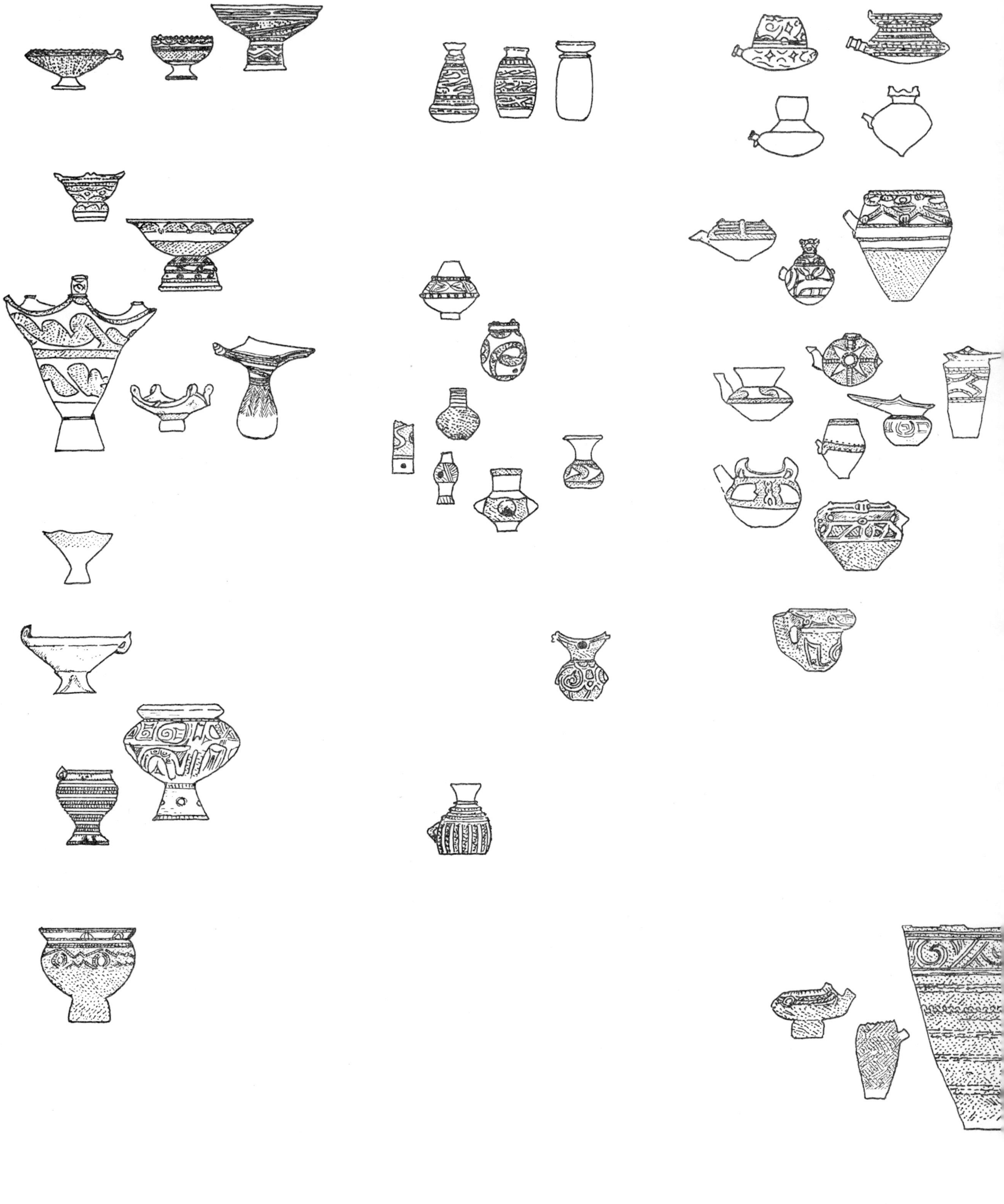

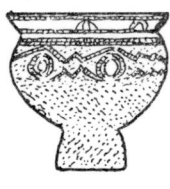

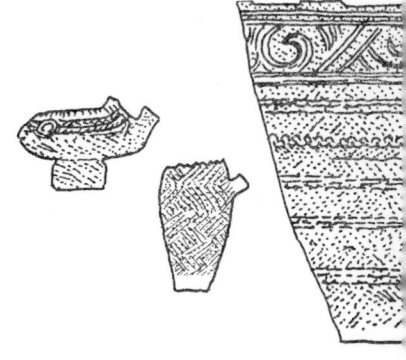

Bibliography and Chapter Notes

For fuller bibliographies the reader is referred to the publication by the Archaeology Society, *Kōkogaku Zasshi Sōmokuroku (General Index to Archaeological Magazines)*, Tokyo, 1943; Okamoto and Asō, *Nihon Sekki Jidai Sōgō Bunken Mokuroku (Bibliography of the Stone Age of Japan)*, 1958; and Kidder, *Jōmon Pottery of Japan*, 1957, pp. 153–186, in which all items are given in translation. There are also several complete local and regional compilations. Many reports in Japanese journals are accompanied by an English title and occasionally a summary in English, German or French. (*Chapter Notes start on page* 298.)

ABBREVIATIONS

JB   *Jōdai Bunka—Culture of Antiquity*
JGSK   *Jinruigaku Senshigaku Kōza—Symposium on Anthropology and Prehistory*
JGZ   *Jinruigaku Zasshi—Journal of Anthropology*
KB   *Kodai Bunka—Ancient Culture*
KGZ   *Kōkogaku Zasshi—Journal of Archaeology*
NK   *Nihon Kōkogaku—Japanese Archaeology*
SGZ   *Shizengaku Zasshi—Journal for Prehistory*
SJ   *Sekki Jidai—Stone Age*
SKG   *Senshi Kōkogaku—Prehistoric Archaeology*

Akaboshi, N., and N. Sakazume, "Kanagawa-ken Miura-gun Misaki-chō Moroiso kaizuka ni okeru tateana jūkyoshi hakkutsu ni tsuite," (On the excavation of pit-dwellings in the Moroiso shell-mound, Misaki-chō, Miura County, Kanagawa Prefecture), *SGZ*, X–3, 1938, 25–38.

Asō, M., "Jōmon doki no hensen ni okeru zenki jōmon doki," (The position of the type termed Early Jōmon in the development of Jōmon pottery), *Saiko Bunka* (West Suburbs Culture), VII, 1954, 27–30.

Beardsley, R. K., "Japan Before History: A Survey of the Archaeological Record," *The Far Eastern Quarterly*, XIV–3, 1955, 317–346.

Bunkazai Hogoiinkai (Commission for the Protection of Cultural Properties), *Yoshigo Kaizuka* (Shell-mounds of Yoshigo), Tokyo, 1952.

—— *Ōyu-machi Kanjō Resseki* (Stone Remains of Ōyu-machi), Tokyo, 1953.

Crane, H. R., and J. B. Griffin, "University of Michigan Radiocarbon Dates V," *Radiocarbon Supplement*, 2, 1960, 31–48.

Egami, N., T. Sekino and K. Sakurai, *Tate-shi* (Tate Sites), Tokyo, 1958.

Esaka, T., "Jōmon bunka ni tsuite," (On the Jōmon culture), *Rekishi Hyōron* (History Review), 13 serial articles in issues 23–35, 1950–52.

—— *Jōmon Bunka: Senshi Jidai*, II (Jōmon Culture: Prehistoric Period, II), Tokyo, 1957.

—— "Jōmon bunka no jidai ni okeru shokubutsu saibai kigen no mondai ni kansuru ichikōsatsu," (On the possibility that vegetable cultivation originated in the Jōmon period culture), *KGZ*, XLIV–3, 1959, 10–16.

Fujimori, E., *Idojiri*, Tokyo, 1965.

Fujimori, E., and Y. Mutō, "Chūki jōmon doki no chozōkeitai ni tsuite," (On storage vessels of Middle Jōmon), *Kōkogaku Techō* (Handbook of Archaeology), 20, 1962, 1–6.

Fujita, R., (ed.), *Nihon Kōkogaku Jiten* (Dictionary of Japanese Archaeology), Tokyo, 1963.

Gotō, S., "Jōko jidai no jūkyo," (Dwellings of ancient times), *JGSK*, 15, 1940, 1–79; 16, 1941, 80–156; 17, 1941, 157–208.

—— (ed.), "Horinouchi kaizuka hakkutsu," (Excavation of the Horinouchi shell-mound), *JGZ*, LXV–5, 1957 (entire issue).

Groot, G. J., *The Prehistory of Japan*, New York, 1951.

Groot, G. J., and Y. Shinoto, *The Shell Mound of Ubayama*, Ichikawa City, 1952.

Hasebe, K., "Rikuzen Ōbora kaizuka hakkutsu chōsa shoken," (Personal observation on the excavation of the Ōbora shell-mound in Rikuzen), *JGZ*, XL–10, 1925, 340–360.

—— "Entō doki bunka," (Cylindrical pottery culture), *JGZ*, XLII–1, 1927, 28–41.

—— "Jōmon to ketsubaku sūhai," *NK*, 1–2, 1948, 1–3.

Iijima, I., and C. Sasaki, *Okadaira Shell-mound at Hitachi*, Memoirs of the Science Department, University of Tokyo, 1883.

Ishida, E., and S. Izumi, *Nihon Nōkō Bunka no Kigen* (The Origins of Japanese Agrarian Culture), Tokyo, 1968.

Ishizawa, T., T. Sato, T. Takeda and H. Tachibana, *Hokkaido no Senshi Bunka* (The Prehistoric Culture of Hokkaido), Asahikawa Regional Museum, 1960.

Kamaki, Y., (ed.) *Nihon no Kōkogaku II: Jōmon Jidai* (Archaeology of Japan II: Jōmon Period), Tokyo, 1965.

Kashiwara Kōkogaku Kenkyūjo (Kashiwara Archaeological Institute), *Kashiwara*, Nara, 1961.

Katō, M., and Y. Sasaki, "Yamagata-ken Ichinosawa iwakage iseki," (Ichinosawa rock shelter in Yamagata Prefecture), *JB*, 31–32, 1962, 33–47.

Kawaguchi, S., "Minami Kyushu Jōmon-shiki bunka no kenkyū," (Study of Jōmon type culture in south Kyushu), *Kagoshima Kōkogakkai Kaihō* (Reports of the Kagoshima Archaeology Society), 3, 1953, 6–20.

Kida, T., and S. Sugiyama, *Nihon Sekki Jidai Shokubutsusei Ibutsu Zuroku* (Plates Illustrating the Vegetal Remains of the Japanese Stone Age), Tokyo, 1932.

Kidder, J. E., "The Kamegaoka Vessels in the City Art Museum, St. Louis," *Artibus Asiae*, XVI–3, 1953, 198–208.

—— *The Jōmon Pottery of Japan*, Ascona, 1957.

—— "The Stone Circles of Ōyu," *Archaeology*, II–4, 1958, 232–238.

—— *Japan Before Buddhism*, London and New York, 1959.

—— "Pre-pottery and Jōmon Pottery Relationships on the I.C.U. Campus, Tokyo," *Artibus Asiae*, XXII–1/2, 1959, 79–94.

Kidder, J. E., and S. Koyama, "C–14 nendai kara mita jōmon jidai no hennen," (C–14 implications for Jōmon period chronology), *JB*, 37, 1967, 1–6.

Kiyono, K., *Nihon Genjin no Kenkyū* (Study of Japanese Primitive Man), Tokyo, 1925.

——*Nihon Sekki Jidai-jin Kenkyū* (Study of Japanese Stone Age Man), Tokyo, 1928.

——*Nihon Jinshu-ron Hensen-shi* (History of Change of the Japanese Race), Tokyo, 1944.

Kobayashi, H., "Kyushu no jōmon doki," (Jōmon pottery of Kyushu), *JGSK*, 11, 1939, 1–48.

Kokugakuin Daigaku Kōkogakkai (Archaeological Association of Kokugakuin University), *Mudoki Bunka kara Jōmon Bunka no Kakuritsu made* (From the Non-ceramic Culture to the Establishment of the Jōmon Culture), Tokyo, 1962.

Komai, K., *Otoe: Hokkaido Kanjō Resseki no Kenkyū* (Otoe: Study on the Stone Circles of Hokkaido), Tokyo, 1959.

Komura, H., *Tōkai no Senshi Iseki* (Prehistoric Sites of Tōkai), Nagoya, 1963.

Kōno, H., and T. Natori, "Hokkaido no senshi jidai," (Prehistoric period of Hokkaido), *JGSK*, 6, 1938, 1–41.

Kōno, I., *Jōmon Doki no Hanashi* (The Story of Jōmon Pottery), Tokyo, 1953.

Koyama, F., (ed.), *Sekai Tōji Zenshū* (Catalogue of World's Ceramics), I, Tokyo, 1958.

Kusama, S., and Y. Yoshida, *Iwate-ken Morioka-shi Hataino Iseki Chōsa Hōkoku* (Report on Investigation of the Site of Hataino, Morioka City, Iwate Prefecture), Morioka City Industry-Cultural Museum, Morioka, 1960.

Matsumoto, H., "Notes on the Stone Age People of Japan," *American Anthropologist*, (new series), XXIII-1, 1921, 50–76.

Matsumoto, N., R. Fujita, J. Shimizu and T. Esaka, *Kamo Iseki* (Remains of Kamo), Tokyo, 1952.

Matsumura, R., I. Yawata and R. Koganei, *Shimofusa Ubayama ni okeru Sekki Jidai Iseki* (The Stone Age Remains at Ubayama, Shimofusa), Papers of the Anthropological Institute of the Imperial University of Tokyo, 5, Tokyo, 1932.

Mitsumori, S., "Senshi jidai no seibu Nihon" (The prehistoric period of west Japan), *JGSK*, 1, 1938, 1–33; II, 35–72.

Miyasaka, E., *Togariishi*, Kayano, 1957.

Miyasaka, M., "Aomori-ken Korekawa-mura Ichiōji shizen jidai iseki chōsa hōkoku," (Report on the investigation of the prehistoric period remains of Ichiōji, Korekawa village, Aomori Prefecture), *SGZ*, II–6, 1930, 1–20.

Mizuno, S., and Y. Kobayashi, *Zukai Kōkogaku Jiten* (Illustrated Dictionary of Archaeology), Tokyo, 1959.

Morse, E. S., *Shell Mounds of Omori*, Memoirs of the Science Department, University of Tokyo, 1879.

Nakamura, K., *Umataka*, Nagaoka Municipal Museum of Science, 1958.

—— *Kosegasawa Dōkutsu* (Kosegasawa Cave), Nagaoka Municipal Museum of Science, 1960.

Nakayama, E., *Irimi Kaizuka* (Shell-mounds of Irimi), Anthropological Institute, Nanzan University, Nagoya, 1955.

Naora, N., *Kinki Kodai Bunka Sōkō* (Investigations of the Ancient Culture of Kinki), Tokyo, 1943.

Nihon Kōkogaku Kyōkai Dōketsu Iseki Chōsa Tokubetsu Iinkai (Special Committee of the Archaeological Association of Japan for the Investigation of Remains of Caves), *Nihon no Dōketsu Iseki* (Remains of Caves in Japan), Tokyo, 1967.

Ōba, I., "Honpō jōdai no dōketsu iseki," (Early Japanese cave sites), *SGZ*, VI–3, 1934 (entire issue).

Ōba, I., (ed.), *Hiraide*, Tokyo, 1955.

Okamoto, I., and N. Akaboshi, *Yokosuka-shi Hakubutsukan Kenkyū Hōkoku* (Report of Research of the Yokosuka City Museum), 1, (Kayama shell-mound), Yokosuka City Museum, 1957.

Okamoto, I., and M. Asō, *Nihon Sekki Jidai Sōgō Bunken Mokuroku* (Bibliography of the Stone Age of Japan), Tokyo, 1958.

Ōyama, K., *Kanagawa-ken Shimoaraiso-mura aza Katsusaka Ibutsu Hōganchi Chōsa Hōkoku* (Report of Excavation of the Remains of Katsusaka, Shimoaraiso village, Kanagawa Prefecture), Brief Reports of the Prehistoric Society, 1, 1927.

Ōyama, K., "Vorläufiger Bericht über die Chronologie der Jōmon-Kultur der Steinzeit im Kantō (Mittel-Japan)," *Praehistorica Asiae Orientalis*, I, Hanoi, 1932, 77–90.

Ōyama, K., K. Ikegami and T. Ōgyū, "Chiba-ken Chiba-gun Miyako-mura Kasori kaizuka chōsa hōkoku," (Report on the investigation of the Kasori shell-mound in Miyako village, Chiba County, Chiba Prefecture), *SGZ*, IX–1, 1937, 1–68.

Ōyama, I., I. Kōno, K. Ikegami and S. Sugiyama, "Aomori-ken Sannohe-gun Korekawa-mura Nakai sekki jidai iseki," (The Stone Age remains of Nakai, Korekawa village, Sannohe County, Aomori Prefecture), *SGZ*, II–4, 1930 (entire issue).

Ōyama, K., M. Miyasaka and K. Ikegami, "Jōmon-shiki sekki jidai no hennengaku teki kenkyū yōhō," (Preliminary report on the chronological study of the Jōmon-type Stone Age), *SGZ*, III–6, 1931 (entire issue).

Saito, T., *Nihon Kōkogaku Zukan* (Illustrated Japanese Archaeology), Tokyo, 1955.

Sakakibara, M., "Sagami-koku Moroiso sekki jidai iseki chōsa hōkoku," (Report on the investigation of the Stone Age remains of Moroiso, Sagami province), *KGZ*, XI–8, 1921, 443–465.

Sakazume, H., "Jōmon bunka ni okeru kamekansō no kisoteki kenkyū," (Basic study on jar-burials in the Jōmon culture), *Risshō Daigaku Bungaku Ronsō* (Journal of Literature of Risshō University), IX, 1957, 88–109.

Sakazume, N., "Nihon genshi nōgyō shiron," (A tentative theory on primitive agriculture in Japan), *KGZ*, XLII–2, 1957, 1–12.

—— *Nihon Jōmon Sekki Jidai Shokuryō Sōsetsu* (Synthetic Study of Subsistence in the Japanese Jōmon Stone Age), Kyoto, 1961.

Serizawa, C., *Sekki Jidai no Nihon* (The Stone Age of Japan), Tokyo, 1960.

—— "Jōmon doki no kigen," (The origins of Jōmon pottery), *Shizen*, XVII–11, 1962, 28–35.

Shimizu, J., *Kamegaoka Iseki* (Remains of Kamegaoka), Keio University, Yokohama, 1959.

Suenaga, M., *Miyataki no Iseki* (Remains of Miyataki), Kyoto, 1944.

Suenaga, M., and T. Kojima, *Nara-ken Sōgō Bunka Chōsa Hōkokusho: Yoshinogawa Ryūiki* (Report of Cultural Investigations along the Yoshino River, Nara Prefecture: Archaeology), 1954, 289–352.

Sugihara, S., *Nihon Kōkogaku Kōza: Jōmon Bunka* (Symposium on Japanese Archaeology: Jōmon Culture), 3, Tokyo, 1956.

—— *Gumma-ken Iwajuku Hakken no Sekki Bunka* (The Stone Age Culture of Iwajuku, Gumma Prefecture), Meiji University, Tokyo, 1956.

Sugihara, S., and C. Serizawa, *Kanagawa-ken Natsushima ni okeru Jōmon Bunka Shotōno Kaizuka* (The Shell-mounds of the Earliest Jōmon Culture at Natsushima, Kanagawa Prefecture), Meiji University, Tokyo, 1957.

Sugiyama, S., *Jōmon Doki* (Jōmon Pottery), Nihon Kōkozuroku Taisei (Corpus of Ancient Designs), XIV, Tokyo, 1931.

—— *Nihon Genshi Seni Kōgei-shi* (History of Primitive Japanese Textile Handicraft), 2 vols., Tokyo, 1942.

Takahashi, K., "Jimmu-ryō nishi hakken no sekki jidai iseki," (A Stone Age site found to the west of the Tomb of Emperor Jimmu), *Kōkokai* (Archaeology), IV-7, 1904, 7–10.

Tanikawa, I., "Moroiso-shiki doki no kenkyū," (Research on Moroiso type pottery), *KGZ*, XIV-9, 1924, 546–551; XIV-11, 679–689; XV-1, 1925, 26–50.

Terashi, M., *Minami Kyushu no Jōmon Doki* (Jōmon Pottery of South Kyushu), Ōguchi, 1954.

Torii, R., *Senshi oyobi Genshi Jidai no Kamiina* (The Prehistoric and Protohistoric Periods of Kamiina), Tokyo, 1926.

Tozawa, M., "Jōmon bunka kigenron no keifu," (History of the theories of the origins of the Jōmon culture), *Nihon Kōkogaku no Shomondai* (Various Problems of Japanese Archaeology), Tokyo, 1964, 1–15.

Tsuboi, K., *Ishiyama Kaizuka* (Shell-mounds of Ishiyama), Kyoto, 1956.

—— *Nihon Rekishi 1: Genshi oyobi Kodai* (History of Japan 1: Primitive and Ancient), Tokyo, 1962.

—— "Kumamoto-ken Goryō kaizuka," (The Goryō shell-mound in Kumamoto Prefecture), *SJ*, 8, 1967, 42–52.

Tsunoda, B., and S. Mitsumori, "Senshi jidai no tōbu Nihon,"(The prehistoric period of east Japan), *JGSK*, 12, 1939, 1–100.

Umehara, S., *Kyoto Kitashirakawa Ogura-chō Sekki Jidai Iseki Chōsa Hōkoku* (Report of Research on the Stone Age Site of Ogura-chō, Kitashirakawa, Kyoto), Report of Research on the Famous Historical Places in Kyoto Prefecture, XVI, Kyoto, 1935.

Watanabe, M., "Jōmon chūki nōkō-ron kankei shuyō bunken mokuroku," (Bibliography on Middle Jōmon agriculture), *KB*, XV-5, 1965, 141–143.

Yagi, S., "Sōshū Moroiso sekki jidai iseki no doki," (Pottery from the Stone Age site of Moroiso, Sōshū ([Sagami]), *JGZ*, XIII-139, 1897, 18–26.

Yagi, S. and S. Shimomura, "Shimōsa-koku Katori-gun Atamadai kaizuka kenkyū hōkoku," (Report of research on Atamadai shell-mound, Katori county, Shimōsa province), *JGZ*, IX-97, 1894, 254–285.

Yamanouchi, S., "Kantō kita ni okeru senidoki," (Fiber-tempered pottery in the Kantō and north), *SGZ*, I-2, 1929, 1–30.

—— "Iwayuru Kamegaoka-shiki doki no bumpu to jōmon-shiki doki no shūmatsu," (The distribution of the pottery of the so-called Kamegaoka type and the last stage of Jōmon-type pottery), *KB*, I-3/4, 1930, 139–157.

—— "Nihon enko no bunka," (The very early culture of Japan), *Dolmen*, I-4, 1932, 40–43; I-5, 85–90; I-6, 46–50; II-2, 49–53.

—— "Jōmon doki no shūmatsu," (The last stage of Jōmon pottery), *Dolmen*, I-6, 1932, 46–50; I-7, 49–53.

—— "Jōmon doki keishiki no saibetsu to taibetsu," (The main divisions and subdivisions of Jōmon pottery), *SKG*, I-1, 1937, 29–32.

—— *Nihon Senshi Doki Zufu* (Atlas of Japanese Prehistoric Pottery), Institute of Archaeology, Faculty of Letters, Tokyo Imperial University, 12 parts, 1939–41 (reprinted 1967).

—— *Nihon Genshi Bijutsu 1: Jōmon-shiki Doki* (Primitive Arts of Japan 1: Jōmon-type Pottery), Tokyo, 1964.

Yawata, I., *Kitasaku-gun no Kōkogakutei Chōsa* (Archaeological Research in Kitasaku County), Nagano City, 1934.

—— *Nihon-shi no Reimei* (The Dawn of Japanese History), Tokyo, 1953.

—— (ed.) *Sekai Kōkogaku Taikei 1: Nihon*, I (World Archaeology Series 1: Japan, I), Tokyo, 1959.

—— *Jōmon Doki Dogū* (Jōmon Pottery and Clay Figurines), Tokyo, 1962.

—— "Katsusaka-shiki bunkaken no chūshin," *Shinano*, 17-5, 1965, 325–329.

Yonemura, K., *Moyoro Kaizuka* (Moyoro Shell-mound), Tokyo, 1950.

Yoshida, I., *Yokohama-shi Shōmyōji Kaizuka* (Shōmyōji Shell-mound of Yokohama City), Reports of Research of the Musashino Regional Museum, Tokyo Prefecture, I, Tokyo, 1960.

Yoshida, Y., "Kamekan to omowareru jōmon bunka chūki no doki gun," (Jars excavated from Middle Jōmon culture sites), *SJ*, 3, 1956, 37–44.

INTRODUCTION

1. Morse, *Shell Mounds of Omori*, 1879; reprinted in 1968 along with other Morsiana.
2. Ōyama, *Kanagawa-ken Shimoaraiso-mura aza Katsusaka . . .*, 1927.
3. Okamoto and Aso, *Nihon Sekki Jidai . . .*, 1958, pp. 77–105, 124–135.
4. See a series of reports on excavations of shellmounds in *SGZ* starting in 1929; chronological synthesis appeared in *SGZ*, III-6, 1931, and in a German version: "Vorläufiger Bericht über die Chronologie der Jōmon-Kultur . . . ."
5. Kiyono, *Nihon Genjin no Kenkyū*, 1925; *Nihon Sekki Jidai-jin Kenkyū*, 1928; a series of articles in

JGZ between 1926–28, sometimes with coauthorship; in *KGZ* between 1929–31; and for his more professed views, *Nihon Jinshu-ron Hensen-shi*, 1944.

6. Yagi and Shimomura, "Shimōsa-koku Katori-gun Atamadai kaizuka . . . ," 1894.
7. Matsumoto, "Notes on the Stone Age People of Japan," pp. 53, 56.
8. Yagi and Shimomura, *op. cit.*
9. Yamanouchi, "Jōmon doki keishiki no saibetsu to taibetsu."
10. Groot, *Prehistory of Japan*, pp. 6–9, 21 ff.
11. Beardsley, "Japan Before History," *Far Eastern Quarterly*, XIV-3.
12. Kidder, *The Jōmon Pottery of Japan*, p. 4.
13. Kidder, *Japan Before Buddhism*, p. 35ff.
14. For example, foldout chart of Jōmon pottery typology, Yawata (ed.), *Sekai Kōkogaku Taikei 1: Nihon*, I.
15. Yawata, *Jōmon Doki Dogū*, p. 14.
16. At Loc. 1 B, I.C.U. site, 66 base sherds of the Horinouchi type were recovered; all belonged to different vessels. Only eight (12%) are mat-marked; see Kidder, "Pre-pottery and Jōmon Pottery Relationships . . . ," pp. 92–93.
17. Yamanouchi, *Nihon Genshi Bijutsu*, 1, p. 150.
18. Fujimori, *Idojiri*, p. 94.

EARLIEST JŌMON

1. As a mark of the change that has taken place, Serizawa, *Nihon Sekki Jidai*, 1960, is the first to put the real stamp "Made in Japan" on the Jōmon culture.
2. Kidder and Koyama, "C–14 nendai kara mita jōmon jidai no hennen," for listing and plotting of C_{14} dates and the resulting picture of anachronistic chronological and regional relationships.
3. Ōba, "Honpō jōdai no doketsu iseki," pp. 56–58. Caves were probably used for shelter during brief hunting stops, as refuges and for burials, but not as normal living places. The survey was basically intended to check caves for Paleolithic remains.
4. Sugihara, *Gumma-ken Iwajuku Hakken no Sekki Bunka*.
5. For instance, this idea, originally conveyed to me by Mr. Yamanouchi, is reflected in his section on pre-pottery and early pottery period stone tools in *Nihon Genshi Bijutsu*, p. 140.
6. Not yet reported professionally.
7. Nihon Kōkogaku Kyōkai, *Nihon no Dōketsu Iseki*, Fukui, pp. 260–265; Kamikuroiwa, pp. 229–236; Hibakoiwa Lower, pp. 55–59.
8. Nakamura, *Kosegasawa Dōkutsu*, Pls. 16, 17, 19, 20; Kato and Sasaki, "*Yamagata-ken Ichinosawa Iwakage Iseki*," plate.
9. Yamanouchi, *Nihon Genshi Bijutsu*, p. 154, says the rolling techniques—sticks, cords, cord-wrapped sticks—are so characteristic of Japan, they should have been developed and expanded in variety inside Japan itself. Esaka in (Yamanouchi ed.) *Nihon Genshi Bijutsu*, p. 161, places the origin of this rouletting in the eastern Chūbu or western Kantō while Inaridai pottery was being made in the southwest part of the Kantō Plain.
10. First presented by Serizawa to the Japan Archae-

ological Association meeting in 1959; Crane and Griffin, *Radiocarbon Supplement*, 1960, p. 45.
11. At the Jaōdo cave, Iwate Prefecture, cord-marked pottery was in the lowest level—Level VII, called middle Earliest—accompanied by rouletted and plain pottery; shell-scraped pottery does not occur in Level VII: Nihon Kōkogaku Kyōkai..., *Nihon no Dōketsu Iseki*, pp. 77, 81. Admitting to uncertainties in Hokkaido, Yoshizaki in (Kamaki ed.) *Nihon no Kōkogaku* II: *Jōmon Jidai*, p. 34, suggests that shell-scraping and marking may be the earliest, cord-marking possibly a little more recent.
12. This reflects my feeling regarding shape and decoration. Yoshizaki, *op. cit.*, p. 31, places it about middle Earliest; Esaka, foldout chart in (Yamanouchi ed.) *Nihon Genshi Bijutsu* has it at the beginning of Earliest, possibly extending back into Subearliest.
13. Esaka in (Yamanouchi ed.) *Nihon Genshi Bijutsu*, p. 160.

EARLY JŌMON

1. Ōyama, "Vorläufiger Bericht über die Chronologie der Jōmon-Kultur..."
2. Gotō, "Jōko jidai no jūkyo," *JGSK*, 15, 1940, pp. 22–24.
3. *Op. cit.*, pp. 26–28.
4. Matsumoto, Fujita, Shimizu and Esaka, *Kamo Iseki*.
5. Hasebe, "Entō doki bunka."
6. Yamanouchi, "Kantō kita ni okeru senidoki."
7. For what may be the most recent attempt to outline the traits of successive types, see Fujita (ed.), *Nihon Kōkogaku Jiten*, p. 321.
8. Nakayama, "Higo-koku Uto-gun Hanazono-mura..."
9. Yagi, "Soshū Moroiso sekki jidai iseki no doki ..."
10. Sakakibara, "Sagami-koku Moroiso . . . ," 1921; Tanikawa, "Moroiso shiki doki no kenkyū," 1924-25; Akaboshi and Sakazume, "Kanagawa-ken Miura-gun Misaki-chō Moroiso kaizuka . . . ," 1938.
11. For instance, see Fujita (ed.), *op. cit.*, p. 537.

MIDDLE JŌMON

1. Miyasaka, *Togariishi*, p. 217; he discovered 33 pit-dwellings at Togariishi and 28 to the north across the river at Yosukeone. Saito, *Nihon Kōkogaku Zukan*, 2 (III), 11, speaks of a large settlement of a few hundred dwellings. Similar protracted excavations at other sites would presumably yield far more pits than are now known.
2. Ōyama, *Kanagawa-ken Shimoaraiso-mura aza Katsusaka Ibutsu . . .* , pp. 9, 18, 32.
3. Kida and Sugiyama, *Nihon Sekki Jidai Shokubutsu-sei Ibutsu Zuroku*, Pls. 5, 6 for nuts; Sakazume, *Nihon Jōmon Sekki Jidai Shokuryo Sōsetsu*, pp. 272–274: grapes, persimmons, musk melon, peaches, etc.
4. Sakazume, "Nihon genshi nōgyō shiron," represents the first serious effort to examine all aspects of the culture from these viewpoints. He

included the manipulation of nut and fruit bearing trees within his broad definition of "agriculture."

5. Esaka, "Jōmon bunka no jidai ni okeru shokubutsu saibai kigen no mondai ni kansuru ichikōsatsu."
6. Fujimori, *Idojiri*, pp. 139–142.
7. The Goryōgadai type is normally listed as the very earliest type of Middle Jōmon, contemporary with Shimoono. The distribution of the former is essentially in the southern Kantō, and its contribution toward the Katsusaka style, presumably mountainous in origin, is probably only minimal; the feeling of continuity in developments, however, is very strong, as reflected in Yamanouchi's claim that all decorative developments have their roots in earlier types: Yamanouchi, *Nihon Genshi Bijutsu*, p. 157.
8. Fujimori, *op. cit.*, p. 80.
9. Esaka in (Yamanouchi ed.) *Nihon Genshi Bijutsu*, p. 167.
10. Kidder, *The Jōmon Pottery of Japan*, p. 47.
11. Yawata, "Katsusaka-shiki bunkaken no chūshin," p. 5.
12. Yamanouchi (ed.), *Nihon Genshi Bijutsu*, p. 152.
13. Fujimori and Mutō, "Chūki jōmon doki no chozōkeitai ni tsuite."
14. Kusama and Yoshida, *Iwate-ken Morioka-shi Hataino Iseki Chōsa Hōkoku*, p. 7.
15. Fujimori in (Yamanouchi ed.) *Nihon Genshi Bijutsu*, caption for Pl. 134, p. 181.
16. Esaka in (Yamanouchi ed.) *Nihon Genshi Bijutsu*, p. 164; for instance, at Tsukayama, Suginami Ward, Tokyo.
17. Esaka, *op. cit.*, p. 165.
18. Yoshida, "Kamekan to omowareru jōmon bunka chūki no doki gun," 1956.

Late Jōmon

1. Nishimura in (Kamaki ed.) *Nihon no Kōkogaku* II, p. 340.
2. Tsuboi, *Nihon Rekishi: Genshi oyobi Kodai*, 1, p. 132.
3. Kamura, *Tōkai no Senshi Iseki*, pp. 267–270.
4. Bunkazai Hogoiinkai, *Ōyu-machi Kanjō Resseki*.
5. Kidder, "The Stone Circles of Ōyu."
6. Kidder and Koyama, *op. cit.*, p. 3, as of August 1966. No significant change in this pattern has emerged with the publication of more recent results.
7. Yoshida, *Yokohama-shi Shōmyōji Kaizuka*.
8. Gotō, "Horinouchi kaizuka hakkutsu," 1957.
9. Isozaki in (Yamanouchi ed.) *Nihon Genshi Bijutsu*, p. 167.
10. Terashi, *Minami Kyushu no Jōmon Doki*, p. 8.
11. Yamanouchi, "Jōmon doki keishiki no saibetsu to taibetsu," 1937, gives for Late Jōmon: Angyō 1, 2; for Latest Jōmon: Angyō 2–3, 3; in the chart at the back of Yawata, *Sekai Kōkogaku Taikei*, 1959, Angyō 2 and 3a are listed as Latest

Jōmon; the foldout chart in the back of Yamanouchi (ed.), *Nihon Genshi Bijutsu*, 1964, gives only Angyō 3a, 3b and 3c in Latest Jōmon; the foldout chart in the back of Kamaki (ed.), *Nihon no Kōkogaku* II, 1965, lists them as follows: Late Jōmon: Angyō I, Angyō II; Latest Jōmon: Angyō IIIa, Angyō IIIc.

Latest Jōmon

1. When the Tsugaru Castle was under construction in 1623 the spot came to be called Kamegaoka—"pottery hill"—because of the quantity of sherds that kept appearing. During the Edo period the character *kame* for pottery was changed to *kame* for turtle, often considered to be more auspicious and aesthetic.
2. Hasebe, "Rikuzen Ōbora kaizuka . . . ."
3. See Yamanouchi, *Nihon Senshi Doki Zufu*, vols. 3, 4, 6, 7, 1939–40. Isozaki seems to be the first to record this last development, in (Yamanouchi ed.) *Nihon Genshi Bijutsu*, p. 170.
4. Tsuboi in (Ishida and Izumi) *Nihon Nōkō Bunka no Kigen*, p. 120, says that it might be worth investigating connections since Jōmon and Late Chou lacquer is usually red while Yayoi and Han lacquer is usually black.
5. I elaborated on this view in detail in "The Kamegaoka Vessels in the City Art Museum . . . ," pp. 202–208.
6. Yamanouchi (ed.), *Nihon Genshi Bijutsu*, p. 151.
7. By a process of correlation it is claimed that while Ōbora A was in style in the north, Yayoi pottery could not have occurred in southwest Japan. Ōbora A is found with many of these pottery types. As late as Kurozuchi B II in the Inland Sea region, with which Ōbora A is found, there is no associated Yayoi pottery; see Isozaki in (Yamanouchi ed.) *Nihon Genshi Bijutsu*, p. 172, quoting studies by Kamaki and Esaka.
8. Frequently repeated by Komai; for instance, see *Otoe*, English résumé, p. 3.
9. Egami, Sekino and Sakurai, the authors of *Tateshi*, conservatively make no such claims for the type of fortifications they investigated, known in northeast Honshu as *tate*, in Hokkaido as *chashi*. I would, however, suggest a possible correlation. The oldest material found with these sites is Haji and Sue pottery of the Tomb period.
10. Takahashi, "Jimmu-ryō nishi hakken no sekki jidai iseki," 1904.
11. Tsuboi, "Kumamoto-ken Goryō kaizuka," p. 45; among the 519 Goryō type sherds, 70.72% come from pots, 22.74% from bowls; 1.54% of the other pottery is rouletted, 1.54% Nishibira type, 3.28% Mimanda type, and 0.19% Sugigami type.
12. Sakazume, H., "Jōmon bunka ni okeru kamekanso . . . ," pp. 91–93.
13. Yonemura, *Moyoro Kaizuka*, English résumé, p. 5.

Index-Glossary

abalone shell, Pls. *299–300*

acorns, 90

adornment, personal, 46

agriculture, 90, 95, 98, 169, 171

Ainu, 9, 10, 231, 236

    embroidery, Pl. *346*

Akamidō (赤御堂) *type site*, Pls. *25, 26*

Akitacho (秋多町) site, Pl. *134*

altars, 89

Amataki (雨滝) site, Latest, Pls. *357, 363, 364, 367, 372, 373*

Anadara granosa, 45, 47

Anadara subcrenata, 26, 276

Angyō (安行) shell-mound, Saitama Prefecture, *type site*, Late to Latest, sometimes listed with as many as five subtypes, 175, 178, 179, 226, 231, 234; Pls. *308–315, 317–319, 394, 396, 399–406*

anklets, wild boar bone, 170

Anthropological Society of Japan, 174

antler objects, 226

Arami (荒海) shell-mound, *type site*, late Latest, incised, 234; Pls. *371, 387, 408*

Aramichi (新道) *type site*, early Middle, mixed techniques, 91, 279; Pls. *111, 112, 119*

arrowheads, stone, 46, 169

Asahi (朝日) shell-mound, 54; Pl. *VIII*

Asahi (朝日) site, Latest, Pl. *396*

Asahichō (朝日町) site, early Middle, Pl. *113*

asphalt, Pl. *361*

Asukayama Park (飛鳥山公園) shell-mound, early Early, Pl. *71*

Ataka (阿高) shell-mound, *type site*, early Middle, grooved, 23, 98, 99; Pls. *229, 335, 336*

Atamadai (or Otamamadai) (阿玉台) shell-mound, *type site*, early Middle, mixed techniques, 95, 98; Pls. *106–110, 117*

axes, 169

    chipped, 46

Aya (綾) *type site*, Late, incised, 99; Pls. *329, 335*

Banki (晩期), Latest Jōmon period

barrel-shaped vessels, 91, 94, 230; Pls. *147–154*

baskets, 227

    lacquered, Pl. *359*

Batōchō (馬頭町) site, Late, Pl. *277*

beads, 226

Beardsley, Richard, 11

bells, Yayoi bronze, 230

Biwa lake-bottom (琵琶湖々底) site, Earliest to Late, Pls. *228–330*

bone

    arrowheads, 169

    fishhooks, 46

    objects, 226; Pl. *381*

bones

    animal, 169, 170

    containers for, 230

    fish, 169

    painted, 230

Botan-batake (ボタン畑) site, Latest, Pls. *353, 380*

bottles, 16, 178, 227, 231; Pls. *254, 357, 358*

bracelets, shell, 170

"bread," 90; Pl. *174*

bronze

    bells, Yayoi, 230

    Han dynasty, 227

buckwheat, 394

burials, 235; Pls. *91, 330*

burial furniture, 9, 170, 230; Pls. *289, 343, 346*

burial practices, 9, 99, 170

burial vessels, 99, 100, 235; Pls. *175, 176, 179, 205–206, 263, 354–355, 419, 425–429*

burnishing, 16, 178, 225, 230, 235

"cake decoration" style, 99; Pls. *61–62, 88, 173, 175, 177, 180, 209*

canoes, 46, 169

Carbon$_{14}$ dating, 12, 17, 18, 22, 23, 26, 89, 170, 171; Pls. *6, 11*

carving, 231; Pls. *368, 372*

cerithidea, 276

chalice shape, 91

chert, 169

chestnuts, 90

Chiami (千網) *type site*, Gumma Prefecture, late Latest, mixed techniques, 234; Pl. *408*

China, 17, 236

    lacquer, 227

Chōjayashiki (長者屋敷) site, Latest, 370

Chōjagahara (長者ヶ原) *type site*, Niigata Prefecture, early Middle, applied strips

Chōshichiyachi (長七谷地) shell-mound, *type site*, late Early, 27; Pls. *25, 26*

chronology, 17, 18, 45, 46, 50, 51, 170, 171, 179

Chūki (中期), Middle Jōmon period

cinnabar, 227

clay, 14, 23, 54, 94, 95, 98, 99, 178, 179, 226, 231, 234, 235; Pls. *15, 34, 39, 98, 113, 123, 130, 137, 148, 150, 152, 156, 177, 178, 202, 235, 274, 290, 334, 410–412, 419, 420, 423*

    colors, 15, 23, 50, 54, 95, 99, 171, 178, 179, 226, 234, 236, 280; Pls. *1, 20, 22, 29, 36–38, 40, 54, 55, 73, 90, 103, 123, 130, 149–150, 152, 156, 160–163, 172, 177, 178, 211, 217, 222, 225, 228, 230, 233, 235, 238, 248, 252, 266, 312, 320, 327, 328, 332–334, 336, 340, 350, 354–355, 387–389, 392, 403, 407, 410, 411, 420, 422, 424, 429*

climate, 45, 46, 90, 174

"cloud-scroll," pattern, 227; Pls. *365–366, 376, 380*

coastal cultures, northern Asian, 236

coil forming, 1, 14, 19, 84

combs, lacquer, 227

combing, 235; Pls. *177, 192, 262*

communities, 15, 17, 174, 175, 278

cooking pots, 14, 23, 45, 46, 51, 54, 55, 91, 174, 179, 231, 234; Pls. *12, 25, 49, 51, 58, 64, 68, 72, 73, 76, 88, 111, 119, 204, 211, 256, 262, 292, 307, 312, 322, 352, 378, 398, 405*

cord-marking types (*overleaf*)

zone cord-marked, Pl. *II*

Minebata (峯畑) site, Middle, Pl. *157*

mirrors, Chinese bronze, 227

Mito (三戸) shell-mound, Kanagawa Prefecture, *type site*, Earliest, incised,

Mitsuhashi (三橋) site, Earliest, Pl. *27*

Miyaji (宮地) site, Middle, Pl. *217*

Miyanomae (宮ノ前) site, Middle, Pl. *180*

Miyanoshita (宮ノ下) site, Middle, Pl. *128*

Miyasaka, Eiichi, 105

Miyataki (宮滝) *type site*, late Late, mixed techniques, 179, 234; Pl. *321*

Mizonokuchi (溝ノ口) site, Late, Pl. *321*

Mizuko (水子) shell-mound, Saitama Prefecture, *type site*, middle Early, cord-marked

molluscs
  Anadara granosa, 45, 47
  Anadara subcrenata, 26, 276
  Pecten yesoensis, 45

Momoishichō (百石町) site, Latest, Pl. *351*

Monomidai (物見台) *type site*, Aomori Prefecture, Earliest, shell-marked, 26

Monzen (門前) shell-mound, *type site*, late Middle to Early Late, mixed techniques, Pl. *204*

Moroiso (諸磯) shell-mound, *type site*, late Early, three subtypes, mixed techniques, 12, 46, 54, 91, 98; Pls. *58, 63, 77–79, 81, 82, 84–86, 92*

Morse, Edward S., 9, 10

motifs
  anthropomorphic, 91
  deer, 216
  dragonfly, Pl. *172*
  floral, 226
  frog, 95, 279; Pls. *105, 149–151*
  sluglike, 95
  snake, 94, 99, 279; Pls. *105, 124–125, 127–129, 133, 156, 172, 201*
  zoomorphic, 91, 227, 236

Motosumiyoshiyama (元住吉山) *type site*, late Late, pseudo-cord-marked, Pl. *322*

Moyoro (最寄) shell-mound, Hokkaido, Okhotsk Sea type, 236

Mukoppara (向原) site, Middle, Pl. *167*

Mukoyama (向山) site, Ibaragi Prefecture, Early, 171

"multilinear evolution," 46

Murayama (村山) site, Early, Pls. *77, 78*

Muroya (室谷) cave, *type site*, early Earliest, string-pressed, Pls. *2–5, 31,–46*

Mushiri (ムシリ) *type site*, Earliest to Early, cord-marked, Pl. *49*

Nabeya (鍋屋) site, middle Early, Pl. *97*

Nado (奈土) shell-mound, Latest, Pls. *308, 310, 403*

Nagakubo (長久保) site, late Late, Pl. *240*

Nagamine (長峯) site, Middle, Pls. *107, 148, 216*

Nagamori (長森) site, Latest, Pl. *362*

Nagane (長根) site, early Middle, Pl. *100*

Nagano (長野) site, Early, Pl. *95*

nail-marking (爪形文), bamboo stick-marking, chiefly Early, from Kantō area to Inland Sea, 19, 22, 54, 91, 273, 274, 279; Pls. *9, 91, 112*

Nakagawa (中川) site, Toyama Prefecture, Latest, 230

Nakahara (中原) site, Nagano Prefecture, early Early and early Middle, Pls. *47, 105, 130, 131, 133, 153, 159, 214*

Nakahara (中原) site, Tokyo, Middle, Pl. *III*

Nakai (中居) site, Latest, Pl. *349*

Nakasugao (中巣生) site, Middle, 99, 100; Pl. *175*

Nakatsu (中津) shell-mound, *type site*, early Late, zone cord-marked, 178; Pl. *324*

Nakaya, Jūjiro, 11

Nakayama (中山) site, Latest, Pls. *358, 393*

Namikata (波方) port sea-bottom site, Late, Pl. *328*

Nampukuji (南福寺) shell-mound, Kumamoto Prefecture, *type site*, late Middle, mixed techniques, 178

Nanukaichi (七日市) site, early Late, Pl. *232*

Nanyōji (南養寺) site, Middle, Pl. *138*

Narahara (楢原) site, Middle, Pls. *135, 144, 223*

Narukami (鳴神) shell-mound, Wakayama Prefecture, Middle to Late

Narukamiyama (鳴神山) shell-mound, Middle, Pl. *106*

Nashikubo (梨久保) *type site*, early Middle, mixed techniques, 89; Pls. *105, 118*

Natsushima (夏島) shell-mound, *type site*, early Earliest, string-impressed, 23, 274; Pls. *11–14*

natural objects, models of, 175; Pls. *299–300*

necklace, blue stone, 170

needles, 46, 169

Neinomaru shell-mound, Yahata City, Fukuoka Prefecture, Pl. *325*

Nishibira (西平) shell-mound, *type site*, late Middle, incised, 178, 235; Pls. *330, 339*

Nishigahara (西ケ原) shell-mound, Late, Pls. *267, 305*

Nishiyokono (西横野) site, Early, Pl. *67*

Nittori (荷取) cave, Nagano Prefecture, Earliest, 19

Nojima (野島) shell-mound, *type site*, middle Earliest, mixed techniques

Nonaka (野中) *type site*, Ibaragi Prefecture, early Early, mixed techniques

Nopporo (野幌) type, Pl. *230*

Notogawa Collection, Pl. *24*

Nowata (野渡) shell-mound, early Early, Pl. *72*

Nozuki (野月) *type site*, late Early, shell-marked, 26; Pl. *21*

Nukazuka (糠塚) shell-mound, *type site*, early Middle, stick-marked, Pls. *61–62*

Nunome (布目) *type site*, early Early, herringbone cord-marking, Pl. *45*

Nusamai (幣舞) *type site*, late Latest, mixed techniques, Pls. *341, 346*

oars, 46

Ōbara (大原) *type site*, Early, shell-marked, Pl. *96*

Ōbora (or Ōhora) (大洞) shell-mound, *type site*, Latest, nine subtypes, carved and cord-impressed, 226, 227, 230, 231, 234–236; Pls. *352, 374*
  Ōbora A, 230, 234; Pls. *341, 342, 347, 354–355*
  Ōbora A′, 230, 231, 234, 235; Pls. *356, 389, 425–426*
  Ōbora B, 226; Pls. *347, 351, 352, 381, 384, 392, 393*
  Ōbora B–C, 227; Pls. *347–349, 357, 358, 363, 364, 367, 370, 372, 373, 377, 378, 381, 382, 383, 390–391, 417*
  Ōbora C, 227, 230; Pls. *346, 347, 350, 353, 359–362, 365–366, 368, 369, 374, 376, 379–381,*